HEAVENLY TORAH

Heavenly Torah
As Refracted through the Generations

Abraham Joshua Heschel

Edited and Translated from the Hebrew
with Commentary
by
Gordon Tucker
with
Leonard Levin

continuum
NEW YORK • LONDON

2005

The Continuum International Publishing Group Inc
15 East 26 Street, New York, NY 10010

The Continuum International Publishing Group Ltd
The Tower Building, 11 York Road, London SE1 7NX

www.continuumbooks.com

Library of Congress Cataloging-in-Publication Data

Heschel, Abraham Joshua, 1907-1972.
  [Torah min ha-shamayim be-aspaklaria shel ha-dorot. English]
  Heavenly Torah : as refracted through the generations / Abraham Joshua Heschel ; edited and translated from the Hebrew with commentary by Gordon Tucker with Leonard Levin.
    p. cm.
  Includes bibliographical references and index.
  ISBN 0-8264-0802-8 (hardcover : alk. paper)
  1. Talmud—Theology. 2. Revelation (Jewish theology) I. Tucker, Gordon. II. Title.
  BM504.3.H4713 2005
  296.3—dc22

                                                                          2004021088

Continuum Publishing is committed to preserving ancient forests and natural resources. We have elected to print this title on 50% postconsumer waste recycled paper. As a result, this book has saved:
    53 trees
    2,473 pounds of solid waste
    22,429 gallons of water
    4,858 pounds of greenhouse gases
    9,020 kilowatt hours of electricity
Continuum is a member of Green Press Initiative, a nonprofit program dedicated to supporting publishers in their efforts to reduce their use of fiber obtained from endangered forests. For more information, go to www.greenpressinitiative.org.

Dedication to *Torah min Hashamayim*

To the memory of my mother,
the zaddik Rivkah Reizel,
and
to the memory of my sisters
Devorah Miriam, Esther Sima, and Gittel
who perished in the Shoah

May their souls be bound up in the bond of life.

Dedication to *Heavenly Torah*

To
Rabbi Max Gelb
and
Rabbi Max Routtenberg

May their memory be a blessing.

If you were to place the dwarf on the neck of the giant, who would see for a greater distance? Evidently, the dwarf would, since now the eyes of the dwarf are higher than the eyes of the giant. So do we dwarves ride on the necks of the giants, for we are aware of their erudition, and we delve into it, and are empowered by their wisdom.

—Rabbi Isaiah de-Trani

CONTENTS

FOREWORD

by Susannah Heschel

The years when my father was writing *Torah min Hashamayim* were among the happiest of his life. He used to come home at the end of the day and talk with enthusiasm about how quickly he was writing and how much he was enjoying it. The rabbinic texts were all in his memory, he said, and they were simply pouring out. I imagine that writing the book was very much an experience of remembrance for him, not only of the texts but of his childhood years in Warsaw, when he first began studying them so intensively. It is no wonder that he dedicated this book to his mother and to the three of his four sisters who were murdered by the Nazis.

My father wrote *Torah min Hashamayim* in a surprisingly short period of time. His friends and colleagues were amazed at how quickly he wrote it, given the massive range of texts he discusses in the book. It was the project he turned to in the late 1950s while completing the English translation and expansion of his German doctoral dissertation, published in 1962 as *The Prophets*. Actual publication of *Torah min Hashamayim* took some time; his English publisher, Sonny Bloch of Soncino Press, was determined to produce two handsome volumes, which finally appeared in 1962 and 1965. My father continued with the project, though he was never able to complete the planned third volume during his lifetime; it was published posthumously, based on an incomplete manuscript.

It seems clear that, for my father, *Torah min Hashamayim* was not simply another tome, nor was it a conventional work of scholarship. Rather, it was a *sefer,* a work of religious inspiration that was intended not only for scholars of rabbinic Judaism but also for Jews seeking theological guidance. He was writing a religious text, as his Hasidic ancestors had done, shaping the rabbinic sources to bring to the surface their often subtle and even concealed views on God, revelation, and the nature of interpretation, and at the same time responding to contemporary concerns that only a strict and uncompromising halakhic Judaism was authentic and legitimate. As always in his writings, he sought to demonstrate that a pluralism of religious views stands at the heart of rabbinic Judaism and was the source of Judaism's vitality and vigor.

This is a work of scholarship that redefines the nature of theological interpretation. It is not the sort of scientific research that marks my father's studies of medieval Jewish philosophy, written in the 1930s and '40s, nor does it follow the classical methods of positivist historiography developed in Germany, where he received his academic training. He does not address the historical-critical questions that would require him to date the texts he is analyzing and compare manuscript variants, nor does he contextualize the

Rabbis' statements within the historical and political circumstances of their time. He seeks instead to find religious categories inherent in the rabbinic texts themselves, and he celebrates the wide range of responses offered by those texts to their own questions. Ambiguities and conflicts are valorized by him, rather than reconciled and unified.

Torah min Hashamayim makes a unique contribution to the modern scholarship on rabbinic thought that, since the nineteenth century, has offered broad, sweeping surveys of the subject. In 1857, Abraham Geiger, whose work my father admired greatly, divided rabbinic thought into two tendencies, a Sadducean, which he defined as conservative, aristocratic, and eager to preserve the prerogatives of the Jerusalem Temple's priesthood, and a Pharisaic tendency, dominated by liberal, democratic, and progressive principles and concerned with the broader masses of Jews. Each group produced its own Halakhah, Geiger argued; the Sadducees were strict adherents of the letter of Scripture, while the Pharisees were willing to modify and relax the Halakhah of the Bible in accord with their liberal principles and efforts to make all Israel a nation of priests.

Geiger's worked sparked an interest in rabbinic literature among Christian as well as Jewish scholars in Germany, several of whom wrote studies of rabbinic thought with the goal of demonstrating the Jewish background of early Christianity. In most cases, however, the results were problematic. Emil Schürer, Wilhelm Bousset, Ferdinand Weber, and Gerhard Kittel found parallels between the teachings of the Rabbis and those contained in the Gospels, but invariably claimed that the Jewish teachings were ethically and religiously inferior. Judaism was described as casuistic, moribund, and amoral, with a remote, transcendent God who cared more about deeds than intention.

George Foot Moore, the first American to write a synthetic account of rabbinic thought in 1927, Judaism in the First Centuries of the Christian Era, broke decisively with what he considered a biased Christian scholarship toward rabbinic Judaism. Moore described what he termed a "normative" Pharisaic Judaism promoted by the Tannaim as a religion on its own terms, without comparison to Christianity.

A few years later, in 1938, the American Jewish scholar Louis Finkelstein produced a study entitled The Pharisees, which was guided by the sociological categories of urban versus rural experience. The differences between urban and rural settings, with their concomitant economic, educational, and cultural distinctions, he argued, produced the differences in belief and practice between Sadducees and Pharisees, respectively. In 1969, the Israeli scholar Efraim E. Urbach, in his study The Sages, presented the first Israeli synthetic view of rabbinic thought, comparing the views of the Rabbis with those of classical Greek philosophers. Urbach attempted to present rabbinic thought as unified on central issues of religious concern and to demonstrate similarities between the thought of the Rabbis and classical Greek philosophers; for Urbach, the God of the Rabbis was to be compared with the God of Plato.

While the work of Moore, including his critique of Christian scholarship on rabbinics, was widely appreciated in the United States (though less so in Germany), the biases toward rabbinic Judaism found in Christian New Testament scholarship were not fully eradicated. In more recent decades, it was my father's good friend W. D. Davies who revolutionized New Testament studies by revealing the rabbinic context of Paul's writings. Davies's student, E. P. Sanders, finally developed the definitive demonstration of how nascent Christian texts could be placed in a positive rabbinic context.

The most important shift in scholarship on the Talmud came with the work of Jacob Neusner, a student of my father's. In the 1970s, Neusner introduced to the texts of rabbinic literature methods of historical-critical analysis that had long been standard in other fields. For example, he pointed out that teachings attributed to Rabbis were not necessarily spoken by them but may have been introduced in later generations. Neusner also applied categories of comparative religion to rabbinic religion and introduced rabbinic literature to students of comparative religion. More recently, Neusner has argued that the Talmud is permeated with philosophical argumentation and scientific logic, if it is properly interpreted.

Unlike prior scholars of rabbinic thought, my father was guided not by sociological and historical categories but by theological concerns. He was more interested in the mystical versus rationalist approaches to Scripture taken by the Rabbis and the implications that flow from each than in determining their social location. Nor was my father troubled by a multiplicity of rabbinic views on central theological questions; on the contrary, he was pleased to find differing viewpoints. For him, the school of Akiva was mystical, apocalyptic, radical, uncompromising, enthusiastic, strong, militant, deep, paradoxical, and sweeping, whereas the school of Ishmael was critical, rationalistic, self-limited, clear, dry, measured, balanced, careful, and patient. In the years after the deaths of these Rabbis, my father wrote, the radical ideas of Rabbi Akiva won and the more liberal and measured theology of Ishmael was neglected.

With *Torah min Hashamayim,* my father felt he was not only unearthing the Rabbis' views regarding revelation but also demonstrating that theological concerns could be found in the aggadic texts of rabbinic literature, which were traditionally dismissed as unimportant in comparison to halakhic passages. To some extent, he was also presenting the Rabbis' conflicting tendencies as expressions of much broader relevance. Some of the disagreements of the Rabbis continued in postrabbinic Jewish literature, and some may have also influenced Christian theological development. The two volumes of *Torah min Hashamayim* were published precisely at the time my father was deeply involved in the Second Vatican Council's formulation of a statement regarding the church's relations with the Jewish people, *Nostra Aetate.* Indeed, my father wrote about this in an unpublished letter in German to Augustin Cardinal Bea, president of the Secretariat for Promoting Christian Unity, who served as a liaison between the Second Vatican Council and Jewish leaders. In his letter, my father suggests that "the formulation of the dogmas of biblical inspiration within the church were influenced by Jewish perspectives." The theories of orthodox Protestant theologians of the sixteenth and seventeenth centuries, he writes, may have been influenced by the work of Rabbi Akiva's school, represented by Rabbi Shimon and Rabbi Meir, who formulated a theory of verbal dictation of Scripture, based on Jeremiah 36:18. Rabbi Ishmael, by contrast, represents understandings of revelation more often shared by Catholic and Jewish thinkers.

As was typical of my father, he sought in his letter to Cardinal Bea as well as in his published writings to illumine parallels in the theological and spiritual problems that faced

Jews, Christians, Muslims, and all people of faith. His work bears no scent of apologetics or triumphalism. Commonalities on the level of what he called "depth theology" were important to him, not the doctrinal differences that set people of faith apart. He hoped that *Torah min Hashamayim* would be a source of inspiration that would illumine the richness and depth of Jewish theology. In fact, he always told me that this was the book he hoped his readers would study the most thoroughly.

My mother and I would like to extend our deep thanks to the two Rabbis who initiated the translation of *Torah min Hashamayim*, Rabbi Max Routtenberg and Rabbi Max Gelb. They worked hard and, sadly, were unable to live long enough to complete the very difficult task of translation. Their efforts, however, formed the basis of the magnificent translation carried out by Rabbi Gordon Tucker. Rabbi Tucker's explanatory notes and commentaries constitute an important and very helpful guide to readers who have limited background in rabbinics, and his commitment to this project, which has taken him many years of hard work, will be appreciated by all who study this book.

Finally, my mother and I want to express our appreciation to Frank Oveis, our editor at Continuum, who has dedicated himself for well over a decade to making sure that this book would finally appear in English. Himself a theologian and scholar, he has become a family friend, celebrating Pesach Seders at my parents' home with our friends and family for many years. His devotion to the book has stemmed from his conviction that it is, as he writes, "the greatest work in rabbinics in the 20th century" and the "greatest book I've been associated with in my 31 years in publishing." For your gratifying words and unwavering fidelity to this project, Frank, we thank you.

SUSANNAH HESCHEL
Eli Black Associate Professor of Jewish Studies
Dartmouth College

PREFACE AND ACKNOWLEDGMENTS

Genesis of This Translation

I don't know exactly when I first became aware of Abraham Joshua Heschel's wide-ranging and ambitious work *Torah min Hashamayim Ba-Aspaklaria shel Hadorot* (henceforth *TMH*), of which the present volume is a translation. During my rabbinic training at Jewish Theological Seminary (JTS), it was never assigned, nor was it even mentioned, as far as I can recollect. This, despite the fact that in those days, the seminary's rabbinical curriculum was excessively focused on rabbinic literature and *TMH* set out to explicate and interpret that literature. I shall not speculate directly on why that was so but shall for the present simply note how peculiar that seems to me today. In any event, sometime after I began teaching at JTS (in 1976), I did become aware of the existence of this work (only two of its three volumes had been published by that time), although it still had a minimal impact on me and figured not at all in my teaching.

During the 1980s, I was asked to give a morning Torah lesson at the annual meeting of the Jewish Educators' Assembly. Again, for reasons that I cannot today reconstruct, the assignment somehow sent me to *TMH*, and I based the lesson on a section of the second chapter of the first volume, a section that deals with the phenomenon of rabbinic exegesis that strays far from the plain meaning of the scriptural text. Heschel's exposition here was an eye-opener for me, but not because it contained·references or ideas that I had not seen before (although it did that as well). It was noteworthy, rather, because it identified the existence of this kind of far-flung exegesis—something that every student of Talmud and halakhic Midrash considered to be second nature and one of the basic facts of Jewish intellectual life—to be a puzzle and indeed to be at the crux of the problem of how to understand what Jacob Neusner has called the "myth of the dual Torah."[1] As it turned out, this section of *TMH* was an eye-opener not only to me but to my audience of educators as well, and for weeks afterwards I received comments and requests relating to this lesson and the source from which it came. Trusting my own instincts, and especially those of the professional educators who clearly thought this material to be of enormous conceptual and pedagogic use to them, I decided that this

---

[1] The "dual Torah" refers here to the idea that there is a Written Torah and an Oral Torah. But how these two are related, and if they are in fact a continuum, is both a historical and a theological problem.

mostly neglected work of Heschel's was something that needed to be resurrected and brought to a wider public. In the ensuing years, I began to use it in teaching rabbinic theology at JTS, and rabbinical students invariably had the same reaction, something along the lines of, "Where has this book been all my life, and why has no one insisted that I read it before now?" The idea of doing a translation was born, daunting as it seemed. I had translated a few sections both for the Educators' Assembly and for my students, and it was no simple task (more on this below). But the project came to seem more and more like an obligation.

It was not until 1992 that I was able to get started with any kind of momentum on this project, the difficulty and scope of which I consistently underestimated. By then, the third and final volume had appeared (it was published in 1990 by JTS), and the original was now more or less complete. And so I began.

I was not working in a vacuum. Heschel had published the first volume in 1962, and the second in 1965, both with Soncino Press. During the 1970s, two rabbis, Max Gelb and Max Routtenberg, had lovingly worked on a translation of parts of the two volumes that had appeared. These two scholars had since passed away, and I had their preliminary translation in front of me. It was clear that, although it was for the most part accurate, and although it had a fairly nice style to it, it could not suffice as a vehicle through which to bring *TMH* to a wider readership. For one thing, although *TMH* certainly needed some editorial shortening for the English reader, the Gelb-Routtenberg translation often excised parts that were, in my judgment, crucial for an understanding of Heschel's argument. Second, it also tended to translate Heschel into an idiom and a cadence more familiar to contemporary English prose. This is a subtle and vexing point in translations. On the one hand, one must respect the habits, styles, and expectations of the intended reader, but on the other, form and content are not always neatly separable; and it seemed to me that Heschel, who had written deliberately not in a modern Hebrew idiom but in the thick, metaphor-laden, and free-associational style of rabbinic Hebrew (what is called in Hebrew *leshon hakhamim,* "the language of the Sages"), did so precisely so that the rhetorical form would lead us into the minds of the Sages. Thus, a translation had to try to capture that style without becoming opaque to the modern English reader. Third, missing from Gelb's and Routtenberg's work was any apparatus of commentary that would assist the English reader in following Heschel's intent and in understanding his many learned allusions. Those allusions, a Heschelian trademark, were sometimes stylistic flourishes (though even then, very instructive ones), but often they were quite central to Heschel's point and needed to be flagged for the reader of the translation, even if they couldn't be captured (as they rarely could) by the translation itself.[2] Finally, the Gelb-Routtenberg translation covered only about half of the first two volumes and did not have the third (then unpublished) volume at all.

---

[2] One example of this: in chapter 6, Heschel is discussing the doctrine of divine participation in the pains and travails of human beings, which emerged during the late first and early second century. In the process he gives the essence of this doctrine as follows: "One who asks: 'Why is this exile come

For all these reasons, a new translation would be required. However, out of deep respect for the work of these two rabbis and scholars, both of whom I had been privileged to know, I made commitments to Mrs. Sylvia Heschel that I would try as much as possible to build on the Gelb-Routtenberg translation, where it existed and where that was feasible, and that their efforts would be duly acknowledged. Their work has rarely been incorporated into this translation unaltered. However, even though it cannot be visible to the reader, it has played a role in the formation of parts of the first twenty or so chapters of the present work, and it has often been a silent advisor on what Heschel's intent might have been. Their devotion to bringing this important work to as many eyes, minds, and hearts as possible is herein gratefully acknowledged, as it has been in the dedication of this volume.

Formal and Structural Characteristics of
Torah min Hashamayim

I shall here reflect briefly on four elements of the form and structure of this work. The first concerns the language of the work. Heschel wrote in five languages—English, German, Yiddish, Polish, and Hebrew. The works most familiar to contemporary readers who are not specialists were written in the first two of these languages. But why did Heschel write *Torah min Hashamayim* in Hebrew? It cannot be a sufficient answer to say that the Rabbis of whom he was writing used Hebrew. The prophets spoke a much more beautiful Hebrew, and yet when Heschel wrote about them, it was in German (*Die Prophetie*), and later in English (*The Prophets*). Heschel does not tell us directly why he wrote *TMH* in Hebrew, but two answers suggest themselves. One is that Heschel was writing as a virtuoso of rabbinic literature, not only as a theologian; as such he wished to present this opus in *leshon hakhamim,* the traditional language for works of commentary on the Talmud and Midrash.[3] Second, and potentially much more important, is the

---

upon us?' (should be answered with) 'Upon *us* and not upon *Him*?' One who removes God from the community has denied the very essence of the faith." That Heschel is paraphrasing a well-known passage from the Passover Haggadah here (the question and answer of the Wicked Son) would scarcely escape the Hebrew reader, but it might well escape the English reader of this translation. Even if he/she were familiar with the Haggadah (as most surely are), the translation here might not match the translation of the Haggadah with which the reader is familiar and thus might not ring the associational bell. But, as the translator's note in chapter 6 remarks, the reference to the Haggadah is not incidental to a full understanding here, for while the Haggadah establishes the centrality of horizontal solidarity among members of the people Israel past and present, the doctrine under discussion established as equally central the vertical solidarity of humans with God and God with humans. No translation without annotation could make this critical interpretive point. Other examples abound.

[3] This holds true also in contemporary times, during and even after Heschel's day, as witnessed by the fact that Heschel's JTS colleagues in the Department of Talmud and Rabbinics published their works of commentary (such as Saul Lieberman's *Tosefta Ki-Feshutah,* David Halivni's *Meqorot U-Mesorot,* and many other monographs) in Hebrew.

idea alluded to above that language can play a critical and irreplaceable role in creating a cultural ambience. One could perhaps explicate some things about the intellectual achievements of the Rabbis in English (this translation project, after all, depends on that), but one cannot get the reader into the *processes,* the worldview of the Rabbis, without recourse to their language and its rhetorical conventions.

An example may serve to clarify this point. In *TMH,* Heschel often goes back and forth from one paragraph to the next, describing first the views of the school of Rabbi Ishmael on a certain issue and then the views of the school of Rabbi Akiva. There are occasions on which these "switchbacks" can go on for several pages. The effect of this, particularly when read in English translation, can be dizzying, as "on the one hand" and "on the other hand" alternate numerous times. Contemporary readers, especially English readers, would expect a fairly complete exposition of the views of one of these schools followed by an equally complete exposition of the rival's views. And that is exactly the point: the culture in which English readers live expects a full hearing for each side and then some kind of decision for one or the other based on the evidence. The very rhetoric of our language reinforces this cultural bias. Not so, however, in the culture of the Rabbis. It has been noted often that the Talmud, which abounds in the kind of alternating argument and dialogue that I have described, does not generally expect or provide clear, unequivocal resolutions to the questions it treats. The dialectical process seems more important, and the reader who is used to the style often feels invited not to choose sides but perhaps to attempt a synthesis among the various viewpoints presented.

Heschel spoke directly of rabbinic dialectic in *The Earth Is the Lord's* (1950). In the course of his paean to the faith of the Jews of Eastern Europe, Heschel takes up *pilpul* (dialectic) and what it signified about the hearts and minds of its practitioners. He concluded:

> They did not know how to take anything for granted. Everything had to have a reason, and they were more interested in reasons than in things. . . . It is easy to belittle such an attitude of mind and to call it unpractical, unworldly. But what is nobler than the unpractical spirit? The soul is sustained by the regard for that which transcends all immediate purposes. The sense of the transcendent is the heart of culture, the very essence of humanity. A civilization that is devoted exclusively to the utilitarian is at bottom not different from barbarism. The world is sustained by unworldliness.[4]

This illustrates well from his own writings a very significant sense in which language serves Heschel's strategy in *TMH,* for I contend that he is not asking us to choose between the two theological approaches that he persistently presents to us. Indeed, other formal features of this work (see below) suggest strongly that Heschel did not want to "choose sides" but rather to effect some synthesis for himself. But it is only the language of rabbinics, the kind of Hebrew that he uses in *TMH,* that can adequately bring the reader into that kind of intellectual orientation. This, as has been noted, also presents a formidable, if not insurmountable, challenge for any translator.

---

[4] A. J. Heschel, *The Earth Is the Lord's* (New York: H. Schumann, 1950), 54–55.

The second formal feature concerns Heschel's own poetic style, quite apart from the culture that he was describing. This is well known to readers of his English books, and one finds it in *TMH* as well. A Mormon philosopher I came to know twenty years ago was very taken with Heschel's work. In a letter he sent me after he began integrating some of Heschel's theology into his teaching at Brigham Young University, he noted that "Heschel sings rather than argues"—intending that assessment not pejoratively but descriptively. I can only hope that this translation of *TMH* will preserve some of that associational, alliterative poetic style. It is certainly there in the original.

Third, Heschel presents the reader of *TMH* with an abundance of dyads. We need look no further than some of the headings themselves: "Human Ways and Divine Ways," "The Fashion of Babylonia and the Fashion of the Land of Israel," "Is the Prophet a Partner or a Vessel?" The list goes on and on, and far beyond the mere headings. Dyads are so ubiquitous that they must signify something. My strong sense, as a careful reader of Heschel's works, is that we have here as well one of many windows into the deeper recesses of Heschel's thought. For example, volumes 2 (chapters 17–33) and 3 (chapters 34–41) are primarily a working out of the implications of two concepts that Heschel considered to be inverses living in tension: "The Heavenly Torah" (*Torah min Hashamayim*) and "The Torah is not in Heaven" (*Lo Bashamayim Hi*). Indeed, at the very beginning of chapter 34, he calls these two concepts "two mutually exclusive articles of faith." Most obviously of all, the *entire* work is presented to the reader as an intellectual biography and genealogy of Rabbi Akiva and Rabbi Ishmael, the two "fathers of the world," who are foils one for the other.

This dyadic quality of the work, when considered in tandem with Heschel's other works, gives us a strong hint that, in addition to everything else that Heschel sets out to accomplish in *TMH,* there is also a strong element of intellectual autobiography in it. Rivka Horwitz, in an early review of the first two volumes, put her finger on this: "Often . . . we have the sense that we are facing an impassioned poet who speaks of matters that tug at his own heartstrings."[5]

What are these matters? Perhaps the most central of Heschel's dyads comprises the immanent theology he associates with Rabbi Akiva and the transcendent theology he associates with Rabbi Ishmael. Now the immanent God of Akiva was unquestionably the world in which he grew up. It was the world of *The Earth Is the Lord's.* It was the world of the Ba'al Shem Tov (the founder of the Hasidism into which Heschel was born), of the palpable nearness of God. It was the world that manifestly felt the eternal, all-encompassing truth of Torah, there to be discovered through esoteric exegesis, at which the kabbalists and the Hasidim excelled.

But the transcendent God of Ishmael, on the other hand, was unquestionably the world to which he moved—Vilna, Berlin, Cincinnati, New York. It was the world of Maimonides, as Heschel saw that world. And the neat, almost obsessive categorization of the two major trunk lines in rabbinic and postrabbinic Jewish thought is a chart of his inner struggle with these two worlds. That Akiva's world was his mother's milk, as it

---

[5] Rivka Horwitz, "Iyyun Hadash Bemakhshevet ha-Tannaim," *Molad* 23 (1965): 242.

were, accounts for his confident statement that Akiva had won the hearts and minds of Israel. How could it seem otherwise for a son of Medzibozh (the Ba'al Shem Tov's town)? But the fact that he had moved on to another world also accounts for his *wistful* description of that victory:

> "All depends on luck, even the Torah scroll in the Sanctuary." And lady luck did not smile on Rabbi Ishmael. His hammer reached the anvil all right, but the sound somehow did not reach the ears. He and Rabbi Akiva came along at the same time, but one soon began to gain in power at the expense of the other.[6]

These are words that betray a desire to see an imbalance redressed, to make the fight within Heschel himself fair, without a predetermined outcome. Thus, we have the widely noted "tilt" toward Ishmael in this work. It was a way for Heschel to understand and present his own odyssey. It was not a simple resolution that he was after, however, but a deeper understanding of the tension and its creative possibilities.

This brings us to the fourth formal characteristic of *TMH* that needs to be noted: its often open-ended quality. Neither in its long introduction (chapter 1 in this translation), nor in any of its chapters, nor in the last words of its last chapter does it reach a cadence in which there is a real resolution. Chapter 1 ends on a very enigmatic note: Heschel, having described what he saw as the victory over time of Rabbi Akiva and his theology, notes that the Ishmaelian theology did not die out by any means and that traces of it can be found throughout the Middle Ages. There the long introduction ends, seemingly in mid-sentence, certainly in mid-thought. Most of Heschel's chapters end in questions that prepare us for the stage of inquiry in the subsequent chapter, but hardly wrap up and clinch a thesis in a neat way. Indeed, the end of the work, chapter 41, is almost anticlimactic. Coming shortly after chapters in which Heschel struggles, again indecisively, with the tension between *ancient* as "spiritually more authentic" and *modern* as "intellectually more comprehensive," this "final" chapter simply deals with issues in interpersonal relationships as seen by the Rabbis.

Now to be sure, the third and final volume was not prepared for publication by Heschel himself. For more than fifteen years following his death in December 1972, material that he had planned to include in a third volume sat in manuscript, until it was finally compiled and readied for publication by Rabbi David Feldman. We don't know exactly how Heschel would have brought this work to a close. Moreover, there were persistent rumors that Heschel had more material for the third volume, material that carried over his dyadic analysis into medieval exegesis. He had published an article in the Hebrew periodical *Hadoar*, the caption to which noted that it was among material to be included in a third volume of *TMH*. The content of that article is not to be found in the third volume, nor is any of the other writing that was said to be awaiting editing and publication. A search of Heschel's papers at his home turned none of it up.

It is thus impossible to speak with confidence of the "end" of this work, but it is thoroughly in keeping with everything else about *TMH* (and about the rabbinic literature that it mimics in style) that there be neither an obvious starting point nor a clear end-

---

[6] *TMH,* end of chapter 1.

ing point. In the review cited above, Horwitz also noted about *TMH* that "the dualism maintains itself to the very end of the work." Perhaps most telling of all was an observation by Tamar Kohlberg, in a master's thesis on Heschel and *TMH*, that "these tensions form the foundation of the mode of paradox that characterizes religious existence."[7] Certainly this was true for Heschel, who in *TMH* displayed for us, but did not resolve, his own internal tensions and contradictions. The reader should be advised that Heschel almost certainly intended to be holding up a large mirror for all of us in the process.

Notes on the Content of *Torah min Hashamayim*

For the most part, the content of this long work will speak for itself as the chapters unfold and as prefaces and footnotes guide the reader. Just a few preliminary observations are in order here.

First, *TMH* can be seen on one level as Heschel's contribution to an understanding of Rabbinic Judaism. Indeed, all three volumes bore English title pages that read "Theology of Ancient Judaism," hardly a translation of *Torah min Hashamayim Ba-Aspaklaria shel Hadorot,* but one way of viewing what Heschel was doing here. But if he was doing theology, it was in a mode very unusual for him. He clearly went out of his way to display his erudition and virtuosity in rabbinics, and the abundance of footnotes that he provided here, which range not only over classical rabbinic literature but also over medieval commentaries and codes, ethical literature, kabbalistic works, and works of modern historical scholarship, is highly unusual for his theological works. The notes are a curriculum in and of themselves, and no one who reads *TMH* can doubt that Heschel, in addition to everything else that he embodied and gave to the world, was also very much a master of Rabbinic Judaism.

In another respect, however, the English title pages were, and are, misleading. For it is not just the intellectual and spiritual world of the Rabbis fifteen hundred and more years ago that Heschel is after here. Repeatedly throughout this work, he hints at, and sometimes makes virtually explicit, contemporary issues and theological problems that he considers to be both the direct descendants of the issues the classical Rabbis faced and still very much part of our own time. For example, in chapter 1, Heschel's long introduction to this work, he simply comes out and says the following:

> Intellectual debates and psychological rumblings are the stuff of every generation. Spiritual problems continually shed forms and take on new ones. Before you can understand the intellectual movements of recent times, you must inquire into the chain of tradition that precedes them.

To take another example, in chapter 6 Heschel discusses what he considers to be the radical ideas about God's empathy and vulnerability that he associates with Rabbi Akiva, and then he addresses the reader with these words:

---

[7] Tamar Kohlberg, "Bein Musar le-Teologia be-*Torah min Hashamayim Ba-aspaklaria Shel Hadorot, Da'at* 29 (Summer 1992).

> The Rabbis in the generation we are considering experienced things which others have not seen: the sacking of Jerusalem, the humiliation of the House of Israel, and the profanation of the Holy Name in the sight of the whole world. Stormy eras filled with human agony also harbor troubling thoughts; even the pillars of heaven shudder. And a nation which has been belittled by the nations of the world is likely to verge on belittling the great presumptions: that God is merciful and compassionate, and that God is the great and the powerful.

Can a readership belonging to a generation that has seen or at least heard testimony of Auschwitz ("things which others have not seen") have any doubt that Heschel, in addition to doing rabbinic theology is here also doing post-Shoah theology?

Indeed, we need go no further than the opening words of chapter 1, in which a dichotomy and an antagonism between Halakhah (legal materials) and Aggadah (narrative and theological materials) is set up for the duration of this work. The truth is, *TMH* is about a dichotomy within a dichotomy. The main split in this work is generally taken, with obvious justification, to be the divergences between the schools of Rabbi Ishmael and Rabbi Akiva (more on this presently). Although these schools had their differences in halakhic exegesis, the bifurcation between them that really matters to Heschel in *TMH* takes place within the realm of Aggadah. And it is part of Heschel's task to elevate the study of Aggadah, rehabilitate it, and give it the dignity and sense of gravity that he believed Jewish theology should have in the late twentieth century. In doing so he had to square off against forces that did not see the theological enterprise in the same light he did. Thus, polemical statements such as the following from chapter 1 have also to be understood in a broader and more personal context:

> Wherever you find disparagement of the Aggadah, there you find also religious impoverishment. In the circles of the modern Jewish Enlightenment, too, the scoffers abounded. They did so not because they found its metaphors strange or its maxims outlandish, but because the very essence of its enterprise, that is, treating the fundamental problems of life through the eyes of religious faith, was foreign to those people.

Once again, it is not just the Enlightenment scholars of the nineteenth century whom Heschel is taking to task here but also their intellectual descendants, people among whom he worked, wrote, and taught. So ancient theology it may be, but *TMH* is much more, and it carries within it the kind of drama and immediacy that well-written contemporary theology and spiritual autobiography should have.

Having mentioned now several times the Ishmael–Akiva debate, to which Heschel gives such great prominence throughout *TMH*, a few words must be said about this as well. Heschel may, as noted, set out here to establish his bona fides as an aficionado of rabbinic literature, but he certainly does not set out to do meticulous history. Whether the historical Ishmael in the second century actually said things that are attributed to him by tradition is not Heschel's principal, or even significant, interest. Whether or not every person whom tradition has identified as a disciple of Akiva was in fact schooled in a point of view and a methodology stemming from the historical Akiva is likewise not Heschel's primary interest. In fact, it is hardly of interest at all. This is not to denigrate historical inquiry, but simply to note that Heschel's task here is defined by him as uncovering the major theological modes and patterns of thought that are discernible in the rabbinic world. If it is convenient to associate them, especially because tradition left that door open, with particular personalities and the schools that they undoubtedly influenced, all the better, for we then have a simple and suggestive vocabulary with which to refer to these theologies.

It is important to point this out, because Heschel was often criticized for such sins as an uncritical acceptance of the theories, learned as they were, of nineteenth-century scholars of rabbinics, or of a selective use of rabbinic sources, citing only those that tended to support the identifications of certain positions with the Sage or the school that Heschel proposed. There is no doubt in my mind that Heschel overreached somewhat in this work; that is, he often attempted to have it both ways. He would lead the reader down the admittedly dramatic path of believing that the actual thoughts and struggles of second-century giants were being brought to light, and would at the same time issue caveats such as this one: "sometimes we find the two intellectual subsets included side by side, or intertwined, within a single method. Sometimes one approach appears to have been subsumed by the other, and sometimes they have been synthesized, so that it seems that two rival ways of grasping the world can somehow co-exist within the same mind."[8] Criticisms that focus on the shortcomings of Heschel's more dramatic identifications of certain ideas with the historical Ishmael and the historical Akiva have, therefore, some basis in Heschel's own presentation.

However, there is equally no doubt in my mind that those criticisms miss the point of this work. When Heschel used the traditional designation *avot ha-olam* ("Fathers of the World" or, more correctly, "Fathers of the Age") for Ishmael and Akiva, he was, I am utterly convinced, making another of his ever-present plays on words. *Av* can mean "paradigm" in Hebrew, and *olam* can mean "eternity." For Heschel, Ishmael and Akiva were of interest not as individuals who were the leaders of their world or of their age, but rather only as stand-ins for what are eternal paradigms of religious thought that sometimes war with one another, sometimes complement one another, and always challenge and refine one another. That *must* be kept in mind if this work is to be understood as Heschel himself did. Elsewhere Heschel wrote of his desire not to do "theology" in the classic sense of systematic demonstrations of religious truths, but rather to do "depth theology," that is, an inquiry that begins with the phenomenon of religious belief and seeks to create empathy and identification with it. Similarly, in *TMH*, Heschel does not set out to pinpoint with the historian's precision the genesis of elements of rabbinic theology; rather, he takes those elements as given and invites the reader to see them over and over again, refracted through the generations right down to the present moment.[9] Each reader will, of necessity, judge for himself or herself how Heschel succeeds in creating this empathy for the "eternal paradigms" that he calls Ishmael and Akiva.

---

[8] See chapter 1, pp. 32–42, and the editor's footnote there.

[9] "As refracted through the generations" is actually the literal meaning of the phrase *ba-aspaklaria shel hadorot*, which appears in the title of this work.

Finally, it should be noted that this is no theoretical exercise for Heschel. It is, rather, theology with an urgent practical agenda. Here I shall translate two brief excerpts from a short introduction that Heschel wrote for volume 2 of *TMH* (it does not appear in the body of this translation):

> Is it really appropriate to say "all is well with me" when contempt outside the fold and indifference in the inner circles take their toll, so that there is no peace? Look, and you'll see how powerless we have become to prevent wholesale loss of faith.

> Two have hold of a Tallit—the strict, austere one, and the cynical argumentative one. One says that doubt itself is forbidden by the Torah, and the other vows not to accept any dogma.

Heschel here states openly that his aim in this work is to recover a richness of thought, through the dialectic of the Rabbis' theological paradigms, that would expand Jewish idea space and make room for greater participation in the great conversations about God, faith, and religion that took place in the classical academies. Heschel wrote to expand his own, and his readers', very existence.[10]

What was the Tallit of which Heschel spoke? Classically, the word meant "cloak," and Heschel's formulation here recalls a halakhic rule known to every beginner in rabbinic literature: when two people claim ownership of the same cloak and no other evidence is present, each must swear that he/she owns not less than one half of it, and then they divide the cloak. But Heschel's actual meaning is quite different. The Tallit is literally the prayer shawl, which contains the fringes at the corners that stand for the commandments. Two types argue over those commandments: one takes a rigid, legalistic approach that brooks no compromise, and the other sees no value in what cannot be proven. Heschel looked around and saw two different species of contempt for theology: one was embodied in what he often called "religious behaviorism," according to which the objective certainties of Halakhah were the pinnacle of religious life, and the other was embodied in a philosophical dismissal of the theological poetics of Aggadah. The two types were fighting over Judaism, and Heschel seems to say that each side will have to yield some of its claimed certainty by swearing only to have not less than half of the truth. The remainder of religious truth will have to come out in the less certain paths of Aggadah, of theological reflection.[11] So did Heschel take on, here and elsewhere in *TMH*,

---

[10] This formulation is taken from an article by Irene Harvey entitled "Doubling the Space of Existence," in *Deconstruction and Philosophy*, ed. John Sallis (Chicago: University of Chicago Press, 1987). Harvey quotes Jean Jacques Rousseau (in *Reveries of a Solitary Walker*) as saying that writing will serve to "double the space of my existence." For Heschel, the very act of recreating and putting into words the eternal debates would create what Harvey describes as an "inflation of affect," an awareness of the productivity of the debates, which would expand one's existence by at least a factor of two. *TMH* was in that way intended to expand our theological field of vision.

[11] The form in which Heschel makes this point is, of course, highly significant, because he has taken a halakhic rule and explicated its language so as to make it express a much more global and far-reaching theological point. Halakhah, which often claims hegemony in Judaism, has thus had its very language and vocabulary made into a servant of Aggadah. This technique is employed by Heschel in many places in *TMH*.

fundamentalisms of religion and philosophy and attempt to offer readers a path for achieving faith as Jews always did, by creating a synthesis out of competing impulses.

Or, as he says even more trenchantly in chapter 36, there can be a "covenant between the opposites."[12] Rationality and esotericism compete over the Tallit, but if one is denied, the other does not win; rather, the totality of faith loses. For "one who is blind in one eye does not make the pilgrimage."[13] Only the shift of perspective from the Ishmaelian paradigm to the Akivan paradigm, only that theological parallax effect can give rise to a religious consciousness worthy of the name. To shut one eye is to fail to make a pilgrimage, not to ancient Jerusalem but here and now, to a place of religious vision. And so, seen in this way, *TMH* is, in addition to many other things, an impassioned argument for theological pluralism.

Notes on Translating *Torah min Hashamayim*

Robert Frost is said to have defined poetry as "what gets lost in translation." If this is true, then undertaking a translation of a work such as *TMH* is fraught with danger, for all that we have said until now makes clear how much of Heschel's exposition is inseparable from his poetics. I felt this danger constantly in this project, and it often led to complete rewritings of whole sections. In the end, the importance of the translation outweighed the challenges, however formidable.

Nicholas de Lange aptly described some of the traditional approaches to the enterprise of translation, and it is worth rehearsing them briefly here.[14] Translators have been looked upon as *copyists*, as persons who are to render the original faithfully into the target language and not put themselves into the text. The flaws in this approach are obvious. For one thing, words are far too complex even in the original language to be susceptible to an unambiguous mapping into another language. In addition, there is the matter of capturing not only the meanings of the words but the cultural bells that they ring when put into combination. For example, the daily Jewish liturgy makes direct reference to the Jew's obligation to worship God "*erev va-voker ve-tzahorayim.*" How shall the Hebrew phrase (taken from the Book of Daniel) be translated? Literally, it means "evening, morning, and afternoon." As a description of liturgical sequence, this rendering would be correct, since the Jewish day begins at dusk. However, if the phrase is taken to be an idiom that expresses a joyful carrying out of the obligation to worship at all times, it might better be rendered into English as "morning, noon, and night," for

---

[12] A play in Hebrew on the "covenant between the pieces" that God cut with Abraham as depicted in Genesis 15.

[13] The phrase in its original setting is, again, a halakhic rule that has to do with who is exempt from making the thrice-yearly pilgrimage to Jerusalem. But Heschel will again detach it from its original context and have it make a theological point. See chapter 36 below.

[14] Nicholas de Lange, "Reflections of a Translator," Rabbi Louis Feinberg Memorial Lecture in Jewish Studies, University of Cincinnati, March 1993.

that is an English idiom that expresses the same meaning. There is no correct answer here, and the point is that there is no such thing as a unique faithful copy.

Occasionally, felicitous translations that seemingly accomplish both copying and good style fall into the translator's lap. Such was the case on several occasions in this work. One example comes from the end of chapter 1, where Heschel compares the fame of Rabbi Akiva to "the sun rising in might" (a phrase lifted from the Song of Deborah in Judges 5), and the fame of Rabbi Ishmael to a "*kokhav lekhet.*" *Kokhav lekhet* means a "planet" (because *kokhav* means "star," and *lekhet* denotes movement), but it would hardly be good English style to contrast "the sun rising in might" to "a planet"—nor would it be intelligible to the reader. Fortunately, the word *kokhav* has as one of its various meanings the planet Mercury, and so the translation became: "in every generation [Rabbi Akiva's] fame shines as the sun rising in might. Rabbi Ishmael's fame has been fleeting and mercurial . . . ." The translator here is no mere copyist but exercises some creativity and puts some of his or her own style into the translation.

This more or less disposes of another characterization of translators—as servants who should do their work but never have their presence sensed. The kind of creative solution just described necessarily makes the translator's presence known, at least as a distinctive style develops over the translation. Yet creativity can go only so far. I have seen beautiful renditions of psalms and prayers that are liturgical creations in their own right and are indubitably based on themes in the original but nevertheless have had their connection to the original language all but severed. So I am drawn to what de Lange himself advocates, which is the view of the translator as analogous to a performing musician. A work of art must be brought to life for a contemporary audience, and both the original composer's intentions and desires and the audience's capacities and culture must be respected.

Who is the audience here? This, too, is complex. For one thing, I translate here for scholars who do not have complete, or even partial, control of Hebrew. But I also translate for rabbinic colleagues who have access to the Hebrew but who need to translate Heschel's arguments for their constituents who are not Hebraically trained. In addition, I translate for laypeople who are deeply interested in Jewish theology and who are willing to follow an extended argument such as Heschel offers. This complexity is another factor that makes translation choices difficult. And it did one other thing: Heschel's work, as noted above, contained many learned footnotes. How much depth should be retained in the translation of those footnotes? There was no easy or obvious answer to this question, and it was inevitably a compromise under which multiple sources that essentially duplicated the original citation were generally omitted, and excurses in the footnotes into issues that were strictly tangential to the argument in the text were most often left out as well. So the scholar has a little less than what Heschel meant to offer, but the layperson has more than he or she is likely to pursue.

At any rate, given that I did not have the privilege of being able to consult the author whose work is being translated here, it is my fervent hope that I have been a good performing musician here and that readers of all stripes will be able to hear Heschel's strains throughout.

The Structure of This Edition

For this translation, *TMH* has been subjected to what was deemed to be an essential amount of editing to remove what would, in English, be considered redundancy. It is a well-known phenomenon that Hebrew welcomes repetition and parallelism in ways that English often abhors. Here, too, some balance was called for. The language of rabbinics requires some of the use of repetition and the piling up of proof texts from Scripture. Leaving all this out would have obscured the gateway into rabbinic thought that the language is meant to provide. On the other hand, it was often possible and desirable to keep the repetitions and proof texts to a minimum. Likewise, there were many occasions on which Heschel simply repeated himself, and often those multiply occurring paragraphs could be reduced to one occurrence without loss of clarity or style. In addition, there were instances in which some transposing of material in the original made the flow of the argument clearer, and that liberty was taken as well.

Every effort was made to ensure the accuracy of Heschel's footnotes, many of which were not accurate (often because of typographical errors) in the original.

Finally, I have provided, in addition to this preface, introductions to nearly all of the forty-one chapters, in which the reader is given some essential orientation to what Heschel will be covering in the coming chapter and why. Running throughout the translation is a second level of footnotes that contain my commentary on Heschel's intent, explicate certain concepts and provide some ideas that Heschel simply assumes, and bring features of Heschel's poetics and wordplays to the reader's attention. My introductory comments and notes are set in the typeface of this preface to distinguish them from Heschel's material.

Acknowledgments

This has been a labor of love from the beginning, but it has also depended on the support, encouragement, and direct assistance of many people, whom I take pleasure in thanking.

From the fall of 1992 to the spring of 1994, I benefited from the academic facilities and ambience of Fordham University, where I was a visiting scholar and where this work really began in earnest. The gracious hospitality of many at Fordham is deeply appreciated.

Dr. Ismar Schorsch, Chancellor of Jewish Theological Seminary, provided sabbatical time at the early stages of this project, the value of which he continually endorsed, and I am grateful for his support and encouragement. Needless to say, my long-standing relationship with the seminary and its faculty, and all that I have learned there over the years, appears on virtually every page of this translation and commentary.

Rabbi Wolfe Kelman, of blessed memory, urged me very early on to undertake this translation; and even after his passing, I often heard his voice spurring me on. He is sorely missed, but his contribution is gratefully acknowledged.

Mrs. Sylvia Heschel early on gave her enthusiastic approval to my plans and gave me access to Dr. Heschel's papers in what was an unsuccessful search, alluded to earlier, for additional material that was to have become part of *TMH*. I hope that the opening of *TMH* to a wider audience will bring her satisfaction as well.

Frank Oveis of Continuum understood from the outset the need for a new translation and has been an extraordinarily patient publisher because of his belief in the importance of this product.

My community, Temple Israel Center of White Plains, has not only generously understood my need to take time to do this work and taken pride in seeing it progress, but above all has provided me with many models of educated laypeople for whom this work is, in part, intended. I owe many levels of growth and understanding to what I have learned from my years as Rabbi of this wonderful synagogue. I have also been conscious throughout those years that I am a successor once removed of Rabbi Max Gelb, and thus Temple Israel has two shares in this book.

Rabbi Leonard Levin has been an invaluable partner in this work. He took pains to check all notes and references, made and implemented wise suggestions concerning style, cared for the maintenance of uniformity, designed and collected data for several appendices that will aid the reader enormously, added some of the "second-level footnotes," and, after quickly learning the approaches and methods I had adopted, reworked some of the Gelb-Routtenberg translation and translated blocks of untouched material himself. His collaboration was especially appropriate because Max Routtenberg was his uncle and a major inspiration in his decision to go to rabbinical school, and thus in our having met. It is a pleasure to acknowledge with appreciation his part in this work.

My wife, Amy, and my children, Ethan, Becky, and Micah, and more recently my daughter-in-law, Ariela, have supported me in countless ways, ranging from prodding, to substantive discussions, to empathy when work was slow, and most of all, to time and attention lost to them. My thanks to them, like my love, cannot be quantified, and my prayer is that they will find the product of all those hours to be worthy of their sacrifices.

Much work on this translation and commentary was done over a number of summers in a very beloved setting, the ocean beach in Corolla, North Carolina. The pristine beauty of the sky and sands and the awesome power of the ocean reminded me constantly of Heschel's unique understanding of the role of wonder and "radical amazement" in the religious consciousness, and provided yet another confluence of form and content that characterizes so much of Heschel's work.

The finishing touches finally came in another cherished setting, along the Mediterranean coast of Israel, during a sabbatical from my synagogue. The aura in that place includes not only the physical loveliness of the sea but also the inspiring story of the human, and Jewish, spirit.

To the Creator of all such beauty, and of us all, goes the ultimate debt of gratitude.

TEL AVIV
SIVAN 5763

INTRODUCTION

Human Ways and Divine Ways

The Torah stands on a dual foundation: on Halakhah and Aggadah.[1] The Tannaim already distinguished between the two and thereby recognized Aggadah as an important and unique vocation of Torah. Although it is difficult to define precisely, we can infer much about Aggadah's essence and unique qualities from the ways in which the Tannaim, as well as the Amoraim, characterized it.

Halakhah and Aggadah were each praised in discrete and disjoint ways. "Halakhot constitute the body[2] of Torah."[1] "Not a day passes that the Holy and Blessed One does not innovate some *halakhah* in the heavenly court."[2] According to Rabbi Johanan ben Dahabai, "Whoever says, 'this halakhah does not seem right,' forfeits his share in the world to come."[3][3]

---

[1] Sifre Ha'azinu 317.   [2] Genesis Rabbah 49:2.   [3] ARN A 27.

This chapter is Heschel's own introduction to this work. As such, it did not seem to require any introductory comments by the translator/editor.

[1] Halakhah is those parts of Torah—be it the Pentateuch, or the body of (originally) oral teaching contained in Talmud and Midrash—that are legal in nature. Halakhah can mean the entire corpus of legal material or one particular religious law. The plural halakhot refers to a group of more than one religious law. Aggadah is those parts of the Torah—written or oral—that are narrative in nature. "Narrative"—the best linguistic equivalent of Aggadah—here is meant to include also purported biography, theology, exhortation, and folklore.

Heschel's introductory statement echoes the saying of Simeon the Righteous: "The world rests on a triple foundation: on Torah, on service of God, on deeds of love" (Mishnah Avot 1:2).

[2] The Hebrew here is *guf*. It is sometimes translated in this context as "essence," but Heschel apparently means to suggest to us the more literal meaning, "body," so as to convey the double idea that Halakhah is the body of Torah, that is, its most concrete and immediate form, and that it has a counterpart, which is the "soul" of Torah. This second idea, the body/soul duality in which Aggadah is, by implication, the more important and enduring, was certainly not the intention of the author of the Sifre from which this quotation is taken. It is, however, already found in prerabbinic Jewish thought in the writings of Philo of Alexandria.

[3] Since Heschel has appealed to the idea of *halakhot* being the *body* of Torah, it is particularly apt to quote this statement of Johanan ben Dahabai (a fourth-generation Tanna). For Mishnah Sanhedrin 10:1 tells us that one who denies that the Torah teaches bodily immortality forfeits his share in the world to come. If *halakhot* are bodies of Torah, then it is only fitting that the failure to acknowledge

In Halakhah you find power and might, while in Aggadah there is grace and love.[4] Halakhah has a voice of power—it breaks cedars—while Aggadah is the still, small voice. Halakhah is like a rush of mighty waters; Aggadah, the spirit of God hovering over the waters. Halakhah is the line of defense for the person whose wisdom exceeds his or her works; Aggadah lifts one up above all works.[5] Halakhah is the yoke of the commandments; Aggadah is the yoke of the kingdom of heaven. Halakhah presents the letter of the law; Aggadah brings us the spirit of the law.[6] Halakhah deals with matters that are quantifiable; Aggadah speaks of matters of conscience. Rabbi Isaac ben Phinehas[7] taught: "Whoever possesses knowledge of midrash but not of Halakhah has not tasted the flavor of wisdom; whoever possesses knowledge of Halakhah but not of midrash has not tasted the flavor of fear of sin."[4]

Halakhah speaks in precise terms, while Aggadah speaks poetry. Halakhah is rooted in tradition, while Aggadah is the flourishing of the heart. In Aggadah, a person can easily reveal non-normative views.[8] Perhaps that is why this difference of opinion: One says, "The Merciful desires, above all, the heart." Yet another says, "Do not stray after your heart." Halakhah is fixity and Aggadah is intention.[9] The former says "make your Torah fixed"[10]: "Tanna de-be Eliyahu: Whoever studies *halakhot*

---

[4] ARN A 29.

---

the eternal correctness ("it does not seem right") of *halakhot* would result—via an extension of Sanhedrin 10:1—in a forfeiture of the world to come.

[4] The term here is *hesed*, which is notoriously difficult to translate into English. The oft-employed "loving-kindness" suggests little of substance, and the biblical meaning, to which "keeping faith" is closest, does not begin to capture the multiplicity of meanings that the word took on in postbiblical usage. "Love" will do here to suggest the gentle and accommodating nature of Aggadah.

[5] Another Heschelian play on words. The Hebrew is a rabbinic/liturgical phrase in which *God* is depicted as being exalted above all *creatures*. But the Hebrew for "creatures," *ma'asim*, can also mean, as in biblical Hebrew, "works"—hence the usage here to talk of *people* being lifted up by Aggadah beyond the (mere) realm of works.

[6] Hebrew *lifenim mishurat hadin*, literally, "inside the line of the law." The image is intended to convey a flexibility in which the rigid, objective boundaries defined by Halakhah are softened and sometimes altered, so as to promote a value that may not be subject to objective definition. The term is used primarily in relationships among human beings, to teach the necessity, on occasion, of allowing another person more of a claim on oneself than legally defined boundaries would permit. Here Heschel is using the idea in a broader sense, to suggest a spiritual, and thus somewhat subjective, dimension to religion.

[7] Heschel here identifies him as one of the late Tannaim, but he (or another teacher of this name?) is identified in BT Pesahim 114a with Rabbi Isaac ben Aha, who was a disciple of Rabbi Johanan in the third century.

[8] A delightful play on words. "Non-normative" here translates *shelo kahalakhah*, which literally means "unlike Halakhah"!

[9] This is the dichotomy between *keva* and *kavvanah*, to which Heschel famously appeals in his discussions of Jewish prayer. It is the dichotomy between structure and spontaneity and the tension between them, which Heschel also sees in the relationship between Halakhah and Aggadah.

[10] Advice attributed to Shammai in Mishnah Avot 1:15.

each day is assured of the world to come."[5][11] The latter says, "Do not make your prayer fixed, but rather a plea for mercy and a supplication before God."[12] And Aggadah is like prayer. "Dorshei Reshumot[13] expounded: Do you desire to know the One who spoke and the world came into being? Study Aggadah, for through it you will come to know the One who spoke and the world came into being, and to cling to God's ways."[6] Life's blessing is to be found not in that which can be weighed and measured but rather in that which is hidden from view.

Now since Halakhah constitutes the body of Torah, the survival of Israel's Torah is due to the Halakhah and its structure of mitzvot and good deeds. All the songs and poetry, the philosophy and the theology, are indebted to Halakhah for their endurance. Aggadah is thus inextricably linked with Halakhah and cannot survive without it. Aggadah is like a flame whose existence depends on the glowing coals of Halakhah. Whoever seeks to separate them extinguishes the light of Judaism in the flame. In sum, one who says "I hold only Aggadah" cannot grasp Aggadah itself.

The Sages promulgated the principle "Not the study of but the performance of mitzvot is the essence of virtue."[7] "One whose wisdom is more abundant than his deeds—to what is he comparable? To a tree whose branches are abundant but whose roots are few. A wind can come, uproot it, and overturn it . . . but one whose deeds are more abundant than his wisdom—to what is he comparable? To a tree whose branches are few but whose roots are abundant. All the winds in the world may blow against it, yet be unable to move it."[8] And in the opinion of R. Huna,[14] "Whoever engages exclusively in the study of Torah is like an atheist."[15][9] Thus, the extraordinary efforts on the part of the Sages to guard the ramparts of the tradition by creating fences and hedges to protect the observance of the mitzvot. "To what can this be compared? To a person charged with guarding an orchard. If he guards it from the out-

---

[5] BT Niddah 73a.   [6] Sifre Ekev 49.   [7] Mishnah Avot 1:17.   [8] Mishnah Avot 3:17.
[9] BT Avodah Zarah 17b.

---

[11] These are not just any talmudic words; they are the final words of the Babylonian Talmud.

[12] Advice attributed to Simeon ben Nethanel in Mishnah Avot 2:13.

[13] Dorshei Reshumot, "solvers of enigmas," were apparently a school of allegorists proficient at interpreting the symbolism of language. Who exactly they were is still an enigma in search of a solution.

[14] A Babylonian Amora of the second generation. The title "Rav" (represented as "R.") is a lesser title than "Rabbi." The highest level of rabbinic ordination (indicated by "Rabbi") was limited to the Sages of the Land of Israel and carried with it the theoretical power to decide all cases of law, even capital ones. The Amoraim of Babylonia used the title "Rav" as an indication of slightly lesser status.

[15] The strength of the English formulation captures the sense of the Hebrew that such a person recognizes no divine authority. The reason is, apparently, that such a person approaches Torah as an intellectual exercise rather than as a mandate for how to live. Heschel here sets up the supposition that the Rabbis understood "action" and "good deeds" to be only the patterns of behavior mandated by Halakhah."

side, it is well guarded. But if he guards it from the inside, whatever is within will be secure, while that which is outside will not be secure."[10]

The following problem thus confronts us: this orchard, which we are called upon to safeguard zealously—is it all Halakhah, that is, entirely a matter of deeds? What of Aggadah, the "science" of that which resides in the human heart? What is its place as a component of Torah?

Observe God's Works

It was Spinoza who injected into Jewish thought the idea that Judaism is not a religion but a legal system, and this doctrine courses through the body of modern Jewish thought like venom. But the truth is, one who says "I hold only Halakhah" cannot grasp even Halakhah; and to say that Torah is only Halakhah is to espouse a non-normative view.[16] The Torah begins not with the first legal commandment (Exodus 12:2) but with the creation of the world, the history of humanity, the patriarchal narratives, and even with conversations involving the servants of the patriarchs. It is not only worldliness[17] that is prior to Torah but fear of heaven as well. "Whoever has Torah but no fear of heaven is like a treasurer who has the keys to the inner vault but not to the outer doors. How shall he enter? In this connection, Rabbi Yannai proclaimed: 'Pity the one who has no doorway but nevertheless erects a gatehouse!'"[11] "Woe to those students of the Sages who busy themselves with Torah but have no fear of heaven."[12] Even of the Sabbath it was said: "Do not stand in awe of the Sabbath, but of the One who commanded concerning the Sabbath."[13]

The Sages knew that one could be a "scoundrel within the bounds of the Torah," that is, within the bounds of Halakhah; and thus they said: "Jerusalem was destroyed only because they adjudicated solely on the basis of the laws of the Torah, and they did not practice *lifenim mishurat hadin*."[14][18]

Now what distinguishes legality (*din*) from *lifenim mishurat hadin*? One can coerce compliance with the law but not *lifenim mishurat hadin*. For what is beyond the legal line is subjective and a matter of conscience.

Herewith an example: the secret of the durability of the Jewish people through the

---

[10] BT Yevamot 21a.   [11] BT Shabbat 31 a–b.   [12] BT Yoma 72b.   [13] BT Yevamot 6a–b.
[14] BT Bava Metzi'a 30b.

---

[16] This, again, is a playful pun on the Hebrew *shelo kahalakhah* (see n. [8] above).

[17] Hebrew: *derekh eretz*, which can mean "refinement" or "worldly pursuits." (See Glossary and chapter 8.) That *derekh eretz* is prior to Torah suggests that Torah *assumes* a prior acquisition of good basic human qualities. Here Heschel suggests that the structure of Torah also assumes and supplements a basic and general attitude of religious reverence.

[18] This is the idea, as explicated in the previous section, of bringing others inside one's legally defined boundaries, that is, a supererogatory ethic not fully legislated.

generations has inhered in its power to motivate self-sacrifice. But the question arose: What is sufficiently important to impel self-sacrifice? Should one give one's life for just any commandment? Halakhists nailed down the following principle: "In the case of all prohibitions defined by Torah, a person should obey a human command to violate them rather than be killed, with the exceptions of idolatry, sexual taboos,[19] and murder."[15] That is the defining line of the law. But the Aggadah added the following: "Better for a person to throw himself into a fiery furnace than to shame another person publicly. Whence do we know this? From Tamar."[16][20] That is, it is better to die than to violate the prohibition against public humiliation. But that was not enumerated along with the legally defined exceptions to the general rule; it was not legislated by Halakhah.[17][21]

The divergence of halakhic and aggadic thinking is illustrated also by the different answers given to the question: Whence the principle that danger to life overrides Sabbath laws? What are the halakhic answers? Rabbi Akiva said: "If the apprehension of a murderer supersedes the Temple service,[22] which in turn supersedes the Sabbath,[23] then a fortiori does a threat to innocent life override the Sabbath."[18] Another halakhic answer: "'You shall keep My laws and My rules, by the pursuit of which man shall live' (Leviticus 18:5)—'by . . . which man shall live' and not by which one should die."[19] These answers flow from logical and legal thinking and follow the usual rules of halakhic exegesis.[24]

But when essentially the same question was asked of Rabbi Tanhum of Naveh, while he was preaching in public: "May one extinguish a candle on Shabbat so that a

---

[15] BT Sanhedrin 74a.   [16] BT Sotah 10b.

[17] See, e.g., Maimonides, *Mishneh Torah* I *Hilkhot De'ot* [Laws Concerning Character, i.e., Ethics] 6:8, where this is not given the status of a prohibition for which one must give one's life.

[18] MI Tissa.   [19] BT Yoma 85b.

---

[19] In rabbinic terms, these include biblically defined incest and adultery.

[20] Chapter 38 of Genesis relates how Tamar, Judah's daughter-in-law, was nearly sent by Judah to an execution by burning for violating her bond of sexual fidelity to Judah's third son. But Judah himself was her paramour, and Tamar, rather than simply announcing that fact, left it to Judah to realize from her hints what the truth was and thus own up himself.

[21] The argument here is that self-sacrifice for public humiliation cannot be legally expected of one, even though it is an ideal, because it is in part a subjective matter of conscience and not an objectively definable act. It thus has the hallmark of Aggadah: not enforceable but still, paradoxically, of ultimate importance.

[22] Exodus 21:14 tells us that a murderer may be dragged from the altar itself to face justice, and the Rabbis understood that to mean that even an officiating priest could be so removed. Thus, the sanctity of innocent life overrides even the Temple service.

[23] Notwithstanding the usual prohibition of the use of fire on the Sabbath, daily and Sabbath sacrifices are brought to the altar and burned.

[24] These rules include the a fortiori reasoning reflected in the first answer given here, and the legitimacy of deducing exclusions from words that are strictly superfluous, such as the last clause of Leviticus 18:5.

sick person may get to sleep?" he gave this answer: "A candle is called *ner,* and the human spirit is also called *ner* [as in 'the spirit of man is the lamp (*ner*) of God' (Proverbs 20:27)]; better that the *ner* of a human being [i.e., a candle] be extinguished in favor of the *ner* of the Holy and Blessed One."[20] This is a poetic, impressionistic explanation, the product of Aggadah, which lifts the matter under consideration above the four cubits of Halakhah to sublime, heavenly heights.[25]

The conceptual category Aggadah thus should not be defined purely negatively [e.g., as scriptural interpretations that are nonlegal]; it encompasses not only a literary style but also a method of thought. It concerns itself with what lies beyond the legal line and aspires to matters of ultimate significance and meaning. Thus, the following two answers to the question of how one comes to know the Creator are, although given in different words, identical in content: (1) "Do you desire to know the One who spoke and the world came into being? Study Aggadah, for through it you will come to know the One who spoke and the world came into being, and to cling to God's ways";[21] and (2) Rabbi Meir said: "Observe God's works, for through that you will come to know the One who spoke and the world came into being."[22]

Beyond the Boundaries of Halakhah[26]

In contrast to Halakhah, which sounds a note of strength, Aggadah sounds a note of feebleness. Many have the sense that there is nothing that cannot be demonstrated by appeal to Aggadah. They see it as a kind of game rather than a product of serious thought; its exegeses seem like the playthings of an unrestrained imagination. Why do they seem so? Because people stroll through the garden of Aggadah and muse:

---

[20] BT Shabbat 30b.

[21] Sifre Ekev 49.

[22] Thus writes Maimonides in *Responsa* (ed. Freimann) #347, p. 312 (Bar Ilan database #150). This statement of Rabbi Meir is not to be found verbatim in the extant rabbinic corpus, but Maimonides may be paraphrasing ARN A 37: "Seven qualities minister before the throne of glory, namely, wisdom, righteousness, justice, kindness, compassion, truth, and peace. . . . Rabbi Meir says, 'Why does the verse [Hosea 2:21] say, "And you shall know the Lord"? To teach that whoever has in himself all these qualities, knows the will of God.'"

---

[25] Heschel here notes Rashi's reluctance to accept this nonlegal "ruling" as anything but poetic rhetoric designed to be impressive to the legally untutored.

[26] This translation of the phrase *lifenim mishurat hahalakhah* is used here to remain relatively true to the literal meaning of the Hebrew phrase and to convey Heschel's intent in this section, which is that Aggadah is a deliberate expansion of the narrowly defined horizons of Halakhah. Thus, although the Hebrew tends to be understood as "within the lines of Halakhah," if the realm of ultimate values lies beyond the domain that Halakhah defines for itself, then "beyond" is, in effect, "within."

"My, how lovely is this tree." They never stop to think, "My, how profound are its roots."[27] They see only the flowers and fail to observe the fruits.[28]

Modern scholars have tended to the prejudice that the Sages were concerned exclusively with the practical Halakhah and there was not to be found in aggadic teachings a basic, cohesive theology—that the talmudic Sages theologized in a sober, repressed way, that they were never singed by the fires of doubt and fear, and that they never explored the secrets or rationale of faith.

But ask yourself this: Is it possible that these Sages, whose minds were so hospitable to the most minute problems of Halakhah, were closed to the problems of religious faith and had no concern for the riddle of human existence? That they were heroic warriors on the battlefield of Torah but mere striplings in the arena of religious thought? Can it be seriously maintained that Jewish thought restricted itself to the field of Halakhah alone and did not delve into matters beyond the boundaries of Halakhah?

Whoever sees in Aggadah mind games or intellectual ornamentation does violence to its essence and squanders its riches. Should people say to you: the Sages delved into Aggadah only for its aesthetic value, that they expounded a verse just "because it was there," or that they created mere side-dishes to *halakhot*[29]—don't believe them. To find the true meaning of Aggadah, search deeply into each interpretation. You will find there struggles, worries, and yearnings, eternal problems and contemporary questions, the travails of community and individual that vexed both the Sages and the nation as a whole.

Aggadah is the serious effort of the Sages to provide answers to spiritual questions of loftiest import, individual and societal. But it can be seen in its true light only if one penetrates its soul and hears its struggles. Without such empathy, Aggadah and the resolutions it offers are like a dry crust to a sated person—they are like solutions to nonexistent riddles.

---

[27] A reference to Mishnah Avot 3:7, in which Rabbi Jacob (in some versions Rabbi Simeon) says that one who interrupts his rehearsal of teachings to say "how lovely is this tree" virtually puts his life in jeopardy. Heschel's use of this phrase thus conveys subliminally the idea that admiring only the external beauty of Aggadah and letting it go at that (i.e., considering the visible tree and not the roots) is to commit a mortal sin, for in doing so, the life-enhancing deep meaning of Aggadah is forfeited.

[28] Here we have an implied criticism of H. N. Bialik's characterization of Halakhah and Aggadah in his classic essay by that name (see *Complete Writings of H. N. Bialik* [Tel Aviv: D'vir, 1947], 207). In that essay, much of which is paralleled by Heschel's treatment thus far, Bialik describes Halakhah as the fruit and Aggadah as the flower. Bialik's idea is that Halakhah is the concrete and the nourishing mundane aspect of religion. But without the beautiful flower of Aggadah, who would be motivated to cultivate the plant that produces the fruit? For Heschel, the flower metaphor attributes too much superficiality and evanescence to Aggadah. Heschel wants to suggest that its roots run as deep as do those of Halakhah and that it, too, is a concrete, nourishing fruit.

[29] The Hebrew phrase is constructed of the language of Mishnah Avot 3:18. The image is one of sauces into which bread is dipped. The bread is the mainstay of the meal, and the dips are mere accompaniments that dress it up.

We must be careful, however, not to project our own struggles and meditations on the Sages of the Midrash. The system of thought current among the scholars of this new age is quite unlike that of the ancient Sages of Israel. The latter's thought processes derived from their knowledge of the Torah and were based in the lexicon of Scripture. Their problems were unique to them, and we must not pin on them struggles that are not indigenous to Judaism.

The religious thought of the Sages and the problems that animated them cannot, for example, be compared with the works of the Greek philosophers. Aggadic teachings cannot always be grasped by the tongs of generally accepted philosophical categories. That is why, in this study, my primary aim was not to search for parallels between the opinions of the rabbinic Sages and those of the philosophers of other peoples. My goal has been to strive to understand the words of the Sages on their own terms so that I could clarify their aggadic teachings.

A careful study of Aggadah reveals that behind the scenes you find a complete and comprehensive world outlook. The various opinions and interpretations are linked together as rings in a chain. Stack them, brick upon brick,[30] and you will behold a finished building, a complete structure of religious thought.

But you will understand aggadic teachings fully only if you distinguish well among the various streams that were current in the world of rabbinic thought. The aim of this work is to make such a distinction between the approaches of Rabbi Ishmael and Rabbi Akiva.[31] These sages, denoted "Fathers of the World,"[32] formed

---

[30] Heschel's image here is fascinating and clever. The Hebrew *ariah al gabei ariah* means, literally, a half-brick upon a half-brick (that is, *ariah* denotes a partial brick used to finish off a row of bricks when less than the width of a whole brick remains). The image of the half-brick suggests that each aggadic teaching by itself is incomplete, partial, and unsuited to building; but associating them together ("stacking" them) can produce something of more enduring and cohesive structure. Can it be that Heschel is also intimating that Aggadah without Halakhah is unstable as well, just as a structure made entirely of half-bricks (as opposed to an alternation of full and half-bricks) is cohesive but unstable? Such an interpretation is plausible because in scribal terminology there are two different ways of writing the poetic parts of Scripture: *ariah al gabei ariah* (half-brick upon half-brick, e.g., the Song of Moses in Deuteronomy 32), and *ariah al gabei levenah* (half-brick alternating with full brick, e.g., the Song at the Sea in Exodus 15). Since Heschel is here speaking of Aggadah, which he has already characterized as religion in the poetic mode, the scribal tradition for writing poetry makes a wonderfully apt image.

[31] Heschel here introduces the main protagonists of this entire work, the second-century C.E. Sages Ishmael and Akiva. Throughout, Heschel will be identifying competing positions on a multitude of issues in religious thought as the outgrowth and consequences of the thought of one of these two rabbinic figures.

[32] This is a literal translation of the phrase *avot ha'olam,* and it is usually rendered this way. However, there is an important ambiguity here, of which Heschel is undoubtedly taking advantage. *Olam* can mean "world," but another, more primary meaning is "eternity." Actually there is a second ambiguity here, and that is that *avot,* usually meaning "ancestors" [or "fathers," used here because the protagonists were both male], can also have the more abstract meaning of "progenitor" or "paradigm." Thus, *avot ha'olam* can also mean "eternal paradigms," which is, of course, exactly how Heschel means to interpret the significance of these two Rabbis and their modes of thought. This is a good example of a Heschelian *midrash,* or interpretation, of a common rabbinic term.

and fixed two different methods, which became cornerstones for all subsequent rabbinic teachings.

You recognize a methodology by two characteristics: (1) consistency, and (2) concern with fundamental issues. Both of these characteristics are to be found in the teachings of the two fathers. The thought systems of Rabbis Ishmael and Akiva are contiguous and, at the same time, opposing forces; and the opposition lived on in the history of Jewish thought. Each approach served as a paradigm for a whole line of beliefs and perspectives, and every Sage, consciously or unconsciously, got hooked into one of the two modes of thought.[33] We can thus categorize many later controversies by reference to the thought of the fathers. Whatever a veteran scholar would ever teach, would surely be a restatement of the teachings of one of these two Rabbis, in the language and form appropriate to the age and its external influences.

Do You Desire to Know the One Who Spoke and the World Came into Being?

Aggadic literature is less accessible than other parts of Jewish thought. In the case of Halakhah, there was an ongoing transmission of its teachings from parents to children, from teachers to disciples, from generation to generation, without interruption. But the teachings of Aggadah were impaired and became like a basket without a handle. Its words were largely ignored in the academies. Teachers tended to omit *aggadeta*,[34] and it was taught only when students began to doze off. The treasury of Aggadah served largely as grist for the homiletic mill, as a spice to promote felicity of discourse, but never as a subject of serious study. It was regarded as something trivial—"it's only Aggadah, not a source of practical instruction." Students busied themselves with it at a time that was "neither day nor night."[35] They did not realize that Aggadah too required a mind as "clear as a day brightened by the north wind."[36]

---

[33] Heschel's belief in the fundamental quality of the thought of the Ishmaelian and Akivan schools leads him here to a bit of overstatement, perhaps forgivable under the circumstances.

[34] The Aramaic term for Aggadah. It was and still is common for sessions in Talmud in traditional schools to skip those sections of the Talmud that deal not with matters of law (Halakhah), but rather with narrative, folklore, theology, and so on. Doing this, of course, presents a very skewed picture of the Talmud, and that is precisely the point Heschel is driving at.

[35] Heschel's reference here is to the (somewhat sarcastic) rabbinic comment in BT Menahot 99b that, since Joshua was told that the Torah is to be studied day and night (see Joshua 1:8), the proper time for the study of Greek wisdom would be when it is neither day nor night. So was Aggadah treated in the traditional academies. It was not banned. But given the overwhelming priority of Halakhah, no time could realistically be allotted to it.

[36] BT Eruvin 65a makes this comment about the need for the kind of clarity brought in by a weather front from the north whenever one makes a halakhic decision. Heschel here asserts that understanding the import of Aggadah requires similar clarity of thought. The image chosen here is a perfect refutation of the prevailing practice of relegating Aggadah to the "twilight," that is, neither day nor night.

The Sages who immersed themselves in the profundities of Aggadah were few in number, and the teaching of Aggadah eluded the great masters of Jewish religious thought. Thus, the study of the most sublime matters languished in Israel. The modern Jew, who thirsts for matters of the intellect, finds in the House of Study only a salty crust and meager rations, and thus rejects the meal. Open your eyes and see: we have a table, we have meat, we have a knife—and yet we cannot put anything in our mouths![37] A heavenly voice echoes forth from the treasure-house of Jewish thought, saying: "I have many coins, but none to make currency of them."[38]

As Halakhah is the edifice of Torah, so Aggadah is its underpinning.[39] If the foundations are torn down, of what use are the masters of Halakhah?

In an earlier time it would never have entered anyone's mind to belittle the value of Aggadah. "They said of Rabban Johanan ben Zakkai that he neglected not the study of Bible, nor of Mishnah, nor of Gemara, nor of Halakhah, nor of Aggadah, nor of Tosefta."23 The Tannaim would teach their disciples both Halakhah and Aggadah: "Rabban Johanan ben Zakkai would sit to teach Torah and his disciples would sit before him for the lesson.[40] When the lesson was concluded, he would teach them Aggadah and then Mishnah."24 [41] When the Roman government sent two undercover officers to pose as converts and see what the Torah of Israel was really about, they came to Rabban Gamaliel in Usha, "and they read Scripture, studied Mishnah, and then Midrash of Halakhah and of Aggadah."25

---

23 ARN A 14.   24 TB Lekh Lekha 10.   25 Sifre Haberakhah 344.

---

[37] The expression is taken from a statement of Rabbi Johanan (third-century Amora of the Land of Israel) given in BT Kiddushin 46a. He used it to express frustration at having an apparently clear statement of law which, on analysis, could not be fully understood. Heschel here uses it to express his own frustration at the fact that the rabbinic tradition produced an enormous corpus, but that the neglect of Aggadah created an incoherency and incompleteness that fail adequately to nourish the Jewish soul.

[38] This expression is the one used by Rabbi Akiva, according to the account given in BT Sanhedrin 68a, to mourn the passing of his teacher, Rabbi Eliezer. It is intended to convey a specific sense of loss—in which one has many resources but is missing the element that makes them useful. A person with many coins from all over the earth with no way of making currency of them is rich and poor at the same time. Rabbi Akiva looked at his massive legacy of legal traditions in need of explication the same way. And Heschel here depicts the Divine Presence itself grieving at the absence of the aggadic element that alone can ground and make coherent the halakhic tradition.

[39] Heschel here notes that Maimonides began his code of law with *Hilekhot Yesodei Hatorah* (Laws Concerning the Foundations of Torah), and that treatise dealt with theology and metaphysics, part of the stuff of Aggadah.

[40] It is clear from the context that the lesson was concerned primarily with Halakhah. But—and this is the point—it was not concerned *exclusively* with Halakhah, as the sequel demonstrates.

[41] It is noteworthy that while the study of Halakhah, according to this text, has priority, Aggadah still has precedence even over Mishnah. Apparently, Mishnah is less valued because it is a set of traditions and involves none of the dialectic and analysis that legal decisions and Aggadah both require.

To Rabbi Ishmael, Aggadah was a serious branch of study with its own blessings. With great haughtiness he said to Rabbi Akiva:[42] "Desist from your statements, and move instead to matters concerning plagues and tent-impurities."[43] 26 In other words, he was telling him that, though he was a great master of Halakhah, he was not competent to engage in Aggadah. In the part of the Sifre to Deuteronomy stemming from the school of Rabbi Ishmael, we find preserved this amazing statement: "Dorshei Reshumot[44] expounded: Do you desire to know the One who spoke and the world came into being? Study Aggadah, for through it you will come to know the One who spoke and the world came into being, and to cling to God's ways."27

The literature is in fact replete with profound utterances in praise of Aggadah. On the verse "May God give you . . . grain" (Genesis 27:28), it is said that this refers to Talmud; ". . . and wine"—this refers to Aggadah.28 Such comments are both descriptive and evaluative. It is universally acknowledged that humankind cannot survive without grain—bread is the basic food of humanity. Wine, on the other hand, sometimes induces well-being and sometimes makes one ill. At the same time, "man does not live on bread alone." The Sages of the Land of Israel would denigrate the "foolish Babylonians," who, they said, "eat bread with bread."29 Wine, however, has a quality that bread does not possess. "Bread sustains but does not delight; wine, however, both sustains and delights."30 Similarly: "There is no joy without wine,"31 "One may not recite Kiddush over anything except wine,"32 "The blessing of song should only be recited over wine."33

The master of Halakhah has a crucial task. It is he who determines how Israel should behave, and it is he who dominates their public and private lives. The master of Aggadah has a more modest role, and his domain is only the realm of thought and speculation—matters of the heart that are invisible.[45] It was to the study of

---

26 Midrash on Psalms 104:9.   27 Sifre Ekev 49.
28 Genesis Rabbah 66:3.   29 BT Nedarim 49b.
30 BT Berakhot 35b, Rashi s.v. *veha-ketiv ve-yayin yesamah levav enosh.*
31 BT Pesahim 109a.   32 BT Pesahim 107a.   33 BT Berakhot 35a.

---

[42] When the latter was engaging in overly fanciful aggadic exegesis.

[43] "Plagues" refers to those affections of the skin, garments, and the walls of houses that give rise to high levels of ritual impurity, according to Leviticus 13–14. "Tent Impurities" refers to another high level of ritual impurity imparted by a corpse, when one is under the same roof (i.e., "in a tent") with it. Both of these areas involve some very arcane halakhic rules, and thus a great deal of expertise, but they are about as far from what is usually considered to be the subject matter of Aggadah as one could get.

[44] See n. [13] above.

[45] We have here a reflection of the common view that Judaism has generally been concerned with acts rather than beliefs. While there is more than a kernel of truth in that assertion, it is often taken to extremes, and it is precisely that extreme that Heschel wishes to discredit in these sections of his introduction to this work on rabbinic theology.

Halakhah that the Sages referred when they spoke of "the Oral Torah, which is difficult to learn, and is acquired only through great pains that can be compared to darkness, for it is said: 'The people that walked in darkness have seen a brilliant light'
(Isaiah 9:1)—this refers to the masters of Talmud, who now see a great light, for the
Holy and Blessed One now illumines them with knowledge of what is forbidden and
what is permitted, what is impure and what is pure."[46] [34]

Desist from Aggadah

Even though the Aggadah neither forbids nor permits, nor does it declare impure or
pure, it is still directed at matters that are of ultimate significance. Despite the denigration it suffered by the mouths of the high-handed, the teachings of the masters of
Aggadah were dear to the hearts of the populace, who were eager to hear their words.
When a preacher made his appearance in the House of Study, the people abandoned
the teachers of Halakhah and streamed to hear the words of Aggadah. The Talmud
relates that Rabbi Abbahu and Rabbi Hiyyah bar Abba chanced to find themselves in
the same community. The people forsook Rabbi Hiyyah, the halakhist, and flocked to
listen to Rabbi Abbahu, the aggadist. As a result, Rabbi Hiyyah became depressed and
Rabbi Abbahu sought to console him. "Let me cite you a parable," he said. "There
were two salesmen, one sold precious stones, the other small wares, spindles, pins
and needles, and tubes, which were used by women and poor people. To whom did
the people flock? Obviously, they went to the one who sold small wares."[35]

Of course, this did not endear the aggadists to the halakhists, and the masters of
Halakhah often spoke harshly of their aggadic colleagues. One of the giants of
Halakhah, Rabbi Zeira, a native of Babylonia who emigrated to Eretz Israel, proclaimed the books of the aggadists to be "books of bewitchment."[36] He was noted for
his scrupulous care in transmitting the tradition; he verified the source of every quotation on the grounds that "any teaching that does not have a pedigree is not a valid
teaching."[37] He therefore ridiculed the homilies of the aggadists because they were
not authoritative and were subject to multiple and contradictory interpretations.
Rabbi Abba bar Kahana, a popular preacher, sought to defend the masters of Aggadah
whom Rabbi Zeira had humiliated. He challenged him to ask for an interpretation of

---

[34] Tanhuma Noah 3.

[35] BT Sotah 40a. Rashi there adds the comment "because the prices were low, he had many buyers; he
[Rabbi Abbahu] said this in order to appease him."

[36] PT Ma'aserot 3:10 (51a).　　　[37] PT Shabbat 19:1 (17a).

---

[46] It is, of course, noteworthy that the exegesis here is on a verse in Isaiah that has long been con-
sidered by Christians to be a herald of a "brilliant light" that would sweep away the old legal order of
Judaism. This particular rabbinic exegesis understood the brilliant light to be a guide to living, in which
"God is in the details."

any verse in Scripture. "Why are you provoking us? Ask a question and we will respond." Rabbi Zeira then asked for an interpretation of a particular verse in the Book of Psalms. But Rabbi Abba and his colleague Rabbi Levi answered in such a manner that it actually lowered the prestige of Aggadah in Rabbi Zeira's eyes. His reaction was, "They turned the verse one way, then they turned it another way, and one could learn nothing from it. Jeremiah, my son, desist from Aggadah and fortify yourself with Halakhah, for it is better than all things." He was fond of quoting the aphorism, "Give your soul to nothing except Halakhah."[38]

Those sages who regarded Aggadah as mere side dishes to the main course of Halakhah were pained to see the populace preferring the aggadic homilies, which delighted their hearts like wine, to the lessons in Halakhah, which are the very essence of Torah. They interpreted this trend as a sign of malaise, of spiritual decline. Others attributed the shift in interest from Halakhah to Aggadah as a symptom of the economic situation. Rabbi Levi said, "Formerly everyone had enough for his necessities and people were eager to learn some Mishnah, Halakhah, or Talmud; but now that they do not have enough for their necessities, and still more that they are worn out with the oppression, they want to hear only words of blessing and comfort."[39]

We can get a glimmer of the viewpoint that sees Aggadah as relatively trivial from Rabbi Isaac's famous wonderment, which is cited at the very beginning of Rashi's commentary on the Torah. "Said Rabbi Isaac: By right, the Torah should have begun with 'This month shall mark for you the beginning of the months' (Exodus 12:2), for that was the first commandment given to all Israel. Why then did it begin with Genesis?"[47] [40] Now Nahmanides had this to say about this wonderment: "One may well dispute this question, for there was a great need to begin the Torah with 'When God began to create heaven and earth . . . ,' for that is the very root of the faith; one who does not believe in this, and believes that the world is primeval, denies the very essence of the faith, and such a person has no Torah at all!"

The Fashion of Babylonia
and the Fashion of the Land of Israel

"Out of the rough came something sweet."[48] It was a boon to the Aggadah that it was treated disrespectfully because it did not become fixed.[49] It never became a

---

[38] BT Rosh Hashanah 13a.   [39] Song of Songs Rabbah 2:5; PRK 12:3 (101b).   [40] TB Bereshit 11.

---

[47] The answer cited by Rashi there is that the object was to establish God's ownership over the entire universe, and thus to preempt any complaints from the Gentiles about Israel's being given the Land of Canaan. But it is the fact of the question that is of significance here, that is, the reflexive assumption that the Torah is essentially a book of law and commandments.

[48] This was the riddle that Samson posed to his wedding guests (Judges 14).

[49] This is an important, though subtle, point. That which is studied and revered as a foundation of

"settled Aggadah," of which one was forbidden to dispute or to alter so much as the tail of the letter *yod*. At the same time, the disrespect resulted in the nation directing most of its energy to the construction of glorious towers within the four cubits of Halakhah, while the vineyard of aggadic thought was neglected. The teachings of Aggadah became that which a person tramples underfoot[50] and in various periods it was not studied at all. Let us see what divided the Amoraim of the Land of Israel, who raised and nurtured Aggadah, from the Amoraim of Babylonia, who were not exercised in Aggadah. The earliest aggadic midrashim, such as Genesis Rabbah, Leviticus Rabbah, Lamentations Rabbati, as well as a majority of aggadic sayings in the Babylonian Talmud, have their source in the Land of Israel.

Already among the first generation of Amoraim in the Land of Israel, Rabbi Joshua ben Levi, a great aggadist, complained about those scholars who did not involve themselves in Aggadah. He applied the verse "Because they do not understand the works of the Lord" (Psalm 28:5) to those who do not study Aggadah and therefore do not understand the works of the Lord.[41]

R. Dimi,[51] who traveled frequently between Babylonia and the Land of Israel, would bring sayings and traditions to the Babylonian academies. One of the aggadic expositions he transmitted was an interpretation of Isaiah 3:1: ". . . every prop of food" refers to the masters of Talmud; "and every prop of water" refers to the masters of Aggadah who delight people's hearts like water."[42] There is something novel in this metaphor. The Tannaim used to compare Aggadah to wine,[52] but in R. Dimi's eyes Aggadah is likened to water: "The world can survive without wine, it cannot survive without water."[43]

The contrast between these points of view is revealed by the attitudes of the Babylonian schools and those of the schools of the Land of Israel toward poetry and song. In the view of Rabbi Johanan, one of the outstanding Amoraim of the Land of Israel, "Whoever studies Scripture without melody or Talmud without song, this verse

---

41 Midrash on Psalms 28:5.   42 BT Hagigah 14a.

43 PT Horayot 3:5 (48c). Rabbi Isaac Aboab (late fourteenth century, Spain), in the introduction to his moralistic treatise *Menorat Ha-Maor,* explicates R. Dimi's idea as follows: "Just as a person occasionally needs bread, but frequently needs water, in order to maintain his bodily health, so it is with maintaining the health of the soul. Matters of the commandments are necessary at discrete times, but matters of Aggadah are needed at all times."

---

a civilization will often become the object of such veneration that a taboo develops about tampering with it. Heschel clearly believes that this has happened to Halakhah (as he will elaborate in the latest chapters of this work). In this sense, Aggadah escaped ossification by being considered less important!

[50] Heschel's wordplay continues. The phrase he uses here comes from a commentary on Deuteronomy 7:12, and in its original setting it refers to those commandments that seem so insignificant that they are treated lightly and, as it were, trampled underfoot. Here Heschel applies the phrase not to commandments (part of Halakhah) but to the entire body of Aggadah.

[51] A Babylonian Amora of the third and fourth generation.

[52] See above.

applies to him, 'I gave them laws that were not good and rules by which they could not live'" (Ezekiel 20:25). This poetic utterance seemed strange in the eyes of the Babylonian Amora Abbaye, and he raised the question, "Because one is unable to sing sweetly, you apply to him the verse, 'rules by which he cannot live'?"[44] To the scholars of the Land of Israel the words of Torah were songs; but to the scholars of Babylonia, when you call the words of Torah songs you profane the honor of Torah.

In the opinion of Rabbi Bibi,[53] Torah is referred to as song, as it is written, "Your statutes have been my songs" (Psalm 119:54).[45] At the opposite pole is the great Babylonian Amora Rava, who gave this exposition: "Why was King David punished? Because he called the words of Torah songs. Whereupon the Holy One said to him, 'In my Torah there are words of wisdom, for example, concerning wealth, "You see it, then it is gone; it grows wings and flies away" (Proverbs 23:5)—and you call these words mere songs?' For this reason, I will cause you to stumble in a simple law which elementary school children know."[54] [46]

The contrast between the two schools is also sharply etched in their attitudes toward the performance of mitzvot. The Amora of the Land of Israel Rabbi Simeon ben Lakish states, "The performance of mitzvot requires intention,"[47] while the Babylonian Amora Rava declares, "The performance of mitzvot does not require intention."[48] There is more: In the Mishnah we read, "One stands in prayer only when in a sober mood,"[49] that is to say, in concentration and with reverence. The Tosefta adds this clarification: "One does not pray while engaged in trivial conversation, in a jocular mood, or in a spirit of levity, but only when engaged in words of wisdom."[50] The text in the Talmud of the Land of Israel reads: "words of Torah."[51] In the ensuing discussion, the meaning of "words of Torah" is clarified. It states that even Elijah did not take leave of Elisha without a word of Torah. What were they discussing? Rabbi Ahavah son of Rabbi Zeira said, "the reading of the Shema"; Rabbi Judah ben Pazzi said, "the creation of the world"; Rabbi Yudan son of Rabbi Aivu said, "the consolations of Jerusalem"; and the Sages said, "the chariot vision of Ezekiel." Not one of the four mentions the subject of Halakhah.[55] One would have to conclude from this

---

[44] BT Megillah 32a.   [45] PRK 5:8 (50a).   [46] BT Sotah 35a.   [47] BT Pesahim 114b.
[48] BT Rosh Hashanah 28b. This tendency of thought is further expressed in Rava's view that mitzvot were not given for human enjoyment (BT Rosh Hashanah 28a). Rashi expands on this idea: "They are like the command of a king" (BT Hullin 89a), "like a yoke around one's neck" (BT Rosh Hashanah 28a).
[49] Mishnah Berakhot 5:1.   [50] Tosefta Berakhot 3:21.   [51] PT Berakhot 5:1 (8d).

---

[53] A third-generation Amora of Eretz Yisrael. See Appendix 2 for the time periods and lands of residence of the rabbis of the Tannaitic and Amoraic periods.

[54] The law upon which King David stumbled was the one that is virtually explicit in Numbers 7, that the ark must be carried by shoulder and not on wagons. Because David missed this obvious point, he had the ark brought back to Jerusalem on a wagon, with the resulting tragic death of Uzza (2 Samuel 6).

[55] It is also noteworthy that three of these four (all but the second) are also anachronistic.

discussion that one must not take leave of his fellow man except with a word of Aggadah. Yet the prevailing view in Babylonia was that one should not rise to pray except when having engaged in halakhic study, nor should one take leave of his fellow man except with a word of Halakhah.[52]

The tension between the two communities sometimes expressed itself in harsh terms. Rabbi Johanan stated that vulgarity—a lack of refinement and sensitivity—was a characteristic that left the Land of Israel for Babylonia.[53] In the eyes of the scholars of the Land of Israel, the Sages of Babylonia did not appear adequately prepared to appreciate the fineness of Aggadah. It is related that Rabbi Simlai,[56] who emigrated from Babylonia to the Land of Israel, asked Rabbi Jonathan (possibly it was Rabbi Johanan) to teach him Aggadah. His reply was: "I have a tradition from my fathers not to teach Aggadah to a Babylonian or to a Southerner, for they are vulgar and deficient in Torah."[54] Rabbi Jeremiah, an Amora of the Land of Israel of the third generation, used to disparage the sayings of the Babylonian Sages. He would say, "Those silly Babylonians dwell in a land of darkness, and therefore their teachings are benighted."[55] His opinion of the Babylonian Talmud was not very flattering. Citing the verse, "He has made me dwell in darkness" (Lamentations 3:6), he applied it to the Talmud of Babylonia.[56]

Pumbedita was the seat of the most prestigious academy in Babylonia. Its scholars were noted for their keen minds and sharp wits. It was said, "they could draw an elephant through the eye of a needle," so great were their dialectic powers.[57] Their studies centered on the profundities of Halakhah rather than on the mysteries of Torah. Thus, the final words of the Babylonian Talmud read: "He who studies Halakhah daily is assured a place in the world-to-come."[57] [58]

After the close of the Babylonian Talmud, the subsequent generations of scholars were drawn completely to the study of Halakhah. It was the goal of the Sevoraim and the Geonim[58] to make the Babylonian Talmud the universally accepted legal authority, and they strove to make it known throughout the Diaspora. The concentration was primarily on the halakhic discussions, and except for a few individuals the majority abandoned the field of Aggadah. In the vast literature of the Geonim that has been preserved, Aggadah has been moved into a corner.

[52] See BT Berakhot 31a.   [53] BT Kiddushin 49b.   [54] PT Pesahim 5:3 (32a); see BT Pesahim 62b.
[55] BT Pesahim 34b.   [56] BT Sanhedrin 24a.   [57] BT Bava Metzi'a 38b.   [58] BT Niddah 73a.

[56] A second-generation Amora.

[57] This is the end of Tractate Niddah. This tractate is not the last in the Mishnah, but it is the last on which the Babylonian academies produced Talmud.

[58] The Sevoraim were a group of talmudic scholars about whom little is known beyond the name traditionally given to them. The reference is always to a school or schools active in the editorial completion of the Babylonian Talmud in approximately the sixth and seventh centuries, after the time of the latest named authorities in the Talmud. The Geonim were the heads of the great Babylonian academies in post-talmudic times. Their period of flourishing was from the eighth century through the eleventh.

Various circumstances contributed to the victory of the Babylonian Talmud over that of the Land of Israel,[59] to a point where the latter was almost forgotten.[59] The teachings of the Babylonian Talmud became disseminated throughout the Diaspora. The various communities adopted their method of study and followed their customs and practices, and the strenuous battle between the influence of Babylonia and the influence of the Land of Israel, which lasted for generations, ended with victory for the Babylonians.[60]

The Small Matter:
These Are the Debates of Abbaye and Rava

It was accepted by most Sages that the study of Halakhah was primary and the study of Aggadah was secondary. But love often causes one to step out of line, and because of this a minority of the Sages tipped the scales to the other side and produced statements in praise of Aggadah, as if it were the very heartbeat of Torah. From time to time one hears that there are degrees in the study of Torah and that the esoteric teachings stand higher than the halakhic teachings. It was said of Rabban Johanan ben Zakkai "that he was devoted to the study of Bible, and Mishnah, and Talmud, and Halakhah, and Aggadah, and the fine inferences from Torah and rabbinics, and logical arguments, and the study of equinoxes,[61] and mathematical calculations, and the discourses of the ministering angels, the demons, and the palm trees,[62] and fullers' and foxes' parables,[63] and the large matter and the small matter." The Talmud explains this last phrase: "The large matter—this is the work of the Chariot;[64] the small matter—these are the debates of Abbaye and Rava."[65] [60]

[59] See Louis Ginzberg, *Perushim ve-hidushim ba-Yerushalmi* [Commentary on the Talmud of Eretz Yisrael], 4 vols. (New York: Ktav, 1971), vol. 1.
[60] BT Sukkah 28a.

---

[59] Many of these factors were political, given the ascendancy of Islam and its political centers near the Babylonian academies.
[60] Thus, according to Heschel, with the lasting ascendancy of Halakhah over Aggadah, though (as he has noted) this may have more to do with the post-talmudic drive to codify than with the particular characteristics of the Babylonian academies.
[61] These were important for setting the calendar and the festivals before the calendar was fixed.
[62] Rashi frankly admits in his commentary on this passage that he has no idea what the last three mean. There was, however, a tradition that ascribed wisdom to those who could somehow decipher the "languages" of beings other than humans, and even objects. So Solomon was praised in rabbinic literature, in a midrash on 1 Kings 5.
[63] Aphorisms probably similar to Aesop's fables that expressed basic truths in a homely, narrative way. In the Middle Ages, Jews produced books of fables of this nature.
[64] Referring to Ezekiel's chariot, a perennial symbol of the secrets of the divine nature. Hence, Maimonides (see below) considered this phrase to be referring to "metaphysics," that is, the study of what lies beyond physics.
[65] This seems to be a gross anachronism, since Abbaye and Rava lived in fourth-century Babylonia,

Maimonides, who explained that "the work of creation" means "natural science" and that "the work of the Chariot" means "metaphysics," and who saw in this bold talmudic statement a corroboration of his teachings, reached out and set this statement as a jewel in his great work, the *Mishneh Torah*.[61] [66] But what appeared to the "Great Eagle"[67] as a precious stone became to his successors a stumbling block. There were rumblings among his commentators. Rabbenu Nissim[68] wrote: "Maimonides wrote what he wished here, but would that it had not been written." And Rabbi Yom Tov ben Abraham Ishbili[69] argued that the debates of Abbaye and Rava "are greater matters than all of the pagan sciences;[70] this is the true interpretation, and not as others have interpreted, may God forgive them."

Rabbi Joseph Caro,[71] following the teaching of Rabbi Eliezer Hisma, declared that a knowledge of the natural world is secondary to a knowledge of Halakhah. Rabbi Eliezer Hisma had taught, "The laws relating to sacrifices of birds and to the calculation of menstrual days[72] are the essentials of Halakhah; the study of equinoxes and mathematical calculations are side-dishes to wisdom."[62] Caro comments, "Even though equinoxes and mathematics deal with lofty matters, that is, the heavenly forces, whereas the laws of bird sacrifices are of lesser significance, while the laws of menstrual purification deal with a repulsive subject, nevertheless it is these laws that represent the essence of Torah[73] and the knowledge of equinoxes and mathematics

---

[61] *Hilekhot Yesodei Ha-Torah* 4:13.   [62] Mishnah Avot 3:23.

---

and we are talking here about Johanan ben Zakkai, of the first-century Land of Israel. What the text refers to, however, is the multitude of halakhic issues on which Abbaye and Rava were later to disagree. It is suggested here that it was the greatness of Johanan ben Zakkai that he had mastered all of these halakhic matters, which later were the subject of great doubt even among such giants as Abbaye and Rava.

[66] A fourteen-book work primarily of Halakhah. It begins, however, with the "foundations of Torah" and clearly expresses the view that behavioral norms are not enough for a pious life. True religious faith, and the struggle to achieve it, is the ultimate foundation and goal.

[67] A common nickname for Maimonides, a major medieval Jewish philosopher and codifier in Spain and North Africa in the twelfth century, author of *Guide of the Perplexed* and *Mishneh Torah*.

[68] Nissim ben Reuven Girondi (fourteenth century, Spain).

[69] Thirteenth to fourteenth century, Spain.

[70] That is, the natural sciences that Maimonides learned from the Greeks and the Arabs, and which he also considered to be part of the essential curriculum of Judaism.

[71] Sixteenth-century Safed, author of *Kesef Mishneh* (a standard commentary on Maimonides' *Mishneh Torah*) as well as the authoritative legal code *Shulhan Arukh*. Caro, who is mostly remembered as the leading halakhist of his generation, also authored a mystical diary.

[72] Both of these require rather complicated mathematical calculations, but they relate to concrete matters of Halakhah. The "side-dishes to wisdom" in the next clause are the basis of Heschel's earlier rhetorical jibe at the patronizing attitude toward Aggadah by the devotees of Halakhah.

[73] For they concern such matters of concrete behavioral concern as how to achieve purity through sacrifice, and when marital relations are permissible between husband and wife.

is peripheral to talmudic wisdom. The latter deserves the general name "wisdom," because its central preoccupation is to expound God's laws."[63]

Maimonides, the unsurpassed master of Halakhah, makes this confession: "I find it more congenial to study the principles of religious faith than any other of my studies."[64] In his magnum opus, *Mishneh Torah,* the section devoted especially to religious thought is entitled "The Foundations of Torah." He also emphasized that a knowledge of nature is a prerequisite to a knowledge of God. He believed that the study of Halakhah alone is not sufficient to lead one to a pure conception of God: "I have already met one of the great scholars of Israel who, I swear, was well-versed in Halakhah and who waged many a battle in its behalf since his youth, who was nevertheless perplexed by the problem of God's corporeality—did God have eyes and hands and feet and intestines, as related in Scripture, or was God incorporeal?"[74] [65]

Commenting on Ulla's statement, "From the time the Temple was destroyed, the Holy One's only dwelling place is within the four cubits of Halakhah,"[66] Maimonides notes, "If you take this statement literally it is palpably untrue; it is as though the end-all of existence is to dwell in the confines of Halakhah and to cast away all other intellectual pursuits. In the time of Shem and Eber[75] and subsequently, before there was a Halakhah, shall we say that the Holy One was not involved in the entire universe?[67]

Maimonides had planned to write a separate treatise on Aggadah. Elsewhere he writes,

> The midrash found in the Talmud is not to be regarded as unimportant and insignificant. Much wisdom resides there. For one thing, it includes marvelous riddles and wondrous, delightful tales. More than that, if you ponder them intelligently, you will find there truths of unsurpassed worth, truths that the wise men preferred to conceal and not to reveal to everyone. As for the philosophers in all generations, if you take their teachings literally, you will find statements that are as irrational as anything.[76] [68]

---

[63] Joseph Caro's commentary *Kesef Mishneh* on Maimonides' *Mishneh Torah, Hilekhot Yesodei Hatorah* [Laws Concerning the Foundations of Torah] 4:13.

[64] Commentary on the Mishnah, end of Tractate Berakhot.

[65] See *Guide of the Perplexed,* I:55.

[66] BT Berakhot 8a.

[67] *Essay on Resurrection of the Dead,* ed. J. Finkel (New York: American Academy for Jewish Research, 1939), p. 3.

[68] Commentary on the Mishnah, Introduction.

---

[74] God's incorporeality was virtually axiomatic for Maimonides, and confusion on this point was thus a very elementary error and the sign of a real novice in religious thought.

[75] The characters in Genesis (see the genealogy in chapter 11) who were taken by early rabbinic tradition to have founded the first academy for the study of Torah. Since this was before Mount Sinai, there was (according to Maimonides) no Halakhah yet, and so the study must have been of a different, more fundamental, kind.

[76] Philosophers should not be taken literally, lest we end up with absurdity. And similarly, Aggadah should not be denigrated just because its literal meaning seems far-fetched. Study requires more effort than that.

Maimonides drew a distinction between "Torah wisdom," that is, Halakhah, and "True Torah wisdom," that is, the wisdom of beliefs and opinions, for which the laws and commandments are merely preparatory and serve only to guard and strengthen one's religious convictions.[69] "Those talmudists who believe true ideas that come to them from tradition, who study the actions by which God is served, but who are untrained in the investigation of the roots of Torah, and who have never delved into the study of religious truth," Maimonides compares to those who have reached the area of the king's palace, but who only walk around it and never advance beyond the anteroom.[70] These statements of Maimonides also elicited a reproach against him. "Many rabbinic scholars claim that this reaction was not written by him. However, if it was, it would best be withdrawn from the public; in fact, burning it would be even more appropriate. How dare he say that those who had knowledge of the natural universe are in a higher category than those engaged in religious studies, and that they are the ones to be found in the king's inner courtyard?!"[77] [71]

The charge that the scholars preoccupied themselves exclusively with halakhic studies was heard throughout the generations. From the time of Bahya ibn Pakudah[78] until the time of Israel Ba'al Shem Tov,[79] one hears the complaint that the scholars ignored the "Duties of the Heart"[80] and rejected the study of secret lore or of Aggadah. Bahya taught that the duties of the heart constitute the foundation of all the mitzvot.

> If any damage is done to the foundation, that is, if the link between heart and deed is missing, not a single mitzvah of the positive commandments can be properly observed. Since both the poles and the axis of the deed are built on the intention of the heart, it would be only natural that the study of the duties of the heart should precede the study of the 613 commandments. Moreover, while the latter have a fixed quota, the heart's commandments are infinite in number and we are under constant obligation to perform them, at all times, everywhere, every hour, every minute. People shy away from the duties of the heart and devote their lives to the study of bizarre and abstruse legal discussions. Their minds are filled with the disputations of the talmudic masters, with their innova-

---

[69] See *Guide of the Perplexed,* Introduction to Part I.
[70] Ibid., III:53.
[71] Commentary of Shem Tov ben Joseph Ibn Shem Tov (late fifteenth century, Spain) on *Guide,* ad loc.

---

[77] There are two Ibn Shem Tovs in the history of Maimonidean criticism. The quotation is taken from Shem Tov ben Joseph Ibn Shem Tov, a late-fifteenth-century Spanish commentator on the *Guide,* who is generally sympathetic to Maimonides, though critical on this point. His grandfather, Shem Tov Ibn Shem Tov (fourteenth to early fifteenth century, Spain), was a kabbalist and anti-Maimonidean polemicist.

[78] Eleventh-century Spain, a great medieval moralist.

[79] Eighteenth-century Ukraine, founder of the Hasidic movement.

[80] The name of Bahya's major work. The title reflects Bahya's idea that the commandments are "duties of the limbs"; that is, they involve physical action. But there are other duties, of the heart and mind, that must not be neglected.

tive legal insights, but are blind to those spiritual matters which are of supreme importance and which they are obligated to investigate.[72]

And Rabbi Israel Ba'al Shem Tov is quoted as saying,

The evil inclination does not try to seduce a person that he should not study, knowing that it would be futile. A person who never studies is held in low esteem by his fellow creatures. How, then, does he seduce him? He persuades him not to study those subjects which would inspire in him reverence for God, such as books of moral instruction, or the *Shulhan Arukh,* which would enable him to observe the laws properly. He seduces him to involve himself totally in the study of Gemara with all its commentaries.[81] [73]

We Do Not Regard the Aggadah as Authoritative

The midrashim of the Tannaim, as well as the Talmudim of Babylonia and of the Land of Israel, were hospitable both to Halakhah and Aggadah. Essentially, it never entered anyone's mind to divide the Torah into two separate domains. In an apt metaphor, the Torah is compared to rain: just as the rain descends on all trees and gives each its distinctive flavor, according to its species, so the teachings of the Torah are of one piece that nourishes different branches of learning—Scripture, Mishnah, Talmud, Halakhah, Aggadah.[74]

It was the Babylonian Geonim who made the division between Halakhah and Aggadah, and the majority of them did not include aggadic subjects in their writings and paid it little attention. Moreover, consider this: the editors of the Babylonian Talmud had no intention of creating a fixed code of law, like the *Shulhan Arukh.* On the contrary, in addition to final decisions about law, they were not averse to including the divergent halakhic opinions of the scholars, even those that were rejected. Similarly, we find included in the Talmud many divergent Aggadot, the deviant ones along with the accepted ones, bizarre and incredible Aggadot along with those that are praiseworthy. The Karaites[82] viewed these deviant Aggadot as worthy of derision and ridicule, and this disparagement of the Aggadot led the Karaites to scoff at the entire Talmud. In the controversy between the Rabbanites and the Karaites, it would appear

---

[72] *The Duties of the Heart,* Avodat Ha-Elohim [The Service of God], ch. 4.
[73] *Tzava'at Ha-Rivash* [Testament of the Ba'al Shem Tov].
[74] Sifre Ha'azinu 306.

---

[81] Note that the Ba'al Shem Tov here does not criticize the study of the codes, that is, "the duties of the limbs," as Bahya would have put it, but rather the excessive study of the processes and dialectic of halakhic matters, even when a bottom line was not reached or even desired. That was the hallmark of some of the Lithuanian academies in his own day, with whom he had some ongoing friction.

[82] A Jewish sect, active during the period of the Geonim, that denied the authority of the Oral Law or talmudic tradition. Their name drives from the Hebrew word for Scripture (*mikra*), which they attempted to observe faithfully to the letter.

that the Geonim thought it preferable to demean Aggadah and uphold Halakhah. This may explain their statement: "We do not regard the Aggadah as authoritative."

R. Saadia[83] already noted this principle and R. Hai Gaon[84] elaborated the reason for it: "The teachings of Aggadah do not constitute an ongoing tradition. They are rather the product of an individual preacher's fanciful exposition. They are not precise enough to be regarded as authoritative."[75] It was a ruling of R. Saadia, that one cannot cite a teaching of Aggadah as proof.[76]

It was a difficult day, the one on which they first announced "we do not regard the Aggadah as authoritative." This statement has two facets to it: its pleasant face shows when it is taken as a one-time caution or a caveat to one who seeks wisdom; its nasty face shows when it is taken as a basic principle of Torah.

This Aggadah Is Pleasing,
and This Aggadah Is Not Pleasing

As we have seen, the Babylonian Talmud became revered and sanctified by the people of Israel. The teachings of the Sages were more beloved than the teachings of Scriptures. All instruction was based on the Talmud; people walked by its light and meditated on it day and night. But they did not relate to the entire literature of the Talmud in the same way. In relation to the halakhic portions of the Talmud, the Sages declared, "Whoever says, 'This Halakhah does not appeal to me,' has no share in the world-to-come."[85] [77] However, in all nonhalakhic sections of the Talmud, many scholars did not hesitate to say, "This Aggadah is pleasing, this Aggadah is not pleasing."

For example, Rabbi Judah Halevi[86] was not inhibited from saying: "I concede to you, King of the Khazars, that in the Gemara there are things that I cannot rationalize nor integrate for you in any adequate way."[78] Rabbi Abraham ibn Ezra[87] said

---

[75] *Otzar Ha-Geonim,* Hagigah, p. 59.   [76] Ibid., p. 65.   [77] ARN A 27.
[78] *Kuzari,* end of Part III.

---

[83] Perhaps the best known of the Geonim, Saadia was the head of the academy of Sura in the early tenth century and the first important medieval Jewish philosopher, as well as a talmudist, and a disputant with the Karaites.

[84] Eleventh century, the end of the period of the Geonim.

[85] This phrase, when it appears in rabbinic literature, is almost never to be taken literally. Rather, it expresses in a very strong way the ultimate opprobrium. It is generally directed not at those things that would call forth universal condemnation and disgust, but rather, as in this case, at things that reasonable people might actually do or believe, but which the Rabbis, as a matter of ideology, wished to declare off limits.

[86] Eleventh- to twelfth-century Spanish poet and philosopher, author of the famous work *The Kuzari,* from which Heschel will now quote.

[87] Twelfth-century Spanish exegete of a rationalist disposition.

about Aggadah: "some of it is like fine silk, and some of it is like crude burlap."[79] Maimonides commented on a precious statement of Rabbi Hanina: "Would that all statements were like this one!"[80] but concerning Aggadot on the Messianic Days, he wrote: "A person should not busy himself with aggadic matters, nor spend much time on midrashim on this subject; do not give them any primacy, for they lead neither to reverence nor to love."[81] And Rabbi Abraham ben David[88] admitted that "there are aggadot that lead the mind astray."[82]

In the school of Rabbi Ishmael they interpreted the scriptural verse "Is not my word like fire, says the Lord, like a hammer which breaks the rock into pieces?" (Jeremiah 23:29) to mean that, just as the hammer scatters a multitude of sparks, so from one verse there emerge countless interpretations.[83] While it is agreed that a verse must be understood in the first instance in its literal meaning, it is permissible to expound Scriptures in whatever manner possible. Sometimes these midrashim approximate the literal meaning, and at other times they are to be regarded as allusive.

A good example is the declaration of one of the Sages that the patriarch Jacob did not die.[84] His colleague retorted, "Was it then for naught that the mourners mourned and the embalmers embalmed and the gravediggers buried him?" To which he replied, "I am only interpreting a verse in Jeremiah" (30:10).[89] What the rabbi meant was, "I know full well that Jacob died, but I am trying to interpret the verse in every possible way. It is possible to say that he did not die in the sense that the righteous, even in death, may be deemed alive, for their reputations and the recollection of their achievements endure forever."[85]

It follows from this approach that midrash is irreducibly subjective. A scriptural verse may yield many interpretations, and which interpretation will be adopted will depend on the motive of the interpreter. That motive will arise from matters of loftiest spiritual import: a conception of God, a conception of Torah, a conception of life. Since the essential purpose of Aggadah is to clarify our beliefs and opinions, that goal must guide a Sage's thought when he seeks to interpret scriptural texts. Aggadah,

[79] Introduction to his commentary on the Torah.
[80] *Guide of the Perplexed*, I:59.
[81] Mishneh Torah XIV, *Hilkhot Melakhim* [Laws Concerning Kings] 12:3.
[82] His critical comments to *Mishneh Torah* I *Hilkhot Teshuvah* [Laws of Repentance] 3:7.
[83] BT Sanhedrin 34a.   [84] BT Ta'anit 5b.
[85] BT Berakhot 18a.

[88] Twelfth-century Provence, often known by the acronym Rabad (= RABaD), the compiler of critical and often caustic comments on Maimonides' *Mishneh Torah*.

[89] The verse speaks of Jacob being delivered. The obvious plain meaning here is that the prophet is speaking of the Israel contemporaneous with him and merely using the not infrequent poetic name "Jacob" for the entire nation. However, the exegesis here is a literal one that seeks to conclude that since Jacob will be delivered, the individual Jacob must not have died.

then, is not simply spice[90] for Israel's Torah; it is its foundation and source, and its concepts have fathered many halakhic concepts.

Like Poetic Metaphors

The vineyard of Aggadah was attacked by many despoilers[91] in the Middle Ages. Enlightened scholars given to extremes looked upon it as a collection of thistles and thorns, and as worthless stones. The Christians, for their part, sought to make converts to their faith, so they would intimidate Israel by saying that one can find evidence for the principles of Christianity in the Aggadah. At the same time they would ridicule many aggadic statements that seemed to them to be empty fabrication. Sages of Israel countered in defense that aggadic statements are not to be treated like halakhic statements; many of them were not to be taken literally but rather are to be interpreted allegorically and metaphorically, for they were composed in the first instance "in the manner of poetic metaphors . . . just as poets do." So was Maimonides' opinion. Moreover, Jews are not obligated to believe all Aggadot.

Nahmanides, in his public disputation with the apostate Pablo Christiani (in Barcelona, 1263[92]), said: "We have three kinds of books; one, the twenty-four books of the Bible in which we all believe wholeheartedly; two, the Talmud which interprets the 613 commandments of the Torah—and we believe in these talmudic interpretations; three, we have a book called Midrash,[93] which, in essence, consists of homilies. It is just as if a bishop were to deliver a sermon that appealed to a listener, and it were committed to writing. In the case of such a book of homilies, if one believes it, all well and good, and if one does not, no harm is done."[86]

Similarly, Rabbi Jehiel of Paris, in his disputation with Nicholas Donin (in 1240),[94] said of the Aggadah in the Talmud, "It contains puzzling teachings which a disbeliever, an *apikoros,* or a sectarian, will find hard to believe, but there is no need to defend them. One may believe these teachings or not, as one desires, since no laws are based on them. However, I must say in all certainty that the Sages of the Talmud

[86] *Otzar Vikkuhim* [A Collection of Polemics and Disputations], ed. J. D. Eisenstein (New York, 1928; repr., Tel Aviv, 1969), 89.

[90] Again, Heschel means to reject some of the colorful but ultimately demeaning ways in which Aggadah has been characterized. It is not spice, or side dish, but rather a main course that deserves at least parity with Halakhah.

[91] An image based on Song of Songs 2:15, in which the vineyard is said to be "in blossom." Thus, Heschel is telling us that Aggadah, the vineyard, although often under attack, is fruitful.

[92] The disputation was at the command of King James of Aragon, and although Nahmanides was victorious, he eventually had to leave the Iberian Peninsula for the Land of Israel.

[93] More properly, a set of books—or, better, a genre of literature. See Appendix 4 for a brief description of the "midrashic" works that form the main primary sources for the current work.

[94] Jehiel of Paris was a thirteenth-century Tosafist. The disputation referred to here was ordered

never wrote anything except that which was honest and truthful. If these aggadic statements appear puzzling to those who hear them, is that not also true of the puzzling things in Scriptures?"[87] There were scholars who took exception to Maimonides' view that aggadic teachings are not to be taken literally but are to be regarded as poetic metaphors. Rabbi Judah Loew of Prague[95] expressed this opinion about the homilies of the sages:

> The verse in Genesis 28:11 reads, "And he took one of the stones of the place and put it under his head." This means that the stones quarreled with one another. One stone said, "Let this righteous man rest his head on me," while another said, "let his head rest on me." To those who believe that this represents meaningless speculation on the part of the Sages, that their words have neither rhyme nor reason, I must teach them that these words deal with lofty spiritual matters. How can one look at this verse in the Torah and say it is to be taken literally? What is the Torah telling us when it records the obvious, that "he took one of the stones"? The Torah is depicting a wondrous scene, and each word reflects part of the wonder. Do not think that the interpretation of the sages exhausts that wonder. It is only to introduce beginners into the mystery embedded in the Torah. Know that if you will explore the words of the sages as you would for a hidden treasure, you will find a treasure-house of precious objects which they have stored away. It is the simpleton who looks upon their words as "only homilies."[88]

Another great defender of Aggadah was Rabbi David ibn Zimra (the RaDBaZ).[96] In his opinion, a person must never say that "Aggadah is not true and basic and was not revealed from heaven like the rest of the Oral Torah. . . . Know that in Aggadah there are both revealed and hidden teachings. What is revealed delights the heart; that which is hidden is only for those expert in mystic lore, in the deepest secrets of the universe."[89]

Wherever you find disparagement of the Aggadah, there you find also religious impoverishment. In the circles of the modern Jewish Enlightenment, too, the scoffers abounded. They did so not because they found its metaphors strange or its maxims outlandish but because the very essence of its enterprise, that is, treating the fundamental problems of life through the eyes of religious faith, was foreign to those people. The streams of faith had dried up for them, and any discussion of the relationship between man and God was empty chaff in their eyes. One learned nineteenth-century scholar suggested that "the study of Aggadah was despised by the Sages and they did not look upon a student of Aggadah as a scholar. . . . The very name Aggadah

---

[87] Ibid., 82.
[88] *Gur Aryeh* [Commentary on the Torah], beginning of Parashat Vayyetze.
[89] Responsa of RaDBaZ, Livorno (Leghorn), #232.

---

by Ludwig IX and was occasioned by Nicholas of Donin, who convinced Pope Gregory IX to order the Talmud banned on the grounds that it was both contrary to Scripture and insulting to Christianity.

[95] Sixteenth-century communal leader, polymath, writer in many genres, and mystic.
[96] Sixteenth century, Land of Israel and Egypt.

suggested deceit and fabrication, for it is mere narrative, arising from some inner sources like poetic metaphors which have no relationship to true wisdom."[90]

Rabbi Nahman Krochmal[97] pondered this problem and strove to find a protecting shield for the attacks against Aggadah. In contrast to the "enlightened ones" of the Berlin school, who could find no merit in Aggadah, he suggested:

> The essential subject matter of Aggadah is the focusing and direction of the heart, and its goal is to infuse the masses with piety, with moral instruction and with sound beliefs. To achieve this, they clothed their homilies in words and idioms that ordinary people could understand. . . . The congregations to whom they preached consisted almost wholly of masses of plain people and women,[98] weary exiles exhausted from their week-long labors, who came on Sabbaths and festivals to listen to the Rabbi's discourse. Obviously, such a congregation was not interested in a critical, detailed analysis of Scriptures in order to establish the truth of a particular text.[91]

However, we must refute the assumption of those scholars that Aggadah developed only to supply subject matter for the preachers in their pulpits and that its end goal was to nourish the congregation. The fact is that in many places in the Talmud we find the Tannaim and Amoraim discussing and debating Aggadah in the same way as they dealt with Halakhah. Rabban Gamaliel, president of the Sanhedrin, who wore his crown with haughtiness, and who, it is true, sometimes dismissed some aggadic teachings as too bizarre, nevertheless frequently said, "We still need the interpretation of the Moda'ite,"[92] for Rabbi Eleazar the Moda'ite was the acknowledged expert in Aggadah. In general, the truly great Sages did not primp and preen. They did not, that is, maintain that the halakhic teachings were their special nourishment whereas the aggadic teachings were bread for the poor and ignorant masses.[99]

The critics of the modern age have largely been influenced by the view of Spinoza, adopted by Moses Mendelssohn, which says: Judaism is law, the disciplined life, and not a system of beliefs and opinions. Mendelssohn thus removed Judaism from the domain of religious thought and placed it in the domain of deeds, constricting it to a legal system. "Among all the Mosaic commandments, there is not a single one which utters the words, 'Believe' or 'Do not believe'; all of them say, 'You shall' or 'You shall not.'"

---

[90] See anonymous article "Al Aggadot ha-Talmud" [On the Aggadot in the Talmud] in Jost and Creizenach's periodical *Tziyyon* 2 (1842): 108ff.

[91] *Moreh Nevukhei Ha-Zeman* [The Guide for the Perplexed of the Time], pp. 242, 247.

[92] BT Shabbat 55b; see also BT Megillah 15b.

---

[97] Eighteenth- to nineteenth-century Galicia; one of the foremost figures of the Enlightenment and a major figure in developing the historical consciousness characteristic of Jewish scholarship in the modern era.

[98] Although the description jars today, it is at least understandable in a context in which women were largely uneducated.

[99] As opposed to more contemporary scholars, to whom Heschel's attention now turns.

Moses Mendelssohn's assumption was accepted as basic dogma by the enlightened ones, namely, that peoples of the ancient Near East were not ready to think in abstract terms, and that philosophical studies were strange to them.[93] Judaism and theology were considered to be opposites, and the masters of Midrash were said never to have tried to sort out the various ideas and to arrange them in a logical, systematic order. One cannot find in Aggadah the philosophical or theological system of any of the Sages, certainly not any unified, concrete arrangement of thought.[94]

At the same time, one who reads the various studies and essays that have been written by Jews in the modern era on the masters of Aggadah would receive the impression that they were a model of collegiality and that all gave words of wisdom and morality that were plain to understand, lucid, and easily accepted. It was rather in Halakhah that Sages struggled with and triumphed over one another, with many opposing approaches and many disputes.[100] That is, the impression is given that in the realm of faith and religious thought, all was a single fellowship, with no polemics and no debate, as if they never entered the fray at all.[95]

Superior Aggadot—Mystifying Aggadot

Midrashic literature contains many strange Aggadot. But do we not find strange things in matters of Halakhah as well?[96] One should, therefore, not approach aggadic literature as if it were a last will and testament and invoke the principle that "if part of it is null, then it is entirely null."[97]

The term *strange,* however, requires examination. Teachings that may seem strange to one Sage may be precious and appealing to another. For example, Rabbi Neho-rai[101] expounded on the miracle at the Sea. "When the people Israel passed through the Sea, the infants were thirsty. A mother would stretch out her hand and fill her bottle with salt water, which immediately turned sweet. Yet another miracle took place: a mother would stretch forth her hand beneath the waves and pick figs,

---

[93] See Paul Fiebig's views in his studies of the Gospels and Jesus' parables (Jerusalem: Magnes Press, 1950) cited in Isaak Heinemann's *Darkhei Ha-Aggadah,* chapters 1–2 (citing Max Kadushin's *Organic Thinking: A Study in Rabbinic Thought* [New York: Jewish Theological Seminary of America, 1938]; and Lucien Lévy-Bruhl's 1926 inquiry into the thought of primitive peoples).

[94] *Hebrew Encyclopedia* (Tel Aviv: Society for the Publication of Encyclopedias, 1949-81), *Aggadah,* 1:356.

[95] See, e.g., Samuel Poznanski, *Ma'asei ha-Tannaim* (Warsaw: Ha-Tzefira, 1917),17; and E. Z. Melamed, *Parashiyot Me'aggadot Ha-tannaim* (Jerusalem: Kiryat Sefer, 1954), 58.

[96] See, e.g., Plemo's question to Rabbi Judah the Patriarch: "If one has two heads, on which should the Tefillin be placed?" (BT Menahot 37a).

[97] PT Sanhedrin 2:6 (20c).

---

[100] This is expressing the curious but often true notion that disputes in a subject matter are the surest sign that the subject is being taken seriously—else why dispute?

[101] A second-century sage, sometimes identified with Rabbi Meir, because both Nehorai and Meir are words that denote enlightenment.

pomegranates, peaches and give them to her child." When Rabban Gamaliel received word of this exposition, he sent word to Rabbi Nehorai, "I see that you, too, have joined the mystifiers." To which he replied, "I am only interpreting a scriptural verse which reads, 'These forty years the Lord your God was with you and you did not lack for anything' (Deuteronomy 2:7). If you grant that the day on which Israel crossed the Sea is to be counted in the forty years . . . you must conclude that just as they lacked for nothing in the wilderness so at the Sea they lacked for nothing."[98]

Nevertheless, Rabban Gamaliel himself indulged in scriptural exegesis for the purpose of deriving a lesson from them. He taught, for example, that in messianic times, women would give birth every day, trees would bear fruit every day, the soil of Eretz Yisrael would produce fine cakes. He supported these statements with scriptural verses. But a student scoffed at him and said, "It is written, 'there is nothing new under the sun.'" Whereupon Rabban Gamaliel made every effort to prove to him that such wonders were within the realm of possibility.[99]

One of the great critics of Aggadah was Rabbi Tarfon, a contemporary of Rabbi Akiva and Rabbi Ishmael. It is worth paying attention to his views. He did not give deference to the aggadic teachings of the great aggadist Rabbi Eleazar the Moda'ite, nor those of his colleague Rabbi Akiva, nor those of Rabbi Nehorai.

When they would mystify him with their fanciful expositions, he would praise Rabbi Ishmael, in the presence of his colleagues and say, "I want you to know that he is a great scholar and an expert in Aggadah."[100] In the entire Tannaitic era, only Rabbi Ishmael was singled out as the "expert in Aggadah." If you examine the literature carefully, you will find that the aggadic teachings of Rabbi Ishmael, which were usually transmitted in the name of "the school of Rabbi Ishmael," exceed in number his halakhic teachings in the Talmud.[101]

Rabbi Ishmael, who did not acknowledge Rabbi Akiva's prowess in Aggadah, described the distinction between a master of Talmud and a master of Aggadah in a manner that goes to the root of the subject. He takes the verse in Proverbs, "A rich man is clever in his own eyes" (28:11), to refer to the master of Talmud, "but a perceptive poor man can see through him" (ibid) to refer to the master of Aggadah.[102] That is to say, the master of Halakhah is like the rich man who is impressed with his own wisdom, though it may not be so. The master of Aggadah, however, the poor man, understands the importance of exploring the subject deeply, more so than the Sage. Wealth is no sign of wisdom.[103]

In sum, what we have said is this: it is not possible to speak of aggadic literature as a unitary composition, as a single fabric. Just as halakhic literature reveals various

[98] YS Hukkat 764.

[99] See BT Shabbat 30b.   [100] BT Moed Katan 28b.

[101] See Michael Higger, *Otzar Ha-Baraitot* (in Hebrew), 10 vols. (New York: Rabbinical Assembly and Central Conference of American Rabbis, 1938–48), 3:38ff., 4:35ff.

[102] Ecclesiastes Rabbah 6:2.

[103] Commentary of *Metsudat David* on Proverbs 28:11.

approaches to the legal problems, so we find different approaches in the field of beliefs and opinions. Here we have literalists and here we have mystifiers. Clashes of opinion everywhere—and the reasons for them are profound. It is our aim in this study to demonstrate that these differences are based on two distinct systems of thought as expressed in the two great rabbinic schools, the school of Rabbi Ishmael and the school of Rabbi Akiva.[102]

A Profile of Rabbi Ishmael

Rabbi Ishmael and Rabbi Akiva, the two greatest Tannaim of the third generation,[103] were nicknamed "Fathers of the World."[104] 104 Each of them founded new approaches to exegesis of the Torah and established in Israel schools that bear their names. From these schools came the great halakhic exegeses of the Torah. The Mekhilta of Rabbi Ishmael on Exodus, the Sifre on Numbers, and part of the Sifre on Deuteronomy came from the school of Rabbi Ishmael. And the Mekhilta of Rabbi Simeon bar Yohai on Exodus, the Sifra on Leviticus, the Sifre Zuta on Numbers, and part of the Sifre on Deuteronomy came from the school of Rabbi Akiva.105

The life of Rabbi Akiva and his profile became the subjects of many books and articles,106 but about the life of Rabbi Ishmael our knowledge is scant.107 Scholars have

---

104 PT Shekalim 3:1 (47b).

105 On these identifications, see J. N. Epstein, *Mevo'ot le-Sifrut ha-Tannaim: Introduction to Tannaitic Literature: Mishna, Tosefta and Halakhic Midrashim* (in Hebrew) (Jerusalem: Magnes, 1957), 501ff. The "Midrash Tannaim" on Deuteronomy is also counted as a Tannaitic midrash and is associated with the Akivan school.

106 Among these are Louis Finkelstein, *Akiba: Scholar, Saint, and Martyr* (Philadelphia: Jewish Theological Seminary, 1936); J. S. Tsuri, *Rabbi Akiva* (Jerusalem, 1924); and Israel Konovitz, *Rabbi Akiva: A Complete Collection of his Sayings in the Talmudic and Midrashic Literature* (Jerusalem, 1956).

107 There is some confusion about the identity of Rabbi Ishmael. It is likely that there were two Rabbis named Ishmael ben Elisha. The first was a High Priest who served in the Temple, and the second was his grandson, the colleague of Rabbi Akiva.

---

[102] Despite these citations concerning Rabbi Ishmael's prowess and expertise in Aggadah, Heschel does not mean to suggest that the Aggadah is to be identified with his school. On the contrary, Heschel wants to demonstrate that Aggadah's seriousness already in classical times is signaled by the fact that the two great schools disputed one another on aggadic matters, and that their different approaches to the text showed up in aggadic disputes as well. The praise of Rabbi Ishmael given above is useful to Heschel, however, because (as will be seen) he wishes to rehabilitate the memory and reputation of Rabbi Ishmael, and he will seem to be taking sides with Ishmael often during this long treatise.

[103] Rabbi Akiva's martyrdom in 135 C.E. at the hands of the Romans is related in Jewish tradition and accepted as historical fact. Although Heschel here in his original text tells us, per tradition, that a similar death befell Rabbi Ishmael, recent scholarship debates whether Rabbi Ishmael also died a martyr's death in the same conflict or died a natural death somewhat earlier. See *Encyclopedia Judaica* (Jerusalem: Keter, 1972), 9:83–86, s.v. "Ishmael ben Elisha."

[104] See n. [32] above.

barely treated it, and for this reason we shall here point out a few details concerning his life.

His family hailed from the "landholders of the Upper Galilee,"[108] and he was a son of the High Priest.[105] He experienced his father's service in the Temple, and he recalled "the garments that Abba wore, and the diadem that he placed in the middle of his forehead."[109] Concerning his childhood, it was related:

> It happened that Rabbi Joshua ben Hananiah went to Rome. There he was told about a child from Jerusalem, with a ruddy complexion, beautiful eyes, handsome face, and curly locks, standing in a pillory. Rabbi Joshua went to investigate. As he reached the entrance to the prison, he recited: "Who was it gave Jacob over to despoilment and Israel to plunderers?" (Isaiah 42:24). And the child responded: "Surely, the Lord against whom they sinned, in whose ways they would not walk, and whose Teaching they would not obey" (ibid.). Immediately, Rabbi Joshua began to weep, and he said: "I am certain that this child would be able to give teaching in Israel. I call heaven and earth to witness that I shall not budge from here until I redeem him at whatever price they shall set." And it was related that he did not budge until he had redeemed him for a great deal of money. And it was not many days before he was giving instruction in Israel. Who was he? Rabbi Ishmael ben Elisha.[110]

Among his early masters was Rabbi Joshua ben Hananiah.[111] He also received instruction from Rabbi Eliezer ben Hyrcanus.[112] Likewise, he was a disciple of Rabbi Nehunia ben Hakkaneh, from whom he learned his approach to exegesis of the Torah (by means of generalization and specification).[106] [113]

---

[108] BT Bava Kamma 80a; see *Dikdukei Soferim* ad loc.
[109] Tosefta Hallah 1:10; see also BT Hullin 49a and Ketubot 105b.
[110] BT Gittin 58a; PT Horayot 3:4 (48b).
[111] Mishnah Kilayim 6:2; Avodah Zarah 2:5.
[112] Sifra Tazri'a 68b.   [113] BT Shevu'ot 26a.

---

[105] There has long been confusion surrounding the various places in rabbinic literature in which Rabbi Ishmael is described as "the High Priest" (this is also so in the medieval liturgy about the ten martyrs that is recited on the Day of Atonement). Among some, Rabbi Ishmael is understood to be the grandson of a High Priest who was also named Ishmael ben Elisha, whereas others take the title "High Priest" in a nonliteral way (since Rabbi Ishmael lived several decades after the destruction of the Temple). Heschel here adopts the first point of view, adding that he was also the son of a functioning High Priest and thus is called a High Priest himself (as he would have been, had the Temple remained in operation). Separating historical fact from mythic narrative is always tricky in such questions. See Gershom Scholem, *Major Trends in Jewish Mysticism* (Jerusalem: Schocken, 1941), 356 n. 3; and *Encyclopedia Judaica*, s.v. "Ishmael ben Elisha."

[106] *Kelal u-ferat* ("General and Specific") is a hermeneutic method associated with Rabbi Ishmael. It makes significant but conservative inferences from the fact that the Scripture sometimes speaks in general categories, sometimes in specifics, and sometimes juxtaposes general and specific descriptions of legal cases side by side. By contrast, Rabbi Akiva is associated with the method *ribbui u-mi'ut* ("Expansion and Exclusion"). This more radical method seizes on a variety of common words and nuances in the Torah's language as invitations to expand and constrict the categories under discussion in a very free and sweeping fashion. See Glossary, *ribbui* and *mi'ut*.

Rabbi Ishmael was apparently among those sages who inclined toward accommodation and adaptation and were opposed to rebellion and revolt against the Roman government. Yet even he was touched by the deadly sword, for he was one of the ten righteous men who were cruelly put to death during the Hadrianic persecutions, and who became known as the "ten martyrs." When these righteous men were imprisoned and condemned to death, what did they say to one another? "The time came for Rabbi Ishmael and Rabbi Simeon to be executed, and Rabbi Simeon said to Rabbi Ishmael: 'My master, my heart sinks, because I know not why I am being put to death!' Rabbi Ishmael said to Rabbi Simeon: 'Did it never happen that a man came to you for a judgment or for religious instruction and you put him off until you had finished drinking from your cup, or putting on your shoes, or donning your cloak?' And the Torah says, 'if you afflict, afflict them . . .' (Exodus 22:22)[107]—that is, whether it be a major or a minor affliction. And because of this answer, Rabbi Simeon said to him: My master, you have comforted me!"[114] Or, according to another version, Rabbi Ishmael said to him: "Perhaps you were disturbed while eating a meal, or were roused from sleep when a woman came to ask instruction concerning her menstruation, and whether she was impure or pure, and you told her to go and resume relations with her husband,[108] for you wished to sleep. . . ."[115]

Rabbi Ishmael was beloved and admired among his colleagues. Rabbi Eleazar ben Azariah and Rabbi Akiva called him "my brother."[116] "When Rabbi Simeon and Rabbi Ishmael were killed, Rabbi Akiva said to his disciples: brace yourselves for great suffering, for had any goodness been the destiny of our generation, none but Rabbi Simeon and Rabbi Ishmael would have received it first. Rather, it is revealed and known to the One who spoke and the world came into being, that great suffering is the destiny of our generation, and these two were removed from our midst first, so as to fulfill what is written: 'The righteous man perishes, and no one considers; pious men are taken away, and no one gives thought . . .' (Isaiah 57:1)."[117]

---

[114] MI Nezikin 18. [115] Tractate Semahot [Mourning] 8.
[116] BT Sanhedrin 51b; Mishnah Yadayim 4:3. [117] MI Nezikin 18.

---

[107] The translation given here is that of Everett Fox, in his translation of the Torah, so that the doubling of the Hebrew root 'nh ("afflict, mistreat, or abuse") is evident. The exegesis here is built on that doubling, which is a standard grammatical feature in biblical Hebrew but is here taken as a symbol of the fact that even minimal mistreatments of the unfortunate will not be tolerated. Although the exegesis itself is actually not in Rabbi Ishmael's usual style, the content of the exegesis (namely, that the suffering is a retribution that may seem arbitrary to us) is in keeping with what Heschel will document as an Ishmaelian approach in chapters 6 and 7.

[108] This is a play on words, for the verse in Exodus just cited revolves around the word 'nh, meaning "to mistreat." But onah, which is phonetically very close to this root, can mean "marital relations," and that is how it is applied here, as a cavalier attitude toward a couple's desire to do the right thing, an attitude that may have led them inadvertently into a misdeed.

Two Philosophical Methods[109]

The fact that at a crossroads in Jewish history two "fathers of the world" met, men who were to become trailblazers in religious philosophy, is of major importance. The meeting of intellectual giants of opposing aspirations, who debated on issues of ultimate significance, inevitably laid bare problems in religious faith that the Sages tended to conceal.

Each generation has its exegetes. Each riddle has its solutions; and the deeper the riddle, the more numerous the solutions.[110] The Torah itself can be acquired in two different ways: via the road of reason or the road of vision. Rabbi Ishmael's path was that of the surface, plain meaning of the text. Rabbi Akiva's path was that of the esoteric meaning. And it is clear that they did not construct their methods *ex nihilo.* Such divergences of paths are the work of generations, and these differences did not suddenly appear in the generation of Rabbi Ishmael and Rabbi Akiva. Their source lay in diverse approaches to Jewish teachings, as they were handed down by tradition over the course of whole eras. The nation harbored treasuries of thought, and Rabbi Ishmael and Rabbi Akiva served as mouthpieces for voices and echoes of generations that preceded them. Yet it was also in their schools that these ideas crystallized and took on a form that had been unknown to previous generations. For they were able to channel ancient and powerful intellectual flows and, in so doing, nourish generations yet to come.

We shall not be able to reach the foundation stone of this debate merely through a comparative study, but rather through an intense consideration of the essence of each method, at a depth that transcends individual ideas. Such research will lay out before us that deepest level of thought on which both intellectual movements drew and from which also flowed their debates and contradictions.

Intellectual debates and psychological rumblings are the stuff of every generation. Spiritual problems continually shed forms and take on new ones. Before you can understand the intellectual movements of recent times, you must inquire into the chain of tradition that precedes them.[111] The things about which Rabbi Akiva and

---

[109] In this section, Heschel, who had a great appreciation of music and musical form, writes a true overture to the chapters that follow. Almost every line is a thematic anticipation of some point that will be developed later in the book. Indeed, there is so much overlap that some parts of this section have been excised in this edition to avoid redundancy. But some foreshadowing is quite useful, and in these editorial notes we point out only the most striking anticipations of later issues and topics. The careful reader will be able to pick up many more.

[110] The riddle referred to here is the very nature of Torah, what its essence is and how it communicates to human beings. This is the central issue of chapter 2.

[111] Here Heschel is tipping us off to what is, in many ways, his real agenda in this work, that is, contemporary Jewish issues, such as post-Shoah theology, attitudes to prayer, fundamentalisms, etc. These contemporary issues will sometimes be dealt with overtly in subsequent chapters, and sometimes covertly, but they will always be there.

Rabbi Ishmael disagreed were still the subjects of debates and triumphant disputations among medieval scholars, and they are still on the agenda today.

Everything cycles in the world; and just as the intellectual problems remain with us, so does the tension. The divergences and dissensions between the two "fathers of the world" continued on their way throughout the generations. It is just that sometimes we find discrete methodologies, each internally consistent, and sometimes we find the two intellectual subsets included side by side, or intertwined, within a single method. Sometimes one approach appears to have been subsumed by the other, and sometimes they have been synthesized, so that it seems that two rival ways of grasping the world can somehow coexist within the same mind.[112]

What were Rabbi Ishmael's personal characteristics? Delicacy, intellectual reserve, clear thinking, and sobriety. He sought the middle way, and his words were carefully measured. His emotional equilibrium and his intellectual sobriety did not allow his feelings to sweep him off into extremism. He preferred one small, immaculate measure of understanding to nine measures of extremism; one small measure of lucidity to nine measures of profundity. Paradox was anathema to him, and he expended his energy on clarity and precision, on that which was given to understanding and cognition.[113]

Rabbi Akiva could be credited with seeking out the wondrous; Rabbi Ishmael could be credited with shunning the wondrous.[114] He shook no structural beams;[115] nei-

---

[112] Here Heschel is staking out a kind of "zone of immunity" from potential criticisms about his identifications of certain points of view and methodologies to Rabbi Ishmael and Rabbi Akiva and their schools. Such criticisms were, in fact, forthcoming, but Heschel is here making the claim that one cannot expect major approaches like this to be perfectly distinct from one another. Thus, if there sometimes appears to be a "crossing of the wires," in which an Ishmaelian view shows up in a statement attributed to Akiva or one of his disciples, this disclaimer covers him. But while there is a tactical reason for Heschel making this remark here, it is also no doubt true to a large extent. One need only think of how thoroughly laissez-faire economics and the workings of the welfare state have become intertwined in contemporary Western democracies. This does not imply that there were not, and are not, two distinctly identifiable streams of thought in economics answering to these descriptions. Heschel's claim should be understood similarly.

[113] This is not to say that Rabbi Ishmael is being identified with a devotion to literal meaning. On the contrary, we are speaking here of "plain" or "surface" meaning (the real denotation of the Hebrew *peshat*). Literal meaning may be very far from plain meaning. A good example of this would be the well-known commentary of Samuel ben Meir (RaSHBaM) on Exodus 13:9. RaSHBaM, who was noted as a devotee of plain meaning, taught that the plain meaning of "this shall serve you as a sign on your hand and as a reminder between your eyes" is a metaphorical one. In this case, the literal meaning (adopted by Jewish practice, hence the phylacteries) is *not* the plain or surface meaning. It will be crucial to keep this distinction between literal and plain meaning in mind during all that follows in this work. These issues will be dealt with in chapter 13, "The Language of Torah," especially the sections on *peshat*, *derash*, and *sod*, the modalities of interpretation.

[114] This division of approach will be expanded on in chapter 3, "Miracles."

[115] A reference to Isaiah 6:4, and a metaphor for changing a whole worldview, as the young Isaiah's was changed by seeing the Divine Assembly.

ther did he impose his authority on the text. Among his good qualities was a level-headed caution. Better in his eyes was a single measure of reflection on what is written and given than massive speculation above and beyond to the very limits of apprehension. One who sees Rabbi Ishmael in a dream should "anticipate wisdom."

Rabbi Ishmael's teachings contained straightforward logic, and with it lucidity, simplicity of language, and an aversion to intellectual games. Attributions to him have no superfluity of language or florid expressions. He sought to strip Scripture of anthropomorphisms and to excise unnecessary metaphor and imagery.[116]

But Rabbi Akiva's teachings sought to penetrate to inner depths, with profundity and potency of language. He did not shrink from anthropomorphism, but rather he preserved the concrete in Scripture,[117] cherished imaginative meanings, added metaphorical embellishments, and created images of the supernal world. Instead of a logic that was subservient to surface meaning, he championed free exegesis and intellectual flights.

A poet at heart, and at the same time a razor-sharp genius, Rabbi Akiva was special in that two fundamental qualities were combined in him: poetry and acuity, the esoteric and the analytic. This rugged man wanted to stand in the Divine Assembly, to roll away the veil from the Torah's secrets. He was caught up in matters that mortal reason cannot apprehend, and his words were singed by the torch of desire to discern the uppermost realms.[118]

Rabbi Akiva articulated his thoughts in order to rouse the public, to demand action from them, to be their guide; and he was the first among the heroes in the wars of Torah. He was a man of action, a spokesman for his people, a public servant, and a traveler to lands beyond the sea. At the same time he was a man in whose soul a poetic spirit moved. His heart and mind sang out to the living God, and in his very language he decoded some of the riddles of life and sought out the secret of Israel's existence in the world.[119]

Rabbi Akiva amazed those of his generation with his heroic actions. He did not fear bringing down the wrath of Israel's enemies. He was not wary of danger, and he taught many how to revolt and fight, and how, if necessary, to give their lives for the commandments. A triumphal tune sounded in the sanctuary of Rabbi Akiva.

In the sanctuary of Rabbi Ishmael there was a still small voice.[120] He was moder-

---

[116] That is, the Ishmaelian approach sees words as primarily denoting things rather than serving as symbols for many layers of meaning. The fundamental Ishmaelian and Akivan approaches to language will be discussed in chapter 2. Their approaches to anthropomorphisms in Scripture will be treated in chapter 12.

[117] For example, Akiva would accept and preserve anthropomorphisms that were the literal (but not plain) meaning of Scripture.

[118] This anticipates Heschel's treatment of rabbinic mysticism in chapters 15–16.

[119] Rabbi Akiva's messianic activism will be discussed in the last section of chapter 11.

[120] As a reference to Elijah's epiphany at Mount Horeb given in 1 Kings 19, this is meant to suggest that Ishmael was not given to zealotry (just as Elijah's zealotry was the subject of God's lesson to him in that revelation).

ate in all things, be they heavenly matters or mundane matters concerning his people. Just as he guarded against extremism in exegesis, so did he criticize those who went to excess in demanding martyrdom, for too much victimization was likely to hamper severely Israel's chances of survival. The world is built on compassion, not on heroism. He, too, taught many, and his lesson was: this is not the way.[121]

The teachings of Rabbi Akiva, who dealt with metaphysics and who entered the *Pardes,* inclined toward a sense of mutual empathy with God. It was not just Israel whom God redeemed from Egypt. "As it were, You redeemed Yourself."[122] He taught that the participation of the Holy and Blessed One in the life of Israel is not merely a mental nod, a measure of compassion born of relationship to God's people. The pain of compassion amounts to pain at a distance; it is the pain of the onlooker. But the participation of the Holy and Blessed One is that of total identification, something that touches God's very essence, God's majestic being. As it were, the afflictions of the nation inflict wounds on God. "Wherever Israel was exiled, the Shekhinah accompanied them . . . and in the future, when they will return from exile, the Shekhinah will, as it were, accompany them as well." The Holy and Blessed One is a partner in the suffering of His creatures; He is involved in the lot of His people, wounded by their sufferings and redeemed by their liberation.

In the wake of this reversal there was effected a veritable revolution in religious thought, one that exerted a profound influence through the course of the generations. From time immemorial the people had perceived the salvation of Israel as a human need, a national need, through which, to be sure, God's name would be magnified in the world. But now Rabbi Akiva taught that Israel's salvation is a divine need. From this circle of thought emerged language such as: "The Holy and Blessed One yearns for the prayers of the righteous"; "one whose toil is Torah brings satisfaction to his Creator"; "for God's sake"; "we need each other"; "you should have assisted Me"; "redemption is Mine and yours"; and "Israel's salvation is the salvation of the Holy and Blessed One." Mundane matters have their parallels above. They dared to look, and in so doing, they found that the pains of the nation were indeed paralleled by the pains of the Creator. And thus, instead of bearing their own afflictions, the people began instead to share in the afflictions of Heaven.

Tannaitic literature contains many appellations for the Holy and Blessed One, and they are all in Hebrew. Note that the only such appellation in Aramaic—*rahamana,* the compassionate One[123]—was used by Rabbi Akiva and by his disciple Rabbi Simeon bar Yohai. This nickname was cherished by the Amoraim and is ubiquitous in their sayings.

Foreign to the teachings of Rabbi Ishmael were Rabbi Akiva's ideas that the Holy and Blessed One participated in the pain of His creatures, in the sufferings of individ-

---

[121] This description of Rabbi Ishmael as "countercultural" sets us up for Heschel's description in the next section of this chapter of Rabbi Akiva's victory in the nation's hearts and minds.

[122] The theme of divine participation in human suffering will be expanded on in chapter 6.

[123] Here used in the sense of "empathetic One."

ual Jews and of the nation. Such an idea is not befitting God's dignity and could lead to a denial of the power of the Holy and Blessed One. In Rabbi Ishmael's teachings, it is God's measure of judgment and God's power that are primary, not the measure of compassion.[124]

Rabbi Akiva justified God's ways, the sufferings that God brings on the righteous, and the tranquility in which the wicked dwell. It is an act of kindness that the Creator does for the righteous when God brings upon them injuries and calamities; and it is just that God lets tranquility flow over the wicked in this world. On the contrary, when afflictions did not come [to the righteous], he would say in astonishment: "Could it be that the Master has already enjoyed his reward?" You may say, "there is a righteous person suffering," but in reality, "one cannot argue with the judgments of the One who spoke and the world came into being, because all is truthful and just!" "The world is judged for the good!" A righteous person who suffers from affliction should not say, "it is bad for me." Afflictions are precious, and a truly righteous person does not rebel against them. Instead of saying "a righteous person is suffering," rather say, "in the case of a righteous person, whatever the Compassionate One does is valuable and precious." Why was Moses our Master punished, so that he would not enter the Land? Because he challenged the Most High.[125] The divine pathos was the lens through which Rabbi Akiva saw the world and all that is in it. That which happens in nature is merely an expression of the sufferings on high.

This teaching discomfited Rabbi Ishmael, and he saw in it no adequate answer to the plaintive question: Why does the way of the wicked prosper? Why are there righteous people who suffer? In his school it was taught that Moses, the chief of all the prophets, himself struggled with this problem, demanded an answer from the Holy and Blessed One, but was not granted it. From his school came forth the anguished cry: "Who is like You, God, among the mighty (Exodus 15:11)—who is like You in how you see the humiliation of Your children and remain silent?"[126]

An affinity for afflictions, which was for Rabbi Akiva a major life principle, demands analysis and investigation. Such an affinity is a matter that relates not only to the domain of humans' relationship to God but also to the value that human beings assign to the world itself. In that era a certain outlook gained prominence, an outlook that denigrated this world and emphasized the tension that exists between the transient and the eternal.[127] This world was seen as a place of impurity, and the world to come was the place of purity. Do these two worlds complement each other,

---

[124] This anticipates the first section of chapter 11, "Judgment or Mercy?"

[125] That is, he doubted God's compassion.

[126] This is a play on the similarity of the words *elim* ("the mighty"), and *ilmim* ("the mute"). More on this in chapters 6 and 7.

[127] Thus, the first and second centuries were marked by many messianic movements, as well as by Gnosticism, which also denigrated the sensual world of creation. The relationship of rabbinic theology to dualistic currents in Hellenistic thought will find treatment in chapter 14.

or are they antagonists? Many Sages arose and said that it is not worth it for a person to labor in this world, for the primary life is in the future world.

Rabbi Ishmael was alone in challenging the denigration of the here and now and the contempt for worldly affairs. In Rabbi Akiva's school, they had interpreted "You shall keep My laws and my rules, by the pursuit of which a person shall live" (Leviticus 18:5) to mean "in the world to come." Against this, Rabbi Ishmael expounded, "by the pursuit of which a person shall live—and not die." And in contradistinction to those Sages who were prepared to neglect the transient, and shun worldly trades so as to study Torah, Rabbi Ishmael expounded: "'See, I set before you this day life and prosperity, death and adversity . . . choose life' (Deuteronomy 30:15, 19)—'choose life' means learn a trade."[128]

Rabbi Akiva, who was not inhibited about speaking of heavenly matters in physical terms, and who taught that the Divine Presence literally descended onto Mount Sinai, also taught that the Shekhinah dwells in the west.[129] This point of view apprehends the indwelling of the Shekhinah as a physical habitation and therefore as being subject to degrees. That is, the presence of the Shekhinah in the west is unlike its presence anywhere else. Rabbi Akiva, who entered the *Pardes* and dealt in metaphysics, and about whom the Talmud says: "The ministering angels attempted to throw him out, when the Holy and Blessed One said to them: Leave this sage alone, for he is worthy to look at My Presence," had not a shred of doubt that Moses our Master saw the Divine Image. He was, after all, the one who taught that but for the effects of sin, human beings would have perceived the Divine Image directly, that when Moses spoke the words of Torah he was literally in heaven, and that the Presence descended onto Mount Sinai. Standing at Mount Sinai, the Israelites said to Moses: "We wish to see our Sovereign!" and some say that at Mount Sinai "they saw God face to face."[130]

Rabbi Ishmael, the one who asked: "Is it then possible for mere flesh and blood to give pleasure to the Creator?," the one who, in reaction to the phrase "And God went before them" (Exodus 13:21) asked, "Is it possible to say thus of the one who fills up all of heaven and earth?," rejected the idea that the Shekhinah is limited in space. Instead, he offered the intellectual and spiritual apprehension that "the Shekhinah is everywhere." This principle removes the idea of indwelling from the universe of location and establishes instead that the Shekhinah transcends space.[131]

---

[128] The this-worldly emphasis in Rabbi Ishmael's outlook is the principal focus of chapter 8.

[129] The Temple in Jerusalem (like the Sanctuary in the desert before it) faced west; see chapter 5.

[130] See the description in Exodus 24. On the question of "seeing God," see chapter 16.

[131] Heschel here brings us to the idea that Rabbi Ishmael saw the Presence of God as ultimately transcendent, whereas the Akivan point of view saw the Presence as capable of actual indwelling in our midst, that is, as immanent. See chapters 2 and 14 for the differing use of these terms throughout the book. The question of the "location of the Shekhinah," or whether it can be located at all, is the focus of chapter 5.

Rabbi Ishmael also found that the very word *Presence* bears several meanings, and that the verse "Oh, let me behold Your Presence" (Exodus 33:18) should not be interpreted as referring to something that can be located in space, something that can be apprehended with the sense of sight, but rather as referring to that which is revealed in time. "Presence" means justice and righteousness, which are revealed in history. That is: Moses did not at all wish to see the Shekhinah, but rather yearned to understand the secret of the suffering of the righteous and the prosperity of the wicked.

Rabbi Ishmael grasped the meaning of the verse "for man may not see Me and live" (Exodus 33:20) in its plain meaning, and thus held that Moses our Master did not see the Presence. When the Torah says of Moses, "he beholds the likeness of the Lord" (Numbers 12:8), "likeness" means that which God sees; that is, Moses saw what the Holy and Blessed One sees. Moses was given to "see" God's words but was not given a view of the Shekhinah. According to this approach, Israel said to Moses while standing at Mount Sinai: "We wish to hear directly from the mouth of our Sovereign!"[132] for the Holy and Blessed One sees but cannot be seen.

Rationalism and lucidity of thought characterized the teachings of Rabbi Ishmael. His greatness lay in a congenial straightforwardness amenable to all. Soaring visions marked the teachings of Rabbi Akiva; his language was a ladder planted on earth, ending in heaven. In one system of thought, there was clarity; in the other, profundity. Here, a shunning of the wondrous; there, a thirst to apprehend the hidden and the wondrous.

Here is an example of Rabbi Ishmael's talent for revealing a verse's intent from the surface meaning of a word. It is written: "Whoever sheds the blood of a human, in a human [court] he shall have his blood shed" (Genesis 9:6).[133] Why were the words "in a human . . ." necessary? Along came Rabbi Ishmael and suggested, that even in the case of fetuses in their mothers' wombs, one is liable for shedding their blood, for it is written: 'Whoever sheds the blood of a human, in a human . . . .' "What sort of a human is in a human? You must say it is a fetus in its mother's womb."[118]

---

[118] BT Sanhedrin 57b.

---

[132] The inversion of seeing and hearing here has its antecedent in the text itself, for Exodus 20:15 reports that the people "saw the thunder." In chapters 15 through 18, Heschel examines the influence of apocalyptic thought on the Akivan school and on early rabbinic mysticism. He considers "hearing" to be the central perceptual modality of the biblical prophets and of the Ishmaelian school, while "seeing" is characteristic of the apocalyptists and Rabbi Akiva's school.

[133] The translation given here is intended to make clear the basis of the exegesis in the possibility of re-parsing the sentence so as to read "the blood of a human in a human." Even in this form, it is inexact, because the word "court" must be added to give the sentence sense. In Hebrew, the ambiguity is much more apparent, because the prepositional letter *bet* can have a locational sense ("a human *in* a human, he shall have his blood shed"), or an instrumental sense ("a human, *by means of* a human he shall have his blood shed").

Contrast this with Rabbi Akiva's exegesis: "Whoever sheds blood expunges the Image, for it is said: "Whoever sheds the blood of a human, in a human . . . shall his blood be shed."[119]

That is, the first occurrence of "human" (*adam*) is interpreted by him as the "heavenly *adam*,"[134] and thus the one who kills it expunges the Image.

There are before us two methods for understanding the essence of Torah and prophecy. Often, in halakhic exegesis, Rabbi Ishmael and Rabbi Akiva followed their methods for aggadic exegesis. Rabbi Akiva often departed widely from the plain meaning of the text, because he viewed the text through an esoteric lens. One who locates the Torah in heaven must believe that it has an existence distinct and apart, transcendent;[135] and the Torah that we discourse over on earth is the same Torah that they discourse over in heaven. This point of view sees the Torah as infinite at its core. Its content—that is, that which is visible within the narrow confines of surface meaning—is like a mere drop in the sea. Rabbi Akiva believed that every detail and every stylistic form has a deep significance and a hidden intent.

To Rabbi Akiva, textual teachings were given in order to be expanded upon.[136] One who interprets via the surface meaning alone is like a poor man looking for gleanings.[137] To Rabbi Ishmael, textual teachings were given in order to be understood and to establish traditions,[138] not to be expanded upon. Each verse's plain teaching, which emerges from our rules of logic, is firm and steady, and whoever expands such teachings seeks to restamp the Torah with a die that is foreign to it.

Rabbi Akiva, a man drawn to the esoteric, who was not satisfied with the path of plain reason, felt that the covert in the Torah is far greater than the overt. Thus, he

---

[119] Tosefta Yevamot, end of chapter 8.

---

[134] This is to take the notion of Divine Image (in Genesis 1) very literally indeed. This contrasts, for example, with Philo of Alexandria, a bit more than a century before Akiva, for whom the Divine Image meant rationality. Heschel expands more on the notion of Divine Image in Rabbi Akiva's thought in chapter 14 and sees it as a key instance of the "correspondence of the heavenly and terrestrial."

[135] Extreme caution is called for in interpreting Heschel's language here. In a previous note in this section, we remarked that Ishmael had a transcendent view of the Divine Presence, and Akiva an immanent view. Here Heschel is focusing not on the Divine Image but on the nature of Torah. If the Torah is God's book, and although it is on earth, it is still the book of the immanent God, then the words of the Torah must have qualities that *transcend* the normal canons of language. It is in this sense only that Akiva is here, and in other parts of this work, described as representing transcendence. It is critical that the reader keep this Heschelian ambiguity in mind and the senses straight.

[136] That is, to be uncovered, layers of existing meaning discovered.

[137] That is, seeking a minimal, subsistence level of nourishment.

[138] That is, the text was given for a specific purpose—to communicate instruction to human beings. It is not beckoning to us to discover layers of existing meaning that are not already visible. However, the text does invite us, as does any straightforward set of instructions, to deduce new directives and truths from it, by the use of logic and reason. But that is *construction*, not discovery; and this summarizes the Ishmaelian view.

pursued the mysteries of Torah and found that the letters yield wisdom and reveal matters that reason could never imagine. According to his approach, human knowledge is unlike the knowledge contained in Torah, just as human language is unlike the language of Torah. From every jot and tittle,[139] he would extract mounds and mounds of Halakhot.

Rabbi Ishmael, a man devoted to cool analysis, who had no concern for hidden things and who did not see the Torah as a transcendent existence, walked a straight, direct path. He tested and balanced verses against one another with the scales of logic, with no gimmicks, and explained them straightforwardly. "The Torah speaks in human language" was his guiding principle. The Torah was not given to the ministering angels, and a person can only judge what the eyes of reason see. According to his approach, plain reason is Torah's faithful companion, and the more Torah is brought into harmony with plain reason, the better.

Rabbi Ishmael did not shrink from saying that there are things in the Torah that Moses said on his own authority, and that in many of the instances in which Moses heard things from on high, he transmitted the general meaning and not necessarily the actual words.[140] And just as the Holy and Blessed One left prophets some degree of freedom, in order that they could be partners in prophecy,[141] so did God leave the Sages some degree of freedom,[142] that they might interpret via the thirteen logical rules. It is thus unnecessary for everything to be written in the Torah. Even that which is not explicitly there can be brought to light and derived by logical reason. When they do so, they are paralleling the divine intent.[143]

Over and against this, Rabbi Akiva believed that the expansion of Torah cannot be dependent on the powers of human reason. There is nothing that is not hinted at in the Torah, and there is no Halakhah that has no foundation in the text.[144] All laws are embedded in the Torah and are hinted at by its letters.[120]

---

[120] On the rabbinic text that says, "When Rabbi Akiva died, the arms of the Torah were no more, and the fountains of wisdom were stopped up," Rashi explains: "[this refers to] the depth of insight, and the ability to give support to every nuance of the Oral Torah by the exegesis of texts, and the study of additional letters and language changes in scripture" (BT Sotah 49b).

---

[139] Heschel's phrase here, which literally means "from the tail of every letter," comes from BT Menahot 29b. The translation here is both (a) more in keeping with normal English usage, and (b) in keeping with the talmudic passage cited, since that story makes reference to the crowns (or "tittles") that God was affixing to the letters so that Rabbi Akiva would someday discover their hidden meanings.

[140] Again, because in the Ishmaelian view, the words themselves are not important but only the instructions that they convey. Here Heschel anticipates issues that will be discussed below, particularly chapters 22–24.

[141] This is the central issue of chapter 26.

[142] See chapter 27, sections "Prophecy of the Sages" and "The Power of the Court."

[143] Another explication of the central idea here, which is derivation vs. discovery.

[144] This is the "maximalist" view of "Torah from Heaven," which will be articulated in chapter 31.

Rabbi Ishmael was focused and level-headed, weighing his words carefully and not prone to extreme views. According to him, the Torah sometimes teaches us not only commandments, statutes, and rules but also matters not confined to the boundaries of religion. The Torah does not hesitate to teach things pertaining to culture in general, such as good manners, accepted customs, and social mores that facilitate human life. Rabbi Ishmael's view was that not all the words of Torah are of a single genre. There are words that convey the divine will, and there are words that relate the habits of life. There are things in the Torah that are obligatory, and there are those that are optional, even, on occasion, when they are formulated in the language of obligation. In contrast, Rabbi Akiva considered every single word of the Torah to be commanding and imposing obligation.

When Rabbi Akiva found difficult or strange language in the Torah, his ears would widen,[145] for in his view strangeness in the text was a gateway to the discovery of the Torah's secrets. Rabbi Ishmael's goal was the integrity of the text.[146] The Torah speaks in human language. If there is difficult or strange language in the Torah, then it is a mistake to take it at face value.

Occasionally, when Rabbi Akiva and his disciples came across a difficult text, they would announce: "had it not been written in Scripture, we could not have said it!" but since Scripture wrote it, it could then be said. Rabbi Ishmael, on the other hand, expressed astonishment on such occasions: "Can one really say such a thing!?"[147] and he would then demonstrate that one could not take at face value verses that are not befitting the divine dignity.

Rabbi Ishmael would teach that *raz* [Hebrew: "secret meaning"] is an anagram for *zar* [Hebrew: "bizarre"], for a text should be interpreted according to its plain meaning. But Rabbi Akiva would teach that *peshat* [Hebrew: "plain meaning"] is an anagram for *tippesh* [Hebrew: "foolish"],[148] for the truth cannot be grasped with nothing but the tongs of plain reason. The surface meaning is but one dimension of an esoteric meaning whose full dimensions have been lost, and the plain sense is a veil that eclipses language. In order to remove the veil, you must activate and stimulate the text, and exegete "every jot and tittle."

In Rabbi Akiva's view, human language is insignificant compared to the language of Torah. Secret meanings lurk in the Torah's language, and the events narrated in it are not like everyday events. What does it mean to say that wonders do not conform

---

[145] The Hebrew here is *apharkeset,* which means a funnel; the reference is to the Aggadah in BT Hagigah 3b. The theme will be developed in chapter 12, pp. 231–35.

[146] Literally, "to refine the text," taken here to mean making it into an integral whole, in the manner of a smelter.

[147] This is the first section of chapter 12.

[148] The anagram does not quite work in English, because of the vocalization that is part of English but not part of Hebrew writing; *p-sh-t* and *t-p-sh* have the same letters.

to human reason?[149] It is precisely contradictions that make truth emerge out of the constricted sheath of language.

There were thus two points of view among the Sages: (1) a transcendent point of view, comprising a method of thought always open to the higher realms, striving to understand matters of Torah through a supernal lens; and (2) an immanent point of view, comprising a method of thought modest and confined, satisfied to understand matters of Torah through an earthly lens defined by human experience.[150] These points of view are foundational and paradigmatic, and from them are derived differing conceptions and analyses, rivals to one another. Thus were crystallized two differing methods of understanding the commandments and their underlying purposes. One says: if you sin, what do you do to Him; if your transgressions are many, how do you affect Him? If you are righteous, what do you give Him; what does He receive from your hand?[151] Mortals need God, but surely God does not need the service of mortals! The other says: the Holy and Blessed One needs our service. One says: the commandments were given in order to provide justification to Israel; they were given only in order to refine God's creatures. And the other says: the commandments were given in order to bring pleasure to the Holy and Blessed One. Again, one says: a person makes a pilgrimage three times a year in order to be seen in the Presence of the Lord God; and the other says that just as one comes to be seen, so does one come to see, as a Master anticipates his servant coming to see him.

Rabbi Akiva, who viewed humanity through a heavenly lens, taught that "owing to our sins, people do not have the wherewithal to know the heavenly Image." He was among those Sages who entered the *Pardes*; that is: "they ascended to the firmament." By contrast, Rabbi Ishmael, who viewed humanity through an earthly lens, was not prone to those things that are beyond the ken of human reason; he had no concern for hidden things. The heavens belong to the Lord, but the earth He gave over to humans. The main worry should be about justice and righteousness in this world.[152]

Rabbi Akiva's Victory

At first not all the Sages were pleased with Rabbi Akiva's method, and they criticized his exegeses. Rabbi Tarfon, for example, complained to him with impatience: "Akiva,

---

[149] And are therefore to be discounted.

[150] Here Heschel is using the words *transcendent* and *immanent* (or better: *terrestrial*) in the senses that will be elaborated in chapter 14. For the other use, see especially the editorial notes to chapter 2, section "The Exoteric and Esoteric Personalities."

[151] Based on Job 35:6–7. The question whether worship is for human or divine "need" is the focus of chapter 4, especially the final sections.

[152] This is consistent with the idea that Judaism is primarily concerned with the here and now. But despite that common idea about Judaism, Heschel will claim in the next section that the visionary quality of Rabbi Akiva's thought, not the down-to-earth quality of Rabbi Ishmael's, tended to carry the day.

how long will you keep gabbing with your exegeses?"[121] Rabbi Eleazar ben Azariah and Rabbi Yose the Galilean reproached him: "Even if you were to expand the category all day long,[153] we would not listen to you!"[122] The Sages especially faulted him for his statements on matters of Aggadah. A case in point is his exegesis of the words "bread of the mighty" (Psalm 78:25):[154] "When these words were recited before Rabbi Ishmael, he said to them: Go and tell Akiva, 'Akiva, you have erred!'"[123] As already mentioned above, Rabbi Ishmael once said to Rabbi Akiva: "Desist from your statements and move instead to matters concerning plagues and tent-impurities."[124] Similar things were said to him by Rabbi Eleazar ben Azariah,[125] and Rabbi Judah ben Beteira once said to him: "You will one day have to give an accounting!"[126]

Yet their opposition did not avail them; Rabbi Akiva gained the upper hand. He defeated his colleagues and his detractors, and Rabbi Tarfon eventually said of him: "Happy are you, Father Abraham, that Akiva came from your loins,"[127] and "Akiva, whoever disengages from you disengages from life!"[128]

Rabbi Tarfon also gave us this image of him: "'I saw the ram butting westward, northward, and southward. No beast could withstand him, and there was none to deliver from his power. He did as he pleased and grew great' (Daniel 8:4)—that is Akiva."[129] The generation that succeeded him accepted his ideas. They established these principles: "Rabbi Ishmael vs. Rabbi Akiva—the Halakhah follows Rabbi Akiva"; "The Halakhah agrees with Rabbi Akiva over any one of his colleagues."[130] And there was even one view that "the Halakhah agrees with Rabbi Akiva even over his teacher."[131]

From the days of Moses, the chief of all prophets, there did not arise such an influential person in Israel. His teachings struck roots in the Babylonian academies and became a dominant system of thought in Jewish teaching to this day. Because of its influence, Rabbi Ishmael's approach was pushed aside, and only remnants of it are preserved in the Mekhilta of Rabbi Ishmael, in the Sifre to Numbers, in parts of the Sifre to Deuteronomy, and in scattered parts of rabbinic literature. Mishnah, Tosefta, and Sifra follow the teachings of Rabbi Akiva.[132] The Mishnah, compiled by Rabbi

---

[121] Tosefta Zevahim 1:6.
[122] BT Zevahim 82a; BT Menahot 89a; BT Niddah 72b; Sifra Tzav 33a.
[123] BT Yoma 75b.   [124] Midrash on Psalms 104:9.   [125] BT Sanhedrin 67a.
[126] BT Shabbat 96b–97a.   [127] Sifre Beha'alotekha 75.
[128] Tosefta Mikva'ot, end of chapter 1; BT Kiddushin 66b.   [129] Sifre Hukkat 124.
[130] See BT Zevahim 57a; BT Yoma 75b; Alfasi Gittin chapter 4 and Bava Kamma 7a. However, if the majority differs with him, the Halakhah does not follow him; see BT Eruvin 46b.
[131] BT Ketubot 84b.   [132] BT Sanhedrin 86a.

---

[153] As noted above, Akiva's exegesis often proceeded from a tendency to expand categories on the basis of the slightest textual pretext. In this case, Akiva had been expounding on definite articles and conjunctions in order to expand the number of occasions on which purification offerings would have to be brought. To this exegesis his colleagues objected.

[154] Akiva interpreted "bread of the mighty" to mean that the manna was the food actually consumed by the ministering angels in heaven, a sort of ambrosia.

Judah the Patriarch, was founded on the teachings of Rabbi Meir, who followed in the wake of Rabbi Akiva, whose teachings he embedded in his.[155]

The Men of the Great Assembly said: "Raise up many disciples."[133] But the schools of Shammai and Hillel disagreed over this. The school of Shammai said: "One should teach only someone who is smart, unassuming, of good lineage, and wealthy."[156] But the school of Hillel said: "One should teach anyone, for there were many sinners in Israel who were brought close to the study of Torah, and whose children became righteous, pious, and good people."[134]

Rabbi Akiva, too, opened his school door wide. It was characteristic of him to encourage and to influence many. He would expound and sermonize in public and would also teach Torah to individuals. And as soon as his reputation spread abroad—according to the evidence of his contemporary, Rabbi Dosa ben Harkinas,[135] his fame traveled "from one end of the world to the other"—many disciples flocked to him.

Just as his desire to study Torah knew no bounds, so did his desire to teach Torah know no bounds. When he was imprisoned, and Rabbi Simeon came to him, saying, "Teach me Torah," he said to him, "My son, more than the calf desires to suck, the cow desires to give suck."[136] And when the evil empire[157] decreed that Israel could no longer busy itself with Torah, Rabbi Akiva did not hesitate to violate the decree in public, and he would assemble great crowds and teach Torah.[137] His exertions were rewarded.[158] According to tradition, "Rabbi Akiva had 12,000 pairs of disciples . . . all of whom died in a single period of time . . . and he subsequently raised up seven more . . . and these arose and filled all of the Land of Israel with Torah."

These virtues—unbounded strength that overflowed its banks, courage, and the desire and effort to raise up many disciples—were not the primary virtues of Rabbi Ishmael. From the exegeses of these two men offered for the same verse, you can learn about the difference between the attitude of soul of Rabbi Ishmael, the analytic scholar, and the attitude of soul of Rabbi Akiva, the man of vision. Rabbi Ishmael approached teaching warily and made determinations uneasily. His chief concern was to learn Torah in an enduring way, as if he were never certain that his teachings were firm or that his learning was secure. Such doubts were far from Rabbi Akiva's

---

133 Mishnah Avot 1:1.   134 ARN A 3.   135 BT Yevamot 16b.
136 BT Pesahim 112a.   137 BT Berakhot 61b.

---

[155] Yet Heschel will argue later that in matters of Aggadah, Rabbi Judah the Patriarch often selected the views of Rabbi Ishmael to be expressed in the Mishnah. See, e.g., chapter 14, "The Doctrine of God's Image," where the Mishnah uses the Ishmaelian formulation of "whoever destroys a life destroys a world" instead of the Akivan "reduces the Divine Image."

[156] That is, the school of Shammai emphasized the word "many" in the original phrase. Don't waste time and effort on those who are less likely to absorb learning; attempt to raise as many disciples as you can, by minimizing failures and dropouts. The school of Hillel, however, emphasized the words "raise up," as the sequel shows.

[157] That is, Hadrianic Rome.

[158] The reward inherent in what follows is in the last part, of course; that is, that he eventually succeeded through his disciples to fill the land with Torah.

heart. His chief concern was to raise up disciples. "Rabbi Ishmael said: Although you have learned Torah in your youth, keep learning it in your advanced age, for you do not know which will endure: the former, the latter, or perhaps both. Rabbi Akiva said: Although you have raised up disciples in your youth, keep raising them in your advanced age, for you do not know which the Holy and Blessed One will account to you: the former, the latter, or perhaps both."[138] And indeed, it was the later disciples of Rabbi Akiva—Rabbi Meir, Rabbi Judah, and Rabbi Simeon bar Yohai—who disseminated his teachings in the generation following the persecutions.[139]

"All depends on luck, even the Torah scroll in the Sanctuary." And lady luck did not smile on Rabbi Ishmael. His hammer reached the anvil all right, but the sound somehow did not reach the ears. He and Rabbi Akiva came along at the same time, but one soon began to gain in power at the expense of the other. In the end, it was the approach of Rabbi Akiva that conquered the hearts of Israel and was absorbed into its heritage. It is so woven and intermeshed in the lexicon of Jewish thought that one hardly perceives it as a distinct force. Rabbi Ishmael was made to defer to Rabbi Akiva. Even Rabbi Ishmael's disciples did not always follow in their master's footsteps and differed with him in several places. It was occasionally said: "Rabbi Simeon's disciples influenced Rabbi Ishmael's disciples to hold their views."[140] Two sovereigns cannot share a single crown. Rabbi Akiva illumined the world, and in every generation his fame shines as the sun rising in might. Rabbi Ishmael's fame has been fleeting and mercurial, even to the extent that Maimonides considered him to be one of Rabbi Akiva's disciples![141]

The teachings of Rabbi Ishmael, an original creation without parallel in our ancient literature, did not penetrate into the consciousness of the generations. Only indirectly and unconsciously were many Sages influenced by his mode of thought. Hints of this are found in the work of champions of plain-meaning exegesis in the Middle Ages, and in the rationalist approach of some medieval thinkers. He is like those "whose waters we drink but whose names we do not remember." Yet his principle, "the Torah speaks in human language," became a cornerstone of scriptural understanding, and his views concerning the sacrifices appear again in Maimonides' *Guide of the Perplexed* . . . .[159]

---

[138] Genesis Rabbah 61:3; ARN B 12. [139] Genesis Rabbah 61:3.
[140] See BT Zevahim 119b, and its variant readings.
[141] Maimonides, Commentary on the Mishnah, Eduyot 2:6.

---

[159] The ellipsis in the translation reproduces a sense that Heschel has simply trailed off at the end of this long introductory chapter. Indeed, the original Hebrew printed text has no period here (though this may be simply a typographical error). In any event, a sense is present that this is no real last word on the subject and that the main work ought finally to begin. It is also noteworthy that the very last chapters of this work, as published (the end of volume 3 in the original) also bring us to an ambiguous ending, as if there is destined to be something unresolved and continuing about these considerations. Although such endings fail to satisfy the reader who is looking for a definitive cadence and a clear resolution, there is a satisfying conformity to a deeper truth about the open-endedness of all theological inquiries such as this one.

2

TWO APPROACHES TO TORAH EXEGESIS

Translator's Introduction

Why is this treatment of rabbinic theology different from all others? Others proceed, as one would expect, through the various topics that must be covered in any conspectus of religious thought. Solomon Schechter's *Aspects of Rabbinic Theology,* for example, begins with "God" ("God and the World" and "God and Israel"), then proceeds to the "Election of Israel," the "Kingdom of God," and then to "The Law." Ephraim Urbach's *The Sages* is similarly organized. These and other modern synthesizers of rabbinic theology followed not only common sense but good medieval precedent as well, for Saadia Gaon began the *Book of Beliefs and Opinions* with a discussion of God as Creator and then proceeded to discuss commandment and law, obedience, disobedience, repentance, and so on. Maimonides, for his part, began *The Guide of the Perplexed* with long discussions of the nature of God and its resistance to depiction in language, with proofs of God's existence and unity, with analyses of revelation, prophecy, and similar themes. It is, in fact, wholly natural that a theological treatise would begin with God and then go on to analyze various ways in which God relates to or is made manifest in the world. Heschel, however, begins *Torah min Hashamayim* with a very different issue.

Heschel's question is, What is the nature of Torah? The first chapter of this long inquiry into the religion of the Rabbis is on the subject of philosophy of language—not as in Maimonides' reflection on language, in the context of the essential nature of God but rather as a way of understanding the choices with which we are confronted in deciding how we will treat and read this foundational religious text that we call the Torah. Understanding the reason for this departure from standard practice is critical to appreciating what Heschel is aiming at in this work. The essence of rabbinic Judaism is the location of religious authority in a *text,* and the concomitant elevation of the practice of interpreting that text to as lofty and central a position in the religious life of Israel as prophecy had enjoyed in the biblical age. But whereas the theory of prophecy was one that allowed no choice—the true prophet spoke, of necessity, what God impelled him or her to speak—in the case of scriptural interpretation (*midrash*), the reader and explicator had some degrees of freedom. And thus there were different approaches to just what this foundational text was, how it came to be our Torah, and how it was to be expounded. Heschel wants us in this book to be drawn into the rabbinic mind and worldview. Cataloguing for us the various rabbinic ideas on the nature of God would hardly allow us to do that; it would at best give us the conclusions of some rabbinic debates, but give us no insight as to why the diversities of opinion exist. It is only by getting the reader to consider the most basic of all issues in rabbinic Judaism, the source of the Torah's sanctity and centrality, that Heschel can give us a vicarious part in the grand debates. The very language of the original, a Hebrew thick with rabbinic idioms and allusions to biblical and rabbinic texts, intensifies the empathic identification with the early Rabbis that Heschel is after. A culture's language is the only sure way, if a way exists at all, into that culture's heart and mind. And reading *Torah min Hashamayim* is intended to be not so much a cognitive experience as an empathic one.

So Heschel schematizes the many complex issues surrounding the nature of Torah and its language as classical rabbinic literature often did: as a duality. Here the paradigmatic schools of thought are those of two of the greatest giants of the second century, Rabbi Akiva and Rabbi Ishmael. We are presented at the outset with "Two Approaches to Torah Exegesis." We are not to read this material as a textual historian would, analyzing the factual accuracy of the attributions of statements in the classical texts to the historical Akiva or Ishmael or their disciples. Rather, we are to read as theologians, as those who have accepted the invitation to explore the phenomenology of a scripturally based religion, where text has become oracle, and to consider the explanatory power of the dichotomy that Heschel offers us. Akiva and Ishmael are *avot ha-olam*, in the sense of "eternal paradigms," and the choices they represent have vast ramifications when we finally come to the many subjects that make up any comprehensive theology.

In this chapter, Heschel lays this groundwork patiently but forcefully.

The Torah Speaks in Human Language

R ABBI AKIVA, who extracted from every jot and tittle in the text piles and piles of *halakhot*,[1] believed it impossible that there be in the Torah a single superfluous word or letter. Each word, each letter issues the invitation: "Interpret me!" Even if the rules and conventions of language require that a certain word or letter complete the syntax, it is nevertheless fair game for exegesis. Thus, he interpreted every seeming redundancy, and even the coupling of a verb to its infinitive:[1] "Any-

---

[1] BT Menahot 29b. See also BT Eruvin 21b.

---

[1] A typical construction in biblical Hebrew is the conjoining of a conjugated verb to its infinitive. The grammatical form is generally used to create emphasis in the verb (often rendered into English by expressions such as "I surely did X" or "He will surely be Y"). Akivan exegesis, as depicted here by Heschel, would treat this construction not as an inseparable grammatical unit created for emphasis, but

man, any-man [of the seed of Aaron . . . of the holy-donations he is not to eat, until he is pure]"[2] (Leviticus 22:4)—this is meant to include the uncircumcised;[2] "Cut off, cut off shall that person be"[3] (Numbers 15:31)—"cut off" in this world, "[again] cut off" in the future world.[3] He even interpreted the word "saying" (in "The Lord spoke to Moses, saying"),[4] the letter *vav*[4] in the word *ve-ratza'* ["he shall pierce"] (in "His master shall pierce his ear" [Exodus 21:6]),[5] and in the word *u-vat* ["when[5] the daughter"] (in "when the daughter of a priest" [Leviticus 21:9]).[6] Even particles and prepositions such as *et* [accusative case particle], *gam* ["also"], *akh* ["yet"], and *rak* ["only"] served as grist for his exegetical mill. By contrast, Rabbi Ishmael would interpret scriptural verses in a straightforward and rational way, or through the use of the thirteen logical rules of exegesis, which also reveal what is hidden in the text by rational means. In his view, the seeming redundancies in Scripture do not imply anything substantive, for the Torah uses a style that is in keeping with the conventions of human language; for example, "you had to go, yes, go" (Genesis 31:30); "you longed, longed" (ibid.); "I was stolen, yes, stolen" (Genesis 40:15).[7]

---

[2] PT Yevamot, beginning of chapter 8, 8c.   [3] Sifre Shelah 112.   [4] Sifre Naso 2.
[5] PT Kiddushin 1:4 (59d).   [6] BT Sanhedrin 51b.
[7] PT Shabbat 19 (17a); PT Nedarim 1 (36c). In line with the Ishmaelian approach, many medieval sages taught that it was merely scriptural style to rephrase the same matter in different words. See Abraham ibn Ezra, *Yesod Mora*, section 1, and the commentary of David Kimhi to Isaiah 5:9.

---

as two separate verbs, each with its own substantive meaning to contribute to the sense of the verse. Needless to say, this violates a straightforward understanding of the grammatical rules, but that is precisely the point here: that Akivan exegesis proceeds notwithstanding straightforward rules of logic and interpretation. For a good sense of how this infinitive/finite verb construction sounds in the Hebrew, see Everett Fox's translation of the Torah (*The Five Books of Moses: A New English Rendition with Introduction, Commentary and Notes* [New York: Schocken, 1995]), in which he preserves the redundant sound to which this style of exegesis was sensitive. We adopt Fox's translation in exegeses of this variety, so that Heschel's point is more easily apparent to the English reader.

[2] Everett Fox's duplication ("any-man, any-man") captures the force of the Hebrew *ish ish*. Other, less literal translations include "No man of Aaron's offspring . . . shall eat" (NJV), "What man soever of the seed of Aaron . . . shall not eat" (AV, OJV). This verse is employed by the rabbis as the scriptural source for adding the uncircumcised to the list of those priests disqualified from eating priestly gifts.

[3] Here, too, Fox's translation captures the redundancy of the Hebrew *hikkaret tikkaret*. More idiomatic English translations are, "That person shall be cut off" (NJV); "that soul shall utterly be cut off" (AV, OJV).

[4] Normally the conjunction *and* in Hebrew, vocalized either as *ve-* or *u-*. Another function of the *vav* in biblical Hebrew is to signal a reversal of verb tense from perfect to imperfect or vice versa. That is the case in the example immediately following, in which "he shall pierce" results from a combination of *vav* and the verb "he pierced." This is another example of how what is known to be a mere convention of grammar is nevertheless treated as an opportunity for more expansive exegesis, as if the *vav* were a conjunction intended to *add* something of substance—in this case, that the slave's ear might be pierced not just with an awl, but with a prick, a thorn, or a shard of glass.

[5] Here the *vav*, vocalized as *u-*, has yet another function, which is to express conditionality.

Even in places where synonyms appear in the Torah, it is not intended as a sub-stantive addition, or for any specific purpose. For example: "He shall abstain from wine and any other intoxicant" (Numbers 6:3)—"Now are not 'wine' and 'intoxi-cant' one and the same? Yes, the Torah simply uses two synonymous terms."[8] In short: the Torah speaks in human language.[9]

For Rabbi Ishmael, this principle governs the text of the Torah: when any passage appears in one place and is repeated in another [with some changes], the purpose of the repetition is simply to introduce those changes, and thus it is unnecessary to rein-terpret that which is identical to the original. Rabbi Akiva, by contrast, believed that one must reinterpret the entire passage, not simply the new material.[10] "Exegeses emanating from the school of Rabbi Ishmael are marked by their simplicity. They do not approach the text in a roundabout way, in order to extract laws by whatever means possible; they rather attempt to keep exegesis in line with the surface meaning, and do not interpret mere superfluities and redundancies."[11]

Rabbi Ishmael protested Rabbi Akiva's mode of exegesis. When Rabbi Akiva inferred an important law from the letter *vav* in the phrase *u-vat ish kohen* ["When the daughter of a priest"] ("Brother Ishmael, my exegesis is of the difference between *bat* and *u-vat*"), Rabbi Ishmael said to him: "Shall we condemn this woman to be burnt just because you wish to interpret the letter *vav*?!"[12] On the other hand, Rabbi Ishmael's method of letting the surface meaning suffice and to identify the "natural setting of the text" seemed to some of his colleagues a mark of incapacity and intel-lectual weakness. Once he argued with Rabbi Akiva (who, as noted above, interpreted the particle *et* to signify some substantive addition) as follows: "The text does not read 'When God began to create the heaven [*hashamayim*] and the earth [*ha-aretz*],' but rather 'the heaven [*et hashamayim*] and the earth [*ve-et ha-aretz*]'—but this is simply the natural style of the text." Rabbi Akiva responded: "'This is not a trifling thing for you'[6] (Deuteronomy 32:47)—and if it is trifling, it is so from you, i.e., from your inability to interpret it. *Et hashamayim* is meant to add the sun, moon, stars, and constellations, and *et ha-aretz* is meant to add the trees, grasses, and the Garden of Eden."[7] [13]

---

[8] Sifre Naso 23.   [9] Sifre Shelah 112.

[10] Sifre Naso 2; BT Sotah 3a, cited in the name of the school of Rabbi Ishmael.

[11] J. N. Epstein, *Mevo'ot le-sifrut ha-tannaim* [Introduction to Tannaitic Literature] (Jerusalem: Magnes, 1957), 536.

[12] Rabbi Ishmael held that a priest's daughter who engaged in harlotry was subject to death by [the more severe method of] burning if she were betrothed, but by [the less severe method of] strangulation if she were fully married. For Rabbi Akiva, the allegedly extra *vav* implied that in either case, she would be subject to death by burning. See BT Sanhedrin 51a.

[13] Genesis Rabbah 1:14. The saying "and if it is trifling, it is so from you" was frequently used by Rabbi

---

[6] The text, if taken literally, reads "from you," and that is the basis of the exegesis to be cited.

[7] This is a very interesting and instructive example of how Akiva's method of reading Scripture is a part of a consistent worldview. For the *form* taken by this exegesis on Genesis 1:1 reflects the con-

Things Not Revealed to Moses
Were Revealed to Rabbi Akiva

The minority of the Torah is written; the majority is oral. Many norms were accepted in Israel even though they do not appear in writing in the Torah, and sectarians would vex Israel by denying the authority of such norms.[8] Israel held steadfastly to its ancient traditions, but there arose the necessity to clarify the connection between the Oral Torah and the Written Torah. Do the numerous norms and rules accepted in Israel have any support in the written Torah? According to one point of view, there are a good number of *halakhot* that "have no support." For example: "The release of oaths fly free in the air, and have no support; rather, a sage releases as his wisdom directs.[9] The laws of Shabbat, festive offerings, and Temple trespasses are poor in text but rich in *halakhot,* like mountains suspended by a thread, and they have no support."[14] But this idea threatened to bifurcate Israel's Torah into two separate Torahs.

Akiva. In keeping with his method, it was said: "There is nothing in the Torah, not even a single letter or word (not to mention a whole verse), which does not have multiple meanings, as it is written, 'For this is not a trifling thing for you' (Deuteronomy 32:47), and if it is trifling, it is so from you, for you have insufficiently contemplated it and argued over its meaning" (MTD, p. 205).

[14] Tosefta Hagigah 1:9; Tosefta Eruvin 8:23. Some Sages disagreed and said, "they have support" (BT Hagigah 10a). See also Genesis Rabbah 60:8.

---

viction that everything (or at least *many* things) is already latent in the text and can be discovered/recovered if we know how to read every formal particle of the text, even the usually neglected accusative particle *et*. The *content* of this exegesis, however, is just another version of that conviction that all is latent in what is originally given; for according to this midrash, God created all that was eventually to appear in the world in the very first act of creation at the very first moment of the very first day. All that appeared on (for example) day 3 was already latent in the earth from day 1. All that was created on day 4 was already latent in the heavens from day 1. The creation story as it is given in Genesis 1 is, except for the first instantaneous act of creation, mere activation of what was already there. This way of understanding creation *and* this associated way of understanding the nature of Torah both denigrate the role of history. For the world of events and phenomena, history is a mere activation of preexisting realities, and for the world of ideas, all religious *nova* are mere discoveries of what is preencoded into the text.

[8] Heschel is here undoubtedly referring to such ancient sects as the Sadducees, who by evidence of the ancients did not accept some of the extensions of the meaning of the biblical text ascribed to oral tradition. Such sectaries, however, did not only give rise to polemics in the ancient world. In the Middle Ages, for example, the Karaites also engaged in similar debates with adherents of rabbinic tradition.

[9] Vows and oaths were considered sacred by the Bible, and more than once biblical books stress that, once an oath is taken or a vow made, there is no going back on it. Yet in rabbinic times there arose the institution of having a vow nullified by a Sage if it could be argued that the vow itself was the result of an error of judgment. Where did such an institution come from, seeing that it contradicts the clear intent of the biblical text? That is the subject of the text Heschel cites here.

In this connection, Rabbi Joshua said: "Tongs are made with tongs. What, then, was the nature of the first pair of tongs? It must have been created."[10] That is, the laws of Shabbat are poor in text, "for the Torah merely stated 'you shall not do work,' and 'you shall cease.' From this simple reference to cessation many forms of cessation were derived, just as many secondary categories of labor were derived from the category of "removal from domain to domain."[11] And the Sages created many additional safeguards as well. There were also the laws of Eruv[12] (attributed to Solomon), as well as all the other categories of labor and their derivatives, and rabbinic injunctions. These have no text on which to rely but are rather oral traditions. Indeed, even the thirty-nine primary categories of labor have no text (apart from the account of the Tabernacle) on which to rely. All is learned from "You shall cease from labor."[15]

Rabbi Akiva, with whom the idea that there are norms that are like mountains suspended by threads did not sit well, "made all of Torah into rings,"[16] that is, into a continuous chain.[13] The Written Torah and the Oral Torah are one. All norms are embedded in the Torah; all rules are to be found there. "Turn it over and turn it over

---

[15] *Mara De-matnita*, which interprets Tosefta Eruvin 8:23 according to the view of PT Eruvin 26d. Another explanation of Rabbi Joshua's statement is found in *Hasdei David* on Tosefta Hagigah 1:9 (= 1:11 in the *Hasdei David* edition).

[16] ARN A 18.

---

[10] From the appearance of this idea of the first pair of tongs in Mishnah Avot 5:6, it seems that this was a saying of much more general scope than its application by the Tosefta to the laws of Shabbat. It may perhaps have been a version of a cosmological argument for the existence of a First Cause, already familiar from Aristotle. In any event, it certainly constitutes an argument against the plausibility of an infinitely regressing chain of causes, and the ultimate anchor of all the many and variegated laws of Shabbat is one simple verse that is God-given and is the starting point beyond which no regress is possible or necessary. Although in the sequel Heschel will suggest that Rabbi Akiva would not have taken well to this description of the laws of Shabbat (because, presumably, it detaches them from the text), that may be an overstatement. It is likely that this anchoring of *Hilkhot Shabbat* in the text through the "tongs" argument would have at least minimally satisfied the Akivan program of rooting all *halakhot* in the text.

[11] As will be noted in the sequel, the rabbinic construction of Shabbat provided for thirty-nine primary categories of activity that are prohibited on the Sabbath, and each primary category gave rise to countless secondary categories derived from the primary ones. "Removal from domain to domain" refers to the rabbinic prohibition on transporting objects from a private domain to a public one, and vice versa.

[12] These rules, also not found in the Torah, provide for the extension of the limits on foot travel on Shabbat and for the blending of several private domains into one, both through legal fictions created for these purposes.

[13] Heschel's understanding of "made all of Torah into rings" is not the apparent meaning of the text in ARN that he cites. The context there makes clear the intent that, based on scriptural exegesis, Rabbi Akiva *categorized* the growing body of Jewish law based on scriptural exegesis into systematic domains, thus making possible the thematic structure of the Mishnah. Here Heschel takes some literary license in understanding "rings" not as "thematic realms" but rather as "links in a chain."

again, for all is within it,"[17] said ben Bag Bag.[14] According to this point of view, the majority of the Torah is written, and its minority is oral![18] In Rabbi Akiva's eyes, the Torah was not a lexicon of inert words. The Sages had expounded: "'There is the sea, vast and wide' (Psalm 104:25)—this is the Torah, of which it is said 'its measure is longer than the earth and broader than the sea' (Job 11:9)."[19] Rabbi Akiva took the metaphor to its limits and discovered that just as in the case of the sea the depths greatly exceed the surface, so in the Torah, the latent and the esoteric greatly exceed what is apparent and on the surface. . . .

Rabbi Eliezer and Rabbi Joshua, the teachers of Rabbi Akiva, also busied themselves with exegesis of the Torah and thereby made the Torah more accessible. But Rabbi Akiva surpassed them all with the vigor of his method and the skill with which he revealed hidden meanings in the texts. Rabbi Simeon ben Eleazar compared Rabbi Akiva's work to that of a stonecutter who was chipping away in a mountain range. He took his pickax and sat on a mountainside and chipped out from it small pebbles. People came by and asked him: "What are you doing?" He answered: "I am going to uproot the mountain and fling it into the Jordan." They said to him: "You will not be able to uproot the entire mountain." But he continued to chip away until he reached a very large boulder; he got under it, pried it loose, uprooted it, and flung it into the Jordan, saying: "This is now your place."[15] 20

---

[17] Mishnah Avot 5:22. The same statement is attributed to Hillel in ARN B 27.

[18] In line with Rabbi Akiva's approach, Rabbi Eleazar said: "The majority of the Torah is written, and its minority is oral"; that is, all that is learned by exegesis is included in the written Torah. Contradicting this, Rabbi Johanan said: "The majority is oral, and the minority written" (BT Gittin 60b).

[19] Midrash on Psalms 104:22. Ishmaelian exegeses would typically say, "the text says" or "it tells us that . . ."; that is, the text intends to convey a particular meaning. By contrast, in the Sifra, the language "it tells us that . . ." gives way to "it gives us to learn that . . . ." That language may perhaps underscore the idea that the teaching under consideration is embedded in the text's deep structure. See Wilhelm Bacher, *Erkei Midrash Hatannaim* [Lexicon of Rabbinic Exegetical Terminology] (Tel Aviv: Rabinowitz, 5683/1923; translated from the German *Die exegetische Terminologie der jüdischen Traditionsliteratur* [Leipzig 1899/1905; repr., Darmstadt: Wissenschaftliche Buchgesellschaft, 1965]), s.v. *higgid*, p. 23.

[20] ARN A 6.

---

[14] A Tanna of the very early period, of whom we have few attributed statements and of whom little is known.

[15] The sense of this image of Rabbi Akiva is unclear. One possible reading, consistent with what is being developed here, is this: Rabbi Akiva's enterprise is depicted as one of *reconfiguring* the elements of a tradition that are already in place. He is attempting to *move* the mountain, not to level it. And in moving it, a boulder once embedded in the middle of the mountain may, in the reconfiguration, become the base of the mountain. Indeed, on this reading, it is plausible that the mountain should be understood to be Sinai, where the original configuration was set. The Jordan then represents the entry into a new phase, that is, the transition from the desert to a new political reality in the Land, a reality that may require new insights to be drawn out from the Sinaitic tradition, but *not* entirely new teachings. This image, then, reinforces both the idea that all that may ever be needed was put into God's original teaching at Sinai, and that the rabbi's role is not to *innovate* but rather to know how to *discover* within the body of tradition those ideas which have not previously been noted but which now

His contemporaries marveled at his wisdom and powers of interpretation, for his exegeses brought to light countless matters out of the text of the Torah. "Things not revealed to Moses were revealed to Rabbi Akiva."[21] Many scriptural verses that the early Tannaim could not expound found their interpretations in the hands of Rabbi Akiva. Of the many *halakhot* that had been denigrated, Rabbi Akiva said, "I will see to it that the words of the Sages stand firm."[22] Thus did many enigmatic usages and ancient traditions find scriptural support. Sometimes, he would even expound a verse and find that the result conformed to the received *halakhah*.[23]

With respect to verses from which Rabbi Ishmael could infer nothing, Rabbi Akiva was able to plumb their depths and thus to find bases and justifications for *halakhot* of the Oral Torah. As already noted, such exegesis was not unknown prior to him, but he went far beyond his predecessors and developed this procedure into a comprehensive system. He interpreted every unusual part of speech, all redundancies, and each conjunction and preposition and extracted from all of them new laws.

Rabbi Ishmael observed that not only are there many norms that "have no support"[16] [24] but also norms that contradict the plain meaning of the text ("Halakhah circumvents the text"[25]), and even some that cannot claim textual support even with the use of the exegetical rules ("Halakhah circumvents midrash"[26]).

Of the thanksgiving sacrifice we read in Scripture: "he shall offer together with the sacrifice of thanksgiving unleavened cakes with oil mixed in, and unleavened wafers spread with oil" (Leviticus 7:12)—Why is the phrase "with oil" repeated? Said Rabbi Akiva: "Had 'with oil' been mentioned only once, we would have assumed that this requires the one *log* of oil customary with all other meal-offerings. The repetition of 'with oil' creates a limitation—for an expansion followed by an expansion creates a limitation—and thus this offering is limited to a half *log* of oil." To this Rabbi Eleazar ben Azariah retorted: "Even if you proclaim all day long that 'with oil' suggests a limitation or that 'with oil' suggests an expansion I shall not listen to you! The require-

---

[21] Tanhuma Hukkat 8 (ed. Buber 24); Numbers Rabbah 19:6.
[22] Mishnah Oholot 16:1.
[23] See David Zevi Hoffmann, "Le-heker Midreshei ha-Tannaim" [On the Study of Tannaitic Midrashim], in *Mesillot le-Torat ha-Tannaim* [Pathways through Tannaitic Thought] (Tel Aviv, 1928), 11; Sifre Beha'alotekha 75; BT Zevahim 13a. See chapter 27 below, pp. 512–14.
[24] See Epstein, *Mevo'ot le-sifrut ha-tannaim*, 535.
[25] Sifre Re'eh 122 (compare MI Neziqin 2); PT Kiddushin 59d.
[26] PT Kiddushin 59d. See Epstein, *Mevo'ot le-sifrut ha-tannaim*, 535.

---

need to be activated. Each transition in Jewish life, such as the one Akiva's generation was concerned to bring about and stabilize, would then be a "Jordan River" vis-à-vis the established mountain of previously developed tradition.

[16] In BT Hagigah 10a, several authorities maintain that the laws of annulment of vows indeed *have* scriptural support, using Akivan-style exegesis. Whose opinion, then, is represented in the Mishnah, that they are *without* scriptural support? Probably Rabbi Ishmael's, whose opinion informed that of Rabbi Judah the Patriarch on many aggadic matters (see chapter 14 below).

ment of half a *log* of oil for the thanksgiving sacrifice is simply a *halakhah* that was given to Moses on Mount Sinai."[17] 27 Rabbi Ishmael adopted a similar approach. Rather than force-fit a *halakhah* to the text in a manner far from the surface meaning, he would say that the *halakhah* comes to us through oral tradition, and we accept it without textual proof.28

When Rabbi Eliezer ben Hyrcanus, a teacher of Rabbi Akiva, expounded a verse in a nonstandard way, Rabbi Ishmael said to him: "Why, you are saying to Scripture: 'Be silent until I expound your meaning!'"[18] And Rabbi Eliezer replied, "Ishmael, you are a mountain palm" (which, because of its altitude, bears few and inferior fruits; similarly, you seem unable to bear fruitful exegesis).29

One may well wonder at Rabbi Akiva's departure from a literal approach to scriptural exegesis. His method is most commonly explained on psychological grounds, that is, that its basis lies in his temperament and intellectual characteristics. He was acute and sharp, and thus loved that which was complex and keen-edged.30 "It was as if he had an innate compulsion to search for textual justifications for *halakhot* in farfetched, dialectical ways, even when he could achieve the same result in ways far less tortured and forced."31

This description, however, conceals more than it reveals. Shall we say that just because Rabbi Akiva was exceedingly sharp he would suspend mountains by a thread? That because he had a keen intellect he would interpret the Torah illogically? Or that because he was such a brilliant dialectician, he did not set the plain truth as his standard? The fact is that Rabbi Akiva's ideas about legal exegesis are part and parcel of a unique and comprehensive worldview. So we must ask: What were its underpinnings?

Two Approaches to the Essence of Torah

Judaic scholars, primarily David Zevi Hoffmann, identified well the characteristics that distinguish the teachings of Rabbi Ishmael from those of Rabbi Akiva.32 But they

27 Sifra Tzav 34d–35a.
28 Epstein, *Mevo'ot le-sifrut ha-tannaim,* 536.
29 Sifra Tazri'a 68b.
30 In BT Eruvin 13a, we read: "Rabbi Akiva said this only to sharpen his students' wits."
31 See J. H. Weiss, *Dor Dor Ve-Doreshav* (Tel Aviv 1957), part 2, p. 102.
32 Concerning the exegetical differences between Rabbi Ishmael and Rabbi Akiva, see D. Z. Hoffmann

[17] The Ishmaelian view here being expressed by Rabbi Eleazar ben Azariah could be paraphrased as follows: "Better to accept the notion that there are multiple sources of religious authority (e.g., the written text and a separate oral tradition), than to be forced into violating the standard logic of textual reading and interpretation."

[18] That is, the meaning of the verse is *indeterminate* until it is determined by the reader. In this case, the intent was certainly that the determination is made by an *authorized* reader, that is, a member of the rabbinic inner circle, the definition of which is not entirely clear.

defined the differences as pertaining only to legal matters. In matters of Aggadah, they found "few differences."[33] Conventional wisdom was that "Tannaitic exegeses exhibited differences only in halakhic matters, but in Aggadah, there were at best minor differences."[34] But an abundance of evidence is at hand that the two schools diverged as well on the most lofty philosophical matters. They dealt as intensely with biblical narratives as they did with passages of legal import. They dwelt on each and every text and investigated theological issues just as they did matters of practical *halakhah*. And the differences between these two schools in matters of faith and belief are weighty indeed. One could almost say that the methodological divergences in halakhic exegesis that we have already mentioned have their basis in two distinct points of departure concerning the very principles of religious thought. Indeed, we have before us two approaches to understanding the essence of Torah and prophecy. In many instances of halakhic exegesis, Rabbi Akiva and Rabbi Ishmael simply follow their methods in aggadic exegesis. Rabbi Akiva often took flight from the plain meaning of the text, because he viewed scripture through an esoteric lens. One who determines the existence of Torah to be a heavenly one believes, *ipso facto*, in a separate, transcendent existence of the text. The Torah over which we debate on earth is also debated in heaven. Such a view sees the Torah as essentially infinite. Its content, as it is perceived in the narrow confines of the text's plain meaning, is but a drop in the ocean. Rabbi Akiva held that every detail, and every stylistic form, has a deep meaning and an esoteric intent. We shall return to this presently.

In Rabbi Akiva's approach to Torah, there is a vast expanse separating the upper realm of the universe from the lower realm. The Torah was written and abides in the supernal world, and Moses ascended to the upper realm and brought it down to earth. The Torah, God's instrument in creating the world, unifies the two realms. Its arms embrace both worlds. Is it, then, conceivable that this Torah speaks in the language of human beings?

What is the distinction between the language of Torah and human language? Human beings distinguish between form and content. There are words that add nothing to the substance of a thought but are uttered because the conventions and rules of language so dictate; their contribution is aesthetic rather than instructive. God's ways, however, are not human ways. With God, form is nonexistent; there is

and H. S. Horowitz, in *Mesillot le-Torat ha-Tannaim;* Epstein, *Mevo'ot le-sifrut ha-tannaim,* 521ff.; see also the bibliography in L. Finkelstein, *Mavo le-masekhtot Avot ve-Avot de-Rabbi Natan* [Introduction to the Treatises Abot and Abot of Rabbi Nathan] (Hebrew with English summary; New York: Jewish Theological Seminary, 1950), 57 n. 96. Compare Y. Neubauer, "Halakhah u-midrash halakhah" [Halakhah and Halakhic Midrash] *Sinai* 22 (Fall 1947): 49–80; and E. Z. Melamed, *Midreshei Halakhah shel Ha-Tannaim ba-Talmud ha-Bavli* [Halakhic Midrashim of the Tannaim in the Talmud Bavli] (Jerusalem, 1943); Bacher, *Erkei Midrash Hatannaim.*

[33] See D. Z. Hoffmann's preface to his edition of MSY (*Mekhilta de-Rabbi Shimon bar Yohai*), p. xi; see also *Mesillot le-Torat ha-Tannaim,* 46–47.

[34] Samuel Poznanski, *Ma'asei ha-Tannaim* (Warsaw: Ha-Tzefira, 1913). Epstein also believes that aggadic material in the MSY is "substantially identical to that in the MI (*Mekhilta de-Rabbi Yishmael*)" (*Mevo'ot le-sifrut ha-tannaim,* 738; compare what he says on p. 565).

only content.[19] Every letter, every word, whether expanding or limiting a subject, is intended to teach a lesson. Each idiom instructs and clarifies. There is no form here; all is content, all is instruction. Just as heaven is loftier than earth, so the language of Torah is loftier than the language of human beings. And our rational powers are insufficient to grasp the esoterics of Torah; they cannot be handled with the tongs[20] of logic alone.

In Rabbi Akiva's view, textual teaching exists for expansion. One who confines exegesis to the surface meaning is like a poor man looking for gleanings. Torah must not be fixed. The text should be treated as is any living organism that will not remain inert and that has multiple facets. For there is life in the text, and it can grow and bear fruit. The Torah exists both in heaven and on earth, and in Rabbi Akiva's own words: "Just as halakhah is debated on earth, so is Halakhah debated in heaven."[35] And according to Rav Yehudah ben Yehezkel, "Not a day goes by in which the Holy and Blessed One does not innovate some *halakhah* in the heavenly court."[36] New understandings continually break forth and ascend out of the hidden depths of the Torah.

In the view of Rabbi Ishmael, textual teaching exists to establish tradition and to facilitate understanding; it is not for expansion. The plain meaning, which arises out of the standard rules of interpretation, has a fixity; and one who engages in expansive exegesis distorts the Torah and ascribes to it alien intents. Just as one receives reward for expounding, so is there reward for desisting.[21] The text's existence depends on fixity. Thus, Rabbi Ishmael's way is that of apprehension, not expansion.

The Exoteric and Esoteric Personalities

Rabbi Akiva's entire temperament was upward-directed, and as between heaven and earth, heaven always took precedence. He did not shrink from concrete descriptions

---

[35] Tanhuma Shemot 18.
[36] Genesis Rabbah 49:2.

---

[19] This thought, as expressed by Heschel, has a distinctly medieval flavor. See, e.g., Maimonides' *Guide of the Perplexed*, I:68ff., in which it is argued that God is prior to, and transcends, the normal distinctions between subject and object, between form and substance. Here the notion is that divine language does not exhibit the usual form–content distinction of human language, and though it may be expressed here in a somewhat anachronistic, overly systematic way, Heschel seems to have captured an important aspect of the basis of this Akivan style of exegesis.

[20] The use of the word *tongs* recalls the text from Tosefta (Hagigah and Eruvin) cited at the beginning of the previous section.

[21] The reference is to BT Pesahim 22b, in which the rhyming relationship of the Hebrew *derishah/perishah* (here translated "expounding/desisting") is exploited in order to suggest that there are limits to how far one may read esoteric meanings out of texts without treading on theologically thin ice. Tellingly, it is Rabbi Akiva who appears there to argue that no such limit need be reached.

of the divine realm: "Moses was in heaven when he promulgated the Torah"; "The Holy and Blessed One telescoped the lower and upper heavens, and thus did the Presence descend on Mount Sinai." He would expound in ways that caused his colleagues to rebuke him. By contrast, Rabbi Ishmael taught that the Presence did not descend and that Moses achieved only the intimacy of words; Rabbi Ishmael apparently dissented from the view that Moses actually ascended into heaven. He carefully weighed his words and attempted always to reconcile those verses whose language did not comport with the Glory of the Holy and Blessed One.[22]

Rabbi Akiva, the esoteric personality who was not satisfied with straightforward rationality, was possessed of an intuition that what is secreted within the Torah far outweighs what is there on the surface. Having searched out the Torah's secrets, he found that its very letters wisen and enlighten in ways inaccessible to reason. His method demonstrates that just as human language is a pale projection of the Torah's language, so are human ideas compared to the ideas latent in Torah.

Rabbi Ishmael, who was possessed of a more reflective and critical personality, who would have no truck with esoteric matters and did not see a transcendent substance in the Torah,[23] proceeded in a straightforward manner. He assessed and weighed Scripture with scales of logic, eschewing sleight of hand, and interpreted it directly. The principle "the Torah speaks in human language" was his guiding light. He was disposed to ascertain the natural setting of Scripture, and he submitted to the plain meaning of the text as it presents itself to the human mind and reason. The Torah was not given to the angels, and a person is responsible only for that which the eye of his reason can discern. His method demonstrates that direct reason is the Torah's best companion, and the more that the Torah can be harmonized with such reason, the better. Rabbi Ishmael did not shrink from asserting that Moses spoke certain things on his own authority and that in many instances in which Moses was spoken to from on high, he transmitted only the intent of what he heard, not the exact lan-

---

[22] Heschel introduces here another difference between the Akivan and Ishmaelian views, which will become extremely important in succeeding chapters. The Akivan view promotes the idea of divine *immanence,* that is, that the divine remains and inheres in all of creation and, in particular, dwells in the midst of the world of human activity. Heaven and earth are not, on this view, opposite sides of a sharp and impermeable boundary—hence the description of Moses ascending to heaven. And hence the idea that the Torah, which may *look* like a text in human language, is actually a divine object, written in God's language, as it were. The Ishmaelian view, by contrast, insisted on the *transcendence* of God and thus on the impermeability of the boundary between heaven and earth. The biblical text is a projection of the infinite divine realm on the finite dimensions of the human domain, but it is not, and cannot be, the entire truth about God. Thus, finally, it follows that other sources of divine truth, including our powers of reasoning and derivation, must be acknowledged and respected.

[23] This use of the word *transcendent* should not create confusion in the light of the substance of the previous note. The Ishmaelian view promotes the transcendent nature of *God* and, as a consequence, denies that the text of the Torah has a transcendent quality. It is intended for human readers and does not capture the reality of the transcendent, divine realm. See also chapter 14 for Heschel's use of these terms.

guage. Just as the Holy and Blessed One allowed prophets some autonomous space, so that they became partners in prophecy, so did God allow the Sages an autonomous domain, in which they could apply the rules of exegesis. Thus, it is unnecessary to assume that *everything* is contained in Torah, for that which it lacks can be derived or constructed by the Sages via logic. In so doing, human thoughts become the intent of divine thoughts. Rabbi Ishmael even expanded this notion into a comprehensive theory of exegetical principles.[24]

In the School of Rabbi Ishmael, it was frequently asked: "Since I can infer this by logic, why was it written?"[37] That is, if something can be derived via the exegetical rules, why was it necessary to make it explicit in the text? An alternative formulation was: "The text made this explicit because one could not otherwise infer it."[38] Of particular importance was the principle of *kal vahomer* (*a fortiori* reasoning), which heads the list of the thirteen exegetical principles, just as it had Hillel's list of seven principles. Rabbi Ishmael enumerated those scriptural verses that themselves include such reasoning,[39] and even taught that Moses our Master broke the tablets because of a *kal vahomer* inference.[40] In sum, human reason is a worthy and reliable tool.

By contrast, Rabbi Akiva believed that the unfolding of Torah is not dependent on the powers of human reason. There is nothing that is not already latent in Torah; there is no *halakhah* that lacks a basis in the text. All laws are embedded in the Torah and are encoded into its letters. Indeed, a demonstration based on revealing that which is latent in the text has greater value and potency than one based on a logical inference such as *kal vahomer*.[41]

In connection with the Paschal sacrifice, we are forbidden to "cook it with water" (Exodus 12:9). Water is thus forbidden; can one infer a prohibition to cook it in other liquids? Rabbi Ishmael said: "By *kal vahomer*: If water, which does not dilute the meat's taste, is forbidden, how much more so other liquids, which do dilute the meat's taste." But Rabbi Akiva sought to extract from the text itself even a matter that could be derived by *kal vahomer*. He extracted this law from the doubling of the language in the phrase "boiled, boiled in water" (ibid.).[42]

---

[37] MI Nezikin 14; Sifre Naso 26.

[38] MI Nezikin 11.

[39] Genesis Rabbah 92:7.

[40] PT Ta'anit 68c. Compare the language of Rabbi Ishmael in BT Shevu'ot 14a: "thus does logic require."

[41] "You may have refuted the logical argument, but how have you refuted the text?" (Sifra Behukotai 113b). See Louis Finkelstein, *Akiba: Scholar, Saint and Martyr* (Philadelphia: Jewish Publication Society; New York: Meridian, 1936; repr., 1962), 308.

[42] MI Pisha 6. Another example: "What of the case of theft [of a bailment]? 'If it was stolen, yes, stolen

---

[24] The list of thirteen exegetical principles associated with the school of Rabbi Ishmael appears in the so-called Baraita of Rabbi Ishmael, which comprises the introductory chapter of the Sifra (the Tannaitic Midrash on Leviticus). A concise version of this passage (without the accompanying case examples) appears in the preliminary daily service in most traditional Jewish prayer books.

A Restrained Faith—
And a Gaze through the Heavenly Lens

As we shall see presently, Rabbi Akiva was of the opinion that our Master Moses transmitted the divine words to Israel in the exact form in which he heard them. By contrast, Rabbi Ishmael taught that even when Moses said, "Thus says the Lord," he was not transmitting God's words with exactitude.[43] Does this difference not reflect two distinct conceptions of the fundamentals of the faith?

Rabbi Akiva and Rabbi Ishmael disputed each other on the questions of whether our Master Moses did things on his own authority and whether certain matters of law eluded him. Rabbi Ishmael is supported by the surface meaning of the text, and, as we shall see presently, the substance of his view was already known before him to Philo of Alexandria. What compelled Rabbi Akiva to depart from the plain meaning and to dispute this view, that is, to maintain that every single word in the Torah was received by Moses from on high and that Moses said nothing on his own authority? Undoubtedly, he felt that intertwined with this issue is a matter of supreme importance: the essential nature of the Torah.

We will also demonstrate below that the original denotation of the term *the heavenly Torah* was the Ten Utterances heard at Mount Sinai, but that Rabbi Akiva expanded the term to include all of the words of the Pentateuch. "I spoke to you from the very heavens" (Exodus 20:22) referred, on this view, to the entire Torah. Every passage in the Torah is from heaven. The Torah was given in its entirety, in one fell swoop: its generalities and its particularities all were given at Sinai, and subsequent teachings were simply reiterations. The Akivan teaching on the giving of the Torah makes no distinctions based in history; it cannot differentiate between earlier and later strata. The giving of Torah is beyond time and perhaps even transcends human space: "Moses was in heaven when he promulgated the Torah."[25]

---

away from him, he is to pay it back to its owner' (Exodus 22:11)—What of the case of loss? 'But if . . .' (ibid.) ['but' is the rendition of the allegedly superfluous letter *vav*] comes to include the case in which the bailee lost the object. Such is the argument of Rabbi Akiva. What about Rabbi Ishmael? So it was taught in the school of Rabbi Ishmael: If in the case of theft, which is close to an act of God, we are told that the bailee must pay, how much more so in the case of loss, which is not very close to an act of God [i.e., seems to be closer to negligence]!" Rabbi Akiva, who expounds apparent superfluities of language, uses the *vav* as the source of the law concerning loss; Rabbi Ishmael, who does not expound such small points of language, derives it instead by *kal vahomer*. See PT Shevu'ot 38b–c.

[43] See chapter 23.

---

[25] As we saw above, this language serves to underscore the permeability, on the Akivan view, of the supposed boundary between heaven and earth, and that permeability is consistent with the immanence of the divine. Here the language that places Moses in heaven at the time of giving the Torah serves to underscore the related idea that the Torah is not primarily a human document, but is rather divine through and through and thus of infinite dimension.

By contrast, Rabbi Ishmael strove to grasp Torah with the tongs of logic. According to his view, Moses was not given the Torah in one fell swoop: generalities were given at Sinai, but the particulars were transmitted in the Tent of Meeting.[26] Unencumbered by excessive passion, Rabbi Ishmael rooted himself in the meanings of words and answered only to lucid reason. The plain meaning was his medium, and he especially undertook to give a naturalistic reading to much that appeared miraculous.

Rabbi Ishmael—who had said to Rabbi Akiva, "Desist from your statements, and move instead to matters concerning plagues and tent-impurities!"[27]—was the author of the proverb "Whoever wishes to acquire wisdom should busy himself with monetary laws; there is no greater specialty in Torah, for they are like an ever-flowing fountain."[44]

What did Rabbi Ishmael intend in likening monetary laws to an "ever-flowing fountain"? As we shall see presently, there are two approaches to the study of Torah. According to one approach, all was given to Moses, and there is no room for innovation; ours is only to transmit what has already been given. To what can a Sage be compared? To a limed pit, which does not lose a drop of water.[28] According to the other approach, however, not all was given to Moses, and we are given to extract more than what was spoken to Moses at Sinai. To what, then, does the Sage compare? To an ever-flowing fountain,[29] or perhaps to a well, which can bring forth more water than is put into it. Perhaps intimacy with monetary laws, that is, the order of Nezikin (Damages),[30] seemed to Rabbi Ishmael to be like the pouring forth of water from a powerful fountain.

Rabbi Zevi Hirsch Chajes[31] described the study of monetary laws similarly. In the entire Order of Damages, it is very uncommon for laws to be related directly to scriptural verses:

---

[44] BT Berakhot 63b; BT Bava Batra 175b.

---

[26] The Tent of Meeting is the enclosure in which Moses received continuing communication from God in the wilderness after the revelation on Mount Sinai. It is generally (but not always) identified with the Tabernacle.

[27] In BT Hagigah 14a and BT Sanhedrin 67b, this advice to Rabbi Akiva (that he confine his expansive exegeses to areas of mundane Halakhah and not to theologically laden topics) is attributed to Eleazar ben Azariah, not Rabbi Ishmael. See beginning of next chapter.

[28] This description is the one given in Mishnah Avot 2:11 of Rabbi Eliezer, one of Rabbi Akiva's teachers. As applied to Rabbi Eliezer, it apparently referred to both a prodigious memory, an abiding respect for tradition, and the need to pass it on intact. In the present context, it is meant to connote not just a respect for tradition but also a rejection of the legitimacy of interpreting it creatively, with one's rational powers.

[29] This is the description, in the same passage of Mishnah Avot, of Rabbi Eleazar ben Arakh. In each case, it seems to be used to connote an impressive measure of creativity.

[30] Nezikin [Damages], the fourth of the six orders of the Mishnah.

[31] Prominent Talmudist, nineteenth-century Galicia.

Scour all of tractate Bava Batra, the largest of all tractates, and you will not find many laws associated with scripture or even with long-standing tradition. All of the laws and rules given there are what the Sages constructed via logical reasoning and from established practice, i.e. what was accepted procedure in, for example, sales and acquisitions, or damages to abutting properties. They are commentaries on the primary mitzvah of the Torah, to wit that the court should adjudicate fairly with respect to damages and claims. Thus it is written: "Do what is right and good in the sight of the Lord" (Deuteronomy 6:18). . . . The majority of the legal presumptions created by the Sages, which served as their foundation for all teaching in this area, all revolve around their familiarity with human nature and social mores, their understanding of social relations, and their realism.[45]

Rabbi Akiva saw this world through a heavenly lens. He saw before him "the ledger open, and the hand recording."[46] The revealed and the hidden were for him one. But Rabbi Ishmael's way was more modest: his straight reason did not depart from plain meanings. He spoke in human conceptual categories and kept cosmic secrets under wraps. What business has anyone with the secrets of the Holy and Blessed One?

Could There Be Anything That Is Not Hinted At in the Torah?

In Rabbi Akiva's style, Rabbi Johanan[32] asked in astonishment: "Could there be anything in the Hagiographa[33] that is not hinted at in the Torah?" (Rashi comments: "The Pentateuch is the foundation of the Prophets and the Hagiographa, and the latter must thus always be dependent on the Torah."[47] [34]) Consistent with this point of view, he taught: "The Prophets and Hagiographa will eventually become null, but the Five Books of the Torah will never be nullified."[48] It is frequently asked in the Baby-

---

[45] Zevi Hirsch Chajes, *The Student's Guide through the Talmud* [Hebrew: *Mevo Hatalmud*] (London, 1952), 119 (chapter 15).
[46] Mishnah Avot 3:17.
[47] BT Ta'anit 9a (Rashi ad loc). See also Numbers Rabbah 10:6.
[48] PT Megillah 70d.

---

[32] An Amora of the third century, Land of Israel.
[33] *Hagiographa* is the third part of the Hebrew Bible, which is conventionally divided into Torah (Pentateuch), *Nevi'im* (Prophets), and *Ketuvim* (Hagiographa). The initial letters of the Hebrew words form the acronym TaNaKh, often used to refer to the entirety of the Hebrew Bible. But there is a clear hierarchy here: the Torah, which in the rabbinic view is of direct divine origin, is the preeminently authoritative part of the Tanakh.
[34] The context here is a talmudic discussion of a verse in Proverbs that is understood as describing how people typically blame their just deserts on God. The surprise that only the Hagiographa contain such a fundamental lesson is answered by the observation that the Pentateuch does indeed hint at this when it notes that Joseph's brothers blame their troubles in Egypt, obviously brought on by their guilt for the sale of Joseph, on God (Genesis 42:28).

lonian Talmud: "What source is there for this matter in the Torah? What is the source of this rabbinic saying?" Indeed, even of folk proverbs it was asked: "What is the source for this popular saying?"[49] The Zohar expanded this principle explicitly: "There is not the slightest word which cannot be found in the Torah."[50]

By contrast, Rav Hisda[35] said: "This matter [that an uncircumcised priest[36] may not serve in the Temple] is not derivable from the Torah of Moses, and is learned only from the Prophet Ezekiel." Rav Ashi[37] dissented from this view and insisted that Ezekiel created no innovation: this law was received orally at Mount Sinai, and Ezekiel merely wrote it down.[51] Yet Ravina, Rav Ashi's colleague, said: "This matter was not derived from the Torah of Moses but is known from tradition."[52] Note also that laws of acquisition, rules concerning proselytes, and the wedding liturgy are all said to be learned from the Scroll of Ruth.[38] [53]

This entire issue is derivative of the problem that exercised Rabbi Akiva and Rabbi Ishmael—that is, whether or not all of the *halakhot* and legal procedures accepted as authoritative oral teaching are rooted in the text of the Torah and thus "have support." It was raised anew in connection with those exegeses that were known by the name *asmakhta*.[39]

On occasion, the Sages expounded a verse in the Torah and said that the exegesis was not a conclusive proof of the legal point at hand but merely a support; that is, the matter at hand is not latently embedded in the deep meaning of the text. The prevalent language in such cases is: "it is a rabbinic enactment, and the text is a mere support [*asmakhta*]." According to Maimonides, such matters "have no hint at all in the

---

49 BT Bava Kamma 92a–93a lists thirteen proverbs, each with this formula.
50 Zohar, Pinehas, 221a. See Nitzotzei Zohar, ad loc.
51 BT Sanhedrin 22b.
52 BT Rosh Hashanah 7a.
53 BT Bava Metzi'a 47a; BT Yevamot 47b; BT Ketubot 7b.

---

[35] A Babylonian Amora of the latter part of the third century.

[36] That a priest who had so violated the fundamental norm of circumcision could even be considered as a Temple officiant may seem impossible. But the Rabbis had in mind a case where circumcision was medically contraindicated, as when two older brothers had already died as a result of circumcision. In rabbinic law, such situations exempted one from circumcision, but the question remained: Is the presence of a foreskin nevertheless such a physical stigma that it would disqualify such a priest from the privilege of serving in the Temple?

[37] A Babylonian Amora of the fourth to fifth centuries.

[38] The Scroll of Ruth is contained in the Hagiographa. The point being made is that some very basic monetary, religious, and liturgical standards do not have their source in the Pentateuch.

[39] The word *asmakhta* comes from the root meaning "support" and apparently means to suggest that the textual basis for the exegesis gives support to the norm or rule at hand. In the sequel, the question will be raised: How literally should this notion of support be taken? Is the text in such cases merely an associational hook, or can it be considered the derivational source of the law?

Torah, but the law is associated with the text as a mnemonic sign, to facilitate its being known and remembered. But it is not the true meaning of the verse, and it is this that the phrase 'the text is a mere support' always means."[54] This view, that such exegeses were essentially mnemonic devices, was stated prior to Maimonides by Judah Halevi, who said the following concerning the exegesis of the verse "And the Lord God commanded the man, saying" (Genesis 2:16):

> It is an indicator of the seven Noahide commandments.[40] "Lord" refers to the prohibition on blasphemy; "God" refers to the prohibition on idol worship; "commanded" refers to the maintenance of a legal system; "the man" refers to the prohibition on murder; "saying" refers to the prohibition on incest and adultery. . . .[55] [41] This verse is very far from all of these matters. But it is popularly accepted that these seven commandments are associated with this verse, which serves as an *aide-memoire*.[56]

The following bold opinion was reported in the name of the Maharil:[42]

> Whenever it is said, "it is a rabbinic enactment, and the text is a mere support," this is what it means: it is certainly a construction of the Rabbis, who then sought out and found a scriptural support. They then associated their enactment with the text in order to strengthen it, so that people would believe it was biblically ordained, and would thus give it weight, and not come to disdain and treat lightly enactments of the Sages.[57]

Against those who claimed that supports [*asmakhtot*] were mere indicators, the Ritba[43] held that

> whatever has support from a verse thereby has the approval of the Holy and Blessed One . . . this is clearly true. It is not so that such textual support is a mere indicator given by the Sages, and is not the intent of the text. God forbid! Let such opinions be forgotten and never expressed, for they are heretical. Rather, the Torah makes its views known and empowers the Sages to enact certain things should they see fit . . . therefore, you will

---

[54] Introduction to the Mishnah, ed. Mosad Ha-Rav Kuk, *Ramban La-Am* XVIII, 34. See also a similar assertion in *Guide of the Perplexed,* III:43.

[55] See BT Sanhedrin 56b.

[56] *The Kuzari,* 3:73.

[57] *Sefer Maharil,* "Gleanings," 70 (ed. Shelomo Spitzer; Jerusalem, 1989), 629.

---

[40] The Seven Noahide Commandments are a rabbinic construct according to which all human beings (or, in some views, all who reside in the Land of Israel), Jew or Gentile, are held responsible for certain basic rules of civilized living. The usual number of these is seven, but there are alternative lists and numbers.

[41] The list continues with the sixth and seventh commandments, that is, the prohibitions against theft and against eating limbs torn from a live animal. The prohibition of theft is derived from the permission "Of every tree of the garden you are free to eat" (hence, whatever I do not grant you, you may not take, for that is theft). The seventh commandment is alternately derived from this same verse, or from Genesis 9:4: "You must not, however, eat flesh with its life-blood in it."

[42] Rabbi Jacob ben Moses Moellin, leading authority of fourteenth- to fifteenth-century Germany.

[43] Rabbi Yom Tov ben Abraham Ishbili, a major legalist of thirteenth- to fourteenth-century Spain.

always find the Sages providing some evidence, or hint, or support for their statements in the Torah, so as to demonstrate that they do not innovate of their own accord. All of the Oral Torah is at least hinted at in the Written Torah, which is perfect, and not, God forbid, lacking anything.[58]

In general, the Sages followed Rabbi Akiva's view that all *halakhot* are at least hinted at in Torah. "Study it and review it; you will find everything in it." This viewpoint was expanded to the point that even secular wisdom, such as natural science, was deemed to have been revealed to Moses and hinted at in the Torah. It was taught in the school of Rabbi Akiva: "he is trusted throughout My household" (Numbers 12:7)—"I revealed to him[44] all that is above and below, all that is in the waters or on dry land."[59] One who is busied with the wisdom of Torah gains much, including access to all other wisdoms. "There is nothing that is not hinted at in the Torah."

[58] Ritba, Novellae to BT Rosh Hashanah 16a. The MaHaRaL, Rabbi Yehuda Loew of Prague (sixteenth century), expressed a similar point of view about the reality of the biblical sources and derivations of laws stated by the Rabbis. See *Be'er Hagolah,* 1.

[59] Sifre Zuta, p. 276.

[44] The subject here, as in the verse in Numbers 12, is Moses.

3

MIRACLES

Translator's Introduction

Having described Rabbi Ishmael's and Rabbi Akiva's different approaches to interpreting the Torah, Heschel now turns to another aspect of their outlooks: their interpretations of the world, particularly with reference to miracles. There are analogies between the Torah and the world. Just as the language of Torah can be thought of as natural or supernatural, so can the events of the world. Indeed, each is equally the creation and self-expression of God. The style and manner of divine creative activity (and our hermeneutic for understanding it) would naturally be the same in the one case as in the other.

In Rabbi Ishmael's view, God revealed the Torah and created the world, *and endowed each with its own autonomous nature and logic.* The Torah follows the canons of human discourse; the world follows its natural course. Human beings can understand both with their natural reason. The events narrated in Torah follow the pattern of the natural world for the most part and are preferably to be interpreted on that basis. Of course, if the Torah says explicitly that God brought the Israelites through the sea dry-shod, or fed them with manna, this cannot be denied, but it can be interpreted in a manner as compatible as possible with the natural order of things.

Where Rabbi Ishmael sees order, Rabbi Akiva sees miracles. Every word in the Torah is a divine utterance containing unique and infinite levels of meaning; every event in the world is similarly a unique disclosing of divinity, with layer upon layer of reality not immediately apparent to reason. Just as every word in the Torah's legal passages yields heaps and heaps of laws through deft exegesis, so every word in the narrative portion intimates miracles upon miracles beyond those explicit in the text. One might extrapolate the same approach to daily living: where Rabbi Ishmael would see the world as autonomous, following the course that the transcendent God set for it, Rabbi Akiva would experience every day, every minute, every experience as another miracle and as evidence of the direct flow of divine immanence.

65

Marvelous Deeds

W HEREAS RABBI AKIVA interpreted the events of Moses' generation as miracles brought about by the hand of God, Rabbi Ishmael looked for a simpler explanation and did not hesitate to say that they were ordinary occurrences.

It says in the Torah, "Moses took one-half of the blood and put it in basins, and the other half of the blood he dashed against the altar" (Exodus 24:6). The Tannaim asked, "How did Moses manage to divide the blood exactly in half?" Many offered miraculous explanations. Rabbi Judah ben Ilay said, "The blood divided of itself." Rabbi Nathan said, "Half of it turned miraculously black, while half remained red." Rabbi Isaac said, "A voice spoke to Moses from Mount Horeb, telling him, 'This marks the halfway point.'" Ben Kappara said, "An angel came down from heaven in Moses' likeness and divided it." Rabbi Lazar said, "The archangel Michael came down from heaven, took Moses' hand and told him, 'This marks the halfway point.'"[1] The *Mekhilta of Rabbi Simeon bar Yohai* cites only one view, that the blood divided of itself.[2] The only Tanna who holds that Moses performed the division himself, without miracles, is Rabbi Ishmael: "Moses was *expert* in the regulations of blood and its division."[3] Moses determined the quantity himself, as it says, "Not so My servant Moses, he is trusted throughout My household" (Numbers 12:7).[1] [4]

One can find many instances of the Ishmaelian school's naturalistic understanding of Torah narratives. The Mekhilta explains Moses' taking the bones of Joseph out of Egypt (Exodus 13:19): "How did he know where Joseph was buried? It is said that Serah the daughter of Asher was a survivor of that generation, and she showed Moses the site of Joseph's grave."[2] [5] But Moses Isserles expressed surprise that the Mekhilta

---

[1] MTD, p. 57.   [2] MSY on Exodus 24:6, p. 220.   [3] Leviticus Rabbah 6:5.

[4] MTD, p. 57. Jacob Mann cites a rare tradition according to which another Tanna also gave a natural explanation: "Rabbi Judah said: He brought scales and weighed out equal portions on the two sides, and took one portion" (*The Bible as Read and Preached in the Old Synagogue*, vol. 1 [Cincinnati: Hebrew Union College; Philadelphia: Jewish Publication Society, 1940], 250.

[5] MI Beshalah intro.

---

[1] Heschel adds: "The use of this verse to prove the point is puzzling here. The verse is cited elsewhere to support the point that even when Moses acted on his own authority, God ratified his decision" (see chapters 22–23.) Actually, this case proves the point. Human initiative and expertise are often necessary to intuit and carry out God's will—whether to effect an accurate division of the sacrificial blood or an equitable distribution of the world's resources. The "trusted" servant fulfills the divine mandate faithfully and resourcefully in either case.

[2] Of course, Serah's survival to the time of the Exodus (by biblical chronology, she would have been the generation of the grandparents of Moses, who was eighty at the time of the Exodus) could

does not cite the alternate rabbinic tradition, that Moses knew this through his prophetic powers.[6]

The Ishmaelian school even tried to give a rational account of the great miracle of the splitting of the Sea: "'[God] turned the sea to dry ground'—but not totally dry, only somewhat dry. 'The waters formed a wall'—rather like something resembling a wall."[7] The medieval exegete Hizkuni[3] follows this approach: "The Israelites did not cross the sea from one side to another. . . . Rather, they entered only far enough for the Egyptians to follow them and drown, then came back in a semicircle, starting and ending in the wilderness of Etham."[4] [8]

On the other hand, you will find that Rabbi Akiva tried to magnify the miracles that were done for Israel. According to the Mishnah, the Holy One inflicted ten plagues on the Egyptians in Egypt, and ten at the Sea.[9] Rabbi Akiva came and extended an argument introduced by Rabbi Eliezer, to show that the Egyptians suffered fifty plagues in Egypt, and 250 at the Sea.[10]

"The Israelites journeyed from Raamses to Succoth" (Exodus 12:37)—the Sages interpreted "Succoth" as a place-name, but Rabbi Akiva said that it refers to the clouds of God's glory.[11]

"The Lord disposed the Egyptians favorably toward the people, and they let them have their request" (Exodus 12:36). Rabbi Ishmael said, "Understand this literally—as soon as the Israelites asked, the Egyptians gave it to them." Rabbi Eliezer ben Jacob said, "The people were endowed with prophetic powers and asked the Egyptians for specific articles in their hidden places, and the Egyptians brought them out and gave them."[12]

"The frog[s] came up and covered the land of Egypt"—Rabbi Akiva said, "One frog came up [and reproduced] and covered the whole land of Egypt. Rabbi Eleazar ben

---

[6] BT Sotah 13a; Novellae of MaHaRShA ad loc.; Isserles, *Torat Ha'olah*, 3:47.

[7] MI Beshalah 5, YS 234 (*Zayit Ra'anan* ad loc).

[8] Hizkuni on Exodus 14:22.

[9] MI Beshalah 4; Avot 5:4.

[10] MI Beshalah 6; MSY, p. 69; Haggadah of Passover.

[11] MI Pisha 14; MSY, p. 47; Song of Songs Rabbah 1:8.

[12] MI Pisha 13; MSY, p. 31.

---

also be seen as somewhat miraculous. But such a "miracle" is an extension of normal events (e.g., longevity) and as such has a more naturalistic quality to it than does a supernatural revelation or other intervention.

[3] Hezekiah ben Manoah, thirteenth-century commentator of Rashi's school.

[4] Hizkuni's explanation coincides remarkably with the modern theory that the Sea of Reeds was an inlet along Egypt's Mediterranean shoreline. See EJ 6:1043; also John Bright, *A History of Israel* (Philadelphia: Westminster, 1959), 112. It is also supported by Numbers 33:7–8, which mentions Etham both before and after the crossing of the Sea.

Azariah retorted, "Akiva, what business have you with Aggadot? Desist from your statements and move instead to matters concerning plagues and tent-impurities!"[5][13]

Miracle of Manna

The marvel of manna was greater than any other. Most miracles were short-lived, but the manna stayed with Israel forty years.[14] Even after it was gone, wonder and amazement about it remained. The miracle of one generation became a beacon for all.

Often the recipient of a miracle does not regard it as such.[6] Those who ate manna did not celebrate it in song, as they later sang over the well. They spoke disparagingly of it, so they were not privileged to sing about it.[15] The Tannaim came and sang the song. All of the hyperbole in their exegeses concerning the manna were songs of celebration. Other Sages, who found such hyperbole unsettling, opposed them. The one thought that the more marvels you add, the better; the other thought that the miracles recounted in the text are enough, and whoever adds, detracts.

Already in the second generation of Tannaim (80–120 C.E.), it is told that Rabbi Tarfon and the Sages were seated together, and Rabbi Eleazar the Moda'ite sat before them. Rabbi Eleazar expounded, "The manna was sixty cubits high." They replied, "Moda'ite, will you never cease to astound us!"[16] They discussed the verse "Bake what you would bake, and boil what you would boil" (Exodus 16:23). Rabbi Eleazar interpreted this verse: "Whoever wished for baked goods would taste in the manna all the baked goods in the world; whoever wanted cooked dishes would taste in it all the cooked dishes in the world"—even without baking or cooking it. Rabbi Joshua ben Hananiah disagreed: "Whoever wanted to bake it, baked it; whoever wanted to cook it, cooked it."[17]

---

13 BT Sanhedrin 67b.   14 Ibn Ezra, Short Commentary on Exodus 16:15.
15 Exodus Rabbah 25:7.   16 MI Vayyassa' 3.
17 MI Shirah 4 (see variants according to Horowitz); Lekah Tov on Exodus 16:23. See also MSY, p. 113: "'Today you will not find it on the plain' (Exodus 16:25)—Rabbi Joshua said, 'You will not find it today, but you will find it tomorrow.' Rabbi Eleazar Hisma said, 'You will not find it in this world, but you will find it in the world to come.'"

---

[5] Rabbi Akiva's midrash plays on the use of the grammatically singular noun for frog, which a more commonsense interpretation would understand as a collective noun. Rabbi Eleazar's humorous put-down suggests that Akiva's subtle ingenuity is best spent on the most technical subjects of laws of impurities, but leads to wild improbabilities in aggadic midrash. There is also a play on words in the talmudic passage cited here. For Akiva was embellishing the second plague—frogs. And the Hebrew for "plague" (used in reference to the tenth plague in Egypt) is nega'. That is exactly the word that is used in telling Akiva to confine his expansive exegesis to matters of "plagues," that is, the affections and eruptions that engender impurity, as described in Leviticus 13–14.

[6] Literally, "The recipient of a miracle does not recognize his miracle" (BT Niddah 31a). Heschel deplored the atrophy of the miraculous sense in the modern age. Here he sees it as a recurrent human failing, of which the Israelites in the wilderness were also guilty. The Akivan celebration of miracle, extreme though it may sometimes be, is a welcome corrective.

Following in Rabbi Eleazar's path, Rabbi Akiva taught: "Manna was the food that the ministering angels ate." He cited the passage, "He rained manna upon them for food, giving them heavenly grain; each man ate the bread of the mighty ones" (Psalm 78:24–25). He took "heavenly grain" literally and interpreted "the mighty ones" to mean the angels. When these words were reported to Rabbi Ishmael, he said, "Go back and tell Akiva, 'Akiva, you have erred! Do angels indeed eat?' Even Moses refrained from eating for forty days when he communed with God! Read not *abbirim* —'mighty ones,' but *lehem ebarim*—food that is absorbed by the 248 limbs."[7] [18]

"And the Lord said to Moses, 'I will rain down bread for you from the heavens. . . .'" The *Mekhilta of Rabbi Ishmael* interprets this in light of the verse, "The Lord will open for you His bounteous store, the heavens" (Deuteronomy 28:12). "*Shamayyim* (heavens)" is an epithet for God, the Heavenly One. "Bread of the Heavenly One" means bread by the agency of God, not spatially coming from heaven. Would you imagine that God would actually open the heavens? Rather, these verses speak of God's blessing, the symbolic storehouse of goodness. So too, "bread from heaven" connotes bread from God's storehouse of goodness, which is found everywhere. "Look down from Your holy abode, from heaven" (Deuteronomy 26:15)— when Israel fail to perform God's will, God seals off the store of goodness, and they die of hunger; but when they perform God's will, God opens the storehouse.[19]

However, most of the sages took "bread from heaven" in its literal, spatial sense. Even the *Mekhilta of Rabbi Ishmael,* which includes his interpretation "bread of the Heavenly One," also cites the differing view of Rabbi Simeon ben Gamaliel: "God reversed the order of creation, making the upper realms lower and the lower realms upper. Normally bread grows from the earth, and dew descends from heaven. But here bread comes down from heaven, and dew comes up from the earth." Here "bread from heaven" is taken literally.

According to Tannaitic teaching,[20] manna was among the ten things created at twilight of the first Sabbath. The Jerusalem Targum also holds that manna was set aside from that point on for the intended use of Israel.[21] According to the "Rashi" commentary on Avot, it was stored "on high." Others said that God invested the air

---

[18] BT Yoma 75b.

[19] MTD on Deuteronomy 26:15, p. 177. This midrash plays on the redundancy of "Your holy abode . . . from heaven." "Your holy abode" does indeed refer to the spatial heavens from which God looks down. "From heaven" must therefore mean something else: the source of God's goodness, from wherever it may come.

[20] Mishnah Avot 5:6; MI Vayyassa' 5; Sifre Haberakhah 355.

[21] Jerusalem Targum on Exodus 16:4.

---

[7] The meaning of Ishmael's exegesis here is that the manna was completely digested by the limbs of the body and left no waste products. Again, this is something that we might consider "miraculous" as well, but here too it is an extension of naturally occurring processes (i.e., very complete digestion) that were known to occur. Thus, this too has a naturalistic air to it that is very different from declaring the manna to be a heavenly ambrosia.

of the heavens with the power to rain bread from heaven for Israel when they were in the wilderness.

These two differing approaches to miracles are found in many other Tannaitic passages. Consider their exegesis of the war with Amalek: "'Whenever Moses held up his hand, Israel prevailed' (Exodus 17:11)—Moses stopped the sun in its course, as it is written: 'When he held his hand up high, sun and moon stood still' (Habakkuk 3:10–11)."[8] And it is similarly written: "Stand still, O sun, at Gibeon, O moon, in the Valley of Aijalon!" (Joshua 10:12).[22]

Rabbi Ishmael interpreted differently: "Did Moses' hands indeed strengthen Israel or weaken Amalek? Rather, whenever he raised his hands heavenward, Israel looked to him and had faith in the One Who commanded Moses to act, and the Holy One performed works of might for them." Similar interpretations are given of the bronze serpent (Numbers 21:9) and the blood that the Israelites placed as a sign on their homes prior to the Exodus (Exodus 12:13).[23] Rabbi Judah the Patriarch[9] incorporated this exegesis into the Mishnah.[10]

[22] Tanhuma Tetzaveh 9; see Tanhuma Beshallah 28.
[23] MI Amalek 1; MSY, p. 121.
[24] Mishnah Rosh Hashanah 3:8.

---

[8] The first clause in the quotation from Habakkuk is very obscure. *Rom* ("high") may be a noun, as in NJV: "The sky (*rom*) returns the echo." Even if taken as an adverb ("on high"), the subject of "held his hand on high" is variously taken to be the deep (OJV) or the sun (NEB), but only by the wildest stretch can this refer to Moses, who is not mentioned in the passage. Characteristic of this midrash is that it is not satisfied with the miracle already described in the text (that the raising of Moses' hands aided the Israelites to victory); it has to add another.

[9] This is the first of several evidences that Heschel cites that Judah the Patriarch, in compiling the Mishnah, tended to adopt Rabbi Ishmael's outlook in aggadic matters.

[10] We refrain from giving a full translation of the final Hebrew section of this chapter, "How Many Utterances Did They Hear at Mount Sinai?" The gist can be adequately given in this footnote: Heschel establishes that Rabbi Ishmael holds that only the first two utterances of the Ten Commandments ("I am the Lord . . ." and "You shall have no other gods before me") were spoken by God. Since the remainder of the Commandments refer to God in the third person, it makes arguably good sense that they were spoken by Moses. Rabbi Akiva maintains that all ten Commandments were spoken by God. This breakdown of opinion follows the pattern already established in the foregoing examples, that the school of Rabbi Ishmael sought to minimize claims of supernatural events, while the school of Rabbi Akiva sought to maximize them.

In Rabbi Ishmael's world, the ordinary predominates. In Rabbi Akiva's, the numinous and divine are so abundant as to become the norm.

4

THE TABERNACLE AND THE SACRIFICES

Translator's Introduction

In this chapter, Heschel now guides us down yet another corridor in the intricate mansion of rabbinic thought. The spaces to which we are here led are of particularly crucial importance to the understanding of both Jewish law and Jewish ritual. The actual texts that Heschel illuminates in this chapter revolve largely around the sacrificial system in the Temple, for that was the premier ritual known to the ancient Rabbis. But that should not distract the modern reader: what is being highlighted in this chapter is a timeless debate about law and ceremony that continues to this day, even though the context has changed considerably.

The first section, entitled "The Imperative That Undergirds All the Mitzvot," seems to contain a surprising turn. Heschel begins with a very brief summary of rabbinic attempts to epitomize all of the commandments in a single rule or principle (itself a fascinating subject), and, in doing so, some of the things he has asserted concerning the Ishmaelian and Akivan views seem almost to reverse themselves. On the one hand, Ishmaelians are here associated with the view that obedience to God is the primary, generative command and that the road from there to the rest of religious law is not a direct, deductive, rational one, whereas Heschel has already accustomed us to thinking of Ishmaelians as valuing human rationality in religious thought. Similarly, Akivans are in this section associated with the view that a single command of love (i.e., the so-called golden rule implicit in Leviticus 19:18) can generate all of the mitzvot by a kind of moral deduction. Or, as Heschel puts it, the Akivans believed that the reasons for the divine commandments could be best discerned "through a moral and rational lens." Of course, we have previously come to look at the Akivans as rejecting the power of human reason fully to encompass Torah.

As the Rabbis would have said, however, there is no contradiction here. Perhaps better, this section demonstrates to us that the line that divides the Akivan from the Ishmaelian worldview is not the line between rationality and mysticism. Rather, the dividing line is that which separates what I shall call "religious essentialism" from "religious conventionalism." In other terms, Ishmaelians and Akivans part company most fundamentally on the issue of whether and how religious texts, commands, and rituals have *essential* force or *conventional* force. Are they inherently sacred or authoritative because of their very structure or content, or do they rather serve some other end through a form that is, ultimately, a matter of arbitrary convention? Akivans are essentialists, says Heschel, and we can recognize that as being consistent with what we have already seen them say on the issue of the nature of Torah, the inherent, almost magically infinite properties of the letters and even the tittles! By contrast, Heschel portrays the Ishmaelians as conventionalists, and that too echoes their views about the text of the Torah. Human rationality was important for the Ishmaelians in exegesis because the words were really there to *serve* human ends, to bring us closer to God; and they had to be used in the only way the human mind could—through reason.

In this chapter, the essentialist-conventionalist debate continues. The Akivan point of view, true to itself, claims that the mitzvot are a tightly structured and inherently important reflection of the divine will itself, and that understanding what the starting point is (e.g., Leviticus 19:18) can enable us to find our way through the entire web of commandments. Ishmaelians, however, take a point of view perhaps more familiar to students of secular legal systems. They put forward what is called in jurisprudence a "basic norm." The starting point of the system of mitzvot is not a specific law, but rather an overarching imperative, to wit, the imperative to eschew idolatry and obey God. That is the goal that the system of mitzvot is designed to serve, but the individual mitzvot can no more be derived from that basic norm than can the Internal Revenue Code be derived from the preamble to the U.S. Constitution. Thus, in this Ishmaelian, conventionalist view, the commandments are not inherently efficacious, but only as they together serve to promote and concretize the overarching imperative (and as they are hallowed through use).

Through this brilliant and insightful extension of the Akivan-Ishmaelian division, Heschel here explicates for us why rabbinic literature exhibits ambivalences on the significance of the mitzvot and of the sacrificial cult specifically. The seemingly trivial debate over whether the golden calf came first or the building of the Tabernacle came first takes on far-reaching importance, and we can sense the ramifications of this ancient rabbinic debate for contemporary struggles with the meaning of religious command and ritual. Indeed, Heschel does one more thing: he makes it clear, through his references to later rabbinic and philosophical literature, that the potentially subversive conventionalist view was by no means a "fluke," but instead survived and even became the cornerstone of Maimonides' understanding of Jewish worship in the Middle Ages. The implications of all of this for such current topics as liturgical reform are easily drawn out.

Two final introductory notes: Heschel's section titles in this chapter are, when not neutral, reflective of the Ishmaelian point of view (see the first two sections especially). For now, one can only speculate on what this might signify concerning Heschel's own preferences on this subject. Further, Heschel's ubiquitous and delightful wordplay and allusions should not be missed. Most notable here is his paraphrase, in the first section, of the rabbinic statement that "everything stands in need of luck, even the Torah in the ark," apparently to lament the fact that psychological considerations have tended to eclipse the Ishmaelian teachings on this subject.

The Imperative That Undergirds All the Mitzvot

THE RABBIS DISTINGUISHED between commandments that overarch and encompass all of Torah and commandments that are specific. This led them to speculate: Can one find a general principle that all the mitzvot serve? Rabbi Eleazar the Moda'ite suggested one that would support all the mitzvot: "'. . . Heed the Lord your God' (Exodus 15:26)—This is a principle that encompasses all of Torah."[1] Rabbi Eleazar was not suggesting a principle from which the contents and justifications of all mitzvot follow by logical deduction. On the contrary, he was telling us not to rely on reason. Rather, wisdom begins with the acceptance of the yoke of mitzvot. What does God want of you? To attend to His voice, to obey.

On the other hand, there is a tendency among other Rabbis to view the mitzvot and their moorings through a moral and rational lens. For example, Rabban Johanan ben Zakkai explained logically why the Torah dealt more stringently with the burglar than with the robber (the burglar must return twice what he stole). Rabban Johanan's explanation is both moral and logical: the robber who steals openly demonstrates brazenness before God and human beings, while the burglar who enters stealthily demonstrates brazenness before God and fear of human authority.[2]

Or another: Hillel's famous aphorism that the entire Torah is nothing but a commentary on the imperative "Love your neighbor as yourself" (Leviticus 19:18), is also an answer to the search for a general principle that all the mitzvot serve.[3]

Rabbi Akiva followed suit and also proposed a moral/rational principle that serves as a foundation for "a multitude of mitzvot." Truth to tell, there is nothing but a change in formulation dividing the statements of Hillel and Akiva from one another: one defined the fundamental principle as a positive imperative, and the other as a negative imperative. That is, Rabbi Akiva said: "'Love your neighbor as yourself'—this is the major principle of the Torah" (the positive formulation). Ben Azzai (a contemporary of Akiva), however, added an important twist of his own: "'This is the record of the descendants of Adam' (Genesis 5:1)—this is an even more major principle."[4]

All agree that these principles are keystones in the edifice of rabbinic thought. But consider: Can these principles (e.g., Hillel's, Akiva's, or Ben Azzai's) really generate all the mitzvot? Perhaps that could be imagined in the case of commandments governing interpersonal relationships, but could that possibly be said of commandments between a human being and God? It seems that Rabbi Ishmael attempted at least to fix a point in the midst of a chaotic field. In his view, it is the prohibition on idolatry

---

[1] MI Vayyassa' 1;   [2] MI Nezikin 15.

[3] "What is hateful to you, do not do to your fellow" (BT Shabbat 31a). This negative paraphrase of the golden rule is found also in Tobit 4:15, in Philo, and in the Jerusalem Targum to Leviticus 19:18 (Isaac Heinemann, Ta'amei Ha-Mitzvot [The Reasons for the Commandments] [Jerusalem, 1954], 34).

[4] Sifra Kedoshim 89b, RABaD's commentary ad loc. ARN B 26 cites Rabbi Akiva's maxim in a manner reminiscent of Hillel's: "What you hate with respect to yourself, do not do to your fellow."

that ultimately serves as generator of many, many mitzvot governing relations between persons and God. But the process of derivation is not a logical one, but rather a historical one, rooted in the nature of Scripture and in the realities of life. So Rabbi Ishmael hinted to us in many places, though it wasn't until Maimonides[1] that the hints were made more explicit.

Rabbi Ishmael's point of departure was a historical event: until the Tabernacle was built in the desert, the Israelites were addicted to idolatry.[5] We have evidence for this in the text itself: ". . . that they may offer their sacrifices no more to the goat-demons after whom they stray" (Leviticus 17:7), which was understood in the school of Rabbi Ishmael as follows: "It is not clear why 'no more' appears in this verse. Why, indeed, was 'no more' said? Because they in fact *had* sacrificed to such demons."[6] In other words, the verse spoke of reality, not of theory.

It is a mere platitude that the prophets of Israel chided their contemporaries concerning this sin of idolatry, and in spite of that the Israelites sank into corruption. "The Land of Israel was not made desolate (in the First Commonwealth) until seven *batei din* [religious courts] committed idolatry."[7] But here is further substantiation for the Ishmaelian view: in contradistinction to the common view, that in the Second Commonwealth there was no active inclination toward idolatry (since the Men of the Great Assembly prayed successfully for control over it),[8] the school of Rabbi Ishmael held that this inclination still held sway in Israel. In that school, Numbers 15:39 was interpreted so: "'so that you do not follow your heart'—this is sectarianism; '. . . and eyes'—this is lewdness; '. . . in your lustful urge'—this is idolatry, as it says (Judges 8:33), 'they lusted after the Be'alim.'"[9]

The rest follows. For it was taught in the school of Rabbi Ishmael: "What commandment was spoken by God and also through Moses? . . . which commandment was given first (at Mount Sinai)? Clearly, it was (the prohibition on) idolatry."[10] "'Because he has spurned the word of the Lord' (Numbers 15:31)—this refers to the idolator."[11] And: "(The prohibition on) idolatry is equal in weight to all other commandments."[12]

---

[5] TB Aharei 17.

[6] Sifre Korah 116. MI Beshalah 6 says, "'But the Israelites had marched through the sea on dry ground' (Exodus 14:29)—at that point, the ministering angels remarked in amazement, 'Mortals who have worshiped idols are privileged to pass through the sea on dry ground!?'"

[7] BT Gittin 88a.   [8] BT Yoma 69b.

[9] Sifre Shalah 115. See BT Kiddushin 49b: "If one betroths a woman 'on condition that I am wicked,' then even if he is very righteous, she is betrothed, for it is possible that at one time he may have had an idolatrous thought."

[10] BT Horayot 8a–b. See *Otzar Habaraitot* (in Hebrew), ed. Michael Higger, 10 volumes (Rabbinical Assembly and Central Conference of American Rabbis, 1938–48), 3:96ff.

[11] Sifre Shalah 112.

[12] MI Pisha 5; Sifre Shalah 111. See Rashi on Exodus 23:13: "Idolatry is ranked as equal to all the mitzvot, and whoever avoids it scrupulously is regarded as having observed them all."

---

[1] Maimonides: see chapter 1 n. [67] above.

Rabbi Ishmael said: "Biblical laws sometimes display stringencies, and sometimes leniencies."[13] But see just how stringent Rabbi Ishmael was in the matter of idolatry. For Scripture says with respect to a *get* [writ of divorce] that a man must find in his wife "something obnoxious," and he then writes her a writ and sends her away from his house. Early on, there was a difference between the schools of Shammai and Hillel on the definition of "something obnoxious."[14] Now Rabbi Akiva held that "something obnoxious" is an "unseemly thing." But, by contrast, Rabbi Ishmael asserted that "something obnoxious" means "thoughts of idolatry."[15] And this Baraita appears in the Babylonian Talmud in this form: "'you are lustful'—this refers to thoughts of idolatry."[16]

The school of Rabbi Ishmael explicitly taught that this matter (idolatry) is a cornerstone of the faith: "Scripture singled out this commandment of all of the commandments written in the Torah and all mitzvot are commentary to this one mitzvah. Just as one who violates all mitzvot divests oneself of the yoke (of heaven), nullifies the covenant, and shows contempt for the Torah, so does one who violates this one commandment divest oneself of the yoke, nullify the covenant, and show contempt for the Torah. And what is this commandment? It is (the prohibition of) idolatry . . . for anyone who acknowledges the validity of idolatry denies all the Ten Commandments . . . and all who deny the validity of idolatry acknowledge the validity of the entire Torah."[17]

Pay attention to the stylistic details here. The usual language in Tannaitic midrash is, "Scripture comes and teaches" or "Scripture comes to teach"; but in this instance, the language is: "all mitzvot are commentary to this one mitzvah." Shall we say that the intention of this assertion is to teach simply that the prohibition against idolatry is equal in importance to all other mitzvot? Is it not more logical to assume that something deeper lurks here, viz., that all other commandments are there to distance Israel from idolatry?

In just such a fashion did Maimonides understand these words of Rabbi Ishmael: "You already know from the Torah's words in many places that the primary intention of the entire Torah was to remove idolatry and expunge its memory . . . and all that it (the holy Torah) brings to bear on this subject, all revolves around removing all such (idolatrous) ideas from the heart."

The evidence from rabbinic literature that Maimonides brings for this is the statement from the school of Rabbi Ishmael: "anyone who acknowledges the validity of

---

[13] PT Berakhot 3b; Sanhedrin 30b.

[14] BT Gittin 90a; Sifre Tetzei 269.

[15] MTD, p. 148; note "aleph" of Hoffmann ad loc.; and W. Bacher, *Aggadot Ha-Tannaim*, volume 1, part 2, p. 16, n. 3.

[16] BT Berakhot 12b.

[17] MI Pisha 5; Sifre Shalah 111, Re'eh 54.

idolatry denies the validity of the entire Torah, and all who deny the validity of idolatry acknowledge the validity of the entire Torah. Understand this."[18]

There is scarcely a statement in all of rabbinic literature that has gained as much
praise and fame as the principle of Rabbi Akiva ("Love your neighbor as yourself—this
is the major principle of the Torah"); it is an aphorism known even to the youngest of
schoolchildren. Yet everything stands in need of luck, even a fundamental principle
of the Torah! Rabbi Ishmael did not have that good fortune, and his principle was not
favored with luck. But then, perhaps it is not luck after all, but a matter of human
psychology. One who speaks of love as a fundamental enjoys the empathy of other
persons; but one who declares that human beings are naturally idolatrous will be
summarily silenced. . . .

The Command Concerning the Tabernacle
Followed the Sin of the Golden Calf

Without the Tabernacle, there can be no sacrifices. Rabbi Ishmael, whose concern
was to emphasize how sacrifice warded off idolatry, understood that the command to
build the Tabernacle, on which depend all the sacrifices, was not given until after the
Israelites created the golden calf. What forced Rabbi Ishmael to postdate the building
of the Tabernacle? It must be a reflection of the conviction that this command did
not enter the divine mind until Israel sinned. At that point, when it was clear that
they were prone to idolatry, the command was given to build a Tabernacle and to
bring sacrificial animals to the officiating priests. The section dealing with the Tabernacle—"Let them make me a sanctuary that I may dwell among them" (Exodus
25:8)—appears in the Torah before the sin of the golden calf (Exodus 32:1ff.). In the
Midrash (Tanhuma Terumah), it was asked: "When was Moses given these instructions concerning the Tabernacle? On the Day of Atonement itself [when the Holy
and Blessed One was reconciled to Israel and delivered the second tablets], even
though in the text the command to build the Tabernacle precedes the golden calf
[which occurred in the month of Tammuz]. Rabbi Judah ben Shalom[2] said: 'There is
no exact chronological order in the Torah, as it is written, "Her course turns this way
and that, and what does she care?" (Proverbs 5:6)—the pathways of Torah, and its
pericopes, are displaced.'"[19] According to this, Moses was commanded concerning
the Tabernacle after the creation of the calf.

This idea, rooted in the methodological principle of Rabbi Ishmael that there is no
reliable chronological order in the Torah, was in fact expressed by Rabbi Ishmael. The

[18] *Guide of the Perplexed,* III:29.
[19] Tanhuma Terumah 8, Tissa 31, Pekudei 2; Exodus Rabbah 51:4.

---

[2] Judah ben Shalom: fifth-century Amora, Israel.

Gentiles were depicted as saying that since Israel sinned, the Holy and Blessed One had irrevocably rejected them.[3] [20] Rabbi Ishmael came and expounded:

> The Tabernacle of the testimony—it is a testimony to one and all that the Holy and Blessed One was reconciled to Israel. To what can this be compared? To a king who married and loved his wife exceedingly but later became angry with her and spurned her. Her acquaintances kept telling her that he would never return to her. But after a time the king was reconciled to her; he entered her residence and ate and drank with her, but her acquaintances still did not believe that he had been reconciled to her. When, however, they smelled the royal perfumes on her, they immediately knew that reconciliation had indeed occurred. So did the Holy and Blessed One love Israel, bring them to Mount Sinai, give them the Torah, and call them royalty. After forty days they made a calf. At that moment the Gentiles said: the Holy and Blessed One will never take them back. But when Moses stood and prayed on their behalf, the Holy and Blessed One said to him: "I pardon, as you have asked. Moreover, My presence will dwell with them, in their midst, so that all will know that I have pardoned."[21]

Also according to Seder Olam (attributed to Rabbi Yose ben Halafta[4]), Moses descended from the mountain on the Day of Atonement, "and informed them that God had been reconciled to them . . . and afterwards all the Israelites approached Moses and he gave them all the commands he had received from God on Mount Sinai. What did he command them? He commanded them to build the Tabernacle."[22]

This notion would surely not have sat well with Rabbi Akiva. According to his view, the entire Torah was given together, in one fell swoop: its generalities and its particularities all came from Sinai. And when Moses received the tablets, he received all of the commandments, including the commands concerning the Tabernacle and the sacrifices.

Note to what lengths Rabbi Akiva went in speaking of the value of the Temple. Unlike Rabbi Ishmael, who viewed the value of the Tabernacle in an anthropocentric way (i.e., "it is a testimony to one and all that the Holy and Blessed One was reconciled to Israel"), Rabbi Akiva praised the Temple as the very majesty of God. Thus did he expound the verse (1 Chronicles 29:11): "'Yours, God, are greatness'—this is the splitting of the Reed Sea, 'and might'—this is the killing of the firstborn, 'and splen-

---

[20] Tanhuma Pekuday 2, 6: "The nations of the world taunt Israel: 'You have made the golden calf!'" (Leviticus Rabbah 27:8).

[21] YS Pekudei 414; Tanhuma Terumah 8; TB Pekudei 2; Midrash on Psalms 3:6.

[22] Seder Olam Rabbah 6. See Exodus Rabbah 33:3: "'I was asleep, but my heart was wakeful' (Song of Songs 5:2)—I was asleep when worshiping the golden calf, but the Holy One knocked at my door, saying 'Make Me a sanctuary!'"

---

[3] This, of course, was to become a common Christian polemic against Judaism.

[4] Yose ben Halafta: second-century Tanna. The ascription of Seder Olam (Rabbah) to Rabbi Yose is fairly ancient and is found in BT Shabbat 88a.

dor'—this is the giving of the Torah, 'and triumph'—this is Jerusalem, 'and majesty'—that is the Temple."[23]

In the school of Rabbi Ishmael they expounded: "'that goodly mountain'[5] (Deuteronomy 3:25)—this is Jerusalem."[24] By contrast, they expounded in the school of Rabbi Akiva: "'that goodly'[6]—this is the Temple, of which it is said 'that goodly mountain.'"[25]

The opinion of Rabbi Simeon ben Yohai,[7] the student of Rabbi Akiva, is diametrically opposed to that of Rabbi Ishmael. According to Rabbi Ishmael, the Tabernacle came to serve a human need—"it is a testimony to one and all . . ."—and it was built to benefit humanity. According to Rabbi Simeon, who holds that "the sanctuary below faces the sanctuary above,"[26] and that on the day that Moses erected the Tabernacle below, "he erected another Tabernacle along with it above,"[27] the Tabernacle came to serve a divine need.[8] And in a famous Baraita, the Tabernacle is included among those things that predated the creation of the world.[28]

This is further hinted at by the fact that Rabbi Simeon ben Yohai opposed Rabbi Ishmael's interpretation of the language "the Tabernacle of testimony (edut)," and

---

[23] BT Berakhot 58a. Contrast with R. Shela's homily there: "'Greatness'—this is creation; 'and might'— this is the Exodus; 'and splendor'—this is the stopping of the sun and the moon for Joshua; 'and triumph'— this is the fall of Rome; 'and majesty'—this is the war over the wadis of the Arnon. Elsewhere, R. Isaac agrees with Rabbi Akiva: "God's 'glory' refers to the Temple" (Genesis Rabbah 3:4).

[24] Sifre Pinehas 134; Tosefta Berakhot 6:1.

[25] Sifre Zuta, p. 265; MI Amalek 2; Finkelstein's notes to Sifre Devarim 28.

[26] Tanhuma Pekudei 2.   [27] Numbers Rabbah 12:11.   [28] BT Pesahim 54a.

---

[5] NJV: "That good hill country." In the context of Moses' request to God, it seems to refer to all the hill country of the Promised Land. In the midrashic use, it refers to a specific mountain: either the heights of the city of Jerusalem or (more narrowly) Mount Moriah, within the city of Jerusalem, on which the Temple stood.

The difference between Rabbi Ishmael's interpretation and Rabbi Akiva's is subtle but significant. Rabbi Ishmael appreciates Jerusalem in its totality—the religious and earthly aspects complementing each other. Rabbi Akiva values especially the sacred aspect, for the link it provides with the heavenly realm. This difference will be spelled out more in chapter 14, "Transcendental and Terrestrial Perspectives."

[6] That is, with the definite article, which is conveyed by the Hebrew letter heh and is included in the English "that" (as opposed to "a goodly mountain").

[7] Simeon ben Yohai: fourth-generation Tanna, associated with the Tannaitic midrash Mekhilta de-Rabbi Shimon ben Yohai, which generally expresses the views of Rabbi Akiva's school.

[8] The notion of a "divine need" (tzorekh gavoah) is daring and paradoxical, especially in the light of the accepted medieval concept (embraced by Judaism, Christianity, and Islam alike) of God's utter perfection and self-sufficiency. Heschel took the notion of divine need to heart as a cornerstone of his own theology, as the title of his central work, God in Search of Man, testifies. He derived it from the Jewish mystical tradition, mediated through his Hasidic upbringing. Here he finds its source in the Akivan outlook.

The connection of this idea with the rest of this section is fairly straightforward: if the Tabernacle came only to correct idolatrous impulses, then it came to serve a human need and only proved necessary after the golden calf. But if God needs and yearns to be recognized and worshiped by humankind, then the necessity of the Tabernacle was present from the beginning, and it was part of the unalterable divine plan, which was revealed at Mount Sinai immediately after the Exodus.

said: "the Tabernacle of testimony"—"don't read *edut* in the sense of testimony, but rather in the sense of teaching [as in] 'these are the testimonies and the statutes' (Deuteronomy 4:45)."[29]

Over and against the approach of Rabbi Ishmael, there survived an alternate idea, that the command to create the Tabernacle preceded the making of the calf, as is the order of the text of the Torah. "A tradition came back with the exiles, which they proceeded to teach, that God jumped over the sin of the calf, and preceded it with the creation of the Tabernacle."[9] [30] According to Seder Eliyahu Rabbah as well, as soon as "Israel accepted the sovereignty of heaven with joy and said 'all the things that the Lord has commanded we will do' (Exodus 24:7), the Holy and Blessed One immediately said to Moses: 'Tell the Israelite people to bring Me gifts' (Exodus 25:2)."[31] And so also is the opinion of the Zohar.[32]

It is possible that Rabbi Ishmael's position implies that, were it not for the Israelites' predisposition to idolatry, they would not have been commanded to sacrifice to God; and had they not made the calf, they would not have been commanded to build the Tabernacle.[33] Rabbi Benaiah,[10] who was apparently from the school of Rabbi Ishmael, taught along these lines: "Israel having engaged in idolatry was liable to destruction. The gold of the Tabernacle came to atone for the gold of the calf."[34] But Rabbi Joshua ben Levi,[11] opposing this view that the Tabernacle was built only because of the sin of the calf, held: "The Holy and Blessed One stipulated to the Israelites in Egypt that they would be taken out from there only on condition that they build God a Tabernacle so that the Shekhinah could dwell among them."[35]

Consistent with Rabbi Ishmael's train of thought, Rabbi Levi[12] taught:

Why was the bovine listed first among the sacrifices [in Leviticus 1]? . . . It can be analogized to a noblewoman who was slandered by someone high in the royal family. The king

---

[29] YS Beha'alotekha 723.   [30] Song of Songs Rabbah 1:12.   [31] SER p. 85.

[32] Zohar Pekudei 224a.

[33] Indeed, there was an ancient view that sacrifices went back to Adam. According to Rabbi Eliezer ben Jacob, Adam offered sacrifices at the site of the Temple altar in Jerusalem (Genesis Rabbah 34:9). Similarly: "'The Lord God took the man and placed him in the Garden of Eden, *le'obdah uleshomrah*' [NJV: "to till it and tend it"]—read *le'obdah* to mean to offer sacrifices [< *avodah* = ritual worship]" (ibid. 16:5). Against this view, Rabbi Ishmael interpreted *le'obdah* to mean study, and *leshomrah* to mean the observance of mitzvot (Sifre Ekev 41).

[34] Sifre Devarim 1; PT Shekalim 45d; Midrash Aggadah, beginning of Vayyakhel; Lekah Tov, proem to Vayyakhel.

[35] PR 18b, Friedmann's note ad loc.; Tanhuma Naso 22; Numbers Rabbah 12:6; Midrash on Psalms 114:5.

---

[9] This text may not exactly illustrate Heschel's point here. The sense seems to be that, although the sin preceded the instructions for the Tabernacle (the Ishmaelian view), God rewrote the Torah, by "jumping" the Tabernacle over the sin so as to give the *impression* that it preceded the sin.

[10] Benaiah: first- (transitional) generation Amora, Israel.

[11] Joshua ben Levi: first-generation leading Amora, Israel.

[12] Levi: second- to third-generation Amora, Israel.

investigated and found the charges baseless. What did the king do? He made a great feast and sat her at the head of the table, in order to publicize that he had investigated and found the charges baseless. So here, since the Gentiles were saying to Israel, "you made the calf," and the Holy and Blessed One had investigated the matter and found it baseless,[13] the bovine was put at the head of the sacrifices.[36]

Rabbi Joshua ben Levi transmitted a homily in the name of Rabbi Simeon bar Yohai, who, like his teacher Rabbi Akiva, expounded the word *et* in the verse: "On the day that Moses finished setting up the Tabernacle" (Numbers 7: 1)—"it does not say *lehakim mishkan,* but rather *lehakim et hamishkan.* What was set up with it?[14] The world was set up with it. For until the Tabernacle was set up, the world tottered; once the Tabernacle was set up, the world became well-founded."[37]

According to the approach of Rabbi Simeon, "when the Holy and Blessed One created the world, He desired a dwelling below just as one existed above."[38] But the sins of humanity caused the Shekhinah to depart from the world. Rabbi Simeon thus taught that the dwelling of the Shekhinah in the Tabernacle was not a *novum,* but rather "something which had been, which ceased for a long time, and which returned to its original state."[15] [39]

This dispute [concerning the Tabernacle] is reflected also in the interpretations of "This is my God Whom I will enshrine (*ve-anvehu*)" (Exodus 15:2). According to Rabbi Yose of Damascus,[16] the Israelites at the Sea said: "Whom I will enshrine"—"I will create for God a Temple." But Rabbi Ishmael, in contrast, interpreted: "*ve-anvehu* is related to the word *noi* (beauty)—I will offer God beauty through mitzvot."[17] [40]

---

[36] TB Emor 15.   [37] PRK 6a.   [38] TB Naso 24.   [39] PR 18b.   [40] MI Shirata 3; MSY, p. 79.

---

[13] Because they had remorse and would be willing to worship God exclusively in the Tabernacle.

[14] According to the Akivan principle of *ribbui* (expansive reading), the presence of the word *et* should hint at something additional not mentioned in the verse, that is, something in addition to the Tabernacle that was also established along with it. The word *lehakim* is the causative verb from the root *kum,* whose range of meaning includes "stand, be set up, stand firm, endure." Thus, through the very action that the Tabernacle was set up, the world was established on a firm basis, to endure securely.

[15] In Rabbi Simeon's view, the manifestation of God in the world through the Tabernacle (or later, the Temple) is part of the right, established, and eternal order of things. The absence of God (or the absence of the Tabernacle/Temple) is the exception, rather than the norm. The Tabernacle is not merely a human convention but the right, fitting, and unalterable form through which the content of the Divine Presence (Shekhinah) is manifested. The heavenly prototype of the Tabernacle (see chapter 14) is symbolic of the eternity of this concept.

[16] Yose of Damascus: third- to fourth-generation Tanna.

[17] This example is adduced in chapter 12 as an expression that Rabbi Ishmael considered (in the concrete sense) to be not befitting God's dignity. The notion of localizing God in a specific place (see next chapter) or tying God's essence necessarily to a specific sacred architecture or ritual was offensive to Rabbi Ishmael's notion of God's absolute transcendence. In this respect, Rabbi Ishmael may have pointed the way to Maimonides' notion of the "negative divine attributes," that is, that God is totally beyond the power of our words or concepts to specify or grasp.

Consider, and you will see that they taught in the school of Rabbi Ishmael: "He said to Aaron, 'take a calf' (Leviticus 9:2)—let the calf come and atone for the making of the calf."[41] By contrast, we have preserved a homily in the style of Rabbi Akiva: "'Take a young bull of the herd' (Exodus 29:1)—to atone for you with respect to the future [for the creation of the calf which Aaron will make], as it is written: 'He said to Aaron, "take a calf of the herd for a sin offering"' (Leviticus 9:2)."[42]

On this subject, there were disputes also in the Middle Ages.[18] Rashi[19] accepted the view that the making of the calf preceded by many days the command to make the Tabernacle.[43] And Rabbi Obadiah Sforno[20] held: "For prior to the sin of the calf, right after the giving of the Torah, Israel did not need all this . . . and they were not commanded concerning the Tabernacle, its vessels, its priests and service corps, nor concerning any public or private sacrifices, until after the making of the calf. As God said: 'For when I freed your ancestors from the land of Egypt, I did not speak with them or command them concerning burnt offerings or sacrifices' (Jeremiah 7:22)."[44]

Rabbi Isaac Abravanel[21] also held this view:

When Israel left Egypt, came before Mount Sinai, and heard the Torah and commandments, God did not command them at all concerning sacrifices, but rather concerning matters of faith and meritorious deeds that they were to perform. However, when they made the calf and God saw their evil inclination . . . it became necessary to prepare for them a salve or antidote for this illness . . . thus came the commands concerning sacrifice . . . and thus it is said . . . "For when I freed your ancestors from the land of Egypt, I did not speak with them or command them concerning burnt offerings or sacrifices" (Jeremiah 7:22)—this refers to the assembly at Mount Sinai, and the acceptance of the

---

[41] Sifra Shemini 43c; TB Shemini 6.

[42] Exodus Rabbah 38:3. The bracketed explanation is that of *Mattenot Kehunah* ad loc. R. Samson of Sens objected: "Isn't it well known that the golden calf preceded [the laws of the Tabernacle]?" We respond: According to Rabbi Ishmael, yes, but not according to Rabbi Akiva.

[43] Rashi on Exodus 31:18, 33:11.

[44] Sforno, *Kavvanot ha-Torah* [The Purposes of the Torah], printed with the Introduction to his Commentary to the Torah.

---

[18] Here, as elsewhere in this work, Heschel makes extensive reference to the lineup of views of the major medieval Jewish thinkers on the same issues that engaged the Tannaitic masters. Even though his starting point is the depiction of the theological positions articulated in the classical rabbinic period (second to fifth centuries C.E.), he is ultimately concerned with the gamut of normative expressions on these topics from the entire spectrum of Jewish thinkers speaking within the tradition, up until fairly recent times (but excluding those "modern" thinkers who, from Moses Mendelssohn on, took their basic intellectual assumptions from the Enlightenment or modern secular philosophy). Thus, Heschel demonstrates that we do not have to step outside the tradition into modernity to find a plurality of Jewish viewpoints; we find this plurality within the tradition itself, in all periods.

[19] Rashi: France, eleventh century, the dean of medieval biblical commentators.

[20] Sforno: Italy, sixteenth-century biblical commentator.

[21] Abravanel: Spain, fifteenth-century statesman, philosopher, and biblical commentator.

commandments recounted in the sections *Yitro* and *Mishpatim,* in which God did not command them concerning burnt offerings or sacrifices."[45]

In contradistinction to this, Nahmanides[22] holds, as does the Zohar, that Moses received instruction concerning the work of the Tabernacle before the making of the calf. Once they sinned, Moses thought that all commands might be nullified. But when the Holy and Blessed One was reconciled to them "and promised them that the Shekhinah would dwell in their midst, Moses knew that the mitzvah of the Tabernacle remained firm."[46]

And Rabbi Abraham Azulai[23] wrote concerning this:

and even though there is apparent difficulty in what our blessed Rabbis said, namely, that the Tabernacle came to atone for the calf, it is nevertheless obvious that God's whole desire and longing is to cause the Shekhinah to dwell below. And when Israel came to believe after they had made the calf, that there could no longer be any indwelling of the Shekhinah, they were then commanded with the work of the Tabernacle, and they knew that they had been forgiven. . . . all this the Holy and Blessed One did in order to prepare the antidote in advance of the disease.[47]

Why Sacrifices?

The Torah says by way of explanation of the sacrificial system: "This is in order that the Israelites may bring the sacrifices, which they have been making in the open, before the Lord, to the priest, at the entrance of the Tent of Meeting—and turn the fat into smoke as a pleasing odor to the Lord;[24] and that they may offer their sacrifices no more to the goat-demons after whom they stray.[25] This shall be to them a law for all time, throughout the generations" (Leviticus 17:5–7).

[45] R. Isaac Abravanel, commentary on Jeremiah 7:21.

[46] Nahmanides on Leviticus 8:2, Exodus 35:1, Leviticus 25:1, and Deuteronomy 10:10. According to this view, "Moses transmitted the command to build the Tabernacle, when he chose to do so." Also, according to Joshua ibn Shuaib's sermons on Vayyakhel and Pekudei, the commandment of the Tabernacle preceded the breaking of the tablets.

[47] *Or Ha-hammah* on Zohar Pekudei 224a, also *Zohar Hai* ad loc.

---

[22] Nahmanides: Rabbi Moses ben Nahman (acronym: RaMBaN), Spain, thirteenth-century talmudist, kabbalist, and biblical commentator. It is significant for Heschel's schema that Nahmanides, one of the seminal thinkers of medieval Jewish mysticism, usually agrees with or develops the viewpoints of the school of Rabbi Akiva.

[23] Abraham Azulai: seventeenth-century kabbalist, Morocco and the Land of Israel.

[24] This seems to be in line with the Akivan view that the ritual is no mere convention designed for human needs, but is intrinsically desired by God in all its particulars for its own sake.

[25] This seems to be in accord with the Ishmaelian view expressed earlier that the primary purpose of all the mitzvot is to combat idolatry.

There are three elements in this scriptural statement discussed by the Sages in evaluating the institution of sacrificial worship. (1) The Torah sought to wean the people away from their idolatrous practices and forbade all sacrifices outside the central sanctuary. (2) The Lord desired these sacrifices for Himself, because they are a pleasing odor to Him. (3) The command to offer sacrifices is not a temporary one, but is a law for all time, throughout the generations—that is, forever.

The schools of Rabbi Ishmael and Rabbi Akiva centered their debate on the question, Were the sacrifices instituted to satisfy the needs of the people or God's needs? In the school of Rabbi Ishmael, the phrase "a pleasing odor to the Lord" (Numbers 18:17; 28:6) is meant to be understood in a spiritual sense.[26] It means that God was pleased with the fulfillment of His commandment to offer the sacrifice to Him, as we find in the Midrash, "I have great satisfaction that they performed My will as I instructed them."[48]

In the school of Rabbi Akiva, "as a pleasing odor" was taken literally. We learn that from the fats of the animals there emerged a fire of pleasing odor that gave satisfaction to the Holy and Blessed One.[49] In this spirit, the Mekhilta of Rabbi Simeon ben Yohai proclaims the superiority of the true God to the idols: "'Their idols . . . have noses but cannot smell' (Psalm 115:4–6). But the One Who by His word created all, is not so! Rather, 'The Lord smelled the pleasing odor . . .' (Genesis 8:21)."[50]

Both schools had to contend with the principle that "there is no eating or drinking with respect to God." The Psalmist asked rhetorically, "Do I eat the flesh of bulls, or drink the blood of goats?" (Psalm 50:13). So the question stood: "Why [asks God] do I tell you to bring sacrifices to Me?" The school of Rabbi Ishmael answered, "Only in order to do God's will, as it says, 'Sacrifice so that it may be accepted on your behalf' (Leviticus 19:5)."[51] But there was also an Akivan response to this question: "God said, 'The only thing I want from your sacrifices is the odor, and it will be to Me as if I had food and drink,' as we read in the Torah, 'My food which is presented unto Me for offerings made by fire of a sweet savor unto Me, shall you observe' (Numbers 28:2)."[52] From this view, the sacrifices were commanded to satisfy God's need.

---

[48] Sifre Shelah 107.   [49] Sifre Zuta, p. 324.   [50] MSY, p. 92.

[51] Sifre Pinehas 143; BT Menahot 110a and Rashi ad loc.: "*Liretzonkhem* [lit., 'at your will,' 'for your favor'] means, for your own need, that you may fulfill My commands and atonement will thereby be effected for you."

[52] Tanhuma Tetzaveh 14; PRK 59a, 60a.

---

[26] The word here is *ruhani*, an obvious pun on the word *reiah*, "odor." Similarly, in the quotation from the Sifre that follows, the English "satisfaction" renders the Hebrew *nahat ruah*, "an easing of the spirit." Thus does Ishmael transmute *reiah* into *ruah*, and the literal and concrete into the spiritual. As in all rabbinic debates, each party must find an alternative explanation for the proof texts supporting the other side of the argument, and it is characteristic that Rabbi Ishmael interprets one of the favorite Akivan proof texts in a nonliteral sense.

[Note: These paragraphs on the general outlooks of the schools on this question are transposed in this translation from the beginning of the next subsection, for the sake of clarity.]

In the view of Rabbi Ishmael, the sacrificial system was instituted primarily to keep the people far from idolatry. Support for this view may be found in the comments of the sages on the command to offer the paschal lamb (Exodus 12:1ff.). In the Midrash, the question is raised: Why did the command to purchase the paschal lamb precede its slaughtering by four days? The answer is: Because the people were steeped in idolatry. . . . therefore, He said to them, "Withdraw yourselves from idol worship and heed the commandments."[53] You may ask, since there were so many other commandments to fulfill, Why was this particular one regarded as so efficacious?[54] The answer is: Because the lambs were worshiped as gods in Egypt, God said to Moses, "I swear that the Israelites will not leave here until they slaughter the gods of Egypt before their very eyes. In this way I will teach them that their gods are worthless."[55] Rabbi Akiva does not associate the command to slaughter the paschal lamb with withdrawing from idolatrous practice. He interpreted the verse "Pick out[27] and take lambs for your families" (Exodus 12:21) to mean: "'Pick out' refers to those who possess lambs; 'take [acquire]' refers to those who do not possess any."[56]

Further support for the view of Rabbi Ishmael may be adduced from the account in the Torah that depicts the people lusting for meat. When were the people granted permission to eat "meat of craving"[28] (i.e., to eat meat as daily fare rather than as a ritual obligation)? According to Rabbi Akiva, the Israelites had never been forbidden to eat meat. Rabbi Ishmael, however, stated that when the Tabernacle was erected, they

---

[53] MI Pisha 5.
[54] So asks the *Zayyit Ra'anan* (Venice, 5503/1743), p. 15b.
[55] Exodus Rabbah 16:3.
[56] MI Pisha 11 anonymous view, MSY, p. 25, citing Rabbi Akiva.

---

[27] The verb doublet *mishkhu u-kekhu* (Fox: "Pick out, take") in Exodus 12:21 is redundant. The Ishmaelian exegesis therefore interprets the first word (*mishkhu*, "draw") in a reflexive sense: "withdraw yourself" (from what? from idolatry). Rabbi Akiva, for whom the lamb was intrinsically important, had to interpret away the redundancy differently: pick one out if you already have a lamb, and acquire one if you do not. The verb [*la*]-*kakh* had the meaning of property acquisition (especially, through purchase) in rabbinic Hebrew.

[28] "Meat of craving" (*besar ta'avah*) has either a negative or a neutral connotation, depending on context. In Numbers 11:1–35, God is angry at the people for demanding meat in the middle of the wilderness march, and those who die in the ensuing plague are buried at Kibroth-hataavah (which name means, "the graves of craving"). But in Deuteronomy 12:20, the permission to eat meat at discretion is granted with the phraseology, "When . . . you say, 'I shall eat some meat,' for you have the craving (*ki te-aveh nafshekha*) to eat meat, you may eat whenever you wish (*bekhol avat nafshekha*)."

This duality of treatment in the Torah foreshadows the divided attitudes of Rabbi Ishmael and Rabbi Akiva on the subject. The key text for Rabbi Ishmael is Leviticus 17, cited at the beginning of this section. Read in detail, this chapter both institutes the sacrificial system of the Tabernacle and prohibits slaughtering meat to the "goat-demons" outside the camp. Rabbi Ishmael deduces from this that, in the wilderness, eating nonsacrificial meat led the people to idolatry—his central theme! Rabbi Akiva, however, read this chapter emphasizing the positive motive of offering the "sweet savor" of the sacrifices. Thus, he did not associate "meat of craving" with idolatry and was more permissive toward it even during the period of the wandering.

were prohibited from eating any meat slaughtered away from the Tent of Meeting. They were permitted only sacrificial meat during their entire stay in the wilderness. When they entered the land of Israel, the prohibition was lifted.[57] He explains this prohibition on the basis of the people's craving for idolatry; they would regard the animals they slaughtered as an offering to the gods. Therefore, in order to keep them from idolatry, Moses ordered them to bring their offerings to the Tent of Meeting and to the priest, who would slaughter the animals as sacrifices to God.[58]

This connection was elucidated by a parable, quoted by Rabbi Phinehas[29] in the name of Rabbi Levi:

> A prince became wayward, and got in the habit of eating carrion meat. The king said, "Let him eat regularly at my table, and he will *ipso facto* foreswear it." Similarly, since the Israelites were addicted to idolatry in Egypt, and would bring their sacrifices to the goat-demons, so they later brought their sacrifices to the local shrines[30] and were punished as a result, so the Holy and Blessed One said, "Let them bring their offerings at all times in the Tent of Meeting, and thus they will separate themselves from idolatry and be saved."[59]

The view that in messianic times the elaborate sacrificial system would be abolished is stated by the same Rabbi Phinehas and Rabbi Levi, and by Rabbi Johanan as well, all in the name of Rabbi Menahem of Galliah:[31] "In the time to come, all the sacrifices will be abolished, except for the thanksgiving sacrifice."[60] The scholars of the Middle Ages sought to explain this astonishing statement. Rabbi Abraham ben David of Posquieres[32] commented: "The Temple and Jerusalem will, in time to come, be transformed into another kind of holiness to the glory of the eternal God. So it was given to me as an esoteric revelation that comes to the God-fearing."[61] In the Midrash, the Sages hinted that in the days of the Messiah there will be no further need for sacrifices. God says to Israel: "In this life, you made your contributions to the Tabernacle, which, in turn, made atonement for your sins, but in the future life, My love for you will be a freewill offering."[62] Similarly, we have the statement, "The

---

[57] Sifre Re'eh 75; BT Hullin 16b.   [58] Tanhuma Aharei 11; TB Aharei 17.

[59] Leviticus Rabbah 22:8.

[60] Leviticus Rabbah 9:7; 27:12. The commentary *Yefeh To'ar* by Mordecai Jaffe (Constantinople, sixteenth century) dissents: "This is inconceivable! For the main purpose of the sacrifices is for the future, and it is for their sake that the Temple will be rebuilt (speedily in our days), as Ezekiel prophesied!"

[61] RABaD, glosses to Maimonides' *Mishneh Torah, Bet Ha-Behirah* [Laws of the Temple] 6:14.

[62] Tanhuma Pekudei 9.

---

[29] Rabbi Phinehas (ben Hama ha-Kohen): fourth-generation Amora, Land of Israel.

[30] "Shrines" (*bamot*, translated in AV and OJV as "high places" in 2 Kings 12:4 and passim) is a reference to the local worship outside Jerusalem in the later monarchical period, forbidden by Deuteronomy 12:2–16.

[31] Menahem of Galliah: fifth-generation Tanna.

[32] RaABaD, Provence, twelfth-century talmudist, commentator, and polemicist.

Holy and Blessed One said, "In this world you achieved atonement through sacrifice, but in the world to come, I will blot out your sins without sacrifice," as the verse reads, "Even I will blot out your transgressions for My sake" (Isaiah 43:25).[63]

The Value of Sacrifices

The basic difference in attitude to the sacrificial system may be summarized thus: In the school of Rabbi Ishmael the view was, "Not for My sake do you offer sacrifices, but for your sakes, to satisfy your needs. For My part, I am pleased that having given you the commandment, you fulfill My will, and I shall reward you."

In the school of Rabbi Akiva, the view was, "I desire nothing else but the sacrifices. Their sweet savor brings delight to Me."

Rabbi Ishmael's view is reflected in an exposition preserved in a later source. It is told that God did not want them to erect a Tabernacle to Him in the first place, and He did not issue the command to build it until the people Israel entreated Him to do so. "Why did they want the entire ritual of the Tabernacle?" The people said to the Holy and Blessed One: "Master of the universe, the sovereigns of all the nations have a tent, a table, a menorah, incense offerings. Every king has need for those rituals in his kingdom. You are our Sovereign, our Redeemer, our Savior—should You not have all these rituals of kingship so that all the nations of the world will know that You are our Sovereign?" The Holy and Blessed One replied: "They who are flesh and blood need all this, but I do not need it. I have no need for food or drink and I do not require any light. My servants can testify to that; the sun and moon which illumine the whole earth—they get their light from Me." However, the people continued to entreat Him, so God finally said to them, "My children, if you feel this way, then do as you please, but you must do it only in accordance with My instructions. Build Me a house, as it is written, and they shall make Me a sanctuary (Exodus 25:8)—also a menorah, a table, and an altar on which to offer incense."[64]

Rabbi Akiva's view is reflected in the following exposition: The verse reads, "I have likened you, my darling, to a mare in Pharaoh's chariots" (Song of Songs 1:9). The term "my darling" (ra'yati) is derived from the root ra'o, to feed. God compares Israel to one who feeds Me. Israel will feed Me daily with two sacrifices, as we read, "You shall offer one lamb in the morning and one in the evening" (Exodus 29:39).[65]

Another exposition that supports Rabbi Akiva's view is based on the verse "The righteous eats to satisfy his desire"[33] (Proverbs 13:25). This refers to the Holy One,

---

[63] Tanhuma Shemini 4.   [64] Midrash Aggadah, Terumah, p. 170.
[65] Song of Songs Rabbah 1:9.

---

[33] Desire, Nefesh. This Hebrew word (which in medieval philosophy became "soul," with all its dualistic connotations) had the original biblical connotation of "life, person, breath" (see especially Psalm 69:2: "The waters have reached my neck [nefesh]"). The Akivan exegesis plays correctly on that

Who said to the people Israel: My children, you offer Me many sacrifices, but I derive pleasure only from the odor, as the verse reads, ". . . of a sweet savor unto Me shall you observe to offer in its due season" (Numbers 28:2).[66]

But consider the distinction that is put forth in another text between the view expressed in the Torah and the view expressed by God concerning sacrifices. Wisdom was asked, "What is the punishment for a sinner?" She answered, "The individual who sins shall be put to death." The Torah was asked, "What is the punishment for a sinner?" She answered, "Let him bring a guilt-offering and his sin will be atoned." God was asked, "What is the punishment for a sinner?" He answered, "Let him do penance and his sin will be atoned."[67]

This exposition is in harmony with the view expressed in the school of Rabbi Ishmael: You offer sacrifices not for My sake but for your sake. In other words, do what is pleasing to you.[34]

The Advantage of Sacrifices

The institution of sacrifices played such a central role in the worship of God that many of the Sages were saddened when it came to an end with the destruction of the Second Temple. They sought consolation in various ways. Some looked to other commandments in the Torah as substitutes. It is related that Rabban Johanan ben Zakkai was walking and Rabbi Joshua was running behind him crying, "Woe unto us, for we have lost our House of Life, the place where we could atone for our sins." Rabban Johanan turned to him and said, "Fear not, we have a substitute to atone for our sins." "What is it?" Rabbi Joshua asked. Rabban Johanan answered him with a scriptural verse, "It is loving-kindness I desire, not sacrifice" (Hosea 6:6).[68] Another Sage declared, "God prefers the study of Torah to burnt offerings."[69] Another said, "Prayer is more important than sacrifices."[70] The Midrash says: One who performs deeds of charity is worthier than one who offers all the sacrifices.[71] And Rabbi Joshua ben Levi[35] taught: One who is downcast in spirit is deemed as though he had offered every sacrifice in the ritual.[72] Rabbi Isaac[36] consoled himself with this thought:

---

[66] PRK 60a.   [67] PRK, Shuva 158b.

[68] ARN A 4, B 8. BT Bava Batra 10b has: "Just as the sin-offering atones for Israel, so deeds of righteousness atone for the nations of the world."

[69] ARN A 4.   [70] BT Berakhot 32b.

[71] Deuteronomy Rabbah 5:3. See God's consolation to David in the story just cited.

[72] BT Sanhedrin 43b.

---

original meaning: "The Righteous [i.e., God] eats to satisfy His inhalation," and for this requires only the savory fragrance, not the gross meat of the sacrifice.

[34] That is, build a Tabernacle, but do it My way, in a controlled way, a way that will wean you from idolatry and serve your purposes.

[35] Isaac: second- to third-generation Amora, Land of Israel.

[36] Joshua ben Levi: second- to third-generation Amora, Land of Israel.

when one studies the law of the sin-offering, he is deemed to have brought a sin-offering; when one studies the law of the guilt-offering, he is deemed to have brought a guilt-offering.[73]

Yet, despite all such statements as: "In time to come, the sacrificial system will be abolished," or, "In the world to come, I will blot out their sins without sacrifices,"[74] the people of Israel prayed for the restoration of the Holy Temple and the reinstitution of the sacrificial system.[75] Normal conversation on earth centers on such questions as: "Did you till the soil or not?" "Did the orchard produce a good fruit crop?" And the normal prayers of human beings also focus on material needs, "May the good earth be productive, O my Master. May we be blessed with a good harvest, O Lord." But the prayers of the people Israel were directed to the Holy Temple. "O, my Master, may the Holy Temple be rebuilt." "Oh, when will we see the Temple rebuilt?"[76] Even in everyday conversation, it was customary to offer the hope, "May the Temple speedily be rebuilt." In the course of a homily that Rabbi Akiva was expounding on the reason for the sacrifices, he said, "Bring an omer of barley on Passover, for that is the barley season, and your produce will be blessed. Bring the first of your wheat (two loaves) on Shevuot, for that is the wheat season, and your fruit will be blessed. Observe the water libation on Sukkot, for that is the rainy season, and everything will be blessed through the rain.[77] And it was Rabbi Akiva who added this petition to the Passover Haggadah: "[May we be] joyous in serving You, and in the renewal of Your Temple. There we shall eat of the paschal sacrifices and other offerings, the blood of which shall be dashed on the wall of Your altar, that they be accepted."[78]

Worship in the Temple

Why did the Sages regard the service in the Temple as of major importance? Many of them rejected Rabbi Akiva's notion that God had a need for this service. They counseled, "Don't be led astray by your evil inclination to think it's God who needs the light!"[79] The case of the Temple lamp was grist for their mill. Just as Rabbi Ishmael had taught that the Tabernacle was erected not for the sake of God, but to give notice to the world that God was reconciled with Israel, so they explained the reason for the menorah. It was not that God needed the light, but it served as witness to the whole world that God's Presence dwelt among the people Israel.[80]

This view is reflected in a midrash: The people asked God, "You instruct us to kindle light for You? You are the light of the world; the light dwells with You. Yet You

[73] BT Menahot 110a.

[74] Cited above (Leviticus Rabbah 9:7, 27:12; Tanhuma Shemini 4).

[75] Note, however, that the prayer at the end of the Amidah, "May it be Your will that *the Temple* be rebuilt speedily in our days," revises the language of its original, "that *Your city (Jerusalem)* be rebuilt" (Avot 5:20).

[76] Genesis Rabbah 13:2.   [77] Tosefta Rosh Hashanah 1:12.

[78] Mishnah Pesahim 10:5, as it appears in PT.   [79] TB Tetzaveh 4,5.   [80] BT Shabbat 22b.

instruct us, let the seven lamps throw their light forward to the front of the menorah!" (Numbers 8:2). The Holy and Blessed One replied, "It is not that I have need of your light but rather that you cast your light toward Me, even as I have cast My light toward you. In this way, I raise your prestige among the nations, who will say, See how the people Israel bring light to Him who gives light to the world."[81]

But the Ishmaelian approach did not satisfy all the Sages either. Are we to explain the Temple service, which is a communion between humans and God, as something required by political considerations between Israel and the nations?

We are caught in a paradox. The one side asks dismissively, "Does God need the light?" The other side addresses God in wonder, "You give light to all and sundry, yet You desire the light which Israel offers You!" The Sages put this exclamation of wonder in Job's mouth: "Master of the world! Heaven and earth are in Your power, yet 'You yearn for Your own handiwork' (Job 14:15)!"[82]

Answers belong to God. In matters of ultimate import, the question may itself be the answer. The very institution of the Temple worship cannot be weighed in the scales of reason. One should not fear paradox. But Job's insight provides a sure tool with which to work toward a synthesis of the two approaches.

"You call, and I answer You, You yearn for Your own handiwork"—Israel says to the Holy and Blessed One, "You command, and I will obey, yet You yearn for Your own handiwork! You carry the burden of the whole world, but You command the Kohathites to carry the ark of Your glory. You feed the whole world but You command us to offer You "the bread of My sacrifice." You illumine the whole world, but You order us to kindle a perpetual lamp. We see light in Your light, yet you tell us to kindle candles.

The Holy One explains, "It is not that I have need of the light of human beings— for with My light I illumine the whole world—but I want to enhance your prestige and make you merit reward."

Elsewhere we find: "God guards His world but He commands Israel to guard Him, as we read, 'And those who encamped before the Tabernacle kept guard over the Sanctuary' (Numbers 3:38–39)."[83]

Rabbi Johanan taught that Moses was overcome with astonishment at three divine pronouncements: "Let them make me a sanctuary, that I may dwell among them" (Exodus 25:8). "Bring Me My offering, My food" (Numbers 28:2). "Each shall pay a ransom for his soul" (Exodus 30:12). Can the infinite God be contained within a sanctuary? Can the Provider of all the world be provided for? Can the soul of infinite worth be ransomed by all the gold in the world?

Nevertheless: "Make it twenty boards by twenty by eight, and I will meet with you there and speak to you from between the cherubim." "One lamb in the morning, and one in the evening." "Half a shekel by the sanctuary weight as an expiation for your souls."[84]

---

[81] TB Beha'alotekha 5.   [82] Leviticus Rabbah 31:3.   [83] Exodus Rabbah 36:4.
[84] TB Naso 19; Numbers Rabbah 12:3; Midrash on Psalms 91:1; PR 84b.

In the incisive thrust of the questions, we hear the voice of Rabbi Ishmael. In the answers given by Rabbi Johanan, however, we recognize Rabbi Akiva's simple trust in the marvels of the divine wisdom.[37]

The Debate over the Purpose of Sacrifices

The debate on sacrifices was raised to new levels of intensity during the Middle Ages by the teachings of Maimonides. He followed the view of Rabbi Ishmael that the people Israel had become habituated to offering sacrifices to the gods, like the peoples about them. Had God prohibited all manner of sacrifices, then the people would have become guilty of idolatry. "It is contrary to human nature to relinquish what has become habitual practice."[85] God, therefore, permitted the offering of sacrifices but insisted that they must be offered in God's name. In this way, God would deter them from idolatrous worship. Maimonides stated his position very clearly: "The service in the Temple was not arranged, or more properly not sanctioned, except for the express purpose of keeping the people far away from idolatry."[86] This point of view aroused a strong protest among many scholars. Nahmanides wrote in rebuttal: These are erroneous statements. . . . They make of God's table an abomination . . . they appeal only to the wicked and the simpletons of the world. The Torah states specifically that the sacrifices are "bread of the fire-offering of sweet savor. . . ." It is unthinkable that they should be regarded as of no value or delight. Only in the opinion of fools can they be looked upon as a rejection of idolatry.[87]

Moses Narboni,[38] in his commentary on the *Guide,* defended Maimonides against these charges. What Maimonides meant, he explained, was that God found a way of accommodating a habitual practice by commanding the people to worship Him with those very rituals with which they had been accustomed in idolatrous worship. This does not negate the fact that offering a sacrifice is, in truth, a way of worshiping God.[88]

Gersonides[39] also expressed a similar view: The Torah frequently utilized one

---

[85] Maimonides, *Guide of the Perplexed,* III:32.
[86] Maimonides, *Guide of the Perplexed,* III:32; also Heinemann, *Ta'amei Ha-mitzvot,* p. 85.
[87] Nahmanides, Commentary on Leviticus, 1:9.
[88] Narboni, Commentary to *Guide,* 3:33.

---

[37] Thus, Rabbi Johanan has effected a synthesis. However, in MI Pisha 16, the same questions are raised, but the answer is more prosaic: "To receive one's reward for doing them." This reflects a more Ishmaelian orientation.

[38] Narboni (Moses ben Joshua of Narbonne): Provence, fourteenth-century philosopher and commentator on Maimonides.

[39] Gersonides: Rabbi Levi ben Gershon (RaLBaG), Provence, fourteenth-century philosopher and biblical commentator.

commandment to serve various purposes, as we have seen in the case of the Sabbath ... the same is true of sacrifices; one of the purposes was to distance them from the custom of offering idolatrous sacrifices. The Torah states this explicitly in Leviticus 17:5–7. This may also have been one of the purposes in erecting the Tabernacle and assigning the priests to this form of service. Nevertheless, it is not correct to believe that there was no value in service in and of itself. Were that the case, the order of the service would not have been given in such detail.[89]

Rabbi Isaac Abravanel,[40] in his introduction to the Book of Leviticus, states that there is great support for the views of Maimonides in the Torah, the Prophets, the Writings and the teachings of the Sages. What Maimonides wrote is to be regarded not as erroneous statements but as sacred teachings.[90]

The statement in Jeremiah 7:22, "For when I freed your fathers from the land of Egypt, I did not speak with them or command them concerning burnt offerings or sacrifices," in the view of the Sages, underscored what He did command them, namely, "There He made for them a fixed rule and ordinance" (Exodus 15:25). This refers to the laws of the Sabbath which He gave them in Marah. He did not, however, give any instructions there concerning the offering of sacrifices.

Rabbi David Kimhi[41] interprets this verse, in the spirit of Maimonides, to mean that the crucial element in God's commandment was not the offering of sacrifices but the obeying of God's will, as in Jeremiah 7:23: "Do my bidding, that I may be your God and you will be My people." It was on this basis that God gave them the Torah. In the Ten Commandments, which represent the quintessence of the Torah, there is no mention of burnt offerings and sacrifices. Even when the Torah deals specifically with the sacrificial rites, God does not state it as a command; rather, the verse reads, "When any of you presents an offering ..." (Leviticus 2)—should a person of his own free will present an offering, then this is the procedure.

The daily offerings, issued as commands, were for the glory of the Temple and were of a communal nature. God did not order individuals to offer sacrifices in the manner in which He commanded them to deal justly or to observe the other laws. God commanded an individual to offer a sacrifice only when he had sinned unwittingly. As for the daily offerings and the building of the Temple for worship, we may agree with our great teacher Moses ben Maimon that its purpose was to redirect the building of sanctuaries for idolatrous practices to the worship of God, thereby blotting out idolatry from the people.[91]

[89] Gersonides, Commentary to Leviticus (Tzav), Mosad ha-Rav Kuk edition (Hebrew), p. 105.
[90] Abravanel, Commentary to Leviticus, Introduction.
[91] David Kimhi, Commentary on Jeremiah 7:22.

[40] Abravanel: Spain, fifteenth-century philosopher, statesman, and commentator.
[41] Kimhi: Provence, twelfth–thirteenth centuries, biblical commentator.

Nahmanides raised an interesting question in his critique of Maimonides: If it is indeed a fact that they were given the sacrificial system to keep them far from idolatry, why did Noah offer a sacrifice when he came out of the ark—a time when there was no idolatry? Moses Narboni, in his commentary, refuted this argument. "It is not true that idolatry did not exist at that time; wherever man is to be found in this universe, there you will find idolatry."[92]

Philo[42] had asked this same question, "Why did Noah build an altar, since he was not commanded to do so?" The answer may be found in a midrashic comment on the verse "Give instruction to a wise man and he will be still wiser, teach a righteous man and he will increase in learning" (Proverbs 9:9). This applies to Noah. How? God instructed him, "Of every living thing of all flesh, you shall bring two of every sort into the ark . . . take with you seven pairs of all clean animals" (Genesis 6:19; 7:2). When he left the ark, "Noah built an altar to the Lord" (Genesis 8:20). How are we to understand va-yiven, "he built"? It means he pondered the matter (va-yitbonen) and concluded that the reason God required a greater number of clean animals than unclean animals is that God wanted me to sacrifice to Him. Immediately, the Torah relates, "And he took from all the clean animals . . . and he presented burnt offerings on the altar" (Genesis 8:20). "A wise man hears the instruction, fulfills it, and then adds to it."[93]

[92] Narboni, Commentary to *Guide,* 3:32.
[93] Exodus Rabbah 50:2.

[42] Philo ("of Alexandria," also called "Philo Judaeus"): first-century Hellenistic Jewish philosopher.

THE ABODE OF THE SHEKHINAH

Translator's Introduction

Is God present in some places more than in others? Is God's Presence attributed to certain places by convention, or is it in the nature of things?

Mircea Eliade illustrated (in *The Sacred and the Profane: The Nature of Religion* [New York: Harcourt Brace, 1959], chapter 1) how the sanctification of place is common to many cultures. In a typical case, a tribe would build an altar or a totem pole in the middle of its own campsite and would consider it to be the "navel of the earth," the geographic center of the cosmos where earth and heaven meet. The Babylonian *ziggurat* (satirized in the story of the Tower of Babel in Genesis) was conceived of as just such a celestial-terrestrial meeting point. So was Jacob's ladder (cited by Eliade), on which the angels passed back and forth between earth and heaven. Indeed, the rabbinic midrashim relocated Jacob's ladder from Beth El (the site recorded in Genesis 28:19) to Jerusalem in order to reinforce the centrality and uniqueness of what was to become the primary focus of Jewish spirituality.[1] For it was in Jerusalem, on the Temple Mount, that they located the Foundation Stone (later identified with the massive boulder now in the Dome of the Rock), from which the world was traditionally created. It was there that Adam brought an expiatory offering after the sin of Eden. It was there that Abraham bound Isaac and extracted the pledge of the eternal covenant. It was there that the First and Second Temples stood. And it is there where (according to tradition) history will find its culmination with the establishment of the messianic kingdom.

But Heschel values the sanctification of time over space. He argues elsewhere (in *The Sabbath: Its Meaning for Modern Man* [New York: Farrar, Straus & Giroux, 1951]) that he considered sanctification of space to be more characteristic of pagan spirituality, while Judaism preferred to create the Sabbath, a sanctuary in time. In the present chapter, Heschel credits Rabbi Ishmael with conceiving of omnipresence as a divine attribute, thus breaking new ground in the conception of God. To be sure, Jewish tradition would continue to prefer to pray toward Jerusalem, the site of the Temple; but a minority view, which Heschel cites here, legitimates praying in any direction, for God is everywhere.

---

[1] See Genesis Rabbah 69:7, and Rashi on Genesis 28:11.

This would support the view that the sanctity of Jerusalem is conventional, the product of contingent historical development, not intrinsic to the nature of things.

Yet is there a danger that, if we say God is everywhere, we will be less likely to experience the Divine Presence anywhere? Is there a virtue in singling out a particular place as the locale of the Shekhinah? Does it help to focus our spiritual seriousness if we regard a particular site (even one marked by a physical designator, such as the controversial Cherubim) as intrinsically sacred, beyond the power of convention or history to alter? Here, too, Heschel sets the two views side by side and leaves the choice to us.

The Shekhinah in the West, or Everywhere?

"THE WHOLE EARTH is filled with God's presence"—"His glory fills the world." This outlook logically should leave no room to inquire, "Where is the place of God's glory?"[2] Nevertheless, you find this question side by side with this outlook and intertwined with it. The assumption is that God's glory fills the world but is not present in every part in equal measure. Even more, presence is sometimes taken to mean localization, so that people tend to the view that the reality of God in the world means that God is found in a particular place, as if God's Presence (Shekhinah) is spatially bounded.

Rabbi Akiva, who had no compunction about speaking concretely about supernal realities and taught that God's glory descended on Mount Sinai, taught also that the Shekhinah abides in the west, that the west is its preferred locale.[3] This is the way taken by Rabbi Joshua ben Levi, who said, "Let us be grateful to our predecessors, who taught us the proper direction of prayer."[4] 1 This view emphasizes that sanctity per-

---

1 BT Bava Batra 25a; PT Bava Batra 13c.

---

[2] All three quotations are from the Kedushah, the portion of the prayer service declaring the sanctification of God (see Hertz, *Authorised Daily Prayer Book* [New York: Bloch Publishing, 1948], 529); the first is originally from Isaiah 6:3.

[3] The original context of this remark (in Tractate Bava Batra) is a discussion about where a tannery may be located in relation to a town. All authorities agree that it should not be located to the west of the town, presumably because the prevailing westerly winds would carry odors to the residential district. But another interpretation is offered, namely, that the west possessed special sanctity, being the abode of the Shekhinah.

[4] The proof text cited is from Nehemiah 9, in which the "host of heaven" are said to prostrate themselves before God. Since the heavenly bodies rise in the east, they would appear to be shining forth and doing homage toward that which is opposite them, that is, in the west. It might strike English readers as very odd that the Shekhinah would be said to be in the west, since it is virtually axiomatic that one faces east in order to pray. But note that it is only from North America, southern Europe, and North Africa that Jerusalem can be said to be in the eastern direction (though this reached Central and Eastern Europe as well, geography notwithstanding). But the ancient Temple was built on an east–west axis, with the entrance at the eastern end and the Ark at the western end. Thus, the natural inclination for a Temple attender would be to think of the Presence as being in the west.

tains to a special place. Whoever prays should face the Temple.[5] Thus, Daniel prayed toward Jerusalem (Daniel 6:11), and, in Ezekiel's words, "And there, coming from the east . . . was the Presence of the God of Israel"[6] (Ezekiel 43:2).

It was Rabbi Ishmael who asked, "Is it indeed possible for mortals to enshrine their Maker?" He rejected the notion that God's presence is spatially bound and counterposed the spiritual-intellectual conception that "the Shekhinah is everywhere."[2] This idea broke new ground in the world's conception of God. The view that the Shekhinah is everywhere removes the notion of Divine Presence from a spatial conceptual framework and establishes that the Shekhinah transcends place. In this vein, Rabbi Yose ben Halafta (who was in many respects close to Rabbi Ishmael's way of thinking) said, "The Holy One is the place of the universe, but the universe is not His place."[3]

The Amoraim R. Hoshaya and R. Sheshet also followed Rabbi Ishmael's approach and therefore were not particular about the direction of prayer. Thus R. Sheshet, who was blind, instructed his valet, "Find me a place to pray, in any direction."[4]

All this should help to clarify for us the magnificent midrash in the Mekhilta of Rabbi Ishmael: "'See, I stand before you there on the rock in Horeb' (Exodus 17:6)—The Omnipresent[7] said to Moses: 'In every place where you find human footprints, I am there before you.'"[5] This midrash combines four separate wordplays: (1) *omed* ("standing") is spelled without the *vav* and can therefore be read *amad* ("[one] stood"); (2) *tzur* ("rock") suggests *tzurah* ("form [impression, footprint]"); (3) *lefanekha* ("before you") is transferred from the spatial to the temporal sense (i.e., before you came here); (4) *sham* ("there") suggests not here in Horeb but out there in the world. Thus, a verse that apparently pins down a specific location for the Divine Presence is midrashically transformed to teach that God is present in every time and place.[6]

---

[2] BT Bava Batra 25a.   [3] Genesis Rabbah 68:9.
[4] BT Bava Batra 25a; Tosafot ad loc., s.v. *lekhol*.   [5] MI Vayyassa' 6.
[6] *Sekhel Tov* on Exodus 17:6, *Me'ir Ayyin* ad loc. Compare Philo, *Allegory of the Sacred Laws*, 2.2.4; G. F. Moore, *Judaism in the First Centuries of the Christian Era: The Age of the Tannaim* (Cambridge: Harvard University Press, 1927–30), 1:372.

---

[5] The Talmud (Berakhot 30a) spells this out in more detail: Whoever is outside the Land of Israel should face the Land of Israel. Within the Land of Israel, one should face Jerusalem. Within Jerusalem, one should face the Temple. Within the Temple, one should face the Holy of Holies (at the western end of the central sanctum). Within the Holy of Holies, one should face the Cherubim. The last possibility, taken literally, could only apply to the High Priest on Yom Kippur. But it undoubtedly was included here for rhetorical purposes, in order to take the sequence to its logical conclusion.

[6] The idea presumably is that the Presence was coming *from* the east to settle in the west.

[7] *Hamakom* (literally, "the Place"), a common rabbinic epithet for God. It is conceptually connected with the statement of Yose ben Halafta previously cited, to the effect that God is the place of everything else, not vice versa. This epithet is used here, not by accident, as part of a play with the next words, *kol makom* ("in every place," i.e., everywhere). As the point of the midrash is to stress God's omnipresence, so the narrator selects the name of God that highlights it.

The desire to purge the notion of Divine Presence of its spatial connotations is reflected and highlighted in several sayings of the school of Rabbi Ishmael:

> You find that whenever Israel is enslaved, the Shekhinah is with them, as it says, "In all their troubles, God is troubled" (Isaiah 63:9). This refers only to communal suffering. Where do we learn about individual distress? From the verse, "When he calls on Me, I will answer him; I will be with him in distress" (Psalm 91:15). Thus, wherever Israel is exiled, the Shekhinah is with them.[8] 7

Similarly: "God's messengers are not like the messengers of mortals. The latter need to return to their senders to report back to them. But not so Your messengers; wherever they go, they are present before You, and say, 'We have performed Your mission,' as it says, 'Do I not fill heaven and earth?'" (Jeremiah 23:24).8

Rabbi Yose ben Halafta joined Rabbi Ishmael in opposing apocalyptic[9] ideas and in trying to free people from the notion that the Divine Presence is dependent on place. It is written: 'The Lord came from Sinai' (Deuteronomy 33:2). Shall we say that the Divine Glory is fixated on Sinai, and comes from Sinai to give Torah to Israel? Rabbi Yose said: "Read rather: 'The Lord came *to* Sinai.'"9 Moreover, Mount Sinai, the site selected for that most glorious and awesome encounter, is proof to all and sundry that there is no place in the world to which the highest sanctity is permanently and inalienably linked. For even Mount Sinai enjoyed that sanctity only for that time. Rabbi Yose also established the principle: "The place does not honor the person, but the person honors the place. So long as the Shekhinah rested on the mountain, we read: 'Whoever touches the mountain shall be put to death' (Exodus 19:12). But as soon as the Shekhinah departed, all were permitted to go up onto the mountain."10

Rabbi Yose similarly explained the term *makom* ("place"), which the tradition uses as an epithet of God: "We do not know if the Holy One is subordinate to the universe or if the universe is subordinate to God, until God says to Moses: 'Here is place with

---

7 MI Pisha 14; Sifre Beha'alotekha 84.
8 MI Pisha, introduction.
9 MI Bahodesh 3.
10 MI Bahodesh 3; BT Ta'anit 21b.

---

[8] This very exegesis, which produces the idea of the Shekhinah going into exile, is cited in the next chapter as being reflective of an *Akivan* view on God's participation in the sufferings of Israel. Thus, as we noted above in the preface, one cannot take with the utmost seriousness the idea that statements cited from rabbinic literature are actually being identified with particular schools of thought. On the other hand, if we are speaking about competing theological paradigms, then one and the same verse and exegesis may be paradigmatic of a sober and rationalistic view when it comes to locating the Divine Presence (e.g., it is unlocatable), and of a mystical view about participation in human sufferings (e.g., the Shekhinah moves into exile with us). The importance of keeping in mind Heschel's real agenda, even when his words seem to suggest otherwise(!), cannot be overestimated.

[9] Heschel means "apocalyptic" in the sense of "influenced by the apocalyptic literature." Proto-mystical themes are prominent in the apocalyptic writings of the Pseudepigrapha. For an extended discussion of the affinity of the apocalyptists and Rabbi Akiva's school, see below, chapters 15 and 17.

Me' (Exodus 33:21)—God is the place of the universe, but the universe is not God's place. Thus, the universe is subordinate to God, and not the reverse."[11]

But we find a different interpretation of the name *Makom* attributed to Rabbi Akiva:[10] "Why is God called *Makom*? Because in every place where the righteous stand, God stands with them, as it is written: 'In every place (*makom*) where I cause My name to be mentioned, I will come to you and bless you' (Exodus 20:21). And it is written: Jacob reached the *makom,* and H/he lodged there"[11] (Genesis 28:11).[12]

In the teaching of Rabbi Levi you find an attempt to reconcile the views of the Shekhinah's omnipresence with its localization in the Tent of Meeting. R. Joshua of Sikhnin quoted him: "What was the Tent of Meeting like? Like a cave by the sea. The sea raged and flooded the cave; the cave was filled, but the sea was not diminished. Similarly, the Tent of Meeting was filled with the radiance of the Shekhinah, but the world lost nothing of the Shekhinah."[13]

However, R. Joshua ben Levi (who said, "The Shekhinah is in the west"), gave a different parable:

> "Do I not fill heavens and earth?" (Jeremiah 23:24). One might think that God's glory fills the upper and lower realms. But does it not say, "When I behold Your heavens, the work of Your fingers, the moon and stars that You set in place . . . ?" (Psalm 8:4). They are only the traces of the manipulation of God's finger. It is like a king who stretched a drapery over the opening of his palace and said, "Whoever is wise, describe this drapery! Whoever is rich, make one like it! Whoever is mighty, reach up and touch it!" Thus the Holy One stretched out the heavens like the membrane of the eye, as it says, "Who spread out the skies like gauze" (Isaiah 40:22). He stretched it as a drapery and said, "Whoever is wise, explain this! Whoever is rich, make one like it! Whoever is mighty, reach up and touch it!"[12] [14]

---

[11] Midrash on Psalms 90:10; Genesis Rabbah 68:9.

[12] PRE 35, also Midrash on Psalms 90:10.

[13] Song of Songs Rabbah 3:15. The text continues: "When did the Shekhinah take up residence in the world? On the day that the Tabernacle was set up."

[14] Midrash on Psalms 19:6.

---

[10] The midrash cited here (Pirkei de-Rabbi Eliezer) is very late (seventh to eighth century), so the attribution to Rabbi Akiva is historically questionable. In any case, the view cited here is analogous to that of Rabbi Ishmael above: wherever Israel is in distress (or wherever the righteous stand), God is present, that is, potentially everywhere. Thus, Heschel fails to establish here a clear-cut, consistent difference between the two schools on the question of God's omnipresence.

[11] The implied midrash on this verse plays on three ambiguities: (1) *vayifga'* = arrived (geographically) or reached out (in prayer); (2) *makom* = the place (Beth El) or God; (3) "he" (subject of *vayyalen,* "he lodged") is Jacob or God. Thus: (a) Jacob reached the place (Beth El) and he lodged there, or (b) Jacob reached out (in prayer) to the Makom (God), and God lodged there.

[12] The difference between the two parables is far from clear. R. Joshua ben Levi seems to emphasize that the world is not necessarily a sign of God's *presence,* but only of God's *handiwork.* On the one hand, this would leave open the question of the site of God's presence. On the other hand,

From Where Did the Shekhinah Speak to Moses?

To answer this question we have two contradictory texts. One text says, "There I will meet with you, and I will speak to you—from above the cover, from between the two Cherubim" (Exodus 25:22). Similarly, we read, "[Moses] would hear the Voice addressing him from above the cover that was on top of the Ark of the Pact between the two Cherubim" (Numbers 7:89). The other text says, "A regular burnt offering throughout the generations, at the entrance of the Tent of Meeting before the Lord. For there I will meet with you, and there I will speak with you" (Exodus 29:42). About these two texts, the Tannaim argued.

Rabbi Akiva said, "The divine utterance came to Moses not from the Tent of Meeting, nor from over the whole of the Ark-cover, but only from between the two Cherubim."[15] Rabbi Eliezer the son of Rabbi Yose the Galilean elaborated on this view: "I might think that the Shekhinah never came down to earth at all, as it says, 'From the heavens [God] let you hear His voice to discipline you' (Deuteronomy 4:36). And: 'You yourselves saw that I spoke to you from the very heavens' (Exodus 20:19).[13] How, then, do I understand the verse 'When Moses went into the Tent of Meeting . . . [he would hear the Voice addressing him from . . . between the two Cherubim]'? (Numbers 7:89). A kind of corridor of fire descended from heaven to the space between the Cherubim, and spoke to him."[16]

The outlook of Rabbi Akiva, according to which the Shekhinah's "preferred locale" was in the west, was accepted by many Sages. They considered the Cherubim to be the special site where the Shekhinah abided. "'My beloved to me is a bag of myrrh lodged between my breasts' (Song of Songs 1:13)—this is the Shekhinah abiding between the

---

[15] Sifra Vayikra 4a; Sifre Naso 58.
[16] Sifre Zuta, p. 254.

Joshua ben Levi has already been seen to locate the Shekhinah in the west, and in any event each parable expresses in similar terms how we and our familiar world are dwarfed by God's immensity. Once again, it is questionable whether Heschel has succeeded in demonstrating a hard-and-fast contrast between the two schools on the question of God's omnipresence. At most, we might say that the Ishmaelian school fastidiously avoided any expressions that seemed to localize God's presence, whereas the Akivan school embraced both the ideas of God's omnipresence and God's local manifestation, without being bothered by the inconsistency.

[13] This was indeed a characteristic Ishmaelian view (see chapter 19 below). According to Rabbi Ishmael, only the voice descended, not the Shekhinah. In fact, this debate predates early rabbinic times, since it appears already in the Bible. Parts of the Bible, e.g., the Priestly narrative at the end of Exodus, conceive of God's Presence (kavod) as dwelling directly in the Sanctuary. But other parts, notably those stemming from the Deuteronomic school, hold a view of God's Presence being in heaven, and the Sanctuary being a place for communication. This second is obviously quite similar to what Heschel has here identified as the Ishmaelian view.

two Cherubim."[17] Rabbi Nathan said, "The Cherubim are as dear as heaven and earth, since they are the abode of the Holy One. The Shekhinah is positioned above and between the two Cherubim."[18] Bezalel was so called, because *betzel-el* means "in the shadow of God"; a shadow is a resting place, and he fashioned the resting place of God between the two Cherubim.

Rabbi Ishmael, who thought that the Shekhinah abides everywhere, seems to have rejected the notion that the Cherubim are the abode of the Holy One. As we saw, the sages of Rabbi Ishmael's school tried to purify the notion of the Divine Presence of spatial attributes. They liked to quote the verse, 'Do I not fill heaven and earth?' (Jeremiah 23:29). It is likely that they were sensitive to the problem discussed in the dialogue between the Samaritan and Rabbi Meir: "Is it possible that the One who fills heaven and earth spoke to Moses from between the poles of the Ark?" Rabbi Meir replied, "Bring me large mirrors." He brought them. "Look at your reflection." He saw, and it was big. "Now bring me small mirrors." He brought them. "Now, look at your reflection." He looked, and it was small. "If you, who are mere mortal, can change yourself at will, how much more the One who spoke and brought the world into being! If God wants, God fills heaven and earth, and if God wants, He speaks to Moses from between the poles of the Ark."[19]

The Samaritan interlocutor in this dialogue criticized the faith in the possibility of prophecy, and also the notion of divinity implied by prophecy. How will the infinite God speak to finite mortal man? The Holy One knows no spatial boundary, so how will He allow Himself to be constrained between the poles of the Ark? Rabbi Meir replied that just as the reflection emanates from the body, but may be large or small, so the Holy One fills heaven and earth but also dwells between the poles of the Ark. The Holy One contracts His presence and appears to the prophet. This answer agrees nicely with the view that the Holy One descended on Mount Sinai in glory; that is, when God wishes, God descends on any particular place with its dimensions.

Rabbi Simeon ben Azzai took this approach one step further: "See the consequences of God's love for Israel: this immense glory, which fills heaven and earth, was forced to appear to speak over the curtain between the two Cherubim!"[20] And the Amora R. Aniya bar Susi said, "Sometimes the world and its fullness cannot contain God's glory, and sometimes God speaks with a person from between the hairs of her head. Thus we find written, 'The Lord answered Job from the *se'arah*' (Job 38:1)—read not '*se'arah* = whirlwind,' but '*se'arah* = hair'—from between the hairs of Job's head."[21]

Out of the idea that the spiritual, which is not delimited, can sometimes limit and constrict itself so as to dwell between the poles of the Ark or between the Cherubim, there came this statement: "The Holy One reduced His Shekhinah in the Tabernacle,

[17] Song of Songs Zuta 1:13.
[18] Numbers Rabbah 4:13; Tanhuma Vayakhel 7.
[19] Genesis Rabbah 4:4.
[20] Sifra Vayyikra 4a.
[21] Genesis Rabbah 4:4.

within the Ark which Bezalel had made, as it says, 'Here is the Ark of the covenant, the Lord of all the earth' (Joshua 3:11). Thus the Holy One was within the Ark."[22]

This paradox, that the Supreme Being was revealed in specific places of finite dimensions, was foreign to Rabbi Ishmael's way of thinking. Truth does not vary; the glory of God always fills heaven and earth. Just as he opposed the idea of God's descent onto Mount Sinai, so it seems he opposed the idea of the Shekhinah's taking up residence between the Cherubim. Perhaps for that reason, his students taught that the Shekhinah would speak "from next to the altar of the burnt offering," as it says, "A regular burnt offering for your generations, by the opening of the Tent of Meeting, where I will meet with you to speak to you" (Exodus 29:42).[23]

One may well ask: What advantage was gained by this emendation? What difference does it make whether God appeared between the Cherubim or next to the altar? There is a constraining of the divine manifestation in either case, but the difference is indeed great. According to the approach of Rabbi Akiva, which is based on Merkavah mysticism, the Shekhinah dwells permanently between the two Cherubim, for that is its proper abode, the place dedicated to it. In contrast, Rabbi Ishmael's approach stipulates that the divine utterance happened to come to Moses at the entrance to the tent of meeting, next to the copper altar, a place of no particular significance, and not the Holy of Holies. The presence of the Shekhinah is not confined to a particular place and follows no set rules. In the event, the utterance came to Moses at a place of special significance for Moses, but not of special significance for the Shekhinah.

The Cherubim

The Cherubim, which were over the Ark of the Covenant, were objects of supreme importance to the Sages who discoursed on the divine chariot. Hezekiah's prayer contains reference to "the God of Israel, enthroned on the Cherubim" (Isaiah 37:16). Ezekiel, who in his first vision of the chariot saw the creatures that bore the chariot, saw in his second vision that "they were cherubs" (Ezekiel 10:20).[24] Even early exegetes drew the inference that the Cherubim of the Ark of the Covenant were a representation of those of the chariot: "the figure of the Chariot—the cherubs—those with outspread wings screening the Ark of the Covenant of the Lord" (1 Chronicles 28:18)[25] [14] According to Josephus, Moses saw the image of the Cherubim engraved

---

[22] Tanhuma Vayyakhel 7.

[23] YS Pekudei 427.

[24] Ben Sira praised Ezekiel, for he "had a vision of the Glory, which was revealed enthroned on the chariot of the Cherubim" (Ecclesiasticus 49:8). See also the Ethiopian *Book of Enoch*, 14:11; 20:7; 61:10, 71.

[25] Zunz (1832), Hebrew version *Ha-Derashot be-Yisrael*, p. 72. The sixteenth-century commentator

---

[14] Here is an example of a later book of the Bible developing and interpreting ideas from earlier biblical books—the rabbinic midrashic method in embryo. This phenomenon was called "inner-biblical

in the throne of God.[26] And R. Abahu cited the Cherubim as an instance of the principle that heavenly and earthly entities correspond to each other.[15] [27]

In the Temple period, the Cherubim were regarded as a symbol and evidence of God's love for Israel: "When Israel went on pilgrimage during the festivals, they would roll back the curtain and show them the Cherubim, which were embracing one another, and say, 'See how beloved you are of God, as the love of man and woman!'"[16] [28] In the Amoraic period, they would say that when Israel performs God's will, the Cherubim face each other, as a sign of God's love for Israel; but when they do not perform God's will, they face the wall—all miraculously.[29] When the Shekhinah departed from the Temple, it did so in ten stages: "from one cherub to the other, then to the threshold of the Temple," and so on.[30]

All this detailed imagery of the Cherubim fits well with the outlook of Rabbi Akiva, who did not conceive of the Shekhinah as pervading all space, and for whom the Song of Songs was so precious as a parable of the love between God and Israel. On the other hand, Rabbi Ishmael struggled against the very fact that there were Cherubim in the Temple. This may be one reason he placed the seat of God's colloquy with Moses outside, next to the altar.

Late sources say, "they inquired of the Cherubim: were they not idols?"[31] The Holy One said to Moses: "Make two Cherubim" (Exodus 25:18), but did He not also command, "You shall not make for yourself any sculptured image" (Exodus 20:4)?[32] There is solid evidence that Rabbi Ishmael also found this hard to swallow.

In the Mekhilta of Rabbi Ishmael we find the exegeses: "'You shall not make any likeness of what is in the heavens above'—that is, not an image of angels, *nor an image of Cherubim,* nor an image of wheels."[33] "Rabbi Ishmael said: 'You shall not make an

---

Eliezer Ashkenazi, in his *Ma'asei Hashem* (*Ma'asei Bereshit,* chapter 19) suggests that the "wheels" referred to in 1 Kings 7:33 corresponded also to the wheels of the divine chariot.

[26] Josephus, *Antiquities* 3.6.5.

[27] Midrash Aggadah on Exodus 26:7; see also Zohar I, 58a and 22a.

[28] BT Yoma 54a. See below, chapter 10, "Cleaving," n. 7.

[29] BT Bava Batra 99a.

[30] PRK 114b; see variants in BT Rosh Hashanah 31a, ARN A 34.

[31] "Commentary of R. Joseph Hamekane," published in *Birkat Abraham* (Hebrew volume of Festschrift for Abraham Berliner [Frankfurt, 1903]), 80–90, here 83.

[32] Midrash Aggadah on Exodus 25:18.

[33] MI Bahodesh 6. See Targum Pseudo-Jonathan, where the Cherubim are omitted.

---

exegesis" by Nahum Sarna, and was analyzed in detail in Michael Fishbane's book, *Biblical Interpretation in Ancient Israel* (Oxford: Oxford University Press, 1985).

[15] This principle is developed at length in chapter 14 below.

[16] The significance of this purported reminiscence is heightened by the reader's assumed knowledge that this procedure would contradict all known Temple norms. How could the pilgrims, who surely included non-priests, be allowed close enough to the veil shielding the Ark to be able to see it when the veil was removed? No Israelites were ever allowed that close. And this is to say nothing of the fact that even the High Priest on Yom Kippur was to be shielded from visual contact with the Ark by a cloud of incense smoke. The impossibility, paradoxically, makes the description that much stronger.

image of My servants who serve before Me in the heavens—not an image of angels, nor an image of wheels, *nor an image of Cherubim.*[34] "'Do not make gods of silver, nor gods of gold'—why do I need this? Has it not already been stated, 'You shall not make for yourself any sculptured image'? Rabbi Ishmael says: Since it says, 'Make two Cherubim of gold,' I might think that once such are permitted in the Temple, they would not be culpable even in the outlying areas. Therefore the text reiterates, 'Do not make gods of silver nor gods of gold' [to emphasize that they *would* be culpable]."[35] Another interpretation: Since the text permits two Cherubim [in the Temple], I shall go ahead and make four! Here too the injunction "Do not make gods of silver, etc." comes to prohibit, within the confines of the sanctuary, anything more than the two Cherubim which were explicitly permitted. Anything additional is tantamount to idolatry.[17] [36]

When the First Temple was destroyed, the surrounding nations taunted Israel on this account. "R. Isaac began his discourse, 'We were shamed, we heard taunts; humiliation covered our faces, when aliens entered the sacred areas of the Lord's House' (Jeremiah 51:51). When the Babylonians captured Jerusalem, Ammonites and Moabites entered the city with them. They came into the Temple and saw the two Cherubim there. They took them and put them in a cage and paraded them through the streets of Jerusalem, saying, 'Did you say that this nation is innocent of idolatry? See what we have found here! See what they worshiped! They are no different from the rest of us!' In that hour, the Holy One swore to eradicate their stench from the earth."[37]

Later sources attempted to reconcile the contradiction between the Cherubim and the prohibition of images. They said, "You shall not make *for yourselves* images, but *for Me* you shall make them." Similarly, no work shall be done on the Sabbath, but a special offering was required on that day—a contradiction, to be sure, but "they were said with a single intention."[38] "The same mouth that forbade also permitted."[39] [18]

---

[34] MI Bahodesh 10.   [35] Midrash Haggadol on Exodus 20:23, p. 441.
[36] MI Bahodesh 10; Zeh Yenahamenu ad loc.
[37] Lamentations Rabbati, Proem 9; PRK 138a. See also BT Yoma 54b: "Resh Lakish said: When the foreigners entered the Temple, they saw the Cherubim embracing each other. They brought them out into the street and said, 'Israel, whose blessing and curse are effective on others, occupy themselves with these?' They immediately despised them, as it says, 'All who admired her despise her, for they have seen her disgrace'" (Lamentations 1:8).
[38] Midrash Aggadah on Exodus 25:18 (perhaps originally included in MI Bahodesh 16 on Exodus 20:8); Lekah Tov on Exodus 20:7.
[39] See Hizkuni on Exodus 25:18: "Even though God said, 'You shall not make yourself a sculptured image,' here He permits the form of Cherubim, since they are made not for worship, but for the Shekhinah's resting place."

---

[17] The implication is: Even the two Cherubim that were permitted are under the suspicion of being quasi-idolatrous; the suspicion is suspended—but not erased entirely—by the scriptural command to make them.

[18] Heschel takes this phrase from the context of self-referential testimony in marital law, especially BT Ketubot 22a: a woman who offers in testimony that she was married but is now single is believed.

Other Sages tried to reconcile the contradiction more explicitly: "The Torah only forbade representations of what is in the heavens above and in the earth beneath, but the Cherubim, consisting only of faces and wings, correspond to no existing being either in heaven or on earth." Another Sage said the prohibition of images extends only to those that are seen regularly, but the Cherubim are hidden from view, inasmuch as they were put in a place where no one entered, except for the High Priest once a year.[40] R. Isaac Abravanel explained: "The Cherubim did not violate the ban on idolatrous images, for this forbade the making of images in order to worship them or to serve as an intermediary between the worshipers and their gods, as the text specifies, 'You shall not bow down to them or serve them' (Exodus 20:5). But the Cherubim were not made for that purpose."[41]

According to Maimonides, belief in angels is a prerequisite for belief in prophecy, for prophecy is brought about through the agency of the angel: God commanded to make the form of *two* angels on the Ark (and not just one), to confirm the belief in angels in the minds of the people.[42]

The view that the achievement of the prophets came about through the agency of the Cherubim was widespread in the Middle Ages.[43]

---

[40] "Commentary of R. Joseph Hamekane," loc. cit.

[41] Abravanel, Commentary on Exodus 25:10.

[42] *Guide of the Perplexed*, III:45. One cherub might have been mistaken for the image of the deity; two Cherubim indicated a plurality of servants subordinate to the deity.

[43] See Rashba, Responsa I 94, and Meir Ibn Gabbai, *Avodat ha-kodesh, Sitrei Torah* 22. See also Abraham Joshua Heschel, "Did Maimonides Believe He Merited Prophecy?" in *Louis Ginzberg Jubilee Volume* (New York: American Academy for Jewish Research, 1945), Hebrew section, pp. 159–88, p. 174 n. 92. The essay is available in English translation in Abraham Joshua Heschel, *Prophetic Inspiration after the Prophets: Maimonides and Other Medieval Authorities,* ed. Morris M. Faierstein (Hoboken, N.J.: Ktav, 1996).

6

TEACHINGS CONCERNING THE SHEKHINAH

Translator's Introduction

The nine sections that make up this chapter bring us to the subject of the relationship between God and Israel. The Shekhinah, or Divine Presence, was a concept employed by the Rabbis of the classical period when, in their discourses, they spoke of liaison between the infinite God and finite humanity. Of particular importance was the link between God and God's nation, partners to the covenant. But what was the nature of that link?

The question takes on its greatest poignancy when one considers the anguish and suffering that characterize many periods of Jewish history. What does, or should, a theory of Shekhinah teach with respect to the effect of Israel's suffering on the heavenly realm? In the ensuing chapters, Heschel's strategy will once again be to demonstrate that the traditions and texts of Rabbinic Judaism owe their complexity and ambivalence on the subject to the interweaving of two very different points of departure with respect to the role of the Shekhinah during times of distress.

The Akivan and Ishmaelian paradigms again take center stage. The former, consistent with its core belief in the immanence of the divine, understands the prophets' intimations of the divine pathos quite straightforwardly. The Shekhinah is the mysterious medium of the divine *identification* with Israel. Parity is the major motif for the Akivans here. God and Israel are both in need of redemption, for the Shekhinah goes into exile with Israel, and even God is depicted as being chained! Heschel describes this teaching as a revolution in religious thought, and so it is, for it thoroughly correlates the fate of God with the fate of Israel. As one of the ancient homilies he quotes in this context puts it: "If you are My witnesses, then I am God, but if you are not My witnesses, then I am, as it were, not God." And God must, as it were (see n. [9]), pray for God's deliverance!

Ishmaelians, however, true to their core belief in the transcendence of God, derive significantly different messages from the prophets' words, which were treated as anthropomorphic metaphors. We need God's salvation, but God does not. We need God's support, but God does not need ours. God is aware, God may empathize, but God does not *identify* with our sufferings. The Divine Glory inheres not in God's apparent suffering with us, but rather in God's superhuman and inscrutable silence amid our distress.

Heschel is, in truth, dealing in these chapters with the classical "problem of evil," the theological field known as theodicy. The standard formulation of the problem is the dilemma that the undoubted existence of innocent suffering poses: in its wake, we cannot believe in both God's omnipotence and God's mercy. Heschel argues here that the Ishmaelian view of God's transcendence requires that omnipotence be chosen (just as it had previously been chosen by the author of the biblical book of Job). The Akivan position, in stressing the immanence of God, is, by contrast, led to choose mercy (even at the price of God's absolute power).

These are excruciatingly difficult theological questions, and Heschel suggests that the cryptic talmudic story concerning the four Sages of the second century who entered the *Pardes*—the "Orchard"—should be understood in this light. They struggled with the problem of theodicy. One died, one went mad, one lost his faith; and only one—Rabbi Akiva—entered and exited in peace. Heschel's message is clear: confrontation with this religious problem can destroy life. It can drive one mad. It can destroy faith. Perhaps only a passionate belief in the divine identification with our travails can enable one to struggle and emerge in peace. One final note: Heschel warns us that these dark theological musings, which always teeter on the brink of heresy, cannot be comprehended from the detached perspective of an outsider. Sorrowful times bring forth bold religious doctrines. It can hardly be doubted that Heschel is here not only guiding us through the theologies of the second century, but illuminating a path for theology in the twenty-first century as well.

Redemption Is Mine and Yours

A MONG THE FUNDAMENTALS OF THE FAITH is the idea that the Holy and Blessed One participates in the sufferings of Israel. Conversely, when Israel "dwells in joy, there is joy for God."[1] This concept of the divine pathos, as expressed by the prophets of Israel, bestirred hearts to participate in the pain of the Holy and Blessed One and shaped the inner character of the prophet as one who empathizes with the divine pathos.[2]

The prophets spoke of God's participation as emotional reaction, as feeling, but the Tannaim described God's participation in the woes of Israel in terms such as: "The Shekhinah descended into exile with them." For example, Rabbi Eliezer raised the question, "Why did the Holy and Blessed One, in revealing Himself from the highest heavens, speak to Moses out of the thornbush? Because just as the thornbush is the lowliest of all the trees in the world, so the people Israel had sunk to the lowest

---

[1] MSY on Exodus 17:15, p. 126.

[2] See Heschel, *Die Prophetie* (1936), 127ff.; in English, Heschel, *The Prophets* (New York: Harper & Row, 1962), chapters 12, 18, 28 (in the 1971 paperback edition, vol. 2, chapters 1, 7, and 17).

level of degradation and the Holy and Blessed One descended with them and redeemed them, as it is written, 'I have come down to rescue them from the Egyptians' (Exodus 3:8)."[3]

The Sages of the second generation of the Tannaim used words such as "descent" only as further explanation of the concept "I am with him in suffering." "The Shekhinah descended with them" was to be understood as saying that it shared their lot—that is, as signifying empathy. But along came Rabbi Akiva, who taught that the participation of the Holy and Blessed One in the life of Israel is not merely a mental nod, a measure of compassion born of relationship to God's people. The pain of compassion amounts to pain only at a distance; it is the pain of the onlooker. But the participation of the Holy and Blessed One is that of total identification, something that touches God's very essence, God's majestic being. As it were, the afflictions of the nation inflict wounds on God.

Rabbi Eliezer said: "Idols crossed the Sea with the Israelites. How do we know? For it says 'whom you have redeemed for yourself from Egypt, people and their gods'" (2 Samuel 7:23). Said to him Rabbi Akiva: "Heaven forbid! Should you understand the verse that way, you would be making the holy into the profane.[1] What, then, is the intention of 'whom you have redeemed for yourself from Egypt'? As it were, You have redeemed Yourself [for You were also in Egyptian exile]."[4]

Rabbi Akiva's very style demonstrates his realization that this daring concept could upset the applecart and invite denial of God's omnipotence and compassion. He homiletically alluded to the possibility of just such a denial: "They have spoken falsehood[2] against me" (Hosea 7:13)—"Now how has falsehood been spoken against the Holy and Blessed One? Rabbi Akiva expounded: They have said, was it for our sake that God was concerned with our redemption? He was concerned with Himself! God redeemed Himself, not us, for it was said: 'whom you have redeemed for yourself from Egypt, a people and *its God.*'"[3] [5]

---

[3] MSY on Exodus 3:8, p. 1. A similar statement is made there by Rabbi Eliezer's colleague Rabbi Joshua.
[4] PT Sukkah 4:3 (54c); MI Pisha 14; Sifre Beha'alotekha 84.
[5] Exodus Rabbah 42:3.

---

[1] Rabbi Akiva understood ve'elohav ("their gods") as "their God," for in Hebrew there is no distinction between "God" and "gods." They are rendered by the same Hebrew word, and Hebrew, of course, has no capital letters. Thus, there is always a potential ambiguity about the descriptive term "God." When the Hebrew word elohim (or any of its inflected forms) refers to the One God, then it is a holy name that may not be erased from the text. It is to this that Akiva is referring in this passage.

[2] NJV: "plotted treason."

[3] Rabbi Akiva treads a fine line here. He wishes to assert that God makes Himself vulnerable by participating in Israel's suffering and redemption. He must then defend against the charge that in that vulnerability God's primary concern in the Exodus was to save Himself, and Israel only as an afterthought. The problem is analogous to that raised in Christian theology by the teaching of the divine Son's humanity and suffering on the cross: How can the person of God be humanized, to facilitate

Rabbi Akiva's disciple Rabbi Meir followed his teacher in teaching this bold concept: "*Thus the Lord delivered* [*vayyosha'*] *Israel that day*" (Exodus 14:30)—"[the Hebrew consonants can be read as if it were] written *thus the Lord was delivered* [*vayyivvasha'*]—when Israel is redeemed, God is, as it were, also redeemed."[6] In another context, Rabbi Meir expressed the same thought: "Redemption is mine and yours, and I, as it were, was redeemed with you, as it is said: 'whom you have redeemed for yourself from Egypt, a people and its God.'"[7]

In the wake of this reversal there was effected a veritable revolution in religious thought, one that exerted a profound influence through the course of the generations. From time immemorial the people had perceived the salvation of Israel as a human need, a national need, through which, to be sure, God's name would be magnified in the world. But now Rabbi Akiva taught that Israel's salvation is a divine need, and God's needs take precedence over human needs. There is yet more: according to the classical theology, salvation was conditional on Israel's merit, but folded into Rabbi Akiva's doctrine is the idea that salvation is the concern and need of the Holy and Blessed One, in all the divine glory, and thus would have to come even in the absence of merit.

> The verse reads: "For soon My salvation shall come" (Isaiah 56:1). It does not say "your salvation" but "My salvation."[4] Were this not written, we could not have uttered it: The Holy and Blessed One said to Israel, "If you lack merit, I shall, as it were, do it for My own sake. For whenever you are in distress, I am there with you, as it is said: 'I will be with him in distress; I will rescue him . . . and show him My salvation' (Psalm 91:15–16), that is, I am My own redeemer."[8]

What was this revolutionary concept of Rabbi Akiva? A momentary flash of inspiration? Light words of consolation? Or perhaps some random theory without roots in

[6] TB Aharei 13; Numbers Rabbah 2:2.   [7] Exodus Rabbah 15:12.   [8] Exodus Rabbah 30:24.

---

empathic identification, without either jeopardizing divine omnipotence or, worse, inviting a sense of human moral weakness to enter the divine description (this seems to be Akiva's concern here).

[4] In its plain sense, this verse can, of course, still be understood in a sense compatible with the notion of an omnipotent, impassive God: "Soon My salvation [which I work upon you] will come." God is the rescuer, and Israel is the rescued. The author of this midrash was surely aware of this natural interpretation, and thus his inversion (making God the recipient of salvation) is all the more daring.

These citations from Exodus Rabbah (a later compilation of the material of Exodus Tanhuma, and of early medieval date, perhaps ninth century) come centuries after the Tannaitic period. The last excerpt is anonymous. Yet there is an essential continuity of thought between them and the passages from MSY and PT cited at the beginning of this chapter. Does the attribution, "Rabbi Akiva said," in a later work represent an authentic tradition, preserved for centuries? Or is it pseudepigraphic, in the manner of such attributions in the Zohar? Whichever was the case, it seems that the figure of Rabbi Akiva became a literary persona in the midrashic and early mystical literature. It is no accident that the sayings attributed to him, whatever their origin, express a common outlook, which on this topic constituted one of the classic and pervasive Jewish responses to the sufferings of exile.

the soil of Torah? Make no mistake about it. This concept has a powerful parentage in the soul of Israel, permeated with faith and burdened with suffering. It is as though it had lain dormant as a sediment in the soul, in the deepest strata of thought, and then suddenly burst forth out of the depths, to illuminate the whole world.

Formerly in Israel, they made a distinction between two domains: the singular domain, that is, the domain of the single One of the universe, and the public domain of peoples and nations.[5] Along came Rabbi Akiva and his cohorts and taught: the two domains are, in fact, one. Formerly, it was believed in Israel that the relationship of the universe to human history is best described by these words ascribed to God: "What is Mine is Mine, and what is yours is yours."[6] That is to say, suffering and exile are your portion; compassion and deliverance are My role. That is the plain meaning of Scripture. Were there anything more hidden in the divine nature, it could not be thought, let alone expressed. But along came Rabbi Akiva and revealed the secrets of the Holy and Blessed One: the universe and human history are related according to the following saying: "What is Mine is yours, and what is yours is Mine." "Redemption is Mine and yours."

This approach is an alloy of sorrow and triumph; it both burdens and comforts. It illuminates an exceptional, higher dimension possessed by all things and all actions. And all succeeding generations, theologians and simple folk alike, walked to its light, and were nourished by its radiance.

The Exile of the Shekhinah

Rabbi Akiva also deepened the concept of the exile of the Shekhinah. He declared: "wherever Israel was exiled, the Shekhinah accompanied them. They were exiled to Egypt, and the Shekhinah accompanied them . . . they were exiled to Babylonia, and the Shekhinah accompanied them . . . they were exiled to Eilam, and the Shekhinah accompanied them . . . they were exiled to Edom, and the Shekhinah accompanied

---

[5] Here Heschel is playing on the distinction, most relevant in Shabbat law, between the *physical* private (literally, individual) and public domains. They are called, respectively, *reshut hayahid* and *reshut harabim*. Here he uses this common terminology to refer to domains of thought and emotion, and *yahid* is taken to mean not "private," as in "individual," but the "divine," as in "Individual," the One.

[6] A rather remarkable formulation by Heschel, since it is a phrase used in Mishnah Avot 5:10 to describe one who is of "average moral character." Indeed, the Mishnah goes on to say that some consider those who say "what's mine is mine, and what's yours is yours" to be exhibiting moral characteristics of the city of Sodom! Unflattering as it is, especially when ascribed to God as well as to Israel, it serves Heschel's purpose in that it highlights why Akiva could not abide such a doctrine. Now Akiva's replacement, namely, "what's mine is yours, and what's yours is mine" is considered by the Mishnah to be characteristic of a boor! But since we are talking about two parties, Israel and God, who both make the same assertion, the Akivan point of view seems to be saying that both parties to this relationship say "what's mine and what's yours are both yours," and that, we are told, is characteristic of the pious.

them[7] . . . and in the future, when they will return from exile, the Shekhinah will, as it were, accompany them as well, as it is said: 'Then the Lord your God will return (*shav*)' (Deuteronomy 30:3)—it does not use the causative 'return' (*heshiv*), but the simple intransitive 'return' (*shav*)."[9]

The Amoraim, first and foremost Rabbi Abbahu, quoted other scriptural passages that teach that Israel's salvation is the salvation of the Holy and Blessed One: "my heart will exult in Your deliverance" (Psalm 13:6)—"Your salvation is ours."[10] "And come [*u-lekhah*] to our help!" (Psalm 80:3), was expounded as if the text had been written *u-lekha*, that is, "all salvation is Yours."[11] "He redeems me unharmed [*beshalom*] from the battle against me; it is as though many are on my side" (Psalm 55:19)—what means "He redeems me *beshalom*"? "Said the Holy and Blessed One: I consider whoever busies himself with Torah and acts of kindness, and prays with a community, to have redeemed Me and My children from among the nations of the world."[12] "I will free you [*vehotzeiti etkhem*] from the labors of the Egyptians" (Exodus 6:6)—"vocalize as '*vehutzeiti itkhem*'—I will be freed with you."[13]

Rabbi Simeon ben Yohai[8] formulated a parable concerning God's bond, as it were,[9] to His people Israel: "Who built His chambers in heaven and founded His vault on earth" (Amos 9:6)—"It is analogous to a person who tethered two ships together with anchor chains and iron moorings, put them out to sea, and built a palace on them. The palace endures so long as the ships are tethered to one another; were the ships to float apart, the palace could not endure. So it is here: when Israel fulfills God's will, the chambers of heaven are built up, but when Israel does not, God's vault, as it were, founders on earth." In a similar vein: "'This is my God and I

[9] MI Pisha 14.
[10] Midrash on Psalms 13:4; see also 91:8.
[11] Midrash on Psalms 80:3; see also Leviticus Rabbah 9:3.
[12] BT Berakhot 8a.
[13] The piyyut "Kehosha'ta Elim" by Eleazar Kalir, in the Hoshanot for Sukkot, traditional Jewish prayer book.

[7] The proof texts come, respectively, from 1 Samuel 2:27, Isaiah 43:14, Jeremiah 49:38, and Isaiah 63:1.
[8] A disciple of Rabbi Akiva, later portrayed by the author of the Zohar as the heroic progenitor of Kabbalah.
[9] The word *kevayakhol* ("as it were"), used here by Heschel, is one of the keys to midrashic spirituality. Used generally in connection with daringly anthropomorphic parables of God, it reminds the listener at the same time that these images are to be understood not literally but symbolically. This double take can be applied to the whole gamut of "outrageous" anthropomorphic expressions of the Akivan school. The word *zikkah* ("bond"), which Heschel qualifies here, is used in halakhic literature to refer to a prenuptial bond, for instance, that pertaining between the partners in levirate marriage before consummation of the marriage: the relation between God and Israel is analogous to the bridal relationship, but also different (because of the radical inequality of the partners). The same expression ("as it were") is used in Rabbi Simeon's parable to qualify the implication that Israel's disloyalty in fact impugns the Divine Glory and causes God's palace to founder.

will glorify Him' (Exodus 15:2)—if I acknowledge God, God is in fact glorious, but if I do not acknowledge God, God is, as it were, glorious in name only [or God, of blessed Name, is, at it were, not glorious]."[14] Likewise: "'For the name of the Lord I proclaim; Give glory to our God!' (Deuteronomy 32:3)—if I proclaim God's name, God is great, but if not, God is, as it were . . . ." Likewise: "'So you are My witnesses—declares the Lord—and I am God' (Isaiah 43:12)—if you are My witnesses, then I am God, but if you are not My witnesses, then I am, as it were, not God."[15]

Had this doctrine not been taught, we could not have articulated it ourselves, for it entails the transcendent significance of human actions. Note that according to Rabbi Simeon's doctrine, an idolator causes "a defect on high."[16]

Ani Va-Ho Hoshi'a Na

The Tanna of the Mishnah teaches: "Each day [of the festival of Sukkot] they would encircle the altar and recite 'O Lord deliver us; O Lord let us prosper' [ana adonai hoshi'a na . . .]. Rabbi Judah said, [they would recite] 'ani va-ho, deliver us' [ani va-ho hoshi'a na]."[17]

What is the nature of the disagreement between the Tanna of the Mishnah and Rabbi Judah? The Babylonian Talmud[18] tells us that ho is a designation for the Holy and Blessed One.[10] So did Rabbi Nathan of Rome[11] explain it: va-ho refers to the Holy and Blessed One; He too, as it were, is in need of deliverance. [Thus read:] "I and You, may You deliver us both."[19] Even Maimonides[12] testifies to the currency of this understanding: "Several of the Geonim said that the intent of Rabbi Judah's formula was to convey that deliverance is sought by the One who is in distress with me."[20]

It was in this sense that the Talmud of the Land of Israel understood Rabbi Judah's statement and supported his view with scriptural verses that teach that God, as it

---

[14] Sifre Haberakha 346. See Meir Friedmann (Ish Shalom)'s comment: "When Israel disobeys, God is disgraced in the world" (his edition of Sifre, p. 144, n. 3 ad loc).

[15] PRK 12:6 (102b).

[16] BT Sanhedrin 74a. See A. Kaminka, "The Esoteric Thought of Rabbi Simeon bar Yohai," in Sefer Klausner: Articles in History and Literature Presented to Professor Joseph Klausner (in Hebrew) (Tel Aviv, 5697/1937), 171–80.

[17] Mishnah Sukkah 4:5.   [18] BT Shabbat 104a.

[19] Otzar Hageonim, Responsa, on Sukkah 45a. The Hebrew is vocalized here as hu, that is, "he," and is taken to be a formal mode of address in which the third person is used instead of the second person.

[20] Maimonides, Commentary on Mishnah Sukkah 4:5. See also Rabbenu Hananel's commentary on BT Sukkah 45b.

---

[10] Apparently because this enigmatic word is just the middle two letters of the Tetragrammaton.

[11] The talmudic lexicographer of the eleventh century, author of the Arukh.

[12] Who himself vehemently condemned such ascriptions of emotion and vulnerability to God.

were, is delivered along with Israel.[21] [And it was quoted] in the name of the Tanna Hananiah the nephew of Rabbi Joshua:[13] 'I am the Lord your God *who brought you out* [*hotzeitikha*] of the land of Egypt, the house of bondage' (Exodus 20:2)—"[the Hebrew consonants can be read as if it were] written *who was brought out with you* [*hutzeitikha*]—as it were, I and you both left Egypt."[22] On the basis of this interpretation Elazar Kalir composed his liturgical poem "*kehosha'ta elim.*"[14]

Rabbi Judah the Patriarch[15] attempted to keep the Mishnah free of esoteric doctrines as well as of opinions and expressions that were not compatible with God's dignity. Perhaps that is why he gave as the anonymous[16] position that claimed that in the Temple the formula used on Sukkot was "O Lord, deliver us." Yet Rabbi Judah, the principal disciple of Rabbi Akiva, taught, in the tradition of his master, that the recitation on Sukkot was "I and You, may You deliver us both." Which opinion was considered normative? Maimonides ruled in accordance with the Tanna of the Mishnah, and it would appear that this was the practice in earlier generations.[23] However, Rabbi Isaiah Berlin[17] expressed astonishment at the practice in his time[18] to recite, during the *hakafot,* "I and You, may You deliver us both"![24]

We Need Each Other

The school of Rabbi Ishmael set out to reinterpret scriptural expressions that did not comport with the divine honor; all the more so were they wary of applying human terms to the singular One of the universe. In contrast, those of the school of Rabbi Akiva did not shrink from resorting to the language of emotions when referring to the Creator. Note the following: It was taught in the school of Rabbi Ishmael: "The Holy and Blessed One said to Israel, 'My children, I have created the evil impulse than which there is none more evil. However, if you will engage in the study of Torah, it

[21] PT Sukkah 4:3 (54c), citing Psalm 80:3; Zechariah 12:7.
[22] Ibid., and also PR 110a.
[23] *Mishneh Torah, Hilkhot Lulav* [Laws of the Palm Branch] 7:23.
[24] See his commentary, "*Nimmukei Hageriv*" in *Otzar Ha-tefillot* (Sephardic Liturgy) (New York, 1915; repr., Jerusalem, 1960), vol. 2, part 2 (Festivals), pp. 5b–6a (Hoshanot).

---

[13] Hananiah, the nephew of Rabbi Joshua, was noted for his explication of Rabbi Akiva's approach to the concept of "the heavenly Torah." See PT Shekalim 49d, cited below in chapter 29, "All the Commandments Written on Tablets."

[14] For the Hosha'not each weekday of Sukkot. In it, Kalir reads Exodus 6:6 in the same way, so as to involve God as a participant in the Exodus.

[15] Compiler of the Mishnah.

[16] And thus more authoritative.

[17] Isaiah Berlin: Germany, eighteenth-century talmudist.

[18] And still current today.

will not have dominion over you.'"[25] In Rabbi Akiva's school it was taught: "'If you follow My laws'" (Leviticus 26:3)—"this teaches us that God *yearns* for Israel to labor in the Torah."[26] For "the term *im*—"if"—is nothing but a plea."[27] One school views the study of Torah as a gift of wise counsel. The other views it as the object of God's deepest yearnings.

We may infer from the statement "God yearns for Israel to labor in the Torah" that those who labor in the Torah bring, as it were, blessing to the One on high. But what is merely hinted at in this statement is given explicitly in an Amoraic teaching: "The Holy and Blessed One said to Israel, 'Both you and I are happy when you obey the teachings of Torah.'"[28] "When are we both happy? When you observe My Torah, as it is written, 'If you follow My laws.'"[29]

The expression "God yearns" served as a paradigm for a variety of statements. Rabbi Simeon ben Yohai taught, "When the Holy and Blessed One created the world, He yearned to have a dwelling place on earth as He had in heaven."[30] He also said, "Each and every day the Holy and Blessed One commanded Moses, 'Speak to the people Israel, command the people Israel.' So much did God yearn to mention the name Israel on every possible occasion."[31] In answer to the question, "Why were the matriarchs barren?" Rabbi Johanan answered, "Because the Holy and Blessed One yearns for the prayers [of the righteous]."[32]

One thought generates another. If God experiences desire, God must also experience the emotion of satisfaction. Rabbi Meir, a disciple of Rabbi Akiva, taught: "Happy is he who was reared in Torah, whose toil is Torah, and who thereby brings satisfaction to his Creator."[33] He also taught the statement in the Mishnah: "When a person is in pain, what does the Shekhinah say? 'My head, my arm, they hurt.'"[34] And it was given in the name of Rav:[19] "There are three watches in the night, and in each of them the Holy and Blessed One sits roaring like a lion, saying: 'Woe to me that I destroyed my house and burned my Temple [and exiled my children] among the nations.'"[35]

Out of this intellectual milieu there emerged the remarkable utterance of Rabbi Eleazar Ha-Kappar, a contemporary of Rabbi Judah the Patriarch: "My Torah is in your possession; the end of days is in Mine. We therefore need each other. Just as you

---

[25] Sifre Ekev 45.   [26] Sifra Behukotai 110c.   [27] BT Avodah Zarah 5a.

[28] Fragment of midrash on Psalm 34, from Jacob Mann, "Some Midrashic Genizah Fragments," *Hebrew Union College Annual* 14 (1939): 303–58, here 325.

[29] Leviticus Rabbah 35:3.

[30] TB Naso 24. See also Numbers Rabbah 10:1, concerning God's yearning to create the world.

[31] Leviticus Rabbah 2:5. See also BT Sotah 38b, that God yearns to hear the priestly benediction.

[32] Genesis Rabbah 45:4; see also BT Yevamot 64a and Midrash on Psalms 116:1.

[33] See Ein Ya'akov on BT Berakhot 17a.   [34] Mishnah Sanhedrin 6:5.

[35] BT Berakhot 3a (see *Dikdukei Soferim*).

---

[19] Babylonian Amora, third century.

need Me to bring about the end of days, I need you to fulfill the Torah, and thus to bring near the rebuilding of My House and of Jerusalem."[36]

In the phrase "we need each other" is embedded the concept of Israel's power to diminish or enhance God's might. This opinion, which served as a cornerstone of kabbalistic teaching, is already alluded to in a homily in Sifre: "You neglected the Rock that begot you" (Deuteronomy 32:18). The word *teshi* ("neglected") can be understood in relation to the word *teshishut* ("feebleness"), whence the interpretation "You weaken the power of the One on high."[20] [37]

According to Rabbi Joshua ben Levi, God Himself revealed to Moses this secret, that it is possible for mere flesh and blood to increase the power of God. "When Moses ascended to heaven, he found the Holy and Blessed One affixing crowns to the letters of the Torah. As Moses stood there silently, God said, 'Is there no greeting of "peace" in your town?' To which Moses replied, 'Shall a servant extend a greeting before His master does?' God answered, 'Yet you should have assisted me.' Whereupon Moses cried out, 'Let my Lord's power become great, as You have declared.' (Numbers 14:17)."[38] According to the Zohar, this idea is also implied in the verse "Give might to God" (Psalm 68:35).[21] [39]

The depths of Scripture thus yielded powerful figures of speech that expressed secrets and mysteries that the ear can barely assimilate. But thus were new paths blazed in Israel's religious life; and once this was firmly acknowledged and the thinking matured, the expounders of esoteric doctrines shed their inhibitions and opened their minds without fear.

---

[36] PR 31:5 (144b).
[37] Sifre Ha'azinu 319.
[38] Shabbat 89a. Zunz (1832) considers the Baraita in BT Berakhot 7a, in which God is depicted as asking Rabbi Ishmael for a blessing, to be very late in the talmudic period (Hebrew version, *Ha-Derashot be-Yisrael,* 329 n. 45).
[39] Zohar Bo 32b.

---

[20] The doctrine that Heschel is discussing here is the doctrine of theurgy, based on the idea that human actions can affect or even manipulate the divine. Theurgy became quite important in medieval Kabbalah, but it was already present as an idea in much earlier periods. Heschel discusses this in various places, including his very last work, the posthumously published *A Passion for Truth* (New York: Farrar, Straus & Giroux, 1973), in which he noted that the famous nineteenth-century Hasidic Rebbe of Kotzk took a dim view of theurgy, just as Ishmaelians had done so many centuries earlier. Indeed, there are more parallels between Heschel's being drawn to Ishmael and to Kotzk than can be explicated here.

[21] The plain (though not literal) meaning is, of course, as the NJV renders it: "Ascribe might to God"; that is, we are to "give" something to God, but it is not the strength itself, as the Akivan reading has it, but rather the appellation of strength.

Does God Really Need Support?

This mode of thought was vigorously opposed by some of the Sages.[22] How could it ever enter one's mind that God needs human assistance? Consideration will reveal how much the Sages struggled with this problem. It seems as though this polemic adjoined itself to the murmurings of religious thought in every generation. And each mode of thought that emerged bore the stamp of one or the other of these two positions. We shall here confine ourselves to the talmudic period.

Two standpoints crystallized. One maintained: "If you sin, what do you do to Him? . . . If you are righteous, what do you give Him?" (Job 35:6–7). Human beings need God, but God does not need the service of human beings. But the opposing standpoint maintained that the Holy and Blessed One needs our service; the righteous enhance the power of God.

Both standpoints made their way into subsequent generations. It is said of Noah: "Noah walked with God" (Genesis 6:9), while it is said of the patriarchs: "The God *before* whom my fathers Abraham and Isaac walked" (Genesis 48:15). "Rabbi Johanan[23] said: The relationship of God to the patriarchs may be likened to that of a shepherd whose flock walks before him. But Rabbi Simeon ben Lakish[24] said to him: Sheep always needed a shepherd [and thus, of what new significance is the statement about the patriarchs]! A more apt analogy would be to a prince who travels and whose retinue marches before him, giving evidence of the prince's splendor. Thus did the patriarchs walk before God." On what point do they differ? "Rabbi Johanan's opinion is that we need His glory, and Resh Lakish's opinion is that He needs our glory."[40] What is a prince without a retinue?

This debate is repeated in the context of the revelation at Sinai. According to one source, the Holy and Blessed One said to His angels, "If Israel were not to accept the Torah, neither you nor I would have a place in which to dwell."[41] The acceptance of the Torah, in this view, was a matter of divine self-interest. Other Sages, however, expressed a contrary opinion: The Holy and Blessed One said: "When you study the Torah you do well for the world, because but for the Torah the world would revert to being unformed and void."[42]

Now the first view expressed the thought that Israel did God a favor by accepting the Torah.

[40] Genesis Rabbah 30:10; TB Lekh Lekha 26.
[41] PR 20:4 (97a).
[42] Deuteronomy Rabbah 8:5; see also Leviticus Rabbah 23:3.

---

[22] Especially those of the school of Rabbi Ishmael.

[23] The most prominent Amora of the Land of Israel in the third century.

[24] Rabbi Simeon ben Lakish (called "Resh Lakish," through a corruption of the abbreviation "R.Sh.") was a third-century Amora of the Land of Israel, a student and primary colleague of Rabbi Johanan.

The Sages taught that which is difficult to hear: To what does God compare? To a ruler who had a precious gem that he deposited with a dear friend. He said to him: Please take care of it and guard it properly. For if it is lost, you will not have the wherewithal to repay me, and I too have nothing with which to replace it, and you will thus have sinned against yourself and me. So do well by both of us, and guard it properly. Thus said Moses to Israel: "If you preserve the Torah, you do a favor not just to yourselves, but to me *and* to yourselves."[43]

The words are here put in Moses' mouth, but it is clear that he speaks for God.

Now Rabbi Ishmael, who attempted to reconcile all scriptural language that did not comport with the divine honor, certainly would not have adopted this entire approach, neither its substance nor its style.

In the school of Rabbi Ishmael, they interpreted this verse: "'Curse Meroz!' said the angel of the Lord. 'Bitterly curse its inhabitants, because they came not to the aid of the Lord, to the aid of the Lord among the warriors'" (Judges 5:23). They said: "Whoever aids Israel, it is *as if* he aided the One Who spoke and the world came into being."[44] This interpretation is an answer to the question of astonishment [which appears not in this text, but elsewhere]: "because they came not to the aid of the Lord"—"does God then need the aid of others?!"[45] Or, in yet another formulation: "Does God really need support?"[46]

Note another interpretation that has already been brought earlier: "Outside the veil of testimony in the Tent of Meeting" (Leviticus 24:3)—"It is a testimony to one and all that the Shekhinah dwells in Israel. And should you think that I need its light: for the forty years that the Israelites traveled through the desert they walked only by *My* light. Rather, it is a testimony to one and all that the Shekhinah dwells in Israel."[47]

From start to finish, this interpretation betrays the language of Rabbi Ishmael, who here explains the Menorah in the same way that he explained the meaning of the erection of the Tabernacle.[48] The idea that the Holy and Blessed One needs humanly generated light is here rejected, just as the idea that God needs firewood, the Tabernacle, and the sacrifices had been rejected.

Consider the gulf between the doctrine of Rabbi Akiva and his disciples, who spoke of the salvation of the Holy and Blessed One as something affecting the very divine essence ["if you are not my witnesses, I am, as it were, not God"], and the doctrine of Rabbi Ishmael, who did not speak about the *essence* of the Holy and Blessed One, but only about His *relationship* to Israel. "It was taught by Rabbi Ishmael: 'You shall not

---

[43] Deuteronomy Rabbah 8:5.
[44] MI Shirata 6; Sifre Beha'alotekha 84.
[45] Anonymously, Tanhuma Beshallah 16.
[46] Tanhuma Vayyehi 5, citing Rabbi Simeon ben Yohai.
[47] BT Shabbat 22b; BT Menahot 86b.
[48] MI Pisha 16.

copy the practices of the land of Egypt . . . or of the land of Canaan . . . I the Lord am your God' (Leviticus 18:3–4)—and if not, I am, as it were, not *your* God."[25] 49

"For thus says the Lord of Hosts . . . 'Whoever touches you touches the pupil of his own eye'" (Zechariah 2:12). According to Rabbi Eleazar, the son of Rabbi Yose the Galilean, the meaning of the verse is that whoever harms Israel harms himself: "it is as if he extends his finger into his own eye and gouges it out. But Rabbi Simeon [bar Yohai] said to him: Not so. The verse speaks of the Holy One,"50 that is: whoever harms you has, in effect, touched the pupil of the Holy and Blessed One. The opinion of Rabbi Simeon, that the verse speaks of the upper realm, is based in the doctrine of Rabbi Akiva that God, as it were, is injured by the afflictions of the nation.

If My People Does Not Enthrone Me on Earth . . .

In the school of Rabbi Akiva, God's bond to Israel is one of intimate empathy. God, as it were, is linked to Israel with bonds of love, participating in its suffering and redeemed by its salvation. Such a bond belongs to the inner realm of the heart. But other Sages saw the bond as a moral imperative; God is, as it were, compelled by the very words of His oath to the patriarchs to be faithful to the covenant concluded with them. Such a bond belongs to the outward realm of the will. The first point of view stresses the divine pathos; it speaks of the bond in the dynamic terms of feeling. The second stresses the covenant; it speaks of the bond in the static terms of obligation. The first sees the bond as a connection to the ever-present Israel, and the second sees the bond to Israel as the deserts of the patriarchs.

Two exegeses exemplify these points of view: "The words that came to Jeremiah from the Lord . . . when he was chained in fetters among those from Jerusalem . . . who were being exiled" (Jeremiah 40:1). It should have read "I" rather than "he."[26] Said Rabbi Aha: "As it were, both of them[27] were chained in fetters."51 By contrast, others expounded: "A king is held captive in the tresses" (Song of Songs 7:6)—"He bound himself by oath to make His Presence dwell in the midst of Israel."[28] "Thus he cannot violate His oath."52

49 Leviticus Rabbah 23:9 (Margoliot version).
50 Midrash Haggadol on Numbers 10:35, p. 243.
51 Lamentations Rabbah, Prologue 34
52 Song of Songs Rabbah 7:6; TB Nitzavim 6.

---

[25] That is, there is a huge difference between saying "I am not God" and "I am not your God"!

[26] That is, although the formal superscription of the verse mentions Jeremiah by name, Jeremiah, the author of this book, should have described his plight in the first person, that is, "when I was chained in fetters." Why the third person?

[27] That is, Jeremiah and God.

[28] The play on words here is as follows: *rehatim* ("tresses") can also be understood via a grammatical root referring to hasty speech; in this case, an oath given, perhaps hastily but nevertheless binding, and thus "captivating."

Often verses in which prophets speak of themselves were interpreted by some Sages as the words of the Holy and Blessed One: "Because my people is shattered I am shattered; I am dejected, seized by desolation" (Jeremiah 8:21). This verse was interpreted by some Sages as the words of the Holy and Blessed One:

> Had not the verse said it, the tongue uttering it would have deserved dismemberment. But the ancients have set the precedent. It is analogous to a young prince who attempted to lift a heavy rock. As he lifted it, it fell and crushed him. When the king heard that his son had been crushed, he began to cry: "I've been crushed!" The palace guard, uncomprehending, said to him: "Your son has been crushed. Why do you say that *you* have been crushed?" Such was the reaction of the Holy and Blessed One, as it were: "Because My people is shattered I am shattered; I am dejected, seized by desolation.'"[53]

Why do the ministering angels declare, "His presence fills all the earth!" (Isaiah 6:3)? "Because the Supreme King of Kings, the Holy and Blessed One, says, "If My glory is not on earth, then My name is neither on earth nor in heaven. If My people does not enthrone Me on earth, then it is as though I have no Kingdom in heaven."[54] According to Rabbi Johanan: "The Holy and Blessed One said: I shall not enter the heavenly Jerusalem until I have entered the earthly Jerusalem."[55]

In times of trouble and distress they knew and believed that just as there is weeping on earth so is there weeping for God above. "As Israel went into exile, with the Temple in ruins and the Sanhedrin uprooted, the Holy and Blessed One cried bitterly for them all."[56] Rabbi Tanhuma the Great preached as follows: "'And do you speak to them thus: Let my eyes run with tears, day and night let them not cease' (Jeremiah 14:17)—now the text was not explicit as to whether it was the prophet who said 'let my eyes run with tears' or not. But since it goes on to say 'day and night let them not cease,'[29] and since flesh and blood cannot cry day and night, we must conclude that the verse speaks of the weeping of the Holy and Blessed One, who alone does not sleep."[30] [57]

---

[53] Lamentations Zuta 1:18, p. 139.
[54] *Aggadat Shir Hashirim,* ed. Schechter, line 216ff. (corresponds to Song of Songs Zuta 1:1, ed. Buber, p. 4a).
[55] BT Ta'anit 5a.
[56] PR 28:1 (134b).
[57] PR 29:1 (136b).

---

[29] And see also Jeremiah 8:23.
[30] The notion that God weeps is another species of theurgy (see n. [20] above). One of the texts always appealed to comes from Jeremiah 13:17—"For if you will not give heed, My inmost self must weep, because of your arrogance . . . ," where "inmost self" renders the Hebrew *mistarim,* which generally denotes a secret place. This led rabbinic aggadists to teach that God has a secret place called *mistarim,* to which God repairs in order to weep.

Heavenly Afflictions

Does not this doctrine[31] diminish our image of the divine and limit our belief in the Creator's omnipotence? Moreover, shall we say that the God of Israel, Who is the nation's source of power and courage, needs *Israel* to give Him strength? The true nature of this standpoint cannot in truth be grasped by a person who can calmly look in from the outside.[32] The Rabbis in the generation we are considering experienced things that others have not seen: the sacking of Jerusalem, the humiliation of the House of Israel, and the profanation of the Holy Name in the sight of the whole world. Stormy eras filled with human agony also harbor troubling thoughts; even the pillars of heaven shudder. And a nation that has been belittled by the nations of the world is likely to verge on belittling the great presumptions: that God is merciful and compassionate and that God is the great and the powerful. If there is mercy, there surely is no power; and if there is power, there surely is no mercy![33] For could one maintain that the Holy and Blessed One empathizes well but does not carry through?[34]

Now in the school of Rabbi Ishmael they expounded: "Who is like You, God, among the mighty [*ba-'elim*]" (Exodus 15:11)—"Who is like You, God, among the *mute* [*ba-'ilemim*], who is like You in how you see the humiliation of Your children and remain silent?"[58]

---

[58] MI Shirata 8.

---

[31] That is, the Akivan doctrine of God weeping, and in general being vulnerable to our sufferings and travails.

[32] The Hebrew rendered here by "calmly look in from the outside" is distinctive, and Heschel uses it for a definite reason: The Sage Ben Zoma was one of the four who were said to have entered the *Pardes,* that is, to have delved into esoteric doctrines. In describing the ill fate that befell him, the Talmud tells us that he "looked in" and was stricken. The Hebrew word used here is the same distinctive one as is used there. Moreover, the Talmud goes on to quote a senior colleague of Ben Zoma as evaluating his behavior after the *Pardes* incident as being "outside"—a word again echoed exactly in Heschel's sentence here. By the use of language that conjures up the memory of Ben Zoma, and, as will be seen, the other three who entered the *Pardes,* Heschel foreshadows what he will make explicit two chapters hence: his conviction that the *Pardes* was nothing other than a grappling with the problem of suffering, with which we are now dealing.

[33] With these words, Heschel is concisely expressing the classic dilemma known as the "problem of evil." God's omnipotence and beneficence cannot simultaneously be reconciled with the magnitude of suffering in the world. Famously, David Hume gave a similarly concise and rhythmic formulation in English: "Is he willing to prevent evil, but not able? Then he is impotent. Is he able, but not willing? Then he is malevolent. Is he both able and willing? Whence then is evil?" (*Dialogues Concerning Natural Religion,* ed. Nelson Pike [Indianapolis: Bobbs-Merrill, 1970], part 10, p. 88).

[34] Heschel's formulation of this question is deliberately constructed so as to echo a famous rejoinder to Ben Azzai, a bachelor who preached on the importance of the obligation to raise a family. The homily brought forth the stinging ironic response from his colleagues: "You preach well but do not carry through!" (see BT Yevamot 63b). The significance of invoking Ben Azzai in this way is that he was the second of the four Sages who entered the *Pardes.* It is said that he "looked in and died."

But Rabbi Akiva and his cohorts believed that it is better to limit belief in God's power than to dampen faith in God's mercy. *"Ani va-ho hoshi'a na"*—we are *both* in need of salvation. Is it not, ultimately, *praise* to say of God "He was chained in fetters" rather than to blaspheme in the manner of Elisha ben Abuyah and say: "Where is the good coming to this child? Where is the longevity coming to this child?"[59] [35]

Rabbi Akiva saw the world through the lens of the divine pathos. Even natural occurrences only express the afflictions of heaven.

> Baltza asked Rabbi Akiva, "How are earthquakes caused?" He replied, "When the Holy and Blessed One beholds the heathen temples and their worshipers enjoying peace and prosperity in this world, and he sees His Temple destroyed, in the hands of idolaters, He becomes jealous and begins to roar. Immediately, heaven and earth tremble." So it is written, "And the Lord will roar from Zion, and shout aloud from Jerusalem so that heaven and earth tremble." (Joel 4:16)[60]

The same thought was expressed by the Amoraim in a different form. They said, "When the Holy and Blessed One recalls His children and their suffering among the nations of the world, two of His tears fall into the ocean and the reverberation is heard from one end of the earth to the other."[61]

When the Holy and Blessed One revealed Himself to Moses at the thornbush, He said to him, "Do you not sense that I dwell in sorrow just as my people Israel dwells in sorrow. Know that in speaking to you here in the midst of the thorns, I participate in their suffering."[62] "May the Lord answer you in time of trouble" (Psalm 20:2), means "it is a time of trouble for heaven and earth."[63]

Now if the Holy and Blessed One shares in the pains of mortals, how much more so is it incumbent on us to take our share in the pains of the Holy and Blessed One. Moreover, whenever there is misery in the world, one should know that there is misery on high just as there is misery below. It was, apparently, to this idea that Rabbi Eleazar Hakkapar (of the generation of Rabbi Judah the Patriarch) alluded when he said: "Whoever attaches the Name of Heaven to his pain will in the end have his sustenance doubled."[64] That is, when a person is enduring pain, he should connect the pain of the upper world with his. This is, indeed, a mode of prayer in Israel: "Master

---

[59] PT Hagigah 2:1 (77b).   [60] Exodus Rabbah 29:9.   [61] BT Berakhot 59a.
[62] Exodus Rabbah 2:5.   [63] Midrash on Psalms 20:3.
[64] BT Berakhot 63a. See Maharsha, Hidushei Aggadot.

---

[35] The story alluded to here is briefly as follows: Elisha ben Abuyah saw a boy obey his father's command that he climb a tree and take the eggs from a nest after sending the mother bird away, in accordance with the law in Deuteronomy 22:6–7. That law and the rule of honoring one's father carry explicit promises of long life. When the child fell from the tree and died, Elisha ben Abuyah uttered this statement in despair of divine justice and mercy. Elisha ben Abuyah, who is said to have subsequently committed apostasy, is the third of the Sages who entered the *Pardes*. The fourth we have been encountering all along. He was Rabbi Akiva, and he was the only one said to have entered and left in peace.

of the Universe, can it be that you are pleased that we are in distress? You are the one who wrote "I will be with him in distress" (Psalm 91:15). Now I am in distress. Can you be pleased?"[65]

This doctrine, which originated in the school of Rabbi Akiva, established a connection between heavenly and worldly afflictions. The Holy and Blessed One is a partner in the suffering of His creatures; He is involved in the lot of His people, wounded by their sufferings and redeemed by their liberation. This response[36] constitutes a sublimation of human suffering. It elevates the mystery of suffering above and beyond the human realm, and seeks to nullify the afflictions of mortals before the afflictions of Heaven.

The people Israel were exiled twice from the land of Israel: first, the ten tribes, and then, the tribes of Judah and Benjamin. What was God's reaction to Israel's troubles? Three answers were given to this question. According to some Sages, the Holy and Blessed One uttered lamentation and said, "Alas! Lonely sits the city!" Rabbi Johanan said, "When the ten tribes were exiled, the Divine Presence participated in their anguish, but when Judah and Benjamin were exiled, the Holy and Blessed One assumed personal responsibility, as it were, for their sins." Rabbi Simeon ben Lakish said, "When the ten tribes were exiled He lamented; when Judah and Benjamin were exiled, He said, 'I have no more strength to lament.' Whereupon He called for the professional keeners to join Him in His sorrow."[66] Rabbi Simeon ben Lakish's lesson goes beyond that of the Tannaim. For they taught that the Holy and Blessed One participates in the suffering of Israel, but he taught that the Holy and Blessed One invites Israel to share in *His* suffering.

Many Sages attempted to sweeten the decree of exile. Some sought to do this by explaining it *logically* (i.e., "for our sins we were exiled from our land"[37]). Some, however, sought to accept afflictions lovingly. Rabbi Akiva, for his part, did not rebel against afflictions. On the contrary, "A person should be happier with afflictions than with comforts."[67] He answered the question that he himself had posed: What is the meaning of sufferings? They are both ours and His, and thus salvation is both ours and His. One who asks: "Why is this exile come upon us?" (should be answered with) "Upon *us* and not upon *Him?*" One who removes *God* from the community has denied the very essence of the faith.[38]

[65] Aggadat Bereshit, 66.   [66] Lamentations Rabbah, Prologue 2.   [67] Sifre Va'ethanan 32.

---

[36] That is, to the problem of suffering.

[37] From the Musaf prayer on the Festivals. It can be thought of as a "sweetening" in the sense that it offers an explanation—and, at that, an explanation that even as it accuses us of wrongdoing holds out the hope that we can correct the problem with our own efforts.

[38] The language here is rightly reminiscent of the question and answer of the Wicked Son, as they appear in the Passover Haggadah. In the Haggadah, the crucial ideology is the horizontal solidarity of all Israel, and the Wicked Son's transgression is removing himself from that solidarity. Here the crucial ideology is the vertical solidarity of God and Israel in the "vale of tears," and the ultimate transgression is to remove *God* from that solidarity.

But don't we still have an unresolved question? For there is an obvious contradiction between the belief in God's omnipotence and the belief that He, too, is in need of salvation. Perhaps the resolution is this: just as the Creator, whose glory fills the universe, contracted His Shekhinah between the two staves of the Ark in order to reveal His words to Moses, so did God compress His Shekhinah into the *history* of Israel so that He might be revealed to His chosen nation as they went into exile together. Between mercy and power, mercy takes precedence—and to the mercy of Heaven there is no limit!

Certainly, this doctrine was no song of joy. But then the times were not made for song. God's creatures were drowning in sorrows—do you expect a song?[39] This doctrine is one of lament and woe, but it is a lament that contains great comfort.

For this is yet another mundane matter that has its lofty parallel above. They dared to look,[40] and in so doing, they found that the pains of the nation were indeed paralleled by the pains of the Creator. Thus, instead of bearing their own afflictions, they began instead to share in the afflictions of Heaven.

Make Atonement for Me

Consider carefully the exegesis of Rabbi Akiva's colleague and student, one of the Sages who entered the *Pardes*:

> Simeon ben Azzai noted this contradiction: It is written, "God made the two great lights" (Genesis 1:16), and it is also written, "the greater light to dominate the day and the lesser light to dominate the night" (ibid.)! The moon addressed the Holy and Blessed One: "Master of the Universe—can two monarchs really share a crown?" The Holy and Blessed One responded to her: "Go and diminish yourself." She addressed God again: "Master of the Universe, shall I diminish myself for having spoken appropriately?!" God said to her: "Go, and your domain will be both day and night." She addressed God again: "Master of the Universe, of what use is a lamp at high noon?" God said to her: "Go [knowing that] Israel will calculate their days and years according to you." . . . Her feelings were still not assuaged. Said the Holy and Blessed One: "Make atonement for Me, for My having diminished the moon."[68]

---

[68] Quoted in the name of Simeon ben Azzai in YS Bereshit 8, also in Aggadat Hatannaim, and in various manuscripts. See *Dikdukei Soferim,* BT Hullin 60b.

---

[39] An obvious reference to the famous Midrash in which Egypt, rather than Israel, is the subject. With the Egyptians drowning in the sea, God silenced the singing angels, saying that a moment at which God's creatures are drowning in the sea is no moment for song. Now if God reacted that way to the drowning of the Egyptians, how much more so would God not expect a tidy, lyrical theology when Israel is drowning in sorrow.

[40] Again, the word used to describe the actions of Ben Zoma (and Ben Azzai as well) in the *Pardes.*

In the period of the Amoraim, textual support for this legend was found in the Torah. Said Rabbi Phinehas: "In the case of all the sacrifices, it is written: 'and one goat for a sin offering'; but on the New Moon, it is written: 'and one goat as a sin offering for the Lord' (Numbers 28:15).[69] [41] Said the Holy and Blessed One: 'I am the One who caused him [i.e., the sun] to encroach on his fellow's domain.'"[70] In the words of Rabbi Simeon ben Lakish: "Said the Holy and Blessed One: this goat shall be atonement for My having diminished the moon."[71]

Certainly, this exegesis would have been alien to the worldview of Rabbi Ishmael. Go see how the school of Rabbi Ishmael understood the matter of the goat on the New Moon: "And one goat as a sin offering for the Lord"—this sacrifice "comes to atone for the graves of the Deep." That is: if a grave is deeply sunk in the ground, and a person walks over it, and then enters the Holy Place—this is an impurity known only to God, and this goat atones for it.[72] This sacrifice is not to make atonement for any person, since this impurity is one that is known "neither at the beginning nor at the end."[73] Thus, "it comes only to atone for the impurity of the Holy Place[42] and its holy objects."[74]

Superficially, there would appear to be some similarity between the idea that the Holy and Blessed One needs atonement and the idea that Israel's salvation is also God's salvation. Actually, however, the two concepts are far apart. Rabbi Akiva is extolling[43] God's attribute of compassion in that God participates in Israel's anguish and identifies with His creatures. Ben Azzai is questioning God's attribute of justice. The moon pleads its cause before the divine Throne of Justice and, in his exposition, Ben Azzai vindicates its claim that the verdict is not a just one. Rabbi Akiva's teaching deals with Jewish history, with matters between human beings and God. Ben Azzai's teaching deals with the work of creation, with matters between nature and God. On matters between human beings and God, human beings have

---

[69] The plain meaning: "dedicated to God," as in Leviticus 16:9.
[70] Genesis Rabbah 6:3.
[71] BT Hullin 60b.
[72] Sifre Pinhas 145, and the commentary "Zera' Avraham."
[73] Mishnah Shevuot 1:4.
[74] BT Shevuot 9a, in the name of Tanna de-ve Rabbi Ishmael.

---

[41] It is, of course, on the New Moon, that the moon is at its "smallest," its most deficient. Note that the plain meaning of "a sin offering for the Lord" is quite straightforward. That is, the goat is offered to the Lord, not on behalf of the Lord. Still, the Hebrew does bear both interpretations as well as others, and a choice must be made.

[42] And thus, "for the Lord" means "for the Temple" and/or "for a sin knowable only by God," but not "for the Lord's transgression"!

[43] Literally, "affixes crowns to," a reference to the story in BT Menahot 29a, in which Moses finds God affixing crowns to the letters of the Torah and is told that Rabbi Akiva will someday understand their significance. Heschel no doubt uses this phrase to remind us of the connection between Akiva's views on the Shekhinah and his general, esoteric approach to exegesis.

standing. On matters that do not affect human beings—"what business have you with these heavenly secrets?"[44]

"Had not the verse said it, the tongue uttering it would have deserved dismemberment. But the ancients have set the precedent."[75] The verse says, "'The Rock!—His deeds are perfect, yea, all His ways are just' (Deuteronomy 32:4), and you say that He needs atonement? That at the beginning of each and every month a he-goat sin offering is brought for God to atone for the diminution of the moon?!"

Of Ben Azzai, who was both student and colleague of Rabbi Akiva, it was said: "'Let us savor your love more than wine' (Song of Songs 1:4)—this refers to Rabbi Akiva; 'sincerely they love you' (ibid.)—this refers to Ben Azzai and his colleagues."[76] He was one of the Sages who entered the *Pardes*; he "looked in and died, and Scripture says of him, "the death of His faithful ones is grievous in the Lord's sight" (Psalm 116:15).

Ben Azzai based his thinking on the view that the sun and moon 'were both created to illumine the earth'[77] but that later there was a change in the plan of creation. Other Sages, however, rejected this view. Rabbi Johanan and Rabbi Haninah said, "Only the sphere of the sun was created to illumine the earth. Why, then, was the moon created? This was for the purpose of sanctifying the new months and years."

A Defect in the Work of Creation

Nevertheless, many things are wrapped up in the saying of Ben Azzai: a heavenly transgression, sin and defect in the work of creation, the power of a human being to make atonement for a heavenly transgression. The idea of sin in the work of creation was taught not only in connection with the moon but also in connection with other works of creation, that is, the trees and the waters.

"Thus said the Holy and Blessed One: 'Let the earth sprout vegetation . . . fruit trees . . . that bear fruit' (Genesis 1:11). The language[45] suggests that just as the fruit was intended to be edible, so the tree was meant to be edible [and that their tastes were to be identical]. But the earth did not do so, for we read: 'The earth brought

---

[75] Lamentations Zuta 1:18, p. 139.
[76] YS Song of Songs 982.
[77] So thought Rabbi Simon, Genesis Rabbah 6:1.

---

[44] Thus, according to Heschel, we have here the negative version of the theology formulated positively by Rabbi Akiva. Given the suffering in the world, Rabbi Akiva sought to emphasize God's empathy, to "affix esoteric crowns" to the attribute of mercy. Ben Azzai saw the negative side and attributed some of the suffering to a "transgression" on God's part. Heschel apparently sees this as an unnecessary and dangerous extension of the doctrine. Perhaps, as the text following suggests, he sees it as a reason why Ben Azzai, like Elisha ben Abuyah, did not leave the *Pardes* in peace.

[45] That is, rather than saying simply "trees that bear fruit," the verse added the apparently superfluous word "fruit" before "trees." The inference drawn is that the trees and the fruit were to have a strong identity with one another.

forth . . . trees . . . bearing fruit' (Genesis 1:12). The fruit could be eaten but not the tree." [Therefore, the earth was punished for its transgression at the same time that Adam was punished for his transgression.][78]

Regarding the waters: On the second day of creation, the Holy and Blessed One said: "Let there be an expanse (raki'a) in the midst of the water, that it may separate water from water. God made the expanse, and it separated the water that was below the expanse from the water which was above the expanse" (Genesis 1:6-7). "God said to the waters: divide yourselves into two halves; one half shall go up, and the other half shall go down; but the waters presumptuously all went upward. Said to them the Holy and Blessed One: I told you that only half should go upward, and all of you went upward?! Said the waters: We shall not descend! Thus did they brazenly confront their Creator. . . . What did the Holy and Blessed One do? God extended His little finger, and they tore into two parts, and God took half of them down against their will. Thus it is written: 'God said, let there be an expanse (raki'a)' (Genesis 1:6)—do not read 'expanse' (raki'a), but 'tear' (keri'a)."[79] [46]

Another midrashic version of the division of the waters:

> The reason Scripture does not say "and God saw that this was good" after the account of creation on the second day is because there was division. For when the waters consigned to the lower sphere were separated from the waters of the upper sphere they cried bitterly, for now they would be residing in an impure region. The Holy and Blessed One said to them: "If you will be appeased, I will command that you be used for the ceremony of the water libation." They were not appeased, however, because that took place only once in the year. Thereupon, God made a covenant that their waters would be used in the rite of salting the sacrificial offerings, as it is written, "You shall season your every offering of meal; you shall not omit from your meal offering the salt of your covenant with God" (Leviticus 2:13). But since there was division on that day, "this was good" was not said thereon.[80]

---

[78] See Genesis Rabbah 5:9.

[79] Midrash Konen, *Otzar Midrashim*, p. 254.

[80] *Hadar Zekenim* (parallel commentaries of the Tosafists and Rabbenu Asher), Bereshit; see also Rashi on Leviticus 2:13.

---

[46] The Hebrew *keri'a* is an anagram of *raki'a*. This is quite an impressive Midrash, coming from the early medieval collection known as Midrash Konen. This passage makes obvious analogies between God's creation and human birth. Both involve waters breaking, both involve pain and a tear. The tear in the waters was necessary to create space in which life could develop, and the tear of birth is necessary for the baby to begin an independent life. *Keri'a* is the rite for the dead, when Jewish law requires the tearing of clothing. The message then is twofold: the tear of death is just the continuation of the tear of birth. Both are necessary for life to continue, and we are powerless to change that. The other message is that God is as much bound by these truths as we are. God also could not create without a day of division and tearing, and thus we and God are both in need of comfort and strength in the wake of the cruelties of nature.

According to this version, it is clear that the waters rebelled against their Creator not out of competitiveness or jealousy but rather out of protest against the partition made by the Holy and Blessed One between the upper and lower realms.

But the division that the Holy and Blessed One applied to the upper and lower waters struck the Sages as an act on which the very destiny of the world depended. Many in the generation of Ben Azzai and Rabbi Akiva debated this point. One Roman woman asked Rabbi Yose ben Halafta: "Why was 'it was good' not said on the second day?"[81] And Rabbi Meir, student of Rabbi Akiva, said: "Schism is lamentable, even when it makes the world habitable. It is written: 'God made the expanse, and it separated the waters'—and since division between the waters is written of there, 'it was good' was not written there."[82]

Four entered the *Pardes*: Rabbi Akiva, Ben Azzai, Ben Zoma, and Elisha ben Abuyah. It seems to me that not only Ben Azzai, but Ben Zoma and Rabbi Akiva as well, struggled with this problem concerning sin and defect in the work of creation.

"Ben Zoma looked in and was stricken." He conjectured that, despite the division of the waters, the upper waters are not very far removed from the lower waters:

It happened that Rabbi Joshua ben Hananiah was walking along the avenue and encountered Ben Zoma. Ben Zoma did not extend greeting to him, so Rabbi Joshua inquired, "Whence do you come and where are you going?" Ben Zoma replied, "I was pondering the creation of the universe and I have concluded that there was scarcely a handbreadth's division between the upper and lower waters. For we read in Scripture, 'The spirit of God hovered over the waters' (Genesis 1:2). Now Scripture also says: 'like an eagle who rouses his nestlings, hovering over his young' (Deuteronomy 32:11). Just as an eagle, when it flies over its nest, barely touches the nest, so is there barely a handbreadth's distance separating the upper and lower waters." Rabbi Joshua then said to his students: "Ben Zoma is already outside." And only a short time passed before Ben Zoma left this world.[83]

And Rabbi Akiva instructed his colleagues who entered the *Pardes*: "When you reach the area of the pure marble stones, do not say 'water, water,' for it is written: 'He who speaks untruth shall not stand before my eyes' (Psalm 101:7)."[84] This cryptic statement possibly contains some allusion to the subject of the controversy surrounding the separation of the upper and lower waters.

The common element in all these legends is this: the idea that the sin of the first human being was not the first of the sins; prior to his sin, some of the forces of nature had already become corrupted. It would seem that the problem of evil should not be forced entirely into the human realm alone. There is a defect in the work of

---

[81] Genesis Rabbah 4:7.
[82] *Mishnat Rabbi Eliezer*, ed. H. G. Enelow (in Hebrew) (New York: Bloch, 1933), 79. Genesis Rabbah 4:7 in the name of Rabbi Haninah and Rabbi Tavyumi.
[83] Tosefta Hagigah 2:6; PT Hagigah 2:1 (77a–b); BT Hagigah 15a; Genesis Rabbah 2:4.
[84] BT Hagigah 14b.

creation. We should not, however, compare these legends to the mythologies of many other nations concerning creatures that rebelled against their creator. It is more likely that the teaching contained in these legends approximates the views of the Gnostics.[47]

---

[47] In that evil and corruption are considered to be inherent in the (physical) world of creation.

ז

AFFLICTIONS

Translator's Introduction

Having dealt with the diverse paths down which our two models of religious thought take us with respect to God's relationship to human suffering, Heschel now proceeds to explore the correlative aspect of this far-reaching religious issue, namely, the ways in which human beings relate to that suffering. Is travail redeemable, in the sense of carrying within it the possibility of some higher understanding or of a more intense experience of life, or is it ultimately pointless? A nihilistic point of view would see suffering as meaningless, a curse that must be endured for no purpose other than that it is there. But the Rabbis were no nihilists, and thus they saw, albeit in different ways, redemptive aspects of suffering. Once again, we will be offered in the ensuing chapters a dichotomy, two attitudes toward human misery, each with its own logic and integrity, and each traceable, as Heschel presents the textual traditions, to our primary division between the Ishmaelian and Akivan paradigms.

One attitude toward afflictions views them as a manifestation of divine justice. It is evident in such statements as this commentary on Psalm 36:7: "The righteous who accept the Torah receive God's lofty beneficence, while the wicked who reject the Torah receive God's profound judgment." This provides a neat and rational scheme for understanding the role of suffering in the world: it is a natural and inevitable result of rebellion, retribution for insubordination to divine authority. This is the gist of the Jewish burial service to this day, known as *tzidduk hadin* ("the justification of divine judgment"); consistent with this attitude, God is depicted as perfect, infallible, and demanding of human subjects. Ours is to accept in faith and resignation, as Job ultimately did, that which we cannot fully apprehend.

The second attitude brought to our attention in these chapters does not dispute the idea that suffering may be connected with sin, but it considers its primary purpose to be elsewhere. Its objective is not so much purification from sin as it is the goal of drawing human beings closer to God. Much more than a means of atonement, afflictions can actually create a bond with God. That is why, in this point of view, afflictions are spoken of as having advantages, and the Torah itself is said to be acquired only through affliction. Consistent with this attitude, God is depicted as being vulnerable, empathetic, and seeking solidarity. Thus, the acceptance of suffering in this view is not the resigned and

127

muted acceptance of Job, but rather the more positive and uplifting acceptance born of that solidarity and of the exhilaration of sharing in God's experience, as it were.

The first attitude is clearly, to Heschel, that which follows from the postulation of a transcendent God, hierarchically above us and removed from our realm. No wonder that it is repeatedly associated with the school of Ishmael, and why that school was the source of a description of God as demonstrating a majestic muteness in the face of human anguish (see the previous chapter as well). Such divine silence is a praise only if one's starting point is the centrality of the vertical hierarchy relating humans and God, for then it demonstrates with brutal clarity just how high above our finite stage of action God dwells. To use a phrase in a somewhat nonstandard way, this silent God is the *unmoved mover.*

Heschel, as can easily be anticipated, sees the second attitude as typifying the Akivan view. A focus on the immanence of the God of Israel means that sufferings can and must be seen as more than the immediate pain that they inflict. For one thing, the school of Akiva had a demonstrable openness to the construct of the future world and thus could see even the expiatory role of suffering as an infinitesimal travail in a finite world that sets the table for eternal bliss in the infinite future world. But most important, solidarity and participation are, in this Akivan view, the keys to salvation. Sufferings are "afflictions of love," that is, afflictions that generate love—love for the God Who participates in the world's travails, and for the world itself. This empathetic God is, to rework the old phrase in a way that Heschel loved, the *"most moved mover."* A Mishnah in Tractate Berakhot, chapter 9, instructs us to thank God for the evil as well as for the good; both have their effect in helping us love God and the world. In the Akivan view, evil does not exist in the absolute sense but only in the world of unenhanced human perception.

Was Akiva, whose attitudes gave rise to such views, who called afflictions "precious," and who, by talmudic tradition, accepted martyrdom from the Romans willingly, simply a masochist? Heschel is sensitive to this problem and takes pains to assure us that Akiva did not value suffering per se, but only as a means toward a greater end, the perception of the close bond between Israel and God. Centuries later, Benedict Spinoza would also be seen in a similar light for his assertions that evils were the result of human perception and for his urgings that we transcend our pains through a higher, intuitive understanding of the unity of reality. Lewis Feuer called this "gallows humor written into a metaphysics," and a "strain of masochism." Spinoza was, of course, no Akivan, and his necessary God devoid of personality is light-years away from Akiva's God of empathy. But surely they have this in common: the belief that there can be an uncommon joy in conjoining one's primary sensations of pain to a greater totality, and in feeling oneself to be part of a whole that has to it an ultimate and encompassing unity. This is not masochism, but rather an interpretation of nature and experience that bootstraps us to higher levels of awareness and understanding. It is not a response to suffering likely to appeal to many, but it has a coherence and a power to it, and Heschel here demonstrates just how deep are its roots in rabbinic tradition.

This brings us to an apprehension of yet another connection between these attitudes toward afflictions and our primary paradigms. In these chapters, Heschel is, in effect, giving us a recapitulation of that with which we began: a fundamental divergence on the question of how we read. Here what is being read is not texts in the usual sense, but rather experience itself. True to form, the Ishmaelian paradigm insists on a naturalistic, commonsense reading of experience; pain must be seen for what it is and must be explained logically, as a just retribution from the Master above. The Akivan paradigm requires that experience, like scriptural texts, be read with an esoteric exegesis. Our experiences of pain and affliction are to be seen as codes for a deeper reality, in which the immanent God and we are partners and coparticipants. Martyrdom itself can follow from this intense solidarity with the immanent God, and it is undoubtedly an Akivan point of view that is reflected in the Fourth Gospel's celebrated statement that "There is no greater love than this, that a man should lay down his life for his friends" (John 15:13). For one who speaks of afflictions that generate love for God and the world, the "friend" is God.

One final note for now: the Ishmaelian reading of experience is, like all logical readings, subject to refutation and falsification. Thus, although this attitude preaches the resigned acceptance of Job and the pious expressions of faith in the unknowable divine justice, it is forever challenged by the apparent injustice of human travail. There is thus a restlessness, perhaps even a resentment, for those who see suffering as the judgment of the transcendent God. Questions of faith abound, and as Heschel shows us, there can even be sardonic equations of our status with that of a Canaanite slave, whose master has ultimate power but who can look forward to freedom from that power when the master's discipline becomes excessive and unjust.

Akiva's esoteric reading of experience is, like all such exegesis, not subject to such refutation or challenge. It posits a different level of awareness and an ultimate unity that reveals problems of theodicy to be pseudoproblems. It also posits an eventual revelation of justice and equity in a future world. In other words, the Akivan paradigm deals with the apparent anomalies of experience through a fundamental shift of the axioms.

Here, as in the previous section, Heschel's exposition makes it clear that the Akivan paradigm dominates in his own thought on these critical religious issues. The section headings are nearly all Akivan phrases, and his explication of the Akivan attitude far outstrips its counterpart in sheer quantity. This is not primarily the case throughout the rest of this long work, and it perhaps suggests that the "space" and the autonomy afforded us by the transcendent God are unsatisfying as a response to the primal and terrifying experience of the world's large repertoire of torments. The hovering, encompassing presence of the immanent (and vulnerable) God may be the image that draws Heschel, and us, more powerfully in the wake of such challenging experiences.

Let a Person Rejoice More in Affliction
Than in Fortune

NONE OF ISRAEL'S SAGES in that era probed more deeply into the mystery of human affliction than did Rabbi Akiva. He noted the following distinction between the Gentiles and the community of Israel: "when good fortune shines on them, they honor their gods . . . when adversity comes upon them they curse their gods. But with Israel, when I bring them good fortune they give thanks, and when I afflict them they also give thanks."[1] Moreover, not only did Rabbi Akiva forbid us from questioning the actions of the Holy and Blessed One—for everything He does is grounded in truth and in justice[2]—he believed that afflictions can be a *reward* and not merely a punishment.

He would say: A king had four sons.[1] Upon being struck, one was silent; one protested; one begged for mercy. The fourth said to his father: "Yes, strike me!" Abraham was stricken and was silent, for it says, "Take your son, your favored one, Isaac, whom you love, and go to the land of Moriah and offer him there as a burnt offering" (Genesis 22:2). He could have said: "Just yesterday you said to me 'for it is through Isaac that offspring shall be continued for you' (Genesis 21:12)." But he was silent, for it says, "So early next morning, Abraham saddled his ass and took with him two of his servants and his son Isaac" (Genesis 22:3). Job protested when he was stricken, for it says, "I say to God, 'Do not condemn me; let me know what You charge me with'" (Job 10:2). Hezekiah begged for mercy when he was stricken, for it says, "Hezekiah . . . prayed to the Lord" (2 Kings 20:2). Others say that he also protested, for it says, "I have done what is pleasing to You" (2 Kings 20:3). King David said to his Father, "Yes, strike me!" for it says, "Wash me thoroughly of my iniquity and purify me of my sin" (Psalm 51:4).[3] Now Rabbi Akiva saw David's way as the exemplar. It was characteristic of Rabbi Akiva to love afflictions, and not gratuitously did he instruct his generation: "Let a person rejoice more in affliction than in fortune."[4]

"Any teaching worth its name has a pedigree." Rabbi Akiva was for twenty-two years a disciple of Nahum of Gimzo and adopted his expansive method of scriptural exegesis.[2] From him he learned lessons in piety, and it was in his spirit that Rabbi Akiva preached to his contemporaries: "Afflictions are precious!"[5]

---

[1] MI Bahodesh 10.   [2] MI Beshallah 6.
[3] Tractate Semahot 8:11. See Midrash on Psalms 26:2, and Buber's note ad loc.
[4] Sifre Va-ethanan 32.   [5] MI Bahodesh 10; BT Sanhedrin 101a.

---

[1] Rabbinic parables typically depict God as a mortal king and human beings as the king's children or subjects.

[2] Literally, the exegetical method based on "inclusion and exclusion," which could expand categories almost indefinitely on the basis of relatively minute clues in the text. This is usually contrasted with what was considered the more structured and hence limited method of "the general and the particular," favored by Rabbi Ishmael.

What was the teaching of Nahum of Gimzo? His colleagues described him as totally blind and as an amputee in all four limbs, and his body was also infected with sores. When his pupils inquired how a man so saintly could be so terribly afflicted he replied, "My children, I brought all this upon myself. Once I was on my way to visit my father-in-law and I had three asses laden with gifts—one with food, one with drinks, and one with all kinds of delicacies. I encountered a poor man covered with sores, and he said: 'Rabbi, give me sustenance.' I replied, 'Wait until I unload the asses.'[3] By the time I had finished unloading, the man had already died. I threw myself down and said, 'May my eyes that had no pity on yours become blind. May my arms and legs that had no pity on yours become stumps.' Yet I had no peace of mind until I said, 'May my whole body be covered with sores.'" His disciples cried, "Woe to us that we see you in this condition." He replied, "Woe to me had you not seen me in this condition."[6]

Once Rabbi Akiva came to visit him and exclaimed, "Woe to me that I see you in this condition: blind, amputated, lame." Nahum of Gimzo replied: "Woe to me that I see you *with* arms and legs." Rabbi Akiva replied: "Are you uttering a curse on me?" Said Nahum, "And are you spurning afflictions that you say 'Woe to me, because of your afflictions'?"[7] In time, Rabbi Akiva came to accept the view of his teacher and adopted his embrace of afflictions.

The Talmud relates:

When Rabbi Eliezer became ill, his disciples came to visit him. Said Rabbi Eliezer, "There is a fierce anger on the face of the earth." They all began to weep, except Rabbi Akiva, who laughed. They asked, "Why do you laugh?" He retorted, "Why do you weep?" They replied, "Can one behold the holy Scroll of the Torah in agony and not weep?" Rabbi Akiva replied, "And that is why I laugh. Were I to see that my master's wine has not soured, his flax has not been smitten, his oil has not become putrid, and his honey has not fermented, I would think, is it possible, God forbid, that my teacher has received his reward in this world? But now that I see my master suffering, I am happy." Rabbi Eliezer asked, "Akiva, is there anything in the entire Torah I have overlooked?" Rabbi Akiva replied, "You, my master, have taught us: 'For there is not one good person on earth who does what is best and doesn't err' (Ecclesiastes 7:20)."[8]

Rabbi Akiva taught: Let a person not be nasty in prosperity nor receive adversity against his will. Let him be gracious both in prosperity and in adversity.

---

[6] BT Ta'anit 21a.   [7] PT Shekalim 5:6 (49b).

[8] BT Sanhedrin 101a. See also Midrash on Psalms 16:2, that no one is judged holy, however righteous, until his death.

▬▬▬▬

[3] That is, Nahum intended to continue to his father-in-law's house, unload the asses, and then return immediately to look after the needs of the pauper. Assuming that his destination was a relatively short distance, as we must (else Nahum would come across as uncharacteristically hardhearted, and the point of the story would be lost), this seems a reasonable thing to do. It did, however, have a tragic ending.

He expounded as follows: "You shall love the Lord your God with all your heart and with all your soul and with all your might" (Deuteronomy 6:5)—"'With all your soul' having been said, is not 'with all your might (me'odekha)' trivial? Why is 'with all your might' then said? It rather means that God is to be loved irrespective of what measure (midah) He metes out to us."[4] 9

Should you ask: Why "let a person rejoice more in affliction than in fortune"? What is the value of affliction? For one thing, "there is not one good person on earth who does what is best and doesn't err." "Were a person to have prosperity all his life, his sins would never be atoned for. How does he gain atonement? Through affliction." But besides providing atonement, afflictions are doubly advantageous, for nothing so well restores a person to decency. King Manasseh did evil in the sight of the Lord all through his reign. Now is it possible that his father Hezekiah, king of Judah, who taught everyone Torah, neglected to teach his own son Manasseh? "But all of his father's teaching, and all of his efforts, had no effect on him until he met with affliction. . . . 'in his distress, he entreated the Lord, his God, and humbled himself greatly before the God of his fathers' (2 Chronicles 33:12). Thus, afflictions are precious!"10

Imagine: Rabbi Akiva, whose blood boiled and churned with love of Torah, who regarded the study of Torah as the summum bonum, who, in the wake of the empire's decree banning the study of Torah, assembled great throngs for just that purpose and declared: "just as water is the fishes' life medium, so is Torah Israel's life medium,"[5] now preaches: "all of his father's teaching, and all of his efforts, had no effect on him until he met with affliction!" The virtue of Torah is exceedingly great, but there are times when a person cannot draw near to the Holy and Blessed One except through afflictions.

Thus, one of Rabbi Akiva's most junior pupils, Rabbi Eliezer ben Jacob, declared: "When a person suffers afflictions, he must express gratitude to the Holy and Blessed One. Why? Because it is his afflictions that draw him to the Holy and Blessed One."11 Indeed, the Torah itself cannot be acquired except through affliction.

Rabbi Akiva's approach entered the repository of the nation's soul. They believed that the Holy and Blessed One examines the conduct of the most righteous down to a minute handbreadth, that there is no suffering without iniquity,12 and that the Holy

---

9 YS Va'ethanan 837.   10 Sifre Va'ethanan 32.
11 Tanhuma Tetze 2.   12 BT Shabbat 55a.

---

[4] The assumption behind the question was that me'odekha meant "your possessions." The answer plays on the phonetic closeness of me'odekha and midah.

[5] The reference here is to an incident related in BT Berakhot 61b: Rabbi Akiva was teaching Torah publicly, in defiance of the Romans' decree, and one Pappus ben Yehuda expressed astonishment at his lack of fear. Rabbi Akiva responded with a parable in which fish tell a hungry fox that they prefer the danger of the fishermen's nets in the water to life outside the water because water is the sine qua non for their survival.

and Blessed One afflicts the righteous in order to purge them. Just as the smith puts the silver in the fire and the gold in the furnace, so the Holy and Blessed One purges the righteous, each in accordance with his dignity (or, in another version, in accordance with his endurance).[13]

So it was taught in a Baraita: "They who serve God with love and rejoice in their afflictions are praised in Scripture as follows: 'May His friends be as the sun rising in might' (Judges 5:31)."[14] And Rabbi Joshua ben Levi commented: Whoever rejoices in his afflictions helps bring salvation to the world.[15]

All That the Holy and Blessed One Does Is for Good

This approach to suffering apparently reverses natural instincts and turns the tables thoroughly. It says that good is evil and evil good, that afflictions are precious and pleasures bitter. However, one who interprets Rabbi Akiva's approach in this fashion misrepresents it. The love of affliction taught by Rabbi Akiva is not an unconditional love, as if suffering were a good *per se*. Love of affliction flows from love of the Holy and Blessed One, a love that brings with it both fortune and adversity. Both come from God, from Whom no evil emerges. What may be regarded as evil by earthly creatures is, in the divine scheme of things, good.

It was taught in the name of Rabbi Akiva: "A person should habituate himself to say, 'All that the Holy and Blessed One does is for good.'"[16] Should one presume to say: "if it is a good accompanied by pleasure, I will accept it; if it is a good accompanied by affliction, I will not accept it"? The Mishnah has established the rule: A person must bless God for evil, just as one blesses God for good."[17] As for Rabbi Akiva, who perceived things through a heavenly lens, he saw only the good—and considered evil to be a product of human perception. In his view, there was no basis for the question, Why does evil befall the righteous? Afflictions are precious, and the righteous do not rebel against them—to them whatever God does is precious and beloved.

This approach to affliction applies only to individual suffering. Rabbi Akiva accepted his own afflictions in love and even told Rabbi Eliezer, who was also sorely afflicted, "Let a person rejoice more in affliction than in fortune." See, however, how his soul was in anguish when he sensed that great troubles for his people were drawing near:

> When Rabban Simeon ben Gamaliel and Rabbi Ishmael were martyred, Rabbi Akiva told his disciples: "Prepare yourselves for adversity, for if fortune had been ordained for our generation, Rabban Simeon ben Gamaliel and Rabbi Ishmael would have been the first to receive it. It is obviously well known to the One who spoke and the world came into being that great adversity is ordained for our generation, and He therefore removed these righteous men from our midst, for it is said, 'The righteous man perishes, and no one

---

[13] PR 43:5 (181a).   [14] BT Shabbat 88b.   [15] BT Ta'anit 8a.   [16] BT Berakhot 60b.
[17] Mishnah Berakhot 9:5.

considers; pious men are taken away and no one gives thought that because of evil, the righteous was taken away' (Isaiah 57:1). Now adversity is about to come upon us."[18]

There is no doubt that the principle, "whatever God does is for the best," is as appropriate for the group as for the individual.[6] That is why our Sages said: "The afflictions that God brought upon Israel were for their good," and "Afflictions come upon Israel only for their good and because of God's love for Israel."[19] Nevertheless, who can accept other people's affliction with love? On the verse "yet He does not remit all punishment (*venakkeh lo yenakkeh*)" (Exodus 34:7),[7] Rabbi Akiva taught as follows: "'*venakkeh*' [literally: 'He will remit punishment'] refers to matters between you and Him; '*lo yenakkeh*' [literally: 'He will not remit punishment'] refers to matters between you and your fellow human being."[20] Now if the Holy and Blessed One cannot grant pardon for the injury or affliction that one person brings upon another, surely we mortals cannot grant it.[8] "When a community is in agony, the individual is obligated to share in that agony."[21]

It is thus well to distinguish between two sorts of afflictions affecting the righteous: afflictions whose purpose is retribution for transgressions and afflictions that a person accepts in order to avoid violating the will of the heavenly Father. The first are afflictions of punishment; the second are "afflictions of love," be it a person's love for God or God's love for that person.[22]

It is likely that Rabbi Akiva sensed that it was impossible to achieve perfect love of God except through suffering, for a person cannot truly taste of the love of God until

---

[18] MI Nezikin 18.   [19] Midrash on Psalms 73:1; SEZ 11 (p. 191).
[20] Sifre Zuta, p. 248.   [21] BT Ta'anit 11a.
[22] It is given in the name of Rava (or Rav Hisda): "If a person has afflictions come upon him, he ought to examine his deeds . . . if, upon examination, he has found nothing, he should attribute it to neglect of Torah. And if he cannot so attribute it, he should know that they are afflictions of love," that is: afflictions associated with a person's love for God (BT Berakhot 5a). The conventional understanding of the phrase follows Rashi: "The Holy and Blessed One afflicts him in this world, even if he is without transgression, so as to increase his reward in the future world even beyond his merits."

---

[6] This does not conflict with what has just been said. Heschel is noting here that the judgment that affliction is ultimately for the good is equally valid irrespective of whether the sufferer is an individual or the nation. In the previous paragraphs, however, he made the entirely consistent point that one may accept one's own afflictions with joy and in love, but it is unseemly to react similarly to the general suffering of the group. See immediately below.

[7] The biblical Hebrew here is a combination of an infinitive (*naqqeh*) and a negative finite verb (*lo yenaqqeh*), which together create an unbreakable emphatic form. Rabbi Akiva's exegesis here treats the phrase as if it were constructed of two finite verbs, one positive and one negative, which thus create a contradiction (in English, it would be rendered by the obviously awkward "He remits and does not remit"). This is not evidence of rabbinic ignorance of biblical grammar, but rather a conventional creation of an opportunity for reading more into and out of a biblical text.

[8] That is, we cannot be expected to accept with equanimity the injury done by a second party to a third. Concerning injuries done to *us*, however, we are presumably expected to be more charitable and forgiving.

he is prepared to mock death itself for the glory of God's great name. From this standpoint, the greatness of afflictions is not only because they cleanse a person's sins, but because within them there is human participation in the afflictions of heaven. No one truly understands the meaning of love, nor does one even know whether he is in love, except through affliction.

It is related of Rabbi Akiva that he was being tortured by the Romans in the presence of the wicked Tinius Rufus just as the time for reciting the Shema arrived. He began the recitation with joy. Said Tinius Rufus: "Old man, are you a sorcerer [who can make himself immune to affliction], or are you merely showing your contempt for afflictions?" Rabbi Akiva replied, "I am neither. But I have always recited this verse: 'You shall love the Lord your God, with all your heart and with all your soul and with all your might' (Deuteronomy 6:5). And each time that I recited it, I was overcome by sadness, wondering when I would ever be able to love God all three ways. I had already fulfilled two of the three: I loved God with all my heart, and with all my possessions. But I had not yet experienced love with all my soul. Now it has been given me to fulfill 'and with all your soul,' at the very time of the recitation of the Shema, and I feel no hesitation. That is why I recite the Shema joyfully."[23]

Not all the Sages shared Rabbi Akiva's views concerning love of afflictions. We have on record the words of Sages who were stricken and, like King Hezekiah, begged for mercy. Rabbi Hiyya bar Abba, Rabbi Johanan, and Rabbi Eleazar[9] were each asked: "Are your afflictions beloved of you?" and each answered: "Neither them nor their rewards!"[24] Rava's habitual prayer included this line: "May it be Your will . . . that I abstain from further sin, and cleanse the sins I have already committed before You, though not by means of affliction."[25] He was also of the opinion that the sacrificial goat offered on the Day of Atonement served as a shield against afflictions.[26] And according to Rabbi Hoshaiah,[10] the patriarch Jacob said: "May He Who in days to come will call a halt to afflictions, call a halt to my present afflictions."[27]

Who Is like You, Who Sees the Humiliation of Your Children and Remains Silent?

What was Rabbi Ishmael's view regarding afflictions? It is clear that he did not accept Rabbi Akiva's thesis that afflictions are precious, and his approach is hinted at in sev-

[23] PT Berakhot 9:7 (14b).   [24] BT Berakhot 5b.   [25] BT Berakhot 17a.
[26] BT Shevu'ot 8b.   [27] Genesis Rabbah 92:1.

---

[9] Rabbi Hiyya bar Abba was a third-generation Amora from Babylonia who moved to Israel. Rabbi Johanan was a leading second-generation Amora in Israel. Rabbi Eleazar (ben Pedat) was a second-generation Amora from Babylonia who moved to Israel, a disciple-colleague of Rabbi Johanan.
[10] Third-generation Amora from Babylonia who moved to Israel.

eral passages on the subject. The basic difference between the two Sages' positions hinges on their views of God's way of relating to the righteous. It was Rabbi Ishmael's belief that for their acceptance of the Torah, the Holy and Blessed One deals charitably with the righteous; and for their rejection of the Torah, He deals with the wicked with the most profound strictness.[28] Rabbi Akiva, by contrast, maintained that He deals with both with profound strictness![11] The Holy and Blessed One is strict with the righteous, "and exacts retribution for the few wrongs that they commit in this world, in order to reward them fully in the future world; and He grants ease to the wicked, rewarding them for the few good deeds they have performed in this world, in order to exact retribution from them in the future world."[29]

Rabbi Akiva vindicated the Master of the Universe concerning the adversity visited on the righteous and concerning the easy existence enjoyed by the wicked. The Creator, in his view, does the righteous a favor when He visits plagues and misfortunes on them, and He is just when he grants ease to the wicked in this world. Rabbi Akiva never questioned the ways of the Holy and Blessed One. He did not ask abjectly, as did Jeremiah in his day, "Why does the way of the wicked prosper?" nor did he struggle with the problem of "the afflictions of the righteous in this world." On the contrary, when afflictions did not come, he would entertain the unthinkable thought: "Perhaps, God forbid, my Master has already received His reward?"

You, the onlooker, may say "he is righteous, and evil befalls him!" but the righteous person himself, plagued with afflictions, does not say "It goes ill with me." Afflictions are beloved, and the righteous person does not resist them. Rather than saying, "He is righteous, and evil befalls him!" one ought to say, "He is righteous, and thus all that God does is precious and beloved to him."

"Your beneficence is like the high mountains; Your judgments like the great deep" (Psalm 36:7)—"Said Rabbi Akiva: You act beneficently with us for the future world, because we have accepted Your judgments in this world."[30]

This theodicy, which served Rabbi Akiva as a shield against the dread of adversity, is an outstanding feature of his worldview, which was so embedded in things heavenly, and engaged in speculation on the future world. But this theodicy did not sit well with Rabbi Ishmael, who did not find in it an adequate answer to the plaintive questions: Why does the way of the wicked prosper? And why are there righteous people whom evil befalls? Rabbi Ishmael, in his belief that the Holy and Blessed One deals strictly with the wicked but acts charitably with the righteous, nullified the very basis on which Rabbi Akiva's teaching was built. Just how much the school of Rabbi Ishmael was given over to the problem of "the afflictions of the righteous in this world" can be inferred from the fact that they taught that Moses, the greatest of the

[28] Genesis Rabbah 33:1.   [29] Tanhuma Emor 5, TB Emor 7.   [30] TB Noah 8.

[11] This theme is expanded in chapter 9 below.

prophets, asked about it abjectly, and requested: "Let me behold Your Presence!" (Exodus 33:18).[31] But though he requested, it was not granted to him.[12]

Rabbi Akiva vindicated the Master of the Universe, and any untoward thought concerning the ways of the Holy and Blessed One was for him virtually a criminal act: Why was it that Moses our Master was punished with not entering the Land? Because he reproached God. The faithful shepherd saw Israel's travail in Egypt and stood before the Holy and Blessed One and said: "What do You care about those who are crushed under these buildings?"[32] Like Moses in his day, Rabbi Ishmael saw the travails of Israel and did not accept his people's afflictions with love. From his academy arose the painful cry: "'Who is like You, God, among the mighty [ba'elim]'—Who is like You among the mute [ba'ilemim]! Who is like You in how you see the humiliation of Your children and remain silent!"[33]

But Rabbi Akiva, who taught: "Let a person rejoice more in affliction than in fortune," rebuked one of his contemporaries for complaining in the manner of Job: "Rabbi Pappus[13] expounded: 'He is one; who can dissuade Him? Whatever He desires, He does' (Job 23:13)—You are the sole judge of all creatures, so no one can argue with Your judgments!" That is, Job's complaint was this: One could argue with the judgments of the Holy and Blessed One, except that human beings are powerless to do so; were they to have the power, they could refute God's judgments. Rabbi Akiva protested this interpretation and said to him: "Enough, Pappus!" Pappus replied: "And how do you understand 'He is one; who can dissuade Him?'" Said Rabbi Akiva: "One cannot argue with the judgments of the One who spoke and the world came into being, because all is truthful and just!"[34]

In a similar vein it was said: "His deeds are perfect" (Deuteronomy 32:4). —"His deeds are flawless with respect to all creatures, and one could not find the slightest falsity in His acts. No one can legitimately ask: Why did the generation of the flood deserve to drown? Why did the generation of the Tower of Babel deserve utter dispersion? Why did the people of Sodom deserve to be engulfed in fire and brimstone? Why did Aaron merit the priesthood? Why did David merit the throne? Why did Korah and his cohorts deserve to be swallowed by the earth? For Scripture says, 'all His ways are just' (Deuteronomy 32:4)."[35][14]

---

[31] Sifre Beha'alotekha 103.   [32] Exodus Rabbah 5:22.   [33] MI Shirata 8.

[34] MSY, p. 68. In Avot 3:16, Rabbi Akiva similarly concludes: "And the judgment is a true one."

[35] Sifre Ha'azinu 307.

---

[12] The conclusion that it was not granted to him to know the secret of afflictions is taken for granted here. It is made explicit in a related passage in BT Berakhot 7a.

[13] Pappus ben Judah, third-generation Tanna, imprisoned by the Romans with Rabbi Akiva. The two are often paired in aggadic debates.

[14] It is to be noted that the questions posed in this text come from both sides. That is, it is acknowledged that apparently undeserved fortune is religiously as vexing a problem as is apparently

Yet you find that Rabbi Joshua ben Hananiah did harbor critical thoughts about the heavenly judgment. He went to Rome and saw there marble columns wrapped in thick carpets, so that they would not crack from expansion in summer, or from contraction in winter. Upon exiting the palace, he encountered a man who was lying in between two reed mats. To the columns he applied the verse "Your beneficence is like the high mountains" (Psalm 36:7) —when You give You bestow lavishly; to the pauper he applied the verse "Your judgments[15] like the great deep" (Psalm 36:7) —when you strike, you do it rigorously.[36]

This question of supreme importance occupied Sages also in the period of the Amoraim. Rabbi Hama bar Hanina[16] decreed a fast during a drought, and no rains came. He said: "O firmament, becloud yourself!" but the heavens did not cloud up. He said: "How ruthless is the firmament!" and the heavens clouded up, and rain fell. Rabbi Levi[17] decreed a fast, and no rains came. He declared before God: "Master of the Universe: You have ascended and seated Yourself on high, and You take no pity on Your creatures!" and rain fell, but Rabbi Levi became lame. Rabbi Eleazar[18] deduced from this: "Let a person not reproach God, for a great man once did so, and he became lame." Who was that? Rabbi Levi.[37]

The Sages were often not at peace concerning afflictions. "Rabbi Johanan would begin crying when he encountered this verse: 'When the many evils and troubles befall them' (Deuteronomy 31:21)—what hope is there for a servant whose master plans evils and troubles for him?"[38]

The Advantage of Afflictions

Rabbi Ishmael did not deny the value of afflictions. He taught that afflictions cleanse a person's sins.[39] In his academy, Aaron was praised for his silence after his sons' deaths, "as the righteous are wont to vindicate God's judgment."[40] Yet not only did

---

[36] Leviticus Rabbah 27:1. See Margoliot's note, p. 617.

[37] BT Ta'anit 25a.

[38] BT Hagigah 5a.

[39] BT Yoma 86a. According to Rabbi Nehemiah (fourth-generation Tanna), afflictions are more acceptable than sacrifices, since sacrifices affect only a person's money, while afflictions affect the body (MI Bahodesh 10).

[40] Sifra Shemini 45a (Mekhilta Demilu'im).

---

undeserved affliction. Aaron had, after all, made the golden calf. David committed (or was accessory to) both adultery and murder, and yet Aaron got the high priesthood and David got what Saul could not: an unbroken dynasty on the throne.

[15] "Judgments": NJV "justice." But as this story illustrates, the classic Midrash on this verse understands mishpatekha as referring to the severity of God's decrees; the question of their justice is another matter. See the beginning of chapter 9 below.

[16] Second-generation Amora, Land of Israel.

[17] Second- to third-generation Amora, Land of Israel.

[18] See n. [9] above.

he not put them on a pedestal or crown them with praise; he treated them resentfully. Sometimes a remark made in passing proves more powerful than a direct declaration. And in the Mekhilta of Rabbi Ishmael the biblical law of the Canaanite slave (Exodus 21:26–27)[19] is thus expounded: "If his master, in disciplining him, knocks out his tooth, blinds his eye, or damages any important external organ, the slave acquires his freedom as a result of his affliction." Rabbi Ishmael—or Sages in his academy—saw in this law of the relationship between a Canaanite slave and his master a paradigm for the relationship between human beings and God. "Is it not a matter of *a fortiori* reasoning: if one acquires freedom through the inflictions of a mortal, how much more so when the inflictions are of heaven. And thus it is said: 'The Lord punished me severely, but did not give me over to death' (Psalm 118:18)."[41] Here is a statement rich in form and in content! Indeed, there is more here than is made explicit: human beings are in the hands of heaven as a Canaanite slave is in the hands of his master! Such an analogy could certainly not have set itself in the heart of Rabbi Akiva. And even the substance of the analogy—that rather than accepting afflictions in love one might harbor hopes of freeing oneself from them entirely—is as far from the thought of Rabbi Akiva as east is from west. According to Rabbi Akiva, "let a person rejoice more in affliction than in fortune";[42] that is, it is advantageous for a person to be plagued with afflictions. In Rabbi Akiva's academy it was taught that the Holy and Blessed One participates in the pain of His creatures, the suffering of individuals and of His nation. Moreover, when a person dwells in pain, he ought to conjoin the pain of heaven to his own.[43]

In Rabbi Akiva's view, there is, besides their power to atone for sins, an advantage to afflictions that doubles their value: there is nothing that so well restores a person to the right path.[44] In this vein Rabbi Berechiah[20] stated: "The Holy and Blessed One associates His Name with living persons only when they suffer afflictions."[45] Others say that rains fall only because of merit earned through afflictions.[46] And according to R. Huna,[21] God's "very good" (Genesis 1:31) pronounced at the end of creation refers to the measure of affliction in the world.[47]

Note this: Rabbi Ishmael wept over the poverty of the people Israel, while Rabbi Akiva sang the praises of poverty: "Rabbi Ishmael wept and said: The daughters of Israel are beautiful, but poverty has disfigured them."[48] Rabbi Akiva, however, declared that poverty is as becoming to Israel as a red ribbon on the head of a white

---

[41] MI Nezikin 9.   [42] Sifre Va'ethanan 32.
[43] See above, chapter 6, "Heavenly Afflictions."
[44] BT Menahot 53b; BT Sanhedrin 101b.   [45] Genesis Rabbah 94:5.
[46] PT Ta'aniyot 3:3 (66c).   [47] Genesis Rabbah 9:8.   [48] Mishnah Nedarim 9:10.

---

[19] Actually, the biblical text simply says "slave." The Rabbis, however, made a distinction between Hebrew slaves and "Canaanite" slaves (i.e., slaves acquired from any non-Israelite nation). Different laws applied to each, and Exodus 21:26–27 was understood as applying to the Canaanite slaves.

[20] Fourth-generation Amora, Land of Israel.

[21] Second-generation Amora, Babylonia.

horse.[49] In the same spirit, it was subsequently said: "The Holy and Blessed One scrutinized all the virtues and found poverty to be the best gift for Israel."[50]

Can This Be Torah and Its Reward?

It is settled doctrine in Jewish teaching that "the Creator, blessed be His Name, rewards those who observe the mitzvot and punishes those who transgress God's will. The plain meaning of this doctrine is a belief in the reward of the righteous in this world.

But how can belief in this idea—fundamental principle of the Torah that it is—stand up in the face of experiences that turn such thinking upside down? There is scarcely a generation devoid of afflictions, and there are daily occurrences that challenge and undermine this belief. How much greater the challenge when a general catastrophe comes and affects the righteous even more than the wicked.

The generation of Rabbi Ishmael and Rabbi Akiva was full of cruelty and atrocity. Rabbi Levi, quoting Rabbi Idi,[22] assessed those events as follows:

> The sufferings that Israel shall have endured may be divided into three equal parts: one part was the lot of the patriarchs and all subsequent generations;[23] one part was the lot of the era of the Hadrianic persecutions; and the third part will be the lot of the generation of the messianic king.[24] What occurred during the Hadrianic persecutions? The Romans took iron balls and brought them to a white heat. They then put them under the armpits of their victims, thereby slowly torturing them to death. Or they would take bunches of reeds and drive them under the victims' fingernails. Thus, many of them died, in sanctification of the Name of God.[51]

The Sages of that generation observed all this in utter consternation: "Consider the foreign pagans, worshiping idols, offering incense to their gods, who live in peace and security; and look at us—our holy Temple, God's footstool, is consumed in flames."[52] Rome rules the world, and God's people are plagued with affliction. Each succeeding day brings increased suffering. What is Jewish existence like? "A prospective proselyte should be addressed so: 'Do you not know that at present the people Israel is perse-

---

[49] Leviticus Rabbah 35:6.
[50] BT Hagigah 9b. On the virtues and rewards of poverty, see Midrash on Psalms 5:2.
[51] Midrash on Psalms 16:4.   [52] BT Makkot 24a.

---

[22] Second-generation Amora, Land of Israel.

[23] That is, with the exception of the generation of the Hadrianic persecutions—see immediately below.

[24] This reflects the common belief that there will be substantial suffering and travail in the period leading up to the advent of the end of days (the so-called birth pangs of the Messiah). See BT Shabbat 118a, BT Sanhedrin 98b, and especially Mishnah Sotah 9:15. On the composition of the latter passage, see J. N. Epstein, *Introduction to the Text of the Mishnah*, vol. 2 (Jerusalem: Magnes Press, 1964), 976–77.

cuted and oppressed, despised, harassed, and overcome by afflictions?'"[53] The people were generally beaten down, but the finest among them, those who continued to fulfill the commandments despite the imperial decrees, suffered a double measure of affliction. Is this the reward of a people that remains faithful to its God and His covenant? Where is the God of justice? Some say: Elisha ben Abuyah became an apostate when he saw the tongue of Hutzpit the Interpreter [one of the ten Sages martyred by the Romans] lying in a dunghill, and he cried: "Shall a tongue which uttered pearls of wisdom now lick filth!"[54] [25]

Legend has it that when Moses ascended heaven, God showed him Rabbi Akiva, who would in the future extract mounds of laws from the mere tips of the Torah's letters. Moses asked, "Master of the Universe, such a person exists, and you convey the Torah through me? God responded: Silence! Such is My will. Moses then said: Since you have shown me his great teaching, now show me his reward. God told him to turn around, and he saw Akiva's flesh being weighed out in a meat market. Moses asked: Master of the Universe, can this be Torah and its reward?! God responded: Silence! Such is My will!"[55]

This consternation at the death of Rabbi Akiva was essentially the consternation of his generation at the lot of the entire people, and Rabbi Akiva himself was overwhelmed by it. The resolution he offered had its basis in the new twist that he gave to teachings on reward and punishment.

Rabbi Akiva's consciousness was ever directed upward, and he could not abide the conventional point of view on the reward of the righteous. In his academy it was expounded: "You shall keep My laws and My rules, by the pursuit of which man shall live" (Leviticus 18:5); —"'shall live' refers to the future world. Should you think that it refers to this world? But he will surely die. Thus, the phrase 'shall live' must mean in the future world."[56] This standpoint also necessitated the following teaching: "'that you may long endure, and that you may fare well' (Deuteronomy 5:16)—in the future world. Should you think that it refers to this world? But he will surely die. Shall we say that the reward of the righteous is serenity in this world? Can this be Torah and its reward?! A puny reward in a 'place of impurity' for devotion to Torah whose source is purity?!"[57] Any reward given in this world is a mere puff of wind!

Rabbi Akiva described life in this world with a metaphor: "Everything is a loan against a pledge; a net is spread over all the living. The shop is open, the shopkeeper extends credit, the ledger is open, the hand records, whoever would borrow may do so; the collectors make their rounds daily, they exact payment from everyone, with or without consent; they have a reliable record."[58] There is no mention here of any reward. The central point seems to be that "they exact payment from everyone, with

---

[53] BT Yevamot 47a.   [54] BT Hullin 142a.   [55] BT Menahot 29b.   [56] Sifra Aharei 85d.
[57] For this use of "place of impurity," see BT Kiddushin 40b, cited in Rabbi Eleazar ben Zadok's parable in chapter 8.
[58] Mishnah Avot 3:16.

---

[25] This story is an alternative tradition to the more common tale of Elisha's apostasy. See below, and chapter 6 above ("Heavenly Afflictions").

or without consent." You might ask: Where is the reward for the commandments? Surely the Holy and Blessed One does not cheat any creature of his wages? With respect to this, Rabbi Akiva said: "The wicked are compensated in full, and the righteous are compensated in installments. The wicked are compensated in full, as though they had observed the Torah willingly and had never been guilty of any evil deed. The righteous are given a small installment, as though they had observed the Torah grudgingly and had never performed any good deeds. Thus, each receives a small payment, and for each, the major recompense is reserved."[59]

This was the key to Jewish survival—the acceptance of affliction with love. The people neither spurned its God nor rebelled against Him. It waited patiently for redemption—even though the steps of the redeemer are slow in coming. Yet there was one who spurned afflictions and rebelled against the God of Israel.

According to an opinion referred to above, Elisha ben Abuyah became an apostate because he concluded that there is no reward for the righteous! "He saw a man climb to the top of a palm tree on the Sabbath and take fledglings out of a nest along with the mother.[26] He descended from the tree without incident. After the Sabbath concluded, he saw another man climb to the top of the palm tree and take fledglings only after sending the mother away. As he descended, a snake bit him and he died. Said Elisha: It is written, 'Let the mother go, and take only the young, in order that you may fare well and have a long life' (Deuteronomy 22:7).—Well, how did it fare well with this man? Where is his long life? But Elisha did not know Rabbi Akiva's exegesis of this verse: 'that you may fare well'—in the world in which all is well; 'and have a long life'—in the world which is eternal."[60]

But this point of view was not universally accepted. Jonathan ben Uzziel[27] translated the verse in Deuteronomy as follows: "in order that you may fare well in this world and have a long life in the future world."[28] And there is much evidence at hand that Rabbi Ishmael—whose exegesis rendered 'by the pursuit of which man shall live' (Leviticus 18:5) as "live by them, and not die by them"[61]—did not concede to

---

[59] ARN A 39, according to the emendation of Schechter.

[60] Ecclesiastes Rabbah 7:8; Ruth Rabbah 6:4. In many other texts the author of the exegesis is not Rabbi Akiva but Rabbi Ya'akov. It is most likely the result of a scribal error for Akiva, but in any event, the essence of this exegesis is certainly consistent with other statements of Akiva.

[61] Sifra Aharei 86b.

---

[26] An act explicitly forbidden by Scripture in Deuteronomy 22:6. Doing this on the Sabbath seems to have compounded the crime. In any event, climbing the tree on the Sabbath violated at least the spirit of the day of rest and put the climber at risk of one or more genuine violations of Sabbath law.

[27] Author of a first-century rendition of the *Prophetic* books into Aramaic. In attributing the translation of Deuteronomy 22:7 here quoted to Jonathan ben Uzziel, Heschel is simply following the attribution traditionally given in texts of the Torah and commentaries. It is, however, generally assumed to be an erroneous attribution of what is in reality a "Jerusalemite Targum."

[28] That is, this Targum asserts the availability of reward, though not the entire reward, in this world.

Rabbi Akiva on this point either. He, after all, taught that the Holy and Blessed One acts beneficently with the righteous who accepted the Torah and does not deal with them with profound strictness. Following the plain meaning of Scripture, Rabbi Ishmael believed that the righteous are promised their reward in this world.[29]

This difference of opinion extended into subsequent generations. Rabbi Akiva's view was adopted by Rabbi Jacob[30] (the nephew of Elisha ben Abuyah), Rabbi Joshua ben Levi, and many other Sages. Rabbi Ishmael's view was adopted by Rabbi Judah the Patriarch and Rabbi Nathan.[31]

"There is no reward for the commandments in this world"[62] was the principle established by Rabbi Jacob in a famous passage. In a similar vein, Rabbi Joshua ben Levi expounded: "What is the meaning of the verse 'with which I charge you this day' (Deuteronomy 6:6)?—they are to be done this day, and not done tomorrow; they are to be done this day, but not to be rewarded this day."[63] [32]

Rabbi Judah the Patriarch, however, followed Rabbi Ishmael's path in his teaching in the Mishnah: "These are the deeds the fruits of which a person enjoys in this world, while the principal is laid up for him in the future world: honoring parents, doing deeds of loving-kindness, attending the house of study punctually morning and evening, providing hospitality, visiting the sick, helping the needy bride, attending the dead, probing the meaning of prayer, and making peace between one person and another—and the study of Torah is equal to all of them."[64] And whereas Rabbi Jacob had said: "For each and every commandment for which the Torah promises reward, the reward depends on resurrection,"[65] Rabbi Nathan said: "For each and every commandment of the Torah, its reward comes in this world; as for the future world, there is no calculating what lies in store!"[66]

---

[62] BT Kiddushin 39b; BT Hullin 142a.

[63] BT Avodah Zarah 3a.

[64] Mishnah Peah 1:1. The Tosefta, however, has a different formulation: "These are the deeds for which one receives some retribution in this world, though the principal is reserved for the future world" (1:2).

[65] BT Kiddushin 39b.

[66] Sifre Shelah 115; BT Menahot 44a.

---

[29] Which would, of course, account for the echoes of protest in statements attributed to the Ishmaelian school on matters related to suffering.

[30] Fourth-generation Tanna.

[31] Rabbi Nathan (the Babylonian), fourth-generation Tanna.

[32] The two inferences here flow from two different possible emphases in reading the text. If *this day* is emphasized, then it asserts that the charge is to act *now*, not tomorrow. If *I charge you* is emphasized, then it asserts that we are being *charged* in the here and now but not *rewarded* in the here and now.

8

TORAH AND LIFE

Translator's Introduction

The central theme of the present chapter is balancing the claims of the sacred and profane realms, of Torah and the world. This theme is developed in a number of different areas, from martyrdom, Torah versus livelihood, to judicial priorities and worldly pleasures. In the latter half of the chapter, we hear from a broad array of authorities not clearly identified as belonging to the Akivan or Ishmaelian schools. Nevertheless, the general lineup of views can be discerned. Rabbi Ishmael is the proponent of moderating the claims of Torah and balancing them against the claims of mundane life, while Rabbi Akiva is extreme in his devotion to Torah even unto death and considers this world merely a prelude or preparation for the world to come. Rabbi Akiva's disciple, Rabbi Simeon bar Yohai, takes the most extreme antiworldly stance; according to legend, he studied Torah with his son in a cave for twelve years during the Roman persecutions and had only bitter words for those who shouldered the burden of the mundane world.

The key question is the relation of the terms "Torah" and "life." Is Torah the sole imperative and life only a means to fulfilling its peremptory demands? Or did God imbue the world with value as well? Did God establish another realm, less sacred but still valuable, with its own autonomous rules—the realm of derekh eretz, of material livelihood, common etiquette, and sensual enjoyment—which also makes legitimate demands on us? If the claims of Torah are exclusive and absolute, then all the Akivan conclusions follow: martyrdom is a positive goal; all the words of Torah are binding, not discretionary; study is more important than livelihood; the pleasures of life are suspect. On the other hand, if the value of this world is granted, then the claims of derekh eretz must also be weighed: survival, where justifiable, is preferable to martyrdom; some commands of Torah are discretionary, or simply good advice; study and livelihood should be balanced; the pleasures of life are legitimate and fulfill part of the purpose of creation. In this chapter, it seems that Heschel's sympathies are with Rabbi Ishmael and the path of balance and moderation.

This is the time to point out to the reader what seems to be a structure to the opening chapters of *TMH*. Thus far we have been taken by Heschel through discussions of textual hermeneutics (chapter 2) and a sequence of theological topics, all of which pertain to God's appearance in and relationship to the world and the human beings in it. Chapters 3–7 dealt with divine miracles, with God's role in the Sanctuary, with the location of the Divine Presence, and with divine pathos amid human suffering. In this chapter, we reach a plateau by moving beyond theoretical theological issues to hard-nosed issues of how one can live a human life and be true to Torah's demands. As we move on to subsequent chapters, a reverse, or chiastic, structure will reveal itself. That is, beginning with chapter 9, there will be discussions of theological issues once more, but this time reversing the focus to concentrate on human initiatives in reaching toward the divine. By chapters 12 and 13, we will be back to our starting point, talking once again about textual issues.

In the preface we noted that Heschel constantly attempts to use rabbinic language and style to evoke an authentic feeling of the culture of the Rabbis. Just as rabbinic literature generally knows of no clear starting or ending point, so does this structure of at least the first thirteen chapters give us a sense of coming full circle and recognizing the interdependence of the many ideas that will have by that time been classified as Akivan or Ishmaelian. Heschel spins for us a web; he weaves a tapestry, rather than constructing a linear argument. As my friend said (see the preface), he continues to sing rather than to argue.

They Loved You—Unto Death

IN RABBI AKIVA'S HEART burned a boundless love for God. How should one love God? Rabbi Akiva answered by interpreting: "'Therefore do maidens love you' (Song of Songs 1:3)—read not *alamot* 'maidens,' but '*ad mot*'—unto death."[1] 1 He preached self-sacrifice and martyrdom in public. In answer to the question why the tribe of Judah was invested with royalty, he answered, because they risked their lives to sanctify God's name at the sea. "'Judah became [God's] holy one'—making God's name holy by jumping into the sea in advance of the others, thus deserving 'of Israel his dominion'" (Psalm 114:2).[2] 2 According to Rabbi Akiva, Hananiah, Mishael,

---

1 MI Shirata 3.

2 Tosefta Berakhot 4:18. See Saul Lieberman, *Tosefta Ki-feshuta* (Jerusalem: Jewish Theological Seminary of America, 1992), I, 71.

---

[1] The midrashic rereading of *alamot* as *ad-mot* may seem to be a long stretch. However, it was commonly held that there was interchangeability among groups of letters that were anatomically related. The dental *dalet* and the lingual *lamed* were considered close enough to be interchangeable, as they are for purposes of this midrash. See Rashi on Leviticus 19:16.

[2] This is a subtle play on Psalm 114:2. "Judah became His holy one" is generally understood to refer to the location of the Temple in the territory of the tribe of Judah. But Rabbi Akiva connected *kodsho* ("his sanctuary" or "holy one") with *kiddush ha-Shem*, sanctification of God's name (i.e., martyrdom). He also reinterpreted the second half of the verse. Rather than understanding it in terms of Israel's being God's "kingdom of priests," he interpreted it to refer to the bestowal of kingship on the

and Azariah sang Hallel when they were thrown into the fiery furnace at Nebuchadnezzar's decree.[3] 3 Self-sacrifice was not optional but mandatory. It was taught in Rabbi Akiva's school: "[God says,] I brought you out of Egypt on condition that you should lay down your lives for the sanctification of My name."[4]

When the Roman government, in the days of Rabbi Akiva and Rabbi Ishmael, issued edicts against the practice of Judaism calculated to undermine the morale of the people, many were forced to transgress their religious obligations. Rabbi Nathan, who lived during the persecution, in commenting on the verse "unto those who love Me and keep My commandments" (Exodus 20:6) said this refers to those who live in the land of Israel and risk their lives to observe the mitzvot. When asked, "Why are you being led out to be decapitated?" they reply, "Because I circumcised my son." "Why are you being led out to be burned?" "Because I read the Torah."[5]

There developed a prevailing view that offering one's life as a sacrifice on the altar of martyrdom was *not* an obligation. "On the contrary, if one could flee from danger, or ransom one's life in any way possible, even by relinquishing all of one's wealth, one should choose that path and not be killed."[6] But Rabbi Akiva did not subscribe to this view. He yearned all his life to give his life for martyrdom. He said, "All my life I was troubled by the verse, '[You shall love the Lord . . .] *with all your soul* (Deuteronomy 6:5)'—even though God takes your soul.[4] I wondered, when will I have the opportunity to fulfill this mitzvah?"[7]

But not all the Sages agreed with Rabbi Akiva. In order to set guidelines, they posed the problem: To what lengths is a person obligated to go in order to sanctify God's name? They considered the matter from three angles: (1) Are we obligated to suffer death (rather than transgress) for *every* mitzvah in the Torah? (2) Are we obligated to undergo martyrdom when the transgression is to be performed *in private?* (3) Is the obligation to undergo martyrdom fulfilled only through death, or can it be fulfilled through suffering?

---

3 BT Pesahim 117a.   4 Sifra Emor 99d.   5 MI Bahodesh 6.

6 This is the apt formulation of Isaiah Horowitz (seventeenth century, Poland), *Shnei Luhot Ha-Berit, Sha'ar Ha-Otiot* "Aleph" 21. See also Hayyim Azulai, *Petah Einayim* on Eruvin 53a.

7 BT Berakhot 61b.

---

tribe of Judah in reward for their self-sacrifice. Furthermore, the Psalm continues with the words "the sea saw them and fled . . . ," and thus the connection between Judah and the Reed Sea was also a natural one to make. Indeed, this midrash is referring to a widely held tradition that the sea did not split until Nahshon, the chieftain of the tribe of Judah, plunged in and nearly drowned. That was Judah's sacrifice.

[3] The story appears in Daniel 3.

[4] Ironically, Akiva is here hitting the true meaning of the biblical word *nefesh*. In postbiblical usage, it eventually came to mean "soul," but in the Bible it referred only to physical life. Loving God with all one's *nefesh*, then, would have meant loving God with all of one's life force, not with one's nonphysical soul. Akiva's interpreting it as an exhortation to yield physical life in martyrdom is thus completely consistent with that biblical meaning.

It was in this period that the Sages met in conclave in the house of Nitzeh in Lydda and decided that if someone is ordered to transgress any mitzvah of the Torah, on pain of death, he should transgress and not suffer death, except for idolatry, adultery/incest, or murder.[8] But we find that even as these Sages were restricting the obligation to martyrdom to apply only to these three mitzvot, Rabbi Akiva was braving death by teaching the Torah in public. Rabbi Hanina ben Teradyon followed his example. As to death and suffering, Rabbi Akiva believed that there was no distinction and that both may be classed as martyrdom. In the matter of public or private transgression, Rabbi Akiva maintained that there was no distinction and that in both situations martyrdom was mandatory. Rabbi Ishmael, however, limited the obligation to martyrdom to public transgression only.

In a later generation, Maimonides understood "transgress and do not be murdered," as an obligation, not an option: "If he chose to die rather than transgress, he is guilty for his own life."[9] By risking his life to teach Torah in defiance of the imperial decree, Rabbi Akiva was at the very least taking on a great personal stringency. Rabbi Joshua ben Korhah applied to him the verse, "Bring in My devotees, who made a covenant with Me over sacrifice!"[10] (Psalms 50:5).[5]

On the other hand, Rabbi Yose ben Kisma rebuked Rabbi Hanina ben Teradyon for taking the path of martyrdom: "Brother Hanina, don't you know that this nation was appointed by heaven to rule? Even though they have destroyed God's abode and slaughtered God's devotees, still they prevail! Yet I hear you still teach to the crowds in public, with the Torah scroll resting on your bosom?" "Compassion will come from heaven." "I speak sensible words to you, and you say compassion will come from heaven? I shall be surprised if they do not burn you alive, together with the Torah scroll!"[6] [11] Perhaps the harshest rebuke to Rabbi Akiva's approach has been preserved in the following statement: "This has been transmitted to me from the Court of Law presided over by Samuel of Ramah,[7] that no *halakhah* may be quoted in the name of one who surrendered himself to martyrdom for the sake of words of Torah."[12]

The tortures that Rome inflicted on those who defied its edicts are too horrible to mention. Rabbi Hiyya bar Abba (a third-generation Amora) declared, "If I should be

---

[8] BT Sanhedrin 74a.
[9] *Hilkhot Yesodei Ha-Torah* [Foundational Principles of the Torah] 5:1. However, the commentators on Maimonides debate the issue at length.
[10] BT Sanhedrin 110b.   [11] BT Avodah Zarah 18a.   [12] BT Bava Kamma 61a.

---

[5] The word *hasid* ("devotee") in this verse often has the connotation in rabbinic literature of one who takes on personal obligations beyond the letter of the law. Of course, this midrash understands the "covenant over sacrifice" to mean martyrdom.

[6] According to tradition, Rabbi Hanina ben Teradyon indeed suffered martyrdom in this manner, burned while wrapped in the Torah scroll. Of course, the story of Rabbi Yose's rebuke (at least in its details) may have arisen later, in response to the event.

[7] That is, the prophet Samuel.

ordered to give my life in martyrdom, I would do so only if they agreed to kill me immediately. Had I lived at the time of the Roman persecutions, I would not have been able to endure the torture. What did they do? They brought iron discs, made them red hot and put them under their armpits until they expired. Or, they brought reeds and put them under their fingernails till they expired."[13] Rav, the first Amora in Babylonia, acknowledged that it is easier for a person to go to his death than to endure prolonged suffering. He declared: "If Hananiah, Mishael, and Azariah would have had to endure flogging, they would have worshiped the idol."[14]

Rabbi Akiva, who rejoiced in his martyrdom, taught publicly that suffering for God's sake is a precious thing, and as he preached so he practiced. He would not acknowledge any limit to human suffering. More than this, while the Sages established the principle that the preservation of life takes precedence over all the mitzvot except the three major ones, he would give his life rather than violate even a rabbinic enactment. Referring to the ritual of washing one's hands, he said, "Better that I yield up my life than transgress the ruling of a colleague."[15]

That One May Live by Them—And Not Die by Them

Take note that Rabbi Ishmael, who regarded the prohibition against idolatry as the central commandment of the Torah, nevertheless declared that if one is ordered to worship idols in private or be killed, he may transgress the commandment to save his life. The Torah says, "that one shall live by them" (Leviticus 18:5)—and not die by them. Can this be extended to include public transgression? No, for Scripture reads, "You shall not profane My Holy Name, that I may be sanctified in the midst of the people Israel" (Leviticus 22:32)—if you sanctify My name, I shall sanctify My name through you.[16]

Both Rabbi Ishmael and Rabbi Akiva underwent martyrdom,[8] yet their responses to this tragic experience were poles apart. The one wept, the other rejoiced.

Rabbi Ishmael was seized by the Roman authorities together with his colleague Rabban Simeon.[9] They were both condemned to death, and Rabbi Ishmael wept.

[13] Song of Songs Rabbah 2:7.   [14] BT Ketubot 33b.   [15] BT Eruvin 21b.
[16] Sifra 86b. Sifra 85a gives the Akivan interpretation of the same verse: "that one shall live by them *in the world to come.*" The same view is found in Targum Onkelos, Targum Yerushalmi, and Rashi. But the whole notion of reward in the world to come does not appear in the corpus of Rabbi Ishmael's teachings.

[8] Current scholarship doubts whether Rabbi Ishmael indeed underwent martyrdom. (See *Encyclopedia Judaica*, s.v. "Ishmael ben Elisha.") Heschel, however, follows here the consensus of the rabbinic tradition, as preserved, for instance, in the Yom Kippur martyrological poem "*Eileh Ezkerah.*"

[9] "Rabbi" means "my master." "Rabban," on the other hand, means "our master," and was the title held by the Patriarch in each generation. Some of the legends about the martyrdom of Rabbi Ishmael have him being martyred with Rabban Simeon ben Gamaliel, the son of the head of the academy in Yavneh after the destruction of the Temple.

Rabban Simeon said, "Why do you weep, Master? Two more steps and you will rest in the bosom of the righteous." To which Rabbi Ishmael replied, "I do not weep for our death; I weep that we are being executed as though we were murderers or Sabbath transgressors."[17]

When Rabbi Akiva was led out to execution, it was the hour for reciting the Shema. As they were scraping his flesh with iron prongs, he was reciting the Shema, smiling as he attested to the kingship of God. His disciples, in wonderment, exclaimed: "Is this the extent to which one goes in accepting martyrdom?" And he told them, "All my life I waited to fulfill the commandment 'You shall love the Lord your God with all your soul'—even if He takes your soul. I wondered when I would have the chance to fulfill this commandment. Now that I have the chance, should I pass it up?" Rabbi Akiva prolonged the word *ehad* ("One"), until his soul departed.[18]

Rabbi Akiva astounded his contemporaries with his heroic deeds. He dared to stand up against Israel's enemies, inciting their anger against himself. He did not fear danger and set a personal example of readiness to sacrifice his life for the Torah. In Rabbi Akiva's temple[10] one heard the voice of triumph.

Rabbi Ishmael was cast in a different mold. In his temple was heard the still, small voice.[11] In all matters he displayed great caution, whether of divine or national concerns. Just as he tried to shield the Torah from those who indulged in fanciful interpretation, so he sought to warn the people Israel against those who made wild claims for martyrdom. He believed that by despising the sacredness of human life they were placing the survival of the nation in jeopardy. He taught that the world would be built by loving-kindness, not by deeds of derring-do. In his own way, he set a personal example and taught, concerning martyrdom, this is not the way![12]

Between the Extremes

The daring principle "Torah speaks in human language" described not only a hermeneutic for understanding the Torah. It also served as a way of conceiving of the divine–human relationship. Rabbi Akiva taught that not only did the Sinaitic voice resound with divine power, but Moses' voice also spoke to Israel with the same

---

[17] Semahot 8:8; ARN B 41.   [18] BT Berakhot 61b.

---

[10] The word is used here to denote his domain of sacred teachings. The phrase "voice of triumph" is borrowed by Heschel from the account of the golden calf in Exodus 32 and is intended to describe Akiva's triumphalism.

[11] Intended as a contrast to the voice of triumph, it connotes minimalism and is taken from the story of Elijah at the cave at Mount Horeb, as told in 1 Kings 19.

[12] "This is not the way"—originally a casual remark of the prophet Elisha (2 Kings 6:19), this phrase was made famous as the title of the first essay of the Zionist writer Ahad Ha-Am, advocating a major revision of policy.

power. Over and against that, in Rabbi Ishmael's school they taught that God speaks to humans in accordance with their capacity to hear; the Shekhinah spoke with Moses' voice.[13]

A favorite saying of Rabbi Ishmael was: "The burden is according to the capacity of the camel."[19] By this he meant that the Torah did not place burdens on the people that were beyond their capacity to carry. "Do not impose a hardship on the community that the majority cannot endure."[20] Rabbi Ishmael tried to avoid the stringencies of the school of Shammai.[14][21] In new cases that arose in his generation, he generally followed the lenient view, while insisting that whoever wished to impose stringency bore the burden of proof.[22] In his view, there were laws in the Torah that were purely optional, and he would not classify them as either positive commandments or prohibitions. In this category he placed the call to martyrdom. He did not regard it as mandatory for a person to martyr himself rather than transgress a Torah commandment (except for the three major ones — and idolatry only as a public act).

The Men of the Great Assembly[15] taught: "Make a fence to protect the Torah."[23] Accordingly, the rabbis enacted various regulations to prevent the people from transgressing Torah commandments.[24] But they lamented one occasion[16] on which the Rabbis made numerous enactments: "That day was as tragic a day for the people Israel as the day when they sinned with the golden calf."[25]

"That day" refers to the time when the disciples of the two great schools of Sham-

---

[19] Sifre Pinhas 135. Genesis Rabbah 19:1; see note ad loc. in J. Theodor edition (Jerusalem: Wahrmann, 1965), p. 170: "the wiser the man, the more suffering is laid on him."
[20] BT Bava Batra 60b, Horayot 3b.   [21] BT Berakhot 11a.   [22] Mishnah Yadayim 4:3.
[23] Mishnah Avot 1:1.   [24] BT Berakhot 4b.
[25] PT Shabbat 1:4 (3c), BT Shabbat 153b, Rashi and Tosafot s.v. *bo bayom gadeshu se'ah*. See also M. Lerner, "Die Achtzehn Bestimmungen," in *Magazin fuer die Wissenschaft des Judentums* 9 (1882): 113–44; 10 (1883): 121–56; and Isaak Halevy, *Dorot Ha-rishonim* [A History of Israel] (in Hebrew) (Pressburg/Frankfurt, 1897), part 1, vol. 3, pp. 580ff.

---

[13] The parallel between textual hermeneutic and principles for living that we have suggested is clearly enunciated here. Rabbi Akiva taught that the Torah speaks with a divine voice, and we must respond with divine heroism by embracing martyrdom. For Rabbi Ishmael, on the other hand, the Torah speaks with a human voice and demands only a proportionate human response from us in return.

[14] The schools of Hillel and Shammai diverged from one another on a host of issues throughout the first century, and generally (though not always) the school of Shammai held the more stringent position. See below.

[15] This term is applied by tradition to the communal leadership from Ezra to the conquest of Alexander, though we know nothing about this body. "Assembly" (*keneset*) was translated into Greek as *synagōgē*, thus indicating the Rabbis' conception of their own historical continuity with this body.

[16] Heschel suggests that there was a danger that, in their zeal, the "fence-builders" would occasionally make too many fences to protect the Torah—creating a burden too heavy for the people to carry. See Rabbi Yose's comment several paragraphs hence. This actually happened in the case Heschel now cites, and he develops this point further in chapter 37, "Against Multiplying Rules."

mai and Hillel met in the upper chamber of Hananiah ben Hezekiah, where they voted on a number of issues. The school of Shammai outnumbered the school of Hillel, and they passed eighteen enactments. They were all fences to protect the Torah. For example, there was a prohibition against reading at the light of the Sabbath lamp, lest one grasp the lamp and tilt it to increase the flow of oil to the wick (a forbidden act). Or, they enacted a prohibition against eating the cheese made by gentiles (for fear it would encourage socializing and ultimately might lead to intermarriage).

Obviously, there were Sages who were pleased with these precautionary enactments. Rabbi Eliezer commented: "On that day they filled the measure to overflowing," establishing high fences to prevent transgressions of the Torah. There were many, however, who were unhappy. Rabbi Joshua ben Hananiah said: "On that day they made the measure deficient."[17] By multiplying hedges and fences that people cannot possibly live by, they are causing them to transgress the laws of the Torah.

It would seem that Rabbi Ishmael was among those who opposed the enactments. He questioned Rabbi Joshua about the prohibition against gentile cheeses, but Rabbi Joshua diverted him to another subject. Various arguments were advanced against the eighteen enactments. One Rabbi declared that it was the creation of just such a fence that led Adam to sin.[18] Rabbi Yose said, "Better a firm wall of only ten handbreadths than a tottering fence of a hundred cubits."[26] On the verse "Do not add to His words, lest He indict you and you be proved a liar" (Proverbs 30:6), Rabbi Hiyya commented, "You must not make the fence greater than the root matter,[19] lest it fall and trample the shoots."[27] Hezekiah commented, "Whoever adds, diminishes."[28]

Rabbi Ishmael was a man who avoided extreme positions. For him the correct path to follow is the middle road. In this respect, he followed the example of the great Tanna, Rabbi Joshua ben Hananiah. It is related that when the Temple was destroyed, many Jews took the path of asceticism, by abstaining from meat and wine. Rabbi Joshua asked, "Why do you refrain from meat and wine?" They replied, "How can we eat meat when the altar on which meat was sacrificed has been destroyed? How can we drink wine which was offered as a libation on the altar and now is no more?"

---

[26] ARN A 1.   [27] Genesis Rabbah 19:3.   [28] BT Sanhedrin 29a.

---

[17] For the possible interpretations of this enigmatic statement, see chapter 37, n. [3].

[18] The story as told in ARN A 1 is that Adam, having been instructed by God not to eat of the Tree of Knowledge, decided to make the prohibition more stringent and told Eve that they were not permitted even to touch the tree. This gave the serpent the opening he needed. He touched the tree, and of course nothing happened, and this discredited everything that Adam had told her.

[19] "Root matter"—'ikkar (literally, "root"; figuratively, "essence" or "principal concern"). Rabbi Hiyya's saying is wholly consistent on the symbolic level and clear in its application. A garden fence must be on the same scale as the plants it guards (of which the plant-root is a handy measure), or by falling down it would ruin the plants. Similarly, a protective legal enactment should be proportionate to the primary law it seeks to protect, or it will cause more harm than good.

Rabbi Joshua then challenged them, "In that case, we should no longer eat bread, since there are no longer any meal offerings." They replied, "That's right. We shall refrain from bread and eat fruit instead." Rabbi Joshua said, "Oh, no, you can't do that, for we are no longer able to offer up the first fruits." They countered: "That applies only to the seven species of fruit enumerated in the Torah; we shall eat the other fruits." Rabbi Joshua pursued the matter further and said, "You'll have to give up water since we can no longer perform the water libation." This time they were silent. Rabbi Joshua continued, "Listen, my children, not to mourn at all is impossible, for the loss has indeed happened. But it is also impossible to establish excessive rules of mourning, for we do not impose hardships on the community that the majority cannot bear."

Rabbi Ishmael said this and more: "From the day that the wicked empire took control of us and decreed evil and harsh decrees, banning Torah and the observance of commandments, and forbidding us to practice circumcision. . . . logic would have required that we not get married or have children. But then the seed of Father Abraham would die out of its own accord. So leave Israel be: better that they sin inadvertently than deliberately."[29] [20]

Scripture testifies that it was customary to consult physicians.[30] But in the generation we are talking about, some adopted the view that in time of illness one should not seek medical help but should turn to God for divine compassion. Rabbi Judah's comment "the best of physicians is destined for Gehenna"[21] [31] may have had its basis in the suspicion of physicians common to the Hellenistic age.[32] The school of Rabbi Ishmael, however, taught that in time of illness one should consult a physician. They interpreted the verse "and shall cause him to be thoroughly healed" (Exodus 21:19) as scriptural authorization for a physician to practice medicine.[33] This came to counter the view that "God smites and God heals,"[34] or "God alone is the healer of all flesh."[35]

The same debate extended to the question of balance between working for a liveli-

---

[29] BT Bava Batra 60b.
[30] See Jeremiah 8:22: "Is there no balm in Gilead? Can no physician be found?"
[31] Mishnah Kiddushin 4:14.
[32] Joseph Heinemann, *Darkhei Ha-aggadah* [The Ways of Aggadah] (in Hebrew) (Jerusalem: Magnes Press, 1970), 229 n. 72, and p. 86.
[33] BT Berakhot 60a, Bava Kama 85a.
[34] Rashi commenting on cited passage in Bava Kama 85a.
[35] Nahmanides on Leviticus 26:11.

---

[20] This statement concedes that there may be something unseemly about bringing children into a world where they will be forced to abandon the covenant, but at the same time is willing to live with this "sin" because it is necessary for the continuation of the national life.

[21] That is, hell.

hood and devoting one's time to the study of Torah.[22] In this debate, the comment of Abaye is apropos: "Many have followed the advice of Rabbi Ishmael [to engage in both] and have been successful; others followed the advice of Rabbi Simeon bar Yohai [to engage only in Torah study] and were not successful."[36] Similarly, Abaye accepted the view of Rabbi Ishmael on the subject of medical help and rejected the opinion of those who claimed there was no value in medicine.[37]

The Torah Speaks of Worldly Ways

Rabbi Ishmael enunciated the principle "The Torah speaks of worldly ways [*derekh eretz*]."[38] [23] That is to say, at times Torah does not just teach us commands and laws, but also matters outside the religious domain. Torah can also provide guidance on matters pertaining to general culture, such as mores, customary behavior, and social amenities that are useful in the life of all humanity. When a midrash cites the maxim "Torah teaches *derekh eretz*," it means the verse in question comes to teach not a law but something from this broader area of practical worldly competence.[39] "God called out, 'Aaron and Miriam!' The two of them came forward [but not Moses]" (Numbers 12:5)—"this comes to teach conversational etiquette."[24] [40] When one suffers injury at the hand of a fellow man, "He shall pay for his idleness and his healing" (Exodus 21:19)—"from this we infer that whoever is ill should rest from his work and devote himself to being cured."[41]

Rabbi Ishmael divided the Torah into two major blocks. One deals with laws and mitzvot, which are obligatory and must be fulfilled. The second deals with the general area of deportment, etiquette, rules of social behavior. These are teachings that may be classed as optional; the individual is free to make his choices. At times the language of Torah may seem to imply obligation when in actual fact it is optional. To

---

[36] BT Berakhot 35b.   [37] BT Berakhot 60a.   [38] Sifre Ekev 42.

[39] See Sifre Ki Tetzei 215 (ed. Finkelstein) n. 248 ad loc; Wilhelm Bacher, *Erkhei Midrash Hatannaim* [Lexicon of Rabbinic Exegetical Terminology] (in Hebrew) (Tel Aviv: Rabinowitz, 5683/1923), entry *derekh eretz*, p. 18ff.

[40] Sifre Beha'alotekha 102. See also MI Beshalah (end of introduction), Nezikin 6, Bahodesh 2; Midrash Haggadol on Exodus 19:8; MTD, p. 128. The same applies to the order of prayer, prefacing petitions with words of praise (Sifre Beha'alotekha 105), or to those setting out on a journey, that they should be efficient (MI Pisha 7).

[41] MI Nezikin 6.

---

[22] This question will be discussed in detail later in this chapter in the section entitled "They Neglect Eternal Life and Busy Themselves with Temporal Life."

[23] See introduction to this chapter, and glossary.

[24] The etiquette being, roughly, "Don't come to enter a conversation unless and until you are specifically called."

Rabbi Akiva, however, every single word of Torah was a commandment and carried with it obligation.[42] For Rabbi Akiva, in the parameters of Torah there existed only "You shall" and "You shall not."

An illustration: "If any man's wife has gone astray . . . in that a man has had carnal relations with her unbeknown to her husband . . . *and a fit of jealousy comes over him*" (Numbers 5:11ff.). On this last phrase, Rabbi Ishmael commented: "Optional." Rabbi Akiva, however, commented: "Obligatory"—that is, it is the obligation of Jewish husbands always to be jealous of their wives, to deter them from immoral conduct.[43] The Babylonian Talmud accepted the ruling of Rabbi Akiva, and in his code of law Maimonides also decided in favor of Rabbi Akiva.[44] [25]

Another illustration of the different views is to be found in the case of the city whose inhabitants had been subverted to idolatrous worship. The Torah states, "put the inhabitants of that town to the sword" (Deuteronomy 13:16). Rabbi Akiva declared: "it is obligatory to slay them—there is no choice." Rabbi Ishmael, however, stated that it is optional.[45] Rabbi Ishmael restricted the law further. The verse reads, "gather all its spoil into the open square and burn the town and all its spoil" (13:17). Said Rabbi Ishmael, "If the town has no open square then it cannot be classified as a subverted town and it is not to be burned."[26] Rabbi Akiva responded, "If it has no square, then you build one!"[46]

---

[42] J. N. Epstein, *Mevo'ot le-sifrut ha-tannaim* [Introduction to Tannaitic Literature] (in Hebrew) (Jerusalem: Magnes Press, 1957[?]), 534. But see Sifra Vayikra 4a s.v. *ki yakriv*—" 'When any of you presents an offering' (Leviticus 1:2)—this is optional."

[43] BT Sotah 3a.

[44] Mishneh Torah, *Hilkhot Sotah* [Laws of the Unfaithful Wife], 4:18.

[45] MTD, p. 69, Hoffman's note ad loc.

[46] BT Sanhedrin 45b.

---

[25] Heschel cites additional instances of this difference of policy, also from BT Sotah 3a: Commenting on Leviticus 25:46, Rabbi Ishmael held that keeping the Canaanite slave in perpetual servitude was optional, while Rabbi Akiva held it was mandatory. Applying Leviticus 21:3 to whether one engaged in another mitzvah should interrupt it to attend to burying a close relative, Rabbi Ishmael said it was optional; Rabbi Akiva that it was mandatory.

Heschel also cites a charming case of Rabbi Ishmael's leniency (and pro-feminism) unconnected to the present issue: "A man vowed to derive no benefit from his niece [that is, he was married to his sister's daughter—a common and much-approved match—and in a fit of anger swore that he would no longer have sexual relations with her. The task became to find a way to release him from this vow so that he—and she—could find sexual fulfillment again]. They brought her to Rabbi Ishmael's house and he had them give her a makeover. Rabbi Ishmael then asked him, "My son, is *this* the woman from whom you vowed to have no benefit?" He replied, "No." Rabbi Ishmael then permitted her to him [annulling his vow]. It was then that Rabbi Ishmael wept, saying, "The daughters of Israel are beautiful, but poverty makes them ugly!" When Rabbi Ishmael died, the daughters of Israel sang an elegy for him, applying to him the verse: "Daughters of Israel, weep over Saul, who clothed you in crimson and finery, who decked your robes with jewels of gold!" (2 Samuel 1:24) (Mishnah Nedarim 9:10).

[26] The exegesis here is, in method, of an Akivan nature. That is, an Ishmaelian reading would have taken the "open square" to be merely a reference to what towns usually have, and not a legal

In this connection we may note the statement in the Tosefta: there never was a subverted town and there never will be one. The Torah simply included it for academic purposes.[27] Rabbi Simeon bar Yohai, disciple of Rabbi Akiva, rejected this view. He interpreted the verse "and burn the town and all its spoil as a whole-offering to the Lord your God"—this means the Holy One said, 'If you fulfill the law of the subverted town, I will regard it as if you had brought a total burnt offering to Me.'"[47]

Rabbi Ishmael followed this principle in interpreting the Torah: whenever the literal sense of the verse is not a command but rather implies an option, it is to be taken in its literal sense. Based on this, he declared, "Every 'im—'if'—in the Torah refers to a discretionary act, except in three instances."[48]

They Neglect Eternal Life
and Busy Themselves with Temporal Life

In order to understand Rabbi Akiva's celebration of suffering we must be aware of the prevailing view of man's relationship to the world he lived in. In general there existed a derogatory view of the universe, a view that underscored the basic tension between life ephemeral and life eternal. In the simplest terms, the Sages regarded this world as the locus of impurity and the next world as the abode of purity. Were these two worlds complementary or antithetical? Their answer: this world is not worth man's labors. The true meaning of life is to be found in the future world. Scripture states: "You shall keep My laws and statutes, that you may live by them" (Leviticus 18:5)—"live by them" refers to life in the world to come.[49] This was taught in the school of Rabbi Akiva.

[47] Mishnah Sanhedrin 10:6.
[48] MI Bahodesh 11. These three are to bring firstfruits (Leviticus 2:14a—but see 2:14b), to lend to the poor (Exodus 22:24—but see Deuteronomy 15:10), and to build an altar (Exodus 20:22—but see Deuteronomy 27:5-6). In each case, the command is specified conditionally in one place, but unconditionally in another.
[49] Sifra Aharei 85d.

---

requirement. However, the conclusion reached by this exegesis is a moderate one that in Heschel's scheme is in keeping with the Ishmaelian temperament, if not with their canons of interpretation. The effect is to limit the amount of official zealotry in the policing of idolatry. Nevertheless, it is worth noting that Akiva is quoted in Mishnah Makkot 1:10 as doing something similar for the execution of capital punishment on individuals. Once again, the dividing line, so clear conceptually, becomes murky when we try to fit it into all that we know of the historical personages.

[27] "For academic purposes"—literally, derosh ve-kabbel sakhar—"study it and receive your wage"! What the phrase means precisely is unclear, but it may be trying to convey the idea that the struggles, both exegetical and moral, that the Sages had with it provide a worthy edification when studied.

Both the depreciation of this world and the justification of suffering are expressed in the following saying of Rabbi Eleazar ben Zadok: "To what may the suffering righteous in this world be compared? To a tree whose trunk and roots stand in a clean place, but whose crown extends to an unclean place. Once the crown is chopped off, the remainder stands in a clean place."[28] 50

The sole goal of life, in the view of these Sages, is to perfect one's conduct so as to be worthy of the world to come. They taught: "This world is a foyer that leads to the world to come; improve yourself in the foyer so that you may be worthy to enter the main hall.[51]

What form is this self-improvement to take? This was a subject of long debate among the Sages. The Talmud related that Rabbi Tarfon and a group of venerable Sages were gathered in the home of Nitzeh in Lod (Lydda), where they debated this question: Which activity is more important (in this world), the study of Torah or the practice of good deeds (performing the mitzvot of the Torah)? Rabbi Tarfon's view was: the practice of good deeds. Rabbi Akiva's view: the study of Torah. After lengthy debate, the Sages reached the following conclusion: the study of Torah is greater, for study leads to the performance of good deeds.[52]

It is clear that in Rabbi Akiva's view the study of Torah is more important than its practice. The conclusion at which the Sages arrived in no way negates his view; on the contrary, it simply expands it. Not only is the study of Torah the highest good *per se;* it has the added benefit of leading one to the fulfillment of the mitzvot.

As a corollary to this dispute, another important issue was debated. In trying to achieve the good life in this world, which path should a person choose? Should one be involved completely in the study of Torah, or should one engage in a gainful occupation? At first blush, the answer would seem obvious: the study of Torah is primary, since it leads to life eternal; engaging in work satisfies only temporal needs. Nevertheless, in the academy of Rabban Johanan ben Zakkai, at Yavneh, the Sages are quoted as saying: "I, who study Torah, am a creature of God, and my fellow human being, an illiterate peasant, is a creature of God. My work is in the city, his is in the field. I rise early to perform my tasks; he rises early to perform his. Just as he does not presume to do my work, I do not presume to do his. Will you say I do much and he

---

50 BT Kiddushin 40b.   51 Avot 4:16.
52 BT Kiddushin 40b.

---

[28] "Clean" and "unclean" here refer to categories of ritual purity, and the view being expressed is that this world is ritually impure, at least in relation to the next world. This makes good sense as a metaphor when one remembers that the source of the highest form of impurity is contact with the dead. This world is a place of mortality, and thus of impurity. The next world, where there is no death, is thus pure. The decapitation in this analogy is also apt in terms of the Roman executions in rabbinic times. For the righteous to be killed in this world, then, is to effect a transition from the impure to the pure.

does little? We have learned: whether one does much or one does little, it is the same, provided he directs his heart to heaven."[29] 53

However, not all the Sages accepted this view. There developed an opposing view that looked upon this world in disparaging terms and that emphasized the contradictions and tensions between this world and the next. The chief spokesman for this point of view was Rabbi Simeon bar Yohai, a disciple of Rabbi Akiva, who, like his master, praised the virtues of suffering and poverty.[54]

Said Rabbi Simeon: "Had I stood at Mount Sinai when the Torah was given to Israel, I would have requested the Holy and Blessed One to provide man with two mouths, one for the study of Torah and one for all his other needs."[55] He trembled when he saw people attending to their business as usual, engaging in trade and commerce, toiling at their daily tasks. "The whole world is not worth one single word of Torah,"[56] yet people are sunk in the life of this world.

Rabbi Simeon was one of the severest critics of Rome and ridiculed those who praised its culture. When the ruling powers became aware of his denunciations, they sentenced him to death. However, he succeeded, together with his son, in escaping from the authorities. They hid in a cave where, according to the Aggadah, they lived for twelve years. They subsisted entirely on the fruit of the carob tree and their skins became encrusted. When Rabbi Simeon finally emerged from the cave, he saw people in the field engaged in ploughing and sowing. Whereupon he exclaimed: "They forsake eternal life and busy themselves with the concerns of this world." It is related that whatever he and his son cast their eyes upon was immediately burnt. Whereupon a heavenly voice cried: "Have you emerged to destroy My world? Return to your cave!"[57]

Rabbi Simeon not only despised the culture of Rome; he despised those engaged in the work of society. He is quoted as saying: "One who is reviewing his studies while strolling and interrupts them to remark: what a beautiful tree, or what a lovely field, is equated to one who is guilty of a capital offense."[30] 58 For him life in this world reduced itself to the question: Torah or culture? Eternal life or ephemeral life? The choice is between these two patterns alone; there is no third, no middle. Another way

---

53 BT Berakhot 17a.
54 See BT Berakhot 5a ("Torah, the land of Israel and the world to come are attained only through suffering"), and Exodus Rabbah 52:3 ("if it's gold you want, take it, but it comes at the cost of your eternal reward").
55 PT Berakhot 1:5 (3b).   56 The saying is Rabbi Berechiah's (PT Peah 1:1 [15d]).
57 BT Shabbat 33b; PRK 88b.   58 Avot 3:7.

---

[29] This last phrase is used in Mishnah Menahot 13:11 in connection with the sacrifices—conveying the thought that whether one can afford a large or a small sacrifice, the heart's intention is what is important. The use of this phrase, then, suggests in this context that the laborers of the world are also making sacrifices, of the kind that they are capable of.
[30] In some texts, it is attributed to Rabbi Jacob.

of putting it was: Torah study is possible only for those who eat manna—that is, they do not work for a living but are sustained by others.[59]

There were other Sages who shared Rabbi Simeon's views. Rabbi Nehorai is quoted as saying: "I reject all the trades in the world—I will teach my son only Torah."[60] Similarly, Rabbi Nehunya ben Hakkaneh, a contemporary of Rabban Johanan ben Zakkai declared: Whoever accepts the yoke of Torah will be spared the burdens imposed by the kingdom[31] and of earning a livelihood; but whoever throws off the yoke of Torah will have to bear the burdens imposed by the kingdom and of earning a livelihood.[61]

In a similar vein, the comment was made: Why was the Torah given in the wilderness? Because "just as the wilderness is not tilled or sown, so one who accepts the yoke of Torah is relieved of the burdens of citizenship and of earning a livelihood."[62]

The movement to reject gainful work and to dedicate one's time fully to the study of Torah struck root in the lives of many people. It is told of Elisha ben Abuyah, the apostate, that he would barge into a classroom and cry to the children who were studying Torah: "What are you doing here? Go out and earn a livelihood; become a builder, a carpenter, a hunter,[32] a tailor!"[63]

The prevailing outlook, which emphasized the primacy of Torah study, did not necessarily abrogate the value of work. In principle, everyone acknowledged the merit of work and the evil of idleness. Shemaya, the head of the Sanhedrin at the end of the Hasmonean era, declared categorically: "Love work!"[33] [64] Rabbi Akiva, too, and many of his contemporaries, lauded the value of work.[65] Nevertheless, Rabbi Ishmael was the sole voice that spoke out against the derogation of this world and of working for a livelihood.[34] He preached against those who relinquished the duties of earning a livelihood and engaged exclusively in Torah study. He quoted Scripture: 'See, I set before you this day life and prosperity, death and adversity. . . . Choose life' (Deuteronomy 30:15–19). This means, choose a trade."[66]

It was against views like those of Rabbi Simeon bar Yohai that Rabbi Ishmael taught: "Conduct your life according to the conventions of society."[35] He brought proof for his teaching from the Torah itself: "It is written, 'You shall gather in your grain, wine, and oil' (Deuteronomy 11:14). Why all these details? Because elsewhere

---

[59] MI Vayyassa' 2, in the name of Rabbi Simeon.   [60] Mishnah Kiddushin 4:14.
[61] Avot 3:5.   [62] Tanhuma Hukkat 21; TB Hukkat 49.
[63] PT Hagigah 2:1 (77b).   [64] Avot 1:10.   [65] ARN A 11.
[66] PT Peah 1:1 (15c); PT Kiddushin 1:7 (61a).

---

[31] The burdens referred to here would include military service, public labor, and taxes.

[32] Or, perhaps, a fisherman.

[33] In Mishnah Avot, Shemaya is identified as one of the teachers of Hillel and Shammai.

[34] "Working for a livelihood": Here the term is derekh eretz, with all the implications discussed in the previous section.

[35] "Conventions of society": Again, the Hebrew term is derekh eretz.

in Scripture we read, 'This book of the Torah shall not depart from your mouth' (Joshua 1:8). This can be taken in its literal sense; that is, we are obligated to study Torah day and night, and we are forbidden to engage in any other activity. Therefore the Torah commands us specifically, 'you shall gather in your grain, wine, and oil.' You must live in accordance with the ways of the world." Rabbi Simeon expressed the exact opposite view when he declared, "Is it possible (to study Torah)? If a man ploughs in the ploughing season and sows in the sowing season and threshes in the threshing season and winnows in the season of the wind, what then is to become of the study of Torah? We must, therefore, have faith that when the people of Israel perform God's will (that is, devote themselves exclusively to the study of Torah), their work will be performed by others."[67] Torah study demands the total commitment of one's life.

On the verse "This book of the Torah shall not depart from your mouth and you shall meditate therein day and night," Rabbi Samuel bar Nahmani gave this interpretation, in the name of Rabbi Jonathan: God did not issue this as a command to Joshua, but rather as a blessing. He assured him that the Torah transmitted to him through Moses, would never depart from him and would be with him day and night.[36]

In the school of Rabbi Ishmael it was taught: The study of Torah is not an obligation that excludes other duties; nor may you exempt yourself from Torah study because of your other responsibilities. One must find a proper balance between Torah study and worldly duties.[68] [37]

The difference between the views of Rabbi Ishmael and Rabbi Simeon bar Yohai may be explained by their attitude to miracles. It was said of Rabbi Simeon that he was an expert in miracles.[69] Obviously, when he declared that if the people of Israel would devote themselves exclusively to Torah study their work would be done by others, he was relying on miracles. Rabbi Ishmael, as we noted above, interpreted many events in the days of Moses as natural phenomena and not, as his colleague Rabbi Akiva did, as miracles. Evidently, he subscribed to the view: one does not rely on miracles.[70]

---

[67] BT Berakhot 35b. Rabbi Ishmael's view is also captured in the following anonymous aphorism: "*Derekh eretz* comes before all else" (SER p. 1).

[68] See the discussion in BT Menahot 99b.

[69] BT Me'ilah 17a.

[70] BT Pesahim 64b.

---

[36] And thus, it was not an obligation to spend literally every waking hour on Torah, to the exclusion of all else.

[37] See also Rabban Gamaliel III's saying in Avot 2:2: "It is fine to have Torah with *derekh eretz*," and Eleazar ben Azariah's saying in Avot 3:17: "If there is no Torah, there is no *derekh eretz*; if there is no *derekh eretz* there is no Torah."

The Pleasures of This World

The contrast between life in this world and in the world to come was depicted by Rabbi Akiva's followers in exaggerated terms. Life here is of inferior quality; in the future world there is beauty and eternal joy. There goodness prevails daily; here only the darkness of night.[71]

Such a view determined the conduct of life. Rabbi Akiva taught: "Do not bring yourself to laughter for that will lead you to sin." "Merriment and levity lead to lewdness."[72] Rabbi Simeon bar Yohai set it as a rule: a person is forbidden to fill his mouth with laughter in this world. In his view, "this world is a lodging place, while the other world is a home, as it is written: 'their grave (kivram) is their eternal home'" (Psalms 49:12).[38] [73]

On this view, the two worlds were in conflict with one another. Rabbi Judah the Patriarch expressed it very clearly: "One who undertakes to enjoy the pleasures of this world will be deprived of the pleasures of the future world; but one who deprives himself of this world's pleasures will be awarded the pleasures of the future world.[74] And this statement: "God Himself did not take pleasure in His universe, and you are seeking to take pleasure in God's universe?" They supported this view by reference to Scripture: "The verse does not read, 'The Lord rejoiced in His works,' but, 'The Lord will rejoice in His works' (Psalm 104:31)." This means that God will rejoice in the good works of the righteous in the future world.[75]

It would almost appear that the Sages conducted a referendum and decided: Israel has no share in this world;[39] this world was not meant for us to enjoy.[40] It follows then that a person should rejoice more in his suffering than in his prosperity. A gentile said to Rabbi Meir, "You say that this world belongs to us, but that the next world belongs to you."[76] According to the Babylonian Amora Rav, all of creation was

71 "'To proclaim Your steadfast love at daybreak, Your faithfulness each night' (Psalm 92:3)—by virtue of our ancestors' faith, who believed in You in this world which is wholly night, we merit the world to come, which is all daybreak" (MI Beshallah 6, MSY, p. 70). Rabbi Meir interpreted Ruth 3:13: "Stay for the night"—"in this world, which is all night" (Ecclesiastes Rabbah 7:8; see also BT Hagigah 12b, where a similar comment is attributed to Rabbi Simeon ben Lakish).

72 Avot 3:13.   73 BT Berakhot 31a; BT Mo'ed Katan 9b.   74 ARN A 28.

75 PRK 26:3 (171a); TB Aharei 3.

76 PRK 6:2 (59b). See SEZ p. 26, where Jacob and Esau are said to have divided the two worlds similarly

---

[38] The Masoretic text gives kirbam, and Simeon bar Yohai constructed this midrash by reading, via a metathesis of two Hebrew letters, kivram, that is, "their grave." Interestingly, scholarly opinion today supports this reading, and so NJV gives "their grave" as the translation of the Masoretic text, and so it appears in the translation of Heschel given here.

[39] A reversal of the common saying: "All Israel has a share in the world to come" (Mishnah Sanhedrin 10:1).

[40] An allusion to the talmudic debate, whether the mitzvot were meant for us to enjoy or not (BT Eruvin 31a, etc.).

brought into being to serve the combined needs of King Ahab and Rabbi Hanina ben Dosa. This world was created for Ahab, and the world to come for Rabbi Hanina.[41] 77 In line with this thought we have the popular saying: Woe unto him on whom fortune smiles.78

Not everyone shared this dismal view of life in this world. We have the outlook of Rabbi Johanan, who taught: "If a man is worthy, he inherits two worlds, this one and the future world."79 This is also the opinion of Rav Nahman, who said: "Esau[42] counts time by the sun which rules by day but not by night. So Esau enjoys this world, but has no share in the world to come. Jacob counts time by the moon, which is small; but just as the moon rules by night and day, so Jacob has a portion in this world and the world to come."80

In the generation of Rabbi Ammi (or Rabbi Hanina), the Sages would take leave of each other with this blessing: "May all your needs be provided in your lifetime and may your latter end lead you to life eternal."[43] 81 The disciples of Rabbi Jonathan quoted this interpretation in his name: "'He has set the world in their heart' (Ecclesiastes 3:11)—this means God put the love of *this* world into their hearts, that they engage in developing the resources of the world."[44] 82

---

in their mother Rebekah's womb. The gentile in the one case, and Esau in the other case, symbolize Rome, the pagan empire of the ancient world.

77 BT Berakhot 61b; see on Rabbi Hanina, BT Ta'anit 24b: "Every day a heavenly voice proclaims, 'The whole world is sustained for the sake of My son Hanina, and My son Hanina subsists on a kab (about one and one-half quarts) of carob a week!'"

78 Zohar, Ra'aya Mehemna Pinhas 232b.

79 Leviticus Rabbah 14:1; Genesis Rabbah 8:1.

80 Genesis Rabbah 6:3.   81 BT Berakhot 17a.   82 Ecclesiastes Rabbah 3:3.

---

[41] The reader will be familiar with the idea that Ahab was a prototype of wickedness (as was his wife Jezebel), and it is thus natural that the text quoted would say that the good but transient things of this world were created for him. His wealth and power as king of Israel were his entire, fleeting quota of pleasure. As for Rabbi Hanina ben Dosa, we know little about his life, and have very few of his teachings, but there were many rabbinic legends about his piety, his ability to call forth miracles, and especially his poverty. These three traits combine to form a prototype of the righteous person who has used up none of his large allotted quota of pleasure on the ephemeral stage of this world.

[42] In rabbinic terminology, Esau (and, what is equivalent, Edom) is Rome, here used not so much as the name of the particular empire, but as a symbol for the entire gentile world.

[43] The prayer literally says: "May you see your world (or your eternity) in your lifetime, and may your latter end lead you to the life of the coming world." Here, Heschel is interpreting this prayer to be affirming this world and its mundane pleasures ("all your needs"). But the idea of eternity being achieved in one's lifetime captured the imagination of many interpreters in the medieval period. Part of the fascinating history of the opening phrase of this prayer is detailed in Gerson D. Cohen, "The Soteriology of Rabbi Abraham Maimuni," reprinted in *Studies in the Variety of Rabbinic Cultures* (Philadelphia: Jewish Publication Society, 1991).

[44] NJV renders this difficult verse: "He also puts eternity [*olam*] in their mind." *Olam* in biblical Hebrew generally means unending time, that is, eternity. The midrashic choice to interpret as meaning *this* world is unusual and pointed.

The opposite point of view is expressed in the preaching of Rav Nahman bar Rav Hisda, in the Akivan vein: "How fortunate are the righteous when the suffering that the wicked will endure in the future comes upon them in this world; alas for the wicked who receive in this world the rewards reserved for the righteous in the future world!" To which Rava retorted: "And if the righteous are privileged to enjoy the fruits of both worlds, should they be hated? I would rather say: How fortunate are the righteous when they receive the same rewards in this world as the wicked do (as well as the rewards in the future world); alas for the wicked who receive the same chastisements in this world as the righteous do (as well as in the world to come)."[83]

This debate is further elaborated in the discussion of the Sages on the "vows of the Nazirite"[45] and the commandment "rejoice in your festival." In the case of the Nazirite, Scripture reads, "and he shall make atonement for him for the guilt he incurred through the corpse" (Numbers 6:11).[46] Rabbi Eleazar Ha-Kappar raised the question, "On whose corpse did he sin that he requires expiation? He sinned against his own body in that he deprived it of wine. We may, therefore, draw this logical inference: if it is a sin against one's own body to deprive it only of wine, how much greater the sin if one denies himself all the pleasures of life."[47] [84] Rabbi Eleazar [ben Azariah] came to a different conclusion: "The verse reads, 'He shall be holy, he shall let the hair of his head grow long' (Numbers 6:5). We can argue logically, if one who denies himself but one thing is called holy, surely one who denies himself all of life's pleasures must be called holy."[85] So we find in Sifre Zuta: "Because he took the vows of a Nazirite to separate himself from society and to live in a state of purity, he is designated as holy. More than this, Scripture equates him with the prophets, as we read, 'and I raised up your sons to be prophets and your young men to be Nazirites' (Amos 2:11)."[86]

In similar vein, we read in the Talmud: "When a city is surrounded by enemy

---

[83] BT Horayot 10b.

[84] BT Ta'anit 11a; also in Sifre Naso 30, with Rabbi Ishmael giving another interpretation. The view is attributed to Simeon the Just (high priest, third-century B.C.E.[?]) in PT Nedarim 36d. See also SER p. 69: "Whoever despises good living in this world, it is a bad sign for him."

[85] BT Ta'anit 11a.   [86] Sifre Zuta, p. 242.

---

[45] The Nazirite takes a vow to live a life of abstinence for a specified period of time. As detailed in Numbers 6, the taboos for a Nazirite include wine, haircutting, and coming into contact with the dead.

[46] The phrase rendered by NJV as "through the corpse" literally reads "concerning the *nefesh* [i.e., the living being]." The plain meaning, captured by NJV, is that the Nazirite sinned (inadvertently) when he unavoidably came into contact with a once living being that was now dead. But the verse never specifies just which *nefesh* it is against which the Nazirite sinned. And thus, the coming midrash attributed to Eleazar Ha-Kappar takes the verse to be referring not to a special case in which the Nazirite unavoidably found himself touching a corpse, but rather *every* case of a Nazarite vow, in which the one taking the vow sins against his own life by the abstinence he/she observes.

[47] The custom of the Nazirite vow became rare in postbiblical times. In the anecdote of Simeon the Just referred to in Heschel's footnote (PT Nedarim 36d), he testified that in his office as High Priest, he officiated at only one such ceremony in his lifetime.

troops, or is threatened with a flood, an individual is permitted to impose a fast upon himself. Rabbi Yose demurred; an individual may not undertake a private fast. He may become incapacitated for work and become dependent on the mercy of a public that may not be sympathetic." Rabbi Judah supported the view of Rabbi Yose by citing an interpretation of Rav on the verse 'And man became a living soul' (Genesis 2:7): according to Rav, the Torah is saying to man: "the soul that He gave you, keep it alive."[87] The Amora Samuel,[48] too, following the teachings of Rabbi Joshua and Rabbi Yose, declared, "One who afflicts himself by fasting is called a sinner."[88] He once remarked to his student R. Judah,[49] "Seize it, genius,[50] and eat, seize it and drink, for we are attending a feast in this world, which we must soon leave."[89] Rashi explained this statement of Samuel to mean, "If you have the means whereby to enjoy yourself, do not wait till the morrow, for you may not live until then and you will have deprived yourself of the pleasure. This world that we must all leave: today it is here, tomorrow it is gone, like a wedding feast, which quickly passes."[90] And R. Hezekiah Ha-Kohen quoted Rav as saying: "A person will someday have to account for everything he saw but did not eat."[51] [91]

With regard to the commandment to rejoice in the festival, the Talmud illustrates the conflicting views with this account: Rabbi Eliezer was lecturing to his disciples on a festival day, expounding the laws of the festival. As he continued, hour after hour, his listeners departed one by one, to partake of the festival meal. Rabbi Eliezer rebuked them, saying, "They are forsaking life eternal to satisfy themselves with temporal pleasure." The Babylonian Amoraim expressed astonishment at this remark of the great Sage of Eretz Yisrael and raised the question: "Is it not a commandment in the Torah to rejoice in the festival?" Some of them, in defense of Rabbi Eliezer, suggested that in his view it was only optional to rejoice in the festival, not obligatory. One is given the choice on a festival to eat and drink or to sit and study. You choose between rejoicing for God's pleasure or for your own. Rabbi Joshua ben Hananiah, however, insisted that we are not confronted by a choice; we can do both. Our time should be spent (on a festival day) half in eating and drinking and half in study.[92]

This debate continued throughout the Amoraic period. Rabbi Samuel bar Nahman[52] declared, "Sabbaths and festivals were intended to be observed primarily by

[87] BT Ta'anit 22b.   [88] BT Ta'anit 11a.   [89] BT Eruvin 54a.
[90] Rashi ad loc.   [91] PT Kiddushin 4:12 (66b).   [92] BT Pesahim 68b.

[48] First-generation Babylonian Amora, colleague of Rav.
[49] R. Judah bar Ezekiel, second-generation Babylonian Amora. Note that the Babylonian Amoraim were generally known by the lesser title "Rav" (indicated here by the abbreviation "R."), whereas the Tannaim and Palestinian Amoraim were known by the more distinguished title "Rabbi."
[50] A word that is usually used sardonically, as here when a teacher is conveying some basic information to a student.
[51] "Eat" is here undoubtedly meant very broadly, as if he had said that we will have to account for all the pleasures of which we did not avail ourselves.
[52] Second- to third-generation Amora, Land of Israel.

eating and drinking," while Rabbi Hiyyah bar Abba[53] stated, "Sabbaths and festivals were intended solely for the study of Torah.[93] Rabbi Eleazar said, "It is universally acknowledged that on the festival of Shavuot, where the Torah explicitly states, "It shall be a sacred occasion *for you*" (Leviticus 23:21), we observe it for our personal pleasure, since this was the day on which the Torah was given." Rashi comments: "We must celebrate by eating and drinking to demonstrate that this day on which the Torah was given is accepted by Israel." Rabbah[54] said, "The same is true for the Sabbath; it is a day given for personal pleasure, as we read, 'You shall call the Sabbath a delight'" (Isaiah 58:13). R. Joseph[55] added: "All acknowledge that the Feast of Purim is to be devoted to one's personal pleasure." In the opinion of Rabbi Hiyyah bar Rav of Difti,[56] "One who eats and drinks on the eve of Yom Kippur, is rewarded as though he had fasted both on the ninth and tenth day of Tishrei.[94]

We should note that the essential elements of this subject had already been debated in the days of Hillel and Shammai. Hillel the Elder taught: All your deeds should be for the sake of Heaven.[95] When Hillel was about to leave a place, he would be asked, "Where are you going?" He would reply, "I am going to perform a mitzvah." When the questioner would persist and ask, "Which mitzvah?" he would reply, "I am going to the toilet." "Is that a mitzvah?" "Yes, for thereby I am protecting my body from injury." On other occasions, his reply was, "I am going to the bathhouse, for it is a mitzvah to keep the body clean." He expanded further on this: "The statues in the king's palaces are washed and scoured by a specially appointed person who is amply compensated for his work and is greatly praised by all the great in the kingdom. Why, then, should I not do at least as much, since I was created in the Image and the Likeness, and cleanse my body with scrupulous care."[96]

Shammai expressed the opposite view. "He said rather, 'Let one fulfill his obligations to this body.'"[57] [97] He spoke disparagingly of man's physical appetites, and he behaved as one who, reluctantly, is being forced to enjoy himself.

Rabbi Eliezer ben Hyrcanus shared the views of Shammai. He said that when he experienced any of the bodily pleasures he felt as if he were being coerced by a demon.[98] When Rav saw Rav Kahana cleansing his head, he said, "Torah will not be found in one who enhances his life in its presence."[58] [99]

---

[93] PT Shabbat 15:3 (15a).   [94] BT Pesahim 68b.   [95] PR 115b.
[96] ARN B 30; Leviticus Rabbah 34:3.   [97] ARN B 30.   [98] BT Nedarim 20b.
[99] BT Sanhedrin 111a.

---

[53] Third-generation Babylonian Amora who moved to the Land of Israel.

[54] Rabbah (bar Nahmani): third-generation Babylonian Amora.

[55] R. Joseph (ben Hiyya): third-generation Babylonian Amora, colleague of Rabbah.

[56] Fourth- to fifth-generation Babylonian Amora.

[57] The sense of Shammai's statement clearly is that one should do what is minimally necessary to care for the body and move on to more important, more enduring things.

[58] The story has Rav quoting the verse in Job 28:13, which states that Wisdom "cannot be found

There were some rabbis who believed that to derive pleasure from this world is as wicked as benefiting from sacred property. So, concerning fruit in its fourth year, the Torah states, "In the fourth year, all its fruit shall be set aside for jubilation before the Lord" (Leviticus 19:24). The Sages interpreted "jubilation" to mean that one must recite blessings before and after eating the fruit. From this, Rabbi Akiva derived the rule: one must not taste any food before reciting a blessing.[100] The Tosefta reinforces this rule with the scriptural verse, "'The earth is the Lord's and all that it contains (umelo'ah)' (Psalm 24:1)—one who derives pleasure from this world commits a trespass."[101] The word "trespass"—ma'al[59]—is associated with making personal use of sacred property. Therefore, one who derives pleasure from this world is considered as though he trespassed against sacred property. However, by the power of the blessing he recites, he redeems God's produce from its sacred status and makes it permitted for human use.[102]

Rabbi Judah the Patriarch is lauded in the Babylonian Talmud for his asceticism. It is told of him that when he was on his deathbed, he held up his ten fingers heavenward and said: "Master of the Universe, it is well known to You that I toiled in the Torah with all ten fingers, but derived no personal benefit from even one little finger."[103]

Happy Is the World
over Which the Holy and Blessed One Rules

While the Sages disparaged the pleasures of this world, they never spoke with contempt of the world itself. The world God created is a pleasant one, but behold what has happened to it at the hands of tyrants who ruled over it. As they put it, "the wine in the barrel was clear but you fouled it." They did not turn their backs on the physi-

---

[100] Sifra Kedoshim 90b.   [101] Tosefta Berakhot 4:1.   [102] PT Berakhot 6:1 (9d).
[103] BT Ketubot 104a.

---

in the land of the living." The meaning of the exchange, as Heschel reads it, is that Rav is setting up a dichotomy between Torah (Wisdom), on the one hand, and the pleasures of life, on the other. Torah will not be found if the pleasures of this life are too prominent, for as in Rav Kahana's case, time spent on luxuriating in this world is time taken away from the Torah, which is eternal.

[59] The midrash obviously connects the words melo'ah ("fullness") and ma'al ("trespass"), even though equating them requires transposing two root consonants as well as interchanging the gutturals aleph and 'ayin. There is, nevertheless, a phonetic similarity that is being exploited here. Taking such liberties with the text was not uncommon in rabbinic exegeses. These practices raise anew the questions of the nature of the text and its interpretation, which were discussed in chapter 2. Did the authors of these exegeses think they were drawing out lessons that were objectively present in the text, or that the expositor was privileged to exercise such license in any case? Or was it merely playful association, calculated to stimulate memory in the listener while teaching a pointed lesson? This, too, was the subject of debate for the later medieval interpreters of earlier rabbinic exegesis.

cal universe which the Holy One had created. They would have rejected the views expressed by Maimonides in the *Guide of the Perplexed* that man's corporeal frame is dark matter, obscure and turbid, and serves as a curtain that separates us from God; that "our tactile sense is an embarrassment to us"; that "the repair of the soul can only be achieved by destroying the body."[60] 104

The Sages never ceased to sing the praises of God's physical universe. What they despised was the historic experience—the ugliness and wickedness of human deeds. They did not regard the normal activities of life on earth as despicable and degraded; however, they distinguished between activities that had enduring value and those of an ephemeral nature. Even to Rabbi Ishmael the pleasures of this world were classed as temporal, and the study of Torah, enduring.[105]

Rabbi Akiva used to expound to his pupils on the beauty of nature and would cite the verse "How manifold are Your works, O Lord, You have made them all with wisdom"[106] (Psalm 104:24). He would also praise the good deeds of humankind. The midrash relates that on one occasion the tyrant Tinius Rufus, a Roman commander in the days of Hadrian, asked Rabbi Akiva, "Whose works are more pleasant, those of God or of mortals?" Rabbi Akiva answered, "The works of humanity are more pleasant." Rufus then queried, "But look at heaven and earth, could human beings have fashioned them?" Rabbi Akiva replied, "We are not discussing matters that are beyond mortals' powers to control but those that are within their realm of competence." "Very well," said Rufus, "then tell me, why do you practice the rite of circumcision?" "I knew you would get to that subject," said Rabbi Akiva, "and I anticipated you by saying that people's works are more pleasant than God's. Here, look at these sheaves of grain and at these cakes: these were made by God and these by people." Rufus, however, retorted, "these cakes are not more pleasant than the sheaves of grain."[107]

In exploring this subject you will find that, unlike other systems, there is absent from rabbinic teaching any suggestion that this world represents a descent or decline from other higher realms. There were Sages who declared that this earthly world is more beloved by God than the supernal world. Rabbi Simeon bar Yohai stated, "When God created the universe, He yearned to have a dwelling place on earth as He

---

104 Maimonides, *Guide of the Perplexed*, III:9; Introduction to the Mishnah.
105 BT Berakhot 48b.
106 Sifra Shemini 52b; BT Hullin 127a.
107 Tanhuma Tazri'a 5.

---

[60] The view described here as being generally rejected by rabbinic culture was common enough in Greek culture. The idea that the physical world is the source of corruption is prominent already in Plato's *Timaeus*, and is also easily discernible in Philo of Alexandria. Not until medieval times did it achieve any real currency in mainstream Jewish philosophical circles.

had in heaven."[61] 108 Rabbi Samuel bar Ammi[62] said, "From the very beginning of creation the Holy One yearned to dwell with His creatures on earth."109 As to God's relationship to the world, the Sages interpreted the phrase "a God of faithfulness" (Deuteronomy 32:4) to mean, God had faith in the world and created it.110

Rabbi Isaac ben Merion[63] found a special nuance in the verse "These are the generations of the heaven and the earth when He created them" (Genesis 2:4): "It is as though the Holy One were boasting of His works and saying, 'Look at the marvelous world I created.' If the Creator praises His works, who may disparage them? If the Creator lauds His creation, who may find fault with it? The truth is, this world is beautiful and desirable!"111

From one single statement we learn of the love of the universe in the hearts of the Sages: "When a man sees a beautiful pillar, he exclaims, 'Praised is the quarry from which this was hewn. The entire world is beautiful—praised is the One who hewed it and created it by fiat! Happy are you, world, that the Holy and Blessed One rules over you!'"112

---

108 Tanhuma Naso 24.   109 Genesis Rabbah 3:9.   110 Sifre Ha'azinu 307.
111 Genesis Rabbah 12:1.   112 Exodus Rabbah 15:22; also, Genesis Rabbah 12:1.

[61] As the arguments in chapter 4 above make clear, this is perfectly consistent with the Akivan view on the matter.
[62] Third-generation Amora, Land of Israel.
[63] Third-generation Amora, Land of Israel.

In Awe and Trembling

Translator's Introduction

Chapter 8 marked the "worldly" perigee in Heschel's chiastic theme development of Volume 1. In chapter 9 he is heaven-bound once more, resuming the theme of divine–human relationship from chapters 4–7.

Popular Jewish tradition sees Rabbi Akiva as the eternal optimist, laughing over the ruins of Jerusalem because he foresees its eventual redemption.[1] Heschel surprises us here with another face of Rabbi Akiva, despairing over the human inability to act righteously enough to avoid God's severe decrees. This image strikes one as a foreshadowing of Augustine's theological pessimism. Rabbi Ishmael's countervailing cheerfulness will remind the theologically well versed of the Pelagian heresy, that human beings are indeed capable of achieving salvation through good works. Yet the optimist/pessimist and Augustinian/Pelagian dichotomies, though suggestive, are each misleading and incomplete.

In fact, Rabbi Akiva plumbed both the depths of gloom and the heights of ecstasy. What provoked his gloom? He despaired of the human ability to fulfill God's expectations. This, in turn, was linked to his maximal reading of what God wanted from us. He took a maximal reading of the Torah itself, finding many more mitzvot in it, with his keen and creative reading, than the more minimalist Rabbi Ishmael was willing to find. Then, in addition, he took the view that we are expected to perform *all* of the mitzvot, not only some, not only 51 percent. This was a heroic and demanding view of the human calling. As a result, however (as we shall see here), it led almost inescapably to the conclusion that we are bound to fall short, and to fail to fulfill to the letter what God wants of us. Put this way, Akiva's despair shares something with the Pauline critique of the Law. Of course, for Akiva, it was certainly not a critique, at least not of the Law. In addition, there is the tendency (which we see in Augustine, and which Feuerbach pointed out in his critique of Western theism), to compensate for human inadequacy with divine superadequacy: where human beings fall short, God takes over and completes the work of redemption, and for this we should be optimistic. But unlike Paul and Augustine, Rabbi Akiva will not let us off the hook. He is thoroughly committed to

---

[1] BT Makkot 24b; see chapter 11 below for a similar tale from the same talmudic passage.

Torah and mitzvot. Human beings are not totally without saving works. Torah is, after all, the bread and butter of Rabbi Akiva's existence; the mystical vision[2] will be but the icing on the cake. We will do whatever we can, studying and fulfilling the Torah in love down to our last dying gasp, and even though we fall short, "the world is judged in goodness."[3] When we have done our best, God will fill in the rest. But before we get to that point, we must be totally honest and realize that in the light of God's true gaze, our deeds are imperfect, our motives questionable, our performance flawed.

While Rabbi Akiva defined *middat hasidut,* setting the norm for the pious elite, Rabbi Ishmael defined a standard that was more practicable for the *beinoni,* the average Jew. Not performance of all the mitzvot, but full devotion to even a single mitzvah, was the minimum goal. If the majority of one's deeds inclined toward the side of merit, this was satisfactory. Adoption of this view by Maimonides made it the generally accepted criterion.[4]

On atonement and repentance, too, the division of opinion is on the question of human self-sufficiency. To say that repentance is required, puts the burden of effort on human mortals. But to say that atonement follows automatically from the performance of prescribed rituals (even where repentance is lacking), is to affirm that the divine power steps in where human efforts fall short.

Jewish tradition ultimately adopted here a synthesis (not always elegant) of the two views. Throughout the Day of Atonement,[5] the liturgy bemoans the burden of sin we labor under, and our inadequacy to measure up in God's sight. But at the end of the day, in the Ne'ilah (Closing) Prayer, the burden of sin is gone; the Jew is confident of having achieved forgiveness, by a combination of human repentance and divine mercy, and proceeds forward refreshed, optimistic about our power to do good in the world under God's guidance.

Even to the Great Deep

ONE SENSES IN RABBI AKIVA'S TEACHINGS a great tension between human beings and God. How shall one adequately take care to follow God's will? "Rabbi Johanan would weep when he reached this verse: 'He puts no trust in

---

[2] See chapters 15–16.

[3] See chapter 11.

[4] Maimonides, *Mishneh Torah* I, *Hilkhot Teshuvah* [Laws of Repentance] 3:4.

[5] This chapter will deal with the divergence of opinion on the very nature of Yom Kippur, the Day of Atonement. On the one hand, the day is said by some to effect atonement by its mere passing on the calendar. At the same time, others insist that one who does not activate the power to repent that lies within cannot be forgiven. For a modern, harmonizing yet compelling reading of those divergent opinions, see Joseph Soloveitchik, *'Al Ha-Teshuvah: devarim shebe-'al peh* [On Repentance] (in Hebrew) (Jerusalem: ha-Histadrut ha-Tsiyonit ha-'Olamit, 735/1975). See Pinchas H. Peli, *Soloveitchik on Repentance* (Mahwah, N.J.: Paulist Press, 1984).

His holy ones; the heavens are not guiltless in His sight' (Job 15:15). If God will not trust the holy ones, whom will God trust?" Earlier, Rabban Johanan ben Zakkai[6] had said: "Woe to us that Scripture has made venial sins weigh on us as heavily as grave ones."[1] In truth, Rabbi Ishmael and Rabbi Akiva both struggled with this tension, and each of them sought enlightenment from the same verse: 'Your beneficence is like the high mountains; Your judgments[7] like the great deep' (Psalm 36:7). But they perceived two different moods in the verse. Rabbi Ishmael perceived an upbeat, cheerful mood, while Rabbi Akiva perceived a gloomy, melancholy mood. For Rabbi Ishmael said: "For the righteous who accept the Torah which was revealed on the high mountains, God's beneficence will soar to the peaks of the high mountains; but with the wicked who do not observe the Torah which was revealed on the high mountains, God will reckon all the minutiae down to the great deep." Rabbi Akiva retorted: "With both the righteous and the wicked, God reckons all minutiae down to the great deep!"[2]

Human beings may be close to God, but nevertheless, "Can there then be comradeship with Heaven?"[3] Rabbi Judah ben Tema would say: "Love Heaven, but fear Heaven."[4] For the Bible says: "the Lord your God is a consuming fire, an impassioned God" (Deuteronomy 4:24).

Similarly, the school of Rabbi Akiva interpreted this verse: "Do not defile yourselves in any of those ways" (Leviticus 18:24)—"Whether you defile yourself in all of those ways, or only in some of them . . . for when I open the ledger, I shall demand payment for all of them."[5]

Rabbi Johanan expounded in the same vein as Rabbi Akiva on this verse: "You are awesome, O God, in Your holy places" (Psalm 68:36)—"Do not read, 'Your holy places (mikdashekha)' but 'those who are sanctified by You (mekudeshekha).'" When is God awesome? When God judges the saints strictly, God is feared, exalted, and praised."[8] [6] It is in the nature of a human being to be more revered by those who are far from him than by those near to him. Not so with the Holy and Blessed One; God is revered by those who are near even more than by those who are far.[7]

---

[1] BT Hagigah 5a.   [2] Genesis Rabbah 33:1.   [3] BT Berakhot 34a.   [4] ARN A 41.
[5] Sifra Aharei 86b-c.   [6] BT Zevahim 115b.   [7] MSY, p. 93; MI Shirata 8.

---

[6] First-generation Tanna, founder of the Yavneh Academy, font of Tannaitic scholarship.

[7] "Judgments": NJV "justice." In the original psalm, the terms tzedakah and mishpat are understood synonymously, as God's beneficent attribute of justice. But the classical midrashim on this verse understand tzedakah as beneficence (whether deserved or not), and mishpat as "judgment" in the negative sense, that is, God's severe decrees (whether deserved or not). This understanding underlies all the interpretations in this section.

[8] This thought is very similar to the standard rabbinic reading of Leviticus 10:3—"Through those near to Me I show Myself holy,"—spoken by Moses on God's behalf just after the death of Aaron's two eldest sons. Those who are closest to God, by virtue of their piety and spirituality, are more exposed physically and morally to the danger of being in the Divine Presence. This reading of Leviticus is based on the idea that Nadav and Avihu were righteous men, a position that not all Rabbis shared.

Rabbi Akiva's soul was seized with trembling and terror; he felt as if he personally were standing at the foot of the mountain that God held over Israel's heads like a tank.[9] "How awesome is this place!"[10] "Devouring fire preceded Him, it stormed around Him fiercely" (Psalm 50:3). The Holy and Blessed One reckons all minutiae with his righteous ones down to a hair's breadth.8 [11] Who can be acquitted in God's court? The mountain is suspended overhead and the great deep lies below. In what can a mere mortal put his trust? Before him—a consuming fire. And behind him . . . ? A person can be indicted for the smallest, most venial misdeeds; can he dare to say: "But I've acted righteously?"[12] Depending on his merits seems to him like leaning on a broken reed. Molehills loom like towering mountains.

Against this view, which goes hand in glove with the idea that, with the righteous, God reckons all minutiae, "even to the great deep," the midrash brings the view of a school of allegorists known as "Doreshei Reshumot":[13] A person is judged on the basis of a majority of his deeds. Therefore, a person should always regard himself as half innocent and half guilty. By performing one mitzvah he tips the scale to the side

---

8 BT Yevamot 121b.

---

[9] Heschel is here referring to the legend given in BT Shabbat 88a that at the time of the revelation at Mount Sinai, God uprooted the mountain, held it over the people's heads, and said: "If you accept the Torah, all well and good, but if you do not, this place will be your grave." This colorful but difficult midrash expresses the sense of compulsion that some Rabbis associated with the mitzvot, even as they celebrated the human will that freely chooses God. The image apparently struck Heschel as fitting what he describes as the Akivan sense of intimacy with God, alloyed with the fearfulness of such proximity to the very source of holiness. That fear and joy can be two sides of the same coin when dealing with the Divine is, again, part of the story of the deaths of Nadav and Avihu (Leviticus 10) and the death of Uzzah, when David was bringing the Ark back to Jerusalem (2 Samuel 6).

[10] This is a quotation from Genesis 28:17, in which Jacob expresses awe and fear at being in the presence of the God who has just, in very intimate terms, promised him blessing and prosperity. Again, Heschel's intent is to show, through biblical and midrashic allusion, how intertwined are the feelings of intimacy with God and fear of God's Presence.

[11] The word for "hair" here is se'arah, which is a homonym of the word for "storm" in the verse from Psalm 50 being expounded in this passage. So, while the Psalm is describing a wondrous revelation of God, it is read by rabbinic tradition as a description of the danger of standing in God's presence ("devouring fire"), a danger that is not physical, as evoked by the image of a storm, but rather moral, since God will hold those closest to Him to a very fine scrutiny ("down to a hair's breadth"). This same wordplay figures in a midrash on Job 9:17—"He crushes me for a hair (se'arah); He wounds me much for no cause." Job is complaining about God's having visited affliction on him for at most a trivial infraction (for he knows he hasn't committed a great sin). But BT Bava Batra 16a (and the Aramaic and Syriac Targums as well) reads it as "He crushes me with a storm (se'arah)," and takes it as an allusion to God's rebuke to Job "out of the whirlwind (se'arah)" in chapters 38ff.

[12] This argument foreshadows future chapters in which totalism in Halakhah is associated with the Akivan view.

[13] Doreshei Reshumot: "Solvers of enigmas" (following Wilhelm Bacher's understanding of rasham in Erkei Midrash Hatannaim [Lexicon of Rabbinic Exegetical Terminology] [Tel Aviv: Rabinowitz, 5683/1923; translated from the German Die exegetische Terminologie der jüdischen Traditionsliteratur; Leipzig, 1899/1905; repr., Darmstadt: Wissenschaftliche Buchgesellschaft, 1965]). Who exactly they were, is still an enigma in search of a solution.

of innocence; if he commits one transgression, woe to him, for he has tipped the scale to the side of guilt.[9] [14]

Some of the greatest Amoraim also struggled with this Akivan idea: "Assuredly, Sheol has opened wide its gullet, and parted its jaws for lack of a precept" (Isaiah 5:14)[15]—"Said Resh Lakish: It [Sheol] threatens one who leaves out even a single precept. Said Rabbi Johanan: The Master [i.e., God] is offended by your speaking of such a person that way.[16] Rather, it means that even if one has observed none but a single precept (he is saved from Sheol)."[10] According to Resh Lakish, one can descend to Gehinnom for one sin; according to Rabbi Johanan, upholding a single precept saves one from Gehinnom.

Both of these approaches were taught in a single context: the extreme view appears in the Tosefta, and the moderate one appears in the Mishnah. The Tosefta says: "Whoever fulfills a single commandment is treated well, his life is prolonged, and he inherits the Land; and whoever commits a single transgression is treated badly, his life is shortened, and he does not inherit the Land."[11] The Mishnah's first clause is like the Tosefta's. But it ends thus: "and whoever does not fulfill a single commandment is not treated well, his life is not prolonged, and he does not inherit the Land."[17] [12] According to the plain meaning, if a person kept a single commandment, he merits all these blessings.[13] Indeed, it is told of the compiler of the Mishnah:

---

[9] Ecclesiastes Rabbah 10:1, on the verse: "Dead flies turn the perfumer's ointment fetid and putrid" (Ecclesiastes 10:1). Simeon ben Azzai asked: "Does even one fly spoil the ointment? Does even one sin doom an otherwise virtuous person?"

[10] BT Sanhedrin 111a (as elaborated in Ein Ya`akov, of Jacob ben Solomon ibn Habib, 15–16th century Spain and Salonika).

[11] Tosefta Kiddushin 1:13.

[12] Mishnah Kiddushin 1:10.

[13] I am interpreting the Mishnah as the Gemara (Kiddushin 39b) does in its initial question. This inter-

---

[14] Heschel here reminds us that the terror of even minor imperfections was hardly a unanimous view. The view given here, although it still demands great vigilance of human beings, is a much less pessimistic and terror-ridden view than the one Heschel has attributed to the school of Rabbi Akiva. The Mishnah in Kiddushin 1:10, to be discussed presently, is a clear example of this.

[15] NJV renders the end of this verse "and parted its jaws in a measureless gape." The last words in the Hebrew are li-veli hok, which literally means "for lack of a precept." It is on this more literal reading that the ensuing exegesis depends. The dispute will be over whether death threatens when even a single precept is violated or only when not a single precept is observed.

[16] The sense may also be that God bristles at being depicted as wielding such an impossibly strict yardstick. See the epilogue to the Book of Job (chapter 42), in which God tells Job's three friends (who have insisted that God is meting out appropriate punishment to Job) that He is incensed at them for not speaking of God as truthfully as Job (with all his protests of innocence) did.

[17] The exegesis of the two Tannaitic sources is difficult and challenging here. In particular, the Tosefta seems to be internally contradictory. In addition, it is quite likely that the Tosefta and Mishnah are really equivalent and simply reflect two different ways of expressing the same thought. In any event, the rabbinic exegesis exists on its own plane and is there, as always, to reflect processes of theological thought that exist independently of the text.

"Rabbi [Judah the Patriarch] cried and said: one can earn eternity in a single moment!"[18] 14 In these passages, Rabbi Judah the Patriarch is following the position of Rabbi Ishmael, who believed that with the righteous who observe the Torah, the Holy and Blessed One deals charitably and does not reckon all minutiae down to the great deep.

Mitzvah's Reward

What are we? Of what value our lives? Our pieties? Our virtues? "All our virtues (are) like a filthy rag" (Isaiah 64:5). We do not plead before You on the basis of our virtue, for we are poor in deeds. Can we possibly claim to fulfill this verse: "He who walks in righteousness, speaks uprightly, spurns profit from fraudulent dealings, waves away a bribe instead of grasping it, stops his ears against listening to infamy, shuts his eyes against looking at evil" (Isaiah 33:15)?[15] Rather, "all depends on the merit of the ancestors"—a theme repeated again and again in the exegesis of the school of Rabbi Akiva.[16]

By contrast, the school of Rabbi Ishmael stressed the value of the deeds of each generation and underscored the doctrine of reward and punishment. They said: "Logically, it would seem that if the non-Jews who worshiped idolatry are permitted to live because of the merit of Noah,[19] then we certainly deserve to be rewarded because of the merit of Abraham, Isaac, and Jacob. But Scripture says: "If *you* will faithfully observe all this Instruction" (Deuteronomy 19:9)—you live as a reward for commandments done; you do not live by the merit of the ancestors."[17]

Note the following difference in exegesis. The Mekhilta of Rabbi Simeon bar Yohai: "'Thus shall you say to the House of Jacob' (Exodus 19:3)—all comes by Jacob's merit —'and declare to the children of Israel' (ibid.)—all comes by Israel's merit."[20] 18 The

pretation is also given by Maimonides in his commentary on Mishnah Makkot 3:15. Note that Maimonides, in commenting on *this* Mishnah (Kiddushin 1:10), offers a different interpretation.
14 BT Avodah Zarah 18a.
15 MSY, p. 144.
16 MSY, pp. 38, 106.
17 "Mekhilta to Deuteronomy" 12:31–13:1, printed in MTD, p. 62, and note 9 ad loc.
18 MSY, p. 138.

---

[18] The context of the passage is the legend that a small act of kindness on the part of the cruel executioner of Rabbi Hanina ben Teradyon (allowing him to die faster) earned the executioner a place in the world to come. Rabbi Judah the Patriarch cried at hearing this legend, presumably because it tended to cast doubt on the value of what he had devoted his entire life to, that is, constant study and observance of God's laws. Why labor in this way if divine grace can intervene even for an act of lessening cruelty. How would Rabbi Judah be distinguishable from the Roman executioner?

[19] Perhaps just by virtue of being Noah's descendants, or by virtue of observing the "seven Noahide commandments."

[20] "Israel" here is, of course, taken to mean Jacob, whose name had been changed to Israel. Thus,

Mekhilta of Rabbi Ishmael: "'Thus shall you say to the House of Jacob' (Exodus 19:3) —these are the women—'and declare to the children of Israel' (ibid.)—these are the men."[21] 19

Rabbi Akiva deprecated the value of even his personal merit. He told this story of himself: "This happened when I was an apprentice before the Sages. I walked out early one morning and found the body of a man who had been killed. I moved him for a distance of three Sabbath limits[22] until I brought him to a place where I could bury him. When I reported this to my teachers, they told me that I had erred and that each step I had taken would be accountable as if I had shed blood.[23] I then made this logical deduction: If when I intended to perform a mitzvah I became culpable, how much more so if I had intended to neglect or violate a mitzvah." Whenever people reminded Rabbi Akiva of this experience, he would reply, "This was the beginning of my acquiring merit."[24] 20

In the opinion of Rabbi Akiva, it is not just one who commits a transgression who needs atonement and forgiveness, but even one who *intended* to transgress but did not succeed in doing so. When Rabbi Akiva came to the following verse, he wept: "Her husband has annulled them, and the Lord will forgive her" (Numbers 30:13).[25] He commented: "if one intended to eat swine's flesh and ate sheep's flesh

19 MI Bahodesh 2.   20 Tractate Semahot [Mourning] 4:19.

---

the verse is read as the biblical parallelism that it is, but with Jacob and Israel referring to the patriarch himself.

[21] That is, the school of Rabbi Akiva (represented in the Mekhilta of Rabbi Simeon bar Yohai) underscores again the centrality of the merit of the ancestors, while the Mekhilta of Rabbi Ishmael has the commandments urgently addressed to the women and men actually standing at Mount Sinai—for their destiny is dependent on *their* observance of those commands.

[22] This is a standard unit of measurement in rabbinic terminology, and it has nothing to do with Sabbath laws here. The Sabbath limit is the distance one is permitted to walk on the Sabbath past the end of the inhabited area in which one resides. It is two thousand cubits, slightly less than one kilometer.

[23] The problem here is that an unattended dead body, a *met mitzvah*, acquires the ground that it is lying on and should be buried right there (BT Eruvin 17b). By moving the body the distance of three Sabbath limits (six thousand cubits, or almost two miles), Rabbi Akiva, with the best of intentions, caused inadvertent distress and disgrace to the dead body. Indeed, since it had been killed, moving it surely caused more blood to flow from the body, and thus the conclusion that what he had done was tantamount to "shedding blood."

[24] That is, knowing just how prone one is to failure is the beginning of piety.

[25] The verse deals with the annulment of a woman's vow by her husband. Rabbi Akiva's interpretation is based on the following reading of the verse: it says "the Lord will forgive her" because she is in *need* of forgiveness. Why? Because even though there was no vow—it having been annulled—she didn't know that and *thought* she was violating the vow. Thus, even unexecuted bad intentions also make one incur guilt. This very stringent point of view clearly contradicts the principle articulated elsewhere (always anonymously) that "God does not conjoin evil thoughts to acts" (see BT Kiddushin 39b and Hullin 142a, and PT Peah 1:1). That is, since a basic principle of most systems of criminal law

instead, and nevertheless the Torah decrees that he requires atonement, how much more so if one intended to eat swine's flesh and in fact ate swine's flesh!" Likewise, he wept at the following verse: "And when a person without knowing it sins, and then realizes his guilt, he shall be subject to punishment" (Leviticus 5:17).[26] He commented: "If one intended to eat permitted fat but ate suet instead, and the Torah nevertheless decrees that he needs atonement, how much more so if one intended to eat suet and in fact ate suet!"[27] In this vein, Issi ben Judah[28] said, "And when a person, without knowing it, sins . . . he shall be subject to punishment—for this (that one is guilty even if he sins unintentionally), all the grief-stricken must grieve."[21]

A Net Is Spread over All the Living

Rabbi Akiva would say, "Everything is a loan against a pledge and a net is spread over all the living."[22] The net, that is, of the Angel of Death, for no person is able to elude the day of death or the day of judgment, as we read in Scripture, "And a man cannot even know his time. As fishes are enmeshed in a fatal net, so men are caught at the time of calamity" (Ecclesiastes 9:12).

Some of the Sages of Israel took the scriptural promise "that your days may be lengthened" (Deuteronomy 6:2) at face value, and they taught that if a person is deemed worthy, years are added to his life (beyond the quota set at birth). Rabbi Akiva, however, declared: "If he is found worthy, he will complete the years apportioned to him."[23]

Rabbi Akiva said: "Why do some Sages die prematurely? Not because they commit adultery, or steal, but because they interrupt their studies to indulge in frivolous con-

---

[21] BT Kiddushin 81b.
[22] Mishnah Avot 3:16.
[23] Ecclesiastes Rabbah 3:4.

---

requires that there be both a bad act and an evil intention, an evil thought in and of itself cannot engender liability unless it is conjoined to an act. This, we are told elsewhere, is what God does not do. The Akivan view in Heschel's exposition here, however, will be seen to hold that both bad acts without bad intention (the present case) and bad intentions without bad acts (see the sequel) can engender liability. This is radical indeed.

[26] The punishment referred to in the Torah is a sacrificial offering that one must bring under such circumstances. The biblical view requires expiation at the altar for unintentional offenses. It is this that Rabbi Akiva is reacting to.

[27] The prohibition against eating "any fat [helev]" (Leviticus 3:17) was understood to apply to the fat of the kidneys and intestines, which were burned on the altar. Permitted fat (such as that of the muscles) was designated by a different name (shuman). Though similar in appearance, they had very different legal-ritual implications. Thus, it was easy to eat the one thinking it was the other.

[28] Fifth-generation Tanna, also called Joseph the Babylonian. See BT Pesahim 113b for list of his other cognomens.

versation. Moreover, they do not resume their studies where they interrupted them."[29] 24

Rabbi Akiva's view was this: "He who studies Torah for other than its intended purposes, it were better had he been smothered by his own placenta, for Scripture says: 'You shall observe My commandments and perform them' (Leviticus 22:31). The commandments were given to be performed and for no other purpose.[30] 25

"Because he has spurned the word of the Lord . . . cut off, cut off, shall that person be" (Numbers 15:31):[31] "One who says that the whole Torah was spoken by the Holy One, but for one verse spoken by Moses on his own—this is the meaning of "he has spurned the word of the Lord"; "Cut off, cut off, shall that person be": He shall be cut off in this world, and he shall be cut off in the coming world. So Rabbi Akiva. Rabbi Ishmael said to him: Now since it says (in Numbers 15:30) "that person shall be cut off," shall I infer that there are *three* cuttings off in *three* worlds?! How then should I understand "cut off, cut off, shall that person be"? The Torah speaks in human language."[32] 26

Indeed, we find not a single place in which Rabbi Ishmael denies any person his share in the coming world. By contrast, Rabbi Akiva was wont to deal with the laws governing the coming world. The Mishnah states: All Israel have a share in the coming world . . . but these are the ones who have no share in the coming world: one who says, the Torah does not teach resurrection of the dead;[33] the Torah is not from heaven;[34] and the Apikoros.[35] Rabbi Akiva added: "Even one who studies the non-

---

24 ARN A 26.   25 Kallah Rabbati 5, Higger edition, p. 276.   26 Sifre Shalah 112.

---

[29] That is, these afflictions happen because of the most trivial of sins. More precisely, the point is that there are no trivial sins.

[30] "For other than its intended purposes" is our rendering of the Hebrew *shelo lishmah*, often translated as "not for its own sake." Akiva's view given here, at least, shows the inadequacy and inaccuracy of the usual translation. According to this view, at least, when the Rabbis spoke of the study of Torah *lishmah*, they were not speaking of study "for its own sake" detached from practice, but the very opposite, that is, study for the purpose of performing the commandments. That is Torah "for its intended purpose."

[31] The translation given here combines the NJV with the Fox translation in order to make the exegesis clear.

[32] This is the now familiar principle of Rabbi Ishmael, according to which such repetitions as *hikkaret tikkaret*, that is, "cut off, cut off" are mere conventions of human language and do not conceal some additional divine message.

[33] The sanction is invoked not on those who deny resurrection but on those who deny that the Torah teaches it. Since the Torah clearly does not speak in any explicit way of resurrection, it was a matter of faith, not just of intelligent reading, that this doctrine was covertly to be found in the Torah. Community discipline in matters of faith were often handled, at least rhetorically, in the harsh ways in which this Mishnah does.

[34] The phrase here in the Mishnah is the title of Heschel's book, that is, *Torah Min Hashamayim—Torah from Heaven*. Heschel will deal with the spiritual implications of this doctrinal statement in the Mishnah in chapter 34.

[35] Literally, "Epicurean." Though it is not perfectly clear what the Mishnah means by this term

canonical books; one who utters incantations over a wound, by reciting from Scripture, "I will not bring upon you any of the diseases I brought upon the Egyptians, for I the Lord am Your healer" (Exodus 15:26).[36] 27 He also disagreed with Rabbi Eliezer ben Hyrcanus and insisted that the generation of the wilderness would not be vindicated on the day of judgment and would receive no share in the coming world,[37] and further, that the lost Ten Tribes would never return to the land and that they, too, had forfeited their share in the coming world.28

If Rabbi Akiva was strict regarding mitzvot between humans and God, he was even more so in the case of mitzvot between human beings and human beings. The verse says: "yet not clearing, clearing the guilty" (Exodus 34:7).[38] Rabbi Akiva expounded: "One phrase says 'clearing (nakkeh)' and one phrase says 'not clearing (lo yenakkeh).' How can this contradiction be reconciled? 'Clearing' refers to the mitzvot between human beings and God. 'Not clearing' refers to the mitzvot between human beings and human beings."[39] 29

If you believe that the Holy and Blessed One deals severely with the righteous and also does not pardon the transgressions between humans and humans, who can stand up in court before God? Matters between human beings and human beings apply in all places and at all times and can ensnare a person even in times of bereavement.[40] Is there anyone in the world so righteous who does not have two handfuls of sins, committed knowingly and unknowingly? This prompted the Sages to say, "If

27 Mishnah Sanhedrin 10:1. The Tosefta (12:10) adds: "Even one who raises his voice to sing the Song of Songs in the taverns, as a common ballad."
28 Mishnah Sanhedrin 10:3; Tosefta Sanhedrin 13:10.
29 Sifre Zuta p. 248.

here, we do find in Midrash on Psalms 1:5 an equation of the "wicked" with those heretics who say that "the world is an automaton (i.e., self-moving)." This view, which rejects ongoing Divine Presence in the world and is thus rejected by the Rabbis, does fit classical Epicureanism as articulated, for example, by Lucretius in De Rerum Natura.
[36] There were others Rabbi Akiva excluded, as reported in other texts, from a share in the world to come: one who chants the Song of Songs in taverns and transforms them into secular love ballads; the spies Moses sent to scout the land of Canaan; Korah and his rebellious followers.
[37] Another amazing and radical idea, even if not meant literally, for it would be denying redemption to the very people who received revelation at Mount Sinai! This is as good a measure as any of how far Akiva's rhetoric would take him.
[38] Once again, the Fox translation is used in order to bring out the doubling of the Hebrew verb on which the exegesis is based.
[39] The more common exegesis based on the splitting of nakkeh and lo yenakkeh goes in a very different direction and states that God clears those who repent and does not clear those who do not repent, a clearly Ishmaelian view under the present scheme (see BT Yoma 86a).
[40] The reference here is to the onen, a person who has lost a first-degree relative and who has not yet buried the deceased. The onen is exempt from virtually all ritual commandments, yet is still subject to all the demands that the Torah makes in terms of relating to other people. Thus, even a person who is subject to very few commandments can incur severe guilt for neglecting these interpersonal commands.

You want the world to endure, you cannot apply the rule of strict justice; if You insist on justice, then You must write off the world!"[30]

Apparently, even Rabbi Akiva was induced to let up on this principle. In Psalm 15, some of the mitzvot between humans and humans are enumerated: "Lord, who may sojourn in Your tent, who may dwell on Your holy mountain? He who lives without blame, who does what is right, and in his heart acknowledges the truth; whose tongue is not given to evil, who has never done harm to his fellow or borne reproach for his acts toward his neighbor; for whom a contemptible man is abhorrent, but who honors those who fear the Lord; who stands by his oath even to his hurt; who has never lent money at interest or accepted a bribe against the innocent. The man who acts thus shall never be shaken."

> Whenever Rabban Gamaliel[41] read this verse he would weep, saying, What man can observe all these deeds? Rabbi Akiva replied: Which divine measure is greater, that of goodness or of punishment? We know the measure of goodness is five hundred times greater than the measure of punishment. Consider this, if a man comes in contact with an insect, even no larger than a lentil, he becomes as impure as if he had touched all the insects in the world. Does it not follow that if one observes a single one of these mitzvot, it is as though he had performed them all? The verse says that one who fulfills all of these commandments will never be shaken, and if one fulfills one of them, it is as if he fulfilled them all! Whereupon Rabban Gamaliel said, "You have comforted me, Akiva, you have comforted me."[31]

In this exegesis, Rabbi Akiva outdid himself and contradicted himself.[42] But it is clear that had he taken a strict and severe understanding of this psalm, no one would have a leg to stand on. All Israel is supposed to have a share in the coming world. But if you say that only one who does *all* of these is unshaken forever, there could be no hope for any creature on earth.

In contrast to Rabbi Akiva's view, Rabbi Ishmael used to say: "You need not take on the task of fulfilling the *entire* Torah, though you are never free to abandon it. Rather, whoever adds more and more accumulates much reward."[32]

Rabbi Ishmael thus erred on the side of kindness, while Rabbi Akiva showed excessive zeal[43] in his love of the mitzvot. The mitzvah of visiting the sick is a rabbinic regulation. Yet Rabbi Akiva took an extreme position and declared, "Not visiting the sick

---

[30] Genesis Rabbah 49:9.   [31] Midrash on Psalms 15:7.   [32] ARN A, 27.

---

[41] Second-generation Tanna and patriarch of the Academy.

[42] By saying that even one of the meritorious acts enumerated in Psalm 15 would be sufficient.

[43] "Erred" (Hebrew *natah*, "to incline, stretch, deviate"); "zeal" (Hebrew *kin'ah*). It is not clear from Heschel's choice of words whether he is neutrally balancing Rabbi Ishmael's leniency and Rabbi Akiva's stringency, or condemning their extreme advocacy as diverging in opposite directions from the golden mean. We may infer, however, from Heschel's general method that he saw aspects of truth in each approach, but valued most of all the synthesis that can combine both truths in a more complex alloy.

is equivalent to committing murder."[33] With this statement, he wiped out the distinction between major and minor mitzvot.[34] According to the Sages, there is capital liability for the transgression of Torah commandments but not of rabbinic legislation.[35] Rabbi Akiva, however, in his extreme zeal, declared that there is capital liability as well for those who transgress rabbinic injunctions.[44]

A story is told in the Talmud concerning Rabbi Akiva's incarceration by the Romans. Rabbi Joshua ha-Garsi[45] would come to the prison to minister to his needs. It was his custom to bring him a measure of water for washing and drinking. One day, the prison guard said to him, "You have brought much water today. Are you trying to undermine the prison walls?" He spilled out half and gave him the remainder. When Rabbi Joshua recounted to Rabbi Akiva what had happened, he said sadly that now there was not enough water for both ritual washing and drinking. Whereupon Rabbi Akiva said, "Give me water to wash my hands." Rabbi Joshua protested, "There is barely enough water for drinking, let alone for ritual washing." He tried to persuade him under the circumstances to waive the ritual requirement. But Rabbi Akiva could not be swayed. "I have no choice. To forgo ritual washing is a capital offense. Better that I be responsible for my own death than transgress an injunction of my colleagues." He tasted no food until Rabbi Joshua brought him water for ritual washing. When the Sages heard of this, they exclaimed, "If this is how strict he is in his old age, how much stricter he must have been in his youth; and if this is how scrupulous he is in prison, how much more so when out of prison!"[36]

Repentance and Atonement

One of the basic tenets of Judaism is the belief in God's mercy and compassion and His readiness to pardon the sinner. "It is impossible that a person should remain totally free from sin or iniquity. . . . But if he believes that it is impossible to make good his error, then he will persist in the wrong course and pile felony upon misdemeanor."[37] Rabbi Berechiah counted among the heretics one who denies that the Holy and Blessed One accepts penitents back in love.[38] But sometimes people despair of the efficacy of repentance. Such a one was Elisha ben Abuyah, dubbed *Aher* ("the

---

[33] BT Nedarim 40a.
[34] See Mishnah Avot 2:1: "Be as attentive to a minor mitzvah as to a major one."
[35] According to Sifre Shofetim 154.
[36] BT Erubin 21b.
[37] Menahem Me'iri (thirteenth century, Provence), "Essay on Repentance," pp. 23ff.
[38] Aggadat Bereshit 53.

---

[44] But in practice, he was opposed to ever applying the death penalty, even though theoretically he believed people deserved it. Here is his ambivalence at work again—strict on the one hand, loving on the other.
[45] Third-generation Tanna.

Other One") by his colleagues, who said to himself, "Once a person has forfeited the next world, let him go and enjoy this world." He imagined that a heavenly voice had summoned all sinners to repentance, himself excluded.[39]

It was the accepted view in Jewish teaching that the pardon of sins consisted of two elements, repentance and atonement, each distinct from the other. Repentance was a human responsibility; atonement was God's. Repentance was a precondition to atonement. The sinner could not achieve atonement unless he first repented. Some Sages, however, held that atonement was independent of repentance. The forgiveness of sin was *grace* bestowed by the Holy and Blessed One, regardless of the sinner's repentance.

During the period of the Hebrew Prophets, there was a prevailing view among the people that atonement could be achieved without repentance. There were sinners in ancient Israel who would grasp the posts of the altar, offer up their sacrifices and believe that this was sufficient to gain them atonement—without any act of repentance. The Prophets denounced these sinners and proclaimed: "Would the Lord be pleased with thousands of rams, with myriads of streams of oil?" (Micah 6:7). Or, "Does the Lord delight in burnt offerings and sacrifices as much as in obedience to God's command? Surely, obedience is better than sacrifice, compliance than the fat of rams" (1 Samuel 15:22). The Prophets were unanimous on this subject: atonement cannot be achieved without repentance. Hosea's call to Israel was: "Return, O Israel, to the Lord your God" (Hosea 14:2).

The Sages accepted the view of the Prophets and indulged in extravagant praise of the virtue of repentance. Do not imagine that the Sages were thereby seeking to lighten the burden of sinners. On the contrary, they were making it heavier. Is repentance, then, a trivial matter? It penetrates deep into a person's inner soul. There it is examined very carefully by God, who studies the deepest motivations of the heart. He knows how deceitful the human heart can be, how fallible (see Jeremiah 17:9). Who can trust the promptings of his own heart? The heart is such a fragile, perishable instrument that God had to create another instrument for man to achieve atonement—repentance.

There were Sages who were troubled by the human predicament. There were countless human beings who transgressed God's will and departed from this earth without repentance. Does this mean there is no hope for them in the next world? Some of the Sages declared that atonement can be achieved independently of repentance. We read in Scriptures, "Absolve Your people Israel whom You have redeemed" (Deuteronomy 21:8). When the verse says, "absolve your people," it refers to the living; "whom You have redeemed" refers to the dead. Hence we learn that even the dead require atonement.[40]

Rabbi Meir, a disciple of Rabbi Akiva, subscribed to the view that atonement does

---

[39] BT Hagigah 15a: "I have heard from behind the curtain, 'Return, rebellious children (Jeremiah 3:14)' —all except that renegade!"

[40] Sifre Shofetim 210; BT Sanhedrin 47a.

not require repentance. He taught, "So great is the act of repentance, that if but a single person repents, God pardons not only him but the sins of all the world."[46] [41] In similar vein, Rabbi Johanan taught, "The nations of the world do not realize what they lost when the Temple was destroyed. When it stood, the altar made atonement for them as well, now who will make atonement for them?[42] So Rabbi Hiyya bar Abba said, "Just as Yom Kippur atones for man's sins, so does the death of the righteous."[43] No mention is made of repentance as a precondition for atonement.

Yom Kippur was the day set apart for pardon and atonement. Scripture reads, "'For on this day atonement shall be made for you to cleanse you of all your sins; you shall be clean before the Lord' (Leviticus 16:30). In the Temple service on Yom Kippur, the High Priest laid both his hands on the head of the live goat and, in behalf of all the people, confessed the iniquities and transgressions of the Israelites (see Leviticus 16:21). And when he was done, the people responded, "Blessed is the name of His glorious kingdom for ever and ever."[44] But it is clear that whoever confessed was repentant of his sins. This is alluded to in the Book of Jubilees (5:17, 18)—the forgiveness of sins on Yom Kippur was accompanied by repentance.

It would seem that the preponderant view is the one expressed by the Sages in this statement: "The sin offering, the guilt offering, death, and Yom Kippur do not bring atonement without repentance. We derive this from the word akh ("however," Leviticus 23:27), which always implies a limitation. Here the limitation is on atonement— if there is repentance there is atonement; otherwise, there is no atonement."[45] Rava said: "Be not like those fools who sin and bring their offerings but do not repent."[46]

However, no less a renowned teacher than Rabbi Judah the Patriarch rejected the view that Yom Kippur gives atonement only to repentant sinners. He declared: "Yom Kippur atones for all the transgressions cited in the Torah, whether one repents or not."[47] There are a few exceptions to automatic atonement: one who rejects the authority of the Torah; one who contemptuously perverts the meaning of the Torah; one who obliterates the sign of the covenant (circumcision).[47] These cannot achieve atonement without repentance.[48] Rabbi Judah is of the opinion that the power of atonement is greater than the power of repentance. "Repentance needs Yom Kippur; Yom Kippur does not need repentance."[49]

---

[41] BT Yoma 86b.   [42] BT Sukkah 55b.   [43] Leviticus Rabbah 20:12.   [44] Sifra Aharei 82a.
[45] Sifra Emor 102a.   [46] BT Berakhot 23a.   [47] BT Yoma 85b, 87a.   [48] Ibid.
[49] Ibid.

---

[46] This, too, of course, is a far-reaching sentiment, even if it can be seen as a rhetorical overstatement for emphatic purposes. The idea of vicarious atonement obviously took on the ultimate importance in Christianity, but it is certainly not unknown in Jewish sources prior to that. The Rabbis themselves noted that the biblical system of sacrifice could be characterized as "the priests eat [the sin offerings] and the owners [of the animals] are atoned for." See, e.g., Sifra on Leviticus 10:17.

[47] This refers to those who literally obliterated the evidence of circumcision from their own bodies through surgery.

Rabbi Judah was not alone in his approach that it is the essential character of the day itself (Yom Kippur) that provides atonement. On the verse "For on this day atonement shall be made for you" (Leviticus 16:30), the Sages said, this refers to the sacrifices offered on that day. Suppose there were no goat to offer as a sacrifice, could atonement be attained? The verse is very explicit, "on this day"—it is the day itself that atones.[50] Again, no mention is made of the need for repentance.

Maimonides, in his Mishneh Torah, agrees with the majority of Sages that atonement cannot be achieved without genuine repentance. However, Yom Kippur does provide automatic atonement for the transgression of minor commandments.[51]

In the school of Rabbi Akiva, it was taught: "As for all the other transgressions cited in the Torah, . . . the goat of atonement and Yom Kippur grant absolution."[52] This Baraita, which makes no mention of repentance, was incorporated verbatim in the Mishnah of Rabbi Judah the Patriarch.[53] It seems as well that the Babylonian Talmud took the Mishnah to be saying that repentance is unnecessary, and that this is the official view of Rabbi Judah the Patriarch. Yet we find in Sifra, along with the passage that we have identified with the view of Rabbi, a contradictory passage.[48] The question is raised, "Is it possible that Yom Kippur atones for the repentant and the unrepentant alike? We may deduce, by logical inference, that this is not so. Since when one brings a sin or guilt offering it must be accompanied by repentance, does not Scripture say, 'the sacrifice of the wicked is an abomination' (Proverbs 21:27)? How then, can the Yom Kippur sacrifice alone atone for a person's sins?"[54]

The subject of repentance and atonement is like a tree whose roots are intertwined and whose branches proliferate. A scholar who devoted himself to this field of study usually concentrated on a single branch of the tree. Rabbi Ishmael was the sole scholar who carefully examined and encompassed all aspects of the subject. He noted all the problems and contradictions that were embedded in the study of repentance and atonement. Thus, one text states that repentance is the atoning agent; another says it is Yom Kippur. In one place we learn that death absolves us of our sins; in

---

[50] Sifra Aharei 83a.

[51] Maimonides, Mishneh Torah I, *Hilkhot Teshuvah* [Laws of Repentance] 1:2–3. Many of Maimonides' commentators took issue with the leniency of this view.

[52] Sifra Aharei 82a.   [53] Mishnah Shevu'ot 1:6.   [54] Sifra Emor 102a; BT Shabuot 12b.

---

[48] It is hard to tell how much one should make of this "contradiction." The passage in Sifra 82a emphasizes that the goat and Yom Kippur atone effectively. The passage in 83a emphasizes that Yom Kippur atones "by itself," that is, without the goat. The passage in 102a repeats this last thought, but adds the qualification that repentance is also necessary. The view that atonement takes place automatically, without repentance, is not explicit in the Sifra but is ascribed to Rabbi Judah the Patriarch in the Babylonian Talmud, along with the first two views in the Sifra. It is only by bringing in the evidence of the Babylonian Talmud that an apparent contradiction develops. Evidently Rabbi Judah the Patriarch adopted most of the anonymous views of the Sifra on these issues but differed from them on whether repentance is mandatory.

another it is suffering. One source comforts us with the thought that repentance conquers all; another tells us that the sinner has no hope for pardon. Rabbi Ishmael sought to resolve these seeming contradictions.

According to Rabbi Ishmael, there are four elements in the subject of atonement. We read in Scripture, "Turn back, rebellious children" (Jeremiah 3:14, 22), from which we learn that repentance brings forgiveness. A second verse reads, "For on this day atonement shall be made for you" (Leviticus 16:30), from which we learn that Yom Kippur brings atonement. A third verse reads, "This iniquity shall never be forgiven you until you die" (Isaiah 22:14), from which we learn that death brings absolution. In a fourth verse we read, "I will punish their transgression with the rod, their iniquity with plagues" (Psalms 89:33), from which we learn that suffering brings forgiveness.

How are these four passages to be reconciled? When a person is guilty of a sin of omission and repents, he is immediately forgiven. When a person is guilty of a sin of commission, repentance alone cannot expiate it. Judgment is suspended until Yom Kippur arrives and atonement is granted. When a person commits a transgression that is a capital offense, whether in a heavenly or in an earthly court, repentance cannot postpone the punishment, nor can Yom Kippur bring pardon. However, repentance and Yom Kippur together qualify for half a pardon. The other half is achieved through the chastisements of suffering. When a person is guilty, by his actions, of the desecration and profanation of God's name, neither repentance, nor Yom Kippur, nor suffering can cleanse him of his guilt. Repentance and Yom Kippur postpone the punishment, and suffering followed by death complete his atonement. Rabbi Judah the Patriarch said, "I might have thought that the day of death does not bring atonement, but when Scripture says, "When I have opened your graves and lifted you out of your graves" (Ezekiel 37:13), I realized that death does bring absolution."[55]

There were basic differences on this subject in the schools of Rabbi Ishmael and Rabbi Akiva. Rabbi Akiva had faith in the atoning power of suffering and of Yom Kippur, even without repentance. To Rabbi Ishmael, even suffering does not atone unless it is combined with repentance. While Rabbi Akiva places the decision of atonement in the hands of God, Rabbi Ishmael places it in the hands of man.

These differences are based on two distinct world outlooks. In Rabbi Ishmael's view, the world is judged by law. "It becomes God that He is the guardian of the law and He shows no special favors to any person." It is up to us to make the crucial decision—to obey the law or transgress it. And if we transgress, there is no pardon without repentance. In the view of Rabbi Akiva, the world is judged by God's goodness and mercy. The decisions in our most vital interests lie with God, not with us. "Length of life, the blessing of children, a secure livelihood—these do not depend on whether a person is worthy or not, but entirely upon supernatural forces."[56] Rabbi Samuel bar

---

[55] MI Bahodesh 7; Tosefta Yoma 4:6-8; PT Yoma 8:7 (45b).
[56] BT Mo'ed Katan 28a.

Nahmani[49] expressed this belief in these words: "The dew does not descend on earth because of man's merit."[57] Everything depends on God's mercy. Repentance is not the only peg on which to pin one's hopes. There can be atonement without repentance.

It would follow, according to Rabbi Ishmael, that should Israel not repent, it will never be redeemed; whereas in Rabbi Akiva's view, Israel will be redeemed even if they never repent.[58] The salvation of Israel is the concern of the Holy and Blessed One alone. Said the Holy and Blessed One to Israel: "If you have no meritorious deeds to bring Me, then I will redeem you for My own sake."[59]

Rabbi Akiva made the following exposition: "Fortunate are you, O Israel! Before whom are you purified? Who purifies you? Before your Father in heaven, as we read in Scripture, 'I will sprinkle clean water upon you and you shall be clean' (Ezekiel 36:25). It is also written, 'The Lord is the hope of (mikveh) Israel' (Jeremiah 17:13).[50] Just as a mikveh (ritual pool) cleanses the impure, so does the Holy and Blessed One cleanse Israel." Rabbi Akiva is teaching us that even when a person is not awakened to repentance, the Holy and Blessed One will act, as the prophet Ezekiel said, "Not for your sake will I act, O house of Israel . . . and I will sprinkle clean water upon you."[60]

Did They Believe—Or Not?

In the school of Rabbi Akiva they believed that all is in the hands of Heaven. The Torah, in all of its details, is heavenly, and the prophet is nought but a vessel to receive its inspiration. Over and against this, they believed in the school of Rabbi Ishmael that there were things that Moses did on his own authority, and that the prophet is a partner in prophecy, not merely a receiving vessel.[61] Wrapped up in these differences are different ways of apprehending human nature. In the school of Rabbi Akiva it was taught that the Israelites were deficient in faith, and that even at moments beyond conception, such as the splitting of the Sea of Reeds or the standing at Mount Sinai, they did not have full-hearted faith. This point of view was disputed

[57] PT Berakhot 5:2 (9b)—That is, rain is withheld on account of sin, but dew is given unconditionally, by God's grace.

[58] See BT Sanhedrin 97b, where the disputants are Rabbi Eliezer and Rabbi Joshua.

[59] Exodus Rabbah 30:24.

[60] Mishnah Yoma 8:9.

[61] These issues will be treated in depth in chapters 22 and 27.

[49] Second- to third-generation Amora, Land of Israel.

[50] The exegesis here is going to depend on the homophonic identity of mikveh, a combined (possessive) noun form meaning "hope of" and mikveh, a nominative case noun meaning "pool of water" and especially, a purifying ritual bath.

in the school of Rabbi Ishmael, where Israel's actions were interpreted so as to flatter them, not denigrate them.

We read in the Mekhilta that as a reward for the faith the people had in God, the Holy Spirit rested upon them and they sang the song, as it is written, "And they believed in the Lord. . . . Then Moses and the people Israel sang" (Exodus 14:31–15:1).[62] It is clear that this exposition corresponds to the views of Rabbi Ishmael. According to Rabbi Akiva it was Moses who sang the entire song and the people simply followed him. Moses began, "I will sing unto the Lord . . ." and the people repeated the words, as is our custom in reciting Hallel in the synagogue.[63] But Rabbi Nehemiah said, "The Holy Spirit descended on Israel, and they sang the song as a person who reads the Shema."[64] "Moses began each verse, and the people completed it after him."[51] [65]

Did Israel believe, or not? The students of Rabbi Akiva themselves disagreed on this. Rabbi Meir proposed this version: When the tribes of Israel stood at the sea, each tribe said, "We will go down first." While they were wrangling, the tribe of Benjamin jumped into the sea first. Rabbi Judah proposed a somewhat different version: When they stood at the sea, one tribe said, "We will not go down first," while another said, "We will not go down first." While they were arguing, Nahshon ben Aminadab[52] jumped into the sea as the waves came over him.[66]

According to the version preserved by the Gaon of Vilna,[53] Rabbi Akiva also held that each tribe said "we will not go down first." We also find in a midrash this statement by Rabbi Akiva: "The people Israel were about to enter the sea but turned back, fearful that the waters would overwhelm them. The tribe of Benjamin, however, persisted in going ahead, whereupon the tribe of Judah pelted them with stones. It was then that Nahshon jumped into the sea and sanctified God's name in the sight of all the people."[67] [54]

---

[62] MI Beshalah 6 (end) 1.   [63] MI Shirata 1.   [64] MI Shirata 1; MSY, p. 72.
[65] Tosefta Sotah 6:2.   [66] MI Beshalah 5.
[67] PRE 42; Lieberman, *Tosefta Kifeshuta*, Berakhot, p. 70.

---

[51] According to Rabbi Akiva, all the words of the Song of the Sea were initiated by Moses, and the people repeated after him. According to Rabbi Nehemiah (of the school of Rabbi Ishmael), the people were also inspired and came up with the second half of each verse on their own. These views are cited here for their bearing on the question, whether humans can achieve merit on their own. In chapter 28 ("Did the Holy Spirit Rest Only On Moses?"), the same views will be cited in connection with a different question, namely, the respective roles of God and human beings in the composition of the Torah. This is one example of how the topics of volume 2 of the original *TMH* (the process of revelation) are organically related to those of volume 1 (the nature of the divine–human relationship in general).

[52] The chieftain of the tribe of Judah.

[53] Rabbi Elijah "the Gaon" of Vilna, eighteenth-century talmudic scholar and intellectual exemplar.

[54] The version Heschel cites from Pirke de-Rabbi Eliezer seems to strive for an artificial harmonization of the contending views, whether the people en masse or a lone individual had the faith to

Rabbi Akiva was a man of various temperaments. He extolled the potential of humanity, while judging actual human achievement harshly. His vital powers had their source in a heart full of love and compassion, yet he said, "It is not the business of the law to show mercy."[68] He taught that man was so exalted that if it were not for his sin he would have seen the likeness of God. His enduring message was: the central doctrine of Torah is contained in the verse, "You shall love your neighbor as yourself" (Leviticus 19:18).

Yet the same Rabbi Akiva declared: "The generation of the wilderness will not be vindicated in the divine court of justice—they will have no share in the world to come." This harsh judgment of Rabbi Akiva (also by Rabbi Judah the Patriarch) was rejected by the majority of Sages who ascribed great merit to the people of that generation. Rabbi Eliezer said: They have a share in the world to come.[69] Commenting on the verse "Happy are they whose way is blameless" (Psalm 119:1), our Sages said this refers to the generation of the wilderness, who were blameless and pious.[70] Rabbi Eliezer expounded: "Bring in my devotees, who have made a covenant with Me over sacrifice" (Psalm 50:5)—this teaches us that Israel accepted the Torah wholeheartedly.[71]

In the school of Rabbi Akiva it was taught that the people accepted the Torah as a result of threats and coercion. When Scripture says, "They stood at the very foot[55] of the mountain" (Exodus 19:17), it means that God inverted the mountain over their heads like a huge tank and said, "If you accept my Torah all will be well; if not this will be your burial place."[72]

According to Rabbi Ishmael, Israel accepted the Torah voluntarily. When the people gave precedence to "we will do" over "we will obey,"[56] a divine voice was heard to say, "O, My children, who revealed this secret to you, which only the angels know how to use?"[73] Similarly, in the Mekhilta there is this comment on the verse "the people replied in unison" (Exodus 19:8)—it was not said hypocritically, nor did they consult with each other, but all of them made up their mind alike.[74] So Rabbi [Judah the Patriarch] declared: "This is told in praise of the people that when they stood at

---

[68] In other words, do not bend the letter of the law (of inheritance, etc.) to show favoritism to the needy; the law is the law (Mishnah Ketubot 9:2–3; see Exodus 23:3, and Targum Onkelos on that verse).
[69] Mishnah Sanhedrin 10:4.   [70] Midrash on Psalms 119:1.   [71] Midrash on Psalms 119:1, 4.
[72] MSY, p. 143; BT Shabbat 88a.   [73] BT Shabbat 88a.   [74] MI Bahodesh 2.

---

take the initiative to cross the sea. This harmonizing version seems to blur Heschel's question rather than shed additional light on it.

[55] Be-tahtit ha-har, which can also be understood literally, "underneath the mountain," that is, with the mountain directly over them.

[56] The reference is to Exodus 24:7 ("all that the Lord has spoken we will do and obey"). Tradition considered this to be the moment of greatest faith and devotion on the part of Israel, especially since the Hebrew can be read to mean "we will do and we will listen"; that is, the commitment to obey came even before they heard all of the instructions, so great was their faith in the goodness and justice of God.

Mount Sinai they were all of one mind, to accept the Kingship of God with rejoicing."[75]

The Sages who believed that the people of the wilderness generation possessed little faith interpreted the verse "we will do and obey" in a manner disparaging to the people. This is how they saw it:

> We find Israel standing at Mount Sinai trying to deceive God. They did so by uttering the words "we will do and obey," thus winning God over to their side, as the verse indicates, "O, would that they were of this mind always to fear Me" (Deuteronomy 5:26). Does this mean that it is possible that God does not know when He is being deceived? Not so. We read in Scripture, "Yet they deceived Him with their speech, lied to Him with their words; their hearts were inconstant toward Him; they were untrue to His covenant" (Psalm 78:36–37).[57] Nevertheless, knowing all this, we read, "He is compassionate, forgiving iniquity and will not destroy" (Psalm 78:38).[76]

Rabbi Akiva even went so far as to say that Moses himself did not possess perfect faith. At times he spoke as if he did not believe that God could provide the people in the wilderness with their needs. He was thereby guilty of profaning God's name in private, though Scripture covered up for him. On this subject, Rabbi Akiva's ardent disciple Rabbi Simeon bar Yohai sharply disagreed with his teacher. "God forbid that this should even enter that righteous man's mind! Can you conceive that Moses, of whom God said, 'Not so Moses, he is the most trusted of all my servants' (Numbers 12:7) should say that God cannot provide for us and for our cattle?"[77]

Rabbi Ishmael had a different understanding of Moses' manner of speaking to God. For example, Scripture tells us that when Moses returned from his first mission to Pharaoh, he said to God, "Why have you dealt ill with this people? Why did You send me? Since I came to Pharaoh to speak in Your name . . . You have not delivered this people at all" (Exodus 5:22–23). Rabbi Ishmael did not see anything disrespectful in Moses' speech. He simply told God the facts, describing the situation exactly as it was.[58] Rabbi Akiva, however, insisted that Moses was reproaching[59] God and

---

[75] MI Bahodesh 5.   [76] Tosefta Bava Kamma 7:9.   [77] Tosefta Sotah 6:6.

---

[57] That is, God knew that He was being deceived by the people, for how else would David (the presumed author of the Psalms) have known this? God must have inspired him with the knowledge.

[58] This is consonant with Rabbi Ishmael's general outlook, that some things that happen in the world are simply God's decrees and not necessarily just. By contrast, Rabbi Akiva believed that everything that happens is for the good and that one should accept even sufferings in love; hence, by complaining vociferously about Israel's suffering in Egypt, Moses showed imperfect piety—as did Job (see below).

[59] "Was reproaching" *hitiah devarim kelapei ma'lah* (literally, "threw [plastered] words at Heaven"). We have come across this same phrase elsewhere: Rabbi Eleazar warned, "Do not reproach God, for 'Let a person not reproach God,' for a great man once did so, and he became lame." Who was that? Rabbi Levi. (See above, pp. 135–38, chapter 7, section "Who Is Like You, Who Sees the Humiliation of Your Children and Remains Silent?") At the very least, in the view of Rabbi Akiva and Rabbi

insinuating, "What do you care about those who are being immured in the build-ings?"[78] "What kind of Deliverer? What kind of Redeemer?"[79] That is why the Holy and Blessed One said to Moses, "I swear, by divine decree, that you will not enter Eretz Israel." Why was God so angry? Because Moses presumed to say, "Since I came to speak to Pharaoh in Your name it has worsened for this people." Rabbi Eleazar the Moda'ite objected to Rabbi Akiva's interpretation and said, "It is forbidden to think that this saintly man would speak in such fashion to God."[80] [60]

[78] Exodus Rabbah 3:9; 5:22.   [79] Midrash Haggadol on Exodus 5:23.
[80] MSY, p. 6

Eleazar ben Pedat, both Moses and Rabbi Levi (as well as Job) exceeded the boundaries of propriety in advocacy of a just cause. Rabbi Ishmael would probably have dissented in all these cases.

[60] And so, we end with a divergence on whether human faith and initiative can ever be sufficient to have a redeeming effect.

10

DUTIES OF THE HEART

Translator's Introduction

In this chapter Heschel asks: How did Rabbi Ishmael and Rabbi Akiva interpret the commands, to "love" God and to "cleave" to God? This question is at the heart of the divine–human relationship. Their answers flow from their different conceptions of God (discussed in chapters 4–7) and of human self-sufficiency (discussed in the previous chapter).

For Rabbi Ishmael, God is majestic and remote, and humans are more or less able to achieve a good record on their own, through mitzvot and repentance. To take the notion of "loving God" literally, then, is somewhat offensive to the divine dignity and not necessary from the human side. It is therefore to be understood symbolically. We have our marching orders, and we show loyalty to God by carrying them out. We do not aspire to look God directly in the face. Rather, our impulse to religious communion is channeled into the social-ethical sphere. We cleave to God by doing God's work on earth, by caring for our fellow creatures.

Rabbi Akiva conceived of God with a more human face and conceived of humans as being needier. The imperative to "love" and "cleave" to God comes directly to fill the void and sense of inadequacy depicted as the Akivan view in the last chapter. Even though we human mortals are inadequate and unworthy, God is ever near and approachable, the Lover of the Song of Songs seeking us, His beloved. Rabbi Akiva had no problem understanding the notions of "loving" and "cleaving" in a direct, literal sense. The personal interplay between God and the individual was key to Akivan spirituality. It will lead us ultimately to the mystical quest (discussed in chapters 15–16).

Heschel obviously valued both approaches. His lifelong pursuit of social justice followed the Ishmaelian view that love of God must be expressed by doing God's work in this world. But his studies of the phenomenology of prophetic experience, of Hasidism, of prayer, and of rabbinic theology sought to see the divine–human encounter as a reality through which God meets every one of us directly on a personal level.

Heschel's title for this chapter, "Duties of the Heart," is the standard Hebrew title of a classic philosophical and moral work of the eleventh century by the Spanish Rabbi Bahya ibn Pakuda. Bahya's work contrasts the "duties of the heart" with the "duties of the limbs," that is, with those performative mitzvot that we do with our physical being. One can habituate one's physical self to do certain things that are obligatory and even to avoid and shun those things that are prohibited. But it is the heart, the intellect, the psyche that sets human beings apart from the rest of creation, and it is therefore only the completion of the "duties of the limbs" with the "duties of the heart" that truly fulfills human obligations to God. Love, trust, belief, and other emotional affects are not only part of religion, according to Bahya—they are the essence of religion. This is much like what Heschel will be attributing here to Akiva: the idea that mitzvot are obligatory and important but are ultimately a means to generate love for God, the true aim of religion. The Ishmaelian view, by contrast, saw exhortations of love in the Bible as means toward the real aim, which was good and right living, in the realm of action.

This, too, is a matter Heschel considered to be of great relevance to the age in which he lived. In the post-emancipation period, reformers had defined Judaism in terms of faith, but had removed so many of the "duties of the limbs." In reaction (Heschel would have said "overreaction"), counter-reformers had stressed the performance of mitzvot in all their fine details to an excessive degree, often to the exclusion of the emotional affect that should undergird it. Once again, Heschel's real agenda is the coaxing of an authentic and spiritually productive synthesis.

Cleaving to God (*Devekut*)

"**A**ND YOU WHO CLEAVE to the Lord your God are alive, all of you this day" (Deuteronomy 4:4). "Love the Lord your God; walk in His ways and cleave to Him" (Deuteronomy 11:22). "And you shall love the Lord your God with all your heart" (Deuteronomy 6:5). How did the Sages understand the ideals of loving and cleaving to God?

In the plain literal sense, "cleaving to God" means attaching oneself to the Shekhinah. That is apparently how Rabbi Akiva took it. But Rabbi Ishmael's school tried to interpret texts that in their view did not accord sufficient dignity to God in more commonsense terms. Since it did not seem reasonable to them that humans could actually have direct communion with the Shekhinah, they divorced this verse from its literal sense. We therefore find two understandings of this mitzvah, one ethical (expressed in deed), and one religious-spiritual (expressed in personal attachment to God). The first transfers the demand from the human–divine relationship to the social realm. The second takes it in its literal sense, as an obligation of the heart, a mitzvah between the individual and God.

In the school of Rabbi Ishmael, the scholars expressed surprise at the literal interpretation of the verse "to cleave to Him." They asked, "How is it possible for man to rise heavenward and to cleave to fire? Does not Scripture say, 'The Lord your God is a consuming fire' (Deuteronomy 4:24); or 'His throne was fiery flames' (Daniel 7:9)? It can only mean that we are commanded to cleave to the Sages and their disciples."[1]

---

[1] Sifre Ekev 49.

In this spirit, it was taught that cleaving to God means giving one's daughter in marriage to a scholar, engaging in trade in behalf of scholars, or enabling scholars to benefit from one's property. Scripture considers these as cleaving to the Divinity.[1] 2

In like manner, they expounded the verse "After the Lord your God you shall walk" (Deuteronomy 13:5)—"Who can possibly walk in His ways? Is it not written, 'The Lord is in the whirlwind and the storm is His way' (Nahum 1:3); or, 'Your way is in the sea and Your paths in the great waters' (Psalm 77:20)? Moses said to them, this is not what I told you. Rather, His ways are ways of compassion and truth, as it is written, 'All God's ways are mercy and truth'" (Psalm 25:10).3

This interpretation is to be found also in the teaching of Rabbi Hama ben Rabbi Hanina,[2] who asks in the style of Rabbi Ishmael: "The verse says, 'You shall follow the Lord your God' (Deuteronomy 13:5). Is it possible for man to follow Divinity? It means, therefore, that man must imitate the divine attributes of the Holy and Blessed One. Even as He clothes the naked, so shall you do likewise; even as He visits the sick, so shall you, etc.[3] 4

Rabbi Akiva, in contrast, understood the term *devekut* ("cleaving") as an inner, spiritual experience. He rejected the notion that cleaving to God means to walk in the ways of compassion and truth. "When one attaches oneself to that which is impure," he taught, "an impure spirit rests upon him; but when one cleaves to the Shekhinah, a holy spirit rests upon him."5 In harmony with this teaching, the school of Rabbi Akiva expounded the verse, "Unto Him shall you cleave" (Deuteronomy 13:5), "separate yourself from idolatry and cleave to God."6

There were other Sages who followed this line of interpretation. The Babylonian Amora Rav gave this exposition of the verse "And you who cleave to the Lord your God" (Deuteronomy 4:4): "It may be compared to two dates that are attached one to

---

2 BT Ketubot 111b; Tanhuma Matot 1; Numbers Rabbah 22:1.
3 Midrash on Psalms 25:11; MTD, p. 64.
4 BT Sotah 14a. Rabbi Hama adds that God buries the dead, for example, Moses. But Rabbi Ishmael held that Moses buried himself. See Sifre Naso 32.
5 BT Sanhedrin 65b; MTD, p. 110; Sifre Shofetim 173.
6 Sifre Re'eh 85.

---

[1] Both Rabbi Ishmael and Rabbi Akiva connected love of God with ethical conduct, but with different emphases. Rabbi Ishmael cannot conceive of an act of loving God apart from ethics. Our ethical conduct is itself the one and only expression of our love for God. For Rabbi Akiva, love of God is separate, mystical, and primary, but flows into ethical conduct as its consequence.

[2] Second-generation Amora, Land of Israel.

[3] That God clothes the naked is learned from what Genesis 3:21 reports about God making leather garments for the unclad Adam and Eve. That God visits the sick is an inference: at the end of Genesis 17, it is reported that Abraham circumcised himself at an advanced age, and the beginning of chapter 18 reports that three men, who obviously had the authority to speak in God's name, came to Abraham's tent as he was sitting near the entrance. The implication? Abraham was sitting in recuperation from his surgery, and God sent emissaries to visit him in his sickness.

the other."[7] The Amora of the Land of Israel Rabbi Simeon ben Lakish, understood *devekut* to mean joining one's heart and soul with the Divine. He said, "With three terms of endearment God manifested His love to the people of Israel: *Devekah* ("cleaving"), *Hashikah* ("yearning"), *Hafitzah* ("desiring"). Cleaving, in the verse 'you who cleave to the Lord your God'"[8] (Deuteronomy 4:4).

In a rather startling midrash, in the spirit of Rabbi Akiva's teaching, Israel's love for God is compared to the love of Shechem for Dinah, Jacob's daughter. "It is written, 'And Shechem loved the maiden' (Genesis 34:3). We only realize the extent of his love when we learn that he gave his life for her. That is the true meaning of love. Of Shechem we read, 'And his soul cleaved to Dinah, daughter of Jacob' (Genesis 34:3). Now of Israel the verse says, "'And you who cleave to the Lord your God. . . .'"[9] Our Sages compared Israel's cleaving to the Holy and Blessed One to Shechem's cleaving to Dinah.

The individual's close identification with God is emphasized in Rabbi Akiva's teaching that he who spills another man's blood is deemed by Scripture to have diminished the Divine image.[10] In his school they gave this homily on the verse "I shall walk in your midst" (Leviticus 26:12): "This may be compared to a king who went for a stroll in the garden with his tenant. The tenant sought to hide himself and the king asked, 'Why are you hiding from me? I am just like you.' So, too, will the Holy and Blessed One stroll with the righteous in the Garden of Eden in time to come. The righteous will be frightened in His presence, and the Holy and Blessed One will say, 'Why are you frightened of Me? I am just like you!'"[11]

In sum, we see that two views became crystallized in the course of time on the subject of what path one must follow to become Godlike. One view held that it was a matter of the heart and that one must follow the path of faith. The other view maintained that it was a matter of ethical conduct and that one must follow the path of good deeds. Rabbi Joshua ben Levi expressed the view of many of his colleagues when he said, "Whoever has faith in God will merit becoming like Him, as it is written, 'Blessed is the man who trusts in God and whose trust God is' (Jeremiah 17:7)."[12] The opposite view is found in the statement of Rabbi Levi bar Lahma,[4] who taught, "The Holy and Blessed One said, if you fulfill My commandments you will become like Me."[13] This promise of achieving godliness is not reserved for some distant future

---

[7] BT Sanhedrin 64a. See also BT Yoma 54a: "Rabbi Kattina said: When Israel went up on pilgrimage, the curtain would be removed and they would see the two cherubim intertwined, and they would be told, 'See, you are as beloved to God as the love of man and woman!'"

[8] Genesis Rabbah 80:7.

[9] TB Vayyishlah 20.

[10] Genesis Rabbah 34:14; compare Avot 3:14.

[11] Sifra Behukotai 111b.

[12] Deuteronomy Rabbah 5:9.

[13] See Deuteronomy Rabbah, ed. Lieberman, p. xviii.

---

[4] Third-generation Amora, Land of Israel (textual variant has "Levi bar Hama").

date. It can be fulfilled now. The verse reads, "My soul thirsts for God" (Psalm 42:3). "If you can recapture the state of godliness that you achieved at Sinai, which led me to say of you, 'I thought you were Godlike, children of the Most High' (Psalm 82:6); if you will clothe yourselves in the garment of godliness worn by Jacob, then, *veyitten lekha ha-elohim* (Genesis 27:28) read not, 'God will grant you,' but 'He will grant you godliness.'"[5] 14

Love of God (*Ahavah*)

The Torah teaches, "You shall love the Lord your God" (Deuteronomy 6:5). The simple meaning of the command is that the love of God is the longing of the soul for its Creator. It is a matter of the heart. So Rabbi Akiva understood it and taught it. Rabbi Ishmael, as in his interpretation of *devekut* ("cleaving"), explained love as the attribute of those who perform good deeds. There are two ways of observing a mitzvah: to perform it out of fear, or to perform it out of love. When we are instructed, "You shall love the Lord your God," we are commanded to act out of love. It also means that we must make God beloved by His creatures, as father Abraham did when he converted people and "brought them under the wings of the Shekhinah."[6] 15 Rabbi [Judah the Patriarch] interpreted the verse, "And these words which I command you this day shall be upon your heart" as follows: "Take these words to heart, thereby you will recognize your Creator and you will cleave to His ways."16

The school of Rabbi Ishmael extended this thought further, namely: through you the name of God will become beloved. How? When a person reads and studies Scripture, when his conversation with people is pleasant, when his business in the marketplace is fair and his transactions are honest, people will say about him: "How fortunate is he who studied Torah; how blessed are his father and teacher who taught him Torah."

Rabbi Ishmael, a man of well-balanced judgment, did not allow himself to be swept away by his emotions. To him the vital center of religion is not spiritual love

---

14 YS Psalms 741 (on Psalm 42).   15 Sifre Va'ethanan 32.   16 Sifre Va'ethanan 33.

---

[5] In the conventional interpretation of this verse, *elohim* (God/godliness) is the subject of the verb "to give." In the midrashic interpretation, the subject–object relationship is reversed: *elohim* (godliness) is the object, and the subject "He" (God) is understood.

[6] The notion that Abraham and Sarah made converts to monotheism in Mesopotamia is derived from a nonidiomatic reading of Genesis 12:5, which tells us that Abram and Sarai set out for the land of Canaan with "all the wealth that they had amassed, and the persons that they had acquired in Haran." Now the last phrase apparently means members born into the family (though not to them directly; Sarai was, after all, barren) and/or male and female servants whom they acquired. However, the Hebrew phrase could also be rendered as "the souls that they made in Haran," and it is this reading that led some Rabbis to conclude that they "made souls," that is, converted pagans, in Haran.

but good deeds. To cleave to God, to love God, means to walk in His ways. Man's relationship to God is a distant one. God is in the heavens and you are on earth. Therefore, let your words about God be few, your deeds many. Rabbi Akiva, a man whose soul longed for a vision of God and communion with Him, emphasized man's close, intimate relationship with God. He said of himself, "I love Him with all my heart and with all my possessions. As for loving God with all my soul, it has not been examined yet."[17]

These differing views on the love of God are clearly illustrated in their interpretation of the death of Aaron's two sons, Nadab and Abihu. Scripture says, "Now Aaron's sons, Nadab and Abihu, each took his fire-pan, put fire in it, and laid incense on it; and they offered before the Lord alien fire, which He had not enjoined upon them. And fire came forth from the Lord and consumed them, and thus they died at the instance of the Lord" (Leviticus 10:1-2). The cause of death would seem to be that they had placed "alien fire" on the altar, something that God had not enjoined them to do. According to Rabbi Akiva, this means they took fire from the stove in their home and not from the holy fire of the altar.[18] The phrase "which He had not enjoined upon them" means that they took this action independently without consulting Moses, their teacher.[7] [19]

This event was understood differently in the school of Rabbi Ishmael. They described it as follows: "The Torah says, 'and a fire came forth from the Lord.' When the people of Israel beheld a new fire descending from above, consuming the burnt offering and the fats, they fell upon their faces and praised heaven. Nadab and Abihu, too, when they saw the new fire, in their excitement "each took his firepan" and decided to heap love upon love. It was their intense fervor and excessive love that brought this tragedy upon them. Love can engender a frenzy that will lead one from the straight path."[20] Rabbi Ishmael could find no words of praise for their zeal and enthusiasm. As a matter of fact, he interpreted the term "alien fire" to mean they had entered the sanctuary in a state of intoxication, the fire caused by the intoxicating heat of wine. Their joyous exuberance derived from such "alien fire."[21]

Rabbi Akiva thought deeply about matters in the domain of the heart. He demanded unconditional faith, without hesitations or vacillations. He even judged

[17] PT Berakhot 9:7, 14b.
[18] Leviticus Rabbah 20:8; see note of Margaliot, p. 461.
[19] Midrash Haggadol on Leviticus, p. 187.
[20] Sifra Shemini 45c (Mekhilta Demiluim 32).
[21] Malbim, Ha-Torah veha-Mitzvah on Leviticus 10:1.

[7] According to the sources Heschel cites, both Rabbi Akiva and Rabbi Ishmael viewed Nadab and Abihu's sin as a tragic error, not a malicious rebellion against God. Rabbi Ishmael saw it as an excess of enthusiasm, welling over from the enthusiasm of the people for the consecration of the Sanctuary (Leviticus 9:24). Rabbi Akiva could not agree with this interpretation, since for him enthusiasm in the service of the Lord was good and knew no excess. He was therefore driven to interpret "alien fire" in a more technical, ritualistic sense.

Moses harshly when he discovered that the faith of this faithful shepherd was not perfect. Furthermore, he practiced what he preached.[8] He probed deeply and searched his own soul to learn whether his love of God was wholehearted. He learned that he was able to demonstrate his unquestioning faith and his unconditional love of God, at the time of his supreme testing, when the Roman authorities led him to his martyrdom, scraping his flesh with iron combs.[22] [9]

Yet the soul of Rabbi Akiva was seized with fear and trembling at the same time that there burned in his heart a limitless love of God. Could these contradictory emotions reside in the same person? Our Sages recognized this paradox. One verse teaches us, "You shall love the Lord your God," and another teaches, "You shall fear the Lord your God" (Deuteronomy 10:20).[10] They commented as follows: "There can be no love where there is fear; there can be no fear where there is love. There is one exception—man's relationship to God. Only God can stir in man love and fear at the same time."[23] Rabbi Judah ben Tema[11] taught: "Love God and fear God; tremble and rejoice in His commandments."[24] At the beginning of Seder Eliyahu Rabbah we read, "My fear flows from my joy, and my joy from my fear. But my love transcends them both."[25]

The sayings of the Sages concerning God's love of Israel are more numerous than those about Israel's love of God. We see revealed in this a basic characteristic of the thought and belief of Israel. Scripture says, "But they that love Him are as the sun when it rises in its strength" (Judges 5:31). Rabbi Simeon bar Yohai commented, "Who is greater? He who loves the King or he whom the King loves? It is clearly he whom the King loves, as it is written, 'And He loves the stranger.'"[26]

My Beloved Is Mine and I Am His

The earliest Sages felt that there were many passages in the Song of Songs that were difficult to accept. A later report says, "At first, the Sages declared that the books of

[22] PT Berakhot 14b.   [23] Sifre Va'ethanan 32.
[24] ARN A 41.   [25] SER 3.   [26] MI Nezikin 18.

---

[8] The Hebrew here, *na'eh doresh ve-na'eh mekayyem* is the very phrase used in its negative form of Akiva's colleague Simeon ben Azzai, who was criticized for not practicing what he preached when he taught that failing to have and raise children was tantamount to a diminution of the divine image in the world. Ben Azzai was a bachelor. Now the fact that ben Azzai was said *not* to practice what he preaches, and Akiva is described otherwise here, is Heschel's subtle way of reminding us again of the hegemony that Akiva enjoyed with respect to even his most distinguished contemporaries and colleagues.

[9] Rabbi Akiva's martyrdom is clearly one of the touchstones of Heschel's portrait of him, uniting as it does the themes of suffering, extreme devotion to Torah, and loving God "even if God should take your soul." See chapters 7–8 above.

[10] We have departed from the NJV translation here in order to accentuate that which is the focus of the midrash on the two verses taken together, namely, the uneasy juxtaposition of love and fear.

[11] Tanna of uncertain date.

Proverbs, Song of Songs, and Ecclesiastes were to be hidden from the public, since they were only parables and do not belong in Sacred Writings. These books lay hidden from the public until the Members of the Great Assembly interpreted them to everyone's satisfaction."[27] When the Mishnah was edited, it stated: "Song of Songs and Ecclesiastes make the hands unclean."[12] Rabbi Judah, disciple of Rabbi Akiva said, "Song of Songs renders the hands unclean, but the status of Ecclesiastes is still in dispute." Rabbi Yose, however, who was close to the views of Rabbi Ishmael in many matters, declared, "Ecclesiastes does not render the hands unclean, but the status of Song of Songs is still in dispute." Whereupon Rabbi Akiva rose and said, "Heaven forbid! No one in the household of Israel ever dared dispute the status of Song of Songs. The whole world was not as worthy of being created as on the day in which Song of Songs was given to Israel. For all of Writings are sacred, but Song of Songs is the most sacred of all."[28]

The following remarkable statement is preserved: "Rabbi Akiva said, 'If nothing had been given to us of Torah but the Song of Songs it would have been a sufficient guide for human conduct.'"[13] [29] A tale is told of Rabbi Akiva that he was once expounding on Song of Songs and when he came to the verse "Let him kiss me with the kisses of his mouth," Rabban Gamaliel wept. His disciples asked, "Why are you weeping?" and he answered, "Because it is forbidden to expound on the Vision of the Chariot even if only one disciple is present."[14] [30] This raises the interesting question: Did Rabbi Akiva interpret the Song of Songs as though it were a chapter in the Vision of the Chariot?[15] [31]

---

[27] ARN A 1.   [28] Mishnah Yadayim 3:5.
[29] Song of Songs Zuta 1:1 (ed. Buber, p. 4).
[30] In a Yemenite manuscript cited in *Festschrift zum achtzigsten Geburtstag Moritz Steinschneider* (Leipzig, 1896; reprint, Jerusalem: Makor, 1970), 52. See also Zohar, Terumah, 144a on the esoteric significance of the Song of Songs.
[31] See Lieberman, *Midreshei Teiman*, 14.

---

[12] It is clear from the discussion in Mishnah Yadayim that the Rabbis regarded sacred literature as "making the hands unclean," while secular books did not. The reasons are not stated. One explanation is that they wished to establish a conceptual and practical boundary between the domains of sacred study and food handling. Food consecrated for the priests (terumah) had to be kept ritually pure. And other pietists in the rabbinic community, even if they were not priests, often voluntarily took on the same eating restrictions that the priests observed. By storing food and scrolls separately, they probably protected the latter against the encroachments of rodents.

[13] This encomium of the Song of Songs seems to declare again Rabbi Akiva's priority of the religious over the ethical. First comes the divine–human relationship, conceived of as a love affair. If we truly love God as the Song of Songs tells us, we cannot fail to behave properly as a result. Ethics will flow naturally and inevitably as a consequence from the true love of God. This is the opposite of Rabbi Ishmael's emphasis, as articulated above.

[14] The rule to which Rabban Gamaliel was referring is given in Mishnah Hagigah 2:1.

[15] The implication would be that the Song of Songs speaks allegorically not merely of the historic relationship between God and Israel but also of the mystical vision of God (for which the Rabbis saw

What did Rabbi Akiva perceive in the Song of Songs that moved him to exalt and extol the scroll of Song of Songs so extravagantly? You cannot understand him unless you grasp that there is more to his words than meets the eye. His one statement divides into two:[16] (1) "The whole world was not as worthy of being created as on the day in which the Song of Songs was given." The congregation of Israel is compared to a bride, and the Holy and Blessed One to her lover. The bride leans on her lover, and the lover is bound to her by passionate love. (2) "For all of Writings are sacred, but Song of Songs is the most sacred of all." That is, all good acts are holy, but the love of God is the holy of holies. Here Rabbi Akiva reveals the secret of his heart's meditation, of his deep longing for God. The whole world was never as worthy as it was when love was revealed. And the Song of Songs is the parable about the love between the congregation of Israel and the Holy and Blessed One.[32] [17]

The love of God burned in the heart of Rabbi Akiva like an enkindling flame. With such an incandescent love, he longed all his days to die a martyr for the sanctification of God's name. And just as he was to die passionately, so did he live passionately. He lived at a time when the people of his generation "were full of sorrow, oppressed, ruined, and driven to madness from all the suffering that had befallen them."[33] The Psalmist declared: "For Your sake, we were killed all day; we were considered as sheep for the slaughter" (Psalm 44:23). Nevertheless, they did not rebel because of their suffering, nor did they reject their covenant with God. They all had the option of assimilation among the nations and enjoying a peaceful life of calm and security. How can you account for such a faith?

The answer is given in a midrashic poem by Rabbi Akiva in which he reveals the mystery of Israel's faith. In this poem our eyes behold a transcendent holiness. Its very stillness speaks its praise.

---

[32] This view preceded Rabbi Akiva. See Song of Songs Rabbah 1:12: "They brought this book out of them from the Exile and studied it, so when they sinned with the golden calf, it was preceded by the instructions for the Sanctuary."

[33] BT Yevamot 47a.

Ezekiel's vision of the Divine Chariot in Ezekiel 1 as the prototype). Maimonides would later use the phrase "the work of the Chariot" as a synonym for "metaphysics," that is, the study of that which transcends the world of physics.

[16] Here again Heschel is using a rabbinic phrase that he expects his readership to be familiar with. It is said of God's words, on the basis of Psalm 62, "One thing God has spoken, two things have I heard." The phrase is intended to suggest that there is more hidden in words of Torah than is there on the surface—there is at least double the meaning that one would immediately see in the words of God. See chapter 2 for a deeper exposition of this idea. But here Heschel cleverly applies the phrase to the words of Akiva himself, for it was Akiva who was, in his scheme, the champion of the idea that there are untold hidden layers of meaning in Scripture.

[17] Heschel adds: Who composed the Song of Songs? Many Sages attributed it to King Solomon, taking literally the biblical superscription—"A Song of Songs, which is Solomon's." But Rashi follows the Yalkut and Midrash Rabbah in interpreting "Shelomoh—the Master of Peace"; that is, God Himself composed it.

"This is my God and I will glorify Him." (Exodus 15:2)

I shall speak the praise of the One Who spoke and the world came into being,
    in the presence of the nations of the world.

For the nations ask Israel: "What is your beloved more than any other that
    you adjure us?" (Song of Songs 5:9)—

That you die for His sake; that you allow yourselves to be killed for His sake?[18]

Why, you are beautiful and heroic—come and mingle with us!

And Israel answers the nations of the world: Do you recognize Him?

Let us recount His praises to you.

"My beloved is fair and ruddy . . . his head is the finest gold;

. . . This is my beloved, this is my friend." (Song of Songs 5:10, 11, 16)

When the nations hear Israel's praise of the One Who spoke and the world
    came into being, they say:

Let us go with them.

"Where has your beloved gone . . . where has your beloved turned that we
    may seek him with you?" (Song of Songs 6:1)

The people of Israel answer: You have no part in Him, "My beloved is mine,
    and I am His" (Song of Songs 2:16); "I am my beloved's and my beloved
    is mine." (Song of Songs 6:3)[34]

One aspect of this poem displays Rabbi Akiva's strength, another his weakness. In his time, the relationship between Jews and Gentiles was one of enmity, both covert and overt. Many of Israel's neighbors sided with Rome and helped her to quell the Bar Kokhba revolt. Indeed, the people of Israel were "full of sorrows, oppressed, and driven to madness. Rabbi Akiva's remark, "you have no part in Him," was made in a mood of depression. His strength failed him[19] and the vision of the prophets escaped him: "Many peoples shall go up and say, Let us go up to the Mountain of the Lord, to the house of the God of Jacob; and he will teach us of His ways and we will walk in His paths" (Isaiah 2:3); or, "In that day shall Israel be the third with Egypt and Assyria, a blessing in the midst of the earth; for the Lord of Hosts has blessed him saying: blessed be Egypt my people and Assyria the work of My hands and Israel Mine inheritance" (Isaiah 19:24-25).

Rabbi Akiva's harsh utterance must be taken together with his extremely severe

---

[34] MI Shirata 3. See also BT Hagigah 16a, according to which Rabbi Akiva interpreted the passage "My beloved is fair and ruddy" referring to God, and was thus saved.

---

[18] A play on al ken 'alamot ahevukha, "therefore do maidens love you" (Song of Songs 1:3), revocalizing 'alamot ("maidens") as 'al mot (or emending it to 'ad mot, "unto death")—"therefore they love you unto death." See the beginning of chapter 8.

[19] As the sequel will show, Heschel is here reacting to the extreme particularism and exclusivity that are evident in these lyrics attributed to Akiva, in contrast to the generous universalism of some of the prophets of Israel. Here Heschel the admirer of the prophets and Heschel the admirer of the Rabbis encounter each other.

utterances about his own people. Thus, he declared "The generation of the desert has no share in the world to come and they will not appear in Judgment Day." Or, "The ten tribes will never return to the fold of Israel."[20] 35 However, Rabbi Johanan's comment on Rabbi Akiva's judgment concerning the generation of the desert, applies also to his opinion regarding the nations of the world. He said, "Rabbi Akiva here abandoned his customary generosity."36

It is a well-established principle in the Torah that water transforms man from a state of impurity to a state of purity. Rabbi Johanan ben Zakkai taught: "I swear that a corpse does not cause impurity and that water (i.e., the water containing the red cow's ashes) does not purify, but such is the decree of the One who is the King of Kings of Kings."[21] 37 To this Rabbi Akiva added: There are times when man achieves a state of purity without any outside help; the Holy and Blessed One, Himself, in all His glory, removes the filth from him. He said, "How fortunate are you, O Israel . . . Who purifies you? It is our Father in Heaven, as it is written, 'And I will pour pure water over you, and you shall be purified' (Ezekiel 36:25). It is further written, 'The Lord is the hope (mikveh[22])—of Israel' (Jeremiah 17:13). Even as the mikveh—the pool of water—purifies those who are impure, so does the Holy and Blessed One purify Israel."38 This homily is a poem of love for the people Israel whose God is close to them, a most precious song about the intimate relationship between the Holy and Blessed One and the congregation of Israel. What a lofty concept!

The school of Rabbi Ishmael also dealt in depth with the mystery of purification but were satisfied with a much more modest concept. They taught: the words of Torah are compared to water. Just as water raises the status of the impure to purity, so too do the words of Torah.[23] 39

---

35 Mishnah Sanhedrin 10:3.   36 BT Sanhedrin 110b.   37 PRK 40b.
38 Mishnah Yoma 8:9.   39 Sifre Ekev 48.

---

[20] See pp. 175–79 above, "A Net Is Spread over All the Living." The argument here, on the surface, is that if Akiva was so harsh on his own people, then it is hardly surprising that he would be harsh on the nations that were persecuting his people and would be led to say, "You have no part in Him." However, it may be that Heschel is saying the reverse; that is, since Akiva has been known to say harsh things even about his own people, such rhetorical utterances ought to be taken with a grain of salt.

[21] The epithet "King of Kings of Kings," which sounds awkward in English, is a typical rabbinic appositive for God, quite common in Jewish liturgy ever since. It was apparently intended to one-up those earthly rulers (e.g., in Persia) who had taken to calling themselves "King of Kings."

[22] See above, chapter 9, n. [50].

[23] That is, the Torah is a means of creating purity among human beings. This is close to Rabbi Johanan's statement quoted in the previous paragraph, and also consistent with the Ishmaelian idea that the Torah is a tool given to human beings in order to help them live a life in keeping with God's will. It differs from the Akivan concept that the Torah is of divine character itself.

Mitzvot Dependent on the Heart

According to Rabbi Akiva's teachings, love and cleaving to God are matters given to the heart. Love is not an attribute of an action;[24] it is an action in its own right. Love is no means to some other act. On the contrary, acts are means to love. In Rabbi Akiva you will find an intoxication, involving all his powers, with the service of God and a cleaving to the divine that knows no bounds, even to the point of giving his life. According to the teaching of Rabbi Ishmael, however, love and cleaving to God are, in fact, means to righteous action. To love God means to act out of love; to cleave to God is to walk in God's paths. Rabbi Ishmael removed from love and cleaving all intangible characteristics and defined them as prescriptions for action.

It is interesting to note the reversal of roles between Rabbi Akiva and Rabbi Ishmael in regard to mitzvot linked to the heart.[25] Here the school of Rabbi Akiva insists on a strict literal interpretation: to love God and to cleave to Him mean exactly what they say. The school of Rabbi Ishmael, in this category of mitzvot, shies away from the literal interpretation; to love God and to cleave to Him mean to perform worthy deeds, to walk in His ways.

We see how these differing views are applied to the process of exegesis. The verse reads, "This is my God and I will glorify Him" (Exodus 15:2). How do you glorify God? Rabbi Ishmael sees it as a call to action and says, "Perform beautiful deeds before Him, . . . I will make myself attractive before Him with worthy acts; I will acquire a beautiful Lulav, a beautiful Sukkah, beautiful *Tzitzit* (fringes), beautiful Tefillin (phylacteries). Rabbi Akiva interpreted it literally, "Be expansive in speaking the praise and splendor of the One who spoke and the world came into being."[40]

Or consider the interpretation each gives to the commandment "You shall not covet" (Exodus 20:14). In Deuteronomy, we have the variant "You shall not crave . . ." (Deuteronomy 5:18). In the school of Rabbi Ishmael they made no distinction between the two expressions "covet" and "crave"; they have but one meaning. He who covets or craves in his heart but does not act upon it, is not guilty of any transgression. The Torah simply "said the same thing in two different ways."[41]

In the school of Rabbi Akiva a distinction was made between the two terms "covet" and "crave." They taught that craving is a matter of the heart while coveting involves

[40] Tractate Soferim 3:17 (p. 133); MI Shirata 3.
[41] See Sifre Naso 23.

---

[24] What Heschel has in mind here is the Ishmaelian idea that "loving God" means performing good acts lovingly (note the adverbial use).

[25] We have earlier pointed out that this is not really a reversal, for Ishmaelian "plain meaning" exegesis does not mean "literal exegesis." On the contrary, sometimes the plain meaning is precisely *not* a literal meaning. Thus, the fact that the Ishmaelian view on loving God is action oriented and not what loving a human being might mean, is not at all surprising.

action. By using both expressions the Torah teaches us that they are to be equated and the one who craves only in thought is as guilty of violating the commandment as one who performs the deed itself.[26]

The midrash probes more deeply into the subject of coveting. The question is raised, Is the person who expresses his coveting orally to be deemed guilty? The answer is found in the verse "You shall not covet the silver and gold on them [the idols] and take it for yourself" (Deuteronomy 7:25). Just as in this case he must take action before he is deemed guilty, so the one who covets only with words is not guilty until he performs an actual deed.[42]

In contrast, the school of Rabbi Akiva taught that "you shall not covet" and "you shall not crave" are two distinct commandments and one is deemed guilty of transgression for each one separately. When a person craves his neighbor's house, or wife, or furniture, or any other possession that he could acquire by purchase; once his heart has seduced him to crave it, he has thereby violated a scriptural prohibition. Craving is a matter of the heart alone, but when he goes about trying to buy that which he craves, pleading, begging, cajoling the owner, then he has transgressed both commandments, "You shall not crave" and "you shall not covet."[43]

This dispute was also carried over to the prohibition "You shall not commit adultery" (Exodus 20:13). According to the school of Rabbi Ishmael, it refers only to the act itself, whereas in the school of Rabbi Akiva it was taken as a warning against even contemplating such a sinful act.[44] An interesting midrash takes this thought further: How do we know that when one is eating from his own platter and imagines himself eating from his neighbor's platter, or one is drinking from his own cup and imagines himself drinking from his neighbor's cup,[27] that he is committing an act he has been forewarned about? We may derive it from the commandment "You shall not commit adultery."[28] [45]

---

[42] See Ibn Ezra on Deuteronomy 5:18; MI Bahodesh 8.

[43] Maimonides, *Mishneh Torah, Hilkhot Gezelah Va'avedah* [Laws of Theft and Loss] 1:10–11; *Sefer ha-Mitzvot* (ed. Lavin), p. 265.

[44] BT Niddah 13b.

[45] MSY, p. 153. Compare Matthew 5:28.

---

[26] Again, Rabbi Akiva is seen to diverge from the general principle that God "does not conjoin actions to evil intent," that is, does not project actions from intentions, so as to create a sanctionable combination of evil intent and bad act. Akiva, by contrast, countenances the idea that God will punish even evil intentions by themselves. See the note in chapter 9, n. [25].

[27] "Eating" and "drinking" are here euphemisms for marital relations.

[28] Thus, Akiva would condemn "adultery in the heart" as a punishable sin. Comparing this to the "antinomies" in Matthew 5, we find that this position is consistent with the stringent stance attributed there to Jesus on the matter of "adultery in the heart." On the other hand, it is interesting to note that whereas the antinomies declare that divorce may take place only on grounds of unchastity (a position taken by the school of Shammai), Rabbi Akiva takes an extraordinarily liberal position on what are grounds for divorce (see Mishnah Gittin 9:10).

The Sages discuss other transgressions that are linked not to direct actions but to inner emotions of the heart. The Torah says, "You shall not take vengeance nor bear a grudge" (Leviticus 19:18). In the school of Rabbi Akiva they asked: How far does this prohibition extend? If one says to another, "Lend me your scythe," and he refuses. The following day the latter says to the former, "Lend me your axe," and he replies, "I will not lend it to you, just as you would not lend me your scythe"—that is a violation of the law, "You shall not take vengeance."

How far does the prohibition "You shall not bear a grudge" extend? If one says to another, "Lend me your axe," and he refuses. The following day, the latter says, "Lend me your scythe" and the other replies, "Here it is, you can have it, for I am not like you who refused to lend me your axe"—that is a violation of the law, "You shall not bear a grudge." Even though he does not express his feelings of vengeance or bearing a grudge in so many words, he is deemed guilty, "For the Holy and Blessed One examines the heart and searches the secrets of the soul."[29] 46

In similar vein, the Sages of the school of Rabbi Akiva interpreted the verse "You shall not hate your kinsman in your heart" (Leviticus 19:17) to mean that it refers only to the hatred that is nurtured in one's heart and not to any overt acts such as cursing or beating or slapping him.[47]

According to this view, the prohibition against taking vengeance applies not only to inflicting pain or physical hurt on one's neighbor but to hurting the feelings of one's fellow man. Thus was it interpreted by Maimonides and by the author of *Sefer Ha-Hinukh*.[30] 48

Rabbi Akiva himself was a living example of this teaching. Rabbi Johanan ben Nuri[31] testified, "I call heaven and earth to witness that on more than five occasions, because of my complaints, I was the cause of Akiva being rebuked by Rabban Gamaliel in the academy in Yavneh. After each and every incident Akiva loved me more than ever, in keeping with the scriptural admonition, 'Do not reprove the scorner lest he hate you; reprove a wise man and he will love you.'"[49]

The Talmud relates that once when there was no rain in Israel, Rabbi Eliezer ben Hyrcanus offered twenty-four blessings in praise of God, but was not answered. Rabbi Akiva approached the Ark after him and prayed, "Our Father, our King, we have no

---

46 Sifra Kedoshim 89b.
47 Sifra Kedoshim 89a.
48 See *Mishneh Torah* I, *Hilkhot De'ot* [Laws Concerning Character] 7:7, and *Sefer Ha-Hinukh* 241.
49 Sifre Deuteronomy 1.

---

[29] This is a fine appreciation of the stratagems of interpersonal retaliation! In a simple tit-for-tat, Reuben refuses to grant Simon a favor because of Simon's previous niggardly behavior. In the more subtle case, Reuben grants the favor but exacts a moral cost by vaunting his superiority. At the highest standard of ethical perfection, even this is reprehensible.

[30] *Sefer Ha-Hinukh* is a work stemming from thirteenth-century Spain, often erroneously attributed to Aaron Halevi of Barcelona, that explicates the commandments.

[31] Third-generation Tanna.

King but You! Our Father, our King, for Your sake have mercy upon us," and the rains came.[32] As the Rabbis began to murmur,[33] a heavenly voice was heard to say: "It is not that one is greater than the other that his plea was answered. It is because Rabbi Akiva is forbearing toward those who hurt him and does not retaliate, while Rabbi Eliezer is not."[34] 50

Rabbi Akiva's personal conduct approximated the teachings of the pious that we find in a well-known Baraita: They who suffer insults and do not retaliate; who are put to shame and do not answer in kind; who do what is right out of love and cheerfully accept suffering, of them Scripture says, "They who love him will be like the sun in all its power" (Judges 5:31).[35] 51

There were other Sages who did not share this view. Rabbi Simeon ben Jehozadak[36] taught: "Any scholar who does not avenge his injury or nurture hatred in his heart as a serpent, is not a true scholar." In the Babylonian Talmud it is demonstrated that if one's fellow man inflicted bodily pain on him, it is permitted to keep it in one's heart and to remember it.[52]

The basic difference between Rabbi Akiva and Rabbi Ishmael regarding "the duties of the heart" stems from their understanding of the fundamental teaching of the Torah. As we have noted above, to Rabbi Ishmael the core teaching of the Torah is the prohibition against idolatry. Our duty to God is to refrain from transgressing his commandments. To Rabbi Akiva, the core teaching of the Torah is the mitzvah "You shall love your neighbor as yourself." Love is an emotion of the heart, and we must rule over our heart's emotions. Just as the mitzvah "You shall not hate your kinsman in your heart" does not refer to deeds but instructs us to banish the emotion of hatred

50 BT Taʻanit 25b.   51 BT Gittin 36b.   52 BT Yoma 22b–23a.

---

[32] The prayer "our Father, our King" (Avinu Malkenu), here attributed to Rabbi Akiva, has become a staple of the Jewish penitential liturgy. In the course of time, the Avinu Malkenu liturgy expanded (as liturgy is wont to do) far beyond the original two verses given here. It is noteworthy that Akiva's doublet expresses a mutuality between God and human beings so characteristic of his thought. God is asked to answer our prayers both because (i) we have no one else to turn to (i.e., our fate is in God's hands), and because (ii) God's honor depends on our success (i.e., God's fate is in our hands).

[33] Presumably about Akiva's apparent effrontery in one-upping his teacher, Rabbi Eliezer.

[34] The most famous instance of Rabbi Eliezer not being forbearing is the well-known story (told in BT Bava Metzia 59bff.) of his being overruled in the academy on a matter of law even though he had successfully demonstrated through various wonders that heaven was on his side. According to that story, he was considered enough of a threat that he was banned from the rabbinic community. Rabban Gamaliel was his brother-in-law but was also the Patriarch and presumably had to approve such a ban. The story reaches its conclusion with the still-wounded Eliezer praying for retribution against his enemies and Rabban Gamaliel suffering the consequences. The contrast here seems to be that Rabbi Akiva was known for accepting his afflictions.

[35] Heschel's use of this phrase from the Song of Deborah here in connection with Rabbi Akiva recalls his description of Rabbi Akiva's teachings at the very end of chapter 1.

[36] First-generation Amora, Land of Israel.

in our heart, so the injunction "You shall love your neighbor as yourself" refers not to any action but to the love we must nurture in our heart.

To Rabbi Akiva and his followers, from the time a person thinks of committing a sin, he is considered as having broken faith with God. As Rabbi Simeon bar Yohai put it, "wrong originates in the hearts of those who are thinking about it" (it was because Abraham was doubting the divine justice that he was commanded to bring his son Isaac as a sacrifice).[53] Such sinful thoughts require atonement. Rabbi Akiva warned against falling into the clutches of the *Yetzer Hara*, the evil inclination. "At first it appears like the thin thread of a spider-web, but at the end it is as thick as the rope of a ship, even as Scripture says, 'Woe unto them that draw iniquity with cords of vanity and sin with a cart-rope'" (Isaiah 5:18).[54]

Intention (*Kavanah*)

Linked to the duties of the heart is the subject of intention—intention in prayer and in the performance of a mitzvah.[37] In both instances the focus is on directing one's thoughts to the Holy and Blessed One. The Mishnah teaches: When one is reading the Torah Scroll and it is the time for reciting the Shema, if he intended while reading this passage to fulfill his obligation to recite the Shema, then he has fulfilled the mitzvah.[55] And the Tosefta states: "When praying, one must direct one's thoughts."[56] The Babylonian Talmud, however, provides a different version: "When praying one must direct his thoughts to heaven."[57] This second version corresponds to the teaching in Mishnah Berakhot, where it states: "The early Hasidim would devote one hour to contemplation before praying, in order to direct their thoughts to God." Note that this utterance does not imply that they removed from their minds all their troubles and disturbing thoughts to concentrate on their prayers, "for otherwise the text would have stated so specifically. Intention in prayer means directing one's thoughts to God, expunging from their hearts all worldly pleasures and delights and concentrating on extolling God."[58]

Thus Maimonides explained this teaching according to the statement of Rabbi

---

[53] TB Lekh Lekha 13.   [54] Genesis Rabbah 22:6; BT Sukkah 52a.
[55] Mishnah Berakhot 2:1.   [56] Tosefta Berakhot 3:6.   [57] BT Berakhot 31a.
[58] Rabbenu Jonah (Gerondi, thirteenth century, Spain) on Berakhot, ch. 5, 21a, "*kedei* . . . ."

---

[37] The notion of *kavanah* ("intention," or "direction of thought") has at least two distinct senses in Jewish religious observance: (1) In the performance of mitzvot generally, it refers to performing an action with the specific intention of fulfilling the religious requirement. For instance, if one happened to hear a ram's horn blown on Rosh Hashanah, but did so without the awareness that it is a religious duty specific to that day, one must hear it again with that significance in mind. This is generally something that is stressed much more in postbiblical than in biblical thought. (2) In the case of prayer, it refers to attending to the meaning of the prayers and concentrating one's attitude on worship of God.

Simeon Hassidah:[38] "When one is engaged in prayer one must see oneself as if one were standing in the presence of the Shekhinah, as it is written, 'I set God before me always' (Psalms 16:8)."[59] And in his will, Rabbi Eliezer instructed just before he died, "When you are engaged in prayer, know before whom you stand."[60]

The second version comports well with the views of Rabbi Akiva, who generally was drawn in thought and deed to the pietists. Indeed, pious attitudes were characteristic of him: a longing for sanctifying God's Name, loving acceptance of affliction, impassioned prayer, and a tendency to waive his own honor. They said of him: "When he would lead a congregation in prayer, he would pray concisely and leave the reader's table, so as not to inconvenience the congregation. But when he would pray by himself, one could leave him in one corner of the room and later find him in another corner, because of his abundant bowing and kneeling."[61]

Note that the school of Rabbi Akiva, which stressed the matter of intention, expounded as follows: "It says in the case of a burnt offering of a land animal, 'of pleasing odor to the Lord' (Leviticus 1:9), and in the case of a burnt offering of a bird, 'of pleasing odor to the Lord' (Leviticus 1:17), and in the case of a grain offering, 'of pleasing odor to the Lord,' all to teach us that whether one gives much or gives little, it is the same as long as one's thoughts are directed to Heaven."[62]

Study and Deed

The tendency to see obligations of the heart as equivalent to the performance of mitzvot is closely connected with the view of those Sages who held that the merit of performing a mitzvah is greater than that of studying Torah. Rabbi Akiva was one of the Sages who did not accept this judgment. At the conference of Sages in the attic of the house of Nitzeh, this question was debated and Rabbi Tarfon declared, "The performance of mitzvot is greater." But Rabbi Akiva retorted, "The study of Torah is greater." The Sages finally came to this conclusion: "Study of Torah is greater because it leads to performance of good deeds."[63] Nevertheless, there were those who would not yield to Rabbi Akiva's view. Rabban Simeon ben Gamaliel said, "Not study is the essence, but the deed."[64] Also his son Rabbi Judah the Patriarch declared, "The deed takes precedence over study."[65] Abba Saul[39] expressed a similar opinion.[66]

---

[59] BT Sanhedrin 22a.   [60] BT Berakhot 28b.   [61] BT Berakhot 31a.
[62] Sifra Vayyikra 9b. See also Mishnah Menahot 13:11.
[63] BT Kiddushin 40b.   [64] Avot 1:17.
[65] PT Pesahim 3:7, 30b.   [66] Tractate Semahot 11:7.

---

[38] Second-generation Amora.

[39] "Abba" was a title used in the early period for masters and teachers. It means "father" and is clearly closely connected with the rabbinic ideology that tends to treat parents and teachers as equivalents (both are creators and shapers of the human being). As a title for a religious leader, it was adopted by the church as well.

Following the line of his teacher Rabbi Akiva, Rabbi Meir taught: Just as light is superior to darkness, so is the study of Torah superior to performing mitzvot. Rabbi Johanan, too, declared that study of Torah is greater, for relative to Torah, a performative mitzvah is like a candle compared to the sun, as it is written, "For the commandment is a lamp, Torah is [a] light" (Proverbs 6:23).[40]

Another debate emerged from these two divergent views on the subject of man's trial before the heavenly tribunal on the Day of Judgment. According to Rava, the first question addressed to him will be, "Have you dealt honestly in the conduct of your business?" And then he will be asked, "Did you set fixed times for the study of Torah?"[67] R. Hamnuna,[41] however, stated, "Man's trial will begin with an examination of his study of Torah."[68] The view of Rabbi Ishmael is found in an exposition of the school on the verse "You shall do what is upright in His sight" (Exodus 15:26). They teach: "This refers to man's conduct in business matters, and we derive from this that he who conducts his affairs honestly wins the approval of his fellow man and is regarded as having performed all the commandments of the Torah."[69]

Plato taught in the name of Socrates that the unexamined life is not befitting human beings. Rabbi Akiva taught that life without Torah is simply not possible. It is not a matter of degree or even quality; it is the very source of life. The Talmud relates that when Rome issued its decree prohibiting the study of Torah, Pappus ben Judah approached Rabbi Akiva while he was teaching Torah in public. "Akiva," he asked, "are you not afraid of the mighty empire?" To which Rabbi Akiva replied, "Let me cite you a parable. A fox was walking along the bank of a river and he saw fish scurrying together from one place to another. Said the fox, 'From what danger are you running?' They replied, 'From the fishermen's nets.' Whereupon the fox said, 'Why don't you come here on dry land and we will live peacefully together as our forebears did?' And the fish said, 'They call you the cleverest of the animals? You must be a fool. If we are in fear in our natural environment where we live, how much more so if we were to leave it for a place that spells certain death.'" So with us. Now that we study Torah, of which it is written, "It is your life and length of days," we find ourselves in this situation; if we abandon it how much greater the danger in which we will find ourselves.[70]

To Rabbi Akiva, reverence for Torah was synonymous with reverence for God.

---

[67] BT Shabbat 31a.   [68] BT Kiddushin 40b.   [69] MI Vayyassa 1.
[70] BT Berakhot 61b.

---

[40] The translation here departs from NJV in two ways: "the instruction (Torah)" is rendered here as "Torah" in English as well, and "a" is placed in brackets. This captures the midrashists reading of the verse, to mean that, whereas commandments are lamps that give light—that is, they are discrete sources of light like a lamp—Torah is light itself.

[41] R. Hamnuna was the name of several Babylonian Amoraim in the first through fourth generations.

Rabbi Simeon ha-Imsoni sought to expound every *et*[42] in the Torah. When he came upon the verse "You shall fear *et* the Lord your God" (Deuteronomy 10:20), he abandoned the project, asking: "Whom can I add to Him as worthy of our fear?" When Rabbi Akiva arrived, he expounded, "You shall fear *et* the Lord your God"—add the Sages of the Torah.[71] But there is another tradition in which Rabbi Akiva expounded the *et* in this verse to mean, "You shall fear the Lord your God—and his Torah." In both traditions we have Rabbi Akiva's conviction that "the teachings of the Torah and the teachings of the Sages will live forever, to all eternity."[72]

[71] BT Pesahim 22b.
[72] ARN A 3.

[42] The word et in Hebrew is the signal of the definite direct object. It is normally untranslated in English, where the direct object relation is indicated by word order. Rabbi Ishmael would adopt here the approach, "The Torah speaks in human language"; that is, this is how Hebrew idiom works, and no additional significance need be drawn from it. Rabbi Akiva, however, found here another opportunity to exercise his predilection to find additional meanings in each detail of the text of the Torah.

ISSUES OF SUPREME IMPORTANCE

Translator's Introduction

The Hebrew title *Devarim ha-omedim be-rumo shel 'olam* (literally, "things that stand in the height of the universe")[1] recalls for the reader associations of the angels in heaven,[2] or matters of highest sanctity. Heschel may also have had Paul Tillich's phrase "ultimate concern" in the back of his mind.

Up to this point, Heschel has been very close to what he called "depth theology," the emotionally freighted life situations that call forth religious responses, as opposed to cerebral theological doctrine. Human suffering, the Shekhinah's participation in Israel's history, trembling at one's moral inadequacy, cleaving to God—these are all theological issues of the heart and the emotions. Perhaps the title of this chapter indicates that he wanted to deal here with more "exalted" topics, the classical theological problems to which the more elemental religious experiences give rise when filtered through philosophical reason. Indeed, he presents us with three such issues here—providence, foreknowledge versus choice, and eschatology. What do they all have in common? They all concern the role that human beings play in the unfolding of events in this world and in the future. Can we challenge God's justice? Do we play a role in determining events on earth? Can we play a role in the unfolding of history's end or fulfillment? The schools of Ishmael and Akiva will be quoted amply on these subjects, though the differences in approach are not nearly as clear-cut as they often are in Heschel's unfolding argument. But then, these are issues that "stand at the heights," and they can hardly be expected to be anything but complex and resistant to simplification.

On the question of Divine Providence, Heschel revisits the issues of chapter 7 with one new factor emphasized: the arbitrary nature of "fate-like" events that happen in the world. Whether one invokes the ancient image of Fate (transposed to a monotheistic framework as God's inscrutable decrees), or the more modern issues of physical determinism or chance, it is generally recognized that certain nonmoral factors (such as genetic endowment, the weather, and the accidents of social and economic opportunity)

---

[1] From BT Berakhot 6b, where the context leads Rashi to comment, "Such as prayer, which ascends heavenward." In BT Megillah 14a, it has a more earthly connotation: Elkanah, Samuel's father, was "of the highest [elite] of the world," being descended from Korah.

[2] As the daily morning liturgy uses the term.

play a part in human events. Rabbi Ishmael tries to show how the play of these factors is at least partly compatible with divine justice, and where no such explanation can be given, he gives a stoic-like shrug: "That's how God decreed it." Rabbi Akiva, on the other hand, has the wild card of being able to accept all sufferings with love, as evidence of God's concern, or as an opportunity for divine participation in our lot.

In the section entitled "Divine Foreknowledge and Human Choice," we see how far the early Rabbis were from formulating abstract philosophical issues in all their complexity. Indeed, only the maxim attributed to Rabbi Akiva, "All is foreseen, yet freedom of choice is granted," rises truly to the level of philosophical reflection (and both its exact meaning and its attribution to Akiva are debatable). For the rest, we have only expression of fundamental (one might say, existential) attitudes of the Rabbis on the question of choice and destiny. It would be up to the medievals to develop coherent philosophical positions on the basis of these materials.

It is perhaps on the question of eschatology that the hidden agenda of theodicy-laden questions speaks loudest. For if Rabbi Akiva truly and fully accepted suffering as a mark of divine love and poverty as a beauty mark on the body of Israel, then it seems he should have accepted with resignation the yoke of subordination to Roman power. Instead, it is said that he hailed Simeon bar Kokhba as the Messiah. Was this simply an expression of the optimistic side of his personality? Was it an expression of his belief in miracles? Was it because religious ideas could not remain ethereal notions for him, but had to take on flesh and blood (just as the Shekhinah had to have a definite geographical abode)? Was it because every word of Scripture had to have concrete instantiation in deed? Was it because (as Heschel suggests) his restless personality could accept no limits, either in textual exegesis or religious quest or history?

In any case, it seems that for him justice could be postponed, but to defer it indefinitely would be to deny it, and come it must, by God's will, "speedily and in our days." The redemption of Jerusalem was not a vain prophecy, but an imminent reality. God would right wrongs sooner rather than later.

But in the end, this immediate answer to the problem of divine justice was denied him. Only in the aftermath of defeat did he give the ultimate proof of his devotion to God, a devotion unto death.

Decrees or Mercy?

WE HEAR THE VOICE of anguished despair in Rabbi Ishmael's saying, "Life is a revolving wheel."[1] The world is like the waterwheel of a cistern: the lower buckets ascend full, the higher descend empty.[2] So, too, the rich

[1] BT Shabbat 151a.   [2] Leviticus Rabbah 34:9; Exodus Rabbah 31:14.

are never safe from imminent poverty. The Torah tells you to put a parapet on your roof (Deuteronomy 22:8), to teach you in how many ways a person can meet judgment, as it is said, "And a man cannot even know his time. As fishes are enmeshed in a fatal net . . . so men are caught at the time of calamity when it comes upon them without warning" (Ecclesiastes 9:12).[3] 3

Rabbi Akiva taught otherwise: "All is foreseen, and free will is given, and the world is judged in goodness."[4] Compassion is key. Better to limit belief in God's power than to dampen faith in God's mercy.[4] Rabbi Akiva viewed all history through the lens of trust in God's mercy. God participates in His creatures' suffering; it is as if God were wounded by the afflictions of Israel, God's people. If Israel is in exile, the Shekhinah is with them. When Israel is redeemed, God is redeemed.

The world is judged in goodness. God does not withhold any creature's reward, even from those who oppose the divine will. Once Rabban Gamaliel, Rabbi Eleazar ben Azariah, Rabbi Joshua, and Rabbi Akiva were traveling together on foot. From a great distance away (120 mil[5]) they heard the noise of a large, bustling Roman community. They began to weep, except for Rabbi Akiva, who was laughing. They said: "Why do you laugh?" And he said, "Why do you weep?" They replied, "Here are these pagans, who bow to their gods, burn incense in astral worship, and they live in peace and security, while we: the House that is our God's footstool is destroyed by fire. How can we not weep?" To which Rabbi Akiva responded, "And I laugh because if this is the recompense of those who transgress His will, how much greater must be the recompense of those who obey His will."[5]

"Precious are afflictions." And: "The world is judged in goodness." With the first of these principles, Rabbi Akiva found the solution to the question of the misfortunes of the righteous. If afflictions are precious, we need not ask why they come upon the righteous. And with the second principle, he found the solution to the question of the

---

3 Sifre Ki Tetze 229.   4 Mishnah Avot 3:15.
5 BT Makkot 24a.

---

[3] Heschel had paraphrased Rabbi Ishmael's statement in the Sifre here as "a person does not know how he will meet judgment," a rendition that required the addition of three bracketed words. However, the Sifre reads straightforwardly if we assume that the point here is this: The Torah literally says that the parapet is to prevent "the faller" from falling from the roof. This teaches us that the one who might fall from the roof is someone who would be destined to take such a fall. So even as we are instructed to prevent our own premises from being the site of such an occurrence, we are reminded that certain things are sometimes fated to happen. Yet we are not, as Ecclesiastes says, generally privy to such information until after the fact.

[4] This is a phrase that Heschel has already used of Akiva in chapter 6.

[5] A "mil" is two thousand cubits, and a cubit is about eighteen inches. Thus, 120 mil would literally be about seventy miles. It is, of course, more natural to take this distance not literally, but as a conventional definition of a "long distance," even as 120 often functioned in antiquity as a large round number (it was, for example, Moses' life span).

prosperity of the wicked.[6] If God compensates the wicked in this world "as if they were observant of the Torah with nary a defect,"6 then we need not ask, why the wicked prosper.[7]

The whole Akivan notion of God's participation in human suffering—in the suffering of individuals and of the people—was foreign to Rabbi Ishmael's teaching. In his view, this notion did not befit God's dignity and could lead to a denial of God's power. For him, God's justice and power are key, not God's compassion. Even when searching for an example of God's compassion, Rabbi Ishmael took it from the realm of jurisprudence; "a person may ransom himself from Heaven for money."[8] Rabbi Akiva said: "Dear is humanity, created in God's image!"7—while in Rabbi Ishmael's school, they taught, "A single individual is equal in value to the rest of creation."8 [9] Rabbi Akiva declared, "Precious are the people Israel, for they are called God's children,"9 while Rabbi Ishmael expressed the view, "Man's relation to God is as a servant to his master."[10] 10 As against Akiva's view that God Himself suffered along with the people Israel, Rabbi Ishmael decried the failure of God's compassion: "Who is like You among the mutes?"[11] Who is like You, O Lord, Who witnesses the humil-

---

6 See statement of Bar Kappara, BT Nedarim 50b, Rashi ad loc.
7 Mishnah Avot 3:14.   8 MI Bahodesh 4.   9 Mishnah Avot 3:14.
10 MI Nezikin 9.

---

[6] This was at least as knotty a question as the first. Indeed, Jeremiah was famously bothered by the second problem especially: "You will win, O Lord, if I make claim against You, yet I shall present charges against You: Why does the way of the wicked prosper? Why are the workers of treachery at ease?" (Jeremiah 12:1).

[7] The essence of the resolution here is, apparently, that even the most incorrigibly wicked have redeeming qualities, and since God judges the world in goodness, God gives them the reward for those redeeming qualities in this world. Thus is their reward "used up," so to speak, and the righteous can thus be reassured that justice will prevail in the fullness of time, that is, in the future world.

[8] God compassionately allows the owner of an ox that has habitually gored and now killed someone to ransom his life with a monetary payment. Of course, the ox is put to death. But although the owner must share in the responsibility, because of his negligence in not guarding the animal, the Torah allows him the out of monetary ransom. In general, ransom for capital crimes was not allowable, but in this case, the owner did not, after all, participate in any active way in the crime. Heschel's point here is that Ishmael's example of compassion is still one that can be understood as a sort of strict justice, for it follows a certain jurisprudential logic.

[9] The context here is the warning concerning the possible fatal consequences of getting too close to Mount Sinai during the revelation. To have even a single individual lose his life would be to have "many of them perish" (Exodus 19:21). The contrast with Rabbi Akiva seems to be this: Whereas Rabbi Akiva spoke readily of people being made in God's image, and thus stressed the similarity and bond between human beings and God, Rabbi Ishmael understood human uniqueness in a more straightforward way—every life is special, compared to other humans (not compared to God).

[10] Again, this expresses the transcendence of God and the fact that we are subordinate to God and not vice versa.

[11] A creative misreading of Exodus 15:11, substituting ilmim ("mutes, silent ones") for elim ("the gods, the mighty"). See chapter 7 above.

iation of His children and is silent?[11] Other Sages would ask, Where is God's power? In Rabbi Ishmael's school, they asked, Where is His compassion?[12]

Following the Akivan approach, Rabbi Meir taught: "What is the response of the Shekhinah when a human being suffers? It says, "My head hurts, my arm hurts.""[13] We learn from this that if God is pained when the blood of the wicked is destroyed, how much more so when the blood of the righteous is spilled."[12] In contrast, Rabbi Ishmael expounded: "The Lord spoke further to Aaron: Now I, here, I give over to you the charge of my contributions"[14] (Numbers 18:8)—"'Now I' means willingly, and 'here' means joyfully . . . but his disciples said to him: But Master, another verse says 'Now I, here, I am bringing the flood of waters upon the earth' (Genesis 6:17)—shall we say here too that there was joy before God at the flood? He said to them: Yes, God was glad for His enemies to perish from the world."[13]

Also extending Rabbi Akiva's views, the Sages commented, "When the Egyptians were drowning in the sea, the ministering angels were about to burst into song. The Holy and Blessed One rebuked them, saying, My creatures are drowning in the sea, and you rejoice?"[14] "Surely if God is so concerned with those who transgress His will, how much more so with those who obey His will."[15] Other Sages gave a different exposition of this event. "The people were in great distress when they reached the sea. At the same time, the ministering angels were preparing to chant their daily hymns of praise to the Lord. God rebuked them and said, "My people are in great distress and you come to sing My praises?!"[15] This homily corresponds closely to the exposition in the Mekhilta. It states, "At this critical moment Moses prayed at length to God. Whereupon God rebuked Moses and said, 'My beloved ones are drowning in the water, and the sea closes on them and the enemy gives chase, and you offer lengthy prayers?'"[16]

Rabbi Akiva taught that it was forbidden to argue against the decree of the Creator, for everything God does is with truth and justice. It was in his mode that Rabbi Meir

---

[11] MI Shirata 8.   [12] Mishnah Sanhedrin 6:5.   [13] Sifre Korah 117.

[14] BT Megillah 10b.

[15] So ends the talmudic passage according to the reading attested by Rabbi Solomon ben Ha-Yatom (Italy, eleventh–twelfth centuries). See also Rabbi Akiva's statement quoted above from BT Makkot 24b.

[16] MI Beshalah 2.

---

[12] That is, to point out that God's compassion is not always evident, for it is not the most prominent divine quality.

[13] Literally, the Hebrew means "I feel light at my head, I feel light at my arm." This, however, is a euphemism for feeling "heavy," that is, feeling pain.

[14] This and the next cited verse are translated here in an eclectic manner, following neither NJV nor Fox precisely, so as to bring out in English the identity of language that prompts the pivotal question from Rabbi Ishmael's disciples.

[15] That is, it was Israel's distress that was of concern to God at that moment, not the Egyptians' distress.

said: "As a person measures out, so it will be measured out to him."[17] That is, "The method of the Holy and Blessed One is always measure for measure."[18]

But Rabbi Ishmael protested against suffering. He believed neither that it was possible to comprehend God's actions on the basis of common sense nor that those actions could be explained according to the principles of righteousness and justice. Various scriptural verses articulated this view. Job said, "See, God is greater than we can know" (Job 36:26). The author of Ecclesiastes observed, "In my own brief span of life, I have seen both these things: sometimes a good man perishes in spite of his goodness, and sometimes a wicked one endures in spite of his wickedness" (Ecclesiastes 7:15). In another passage he comments, "For all this I noted, and I ascertained all this: that the actions of even the righteous and the wise are determined by God. . . . For the same fate is in store for all: for the righteous, and for the wicked; for the good and pure, and for the impure; for him who sacrifices, and for him who does not; for him who is pleasing, and for him who is displeasing; and for him who swears, and for him who shuns oaths' (Ecclesiastes 9:1–2). In this spirit Rabbi Ishmael said, "Man's life is a revolving wheel."

There were two approaches to this issue. The one, Rabbi Akiva's, maintains that everything that happens is in accord with God's truth and justice. The other, Rabbi Ishmael's, maintains that everything happens in accordance with God's decrees.

In line with Rabbi Akiva's view, Rabbi Ammi[16] sought to explain the cause of untimely death. "Death is always a consequence of sin, and there is no suffering except as punishment for transgression."[19] Those who held the Ishmaelian view gave this response to Rabbi Ammi: "The ministering angels said to the Holy and Blessed One, 'Master of the Universe, why did Adam, the first man to be created, die?' God replied, 'Because he did not obey My commandments.' The angels continued, 'But Moses did obey Your commandments, yet he died?' To which God replied, 'It is my decree, which applies equally to all men, as it is written, "This is the law, when a person dies in a tent"'"[20] (Numbers 19:14). The cause of death is a closed and hidden matter. No one knows or understands its cause or meaning. It is something that happens to the righteous as to the wicked, to the pure and to the impure.[17] [21]

---

[17] BT Sanhedrin 100a, and similarly in Mishnah Sota 1:7.
[18] BT Sanhedrin 90a.   [19] BT Shabbat 55a.   [20] Sifre Ha'azinu 339.
[21] BT Shabbat 55b.

---

[16] Third-century Amora, Land of Israel.

[17] The verse from Numbers 19:14 would suggest this in several ways. First, it prefaces mention of the death of "a person" (i.e., any person) with "This is the law." That is, it is a universal, impersonal law of nature that death strikes us all. Situating the death in a tent, that is, in a private place hidden from public view, would also hint at the secret nature of death, that its reasons are hidden from public view. Finally, all of Numbers 19 deals with matters of purification, through the ash of the red cow, that are quintessentially nonrational and impossible to explicate logically. It is also noteworthy that this midrash starts from the assumption that Moses was free of sin. This is not the plain meaning of the Torah's account, but it is a theme that recurs in certain rabbinic midrashim.

The power of the Divine decree is reflected in the following midrash. The verse reads, "Ascend . . . and you shall die on top of the mountain" (Deuteronomy 32:49–50). Moses said to the Master of the Universe, "Why am I to die? Would it not be better for the people to say of me, 'Moses is good' out of personal knowledge than as mere rumor? Would it not be better for people to say, 'This is the Moses who led us out of Egypt, divided the sea for us, caused manna to descend from heaven and performed many miracles for us and mighty deeds' rather than to say, 'Moses was like that, Moses did such and such'?" God silenced Moses and said, "Stop that, Moses! This is My decree, which applies to everyone alike, as it is written, 'this is the law, when a person dies in a tent' (Numbers 19:14), and it is written, 'And this is the law of man, O Lord God'" (2 Samuel 7:19).[18] 22

Everything has concealed within it its opposite, and often things proceed to unfold in a direction contrary to what is expected. Rabbi Akiva preached the doctrine that the world is judged in goodness, yet his own martyrdom would seem to refute and destroy this thesis. The Sages of Israel, in later generations, grew weary in their struggle to find justification for his brutal death and were forced to resort to the explanation that it was the divine decree that we must accept in faith. They said, "Moses himself saw in a vision how they were weighing out his flesh in a market and cried to God, 'Master of the Universe, is this the Torah and this its reward?' And God replied, 'Be silent. This is what I have decreed.'"[19] 23

These two approaches are found in the Amoraic period, in alternative interpretations of a puzzling Mishnah: "If the prayer leader says, 'Your mercies extend to a bird's nest' (alluding to the command to drive away the mother bird before taking her eggs—Deuteronomy 22:7), he should be silenced."24 The first interpretation is along Akivan lines: "One who says this is saying, 'You have mercy on birds, but not on me!' and he thereby challenges God's justice."25 The second view is characteristic of the

22 Sifre Ha'azinu 339.   23 BT Menahot 29b.
24 Mishnah Berakhot 5:3.   25 PT Berakhot 5:3 (9c).

---

[18] The connection of the verse in 2 Samuel to the subject at hand is not transparent. A suggested connection is this: it comes as part of a dialogue between David and the prophet Nathan, in which David is expressing gratitude for God's granting his line an eternal covenant of kingship over Israel. Nathan, of course, had just told David that he would not be able to build a Temple, but that his son who would succeed him on the throne would do so. David's expressing gratitude at that juncture would then lend itself to the interpretation that he was reconciled to the fact that he would not complete all that he wished to do because mortality is "the law of man." In this way, it is particularly apposite to Moses' plea, since God had to get Moses to the same reconciliation with the inexorable law of death that David would later have to accept.

[19] That is, the response to the puzzlements about Akiva's suffering and martyrdom was decidedly Ishmaelian in tone! This was precisely Heschel's intended point in this discussion about how everything conceals a bit of its opposite. As we have pointed out repeatedly, the "dichotomy" between Ishmael and Akiva is delineated in this work always as a way of showing how complex is a tradition that constantly navigates between and among their signature views.

Ishmaelian school: "He erred in proclaiming that God's ways are merciful, when in fact they are only arbitrary decrees."[20] 26

Rabbi Akiva never doubted God's justice, and he taught, "One may not challenge the One Who spoke and the world came into being on His judgments, for they are carefully weighed and measured and meted out with justice." Rabbi Ishmael, however, regarded God's justice as awesome and terrifying. Both accept that God's decrees originate in justice and equity. But justice is one thing, and the effects of the decree are quite another. The decree, when it issues from the ruler, can throw off the demands of justice and can become like floodwaters that sweep through and destroy and annihilate everything in their path.[21]

Thus, in the school of Rabbi Ishmael, they gave this exposition of the scriptural account of the slaying of the first-born in Egypt: The verse reads, "None of you shall go outside the door of his house until morning" (Exodus 12:22). They said, "Once permission is given to the Destroying Angel to carry out his task, he makes no distinction between the righteous and the wicked, as it is written, '[Thus said the Lord:] I am going to deal with you! I will draw my sword from its sheath, and I will wipe out from you both the righteous and the wicked' (Ezekiel 21:8)."[22] 27

"Remember [Deuteronomy 5:12: "Observe"] the Sabbath day and keep it holy" (Exodus 20:8). From the differences in how these verses were interpreted in the Ishmaelian and Akivan schools one also gets a strong sense of the different characters of their thought. In the Ishmaelian school they expounded: "'Remember' refers to what precedes it, and 'Observe' refers to what comes after it. From this it was derived that one must add from the mundane to the holy.[23] It is analogous to a wolf that creates

---

26 BT Berakhot 33b.　　27 MI Pisha 11.

---

[20] This brings up the issue of ta'amei ha-mitzvot—the rationalization of the commandments—which has been a constant issue in Jewish thought since talmudic times. See further discussion in chapter 14.

[21] Heschel's reference in using the Hebrew words translated here as "issues from the ruler" is clearly to Ecclesiastes 10:5: "as great as an error committed by a ruler." As understood in rabbinic tradition, that verse meant to point out that decrees sometimes have unintended effects that cannot be taken back once they have the authority of the ruler behind them. Among the clearest examples of this in rabbinic literature are BT Ketubot 23a, PT Shabbat 14d, and Genesis Rabbah 74. Thus, the view attributed to the Ishmaelians here is that God's decrees always originate in justice, just as rains may be sent to water deserving fields, but also have unintended consequences, just as the rains produce floods that are destructive. BT Bava Kamma 60a also expresses (in the name of Rabbi Jonathan) this thought when it says that destructive forces enter the world only because of the wicked, but often their destructive effect is experienced also, or even especially, by the righteous. The alert reader will note that this view accepts the possibility of God being unaware of the eventual consequences of a just decree and thus seems to run afoul of Heschel's insistence that Ishmaelians never call God's power into question.

[22] Rabbi Akiva, by contrast, gave another interpretation of the night of the Exodus that focused instead on the fact that the Destroyer spared the Israelites, that is, reflected divine mercy.

[23] The halakhic rule is that some of the day before and the day after, even if a minimal amount, should be added to the sanctity of the Sabbath.

agitation some distance in front of him and some distance behind."[24] 28 Don't dismiss this analogy, for it reveals something about the character of its author. This analogy, which compares the Sabbath to a wolf, fits the Ishmaelian saying that human beings are in the hands of heaven as a servant in the hands of the master. By contrast, consider the words of Rabbi Akiva's disciple: "Rabbi Simeon bar Yohai taught: The Sabbath spoke before the Holy and Blessed One and said, 'Master of the Universe, every day has its partner, but I have no partner.'[25] The Holy and Blessed One said to her, 'The congregation of Israel will be your partner.' And so it was that when Israel stood at Mount Sinai, the Holy and Blessed One told them to remember what had been said to the Sabbath: 'Remember the Sabbath day.'"29 The end of the verse is "and keep it holy," and holiness is the language used in marriage.[26] Thus, in this interpretation, the Sabbath is depicted as the lover or partner of the people Israel.

Divine Foreknowledge and Human Choice

Josephus relates that the Essenes, the Sadducees, and the Pharisees held differing views on the seeming contradiction between a human's freedom of choice and God's absolute decrees.30 These differences persisted in the era of the Tannaim. Rabbi Akiva stated it flatly as a paradox: "All is foreseen, yet freedom of choice is granted."31 [27] All of our deeds, past and future, are known to God. But we should not conclude from this that since God knows what a person will do, that person is forced on that account to be righteous or wicked. Rather, everyone is free to choose between good

---

28 MI Bahodesh 7.　　29 Genesis Rabbah 11:9.
30 See George Foot Moore, *Judaism in the First Centuries of the Christian Era, the Age of the Tannaim*, 3 vols. (Cambridge, Mass.: Harvard University Press, 1927–30), 1:457, 3:139.
31 Mishnah Avot 3:15.

---

[24] As Heschel will point out, the image of agitation on both sides of the wolf is a violent picture that is jarring when used in connection with a symbol of peace such as the Sabbath. It seems to bespeak a focus on the restrictions that the Sabbath imposes and on the severity of the penalty for violating it.

[25] That is, since there are an odd number of days, the last day of the week cannot be paired off.

[26] That is, the Hebrew term for marriage is *kiddushin*, a word that comes from the same root as "holy."

[27] The word *tzafui* in Rabbi Akiva's aphorism is ambiguous. The medievals interpreted it as "foreseen" and understood Akiva to be expressing the paradox that even though God foresees what we are going to do, we still choose freely among alternative courses of action. It is possible that it meant simply "observed"; that is, God observes what we do, even in our most private quarters and compensates us depending on the use we make of our free choice. Another reading, *tzafun*, yields the meaning, "Everything is hidden, and free choice is given. . . ." Another ambiguity here involves the attribution to Akiva, for it is not explicitly attributed in Mishnah Avot; rather, it is inferred from the fact that it follows an attribution to Rabbi Akiva in an earlier Mishnah, with no attribution to another sage intervening.

and evil and is under no compulsion to act one way or the other. Rabbi Akiva's statement both fixes an idea and uproots it;[28] it is paradoxical, and in that way conforms to the pattern of his thought. Rabbi Ishmael preferred a more straightforward style of thought and avoided such intricacies. He never mentions the concept of freedom of choice, but speaks of certain matters that have been predestined and decreed since the six days of creation.

"Life is a revolving wheel." It is beyond a person's power to determine his or her destiny. An ancient decree governs one's life. Thus, in the school of Rabbi Ishmael they expounded as follows:

> "When you build a new house you shall make a parapet for your roof, so that you be not guilty of bringing blood upon your house, if the faller should fall from it" (Deuteronomy 22:8). Note that the Torah calls him *hanofel* (the Faller), for he was designated at the time of creation to be a faller from that roof. But he in fact did not fall [since the parapet, built by the righteous homeowner, prevented the fall]. Why then, does the Torah call him "the faller"? It teaches us that merit results from the actions of the meritorious, and evil results from the actions of the evil.[29] 32

Another application of this view of the school of Rabbi Ishmael is to be found in their exegesis of the law of the unintentional killer. Scripture says, "if he did not do it by design, but it came about as an act of God" (Exodus 21:13). Why would God do such a thing, and arrange that he kill a person unintentionally? This is the case respecting which David cited "the ancient proverb . . . wicked deeds come from wicked men" (1 Samuel 24:14).[30] What is the case? Two people were guilty of homicide, one who killed intentionally and one unintentionally. In both cases there were no witnesses to the deed, hence the intentional killer was not executed and the accidental killer did not go into exile to a city of refuge.[31] It is here that God intervenes. The intentional killer is sitting at the foot of a ladder; the unintentional killer is at the top of the ladder and accidentally falls down and kills the man below. Since there

---

32 BT Shabbat 32a.

---

[28] Another splendid example of Heschel using halakhic vocabulary to describe aggadic issues, especially those he considers to be of "supreme importance." "Uprooting" ('akirah) and "setting" (hanahah) are the actions that describe the technical legal meaning of transporting something from one domain to another on Shabbat, thus violating Shabbat. Here, however, the terms are used not of objects but of theological concepts.

[29] This is a noteworthy combination of predestination and free will. The idea is that people do have some destiny that they are headed for, but that sometimes righteous action can make the "world line" of that individual swerve toward a more positive outcome, and wicked action can have the opposite effect. In this case, the righteousness of the maker of the parapet, who has fulfilled the divine command, postpones or even averts the decree that hung over the "faller."

[30] By "the ancient proverb," the Midrash understands, "the proverb of the Ancient One (God), that is, the Torah, in this very verse (Exodus 21:13).

[31] As is prescribed for the accidental homicide; see Numbers 35.

were witnesses, the unintentional killer must now flee to the nearest city of refuge, while the intentional killer receives his due punishment.[33] In similar fashion, the school of Rabbi Ishmael taught that it had been ordained at creation that Bathsheba would be the spouse of King David. However, he could not wait until she became his legitimate wife and he enjoyed her as an unripe fruit.[34] These two examples of the unintentional killer and of David and Bathsheba served as proof texts for those who believed that human beings' deeds are predetermined.

The Sages differed as to how far this principle of predestination extended. According to one view, the angel appointed to supervise the birth of a child takes a drop of semen and brings it before God. He asks, "What shall this drop become? Will this one born be strong or weak, wise or foolish, rich or poor?" However, he does not ask whether the child will grow to be righteous or wicked—that is not predetermined.[35]

Rabbi Akiva taught: God set before Adam two paths, the path of life and the path of death. Which did he choose (out of his own free will)? The path of death.[36] But in the school of Rabbi Ishmael it was taught: No man is seized with jealousy of his wife unless he is invaded by a spirit, as it is written, "A spirit of jealousy comes upon him" (Numbers 5:14). By the term "spirit" our Sages understood an impure spirit that descends on a man by heaven's decree. In keeping with this view, Rabbi Simeon ben Lakish declared: No man commits a transgression unless a spirit of folly entered into him.[32] [37]

Here, then, we have these two schools of thought. One school teaches: God judges the world with goodness and compassion, the other says, the world is ruled by divine decree. In the school of Ishmael they gave this exposition of the verse, "Would that they always be of such a mind to fear Me and keep all My commandments that it might be well with them and their children forever" (Deuteronomy 5:26): "Were it possible to recall the Angel of Death, I would recall it, but the decree has already been issued [and cannot be revoked]."[33] [38]

Rabbi Judah, a disciple of Rabbi Akiva, expressed the opposite view in his exposition of the verse "The writing was God's writing, incised upon the tablets" (Exodus 32:16): "Do not read *harut* (incised) but *herut* (freedom), that is, freedom from the Angel of Death." For "when Israel stood at the foot of Mount Sinai and declared, 'we will do and obey' (Exodus 24:7), at that moment the Holy and Blessed One sum-

[33] Rashi on Exodus 21:13; MI Nezikin 4; BT Makkot 10b.
[34] BT Sanhedrin 107b.   [35] BT Niddah 16b.   [36] MI Beshalah 6.
[37] BT Sotah 3a; see Maharsha (Rabbi Samuel Edels) ad loc.
[38] MI Bahodesh 9.

[32] That is, some things are not completely in our control, as if we are fated to do certain things because we are invaded by certain spirits.

[33] Note again the theme of God being unable to revoke a decree that He issued, even though it had consequences that were distasteful to God. As we have already pointed out, this does not sit well with the usual Ishmaelian view about God's power.

moned the Angel of Death and said, 'You are not to have dealings with this people.'"[39]

Rabbi Yose limited human beings' freedom of choice. He taught: "God removes the evil inclination from the righteous and provides them with a good inclination; God removes the good inclination from the wicked and gives them an evil one. To those who are neither righteous nor wicked, God gives both inclinations (and the freedom to choose)."[34] [40]

Rabbi Hanina taught: "Everything is in God's power, except the fear of God."[41] Rabbi Hamnuna, however, taught: King Hezekiah, through the power of the holy spirit, knew that a decree had been issued at the time of the birth of his children that they would not be God-fearing.[42]

The Ultimate Wonder

Rabbi Ishmael was like the slow, trickling waters of Siloam; Rabbi Akiva was like a torrential stream. Rabbi Ishmael's qualities were modesty and punctiliousness, restraint and caution, moderation and patience. By contrast, Rabbi Akiva was all yearning and striving, insatiable appetite, unquenchable thirst.

Rabbi Akiva felt hemmed in[35] by the constraints of the plain sense of the text, by the conception of God provided by ordinary faith and obedience to mitzvot. He also felt cramped by ordinary historical process. He was weary of the burden of exile; his spirit bridled, his patience broke. Many waters cannot quench love; and so, too, the prophet's warning, "If he tarries, wait for him," did not assuage his soul-felt longing for speedy redemption. It was an established tradition in Israel that the time of the coming of the Messiah is hidden and covered in secrecy. But Rabbi Akiva peered "behind the curtain" and announced that the advent of the Messiah was imminent, the end of days was near at hand. He quoted the prophet Haggai (2:6), "In just a little while longer I will shake the heavens and the earth."[43]

His strong influence provided powerful support for the uprising against Roman rule led by Bar Kokhba. His disciple Rabbi Simeon bar Yohai quoted his master as say-

---

[39] Song of Songs Rabbah 8:3.   [40] ARN A 32.   [41] BT Niddah 16b
[42] BT Berakhot 10a.   [43] BT Sanhedrin 97b.

---

[34] There is, of course, some deep psychological insight in this statement, as Maimonides would note centuries later. Habituation to righteous acts creates a good instinct, and habituation to wickedness creates an evil instinct. Choices can become self-fulfilling and thus create the illusion (or perhaps the reality) of coercion.

[35] *Tzar lo hamakom*, literally: "the place was too narrow for him," a graphic expression of impatience. This expression alludes to two classic texts: Isaiah 49:20: "The children you thought you [O Zion] had lost shall yet say in your hearing, 'The place is too crowded for me'"; and Mishnah Avot 5:5: "Ten miracles were performed concerning the Temple [the last of which was that] no one ever said during the pilgrimage festivals, 'It is too crowded for me to lodge in Jerusalem.'"

ing, "the verse 'A star rises from Jacob' refers to Bar Koseva (Bar Kokhba[36]) and when he saw him in person, he exclaimed, 'Here is the King Messiah!'" Rabbi Johanan ben Torta,[37] however, said to him, "Akiva, grass will grow on your cheeks before the Messiah arrives."[38] 44

In the school of Rabbi Ishmael the view was that the ultimate wonder[39] is shrouded in secrecy and those who seek "to hasten the end" are guilty of violating the "oath."[40] The Mekhilta of Rabbi Ishmael teaches that there are seven things that are hidden from a person's knowledge: the day of death, the day of comfort, the strictness of God's judgment, how he will earn his livelihood, what another person's thoughts are, when the kingdom of David will be restored, and when the wicked kingdom will be uprooted.45 Those who long for the redemption must content themselves with the faith that the Guardian of Israel is also the Guardian of the end of days. Thus, they expounded the verse, "The Lord bless you and guard you" (Numbers 6:24) to mean that He will guard for you the advent of the Messiah.[41] So, too, they cite the verse, "Watchman, what of the night, watchman, what of the night? The watchman says, morning will come even as the night comes" (Isaiah: 21:11–12).46

It was a common practice of the Sages to search in Scriptures for allusions to contemporary events. There are various midrashim that tell us that, while in Egyptian bondage, the tribe of Ephraim calculated the time of liberation and concluded that the hour had come. What did they do? They assembled their forces, went to war with the Egyptians, and were soundly defeated, suffering many casualties.47 In this connection, the School of Rabbi Akiva gave this exegesis: "The peoples hear, they tremble; agony grips the dwellers in Philistia" (Exodus 15:14). Why were they terrified? The people of Philistia said, "Now they are coming to compensate for the blindness of their father Ephraim, as it is said, 'The children of Ephraim were archers armed with the bow, yet retreated in the day of battle'" (Psalm 78:9).48 In the school of Rabbi Ishmael, they quoted this homily as well, but they added a derogatory twist at the end: "they retreated in the day of battle" because they violated the prohibition against cal-

---

44 PT Ta'anit 4:5, 68d.   45 MI Vayyassa' 5.   46 Sifre Naso 40.
47 Song of Songs Rabbah 2:20; Exodus Rabbah 20:21; YS Beshalah 226.
48 MSY, p. 97. Possibly noshekei romei keshet was taken as an allusion to Rome.

---

[36] Bar Kokhba's original name was Simeon bar Koseva. It was changed honorifically to "Bar Kokhba" ("son of the star," a reference to Numbers 24:17 "a star rises from Jacob"). Then after his defeat people derogatorily called him "bar Koziva" ("the fraud").

[37] Third-generation Tanna, colleague of Rabbi Akiva.

[38] A rather colorful and almost vulgar way of dismissing Akiva's enthusiastic assertion. Johanan ben Torta's expression is more or less equivalent in meaning and tone to the English "you'll be pushing up daisies."

[39] The phrase as used here means to refer to the coming of the Messianic Age.

[40] See the paragraph below for an explanation of this "oath."

[41] That is, although you cannot know when it will be, you can trust that God is keeping it in store.

culating the end of days and "the Oath."[49] What oath did they violate? We find the answer to what is hinted at here given explicitly in another place: "God imposed four oaths against Israel . . . that they shall not rebel against the established government and they shall not seek to hasten 'the end of days.'"[50]

Indeed, the Sage Rabbi Yose ben Halafta, who shared many of Rabbi Ishmael's views, taught: "He who seeks to calculate the time of redemption forfeits his share in the world to come."[51]

"Rabbi Nathan said, 'The following verse pierces and plumbs the very depths: "For there is yet a prophecy for a set term, a truthful witness for a time that will come. Even if it tarries, wait for it still; for it will surely come, without delay"' (Habakkuk 2:3). Not as our rabbis interpreted according to Daniel (7:25)—'a time, times, and half a time,' nor as Rabbi Simlai[42] interpreted, 'You have fed them tears as their daily bread, made them drink tears threefold' (Psalm 80:6), nor as Rabbi Akiva interpreted, 'In just a little while longer I will shake the heavens and the earth' (Haggai 2:6), but the first kingdom will be seventy years, and the second kingdom fifty-two years, and the kingdom of Ben Koziva two and a half years."[52] [43]

The clash of views among the Sages on this subject came at a time of great crisis and upheaval. A large segment of the people were seized with fanatical zeal and obsessed with the idea of overthrowing the Roman tyranny by force. Rabbi Akiva, who believed the time of redemption had come, was among those Sages who rejected any compromise and preached rebellion. Rabbi Ishmael appears to have been among those who warned against confrontation and preached submission to Roman decrees by avoiding public protests and practicing forbearance until the angry storm would subside. They opposed the rebellion and preferred to make accommodation to reality.

[49] MI Shirata 9.
[50] Song of Songs Rabbah 2:7; also BT Ketubot 111a. The other two are "not to reveal their secrets to the Gentiles, and not to return from exile in one large bloc [presumably, before God wills it].
[51] Derekh Eretz Rabbah 11.
[52] BT Sanhedrin 97b.

---

[42] Second-generation Amora, Land of Israel. Apparently the ensuing discussion is not part of the Tanna Rabbi Nathan's statement, but a later talmudic comment juxtaposing various other views.
[43] Note the following play on words: "Truthful witness" in Habakkuk is: lo yekhazev (will not lie). The derogatory epithet "Ben Koziva" (with which Bar Kokhba was dubbed by his opponents) means "the Fraud," from the same verbal stem kzv.
The entire midrash here is predicated on the rejection of the various attempts that had been made to calculate the messianic advent. As Rashi reads the passage in BT Sanhedrin 97b, "The Rabbis" used the words of Daniel to calculate a time of fourteen hundred years; Rabbi Simlai calculated, on the basis of Psalm 80, a time of 1410 years; and Rabbi Akiva used the prophet Haggai's words to suggest that the Messianic Age was imminent. But Rabbi Nathan looked into "the depths." For him, there was a "little while" not to the Messianic Age but rather for the enjoyment of Jewish sovereignty: seventy years under the Hasmoneans, fifty-two years under Herod, and two and one-half years under Bar Kokhbah. Then it would be an indefinite wait until the Messiah's arrival, and calculation was futile.

A popular proverb declared: When it is the fox's time to be ruler, all animals must bow to him.[53] This appears to have been the opinion of Rabbi Joshua ben Hananiah, to whose thought Rabbi Ishmael was close.[54]

On submitting to the ruling power, Rabbi Ishmael gave this exposition of the verse, "So the Lord spoke to Moses and Aaron *in regard to* . . . Pharaoh King of Egypt" (Exodus 6:13)—this means that God instructed them to show the respect due to royalty.[55] He is also the author of the saying, "Be submissive to a superior, and affable to a junior."[56]

Among the cautious Sages of that generation you also find Rabbi Yose ben Kisma, who said to Rabbi Hananiah ben Teradyon,[44] the one who "organized public gatherings" to teach Torah at a time when the ruling powers prohibited such gatherings, "My brethren, do you not understand that it was heaven that ordained that this nation rule over us?"[57] And the saying of Rabbi Yose bar Hanina,[45] of a later generation, illustrates the evolution of sentiment on this issue over time: "The Holy and Blessed One has imposed two oaths, one for the people Israel: do not rebel against the established government; one for the ruling power: do not impose too heavy a burden upon Israel."[58]

---

[53] BT Megillah 16b.

[54] See Genesis Rabbah 64:10: Rabbi Joshua was charged with pacifying the Jewish gathering at Beit Rimmon after the Romans withdrew permission to rebuild the Temple. He told them the parable of the crane who picked out a bone from the throat of a lion, and on asking for his reward, was told, "Be grateful that you had your head in the lion's mouth and still escaped unharmed!"

[55] MI Pisha 13.

[56] Avot 3:12.

[57] BT Avodah Zarah 18a.

[58] Song of Songs Rabbah 2:7. The continuation is pregnant with significance: "For if they impose too heavy a burden on Israel, they will bring about the redemption prematurely." Compare also BT Ketubot llla, cited above.

---

[44] Yose ben Kisma and Hananiah (a.k.a. Hanina) ben Teradyon were third-generation Tannaim.

[45] Second-generation Amora, a century later.

12

SCRIPTURAL LANGUAGE NOT BEFITTING GOD'S DIGNITY

Translator's Introduction

In this chapter and the next, Heschel closes the circle and returns to the issue of theological language, which he treated in chapter 2, but he has covered a lot of ground in between. The theological ideas with which he has acquainted us in the intervening chapters inform the discussion of textual-hermeneutic issues, which is resumed here.

Rabbi Ishmael has hitherto been presented as the advocate of a commonsense reading of the Torah text. The text means what it says. "The Torah speaks in human language," so redundancies are simply a stylistic feature, not to be loaded with a lot of hyperinterpretive baggage. But Rabbi Ishmael also has certain definite theological ideas. God is abstract, transcendent, remote, not emotionally involved with us in a direct way. What if it should turn out that the Torah text, on which Rabbi Ishmael relies, lends credence in many places to a passionate, involved God in the Akivan mold? Rabbi Ishmael might then have to resort to symbolic or metaphorical reading of those biblical passages, in order to reconcile them with his theological notions. He might have to depart from his preferred exegetical mode, in order to salvage his theology.

Does it follow, then, that Rabbi Akiva's treatment of the same anthropomorphic passages will be more literal? Possibly, but not necessarily. In some cases, "literal" may be an apt designation of the Akivan treatment ("the idols cannot see, speak, or smell, but our God can," etc.). But sometimes the Akivan exegesis is as fanciful and prolific in these theological contexts as we have been accustomed to expect from him. What is the difference, then, between the Ishmaelian and Akivan exegesis, when neither hews to the plain literal sense?

The difference is important but hard to characterize. We may attempt to express it by saying that Rabbi Ishmael wants to play down the anthropomorphism, while Rabbi Akiva wants to play it up. To Rabbi Ishmael, the truth behind the words is at bottom inexpressible, and the expressions we have in the Torah are but a concession to the weakness of human understanding. Heschel has already in chapter 1 alerted us to the Ishmaelian quality of some of Maimonides' philosophy in the Middle Ages, and that will come through here as well, since Maimonides preeminently argued for the limits of language in describing the divine. Our expressions are "conventional" (in the sense discussed in chapter 4)—one may just as well use one symbolic means of expression as another, for they are all inadequate except as means of pointing beyond themselves, to the transcendent, abstract reality beyond all human words and conceptions.

By contrast, we have the Akivan formula, "Were it not written, we could not say it!" But it **is** written thus, and so we must take it as a necessary, unalterable revelation of some secret of the infinite divine mystery. The accompanying exegesis will then expand on the biblical figure and end up with an even more extravagant image than the original ("as a nursing mother leaning over her child and suckling him," etc.). This approach has been called *hyperliteralism* by modern students of Jewish mysticism; the text is taken as meaning more than what the words say, not less.

Heschel coined the phrase "the prophetic understatement" in *God in Search of Man*. In that context, he cited the Ishmaelian maxim, "the text adapts itself to what the human ear can hear." But this Heschelian concept is truly the intellectual child of both the approaches discussed in this chapter.

Can Such a Thing Be Said?

RABBI ISHMAEL, THE RATIONALIST, attempted to reinterpret, in a way that would be acceptable to the rational mind, those scriptural passages not befitting God's dignity. These fall into the following categories:

(a) References to God as having spatial location ("pass over," "the Lord went," "I will pass through the land of Egypt," "I will see the blood," "I will enshrine [God]").

(b) References to God as having sensory organs ("the ears of the Lord"), bodily needs (such as rest), or emotions (jealousy).

(c) Other expressions impugning God's uniqueness or transcendence ("Who is like You among the gods?" "The Lord is a man of war," "I bore you upon eagle's wings").

In these instances, Rabbi Ishmael gave spiritual or metaphorical interpretations.[1]

It says of the original Pesah event: "And the blood on the houses where you are staying shall be a sign for you: when I see the blood, *ufasahti* (I will pass over) you" (Exodus 12:13). In the school of Rabbi Akiva this word *ufasahti* is understood graphically: "Were it not written, we could not say it! God is portrayed as a nursing mother

---

[1] This is in keeping with the "plain-meaning" approach to Scripture, which is certainly not identical with a "literalist" approach. That is, the plain meaning may in fact be a metaphorical one and not a literal one.

leaning over her child and suckling him."[1] However, Rabbi Ishmael took it in an abstract sense, "I shall have mercy," as in the verse "As birds hovering, so will the Lord of Hosts protect Jerusalem, shielding it and saving, protecting (*pasoah*) and rescuing" (Isaiah 31:5).[2] 2

Or consider the verse: "The Lord went before them in a pillar of cloud by day, to guide them along the way" (Exodus 13:21). Rabbi Yose the Galilean interpreted this verse literally: "Were it not written, we could not say it! It is like a father who holds a lantern for his son, or a master who holds it for his servant."[3] When a mortal human being acquires a servant, it is the servant who holds the lantern to light the way for his master. Not so with the Holy and Blessed One, Who holds the lantern aloft to light the way for Israel.[4]

But in the school of Rabbi Ishmael we find a different approach. They expressed their astonishment: "How is it possible to say 'The Lord went'? Did not the prophet say long ago about God, 'Do I not fill heaven and earth' (Jeremiah 23:24)? Is it not written, 'the whole earth is full of His glory' (Isaiah 6:3)? How can we say of God, 'He went,' which implies going from one place to another, when in fact, His glory is everywhere?"[5]

In the last passage, the question was raised but the answer was omitted. But in the next case, we find the answer without the question. A verse says, "I [the Lord] shall pass (*ve'avarti*) through the land of Egypt' (Exodus 12:12). Rabbi Judah, a disciple of Rabbi Akiva, understands this verse literally and elaborates: "Like a king going from place to place."[6] How does Rabbi Ishmael understand it? We may infer his question from his solution: "'*Ve'avarti*—I will impart my *evrah* [wrath] upon the Egyptians,' as we find in the verse 'He sent upon them the fierceness of His anger, wrath [*evrah*], indignation, and trouble'" (Psalm 78:49).[3] 7

Consider as well this verse: "When I see the blood [I shall pass over you]" (Exodus 12:13). Onkelos interprets it literally, "when I actually see the blood of the paschal lamb." And there is yet another interpretation that expands the meaning to include the blood of circumcision, which was mixed with the blood of the paschal lamb and smeared upon the doorposts.[8] A late midrash elaborates on this. "When the Holy One passed through to smite the Egyptians and saw the blood of the covenant and the blood of the paschal lamb, He was filled with compassion for Israel, as it is said,

---

[1] MSY, p. 27.   [2] MI Pisha 7.   [3] MSY, p. 47.
[4] Tanhuma, additions to Shelah 11; Exodus Rabbah 25:6
[5] MI Beshalah, intro.   [6] MI Pisha 7, 11; MSY, p. 14.   [7] MI Pisha 7.
[8] Jerusalem Targum (traditionally ascribed to Jonathan ben Uzziel).

---

[2] See NJV on Exodus 12, in which it is noted that *psh* may, in fact, mean "protection."

[3] Thus, the Ishmaelian exegesis uses the coincidence in root between "passing" and "wrath" [each comes from the root '*vr*] to move away from the literalist meaning that implies movement on God's part, and instead embrace a more plain, but metaphorical meaning that denotes a wrathful violence that will result for the Egyptians.

"When I passed by you and saw you wallowing in your blood, I said to you, 'In your blood, live; yea, I said to you, in your blood live'" (Ezekiel 16:6).[9]

Rabbi Ishmael had a completely different perspective on the verse "When I see the blood." He raised the question, "Is not everything revealed to Him? Is it not written, '[God] knows what is in the darkness and light dwells with Him'? (Daniel 2:22). What, then, is the significance of 'When I see the blood'? It means that as a reward for performing this mitzvah God is manifested to Israel and has mercy upon them. For the root *psh* means nothing more or less than "to have compassion."[4] "When I see" means "when I know," and "the blood" refers to the performance of the mitzvah.[10]

Similarly, the verse "This is my God *ve'anvehu* (and I will enshrine Him)" (Exodus 15:2) presented a difficulty. What is the meaning of the word *ve'anvehu?*[5] Onkelos derived it from *naveh,* a dwelling place, and translated it, "I will build Him a Sanctuary." Rabbi Ishmael, however, argued, "How is it possible for mere mortals to enshrine their Creator?"[6] He therefore derived *ve'anvehu* from *noi* ("beauty") and interpreted: "I will beautify God with mitzvot—I will make for God a beautiful palm branch, a beautiful Sukkah, beautiful fringes, beautiful prayers."[7] [11]

---

[9] PRE 29; Numbers Rabbah 14:12.   [10] MI Pisha 7, 11.   [11] MI Shirata 3.

---

[4] This is the equivalent here of "protection," the alternate translation given above.

[5] The Rabbis' puzzlement over this word was not theirs alone. There is a similar range of divergence in the various English translations: "I will prepare him an habitation" (AV), "I will glorify Him" (NEB, OJV), "I will enshrine Him" (NJV).

[6] That is, the whole idea of building a place to house God is absurd.

[7] Heschel includes the following additional examples of reinterpretation:

"The people complained bitterly in God's ears" (Numbers 11:1)—[But are we to believe that God has ears? No, rather this language expresses the people's urgency:] "This indicates that it was their purpose to be heard by God. It is like a man cursing the king, who was warned, 'Be quiet, the king may hear you!' He replied, 'Maybe I want him to hear me!'" (Sifre Beha'alotekha 85, version of *Midrash Hakhamim*).

"God rested on the seventh day" (Exodus 20:11)—"But does God experience weariness? 'He never grows faint or weary'! (Isaiah 40:28). 'By the mere word of the Lord the heavens were made'! (Psalm 33:6). Rather, God, as it were, had it recorded that He created the world in six days and rested on the seventh"—even though that was not to be taken literally (MI Bahodesh 7).

"Who is like You, O Lord, among the gods?" (Exodus 15:11). This verse troubled the ancients. Was it likely that Moses and the Israelites ascribed reality to the pagan gods? Onkelos paraphrased rather than translated: "There is none but You, for You are the God, the Lord!" The Mekhilta of Rabbi Ishmael, however, says that the Israelites here were giving voice to the reaction of the Gentiles: "And not only did the Israelites praise God in song, but also the nations of the world, when they heard that Pharaoh and the Egyptians perished in the sea, that their hegemony was abolished, and that their idols suffered judgments. At that, they too foreswore their idols and opened their mouths in acknowledgment of God, saying, 'Who is like You, O Lord, among the gods?'" (MI Shirata 8). Elsewhere is preserved the midrash: "This verse was said by Pharaoh when he heard the Israelites praising God in song at the Sea" (*Midrash Aggadah* ad loc.).

Another troubling verse that appears in the Song at the Sea of Reeds is: "The Lord is a man of war, the Lord is His name." According to Rabbi Judah, a disciple of Rabbi Akiva, the verse tells us "that God revealed Himself to them in all His armor, as a warrior girded with a sword, as a horseman in a coat of armor and helmet, holding a spear, wearing breastplate and shield." Although the Holy and Blessed One had no need for these accoutrements, this is how He appeared to them.[12] Another unattributed exegesis holds that "The Lord is His name" comes to teach us that this is the same God who later appeared to them at Sinai in the appearance of a loving elder, as it is said, "and they saw the God of Israel: under His feet there was a likeness of a pavement of sapphire" (Exodus 24:10). "The Lord is His name" comes to prevent us from concluding that the different guise implies a different God.[13] This must be an Akivan view, for as we shall see later on, the school of Rabbi Ishmael did not take the story of Israel seeing God in Exodus 24 literally.

Rabbi Ishmael's interpretation was as follows:

> "The Lord is a man of war"—Can such a thing be said? Does it not say: "For I fill both heaven and earth, declares the Lord"? (Jeremiah 23:24). And: "Holy, holy, holy! The Lord of Hosts! His presence fills all the earth!" (Isaiah 6:3). And: "There was the Presence of the God of Israel, and the earth was lit up by His Presence" (Ezekiel 43:2). What, then, does this verse, "The Lord is a man of war" come to tell us? In effect, God says to Israel, because of your love for Me and because you have become holy by performing My mitzvot, I will sanctify My name through you, as it is written, "Though I am God, and not a man, yet I, the Holy and Blessed One, am in your midst" (Hosea 11:9)—I sanctify My name by you.[8] [14]

If you wish to fathom the meaning of this exegesis, give full weight to the prophetic texts cited here, which are absent from the Akivan sources. The verse from Hosea seems totally to undermine the meaning of the original verse from Exodus. The latter says, "The Lord is a man of war," while the former says, "I am God and not a man." It seems to me that he recommends reading the verse in Exodus as a rhetorical question: "Is the Lord a man of war? (Obviously not!) The Lord is His name." The midrash continues in the same vein: "'The Lord is His name'—God does battle through the power of His name, and has no need of armaments." Another possible reading of the verse is: "The Lord is (God and not) a man of war. The Lord is His name—I do battle with My name."[9]

---

[12] MI Shirata 4.   [13] MSY, p. 81.   [14] MI Shirata 4.

---

[8] That is, God did not appear in human guise at all, but rather, God will establish a connection of sanctity with the Israelites, as a reward for their obedience. Even this connection should have been un-Godlike, but the verse in Hosea opens the door for this minimal humanlike bond. That is all the verse in Exodus 15 means to say when it calls God a man. See also Heschel's explanation immediately following.

[9] Heschel now provides further examples:

"I bore you on eagles' wings"—according to Rabbi Ishmael, this is a metaphor for the swift migra-

In Rabbi Ishmael's school, they sensed that language is incapable of communicating God's truth in all its essence, just as mortals are incapable of hearing the voice of God in all its power. They taught that the text "directs toward the ear that which the ear can hear."[10] 15 In other words, the text accommodates itself to the power of human imagination. This expression is drawn from the midrash on the Sinaitic revelation, of which it was also said: "God imparted to each person according to his or her capacity."16 "Adapting to what the ear can hear" is close to the medieval philosophers' understanding of the Ishmaelian maxim "The Torah speaks the language of human beings"; that is, one should interpret all corporeal figures of speech that refer to God in an allegorical sense. Even though we do not find this particular maxim used in this sense in the Tannaitic or Amoraic literature, we can see from the many places where Rabbi Ishmael labors to give a rational turn to phrases not befitting God's dignity that this usage well fits his overall outlook.

Rabbi Ishmael enunciated another principle: "The Torah speaks in terms of common usage."[11] This motto embodies the notion that not every word in the Torah is meant to teach hard and fast law. Sometimes the text just comes to teach us common courtesy and accepted usage. It was later used by teachers of aggadah to explain scriptural passages that were not in keeping with God's dignity. Thus, in the story of the Tower of Babel, we read, "And God descended to see the city and the tower" (Genesis 11:5). Again the well-known question of Rabbi Ishmael was raised: "Is not everything revealed to Him? Why the need to descend and see?! Scripture, however, intends to teach us proper conduct toward our fellow man. One must not jump to hasty conclusions in matters of law, nor may one express an opinion on a matter before seeing it."[12] 17

---

15 MI Bahodesh 4.   16 MI Bahodesh 9.   17 TB Noah 28.

---

tion of the Israelites from Raamses to Sukkoth; the Akivan interpretation is that the ministering angels —and even God—carried them to assist them on their journey (MI Pisha 14; MI Bahodesh 2, 9).

"Advance, O Lord, may Your enemies be scattered, and may Your foes flee before you!" (Numbers 10:35). In the school of Rabbi Ishmael, they asked: Is anyone, indeed, the enemy of God? Rather, whoever is an enemy of Israel is regarded as an enemy of God (Sifre Beha'alotekha 84).

"God put Abraham to the test" (Genesis 22:1). Was God unable to foresee the outcome in advance? Rabbi Yose the Galilean said: God did this to elevate Abraham in the eyes of others (connecting nissah ["tested"] with nes ["banner," e.g., the banner of a ship] (Genesis Rabbah 55:6). Rabbi Joshua had already anticipated this view of Rabbi Ishmael. See MI Vayyassa' 1 (on vesham nissahu), also MI Bahodesh 9.

[10] See the full midrashic context of this maxim at the end of this section of the text. Heschel cites this midrashic passage elsewhere as an example of "prophetic understatement." See God in Search of Man, 183 n. 2.

[11] "Common usage"—Hebrew: derekh eretz ("the way of the world"). Here is another facet of this far-reaching concept that was addressed at greater length in chapter 8 above.

[12] Indeed, it is a common expression in Jewish jurisprudence that "a judge has only what his eyes see." The phrase not only entitles a judge to utilize subjective judgment in rendering a decision [its

Philo, the Alexandrian philosopher, had already given this exegesis and even included the phrase "the giver of the Torah spoke the language of human beings." Here are his words: "'And God descended to see the city and the tower'—these words must be understood metaphorically. The giver of the Torah uses human language when speaking of God, who transcends humanity, in order to teach us, the students, a particular lesson." Moses was aware of God's knowledge of both past and future events, but he described God's visit to the city and the tower in order to teach us not to jump to conclusions, not to rely on mere assumptions, and to instruct us that "those who have not witnessed personally things far removed from them must not hastily reach conclusions or rely on unfounded assumptions."[18]

There are other passages in Scripture that seem to cast doubt on God's attributes of justice and righteousness, and the Sages of the midrash struggled to explain them. Thus, in the story of the Exodus we read, "the Lord struck down all the firstborn . . . from the firstborn of Pharaoh who sat on the throne to the firstborn of the captive in the dungeon, and all the firstborn of the cattle" (Exodus 12:29). In the school of Rabbi Ishmael, the question was raised, "of what sin were the captives guilty? As for the cattle, can we say they sinned?"[19] Or, with regard to exterminating all Amalekites, they asked "True, the men may have sinned against Israel and deserved to be punished, but why the women and the children and the cattle?"[13][20]

The Sages, in seeking some rationale, placed certain limitations on God's exercise of strict justice. On the verse "For I, the Lord your God, am a jealous God" (Exodus 20:5), they gave this interpretation: "I will jealously punish those who are guilty of idolatry; but with the other transgressions I am a merciful and compassionate God." Or, on the verse "visiting the iniquity of the fathers upon the children" (Exodus

---

[18] See H. A. Wolfson, *Philo: Foundations of Religious Philosophy in Judaism, Christianity, and Islam*, 2 vols. (Cambridge, Mass.: Harvard University Press, 1947), 2:189. Philo's formulation is: "The Lawgiver [*nomothetēs*] uses human language [*anthropologeita*]." Philo gave a similar interpretation of God's "going down" to investigate the case of Sodom in Genesis 18:21 (*Questions on Genesis* 4.24).

[19] MI Pisha 13.

[20] Ecclesiastes Rabbah 7:16; BT Yoma 22b.

---

usual interpretation], but also requires the judge to see for himself what the facts are before attempting to dispose of the case.

[13] This touches on the philosophical problem already formulated (in polytheistic language) by Plato in the dialogue *Euthyphro*: Is God or "good" preeminent? Does God define "the good" by the divine will (and therefore God is not bound by common, human moral considerations), or is God "answerable" to common notions of the good so that God's own actions can be judged by them? Abraham, of course, had apparently done just that in Genesis 18, when he questioned the justice of God destroying the entire population of Sodom and Gomorrah, including those who did not sin. Here as elsewhere, Rabbi Ishmael seems to accord autonomy to human, commonsense, and worldly norms, to which even God is expected to conform. At least, he is willing to raise the question, even though the answer may be that we cannot know the transcendent God's motives. That God must play by the rules of ethics has its counterpart in the assertion by Rabbi Joshua that God must also play by the rules of Halakhah as well. See chapter 34 below.

34:7), they gave this interpretation: "This punishment applies when there is no hiatus between the generations, that is, a wicked father, followed by a wicked son and a wicked grandson, or a destroyer, son of a destroyer, son of a destroyer. When, however, they skip a generation, it does not apply." When Moses heard this explanation, he exclaimed, "On no account! It could never happen among our people—a wicked person, followed by a wicked son and a wicked grandson."[21]

Rabbi Ishmael's approach to these difficult scriptural texts may be summarized by this passage in the Mekhilta: "It was taught in the school of Rabbi Ishmael, 'We match the burden to the strength of the camel.'"[14] [22] Concerning the fire that appeared at the great gathering at Mount Sinai, Scripture says, "Now Mount Sinai was all in smoke, for the Lord had come down upon it in fire; the smoke rose like the smoke of a furnace" (Exodus 19:18). One might infer that it was like ordinary smoke; therefore we are told, "of a furnace." Now we still might think it was like the smoke of an ordinary furnace. But we are told in another passage, "The mountain was ablaze with flames to the very skies, dark with the densest clouds" (Deuteronomy 4:11). Why then does Scripture say "like the smoke of a furnace"? So that the ear would hear what it has the capacity to understand.[15] There are several examples of this in Scripture. The verse reads, "A lion has roared, who can but fear?" (Amos 3:8). This is a strange metaphor for God. After all, who gave the lion strength and power to be feared if not God Himself?[16] However, in order to describe God in a manner that people can comprehend, Scripture uses familiar figures of speech, creatures known by experience. Or, . . . "and His voice was like the roar of mighty waters" (Ezekiel 43:2). Who gave strength and might to the waters? Was it not God? But Scripture describes God by figures known to us from the world God created, so that the ear may comprehend.[23]

[21] MI Bahodesh 6.
[22] BT Sotah 13a.
[23] MI Bahodesh 4.

---

[14] Heschel applies this maxim on many levels. In chapter 8, he saw it as an expression of Rabbi Ishmael's halakhic leniency, that he did not load the people with more duties than they could perform. The midrashic scholar Theodor commented on this, saying that in Rabbi Ishmael's view, God imposed trials and sufferings on individuals in accordance with their capacity to bear them. Here it becomes a principle of textual hermeneutics: the Torah chooses language in accordance with human ability to understand it. Once again, the many levels of theological discourse intersect and illuminate each other.

[15] That is, the image of a smoking furnace is one that is available to most people. If the Torah had merely said that the mountain was ablaze in flames to the very skies, imagination might have failed the average reader.

[16] It thus makes no sense to compare God to that which is a creature of God. The point, of course, is that this objection could be raised to anything at all to which God was to be compared. Either comparisons must be entirely forgone, and with them the very possibility of speech about God, or we must conclude that we are dealing with imperfect metaphors that are there to aid the imagination and understanding.

Were It Not Written, We Could Not Say It!

Nothing reveals a thinker's approach better than the characteristic formulation of his questions. Characteristic of Rabbi Ishmael's school are the questions: "Is not all revealed before God? What use is the blood to the angel or to Israel? Do Moses' hands strengthen Israel or weaken Amalek? Does a bronze snake kill or heal? Did they really eat before God? What sin did the captives commit? Does God really get weary? How can humans call God by name? How can mortals ascend to Heaven and embrace fire?"[17] 24

When Rabbi Akiva found strange or difficult language in the Torah, he opened his ears as wide as a hopper. For him, paradox in the text was a door to hidden truths of Torah. Rabbi Ishmael tried to purify the text of such elements, saying, "Torah speaks in human language," or "it tells only what the ear can hear." To take such strange or difficult parts as literally true was erroneous, in his view.

When Rabbi Akiva and his disciples came upon a difficult scriptural text, they would say, "If this verse had not been written in the Torah, it would be impossible for us to say it."25 Since it is written, however, we not only say it, but these passages, in their literal sense, constitute the very essence of Torah.

Thus, Rabbi Akiva was not afraid to speak of transcendental matters in corporeal terms. We find in his discourse such expressions as: "God pointed this out to Moses with a finger"26; "Manna is the bread that the ministering angels eat"27; "'The birds of the sky dwell upon them' (Psalm 104:12)—this refers to the ministering angels"28; "God bent down the upper and lower heavens so they touched the mountain, and the divine glory descended on Mount Sinai, like a *person* who sets out a pillow at the head of the bed, and like a *person* who speaks with head resting on the pillow."29 All this is characteristic of many of his homilies.

In the Book of Daniel, we are told that Daniel saw in a dream two thrones of justice set up in heaven. On one sat the Holy and Blessed One (Daniel 7:9). Rabbi Akiva was asked, "To whom was the second chair assigned?" And he answered, "One is for God and one is for King David." This daring explanation, which raised David to the stature of having a seat next to the Holy and Blessed One, provoked a sharp comment from Rabbi Yose the Galilean[18] who exclaimed, "Akiva, how long will you continue

---

24 MI Pisha 7,11,13; MI Beshalah 1; MI Amalek 1; PT Eruvin 5:1, 22b; Sifre Ekev 49.
25 MSY, p. 16, p. 27.   26 MI Pisha 1.
27 BT Yoma 75b.   28 Midrash on Psalms 104:9.
29 MI Bahodesh 4.

---

[17] These questions concern the sense we are to make of God's testing humans, of the need to smear the paschal blood on the doorposts, of God resting on the seventh day, and many other passages that ascribe less than omnipotent powers to God.

[18] Third-generation Tanna.

to degrade the Shekhinah to the level of the mundane?"[19] [30] We learn from this that besides this exegesis, Rabbi Akiva produced many others that were bitter pills for Rabbi Yose the Galilean and his colleagues. Rabbi Eleazar ben Azariah also objected to this exegesis and said, "What business do you have dabbling in Aggadah? Go back to studying skin-diseases and tent-impurities!"[20] [31]

Rabbi Akiva's exegeses of the passages relating to the Divine Presence were audacious and astonishing. His images are opaque and strange and can easily lead to heretical conclusions. But it is precisely because of their audaciousness, their exaggerations to the point of irreverence for the divine and distortion of basic doctrines, that we are compelled to examine the text and to realize that they are not to be understood literally.

Thus, for example, he stated, "The Holy and Blessed One revealed Himself (at the Sea of Reeds) riding on a male horse, for it is written, "He mounted a horse (a cherub) and flew" (Psalm 18:11). "The Holy and Blessed One rode, as it were, on a red horse, a white one, and a black one, as it is written, 'You have trodden the sea with Your horses' (Habakkuk 3:15). This means not many horses but one horse of many colors."[32]

Or let us compare two treatments of the same topic: "Who is like You among the gods?" (Exodus 15:11). In the Mekhilta of Rabbi Ishmael, we find: "Who is like You among those whom the others call 'gods' though they have no substance. Of such it is said: 'They have mouths but cannot speak' (Psalm 115:5)—but the Holy and Blessed One says two different things in the same utterance, which is impossible for mortals, as it says: 'One thing God has spoken; two things have I heard' (Psalm 62:12), and: 'Behold My word is like fire, declares the Lord, and like a hammer that shatters rock!'"[21] (Jeremiah 23:29).[33] Against this we find the following continuation of the same passage in the Mekhilta of Rabbi Simeon ben Yohai: "'They have . . . eyes, but cannot see'—but not so the One who spoke and the world came into being; rather, 'the eyes of the Lord range over the entire earth' (2 Chronicles 16:9). "They

---

[30] BT Hagigah 14a.   [31] Midrash on Psalms 104:9; BT Yoma 75b.
[32] Song of Songs Rabbah 1:48; MI Beshalah 6.   [33] MI Shirata 8.

---

[19] That Rabbi Yose the Galilean reacted in this way is, for Heschel, a measure of how daring the exegesis of Akiva was in this instance. For Yose the Galilean was often seen to reflect an Akivan mode of exegesis. And yet here he declines to "go the limit." The Passover Haggadah perhaps reflects a bit of this, in that Yose the Galilean is willing to use exegetical tools to expand the number of plagues from the ten in Egypt to include another fifty at the Sea. But Akiva's expansion far outstrips his: he comes up with fifty in Egypt and two hundred fifty at the Sea!

[20] Areas of Halakhah that are both arcane and, with the Temple destroyed, of no practical application. In such areas, Akiva's expansiveness and unusual interpretations would be of intellectual interest but would cause no harm. In theology, however, Akiva's exegetical pyrotechnics could perhaps lead to misunderstanding or even heresy.

[21] The midrash on this is crucial to the point: Just as a hammer striking a rock causes many sparks to fly, so does one word of the Torah generate many meanings.

have ears, but cannot hear"—but not so our Creator; rather, 'You will listen to the entreaty of the lowly, O Lord, You will make their hearts firm, You will incline Your ear' (Psalm 10:17). 'Noses, but cannot smell'—but not so our God; rather, 'The Lord smelled the pleasing odor' (Genesis 8:21). 'They have hands, but cannot touch'—but not so our Maker; rather, 'My own hand founded the earth' (Isaiah 48:13). 'Feet, but cannot walk'—but not so our Eternal; rather, 'On that day, He will set His feet on the Mount of Olives' (Zechariah 14:4). 'They can make no sound in their throats,' but not so our Holy and Blessed One; rather, 'His mouth is delicious' (Song of Songs 5:16), and: 'Just listen to the sound that comes out of His mouth' (Job 37:2)."[22] 34

Another illustration of this kind of audacious exegesis is found in the comment of Rabbi Akiva on the account of God's anger when Israel sinned with the golden calf. Scripture states that God said to Moses: "Let me alone and I will destroy them" (Deuteronomy 9:14). In the school of Rabbi Ishmael, they expressed astonishment at this phrase, "let me alone"—"Does this mean that Moses was holding on to the Holy and Blessed One as if trying to prevent Him from carrying out His intention?"35 Rabbi Akiva, however, said, "If this were not written in the Torah we could not utter these words. However (since it is written) it teaches us that Moses held on to the Holy and Blessed One as a man holds on to the garment of a neighbor and said to Him, 'Master of the Universe, I will not let go of You, until You forgive and pardon them.'"36

It is clear that when he dealt with these matters, Rabbi Akiva did not speak the language of ordinary human beings, nor present logical concepts where one idea is deduced from another. Here Rabbi Akiva became the mystic and spoke the language of those who delved into the mysteries of the Merkavah.[23] He made use of symbols with hidden meanings and of metaphors to convey certain images and ideas. They are like doves fluttering above the waters; they touch and yet do not touch the subject under discussion.[24]

The life of man is imprisoned in earthly concerns, but his soul opens somewhat to heavenly matters. He is therefore obliged to speak in two tongues, one entirely earthly, the other entirely heavenly. He must, perforce, use two types of idioms. The

---

34 MSY, p. 92.
35 Sifre Va'ethanan 27; Deuteronomy Rabbah 3:15, comment of Rabbi Simon.
36 BT Berakhot 32a.

---

[22] And thus we see that the Ishmaelian exegesis is concerned to glorify God's powers without giving any credence to the anthropomorphic language of Scripture. The Akivan exegesis in MSY, however, concentrates our attention on even more verses that describe God's eyes, ears, arms, and so on.
[23] See chapters 15–16 for detailed examination of this aspect of Rabbi Akiva's teaching.
[24] The last phrase is intended to convey the difficulty in grasping clearly the mystical language that Heschel is ascribing to Akiva. It also recalls the mystery of creation through the image of hovering waters that is the description of God's spirit on the first day of creation. That image is also used by Akiva's colleague Ben Zoma when he is describing some of his own mystical speculations and visions.

earthly idioms are used for all those matters that are within his control, things that he can feel and touch, and things that his mind can grasp and his imagination encompass. He coins the heavenly idioms to express his sense of the sacred, never to be used for any practical purpose but for contemplation alone.[25] They belong in the realm of faith and are beyond the reach of the rational mind. In the realm of thought, we must accept the idea that there are two domains, two lexicons, and one domain should not overlap the other at all.[26] "When the Holy and Blessed One created the world, it was decreed: 'the heavens belong to the Lord, but the earth He gave over to man' (Psalm 115:16). But when God sought to give the Torah, the earlier decree was set aside, and God said: let the lower spheres ascend and the upper descend, and I will begin the process, as it is said: 'The Lord came down upon Mount Sinai' (Exodus 19:20), and further, 'Then He said to Moses, "Come up to the Lord"' (Exodus 24:1)."[27] 37

In Merkavah mysticism they search for the place where heaven and earth embrace. Its language is a ladder set on earth whose head reaches heaven—it is both all earthly and all heavenly. In the idiom of Rabbi Akiva: the revealed things of the world below are on this side and the mysteries of the world above are on the other side.

Rabbi Akiva's turbulent soul yearned to reach the gates of heaven, even to enter the chambers on high. He struggled mightily with all his intellectual powers and wrestled to uncover the secrets of the universe with all the strength he possessed. The roots of his struggle lay in the longing of his spirit, while the branches had their source concealed in his soul. Visionary teachings came from the tongue of Rabbi Akiva, but all have been forgotten in the flow of time. We do not possess the power to open what has been closed nor to revive what has been lost to memory. The wells have been blocked. The encounter with angels has ceased, the ladder has been broken. No one

---

37 Tanhuma Va'era 15; Exodus Rabbah 12:4.

---

[25] The phrase Heschel uses here is precisely the one that is used in halakhic discussions of the Hanukkah candles. Their light is not to be used for any practical purpose—they are only to be seen and contemplated. The aptness of this wordplay here is evident when we consider that what the Hanukkah candles are supposed to evoke is our contemplation of the miraculous.

[26] Once again, Heschel brings in a midrashic phrase to express his point. When Moses asked that he be allowed to live a bit longer, even if Joshua were to be leading the people, God is said to have told Moses that "one domain [i.e., one era of leadership] may not overlap another by even a second." The same phrase is used here not for human dominion, but rather for the domain of thought.

[27] Heschel has here again given expression to the idea that there are, indeed, two realms of thought and language, and that by rights they are separate from one another. But the act of revelation, the giving of the Torah, is the act that somehow brings the rational and the mystical together. We can distinguish the two threads, but the mystery of religion (at least a religion of revelation) consists in the interweaving of the rational and the mystical in ways that we cannot easily describe. He is suggesting here that Akiva achieved this synthesis. But, taking the wider view of Heschel's agenda in this work, he is again hammering away at his main point, which is that Ishmael and Akiva, who represent differing poles of thought and language, really must be synthesized and combined in order to see and apprehend Judaism whole.

ascends, no one descends. Nothing remains but fragmentary bits of language,[28] mystic idioms with no one to use them. They have been rubbed out and survive only as tokens.[29]

The exalted emotion induced by contemplation of the Divine Presence is antagonistic to human language. The mystics, whose visions are not subject to weight and measurement, cannot survive within the narrow confines of pedantic studies. The source of Rabbi Akiva's power lay in his soaring imagination, far beyond the field of critical thought, in a place where the cutting edge of the intellect cannot reach. ". . . the bounds of expression in all languages are very narrow indeed, so that we cannot represent this notion to ourselves except through a certain looseness of expression."[38] Is it not evident that even those expressions which seem fitting to describe the divine attributes, in reality are utterly futile in relation to God's essence? All the attempts at harmonization and adaptation which give the impression that language has succeeded in depicting reality, are essentially defective. Do we imagine that God's essence can be reduced to our definitions? Whichever way we approach this subject, we are led to the conclusion that our intellectual equipment is very limited—for our ways are not His ways.[30]

Hard to Say, and Impossible to Explain[31]

Many other Sages adopted Rabbi Akiva's manner of speaking, notably Rabbi Yose the Galilean, Rabbi Judah ben Ilay, Bar Kappara, Rabbi Joshua ben Levi, Rabbi Johanan ben Nappaha, Rabbi Simeon ben Lakish, Rabbi Abbahu, R. Hanina, and R. Hama bar Hanina.[32]

"The Lord went before them in a pillar of cloud by day, to guide them along the way" (Exodus 13:21)—Rabbi Yose the Galilean said: "Were it not written in Scrip-

---

38 Maimonides, *Guide of the Perplexed,* I:57.

---

[28] The Hebrew suggests trivial denominations of coins (as "bits" does in the expression "two bits"). Throughout, Heschel has used the Hebrew word for "coin"—a traditional word that denotes an honored liturgical or philosophical form—for the mode of expression of Akiva. Now he says that all that is left are "bits"—not real coins, but trivial subdenominations. This metaphor will be built upon in the next phrase.

[29] That is, unminted coins, bullion without images.

[30] It should not be surprising that Heschel, who began this work with a chapter on language (chapter 2), returns again and again to the problem of expressing truths about God and religion in human language. It is, indeed, the major problem in this work and in Heschel's writings generally.

[31] The exact nuance of this is elusive. It seems to mean: Scripture says something so daring that it is hard for us even to quote the scriptural text in its original language, and harder still to elaborate and unpack the full implications of what it means.

[32] These authorities range from third-generation Tanna to third-generation Amora and include many of the prominent aggadists of this time span. See appendix 3 for precise identifications.

ture, you could not say it—like a father carrying a lantern before his son, or like a master carrying a lantern before his servant."[39] Rabbi Judah ben Ilay said: "Were it not written, you could not say it—it implies that Moses was carried on the wings of the Shekhinah."[33] [40] R. Huna in the name of Bar Kappara said: "Were it not written, you could not say it—'God created the heavens and the earth'—from what? From 'The earth was chaos and emptiness,'" that is, from that chaos and emptiness God made the world, and so there was primal matter prior to the creation of the world.[41]

Here are some more of their audacious interpretations of scriptural verses pertaining to God (always with the motto "Were it not written, you could not say it" in the original source):

"But who requites His enemies before His face to destroy them" (Deuteronomy 7:10)—Rabbi Joshua ben Levi said: "Like a man who carries a burden in front of his face and wants to cast it down."[42]

"He who is generous to the poor makes a loan to the Lord" (Proverbs 19:17)—Rabbi Johanan said: "As it were, 'the borrower is a slave to the lender' (Proverbs 22:7)—and thus God becomes subservient (as a borrower) to the one who gives charity!"[43]

"[God said to Satan:] So you have incited Me against him to destroy him for no good reason" (Job 2:3). Rabbi Johanan said, "Like a human being, who yields to temptation!"[44]

"This is the blessing with which Moses, the man of God, bade the Israelites farewell before he died" (Deuteronomy 33:1). Rabbi Simeon ben Lakish said, "Moses is called ish ha'elohim, the husband of God! Just as a wife faithfully obeys her husband's injunctions, so God faithfully obeyed Moses' injunctions."[45]

"And the Lord was standing over [Jacob in his dream]" (Genesis 28:13)—"Like a father standing over his son and fanning him to revive him from the hot desert wind."[46]

"We can learn that parties to a lawsuit should comport themselves reverentially, for they are, as it were, being judged by God. For Jehoshaphat charged the judges saying, 'Consider what you are doing, for you judge not for man, but for the Lord'" (2 Chronicles 19:6).[34] R. Hama bar Hanina said, "Were it not written, you could not say it—human mortals judge their Creator! The Holy and Blessed One says to the

---

[39] MSY, p. 47.   [40] BT Sotah 13b.
[41] Genesis Rabbah 1:5; see Yefei To'ar and Minhat Yehudah ad loc.
[42] BT Eruvin 22a.   [43] BT Bava Batra 10a; Rashi ad loc.
[44] BT Bava Batra 16a.   [45] PRK 32/Supplement 1 (Haberakhah, 198b)
[46] BT Hullin 91b, Rashi ad loc.

---

[33] The issue here is that a not very farfetched reading of Scripture implies that Moses died in the future territory of Reuven but was buried in the future territory of Gad. How did his corpse get from one territory to another? He must have been carried by the wings of the Shekhinah.

[34] The Hebrew particle l- connotes an indirect object in Biblical Hebrew ("on behalf of the Lord"), but a direct object in Aramaic. In the biblical text, God is the supreme Judge who delegates authority to human judges. In the rabbinic interpretation, God is a party to the suit, as plaintiff or defendant.

judges: 'Comport yourselves reverentially, as if you were judging me.' How so? If a person does a mitzvah for Me, I may decree that he should come into possession of a hundred fields. If you deprive him unjustly of one of these, I will compensate him from My own, and I will reckon that you took it from Me."[47]

Just as they went to extremes with language "that compared the powerful image of God to human forms," so did they not shrink from suggesting that the Master of all creatures is a guarantor for His creatures and accepts responsibility for His children. The Lord said to Cain, "Hark, your brother's blood cries out at Me from the ground!" (Genesis 4:10). "Rabbi Simeon ben Yohai said, 'This is hard to say, and impossible for the mouth to explain!' It is like two gladiators in combat before the king. If the king wished, he could separate them, but he did not. One prevailed over the other and slew him. The dying one wailed, 'Bring suit against the king on my behalf, that he did not have mercy on me!' Read not, 'cries out to Me,' but 'cries out against Me'!"[35] [48]

The verse "The Lord is a man of war," which was so troubling for Rabbi Ishmael, was used by Rabbi Simeon ben Yohai and others as the basis of a new hermeneutic rule, that the word "man" in certain places can be interpreted to mean "God." For example:

"A ready word is a joy to a man, and how good is a thing rightly timed!' (Proverbs 15:23)—Not only a joy to man, but also to God (as when God with His word created light and found it good)! Read ish ("man") = God, on the basis of: "The Lord is a man of war."[49]

Rabbi Johanan expounded: "'Yea, mortal is bowed, and man brought low' (Isaiah 5:15)—the people's sinfulness causes depression to God as well."[50]

Rabbi Joshua ben Levi expounded: "When Jacob blessed his sons, 'May God Almighty dispose the man to mercy toward you' (Genesis 43:14), 'the man' means the Holy and Blessed One."[51]

An anonymous exegesis: "A man, a man whose wife goes astray, breaking faith with him" (Numbers 5:12)—she has broken faith with two "men," the supernal Man (God) and the earthly man (her husband).[52]

R. Aha said, "When Israel was exiled, the nations of the world addressed Heaven: 'Like a sparrow wandering from its nest is a man who wanders from his home'

---

[47] TB Shofetim 6.
[48] Genesis Rabbah 22:9; Midrash Haggadol on Genesis 4:10.
[49] Genesis Rabbah 3:3.   [50] BT Sotah 48a.
[51] Genesis Rabbah 92:3; see Minhat Yehudah ad loc.
[52] TB Naso 9.

---

[35] The difference in the Hebrew is minute: it is the exchange of the silent aleph for the nearly silent 'ayin (from eilai to alai). But the change makes an enormous difference: in the former vocalization, Abel is crying out to God for vindication and vengeance. In the latter, Abel is crying out an indictment against God, who is depicted as having responsibility for His creature.

(Proverbs 27:8), alluding to God's exile from His abode, as it says, 'This is My resting-place for all time' (Psalm 132:14)."[53]

These homilies are a paean to the will to link the lower realm to the higher, by finding in the words of the lower realm references to the higher. Probably the authors of these midrashim took the word *ish* (man) not in the sense of "mortal" but in the sense of "master, lord, ruler," as we use it today in the sense of a dominant persona.

[53] Midrash on Psalms 11:1.

13

THE LANGUAGE OF TORAH

Translator's Introduction

Heschel began the substance of this work (in chapter 2) with a discussion of the differences between the literary hermeneutics of the schools of Rabbi Ishmael and Rabbi Akiva. Now he revisits this issue in order to increase its complexity. Up to this point, he has assumed that the literary aspect (how should one interpret the Torah?) was fairly self-evident, and one was therefore free to delve into the theological aspect (what is the nature of God's self-revelation, if that is how one is to read the Torah?). Here he shows us how much even the literary formulae we have accepted to this point are but the tip of the iceberg.

"The Torah speaks in human language" (according to Rabbi Ishmael). But how does human language speak? A complete answer to this question would require one to develop an entire theory not only of grammar but of rhetoric as well. Can one deduce, from the fact that one said X before Y, that X really occurred before Y? No, the events could have occurred and been narrated in different order. ("There is no chronological order in the Torah"; "reverse the text and interpret it.") Does "human language" include people telling white lies, using hyperbole, speaking in metaphor? Then a document that speaks in "human language" will use all these rhetorical devices at times, and the "commonsense" meaning will not be the literal meaning, but beneath the surface. It is not hard, once these principles have been conceived, to find striking instances of them in the books of the Bible. Heschel shows how the Sages of the Ishmaelian school followed this logic to its conclusions and, in so doing, laid the basis for a sophisticated understanding of what the "plain sense" of the Torah really implied.

The Sages of the Akivan persuasion and the medieval mystical commentators after them had a different theory of how the Torah revealed its content through its form, and this required elaboration as well. If the order of the literary units of the Torah is neither strictly chronological nor random, it must be indicative of some thematic connection between those units. Again, if the later narrative books are not there for entertainment (and how could they be?), they must express hidden religious truths. If the Ishmaelians have explained certain phrases as redundancy, hyperbole, or figure of speech, the mystics must counter this "humanistic reductionism" by showing how every one of these expresses the highest mystical truths.

Thus two textual methodologies were developed and elaborated over the centuries: the one based on grammar and rhetoric, the other on principles of mystical interpretation of the outer form of Torah. The theological stakes of this debate have been indicated in the foregoing chapters but will be spelled out at even greater length in subsequent chapters, especially 22–28. If the Torah speaks in human language, then the divine and human, the necessary and conventional, the heavenly and worldly are all intermingled in it; it is a living organism that grows and develops. If every letter and crown are from the divine mouth and reflect not only human language but divine thought as well, then not only the Written Torah but the Oral Torah is sacred and immutable, and every detail is holy.

Is a compromise or synthesis between these two positions possible? Or must one choose between them? This is the pivotal question that leads from this chapter through many subsequent chapters.

Does the Torah Lack Chronological Order?

R ABBI ISHMAEL'S DISCIPLES were very concerned with the characteristics of language. Their interpretations often address the literal meaning of words and rules of grammar.[1] To a Tanna of the school of Rabbi Ishmael is attributed the principle "Reverse the text and interpret it."[2] Also attributed to his school is the comment "Do you assume that whoever said X also said Y? On the contrary!"[3]

"There is no chronological order in the Torah"[1] was a generally accepted axiom of the school of Rabbi Ishmael. It was fundamental for their determination of the *peshat*, the surface or plain-sense meaning of the text. This was for them nothing more than the fruit of examination and analysis: from a close reading of the content, one can see that there were chapters and verses not arranged in the order in which the words were spoken or in which the events occurred. For this reason, Rabbi

---

[1] For example: (i) "The present tense sometimes refers to what will happen in the future" (MI Pisha 18 on Exodus 12:13). (ii) "'Tomorrow' sometimes refers to the remote future" (MI Pisha 18 on Exodus 13:14). (iii) "The verb *naham* means 'to lead'" (MI Beshalah 1 on Exodus 13:17). (iv) "The noun *ka'at* refers to the pelican (*kik*)" (PT Shabbat 4c). (v) "Why are gourds called *kishu'in*? Because they are hard (*kasheh*) on the body as swords" (BT Berakhot 57a). See chapter 2 on Rabbi Ishmael's principle "The Torah speaks in human language," of which this is an elaboration.

[2] Sifre Naso 15. See MI on Exodus 16:20 cited later in this chapter, under "Homily and Plain Sense (*Derash* and *Peshat*)."

[3] Sifre Beha'alotekha 88.

---

[1] Literally: "There is no early-and-late in the Torah"; that is, what comes first in the order of narration may have occurred later in actuality, and vice versa. The reader will recall the discussion in chapter 4 about the chronological relationship between the instructions for the Tabernacle and the sin of the golden calf.

Ishmael rejected the exegetical technique used by some Sages of finding special meanings in contiguous passages. Rabbi Judah the Patriarch was of the same opinion when he said: "There are many passages linked to each other in the text but in actuality they are as far apart as east from west." Rabbi Akiva, however, stated bluntly, "Every passage that adjoins another has to be learned in conjunction with it."[4]

While Rabbi Ishmael's view was received favorably by many of the Sages, it was found objectionable by those who loved to search for hidden meanings in Scripture. Whoever regarded the Torah from a transcendental perspective, "the precious vessel by which the world was created" (to use Rabbi Akiva's description), recoiled from such critical and analytical statements as "there is no chronological order in the Torah," or "we have a misplacement of passages here," or "this verse was not placed in its proper order." He would argue, "The Torah of the Lord is perfect and you say there is no order in the Torah?! Who gave a mere mortal the authority to put the Torah to the test and to declare, 'This passage was not written in its proper place'? How could it even enter one's mind that the Torah, which is the quintessence of perfection, was not arranged in chronological order?!"

The source of Rabbi Ishmael's principle is to be found in the Mekhilta. We read in the Song at the Sea of Reeds, "The foe said, 'I will pursue, I will overtake, I will divide the spoil' (Exodus 15:19). Clearly, this belongs at the beginning of the Song. Why was it placed here? Because there is no chronological order in the Torah."[5] Also the opening verse in Leviticus 9, which deals with the assumption of duties by Aaron and his priests, properly belongs at the very beginning of the Book of Leviticus. However, because there is no order in the Torah, it was placed here. Similarly, we read in Deuteronomy 29:9, "You all stand this day before the Lord your God." Since this is the start of Moses' farewell orations to the people, it should have been placed at the beginning of the Book of Deuteronomy. Again, since there was no attempt at chronological order, it found its place here.[2][6]

As we have noted, the Sages who rejected this principle of Rabbi Ishmael applied

---

[4] Sifre Balak 131. H. S. Horowitz, in his 1917 edition of the Sifre (Leipzig), suggests the following expansion of Rabbi Judah's saying: "There are passages close in the text but unrelated in topic, and others far apart in the text but close in topic" (note, ad loc.).

[5] MI Shirata 7, MSY, p. 88. The Mekhilta goes on to give many instances of verses that logically should have served as the openings of their respective books: Isaiah 6:1; Ezekiel 2:1; 17:2; Jeremiah 2:2; Hosea 10:1; and Ecclesiastes 1:12.

[6] Ecclesiastes Rabbah 1:12.

---

[2] Additional examples: Rabbi Hezekiah thought that Numbers 9:1 should have started the book of Numbers (because it describes events that took place a month earlier than those described in chapter 1); Rabbi Levi in the name of Rabbi Hama ben Haninah said that Leviticus 14:34 should have started the section on leprous afflictions (because it deals with another affliction, and it should have come before any discussion of the purification from the afflictions); Deuteronomy 31:14 was thought to be the logical start of that chapter (because it is where God tells Moses that his last day has arrived, the logical precursor to the entire chapter).

their exegesis to interpreting contiguous scriptural passages, a method known as
semikhut (thematic juxtaposition). Support for this method was based on the verses
"All His precepts are reliable; they are adjoining[3] for all eternity, they are wrought of
truth and equity" (Psalm 111:7–8). Rabbi Eleazar ben Pedat interpreted this to mean
that we must not doubt the validity of teachings derived from adjoining passages. If
you examine them carefully you will find that they are always in order, teaching truth
and equity.[4] 7

Rabbi Aha[5] made this interesting observation: The fact that there is no chronological order in the Torah testifies that the sacred texts were uttered by the Holy and
Blessed One. Otherwise, people would say, "They are merely fiction, written by someone who used his imagination, in the manner of a person who relates what happened
in his lifetime." He concludes, therefore, that because they lack any chronological
order, they must be the product of the Holy Spirit. Moses wrote them down in the
order in which they were communicated to him through prophecy.8

Rabbi Abraham, the son of Maimonides,[6] in his commentary on Exodus 18:1
declares that both viewpoints—there is a chronological order, there is no chronological order—have validity, despite the apparent contradiction. He points out that there
are passages in the Torah that appear to be out of order, belonging earlier or later, but
a careful examination of the text justifies the order in which they appear. That is,
what appears to be chronologically earlier must in fact be later, if one attends to the
context.[7] However, there are other passages that, upon examination of the context,
clearly reveal that they are not in chronological order.9

---

7 BT Yevamot 4a; BT Berakhot 10a, Rashi and MaHaRShA ad loc.
8 Genesis Rabbah 85:2, statement of R. Huna in the name of R. Aha; *Minhat Yehudah* ad loc.
9 Commentary of R. Abraham on Genesis and Exodus, p. 294.

---

[3] The Hebrew word is *semukhim*. NJV translates: "well-founded." The root *smkh* means "to lean,
support." Adjoining verses are contiguous, as if leaning the one on the other. The precepts in the
verse are reliable; one can lean on them.

[4] Heschel adds that Rabbi Eleazar ben Pedat, whom Rabbi Johanan sought to instruct in the Mystery of the Chariot, also gave a mystical twist to this notion: "'No man knows its *erekh*/arrangement
[NJV: value]' (Job 28:13)—The Torah was given out of order on purpose. If we knew the correct
order, then reading it in that order would empower us to perform miracles and raise the dead. Therefore it was kept hidden from us. But it is known to God, as it says: 'Who like Me can announce, tell
it, and arrange it for Me?'" (Isaiah 44:7; NJV: "and match Me thereby"). Eleazar ben Pedat, who was
devoted to the idea that the order in Scripture was significant, here articulates the idea that it only
seems out of order to us, but that the written structure reflects deeper truths.

Heschel also cites a tradition (Midrash on Psalms 83:2, manuscript) that two Sages sought without
avail to restore the correct order of the Book of Psalms: Rabbi Joshua ben Levi and Rabbi Ishmael.
(Versions differ on the identity of the second Sage.) The tale concludes with the latter Sage's own
teacher citing against him the verse: "They are well-founded [*semukhim*] for all eternity, etc." This dra-
matizes the two approaches to understanding the literary order of Scripture: the one seeking narrative
order, the other looking for thematic juxtapositions.

[5] Fourth-generation Amora, Israel.

[6] Abraham son of Maimonides: Egypt, thirteenth century.

[7] That is, some things have to be anticipated in the text in order to provide a proper context, and

Nahmanides seems to share this viewpoint. In his commentary he states, "The entire Torah follows a chronological order, except where it provides a specific explanation for placing a text earlier or later, depending on the demands of the subject or for other reasons."[10]

"You Just Don't Know How to Interpret It!"

The Sages issued stern warnings that it is forbidden to regard certain books of Scripture as poetry or to treat various passages of Torah as songs to be chanted. They established certain rules, which are cited in a Baraita, "Whoever reads a verse from the Song of Songs and chants it as a song, or one who recites scriptural texts in a tavern for the amusement or entertainment of the people, brings evil upon the world. The Torah, clad in sackcloth, will stand before the Holy and Blessed One and moan, 'Your children have made me into a harp on which scorners play.'"[11]

The Babylonian Amora Rava[8] homilized: Why was King David punished? Because he called the words of Scripture zemirot—songs, as it is written, "Your laws have been songs for me wherever I may dwell" (Psalm 119:54). Said the Holy and Blessed One to David, "These very Scriptures contain the warning, 'You see it, then it is gone; it grows wings and flies away, like an eagle, heavenward' (Proverbs 23:4, 5). And you characterize this as a song?![9] Your punishment will come as a result of your ignorance in a matter that elementary school children know."[10] [12]

The Sages also warned that certain books of Scripture were not to be regarded simply as historical records. Thus, Rabbi Judah the Patriarch and Rabbi Joshua ben Levi established this principle: The Book of Chronicles is not intended to be read as literal history, but its texts are to serve as a basis for religious instruction.[11] [13] It is reported

---

[10] Nahmanides, commentary on Numbers 16:1.
[11] BT Sanhedrin 101a.   [12] BT Sotah 35a.   [13] Leviticus Rabbah 1:3.

---

others must be presented in flashback. This is the Ishmaelian principle again, and it is not surprising to find it in the son of Maimonides, since his father also held to it, as Heschel has previously pointed out.

[8] Leading Amora of Babylonia, fourth generation.

[9] The verse in Proverbs speaks of Wisdom (which, for the rabbinic commentators, is identical to Torah). It seems to say that one cannot grasp it. It is, in other words, no human song, but rather a deep divine secret.

[10] This is a reference to the incident told in 2 Samuel 6:6–9. David should have known that the Ark of the Covenant was to be moved not by cart and oxen but on the shoulders of the Levites as commanded in Numbers 7:9. The death of Uzzah resulted from David's ignorance.

[11] Chronicles often has narratives that are different from, or entirely unknown to, earlier, parallel scriptural passages. Thus, 1 Chronicles 28 reports that God told David that he could not build the Temple because of the wars that he had fought (not present in 2 Kings), and 2 Chronicles 33 reports that King Manasseh of Judah was exiled during his reign, then repented, and was restored to Jerusalem and his throne (unknown to 2 Kings). This idea of Joshua ben Levi solves this exegetical problem.

of Rabbi Simon[12] that he derived homilies from the names in the genealogical lists in the Book of Chronicles.[14]

The Sages also expressed astonishment at some of the things they found in Scripture. Concerning some passages, they said, "These should be burned, like the books of Homer";[15] of others, they commented, "What possible future need can be served by this material?"[16] Nevertheless, they point out that each passage carries a basic message of special significance.

Thus, for example, Rabbi Isaac raises the question, "Since we assume that the essential purpose of Torah is to teach mitzvot, why does Scripture begin with the creation story; it should begin with the first mitzvah, the laws of Passover, 'This month shall mark for you the beginning of the months' (Exodus 12:2)? It is to make known to us the power of his might as a Creator, as it is written, 'He revealed to His people His powerful works, in giving them the heritage of nations'" (Psalm 111:6).[17]

In a similar vein, Rabbi Zeira[13] asks, "Why was the Scroll of Ruth written? It contains no teachings concerning purity or impurity, what is prohibited and what is permitted. However, its basic purpose is to teach us the great mitzvah of acts of loving-kindness and the great reward for performing them."[18]

In general, the Sages believed that mere mortals could have only imperfect understanding of Torah. This Torah, a treasure hidden by the Holy and Blessed One for 974 years before creation and regarded by Rabbi Akiva as "the precious instrument by which the world came into being," how could mortal humans possibly comprehend it? When Job asked, "Where can wisdom be found? What is the source of understanding?"—he was referring to Torah, according to the Sages. Similarly: "No man can set a value on it; it cannot be found in the land of the living . . . it is hidden from the eyes of all living, concealed from the jowl of heaven . . . God understands the way of it; He knows its source" (Job 28:12-13, 21-23). Can you say that mere flesh and blood can encompass its meaning?

In his debates with Rabbi Ishmael, Rabbi Akiva taunted him: "'It is not an empty thing for you' (Deuteronomy 32:47)—meaning that if it is empty, it is *because of you,* for you do not know how to interpret it."[14] [19] But even Rabbi Akiva, to whom every

---

[14] Ruth Rabbah 2:1; BT Megillah 13a, Hullin 60b.

[15] BT Hullin 60b. See also YS Joshua 22, which has the reading "like the books of the heretics [*minim*]," apparently a better reading that was mistaken for *mirus,* or short for *homerus* (= Homer).

[16] Sifre Ekev 37.

[17] TB Bereshit 11; cited by Rashi in his opening comments to the Book of Genesis. For Rashi, the issue was not just the demonstration of God's power but also, and primarily, the establishment of Israel's right to the Land (at a time at when Christians and Muslims were fighting over it!).

[18] Ruth Rabbah 2:14.

[19] Genesis Rabbah 1:14, cited above, p. 49.

---

[12] Second- to third-generation Amora, Israel.

[13] Third-generation Amora from Babylonia who moved to Israel.

[14] The exegesis here revolves about the words *rek hu mikkem* that are embedded in the verse.

crownlet which decorated the letters of Torah had significance, felt that man's intellectual grasp fell short of achieving the goal of complete understanding. Rabbi Simlai[15] declared, "There is no chapter in the Torah that does not hint at the resurrection of the dead, but we do not possess the power to interpret it."[20]

We saw that Rabbi Simeon ha-Imsoni[16] set out to interpret all occurrences of the word et[17] in the Torah as adding something further to the category under consideration,[18] but recoiled from interpreting the verse "You shall revere et the Lord your God" (Deuteronomy 10:20). "Whom else," he asked, "could one dare to revere in addition to God?" Rather than risk blasphemy, he was prepared to retract all the teachings he had derived from the word et in all other places. They asked him, "Rabbi, what will become now of all your other teachings on the word et?" He replied, "As I was rewarded for my interpretation, so I will be rewarded for my retraction." Then along came Rabbi Akiva and gave this interpretation: "'You shall revere et the Lord your God'—from the et, we learn to revere also the Sages of the Torah.[21]

Rabbi Phineas ben Jair[19] taught, "One should search for the teachings of Torah as diligently as one searches for hidden treasures." The Sages expounded Scripture as follows: "It is written, 'His head is finest gold, his locks are curled and black as a raven' (Song of Songs 5:1). 'His head' refers to Torah; 'finest gold' refers to the teachings of Torah; 'his locks are curled' (taltalim) was explained by Rabbi Azariah[20] to mean, 'Even the things that appear only as ornamental strokes in the letters of Torah, possess mounds upon mounds [tillei tillim] of significance, containing hints of numerous teachings and hidden meanings.'"[21] [22]

As for the phrase "black as ravens ['orev]," Rabbi Simeon son of Rabbi Isaac explained that this refers to those passages in the Torah that appear black—that is, repulsive and unbecoming for public discussion, such as the laws pertaining to venereal diseases and plagues. Yet even of these the Holy and Blessed One said they are

---

[20] Sifre Ha'azinu 306.
[21] BT Pesahim 22b; see above, p. 207.
[22] Song of Songs Rabbah 5:10.

Taken out of context, these words mean "it is empty from you." Thus, the interpretation says that the Torah is not empty words (as the verse says in its plain meaning), but that if it appears to be so, it is because of the reader's lack of interpretive ability.

[15] Second-generation Amora, Israel.

[16] In some versions, Nehemiah ha-Imsoni.

[17] Et has no intrinsic meaning, but is merely a grammatical marker for the accusative case; then the object is a definite noun, pronoun, or name.

[18] As, for example, in an exegesis that takes the et in "she conceived and bore et Cain" (Genesis 4:1) to mean that a twin sister was born along with Cain.

[19] Fifth-generation Tanna.

[20] Fifth-generation Amora, Israel.

[21] This is an allusion to BT Menahot 29b, already cited in this work.

'arevot, "pleasing to me," as it is written, "Then the offerings of Judah and Jerusalem shall be pleasing [ve'arvah] to the Lord" (Malachi 3:4).[22] 23

The Sages have an interesting homily on the verse "I am only an alien resident [ger] in the land; do not hide Your commandments from me" (Psalm 119:19). Using the word ger in its later meaning of "convert," they ask, "Did David imply that he was a proselyte? Rather, this verse teaches us that just as one who comes to be converted knows no Torah, so, even though a man's eyes may be open, he possesses no knowledge at all of Torah. Now if David, who composed all these songs and psalms could say of himself, 'I am a stranger in the land,' I know nothing, how much more true it is of us that we know nothing of Torah."24

Basic to the study of Torah (in this view) is not our intellectual grasp but our awareness of the holiness of Torah. Essentially, there is no difference between such passages in the Torah which add to our understanding and those that do not add to it. According to the Sages of the Talmud, "Whoever says this teaching is good, but that one is not, has lost the riches of Torah."25 Based on this view, they taught, "If one has no knowledge of Scriptures or Mishnah, but, in fulfillment of the duty to study Torah, sits all day and repeats the words, 'The sister of Lotan was Timnah'[23] (Genesis 36:22), he is entitled to a reward for studying."26

The Torah Uses Hyperbole

The principle "The Torah speaks in human language" served as the basis of many corollaries regarding Torah language: "The Torah speaks in common usage"; "the Torah speaks of the usual case"; "the Torah speaks figuratively"; "we apply figures to God from His creatures"; "the text says what the person can hear"; "the Torah speaks euphemistically"; "while speaking of one thing, it touches on another"; "this is the idiom of Scripture"; "it adds words for elegance—'that He may magnify and glorify His teaching' (Isaiah 42:21)"; "the Torah speaks deceptively";[24] "the Torah uses hyperbole."[25] In Rabbi Ishmael's school, they pointed out that Torah often speaks in euphemisms, in deference to polite usage.27 They further comment, "The Holy and

---

23 Song of Songs Rabbah 5:14.   24 Midrash on Psalms 119:10.
25 BT Erubin 64a.   26 SEZ 2:3.   27 BT Pesahim 3a.

---

[22] Heschel includes the following afterthought from the same midrash: "The Torah uses some discretion when on subjects that are 'black as ravens.' This is illustrated by the fact that it does not discuss venereal discharges by men and women in the same passage. It treats them in separate paragraphs: 'When any man has a discharge from his member' (Leviticus 15:2), 'When a woman has a discharge of blood' (Leviticus 15:25). The Torah, in other words, exercises derekh eretz in such matters."

[23] A verse that always struck the Rabbis as apparently useless (as indeed, did most of Genesis 36, the genealogies of Esau). See below, chapter 21, "Who Said, 'He Ought Not To Have Written in the Torah . . . .'"

[24] See the next paragraph for an elaboration of this startling assertion.

[25] As when it speaks of cities whose fortifications reach the heavens (Deuteronomy 1:28); see the sequel for an elaboration.

Blessed One used circumlocutions in many Scriptural verses in order to avoid impure language."[28]

There are times, for the sake of higher values, when Torah does not shrink from falsifying the facts. Here are two illustrations. Sarah, in reply to the announcement that she would have a son, said, "With my husband so old?" (Genesis 18:12). But when the Holy and Blessed One quoted her to Abraham, he changed the words to "old as I am." Why? The Holy and Blessed One did this to preserve peace between husband and wife.[29] This homily has its source in the school of Rabbi Ishmael.[30]

When the patriarch Jacob died, the brothers were afraid that Joseph would take vengeance on them. They sent him this message: "Before his death, your father left this instruction. . . . Forgive, I urge you, the offense and guilt of your brothers' (Genesis 50:16–17). Jacob never gave such instructions because he had no such suspicion of Joseph. The brothers invented these words. How many pens were broken, how much ink was spilled in order to include these fictitious words in Scripture?[26] And to what purpose? Rabbi Simeon ben Gamaliel said, "The Torah included these fictitious words to achieve peace between Joseph and his brothers."[27] [31]

Our Sages noted that the Torah frequently uses the language of hyperbole. Rabbi Ammi, who succeeded Rabbi Johanan as head of the academy in Tiberias, established the rule that "Torah, Prophets and Writings all make use of hyperbolic language. An example from Torah is the report of the twelve spies when they said, 'Great cities fortified up to heaven' (Deuteronomy 1:28). Can you take this literally? It is, of course, an exaggeration."[32] It is the language of an ordinary person who is not precise in his language.[33] He is like the person who magnifies the story and keeps adding to his description.

Rabbi Judah ben Simon[28] spoke of the prophetic use of hyperboles. Thus, on the verse "An ox knows its owner, an ass its master's crib, but Israel does not know, My people takes no thought" (Isaiah 1:3)—Is it possible? Are they inferior to the ox or ass? What the prophet is attacking is not their ignorance or stupidity but their obduracy. They repeatedly refused to take heed of God's warnings. They did not try to understand and sinned out of habit.[34]

It is not possible to justify Torah's use of hyperbole except as an expansion of the principle "Torah speaks the language of human beings." This expansion, however,

---

[28] PR 14:5 (57b). A classic example is Genesis 7:2; instead of saying "and of every unclean animal," the text says, "and of every animal that is not clean," adding several extra words in both Hebrew and English.
[29] PT Peah 1:1, 16a.   [30] BT Yevamot 65b.
[31] PT Peah 16a; Rashi on Genesis 50:16.   [32] BT Tamid 49a, Hullin 90b.
[33] Rashi on Hullin 90b.   [34] Leviticus Rabbah 27:8; Margaliot's note ad loc.

---

[26] As if the quills and the ink were reluctant to write something that was not strictly true.
[27] Of course, we would say that the Torah was not at all speaking fictively, but rather reporting truthfully the brothers' deceit. But Simeon ben Gamaliel thought that even giving honor and credence to the brothers' lie would ordinarily be beneath the dignity of the Torah.
[28] Third- to fourth-generation Amora, Israel.

poses some serious problems in scriptural interpretation.[35] When is a verse to be interpreted literally and when is it to be regarded as a metaphor? Rabban Simeon ben Gamaliel[29] dealt with this problem, and, while he accepted the fact that Scripture spoke in hyperboles, he insisted that not all passages that appear to be exaggerations can be interpreted as such. For example, when God said to the patriarch Abraham, "I shall multiply your seed as the stars in the heaven" (Genesis 26:4) or "I will make your seed as the dust of the earth" (Genesis 13:16)—these are not to be taken as hyperboles.[36] The later Geonim also felt that the principle of hyperbole could become a stumbling block to proper interpretation. They declared, "You cannot depart from the literal meaning of the text except when you present adequate proof."[37]

On the other hand, this principle provides freedom for the intellect to roam through Scripture. Torah lends itself to subjective interpretation[30] and all depends on the depth of our understanding of the language of Scripture. There are passages that use precise language and others that use the language of metaphor and hyperbole. The general rule that the interpretation of a text must not depart from its plain meaning applies at all times. However, in passages of the first kind, the plain meaning *is* the literal meaning. But in passages of the second kind, the literal interpretation is not identical with its true meaning. For one who interprets a metaphor as it is formulated is falsifying the text.[31]

Human Beings Speak in the Language of the Torah

This last was the view of some leading scholars in the Middle Ages, namely, that many passages in the Torah are to be understood as metaphors. Saadia Gaon,[32] for example, allows that we should interpret a scriptural passage figuratively in four cases: (1) if it contradicts the evidence of our senses, (2) if it contradicts reason, (3) if it contradicts another verse, or (4) if it contradicts our traditions. Thus, the

---

[35] According to one tradition, King Manasseh pointed to such examples as evidence that the Torah is not wholly divine in origin. See Mahzor Vitry, p. 512.

[36] Sifre Devarim 25.

[37] See the words of Sherira Gaon and Hai Gaon in *Arukh*, entry *Guzmah*.

---

[29] Rabban Simeon ben Gamaliel (II)—fourth-generation Tanna and Patriarch of the Academy.

[30] *Nitenah ha-Torah leshi'urim.* Heschel here uses approvingly the same language with which the Talmud elsewhere objects to vague rules that change with circumstances. This implicitly raises the issue: Ought the Torah to be interpreted flexibly?

(Con:) A law that varies with every time, place, and circumstance is no law.

(Pro:) Human life is complicated and people of intelligence and understanding must have the courage and flexibility to use discretion and apply traditional texts wisely to present-day requirements.

See Heschel's use of the same phrase in chapter 38 under "Stringencies Proliferate" (translated: "Were that so, everything would be relative!").

[31] See BT Kiddushin 49a.

[32] Tenth century, Egypt and Babylonia, first major medieval Jewish philosopher.

verse reads, ". . . for the Lord is a consuming fire" (Deuteronomy 4:24). This cannot be understood literally, for it conflicts with our rational understanding of fire as a created substance, and we must interpret the text figuratively.[38] Maimonides dealt with the hyperbolic language that is frequently found in Scripture and especially with the use of anthropomorphisms. He cites such examples as "beneath His feet" or "written with the finger of God," which are so phrased because the limited comprehension of people can conceive only that which is corporeal.[39]

The traditional aggadists and the kabbalists had a different approach to these scriptural metaphors. While teachers like Saadia pointed to such expressions as "the eye of the earth," "the mouth of the earth," "the corner of the earth," as defying literal interpretation, the aggadists sought to endow these phrases with substantive meanings and symbolic significance. In this view, they are not simply figures of speech but are intended to teach us special lessons. Thus, Rabbi Simeon ben Lakish taught, "Everything that the Holy and Blessed One created in humans, He created its counterpart in the earth. Humans have eyes, and so has the earth, as we read, 'It will cover the eye of the earth'[33] (Exodus 10:5). Humans have mouths, and so has the earth, as we read, 'The earth opened its mouth'" (Numbers 16:32).[40] R. Avin[34] taught, "We have heard that the earth has wings, as we read, 'From the wing of the earth[35] we heard singing'" (Isaiah 24:16).[41]

At the core of these divergent approaches to the metaphorical passages and phrases in Scripture, we have an ideological controversy that has created two camps, the philosophers and the kabbalists. The fourteenth-century kabbalist Rabbi Isaac ben Samuel of Acre made the following observation: "The philosophers declare that the wisdom of the kabbalists is basically heretical for they interpret the literal words of the Torah in corporeal terms. . . . The kabbalists, for their part, regard the wisdom of the philosophers as consisting entirely of negation, telling us only what God is not, namely, that He is not in any way corporeal. They simply do not have the capacity to comprehend the truth of the traditional teachings, unless they can be given proof."[36] [42]

---

[38] Saadia, *Book of Doctrines and Beliefs* 7:1.

[39] Maimonides, *Guide of the Perplexed* I:28; I:46; II:47 and Mishneh Torah, *Hilkhot Yesodei Ha-Torah* [Foundational Principles of the Torah] 1:9.

[40] Ecclesiastes Rabbah 1:4; see Isaac Heinemann, *Darkhei Ha-agaddah* (Jerusalem: Magnes Press, 1954), p. 19.

[41] Ruth Rabbah 5:4; PRK 124a.

[42] Quoted by Gershom Scholem, *Reshit Hakkabbalah* (in Hebrew; 1948), p. 174. See revised English version, *Origins of the Kabbalah* (Philadelphia: Jewish Publication Society; Princeton: Princeton University Press, 1987), 393ff.

---

[33] So literally. NJV: "[The locusts] shall cover the surface of the land," that is, that portion of the land which is visible to the eye.

[34] Third- to fourth-generation Amora (or his son, fifth-generation Amora), Babylonia.

[35] NJV: "From the end of the earth."

[36] This, of course, describes Maimonides perfectly, for among many medieval philosophers who

In the view of the later kabbalists, the statement "Torah speaks in hyperboles" is totally unacceptable. Rabbi Menahem Azariah of Fano[37] did not hesitate to attack this view despite the fact that it was enunciated by the Sages of the Talmud. "God's Torah is perfect, exactly as it is written; God forbid that we regard any of it as exaggerations. The Torah steers clear of metaphors and equivocal speech. There are seventy different aspects of Torah, and each aspect generates various understandings. We often find that one verse clarifies another verse, contrary to the usual rabbinic exegesis. Even with regard to the verse "great cities whose fortifications reach the heavens" (Deuteronomy 9:1), the comment has been made that it is the literal truth. What the verse is telling us is that the earthly borders correspond to the heavenly borders. There are boundary markers in heaven that demarcate the territory of the Land of Israel from that of other nations. The seventy guardian angels who have been appointed to watch over the lands of the nations are stationed two thousand cubits distance from the area of the land of Israel and are not permitted to enter the heavenly borders of Israel."[38] 43

Rabbi Menahem Azariah opposed the view of Nahmanides, who declared that while the Torah reveals its literal meaning to us, it only hints at its secret meanings. He maintained just the opposite: the Torah speaks primarily of heavenly things and only secondarily of things on earth. The hidden meaning of a scriptural text is actually its literal meaning. In his view, Nahmanides was influenced by the dictum "The Torah speaks in human language." On the contrary, human beings speak in the language of Torah. It is all true for the discerning ear.[39]

The noted scholar Rabbi Isaiah Horowitz,[40] author of *Shnei Luhot Habrit,* also takes the side of those who deny that the Torah indulges in exaggerations. He bases his views on the rabbinic interpretation of the verse "for this is no empty thing for

---

43 *Responsa,* Rabbi Menahem Azariah of Fano, No. 73.

---

indulged in what is called "negative attribute theory"—that is, confining our speech about God essentially to what God is not—he was the most famous of all.

[37] Rabbi Menahem Azariah of Fano (sixteenth- to seventeenth-century Italy) propagated the kabbalism of Safed in Europe.

[38] The exegesis here is as follows: the text that we translate here as "whose fortifications reach the heavens" can be read in Hebrew as "whose fortifications are in heaven." Thus, one interpretation says that this is no metaphor; the text merely points out that there are fortifications for these cities in heaven as well—designed to keep the patron angels of the other nations out of this territory, the territory of the Land of Israel.

[39] Rabbi Menahem Azariah insisted also on taking literally the talmudic dictum that all our works are written in a book. Do not all the motions of our body, whether for good or bad, leave traces in the ether? All the good ethereal traces, then, are gathered in Paradise, and all the bad traces in Gehenna, to justify our reward and punishment (*Imerot Tehorot* 2:4, 12).

[40] From sixteenth- to seventeenth-century Poland, moved to Israel.

you"—if it is empty it is from you, that is, it is your fault. What appears as exaggerations pertains only to the realities on earth below, but they are not exaggerations from the heavenly perspective.[41] 44

Horowitz also expressed astonishment at the rabbinic excuse for extra verbiage—"that He may magnify and glorify His teaching" (Isaiah 42:21). "What use would it be to enlarge the Torah with superfluities?" He suggests: "Even though the words in question add nothing to the current passage, they are put there so we may derive some insight for another matter."45

One of the scholars of the Middle Ages[42] expressed amazement at the rabbinic view that the Torah permitted a falsehood for the sake of maintaining peace between Abraham and Sarah. He said, "Heaven forbid that we should say of God that He altered Sarah's words! Have we not been taught that "he who speaks untruth shall not stand before My eyes"? (Psalm 101:7). This scholar suggests that the rabbinic dictum is to be understood as follows: God did not report to Abraham all that Sarah said, only a part of it.46

The Method of Plain-Sense Interpretation (*Peshat*)[43]

The Sages never doubted the value of midrashic-homiletic[44] understanding of the Torah. Indeed, Scripture says that Ezra "dedicated himself to *seek out the meaning*

---

44 *Shnei Luhot Habrit* 412a.   45 *Shnei Luhot Habrit* 409b–410a.
46 Commentary *Ba'alei Ha-Tosefot*, Vayera.

---

[41] Horowitz adds a play on *havai/hevel* ("hyperbole/vanity"): There are seven vanities alluded to in Ecclesiastes 1:2 (for *hevel* appears five times, and two of these are in the plural), and seven mentions of "the voice of the Lord" in Psalm 29. But *hevel* means literally "vapor." The heavenly vapors are the vapors of Torah. "The voice of the Lord shatters the flames of fire" (Psalm 29:7) refers to the supernal vapors of Torah overcoming the earthly vapors of vanity through the revelation at Sinai. Thus, the figures of speech in Torah that appear to be exaggeration or vanity will be seen in their true transcendental light when regarded as revealed truth.

[42] The commentary *Ba'alei ha-Tosafot* is a commentary on the Torah that emanated from the school of the Tosafists, the twelfth- to fourteenth-century Franco-German commentators on the Talmud.

[43] *Peshat* literally means "surface meaning," that is, that which stretches out before us and requires no deep probing. "Surface," however, too often has the connotation of "superficiality," so we use "plain" or "plain-sense" here instead.

[44] Regrettably, no English word captures the connotation of *derash*: an interpretation of the text that goes one step (and sometimes a few steps) beyond the plain meaning (from *darash*, "to search out or inquire," and from which the Hebrew word *midrash* is derived). The distinction between *peshat* and *derash* should be understood along the lines of the distinction made by linguists between the surface and deep structure of a linguistic unit. We use "homily/homiletic" here as a readily understood term. See glossary entries: *derash, midrash*.

[*lidrosh*] of the Torah of the Lord" (Ezra 7:10).[45] The Targum on Judges 5:9 says that even during the troubles of the time of Deborah they did not stop giving homilies on the Torah. Even in Rabbi Ishmael's school we find the aphorism "'Behold, My word is like a fire . . . and like a hammer that shatters rock' (Jeremiah 23:29)—even as a hammer sends out many sparks, so a text lends itself to many interpretations."[47] Nevertheless, they distinguished between homiletic meanings that stand in opposition to the plain meaning of a text, and those that can supersede it.[46] In Rabbi Ishmael's school they taught that there were only three places where the Halakhah overrides the plain sense of the text; in all other cases, the plain sense of the text is decisive.[48] As we have seen, nothing characterizes Rabbi Ishmael's method more than his devotion to the plain-sense meaning of the scriptural text.[47]

Several of the Amoraim enunciated a principle that describes Rabbi Ishmael's method of interpretation. The principle is: A scriptural text never loses its *peshat* (literal meaning). Maimonides points to the recurrent talmudic question, "What is the essential meaning of this text?" as evidence that the Sages distinguished between *peshat* and *derash*. However, Rav Kahana[48] testified, "When I was eighteen years old and had completed the study of the entire Talmud, I still did not know that a scriptural text never loses its literal meaning." This would indicate that this principle was not widely known among the Torah students of his generation.[49]

Rabbi Judah ben Ilay, a disciple of Rabbi Akiva, established the rule: "He who translates a verse literally is a liar, and he who adds to it is a blasphemer and reviler."[50]

---

[47] BT Sanhedrin 34a. See variant in BT Shabbat 88b: "seventy meanings (tongues)."
[48] PT Kiddushin 59d, *Penei Moshe* ad loc.
[49] BT Shabbat 63a; BT Yevamot 11b, 24a.
[50] BT Kiddushin 49a; Tosefta Megillah 3:41. See excursus by M. Kasher in *Torah Shelemah* (New York: American Biblical Encyclopedia Society, 1949–), 17:313ff.

---

[45] It is worth noting that this verse expresses something of historic importance. Previously, the root *drsh* was used for seeking out God, that is, for consulting an oracle, a priest, or a prophet. Now it is being used for the teaching of God, for the Torah. Ezra begins to inquire of a text, and thus are we signaled that the era of prophecy is at an end. Ezra is not prophet but "scribe," a man of the Book.

[46] The distinction is between those texts that can have nonstandard interpretations that are simply of theoretical interest and those very few (according to the school of Ishmael) whose nonstandard interpretations later become their accepted legal meaning.

[47] Heschel notes: "The Hebrew term *mikra meforash* ('explicit text'—which we have rendered 'the plain sense of the text') is peculiar to the teachings of Rabbi Ishmael's school. See Wilhelm Bacher, *Erkei Midrash Hatannaim* [Lexicon of Rabbinic Exegetical Terminology] (Tel Aviv: Rabinowitz, 5683/1923; translated from the German *Die exegetische Terminologie der jüdischen Traditionsliteratur* (Leipzig, 1899/1905; repr., Darmstadt: Wissenschaftliche Buchgesellschaft, 1965]), p. 105, s.v. *paresh*. Also the term *kemashma'o* ("take this in its literal meaning") is characteristic of his school, and 'the Torah spoke with its letters' (i.e., spelled it out in black and white). This may explain the puzzling dictum 'The Torah was given with its letters'" (MI Nezikin 17, MTD p. 60; see Louis Ginzberg's article in M. Braun and J. Elbogen, eds., *Festschrift zu Israel Lewy's siebzigstem Geburtstag* [Breslau: M. & H. Marcus, 1911], 420).

[48] Rav Kahana (III), fourth-generation Amora, Babylonia.

Although Rabbi Judah's dictum referred specifically to translation of Scripture, it was understood to be a warning, also, to those interpreters who relied entirely on the literal interpretation of the text.

Maimonides, in examining the different methods of interpretation, saw a great distinction between those commandments that were derived from a literal interpretation of the text and those that were derived by rules such as the thirteen principles of Rabbi Ishmael or the rules of *ribbui* (expansion) and *mi'ut* (limitation) taught by Rabbi Akiva. In the case of Rabbi Akiva, commandments were derived from the use of certain words like *et* and *gam* and *akh* and *rak*. Maimonides points out that the former derive their authority from Scripture; the latter from the deductions of rabbinic Sages. The former may be classed as the "roots" of the Torah that was given to Moses; the latter are "branches" that grew as a result of the hermeneutics of the Sages. Hence, these rabbinic laws cannot be counted among the 613 commandments—with a few exceptions. As an example, Rabbi Akiva interpreted the *et* in the verse "You shall revere the Lord your God" to mean that the Sages, too, are to be revered. Since this is not literally in the text, it cannot be included among the 613 commandments.[51]

Nahmanides took sharp exception to the views of Maimonides. "God forbid that we regard the midrashic exegesis of the Sages as a violation of the literal meaning of the text. These interpretations are true to the text, and we derive many additional laws from them." The expansion of the meaning of "You shall revere the Lord your God" to include the Sages is perfectly legitimate and does no violence to the literal meaning of the text. Similarly, all the rabbinic laws that are grounded in the text by the methods of *ribbui* and *mi'ut* and similar devices, should be included within the "plain-sense meaning" of the law. The *peshat* is not what those who do not understand rabbinic exegesis say it is; nor is it what the Sadducees say it is. The Torah of God is perfect, with not a single letter extra or missing. Every letter was put there for a purpose, and those homilies which use various features of the text to ground essential laws are not violating the plain sense of the text but revealing it. Wherever the Sages interpreted a metaphorical or allegorical passage, they took both meanings into account, the inner and outer, and regarded both as expressions of the truth. Whenever the homiletic interpretation seems to contradict the literal meaning, it is because the Sages had a tradition that this was the correct interpretation. The rule states: A scriptural text may not lose its literal meaning. It does not say that the text has *only* one meaning. We hold onto both meanings; we cannot ignore either. The text is able to embrace both, because both are true.[49] [52]

---

[51] Maimonides, *Sefer Ha-Mitzvot*, Introduction, Principle #2, and Maimonides, *Responsa*, ed. Friedmann, p. 162, to the effect that even a "law of Moses from Sinai" is considered of rabbinic status if it is derived from the text by means of the thirteen hermeneutic principles.

[52] Nahmanides, glosses on Maimonides' *Sefer Ha-Mitzvot, ad loc.*

---

[49] The notion that rabbinic exegesis actually preserves the original meaning of the text has recently been taken up in earnest by Halivni, in *Peshat and Derash: Plain and Applied Meaning in Rabbinic Exegesis* (New York: Oxford University Press, 1991).

Homily and Plain Sense (*Derash* and *Peshat*)

Do not think that the task of the plain-sense interpreters was simple! The path of *peshat* is one on which the wise may walk without fear, but the naive can stumble on it. We have noted that the interpretations of scriptural verses will vary with the context. We must ponder the nuance of language in each text. Some texts speak precisely, others poetically. The rule that a verse may not depart from its plain-sense meaning applies to both types. However, in passages of the first type the plain-sense meaning is its literal meaning; in the second category, however, the plain-sense meaning is not its literal meaning, so that we may say that he who interprets a metaphor literally is falsifying it. This was the source of the principle that emerged from the school of Rabbi Ishmael: "A single text can have many meanings."[53] This is not so surprising when we realize that many words in popular usage are very complex and have double meanings. How much truer is this of words of wisdom that are divinely inspired.

This will explain why even Rabbi Ishmael on occasion departed from the literal meaning of a text because the content of the passage demanded a different interpretation. Take the case of the woman whose husband suspects her of adultery. According to the Torah, she must drink the water of bitterness. If the test proves her innocent, what compensation may she claim for having undergone such humiliation? Rabbi Akiva quoted the verse that says: "She shall be unharmed and be able to bear children" (Numbers 5:28), and explained, "This means that if she was barren, she will be remembered by God and will give birth." Rabbi Ishmael raised an objection. "If that is what the verse means, would not all barren women pretend to have defiled themselves, thereby rousing the suspicions of their husbands? Then, when proved innocent, they would be rewarded by giving birth. Is this not depriving the honest barren woman of her just reward? Our text means something else. Her reward is: If she gave birth in pain, henceforth she will give birth in ease; if hitherto she gave birth only to females, they will now be males; if her children were dark skinned, now they will be fair; if short, now they will be tall."[50] [54] Here we have one example of Rabbi Ishmael deviating from the literal meaning to avoid an interpretation unacceptable to common sense.[55]

Another instance of Rabbi Ishmael departing from the literal interpretation is found in the case of the man who marries a woman and defames her saying, "I found she was not a virgin." The Torah says, "The girl's father and mother shall produce the

---

53 BT Sanhedrin 34a.
54 Sifre Naso 19.
55 See Wilhelm Bacher, *Agadot Hatanaim* (in Hebrew) (Jerusalem: Devir, 1922–27), 1:12.

---

[50] All of these are reflecting ancient biases (at least in Middle East culture).

evidence of her virginity . . . and they shall spread out the cloth before the elders of the town" (Deuteronomy 22:13–17). Rabbi Ishmael does not take the spreading of the garment literally but interprets it metaphorically, "let the parents present evidence that is as clear as a spotless garment."[56] Rabbi Eliezer ben Jacob,[51] however, disagreed with him and said, "These words are to be understood as written; that is, they are to be taken literally."[57]

Rabbi Ishmael's school also used the rule "Reverse the text and interpret it," which was unknown to Rabbi Akiva's school. We read of the leftover manna that "it became infested with maggots and stank" (Exodus 16:20). The Mekhilta objects: "The text is reversed. Did it first become infested and only later stank? Rather the opposite, as it says later of the manna on the Sabbath: 'It did not turn foul, and there were no maggots in it.'"[58] Other Sages said the events occurred in the order narrated, in miraculous defiance of the order of nature.[59] The debate continued into the medieval period, with Rashi supporting the text-reversal view and Nahmanides the miraculous hypothesis.[60]

According to the Babylonian Talmud, Rabbi Akiva declared that the traditional oral reading of the scriptural text is authoritative, while Rabbi Ishmael declared that the written text is authoritative.[61] [52] It is true that we find that the Ishmaelian school used the principle al tikri—"read not thus, but thus," which based a homily on an alternate vocalization of the consonants of the Hebrew scriptural text. But there is still a great difference between such exegesis and interpretations of the school of Rabbi Akiva, which derived mounds and mounds of halakhot from each tittle on the letters. Al tikri presents an alternative, it is true, but it is one that is still tied to the extant letters.[62]

---

[56] Sifre Tetze 237.

[57] Ibid.; see also Rabbi Judah in Sifre Re'eh 104, and the dispute of Rabbi Johanan and Resh Lakish, BT Sanhedrin 111b.

[58] MI Vayyassa' 4.

[59] Exodus Rabbah 25:10.

[60] Rashi and Nahmanides on Exodus 16:20.

[61] BT Sanhedrin 4b.

[62] See Adolf Rosenzweig, "Die Al-Tikre Deutungen," in Festschrift zu Israel Lewy's siebzigstem Geburtstag (Breslau: M. & H. Marcus, 1911), 204–53.

---

[51] Second-generation Tanna.

[52] The details of the talmudic example of this principle seem very remote from a plain-sense reading of the text no matter whose view we adopt. The Talmud discusses the question: How do we know there should be four chambers in the headpiece of the tefillin (phylacteries)? The word totafot ("frontlets") occurs three times in the Torah in connection with the commandment of tefillin: twice spelled TTFT, and once spelled TTFWT. The reading TTFWT is necessarily plural and is counted as two, while each occurrence of TTFT could be singular and is therefore counted as one: 2 + 1 + 1 = 4. This view is attributed to Rabbi Ishmael. Rabbi Akiva finds that each syllable of the word, tot and fot, means "two" in a different language, and he adds them together. The second-century "plain sense" may in some cases seem close to ours, but in other cases it is maddeningly counterintuitive.

Plain Sense and Mystical Allegory (*Peshat* and *Sod*)

During the Middle Ages there were scholars who devoted themselves to the discovery of the secret meanings hinted at in the Torah. To the literalists, the literal interpretations represent the very essence of Torah, while the study of *sod* (the secret meanings) is of secondary significance. They supported their view with the verse "The secret things belong to the Lord, our God, the revealed things belong to us and our children" (Deuteronomy 29:28). According to Nahmanides, "Scripture tells us what is of concern to us on earth; it only hints at what happens in the upper spheres."[63] In other words, the *peshat* is revealed; the *sod* is but vaguely alluded to in the Torah.

The opposite view was held by those scholars who maintained that the secret teachings were of major importance, while the literal interpretations possessed only secondary value. According to the testimony of Philo, there are students of Holy Scriptures who delve deeply into the metaphorical interpretations of the master teachers. They regard the literal meanings as "symbols of hidden teachings expressed allegorically." The entire Torah may be compared to a living human being: its body is nourished by words that are explicit, but its soul is nourished by ideas that are embedded in the words, invisible to the naked eye.[53] [64]

The kabbalists did not quarrel with those who insisted on the literal meaning of a text; their quarrel was with those who maintained that the Torah teaches us nothing beyond its literal meaning. The Zohar's teaching on this subject clarifies this viewpoint.

> Even as the angels who descend upon earth appear dressed in garments of this world, so is the Torah dressed with human narratives. These narratives are the garments of the Torah. Foolish people, when they see a well-dressed person, look no further. They judge him by his clothes; they regard the clothing as the body and the body as the soul. The truth is, the Torah does possess a body—the mitzvot of the Torah are its body (*gufei ha-torah*[65]). This body is dressed in clothing which consists of the narratives of this world. Foolish people pay attention only to the externals and disregard what is behind it. Those who are more perceptive do not look at the clothes, but at the substance within the garment. The Sages, servants of the Supreme King, who stood at Mount Sinai when the Torah was given, gaze only at the soul of the Torah, which is the essential Torah. In time

---

63 Nahmanides, commentary on Genesis 1:1.
64 Isaac Heinemann, *Darkhei Ha-Aggadah,* p. 179.
65 Mishnah Hagigah 1:8.

---

[53] The dualism of surface and deep meanings that is evident here is of a piece with the thoroughly dualistic nature of Philo's thought, in which body and soul, for example, are quite distinct. The body/ soul distinction thus forms a strict analogy to the point he makes here about meanings. We also see the underpinnings of the allegorical interpretation for which Philo is famous.

to come, the time of redemption, they will be privileged to gaze at the soul which is within the soul of the Torah.[54] 66

The kabbalists were harsh in their condemnation of those who shunned the secret meaning of Torah. We have such statements as, "Such men cause poverty in the world and lengthen the period of exile." Or, "Woe to them that have made the Torah such a parched land because they have banned the study of wisdom and Kabbalah, thereby causing the flow of wisdom to cease."67

The Zohar took as a basic principle that all the Torah is hidden and revealed at the same time. The divine name is a paradigm of this. Just as it is written one way and pronounced another, so the Torah (which they regarded also as a name of God) has one truth on the level of naive understanding, with secret meanings hidden behind every word.68

We read in the Zohar:

Consider the fact that a mortal king would find it beneath his dignity to speak as a commoner speaks, or to use unbecoming language. How can it enter your mind that the King of Kings did not have enough sacred subjects with which to write the Torah and resorted to recording the conversations of commoners like Esau, Hagar, Laban (with Jacob), the words of Balaam's ass, of Balaam, Balak, Zimri, and so on, together with other narrative portions and made them part of the Torah! If this be so, why do we call it "the Torah of truth"; why do we say, "the Torah of the Lord is perfect," or "the Lord's testimony is trustworthy"; "the Lord's judgments are true"? Which Torah is referred to in these statements? It is to the holy Torah in heaven, where every word reveals to us a knowledge of transcendental matters.69

The author of Tikkunei Zohar[55] writes:

Woe unto the foolish creatures, born of woman, whose hearts are sealed off, whose eyes are blind, of whom it is said, "They have eyes but they see not" (Psalm 115:5) the light of the Torah. They are like cattle, they do not understand, they know nothing except the straw of the Torah which is its external cover, and its chaff of which it is said, "Chaff and straw do not require tithing (because they are worthless). The masters of the Torah's secrets cast away the outer shell of straw and chaff and eat the nourishing wheat of Torah concealed within."70

Rabbi Moses Cordovero,[56] the noted kabbalist of Safed, in writing in praise of Kabbalah, denigrated the importance of grammar and linguistics for the understand-

---

66 Zohar Beha'alotekha 152a.   67 Tikkunei Zohar 443; ibid. 430 13b.
68 Zohar Aharei Mot 72a, Mishpatim 95a.   69 Zohar Beha'alotekha 149b.
70 Tikkunei Zohar 469, 114a.

---

[54] That is, even greater secrets and deeper esoteric meanings that will be revealed only in the future.
[55] An anonymous accompaniment to the main body of the Zohar, probably authored in the late thirteenth century in Spain.
[56] Sixteenth-century Safed.

ing of Scriptures. Like other kabbalists before him, he pointed out that the words *peshat* ("plain sense") and *tippesh* ("fool") are spelled with the same letters. While the grammarians have difficulty explaining words with superfluous letters or the difference between *keri* and *ketiv* (where a word is read one way and written another), the student of Kabbalah has no problem clarifying these passages. For example, the verse reads, *tevi'eimo vetita'eimo* ("You will bring them and you will plant them" [Exodus 15:17]). What do we learn from the extra *vav* in *tevi'eimo*? The Holy Spirit spoke here of the subsequent generation, which Joshua had circumcised and to whom was revealed the sacred Name of God, and that the unity of God is expressed with a *vav*. They merited inheriting the land, as it is written, "And your people [*ve'amekh*] are all righteous, they will inherit the land forever" (Isaiah 60:21).[57] This means that to whomever the secret letters of God's name are revealed and he keeps them secret, such a person is called a "righteous person" (a *tzaddik*), and he merits "to inherit the land forever." Thus we see that there is no word or letter in the Torah that does not have a transcendental meaning. Ask a linguist about this verse and he will tell you that the letter *vav* is superfluous and that it is one of seven letters that are normally added to words for stylistic reasons. In our opinion, anyone who says there is a single superfluous letter in the Torah deserves to have his teeth made superfluous. Those who lack a proper understanding of this are robbed of the teachings of the Torah. To them may be applied the verse, "The tears of those who are robbed and have no one to comfort them" (Ecclesiastes 4:1).[71]

---

[71] Moses Cordovero, *Or Ne'erav* 5:2; see Zohar Mishpatim 99b.

---

[57] The *vav* that is rendered as "and" seems to be interpreted here as the distinguishing characteristic of the people that makes them righteous and gives them the merit of entering the land. The generation of the Exodus was circumcised, according to the Book of Joshua, but the next generation that was to enter the land, was not. Only when Joshua circumcised them did they learn some of the secrets that made them righteous and fit to inherit the land. They learned the secret of the unifying *vav* in God's Name. That is the secret of the superfluous *vav* at the end of the word that means "you will bring them in" to the land.

ר14ר

TRANSCENDENTAL AND TERRESTRIAL PERSPECTIVES

Translator's Introduction

The current chapter[1] is the climax of Heschel's theological investigation thus far. In it, he distills what he regards as the single most important point of principle underlying the respective outlooks of Rabbi Ishmael and Rabbi Akiva, which explains their different interpretations of the doctrine "Torah from Heaven."

He finds this issue expressed in its most general form by the third-generation Palestinian Amora Rabbi Abbahu: "Whatever exists on High exists on earth." As in Platonic Idealism, the prototypes of all things are in heaven, and their reflections are on earth. This he dubs the "transcendental" outlook. The "terrestrial" or "immanentist"[2] outlook, by contrast, sees the meaning of the things of this earth not in their correspondence to heavenly prototypes but within the earthly scheme, in their relationship to the cosmic plan. In the "transcendental" viewpoint, a human being is the image of God; in the "immanentist" viewpoint, a human being is a "complete world," a microcosm.

The implications of this distinction will become clear in subsequent chapters. For the "transcendental" viewpoint, "Torah from Heaven" will refer to the doctrine that the earthly Torah is a copy of a heavenly prototype, which is the real "Torah in Heaven." For the "terrestrial" viewpoint, the doctrine will be understood in a more symbolic sense, that our Torah contains teaching from God, who is referred to by the epithet, *Shamayim*—"the Heavenly One."

While the relation of these notions to chapters 17 and following is clear, it is not as obvious how to integrate it with the complex of issues we have seen Heschel developing thus far. We have located the center of this complex of ideas in the contrast between Rabbi Ishmael's abstract, distant God, to whom we relate indirectly and symbolically, and

---

[1] Literally, the title is "The Upper *Aspaklaria* (Lens), and the Lower *Aspaklaria*." Heschel introduces the actual terms "transcendental" and "immanentist" in the third subsection of this chapter. See also chapter 2, the section entitled "The Exoteric and Esoteric Personalities," and the editorial notes there.

[2] "Terrestrial" is better than "immanentist" for describing the Ishmaelian outlook presented in this chapter, and the reader is well advised to make this mental substitution throughout. Again, see the editorial notes in chapter 2, the section entitled "The Exoteric and Esoteric Personalities."

Rabbi Akiva's passionate, accessible God, who participates in Israel's suffering and with whom we can have a direct, personal relationship. How does this typology relate to the terminology of the current chapter?

We may perhaps clarify the issue by asking: How do Rabbi Ishmael and Rabbi Akiva draw the lines between what Franz Rosenzweig saw as the three fundamental entities, God, humanity, and world? For Rabbi Ishmael, there is a clear line to be drawn between God on the one side, and humanity and world together on the other side. The human being is *ben adam,* the earthly creature (from *adamah,* earth). God is "transcendent" or "other," in the terminology we have been using until now; God is the *only* transcendent entity. The boundary between earth and heaven is fixed and impermeable. Even to speak of God as on the "heavenly" side of the boundary is metaphorical (as Heschel will suggest in chapter 20). Humans must find their way of expressing themselves, their strategy for coping, and their frame of reference within limitations posed by this earthly realm. *Derekh eretz* is an essential component of the program for right conduct. This is the "terrestrial" perspective of the current chapter.

For Rabbi Akiva, the picture is more complex. Even if we follow Heschel and ascribe to Rabbi Akiva the Platonic-dualistic outlook that Rabbi Abbahu articulated, it is *the created world itself* that is invested with this duality. "Heaven-and-earth" is the biblical-rabbinic idiom describing the whole of creation. God created two worlds, "this world" and the "world to come," which correspond to each other. To be sure, in all expressions of Platonic dualism (including the Jewish mystical tradition of Kabbalah, which draws heavily on Akivan proto-mysticism), the heavenly realm is closer to the original impetus of creation and therefore is invested more heavily with divine content. But there is a continuous flow from the one to the other. The boundary of heaven and earth is permeable. The heavenly Torah embodies the supernal wisdom. Even if the earthly Torah is only a "fallen fruit" of its heavenly prototype, still every letter and crown in it is the living word of God. The Shekhinah is truly present in certain sites more than others—on the heavenly throne, between the cherubim of the Tabernacle—yet the Shekhinah also suffers exile, and God truly participates in the sufferings of Israel. Thus, *transcendence* is a dimension of the whole heaven-and-earth continuum and system of correspondences described in this chapter; yet God is *immanent* on all levels of the continuum, in the sense we have discussed in earlier chapters. By relating to God Who is immanent in Torah, in mitzvot, in the miracles of daily living (which are all pointers to their heavenly prototypes), we transcend the mere facticity of our earthly existence. This is (to use the terminology of the present chapter) the "transcendental" perspective.

It is well to remember in reading on: in the terminology of this chapter, Akivan = transcendentalist, and Ishmaelian = immanentist.

The Doctrine of God's Image

HUMANITY IS GREAT and precious in God's sight, according to Rabbi Akiva. How so? "Precious are humans, that they were created in God's image. A special affection they have in that it was made known to them that they were created in the Image, as it is written, 'In His image did God make man'" (Genesis 9:6).[3] 1

The person is a reflection of the supernal realm. The human image below corresponds to the Divine Image above. According to Rabbi Akiva, "He who spills human blood, Scripture regards such a person as though he had diminished the Divine Image, as it is written, 'Whoever sheds the blood of man, by man shall his blood be shed; for in His image did God make man' (Genesis 9:6)."2 The midrash cites a parable: A mortal king visited one of his provinces and the people put up a statue and struck coins in his honor. Sometime later, they tore down his statue, destroyed his coins and thus diminished his image.3

We quoted above the example of Hillel the Elder, who washed in the bathhouse, because it was a mitzvah to keep clean the body that was created in the likeness of God.4 For Hillel, the doctrine of man's divine image clarifies the nature of human greatness; for Rabbi Akiva it teaches us about the Holy and Blessed One and the extent to which human deeds affect what happens above ("diminishing the Image"). Moreover, the expression itself, *et ha-demut*, "the Image,"[4] makes it evident that its purpose is not to indicate the nature of humanity but to point to the existence of the Divine. It is in this sense that Rabbi Akiva taught, "Because of his sin, man has no possibility to know what the Divine Image is."5

The ancients saw the reflection of God in all existence. They believed that the different elements of reality were not hermetically self-contained and impermeable. On the contrary, every element was a reflected light of the Divine. All existence was a harmonious reality, its various elements in a mutual relationship. However, there were two approaches to this harmonious reality: one cosmological or immanental, the other transcendental.[5] According to the former, the particular reflects the gener-

---

1 Avot 3:14.　　2 Genesis Rabbah 34:14.　　3 MI Bahodesh 8.
4 Leviticus Rabbah 34:3.　　5 ARN A 39.

---

[3] The idea here is that humans have a distinction above all other creatures, even those that are conscious of their surroundings, because only humans have a sense of *self*-consciousness, that is, consciousness of the self. In Akiva's terminology, we are not only made in the image of God, but we know that we are.

[4] The expression occurs in the phrase *mi'et et ha-demut*, or "diminished the Image."

[5] Heschel here uses the transcendent/immanent dichotomy in the opposite sense from its usage in contemporary theological discourse. For how the different usages are correlated, see the introduction to this chapter and editorial notes in chapter 2, the section entitled "The Exoteric and Esoteric Personalities."

ality *within the earthly realm;* that is, the human microcosm corresponds to the macrocosm.[6] But the transcendentalists taught that all the earthly elements had their counterpart in the supernal world. Thus, man's image and likeness were derived from above; terrestrial man resembled heavenly man.[7]

This striking contrast in the evaluation of human worth is reflected in Rabbi Akiva's view of capital punishment. In the Mishnah we read: "A Sanhedrin that executes one person in seven years is called tyrannical. Rabbi Eleazar ben Azariah taught, 'One in seventy years.' Rabbi Tarfon and Rabbi Akiva declared, 'Had we been in the Sanhedrin, no person would ever have been executed.' But Rabbi Simeon ben Gamaliel said, 'They would have increased the number of murderers in Israel.'"[8]

The doctrine of the image of God has a powerful appeal, for it compares the likeness of the created to its Creator, the image of mortal human to the One who brought the world into being.[6] This likeness is not only the secret of a human being's creation but is part of the very essence of the human's existence. In his very existence a human being is a reflection of the Holy and Blessed One. This daring concept became the basis for many of the popular maxims of the Amoraim. Said Rabbi Simlai,[7] "Man's body comes from the earth but his soul comes from heaven. When he performs the commandments of the Torah and obeys the will of heaven, then he becomes like the heavenly beings."[9] Rabbi Simeon quoted Rabbi Joshua ben Levi as saying, "Whosoever puts his trust in the Holy and Blessed One is privileged to become like unto Him, as it is written, 'Blessed is he that trusts in the Lord, whose trust is the Lord alone' (Jeremiah 17:7). But whosoever puts his trust in idols condemns himself to be like them, as it is written, 'They who fashion them, all who trust in them, shall become like them'" (Psalm 115:8).[10]

The danger of this doctrine, which in effect teaches that man can become like God, was obvious to Rabbi Simeon ben Lakish. To offset it, he was moved to teach: Moses stated two things in the Torah that clarify our relationship to God. We read, "You will always be at the top" (Deuteronomy 28:13). Does this mean that you will be like Me? Impossible! That is why the Hebrew word *rak* (only) is used in this verse, to limit

---

[6] See Louis Ginzberg, *The Legends of the Jews,* 7 volumes (Philadelphia: Jewish Publication Society, 1909-38), 5:64ff.

[7] See Zohar II,76a.

[8] Mishnah Makkot 1:10.

[9] Sifre Ha'azinu 306, comment on *ya'arof kammatar.*

[10] Deuteronomy Rabbah 5:9.

---

[6] Heschel adds: When Rabbi Akiva answered Tineius Rufus that human deeds are preferable to God's, this probably gives an additional nuance to Akiva's doctrine of being created in the divine image (Tanhuma Tazri'a 5).

See also the homily on Leviticus 26:12, cited in chapter 10: When God strolls in the Garden of Eden, and the righteous hide in fear, God will say, "Why are you frightened of Me? I am just like you!" (Sifra Behukotai 111b).

[7] A teacher of the transitional Tannaitic-Amoraic generation.

man's greatness and to teach us that God said, "My greatness is above your greatness." In another passage we read, "Speak to the whole congregation of Israel and say to them, 'You shall be holy for I the Lord your God am holy.' Does this mean you will be holy like Me? When the verse says, 'for I the Lord your God am holy' (Leviticus 19:1). God is telling them, 'My holiness is above your holiness.'"[11]

Not all the Sages agreed with Rabbi Akiva's doctrine of the Divine Image. Many followed the immanentist approach and saw humanity as a reflection of the terrestrial realm, the microcosm balancing the macrocosm of creation. When God told Moses, "Go down, warn the people not to break through to the Lord to gaze, lest many of them perish" (Exodus 19:21), the Mekhilta comments: "Every individual who might perish of them is equal in My eyes to all of creation!"[8] [12]

Though Rabbi Judah the Patriarch followed Rabbi Akiva in legal matters, he adopted Rabbi Ishmael's view in speculative and aggadic areas. Nowhere did he use the language of "divine image" in the Mishnah.[9] Thus, in describing the briefing of the witness in capital cases, the Mishnah tells us one should be especially cautious of erroneously taking a human life, not because (as Rabbi Akiva would have it) we would be diminishing God's image, but because "whoever destroys a single life is as if he had destroyed an entire world."[13] The same passage in the Mishnah goes on to reflect on the creation of the human race. Instead of saying that humans are created in the Divine Image, it says, "God stamped out all humans from the impress of the original Adam (and yet each is unique)." Perhaps this text hints that the primordial Adam was created in the image of God, but the succeeding generations were born in the likeness of that first human prototype. According to another midrash, Adam said to Moses, "I am greater than you, for I was created directly in God's image."[14]

We read, "If a man is found guilty of a capital offense and is put to death and you impale him on a stake, you must not let his corpse remain on the stake overnight, but you must bury him the same day. *For an impaled body is an affront to God*" (Deuteronomy 21:22–23). The interpretations of the last phrase diverge along the same lines we have just seen. One answer is that people will ask, "Why was this man impaled?" And the answer will be, "Because he blasphemed God's name." And thus, the Name of Heaven will be affronted.[10] [15] Rabbi Meir had a different interpretation of this verse,

---

[11] Genesis Rabbah 90:2.   [12] MI Bahodesh 4, ed. Lauterbach.
[13] Mishnah Sanhedrin 4:5; ARN A 31; ARN B 36.
[14] Deuteronomy Rabbah 11:3.
[15] Sifre Ki Tetzei No. 221; Mishnah Sanhedrin 6:4.

---

[8] This reflects a concern with the horizontal bond among creatures on earth, as opposed to the vertical bond between the Creator and creatures that is the concern of the Akivan school. We have already seen this contrast between the horizontal and the vertical bonds in chapter 6.

[9] Except, of course, in the sayings attributed to Rabbi Akiva, and then only in Mishnah Avot 3:14.

[10] The concern here, in other words, is for desecration of God's name, in that the offense against God for which he was executed will have to be retold. This is the classic concern for *hillul hashem*, or the desanctification of God's Name.

which he gave in the form of a parable: "There were twin brothers who were alike in appearance. One became a ruler over the entire world, the other a highway robber. When the latter was impaled on a cross, every passerby would exclaim, "It appears that the king has been impaled." That is why the Torah teaches us that 'an impaled body is an affront to God.'"[16] Here, too, the Mishnah cites the Ishmaelian view, while the Akivan view is preserved in the Tosefta.

We find both views enlisted in support of practical ethics. On the one hand, Rabbi Hanina said, "Whoever strikes the jaw of a fellow Jew is as if he struck the jaw of the Shekhinah."[17] On the other hand, we find a critique of revenge based on the unity of the human race: "If one accidentally cut his hand while chopping meat, would he punish the offending hand by cutting it as well?"[18]

Earthly Beings Have Supernal Prototypes

In the Mishnah we read, "If someone is riding an ass, he should direct his heart to the Holy of Holies in the Sanctuary." The question is raised in the Palestinian Talmud, "To which Holy of Holies does the Mishnah refer?" Rabbi Hiyya Raba[11] said, "He is to direct his heart to the Holy of Holies in heaven." Rabbi Simeon ben Halafta[12] said, "To the Holy of Holies on earth." Said Rabbi Phineas, "The two views are not in conflict with each other. The Holy of Holies on earth is directed toward the Holy of Holies in heaven, as we read, 'The place You made to dwell in' (makhon l'shivtekha, Exodus 15:17)—the word makhon is to be read mekhuvan 'directed,' and the meaning is 'directed toward your abode.'"[13] [19]

So too (as we shall examine later in detail), Rabbi Akiva believed that before the Sinaitic revelation, the Torah existed in heaven as a unitary document,[14] written in heaven and manifest to God. Just as humanity was created in the image of the heavenly God, so the Torah we now have is a copy of the heavenly Torah. We call our Torah "Torah from heaven," because the original Torah is even now in heaven.[15]

---

[16] Tosefta Sanhedrin 9:6; BT Sanhedrin 46b.
[17] BT Sanhedrin 58b.
[18] PT Nedarim 9:2, 41c.
[19] Mishnah Berakhot 4:5; PT Berakhot ad loc., 8c.

---

[11] "Hiyya the Greater," of the transitional Tannaitic-Amoraic generation.

[12] Also of the transitional Tannaitic-Amoraic generation.

[13] In Heschel's original Hebrew text, this paragraph was placed prior to the subchapter heading.

[14] Presumably, this means that it is not unfolding in history, but rather a complete and timeless unit. This contrasts, of course, with the view according to which the Torah was written down "scroll by scroll," a perspective that Heschel will treat in chapter 32.

[15] And thus, it was not created for people, at least not exclusively, or even primarily, for people.

The notion of a Torah literally existing in heaven may seem at first like a strange growth, the chaff and straw of our religious imagination. But on reflection it is simply a particular consequence of a whole systematic way of looking at the relationship of the supernal and the terrestrial realms, which was common in ancient thought. The supernal realm contains the secret and origin of everything terrestrial. The lower realms add nothing new; they derive all their reality from on High. Different ages and cultures developed this fundamental idea in different styles and ways, but they all agreed in establishing a hierarchical relation between the lower and higher realms.

It is interesting to compare the rabbinic views on the Torah's existence in heaven with the teachings of Plato. The Forms, according to Plato, comprise on the one hand the general concepts of things that impinge on the senses; on the other hand they comprise the original images of existence in their pure and most refined form, which transcend the realm of the sensory. The cosmos was created by the demiurge, who, gazing at these ideal Forms, created physical beings by imitating them. Thus, the physical world was created in the forms and images of their ideals. The Forms provide the models for the world of nature. And all that exists in it are reflections of these Forms.

Although we grasp the forms intellectually (as species or genus) through internal reflection, their essential nature is beyond the reach of the world of the senses. Ideals dwell above the arch of heaven.[20] Glaucon, in discussing with Socrates the order of the Republic, says to him: "Do you have in mind that Republic which exists only in thought, for I do not believe that it exists anywhere on earth." Socrates replies, "But in heaven it can perhaps serve as a model for anyone who desires to study it and to constitute himself thereby: for it matters not whether it exists anywhere or not."[21]

Notwithstanding these striking similarities, the basic lines of thought that underlie the doctrine that the original Torah exists in heaven are not at all identical with the Platonic concept of Forms. That which the two have in common, namely, that all things that exist on earth below have their original form in heaven—antedates Plato's work and was already known in Babylonia.

In the light of this general outlook, we can better understand the teaching that certain things were created before the world came into being. Does it not follow, then, that if there are things that antedate the world, they surely have continued to exist after the world was created? These, then, are the supernal prototypes of what exists on earth.

"In the beginning God created heaven and earth." The Mishnah declares: Whoever seeks to find answers to the four mysteries of creation, it were better for such a person not to have been born. What is above? What is below? What came before creation? What will come at the end of time?[22] Notwithstanding this prohibition, the Sages did not refrain from discussions concerning things that were created before the heaven and earth were created. Rabbinic literature is replete with speculations on this

[20] *Phaedrus* 247, see 250.   [21] *The Republic* 592.   [22] Mishnah Hagigah 2:1.

theme.[23] Some of the sources say that these things were actually created; others that they were conceived in thought. Most of the things in question have substantial existence, while two (repentance and the name of the Messiah) are incorporeal. What all the sources have in common is the belief that four things did antedate creation: the Torah, the Throne of Glory, the Holy Temple, and the name of the Messiah. It is probable that the most ancient record knew only of these four things. Such views became more widespread in later generations. R. Shila[16] said, "Blessed is the Merciful One who created the earthly kingdom according to the model of the heavenly kingdom!"[24] Rabbi Abbahu[17] declared, "Whatever exists on High exists on earth. On high there are stars . . . so too there are stars below; on high there are hosts . . . so too there are hosts below; on high there are Ophanim (a variety of angels) . . . so too there are Ophanim below; there are cherubs on high . . . so are there cherubs below; there is a Sanctuary above . . . so too there is a Sanctuary below. There are curtains above . . . so are there curtains below."[25] Rabbi Berechiah[18] expounded the verse "for everything that is in heaven and on earth" (1 Chronicles 29:11)[19] to mean, "You will find that everything the Holy and Blessed One created on High, He also created on earth," and he listed sixteen things. He concluded his lecture saying, "The things that are on earth are more precious than those on High. As you will note, the Creator left all that is above and descended to be with His people on earth, as it is written, 'Let them make Me a Sanctuary that I may dwell among them'" (Exodus 25:8). In the name of Rabbi Hiyya it was said, "As there are songs (at the divine service) on High, so are there songs at the divine service on earth."[26] This outlook provides the foundation for the study of the teachings of the Kabbalah. In many places of the Zohar you will find the statement that the Holy and Blessed One created this world on the model of the world above: "Everything that exists above is replicated below."[27] In the opinion of the Sages, the people brought with them from Babylonia the names of the angels.[28] But we have not yet been able to discover the source of the concept regarding the parallelism between the world above and the world below. This belief is found

---

[23] (a) "Six things were created before the world: Torah and the Throne of Glory were created; the patriarchs, Israel, the Temple, and the name of the Messiah were conceived in thought" (Genesis Rabbah 1:4). (b) "Seven things were created before the world: Torah, repentance, the Garden of Eden, Gehenna, the Throne of Glory, the Temple, and the name of the Messiah" (BT Pesahim 54a; Midrash on Proverbs 8:9). Other lists give different combinations and permutations of the same elements.

[24] BT Berakhot 58a.

[25] Midrash Aggadah, Terumah, p. 169.

[26] PRK 27/26 (ed. Buber 177b, not in Mandelbaum/Braude); Leviticus Rabbah 21:11.

[27] Zohar, Pekudei 221a.   [28] PT Rosh Hashanah 1:2, 56d.

---

[16] First-generation Amora (transitional generation), Babylonia.

[17] Third-generation Amora, Israel.

[18] Fourth-generation Amora, Israel, famed aggadist.

[19] The ensuing exegesis depends on the fact that the Hebrew can be taken literally to mean "for everything is in heaven and on earth"; that is, everything has a double above.

among many peoples. It is possible that it developed in Israel without any external influence.

Transcendental and Terrestrial Perspectives

We have established that whoever said that Torah and the Sanctuary preexisted the world, believed that the heavenly prototypes exist since the creation also. If they believed the Torah exists both in heaven and on earth, they believed also that there is even now a heavenly Temple corresponding to the terrestrial Temple.

The belief in a heavenly Sanctuary is not derived from the Torah. In the building of the Tabernacle we read that Moses was instructed, "Exactly as I showed you—the pattern of the Tabernacle and the pattern of all its furnishings—so shall you make it. . . . Note well, and follow the patterns that are being shown you on the mountain" (Exodus 25:9, 40). What is here stated is that the Holy and Blessed One showed Moses the pattern of the Tabernacle, not the Tabernacle itself. In the Wisdom of Solomon (9:8) we likewise read, "and You commanded to build a Sanctuary on Your holy mountain . . . the pattern of the Holy Sanctuary which You have prepared from the very beginning." This, too, clearly refers to the pattern of the Sanctuary, not to the Sanctuary itself.

This belief in the existence of a Sanctuary or a Temple in heaven was already known to the ancient Babylonians.[29] In the books of the Apocalypse, we also read that when Enoch rose to the highest heaven he saw there "a building made of crystal stones, and between these stones were flames of burning fire."[30] This same concept is also to be found in Rabbi Akiva's school.

Where did the Sages find support for this? "'The place You made to dwell in' (Exodus 15:17)—this is one of the things on earth that replicates the one on High: for the throne below points to the one above."[31] This concept, that the things on earth correspond to the things in heaven, occupies a prominent place in the teachings of Rabbi Akiva. It was he who taught, "Just as we discuss matters of Halakhah here on earth, so are such discussions held on High."[32] Since, according to him, the Holy and Blessed One showed Moses the menorah by pointing with His finger, it indicates that there is a menorah on high.[33]

As we have indicated earlier, two concepts of reality are well known in rabbinic literature, one transcendent, the other immanent. So, too, are these two concepts brought to bear on the divergent interpretations of the secret of the Tabernacle and the Holy Temple. One view declares that the Tabernacle on earth corresponds to the model in heaven; the other says that the Tabernacle and its appurtenances are symbolic of the earth and its contents. The first view is to be found in the school of Rabbi

---

[29] Raphael Patai, *Man and Temple in Ancient Jewish Myth and Ritual* (London: T. Nelson, 1947; reprint, New York: Ktav, 1967), 106ff.

[30] Ethiopic Book of Enoch 70:5.   [31] MI Shirata 10, MSY, p. 99.

[32] Tanhuma Shemot 18.   [33] MI Bo 1.

Akiva, and the second is to be found in the writings of Philo and Josephus[34] and in the school of Rabbi Ishmael.

Rabbi Nehemiah,[20] who in aggadic matters generally followed the view of Rabbi Ishmael, said, "The *ohel mo'ed* (tent of meeting) which Moses built in the wilderness corresponds to the work of Creation. The curtains correspond to heaven and earth; the basin and its stand to the waters; the altar for burnt offerings to cattle; the altar for burnt incense to all the spices. The menorah (candelabrum) corresponds to the sun and moon; its seven branches to the seven stars which serve the world."[35] Rabbi Nehemiah is the Sage who believed that "a single person is as important as all creation."[36]

In accordance with this line of thought, we find it said in various places: "The Tabernacle is as important as the whole world, and as the creation of man, who is a microcosm."[37] "The Tabernacle is as important as the whole world, which is also called the Tent."[38] The Tabernacle was equated with the creation of the world.[39] "Even as in the sky there are stars, so there are the Tabernacle's hooks."[40]

You cannot use biblical exegesis to draw the conclusion that the Tabernacle has equal status with the whole world unless you perceive the world itself as a Tabernacle. This is precisely what Philo says, "One must perceive the world as the exalted and true Sanctuary of God."[41] Search and you will find that even at the school of Rabbi Ishmael there is a hint of the concept that the whole world and its content are the Sanctuary of the Holy and Blessed One. "God says, 'Let them make Me a sanctuary that I may dwell among them' (Exodus 25:8). But it says elsewhere: 'Thus said the Lord: The heaven is My throne and the earth is My footstool; where could you build a house for Me . . . ?' (Isaiah 66:1). But let them build it and be rewarded for their efforts."[42]

According to the followers of the transcendental line of thought, which declares that all things below correspond to things above, it is obvious that the heavens were created first. It is likely, therefore, that those Sages who differed with the whole transcendental approach advanced the opinion that the earth was created first. The controversy between these two views of reality will clarify for us an obscure chapter in ancient theology in which the school of Shammai and the school of Hillel had differing views. One of the questions that Alexander of Macedon asked the Elders of the Negev was, "Were the heavens created first or were the earth and heaven created simultaneously?" They replied, "The heavens were created first, for it is written, 'In the beginning God created the heavens and the earth.'"[43]

---

[34] See quotations in Isaac Heinemann, *Philons Griechische und jüdische Bildung: Kulturvergleichende Untersuchungen zu Philons Darstellung der jüdischen Gesetze* (Breslau, 1932; reprint, Hildesheim: G. Olms, 1962), 1:112.

[35] YS Pekudei 419.   [36] ARN A 31, cited earlier.

[37] Tanhuma Pekudei 3.   [38] Numbers Rabbah 12:16 (12:13 in some editions).

[39] Midrash Tadshei on Baraita of Rabbi Phinehas ben Jair, 2 and 11.

[40] PRK 1:3 (4b-5a).   [41] Philo, *De Specialibus Legibus*, 12.66.

[42] MI Pisha 16. A manuscript variant cites Jeremiah 25:24: "Do I not fill both heaven and earth?"

[43] BT Tamid 32a.

---

[20] Fourth-generation Tanna.

This idea itself was controversial. "The school of Shammai held that the heavens were created first, then the earth. The school of Hillel declared that the earth was created first, then the heavens."[44] The school of Shammai represents the transcendent view, and the school of Hillel represents the immanent outlook. Note that Rabbi Akiva, who represents the transcendent line of thought, taught that the heavens were created first; and Rabbi Ishmael, who opposed that view, leaned toward the thinking of the school of Hillel. Note well that the transcendent outlook was not acceptable to all the Sages. According to Rabbi Johanan, "The Holy and Blessed One said, 'I will not come to the Heavenly Jerusalem until I first come to the earthly Jerusalem.'" In connection with this quotation, which embodies an ancient concept in the transcendent outlook,[45] the Babylonian Sages expressed surprise, "Is there a heavenly Jerusalem?!"[46]

"He who ordains peace in His heavens will ordain peace for us" [from the Kaddish]. This prayer has its roots in the words of Job (25:1): "Dominion and dread are His; He ordains peace in His heights." This verse has been interpreted in two ways. Those who link earthly events with those on high interpret it as referring to the world of angels, but the Sages who refrained from asking "What is above?" explained it as referring to "things on earth."

"He who ordains peace in His heavens" indicates that "those who dwell on high are in need of peace."[47] Rabbi Simeon ben Yohai taught: "Heaven is made of snow and the heavenly creatures are made of fire; yet neither destroys the other."[48] Rabbi Jacob of Kephar Hannah[21] taught: "'Dominion' refers to the angel Michael, and 'dread' refers to the angel Gabriel, who ordains peace in His heavens."[49]

Note that certain Sages understood the words of Job as alluding not to the world of angels but to human beings in this world.[50] Rabbi Johanan commented: "'He ordains peace in His heavens'—the sky is composed of water and the stars of fire, yet they do not injure one another."[51] Rabbi Levi said, "None of the constellations of the Zodiac sees which constellation is before it, only the one behind it, like a man who descends a ladder facing backwards, so that each constellation may claim, 'I was first.' This is how the Creator 'ordains peace in His heavens.'" Other interpretations: "The stars relate to each other with respect and thereby maintain peace." "In all its days the sun never saw the defect in the moon (i.e., the moon's curved crescent is always away from the sun), so as to maintain peace."[52]

---

[44] PT Hagigah 2:1, 77c.

[45] Revelation 21:2–3: "I saw the holy city, new Jerusalem, coming down out of heaven from God. . . . 'Now at last God has His dwelling among men!'"

[46] BT Ta'anit 5a.   [47] Sifre Shofetim 199, Sifre Naso 42.

[48] Song of Songs Rabbah 3:11.   [49] TB Bereshit 13.

[50] See Ibn Ezra on Job 25:1: "In His heavens there is no war, for they are all good. The evil is down below on earth." Contrast Sifre Naso 42: "If peace needs to be ordained even where there is no enmity, competition, hatred, or gossip, how much more so where all these apply!"

[51] Song of Songs Rabbah 3:11.   [52] Deuteronomy Rabbah 5:11; Numbers Rabbah 12:8.

---

[21] Third-generation Amora, Israel.

Reasons for the Mitzvot

The transcendental school developed a theology that is boldly directed toward the heavenly world; the immanentist school arrived at a theology that is much more modest and conservative, content to understand the teachings of Torah as reflecting primarily man's destiny in this world. Each of these two views became the foundation and source of differing concepts and value systems—one in opposition to the other.[22] Thus, two systems of thought were crystallized on the matter of reasons for the mitzvot.

The one system declares: If you sin, what do you do to Him? If your transgressions are many, how do you affect Him? If you are righteous, what do you give Him? Mortal man needs God, but God has no need for mortal man's worship. The other view maintains: The Holy and Blessed One needs our worship of Him, as it is written, "Give might to God" (Psalm 68:35).[23] The immanentist view teaches that the reason for the mitzvot was to bestow merit upon Israel, or that the sole purpose of the mitzvot is to purify human beings. In contrast, the transcendental view maintains that the mitzvot were ordained to bring satisfaction to the Holy and Blessed One.

One view holds that a man makes three pilgrimages a year to Jerusalem for the purpose of being seen by his Master, the Lord. The other declares that just as a man is eager to be seen by his Master, so is the Master eager to see him;[24] man is a servant whom the Master looks forward to seeing. One school of theology teaches that the four species of plants connected with the palm branch (on the Sukkot festival) symbolize four types of people; the other school teaches that the four species refer to God's attributes. One maintains that the sinner causes harm to himself by making his heart insensitive to evil, resulting in a defect in man. The other declares that the sinner diminishes the Divine Image and that, as a consequence, the Holy and Blessed

---

[22] Here Heschel indicates again that these two schools give rise to significant and substantive differences on a host of religious issues. It is, of course, Heschel's main goal to demonstrate how ubiquitous is the central divergence of the schools, in that it shows up in virtually every interesting theological debate throughout the generations.

[23] As noted in chapter 6, the plain meaning of the verse is "Ascribe might to God." That is, it is descriptive of God's power. But here it is taken more literally to mean that we are being exhorted to give or to add might to God, as if God needs our increment of power.

[24] "In the manner that one comes to be seen, so one comes also to see." The Hebrew text of Exodus 23:17 and especially 34:23 attests to an original belief that "three times a year all males shall see the Lord." Certainly by rabbinic times, this was revised to "shall be seen" by revocalizing the word YR'H without changing the written consonantal text. (It should be noted, however, that the presence of et, the accusative particle, makes the passive vocalization, though traditional, grammatically untenable.) Heschel is playing on this dual meaning by ascribing each meaning to one of the rabbinical schools. He is also playing on Hagigah 2b and 4b: "the one-eyed man is exempt from appearing at the Temple, for in the manner that one sees [i.e., with two eyes], so one comes to be seen." See chapters 16 and 36.

One laments: "What pleasure have I in you?" Human sins are responsible for a defect in God.

In keeping with the immanentist view, Rabbi Hananiah ben Akashya[25] taught, "God desired to confer merit upon Israel. He therefore gave them a voluminous Torah and a great many mitzvot."[53] In similar vein, our Sages quote the verse "The way of God is perfect, the word of the Lord is pure" (Psalm 18:31). Since all His ways are perfect, why would God care whether a person slaughters an animal ritually and eats it, or whether he pierces it and eats it? How is this beneficial or harmful to Him? Or what concern is it of God whether man eats the flesh of pure animals or of impure animals? The answer is, "If you are wise, you are wise for yourself, and if you are a scoffer you bear it alone" (Proverbs 9:12), which is to say that the mitzvot were given for the sole purpose of purifying human beings.[26] [54]

This statement does not express the views of all the Sages. You ask, "What concern does God have with the rituals?" He certainly is concerned! You say, "The mitzvot have as their sole purpose to purify human beings?" Some other Sage, however, may tell us that the reasons for the mitzvot are beyond our capacity to grasp. Rabbi Simeon, a disciple of Rabbi Akiva, cited the verse "You are My witnesses, declares the Lord" (Isaiah 43:10). When you are My witnesses, I am God, but if you are not My witnesses, then, as it were, I am not God.[55] In this same vein, the Sages said the following, "Should Israel refuse to accept the Torah, neither I nor they [the angels] would have a home."[56] "As long as the people of Israel do the will of God, they add power to the Mighty One on High."[57] Rabbi Alexander[27] said, "Everyone who studies Torah for its own sake brings peace to the heavenly household and to the household below, as it is written, "If he holds fast to My refuge, he makes peace for Me, he makes peace for Me" (Isaiah 27:5). Rav added, "It is as if he built a palace in heaven and on earth, as it is written, 'I have put My words in your mouth and sheltered you with My hand; I who planted the skies and made firm the earth'" (Isaiah 51:16).[58]

The view that says "the mitzvot were given for the sole purpose of purifying human beings" does not comport with the view that declares that the Holy and Blessed One puts on Tefillin[59] and observes the mitzvot. There is the story about Rabban Gamaliel, Rabbi Eleazar ben Azariah, and Rabbi Akiva, who traveled to Rome and there, in their lecture, said, "The ways of God are not those of mortal man, for mortal man issues a decree and demands that others obey it, but obeys nothing himself, while the Holy

---

[53] Mishnah Makkot 3:16.   [54] TB Shemini 12.   [55] Sifre Haberakhah 346.
[56] PR 20:4 (97a).   [57] PRK 26/25:1 (166a-b).   [58] BT Sanhedrin 99b.
[59] BT Berakhot 6a.

---

[25] Tanna whose saying (here cited) is used to close the customary reading of a chapter of Avot.
[26] The exegesis here depends on reading the word tzerufah in Psalm 18 not as "pure" but as "purifying." God's words, that is, God's commands, purify us; but the actions that are commanded are not inherently important. Their value is conventional, not essential.
[27] Alexander (= Alexandri, cited earlier), second- to third-generation Amora, Israel.

and Blessed One does not act that way." There was a heretic among the listeners, and as the Sages were leaving, he said to them, "Your teachings are nothing but lies. Did you not say that God speaks and acts upon his words? Why then does He not observe the Sabbath?"[28] They answered him, "You most wicked of men! Are you aware of the law that a person is permitted to carry anything in his *private* domain on the Sabbath?" He replied, "I am." Whereupon the Sages said to him, "Everything above and below is God's private domain, as it is written, 'The fullness of the earth is His glory'"[29] (Isaiah 6:3).[60]

Rejecting the immanentist view that the mitzvot were given for the benefit of mankind, Rabbi Akiva and his school taught that man's highest destiny is to bring satisfaction to his Creator. Rabbi Meir, a disciple of Rabbi Akiva, used to say, "Fortunate is he who is reared in the Torah and labors in Torah, thereby bringing satisfaction to his Creator."[61] A well-known anonymous teaching says, "We ask our teachers: One who builds a house, what benediction should he recite? Our Sages, of blessed memory, answered: He should recite the blessing Sheheheyanu ('who has kept us alive to this time') so that he may bring satisfaction to his Creator."[62]

Another illustration of these two views—one immanentist and the other transcendental—is to be found in the comments on the verse "Let them attach a cord of blue to the fringe of each corner . . . that you look at it, and recall all the commandments of the Lord" (Numbers 15:38–39). An anonymous passage in the Sifre for Numbers, whose source is the school of Rabbi Ishmael, provides an immanentist interpretation: "This passage teaches us that whoever observes the commandment regarding fringes is granted merit as if he observed all the commandments of the Torah. We can therefore deduce that he who observes all the commandments is certainly deserving of such merit."

But the transcendental view is expressed by Rabbi Meir, the disciple of Rabbi Akiva: "The verse does not read 'and you shall see *otam*—them (the fringes),' but 'you shall see *oto*—Him.' The verse thus teaches that whoever observes the commandment concerning fringes is considered as if he had welcomed the Shekhinah. For the cord of

---

[60] Exodus Rabbah 30:9.

[61] According to the reading of Ein Ya'akov, BT Berakhot 17a. The standard text attributes this saying to Rabbi Johanan.

[62] Tanhuma Bereshit 4. For a striking example of the immanentist view, see Rabbi Hiyya bar Abba's statement: "It is common practice for a laborer to be paid by his employer, to compensate him for degrading work with mortar and sludge. But the Holy and Blessed One tells Israel, 'I will reward you for *not* degrading yourselves,' as it says: 'You shall not draw abomination upon yourselves through anything that swarms, etc.' (Leviticus 11:43)" (Numbers Rabbah 10:3).

---

[28] The heretic is alluding to the law of the Sabbath that forbids carrying in a public domain. On the Sabbath day as any other, God makes the winds blow, moving clouds and rain from one country to another. By so doing (according to the objection), God violates the law against carrying in public on the Sabbath.

[29] So literally, construing melo as a noun "fullness." Other translations: "The whole earth is filled with His glory" (traditional), "His presence fills all the earth" (NJV).

blue is like the color of the sea, and the sea is like the firmament, and the firmament is like the throne of Glory, as we read, 'Above the firmament over their heads was the semblance of a throne in appearance like sapphire' (Ezekiel 1:26).[63]

Note how the Sages gave two very different interpretations to the Four Species of the Lulav.[30] Rabbi Akiva said, "The citron is the Holy and Blessed One, for *hadar* means majesty, as in, 'You are clothed in glory and majesty' (Psalm 104:1). The palm is the Holy and Blessed One, for we read, 'The Righteous [i.e., God] blooms like a date-palm' (Psalm 92:13). The myrtle is the Holy and Blessed One, for Zechariah had a vision of God 'standing among the myrtles' (Zechariah 1:8). The willow (*arava*) is the Holy and Blessed One, for it says, 'Extol Him who rides the clouds (*aravot*), the Lord is His Name'" (Psalm 68:5).[64]

In contrast, the immanentists explained the Four Species as corresponding to four types of people. The citron, which has fragrance and taste, represents those Jews who have learning and good deeds. The date-palm, whose fruit has taste but whose leaves are without fragrance, represents those with learning but no deeds. The myrtle, with fragrance but no taste, represents those with deeds but no learning. The willow, with neither fragrance nor taste, represents those with neither learning nor deeds. What does the Holy and Blessed One do? He cannot wipe out His people, but he says, "Bind them all together, and let them make up for each other's deficiencies, then I will be exalted. Thus it says: 'God builds His lofts in the heavens—' when? 'when His band is gathered on earth'" (Amos 9:6).[65] [31]

The transcendentalists explained the enormous power of sin by expounding the verse "You neglected the Rock that bore you" (Deuteronomy 32:18). Translating the word *teshi* ("neglected") as similar to *t'shishut ko'ah* ("diminished strength"), they took this text to mean that by following other gods "you are diminishing the power of your Creator."[66] Rabbi Eleazar expounded the verse "Through slothfulness, the ceiling sags" (Ecclesiastes 10:18) to mean because of Israel's slothfulness in neglecting the Torah, the enemy of God (euphemism for God)[32] became weakened (as one who

---

63 Sifre Shelah 115.   64 PRK 28/27:9 (184a); Leviticus Rabbah 30:9, anonymously.
65 Leviticus Rabbah 30:12.   66 Sifre Ha'azinu 319.

---

[30] On the festival of Sukkot (Tabernacles), Jews wave a citron (*etrog*) together with bound branches of palm, myrtle, and willow, based on Leviticus 23:40. *Hadar* was understood to mean citron, either because it is a beautiful, majestic fruit, or because it lingers (*dar*) on the tree. *Aravot* is a homonym, meaning either willows or clouds.

[31] NJV: "Who built His chambers in heaven and founded His vault on the earth." *Aguddah* ("band"; NJV "vault") means either a group of people, a bundle of objects (such as sticks), or a storage room (vault). The homily plays on this ambiguity.

[32] Often, when something is said that expresses some diminution of God, the phrase "God's enemies" is substituted, so as to avoid the direct diminution. This is evident in Scripture as well; for example, Job's wife tells Job to curse God and die with the words "Bless God and die." The same phenomenon occurs with Israel; when some calamity is said to befall Israel, it is often said to befall "Israel's enemies."

lacks sufficient power to save). The root word of *makh* means poor (impoverished) and the word *mekareh* ("ceiling") is a euphemism for God.[67]

The great importance of charity is seen from these two differing perspectives. "He who performs deeds of charity and justice is regarded as if he filled the whole world with kindness."[68] Or: "He who practices giving charity betters not only himself but all mankind."[69] In contrast to this view, Rabbi Aba reports in the name of Rabbi Berechiah, "He who practices *tzedakah* benefits not only the world below but also the world above. Who is it that preserves those who dwell on high and those who dwell below? It is he who gives *tzedakah* with his hand as it is written, "Your beneficence is as high as the heavens, O God" (Psalm 71:19).[70]

On the subject of holiness, Rabbi Ishmael, whose theology is immanentist, declares that Israel's holiness is a precondition of God's attachment to Israel. "'You shall be holy people to Me' (Exodus 22:30)—when you are holy, then you are Mine." Issi ben Judah[33] said, "When God adds a new mitzvah for the people of Israel, he increases their holiness."[71] "You shall keep the Sabbath for it is holy unto you" (Exodus 31:14)—this teaches that the Sabbath increases the holiness of Israel.[72] When a person sanctifies himself but a little, a great measure of holiness is added to him; when man sanctifies himself on earth, he is sanctified from heaven; when he sanctifies himself in this world, he will be sanctified in the world to come."[73] The meaning of all these statements is: holiness is a gift from heaven. The man who lives in holiness sanctifies himself. This concept is part of Israel's accepted traditions. But at the school of Rabbi Akiva they added, "Holiness is also a gift *to* heaven. He who lives a life of holiness increases, as it were, the holiness of heaven. It is written, 'You shall be holy for I, the Lord your God, am holy' (Leviticus 19:2). This means, if you sanctify yourselves, I shall regard it as if you sanctified Me; and if you fail to sanctify yourselves, I shall regard it as if you failed to sanctify Me. We might say that the meaning of the verse is, if you sanctify Me, then I am holy and if not, I am not holy. Therefore, the verse reads, 'for I am holy'—I remain holy whether you sanctify Me or not."[74]

Torah in Heaven and Earth

The theological concept concerning the existence of Torah in heaven did not develop out of the need to find an answer to the question, Where was the Torah before it was given to Moses? Nor did this concept have as its purpose to teach us that there is a special place in heaven, a kind of heavenly library, where the Torah was kept until it

[67] BT Megillah 11a.   [68] BT Sukkah 49b.
[69] Song of Songs 1:13, Buber ed., p. 20.   [70] Leviticus Rabbah 26:8.
[71] MI Kaspa 20.   [72] MI Tissa 1.
[73] BT Yoma 39a.   [74] Sifra Kedoshim 1:1, 86c.

[33] Fifth-generation Tanna (also called Joseph the Babylonian).

descended to earth. The essence of this teaching is simply to tell us that even as there exists a Torah below, so there also exists a Torah above. There is nothing here to suggest "two powers" or two Torahs, a lofty one above and a lesser one below, and that the one below emanated from the one above.[34] This concept can be formulated correctly by stating that the Tannaim believed that the one Torah existed in two forms. There is a difference in locale but no change in content. What the Sages study in the academy below is also studied in the academy on high; there, too, their lips whisper softly in heaven. There is only one truth and an identical content in heaven and on earth. Originally, the Torah existed only in heaven. After the Torah was given to Israel, it exists both in heaven and on earth. This concept is to be found in the teaching of Rabbi Akiva.

"He is One, and who can dissuade him?" (Job 23:13). Rabbi Pappus expounded, "Because He is One and there is none to prevent Him, He will do as He wishes— 'whatever He desires He does'" (Job 23:13). Hearing this, Rabbi Akiva exclaimed, "I swear by your life, Pappus, that you cannot interpret in this manner." To which Pappus responded, "What do you make of this verse?" He answered,

> Even as questions are asked in the academy on earth, so are they asked in the academy in heaven. How do we know that? It is written, "This sentence is decreed by the Watchers: This verdict is commanded by the Holy Ones, so that all creatures may know that the Most High is sovereign over the realm of man and He gives to whom He wishes and He may set over it the lowest of men" (Daniel 4:14). This teaches that even as matters of Halakhah are argued in the academy below, so are they argued in the academy above. How then shall we interpret the verse "He is One and who can dissuade Him"?! When a decision has been made, the Holy and Blessed One enters a place where human beings cannot enter and He puts His seal upon that judgment, as it is written, "He is One, who can dissuade Him? He knows the thoughts of all His creatures and who can oppose His judgments?"[75]

Rabbi Aha[35] said, "When Moses reached the highest heaven, he heard the voice of the Holy and Blessed One, Who was seated, discussing the law of the red heifer and citing a halakhic opinion in the name of he who originally said it: 'Rabbi Eliezer said: The red heifer must be two years old or less, and the beheaded cow[36] must be no older than one year.' Moses was startled and said, 'Master of the Universe, are not the

---

[75] Tanhuma Shemot 18.

---

[34] Heschel is concerned to distinguish this somewhat dualistic view about the Torah from a truly dualistic view, which would be more characteristic of ancient Gnostic thought. Here there is a parallelism, but not a duality that includes contrast. Heschel will modify this assertion slightly toward the end of this chapter, in presenting another view, according to which the earthly and heavenly Torahs are closely related, the former still striving to become the latter.

[35] Third- or fourth-generation Amora, Israel.

[36] This refers to the heifer whose neck is broken in a quasi-sacrificial rite intended to atone for a murder in which the murderer is unknown. It is described in Deuteronomy 21.

worlds above and below yours, yet you quote laws in the name of a mortal scholar?!' And God answered, 'A righteous man will arise in My world who is destined to open his lecture with the laws of the heifer; he is Rabbi Eliezer.'"[76] It was said about Rabbi Abiathar[37] that when the prophet Elijah revealed himself to him, he asked, "What is the Holy and Blessed One doing?" and he answered, "He is discussing the case of the concubine at Gibeah (Judges 19–21). "What was His decision?" Elijah replied, "He said, This is what My son Abiathar says, and this is what My son Jonathan[38] says."[77]

We must emphasize this point, that it was far from the thinking of the Sages to believe that Torah in heaven is different and apart from Torah in our possession, as if our Torah is merely a reflection of Torah in heaven. They firmly believed that an everlasting bond and mutual relationship existed between the two. Eternity rests upon Torah; and because this is so, our enemies and our detractors cannot prevail over us.

Torah, including the teachings of the Sages, contains the words of the living God. That is to say, it is not something uttered once by the Holy and Blessed One, which then becomes an entity by itself, cut off and uprooted from its source. The expression "the living God" means that they live in God. "When a person studies Torah, he acquires a knowledge of God, as it is written, 'Then you will understand the fear of the Lord and attain knowledge of God'" (Proverbs 2:5).[78] According to Rav: "The day has twelve hours divided into three periods. The first period, the Holy and Blessed One devotes to the study of Torah; the second, He sits in judgment on the whole world; and in the third, He is occupied with providing food for the whole world."[79]

Several statements testify that there was a theological concept that gained a following among certain Amoraim, namely, that the Torah that preceded all creation and was the instrument by which the world was created, is not the same Torah that we possess.[39] They claimed that the things that exist in heaven are not like the things on earth; and Torah is no exception. "Rabbi Hinena bar Isaac[40] said: Three things are

---

[76] PRK 4:7 (39b–40a).   [77] BT Gittin 6b.
[78] ARN A 4, p. 9b.   [79] BT Avodah Zarah 3b.

---

[37] Third-generation Amora, Israel.

[38] Second- to third-generation Amora (Israel), Rabbi Abiathar's colleague and discussant in this episode.

This case is all the more amazing because of its detailed circumstances. The dispute concerns whether the concubine's husband (described in Judges 19) alienated her upon finding a fly in his food or a brittle hair on her body. On such a question of historical fact, could there be any doubt in the mind of an omniscient God? Yet the last word of truth, according to this tale, is that it is still in dispute between Rabbi Abiathar and Rabbi Jonathan.

[39] In the succeeding paragraphs, Heschel modifies this assertion in order to show the rabbinic underpinnings of the kabbalistic idea of the supernal Torah that is the perfect, limiting case of the earthly Torah, which will be transformed to perfection only in the fullness of time. The earthly and heavenly Torahs are not in opposition to each other—rather, one yearns for the other.

[40] Third-generation Amora, Israel.

like fallen, unripe fruit—they are surrogates:[41] the surrogate of death is sleep; the surrogate of prophecy—dreams; the surrogate of the world to come—the Sabbath. Rabbi Avin[42] added: The surrogate of the supernal light is the sun; the surrogate of the supernal wisdom—Torah."[80]

Abbaye cites as common knowledge that Job was referring to the Torah when he said, "But from where does wisdom come? Where is the source of understanding? It is hidden from the eyes of all living, concealed from the fowl of heaven" (Job 28:20–21). "No man can set a value upon it; it cannot be found in the land of the living" (Job 28:13). It is clear, based on the view of this interpreter, that Job is referring to Torah in heaven of which no one has knowledge.[81]

The Sages expounded Ecclesiastes 11:8, "Even if a man lives many years . . . let him rejoice" to mean: let him rejoice in Torah. Let him "remember the days of darkness" refers to evil days, "for they will be many . . . as nothing" refers to Torah when studied in this world, which is as nothing compared to Torah of the Messianic Age.[82] When Torah was given, not everything was revealed, but Israel "was assured that God will reveal Himself again to transmit to them its secret reasons and its hidden mysteries, and they will implore Him to keep His promise." This is the promise that Scripture intimates, "Let Him kiss me with the kisses of His mouth" (Song of Songs 1:2).[83] In another source it is stated that in messianic times Elijah "will produce the Book of Yashar, in which our Torah is but one of its poems."[84]

Another expression of this view declares, "From the time Torah was given until the times when the final Holy Temple will be built, we possess Torah as it has been given us, but its full glory has not been revealed. Its preciousness, loftiness, beauty, its awe and dread, its majesty and genius, its splendor, its might and daring, its supreme authority and power—these will not be transmitted until the final Holy Temple will be built and the Shekhinah will dwell within it."[85]

In kabbalistic circles they taught: There is a Torah above and there is a Torah below. The Torah above is in heaven and the Torah below was given to human beings. This is how Rabbi Menahem Azariah of Fano explained the intent of the prayer, "Grant our portion in Your Torah." "Our portion" asks that the new laws we promulgate, based on the Torah below, may also become part of the Torah above. Even as God made known to Israel and its Sages the heavenly secrets, so does He impart to the angels all the innovations in the Torah introduced by mortal men below. When we read of "mighty ones who do His bidding" (Psalm 103:20), it refers to the righteous scholars

---

[80] Genesis Rabbah 17:5.   [81] BT Shevuot 5a.   [82] Ecclesiastes Rabbah 11:8.
[83] Rashi, introduction to Song of Songs.
[84] Aggadot of Song of Songs, ed. S. Schechter, line 1120.
[85] Hekhalot Rabbati ch. 27, Beit Ha-Midrash part 3, p. 104.

---

[41] Heschel's note: "The term *novelot* refers to fruit that falls from the tree before it is fully ripe. It is a metaphoric reference to lesser entities which reflect the fuller, more powerful sources from which they emanate, just as fallen fruit is less than what remains on the tree."

[42] Third- to fourth-generation Amora (or his son, fifth-generation Amora), Babylonia.

who literally fulfill His word by their halakhic innovations in Torah. These are reserved in the treasury of the Ruler of the Universe—Torah in heaven. It is this Torah that is the instrument of His daily craft in creating new heavens and a new earth. The prayer of Rabbi Zeira[43] expressed a similar plea: "May it please You that I will innovate something that is acceptable,"[86] meaning in heaven above and on earth below.[87]

[86] BT Betzah 38a.
[87] Imrot Tehorot, Rabbi Menahem Azaryah of Fano, Hikur Hadin, part II, chapter 14.

---

[43] Third-generation Amora from Babylonia, who moved to Israel.

15 פרד

GO 'ROUND THE ORCHARD!

Translator's Introduction

In this chapter, Heschel sets out for us what he sees as the ambivalent nature of Jewish tradition when it comes to mystical speculation. On the one hand, there is the warning of the Mishnah that speculative thought on the origins and the limits of the world (i.e., metaphysics) is a dangerous betrayal of human responsibility. On the other hand, there are innumerable approvals of metaphysical inquiries by specific Sages, and especially Rabbi Akiva. This emerges as yet another of Heschel's "dualisms": mystical speculation has potentially great religious value, and that value is at the same time counterbalanced by the dangers that it poses.

In addition to cataloguing and documenting the rabbinic ambivalence on the subject, Heschel also contributes a novel idea of his own: that prophecy and apocalyptic thought are historically intertwined, but are essentially mirror images of each other. Both represent connections between the earthly and the supernatural. Both can be ecstatic experiences. But prophecy is ultimately about God reaching out to human beings in order to attend to the repair of the world. Apocalyptic, on the other hand, is about human beings reaching out to heaven in order to see, and perhaps even have a hand in ordering, the supernal realm. In making this distinction, Heschel is also suggesting that prophecy is based in what is a fundamentally optimistic view of this world: it is susceptible to perfection through human agency (with divine inspiration), even though it cannot be one with the transcendent realm of the Creator. Mystical/apocalyptic thought is, by contrast, based in a pessimistic view of the terrestrial world, absent a connection to the divine realm. Apocalyptic thought seeks to connect to the divine realm in order to get beyond what would otherwise be an irredeemable earthly existence. And it is perhaps in this pessimism about the ability of the human world to repair itself that the potential dangers of mystical indulgence reveal themselves. Nevertheless, that "Rabbi Akiva entered in peace and exited in peace" is evidence that engaging in apocalyptic thought while averting its attendant danger of negating this world is possible, even though rare.

One final introductory note: Heschel also connects the yearning for political independence (cf. Bar Kokhbah) with the yearning for a resumption of prophecy. Aside from the psychological connections between the two, this linkage has traditionally been found in Isaiah 1:26 and has been articulated by Maimonides in his *Epistle to Yemen*. A particularly interesting example of a nexus that was made between messianism (i.e., political independence) and prophecy was the attempt to renew rabbinic ordination in sixteenth-century Tzefat.[1]

Rabbi Akiva Was Worthy to See the Glory

ACCORDING TO A TANNAITIC TRADITION, Rabbi Akiva engaged in the study of the Merkavah, the mystic speculations on Ezekiel's vision of the divine chariot.[2] "Many have studied the subject of the Merkavah but have never seen it."[1] Rabbi Akiva, however, was inspired by the vision and saw the chariot. He lectured on the Merkavah in the presence of Rabbi Joshua. In his teachings concerning the prophecy of Moses, you will find that his views are close to those of the apocalyptic visionaries.

These visionaries yearned for a glimpse of what is on high. In the teachings of the Mishnah, there is a statement that is probably directed against such aspirations. "Whoever seeks to know the answer to these four questions, it were better for him not to have been born: What is above? What is below? What was there before? What will be after?" The Mishnah, however, does not forbid the teaching of mysticism; it rather seeks to set guidelines and to limit the number who qualify for such studies: "One shall not lecture . . . on the Merkavah to a single student unless that student is a scholar who can understand with independent mind."[2] "How shall he proceed? The teacher begins with the highlights of the subject and the student agrees."[3] The wisdom of the Merkavah does not depend entirely on tradition or on oral instruction. With regard to acquiring knowledge of the revealed Torah, we praise the scholar who never says anything that he has not heard from his teacher.[3] With regard to acquiring knowledge of esoterics, however, we expect the student to "understand with inde-

----

[1] Tosefta Megillah 4:28.　　[2] Mishnah Hagigah 2:1.　　[3] PT Hagigah 2:1, 77a.

----

[1] See Arie Morgenstern, "Dispersion and the Longing for Zion, 1240–1840," *Azure* (Winter 2002). For an explanation of the phrase "Go 'round the Orchard," see below, the subsection entitled "The Way of Prophecy and the Way of Apocalypse."

[2] Just over a thousand years later, in the twelfth century, Moses Maimonides stated that the area of wisdom covered by the term *Ma'aseh Merkavah*—the work of the chariot—was what philosophers called "metaphysics."

[3] This is how Rabbi Eliezer ben Hyrcanus describes his own virtue; see BT Sukkah 28a. The idea seems to be that in the realm of that which was revealed, e.g., Halakhah, to state that which has not been previously taught is illegitimately to innovate. However, Rabbi Eliezer's teacher, Rabban Johanan ben Zakkai, apparently felt that the power of innovation was as important, if not more important; see Mishnah Avot 2:8.

pendent mind" and to "agree" with his master's teaching.[4] You will find support for this in what the Sages said: "Three scholars lectured on the Merkavah before their masters: Rabbi Joshua before Rabbi Johanan ben Zakkai; Rabbi Akiva before Rabbi Joshua; Hananiah ben Hakhinai[5] before Rabbi Akiva. From that point on, however, minds were no longer receptive.[6]"4

The requirement for qualification refers not only to acquiring information of esoterics orally, or from mouth to ear, but also demands total absorption in the ambience of mysticism. The student does not embrace this knowledge; this knowledge rather embraces the student.

A story is told about Rabbi Johanan ben Zakkai, who was riding on a donkey, while Rabbi Eleazar ben Arakh[7] walked behind him. Rabbi Eleazar said to his master, "My master, teach me one lesson on the Merkavah." His teacher replied, "Have not our Sages taught that it is forbidden to teach one individual the mystery of the Merkavah, unless he is a scholar and can understand it independently?" Rabbi Eleazar then said to him, "Do permit me to expound something on this subject." He answered, "Speak." As soon as Eleazar ben Arakh began to speak about the secret of the divine chariot, Rabbi Johanan descended from his donkey saying, "It is not proper that I shall hear about the glory of my Maker while riding on a donkey." They walked a while and then sat down beneath a tree, whereupon a fire descended from heaven and surrounded them. The ministering angels leapt before them with joy like guests at a wedding who rejoice with the groom. One angel spoke from within the fire saying, "Eleazar ben Arakh, it is exactly as you have explained it—you have revealed the secret of the Merkavah!" Instantly, all the trees opened their mouths and sang, as it is written, "Then all the trees of the forest will sing" (Psalm 96:12). When Rabbi Eleazar ben Arakh finished his presentation of the Merkavah, Rabbi Johanan rose, kissed him on his head and said, "Blessed is the Lord, the God of Abraham, Isaac, and Jacob, who gave Abraham our Father a wise son who can

---

4 PT Hagigah 2:1, 77b; Tosefta Hagigah 2:2; BT Hagigah 14b.

---

[4] Presumably, this does not mean simply to mimic one's teacher, but rather to be consistent with it while using one's independent powers of thought to reveal even more of what had been hidden.

[5] Third- to fourth-generation Tanna, versed in mysticism.

[6] Literally, "clean." The point of this seems to be that the ability to deal in the esoteric matters represented by the chariot was possessed by the greats of the first and early second century, but the chain did not continue. Three generations from Johanan ben Zakkai to Hananiah ben Hakhinai were able to use independent powers of mind to "agree" with their masters and develop the esoteric tradition. But that art was lost.

[7] Second-generation Tanna, attracted to mysticism. He is compared to an "overflowing fountain" in Avot 2:8. There are conflicting traditions as to whether he or Rabbi Eliezer ben Hyrcanus was Rabban Johanan ben Zakkai's favorite student (ibid.). The stories told here are evidence of a relationship of close intimacy between them. Apart from these mystical traditions, he left no substantial body of teaching, and no disciples. Perhaps he was a casualty of mystical burnout, like three out of the "four who entered Pardes (the Orchard)"? See ARNA 14 and BT Shabbat 147b.

lecture on the glory of our Father in Heaven . . . and fortunate are you, Father Abraham, that Eleazar ben Arakh is one of your descendants."[8] 5

In a Baraita, we are taught: "Four entered the Orchard:[9] Ben Azzai, Ben Zoma, Aher (Elisha ben Avuyah[10]), and Rabbi Akiva. Ben Azzai gazed and died; Aher 'mutilated the shoots,'[11] Ben Zoma gazed and was stricken. Rabbi Akiva left unharmed."6

What was the supreme yearning of these four Sages? According to Rashi, there is a hint that they aspired to see the Shekhinah.7 Ben Azzai gazed toward the Shekhinah and died. Scripture refers to him when it says, "The death of His faithful ones is grievous in the Lord's sight" (Psalm 116:15)—It was inevitable that he would die, for it is written, "Man may not see Me and live" (Exodus 33:20). Ben Zoma gazed and was stricken—this means he lost his mind; he went mad at the sight of the startling scenes that were beyond his power to bear.[12] 8

---

5 PT Hagigah 2:1, 77a.   6 BT Hagigah 14b.
7 Rashi, BT Hagigah 13a, on *hen hen ma'aseh hamerkavah*.
8 BT Hagigah 14b, following Rashi and Rav Hai Gaon. Also see BT Hagigah 15b for the next phrase in the text.

---

[8] In ARN A 6, a similar story is told about Eleazar ben Arakh's contemporary and colleague Eliezer ben Hyrcanus. There the subject matter is not explicitly stated to be Merkavah wisdom, although it does describe Eliezer's subject matter as something that "no ear had ever before heard."

[9] "Orchard" (Hebrew *Pardes*, from the Persian; cf. the Greek *paradeisos*): The "garden of divine mysteries," identified with Paradise. Clearly they were involved in some sort of mystical pursuits. Perhaps they sought, through meditative techniques, to enter the realm of the angelic spirits, perhaps to approach the Divine Presence itself. The whole enterprise is a classic test of the idea we have associated with the Akivan school, that the boundary of earth and heaven is permeable. It also anticipates the assertion discussed in chapter 18 that Moses ascended to heaven. Note also our earlier interpretation of Heschel's suggestion that *Pardes* was a preoccupation with the problem of suffering (chapter 6 above).

[10] Elisha ben Avuyah was dubbed "Aher" (the "Other," or Renegade) after turning heretic. There are various incidents related about the cause of his doing so. The most famous, related in chapter 7 ("Can This Be Torah and Its Reward?") tells how he witnessed a boy falling to his death from a tree after performing the twin mitzvot of parental obedience and mercy on animals. The current story suggests that he became intellectually and spiritually disoriented from entering the Orchard. These accounts could be complementary, as Milton Steinberg suggested in his historical novel *As a Driven Leaf* (New York: Bobbs-Merrill, 1939).

[11] An ambiguous expression that could mean, among other possibilities, either uprooting the fundamentals of the faith or corrupting the youth. Both of these possibilities are represented in traditions about Elisha ben Avuyah.

[12] Heschel adds: According to Rabbenu Hananel (BT Hagigah 14b): "Ben Azzai continued to utter names, in hope of seeing through the bright speculum, but died." According to this, he looked through the dark speculum. The *Otzar Hakavod* comments critically on Rashi: "Ben Azzai gazed and died because his soul cleaved truly in great love to those supernal entities that are its foundation, and gazed on the brilliant light, separated from the body and cast off the body altogether. In that hour his soul saw its rest, that it was good, and did not return to its place. Not as those commentators who said he saw the Shekhinah and died, for it says, 'Man shall not see Me and live,' and we would then be placing Ben Azzai's achievement above Moses's."

"Rabbi Akiva ascended in peace and descended in peace. The words of Scripture apply to him: 'Draw me after you, let us run! The King has brought me to His chambers'" (Song of Songs 1:4). The expression "he ascended and descended" supports the view that this is a reference to ascending to heaven. This is how Rashi explains it: "'They entered the Orchard' means they ascended heaven."[9] "The King brought me into His chambers." It is said of the Merkavah mystics that they ascended to heaven and saw the Divine Throne. Rabbi Akiva entered the chambers and palaces on high. Did he see the Divine Presence? According to many of the commentators, Rabbi Akiva was able to leave in peace precisely because he did not destroy the boundaries between heaven and earth nor did he seek to break through to the Divine Presence; he descended in peace because he did not gaze at the Supreme Mystery.[10]

According to the account in the Babylonian Talmud, however, Rabbi Akiva did look at God's Glory. "The ministering angels also sought to push aside Rabbi Akiva (as in the case of Moses, when he ascended to heaven, the angels sought to kill him)."[11] But the Holy and Blessed One said to them: "Let this venerable Sage stay. He is worthy to behold My Glory."[12] In later sources we read: "When Rabbi Akiva began his lectures on the Vision of the Merkavah, his mouth became like Mount Sinai and his voice like a ladder on which angels ascended and descended."[13] [13] "For the eye of Rabbi Akiva beheld the Merkavah in the same manner that the eye of the prophet Ezekiel beheld it."[14]

Just as there were some Sages who criticized Rabbi Akiva for his exaggerations in expounding Torah ("he would expound mountains of laws from the crowns of the letters"[15]), so there were other Sages who expressed high praise for his mastery of the secrets of the Merkavah. Rabbi Huna expounded the verse: "In that day there shall be neither sunlight nor cold moonlight" (Zechariah 14:6)—"The text is written *yekippa-'on*; this suggests that things that are hidden from you in this world will become as clear as though you gazed into a crystal bowl."[14] It is written, "I will lead the blind by a road they did not know, and I will make them walk by paths they never knew. I will turn darkness before them to light, rough places into level ground. These are the

[9] Rashi, loc cit. Rabbenu Hananel disagreed, saying they saw only the imaginings of their own mind, like one peering through a dark speculum.
[10] *Otzar ha-Kavod* (thirteenth century).
[11] Exodus Rabbah 42:4.
[12] BT Hagigah 15b, according to the reading of Rabbenu Hananel.
[13] Zohar Bamidbar 230b.
[14] *Midrash Hillel,* in *Beit Hamidrash* (ed. Jellinek), 6:97.
[15] MaHaRZU (commentary of Rabbi Ze'ev Wolf) on Numbers Rabbah 19:6.

[13] That is, Akiva's voice and his teachings mediated between earth and heaven, a mediation that occurred both at Sinai, when God descended on the mountain, and at Beth El in Jacob's famous dream.
[14] The exegesis seems to turn on the *yod* at the beginning of *yekippa'on*, typically a marker of the third person future tense. That is the *ketiv*, the way in which the word is written in the Masoretic tradition. The *keri*, however, the Masoretes' prescribed pronunciation, substitutes a *vav* for the *yod*, denoting the conjunction that is captured by the word "nor" of the translation.

things I will do—I will keep them without fail" (Isaiah 42:16). The text, however, does not literally say "I will do," but "I have done and have not failed." God is saying that He has already done this for Rabbi Akiva and his colleagues, as Rabbi Aha said, "Secrets that were not revealed to Moses at Mount Sinai were revealed to Rabbi Akiva and his colleagues, as it is written, 'His eyes beheld every precious thing' (Job 28:10)—this refers to Rabbi Akiva."[15] What is stated here are words of such superlative praise for Rabbi Akiva and his colleagues as were never said of any prophet or Sage in the history of Israel. The phrase *niglah lo* "revealed to him," implies a transcendental perception such as is attained only in prophecy or by the Holy Spirit. It is, therefore, correct to say that the language used ("things that were not revealed to Moses at Sinai were revealed to Rabbi Akiva") was intended to teach us not only that Rabbi Akiva attained so profound an understanding of Torah that even Moses did not achieve, but that he achieved mystical illumination beyond that of the greatest of the prophets: "His eyes beheld every precious thing."[16]

"The God Who is invisible to the human eye and hidden from His ministering angels was nevertheless revealed to Rabbi Akiva in the vision of the Merkavah."[17] This daring statement, it appears, was a challenge to the Amoraim, who struggled to comprehend this difficult subject[18] and who asked, "How did he expound (this subject)?" In my opinion the meaning of the question "How did he expound?" is, How did Rabbi Akiva know that he was looking at God's Glory? Rabbah bar bar Hannah cited the verse, *v'ata merivevot kodesh* ("he approached from Ribeboth-kodesh" [= "the holy multitudes"], Deuteronomy 33:2). The word *v'ata* is to be read *ot hu,* "it is a sign." God gave the holy multitude a sign by which to recognize Him. When He revealed Himself at the Sea of Reeds, they immediately recognized Him, as it is written, "This is my God and I will glorify Him" (Exodus 15:2).[19] The rest of this homily supports the view that *ot* ("sign") refers to the sign that enables one to recognize the Divine Glory and not, as others have explained, as a warning not to look at the Divine Glory.[20]

Those who have looked at the Merkavah face a very difficult question. They behold the beauty and the splendor, but how do they know whether they are actually seeing the Divine Glory? "The whole world is full of His Glory . . . where is the place of His Glory?"[21] Great multitudes of angels surround His Throne; how can mortal man

---

[16] PRK 4:7 (39b).

[17] Quoted in Gershom Scholem, *Major Trends in Jewish Mysticism,* The Hilda Stich Stroock Lectures 1938 (Jerusalem: Schocken, 1941), chapter 2, n. 80, from *Heikhalot Zutrati.*

[18] BT Hagigah 16a.

[19] Ibid.; Sifre Haberakhah 343.

[20] For instance, Rashi, Hagigah 16a, on *mai darash.*

[21] Prayer Book, Kedushah of Musaf Service, Sabbath.

---

[15] There is a noteworthy irony here, since there is a tradition, preserved in BT Bava Batra 14b, that Moses was the author of Job, the book from which the proof text for Akiva's superiority to Moses is taken!

know whether he saw an angel or the Divine Glory? "Thousands upon thousands served Him; myriads upon myriads attend Him" (Daniel 7:10). "Can His troops be numbered?" (Job 25:3). "Do you imagine that the ministering angels themselves know where He is?! Has it not already been said, 'Blessed is the glory of the Lord in His place'? (Ezekiel 3:12). They never saw His place!"[22] [16] That is why they expounded, "He is a sign by which His multitudes recognize Him."[23] Although He is among the holy multitudes, He can be recognized.[24] So, too, did they interpret the word *tzevaot*. He is a sign for His hosts.[17] [25]

This subject is explained in the teachings of the Tannaim. "A parable about a mortal king who enters a city and about him is a suite of bodyguards who surround him; to his right and left are strong men; armies are stationed before and behind him. Everyone asks, 'Which one is the king?' since he is a mortal man like themselves. But when the Holy and Blessed One revealed Himself at the Sea and He showed them His troops of ministering angels, they had no need to ask, 'Who is the King?' As soon as they saw Him, they recognized Him and all exclaimed, 'This is my God!'"[18] [26]

Rabbi Akiva is one of the Tannaim of whom it is told, "Rabbi Akiva saw clairvoyantly with the help of the Holy Spirit."[27] According to legend, Elijah revealed himself to Rabbi Akiva and his wife.[28] According to his own testimony, he aspired to "the vision of the Shekhinah," and he wept "because our sins caused us" to be unworthy of this, as it is written, "But your iniquities have been a barrier between you and your God" (Isaiah 59:2). He would weep when he read this verse and said, "If one who fasts so that the spirit of impurity may rest upon him, attains his purpose, then he who undergoes privations so that the spirit of purity may rest upon him, should all the more readily attain his purpose! But what can I do when our sins cause us to fail?"[29] This statement is also found in another version: "If one who cleaves to impurity, the spirit of impurity rests upon him, surely he who cleaves to the Shekhinah should as of right have the Shekhinah rest upon him!"[30]

[22] PR 20:4 (97a).
[23] Midrash Lekah Tov, Haberakhah p. 124.
[24] Sifre, ed. Pardo (*Sifre de-ve Rav la-Rav David Pardo*), 306c.
[25] MI Shirata 1.
[26] MI Shirata 3.
[27] See story in Leviticus Rabbah 21:8 and PRK 27/26 (ed. Buber 176b, not in Mandelbaum/Braude).
[28] BT Nedarim 50a; Midrash on Proverbs 9:2.
[29] BT Sanhedrin 65b, and Rashi ad loc.
[30] Sifre Shofetim 173, where this statement is attributed to Rabbi Eliezer.

[16] The verse in Ezekiel 3:12 is taken as proof of the angels' ignorance. From the fact that they say vaguely, "Blessed is the glory of the Lord in His place," the author of the midrash infers that they do not know God's place, else they would have mentioned it.

[17] Here, the word *tzevaot* ("hosts") is taken as a contraction of *tzava* and *ot*, i.e., "host" and "sign." The point is that the elect have a kind of password by which they can gain access to that which they then see more clearly than anyone else.

[18] That is, the people who experienced the parting of the sea were the elect.

The Way of Prophecy and the Way of Apocalypse

The theology of Rabbi Akiva has two basic concepts of an apocalyptic nature: the ascent of Moses to heaven and the existence of the Torah in heaven in the form of a book. These concepts were well known in the books of the Apocrypha.[19] They emerged from the apocalyptic universe of discourse and left their imprint on the books of the Apocrypha.

The cessation of prophecy was not easily accepted by the people of Israel. It was no trivial matter, but rather a very painful experience. Though the majority of the Sages removed themselves from the source of mystical study and said, "Go 'round and 'round it, but do not approach the Vineyard!"[20] there were those who continued the struggle to enter the Orchard and to ascend to heaven.

Many wrestled with the Holy Spirit and were injured in the process. Apocalyptic thought represented, as it were, a brandishing of the swords in the struggle with God. Even as Bar Kokhba and his followers rose up in revolt against the Roman Empire because they would not willingly surrender the loss of their independence, so the visionaries of the Apocalypse refused to surrender their hope for a return to prophecy.[21] Apocalyptic thinking had its birth in the struggle of those who yearned for prophecy, and the books that they consequently produced had their basis in the belief that the Holy Spirit rested upon its authors and inspired them with the words to inscribe in a book.

The author of the Vision of Ezra, who apparently lived in the Land of Israel after the destruction of the Second Temple, tells us not only that he saw the angel Uriel, who explained to him God's ways and the reasons for the Temple's destruction, but that he heard God's voice speaking to him out of the bush and he implored God to bestow upon him the Holy Spirit so that he could record his visions in a book.[31] The author of the Book of Enoch II (the Slavonic version) relates that he saw God[32] for

31 Vision of Ezra 12:1, 22 (NEB: 2 Esdras 1:4ff.; 4:1ff.; 14:1–26).
32 Enoch II (Slavonic version) 9:4; 22:1.

---

[19] Literally, the "hidden" books. In Hebrew, they were known as the "outside" books, because they were extracanonical, that is, not in the Bible. They included apocalyptic books, but they were by no means all apocalyptic.

[20] Heschel is here adapting a talmudic phrase used in conjunction with the Nazirite, who is under a vow of abstention from wine. "Go 'round and 'round it, but do not get too near the vineyard" is the advice given to the Nazirite. Detour around the vineyard so that you are not tempted to violate your vow. The Pardes represents direct apprehension of the Divine, and the Jews, as it were, were avowed to abstain from prophecy. So the would-be apocalyptist was advised by the Sages to detour around the Pardes, the Orchard, so as to avoid temptation.

[21] A noteworthy analogy that captures the passion of apocalyptic and attempts to explain why such trends in thought were contemporaneous with the kind of political activism represented by Bar Kokhba.

"the Holy Spirit was poured upon him."[33] The author of the Vision of Baruch I relates: "Behold, the heavens opened up and I saw, and strength was given me, and I heard a voice from heaven and He said to me . . . .[34] The Book of Jubilees is also written in the prophetic style, in the form of speech issuing from the mouth of the *sar hapanim* (Angel of the Presence) to Moses our Teacher.[35]

We must understand, however, that prophecy and apocalyptic belong to two distinct spheres. Torah is *sefer toledot adam,* the book of man's history, which records the deeds of mankind and the mitzvot given to human beings. The Prophets dwell not upon what goes on in heaven, but on what happens on earth. The heavens are God's, but the earth God gave to humans. Prophetic thought is characterized by humility, as it confronts the Supreme Mystery of the world. A great principle of Torah is, "The hidden things belong to the Lord our God, but the revealed things belong to us and our children" (Deuteronomy 29:28). "It is the glory of God to conceal a matter" (Proverbs 25:2). "But the Lord is in His holy Abode—be silent before Him all the earth!" (Habakkuk 2:20). When the prophets speak of what they saw in a vision, they reveal one handbreadth while concealing two. When Isaiah saw the King, the Lord of Hosts, seated on a throne in the loftiest heights, he trembled and was stunned. "Woe is me, I am lost! For I am a man of unclean lips . . . yet my own eyes have beheld the King Lord of Hosts" (Isaiah 6:5). This attitude prevailed also in the era of the Talmud, namely, all that a human being can comprehend is but the very edge of God's ways. "If we cannot comprehend even the nature of a storm, how much more impossible is it for us to understand the order of the universe!"[36]

In contrast to the prophets, the devotees of apocalyptic reached out toward the Supreme Mystery of the universe. Apocalyptic is the expression of potential yearnings for the transcendental world. The apocalyptic visionaries were a generation thirsting and longing to strengthen their bonds with heaven. They recoiled from a world that was in the power of evil, a world that had caused the fall of man, and they sought salvation by turning to the supernal world. The prophets taught that humans would find healing and the path to salvation by *teshuvah,* turning back to God. Apocalyptic thinkers, however, did not believe that there could be any improvement in the human condition on this earth.[22]

The goal of the apocalyptic visionaries was to behold the world above and to see that which is hidden from the eyes of those who dwell on earth: the Garden of Eden and Gehenna (hell), the souls of the departed, and the miracles that would occur at the End of Days.[23] They could envision the angels who serve the Lord of the Uni-

[33] Enoch II 91:1.   [34] Vision of Baruch I 22:1.
[35] See Jubilees 1.   [36] Genesis Rabbah 12:1.

[22] That is, there was a certain pessimism about the prospects for improvement in the natural course of events.

[23] Note that all that Heschel enumerates here are the very things forbidden to be considered by Mishnah Hagigah 2:1.

verse, the reward that awaits the righteous, and the punishment that will be meted out to the wicked. There one learns, "What was, what is, and what will be until Judgment Day."[37]

Apocalyptic books did not find a place in the rabbinic curriculum.[24] The Sages of Israel consigned them to the Genizah,[25] saying, "Whoever brings into his home more than the twenty-four books of the canon is bringing confusion into his home."[38] The books were hidden, but the thoughts and the aspirations of the apocalyptic visionaries continued to exert their influence and did not disappear from the teachings of many Sages in the course of history.

They Sought to Suppress the Book of Ezekiel

Moses our Teacher was "a father of Torah, a father of Wisdom, a father of Prophecy."[39] The prophet Ezekiel was a master of the mystic speculations of the Divine Chariot, a master of apocalyptic. His visions opened the door to those who sought to acquire a knowledge of the secrets of the chariot. These became the peg on which the mystics of Israel and of the nations of the world based themselves.[26] Just as the opening chapters of the Torah became the subject of study known as Ma'asei Bereshit ("the Secrets of Creation"), so the vision of Ezekiel became a subject of study called Ma'asei Merkavah ("the Secrets of the Chariot").[27]

Not all the Sages, however, approved of what Ezekiel did in revealing that which would better have been concealed. There is a note of criticism in the comment of Rava, "Everything that Ezekiel saw, Isaiah also saw (when the Holy Spirit alighted upon him). To whom can we compare Ezekiel? To a villager who saw the King. And to whom can we compare Isaiah? To one raised in a big city who is not impelled to report everything, for he was a descendant of kings and raised in a palace; accustomed to seeing royalty, he is not overwhelmed or astonished and therefore is not

---

[37] Enoch 13:2.
[38] Ecclesiastes Rabbah 12:11.
[39] BT Megillah 13a.

---

[24] Hebrew: Bet Hamidrash, "House of Study," that is, the Jewish academy or curriculum of rabbinic studies.

[25] Genizah—storeroom of retired books. Here the implication is that these books were not fit to be studied because of their unorthodox content; they were suppressed. See glossary and chapter 33, the section entitled "Apocryphal Books."

[26] By "peg" here, Heschel means a scriptural verse or verse fragment that serves as even a tenuous source in the Bible for certain modes of thought. In this way, mystics always appealed to Ezekiel's visions as support and precedent for what they attempted to do.

[27] As mentioned in part earlier in this chapter, Maimonides considered these two terms to refer, respectively, to physics and metaphysics.

impelled to tell all."[28] 40 "Moses and Samuel were not like Ezekiel, who disclosed everything he saw . . . therefore Scripture refers to him as *ben adam* ('the son of man'[29])."41

The Sages had grave doubts about the Book of Ezekiel. "Hananiah ben Hezekiah[30] is to be commended highly; were it not for him, the Book of Ezekiel was in danger of being suppressed from the canon." The Sages had misgivings about Ezekiel "because some of his teachings contradicted the Torah"42 and because he opened the door to speculations about the chariot. "The story is told of a child who was reading the Book of Ezekiel at the home of his teacher. When he understood the meaning of the word *hashmal* (electrum), a fire broke out from *hashmal* and consumed him. As a consequence, the Sages sought to suppress the Book of Ezekiel."43

It is an established tradition that Malachi was the last of the prophets. "When the last of the prophets died, Haggai, Zechariah, Malachi, the Holy Spirit disappeared from Israel."44 But according to another opinion that has been preserved, "Jeremiah was the last of the prophets." Do we have a hint in this opinion that there were Sages who wanted to suppress the Book of Ezekiel? Perhaps it is an expression of their desire to separate prophecy from the apocalyptic teachings contained in the Books of Ezekiel, Zechariah, and Daniel? This is what the midrash tells us: "The words of Jeremiah . . . in the territory of Benjamin" (Jeremiah 1:1). Even as Benjamin is the last of the tribes, so is Jeremiah the last of the prophets. But did not Haggai, Zechariah, and Malachi prophesy after him? Rabbi Eliezer's answer is: "They had very brief prophecies." Rabbi Shmuel ben Nahman says: "Theirs was an old prophecy that was preserved by them [and articulated later]."45 [31]

Various scholars warned against speculating on the chariot and on what transcends nature. They cited the words of Ben Sira, "Do not pry into things too hard for

---

40 BT Hagigah 13b; Rashi ad loc.   41 Tanhuma Tzav 13.   42 BT Shabbat 13b.
43 BT Hagigah 13a.   44 Tosefta Sotah 13:3.
45 Midrash Aggadah on Mattot, p. 274; PRK 13:14, 116a.

---

[28] The contrast is between the breathless exuberance with which Ezekiel reports every detail of his vision (in chapter 1 of his book) and the sedate, matter-of-fact report of Isaiah on his vision (in chapter 6 of his book). Heschel here detects a note of "snobbery" with the sedate-tempered Sages identifying with Isaiah, and criticizing the too-revealing provinciality of Ezekiel. If later mystics used Ezekiel as their source, the implication of this critique is obvious.

[29] That is, the phrase "son of man," which is used as a form of address only in the Book of Ezekiel, is seen as opposed to, simply, "man." It thus connotes youth or childishness; in this case, one who speaks in amazement, like a child, at the wonders he saw.

[30] A teacher of the late Second Temple period, contemporary of Hillel and Shammai (first century B.C.E.).

[31] Perhaps what is meant is that he was the last of the prophets of the First Temple. But in any event, in this midrash, it is curious that the question brought to challenge this statement is: "Didn't Haggai, Zechariah, and Malachi prophesy after him?" There is no mention of Ezekiel, who, while he overlapped with Jeremiah, certainly can and should be considered a later prophet.

you, or examine what is beyond your reach. Meditate on the commandments you have been given; what the Lord keeps is no concern of yours."[46] It is told that Rabbi Judah the Prince had an outstanding student who expounded a chapter on the mystery of the Merkavah. Rabbi did not agree with him and he was stricken with boils.[47] In accordance with this discussion, the Mishnah records the opinion of the first-cited Tanna, "It is forbidden to recite the chapter on the Merkavah for the Haftarah." But Rabbi Judah, a disciple of Rabbi Akiva, permitted it.[32] [48]

Did God Reveal the Heavenly Secrets to Abraham or Moses?

A stinging rebuke against the apocalyptic visionaries may be preserved in the words of Rabbi Johanan: "All the prophets prophesied only about the Messianic Days, but as for the world to come, 'no eye has seen, O God, but You'" (Isaiah 64:3).[49] In other words, the eye of the prophet has not seen the Upper World, only God has seen it. However, there was no generally accepted tradition. On the question as to what God revealed to Abraham at the time He made a covenant with him (Genesis 15:9–10, 18), Rabbi Johanan ben Zakkai said, "He revealed to him the secrets of this world but not of the world to come." Rabbi Akiva said, "He revealed to him both this world and the world to come."[50] It appears that the greatest of the Tannaim were involved in discussions on the same subject that was of basic concern to the apocalyptists.[33]

According to Rabbi Johanan's opinion, apocalyptic visions are meaningless, for if God did not reveal the future world even to Abraham, He certainly would not reveal it to those in much later generations. Rabbi Akiva's opinion, however, provides support for apocalyptic teachings.

Even as the Sages differed as to the nature of Abraham's vision, so they differed as to what Moses saw in his vision. At the school of Rabbi Akiva, they taught: "Moses' vision was greater than that which is recorded with regard to Abraham."[51] Not all the Sages, however, agreed with this view.

When God revealed Himself to Moses at the burning bush, Moses hid his face, "for he was afraid to look upon God" (Exodus 3:6). Rabbi Joshua ben Korhah commented: "Moses did not act properly when he hid his face, for had he not done so,

---

[46] Ecclesiasticus of Ben Sira 3:19 (NEB: 3:21-22).
[47] PT Hagigah 2:1, 87a.   [48] Mishnah Megillah 4:10.   [49] BT Berakhot 34b.
[50] Genesis Rabbah 44:22.   [51] Sifre Zuta, p. 319.

---

[32] It is, of course, standard synagogue practice to recite Ezekiel ch. 1 on the first day of the festival of Shavuot.

[33] The word gillah ("revealed") in the Hebrew Bible is translated apokalyptein by the Septuagint (for example, on Psalms 98:2; 119:18).

God would have revealed to him what is above and what is below, what was and what is to be." When Moses finally pleaded with God to show him His Glory, the Holy and Blessed One replied, "When I desired this, you did not; now that you desire it, I do not."[52] According to this view, the very secrets that are the soul's quest of all who devote themselves to mystic knowledge were never revealed to Moses.[53]

A similar comment was made by Rabbi Yose ben Hanina:[34] "How much did the soul of Moses grieve over God's refusal to reveal to him the mysteries of Israel and those revealed to Daniel! He wanted to know when He would visit punishment on Israel's arch enemy, but God did not reveal it to him. Instead, God said, 'Enough!'[35] Thus, God did not reveal to Moses when divine retribution would befall Edom."[36] [54]

They also applied to Moses our Teacher the words of Zophar the Naamatite, "Would you discover the mystery of God?" (Job 11:7). "Who can discover the things in which God reveals Himself? 'It is as high as the heavens'" (Job 11:8). We shall never know how the heavens and the earth were made, for even Moses, who ascended to heaven and received the Torah directly, could not fathom this."[55]

In opposition to this view, the school of Rabbi Akiva taught, "'He is trusted throughout My household' (Numbers 12:7)—I have revealed to him all that is above and below, and all that is in the sea and on dry land."[56] In the spirit of Rabbi Akiva's school, his disciples taught: "He is my trustee even over the ministering angels and the Holy Temple. I have shown him what is before creation and what will be in the future, what was and what will be."[57] Another version states that God revealed to him all the treasures of the Torah, wisdom and knowledge, and the secrets of life. "And God revealed to him what will be in the world to come."[58] Yet another midrash states, "As soon as Moses ascended to heaven, God opened the seven heavens and showed him the Holy Temple on high."[37] [59]

The Sages embellished the last episode in the life of Moses with endless midrashim, and they presented divergent interpretations of what Moses saw when he ascended Mount Nebo before his death. God said to Moses, "Ascend Mount Nebo . . . and view the land of Canaan, which I am giving the Israelites as their holding" (Deuteronomy 32:49). "Moses went up . . . to Mount Nebo . . . and the Lord showed him all the

---

[52] BT Berakhot 7a.
[53] Compare Mishnah Hagigah 2:1, which defines "what is above and what is below," etc. as within the province of mystical knowledge.
[54] Deuteronomy Rabbah, ed. S. Lieberman, p. 20.
[55] Midrash on Psalms 106:2.   [56] Sifre Zuta, p. 276.   [57] YS Beha'alotekha 739.
[58] YS Shemot 173.   [59] PR 20:4 (98a-b).

---

[34] Second- to third-generation Amora, Israel.
[35] The phrase "Enough!" appears in Deuteronomy 3:26 in the context of God's refusal to listen to Moses' pleas that he be allowed to enter the Land of Promise. Here the context is expanded to include Moses' desire to know certain mysteries and certain aspects of the future.
[36] The conventional rabbinic way of referring to Rome.
[37] The issue, put simply, is: Can a mortal know these things? Can one retrace Moses' steps?

land: Gilead as far as Dan, all Naphtali . . . as far as the Western sea" (Deuteronomy 34:1, 2). At first the Sages interpreted this text literally, "God showed him what was far as though it were near, what was not visible as though it were visible—all that is called the Land of Israel."[38] 60 In the course of time, however, a strong tendency developed to enlarge the horizon of what Moses saw. Thus we note the opinion, in the name of Rabbi Eliezer: "God endowed the eyes of Moses with the power to see from one end of the world to the other."61 Even this expanded interpretation did not satisfy all the Sages. Is it likely that with the special powers of sight that God conferred on Moses, he could see only this world?

They therefore increased the range of Moses' vision and declared that God had enabled him to see not only what was distant in space but also what was distant in time. Two homilies have been preserved on this subject, one in the Mekhilta of Rabbi Ishmael and the other in the Sifre on the Torah portion *Vezot Haberakhah*. They are similar in essence except for two important details. According to the Mekhilta, He showed him the Holy Temple, Samson, Barak, Joshua when he reigned, Gideon, David when he reigned, the burial places of the patriarchs, the destruction of Sodom and Gomorrah, Gog and his hosts.[39] 62 In contrast, the Sifre taught that God showed him things that were being built, and then as they were destroyed. He showed him the Holy Temple when it was inhabited and functioned peacefully and then He showed him the enemies who destroyed it; the land as it was inhabited in peace by each tribe and then the oppressors who took possession of it.63

The basic difference between the two views may be reduced to this one element. The two schools derived the various items that Moses saw from the text of Deuteronomy 34:1–3. Take note of how they expounded the words: "The Lord showed him . . . the city of palm trees." In the Mekhilta we read that "He showed him Deborah, as we read: 'She used to sit under the Palm of Deborah'" (Judges 4:5). In the Sifre, however, they expounded our text: "It teaches that He showed him the Garden of Eden with the righteous strolling in it, as we read: 'The righteous bloom like a date-palm'" (Psalms 92:13).

The midrashic elaboration is very important, for it tells us that Moses saw not only what exists and what the future will be in this world; he also looked and saw what was happening in the Garden of Eden. In similar vein, we are told in another midrash that he saw the seven chambers of Gehenna, as well as heaven and the highest heavens.[40] 64

---

60 Sifre Pinhas 135.   61 Sifre Pinhas 136.   62 MI Amalek 2.
63 Sifre Haberakhah 357.   64 Deuteronomy Rabbah, ed. S. Lieberman, p. 52.

---

[38] A midrash in MTD, p. 206, has Rabbi Eliezer claiming that this was a miraculous happening. Indeed, Moses' ability to see the Western Sea (i.e., the Mediterranean) from Mount Nebo would be miraculous, not because of distance but because the mountain ranges in central Canaan would have blocked the sea from sight.

[39] That is, the final, apocalyptic battle

[40] Thus, Heschel has established here a *tendency* to expand Moses' vision.

The Prophet Hears, the Apocalyptist Sees

The prophets hear words from the Almighty and learn what is on the mind of the Holy and Blessed One at that moment. The visionaries of the Apocalypse see words in heaven; they read what is written and engraved, since earliest times, in the books and on the tablets that are in heaven.[41] The prophets speak of what they heard; the apocalyptic visionaries tell us what they read.

Of the prophecy of Moses it is said, "He would hear the Voice addressing him" (Numbers 7:89). But it does not say of him that he saw. On the contrary: "And Moses hid his face, for he was afraid to look at God" (Exodus 3:6). When he pleaded, "Oh, let me behold Your Presence!" the Holy and Blessed One answered, "For man may not see Me and live . . . you will see My back but My face must not be seen" (Exodus 34:18, 23). Only of the seventy elders of Israel is it written: "They saw the God of Israel" (Exodus 24:10). *They* saw . . . but it does not say that Moses personally saw Him.[42]

Israel "heard the voice of the living God speak out of the fire" (Deuteronomy 5:23). "They witnessed the thunder and lightning" (Exodus 20:15), but they saw no image. "You saw no shape when the Lord your God spoke to you at Horeb out of the fire" (Deuteronomy 4:15). In contrast, Balaam says: "The word of him who hears God's speech, who beholds visions of the Almighty, prostrate, but with eyes unveiled" (Numbers 24:4).[43]

Elijah, too, only heard "a soft, murmuring sound" (1 Kings 19:12). When Isaiah came and said, "I beheld my Lord seated on a high and lofty throne" (6:1), Manasseh rebuked him saying, "Your teacher Moses said 'for no man may see Me and live,' and you said, 'I beheld the Lord!'"[65] Isaiah revealed a little of what he saw and concealed much. More was not revealed until Ezekiel came and said, "The heavens opened and I saw visions of God" (Ezekiel 1:1). Daniel, among the earliest in the apocalyptic movement,[44] hears the angel say, "I will tell you what is recorded in the book of

---

[65] BT Yevamot 49b.

---

[41] Notice the contrast with the phrase "at that moment" in the previous sentence. This view of apocalyptic is reminiscent of the view, associated by Heschel with the Akivan school, of the Torah as being primeval.

[42] An astounding comment that follows the literal contours of the remarkable text in Exodus 24 to the conclusion that Moses the prophet could not see what the seventy "apocalyptic elders" were able to see.

[43] It is no accident that Heschel largely quotes Deuteronomy in this paragraph about auditory revelation, for it is that book that insists that the revelation was entirely auditory. Exodus speaks of vision, even if only of lightning and other climatic and seismic events. Deuteronomy speaks only of Israel hearing.

[44] One must assume that Heschel is using this phrase quite loosely.

truth" (Daniel 10:21).[66] At the banquet of Belshazzar, the last king of Babylon, a hand appears and writes in a mysterious script on the wall of the king's palace foretelling the end of his kingdom (Daniel 5:5).[45]

In the opening chapter of the Book of Enoch (Ethiopian version) it is written: "Enoch is a righteous man whose eyes the Lord opened, and he beheld a holy vision in the heaven which the angels showed him" (Enoch 1:2). What is significant is that he sees what exists in heaven, and that it is the angels who show him everything. Enoch relates: "No angels could enter nor behold the Divine Presence" seated on a high throne, "and no mortal could see him" (14:21). Notwithstanding all this, he declares that he saw the Lord's Presence (9:10): "I knew the secret and I read the heavenly tablets, and I have seen the holy books and I found what was written and engraved on them." It is out of these books that he teaches humankind. According to the Book of Jubilees, the *sar hapanim* (Angel of the Presence)[46] says to Moses, "Behold, I tell you not on my own authority but from a written book, inscribed on the heavenly tablets, about the division of the days." In the visions of the night, an angel comes down from heaven bearing seven tablets; "he gave them to Jacob, who read all that was written in them concerning what will happen to him and to his sons in all the future worlds."[67] This distinction is basic and all-important. The prophet hears, the apocalyptic visionary reads. In apocalyptic vision, the image takes the place of the voice.

The task of the prophet is to translate the words uttered by God's voice to his own voice, from the language of divinity to human language, because "you instruct man according to his capacity to comprehend." In contrast, the apocalyptic visionary sees before him the words in the heavenly book, and he has nothing else to communicate but what his eyes see, without change or addition.

On this subject there is a controversy between Rabbi Ishmael and Rabbi Akiva. Of the assembly at Mount Sinai, it is said, "All the people saw the thunder and the lightning" (Exodus 20:15). The Sages were puzzled: How is it possible to see sounds?[47] Rabbi Ishmael explains the text according to common sense and nature. They saw what was visible (the lightning) and heard what was audible (the thunder). Rabbi Akiva, however, finds here one of the miracles associated with the giving of the Torah. "They saw and heard what was visible. They saw a word of fire come out of God's mouth carving itself into the tablets, as it is written: 'The voice of the Lord *hotzev*—

---

[66] According to Rabbi Jeremiah and Rabbi Hiyya bar Abba, Daniel was not a prophet. See BT Megillah 3a.

[67] Jubilees 6:35; 32:21.

---

[45] This tale thus reinforces the idea that Daniel is not really a prophet, but an apocalyptic visionary. We are set up for him to be told something, but in fact he sees something.

[46] Literally, "angel of the face."

[47] The same Hebrew word, *kolot*, can mean "thunder," "sounds," or "voices." The question of which is meant in Exodus 19 and 20 is an important crux in understanding the biblical view of revelation.

carves with[48] flames of fire'" (Psalm 29:7).[68] Rabbi Akiva was of the opinion that the divine voice appeared in an image visible to the sense of sight; the people saw the words and the image of the letters. "Even as they saw the lightning, so they saw the voice."[69]

Prophecy is a phenomenon that takes place between God and the prophet, as with God's utterances to Moses. Rabbi Akiva asked, What existed before the revelation? He expounded on the miraculous nature of God's revelation, which applied not only to Torah given on Sinai but also to Torah in heaven.[49] God's revelation consisted not only in the words that reached Moses but also in the words God spoke to Himself. He taught that when the Holy and Blessed One came down to give Torah to Israel, He first rehearsed it (two or three times) to Himself.[70]

Ben Sira says: "Has anyone ever seen him, to be able to describe him?" (Ecclesiasticus 43:31)[71]—that is to say, no one who saw the Divinity can describe Him truthfully. Even to Moses He revealed only 'a little of His glory.'[72] In the apocalyptic literature, however, it is said that Enoch saw that "the Antecedent of Time[50] was sitting on the Throne of His Glory, surrounded by angels and the righteous."[73] In another section he describes "the Antecedent of Time: His head is white and pure like wool, and His garment beyond description."[51] [74]

God Showed Them with a Finger[52]

According to Rabbi Akiva, Moses had difficulty understanding three instructions from God, and God showed them all with the divine finger: the shape of the new moon, the lampstand for the Tabernacle, and some say also the correct manner of slaughtering animals.[75]

---

[68] MI Bahodesh 9.   [69] MSY, p. 154.

[70] Tanhuma Yitro 15; Genesis Rabbah 24:5; Exodus Rabbah 40:1. Based on a homiletic rendering of Job 28:27, *vayyesapperah hekhinah,* "he proclaimed it after he rehearsed it."

[71] See M. Siegel, *Sefer Ben Sira Hashalem* (Jerusalem: Mosad Bialik, 1958), p. 300.

[72] See Henry J. Wicks, *The Doctrine of God in the Jewish, Apocryphal, and Apocalyptic Literature* (New York: Ktav, 1971).

[73] 1 Enoch, Ethiopian version, 60:2.

[74] Ibid., 71:9.   [75] MI Pisha 1.

---

[48] NJV: "kindles."

[49] That is, the question is: Is Torah a *thing,* or is it a *relation*? Again, this is completely consistent with other Akiva–Ishmael issues that we have encountered.

[50] Literally, the "head of the days."

[51] A contrast is thus drawn between Ben Sira, of the wisdom literature genre, and the Ethiopic Enoch, of apocalyptic genre.

[52] Heschel concludes this chapter on rabbinic mysticism with an excursus on what may at first sight seem to be a minor hermeneutic technicality. According to the Akivan school, the word *zeh* ("this") should be understood, especially in divine utterances, in a quasi-physical sense: "this present object to which I am now pointing as if with my finger." But especially in the case of the lampstand (menorah),

How did this occur in the case of the new moon? We read: "The Lord said to Moses and Aaron in the land of Egypt: '*This* month shall mark for you the beginning of the months'" (Exodus 12:1–2). There was a generally accepted principle that God only spoke to Moses during the daytime, but it would seem here that the moon was present at the time of the communication. Rabbi Ishmael reconciled it by saying that the text alludes to Moses' speaking to the Israelites, pointing out the moon and saying to them, "In the future, when it looks like this, you should declare that the new moon has arrived." It was in this retelling that Moses added the word "this." By contrast, Rabbi Akiva said this was one of the three things that God pointed out to Moses with the divine finger.[76] Elsewhere we are told that God showed Moses the image of the moon in addition to speaking to him—a miraculous addition.[53] [77]

Of the lampstand we read: "According to the pattern (*mar'eh*, 'vision,' 'appearance') that the Lord had shown Moses, so was the lampstand made" (Numbers 8:4). In Rabbi Ishmael's school, they said: "This was said in praise of Moses, that he made the lampstand as God had told him."[78] The emphasis is on the telling and the doing; the exegete makes no reference to any image or seeing.

In contrast, in Rabbi Akiva's school they took advantage of the redundancy of language to claim that God showed Moses the image of the lampstand no fewer than four times: "Moses saw it with its accessories and forgot it; he saw it again; Michael stretched it out before him; he saw it in the process of being made, and then in its completed state."[79] The ambiguity of *ken asah* (NJV: "so was the lampstand made," literally, "so he made it") is exploited to mean: God made it. There is also a play on the word *mikshah* ("hammered work") and *kasheh* ("difficult") to imply that Moses had difficulty with this task (in contrast with the artist Bezalel, who grasped it and executed it instantly).[80]

In later generations, Rabbi Akiva's view was accepted, that the Holy and Blessed One showed Moses the heavenly lampstand. Rabbi Yose said in the name of Rabbi Judah: "An ark of fire, a table of fire, and a lampstand of fire came down from heaven, and Moses saw them and copied them, as it is written, 'Note well, and follow the patterns for them that are being shown you on the mountain' (Exodus 25:40)."[81]

---

[76] Ibid.
[77] MSY, p. 8, cited in Maimonides, *Hilkhot Kiddush Hahodesh* 1:1.
[78] Sifre Beha'alotekha 61.
[79] Sifre Zuta, p. 256.
[80] TB Beha'alotekha 11. (See Buber's notes.)
[81] BT Menahot 29a.

---

which had not been made yet, this raises a question: what could God have been pointing to? The answer is to be found in the theory of supernal prototypes of earthly entities (discussed in chapter 14). If there was as yet no earthly lampstand, God must have been pointing to the heavenly one. Even a simple matter like giving Moses the instructions for building the Tabernacle required a mystical experience.

[53] Miraculous, since Moses was able to see the sliver of moon in the midst of daylight.

According to another view, the Holy and Blessed One showed Moses white fire, red fire, black fire, and green fire, and showed him how to make the lampstand. Moses had repeated difficulty, even with divine assistance. Eventually God instructed him to cast the gold into the fire, and it was made automatically.[82] Elsewhere, we are told that all the sacred implements had their supernal counterparts, which God showed Moses in colored fire.[83]

We are also told that God showed Moses the species of forbidden animals, as it says, "*These*[54] shall be unclean for you from among the things that swarm on the earth" (Leviticus 11:29), and "*These* are the creatures that you may eat from among all the land animals" (Leviticus 11:2).[84] God took each animal in turn and showed it to Moses. This answers the question that Rabbi Akiva had to wrestle with elsewhere: "Was Moses then an expert hunter or herbalist, that he should know all these species?"[85]

Rabbi Johanan learned that God showed Moses not only the form of the moon but the procedure for proclaiming the new month: "The Holy and Blessed One was wrapped in a fringed prayer shawl and stood Moses on one side and Aaron on the other, called Gabriel and Michael as if they were witnesses, and examined them: 'How did you see the moon? Was it before the sun or after it? To the north or to the south? How high in the sky? Which way did it point? How wide was it?'—So shall your descendants intercalate the months and years below on earth: with judges, with witnesses, and a fringed prayer shawl."[55] [86]

In similar fashion, Rabbi Johanan taught: "The Holy and Blessed One showed our patriarch Abraham four things: Torah, the sacrifices, Gehenna, and the kingdoms destined to rule over his descendants."[56] Other Sages said: "The Holy and Blessed One showed our patriarch Jacob the patron angels of Babylonia, Media, Greece, and Rome in their ascendancy and decline."[57] [87]

The following late homily combines two characteristics of Rabbi Akiva's approach: taking letters and words as having concrete significances beyond their simple mean-

[82] PRK 1:3 (4b); TB Shemini 11.
[83] PR 20:4 (98a-b); Song of Songs Rabbah 3:11; PRK 1:3 (4a-b); Tanhuma Vayakhel 3.
[84] TB Shemini 11; Tanhuma Shemini 8; BT Menahot 29a, Tosafot s.v. *sheloshah*; BT Hullin 42a; PR 15:21 (78a); PRK 5:15 (54b).
[85] Sifre Re'eh 102; BT Hullin 60b.
[86] PRK 5:15 (55a).
[87] PRK 5:2 (42b); see also PRK 23:2 (151a) and 23:10 (154b).

[54] The same Hebrew word, *zeh*, is used here and in the following biblical citation.
[55] The procedure described here is essentially that which is prescribed for the rabbinic court in Mishnah Rosh Hashanah 2:6.
[56] All of this is said to have happened during the so-called covenant between the pieces described in Genesis 15.
[57] This is an interpretation given to the dream of the ladder between heaven and earth, described in Genesis 28.

ing and a tendency to describe mystical experiences as visual ones: "Rabbi Akiva said: 'When Israel sang, "Then they will sing . . ."[58] the Holy and Blessed One dressed up in a brilliant robe on which was embroidered every occurrence of the word "then" in the Torah. After they sinned, God tore up the robe. In time to come, God will restore it.'"88[59]

---

88 YS Beshalah 241; see PRK 15:3 (120a), Leviticus Rabbah 6:8.

---

[58] The quotation is actually a superscription to the Song at the Sea (Exodus 15) and is used here as the title of the song.

[59] Heschel thus ends this chapter with a messianic peroration in conformity with the custom of many classical midrashim.

BEHOLDING THE FACE OF GOD

Translator's Introduction

The present chapter can only be considered a continuation of the previous one. Indeed, Heschel here reformulates the idea that mysticism is often related to a dissatisfaction with the world as it is. But his focus alights here on a particular issue in religious mysticism, and that is the quest for a visual experience of God. It is the nature of—and the dangers inherent in—this quest that exercise him now. The duality, familiar to every student of the Hebrew Bible, between *ketiv* and *keri*—between how the text is written and how it is traditionally vocalized—serves him well here. For it is a fortunate circumstance that (unvocalized) Hebrew writes the word *yir'eh* ("shall see") and *yera'eh* ("shall be seen") identically. In fact, in several places in the Tanakh (e.g., Exodus 34:24; Deuteronomy 16:16; Psalms 42:3) the traditional vocalization of the consonants has made sure that we read of the desire to *be seen by* God, and not to *see* God. Is the accepted vocalization the only possible way to read the text? Rabbi Yose ben Halafta's advice to his son seems to suggest that: "Do you wish to see the Shekhinah in this world? Study Torah in the Land of Israel." This is, indeed, the consequence of what we have been calling the Ishmaelian view about God's transcendence. The truly transcendent cannot be seen by human eyes. "Seeing" God can only be a metaphor for the understanding that comes through God's book. And yet there is another point of view to be reckoned with. It is the perspective according to which humans resemble the Creator, and if they merit it, that intimate resemblance can enable them to behold God with the full range of their senses.

So does this difference of opinion lead to different understandings of what Moses' own experience was. According to one view, Moses, being mortal, could only be refused when he asked to see God. But against this came the conviction of other Sages that Moses achieved sufficient distance from sin to be able to see God's Glory. The Ishmaelian–Akivan split thus takes on yet another guise: according to the one, seeing God is in principle impossible for human beings; according to the other, seeing God is only contingently impossible for humans, and it is the nearly irresistible power of sin that stands in the way and disqualifies us from fulfilling the ultimate human quest.

It is not surprising that, if seeing God in this second point of view is tied up with overcoming the power of sin, it would also be intertwined with the ever-present human quest to conquer death. Thus arises a further paradox that Heschel here explores: although the Torah clearly states that one cannot see God and live, the (Akivan) view that affirms the possibility of seeing God understands that text to mean that *if* one were to see God, one would *ipso facto* have vanquished death itself. Indeed, a mystical apotheosis.

It is with this chapter that Heschel concluded volume 1 in the Hebrew original. The speculations on what in fact Moses experienced at Mount Sinai is a natural and perfect transition to volume 2, in which he proceeded to explore the diverse views on the Mosaic revelation and how it should be understood.

Your Face I Will Seek

WHOEVER SEES IN THE AGGADAH merely a mental game, intellectual ornament, or play of the imagination falsifies its essence and forfeits its riches. If someone tells you that the Sages delved into Aggadah for the beautification of mitzvot, to embellish an extra verse and get extra points for study, an hors d'oeuvre to the halakhic main course, don't believe them! If you wish to know the true meaning of their words, search not outside and around the corner, but in the words themselves. In the midrashim themselves you will find the concerns and wrestlings, the flights of thought and yearnings, the eternal problems and timely questions, the communal woes and private agonies that preoccupied the Sages and the nation. The Sages' preoccupation with theoretical issues, with existential questions, with the heart's meditations, was genuine and wholehearted. They turned to God for the answers. The Torah offered higher wisdom, intellectual enlightenment, spiritual guidance. This higher wisdom presented itself in two guises: in the form of explicit statements, and in the form of narratives—the sacred narratives of the Exodus, of the Sinaitic revelation, of the lives of the patriarchs and prophets, and of the events of the End of Days. Torah contains hidden light.[1] If one is worthy, one can be nourished from its radiance.

Among the mystic elite, in the very depths of their soul lay the hidden aspiration to rise to the highest peak of spiritual achievement, namely, to behold the face of the Shekhinah. In the idiom of the mystics, this experience was referred to as "tasting the wine preserved in the grapes from the time of Creation."[2] It may happen that a man

[1] "Hidden light" is the term for the first light of creation (from day 1), more brilliant than the sun (created on day 4), reserved for the righteous to enjoy at the End of Days. It is also identified with the light of mystic enlightenment.

[2] This is a common motif in rabbinic literature, that certain natural things are stored away in their most perfect state for the elect to enjoy in the future. It is similar to the notion mentioned in the previous note, that we enjoy the light created on the fourth day of creation, but the light created on day 1 is a more perfect, all-illuminating light that is secreted away for the righteous to enjoy in the hereafter.

will be deemed worthy of tasting a drop of that wine, but he will experience only a derivative taste.[3] In the Book of Psalms, you hear a voice pleading, "My soul thirsts for God, the living God; O, when will I come and see the face of God? (Psalm 42:3). The prophet Isaiah, who was deemed worthy to behold God, was overwhelmed by the experience and cried, "Woe is me, I am lost! For I am a man of unclean lips and I live among a people of unclean lips; yet mine own eyes have seen the King, Lord of Hosts" (Isaiah 6:5).

To drink much of this wine is harmful, but a little is beneficial. There are some who drink of it and become ill. In the period we are discussing, the number of visionaries increased substantially. It would seem that our Sages were referring to these people when they said, "Since the destruction of the Temple, prophecy was taken from the prophets and handed over to fools and little children."[1]

Our Sages witnessed the apocalyptic movement in its degeneration and declared: "We vow to abstain from tasting the wine; we will have nothing to do with secret studies." They opposed those who craved such studies and those who broke through the wall to the world of the mysterious. From that time on, they were determined to replace the thirst for visions, the soul's longing to gaze upon the glorious Presence, with the thirst for the study of Torah, with the longing to cultivate good character and virtuous deeds. The grammarians changed the vocalization of the word ve'er'eh, 'I will see' to ve'eira'eh, 'I will be seen,' so that the Psalmist cries, "When will I come and be seen? . . ." (Psalm 42:3).

However, there are no guardians over the soul's yearnings.[4] The intellect gives the command but the heart nullifies it.[5] The human soul loathes this wretched world.[6] Despite rabbinic decrees and protests, those who longed to behold the Divine Presence did not cease their efforts and persisted in their quest. And all each side could do

---

[1] BT Baba Batra 12b. See also Midrash on Psalms 7:3: "What is meant by 'Erring and causing to err are from Him' (Job 12:16)? Rabbi Simeon ben Lakish said, 'Prophets and their prophecies'; Rabbi Johanan said, 'Fools and their delusions.'"

---

[3] Heschel's term is *notein ta'am bar notein ta'am*, a legal term in the laws of forbidden foods that denotes the imparting of a taste that is two steps removed from the original. We have often seen Heschel using legal terminology in theological discussions, usually with some symbolic purpose. Here it may be this: the concept of *notein ta'am* has to do with imparting tastes that would ordinarily be forbidden. Use of this term hints at the dangerous nature of seeking God's face. But *notein ta'am bar notein ta'am* is permitted, that is, getting no closer than two degrees of separation may be safe.

[4] Again, Heschel resorts to an adaptation of a rabbinic legal phrase. In this case, it is "there are no guardians when it comes to illicit sexual relations." That phrase asserts that the sexual drive is such that it will override nearly all safeguards. The use of the phrase here suggests that there is a sexual-like energy and passion to mystical yearnings, and they have a similar nonrational power.

[5] Inverted allusion to: "The righteous person decrees, and God fulfills it."

[6] Allusion to the people's cry over the manna: "Our soul loathes this wretched bread" (Numbers 21:5). The point here is that the surface meaning of the world can never satisfy the soul's deepest longings, just as the simple manna could not satisfy the depths of physical hunger.

was protest.[7] The grammarians vocalized, but the visionaries still thirsted. They declared, "I crave not for food and drink but to behold Your face, as it is written, 'My heart says of you, "Seek My face."' Your face, O Lord, I will seek" (Psalm 27:8).[2]

"My soul thirsts for God, the living God—when shall I come and *see the face of God?*" (Psalm 42:3). Israel says to God: "When will You restore the glory, that we would ascend three times each year to Jerusalem and *see the face of the Shekhinah?*"[3] [8]

This chapter of thought was forgotten and suppressed, until only its echoes and nuances remained. What is the lot of the one who is fortunate enough to look behind the veil? How should one comport oneself, to penetrate behind the curtains? Perhaps we find a hint of reaction against this visionary path in the homily: "'Seek His face continually' (Psalm 105:4)—Rabbi Yose ben Halafta said to his son Ishmael: 'Do you wish to see the Shekhinah in this world? Study Torah in the Land of Israel.'"[4]

Modesty befits piety. The modest cover their faces and avoid explicit language. They sublimate their experience of their own divine encounter through homilies on the prophetic heroes of the past. In the traditions about Moses and the generations of the wilderness, who saw the Shekhinah, we find a treasure trove in which the Sages concealed their own private fantasies and longings.[9]

On three separate occasions it is told that the Israelites asked Moses to reveal the supernal mysteries. They asked, "What reward is the Holy and Blessed One going to give us in the hereafter? He responded, "I can only say that you are fortunate as to what lies in store."[5] They asked, "What is the divine judgment on high?" He replied cryptically.[6] They asked, What is the Divine Glory on high? He replied, "Let me tell you a parable. A man wanted to see the king's glory. They told him to go to the king's province. He arrived at the border, and there was a hanging over the entrance gate, set with such brilliant jewels, he fainted at the sight of them. The implication is clear. Try to look up at the sky. If you cannot even gaze at the luminaries in the sky, how infinitely greater would be your helplessness in trying to gaze at the Divine Presence."[7]

This view, that mortals can neither see nor comprehend the nature of the Divine Presence, is associated with the school of Rabbi Ishmael, and many of the Sages

---

[2] Midrash on Psalms 42:3.   [3] PR 1:2 (1b).   [4] Midrash on Psalms 105:1.

[5] Sifre Haberakhah 355.

[6] Sifre Ha'azinu 307: "I cannot say, to reward the deserving and punish the guilty, but even if it were the reverse, He is 'a faithful God, never false'" (Deuteronomy 32:4).

[7] Sifre Haberakhah 355; MTD, p. 221.

---

[7] Yet another halakhic phrase; see, e.g., Mishnah Bava Metzia 6:1.

[8] Heschel also points out that the revocalization *yir'eh/yeira'eh* occurs in Exodus 23:17 and 34:23. The original vocalization implies that on the three pilgrimage festivals, the worshiper sees God; the more conservative revocalization, that the worshiper is seen by God. Rabbi Judah, cited in BT Hagigah 2b, held that both were correct. He was a disciple of Rabbi Akiva, who held that humans can see the Shekhinah. See chapter 14, n. [24].

[9] What follows now is an Ishmaelian understanding of the specialness of Moses, which nonetheless did not include his ability to see the Shekhinah.

accepted it. Rabbi Akiva, however, taught that it is possible for righteous and worthy individuals to behold the Shekhinah. He based this view on the belief that the Creator resembles His creatures; that the human stature is higher than that of the angels; and that Moses, who was even higher, certainly merited to see the Divine Glory.

Devotees of plain meaning were strongly opposed to this (Akivan) view, on the grounds that whoever raises the stature of man to the borders of heaven thereby detracts from the glory of heaven. The attempt to sanctify the profane, reduces the holy to the mundane. They cried in protest, "Akiva, how long will you continue to make of the Shekhinah an ordinary being?" This was a sharp protest not against a particular exposition uttered at a special occasion, but against Rabbi Akiva's entire system of thought.

As we have noted, it was Rabbi Akiva's belief that man became unworthy of comprehending God's image because of his sins. Otherwise, the keys to heaven would have been given to him and he would have known with what the heavens and earth were created.[8] The prophet Isaiah held out hope when he said, "The eyes of the blind shall be opened and the ears of the deaf unstopped" (Isaiah 35:5). In days to come they will be raised to life and hear the words of the Lord. They will gaze upon their teacher and see Him as it is written, "Then your Teacher will no longer be ignored but your eyes will look at your Teacher" (Isaiah 30:20).

"For No Mortal Can See Me and Live"

Nowhere in the Torah do we find Moses saying, as the other prophets did, "I have seen the Lord." This, then, was the basis for the controversy between the schools of Rabbi Akiva and Rabbi Ishmael on the question, Did Moses see God's Glory or image? The text of the Torah itself seems to beg for clarification. When the verse reads, "With him do I speak mouth to mouth, in a vision and not in riddles," and "He beholds the apparition of the Lord" (Numbers 12:8), what is the meaning of "vision" and "apparition"? Or, when Moses requests, "Show me, I pray, Your glory"[10] (Exodus 33:18), what does "glory" mean in this context? Are we to understand that Moses sought to behold the Shekhinah? The Holy and Blessed One's answer was, "You cannot see My face, for no man can see My face and live . . . you shall see My back, but My face shall not be seen" (Exodus 33:20, 23). What is this seeing of the back, which Moses was privileged to see? Are we to take literally the words "no man can see My face and live"?[11]

---

8 ARN A 39.

---

[10] Hebrew: *kavod,* a term that in the Bible generally denotes the luminous presence of God.

[11] The next section will elaborate on the answers to these questions. "Vision" (*mar'eh*) was variously interpreted "the illusion of speech" by the commonsense school, and "mirror of God's Glory"

The controversy of the Sages on this last verse speaks volumes about their attitudes to the divine mysteries. The rationalists[12] insisted that it is beyond mortal man's powers to see God. There is scriptural evidence to support this view. We read, "and Manoah said to his wife: 'We shall surely die because we have seen God'" (Judges 13:22). Rabbi Joshua ben Hananyah expounded this theme as follows: "We can infer, by *a fortiori* reasoning, that humans are incapable of standing in the presence of God's glory. Since the sun, which is only one ten-thousandth part of the celestial creatures that minister to God, is so dazzling that no creature can gaze upon it, how much more so is this true of the Holy and Blessed One, Whose glory fills the entire universe."[9] Seeing God's glory is impossible in principle, *because of the limitations of human nature*.[13]

This view, which sees no exception to the rule that mortals, including Moses himself, cannot behold the glory of God, was unacceptable to those Sages who were eager to gaze upon the chariot. They taught that the patriarch Abraham "saw, on the third day, the Shekhinah standing on the mountain."[14] [10] With regard to the patriarch Isaac, they said that when Abraham bound him on the altar, "he turned his eyes heavenward and gazed upon the Shekhinah. That is when his eyes became dim."[15] [11]

Rabbi Hoshayah said of the patriarch Jacob, "Blessed is a mortal who saw the King."[12] According to Rabbi Abahu, when Simeon the Righteous[16] entered the Holy of Holies, he saw the Holy and Blessed One.[13] It is also related of Ishmael ben Elisha, the High Priest, that he beheld the Lord of Hosts seated on His exalted throne.[14] Similar tales were told of other Sages. They went even beyond this and claimed that Potiphar, Pharaoh's officer who purchased Joseph, and the daughter of Pharaoh who drew Moses from the water, beheld the Shekhinah.[17] [15]

---

[9] YS Tissa 396; BT Hullin 59b-60a.   [10] Aggadat Bereshit 31, p. 63.
[11] Genesis Rabbah 65:10; PRE 32.   [12] TB Bemidbar 22; Numbers Rabbah 4:1.
[13] PT Yoma 5:1, 42c.   [14] BT Berakhot 7a.   [15] Tanhumah Vayyeshev 8.

---

by the mystics. "Apparition of the Lord" was interpreted by the commonsense school to mean that Moses was privileged to see reality from the divine viewpoint, while the mystics took it to mean that he saw the likeness of God. The Ishmaelians understood "Glory of God" to mean God's justice revealed in history and in the hereafter, while the Akivan mystics took it literally to mean the Shekhinah.

[12] That is, those not given to visionary experiences.

[13] And not contingently impossible, because of human sin. Contrast Rabbi Akiva's view, cited at the end of previous section and discussed in chapter 15 and below.

[14] The text says that Abraham saw the place (*hamakom*) from afar. But since *hamakom* is a rabbinic appellation for God (since God is in every place), the verse can be read to mean that Abraham saw God from afar.

[15] Others have different explanations for why Isaac's eyesight became poor. One of these is that the tears of the angels shed in anticipation of his being slaughtered entered his eyes and dimmed them.

[16] Fourth century B.C.E.

[17] In Genesis 39:3, it is said that Joseph's master saw that "the Lord was with him." And in Exodus 2:6, it is written that Pharaoh's daughter opened the basket drifting on the water, and (literally) "saw him, and the boy," and it was taken to mean that she saw the infant Moses and the Presence of God.

Both Rabbi Ishmael and Rabbi Akiva based their views on the verse "No man can see My face and live." Rabbi Ishmael took this literally: the word "man" means "mortal man" and the Hebrew word va-hai "and live" means precisely that. Rabbi Akiva (together with Simeon ben Azzai, one of the four who entered the Orchard) read this verse quite differently. "Man" in this context refers not to mortal man but to "heavenly beings," as in Ezekiel's vision where he says, "as for the likeness of their faces, they had the face of a man" (Ezekiel 1:10). As for the word va-hai, it is the shortened form of v'hayyot ha-kodesh, the celestial creatures, or the angels. The verse means, "No heavenly being, no angel can gaze upon My face." However, those mortals who are deemed worthy may do so.[16]

There is an interesting aggadah that supports the view of the Akivan school that the term "man" refers, at times, to the ministering angels. Rabbi Abahu interpreted the verse "No man shall be in the tent of meeting" as referring to the angels. In the aggadah, it is related that Simeon the Righteous ministered as a High Priest for forty years. In his final year he said to his people, "This year I shall die." They asked him, "How do you know this?" He replied, "Each year when I entered the Holy of Holies there was an old man, wrapped in white garments, who entered together with me and left with me. This year, however, he entered with me but did not leave with me." Rabbi Abahu was asked, "Is it not written, 'No man shall be in the Tent of Meeting when he goes in to make atonement in the holy place, until he comes out' (Leviticus 16:17), and this refers even to angels?" To which Rabbi Abahu replied, "I must tell you that Simeon the Righteous was referring to the Holy and Blessed One."[17]

In sum, Rabbi Akiva and his followers refuted the claim of the literalists who taught that Moses could not have seen the glory of God because the Torah states specifically, "No man can see Me and live." This verse, they insisted, refers not to mortals but to angels. It follows, therefore, that what was denied to the celestial creatures was not withheld from the righteous ones, and most certainly not from Moses. The disciples of Rabbi Akiva taught with complete assurance, that Moses did indeed see the Glory of God.[18]

Did Moses Indeed See God's Image?

Rabbi Ishmael and his school, who generally followed the plain meaning of Scripture, were confronted with certain expressions in the Torah that demanded elucidation. Moses' request, "O let me behold Your Glory [kavod]," was an astonishing demand

---

[16] The radical reinterpretation of "man" to mean "angels" is attributed to Rabbi Simeon the Temanite, in extension of Rabbi Akiva's argument. See Sifra 4a–b; Sifre Beha'alotekha 103, variant according to Midrash Hakhamim, p. 101 line 18, and Horowitz's note ad loc.; YS Vayikra 431.

[17] PT Yoma 42c; BT Menahot 109b; BT Yoma 39b.

---

[18] Heschel adds: There is a parallel to this interpretation in the Ethiopian version of Enoch, according to which the angels could not see God's Glory, but Enoch himself saw God (Enoch 14:20-21; 90:21, 29; 46:1; 47:3).

that puzzled even the Sages of the Middle Ages. Rabbi Samuel ben Meir[19] commented, "How could Moses our teacher even aspire to such a vision? Does not Scripture actually praise him when it says 'he hid his face for he was afraid to look at God' (Exodus 3:6)?"[18] Saadia Gaon declared, "This whole episode about Moses our teacher confuses the minds of some people. How could he possibly make such a request?"[19]

A similar difficulty was posed by the expression, "You will see My back, but My face will not be seen." How can we use the terms "back" and "face" when referring to God? Is it not written, "I fill heaven and earth, said the Lord" (Jeremiah 23:24) or "His glory fills the whole earth" (Isaiah 6:3)? How can we reconcile such lofty prophetic concepts with "seeing God's back but not His face"?[20]

Rabbi Ishmael, therefore, rejected this approach. With remarkable sensitivity to scriptural language, he found that the words *kavod* ("glory"), *ahor* ("back") and *panim* ("face") possessed multiple meanings. He took the words *ahor* and *panim* in this context to refer not to constructs that existed in space, things that could be seen by the human eye, but rather to things that existed in time.[20] *Panim* refers to the present time, while *ahor* refers to that which is last, namely, the future world.[21] As for the word *kavod* in this context it refers not to God's glory, but to His justice and righteousness, which are revealed in the course of history.[22] According to this interpretation, Moses at no time demanded to behold the Shekhinah; he was asking for an explanation of the mystery that haunted him, the suffering of the righteous and the prosperity of the wicked. How could he reconcile this paradox with His justice and righteousness? To which God replied, "You cannot see My justice in the present world, only in the future world."[23] There the wicked will receive their full punishment and the righteous their full reward.

There was yet another scriptural difficulty to overcome. The verse states explicitly, "He beheld the image of God (*temunat adonai*)" (Numbers 12:8). Again Rabbi Ishmael was compelled to abandon the literal meaning. He rendered the word *temunah* not as the form and appearance of something but as an act of contemplation and that it was God, not Moses, who contemplated. The verse is saying, Moses saw and understood what God was contemplating, namely, what He had in store for the righteous and the wicked in the future world. It was the vision of the future world that Moses saw.[21]

---

[18] Commentary of RaSHBaM on Exodus 33:18.

[19] Saadia Gaon, *Book of Beliefs and Opinions,* 2:12.

[20] MI Shirata 4, cited above, p. 227.

[21] See Genesis 11:28, Isaiah 42:43, and MI Bahodesh 6 on *al panai.*

[22] See Isaiah 62:2.   [23] Exodus Rabbah 45:5.

---

[19] Grandson of Rashi, twelfth century.

[20] It is a fact that spatial words such as *ahor* and *kadim* ("backward" and "forward," respectively) also have temporal meanings ("future" and "past," respectively).

[21] This is, of course, not the plain, surface meaning of the verse, but it does make good, nonmystical sense of the verse. This is why Heschel notes that Ishmael was forced to abandon his usual tendency toward a plain-meaning exegesis here. It was a theological necessity.

"He Saw God's Image Immediately"[22]

We may reasonably infer that Rabbi Akiva—who entered the Orchard and engaged in study of the Merkavah, and of whom it was said in the Babylonian Talmud, "The ministering angels sought to drive him out, but the Holy and Blessed One said to them, 'Let this old man be, *he is worthy to behold My glory*'"[24]—did not doubt that Moses saw God's likeness. After all, had he not taught that but for their sins, humans would know the supernal presence; that when Moses declaimed the Torah, he was in heaven; and that the divine glory descended upon Mount Sinai? Though we have no explicit statement on this question from Rabbi Akiva himself, his students Rabbi Simeon ben Yohai and Rabbi Judah ben Ilay did teach that Moses saw the divine glory.

Rabbi Simeon ben Yohai, commenting on "he saw God's image," declared that Moses saw God's image immediately.[25] Elsewhere, Rabbi Simeon is quoted as saying, "When God revealed Himself to Moses in the burning bush, Moses said, 'Master of all the worlds, take an oath on my behalf that whatever I wish to do, You will facilitate.'"[23] [26]

This homily is the basis for an *aggadah* that tells us: Moses said that on Yom Kippur he will see the glory of the Holy and Blessed One. How did Moses know this? He said, "Master of the universe, show me Your glory" (Exodus 33:18). Whereupon God answered, "You cannot see My glory, lest you die. . . . However, because of My oath to you and because of My name which I made known to you, I shall agree to your request. Stand at the entrance of the cave and I shall cause all my ministering angels to pass before you, as it is written, 'I will make all My goodness to pass before you.' When you hear the Name that I have made known to you, I shall be standing there before you. Exert all your strength and stand firmly, do not be afraid." When the angels heard this, they spoke up before the Holy and Blessed One. "We minister to You day and night; yet we are not permitted to see Your glory. Yet this man, born of woman, dares to demand that he see Your glory!" The angels rose in anger and dismay against Moses to kill him. He was near to death when the Holy and Blessed One appeared in a cloud, covered him with the palm of his hand, and saved him. When the Holy and Blessed One had passed, He drew back His hand, and Moses saw the back of the Shekhinah.[24][27]

---

[24] BT Hagigah 15b.   [25] Sifre Zuta, Beha'alotekha p. 276.
[26] PRE 45.   [27] PRE 46.

---

[22] The Hebrew *mi-yad* means just what the English "immediately" means—without mediation. And that is what the midrash that will be cited in the subsection means to say about Moses' apprehension of the Divine.

[23] The significance of this follows.

[24] The reference to Yom Kippur in this *aggadah* is based on the idea—bolstered in several rabbinic texts by a (nearly, but not quite, exact) chronology of Moses' three forty-day stays on Mount Sinai—

Rabbi Simeon ben Yohai also held that sin disqualified Israel from seeing God. Before the sin of the golden calf, they were able to see the Glory of God "whose appearance was as a devouring fire" (Exodus 24:17) and not tremble. But after that sin, they feared even beholding the afterglow of divine radiance from Moses' face when he emerged from the Tent of Meeting after communing with God (Exodus 34:30).[28]

Rabbi Judah, one of Rabbi Akiva's outstanding disciples, who also believed that Moses beheld the Glory, drew a distinction between Moses and the other prophets of Israel. "All the prophets had a vision of God as He appeared through nine specula[25] [aspaklariot] . . . Moses saw God through one speculum, as it is written, 'I speak to him mouth to mouth, clearly and without riddles'" (Numbers 12:8). The Sages drew this distinction: All the prophets saw Him dimly as through a dirty, nearly-opaque speculum, but Moses gazed at Him through a polished speculum, as it is written, "He beheld the likeness of God."[29]

We cannot know with certainty whether the word aspaklaria ("speculum") referred to a reflective mirror or a transparent window glass or lens.[30] In another case, Rabbi Judah seems to teach that Moses had a true vision of the divine glory but not a wholly direct or unmediated one. He saw God through a glass, not face to face. Similarly, according to Rabbi Judah, God revealed Himself to Israel at the Sea of Reeds as an armed warrior (i.e., through the mediation of an image, not a direct communication of the Divine Essence).[26][31]

---

[28] Sifre Naso 1, PRK 5:3 (45a).			[29] Leviticus Rabbah 1:14.
[30] See Rabbi Samson of Sens on Mishnah Kelim 30:2, and R. Hai Gaon in Otzar Hageonim on BT Yevamot 49b.
[31] MI Shirata 4.

---

that Moses descended from the mountain for the third time on the tenth of Tishri, carrying the second tablets and announcing God's forgiveness of the sin of the calf. That day became Yom Kippur, because it was the first act of forgiveness by God for the people as a whole. Moses' beholding God with immediacy on this first Yom Kippur can be seen as being reenacted to some extent by the High Priest entering behind the veil of the Holy of Holies on subsequent Yom Kippurs.

[25] We are following Elliott Wolfson here in translating the rabbinic word aspaklaria by the closest English cognate of the original Latin specularia (see Through a Speculum That Shines: Vision and Imagination in Medieval Jewish Mysticism [Princeton, N.J.: Princeton University Press, 1994]. As Heschel presently notes, it is unclear whether it means "lens" or "mirror," but the metaphoric significance is the same either way: it is a medium through which one perceives the divine light indirectly and therefore imperfectly. A "clear" or "bright" speculum transmits the light as clearly as one may hope to attain; a "dark" or "occluded" speculum transmits it poorly, and therefore one gets only a vague, distorted impression of the divine reality.

Aspaklaria (= Latin specularia) is a keyword of Heschel's book, starting with the Hebrew title ("Torah from Heaven in the Aspaklaria of the Generations"). He tells us here that a glass (whether refractive or reflective) is an imperfect medium of seeing, but the best we have. This would seem to apply equally to the prophets' vision of God and to our own vision of the religious wisdom of the tradition.

[26] Similarly, we might say, religious doctrines, even such a basic one as "Torah from Heaven," can be seen only through each generation's refractors.

Moses and the Angels

As we have seen,[27] the Akivan school applied Exodus 33:23 ("for no mortal shall see Me and live") not to humans but to the angels. And if you object, "it is also written, 'You cannot see My face' (Exodus 33:20), this can be understood not as a physical impossibility but as denying permission (like the use of 'cannot' in certain other legal contexts [Deuteronomy 22:19; 12:17]). So says Rashi: "When I cause My goodness to pass before you, I do not give you permission to see My face."

If you would object, "How could Moses see what the angels could not?" then consider: Moses was no ordinary man, but was comparable to the angels![32] Indeed, he even outranked them.[33] According to Rabbi Meir, even Michael and Gabriel trembled before Moses.[34] So it is conceivable that what was impossible for the angels might be possible for Moses. In fact, we find that the controversy of the schools extends to Moses' status relative to the angels. "He [Moses] is faithful in all My house" (Numbers 12:7)—Rabbi Akiva's school interprets: "even over the ministering angels," while Rabbi Ishmael's school interprets: "except for the ministering angels."[35]

The superiority that Moses had over the angels, in that he was privileged to behold the Divine Presence, was shared by the people Israel. In various midrashim it is pointed out that when the ministering angels sang their hymns of praise to God they did so in a loud voice. Why? Because they were a great distance removed from the Holy and Blessed One and did not know where He was, as it is written, "Blessed is the Divine Glory in His place"[28] (Ezekiel 3:12). But when the people Israel stand in prayer they know that God is near them, as it is written, "He stands at the right hand of the needy" (Psalm 109:31).[36] The angels ask, "Where is the place of His glory?" The people Israel, each one of them, at the Sea of Reeds, pointed with his finger and said, "This is my God and I will glorify Him."[37]

Rabbi Meir, Rabbi Judah, and Rabbi Simeon were all quoted as saying, "The righteous are greater than the ministering angels.[38]

"We Wish to See Our King!"

The question whether the people Israel actually saw the Divine Presence at Mount Sinai was the subject of debate among the Sages. According to Rabbi Judah the Patri-

---

[32] ARN ed. Schechter, p. 157.   [33] YS Beha'alotekha 739; Zohar Pinhas 232a.
[34] Midrash Zuta to Ecclesiastes 9:9, p. 124.   [35] Sifre Zuta p. 276, Sifre Beha'alotekha 103.
[36] YS Va'ethanan 825.   [37] Exodus Rabbah 23:15.
[38] Mishnat Rabbi Eliezer (ed. Enelow) p. 292; Midrash Haggadol to Genesis, ed. Margaliot, pp. 571ff.

---

[27] Earlier in this chapter, pp. 303–5.
[28] The text literally reads "from His place," taken here to mean "some distance from God's place."

arch, when the Israelites stood at the foot of Mount Sinai, they said to Moses, "We wish to hear from the mouth of our King." God replied, "Grant them what they have asked, 'so that the people may hear when I speak to you'" (Exodus 19:9).[39] We learn from this that at Sinai they were privileged only to hear the voice of God but not to see His image. This harmonizes with the scriptural verse "Since you saw no shape when the Lord your God spoke to you at Horeb out of the fire" (Deuteronomy 4:15). Rabbi Johanan, too, was of the opinion that the Israelites asked for nothing more than "we wish to hear from His mouth."[40]

There is another view, however, that was held by some Sages. According to them, the people Israel said to Moses, "We wish to see our King; how can you compare hearing to seeing?" Whereupon God said to Moses, "Grant them their wish," as it is written, "for on the third day the Lord will come down in the sight of all the people on Mount Sinai" (Exodus 19:11).[41] Rabbi Judah bar Ilay, Rabbi Akiva's disciple, taught: In Egypt they saw Him publicly,[29] as it is written, "When the Lord goes through to smite the Egyptians" (Exodus 12:23). At the Sea of Reeds they beheld Him publicly, as it is written, "And Israel saw the great hand" (Exodus 14:31). At Sinai they saw him face to face, as it is written, "The Lord came from Sinai" (Deuteronomy 33:2).[30] [42]

Rabban Gamaliel, president of the Sanhedrin in Yavneh, supplied a different interpretation for the verse "No man can see Me and live." Focusing on the word va-hai, "and live," he stated: The Holy and Blessed One sees, but is Himself invisible; one who claims that he saw God, saw Him with his soul, which withdraws itself from the body. Thus, when Ezekiel saw the divine likeness, he attained this vision in a state of ecstasy or "by divesting himself of all corporeality"—which is as if the soul had departed from the body.[31] [43]

It is told of Rabban Gamaliel that he was asked by a pagan, "Where is God to be found?" He answered, "I do not know." The pagan continued, "Of what avail are all your daily prayers and your wisdom, if you do not even know where He is?" To which Rabban Gamaliel replied, "The Holy and Blessed One sees all His creatures, but they cannot see Him, as it is written, 'No man can see Me and live.' This is what Scripture

---

[39] MI Bahodesh 2.   [40] Song of Songs Rabbah 1:2 (1:14).
[41] MI Bahodesh 2.   [42] Song of Songs Rabbah 3:9.   [43] Tur, Orah Hayyim 98.

---

[29] Although it is not quite the original intent of the midrash cited, the intent here is that it was a public, not an intimate, revelation. Everyone saw the power of God's deeds. But at Sinai, the revelation was intimate, with God's essence, and not just God's power, being revealed. In the original setting, the intent was not so much to separate Sinai from Egypt and the Sea as to separate them all from the privacy of communion at the Tabernacle later on.

[30] Heschel adds: Rabbi Judah held that God appeared in many guises to the Israelites: as a warrior girt with sword, as a knight on horseback, as a spear thrower, an archer, and so on. Possibly we should ascribe to Rabbi Judah also the anonymous midrash that God appeared to the Israelites at Sinai as an elderly Sage (MI Shirata 4, MSY, p. 80ff., MI Bahodesh 5).

[31] The soul-body dualism is quite notable here. It means that this kind of apprehension of God is a "soulful" thing and thus not the stuff of normal everyday life.

is saying when it describes Ezekiel, 'and I saw and fell upon my face' (Ezekiel 1:28); when he saw the Divine Presence, his soul left his body."[32] 44

There is a contrary view, stated anonymously, that declares: "The Holy and Blessed One is at times seen and at times not seen; at times He listens and at times He does not listen; at times He is sought and at times he is not sought; at times He is to be found and at times He is not to be found; at times He is near and at times He is not near."45 This view finds support in the many contradictory scriptural verses we have already seen, which alternately affirm and deny that humans saw God (Exodus 33:11; 33:18; 24:10; 24:17; Deuteronomy 4:12, 16).

Another view holds that individuals see God only at the moment of death. "For man shall not see Me and live"—not during one's lifetime but at death one may see God.46

What did Moses ask of God before he died? Note carefully the two opinions on this question. "When the time came for Moses to leave this world, he said, 'Master of the Universe, I ask but one thing of You before I die: let the gates of heaven and of the depths below be forced open so that all may see that there is none else in the universe besides You.'"47

The other view states: when Moses was about to leave this world, God said to him, "What request do you have to make of Me?" He replied simply, "Master of the Universe, O let me see Your glory." He saw the Almighty, as it is written, ". . . and God showed Him . . ." (Deuteronomy 34:1).48

A precious projection of the world to come emanated from the Babylonian Amora Rav: "The righteous will sit with crowns on their heads and enjoy the Divine Glory."49 Before his death, Rabban Johanan ben Zakkai said, "Is it a mere mortal king that I am about to greet? I am going to greet the King of Kings of Kings, the Holy and Blessed One."50 So Rabbi Simeon ben Yohai declared, "The righteous will greet the Shekhinah in the world to come."51

At the Sea, the Handmaid Saw What Ezekiel Did Not

In Rabbi Eliezer's view: "At the Sea, even the handmaid saw what Isaiah, Ezekiel, and the rest of the prophets never saw." Whereas the prophets described God in veiled imagery, at the sea the people saw God directly. A king may go unrecognized amid the

---

44 Midrash on Psalms 103:5.   45 PRK 24 (ed. Buber 156a, not in Mandelbaum/Braude).
46 Sifre Beha'alotekha 103, Sifra 4a.   47 Deuteronomy Rabbah 11:8.
48 YS Berakhah 964.   49 BT Berakhot 17a.   50 ARN A 25.   51 Sifre Ekev 47.

---

[32] The image of God as the One who sees but cannot be seen, is beautifully captured in a blessing given by a blind man to those who came to pay respects to him (see BT Hagigah 5b): "You have done honor to a face that can be seen but cannot see; may you be privileged to honor the Presence that sees but cannot be seen."

throng of his courtiers and soldiers, but at the sea God acted alone in full view of the people. Rabbi Eliezer based his view on the exclamation "*This* is my God and I will enshrine Him" (Exodus 15:2). Like Rabbi Akiva, he interpreted the word "this" to indicate pointing to some entity that is readily visible.

Note that Moses alone of the prophets saw God directly, for he of course was present at the sea. Some Sages said that even infants saw God. Even fetuses in their mothers' wombs pointed their fingers toward the Shekhinah and said, "This is my God and I will glorify Him."[52]

The Sages sought to find praise and extenuation for the generation in whom glorious events and sin alternated so dramatically.[33] The chapter of the golden calf was read in public only in Hebrew, not in the vernacular. We even hear the view that God's manifestation to them was the indirect cause of their sin. At the sight of the calf, the heavenly hosts demanded, "Master of the Universe, destroy this people! Yesterday they said, 'We will do and obey' (Exodus 24:7); today they say, 'These are your gods, O Israel!' (Exodus 32:4). The Holy and Blessed One replied, 'I Myself caused them to sin, for I showed them My chariot borne on four angelic visages: a man, a lion, an eagle, and an ox.[34] They took the dust from under the legs of the ox, and the result was the golden calf."[35] [53]

The Sin of Sinai

The view that seeing the Shekhinah was not impossible but was dangerous was among those conveyed in a whisper. They looked in Scripture and saw that, when people looked, they were injured.

One verse in particular is troubling and shocking to anyone who reads it: "Then Moses and Aaron, Nadab and Abihu, and seventy elders of Israel ascended; and they

---

[52] PT Sotah 20c.

[53] *Genizah Studies in Memory of Dr. Solomon Schechter* (New York: Jewish Theological Seminary, 1928–29), 1:243; see also Louis Ginzberg, *Legends of the Jews*, 7 vols. (Philadelphia: Jewish Publication Society, 1909–38), 6:52 n. 271.

---

[33] On this subject, see the debate between Rabbi Akiva and Rabbi Eliezer in Mishnah Sanhedrin 10:3. The former concentrates on the desert generation's sin of unfaithfulness to insist that they are barred from the world to come. The latter, appealing to Psalm 50:5, concentrates on the peak events to which they were party and finds it inconceivable that such a generation could be barred from the world to come.

[34] So Ezekiel 1. A similar vision in Ezekiel 10 substitutes "cherub" for the ox.

[35] The deeper meaning of this is that in the very act of seeing God humans are prone to error, and they mistake the part for the whole, the appearance for the reality. The face of the ox is part of Ezekiel's vision of the chariot, yet the ox is cousin to the golden calf. In a similar vein, Arnold Ehrlich (*Mikra Ki-feshuto*) understands Moses' breaking of the tablets as born of a recognition that tangible objects lead people into idolatry. Even the tablets themselves were, according to this, an unacceptable risk.

saw the God of Israel: under His feet there was the likeness of a pavement of sapphire, like the very sky for purity" (Exodus 24:9–10). In Rabbi Ishmael's school they divorced this verse from its literal sense. They connected *livnat* ("pavement") to *levenim* ("bricks"), and found that it referred to God's sympathetic suffering with the Israelites who were forced to lay bricks and mortar in Egypt. This is contrasted with "like the very sky for purity," which is symbolic of redemption.[54] Clearly, the school of Rabbi Ishmael interpreted these verses metaphorically. The elders did not see the Shekhinah, but prophetically intuited that the Holy and Blessed One empathizes with the Israelites' suffering.[36]

In contrast, the Akivan school held that the elders feasted their eyes on the splendor of the Shekhinah. They illuminated the description of the elders' vision by comparing it with Ezekiel's description of the chariot. "They saw the God of Israel" means that they feasted their eyes on the splendor of the Shekhinah. "Under His legs" means they became confused and confounded the supernal and terrestrial realms. "Sapphire pavement" is parallel to "they gleamed like beryl" (Ezekiel 1:16);[37] just as the one had wheels, so the other had wheels. "Like the very . . ." denotes a vague comparison; that is, the text speaks what the ear can hear.[55]

But other Sages did not approve of the actions of the elders and of Nadab and Abihu. Feasting their eyes on the Shekhinah was called the sin of Sinai, for which they were punished with death.[56] Nadab and Abihu were later burned for this. The Sages said that Moses did not look at the Shekhinah in the same spirit when he ascended to heaven.[57] "The elders became light-headed when they ascended Mount Sinai and saw the Shekhinah. As of that day, the elders, Nadab and Abihu deserved to be burned to death. But because the giving of Torah was so dear to the Holy and Blessed One, He did not want to inflict punishment on that day, but deferred it to a later time. Nadab and Abihu were burned when they entered the Tent of Meeting after their ordination, and the elders were burned at Taberah when the people lusted for meat."[58]

Rabbi Judah said: "Whoever translates a verse literally is a liar, and whoever adds to it is a blasphemer." Rabbenu Hananel applied this maxim to our verse as follows: "'Whoever translates a verse literally'—as for instance, 'and they *saw* the God of Israel'—is a liar, for they did not actually see the Shekhinah. 'Whoever adds to it'—as

---

[54] MI Pisha 14; Sifre Beha'alotekha 84.
[55] MSY, p. 221.
[56] YS Beha'alotekha 732; Midrash Aggadah on Exodus 24:10.
[57] TB Aharei 13.
[58] TB Beha'alotekha 27; Numbers Rabbah 15:24.

---

[36] Ishmael's position is that God empathizes but does not participate. See the extended discussion in chapter 6 above.

[37] This is reminiscent of the *Pardes* story (BT Hagigah 14b), in which Akiva warns his colleagues not to have their perceptions confounded by the sight of the "pure marble stones" that they will see.

for instance: 'They saw the *angel* of God'—is a blasphemer, for he ascribes to an angel the praise due to God. Rather translate: 'And they saw the *glory* of the God of Israel.'"[59]

We have here two interpretations representative of our two systems of thought. "They saw the God of Israel"—one view says this means the Shekhinah rested on them; the other says they actually saw the Shekhinah.

The Debate in the Period of the Amoraim

The debate on this topic continued in the period of the Amoraim. Following the Akivan position were Rabbi Johanan, Rabbi Levi,[60] and Rabbi Jonathan,[61] all of whom taught that Moses saw the divine image.[38]

"The Lord passed before [Moses] and proclaimed"—Rabbi Johanan said, "If it were not so written, you could not say it! This teaches that the Holy and Blessed One wrapped Himself in a prayer shawl like a *Shaliah Tzibbur*[39] and showed Moses the order of the prayer service, saying, 'Whenever Israel sins, they should pray according to this arrangement, and I will forgive them.'"[40] [62] He also said, "If there had remained an opening the size of the eye of a needle in the cave where Moses and Elijah stood at the moment of God's revelation, they could not have withstood the light,[41] as it says, "Man cannot see Me and live."[63]

"You shall see My back" (Exodus 33:23) was also interpreted literally. "God removed the palm of His hand from Moses, and he saw the back of the Shekhinah."[64] Rabbi Simeon Hasida said, "The Holy and Blessed One showed him the knot of His tefillin."[65]

The Midrash Aggadah confirms that Moses saw the Shekhinah: Moses was on a higher level than the angels, for they did not know God's place (since they say: "Blessed is the glory of the Lord *from His place*"),[42] whereas Moses spoke face to face

---

[59] BT Kiddushin 49a, Tosafot s.v. *hammetargem*.
[60] PRK 26:9.   [61] BT Berakhot 7a.   [62] BT Rosh Hashanah 17b.
[63] BT Megillah 19b.   [64] PRE 45.   [65] BT Berakhot 7a, Menahot 35b.

---

[38] More precisely, that Moses was capable of seeing the Divine Image. In some of these midrashim, Moses is praised for forgoing that which he was able and entitled to do.

[39] "The community's messenger," that is, one who leads the congregation in prayer—today, a cantor.

[40] This is referring to the central recurring prayer of the Selihot (Forgiveness or Penitential) service that today marks the liturgy of Yom Kippur and the weeks leading up to it. It comes from Exodus 34, the very text that Rabbi Johanan is here expounding.

[41] For this to fit Heschel's point here, we must assume that he is reading the midrash as saying that others, besides Moses and Elijah, could not have withstood the light. That leaves us with the image of Moses and Elijah, empowered to see the full glory of God, nevertheless being satisfied with a small fraction of that Presence. Others, however, could not even have withstood that.

[42] That is, at a distance; see section entitled "Moses and the Angels" above.

with the Shekhinah. Furthermore, the angels had six wings, two of which they used to hide their faces so they would not look upon the Shekhinah, whereas Moses removed his veil before speaking with God (Exodus 34:34).[43] 66

On the opposing side, we hear the view: "Moses did not look at the Shekhinah, but Balaam did so, for it says in Balaam's prophecy: 'He sees the vision of the Almighty' (Numbers 24:4)."67

The Amora Rava also held that Moses did not see the divine image. Simeon ben Azzai was quoted as saying, "I found a scroll of genealogies in Jerusalem, on which was written that the king Manasseh killed the prophet Isaiah." Rava commented on this: "He tried him judicially and executed him. He accused him: 'Moses your teacher said, "No man shall see God and live," yet you say, "I saw the Lord seated on a throne, high and exalted" (Isaiah 6:1)?!'" The Gemara sought to reconcile these texts along the lines of a Baraita: "The prophets saw through a darkened glass, but Moses saw through a clear glass." Rashi comments: "The prophets thought they saw God, though they did not; but Moses saw through a clear glass and knew that he did not see God directly."[44] 68

The Amora R. Hanina said, "In time to come, the Holy and Blessed One will show His glory to all mortals, and will lower His throne to the middle of the firmament. Rabbi Hanina the Elder (a pupil of Rabbi Judah the Patriarch) disagreed: "Is it possible for Him to display His glory thus? It is written, 'Man shall not see Me and live,' and you say He will display His glory to all mortals?!"69

Did the Israelites See God's Glory?

Opinions were also divided as to whether the Israelites saw God's Glory at the Sinaitic revelation. According to Rabbi Levi, "Israel requested two things of the Holy and Blessed One, that they see His Glory and hear His voice, and both were fulfilled, as it says, "You said, 'The Lord our God has just shown us His majestic Presence, and we have heard His voice out of the fire'"70 (Deuteronomy 5:21). Rabbi Phinehas felt the strangeness of this request and interjected: "Do we grant a fool his request? But the Holy and Blessed One foresaw that they would make the golden calf forty days later. He considered: If I do not grant their request, they will plead in their defense

---

66 Midrash Aggadah on Leviticus, proem, p. 3.
67 Midrash Aggadah on Numbers 24:4 (p. 141), 24:16 (p. 144).
68 BT Yevamot 49b; Rashi ad loc.
69 Tanhuma Shofetim 9.   70 Exodus Rabbah 29:4.

---

[43] This is consistent with the biblical account in Exodus 34, according to which the veil was there to protect not Moses but rather the people.

[44] The judicial execution is not the point here, but rather that notion that Moses did not see God. Ironically, it was Moses' clearer vision that made him aware of that!

that they asked for this direct revelation from Me and I did not grant it, and they will plead that it was only because they did not see My image or hear My voice, that they turned to idols! Therefore I will show them My image and speak directly to them."[45] 71

Others said, "When the Israelites said, 'We want to see Him,' the Holy and Blessed One responded, 'I also desire to see you,' as the male lover says to his beloved, 'Let me see your face!'" (Song of Songs 2:14).[72] They also said, "When Israel stood at Mount Sinai to receive Torah, they asked Moses, 'Did you see Him?' He answered, 'Yes.'" They said, "We want to hear His voice," as it says, "Let Him kiss me with the kisses of His mouth" (Song of Songs 1:2). Immediately the Holy and Blessed One revealed Himself to them and said, "I am the Lord your God" (Exodus 20:2). As soon as they heard God's voice, they all died, as it says, "My soul went out when He spoke" (Song of Songs 5:6). The Torah went before the Holy and Blessed One and begged mercy for them, and He restored their souls, as it says, "The Torah of the Lord is perfect, restoring the soul" (Psalm 19:8).[73]

Another version tells that when the Israelites died on hearing the first commandment, the Holy and Blessed One sent down 1,200,000 angels—two angels for each of them. One placed his hand on the person's heart,[46] and the other raised his neck, *so he should see the Holy and Blessed One face to face.* Why? So that if in a succeeding generation any should attempt to lead them astray into serving idols, they should be able to say that they have seen the God that they are to serve.[47] 74

The two tendencies differ also in interpreting Moses' words on the eighth day after dedicating the Tabernacle: "For today the Lord will appear to you" (Leviticus 9:4). According to those who thirst after visions, this was in response to the Israelites' request: "How shall the people of the country acclaim their king, if they cannot see him?"[75] But other Sages understood it as symbolically marking the first time that the Shekhinah dwelt in the Tabernacle, and the full investiture of Aaron and his sons.[76]

---

[71] Exodus Rabbah 41:3.   [72] Song of Songs Zuta 1:2, p. 10.

[73] Exodus Rabbah 29:4 (continuation). In Midrash Aggadah on Leviticus 16:1 (p. 37), it is suggested that Nadab and Abihu met their fate from pursuing a similar desire, only they did not revive. See the section entitled "The Sin of Sinai" earlier in this chapter.

[74] PR 20:4 (98b).   [75] Sifra Shemini 43d (*Mekhilta de-Millu'in*).

[76] Ibid. 44c, RaBaD ad loc.; ibid. 41c.

---

[45] Interestingly, if we conjoin this text to the one cited at the end of the subsection entitled "At the Sea, the Handmaid Saw What Ezekiel Did Not," we get the following result: God tried to prevent the Israelites from having an excuse for building the golden calf by showing them the Divine Image; but it was that very perception of the image that ultimately served as at least partial exoneration for making the calf!

[46] To keep it from failing.

[47] This midrash assumes the well-known doctrine that all souls, past, present, and future, were there at Mount Sinai.

All agree that when the dedication was complete, and fire descended from heaven, the people burst into song, as the psalm alludes, "Sing forth, O you righteous, to the Lord, it is fit that the upright acclaim Him" (Psalm 33:1). But the mystics seize on the particle *bet* in this verse (literally: "Sing forth, O you righteous, *in* the Lord"). This means that they burst into song when they saw the Shekhinah.[48] 77

Abaye said: "No fewer than thirty-six righteous greet the Shekhinah each day (or each generation)."78

"The Lord cause His face to shine upon you" (Numbers 6:25)—In Rabbi Ishmael's school, they interpreted, "May God show you favor." Rabbi Nathan said, "This is the radiance of the Shekhinah."79

Whoever Sees the Divine Presence Does Not Die

The troubling question did not go away: How could some of the Sages believe that the Israelites saw the Divine Presence at Mount Sinai, when Scripture specifically states: "Man may not see Me and live"? One answer is provided in an anonymous interpretation of this verse: "'Man may not see Me,' but if he does, *vehai*, 'he will live'—forever."[49] This interpretation is hinted at in the teaching of Rabbi Levi, one of the scholars in Israel who belonged to the generation that marked the transition from the age of the Tannaim to that of the Amoraim and who was among the close colleagues of Rabbi Judah the Patriarch.[50] Rabbi Levi was of the opinion that at Mount Sinai the Israelites saw "the Divine Countenance, and whoever sees the Divine Presence does not die, as it is written: 'In the light of the King's countenance is life'" (Proverbs 16:15).80 According to one of the commentaries on the Zohar, the Holy and Blessed One said to Moses: "Man may not see Me, but if he merits seeing Me, he will live forever."[51] 81

Rabbi Levi's teaching is linked to Rabbi Judah's line of thought: "'The tablets were God's work and the writing was God's writing, incised upon the tablets' (Exodus 32:16)—do not read *harut*, 'incised,' but *herut*, 'freedom.' Rabbi Judah interprets the word *herut* to mean freedom from the Angel of Death. Rabbi Nehemiah said it means

---

77 Sifra Shemini 44d; Midrash on Psalms 33.
78 BT Sukkah 45b, Sanhedrin 97b.
79 Sifre Naso 11.
80 Midrash on Psalms 68:10; PRK 12:22 (108a); TB Yitro 14.
81 Tikkunei Zohar 69.

---

[48] The *instrumental* meaning of the preposition *bet* has here been changed to the *locational* meaning. In the midst of the Shekhinah, they sang forth.

[49] This thought is similar to God's worry in Genesis 3 about the Tree of Life. Adam is no longer to eat of it, after his sin, but if he were to, he would live forever.

[50] That is, early third century C.E.

[51] It is as if seeing the source of holiness, the *kodesh*, renders one also *kadosh*, and thus eternal.

freedom from subjection to foreign kingdoms. The Sages said it means freedom from human suffering."[82]

A similar view is reported also in the name of Rabbi Eliezer, son of Rabbi Yosi, the Galilean: "When the Israelites stood at Mount Sinai and said, 'We will do and obey,' God called the Angel of Death and said to him, 'You have no power over this nation.'"[52] [83] In the name of Rabbi Yosi it was reported: This was in fact the condition made by the Israelites in accepting the Torah at Mount Sinai, that the Angel of Death would have no power over them, as it is written: "I declare you to be divine beings, all of you are the sons of the Most High" (Psalm 82:6). But because you have been corrupted by making the golden calf, "you shall die as mortal men do" (Psalm 82:7). An opposing view is found in an anonymous statement in the Mekhilta of Rabbi Ishmael: "If it were possible for Me to do away with the Angel of Death, I would have done so, but the decree has already been issued."[53] [84]

Rabbi Levi's opinion is reported elsewhere: "The Holy and Blessed One revealed Himself to them in the likeness of a king's statue that had faces in every direction. A thousand people look at the one statue, and the statue looks at all of them. So it was when the Holy and Blessed One spoke to the Israelites, each one of them reported, saying: 'The Word is addressed to Me.' That is why the text reads, 'I am the Lord your God'; the word 'your' is written not in the plural but in the singular form."[85] Rabbi Hoshaya likewise explained the text: "He saw the likeness of God" (Numbers 12:18) to mean "like a king who reveals himself to a member of his household through his statue."[86]

Moses' Request in the Perspective of the Middle Ages

During the Middle Ages, the Sages of Israel continued to be concerned with the subject of Moses' request to see God's Presence. According to Saadia Gaon, it is altogether wrong to say that Moses asked literally to see the Creator with his eyes, "for this is the path of falsehood."[54] We must rather understand that the Creator has a light that He reveals to the prophets. This assures them that the words of prophecy that they hear come from the Creator. This is the meaning of *Hakavod*, God's Glory.

---

[82] Exodus Rabbah 32:1, 41:7.   [83] Leviticus Rabbah 18:3.   [84] MI Bahodesh 9.
[85] PRK 12:25 (110a).   [86] Leviticus Rabbah 1:14.

---

[52] This is presumably not the same as saying that the Angel of Death no longer has power over *individuals* in that nation.

[53] It is an inseparable part of life. Again, the transcendence that separates God radically from humans is emphasized in the Ishmaelian school.

[54] This is consistent with much of medieval philosophical exegesis, which rejected the literal understanding of anthropomorphisms. See also BT Kiddushin 49a, where it is stated that one who translates biblical verses literally is a liar.

Whoever gazes at this light finds that "his perplexities disappear and his spirit blossoms." What Moses requested was "that the Creator grant him strength to gaze at that light. He answered him that the first glance at the light was blinding, and it was impossible to gaze at it and not die. But He would cover Himself with a cloud or with something similar, to enable him to see the afterglow of that light."[87]

Maimonides is also of the opinion that the Glory of God at times refers to the light that was specially created to reveal God's Glory. It was this special light that was visible to all the Israelites. "How then can we say that God would deny this privilege to the chief of the prophets and say to him, 'You cannot see My Divine Presence'?"[88] In the opinion of Maimonides, "Moses sought to apprehend God through the truth of His existence."[89] That is to say, "he asked that he be given knowledge of the existence of the Holy and Blessed One with the same certainty as knowing an individual person. Once having seen a person's face, his appearance is engraved in his heart, and this man's image is fixed in his mind entirely distinct from other men. So, too, did Moses request that God's existence should be utterly distinct from any other and that he would thereby grasp the truth of His existence as it is in reality. And He, Blessed be He, answered him that it is not in the power of the mind of a living man, composed of body and soul, ever to achieve a full understanding of Divinity. "For there remains a barrier between him and his capacity to comprehend Divinity in its true reality. That barrier is human intelligence, which is attached to the physical body so long as man lives."[55] [90]

Many of the critical scholars asked: How was it possible for the Master Prophet to ask for something impossible to achieve in its own terms? To understand the essence of Divinity is an utter impossibility. The philosopher[56] had stated: "Were I to know God, I would be God." How then was it possible for the teacher of scholars and prophets not to know what even the least of the philosophers knew?[91]

According to Hasdai Crescas,[57] Moses never requested to have knowledge of God's essence. What he asked was for knowledge of God's distinctive attributes,[58] yet this, too, was denied him.[92] The kabbalists took Moses' request literally, but added

[87] Saadia Gaon, *Book of Beliefs and Opinions*, 2:12.

[88] Isaac Abravanel, commentary on Exodus 33:12.

[89] Maimonides, "Eight Chapters" (Commentary on the Mishnah, Introduction to Tractate Avot), chapter 7.

[90] Maimonides, Mishneh Torah, *Hilkhot Yesodei Hatorah* [Foundational Principles of the Torah] 1:10; *Guide of the Perplexed* III:9.

[91] Abravanel, Commentary on Maimonides' *Guide* I:54; Abravanel, commentary on Exodus 33:12.

[92] Crescas, *Or Adonai* 1.3.1, 1.3.3.

[55] Thus, mortal humans cannot ascend all the way to a perception of God. This is the Ishmaelian position taken by Maimonides. But on death, there can be a reuniting with the Divine, when the physical matter falls away, and that soul/body dualism is also a signature issue of the Middle Ages.

[56] The reference is to Joseph Albo, fourteenth- to fifteenth-century Spain, author of *Ikkarim*.

[57] Fourteenth- to fifteenth-century Spain, philosopher and communal leader.

[58] Attributes are the ways in which essences make themselves known, so they are at least one step removed from the essence.

a new dimension to the meaning of *kavod*, glory. When Moses said, "I pray, show me Your glory," he was referring to a higher glory.[93] Rabbi Menahem Recanati[59] explains: There is a glory above the glory that man sees. When Moses says "show me," he means "let me understand" as in the verse "my heart understood" (Ecclesiastes 1:16). "Your glory" in this context refers to the great splendor, the reflective mirror. Moses was seeking to attain an understanding of the inner essence of this glory and how it was different from the lesser glory. Yet it was denied him. Even though his prophecy derived from the great splendor, he only sensed that it came from there, but he never achieved full understanding of its essence.[94]

Bahya ben Asher[60] followed in this line of thought.

> There is a glory above the glory. When Moses received the Torah he achieved seven of the ten Sefirot.[61] He therefore requested that he be permitted to go higher. The glory that he sought is the supreme exalted glory called keter, Crown—the luminous mirror. When he said, "show me," he actually wanted to see it with his naked eye. What made him believe that he could achieve this impossible goal? This greatest of prophets, who went forty days and forty nights without food or drink, believed that he had achieved a stage where his corporal nature had been so impoverished that he could achieve now what can only be achieved when the soul leaves the body. His request was not granted. He was still a mortal man.[62] [95]

The power of Moses' prophecy exceeded that of all the prophets who followed. "There has not arisen a prophet since in Israel like unto Moses" (Deuteronomy 34:10). And yet the Torah itself hints at Moses' limitations. The text does not read, "Who knew the Lord face to face," but rather, "Whom the Lord knew face to face." Similarly, the verse does not say, "Moses spoke to the Lord face to face," but rather, "The Lord spoke to Moses face to face" (Exodus 33:11). The Lord knew and saw Moses face to face; Moses did not know or see God face to face.[63] [96]

[93] Nahmanides on Exodus 33:18.
[94] Recanati, Commentary on the Torah, Ki Tissa.
[95] Rabbenu Bahya, Commentary, Exodus 33:18.
[96] Nachmanides on Numbers 24:1; Hizkuni on Deuteronomy 34:10.

---

[59] Thirteenth- to fourteenth-century Italy, kabbalist and commentator.

[60] Thirteenth-century Spain, commentator and popularizer of Kabbalah.

[61] These are the emanations or mediations from the Divine that play a very prominent role in most Jewish mysticism. The seven lower Sefirot referred to here are particularly important as bridges between the divine and the mundane. But Moses wanted more than the seven lower ones, according to this reading.

[62] Once again, an Ishmaelian point prevailing in medieval Jewish philosophical exegesis.

[63] Once again we have the motif of humans having faces that are seen but do not see, while God's Presence sees but cannot be seen.

THE TORAH THAT IS IN HEAVEN

Translator's Introduction

With this chapter, Heschel began volume 2 in the Hebrew, which was subtitled "Torah from Sinai and Torah from Heaven." The reader will already recognize yet another of the ubiquitous Heschelian dyads here. It is at this point that, having dealt in sequence with a very full array of theological topics on which he believed Rabbinic Judaism harbored a rich and patterned diversity of thought, Heschel proceeded to what was, for him, very much a theological issue of his own day. In order to get a sense of the more focused agenda in the subsequent chapters, it is worth quoting from Heschel's brief introduction to volume 2, which we otherwise do not translate here:

> Two expressions are used in the Mishnah with respect to the Torah: "Moses received Torah from Sinai" and "Torah from Heaven." These two expressions represent two perspectives. . . . The purpose of this study is to unpack the nuances of these expressions—their pedigree, their meaning, their scope. Does "Moses received Torah from Sinai" mean that he received instruction [the literal meaning of "Torah"], but not all of *the Torah* [i.e., the five books]? Were many commandments received later, in the Tabernacle, or in the steppes of Moab? Or does this expression mean that the entire Torah was received at Sinai, with all of its principles and minutiae? Is it even possible that this expression means that the Oral Torah was also received at Sinai?

> Does "Torah from Heaven" mean that the Torah in the form in which we have it [i.e., from Genesis 1:1 to Deuteronomy 34:12] is entirely "from Heaven"? That the words and letters descended from heaven to the ears of Moses? Does this expression mean that the Torah is in every respect a creature of the supernal realm, and that mortals have no part in its creation? Does "Heaven" mean to denote a place, or is it a way of referring to the divine will?

> A penetrating study of the original sources has opened my eyes to the fact that the understanding of the principle "Torah from Heaven" given by Maimonides [i.e., that all words and letters came directly to Moses] was not always fixed and unchallenged. Since time immemorial two different ways of understanding this important principle have coexisted. One is extreme and unyielding; the other is moderate and has give. One closes the door in the face of questioners, and the other offers an open hand to sincere seekers. In the course of the generations, the extreme approach gained the upper hand, and the views of the moderates were suppressed.

It is with this, and with the conviction that his own age was one in which questioners could not be turned away, that Heschel began here to turn his attention to what is the true meaning of the "Heavenly Torah."

Torah: Heaven's Daughter[1]

WHAT IS TORAH'S SUBSTANCE? The answer seems simple, but it is not. Our Sages who were involved in it day and night found it difficult to grasp its essence. They heaped excessive praise on it, realizing at the same time that simply extolling its virtues was secondary to defining its substance. Paeans of praise cannot reflect an essence. "The world and all it contains was created only by the Torah's merit."[1] "When Moses charged us with the Torah as the heritage of the congregation of Jacob" (Deuteronomy 33:4)—read not "heritage" (*morashah*) but rather "betrothed" (*me'orasah*)—for this teaches that the Torah is betrothed to Israel.[2] Such statements of faith still do not solve the riddle: What is Torah's substance?

Part of the answer is found in the view that the existence of Torah antedates not only Moses but also the creation of the world. It is because of the merit of Torah that the world endures. Linked to this concept is the bold and lofty notion that Torah is of greater worth than heaven and earth. This was quoted in the names of two Amoraim, Rabbi Berekhiah and Rabbi Hiyya of Kefar Tehumin: "The entire world is not worth a single word of Torah." Yet even this assessment does not directly answer the question: What is Torah's substance?

The classical philosophers held that there was no distinction in the universe more profound than that between existence and nonexistence. The Tannaim, however, found that the most profound distinction was between heaven and earth, between the supernal and the mundane, transitory world. Even those Sages who did not disparage the importance of quotidian, mundane concerns, nevertheless believed with all their hearts that the profit of one's work in this world was only meaningful if the principal endures to the world to come.

Torah's source is heaven, not earth. It is not simply a book possessed by Israel, with words written on parchment, residing in a holy ark. The concept developed that

---

[1] Genesis Rabbah 1:4.　　[2] Sifre Haberakhah 345.

---

[1] We are tempted—with more than a little justice—to draw a parallel between this notion and the Christian belief in the divine Son. Each uses human imagery for the Divine Logos, the Word proceeding from God, which becomes an archetype and blueprint for the material world (a concept articulated early on by the Hellenistic Jewish philosopher Philo of Alexandria). Although we can take no position here on whether this parallel was consciously apprehended, it is a striking example of similarity-with-difference between Judaism and Christianity.

Torah had not only a heavenly source but a heavenly essence as well. It was regarded as God's darling daughter, and even after she departed from God's domain (where God played with her), her glory and splendor did not evanesce.

With the assembly at Mount Sinai, it descended from the heavens and became the possession of mortals. Rabbi Simon said that this may be compared to a king who had a precious jewel. His son asked for it and the king said, "it is not yours." But the son was obdurate, and he finally gave it to him. So Israel demanded from the Holy One at the Reed Sea that He give them His Torah: "Lord, this is *my* strength (*oz*)!" (Exodus 15:2).[2] God said, "It does not belong to you, it belongs to the heavenly creatures." But they persisted until God finally yielded, as it is written, "The Lord will give strength (*oz*) to His people" (Psalm 29:11).[3]

The Aggadah records the opposition of the angels to transferring Torah to mortal beings. "When Moses ascended to heaven, the angels complained to God, 'What is a mere mortal doing here in our midst?' God replied, 'He has come to receive Torah.' The angels replied: 'You have kept concealed this precious treasure for 974 generations[3] before You created the world and now you want to give it away to a creature of flesh and blood?! O, what is man that You are mindful of him, mortal man that you have taken note of him? O Lord, our Lord, how majestic is Your name throughout the earth, You who have covered the heavens with Your splendor. It is fitting that You give Torah to us in heaven. Why? Because *we* are holy and pure and *it* is pure and holy . . . far better that it remain with us.' The angels contended with the Holy One on this matter, and when the tablets were broken by Moses, they rejoiced and said, Now the Torah will be restored to us."[4]

The Torah apparently came into human possession, but in reality its substance remained lofty and exalted, far above the human domain. When Moses our Master shattered the tablets, "the tablets were broken, but the letters went flying;"[5] "the heavenly writing returned to its place."[6] That is, even while on earth, the supreme nature of its substance did not cease. And for that reason, no conceivable weapon could succeed in destroying it, not even fire.[4] The idea expressed in such *aggadot*,

---

[3] Midrash on Psalms 28:6.   [4] Midrash on Psalms 8:2.
[5] BT Pesahim 87b.   [6] MI Amalek 1; MSY, p. 120; ARN A 41, ARN B 47.

---

[2] This highly compressed midrash takes the following steps: (1) "The Lord [is] my strength and song" (Exodus 15:2)—Rabbi Simon reverses the syntax to turn "Lord" from the subject to a vocative, thus: "Lord, [this is] my strength!" (2) He pairs the mention of "strength" (*oz*) in Exodus 15:2 with Psalm 29:11: "The Lord will give strength to His people," and interprets the two verses as parts of a dialogue. (3) He interprets "strength" in both places to mean "Torah."

[3] This is based on the rabbinic understanding of Psalm 105:8: "He has commanded a word to the thousandth generation." There were twenty-six generations from Adam to Moses. If the generation that received the Torah was the thousandth generation, this implies counting 974 generations prior to the creation of the world. See Rashi on BT Zevahim 116a.

[4] Heschel refers to the story of the martyrdom of Hanina ben Teradyon. The Romans wrapped him in the Torah scroll and burned him at the stake. His students asked him what he saw. He replied, "The parchment is burning, but the letters are flying up!" (BT Avodah Zarah 18a).

that no destructive agent is capable of destroying Torah's substance, has its foundation in the faith that Torah primarily has a supernal abode. And so, after Rabbi Hanina ben Teradyon was burnt, it was said to the executioner: "Do not be troubled about having burnt the Torah. From the moment she left the arena, she returned to her father's house."[5]

In consonance with the view that life in this world is but a preparation for life in the world to come, the opinion was expressed that even study of Torah in the foyer is only a preparation for the full understanding of Torah that people will study in the future world.

Rabbi Abba was quoted as saying: "In fact, Torah need not have been given to the people Israel in this world, for in the next world everyone will learn Torah directly from the Holy One. Why, then, was it given to them in this world? So that when the Holy One will teach them in the world to come, the people will know at least with what subject He is dealing."[6] 7

Torah Was Brought Down from Heaven

The expansion of the concept "Torah from heaven"—from simply the Ten Commandments to all the Five Books of Moses—is the result of a change that took place in the meaning of the phrase "from heaven." This change is rooted in the belief that Torah existed in heaven before it was given to Moses. To quote Rabbi Hananiah bar Hama:[7] "Originally, the Torah was in heaven, as it is written, 'I was with Him as a confidant, a source of delight every day, playing before Him at all times' (Proverbs 8:30). Then Moses ascended, took the Torah and brought it down to earth and gave it

---

7 Tanhuma Ki Tavo, 4.

---

[5] The imagery here also recalls the return of a previously married woman to her father's house in widowhood or after divorce (see Leviticus 22:13). In this case, Torah's father had given her in marriage to Israel (represented here by Hanina ben Teradyon), and Israel was now vanquished (as represented by Hanina's death). In widowhood, therefore, the personified Torah returns to her father's home in heaven.

[6] This view (that we learn Torah in this world in preparation for recognizing it in the world to come) is the inverse of the ancient doctrine of recollection. According to the doctrine of recollection, human souls were created and subsisted in heaven before birth, where they learned the divine wisdom; but at birth, an angel slaps the child and causes her to forget all that she knew. Plato argued for this view in the *Meno* from the sense we often have, when learning something, that we are *recollecting* something we previously knew but forgot. The same doctrine of precognition is found in the rabbinic literature, e.g., Tanhuma Pekudei 3. But in Rabbi Abba's view, we will be recollecting in the world to come that which we learned in this world.

[7] A first-generation Amora of the Land of Israel.

to humankind, as it is written, 'Playing in His inhabited world, finding delight with mankind'"[8] (Proverbs 8:31).[9] 8

This idea was expressed also by R. Bibi (a third-generation Amora of the Land of Israel): "'A season is set for everything, a time for every desired object under heaven' (Ecclesiastes 3:1)—there was a time for *that thing* (Torah) to be *above* the heavens, and now it is to be deposited *under* the heavens!"9

In light of this idea, the phrase "from heaven" underwent a change in content and scope. In content, the new meaning was that the Torah itself actually was brought down from heaven to earth. It no longer meant that God simply made His will known to humans through the process of revelation. In scope: The Torah itself says that the Ten Commandments alone were heard from heaven. But via the belief that the Torah had heavenly substance, it came to mean that the entire Torah was in heaven before being given to Moses and brought down by him.10

Primordial Torah

The concept that Torah existed in heaven before it was given to Moses dovetails with an array of ideas concerning creation. "*Bereshit* God created the heavens and the earth" (Genesis 1:1). The conventional interpretation, according to which the *bet* of *bereshit* means "at (the time of)," so that *bereshit* means "at the beginning," did not satisfy the exegetes of Torah. Already in ancient times they said that the *bet* here is the *instrumental bet,* meaning "by means of." Thus: "By means of *reshit*[10] did God create the heavens and the earth." Now God did not create the world with exertion and labor, but rather with utterances: "With ten utterances was the world created."11

What, then, is *reshit* in that verse? What was in existence before the creation of the

---

8 Midrash on Proverbs 8:9, ed. Buber, p. 30a.
9 Ecclesiastes Rabbah 3:1. See also PRK 12:7 (103a).
10 See Sifre Ha'azinu 306; Exodus Rabbah 46:1; ARN A 1; BT Sanhedrin 59b.
11 Mishnah Avot 5:1.

---

[8] The Hebrew of the last phrase is being read more literally as "My plaything for (or with) mortals."

[9] This is the first of many rabbinic references to Proverbs 8 that Heschel cites in this passage. Originally, Proverbs 8 may simply have been a poetic paean to the importance of "wisdom" in human affairs since time immemorial. Having wisdom speak in the first person ("Through me kings reign . . . The Lord created me at the beginning of His course," etc.) may have been just a literary device, which is repeated throughout the book. The decision to take the personification literally had profound implications for the direction of Western religious thought, both Jewish and Christian. More specifically, equating the Wisdom of Proverbs 8 with Torah was absolutely crucial for the elaboration of the rabbinic doctrine of "Torah from Heaven," as Heschel makes abundantly clear in this exposition.

[10] That is, by means of what had existed from the beginning, primordially.

world? Wisdom. And so the "Jerusalem Targum" renders the first words of the Torah: "With wisdom did God create. . . ."

Support for the preexistence of Wisdom is found in the Book of Proverbs: "The Lord created me [wisdom] at the beginning [*reshit*] of His course, as the first of His works of old. In the distant past I was fashioned, at the beginning, at the origin of earth. There was still no deep when I was brought forth, no springs rich in water, before the mountains were sunk, before the hills I was born" (Proverbs 8:22–25). The idea that God created the world with Wisdom was also preserved in rabbinic literature: "'Wisdom has built her house' (Proverbs 9:1)—this refers to the King of Kings of Kings, who built the entire world with wisdom."[12] Moreover, already in the second century B.C.E. it had been asserted that Torah was the primordial wisdom. This is hinted at in the Book of Ben Sira: "Wisdom was first of all created things" (Ecclesiasticus 1:4). And Wisdom herself said: "I am the word which was spoken by the Most High. . . . Before time He created me, and I shall remain forever. . . . All this is the covenant-book of God Most High, the law which Moses enacted to be the heritage of the assemblies of Jacob" (Ecclesiasticus 24:3, 9, 23).[11]

One of the rabbinic Sages, Rabbi Simeon ben Lakish, declared that the Torah existed two thousand years before the creation of the world. He based this on Proverbs 8:30: "a source of delight every day." The Hebrew for "every day" reads *yom, yom*—day, day. Since a thousand years in God's eyes are but as a day,[12] we may infer that the Torah was a source of delight to God for two thousand years.[13] Indeed, the Torah not only predated the world but was the instrument by which the world was created.[13] [14]

Several other opinions developed from the view that Torah predated creation. One was that the Torah was the instrument that God used to create the world. Another was that God sought counsel from the Torah on whether or not to create human beings. On the verse "God said, let Us make a human . . ." the question arose, Whom was God consulting? Various answers were forthcoming: God consulted heaven and

---

[12] Tosefta Sanhedrin 8:3.   [13] Leviticus Rabbah 19:1.
[14] See Avot 3:14: Rabbi Akiva said: "Dear are Israel, that they were given the precious instrument by which the world was created [i.e., the Torah]."

---

[11] As Heschel indicates, here we see a literary imitation of Proverbs 8, in which the references to Wisdom are glossed by the author as referring to the Torah, through a verbatim quotation of Deuteronomy 33:4. Ecclesiasticus is, of all the apocryphal works, the most akin to the interpretation of Judaism that developed into Rabbinic Judaism, and here it expresses one of the most central tenets of that later development.

[12] The reference is to Psalm 90:4.

[13] See Avot 3:14: Rabbi Akiva said: "Dear are Israel, that they were given the precious instrument by which the world was created [i.e., the Torah]." Akiva brought no proof text for this assertion—it was merely assumed (as it was, for example, at end of Sifre Ekev 48). A proof text was brought only for Israel's having been made aware of this primordial role of the Torah.

earth; the ministering angels. One opinion stated: God consulted the Torah. A late source preserves this dialogue for us. Said the Holy One to Torah, "Let Us make a human in our image and likeness." The Torah replied, "Master of all worlds, the world is Yours. This human You want to create is short-lived, very quarrelsome, and of a sinful nature. If You are not prepared to be patient and forgiving with him, it would be better if he were not created." The Holy One said, "Is it for nothing that I am called 'long-suffering and most compassionate?'"[15]

In the works of the Alexandrian philosopher Philo, Torah is called the Divine Logos, and the Logos is the instrument (*organon*) by which the world was created. Philo distinguishes between Torah as Divine Logos, second only to God in the celestial hierarchy, and Torah, which was given to us on Sinai and is only a reflection of the heavenly Torah. The divine Torah (to be transmitted to humans) had to be dressed in material clothes—words, nouns, verbs, and the like. The rabbinic Sages, too, were seized with the question, In what form did the heavenly Torah exist? Was there no difference between the primordial Torah and the one that is to be found in our possession? Did the heavenly Torah exist in God's mind as thought, or did it sit before God in writing?[14]

We find some hint in Scripture that the Torah was not actually created but that it was an expression of God's will and thought before the creation of the world: "'He gave to Moses when He finished [speaking to him]' (Exodus 31:18); thus says Scripture: 'You went up to the heights [i.e., to heaven], you took spoil [i.e., Torah]' (Psalm 68:19). When human beings seize things, they are gold or silver or clothes; can they seize what is in another's mind? And yet, [God said]: 'You [Moses] have seized what was in My mind!'"[15]16

In Rabbi Akiva's words, the Torah is the instrument through which the world was created. An ancient midrash combines the metaphors of the instrument and the book: "'I [Wisdom] was with Him as a confidant [*amon*]'—the Torah says: 'I was the artisan's tool [*keli umanuto*] of the Holy and Blessed One.' When a king builds a palace, he does not do so unaided, but avails himself of the knowledge of an artisan, and the artisan does not do it unaided, but uses tablets and notebooks so he can see where he must make rooms and passages. Similarly the Holy and Blessed One looks into the Torah and builds the world from it."[17] In this metaphor, the idea that the heavenly Torah has the form of a book is hinted at. The terms for tablets and notebooks—*pinkes* (from the Greek *pinax*) and *diphthera*—were also used by the Sages to

---

[15] PRE 11.   [16] Tanhuma Ki Tissa 17.
[17] Genesis Rabbah 1:4.

---

[14] Heschel notes: There is an echo of this issue in a late exegesis of the word "Torah": "In Greek they call the external appearance *theoria* (= "Torah")"; that is, the Torah was at first hidden in heaven before creation, and later made manifest to Israel (Beit Hamidrash II, p. 23).

[15] In other words, it was not just a thought that was later written down for Israel, but rather something that already existed in writing, even before it became time for it to be given to Israel.

denote the heavenly Book of Remembrance on which human deeds were recorded. Rabbi Akiva spoke of an "open tablet" with a "hand that records" everything a person does.[18]

In Rabbi Ishmael's school there was no mention of the idea that the Torah is the instrument with which the world was created. In more modest language they taught: "Whatever is dearest to God, He created first. Since Torah was dearest of all to God, it was created first, as it says, 'The Lord created me at the beginning of His course as the first of His works of old' (Proverbs 8:22).[19] This exegesis says that Torah was first in order of creation, but not that it was the instrument with which the world was created.[16]

Books in Heaven

Scripture makes no mention of a primordial book in which all human deeds are written. On the other hand, we do find mention of a "book which the Lord wrote," "book of life," and "memorial book." How did the Rabbis understand the nature of these books?

After the episode of the golden calf, Moses said to the Holy and Blessed One, "[if You do not forgive the people's sin,] erase me from the book which You have written!" (Exodus 32:32). Most midrashim and commentators identify this with the "book of life."

We find in Scripture and in liturgy mention of a "book of life" in which people are inscribed for life: "all who are inscribed for life in Jerusalem" (Isaiah 4:3); "Your eyes saw my unformed limbs; they were all recorded in Your book (Psalm 139:16); "may [my persecutors] be erased from the "book of life" and not be inscribed with the righteous" (Psalm 69:29); "your people will be rescued, all who are found inscribed in the book" (Daniel 12:1). Among the Rabbis, Rabbi Johanan speaks of three books opened on Rosh Hashanah: one of the righteous, one of the wicked, and one of average people.[20] According to R. Abbahu: "On Rosh Hashanah the King sits on the throne of judgment, and the books of the living and the dead are opened before Him."[21] This idea is already found in the Book of Daniel: "the court sat and the books were opened" (Daniel 7:10).

It is common for Scripture to speak of human actions being written down in

---

[18] Avot 3:16.   [19] Sifre Ekev 37.
[20] BT Rosh Hashanah 16b.   [21] BT Rosh Hashanah 32b.

---

[16] Even this is not quite what Heschel had said earlier about the Ishmaelian school, that is, that the Torah was a historically conditioned work intended for the freed Israelites. Being first in the order of creation may or may not be consistent with that. But the point once again is not the rigid consistency of *doctrine*, but rather the different views about Torah. Is it prior to the existence of the world, and thus divine, or is it *of* the world, and thus less than divine?

heaven. Malachi calls this a "book of remembrance": "In this vein have those who revere the Lord been talking to one another. The Lord has heard and noted it, and a *scroll of remembrance* has been written at His behest concerning those who revere the Lord and esteem His name" (Malachi 3:16). This is called at one point in the midrash: "The Book of the Holy and Blessed One." The Rabbis picked up this imagery of a book of our deeds. As we saw in the last section, Rabbi Akiva uses the imagery of the active tablet on which the hand writes the record of human deeds.[22]

There was a saying current among the Rabbis, "The Holy One showed Adam each generation and its teachers, its administrators, its leaders, its prophets, its heroes, its sinners, and its saints. In such a generation, so-and-so is to be king; in such a generation so-and-so is to be a Sage." This was variously attributed to R. Simeon ben Lakish in the name of Rabbi Eleazar ben Azariah, and to Rabbi Joshua ben Korhah.[23] No book is mentioned; rather the Holy One showed Adam the coming generations as in a pageant. But other Sages expanded the notion into the Book of Adam.[24] They even connected it with the verse we cited earlier, "Your eyes saw my unformed limbs; they were all recorded in Your book" (Psalm 139:16).[17]

It may appear that the idea of a Torah written and preexisting in heaven could have developed from the concept that was prevalent in Israel, of a book in heaven in which human deeds are recorded. But the difference between the two is profound and fundamental. The heavenly "book of remembrance" is God's private record; no human eye has seen it, nor has it ever come down to earth. On the other hand, the Torah *did* come down to earth, and people study it. Beliefs concerning books and tablets in heaven were common among peoples of the ancient Near East. It is of inestimable importance that Scripture steered clear of the belief that the Torah existed in heaven in the form of a book.[18] The "book of life," or "book of remembrance," is in God's secret domain. The prophets spoke of it, but no eye save God's ever saw it, until the author of Daniel (one of the first apocalyptic visionaries) said, "I will tell you what is recorded in the book of truth" (Daniel 10:21). Even the Rabbis restricted access of this knowledge to Adam, God's direct handiwork.

Ezekiel does tell us that he saw "a hand stretched out to me, holding a written scroll. He unrolled it before me, and it was inscribed on both the front and the back; on it were written lamentations, dirges, and woes" (Ezekiel 2:9–10). But we have only his summary description of the contents of the scroll. The words remain a mystery.

[22] Avot 3:16.
[23] PR 23:1 (115a); ARN A 31; TB Bereshit 28. See J. Theodor and Ch. Albeck's notes on Genesis Rabbah 24:2 (*Midrash Bereshit Rabbah* [in Hebrew] [Jerusalem: Wahrmann Books, 1965]).
[24] Midrash on Psalms 139:6.

---

[17] It would also, obviously, be connected to Genesis 5:1, literally, "This is the book of the descendants of Adam."
[18] The assertion here is that the early belief was that God had private records, but that "the Torah" was not a book, at least not as we have it.

Tablets Written and Set Aside since the Days of Creation

One source of the belief that the Torah was written in heaven before the world was created may be found in the ancient tradition that "writing, the inscription, and the tablets" were among the ten things created at twilight on the eve of the Sabbath of creation.[25] In the language of the Tannaim, the writing on the tablets is called "the writ of heaven."[26] According to Pirkei de-Rabbi Eliezer, "the tablets were created not from earth, but from heaven."[27] The following is consistent with all this: "When Moses ascended to heaven to receive the tablets, *which were written and set aside from the six days of creation* (as it says: 'The tablets were God's work, and the writing was God's writing, incised upon the tablets' [Exodus 32:16]), the angels objected. . . ."[28] This oft-repeated legend tells us that it was only the tablets, which contained the Ten Commandments, that existed from creation.

The alternative view, that the entire Torah was from creation, is reflected in Rabbi Eliezer's homily on the conception of Isaac: "'*And* the Lord took note of Sarah' (Genesis 21:1)—'and' indicates a *ribbui* (expansive interpretation), referring to God's heavenly court. The angels argued, 'Master of the Universe! It is mandatory that You grant this favor to Sarah and Abraham, for otherwise Your Torah will be made false.' Rabbi Judah the Levite expanded the argument: 'Abraham was seventy years old when God promised him, "Your *offspring* shall be strangers in a land not theirs for four hundred years" (Genesis 15:13).[19] Now, the Torah preceded the creation of the world, and in it is written: "The length of time that the Israelites lived in Egypt was 430 years" (Exodus 12:40). The difference is the thirty years that had elapsed, for Abraham was now one hundred years old (as compared with seventy). So unless God granted Abraham offspring immediately, He would render the Torah false."[29] [20]

It was said in Rabbi Samuel ben Isaac's name: "Six things preceded the creation of the world, but the thoughts of Israel preceded everything. It is like a king whose queen had not borne him any children. He was once passing through the market and said,

[25] Avot 5:6; Sifre Deuteronomy 354.   [26] MI Amalek 1; MSY, p. 120.
[27] PRE 46.   [28] ARN A 2.   [29] PR 42:3 (175b).

---

[19] This midrash is stated in somewhat convoluted language. It is based on several notions: (1) Abraham was seventy-five (as the text says) when he left Haran but seventy when he left Ur. (2) The length of the Israelite exile is counted from his uprooting from his homeland at age seventy. (3) At the "covenant of the pieces" related in Genesis 15, God speaks to Abraham about the length of exile of his *descendants,* and since the figure four hundred is used, is must be that Abraham's descendants will appear when he is one hundred years old, or thirty years older than when the exile was counted as 430 years.

[20] This exegesis takes the doctrine of a preexisting Torah to an interesting conclusion. Since the Torah describes the actions of people who lived in created time, then once it is written, the heroes of those narratives (including God) have no choice but to follow the preordained script to the letter. The potential paradoxes involving the doctrine of free will are obvious.

'Buy ink and an inkstand for my son.' His servants said, 'The king must be an astrologer, for if he did not foresee that she would bear him a son, he would not ask us to buy ink and an inkstand for his son.' So, too, if the Holy One had not foreseen that twenty-six generations later Israel would accept the Torah, He would not write in the Torah, 'Command the Israelites,' 'Speak to the Israelites,' and so on."[30] [21]

Torah Written in Heaven

The view that the Torah was already written and available to God in heaven before it was given to Moses is reflected also in the following Tannaitic story: "The Lord said to Moses, 'The daughters of Zelophehad's daughters speak *rightly* (Numbers 27:6) for that is how the whole episode is written before Me in heaven.' Happy is the person whose words are agreed to by the All-Present!"[22] [31]

We have a statement of Rabbi Akiva that testifies to his belief in the preexistence of the written Torah as a unitary document.

It is told of Rabbi Akiva that the cantor called him to read from the Torah scroll in public, and he refused. When his students asked why, he replied, "By the Temple service! I would have read, except that I had not had time to rehearse the portion two or three times. No one should read from the Torah without first rehearsing it two or three times, for even concerning the Holy and Blessed One, Who gives the power of speech to all His creatures, and who had the whole Torah spread out before Him *as a single document,* we learn: 'Then He saw and spoke it; He prepared it and searched it out,' and only afterwards 'spoke it to man' (Job 28:27–28). Thus it says, 'The Lord spoke all these things'—to Himself, and then 'saying'—to the Israelites."[23] [32]

These remarks of Rabbi Akiva are explained in the following responsum of the Geonim: "It is written, 'The Lord spoke all *these* words'—why 'these' words? It implies that the words were written out before God, and He read them from the written text.

---

[30] Genesis Rabbah 1:4.

[31] Sifre Pinhas 134. Two voices are combined in this homily. The reference to the "episode written before God in heaven" seems to be a later addition in the spirit of the Akivan school. But without this gloss, the story line is different: God endorses the suggestion of the daughters of Zelophehad *after* they offer it. This commonsense interpretation is similar to other homilies of the Ishmaelian school.

[32] Tanhuma Yitro 15.

---

[21] Here too the midrash marvels at the paradox that the Torah, conceived of as preexisting creation, contains details of created history, such as the people Israel, which came only later. This has the effect of compressing all of history into a single instant.

[22] We do not give here Heschel's ensuing (and not terribly convincing) argument that this midrash is of composite authorship. The essential point is made, however, that there was a view that the Torah was preexistent in writing and that human history conforms to it.

[23] Of course, this does not necessitate *preexistence, but rather a written-out speech.

Similarly, one who reads from the Torah should have the written text before him."[33]

The procedure of giving the Torah here is similar to the procedure of creation noted earlier. Just as the Holy and Blessed One looked in the Torah and created the world, so here He looked in the written scroll and recited the words to Israel. Furthermore, just as (according to the Akivan view) the Israelites *saw* the words of fire emerge from the divine mouth and inscribe themselves onto the tablets, so the Holy and Blessed One saw the words before speaking them.

The geonic interpretation of *these* (as implying immediate visual perception) follows the pattern of Rabbi Akiva's interpretation of *this,* which we examined earlier. "'*This* new-moon shall be for you . . .'—God pointed out to Moses the form of the new-moon."[34] The Akivan school also took note of the paradoxical language: "All the people *saw* the thunder and lightning"—"they saw even the auditory phenomena."[35] This conception of the Sinai event as a visual revelation is influenced by the apocalyptists: the prophet hears, the apocalyptist sees.

Not all the Sages agreed that the Torah was written in heaven before it was given to Moses. Small differences in language are significant. According to one source, "six things [including the Torah] *were conceived in thought* before the creation of the world."[36] When Mishnah Avot says "writing, the inscription, and the tablets" were created at twilight on the eve of the Sabbath of creation, there is no mention of the preexistence of the written Torah. Another source speaks of Moses ascending to heaven to receive only the tablets, which had been written and laid aside since creation.[37] Yet another source says that the *light of Torah* preceded the creation.[38]

Scripture shows no trace of the view that the Torah was written in heaven before it was given to Moses. This view is first found in the Apocrypha. The notion that the "word of the Lord" has an independent existence can be found in a few scriptural verses—"He sends forth His word to the earth, His command runs swiftly" (Psalm 147:15); "So is the word that issues from My mouth; it does not come back to Me unfulfilled" (Isaiah 55:11). These, however, attest only to the power of God in this world, but give no hint of the independent existence of the word of the Lord in the supernal world. But in the Wisdom of Solomon, we read that during the Exodus, "Thy almighty Word leapt from Thy royal throne in heaven into the midst of that doomed land like a relentless warrior" (Wisdom of Solomon 18:15).[24]

[33] Teshuvot Hageonim, Sha'arei Teshuvah 352.
[34] Discussed above, end of chapter 15.
[35] MSY, p. 154, cited in chapter 15.
[36] Midrash on Psalms 93:3.
[37] ARN A 2.
[38] *Menorat Hamaor* of Israel Al-Nakawa, III, p. 230.

---

[24] Heschel seems to be reacting to the phrase *ha-kol yakhol* in this text. Instead of understanding it as "almighty," he may be taking it as "all-encompassing"—a plausible and legitimate reading.

The Torah Is Fire

According to the Tannaim, the heavenly Torah is no mere idea or mental figment but a real existing being that has made its way from conception to actuality. It is written and exists in the same way that this world does, not as a mere idea in God's mind. We might think that this is a case of overconcretizing the supernal realm. Actually, it is a way of elevating the status of Torah and emphasizing its grandeur and majesty.

Aristobulus[25] already had a problem with the notion "voice of God." He pointed out that sounding one's voice is a physical activity, created by the pressure of forced air from the lungs against one's windpipe. Since God is without body, how can God have a voice?[39] The Tannaim faced the same problem. Since God transcends any similarity to mortals, the divine voice that Israel heard must be different from any creaturely voice. Thus, Rabbi Akiva taught, the voice of the Holy One is of *fire*. This idea was accepted by many Sages and was extended by them to suggest that not only the voice but also the tablets and even the primordial Torah consisted of fire. Thus, in Rabbi Akiva's account of the Sinai event, the people saw *words of fire* emitted from God's mouth carving themselves upon the tablets.[40]

The Torah says that the tablets which Moses received on Mount Sinai were stone tablets. But Rabbi Simeon ben Lakish taught: "The Torah that the Holy One gave to Moses was white fire incised on black fire, made of fire, carved of fire, and given forth from fire, as it says, 'From His right hand He gave them fiery law'"[26] (Deuteronomy 33:2).

The notion that the Torah consisted of fire derived from the notion that the Torah came from heaven. In the words of the Sages, the Holy One "is wholly fire, and His ministering angels are fire."[41] Rav interpreted the word *shamayim* ("heaven") as a combination of *esh* ("fire") and *mayim* ("water"). They therefore portrayed those things that descended from heaven as if they were made of fire: "an ark of fire, a table of fire, and a lampstand of fire descended from heaven. Moses saw them and copied them."[42] Moreover, when Eleazar ben Arakh expounded on the chariot before Rabban Johanan ben Zakkai, "fire descended from heaven and surrounded the trees of the field."[43]

---

[39] J. Gutmann, *Ha-sifrut ha-yehudit ha-helenistit* (Jerusalem: Mosad Bialik, 1958), pp. 192ff.
[40] MI Hahodesh 9.   [41] Midrash on Psalms 90:5.
[42] BT Menahot 29a.   [43] BT Hagigah 14b.

---

[25] Probably a Hellenistic Jew of Alexandria, second century B.C.E. See James H. Charlesworth, ed., *Old Testament Pseudepigrapha,* 2 vols. (Garden City, N.Y.: Doubleday, 1983), 2:831ff.

[26] NJV renders: "Lightning flashing at them from His right." The Hebrew *esh-dat* is unique to this passage and defies easy understanding. The midrash interprets it as a composite of two words: *esh* ("fire") and *dat* ("law"). *Dat* is a word from the Persian period and thus almost certainly does not figure in the actual meaning of Deuteronomy 33:2.

Scripture and the Sages compared many things to fire, including Israel, the scholars, sin, controversy, and temptation.[44] The fire that humans use is not the same as the fire that is the substance of the heavenly angels. And the fire of God's utterance is more exalted than the fire of the angels.[45]

The notion of fire helped the Sages conceive of the manner in which the primordial Torah could have had its existence in heaven: "How was the Torah written? In black fire on white fire, resting on the knee of the Holy and Blessed One."[27] [46]

Heavenly Tablets

The notion of heavenly writings was known among the peoples of the Near East in ancient times and had its source in the intuition of a fate that determined the course of a person's life. This intuition, which gave rise to the Babylonian belief in predestination, found expression in the notion that fate is set down in writing, that at the creation of the world everything was written in the "tablets of fate" (*tup simati*). They also believed that Marduk commissions his son Nabu to record all human deeds.[47]

Belief in fate or predestination was foreign to ancient Israelite religion, which had no place for the concept of "tablets of fate." The verses quoted earlier about a heavenly book were meant poetically.

A fundamental change came into Jewish religious thought with the apocalyptic movement. The prophetic tradition already knew of a supernal realm and of Wisdom dwelling in the secret heights. But they dared not go up to it and look behind the veil. The supernal Wisdom was "hidden from the eyes of all living, concealed from the fowl of heaven" (Job 28:21). "No eye has seen it but You, O God (Isaiah 64:3). Wisdom says, "The Lord created me at the beginning of His course, as the first of His works of old. . . . I was with Him as a confidant, a source of delight every day" (Proverbs 8:22, 30). There is only a suggestion here, no concrete description. The apocalyptic visionaries were not satisfied with suggestions. They asked, What was primordially? What and how was the Torah's mode of existence before it was given to Moses? They filled in the gaps by asserting that there are tablets in heaven, on which the whole Torah is engraved.

The existence of "tablets of heaven . . . the book of all the deeds of humanity and

[44] BT Betzah 25a; Hagigah 27a; Kiddushin 81a; Gittin 52a; Sanhedrin 64a.

[45] PR 33:10 (155a-b).

[46] Midrash on Psalms 90:12

[47] E. Schrader, *Die Keilinschriften und das Alte Testament* (Berlin: Reuther & Reichard, 1903), 400–407; B. Meissner, *Babylonien und Assyrien* (Heidelberg: C. Winter, 1920–25), 125ff.; Leo Koep, *Das himmlische Buch in Antike und Christentum: Eine religionsgeschichtliche Untersuchung zur altchristlichen Bildersprache* (Bonn: P. Hanstein, 1952).

---

[27] That is, as one would hold a book. Fire is the perfect metaphor for God—real, perceptible, incorporeal, powerful beyond human capability, directed upward, capable of both building and destroying, and so on. And only fire can hold fire.

all the children of flesh upon the earth for all the generations of the world"[48] is mentioned frequently in the noncanonical literature. The Ethiopian book of Enoch says that it is inscribed in the "tablets of heaven" that in each generation mortals will sin.[49] These words "were written and sealed above in heaven so that the angels may read them and know that which is to befall the sinners" and also the righteous.[50] According to the Book of Jubilees, the patriarch Jacob saw in a vision at night that "an angel was descending from heaven, and there were seven tablets in his hands. And he gave them to Jacob, and he read them, and he knew everything that was written in them, what would happen to him and to his sons during all the ages."[51] And in the Testament of the Twelve Sons of Jacob, Asher and Levi read in the tablets of heaven what will befall their progeny.[52]

The Book of Jubilees tells that God revealed to Moses at Sinai the subsequent events in Israel's history. The Angel of the Presence read to Moses from the tablets of heaven the record of human history since the creation.[53] Not only human history but also the mitzvot were inscribed on the tablets.[54] That is how the ancients, from Adam to Noah and from Abraham to Jacob, were able to observe the mitzvot even though they had not been revealed publicly in all their details, for they were inscribed on the tablets of heaven, and Enoch (seventh in line from Adam) passed them down to his progeny.[55]

Muhammad also speaks of a "glorious Koran, inscribed on a preserved tablet."[56] The supernal Koran is the "mother book"[57] from which fragments were transmitted to Muhammad and prior prophets by the angel Gabriel. All human deeds are recorded in it, for each person's hand writes her deeds in it. In this book are written God's wisdom and decrees, as well as everything that comes to humans through prophecy.[58]

The people of Mecca, who dismissed Muhammad's prophecy, said they would not believe in him until God would send down a book from heaven.[59] Muhammad retorted, "If We sent down to you a book inscribed on real parchment and the unbelievers touched it with their own hands, they would still say: 'This is nothing but plain magic!'"[60] Muhammad did not say that he himself saw this venerable book. According to the Koran, the "mother book" never came down to earth, but portions were revealed to Muhammad in clear and distinct Arabic by Allah's messenger. The Jewish

---

[48] 1 Enoch 81:1–2, Ethiopian version.
[49] 1 Enoch 107:1.   [50] 1 Enoch 108:7.   [51] Jubilees 32:21.
[52] Testament of Asher 7:5; Testament of Levi 8:14.
[53] Jubilees 1:29; 5:13; 6:29, 31; 16:3; 18:19; 24:33; 31:32; 49:8.
[54] See Jubilees 3:10, 31; 4:5; 15:28; 16:88; 32:10, 28; 49:8; 50:13.
[55] Jubilees 7:38ff.; Ch. Albeck, *Das Buch der Jubiläen und die Halacha* (Berlin: Ch. Albeck, 1930), nn. 5, 6, 20.
[56] Koran 85, "The Constellations" (Penguin edition).
[57] Koran 43, "Ornaments of Gold."
[58] Koran, 6, "Cattle."
[59] Koran 17, "The Night Journey."
[60] Koran 6, "Cattle."

and Christian Scriptures are also parts of the same book, those parts having been given respectively to Moses, John the Baptist, and Jesus.[61] That is why Muhammad called the Jews and Christians "People of the Book."

The Muslims believed in an eternal, divine, preexisting Koran. But this article of faith underwent significant transformation. Originally by "the primordial Word" they meant only the mother book, the heavenly Koran. Eventually they came to iden-tify the Arabic Koran with the Koran inscribed on heavenly tablets and coined the maxim: "Whatever is between the covers of the Book is the word of God." The Mutazilites opposed this view, for an eternal Koran would be co-eternal with God and would detract from God's unity. They therefore understood the "preexistence" of the Koran to imply not eternity but being created before the creation of the world.[28]

Saadia Gaon wrote about those who understood "The Lord *kanani* [acquired me; NJV: created me] at the start of His course" as referring to a preexisting Word that was uncreated, but he argued that they erred in fifteen ways.[62]

Maimonides declared that all Israel agreed that the Torah was created like all other created beings, and came into existence only when God decided to reveal it to Israel. The word that Moses heard was created *ex nihilo* that very moment by God in the same manner that the world and all other creatures were created. If Moses heard a voice, he knew that it was not truly the voice of God, but a voice that God created for the purpose of His revelation.[29] [63]

The Idea of the Preexistence of the Torah
in the Middle Ages

The medievals also wrestled with the question of a preexisting Torah. One starting point of their discussion was Moses' remark at the incident of the golden calf: "Erase me from Your book which You have written" (Exodus 32:32). To what book could Moses have been referring? The Amora R. Nahman ben Isaac[30] had said that this referred to the book of remembrance that people write with their own actions, which was really three books—for the righteous, the wicked, and the intermediate individu-als.[64] Abraham ibn Ezra said that it referred to the heavens, for all decrees are in the

---

[61] Koran 37, "The Ranks"; 19, "Mary."
[62] Saadia Gaon, *Book of Beliefs and Opinions*, I,3, II,6.
[63] Maimonides, *Guide of the Perplexed* I:65.
[64] BT Rosh Hashanah 16a.

---

[28] This is more like the Ishmaelian view given above, at the end of section entitled "Primordial Torah."

[29] Once again, Maimonides is being very Ishmaelian.

[30] Fourth-generation Amora, Babylonia.

arrays of the heavens.[31] [65] RaSHBaM and Hizkuni understood it to mean the book of life.[66]

But Rashi comments: "From Your book—from the entire Torah, so people should not read it and say, I was unable to win forgiveness for them." Did this refer to an already written Torah that was about to be given to Moses, or one still to be written? Nahmanides had difficulty with this verse and declined to opt for a preexistent Torah; instead, he interpreted it as the book of life.

As for three of the ten things created at twilight of the first Sabbath ("writing, the inscription, and the tablets"),[67] there are again different interpretations. The Geonim understood the first of these to mean the art of writing itself.[68] But Maimonides, in his commentary on the Mishnah, wrote: "'Writing' refers to the Torah written before God, in a manner we cannot comprehend (see Exodus 24:12: 'the Torah . . . which I have written'). 'The inscription' refers to the writing on the tablets."[69] [32] Rabbenu Jonah gave the same interpretation, prompting Rabbi Simeon ben Zemah Duran to respond: "This cannot be, for the Torah was created prior to the world, not on the twilight of the first Sabbath!"[70]

A late midrash asks: "On what was the primordial Torah written? On parchment? But the animals had not been created yet, so how could one use their skins for parchment? Maybe on gold or silver? But the metals had not been created, refined, or unearthed! Maybe on wooden tablets? But the trees had not yet been created! So what was it written on? It was written with black fire on white fire and wrapped around the right arm of the Holy One, as it is written: "On His right arm fiery law" (Deuteronomy 33:2).[71]

---

[65] Ibn Ezra on Exodus 32:32; see his commentary on Psalm 69:29.
[66] RaSHBaM ad loc.; see also Isaiah 4:3. Minhat Yehudah ad loc.
[67] See Mishnah Avot 5:6
[68] R. Yehudai Gaon in Otzar Hageonim, Pesahim p. 73ff.; Rabbenu Hananel on Pesahim 54a; Arukh, article ketav; Mahzor Vitri p. 541.
[69] Maimonides, commentary on Avot 5:6, Hebrew text.
[70] Rabbenu Jonah and Magen Avot, ad loc.
[71] Midrash Konen, Beit Hamidrash II p. 23.

---

[31] The majority of medieval thinkers, including Ibn Ezra, believed in astrology, that is, that the configurations of astral bodies determine human affairs. It falls short, however, of strict determinism, since the whole point of the passage is the possibility of erasures. Maimonides and a few others denied such claims.

[32] This seems to contradict the view of Maimonides cited at the end of the last section, that God created the words of the Torah in the act of transmission to Moses. Possibly Maimonides changed his mind between writing the commentary on the Mishnah (as a young man) and the Guide of the Perplexed (at the end of his career). It may also be that ketav (writing) is being taken here very figuratively, to mean a manner of recording without writing. That is part of why it cannot be comprehended.

Rabbi Abraham ibn Ezra ridiculed those Sages who took the idea of Torah's ante-dating creation by two thousand years literally. The statement that seven things[33] were created prior to the world, is of the sort we can neither dismiss as outright false-hood nor understand literally, but "the author knew its secret meaning, for the ancients' words expressed secret meanings by means of proverbs and riddles." How could historical entities such as the Temple and Israel exist prior to the world? How could the passing of two thousand years be measured prior to creation of the lumi-naries? The preexistent Torah is to be identified with Wisdom, "for wisdom is a world in itself, prior to all existing beings, and Torah is truly wisdom, for it is the source of all hidden insight."[72]

Another Sage seconded this point: "'Seven things were created prior to the world' is but a parable, as we can demonstrate. '*Prior* to the world' implies the existence of time, and 'the Temple' implies the existence of space. But if time and space exist, then the world exists! How could Rabbi Eliezer the Great[34] have said something so self-contradictory? For mark what else he says:[35] 'Before the world was created, there was only the Holy One and His Name.'"[73]

On the other hand, R. Moses Taku,[36] who vehemently rejected the approaches of Saadia and Ibn Ezra, wrote that when God came to write the Torah, He wrote the Oral Torah and the Written Torah in the same way it is written in the Humash, whether in the pre-Mosaic generations or after the Sinai revelation. He wrote in it, "The Lord descended on Mount Sinai," "The Lord called to Moses," and so on, and fashioned all its details; He meditated on it and took delight in it. It was a very thick scroll, as it says, "Its measure is longer than the earth (Job 11:9)."[74]

R. Simeon ben Zemah Duran cited the "black fire on white fire" tradition in sup-port of his view that "one must believe that every verse in the Torah, from the start of Genesis to the end of Deuteronomy, is divinely revealed. Even concerning the last eight verses, though one talmudic view says that Joshua wrote them, it is more correct to hold that Moses wrote them through his tears.[37] Even to say that Moses added some verses on his own initiative contradicts the correct view that he wrote it in the same manner as a scribe copies a new scroll from an old one."[75]

---

[72] Abraham ibn Ezra, Commentary on the Torah, Introduction, "alternate method," p. 4.

[73] *Sha'ar Hashamayim, Kerem Hemed* II p. 7, citing PRE 3; see also Rawidowicz edition of R. Nahman Krochmal's works, p. 400.

[74] Ketav Tamim, Otzar Nehmad III, p. 83.

[75] Magen Avot, Leghorn 5545, 29b.

---

[33] As we have seen, this number varies from text to text.

[34] That is, Rabbi Eliezer ben Hyrcanus. This statement is predicated on his being the author of PRE.

[35] What follows comes from PRE 3. And just a few lines later comes the contradictory "seven things . . . ," which includes the Torah!

[36] Thirteenth-century Tosafist and polemicist.

[37] Or, "with his tears," as if the tears served as ink.

A German scholar subsequent to Rashi wrote: "The form of the letters was created during the six days of creation. The primordial Torah two thousand years earlier lacked the form of the letters, but existed in oral form only."[76]

Rabbi Judah ben Barzilai of Barcelona[38] dealt with this problem as follows:

It is not clear to us how the Torah could be created prior to the existence of the world. Any created thing requires space to be present, so if space had not been created, where would the Torah be? Even though God, the Omnipresent, who is called Makom ("place")—for He is the Place of all creatures—could be the place for the Torah, it would seem He would have created a place for the Torah before He created the world. It is also unclear to us how the Torah was created: as a form without matter, or a form with matter even more delicate than the matter of spirits, and similar to them? Many commentators say that the primordial Torah was created only in thought, not actually, out of God's love for those who would someday study, receive, and observe it. For our part, we say the original statement was only offered as a parable and simile.[77]

Rabbi Solomon ben Adret (RaSHBA) took the same position:

When they said the Torah was created prior to the world, they meant that God knew in advance that He would someday give the Torah. If it were to mean that it was written in fire, is not fire a material substance that requires space, and space did not yet exist! Rather, it was present in God's thought, for God created the world for the purpose of the acceptance of the Torah. Black fire and white fire are metaphors for punishment and reward. But if you insist it was actually written, there is no question how it could exist, for God Who is the place for the world and prepared space for the celestial spheres and the earth, somehow provided a place for it before the heavens existed, but we will never fathom His wisdom until He reveals it.[78]

RaSHBA's pupil, R. Joshua ibn Shu'ib, noted that the statement concerning the primordial Torah must be taken allegorically, because "prior to creation, there were no days and years, nor any black and white fire."[79]

Rabbenu Nissim said the seven mentioned things were conceived in thought prior to creation, "for the world would be impossible without them."[80]

Rabbi Jacob ibn Habib said it is clearly obvious that the Torah and other items could not have been actually created prior to the world, for this would contradict the fundamental belief that the Holy One created the world out of absolute nothingness, so how could the Garden of Eden, Gehenna, and the Temple be present? Rather (fol-

---

[76] Commentary on Avot 5:6, attributed to Rashi.
[77] R. Judah ben Barzilai, commentary to *Sefer Hayetzirah* (Berlin, 5645), pp. 88–89.
[78] J. Perles, R. Salomo b. Abraham b. Adereth (Breslau, 1863), Hebrew portion pp. 48–49.
[79] R. Joshua ibn Shuaib, sermon for Shavuot.
[80] Rabbenu Nissim on BT Nedarim 39b.

---

[38] Spain, eleventh to twelfth centuries.

lowing RaSHBA), these refer to the purpose God had in mind when creating the world.[39] 81

Rabbi Joseph Albo extended this argument further. Torah preceded the world in the sense that it was the purpose for which the human race was created, and the purpose (in Aristotelian terms: "final cause") is necessarily prior to the other causes.[82]

R. Ezra, friend of R. Azriel, said the statement concerning the primordial Torah referred to the supernal Torah, from which the written Torah emanated.[83] According to the Zohar, "Torah emanated from the supernal Wisdom";[84] "Torah is located in the supernal Wisdom and is sustained by it, and plants its roots in it in every direction."[85]

R. Isaac Abravanel thought that Torah was like a picture drawn in the supernal Wisdom and that Moses' words were a copy of that divine drawing.[86]

---

[81] Ein Ya'akov, introduction and on Nedarim 29b.

[82] Joseph Albo, *Ikkarim* [Principles (of Faith)] 3:12.

[83] Gershom Scholem, "A New Document Concerning the History of Early Kabbalah" (in Hebrew) in *Sefer Bialik* [Literary and Scholarly Pieces in Honor of Hayyim Nahman Bialik] (Tel Aviv, 1934), section III (articles), p. 159.

[84] Zohar Yitro 85a.

[85] Zohar Kedoshim 81a.

[86] Abravanel, *Mif'alot Elohim* [The Works of God] 1:1. See Moses Isserles, *Torat Ha'olah* [The Law of the Burnt Offering] a philosophical-mystical-allegorical commentary on the Tabernacle ritual, 3:7.

---

[39] This, of course, is now taking for granted the doctrine of *creatio ex nihilo*. But although this is a ubiquitous concept in the Middle Ages, it is not primarily an ancient doctrine. See Jon Levenson, *Creation and the Persistence of Evil: The Jewish Drama of Divine Omnipotence* (San Francisco: Harper & Row, 1988).

18

MOSES' ASCENT TO HEAVEN

Translator's Introduction

In the previous chapter, Heschel began his analysis of the theological doctrine of "Torah from Heaven" by describing a notion that existed in some quarters that there were books in heaven that existed quite independently of any human readership. Such was the case, according to some Jewish Sages, with the Torah itself, for perhaps thousands of years before the freed Israelites reached Mount Sinai. In this chapter, Heschel will conjoin to this idea another one, namely, the idea that Moses at Mount Sinai not only ascended the terrestrial mountain but actually ascended all the way into heaven. This notion is also well attested among some ancient rabbinic Sages. Heschel will now make the contention that it was the conjunction of these two ideas—the human ascent into heaven and the existence of a completed book of the Torah in heaven—that created the doctrine that the entire Torah was brought down to earth, word for word, by Moses. It was this, he suggests that ensured that the otherwise metaphoric idea of *Torah min Hashamayim* took on for some a more literal meaning, that is, that the Torah actually descended intact from heaven.

As intellectual history, it is not possible here to evaluate this claim of Heschel's. Perhaps the dogma of the descent of the biblical text actually developed in this way, or perhaps in some other way. But conceptually it does provide a good analysis of what is substantively contained in the dogma; for it does assume at least a momentary direct connection between earth and heaven and that the Torah existed in toto prior to the Sinai revelation.

Heschel's reading of the sources also reveals that the idea of an ascent into heaven from which one returns is not only not biblical (Enoch and Elijah ascended but did not return to earth) but also does not appear before the early second century, the age of Rabbi Akiva. Moreover, there were strenuous opponents of this interpretation of Moses' encounter at Sinai when it did appear on the Jewish scene. And with good reason, for a safe ascent to heaven, it would seem, could be successfully accomplished only by someone who is, at least in part, of heaven. Thus it is that the idea of the ascent of a human to heaven brings close on its heels the idea of a descent to earth of a heavenly being. The latter, of course, is *the* central tenet of Christianity. This is not the first time we have seen parallels between Akivan ideas in the second century and roughly contemporaneous ideas characteristic of early Christians (and especially Jewish Christians).

Nor is this the first (or the last) time we see controversy over Akivan views being raised and energized by that very parallelism.

———————

Rabbi Akiva's View: Moses Was in Heaven

A FUNDAMENTAL CHANGE took place in the meaning of the phrase *Torah min Hashamayim* (Torah from Heaven). Instead of signifying the Torah (i.e., teaching) that Moses heard from the Heavenly One, it came to mean the Torah (i.e., document) that Moses brought down from heaven.[1] This shift in meaning was based on the belief that Moses actually ascended into heaven—a belief voiced by Rabbi Akiva, but opposed by other Sages.

Though the belief in Moses' ascent had some currency in Israel, it did not bring about a transformation in the doctrine of "Torah from Heaven" until Rabbi Akiva added an additional element: Moses ascended to heaven, *and brought down the Torah from there.* In short, the expanded notion of *Torah min Hashamayim* is the synthesis of two prior doctrines: the preexisting heavenly Torah and Moses' ascent to heaven. It was Rabbi Akiva who stated explicitly: When Moses spoke the words of Torah, he was in heaven.

We read in Scripture the peroration of Moses: "Give ear, O heavens, let me speak; let the earth hear the words I utter" (Deuteronomy 32:1). The prophet Isaiah said similarly, "Hear, O heavens, and give ear, O earth" (Isaiah 1:2). The Sages were astonished: Why did Isaiah see fit to employ the same imagery as Moses? Some drew the conclusion: this teaches us that the words of all the prophets are of equal importance.[1] This view is rare in rabbinic literature. Other Sages read in the subtle differences of language a reflection of their different status: "Moses was very close to heaven; therefore he used the expression, 'Give ear, O heaven.' Since he was distant from earth, he said, 'let the earth hear.' Isaiah, who was distant from heaven and close to earth, reversed the phrases and said, 'Hear, O heavens and give ear, O earth.'"[2] [2] What did the midrash have in mind when it said, "Moses was very close to heaven"? Was it not trying to portray Moses as though he were standing in heaven?[3]

---

[1] TB Ha'azinu 2, p. 51.   [2] Sifre Ha'azinu 306.
[3] See Midrash Lekah Tov, Ha'azinu 54b, also 53b.

———

[1] Heschel pointed out in chapter 3 the ambiguity of *hashamayim* (as meaning either "heaven" or "the Heavenly One [God]"). He reserves his discussion of the multiple meanings of "Torah" for chapter 20 below.

[2] According to this interpretation, the word *ha'azinu* ("give ear") is used when one is close; *shim'u* ("hear") is used when far away.

Though this midrash was terse on the last point, Rabbi Akiva was more expansive: "'Give ear, O heaven . . .'—This tells us that Moses was in heaven when he spoke those words. He spoke as naturally to the heavens as he would with an earthly friend. He saw the earth farther away, so he said, 'let the earth hear.' Isaiah, however, who spoke to the people Israel on earth, said, 'Hear, O heavens' (for they were distant from him), and then addressed the earth (which was close to him) with the words, 'Give ear, O earth.'"[4]

Rabbi Samuel bar Nahman gave this homily in the spirit of Rabbi Akiva: "Why did Moses address both heaven and earth? This may be compared to a general who served two provinces, Persia and Colonia.[3] He arranged for a public feast and said to himself, 'If I invite one, the other will be angry.' What did he do? He invited both. So Moses, a child of earth, but whose stature grew in heaven (as it is written: 'Moses remained in heaven forty days and forty nights,' Exodus 24:18), said to himself, 'If I address the heavens, earth will be angry; if I address earth, the heavens will be angry.' He therefore concluded, 'I will address them both, the heavens and the earth.'"[5]

Moses Ascended to Heaven

In the Torah we find no explicit statement that Moses ascended to heaven. On the verse "And Moses went up to God"[4] (Exodus 19:3), the Aramaic translation by Onkelos renders, "Moses went up before God." The Jerusalem Targum renders, "Moses went up to receive instruction from the Presence," and the Targum attributed to Jonathan ben Uzziel states, "Moses went up to the top of the mountain." Similarly, the Septuagint reads, "Moses ascended the mountain of God."

Moses himself says, "I had ascended *the mountain* to receive the tablets of stone . . . and I stayed *on the mountain*" (Deuteronomy 9:9). Mark well that Scripture often speaks figuratively of heavenly ascent: "If I ascend to heaven, You are there" (Psalm 139:8); "If they ascend to heaven, from there I will bring them down" (Amos 9:2). The patriarch Jacob sees in his dream "a ladder set on the ground and its top reaching the heavens," but only "the angels of God were going up and down on it" (Genesis 28:12).

---

[4] TB Ha'azinu 2.   [5] Deuteronomy Rabbah 10.

---

[3] Jastrow renders: "One a Roman province, and the other a colony."

[4] "And Moses went up to God"—The language of this crucial verse is vague. Its exact meaning depends on where the reader conceives of God as being at the time. It could have meant, "Moses ascended the mountain, *toward God*" (who was either at the top of the mountain or in heaven looking down at the mountaintop). Or it could be taken to mean that God was in heaven and that Moses ascended *to heaven*. All the Aramaic translations that Heschel will cite undercut the second possibility, by stressing that Moses only ascended the mountain, *before (i.e., in the presence of)* God, not *to* God. Apparently, these translators were either unfamiliar with the notion of Moses' ascent to heaven, or they purposely rejected it.

The Sabbath prayers, too, speak of "when Moses stood before You *on Mount Sinai,* then brought down the two stone tablets."[6] Likewise, an early Mishnah says, "Moses received Torah at Sinai," not "from Heaven." Avot de-Rabbi Nathan elaborates: "Moses was sanctified in the cloud and received the Torah from Sinai."[7] Other traditions agree: "On the seventh day after the Ten Commandments, Moses ascended the mountain." "Ben Bathyra[5] said: Moses was occupied on Mount Sinai for forty days."[8]

We find evidence in the Book of Proverbs that in biblical times the people did not think that Moses had ascended to heaven: "Who has ascended heaven and come down?" (Proverbs 30:4). Abraham ibn Ezra comments: "That is to say, there is no person who has the power to ascend the heights of heaven and to descend to earth." However, in the Amoraic period the question in this verse was read not rhetorically but, in all seriousness, as requiring an answer: "Who has ascended heaven? Elijah . . . Or Moses, as it is written: 'Moses went up to God (Exodus 19:3) . . . and Moses came down (19:14)."[9] Indeed, the verse "Moses went up to God" is reticent and suggestive. "The wise know God's hints and God's meaning."[10] But the apocalyptic visionaries were not content with mere hints and declared forthrightly: Moses ascended to heaven.

Moses was not the only one of whom it was said that he went up to heaven. One of the most important motifs in apocalyptic literature is that a few chosen individuals are deemed worthy to ascend to heaven in their lifetime. Scripture speaks of Enoch as follows, "Enoch walked with God; then he was no more, for God took him" (Genesis 5:24). Of Elijah it is written, "When the Lord was about to take Elijah up to heaven . . ." (2 Kings 2:1). But Moses' ascent to heaven was more significant than that of Enoch or Elijah. The latter two ascended to heaven but did not return; they went up at the end of their days on earth and never knew the taste of death. Moses both ascended and descended. However, we do find tales about some chosen few who went up to heaven for a brief stay and then returned. In a late source we find a midrash that tells that God brought Adam to the heights of heaven to rejoice in the joy of Sabbath observance.[11]

In the apocalyptic books, we are told that Abraham, in his deep sleep, was transported to the highest firmament,[12] and that Enoch was shown all the mysteries of

---

[6] Authorized Daily Prayer Book (by Dr. Joseph H. Hertz, New York: Bloch, 1948), 457. This is in the spirit of the verse: "Moses went down from the mountain bearing the two tablets of the Pact" (Exodus 32:15). There is no mention here that Moses brought the tablets down from heaven.

[7] Avot 1:1; ARN A 1.

[8] Jubilees 4:26; PRE 46; PT Ta'anit 4:8 (68b).

[9] PRK 1:4 (5b); Midrash on Proverbs ad loc., p. 104.

[10] Genesis Rabbah 12:1.

[11] *Seder Rabbah Dibereshit* 1:15, collected in *Batei Midrashot* I,27.

[12] G. Nathanael Bontwetsch, *Die Apokalypse Abrahams* (Leipzig, 1897), 2:5, pp. 27ff.

---

[5] Either Joshua ben Bathyra or Judah ben Bathyra II, both third-generation Tannaim.

heaven by the angel Michael, and then returned to earth. After he had instructed his children how to conduct themselves, he returned once more to the upper world of eternal life.[13] In various rabbinic *aggadot* we are told that Moses ascended to heaven four times: (1) God revealed Himself to him at Horeb.[6] (2) He ascended to receive the Torah. (3) When the day of his death was approaching, Moses was brought to heaven, where he was shown what his reward would be and what the future held in store, following which he descended from heaven in joy.[14] (4) Moses did not actually die but ascended to heaven where he continues to serve.[15] Fragments of the lost apocalyptic book Assumption of Moses indicate that this book portrayed the fourth version of Moses' ascent: Moses did not die but ascended to heaven and stands there alongside Joshua and Caleb.[7] [16]

"You Ascended to Heaven, You Took Spoils"

Many distinguished Sages shared the belief that Moses ascended to heaven.[17] They found an allusion to this event in the verses "You ascended the heights, you took spoils" (Psalm 68:19)[8] and "Moses went up to God"[18] (Exodus 19:3). They gave

[13] 1 Enoch (Ethiopian) 71:3. See also 2 Enoch (Slavonic) 13:113. Testament of Levi 2:7-9; 5:1 is reminiscent of Isaiah's vision in chapter 6. The Ascension of Isaiah tells how the prophet ascended the seven heavens and saw Abel and Enoch in the third heaven, also God, and then returned to earth. Apocalypse of Baruch has a similar account of ascent and return.

[14] Manuscript *aggadah* of Moses' death, cited in *Beit Hamidrash* VI, xxii.

[15] BT Sotah 13b; Midrash Haggadol Genesis 5:24.

[16] See R. H. Charles, *The Assumption of Moses* (London, 1897), xiv, 105ff.

[17] These Sages included Rabbi Judah ben Ilay (Exodus Rabbah 42:4); Rabbi Meir (Genesis Rabbah 45:14); and Simeon ben Halafta (Tanhuma, ed. Buber, Vayetzei 7). Rabbi Joshua ben Levi told of the debate between the angels and Moses about whether mankind was worthy to receive the Torah (BT Shabbat 88b). Rav told of Moses inquiring why God was decorating the letters of the Torah with crowns, and being told by God that Rabbi Akiva would turn them to exegetical use (BT Menahot 29b). See also Rabbi Simeon ben Lakish (Exodus 41:5, PR 48:3 [194a]; Tanhuma, ed. Buber, Tissa 12), R. Isaac Nappaha (Midrash on Psalms 18:13, Exodus Rabbah 42:4), R. Abbahu (Tanhuma Buber, Tissa 12), R. Tanhum bar Hanilai (BT Baba Metzi'a 86b), R. Samuel bar Nahmani (Midrash on Psalms 7:6), R. Hiyya bar Abba (Deuteronomy Rabbah 3:11), R. Berechiah (Song of Songs Rabbah 1:55), R. Phinehas (PR 47:4 [191b]), and R. Tanhuma (PR 4:2 [13a]). According to R. Samuel bar Nahman, "Moses originated from the earth but grew up in heaven" (Deuteronomy Rabbah 10:4).

[18] PR 5:3 (15b); PRK 1:4 (5b); BT Sukkah 18a; Ecclesiastes Rabbah 9:12; TB Vayyetzei 7.

[6] That is, from the burning bush.

[7] Heschel does not spell out the implication, but we may infer: even though certain books were excluded from the canon, their ideas persisted underground and found their way into the rabbinic lore. The two crucial Akivan elements in the doctrine of *Torah min Hashamayim* were the existence of a heavenly original of the Torah and Moses' ascent to heaven. Heschel traces both of these elements to apocalyptic influence. Every parallel that Heschel draws between apocalyptic ideas and rabbinic ideas strengthens this connection.

[8] NJV reverses the order of events: "You ascended the heights, having taken captives." According to the rabbinic interpretation, this verse referred to Moses' ascending to heaven and bringing down

similar interpretations to other verses: "One wise man prevailed over a city of warriors, and brought down its mighty stronghold" (Proverbs 21:22);[19] "Gird your sword upon your thigh, O hero; in your glory, win success, and ride on" (Psalm 45:4-5);[20] "Who may ascend the mountain of the Lord? Who may stand in His holy place?" (Psalm 24:3)—obviously, Moses, who ascended to heaven.[9] [21]

There are many *aggadot* connected with the belief in Moses' ascent to heaven to receive the Torah. One of them tells of Moses entering the cloud, which transported him to heaven. On arriving there, he encountered the angel Kemuel, chief of the twelve thousand angels of destruction, who dwelt in the gate of the firmament. He addressed Moses with great anger: "What are you doing in these sacred precincts? You who come from a place of filth dare to enter these pure surroundings? One born of woman presumes to walk in this place of sacred fire!?"[10] Moses replied, "I am the son of Amram, and I have come to receive the Torah on behalf of the people Israel." But Kemuel would not let him enter the gate, whereupon Moses struck him and with one blow destroyed him utterly.[11] [22]

When he entered through the gate into heaven, he found himself amidst angels, celestial beasts, and seraphim (of whom one alone could incinerate the whole world).[12] [23] But the Holy and Blessed One had forbidden any angel or seraph to come anywhere near him.[24] However, according to Rabbi Judah ben Ilai, when Moses was ready to descend with the Torah, the angels sought to kill him. What did he do? He grasped the heavenly throne and the Holy One spread His mantle over him to protect him. He wrestled with them—that is, he debated with them whether Israel was worthy to receive the Torah, and he prevailed.[25]

Sadly, he descended precisely at the time when the people fashioned the golden calf. How did that happen? Before he left them to ascend to heaven, Moses assured the people that in forty days he would bring them the Torah. After six hours of the fortieth day had elapsed and he had not come, the people demanded that Aaron make

---

[19] Midrash on Proverbs 21:22; PR 20:4 (96b-98a).   [20] Midrash on Psalms, ad loc.
[21] Mahzor Vitri, p. 323.   [22] PR 20:4 (96b).   [23] Sifre Ha'azinu 306.
[24] *Midrash of the 32 Attributes,* ed. Enelow, p. 150.
[25] Exodus Rabbah 42:4, 28:1; PR 10:6 (37a); TB Ki Tissa 13.

---

the Torah as a gift to Israel. The "spoils" would have referred, presumably, to a war with the angels. See the sequel.

[9] The midrashim on these verses equate the poetic figures with the story of Moses' ascent as follows: The "city of warriors" is the angelic entourage in heaven; the "mighty stronghold" is the Torah. The "wise man" and "hero" are Moses; the "sword" is Torah; "ride on" alludes to Moses' riding above the clouds. "His holy place" also refers to heaven.

[10] A play on the words *ishah* ("woman"), *esh* ("fire").

[11] It is striking that these motifs reflect a view that somehow revelation required violence. Creation had chaos to deal with. Redemption will, by tradition, have its chaotic and violent prelude. And even Revelation, according to the views brought here, is not free of violence.

[12] "Seraphim" comes from the root *srf,* which means "to burn."

them a god (Exodus 32:1). This was the opportune time for Satan to mislead the people, for precisely at that time Moses appeared suspended between heaven and earth. Pointing their finger at him, the people cried, "This man Moses who brought us out of Egypt, what has happened to him?"[13] 26

Moses was known by ten names. One of them, mentioned first, is Jared.[14] He was given this name because he brought down the Torah from heaven to earth. Another explanation is, because he brought down the Shekhinah from heaven to earth.[15] 27 Jared was the father of Enoch, and according to the Book of Jubilees (4:17–18), he was called Jared[16] because in his time the angels of God descended to earth to instruct human beings how to live justly and righteously with each other on earth.[17]

The Ascent of Enoch

The theme of human ascent to heaven is of great importance in the study of religion, but Judaism demands that humans should know their place. Israel lives by the rule: "God is in heaven, and you are on earth" (Ecclesiastes 5:1). There is a vast distance between heaven and earth, as there is an infinite difference between God and humans. Isaiah derided the king of Babylon for his conceit that he would ascend to heaven (Isaiah 14:13). As we have said, there is no mention in Scripture of Moses having ascended to heaven. The belief in Moses' ascent grew out of the legends that dealt with Enoch's ascent to heaven. These legends, which served as background for the apocalyptic literature, gradually entered the corpus of stories about Moses.

Indeed, the belief in the human ascent to heaven, body and soul, became a cornerstone of the emerging Christian theology. Still, in the second century, many Jewish Sages were unalterably opposed to this doctrine. Nevertheless, the idea was widespread in many circles during the Hellenistic age that after one's death, the human soul ascended to heaven. Closely allied to this doctrine was the belief that the souls of certain privileged individuals ascended to heaven during their lifetimes.28

---

26 Exodus Rabbah 41:7.   27 Leviticus Rabbah 1:3.
28 See W. Bousset, "Die Himmelsreise der Seele," *Archiv für Religionswissenschaft* 4 (1901): 13ff.; see

---

[13] This harks back to the Akivan view of the word *zeh* ("this"). When the people spoke of "This man Moses," they were pointing at his image.

[14] In Hebrew, the root *yrd* (= Jared) means "descend" or, in the causative form, "bring down."

[15] The bringing down of the Shekhinah refers to Moses' having erected the Tabernacle, which became God's dwelling place. See PRK 1.

[16] The epithet "Jared" given to Moses brings to mind the original Jared, the sixth-generation descendant of Adam (Genesis 5:18–20). His son Enoch did not die a normal death but is supposed to have undergone translation to heaven—one of the prototypes of the "ascent to heaven" and therefore fittingly the subject of the next section.

[17] But it didn't work, for the flood had to come three generations later because of rampant corruption. Thus, a "second Jared" was needed, who brought not angels but Torah to civilize human beings.

There were many legends current in Israel that some of the greatest of the early saints never tasted death or burial but were translated to the heavens while they were still alive. Among those were Moses, Enoch, and Elijah. In apocalyptic circles Enoch was very much prized, for, like Elijah, he served as an intermediary between heaven and earth.

The revelation of God's spirit took various forms. In the case of Moses, it was a direct communication "from mouth to mouth." In the case of the last prophets, Zechariah and Daniel, it was through an angel. With the end of prophecy, this kind of divine revelation ended, and in its place we have the revelations of Enoch and Elijah.[18] As "Angel of the Presence," Enoch became guide and interpreter to the apocalyptic visionaries and mystics of the chariot; Elijah served primarily as teacher and revealer of secrets to the Sages of the Talmud.

Neither Elijah nor Enoch experienced death and burial; they bridged the gap between this world and the next. Beloved in life and unseparated in death,[19] they continued to extract heaven's secrets and transmit them to those who hungered for heavenly visions. With regard to Elijah we are told that he was taken up "by a whirlwind into heaven" (2 Kings 2:1). As for Enoch, the scriptural account of his departure can be taken two ways. In his case Scripture seems to conceal more than it reveals. The verse reads, "Enoch walked with God, then he was no more, for God took him." The phrase, "he was no more" is a lovely euphemism for a person's departing from the world, rather than the harshness of the term "death."[29] However, it is also reminiscent of Elijah's ascent to heaven (2 Kings 2:3ff.), and of Utnapishtim in the Gilgamesh Epic (II,196).[30]

Scripture seems to present Enoch's translation as a mark of honor. That is how it was understood by most of the ancients,[31] including several of the midrashic

also the articles cited by H. Schrade in *Zur Ikonographie der Himmelfahrt Christi,* Vorträge der Bibliothek Warburg (Berlin, 1933), 97 n. 1; and Robert M. Grant, *Miracle and Natural Law in Graeco-Roman and Early Christian Thought* (Amsterdam: North Holland, 1952), 179ff.

[29] Compare Psalms 39:34; 103:16; Proverbs 12:7; Job 7:21; 8:22.

[30] On Genesis 5:22, see U. Cassuto, *Me-Adam ad Noah* [From Adam to Noah] (in Hebrew) 1st ed. (Jerusalem, 1944), 164ff.; 2nd ed. (1953), 195ff.; Alexander Heidel, *The Gilgamesh Epic and Ten Old Testament Parallels* (Chicago: University of Chicago Press, 1946).

[31] Ecclesiasticus 44:16, 19; 49:20 (see note of M. D. Segal, p. 307); Jubilees 4:22; Wisdom of Solomon 4:10–11; Josephus, *Antiquities* 1:3.

---

[18] That is, revelations in which Enoch and Elijah would appear to human beings.

[19] Allusion to 2 Samuel 1:23 (David's lament over Saul and Jonathan). This phrase is also used in the martyrology to refer to the saints of Jewish history. Heschel transforms the meaning of the phrase: Elijah and Enoch were not separated from mortal humanity by death, *because they did not die.* Or, more pointedly, they were not separated into body and soul, with only the latter continuing to live. In their cases, both body and soul lived on.

authors,[32] and later by the kabbalists:[33] "Enoch was of the privileged few who entered Paradise in their lives."[34] "Enoch is the archangel Metatron."[35]

However, a dissenting view was expressed by the Alexandrian philosopher Philo, in his exegesis of the verse "and He took him." He interprets this to mean that Enoch had led a dissolute life and that, in the end, God took him and turned him around; that is, he repented of his sinful life and became righteous. According to this interpretation, Enoch died a natural death.[36]

When the Sages engaged in debate with the early Christians, they found it necessary to refute one of their major dogmas by insisting that Enoch was a repentant sinner who did not ascend to heaven. The Christians formulated two basic articles of faith: (1) God or the Logos descended from heaven, took on flesh, and became human; (2) Jesus rose from the dead and ascended to heaven. The second dogma served as a basis for and as proof of the first. As John put it, "No one ever ascended to heaven except the one who came down from heaven" (John 3:13). Rabbi Abbahu, who lived in Caesarea in the third century and frequently debated with the Christian sectarians, said about these dogmas, "If one tells you, 'I am God,' he is a deceiver; 'I am the Son of Man'—he will live to regret it; 'I shall ascend heaven'—he says it but will not fulfill it."[20] [37]

The disciples of Jesus regarded the ascent of Enoch to heaven in his lifetime as of supreme importance. Perhaps for this reason the Sages of Israel insisted that Enoch died a natural death. The debate reached such intensity that Rabbi Hamah bar Hoshiyah, who lived in the third century, declared, "Enoch is not listed in the rolls of the righteous but rather in the rolls of the wicked. . . . Rabbi Aibu said that Enoch was a hypocrite, sometimes righteous, sometimes wicked. Said the Holy and Blessed One, 'I will remove him from this earth while he is still righteous.'"[38] The derogation of Enoch's importance was no trivial matter and was the subject of serious discussion by Rabbi Akiva and his colleagues. But though it is not explicitly stated, we may safely

[32] PRK 23:10 (155a); Leviticus Rabbah 29:11; *Genizah Studies in Memory of Dr. Solomon Schechter*, ed. Louis Ginzberg and Israel Davidson, 3 vols. (New York: Jewish Theological Seminary, 1928–29), 1:103.

[33] Zohar, Genesis 56b; Letters of Rabbi Akiva, *Beit Hamidrash* II,114.

[34] DEZ 1:9 (English 1:18); YS on Ezekiel 367. See J. Theodor and Ch. Albeck's note on Genesis Rabbah 25:1 (*Midrash Bereshit Rabbah* [in Hebrew] [Jerusalem: Wahrmann Books, 1965]).

[35] Targum of pseudo-Jonathan on Genesis 5:24; BT Hullin 60a (Tosafot s.v. *pasuk ze*); Louis Ginzberg *Legends of the Jews*, 7 vols. (Philadelphia: Jewish Publication Society, 1909–38), 5:157.

[36] Philo, *De Abrahamo* 3; *De Premus* 3. Elsewhere, however, Philo seems to favor the opinion that Enoch did not die. See *Quaestiones et solutiones in Genesin* 86.

[37] PT Ta'anit 2:1 (65b), playing on Numbers 23:19: "Will he say it . . . and not fulfill it?"

[38] Genesis Rabbah 25:1. The kabbalists who revered Enoch as a saint took strong exception to these words of Rabbi Hamah bar Hoshaya. See *Ma'amar Hanefesh* of Rabbi Menahem Azariah of Fano, 5:12.

[20] See also YS 766 (uncensored version).

assume, on the basis of Rabbi Akiva's theological views, that he believed in Enoch's ascent to heaven.[21] 39

Moses Did Not Ascend to Heaven

There is compelling evidence that not just Enoch's ascent but also Moses' was a matter of contention among the Sages. This notion, born in the worldview of apocalyptic, was attractive to the visionaries but a thicket of difficulties to the rationalists. Rabbi Yose opposed it vehemently.[22] He set hard and fast boundaries between exalted divinity and unworthy humankind. We learn the thrust of his thought from the polemics he directed against both central Christian dogmas: the ascent of mortals to heaven and the descent of the divine Glory (or Logos) to earth.

This opposition will explain his famous saying, which many struggled so long to understand: "'The heavens belong to the Lord, but the earth He gave over to man' (Psalm 115:16)—Moses and Elijah did not ascend to heaven, nor did the Glory descend to earth. Rather, the Holy and Blessed One said, 'Moses, I now call to you from the top of the mountain, and you will come up,' as it says, 'The Lord called Moses'" (Exodus 19:20).40 The same ambiguous verse, "Moses went up to God," on which were based the *aggadot* of Moses ascending to heaven, Rabbi Yose took in the plain sense: Moses climbed the mountain. He even compared it to the "ascent" of Ezra from Babylonia to Israel.41

Rabbi Yose often spoke up to reinstate correct opinions in the face of erroneous opposing views. He once contradicted Rabbi Akiva thus in a legal context: "So indeed did Rabbi Akiva teach, but the original teaching was otherwise."42 Here, too, Rabbi Yose sought to preserve an original teaching against Rabbi Akiva's innovations. For if

---

39 See Midrash Aggadah, ed. Buber, p. 15, and Theodor's note on Genesis Rabbah 25:1: "Since Enoch was righteous, the Holy One took him from mortals and made him an angel, who is Metatron, and this is a matter of dispute between Rabbi Akiva and his colleagues."

40 MI Bahodesh 4. The Babylonian Talmud states even more emphatically: "The Shekhinah *never* descended to earth, nor did Moses or Elijah ascend to heaven" (BT Sukkah 5a; see also MSY, p. 145).

41 "Rabbi Yose said, 'Ezra was worthy of having the Torah given through him, had not Moses preceded him.' 'Ascent' is mentioned of both: 'Moses went up to God' . . . 'Ezra came up from Babylon'" (Ezra 7:6). Tosefta Sanhedrin 4:5; BT Sanhedrin 21b.

42 Mishnah Sanhedrin 3:4.

---

[21] Thus, Enoch was, for Christians, a paradigm of ascent to heaven, just as Isaac was the paradigm for the sacrifice of the beloved son. Perhaps it is for this reason that, just as Enoch was derogated by some of the Rabbis, the binding of Isaac was generally associated by the Rabbis with Rosh Hashanah rather than with Passover. On the paradigmatics of the binding of Isaac, see Jon Levenson, *The Death and Resurrection of the Beloved Son: The Transformation of Child Sacrifice in Judaism and Christianity* (New Haven: Yale University Press, 1993).

[22] *Shada bei narga*, "swung an axe at it"—a talmudic image of energetically knocking down an opposing view, something like the contemporary English "shot it down."

the belief in the ascent of Moses had been standard among the people, it is doubtful that Rabbi Yose would have opposed it.

How Could a Person Ascend to Heaven?

The idea of Moses' ascent is not mentioned by the Tannaim prior to Rabbi Akiva. We have seen that Rabbi Yose ben Halafta opposed it. There is evidence that the school of Rabbi Ishmael was opposed to the very idea that mortals could ascend to heaven. Earlier we noted Rabbi Ishmael's hesitancy to take the notion of "cleaving to God" literally: "How is it possible for mortals to rise heavenward and cleave to fire?"[23] This midrash continues: "Rather, cleave to the Sages and scholars, and I will count it in your favor *as if you had stormed heaven and taken it by force,* as it says, 'You ascended to heaven, you took spoils'"[43] (Psalm 68:19). Note how this key proof text for the view of Moses' ascent is here taken figuratively: "as if you had stormed heaven."

Many of the rabbinic tales surrounding the Sinai event come to us in two versions, dividing on this issue. Rabbi Samuel bar Nahmani says that when Israel made the golden calf, Moses did not leave a spot *in heaven* that he did not batter [in his rage].[44] Rabbi Joshua said that he did not leave a spot *on the turf of the mountain* unbattered.[45] Some say that Moses composed Psalm 91 when he ascended to heaven;[46] others that he did so on the mountain.[47]

The Amoraim were similarly divided on whether Abraham ascended to heaven. "God brought Abraham outside, and said, 'Look at the heavens'" (Genesis 15:5). Rabbi Joshua of Sikhnin[24] said in the name of Rabbi Levi, "Do you think this means God brought Abraham outside of the world? No! He simply showed him the outer reaches of the heavens." But Rabbi Johanan said, "He lifted him above the dome of the firmament and instructed him to look down on it from above."[48]

There were medieval Sages, too, who refused to accept that Moses ascended to heaven. On the verse "Moses went up to God," the Midrash Lekah Tov[25] interprets: "This means, to the spot on the mountain where the Shekhinah was present." R. Abraham ibn Ezra explains: "Moses did not ascend any higher than the top of the mountain, for that is where God spoke to him."[49] Maimonides wrote in his *Guide:* "Moses ascended to that spot of the mountain to which the created light [symbolizing God's presence] descended. One should not think that God has a location to

---

[43] Sifre Ekev 49.   [44] Midrash on Psalms, ed. Buber, note 36 on Psalm 7.
[45] Ecclesiastes Rabbah 4:3.   [46] Midrash on Psalms 91:1.   [47] TB Naso 27.
[48] Genesis Rabbah 44:12.
[49] See Midrash Lekah Tov and Abraham ibn Ezra's Commentary on Exodus 19:3.

---

[23] See above, chapter 10.
[24] Fourth-generation Amora of the Land of Israel.
[25] A late eleventh-century midrash on the Torah and Five Scrolls by Tobias ben Eliezer (who lived in the Balkans).

which one ascends to Him or from which one then descends. May God be infinitely exalted above such foolish imaginings!"[50] Nahmanides and R. Joseph Bonfils also held that Moses only ascended to the top of the mountain.[51]

On the other hand, R. Yehudai Gaon exclaimed, "See how great Moses was, that he ascended to heaven!"[52] R. Moses Alshekh[26] declared that "Scripture depicts Moses as greater than Elijah. Moses ascended heaven without any outside help, whereas Elijah was brought up to heaven by a fiery chariot and fiery horses with the aid of a whirlwind."[53] R. David Messer Leon[27] wrote: "Let no one argue that Moses did not ascend to heaven! We find written, 'I [God] spoke to you from heaven' (Exodus 20:22), and prior to that is written, 'Moses went up to God' (19:3). This is no mere foolish conceit, but it is unquestionable that Moses did in fact ascend to heaven (a great marvel) and went back down to lead and instruct the people, preserving all the time the perfection that he achieved during his ascent—a great marvel, indeed. He achieved feats through his mastery of the elements of air and water which would be considered proverbially impossible (such as gathering the wind in his hands, or water in his garment)."[54]

R. Joseph Ibn Kaspi[28] interpreted the ascent figuratively: "Moses ascended *intellectually* to the heavens to bring down the Torah." R. Moses Cordovero also had difficulty with the question and responded: "It is impossible for something corporeal to exist on high, as it is for something spiritual to exist on earth (without a body)! If, then, Moses did ascend heaven, he did so by becoming purified. That is to say, he shed his corporeal garment and entered heaven as a pure spirit. This is what the verse means when it says, 'Moses entered into the midst of the cloud' (Exodus 24:18). He actually wrapped himself in the holiness of the cloud, and his flesh was transformed into spirit so that he could experience conjunction with the Divine Spirit. Similarly, when he descended to join the people Israel, he divested himself of his diaphanous garb and came to them clad in worldly form."[55]

---

[50] Maimonides, *Guide of the Perplexed* I:10.

[51] Nahmanides' Commentary on Exodus 19:3; Bonfils *Tzafnat Pa'neah* ad loc. Even the Zohar raises the interpretation, "'And to Moses He said, Come up to the Lord' (Exodus 24:1)—i.e., to heaven"—only to reject it. "'Who ascended to heaven?'—this is Elijah, of whom Scripture truly says that he went up to heaven in a whirlwind" (Zohar Vayakhel 197 and Or Hahamah ad loc.). Zohar Yitro 79a gives yet another interpretation: "Who ascended heaven? The Holy and Blessed One, of whom it is written: 'God ascends midst acclamation' (Psalm 47:6)."

[52] Teshuvot Hageonim, 5624/1864 edition, #45, p. 18b.

[53] Moses Alshekh, *Torat Moshe* on Exodus 19:3.

[54] David Messer Leon, *Tehillah Le-David* I,32.

[55] Cordovero, *Shi'ur Komah* 32. See Zohar, Vayakhel 191a.

---

[26] Sixteenth-century halakhist and kabbalist, Safed.

[27] Fifteenth- to sixteenth-century talmudist and philosopher, Italy.

[28] Thirteenth- to fourteenth-century philosopher, Provence and Spain.

Rabbi Judah Loew (the Maharal) of Prague[29] interpreted the phrase "he ascended on high" to mean that he rose to the state of the celestial beings to receive the Torah. In his corporeal state it would have been impossible for him to receive the Torah.[56] [30]

Rabbi Ishmael: Moses Buried Himself

Most of the tales of Moses' ascent to heaven are connected with his receiving the Torah. Related to these, however, is the tradition (the basis of the lost book Assumption of Moses[31]) that Moses never tasted death, but like Enoch and Elijah entered heaven while yet alive. An anonymous (purportedly Tannaitic) tradition states: "Three ascended and served on high: Enoch, Moses, and Elijah. Moses, as it is written: 'Moses ascended from the steppes of Moab . . .' (Deuteronomy 34:1).[57]

Rabbi Simeon ben Yohai derived this view from the following verse: "'Ascend these heights of Abarim . . . and die on the mountain *to which you ascend'*—you will ascend to heaven, and no one else will ascend with you."[58] Some derive it from the parallel use of the word *sham* ("there") in Exodus 34:28 (when Moses ascended again to receive the second tablets after the golden calf) and Deuteronomy 34:5 (in connection with Moses' death).[59] This view, which was known to Josephus,[60] was not accepted by all the Sages. Even those who believed that Moses ascended to heaven to receive the Torah did not exempt him from death. Lists of nine or thirteen persons who entered Paradise alive do not include Moses.[61]

Who buried Moses? Scripture reports: "*He* buried him in the valley" (Deuteronomy 34:6), but does not specify who buried him. "No one knows his burial place" (Deuteronomy 34:6)—from this we may infer that no other person attended to his burial. Some say the Holy and Blessed One attended to him.[62] Rabbi Judah said, "Moses was carried four miles on the wings of the Shekhinah."[63] Against this view, Rabbi Ishmael responded: "Moses buried himself"[64]—that is, he entered a cave and

---

[56] Maharal, *Tif'eret Israel* 63.

[57] Midrash Haggadol on Genesis 2:24.

[58] MTD, p. 206.

[59] BT Sotah 13b.

[60] Josephus wrote: "Moses wrote about his own death, in order to anticipate those who would dare to say that on account of his great righteousness, he entered heaven alive" (*Antiquities* 4.48).

[61] YS Ezekiel 367.

[62] MI Beshalah, intro.; Sifre Beha'alotekha 106; Deuteronomy Rabbah 9:5.

[63] Tosefta Sotah 4:8; BT Sotah 13b.

[64] Sifre Bemidbar 32.

---

[29] Sixteenth-century talmudist and kabbalist.

[30] Strikingly, the views of Cordovero and the Maharal both suggest that Moses had an "incarnated" and an "unincarnated" form.

[31] Mentioned above, in the second section of this chapter, "Moses Ascended to Heaven."

died there.[65] Thus Rabbi Ishmael opposed the view that Moses our Master was buried in a supernatural fashion.[32]

Maimonides takes a lone stand and writes that Moses' death was "death—for us, as we are missing his presence, but life for him, seeing the higher state to which he ascended. This is as the Rabbis said: Moses our Master did not die but ascended and serves on high."[33] [66]

Elijah's Ascent

It was commonly held among the Rabbis that Elijah did not taste death but entered Paradise alive, based on the scriptural verse "Elijah went up to heaven in a whirlwind" (2 Kings 2:11).[67] Nevertheless, Rabbi Yose was not alone in the opinion that Elijah did not ascend to heaven. The Septuagint and Targum render, "went up *toward* heaven."[68] Josephus wrote of Enoch and Elijah: "They are gone, and no one knows anything about their deaths."[69] Another enigmatic source speaks of concealment: "Since Elijah was concealed, the holy spirit has departed from Israel."[70]

The late midrash Seder Eliyahu Rabbah suggests that Elijah's ascent was spiritual rather than corporeal:

"As they kept on walking and talking, a fiery chariot with fiery horses suddenly appeared and separated one from the other; and Elijah went up to heaven in a whirlwind" (2 Kings 2:11)—they were discussing matters of Torah. The angel who was sent to dispatch them found them engaged in Torah. He said, "Master of the Universe! As long as they are

[65] Abraham ibn Ezra on Deuteronomy 34:6; Rabbenu Hillel on Sifre ad loc.
[66] Commentary on the Mishnah, introduction.
[67] Genesis Rabbah 21:4; DEZ 1:18; Leviticus Rabbah 27:4.
[68] Septuagint: *hōs eis ton ouranon*; Aramaic: *letzit shemaya*.
[69] Josephus, Antiquities 9.2.2.
[70] Tosefta Sotah 12:8. The term *nignaz* ("was concealed") is applied in the rabbinic literature to the ark, the Tent of Meeting, the jar of manna, the Book of Healings, and many other things. We have clear evidence in at least some cases that these did *not* go up to heaven; for instance, Tosefta Shekalim 2:18, Tosefta Sotah 13:1.

---

[32] Rabbi Ishmael was said to have interpreted three passages where there is a direct object but no subject to indicate the reflexive—that is, the subject did the action on itself. The burial of Moses was one of these (". . . buried him there" is taken to mean "he buried himself there"). The other two are in Leviticus 22:16 and Numbers 6:13. See Sifre Numbers 32.

[33] This is an exceptional case in which Maimonides seems outwardly to agree with the Akivan position. But Maimonides evidently took this in a philosophical sense. Maimonides understood immortality as an intellectual union with the active Intellect, based on one's intellectual attainment in this life. He also believed that Moses achieved perfect philosophical understanding, insofar as it is possible for any human being. It followed naturally, therefore, that for Maimonides the complete philosopher (Moses) would achieve the highest level of intellectual immortality after this life—expressed fittingly (perhaps hyperbolically) in the notion that he did not die but entered the higher realm alive. It is of interest to ask whether in his later period Maimonides would have agreed to this formulation, which he offered at the start of his first major work.

engaged in Torah, I have no power over them." "Fiery chariot" refers to the three portions of the Bible; "fiery horses," to the legal and aggadic portions of rabbinic study. "Fire" means Torah.[71]

One of Saadia Gaon's students posed the problem: If the ascent of Enoch and Elijah was merely spiritual, what is so special about them? Do not the spirits of all creatures return to their source? Saadia replied that Elijah rose up some distance into the air in token of his importance, then descended in another place.[72]

R. David Kimhi reported the view that God brought Elijah and Enoch bodily into the Garden of Eden, as Adam had been before his sin. However, he himself believed that the whirlwind raised Elijah to the sphere of fire, where his garments and flesh were consumed, leaving only his spirit, which ascended to God.[73]

R. Isaac Abravanel expressed the view that God miraculously made Elijah's body eternally indestructible, like the heavenly bodies, to facilitate his later appearances to prophets, pious people, and Sages and his eventual heralding of the Messiah. But as Moses' ultimate fulfillment was to cleave to the celestial intellects, he left behind his body, for which he had no further need.[74]

The Zohar asked: How could Elijah ascend to heaven, given that the heavens cannot tolerate even a mustard-seed's mass of corporeal substance from this world? We learn from the case of Moses: "The Presence of the Lord appeared in the sight of the Israelites as a consuming fire on the top of the mountain" (Exodus 24:17). How did Moses approach God? "Moses went inside the cloud and ascended the mountain" (Exodus 24:18). He entered the cloud as if putting on a protective garment, and with this protection he approached the fiery presence of God. Similarly, "Elijah went up to heaven in a whirlwind—he donned the whirlwind as a protective garment and ascended to heaven in it.[75]

R. Moses Sofer combined these views:

> Truth will tell, Elijah never ascended bodily to heaven. Rather, his body and soul separated: the soul rose and serves in heaven among the ministering angels, and the body was refined and abides in the lower Garden of Eden on earth. When the appointed day comes (may it be soon in our days!), his soul will don that holy body, and he will be as any other of the prophets or Sages of Israel, ready to fulfill his appointed role. In the meantime, when he appears bodily to intervene in the affairs of this world, the soul has taken on the body; but when he is present only in spirit (as at a circumcision), he is as an angel. When he appears to a scholar in a vision, one should not be guided by his opinion,

---

[71] SER 5, p. 23; I. Heinemann, *Darkhei Ha'agadah* (Jerusalem: Magness Press, 1970), 81; Louis Ginzberg, *Legends of the Jews*, 7 vols. (Philadelphia: Jewish Publication Society, 1909–38), 6:322 n. 32.

[72] Moshe Zucker, *Al Targum RaSaG la-Torah* (New York: Feldheim, 1959), 106ff.

[73] Kimhi on 2 Kings 2:1. See also Nahmanides on Leviticus 18:5, Deuteronomy 11:22.

[74] Abravanel on 2 Kings, chapter 2.

[75] Zohar Vayakhel 191a. See also RaABaD's introduction to *Sefer Hayetzirah* (Warsaw, 5644/1884), 8: "When the separate intellects, angels or departed ones, prepare to descend to the material world, they put on corporeal embodiment from the four elements in order to appear to earthly beings. . . . This is the mystery of vestment."

for we do not listen to voices from heaven. But when he appears in bodily form, he speaks with the authority of one of the great Sages of Israel, and of this we say: "The Tishbite will resolve all questions and problems."[76]

Cordovero attributed to Moses de Leon the "great and wonderful mystery: You never find in Scripture any mention of Elijah's genealogy, but he is described simply as one of the inhabitants of Gilead. They say he came down from heaven, and his name was recorded in the supernal wisdom. It was to him that God spoke when God said, 'Let Us make a human.' Because he assented,[34] he was privileged to descend later to earth and bear witness: 'The Lord is God' (1 Kings 18:39)."[77] Joseph Caro similarly wrote: "This is the secret of Elijah: He only came to this world in order to proclaim the divinity of the Holy One. He is Metatron. Therefore you will find no mention of his father or mother, or that he married and had children, for he had no need of them."[78] However, Cordovero ultimately rejected this view: "This view is absurd. Even Simeon ben Yohai[35] held that he was human, as did all the Sages of the Talmud. They debated what tribe he came from, but no one suggested that he was an angel in human form."[79]

The Soul's Ascent

In a later period, stories spread about other notables of the Jewish people who ascended to heaven. One tradition has it that Ishmael, son of Elisha the High Priest, ascended by means of the Ineffable Name to inquire if the evil decree laid upon the Jews had been endorsed by God.[80] [36] Others say that Rabbi Joshua ben Levi entered

---

[76] Responsa of Hatam Sofer (R. Moses Sofer), VI,98.

[77] Cordovero, *Pardes Rimmonim*, 24:14.

[78] Caro, *Maggid Mesharim*, Mikketz. The view is also attributed to Abraham Galanti, cited by Abraham Azulai in *Or Hahamah*, Bereshit 1d. But Galanti was one of Cordovero's pupils, which makes the attribution doubtful. See also the mystical work *Leshem Shevo Ve'ahlamah*, I,5,7:2.

[79] Cordovero, *Pardes Rimmonim*, loc. cit., citing Zohar Vayiggash 29a.

[80] Midrash Eileh Ezkerah, Otzar Hamidrashim, p. 440.

---

[34] As we have seen previously, many angels *dissented*.

[35] Cordovero cited the Zohar to determine Simeon ben Yohai's view. According to current scholarly opinion, the Zohar was authored by Moses de Leon in the late thirteenth century. Cordovero accepted the traditional kabbalistic view that it was the creation of Simeon ben Yohai in the second century. All the more interesting, therefore, that he cites the Zohar to refute an opinion attributed to Moses de Leon. What did Moses de Leon really believe? Perhaps the view of Elijah's angelic origin was retrojected onto Moses de Leon by a later author, but we cannot say for sure.

[36] This tradition is extremely ironic in the light of Heschel's major thesis. Is this the same Rabbi Ishmael whom Heschel portrays as the champion of rationalism and opponent of supernaturalism in the Tannaitic period? Heschel even suggests elsewhere (in the Hebrew edition, chapter 2, "The Exoteric and Esoteric Personalities," n. 3) that there were two Ishmael ben Elishas, one a rationalist, the other given to direct communion with the divine glory in the Temple (see BT Berakhot 7a). The more

the Garden of Eden while yet alive.[81] In a third story, the soul of Rabbi Joshua ben Levi's son (R. Joseph) flew upward to heaven. When the son returned, the father asked, "What did you see?" He replied, "An upside-down world, in which the higher are lower and the lower are higher."[37] [82]

Other traditions reflect skepticism toward the idea of ascent. A half-century after Rav's death, it was reported that Rav confirmed the view of Rabbi Hananiah ben Gamaliel that flogging is sufficient expiation for the punishment of "excision." R. Joseph dismissed this report with the comment, "And who has gone up to heaven and brought back word?"[38] When Samuel boasted of his astronomical prowess, "I know the paths of the heavens as well as the paths of Nehardea," they expressed astonishment: "Has Samuel ascended to heaven?"[83]

Some of the rabbis believed that the soul ascends to heaven when a person is asleep. Rabbi Meir taught: "The soul fills the body. While a person sleeps, the soul ascends and draws life from the higher realms."[84] "All the souls go up to God. In the morning, God restores the souls to each individual."[85] The Lurianic circle developed these themes, stressing the spiritual nourishment that the soul derives from the higher realms and transmits to the body. "Were it not for this, the body would not have the strength to endure the supernal light which shines on it from above."[86] It was said that Luria's soul ascended to heaven to learn Torah.[87] And the Baal Shem Tov wrote of his spiritual ascent in a letter to R. Gershom of Kitow.[88]

[81] BT Ketubot 77b. See Leopold Zunz, Ha-Derashot be-Yisrael ve-hishtalshelutan ha-historit, ed. Ch. Albeck (1832; repr., Jerusalem: Mosad Bialik, 1954), 66, 312 n. 96.

[82] BT Pesahim 50a.

[83] Midrash on Psalms 19:4. The same objection was raised against R. Hoshaiah in BT Gittin 84a.

[84] Genesis Rabbah 14:9.

[85] Deuteronomy Rabbah 5:15; YS Va'ethanan 835; Zohar Aharei 67a.

[86] Vital, Sha'ar ha-Hakdamot [Gate of First Principles] (Jerusalem, 5610/1850), 16.

[87] Vital, Peri Etz Hayyim [Fruit of the Tree of Life] (Jerusalem, 1987), 16:1.

[88] Ben Porat Yosef of the Baal Shem Tov's disciple R. Jacob Joseph of Polonnoye (various editions), end.

likely explanation (suggested by Gershom Scholem, Major Trends in Jewish Mysticism, The Hilda Stich Stroock Lectures 1938 [Jerusalem: Schocken, 1941], 356 n. 3) is that because Rabbi Ishmael was a priest (and by some accounts, descended from a High Priest), later mystical traditions (ignoring his expressed views) made him privy to the divine mysteries contained in the Holy of Holies. The Eileh Ezkerah (a version of which occurs in the Yom Kippur liturgy) is a medieval literary creation that dealt freely with earlier traditions. It is ahistorical in making Rabbi Ishmael a victim of the Martyrology of the Ten Sages, when in fact he probably died before that event.

[37] "Higher lower and lower higher"—in all probability, this means that in the "true world," those who lorded it over their fellowmen in this world suffer humiliation, but those who were patient while downtrodden in this world are rewarded and exalted. R. Joseph's father replied: "You saw a clarified world."

[38] Rav was a Babylonian Amora of the "first generation" (approximately 220–250 C.E.), while R. Joseph was of the "third generation" (290–320 C.E.).

THE DESCENT OF THE DIVINE GLORY

Translator's Introduction

The preceding chapter, on the question of humans ascending to heaven, was one of the most pro-Ishmaelian, antimystical in the book so far. Heschel repeatedly stressed that the Torah has no clear basis for the notion of Moses' ascent; that Rabbi Akiva innovated radically in introducing the doctrine; that it was heavily influenced by the apocalyptic visionaries and paved the way for Christianity; that Judaism lives by the rule "God is in heaven, and you are on earth."

How will Heschel balance the positions on the related question of God's descent to earth in this chapter? The first section starts with an evenhanded approach and then concludes on a pro-Ishmaelian note with citation of Rabbi Judah the Patriarch, redactor of the Mishnah. But some surprises are in store. Aristobulus, usually on the rationalist side, supports taking the divine descent on Sinai literally. By the fourth section, the debate is taking place completely within the pro-descent camp, between those who see the descent as real but exceptional and those (notably Simeon ben Yohai) who see it as the normal order of things. The chapter ends with a heart-wrenching sermon by Rabbi Meir coming out in favor of human ascent, to which Heschel's silence seems to give assent.

The second section is the pivot on which the chapter as a whole revolves. Here Heschel names what for him is the central theological issue behind the metaphor of "divine descent": whether revelation is an event in which humans gain enlightenment while the Unmoved Mover remains impassive, or whether it is an important event for God as well. One need read no further than the title of Heschel's *God in Search of Man* to know on which side of this question Heschel stands. God, for Heschel, is not the Unmoved Mover but the Most Moved Mover. Yes, God does descend to meet us at Sinai.

The chapter starts by talking about the *kavod*—the Divine Glory—but it ends by talking about the Shekhinah. It starts on the theme of God's power but ends on the theme of God's love. It is as if Heschel started writing with certain plans in mind but found his heart turned along the way.

Did the Divine Glory Indeed Descend?[1]

THE DESCENT OF GOD'S GLORY to earth was also a matter of debate among the Sages. They saw in this not simply a deviation from the normal order of nature, but rather something that touches the latent structure of the universe. Those Sages who believed that Moses ascended to heaven were the same ones who taught that God descended to earth, as though the two matters were interdependent.

Here, too, Rabbi Ishmael and Rabbi Akiva framed their differences in the interpretation of conflicting verses. One verse says, "You yourselves saw that I spoke to you from the very heavens" (Exodus 20:19). Another verse says, "The Lord came down upon Mount Sinai" (Exodus 19:20). Rabbi Ishmael's Thirteenth Canon of Interpretation says that in such a case, a third verse shall be brought as the tie-breaker. Thus, it says, "From the heavens He let you hear His voice to discipline you; on earth He let you see His great fire" (Deuteronomy 4:36). From this, Rabbi Ishmael concluded that God did not descend on the mountain, but only let the people hear His voice from heaven.

Rabbi Akiva accepted the third verse as decisive but interpreted it differently: "The Holy and Blessed One bent the upper heavens down so that they touched the top of the mountain and spoke to them from the point where heaven and earth touched, as it says: 'He bent the sky and came down, thick cloud beneath His feet' (Psalm 18:10)."[1] Another version added this detail: "The Divine Glory came down and rested on Mount Sinai, as one who sets a pillow at the head of the bed and speaks with his head resting on the pillow."[2]

Rabbi Akiva also debated the issue with Rabbi Eliezer [ben Hyrcanus]. They interpreted the verse "While the king was on his couch, my nard gave forth its fragrance."

---

[1] MI Bahodesh 9. Rabbi Akiva has the last word, even in the Baraita de-Rabbi Ishmael, Sifra 3a.
[2] MI Bahodesh 4.

---

[1] "Glory" is used here to translate the Hebrew *kavod*. The connotations of the word derive from association with the verb *kabbed* ("to honor") and the adjective *kaved* ("heavy, massive"). Key texts are: "See, there is a place near Me. Station yourself on the rock and as My *kavod* passes by, I will put you in a cleft of the rock and shield you with My hand until I have passed by" (Exodus 33:21–22); "The cloud covered the Tent of Meeting, and the *kavod* of the Lord filled the Tabernacle. Moses could not enter the Tent of Meeting" (Exodus 40:34–35); "Holy, holy, holy! The Lord of Hosts! His *kavod* fills all the earth!" (Isaiah 6:3). *The Oxford English Dictionary* (1971) gives as definition 5: "The glory of God: the majesty and splendour attendant upon a manifestation of God." The problem with NJV "Presence" (for *kavod*) is that it makes difficult the differentiation between *kavod* and *shekhinah*. *Shekhinah* emphasizes the love and inner exaltation attendant on God's spiritual nearness; *kavod* emphasizes the numinous power and radiance emanating from the divine majesty. Whether the *kavod* is truly to be identified with God, or is a created manifestation of God, is of course the subject of debate. See especially chapters 5 and 6 above for Heschel's analysis of the positions of the Ishmaelian and Akivan schools on this and related issues.

Rabbi Eliezer said: "Even while the Holy and Blessed King of Kings was resting on His couch in heaven, Mount Sinai beamed forth a column of light." Rabbi Akiva differed: "Even though the Holy and Blessed King of Kings was resting on His couch in heaven, still, 'the glory of God abode on Mount Sinai' (Exodus 24:16)."[3]

Rabbi Eliezer the son of Rabbi Yose the Galilean was a contemporary of Rabbi Yose ben Halafta. All three followed the view of Rabbi Ishmael.[4] Rabbi Judah the Patriarch had great admiration for Rabbi Yose ben Halafta and taught similarly: "It is written, 'The Lord came down on Mount Sinai' (Exodus 19:20)—ought we to understand this literally? Consider, if even the sun, which is but one of God's many servants, can remain in place while radiating its light all over the world, how much more so can the One whose word brought the world into being, do the same!"[5]

The Importance of the Question

This debate was extended to include God's communication with Moses in the Tent of Meeting. The school of Rabbi Ishmael commented on the verse "When Moses entered the Tent of Meeting to speak with Him, he heard the Voice speaking to him from above the ark cover . . . from between the two cherubim" (Numbers 7:89): "This teaches that when Moses entered the Tent of Meeting, *only the voice of God came down from heaven* to the space between the two cherubim, and Moses heard the voice speaking to him from there."[6]

Rabbi Akiva's school pointed out a conflict between this verse and another: "Moses was not able to enter the Tent of Meeting . . . because the glory of God filled the Tabernacle" (Exodus 40:35). How could these two conflicting verses be reconciled? "When the Shekhinah descended to earth, Moses was not able to enter; but when the Shekhinah removed itself from the earth, then Moses entered the Tent of Meeting and God's voice spoke to him."[7]

In the eschatology of 1 Enoch (the Ethiopian version), great importance was attached to God's descent on Mount Sinai. It is stated there that in the End of Days the God of the Universe would descend on Mount Sinai to pass judgment on everyone (1:4–9). God would also come down to Egypt from heaven to rescue the people Israel and to lead them on their journey, "with countenance radiant and glorious, and awesome to behold" (89:16, 22). The apocalyptic Vision of Ezra says (in the vein of Rabbi Akiva): "You [God] folded the heavens and descended to earth" (81:19).[8]

---

[3] Song of Songs Rabbah 1:12; Yefei Kol ad loc.

[4] For Rabbi Eliezer ben Rabbi Yose's views, see Midrash Haggadol on Numbers 7:89. For Rabbi Judah the Patriarch's admiration of Rabbi Yose, see PT Gittin 6:9 (48b).

[5] MI Bahodesh 9. It is well known that Rabbi Judah was careful not to include any apocalyptic doctrines in the Mishnah.

[6] Sifre Naso 58.

[7] Sifre Zuta p. 254, following YS Naso 719.

[8] See F. Rosenthal, *Vier apokryphische Bücher aus der Zeit und Schule R. Akibas* (Leipzig, 1885), 59 n. 3.

Why did some of the Sages avoid the notion of the divine descent? There was one Second Temple philosopher in particular who insisted that our notions of God should be refined. He avoided any concrete descriptions of the deity and interpreted all such concrete descriptions in the Bible allegorically. Yet he hesitated to treat the account of God's descent on Sinai in the same way. He stated that the Lord descended "at the time of giving the Torah, so that all should be in awe of the divine power." God sought to reveal to the world the foundations of true religion. Such a revelation was impossible without a violation of the natural order, and the descent of God onto Mount Sinai was just such a violation. After quoting the scriptural account of the Sinaitic revelation, Aristobulus concludes: "It is clear from this that a divine descent occurred. God Himself, without any intermediary, revealed His greatness by means of all these visions." But Aristobulus did not believe that this was truly a descent of the inner essence of God, for God is everywhere. Rather, this "descent" was a revelation of God's powers to the whole world, outside the normal course of nature.[9]

It seems to me that the debate of the Tannaim on the issue of God's descent to earth does not center on the question whether to attribute spatial movement to the Master of the Universe or not. The basic question is, does the Holy and Blessed One, whose very heavens cannot contain Him, reduce Himself in size to the dimensions of this world? Bound up with this issue is an even more profound matter, namely, what is the nature of God's revelation? Is it verbal communication? Is it the revelation of God's will alone? Or is it an event that affects the Divine Essence?[2]

See how Rabbi Joshua ben Hananiah and Rabbi Eleazar ben Arakh discussed this very question. They both asked: "How is it that the Holy and Blessed One, Who is manifest from the highest heavens, spoke with Moses in a bush?" According to Rabbi Joshua, there was no alteration in the Divine Essence here. The Shekhinah is always with Israel, and the theophany at the burning bush was not a unique event: "When Israel went down to Egypt, the Shekhinah went down with them; when they encamped at the sea, the Shekhinah was with them; when they came to the wilderness, the Shekhinah was with them."[10] On the other hand, Rabbi Eleazar ben Arakh taught that the theophany of the burning bush was an event in the life of the Divine Essence, and an exceptional one at that: "God humbled Himself and spoke from the burning bush."[11]

---

[9] J. Gutmann, *Ha-sifrut ha-yehudit ha-helenistit* (Jerusalem: Mosad Bialik, 1958), 217ff.; I. Heinemann, "Allegory in Hellenistic Jewry," in *Sefer Yohanan Levi* (Jerusalem: Magnes Press, 1949) 51.

[10] MSY, p. 6.

[11] Midrash Haggadol on Exodus, ed. Margaliot, p. 46; MSY, ed. Hoffman, p. 2. MS Halahmi of Mekhilta

---

[2] The Rabbis of the Tannaitic and Amoraic periods (first to fifth centuries C.E.) did not use philosophical language like "alteration of the Divine Essence." They spoke in more poetic and figurative language. It is Heschel's contention throughout this work that through the poetry and imagery they were dealing with theological issues as serious and challenging as their more philosophically sophisticated successors. In this case, Heschel supplies the philosophical terminology that he thinks points at the same problem Rabbi Joshua and Rabbi Eleazar address in the following paragraph. And the issue, to repeat, is whether revelation is an event that answers a need of God as well as the needs of humans.

The problem continued to occupy the Sages. We find that Rabbi Joshua ben Levi dealt with it also. What is revelation of the Shekhinah all about? "Face to face the Lord spoke with you" (Deuteronomy 5:4)—how can the divine face be on the same level as the human face? We must assume one of two things: either the higher partner has become humbled, or the lower partner has become elevated. Which? Scripture tells us: "The Lord came down upon Mount Sinai" (Exodus 19:20). From this, we learn that the higher partner humbled Himself.[12]

The Babylonian Amoraim posed the same problem using another verse: "For thus said He who high aloft forever dwells, whose name is holy: I dwell on high, in holiness, yet with the contrite and the lowly in spirit—reviving the spirits of the lowly, reviving the hearts of the contrite" (Isaiah 57:15). R. Huna said: "I raise the contrite so that he may dwell with Me." R. Hisda said: "I bend my Shekhinah down to meet him." The argument ends with the conclusion: "The second position is more likely. Indeed, we find that the Holy One forsook all the highest mountains and let the Shekhinah rest on lowly Mount Sinai. God came down to it; the mountain did not come up to God."[3] [13]

The notion that God humbled himself by descending to earth was an important element in the theology of Paul the Apostle. He taught that Jesus "even though he bore the divine likeness . . . made himself nothing, assuming the nature of a slave. Bearing the human likeness . . . he humbled himself, and in obedience accepted even death—death on a cross" (Philippians 2:6–8). Perhaps those Sages who taught that the Divine Glory did not descend, recognized that this concept was an essential article of faith among the Christians.[4]

The Controversy Continues

Many rabbinic Sages weighed in on the question of the divine descent on Mount Sinai, and the controversy continued into the Middle Ages as well.[14]

with Berurei Hamiddot (Vilna, 5604/1844), 48a has the reading: "The Holy and Blessed One humbled His Shekhinah." See Hillel's saying: "My humbling is my exaltation, my exaltation is my humbling" (Leviticus Rabbah 1:5).

[12] PR 21:6 (102a).

[13] BT Sotah 5a. A later view disagrees and says that Mount Sinai was uprooted from its place and brought up to heaven (PRE 41).

[14] Proponents of the divine descent (in addition to those mentioned) include Rabbi Joshua ben Levi (PR 21:6 [102a]), Rabbi Johanan (PR 21:5 [100a]), Rabbi Eleazar ben Pedat (YS Yitro 286), R. Isaac Nappaha, and R. Tanhuma bar Abba (Tanhuma Naso 24, YS Jeremiah 279). Opponents include Targum Onkelos

---

[3] See also YS 856 for the classic statement on God's "humility."

[4] In general, the theology of immanence often displays affinities with Christian theology, since it tends to blur the distinction between earth and heaven, between the human and the divine. We have seen this in previous chapters as well. It serves exceptionally well as a theology of suffering but could well give pause to more conventional Jewish theologians.

When the Khazar[5] in Halevi's dialogue asks the meaning of "The Lord descended on Mount Sinai," the Rabbi answers: "This refers to the ethereal spiritual substance called 'holy spirit' or 'glory [*kavod*] of the Lord,' or metaphorically the Divine Name YHWH"[15]—but one should not ascribe spatial descending to the Divine Essence. Maimonides understood divine descent as a metaphor for intellectual or prophetic enlightenment.[16] Similarly Rabbenu Bahya wrote: "'Descent' as applied to God refers to His bestowing intellectual enlightenment, and is similar to 'The Lord *was revealed* to Abraham' (Genesis 18:1). But Scripture calls it 'descent,' for the Shekhinah's self-revelation to the lower realms is a humbling of status for the Exalted One."[17]

The opposing view was expressed in the Seder Eliyahu Rabbah: "He descended from the abode of His radiant glory, from the highest heavens."[18] R. Meir ibn Gabbai elaborated: "The mystery of how God revealed and the people comprehended when the Torah was given is this: *The Divine Glory descended on the mountain.* There is nothing astonishing about this. Did not God Himself say, 'I will go down with you to Egypt'? (Genesis 46:4). Do not be misled by those sowers of confusion who weigh with their deceitful reason the words of Torah that emanate from our blessed Creator and can only be properly grasped from His mouth. All the rest of their words and arguments, which are ostensibly aimed at exalting God, are thus all for nought.[6] Of them the Psalm says: "Who invoke You for intrigue, and lift You up falsely" (Psalm 139:20).[7] What, then, was the purpose of building a Tabernacle and a Temple on earth in the design of the heavenly chariot, if not to provide a dwelling place for Him below such as the one He had on high? We, the believers, descendants of believers, truly believe that God's glory came down on Mount Sinai, for the Torah itself testifies to that fact, and 'The testimony of the Lord is trustworthy' (Psalm 19:8)."[19]

Rabbi Judah Loew of Prague believed that scriptural references to divine descent and approach are not to be understood corporeally.

---

and Jerusalem Targum on Exodus 19:20 (cited in Maimonides, *Guide of the Perplexed* I:27) and the Zohar (Yitro 86a).

[15] Judah Halevi, *The Kuzari* (Jerusalem: Magnes Press, 1977), II,4. See also Saadia Gaon, *Book of Doctrines and Beliefs*, II,7.

[16] Maimonides, *Guide of the Perplexed* I:10.

[17] Bahya ben Asher, Commentary on Exodus 19:20.

[18] SER 17, p. 85.

[19] Meir Ibn Gabbai, *Avodat Hakodesh, Sitrei Torah* 30.

---

[5] A pagan king on a religious search whose dialogue with a Rabbi is the matrix for the *Kuzari* of Judah Halevi.

[6] That is, to say that God cannot descend to earth is to *deny* God's perfection. Similarly, contemporary proponents of the idea that God dictated the Torah word for word to Moses often argue that to deny that God can dictate in human language is to impute imperfection to God.

[7] NJV: ". . . who swear by You falsely." But the literal meaning is what is being expounded here. They try to lift up God by keeping God off earth and in the heavens, but that is a false exaltation because it denies God's power to descend.

God forbid that the Torah be taken corporeally! The Torah speaks in human language, what the ear can hear, but not in a way to cause erroneous belief. Expressions such as "The Lord descended" and the like, are meant relative to the human perspective, for that is how God appears to the human observer, as if He were descending from heaven onto Mount Sinai. But that is not how it is in reality. You will find it is human reason which assigns names to everything, as it says: "The Lord God . . . brought [all the beasts and birds] to man to see what he would call them; and whatever the man called each living creature, that would be its name" (Genesis 2:19). It is marvelous, indeed, that it is we who are called on to give names to the terrestrial creatures, and we name them as they relate to us. Even the name of God is determined by the relationship of God to humanity. Why should we be surprised, then, that it is written, "The Lord descended"? It is human beings who assign words to what happened, and this is a description from the human point of view[8] of the apprehension of the glory of God which occurred at Mount Sinai, for God is present in the manner that one apprehends Him. Perhaps you will say that the notion of God's descent is not in accord with reason? But the human being is not wholly rational, and speaking of God's descent answers to part of human experience. Not that God appears to the recipient *only* as descending, but God is nevertheless experienced (in one aspect) as descending on Mount Sinai, and the person describes what happened as s/he experienced it. This is a basic doctrine of supreme importance, and fitting that it be kept constantly in mind.[20]

In a somewhat later period,[9] the doctrine of divine descent was accepted without criticism. Many authorities attacked Rabbi Yose's view that "the Shekhinah never descended." R. Berekhiah Berakh[10] cites a tradition whose original source escapes me: "Issi ben Judah said: Nadab and Abihu died because there were those in Israel who said the Shekhinah did not descend to earth. The manner of their death (fire descending from heaven) proved that the Shekhinah did indeed descend to earth."[21]

Descent of the Shekhinah in History

As we mentioned earlier, Moses' name "Jared" was significant in two ways: he brought the Torah down to earth, and he brought the Shekhinah down to earth.

---

[20] MaHaRaL, *Tif'eret Israel* 33.
[21] "From the Yalkut," *Zera' Berekh Shelishi,* Vayera (Halle, 5474/1674), p. 16a.

---

[8] The MaHaRaL walks a fine line between affirming that "the Torah speaks human language" and avoiding the implication that "humans wrote the Torah." Even if divinely authored, the Torah can still be telling the story of the divine–human encounter that the human reader will recognize as true to his or her experience.

[9] Heschel here posits a transition in European Jewish thought from critical, philosophically informed acceptance of the tradition to uncritical fundamentalism, and he dates it between the Maharal (1525–1609) and Berekhiah Berakh (d. 1663). This agrees with the analysis of Joseph Davis that there was a flourishing of rationalism in Polish Jewry around 1550–1620, which was eclipsed by the resurgence of Kabbalah shortly thereafter. See "R. Yom Tov Lipman Heller, Joseph b. Isaac ha-Levi, and Rationalism in Ashkenazic Jewish Culture 1550-1650" (diss., Harvard University, 1990).

[10] Seventeenth-century Poland, student of the kabbalist Nathan Nata Spira.

The question of the divine descent (whether Glory or Shekhinah) is an issue of ultimate importance. Rabbi Simeon ben Yohai said, "When the Holy and Blessed One created the world, He wanted a dwelling place on earth as He had in heaven."[22] But human sin caused the Shekhinah's withdrawal from the world. This results in the problem that the world which the Holy One created is empty of the Shekhinah.[11] From these premises follows the eschatological conclusion: *To mend the world, one must restore the Shekhinah to it.*

There are two aspects of the Sinai event: giving the Torah and revealing the Shekhinah. From Sinai proceeds not only instruction but also redemption. Both aspects are important: what was transmitted, and the event itself—the Shekhinah appearing to all Israel. The Sinai event was an attempt to restore the crown to its former estate, to return the Glory to its place.[12]

In contrast to Rabbi Ishmael (for whom the very notion of divine descent should not be articulated), Rabbi Simeon ben Yohai taught (in a way worthy of his master Rabbi Akiva) that no fewer than ten descents[13] of the Shekhinah are mentioned in the Torah. He viewed all human history from the standpoint of the alternating withdrawal and return of the Shekhinah to the world. Given this outlook, the descent of the Divine Glory was not a one-time novel occurrence but the resumption of an interrupted process.

"And it was [*vayehi*], on the day that Moses finished setting up the Tabernacle"[14] (Numbers 7:1)—Rav said: "*Vayehi* indicates a novelty, for the Shekhinah had never abode on earth before." Rabbi Simeon ben Yohai said, "*Vayehi* indicates something that was interrupted but is now resumed. You find that from first creation the Shekhinah was present on earth, as it says, '[Adam and Eve] heard the sound of the Lord God moving about in the garden' (Genesis 3:8). But through the sins of the human race, it withdrew in seven stages: (1) after Adam's sin; (2) after Cain killed Abel; (3) after the generation of Enosh;[15] (4) after the generation of the Flood; (5) after the Tower of Babel; (6) after the sin of Sodom; (7) after the sins of the Philistines.[16] By now, it had retreated to the seventh heaven. Abraham's hospitality

---

[22] TB Naso 24; PR 7:4 (27b).

---

[11] Thus, in some sense, it is no longer God's world. This is a stunningly *simple* retort to any transcendent theology.

[12] This, of course, makes the sin of the golden calf even more scandalous.

[13] These are ten *separate* occasions on which the Shekhinah was said to descend to earth. They are not to be confused with the seven *stages* of withdrawal and return that are to be enumerated next.

[14] This is taken to be Moses' feat of bringing the Divine Presence to earth. For *mishkan* (= Tabernacle) comes from the same root as *Shekhinah*.

[15] Adam and Eve's grandson. This follows the understanding of Genesis 4:26 according to which it was in his generation that idolatry entered into human society.

[16] This refers to the Philistine king taking Sarah when Abraham was in his land; see Genesis 20. This is a bit problematic on two counts. First, since Abraham had said that Sarah was his unmarried

induced it to come down one level, to the sixth heaven. Isaac's readiness to self-sacrifice coaxed it down another level, to the fifth. Jacob's studying in tents brought it down to the fourth heaven. Levi, Kohath, and Amram brought it down three more levels, to the first heaven. Happy are the righteous, who cause the Shekhinah to dwell on earth! It was Moses' achievement to complete this process, as it is written: 'The glory of the Lord filled the Tabernacle' (Exodus 40:35)."[23]

Certain of the Amoraim had a different interpretation of the Sinai event. For them, too, it was more than just giving Torah and mitzvot. It was an upheaval in the established order. "It is as if an emperor had decreed: 'Romans shall not travel to Syria, nor shall Syrians travel to Rome.' So too, when the Holy and Blessed One created the world, He decreed: 'The heavens belong to the Lord, but the earth He gave over to man' (Psalm 115:16). When God prepared to give the Torah, He canceled the original decree, and said, 'The lower may go up, and the higher may come down.[17] I will be the first.' So it says: 'The Lord came down upon Mount Sinai' (Exodus 19:20), and 'Then He said to Moses, "Come up to the Lord"' (Exodus 24:1). Thus, 'whatever the Lord desires He does, in heaven and earth' (Psalm 135:6)."[24]

Consider the difference between this view and Rabbi Simeon's. For Rabbi Simeon, the normal state of the Shekhinah was on earth, for the Holy One wanted a dwelling on earth as on high, but because of human sin the Shekhinah withdrew to the higher realms. Furthermore, the descent of the Shekhinah at the dedication of the Tabernacle was only one of ten such occurrences in history. In contrast, for the author of the last midrash, the normal state of the Shekhinah is in the upper realms, and only at Sinai did the Holy One override the decree and allow the Shekhinah to descend.[18]

As for the Torah itself, was its possession by Israel normal or exceptional?[19] The

---

[23] PR 5:7n (18b); TB Va'era 19, Naso 24.
[24] Tanhuma Va'era 15; Exodus Rabbah 12:4; PRK 12:11 (104b).

---

sister, it is not so clear what the heinous crime was, especially since we are told that Avimelekh never touched her. In addition, the seven stages of withdrawal would seem to have to *precede* all of the stages of reengagement with the Shekhinah. But the events of chapter 20 *are subsequent to* the first redemptive act mentioned by the midrash, that is, Abraham's acts of kindness, which are related in chapter 18. There is a reason why it is said, "Questions cannot be directed to *aggadot*"!

[17] The analogy with the emperor makes it clear that God's sovereignty is at stake. If the domain of the emperor is divided into unconnected regions, then it can hardly count as one enormous empire. Similarly, God's rule over the entire universe required a connectivity between the upper and lower realms. But, Heschel will presently argue, on this view it was just a one-time connection, in order to establish the principle. The normal world order, however, remains as "heaven is heaven and earth is earth, and never the twain . . . ."

[18] That is, as a one-time dispensation.

[19] The last section of this chapter is not strictly unified by topic. Rather, Heschel free-associates among four issues concerning the boundary between the divine and human realms and whether certain "peak moments" are by their nature *exceptional* or rather made rare by human failure: (i) Is the descent of the Shekhinah exceptional or the normal state (from which we fall short due to sin)? (ii) Is the Torah primarily a heavenly entity, or designated for humankind? (iii) Was Moses right or wrong to

parable we cited of Rabbi Simeon[20] suggests that the Torah belonged essentially to the upper realms, and had Israel not pleaded and pressed God for this precious jewel, they would not have received it. In contrast, Rabbi Simeon ben Lakish seems to have thought the Torah was originally designated for humankind: "The Holy and Blessed One set a condition with the works of creation and said to them, 'If Israel accepts the Torah, well and good, otherwise I will return you to chaos.'"[25]

The debate between the prophetic and apocalyptic legacies continued for generations and was expressed in various ways. The rabbis debated whether Moses acted rightly in hiding his face when God addressed him, "for he was afraid to look at God" (Exodus 3:6). "Rabbi Joshua ben Korhah said, 'He did not act rightly, for had he not hidden his face, the Holy and Blessed One would have revealed to Moses what is above and what is below, what was in the past and what will be in the future." Rabbi Hosha'ya the Elder said, "Moses indeed acted rightly, for the Holy One rewarded him and said, 'Since you honored Me by hiding your face, I will keep you by My side forty days and nights, and you will bask in the radiance of the Shekhinah.'"[26]

Was it right for human beings to attempt to ascend to heaven? On the one hand, the Rabbis disparaged the generation of Babel: "They sought to ascend to heaven, but could not."[27] Their intention in building the tower was "to take heaven by storm."[28] On the other hand, Rabbi Meir thought that Jacob could have ascended to heaven and missed a great opportunity by not doing so.

Jacob saw in his dream that "a ladder was set on the ground and its top reached to the sky, and angels of God were going up and down on it" (Genesis 28:12). Rabbi Meir commented: "The Holy and Blessed One showed the Patriarch Jacob the guardian angels of Babylon, Media, Greece, and Rome ascending and descending. God said, 'You, too, may ascend.' But Jacob became frightened and said, 'Is it not likely that just as all of them descended, I, too, will descend?' But God replied, 'Fear not, Israel, if you ascend you will never experience a descent.' Jacob did not believe, and did not ascend."

Rabbi Meir continued: "The verse says, 'For all this, they sinned still and believed not in His wondrous works' (Psalm 78:32). This refers to Jacob, who did not believe and did not ascend. The Holy One said to him, 'Had you believed and ascended you would never have descended. Since you did not believe and did not ascend, your descendants are caught among the nations and entangled among the kingdoms.'"[29]

---

[25] Tanhuma Bereshit 1.   [26] Exodus Rabbah 3:2.
[27] YS Psalms 810.   [28] TB Noah 28.
[29] Leviticus Rabbah 29:2. See also Exodus Rabbah 34:7: "Do not fear; just as I never descend from My greatness, so you and your progeny will not descend from their greatness."

---

hide his face from God? (iv) Is it right or wrong for humans (such as the tower builders of Babel, or Jacob) to aspire to ascend to heaven? By the end, Heschel has come full circle from the theme of divine descent to that of human ascent (the topic of the previous chapter).

[20] At the beginning of chapter 17.

20

TORAH FROM HEAVEN

Translator's Introduction

The title of this chapter (in Hebrew: *Torah min Hashamayim*) is the title of the entire work, and that suggests that this chapter will now truly get down to the business of exploring, against the background that Heschel has drawn for us, what is meant by, and what is packed into, this common phrase, which is still in regular use in our own time. It first appears in Mishnah Sanhedrin 10:1, and that text now becomes a crux, the understanding of which will determine a whole theological edifice. What did the Mishnah mean when it threatened with loss of the world to come those who do not believe in "Torah from Heaven"?

There are several things to be noted here. First is the ambiguity (by no means easily resolved) in the meaning of the word "Torah" in this phrase. Is it, for example, a common noun meaning "instruction," and thus the Mishnah is anathematizing those who reject the idea of Mosaic prophecy entirely? That is certainly a plausible reading, since presumably such a rejection would have nothing to do with the life of Moses *per se*, but rather would express a rejection of the idea that the divine will is made manifest in any way at all to human beings. That would, indeed, be a rejection of a very basic foundational idea of Judaism. There is nothing at all unnatural or forced about reading the Hebrew in the Mishnah this way.

But it is not the only way. For "Torah" could be taken as a proper noun as well, referring to a particular book or corpus. It is true that it would be more natural for the Mishnah, if this were its intent, to prefix the definite article to the word "Torah," but that is hardly *essential*. If this is the intent of the Mishnah, then there is another ambiguity that needs to be resolved, and that is the referent of the word "Torah." Just what text is the Mishnah referring to? It is tempting, because of later standard usage, to take it to mean exactly the five books of the Pentateuch. But again, that can hardly be taken for granted, and Heschel will take us through the possibilities, beginning with the modest one, according to which it refers to the Ten Commandments, and ranging through successive expansions of the referent to encompass far more than the Pentateuch and even Scripture itself.

Another item worth noticing is that the extreme sanction imposed by the Mishnah (i.e., loss of the world to come—a forfeiture of the gift of immortality) already suggests strongly that whatever view the Mishnah is trying to enforce as normative is not at all

368

an obvious view. Failure to accept an obviously true idea may call forth derision or dismissal, but it does not generally call forth excommunication. The latter is reserved for those who do not accept a doctrine that, while not obvious at all, is taken by the anathematizer to be central. Indeed, just as it is not immediately obvious that God speaks to humans through prophecy (it is, in the end, an article of faith), so it is not immediately obvious, even from the narratives in the Torah itself, that the text of the Torah (or certain parts of it) was given verbatim and *in toto* by God to Moses. It is, in the end, an article of faith.

In this chapter, Heschel will draw on all that he has taught us about the Ishmaelian and Akivan approaches to theology in order to identify the former with the minimalist view of what was revealed by God, and the latter with the more maximalist view on revelation. The polemic, as it will be developed by Heschel in many of the subsequent chapters, begins right here.

The Entire Torah at Divine Behest

IN DEVELOPING THEIR DOCTRINE of revealed Torah, the Rabbis made repeated use of the scriptural passage "That person, be he citizen or stranger, who acts defiantly reviles the Lord; that person shall be cut off from among his people. Because he has *spurned the word of the Lord* and violated His commandment, that person shall be cut off—he bears his guilt" (Numbers 15:30–31). What exactly is "the word of the Lord," for whose spurning one merits being cut off? The Sifre cites the view: "Whoever says, 'I accept the entire Torah, except for this one matter,'[1] spurns the word of the Lord. Even someone who says, 'Moses spoke the whole Torah at the divine behest, except for this one matter which he spoke on his own initiative,' spurns the word of the Lord."[1] The author of this view interprets "the word of the Lord" as extending to even a single utterance contained in the Torah.

By contrast, we read in a famous mishnah, "All Jews have a share in the world to come . . . but these have no share in the world to come: the one who says that the

¹ Sifre Shalah 112.

---

[1] "Except for this one matter"—*hutz mi-davar zeh*. The word *davar* is related to—and spelled identically with—*dibber*, "unit of speech." Heschel paraphrases it with *dibbur*, which we have translated as "utterance." Even the English phrase "the word of the Lord" (*devar adonai*) has a collective connotation, for a single word by itself does not express a complete thought. A lot of the discussion in this chapter will focus on precisely how large or small a unit of Torah one must deny in order to fall under the pejorative description of this verse. When Maimonides wants to define this unit as an actual grammatical "word," he uses the more precise term *afilu tevah ahat*, "even one word" (see last section of this chapter).

doctrine of the resurrection of the dead is not found in the Torah, *and that Torah is not from heaven. . . .*"[2] Whoever reads this mishnah with a discerning eye will see that its author only condemned one who rejects *the general principle* that there is Torah from heaven, not one who rejects a single detail.[2] But now we need to clarify what is meant by all the terms in the expression "Torah from heaven."

Torah[3]

The word "Torah" has many meanings. It is frequently used to refer not only to the Scroll of the Torah, or to the Five Books of Moses, but to all of Scripture. When Rabbi Ishmael counted ten instances of a fortiori argument in the "Torah," he cited examples from Samuel, Jeremiah, Proverbs, and Esther.[3] Other Rabbis, citing support for their views from "the Torah," were referring to Psalms, Kings, and the Song of Songs.[4]

Sometimes the term is used in an even broader sense to include authoritative teaching that is derived midrashically from the text: "they came in finally to the High Court in the Chamber of Hewn Stones, from which Torah was propagated to all of Israel."[5]

It includes also the activity of studying Torah: "Any Torah without a worldly craft leads to sin." "[On the contrary,] I would leave aside all worldly crafts, and teach my son only Torah."[6]

It includes the oral traditions (especially legal) as well as written Scripture: "'These are the laws, rules, and *instructions (Torot)*' (Leviticus 26:46): [From the plural form *Torot*] we learn that there were two Torahs given to Israel, one written and one oral. Rabbi Akiva said: 'Only two Torahs? Rather, there were many: This is the Torah of the burnt-offering, this is the Torah of the guilt-offering,' etc."[7] [4]

---

2 Mishnah Sanhedrin 10:1.
3 BT Eruvin 58a.
4 BT Yevamot 4a, Megillah 25b, Sanhedrin 37a.
5 Mishnah Sanhedrin 11:2.
6 Mishnah Avot 2:2; Kiddushin 4:14.
7 Sifra Behukotai 112c.

---

[2] *Ein Torah min hashamayim* is actually ambiguous. Rendered as "there is no Torah from heaven," it supports Heschel's statement here. But rendered as "the Torah is not from heaven," it could be understood as expressing the claim that the Torah *as we have it,* that is, every letter, is not the way it came from heaven. See editor's note below, p. 376.

[3] Heschel will give many meanings to this term here. It should be noted that in the Torah itself, *torah* is a common noun that means "instruction." The word is from the same root as *moreh/morah* ("teacher").

[4] Heschel now adds even further meanings: Sometimes the word *torah* refers to the manner and legal status of an action or object: "[this applies to] taking an article *in the manner of* (*be-torat*) a bribe [but in the current case, he took it as a fee]" (see BT Ketubot 105a); "he has not entered *the state of* (*le-torat*) matrimony at all" (see BT Kiddushin 50b); "[it came to him] *in the status* (*be-torat*) of a trust" (see BT Bava Metzi'a 62a).

Torah (Without Specification) Means
Ten Commandments[5]

However, just as "Torah" was used in the broadest sense, it was also used in a narrow sense to refer to the Ten Commandments alone. Based on the tradition that the second set of tablets was given to Moses on Yom Kippur, the Mishnah refers to that day as the day of giving the Torah to Israel.[6] 8 A Baraita that states, "On the sixth day of the month the Torah was given to Israel," appears elsewhere as, "On the sixth day of the month the Ten Commandments were given to Israel."9 In the Avot of Rabbi Nathan, we read, "Moses received Torah[7] at Sinai. How do we know that he wrote it? Because Scripture states, 'He wrote them on two stone tablets' (Deuteronomy 4:13)."10 It can hardly be supposed that the entire Torah was written on the two tablets.

Note that in the following midrash, Rabbi Ishmael used the word "Torah" to refer to the Ten Commandments: "Moses our Master shattered the tablets, based on a fortiori reasoning: If the paschal sacrifice, a single commandment, is forbidden to aliens (Exodus 12:43), how much more so should the Torah,[8] which includes [by implication] all the commandments!"11

Deuteronomy (17:18–19) commands the king of Israel to write for himself "a copy of this Torah . . . let it remain with him and let him read it all his life." The biblical commentary ascribed to the Tosafists cites the view that "this Scroll of Instruction attached to his arm had written on it only the Ten Commandments. However, this excerpt is called 'the Torah Scroll' because it contains 613 letters."12

---

8 Mishnah Ta'anit 4:8.   9 BT Yoma 4b, Shabbat 86b.
10 ARN B 1; Mishnah Avot 1:1.   11 PT Ta'anit 4:8 (68c).
12 The Commentary *Ba'alei ha-Tosafot* on Deuteronomy 13:20.

---

[5] This is a quotation from Rabbi Moses of Trani, whose position on the subject is articulated in the present subsection.

[6] A glance at the Mishnah will show that this assertion is somewhat overstated. A ceremony described as taking place on Yom Kippur (and also on the 15th of Av) includes a song that speaks of the joy at the giving of the Torah. That is not quite as strong as Heschel's assertion here.

[7] "Torah," not "the Torah." Heschel adds: "This is often interpreted to mean the entire Torah, including the Oral Torah. But this stands in contradiction to Rabbi Ishmael's view that general principles were given at Sinai and the details in the Tent of Meeting" (see chapter 25, section entitled "They Were Trebled in the Steppes of Moab"). But see the end of this section on the Rabbis' inconsistency in the use or omission of the definite article.

[8] Heschel's enlisting this midrash for his thesis depends on some subtle distinctions. Only the Ten Commandments were written on the tablets that Moses shattered. These are presumably referred to as "the Torah." What, then, of the aside that the Torah "includes all the commandments"? The Ten Commandments include all the other commandments *by implication,* as the general principles include by implication all the detailed applications that can be derived from them. See previous note, and Rashi on Exodus 24:12.

The Sibylline Oracle, composed around 140 C.E., actually uses the phrase "Torah from heaven" in the sense of the Ten Commandments: "At Mount Sinai God gave [to Moses] the Torah from heaven, and he wrote all its judgments on two tablets" (3:256).[13]

Rabbi Moses ben Rabbi Joseph of Trani (the "MaBIT")[9] expressed perplexity on the question of whether there are gradations of holiness in the Torah: "On the face of it, it would appear that the highest sanctity pertains only to the commandments and admonitions, not to the narrative and miscellaneous portions. Nor might we regard the Book of Deuteronomy, which contains the addresses of Moses to Israel, as possessing full sanctity. Yet we find that the sacredness of the entire Torah is of one piece, whether it deals with the commandments of God or the marital relations of Cain and his wife. The same scrupulous care applies to all, that they should be written on proper parchment, without an extra or missing letter,[10] and read in synagogue with equal reverence. For it is all the word of the living God, the Sovereign of the Universe, written two thousand years before the creation of our world. All of it contains the names of the Holy and Blessed One."[11] [14]

Nevertheless, at the conclusion of his treatise, the Mabit voices his doubts. "Indeed, narratives such as the lists of kings may contain hidden meaning. But when the Torah quotes the words of ordinary people, such as those spoken between Cain and Abel, or between Lot and the people of Sodom, and many similar ones, we must conclude that these sections possess no sacredness. How can we say they were spoken by God before the creation of the world?"[12] To resolve this dilemma, the Mabit suggests, "When we say that the Torah preceded creation, we are referring to the Ten Commandments, which God revealed to Moses at Sinai. The term 'Torah' without specification refers to the Ten Commandments, because they include the 613 mitzvot, and whoever accepts them, implicitly accepts the entire Torah as well."[15]

The Mabit cites various rabbinic traditions in support of this conclusion. Among

[13] *Oracula Sibyllina* (ed. Al Rzach; Vienna: F. Tempsky, 1891) p. 61; P. Lieger, *Die Jüdische Sibylle* (Vienna, 1908), 29.

[14] Moses of Trani, *Beit Elohim* 33, Venice, p. 336.

[15] Ibid., 64. But see above, chapter 17, section entitled "Torah Written in Heaven," that some Rabbis regarded the narrative sections also as preexisting creation.

---

[9] Safed, sixteenth century.

[10] Traditionally, some words with variable spelling should be written *plene* (with full spelling or even with extra letters) in certain places and *defectiva* (lacking one or more letters) in other places. These local textual peculiarities were to be adhered to scrupulously, without modification, especially as they could be made the basis of legal interpretations.

[11] The idea is a kabbalistic one, that names of God are hidden among the letters of the text of the Torah. Trani says that this is true of narrative parts of the Torah as well.

[12] This is an interesting distinction. Any narrative portions, apart from direct quotations, may have been worded by God and may therefore possess special sanctity. But the quoted words of Cain, Lot, and others were presumably authored by the individuals themselves and are therefore only human. Of course, there is always the possible retort that God knew what words would be spoken.

them is the *aggadah* of Moses answering the objections of the angels, against entrusting the heavenly Torah to mortals. "Do you live among idolators, that you need to be warned against idolatry? Do you work, that you need the Sabbath for rest? Have you a father or mother, that you need to honor them? Have you jealousy and hatred, that you need to be commanded against murder, adultery, and theft?"[16] From this it is evident that the hidden treasure, guarded on high since creation, consisted of the Ten Commandments.

The mishnah we quoted above refers both to the one who says, "The resurrection of the dead is not in *the* Torah," and to the one who says, "Torah is not from heaven." A point might be made about the use of the definite article in the first phrase and its absence in the second. Perhaps "*the* Torah" means the Book we have today, while "Torah" in general refers to prophecy, or the revelation at Sinai, and it is a denial of the latter for which one forfeits eternity. However, one cannot establish fixed rules about the use of the definite article by the Rabbis in relation to the word Torah. Sometimes they use the word "Torah" (without the article) to refer to the Pentateuch, and sometimes, as we find in the Mekhilta of Rabbi Ishmael, the people are standing before Mount Sinai to receive *the* Torah, where it means the Ten Commandments.[17]

"From Heaven"

The word "heaven" (*shamayim*) in rabbinic usage has three meanings. It refers to God, as in "the name of Heaven," "the kingdom of Heaven," "the fear of Heaven," "the judgment of Heaven," "in the hands of Heaven," "for the sake of Heaven."

It refers to heaven itself, the place, as in "our Father in heaven," or "heaven and earth."

It also refers to the will of God. When the Mishnah speaks of a man acquiring a woman "from heaven,"[18] it does not mean that she descended bodily from the sky, but that it was God's will or decree that brought her to him.[13] This usage is also found in the liturgy: in the Kaddish, "may there be abundant peace from Heaven," and in the prayer *Yekum Purkan*, "may salvation arise from Heaven." The use of "from Heaven" as meaning help from God, is especially old. It may stem from the Song of Deborah, "They fought from heaven" (Judges 5:20). Later we find Jonathan, the brother of Judah Maccabee, writing "We have help from heaven" (1 Maccabees 12:15). Similar expressions are to be found in the Gospels (Matthew 21:25; John 3:27).[14]

[16] BT Shabbat 88b–89a.   [17] MI Bahodesh 5.   [18] Mishnah Nedarim 10:6.

---

[13] The reference is to a woman eligible for levirate marriage. The death of her first husband (an "act of God") automatically makes her brother-in-law (the levir) next in line to marry her.

[14] Comparison of traditional and modern translations bears out Heschel's point: "The baptism of John, whence was it? From heaven [Greek: *ex ouranou*], or of men?" (Matthew 21:25 according to

Most likely, in the expression "Torah from heaven," the term "heaven" refers not only to God's will but also to the place of heaven itself.[19] This literal usage is found in other scriptural contexts: "An angel of the Lord called to Abraham from heaven" (Genesis 22:11) etc.[20]

Undoubtedly, the usage of "heaven" in the expression "Torah from heaven" is based on the verses speaking of the Sinai revelation: "I spoke to you from the very heavens" (Exodus 20:19), and "From the heavens He let you hear His voice" (Deuteronomy 4:36). Understanding what "heaven" means here will also help us understand what "Torah" means in "Torah from heaven."

Within scripture, only the Ten Commandments are said to have come directly "from heaven." All the other utterances were said to Moses at Sinai, in the vicinity of Sinai, at the Tent of Meeting, between the cherubim on the ark cover, or in the steppes of Moab. Further, every time the Sages speak of Torah "from heaven," they cite the two verses we have just quoted. For example, the Sifre comments: "'A fiery law to them' (Deuteronomy 33:2): The text compares the words of Torah to fire. Just as fire was given from heaven, so the words of Torah were given from heaven, as it says, 'You have seen that I spoke to you from the very heavens' (Exodus 20:19)."[21] Similarly: "The words of Torah are compared to water. Just as water is given from heaven, so the words of Torah are given from heaven, as it says, 'I spoke to you from the very heavens' (Exodus 20:19)."[22]

The Avot of Rabbi Nathan states: "Three returned to their original place: Israel, the Torah, and the silver and gold [which the Israelites took from Egypt]." The Torah was from heaven (citing Exodus 20:19). It returned to its place, as it says: "You see it, then it is gone" (Proverbs 23:5).[23] Two other sources cite the same midrash. One has, in place of Torah, "the writing of heaven"; the other has "the writing on the tablets."[24] Here, too, is evidence that "Torah from heaven" meant the Ten Commandments.

Many Sages differentiated between "Torah from heaven" and "Torah from Sinai." While the first refers only to the Ten Commandments uttered by God and heard by Israel at Sinai, the many commandments that were said to Moses at Sinai, but which

---

[19] BT Tamid 32a.

[20] See also the angel calling to Hagar (Genesis 21:17), the farmer's prayer for Heaven's blessing (Deuteronomy 26:16), and Solomon's plea for Heaven's attentive regard for human prayer (2 Chronicles 6:23). But see above, chapter 3, on how Rabbi Ishmael interpreted the second of these as referring to Divine Providence everywhere, not just in heaven.

[21] Sifre Berakhah 343.

[22] Midrash on Psalms 1:18. See also Sifre Ha'azinu 306: "Moses called on the heavens to give ear, because the Torah was given from heaven, as it says, 'I spoke to you from the very heavens.'"

[23] ARN B, p. 130; ARN A, p. 133 (where "the heavenly script" replaces "Torah").

[24] MI Amalek 1; BT Pesahim 87b.

AV). In a modern translation, this becomes "The baptism of John: was it from God, or from men?" (NEB).

were not part of the great event, are referred to as "Torah from Sinai" or *halakhah le-moshe mi-sinai*.[15] Some of these are recorded in the Torah, while others were transmitted orally to Joshua. It is not until later, in the days of Daniel and the apocryphal books, that there is mention of God speaking to prophets directly "from heaven" (Daniel 4:28; 1 Baruch 13:1; 1 Enoch 96:3).[16]

The One Who Says,
"Torah Was Not Given from Heaven"

If we interpret "one who denies Torah from heaven" as "one who denies everything," it will help us clarify a puzzling matter in the Tosefta. The Mishnah has stated: "But these have no share in the world to come . . . the one who says, 'Torah is not from heaven.'" The Tosefta adds: "Also one who casts off the yoke, one who undoes the covenant, one who unmasks the face of Torah . . . these have no share in the world to come."[25] The Palestinian Talmud comments on these categories: "'Casting off the yoke' refers to the person who says, 'There is a Torah, but I do not accept it as incumbent on me.' 'Undoing the covenant' refers to the person who stretches his foreskin (to appear uncircumcised).[17] 'Unmasking the face of Torah'[18] refers to the person who says, 'the Torah was not given from heaven.'"[26]

The Rabbis were puzzled: How does "one who says, Torah is not *given* from heaven" differ from "one who says, there is no Torah-from-heaven"? Note that the editor of the Mishnah did *not* condemn one who says that nearly all the Torah is of divine origin, but Moses added something on his own![19] We may say that the Mishnaic for-

---

[25] Tosefta Sanhedrin 12:9.

[26] PT Pe'ah 1:1 (16b); PT Sanhedrin 10:1 (27c).

---

[15] "A *halakhah* given to Moses from Sinai." This classic phrase was commonly used to refer to laws from hoary antiquity that are not found explicitly written in the Pentateuch but were believed to have been transmitted orally from Moses onward. In a famous *aggadah*, Moses is baffled by Rabbi Akiva's intellectual prowess in teaching Torah, but is reassured when he is told that the laws Akiva taught were "a *halakhah* given to Moses at Sinai." See below, chapter 30, under "A *Halakhah* Given to Moses from Sinai," and "Things Not Revealed to Moses."

[16] That is, direct revelation was originally confined to the Ten Commandments and only later was it expanded.

[17] Some hellenizing Jews in the ancient world took steps to disguise the physical evidence of circumcision, so they would not be identified as Jewish when they stripped in the gymnasium or public baths. The "covenant" referred to in this phrase is the covenant of Abraham.

[18] *Megaleh panim ba-Torah* means literally, "revealing face[s] in/of/at the Torah." Debunking is the most derogatory form of revealing. *Panim* ("face") can also mean "aspect" or "meaning." *Shiv'im panim la-Torah*—"[every item in] the Torah has seventy possible meanings." The skeptic or debunker is adept in uncovering those meanings which subvert the traditional outlook. Similarly, *Entdecktes Judentum* ("Judaism Unveiled") was the title of a famous anti-Semitic tract.

[19] This view will be discussed later in this chapter (the "alternate tradition").

mula speaks simply of complete denial of divine revelation of the Ten Command-ments. The Tosefta adds another level. As used in other contexts (such as: "Torah was only *given* for midrashic interpretation to the manna-eaters," "Torah was only *given* to Moses and his progeny"), we find that the Torah as something "given" is under-stood to mean the entire Torah as we have it.

"Unmasking the faces of Torah" can mean showing the differences between its various parts: some came from the divine behest, others from Moses' initiative.[20] When the Palestinian Talmud equates this with one who says, "the Torah was not *given* from heaven," it refers to one who says, not *all* the Torah is of divine origin. Rashi similarly interprets *megaleh panim ba-Torah* as unmasking one's own face toward the Torah: "One who comes to the Torah with naked arrogance and brazen face, like Manasseh[21] who remarked contemptuously, 'Had Moses nothing better to write than that Timna was the concubine of Eliphaz?'"[27]As we shall see, this was a proverbial reference to the view that Moses wrote some parts of the Torah on his own initiative.

Note the categorical language in the Mishnah: "One who says, *there is no Torah-from-heaven*."[22] This refers to one who completely negates the reality of prophecy, and similarly denies the revelation of God's presence at Mount Sinai.[28]

Broadening the Concept

In early times, it was deemed sufficient to believe in "Torah from heaven" in its plain meaning,[23] for even the Sadducees acknowledged the sanctity of the Five Books of Moses. However, when new heretics[24] arose who claimed that the Ten Command-

[27] Rashi on Shevuot 13a, s.v. *megaleh panim*.

[28] This is supported by parallel formulations: "If a court teaches *there is no* law of the menstruant in the Torah, or there is no law of Sabbath, or there is no law of idolatry in the Torah, they are exempt [with

---

[20] This is yet another meaning of the phrase. Heschel here presents the view attributed to Manasseh as if it were an anticipation of the modern Documentary Hypothesis, which "reveals the faces" of the different literary strands that were interwoven by a redactor to produce the current book.

[21] The king in seventh-century Judea, who was the proverbial wicked leader who defied God.

[22] *Ein Torah min hashamayim*. Heschel notes: An alternate phrasing, *Ha-Torah einah min hashamayim* would clearly have meant: "The Torah is not from heaven." But this locution is more typical of mod-ern than of Mishnaic Hebrew. The original Mishnaic formulation is actually ambiguous. In this para-graph, Heschel makes a valid case for understanding it in the Ishmaelian sense. But Akiva is able to quote the very same words and understand them in the broader sense. By translating the phrase into English, we are forced to choose: "There is no Torah from heaven" (Ishmaelian), or "The Torah is not from heaven" (Akivan).

[23] That is, instruction from God.

[24] Most notably, Christians.

ments alone had been given to Moses at Sinai, the Rabbis responded by expanding the scope of the phrase. We saw the maximalist view earlier, in the Sifre's interpretation of "spurning the word of the Lord."[25] We see it also in the difference between two versions of a famous story. In one source, we read: "Quintus, the Roman general, asked Rabban Gamaliel, 'How many Torahs were given to Israel?' He replied, 'Two, one written and one oral.'"[29] The other version reads: "Agrippa, the Roman general, asked Rabban Johanan ben Zakkai, 'How many Torahs were given to you *from heaven?*' He said to him, 'Two, one written and one oral.'"[30]

Consider another example. In Exodus 21:5–6 we read that the bondsman who refuses to go free after his six years of service must have his ear pierced against the doorpost of his master's house. In the Mekhilta of Rabbi Ishmael we read: "Why was the ear, of all organs, selected to be pierced? Rabban Johanan ben Zakkai explained it homiletically: The ear that heard, 'You shall not steal,' and then went and stole,[26] it alone of the organs is pierced."[31] Rabban Johanan makes a clear and distinct assumption in this homily, to wit: All Israel stood at Mount Sinai [including this thief]. And the command that he [and all Israel] heard was one of the Ten Commandments.[27] The Tosefta, however, tells it differently: "Why is the ear pierced? Because it heard at Mount Sinai, 'For it is to Me that the Israelites are servants; they are My servants' (Leviticus 25:55). Since it threw off the yoke of Heaven and took on the yoke of flesh and blood, it did not observe that which it heard."[32] The language here is precise, for Leviticus 25 is said to have been spoken "at Mount Sinai" (Leviticus 25:1).[28]

The Palestinian Talmud combines both versions, while distinguishing between the

respect to the penalties of the Rebellious Elder, for the claims are so far-fetched they would not be believed]" (Mishnah Horayot 1:3).

[29] Sifre Devarim 351. See also BT Shabbat 31a and ARN A 15. But ARN B 29 has: "from heaven."
[30] MTD, 33:10, p. 215.   [31] MI Nezikin 2.   [32] Tosefta Bava Kamma 7:5.

---

[25] Beginning of this chapter.

[26] This interpretation already assumes the ruling of the anonymous Tanna (in BT Kiddushin 14b) that only one who has been sold into slavery by the court for theft is subject to the law of the pierced ear. The basis of the sale of the thief by the court is in these verses: "When a man steals an ox or a sheep . . . he must make restitution; if he lacks the means, he shall be sold for his theft" (Exodus 21:37-22:2).

[27] The eighth, to be precise.

[28] Heschel's point is this: from the Mekhilta we could not conclude that every average Israelite heard any more than the Ten Commandments at Mount Sinai. But the Tosefta at least makes a significant expansion of what was heard by everyone at Mount Sinai on the basis of the simple meaning of the verses in Leviticus 25. At least something other than the Ten Commandments was heard by everyone from God, and this slave is being held responsible for hearing Leviticus 25:55. Note also that this exegesis assumes the position of Rabbi Eleazar in BT Kiddushin 14b, namely, that someone who sold himself into slavery is also subject to the law of the pierced ear. For the crux of this homily is that this slave violated Leviticus 25:55 by *voluntarily* choosing human sovereignty over himself.

Ten Commandments and Leviticus: "the ear that heard *from* Sinai, 'You shall have no other gods besides Me' . . . the ear that heard *before* Sinai, 'for it is to Me that the Israelites are servants.'"[33] Perhaps Rabban Johanan thought that the section from Leviticus was given before the revelation of the Torah at Sinai.[29]

Broadening the scope of "Torah from heaven" did not happen all at once, and the phrase itself was not reinterpreted until the concept had already been established. We can see this by comparing two versions of the same Baraita. At the start of this chapter, we quoted the Sifre: "Someone who says, 'Moses spoke the entire Torah at the divine behest, except for this one matter which he spoke on his own initiative,' spurns the word of the Lord."[34] In the Babylonian Talmud, however, the one who has spurned the word of the Lord is "the one who says, 'Torah is not from heaven.'"[35] The Sifre is older and is forced to use the more explicit language, *kol ha-Torah kulah*, "the entire Torah." The Talmud uses "Torah from heaven" in the later, expanded sense.

The Broadening of the Concept
in Rabbi Akiva's School

We have seen that originally "Torah from heaven" referred only to the Sinai event. In the extended sense, however, it came to mean that all the narratives and mitzvot in the entire Five Books were communicated to Moses at Sinai. It is precisely on this point that the schools of Rabbi Akiva and Rabbi Ishmael differed.

"It has been taught: Rabbi Ishmael said, 'Generalities were spoken at Sinai, details at the Tent of Meeting.' Rabbi Akiva said, 'Generalities and details were spoken at Sinai, repeated at the Tent of Meeting, and trebled in the steppes of Moab.'"[36] The plain sense of these words is that Rabbi Ishmael held that only the general principles of the Torah were revealed at the Sinai theophany; only after the Tabernacle was built were the details communicated to Moses. In contrast, Rabbi Akiva held that all the Torah, with its details and minutiae, was communicated three times, and nothing

[33] PT Kiddushin 1:2 (59d).
[34] Sifre Shalah 112.
[35] BT Sanhedrin 99b.
[36] BT Sotah 37b; Hagigah 6b; Zevahim 115b.

---

[29] Another explanation is simpler. Heschel noted above (see section above entitled "Torah [Without Specification] Means Ten Commandments") that some of God's revelations to Moses occurred *lifnei har sinai*—which we have translated, "in the vicinity of Mount Sinai." Leviticus starts by recounting the laws spoken by God to Moses "from the Tent of Meeting" (Leviticus 1:1), while chapters 25–27 in particular are placed "in/on Mount Sinai" (Leviticus 25:1; 27:34). If the Israelite encampment (including the Tent of Meeting) was at the foot of the mountain, then it was "in Mount Sinai" (broadly construed) but also "before Sinai" (facing the mountain peak). But Heschel cites another version, according to which Rabbi Simeon ben Rabbi said that God declared, "it is to Me that the Israelites are servants" in the course of the Exodus itself, while passing over the houses of the Israelites in Egypt! This corresponds to "before Sinai" in the temporal sense (BT Kiddushin 22b).

new was added at the Tent of Meeting or in the steppes of Moab. Rather, the same generalities and details were repeated a second and a third time.

Rabbi Ishmael said, "Whatever was repeated, was repeated solely for the sake of some new element that was added."[37] Many mitzvot—details—were added at the Tent of Meeting that were not specified at Sinai. The Tosafot and Nahmanides asked in surprise: Wasn't Rabbi Ishmael aware of the tradition, voiced by Rabbi Simlai, that all 613 mitzvot were revealed to Moses *at Sinai?*[38] No, for as RaABaD (R. Abraham ben David)[30] explained, the view that all the mitzvot, their general principles along with their particulars, were revealed at Sinai is not Rabbi Ishmael's view.[39]

Precise as always, Rabbi Ishmael could not affirm that the whole Torah was revealed at Sinai. Only the general principles were from Sinai; the details were from the Tent of Meeting. By his method, you could not speak of "the entire Torah from heaven," for "from heaven" referred to the Sinai event.

Rabbi Akiva, on the other hand, consistently held the view that the entire Torah, with all its details and minutiae, was from heaven—that is, it was given in full at the revelation at Sinai. One example of the broader use of the term is found in the midrash on Deuteronomy 14:7: "'The following, which bring up the cud or have hoofs which are cleft through'—Was Moses then an expert hunter, that he should know all these species? This is a refutation of those who say, *the Torah is not from heaven.*"[31]

The term "Torah from heaven" does not occur in Sifre to Numbers, which is of the school of Rabbi Ishmael, but it appears in the Sifre Zuta of Rabbi Akiva's school: "'And violated His commandment'—this refers to one who says, 'there is no Torah from heaven.'"[40] Rabbi Akiva would not entertain the thought that Moses uttered even one word on his own, or that even one *halakhah* was withheld from him. Rabbi Ishmael, as we shall see later, expressed the view that Moses did speak on his own at times.

In its original sense, the term "from heaven" alluded to the divine, heavenly voice that the Israelites heard, which spoke the Ten Commandments. But we have seen that Rabbi Akiva taught that Moses ascended to heaven and brought down the Torah from there. This was the basis for expanding the concept of "Torah from heaven" to embrace the entire Five Books of the Torah.

[37] BT Sotah 3a.
[38] BT Sotah 3a; Tosafot s.v. *Rabbi Ishmael;* Nahmanides' glosses on Maimonides' *Sefer Ha-Mitzvot*, 1.
[39] Commentary of RaABaD on Sifra, Behar 105a.
[40] See Sifre Zuta to Numbers 15:31.

[30] RaABaD of Posquieres (twelfth-century Provence), in addition to his commentaries on Alfasi and polemics on Maimonides, wrote the definitive medieval commentary on the Sifra, from which this comment is taken.

[31] The idea is that it *must* have been from God, who alone would have known all of the zoological facts. Here Rabbi Akiva applies the term "Torah from heaven" to the dietary laws of Leviticus and Deuteronomy. Clearly, then, he did not restrict it to the Ten Commandments.

We saw earlier[32] that the Torah was counted as one of the "three things that returned to their place." In the original version, adopted by Rabbi Ishmael, Torah in this connection was just the Ten Commandments. Rabbi Akiva applied the extended concept here as well: "When a person learns a chapter[33] and forgets it, it returns to heaven, as it says, 'You see it, then it is gone' (Proverbs 23:5).[41]

"He Has Spurned the Word of the Lord"
—Refers to Idolatry

There is good evidence that the expansion of both the concept "Torah from heaven" and the sanction announced in the Mishnah: "One who denies Torah from Heaven has no portion in the world to come" [to include more than the Ten Commandments] has its source in the school of Rabbi Akiva.

The basis of the disagreement between Rabbi Ishmael and Rabbi Akiva is in the exegesis of Numbers 15:22–31. The passage deals with unwitting sins, whether of the community or of an individual. Nahmanides noted that it is enigmatic, for it does not specify what kind of sins.[42] But the Sifre arrived at a consensus that the first two sections (15:22–29) referred to idolatry.[34] The disagreement focused on the last two verses:

> "But the person who acts defiantly"—that is, who unmasks the face of Torah. "That person shall be cut off," that is, the one who acts willfully, according to Rabbi Akiva. "Because he has spurned the word of the Lord"—that is, the Sadducee—"and violated His commandment"—that is, the Epicurean. Another opinion: "He has spurned the word of the Lord" refers to one who says, all the Torah was at the divine behest, except for one matter which Moses said of his own initiative. Rabbi Ishmael says: It refers to idolatry, for he has spurned the first word that was said at the divine behest through Moses, namely: "I am the Lord your God . . . You shall have no other gods besides Me" (Exodus 20:2–3)."[35]

41 Midrash Haggadol on Exodus 3:22. See also Midrash on Proverbs 23:1, citing Rabbi Ishmael in the first view.

42 Nahmanides, Commentary on Numbers 15:22.

---

[32] See section above entitled "From Heaven."

[33] "Chapter" in rabbinic parlance referred to Mishnah, the preeminent collection of rabbinic law; thus, the concept of Torah that came from heaven [and could thus return to heaven] would include, according to him, the Oral Torah as well.

[34] That is, the sacrifice that is described there is acknowledged by all to be a sacrifice occasioned by a ruling of a governing religious body that unwittingly led the people into an idolatrous practice. This interpretation was made necessary by the fact that this sacrifice differs in its details from what Leviticus 4 prescribes for all erroneous rulings that lead the community into sin. Idolatry was taken to be a special case and the one dealt with in Numbers 15.

[35] Again, Ishmael confines the sanction of these verses, which label the violator a denier of "the word of the Lord" to those who commit idolatry, the first of the prohibitions in the Ten Commandments.

Here we see that, while all the other Sages interpreted the expression "He has spurned the word of the Lord" to yield various novel teachings, Rabbi Ishmael said we should hew to the plain sense of the text. If the rest of the passage is understood to refer to idolatry, we should understand this clause in similar fashion. The view stated earlier in the Sifre understood "the word of the Lord" to mean each and every word in the Torah. Rabbi Ishmael understood it to mean the first utterance of the Ten Commandments. Perhaps Rabbi Ishmael himself originated the view that only the first two verses were heard directly from the divine voice,[43] and therefore are uniquely privileged to be called the "word of the Lord" in the full sense.[44]

The basic lesson of the first Mishnah in Sanhedrin chapter 10 is that whoever denies Torah from heaven has no share in the world to come. This starts from the scriptural text, "that person shall be cut off from among his people," and carries it one step further. This is based directly on Rabbi Akiva's understanding of the text, which is opposed by Rabbi Ishmael. For verse 31 contains the redundant[36] verbal construction *hikkaret tikkaret*: "Because he has spurned the word of the Lord and violated His commandment, *cut off, cut off* shall that person be." Rabbi Akiva interpreted the redundancy: "*Hikkaret*—cut off in this world, *tikkaret*—cut off in the next world." Rabbi Ishmael replied: "Since the previous verse also says 'cut off,' will you therefore deduce that he is cut off three times in three worlds? Rather, this proves that the Torah speaks in human language."[45]

The Sifre records another understanding of "spurning the word of the Lord": one who unmasks the face of Torah. The Talmud cites this view, but with a significant addition: "one who throws off the yoke and unmasks the face of Torah." Rashi comments: "'Throwing off the yoke' refers to one who rejects the first utterance at Sinai, 'I am the Lord your God,' which was heard directly from the divine voice."[46] According to the conclusion of the Talmud, this view is that of Rabbi Judah the Patriarch, the redactor of the Mishnah. This helps explain why Rabbi Judah did not include the more extreme interpretation of "spurning the word of the Lord," that is, one who rejects the divine authorship of so much as a single passage in the Torah. His understanding of "spurning the word of the Lord" is in agreement with Rabbi Ishmael, but his conclusion, "such a person has no portion in the world to come" is in agreement with Rabbi Akiva.

Note that Rabbi Ishmael deviated from the commonly accepted division of the Ten

---

[43] BT Horayot 8a. Note that Rabbi Ishmael also considered the first two verses ("I am the Lord . . . you shall have no other gods") a single utterance.

[44] Note that the Jerusalem Targum follows Rabbi Ishmael's method by translating Numbers 15:31: "For he has transgressed the first utterance which the Lord commanded at Sinai." Rashi and RaSHBaM follow suit in their commentaries.

[45] Sifre Shalah 112; BT Sanhedrin 64b.

[46] BT Shevuot 13a.

---

[36] Redundant, that is, only to one doing Akivan midrash. It is perfectly straightforward biblical style, as Ishmael will argue.

Commandments. It is generally accepted that the first Commandment is "I am the Lord your God," and "You shall have no other gods" is the second.[47] Rabbi Ishmael, however, combines these two into a single utterance. This division is the one adopted also by Philo and Josephus.[48] [37]

An "Alternate Tradition" Extends the Concept Further

The Babylonian Talmud also deals with the concept of "Torah from heaven." We shall present the text in three sections for clarity.

A. Our rabbis taught: "He has spurned the word of the Lord" refers to one who says there is no Torah from heaven. Another interpretation: It refers to the Epicurean.

B. An alternate tradition: "He has spurned the word of the Lord" refers to one who says the Torah is not from heaven.[38] Even one who says, "All the Torah is from heaven except for this one verse, which Moses said on his own," spurns the word of the Lord. Even one who says, "All the Torah is from heaven, *except for this one distinction, deduction, or analogy,*"[39] spurns the word of the Lord.

C. Rabbi Ishmael says: This refers to idolatry. We have a teaching of the school of Rabbi Ishmael: "He has spurned the word of the Lord" refers to the first utterance of the Ten Commandments."[49]

[47] See MI Bahodesh 8; Song of Songs Rabbah 1:2; PT Berakhot 1:8 (3c); PR 21:5 (106b).
[48] Philo, *De Decalogo;* Josephus *Antiquities* 3.5.5.
[49] BT Sanhedrin 99a; YS I, 335, 749.

---

[37] The combination of the first two into one is preserved also, interestingly enough, in the cantillation that is used this day for the public reading of the Ten Commandments in the synagogue.

[38] *Ein Torah min hashamayim.* See n. [22] above, on the ambiguity of this phrase: "there is no Torah from heaven" or "the Torah is not from heaven." The translation here alternates between the two, depending on context.

[39] Three categories of exegesis are enumerated here. *Dikduk* ("distinction") will be discussed below. *Kal vahomer* (deduction, a fortiori) is the argument from a less obvious to a more obvious case. *Gezerah shavah* (analogy) is the argument that if the same words are used in two contexts, the same meanings apply. All three are examples of teachings that are not in the written Torah, but are supplementary to it. They are part of the Oral Torah or Oral Law. The current passage raises acutely the very status of teachings that fall into this category. Are they "rabbinic" (and therefore of less authority than "Torahitic" teachings)? Can they be considered "Torahitic" (deriving from Moses, and even divinely revealed) even though they are not in the written Torah? This recalls a crucial distinction between the assumptions of Rabbi Ishmael and Rabbi Akiva: for Rabbi Ishmael, the greater part of the Torah was in writing, while for Rabbi Akiva, the greater part was oral (see ch. 2 above, pp. 50ff.) It also recalls the debate between Maimonides and Nahmanides, whether the deductions made from the written text on the basis of exegetical principles are to be considered a rabbinic extension of the Torah or integral to the Torah itself (see chapter 13, section entitled "The Method of Plain-Sense Interpretation [Peshat]").

What is the difference between the first and second Baraitot (neither of which is from the school of Rabbi Ishmael)? The first is given in general terms; it speaks of one who denies generally that there is any instruction from heaven.

The second Baraita is radically different from the first. The opening recalls the excerpt from Sifre 112 that we cited at the beginning of this chapter, with an important difference: "All the Torah is at the divine behest" (*mipi hakodesh*) is replaced with: "All the Torah is from heaven" (*min hashamayim*). This is the Akivan extension of the phrase "Torah from heaven" that we have already seen. But note how the author of the second Baraita extends the definition of heresy to one who denies even the "distinctions, deductions, and analogies"! One commentator rightly points out that this blurs the boundary between the written Torah and the oral tradition.[50]

The Sinaitic revelation of the oral traditions is a recurrent theme in the halakhic midrashim of the Akivan school. We find in the Sifra: "'These are the laws, rules, and instructions that the Lord established, through Moses on Mount Sinai, between Himself and the Israelite people' (Leviticus 26:46)—this teaches that the Torah was given together with its legal minutiae,[40] distinctions, and interpretations through Moses at Sinai."[51] To be sure, the school of Rabbi Ishmael also agreed that Moses received more than the written Torah at Sinai, but they never taught that *all* the distinctions and interpretations were given to him. They said, in more restrained language: "'If you will heed the *voice* of the Lord your God diligently' (Exodus 15:26)—this refers to the Ten Commandments—'and do what is *upright* in His sight'—these are the choice *aggadot* that are pleasing to all—'give ear to His commandments'—these are secondary enactments[41]—'and keep all His laws'—these are legal minutiae."[42] [52]

What are *dikdukim* ("distinctions")? Rashi says: "This refers to superfluous letters from which extensions and exclusions of the law can be derived midrashically. For instance, from the extra *hei* in 'the citizens in Israel shall live in booths,' we learn that

---

[50] *Metzaref Lakkesef*, 2:1.
[51] Sifra 112c. See also Sifra 40c, 105a, Sifre Berakhah 343, and Sifre Zuta on Numbers 6:23, p. 247.
[52] MI Vayyassa' 1.

---

[40] *Halakhot* (legal minutiae). This refers to the genre of tradition represented by the Mishnah and Tosefta: detailed lists of the application of the law to various conditions. Though often based on general laws written in the Torah, they go far beyond the written Torah in their specific application. The current midrash (and many others like it) asserts that these were not a later development to supplement the paucity of written text but were revealed from God to Moses and transmitted orally for over a thousand years until they were finally codified by Judah the Patriarch in the Mishnah around 200 C.E.

[41] Hebrew: *gezerot*, that is, protective enactments put in place to guard against infringements of a core law (e.g., that musical instruments not be played on the Sabbath [a *gezerah*], lest one be tempted to construct an instrument [a core Sabbath violation]).

[42] This midrash clearly says that God has enjoined the Israelites in a general way to observe all the varieties of religious law that may be enacted at any time. What is missing is the assertion that all the details of those enactments were present in some form in the Sinaitic revelation.

women are exempt." This is the typical Akivan style of exegesis, as opposed to the Ish-maelian approach that such redundancy is a feature of the human language in which the Torah speaks.

The formulation "whoever says all the Torah is from heaven *except for this one verse*" is also significant and derives from Sifre Zuta, a midrash on Numbers from the Akivan school. It probably hints disparagingly at various heretical views that did pre-cisely that, denying the authority of particular verses. This was an important attempt to define the essentials of Jewish belief. Sifre Zuta distinguishes also between two kinds of heretical dissent: "'He has spurned the word of the Lord'—asking, 'Why was this written?'; 'and violated His commandment'—saying, 'All the Torah is from heaven except for this one verse.'"[53] The one questions the narratives in the Torah; the other is more serious, attacking the mitzvot as well.[43]

Indeed, various Sages asked precisely this question, "Why was this written?" Why did the text bother to tell us that Timna was Eliphaz's concubine?[54] Why did it list all the way stations on the journey of the Israelites in the wilderness?[55] Why did it include the law of executing the rebellious son, which we learn was never applied in reality—just to have the reward of studying it?[56] In Rabbi Ishmael's school, they asked, "What need was there for the people of the world to know this?"[57] But it is clear that there are two senses to such questions: the heretics asked them to mock the tradition, but the Sages asked in an earnest attempt to gain clarification.

Maimonides' Ruling

Maimonides explicitly invoked both the narrow and the broader understandings of "Torah from heaven." In his code, he established: "The Epicurean and Denier of the Torah have no portion in the world to come. . . . The 'Epicurean' includes one who says there is no such thing as prophecy—that is, that no knowledge is communicated between God and human beings—as well as one who denies that Moses was a prophet. . . . 'Denier of the Torah' refers to one who says the Torah is not from God, or that even one verse or one word was said by Moses on his own initiative. It also includes one who denies the interpretations of Oral Law, or rejects those who trans-

---

[53] Sifre Zuta, p. 287.
[54] Sifre Ha'azinu 336.
[55] Midrash Lekah Tov and Rashi on Numbers 33:1–2.
[56] Tosefta Sanhedrin 11:6.
[57] Sifre Ekev 37; Bereshit Rabbati, ed. Albeck, p. 94.

---

[43] The evaluation that mitzvot should be taken more seriously than narratives, is of course endemic to the rabbinic tradition. An important corrective to this bias is provided by Heschel himself in chapter 1.

mit it. Such were Zadok and Boethus."[44] 58 By condemning both, Maimonides came down on the more stringent side.

Maimonides wrote similarly in his "Thirteen Principles," which he included in his introduction to Mishnah Sanhedrin chapter 10: "The eighth principle is that Torah is from heaven. This means that we must believe that the entire Torah in our possession was given by God through Moses our Master. The one who says, 'the Torah is not from heaven,' rejects this. Thus our Sages said: 'Whoever believes that all the Torah is of divine origin except for this one verse, which was said not by God but by Moses on his own has "spurned the word of God."'" 59 Elsewhere Maimonides wrote, "There is no distinction between one who denies the entire Torah and one who denies only a single verse." 60

Is such perfectionism possible? Rabbi Yose the Galilean divided people into three categories: righteous, wicked, and average. Rava said, "People like us are average." At this, Abbaye cried out and said, "The master leaves no hope for life for any creature!" —that is to say, if *you* belong to the average, there is no completely righteous person in the world. 61 Abbaye might rightly have cried out also against the "alternate tradition" in the Babylonian Talmud. If anyone who believes that one verse in the Torah is merely Mosaic and not divine in origin, thereby "spurns the word of the Lord," how many of the great Sages of Israel whose teachings we imbibe and who give us spiritual life, would be condemned by this standard! Abbaye himself, that great pillar on which our Talmud rests, stated specifically that there was not only one verse but many verses in Deuteronomy which Moses said on his own accord. "Beware of Abbaye and his teaching!"[45]

Abbaye was fond of saying,[46] "A person should be intelligently pious, give a soft

---

58 Maimonides, Mishneh Torah I, *Hilkhot Teshuvah* [Laws concerning Repentance] 3:6, 8.

59 "Introduction to Mishnah Sanhedrin chapter 10," ed. Haltzer (Berlin, 5661/1901), 26 (found also in *A Maimonides Reader*, ed. Isidore Twersky [New York: Behrman House, 1972], 420).

60 Responsa of Maimonides, 77.

61 BT Berakhot 61b.

---

[44] Maimonides here cites the supposed views of the Sadducees and Boethusians. These parties in Second Temple Jewry competed for prestige and following with the Pharisees (from whom Rabbinic Judaism derived). They differed famously with the Pharisees on the interpretation of certain laws of the Torah and hence were perceived by the Pharisees as denying the Oral Law. Maimonides followed the rabbinic tradition in supposing that they were founded by (and named for) two individuals named Zadok and Boethus, identified in ARN A 5 as disciples of Antigonos of Sokho (third century B.C.E.). More likely, the Sadducees (whose constituency included the priestly leadership) were named for Zadok, High Priest in the days of King David and King Solomon, whose descendants were singled out by Ezekiel (40:46) for leadership in the restored Temple. The Boethusians probably got their name from Simeon ben Boethus, who was High Priest under Herod.

[45] Pesahim 112b tells the story of a demon who encountered Abbaye and said, "Had they not told me in heaven, 'Beware of Nahmani [Abbaye's given name] and his teaching,' I would have put you in danger."

[46] Heschel's purpose in quoting Pesahim 112b above is to establish Abbaye's authority. He now quotes various sayings in order to communicate Abbaye's personality and general outlook as back-

answer to turn away wrath, and make peace among his family and neighbors, even the stranger in the marketplace. Thus he will be loved on high and amiable below, and welcomed by everyone."[62] He also said: "Go out and see what the people are saying."[63] "Better they should sin out of ignorance than out of malice."[64] "The purpose of the whole Torah is to further peace."[65]

[62] BT Berakhot 17a.   [63] BT Berakhot 45b.
[64] BT Shabbat 148b.   [65] BT Gittin 59b.

---

ground for his lenient approach on the divine origin of the Torah. Prudence, gentleness, responsiveness to the common people, and promotion of peace—all these argue implicitly for moderation, and against maximalist perfectionism.

THE SECTARIANS

Translator's Introduction

In the previous chapter, Heschel noted that the ultimate widening of the referent of the word "Torah" in "Torah from Heaven" was articulated in a Tannaitic reading (embodied in a Baraita in Tractate Sanhedrin) of Numbers 15:31, which speaks of those who "spurn" the word of God. This seems to have brought him, by association, to a kind of interlude, in which he undertakes a discussion of the various unorthodox views on the Torah that were held by those who were labeled "sectarians."

In addition, however, to the prompting from the reference to "spurners" in Numbers 15, there is another reason for Heschel to interpose this chapter here, before proceeding to define the two principal views on "Torah from Heaven." It is important for him to keep his readers from falling into the "genetic fallacy," that is, to draw conclusions and judgments about certain views about the Torah on the basis of some of the sources and adherents of those views.

He speaks here of the general effect of Hellenistic rationalism on the belief structure of the Jews who encountered that world. Revelation and prophecy, especially their particularistic natures in Jewish thought, faced a severe challenge in the Hellenistic world. Precisely because there was also high esteem for Hellenistic culture (many Rabbis had, after all, subscribed to the idea that "the beauty of Japhet [i.e., Greece] shall dwell in the Tents of Shem [an ancestor of Abraham]") the doubts that that culture cast on revelation as a source of truth were all the more serious. The "Denials of Japhet" thus also entered the Tents of Shem.

Now rabbinic tradition identifies at least four different points of view that come in for disapproval and/or condemnation, in at least some texts. Two of these—(a) that revelation is impossible, and (b) that Moses' Torah is a forgery—were articulated in late antiquity by those who clearly sought to undermine Judaism. But the other two—(c) that the Ten Commandments alone were given at Sinai, and (d) that Moses both spoke and did things on his own authority—were of a different kind. Those who were defined as sectarians—whether influenced by Hellenism, Christianity, Gnosticism, or other ideas—may well have articulated notions (c) and (d) as well. But these latter two points of view also found a natural home in the minds of some prominent rabbinic thinkers. They do not, by their nature, necessarily undermine Judaism by attacking fundamentals of the faith. Or so Heschel wishes to convince us in the subsequent chapters. For that reason, he must pause here in chapter 21 to do his "taxonomy of heresies," so that we will know how to distinguish between alien views that destroy the roots and views with perhaps some external influences that nevertheless can, and did, dwell comfortably in the intellectual and spiritual Tents of Shem.

Four Kinds of Unbelievers[1]

ALL THESE RABBINIC TRADITIONS were taught not only to formulate the principles of faith but also to proscribe the sectarians of Israel.[2] Rabbi Simeon Hasida interpreted the verse "'How they were shriveled up before their time, and their foundation poured out like a river?' (Job 22:16). This refers to the brazen-faced, whom the Holy and Blessed One has planted in every generation."[1] "Each generation has its scoffers"[2]—prophets always stood alongside sectarians, believers and heretics together.

The talmudic Sages did not preserve the actual remarks of their opponents. The words themselves were suppressed. Only the rabbis' refutations of them were preserved, and from those replies we hear echoes of the original controversies. Even though the echoes are faint and distant to us now, we sense that they once rang loud and clear to their listeners.

The Sages' discussion of heretical views was not hypothetical, for intellectual edification only. The views they cited were quoted, perhaps verbatim, from the members of the actual sects. The following expressions in the rabbinic literature represent views of their contemporaries, disputing the authenticity of the Torah:

"There is no Torah from heaven."

"Only the Ten Commandments were given to Moses."

"Most of the Torah is of divine origin, but there are things Moses added himself."

"Moses forged the Torah."

---

[1] BT Hagigah 13b–14a.   [2] PT Shekalim 2:7 (47a).

---

[1] There are two words for heretic/heresy which Heschel uses in this chapter. *Kofer* has the sense of "denier, unbeliever," as in *kofer ba'ikar,* "one who denies the basic principle." *Min* (whose root meaning is "species, kind") has the sense of "sect, sectarian." The chapter title, *Haminim,* therefore, should be taken to mean "The [heretical] Sectarians." When Heschel speaks of "heresy" in this chapter, he does not generally express his own evaluation of a given view, but rather that of the Rabbis.

[2] Heschel's use of the rare verb, *lehoki'a* ("proscribe"), recalls Numbers 25:4: "Take all the ringleaders (of the idolatrous faction at Ba'al Pe'or) and have them publicly impaled before the Lord." The sense here is: identify them in order that they may be ostracized from the community.

We recognize here the common coin and household words of sectarian discourse in the rabbinic period. From them, we may infer there were four principal types of heretical thought:

A. Those who said, there is no divine Torah at all, no revelation and no prophecy.

B. Those who said, only the Ten Commandments were given to Moses at Sinai.

C. Those who said, the Torah was said by Moses at divine behest, but he formulated some things on his own.

D. Those who said, Moses forged the Torah; that is, he introduced certain portions which were not at the divine behest.

There are differences among these types. As human faces differ, so do their ways of straying from the accepted path. Their expressions are testimony to spiritual ferment and crisis. This contradicts the accepted view, that Israel of the early rabbinic period was united in perfect faith. The spiritual environment was replete with confusion and agitation, searching and groping. These tensions led the Sages to set the doctrine of the Mosaic Torah in a crystallized form, for protection and security.

The Sages who met in Nitzeh's upper story in Lydda during the religious persecutions,[3] commented on the verse "When I stumble, they gleefully gather; wretches gather against me, I know not why" (Psalm 35:15): "When Israel engage in heresy, that is when the nations of the world rejoice and gather their forces to kill them, taking advantage of their wretched and lame condition." "There is no breaching and no sortie, and no wailing in our streets" (Psalm 144:13)—we pray that we do not have a son or disciple who spoils his cooking in public.[4] 3

Rabbi Johanan Nappaha[4] said, "The Jews were not exiled until they broke apart into twenty-four heretical sects." A third-century source uncovered in Egypt in 1945 reports that there were as many forms of heresy as letters in the alphabet, "and they persist to this day."[5]

---

[3] BT Berakhot 17b.

[4] Rabbi Johanan Nappaha also transmitted the story of Kamtza and Bar Kamtza, the moral of which is that personal animosity and political factionalism caused the destruction of Jerusalem (see BT Gittin 55b).

[5] G. Quispel, "Christliche Gnosis und Jüdische Heterodoxie," *Evangelische Theologie* 14 (1954): 1–11.

---

[3] The meetings in Nitzeh's upper story were the occasion of many important doctrinal discussions. It was the scene of the debate between Rabbi Akiva and Rabbi Tarfon about which was more important, study or action (BT Kiddushin 40b). There, too, the Sages agreed that one should violate any of the mitzvot to save one's life, except for the prohibitions of murder, idolatry, and sexual immorality (BT Sanhedrin 74a). The persecutions referred to are probably those associated with the Bar Kokhba rebellion (132–135 C.E.).

[4] "Spoiling the cooking" was a metaphor for adding too many extraneous ingredients to the recipe of correct Torah learning.

The Denials of Japheth in the Tents of Shem

The Sages were of divided opinion about the value of Greek culture. Bar Kappara appreciated the Greek regard for beauty and applied the verse "May God beautify Japheth, and let him dwell in the tents of Shem" (Genesis 9:27).[5] "They shall speak the language of Japheth (Greek) in the tents of Shem."[6] Rabbi Johanan interpreted: "They shall speak the matters of Japheth in the tents of Shem." Rabbi Hiyya bar Abba said: "The beauty of Japheth shall be in the tents of Shem."[7] "'Without blemish' (Numbers 19:2)—this is Greece."[8]

But the Hellenistic period was one of confrontation between Israel's Torah and Greek culture. The stream of Greek enlightenment, which swept over the Jewish world, was likely to sweep away not just the fruits but the roots as well, leading not just to laxity in observing the mitzvot but to surrender of first principles as well.[6]

The Rabbis understood the threat that Hellenization posed to them. Rabbi Simeon ben Lakish interpreted: "'The earth was unformed'—this is Babylon; 'and void'—this is Media; 'and darkness'—this is Greece, which darkened Israel's eyes through its decrees,[7] saying to Israel: 'Write on the horn of the ox[8] that you have no part in the God of Israel.'"[9] Whoever says that Hellenization was only superficial, a hedonistic gourmandizing or putting on language and manners, has not plumbed the depth of the matter. Hellenization pierced to the core of its adherents, bringing on a crisis of faith. They overthrew the yoke[9] of faith as well as deeds. A culture based on reason

---

[6] PT Megillah 1:11 (71b).   [7] BT Megillah 9b.   [8] PRK 4:9 (40b).

[9] Genesis Rabbah 2:4; on Greece's darkening Israel, see also MI Bahodesh 9.

---

[5] NJV: "May God enlarge Japheth." Bar Kappara understood the Hebrew yaft (= Japheth) as related to yafeh ("beautiful"). According to the genealogy of nations in Genesis 10, Greece (Javan = Ionia) was a descendant of Japheth, and Israel was a descendant of Shem.

[6] Heschel uses the expression, la'akor et hakol ("to uproot everthing"). This is an allusion to Laban's purported threat to completely annihilate Jacob's clan (mentioned in the Haggadah of Passover). It is also a verbal play on kafar ba'ikar—one who denies the root-principle of faith, the belief in One God.

[7] This is probably an allusion to the aggressive Hellenization policy of the Seleucid king Antiochus Epiphanes (176–163 B.C.E.), which led to the Maccabean revolt.

[8] Writing something "on the horn of an ox" was an expression for publicizing it (for an ox would walk around and thus carry the message to the public). What is described here is the Antiochan demand for a public, not just a private, renunciation of the God of Israel. In rabbinic law, a private renunciation might not have necessitated resistance to the point of martyrdom, but a public renunciation did.

[9] Heschel alludes to the two "yokes" of Jewish liturgical tradition: the "yoke of Heaven" (reciting the Shema: "Hear O Israel! The Lord is our God, the Lord alone. You shall love the Lord your God . . ." [Deuteronomy 6:4–9]) and the "yoke of mitzvot" (reciting Deuteronomy 11:13–21: "If, then, you obey the commandments . . ." [see Mishnah Berakhot 2:2]). He calls the first of these "the yoke of faith." Faith in God is the root fundamental on which adherence to observance of mitzvot is based. Hellenization eroded both.

challenged the Torah based on revelation, as the midrash testifies: "'The *shafan* [daman]' (Deuteronomy 14:7)—this is Greece, which brought low the Torah proclaimed by prophets."[10] 10

A story about the Hasmonean period[11] tells how King Antiochus forced an elderly Jew to eat pork and said, "Why do you despise eating the excellent flesh of this animal which nature has provided us with? It is folly to abstain from such pleasures! When will you take leave of your childish philosophy and adopt a more mature outlook?" The Jew replied, "Antiochus, we derive our life from God's Torah! We believe it is wrong to transgress it in any way. But even if our Torah were not really from God, as you imagine, but we believed in it nevertheless, it would still be incumbent on us to maintain our faith in how God is to be revered."11

The name of Moses was familiar to some of the Greeks at the time of Alexander the Great. When Hecataeus of Abdera visited Egypt (ca. 323 B.C.E.), the Torah had not yet been translated into Greek. He reported that at the end of the laws of the Torah was written, "Moses told the Israelites what he had heard from God."12 Hecataeus himself did not dispute this claim, but Diodorus, in a work that is mostly a compendium of Hecataeus, added that Moses said this in order to gain acceptance for his sayings.13

Posidonius (ca. 51–135 C.E.) wrote that Jews valued God's commands more in previous generations than in his own time. Whatever the truth of it, they believed them and accepted them as law. He mentioned that the Greeks also had legislators (Amphiaraus, Trophonius, Musaeus, Tiresias) who spoke in the name of the gods, and so did other peoples. Moses did likewise. Because Moses and the later prophets claimed to be conveying the divine will, their pronouncements were privileged over those of ordinary people.14 But times changed. Philosophers displaced prophets, and in place of blind faith in prophetic words, one now had truth arrived at through rational demonstration.15 Anti-Jewish authors, such as Apollonius, Lysimachus, and Molo, wrote that Moses was a fabricator;[12] he had no divine revelation but deceived

---

10 TB Shemini 14.   11 The Hasmonean Scroll IV,85.

12 F. Jacoby, *Die Fragmente der griechischen Historiker* (Berlin: Weidmann, 1923–58), III A (Commentary), pp. 46–52; Diodorus Siculus, *Diodorus of Sicily, Library of History,* trans. C. H. Oldfather, Loeb Classical Library 279 (Cambridge, Mass.: Harvard University Press; London: Heinemann, 1933–67), 1:321.

13 Jacoby, *Fragmente,* III A (Commentary), 75ff.

14 Ibid., II C (Commentary), 196ff.

15 R. Walzer, *Galen on Jews and Christians* (London: Oxford University Press, 1949), 22. Compare Julian the Apostate, *Against Christianity* (*The Works of the Emperor Julian,* trans. Wilmer Cave Wright, Loeb Classical Library [Cambridge, Mass.: Harvard University Press; London: Heinemann, 1913–23], 3:349ff.

---

[10] The obscure word *shafan* is interpreted as an acronym of *hiSHPil Nevuah*—that which "humbled prophecy." The Rabbis called this kind of midrash *notarikon*. In addition, *shafan* and *yavan* (Greece) had a certain phonetic affinity.

[11] Second century B.C.E.

[12] The midrash of Satan, Moses, and God, cited above (chapter 20, "Torah [Without Specification] Means Ten Commandments"), echoes this accusation.

his followers.[16] Horace considered the Jewish religion a *superstitio prava immodica*,[13] and the medical authority Galen (129–199) compared unscientific medical writers to "Moses, who gave laws to the Jewish tribe, who would write things unsupported by any proof, saying only that 'God commanded,' 'God said.'"[17]

One Who Says,
"There Is No Torah from Heaven"

The basic foundation of Judaism is expressed by the Talmud in the formula "Moses is true and his Torah is true."[18] Whoever denies Moses' prophecy denies prophecy as such. The revelation at Sinai also rests on Moses' reliability: "Moses spoke, and God answered him by a voice" (Exodus 19:19).[14] "'They had faith in the Lord and His servant Moses' (Exodus 14:31)—this teaches you that believing in Moses, the shepherd of Israel, is tantamount to believing in the Creator of the World." Nevertheless, there were those in Israel "lacking in faith" "who did not believe in our Master Moses' words," "who did not listen to Moses" (Exodus 16:20).[19] These are the ones who never ceased clamoring, murmuring, and complaining against Moses, and not against him alone. Questioning the shepherd of Israel is tantamount to questioning God.[20]

"Let lying lips be stilled that speak haughtily against the righteous with arrogance and contempt" (Psalm 31:19). This verse was interpreted as referring to Moses' detractors, who said, "Is it possible that the Shekhinah rests on the son of Amram?"[21] These are the scoffers who questioned prophecy.[22] Rabbi Meir said, "Even at the hour that they said, 'All that the Lord has spoken we will faithfully do,' their mouths said one thing and their hearts another."[23] When the Midianite women seduced the Israelites, they would say to them, "I will not let you be, until you renounce the Torah of Moses."[24] When Moses came to give his farewell address to them after forty years,

[16] Josephus, *Against Apion* 2.13.

[17] Walzer, *Galen on Jews and Christians*, 18, 46–48.

[18] BT Sanhedrin 110a.

[19] MI Beshalah 4; Midrash Lekah Tov on Exodus 16:4. Abraham ibn Ezra comments on Exodus 19:9: "The Egyptians and Indians were both descendants of Ham. Now, the Sages of India argued from their premises that it is not credible that God would speak with man and he would live. When Israel was in Egypt, they encountered people of this persuasion, and some of them doubted Moses' prophecy as a result."

[20] MI Beshalah 6.

[21] Exodus Rabbah 52:2; YS Pekudei 417.

[22] Caro, *Or Tzaddikim*, Pekudei.

[23] Numbers Rabbah 7:4.

[24] BT Sanhedrin 106a; PT Sanhedrin 10:2 (28d): "Renounce Moses's Torah, and I am yours."

[13] A depraved, extravagant superstition.

[14] NJV: "As Moses spoke, God answered him in thunder."

some of them said, "He is out of his mind!"[25] A plain reading of the Korah episode in Scripture makes clear that Korah questioned Moses' prophecy: "Why do you raise yourselves above the Lord's congregation?" (Numbers 16:3). That is how Moses understood their challenge as well: "By this you shall know that it was the Lord who sent me to do all these things; that *they are not of my own devising*. If these men die as all men do, *it was not the Lord who sent me*. But if the Lord brings about something unheard-of, . . . you shall know that these men have spurned the Lord" (Numbers 16:28–30). Such piercing words would not have been called for, had the rebels not sought to overturn everything. The midrashim we have cited make the same point.

The authors of the midrash read Scripture in the light of their own contemporary reality. For them, there was nothing new under the sun. They saw Korah's company as precursors of their own heretics. Just as the Greek historians put timely editorials in the mouths of past heroes, so did the rabbis attribute to Korah the views of later sectarians.[26] "The likes of Korah and his companions are found in every generation."[27] "Korah accused Moses of passing off his own words as God's."[28] "Korah said: 'There is no Torah from heaven; Moses is not a prophet, and Aaron is not the high priest.'"[29]Here is the stark denial of Torah as prophecy, uttered as it were before the writing of the Torah was even completed.

The midrashic authors even had Moses step out of character[15] and say, "If such as these die a natural death, then even I will turn heretic and deny that God sent me," or (in another version) "that there is Torah from heaven."[30] "I am willing to forgive the insult to Aaron and myself, but not the insult to the Torah."

Josephus attributed to Zimri son of Salu (Numbers 25:14) the view that Moses legislated with a view to enslaving the people and aggrandizing himself; that is, he had no revelation but deceived the people.[31] He also attributed to Korah the view that Moses laid onerous laws on the people that he falsely claimed were divine.[32]

Rabbi Simeon ben Eleazar said, "Those who lend at interest lose more than they profit, for they make the Torah a fraud and Moses a fool when they say, 'Had Moses known how much we profit from interest, he would not have forbade it.'"[33] [16]

---

25 YS Deuteronomy 793, citing Yelammedenu.
26 See Isaac Heinemann, *Darkhei Ha-aggadah*, p. 17.
27 MTD 32:7, p. 189.   28 Tanhuma Korah 8.
29 PT Sanhedrin 10:1 (28a); Ecclesiastes Rabbah on 10:1; YS I,752.
30 Numbers Rabbah 18:12; Tanhuma Buber, addendum to Korah, 2.
31 Josephus, *Antiquities* 4.6.11.   32 Josephus, *Antiquities* 4.2.3.
33 Tosefta Bava Metzi'a 6:17; PT Bava Metzi'a 5:13 (10d); BT Bava Metzi'a 75b.

---

[15] For he was usually modest and forbearing.

[16] In other words, Moses did it on his own (and the Torah is thus forged, at least in part); and Moses did it only out of sheer ignorance of the ways of the world of business, and thus he was a fool. It is noteworthy that this is brought as another example of heresy, since it might be said that it is just a giving in to the temptation of quick enrichment. But the attribution of the prohibition to Moses makes it more than that. It becomes a heresy.

Apparently Rabbi Simeon was reporting the denial of the Torah on the part of actual money-lenders of his generation.

The issue of "Torah from Heaven" was also a bone of contention in Jewish–Christian polemics. This will help us understand the remarks of Rabbi Abbahu:[17] "The nations of the world agree with us on two important principles: they agree that the Holy and Blessed One created the world, and they agree on the resurrection of the dead."[34] Significantly, he makes no mention here of "Torah from heaven."[18]

So They Should Not Say,
"These Alone Are from Sinai"

Many rabbinic sayings will attest to the unique status of the Ten Commandments, which the Israelites heard at Sinai. We saw earlier that they were widely taken to include in some way the 613 commandments of the Torah.[35] In the Temple, they would recite the "Ten Utterances" daily, but this custom was abolished in the early synagogue because of "the quarrel of the sectarians."[36] The Babylonian Talmud does not explain what exactly this quarrel consisted in, but the Palestinian Talmud elaborates: "The Ten Commandments should rightly be recited daily in the liturgy. Why, then, do we not recite them? Because of the contention of the sectarians, so they should not say, these alone were given to Moses at Sinai."[37] Rashi explains: "So they should not say the rest of the Torah is not true, for they only read what was heard from the mouth of the Holy and Blessed One at Sinai." It is no small thing that the rabbis should have abolished an ancient liturgical custom. Surely they would not have taken such drastic steps, were it not for a great and present danger.

"They asked Simeon ben Azzai to expound on Lamentations. He interpreted the opening word Eikhah:[19] 'Israel was not exiled until they renounced the One God, and circumcision, which was given in the twentieth generation,[20] and the Ten Com-

---

[34] Midrash on Psalms 19:1.

[35] Views of Rabbi Ishmael and Tosafists above, chapter 20, section entitled "Torah (Withough Specification) Means Ten Commandments." This is also found in Philo, De Decalogo, trans. F. M. Colson, Loeb Classical Library (Cambridge, Mass.: Harvard University Press, 1937), 83.

[36] BT Berakhot 12a. The Nash Papyrus includes the Shema together with the Ten Commandments. See W. F. Albright, "A Biblical Fragment from the Maccabean Age: The Nash Papyrus," Journal of Biblical Literature 56 (1937): 145–76; he thinks this was written in the Hasmonean period.

[37] PT Berakhot 1:4 (3c).

---

[17] Heschel has mentioned Rabbi Abbahu's role in Jewish–Christian polemics above in chapter 18, under "The Ascent of Enoch."

[18] Since he does not mention it as a point of agreement, we may infer that the Christians with whom Rabbi Abbahu debated did not believe in the divine revelation of the entire Torah.

[19] The word eikhah is spelled: aleph (1), yod (10), kaf (20), hei (5). The numerical values of the Hebrew letters are given in parentheses.

[20] There were ten generations from Adam to Noah, and then another ten from Noah to Abraham. See Mishnah Avot 5:2.

mandments, and the Five Books of the Torah, according to the numerical value of the letters in the word *Eikhah*."[38] The commentators objected: Does not the one who denies the One God deny, by implication, the divinely revealed Torah as well? The answer is given: There were various heretical sects; some denied God, others circumcision, still others the Ten Commandments or the revealed Torah.[39]

The Sifra attests: "There are some who do not learn, and do not practice, who despise those who do, and hate the Sages, and do not allow others to practice, but they agree on the commandments that were spoken at Sinai." Such a person apparently rejected the rabbinic tradition but accepted the written Torah. Of such a person, the Sifra adds: "Eventually he will reject even the commandments spoken at Sinai; eventually he will even reject the basic principle."[21] [40] A later source attests: "Woe to those sectarians who reject the *halakhah* and say, 'Only the Ten Commandments were given to Moses.'"[41]

A midrash expounds on the phraseology "Moses addressed the Israelites in accordance with *all* of the instructions that the Lord had given for them" (Deuteronomy 1:3)—"We might have thought that Moses received only the Ten Commandments in prophetic revelation. How do we know that all the utterances in the Torah, together with the deductions, analogies, generalities, specifics, and minutiae were commanded by God (and he did not make them up on his own)? Because it is written, '*all* off the instructions . . . .'"[22][42]

This heresy, too, was attributed to Korah. "Korah assembled the people and said, 'When the Ten Commandments were given to us, every one of us derived the divine teaching from Sinai, and it consisted only of the Ten Commandments. We heard nothing about a bread offering, or a heave offering, or tithes, or putting fringes on our garments. Surely Moses invented these things in order to aggrandize himself and his brother Aaron!"[23] [43] According to this midrash, Korah accepted the Ten Commandments, but rejected the rest of the mitzvot that were received through Moses.

And from early Judeo-Christian sources, we find the following interpretation of a famous saying of Jesus: "'For verily I say unto you, till heaven and earth pass, one jot[24] or one tittle[25] shall in no wise pass from the law, till all be fulfilled' (Matthew

---

[38] Lamentations Rabbah 1.   [39] *Yefei Anaf* ad loc.   [40] Sifra Behukotai 111c.
[41] Midrash Haggadol on Exodus 26:7, p. 590.
[42] Sifre Devarim 2; YS 800, *Zayit Ra'anan* ad loc.
[43] YS I, 752; Tanhuma, ed. Buber, Korah pp. 86–88.

---

[21] Generally, this means the very sovereignty of the one God.

[22] Note the similarity to the "alternate tradition" in BT Sanhedrin 99a, cited in the previous chapter, which articulates the maximalist view.

[23] And the text means literally "to aggrandize." The gifts Korah mentioned were to go to Moses' brother, the priest, and to himself, a Levite. (Korah was, of course, a Levite as well, but he also had Reubenites in his rebellion.)

[24] Greek: "one iota."

[25] The crowns on top of certain letters in the Torah—see BT Menahot 29b.

5:18 [King James Version])—he was alluding to the Ten Commandments [for the numerical value of the letter yod[26] is ten]. But he regarded the laws in Deuteronomy (said by Moses in his own name) as not binding."[44]

He Said, "He Ought Not
To Have Written in the Torah . . ."

The heresy "Moses said some things on his own" was also phrased negatively: "Moses ought not to have written in the Torah. . . ." The substance of this view is discussed in the Palestinian Talmud: "'He has spurned the word of the Lord' refers to one who rejects substantive matters of Torah. Where can we learn that even one who rejects a single scripture, or Targum,[27] or deduction is also condemned? By the continuation: 'and violated His commandment.' An example of a verse: 'And Lotan's sister was Timna' (Genesis 36:22). An example of a Targum (Aramaic translation): 'Laban named it Yegar-sahadutha' (Genesis 31:47). An example of a deduction: 'If Cain is avenged sevenfold, then Lamech seventy-sevenfold'" (Genesis 4:24).[45] [28]

---

[44] *Didascalia Apostolorum,* ed. R. Hugh Connolly (Oxford: Clarendon Press, 1929), chapter 26, pp. 216ff.

[45] PT Sanhedrin 10:1 (27b); *Yefeh Mar'eh* ad loc.

---

[26] The letter Jesus referred to was the smallest letter of the Hebrew alphabet, rendered in Greek as *iota.*

[27] Targum: Rabbinically recognized Aramaic translation of a scripture. (See next note.)

[28] There is an obvious similarity between the list of items included as the "word of the Lord" here and in the "alternate tradition" in chapter 20. Each insists that the rabbinic extensions of the tradition are to be included in the part of the tradition that is sacrosanct. This is evident from the following explication of the items listed:

(a) A "scripture" is the smallest possible unit of scriptural text, even a verse or verse fragment. This rules out the view that there is even one verse that Moses did not write, but does not yet extend to rabbinic interpretations.

(b) "Targum" refers to the authoritative Aramaic translation of the Bible, which often incorporates rabbinic interpretations of the meaning of the text. Thus, anyone who interprets the text contrary to the rabbinically accepted Aramaic translation dissents from the tradition.

(c) "Deduction" (*kal vahomer,* a fortiori) was the first (and most common) of the thirteen principles of interpretation enumerated in the Baraita of Rabbi Ishmael. It is either used here as shorthand for rabbinic interpretation generally, or insists that a certain minimum of rabbinic interpretation be accepted as canonical.

However, the examples given of "Targum" and "deduction" are probably a later, extraneous addition to the original midrash, for they undercut the whole point that rabbinic extension is sacrosanct. In an interpretive tour-de-force, they find examples of a "Targum" and a "deduction" *in the written Torah itself.* Apparently, the original saying generated controversy, for not all the rabbis agreed that rabbinic extensions to the Torah are sacrosanct. The moderates were able to give assent to the saying, by giving it a very narrow interpretation, as applying only to the sanctity of the written Torah, as follows:

(a) "Scripture" was interpreted as narrative (as opposed to law), and they found as an example a verse fragment with apparently nonweighty content.

In what cases would one reject a single scripture? We are told of individuals who disparaged certain narratives of the Torah: "Like King Manasseh, who invented derogatory *aggadot* before the Omnipresent. He said, 'He [Moses] ought not to have written in the Torah, "Once, at the time of the wheat harvest, Reuben came upon some mandrakes in the field"[29] (Genesis 30:14). He ought not to have written, "And Lotan's sister was Timna."[30] Of him, it is written: "You sit with your brother and speak, with the son of your mother you spread scandal"[31] (Psalm 50:20).[46]

The expression "Moses ought not to have written . . ." implies that Moses wrote these passages on his own. Elsewhere Manasseh is mentioned as citing the same passages and commenting, "these are worthless matters, and Moses said them on his own initiative."[47] Apparently the author of these midrashim intended to depict sectarians who accepted the laws of the Torah as being of divine origin, but who belittled the Torah narratives. The citation from Psalm 50 supports this reading, for we find in that context: "And to the wicked, God said: 'Who are you to recite[32] My laws?'" (Psalm 50:16). Whoever belittles the Torah narratives ought not to recite its laws.

[46] Sifre Shelah 112; BT Sanhedrin 99b.
[47] *Mahzor Vitri*, p. 512.

(b) For a "Targum" within Scripture itself, they found the Aramaic name given in Genesis 31:47 as an equivalent for the Hebrew place-name Gal-ed.

(c) For an a fortiori deduction in Scripture, they found the rhetorical example in the Song of Lamech. This example is technically invalid, for reasons discussed below. Still, finding even imperfect examples of a rabbinic trope in the biblical text is very ingenious.

All this is beside the point of the current chapter, which is to illustrate the view (heretical or within the rabbinic mainstream) that certain parts of the *written* Torah are of less-than-divine origin. The *final* version of the midrash in the Jerusalem Talmud does indeed illustrate that view.

[29] The mandrakes were apparently either an aphrodisiac or fertility remedy. The Hebrew *duda'im* (related to *dodim*, love-making) has a more explicit sexual connotation than the English, which may have raised some eyebrows among ancient readers.

[30] Another verse about Timna mentioned in this connection was: "Timna was a concubine of Esau's son Eliphaz" (Genesis 36:12). The remainder of the verse ("she bore Amalek to Eliphaz") is not mentioned, but it may be significant that Amalek was regarded biblically as the arch-enemy of Israel. We can only guess what the Rabbis regarded as particularly derogatory about mention of Timna—That she was a concubine, and thus the verse gives us useless information, gossip even, about sexaul liaisons in Esau's family? That she was a woman mentioned in male genealogies? The ancestress of evil? Another midrash (Tanhuma Vayeshev 1) tells that Eliphaz committed adultery with Seir's wife, who bore their daughter, Timna, whom Eliphaz then took as a concubine; she was thus (in the Rabbis' imagination) the product of adultery and also partner to incest. Who knows, for how many centuries these texts were the subject of inside jokes, lightning rods of scurrilous fantasy? How much of this inside humor is implied in the statement (attributed to Manasseh, but in currency among heretics), that such verses should not have been written? For a more honorable look at Timna, see Rabbi Simeon's comment later in this section (Genesis 36:22).

[31] NJV: "You are busy maligning your brother, defaming the son of your mother." A more radical reading of this ambiguous verse, in line with the scurrilous midrash about Timna, might be: "She dwells with your brother; she is intimate with the son of your mother; she creates scandal."

[32] "To recite"—*le-sapper,* from the same root as *sippur* ("narrative"). The midrashist finds here an allusion to the conjunction of narrative and law in the Torah.

Here, too, the Sages applied the maxim "It is not an empty thing for you" (Deuteronomy 32:47). Rabbi Simeon found the genealogy of Timna worth mentioning, "to let the reader know how highly regarded Father Abraham's family was, that women of royalty would go to such lengths to marry into it."[48]

The *Yefeh Mar'eh* notes that the a fortiori deduction cited by the Jerusalem Talmud from the story of Lamech is invalid by the standards of rabbinic logic.[33] Therefore the reader might think that Moses wrote it on his own, for how would God have told him to write an invalid deduction in the Torah?[49] Even Rabbi Judah the Patriarch declared it to be an invalid deduction.[50]

We are not told the heretics' objection to the Aramaic phrase in Genesis 31:47, "Laban named it Yegar-sahadutha." Maybe they considered it pointless to record two names for the same place.[51] Maybe they considered Aramaic of inferior sanctity to Hebrew. Maybe they argued that an explanatory digression of this sort could not have been part of the original Torah. But R. Samuel bar Nahman took the opportunity to emphasize that this was a way for the Holy and Blessed One to show honor to the Syriac language.[52]

Rabbi Simeon ben Lakish said, "There are many parts of Scripture that seem worthy of being burned,[34] and yet they are essentials of Torah." We read of the Avim who dwelt in Gaza, until the Caphtorim wiped them out (Deuteronomy 2:23)—what difference does it make to us?[35] [53]

Sectarians challenged the Sages with skeptical questions about the stories of Genesis. Perhaps an echo of their arguments is found in the question of Rabbi Isaac:[36] "The Torah ought to have started with the first mitzvah, 'This month shall mark for you the beginning of the months' (Exodus 12:2). Why start with the story of cre-

---

[48] Genesis Rabbah 82:14.   [49] *Yefeh Mar'eh* on Sanhedrin, chapter 11.
[50] Genesis Rabbah 23:4.
[51] *Me'or Ha-afelah* ad loc.
[52] Genesis Rabbah 74:12.
[53] BT Hullin 60b; Rashi ad loc. Deuteronomy 2:10–12 and 2:20–23 digress from the story to give this kind of historical background, much of it obscure. Numbers 21:26–30 is a similar digression mentioned by Simeon ben Lakish.

---

[33] Lamech's deduction ("If Cain is avenged sevenfold, then Lamech seventy-sevenfold") follows the outer form of a rabbinic a fortiori, but violates one of its rules. Correct rabbinic reasoning would allow:

> Cain was a great sinner, killing wittingly.
> Lamech was a lesser sinner, killing unwittingly.
> Cain was given protection: "Whoever kills him, shall be avenged sevenfold."
> Therefore Lamech is entitled to the *same* protection, of being avenged *sevenfold*.

The actual conclusion, that Lamech shall be avenged *seventy-sevenfold*, is rhetorically plausible but (by rabbinic logic) logically flawed, for the rabbinic rule is that the law in the conclusion may be no more stringent than in the original case.
[34] Manuscripts add: Like the books of Homer.
[35] And yet, says R. Simeon ben Lakish, they *are* essentials.
[36] Cited by Rashi in his commentary on Genesis 1:1.

ation?"[54] Why fill the reader's mind with endless names for the same place—
Hermon, Sirion, Sion, Senir? (Deuteronomy 3:10; 4:48). What need do we have to
know all this?[37]

<h1 style="text-align:center">One Who Says,
"Moses Said It on His Own"</h1>

It is generally accepted that the Sadducees and Boethusians agreed on the sanctity of
the Five Books of the Torah but rejected the tradition recounted in Mishnah Avot, of
an Oral Torah transmitted by the Sages. Yet there are signs that the Sadducees also
made some disparaging remarks about Moses, saying that he made up certain laws
for the love of Israel or his brother Aaron.

In the generation of Rabban Johanan ben Zakkai, a Boethusian elder maintained,
"Our Master Moses, out of his love for Israel, arranged that the single day of Shavuot
should always occur on the morrow of the Sabbath, so Israel might enjoy themselves
for two days."[38] [55]

Similarly, it is told in the Scroll of Fasting that the Sadducees (or Boethusians) told
Rabban Johanan ben Zakkai that because Moses loved his brother Aaron so, he told
him not to eat the sacrificial meat plain, but rather with cakes of fine flour, like one
telling a friend, "Have some meat! Have some cake!"[56]

Josephus wrote: "The belief in these scriptures is implanted in the heart of every
Jew from birth, for they are the words of God, and the Jew commits to holding fast to
them and even dying for them if need be."[57] Josephus believed in prophecy and the

---

[54] TB Bereshit 11.
[55] BT Menahot 65a–66a.
[56] *Megillat Ta'anit*, Heshvan 27, *Hebrew Union College Annual* 8–9 (1931–32): 338.
[57] Josephus, *Against Apion* 1.8.

---

[37] So go the sectarian questions.

[38] The technical differences in calendar setting between the two groups were as follows: The
Boethusians counted forty-nine days from the "morrow of the Sabbath" (Leviticus 23:15) occurring in
the week of Passover, taking "Sabbath" in the literal sense, and therefore arrived at the date for
Shavuot always on a Sunday. The Pharisaic-rabbinic party understood "Sabbath" to mean the first day
of Passover, so Shavuot could fall on various days of the week.

What the Boethusian said was tantamount to heresy, for it asserted that Moses composed laws on
his own for the convenience of Israel and was not transmitting the divine word.

The passage goes on to give Rabban Johanan's retort: "Since the Torah says that it is an eleven-day
journey from Horeb [=Sinai] to Kadesh Barnea [the border of the Land of Canaan], why would Moses,
who so loved Israel, have kept them in the desert for forty years?" When the Boethusian complained
that this was a frivolous answer, Rabban Johanan retorted, "Fool! Our perfect Torah should not be
treated on a par with your idle talk!" The Boethusian's heresy was not to be dignified with a serious
answer. There was a serious answer, which follows in the text.

Sinai theophany, yet he wrote that Moses "took it on himself to do what was good in God's eyes, and to give just laws to the nations. . . . Inasmuch as his intention was good, and his actions great and mighty, he rightly thought that God was assisting him and supporting him through His counsel. . . . He believed with all his heart that God guided all his actions and thoughts. . . . Such a man was our lawgiver, no wizard or impostor, as our detractors allege, with malice and guile on their tongue, but a man such as Minos [of Crete] and the other honorable and renowned lawgivers of Greece who followed him. Some of these attributed their laws to Zeus, while others said they received them from Apollo or the Delphic oracle. Perhaps they believed this in all good faith, or perhaps they hoped to sway their followers with these claims."[58] Perhaps Josephus did not reveal his own opinions here, but formulated a position that would be acceptable to his Greek readers.[39]

This view, that Moses said things on his own that were not commanded by God, was expressed especially in connection with the sacrifices and the construction of the Tabernacle. Through the arguments of Moses' critics in that episode, the Sages revealed the views of the sectarians of their own time.

Moses came down from the mountain, reporting that God had instructed him to make a tabernacle, an altar, and all their accoutrements. The people asked, "Who is going to make all this?" He replied, "Bezalel." They then started to clamor against him, "The Holy and Blessed One did not tell Moses to make the Tabernacle through Bezalel, but Moses appointed him on his own! He has made himself king, his brother Aaron High Priest, Aaron's sons next in line to him, Eleazar chief of the Levites,[40] the Kehatites[41] porters of the most holy objects, and now he puts this fellow in charge of Tabernacle construction! Moses puts himself in charge of everything important." Moses replied, "I have done nothing on my own, but God directs every-

---

[58] Josephus, *Against Apion*, 2.161. See Heinemann, "Darko shel Yosefus," *Tzion* 5 (1940): 187 n. 24. A skeptical spirit speaks in Josephus in several places. In discussing the thunder and lightning at Sinai, he wrote: "My readers are free to think of these phenomena as they wish" (*Antiquities* 3.5.2) This disclaimer recurs throughout his work in various forms.

---

[39] Josephus and Heschel both address here the problem of faith claims in a pluralistic culture. (See Peter L. Berger, *The Heretical Imperative: Contemporary Possibilities of Religious Affirmation* [Garden City, N.Y.: Doubleday, Anchor, 1979].) The believer in a particularistic faith, confronted with contrary faiths, applies a skeptical reductionism to them—maybe their "gods" did not really speak to them, but it was all in their minds. He must then pose the same questions to his own faith claims: Did his prophet really have the one truth from the one Source? Josephus seems to resolve this dilemma through a temporizing position: it matters less whether the prophet really had the one truth from the one Source, than that he pursued his mission with the best motives, in the sincere belief that somehow God guided him. Many prophets in many traditions could make the same claim in all sincerity, without contradicting each other. But such a position does tend to stray from the maximalist claim that every word in the Torah is directly from God, and that Moses contributed nothing on his own.

[40] Numbers 3:32.

[41] Moses' clan within the Levites.

thing! 'See, *the Lord* has singled out by name Bezalel!'" Thus Moses observed the maxim "Find favor and approbation in the eyes of God and man" (Proverbs 3:4).

Similarly, the Israelites grumbled against Moses when it was time to set up the Tabernacle, and it would not stand up.[42] They said, "Could it be that the Holy and Blessed One gave Moses an easy task in building a Tabernacle, and Moses himself led us into all this tedium?"[43] The Holy One responded, "Since you grumble at Moses, blaming the outcome on him, place the blame rather on Me, who authorized every step of the process!" Therefore at each stage of the completion of the Tabernacle, the refrain is repeated: "as the Lord had commanded Moses" (Exodus 39:1, 5, 21, 26, 29, 31).[59]

When Aaron's sons came to collect their priestly dues, the breast and right shoulder, Korah stood up against them and asked, "Who told you to take these? Moses? We will give you nothing, for God did not command him this."[60]

We have suggestions in Josephus and Philo that the Essenes disparaged the sacrifices. They would send meal offerings to the Temple in Jerusalem, but no bullocks or doves. Apparently some priests in the Temple were also suspected of denying the value of the sacrifices. This is apparent from the words of Rabbi Simeon: "Any priest who does not believe in the Temple service shall have no portion in the priesthood." Rashi explains: "Any priest who says in his heart, 'All this is a sham, for God did not command us to offer sacrifices, but Moses invented it on his own,' shall not eat of the priestly dues."[61] We know that some sectarians contended that the passages in the Torah dealing with sacrifices were inspired not by the true God but by Satan, and that only the demons desire sacrifices.[62]

It was against such heretical tendencies that Rabbi Simeon ben Azzai argued: "In all the passages of sacrifices in the Torah, we find no mention of any secondary names of God (God, Almighty, Hosts, etc.), but only the Tetragrammaton [rendered 'the Lord'], so as not to give opportunity to the heretics."[63]

When Jesus taught, "What God has joined together, man must not separate," the Pharisees challenged him: "Why then did Moses lay it down that a man might

---

[59] Tanhuma Pekudei 11.

[60] Tanhuma Korah 2.

[61] BT Menahot 18b; Hullin 132b.

[62] Sermons of Clement of Rome, 3.2.24ff., 52ff., 54.2ff. This is supported by a midrash on Deuteronomy 32:38: "Who ate the fat of *their* offerings." See Midrash Tannaim, p. 202.

[63] Sifre Pinhas 143, Sifra 4c in the name of Rabbi Yose. RaABaD explains: "They would argue that since there are many names, there are many gods, each requiring different sacrifices."

---

[42] The Midrashim here describe the difficulty the Israelites at first had in erecting the Mishkan after all the components were finished. One version has it that Moses' sense of sadness that perhaps he himself had not done enough for the Tabernacle was the factor that kept the Mishkan from standing. In any event, the Israelites were annoyed at their inability to finish the work that they had arduously done at Moses' command.

[43] That is, Moses unnecessarily complicated the plans, and that is why they were not completable?

divorce his wife by note of dismissal?" Jesus answered, "It was because your minds were closed that *Moses gave you permission* to divorce your wives; but it was not like that when all began" (Matthew 18:6-8). The Church Fathers saw in this a suggestion that Moses instituted the law of divorce on his own.[64]

In 140, Marcion composed his "Antitheses," in which he impugned the Torah of Israel and advocated its exclusion from the Christian canon. He argued that the Torah was authored by the evil Jewish God, whereas Jesus came to reveal the Supreme God, Who hitherto had been unknown in the world, and to abolish the Torah. It is well known that the Christian church opposed Marcion's view as heretical.[65] The Gnostic Ptolemy of Alexandria (fl. 137-166) wrote a letter to a woman in which he distinguished between the Creator God and the Supreme God. He opposes those who use Jesus' words to prove that the same God authored the Torah and also sent Jesus to the world. Ptolemy distinguished three strata of the Torah: one divinely authored, the second by Moses, and the third added by the elders.[66] This certainly exemplifies the heresy that Moses said some things on his own.

Rabbi Nehemiah projected these heretical views onto the imperial Romans. He told the story: "When Titus entered the Holy of Holies, he cut through the two curtains[44] with his sword and said, 'If there is a god here, let Him "who ate the fat of their offerings" (Deuteronomy 32:38) come and protest. Surely Moses deceived this people, telling them to build an altar and offer sacrifices and libations on it. "Let [this god] rise up to your help, and let him be a shield to you!" (Deuteronomy 32:38)'"[45][67]

Deniers of the Torah

It is no surprise that there were people in Israel who said there is no Torah from heaven. Already in the psalms we hear, "The fool says in his heart, 'there is no

---

[64] P. Dausch, *Die Schriftinspiration: Eine biblisch geschichtliche Studie* (Freiburg: Herder, 1891), 61, 64, citing Origen and Ambrose. See also Rabbi Johanan in PT Kiddushin 58c.

[65] On Cerdo, who denied the Torah, see Adolf von Harnack, *Marcion: Das Evangelium vom fremden Gott: Eine Monographie zur Geschichte der Grundlegung der Katholischen Kirche,* Texte und Untersuchungen zur Geschichte der altchristlichen Literatur 45 (Leipzig: Hinrichs, 1924), 25ff.

[66] *Ptolémée: Lettre à Flora,* trans. Gilles Quispel, Sources chrétiennes 24 (Paris: Cerf, 1949), 50.

[67] Sifre Ha'azinu 327-28.

---

[44] One hung at the entrance to the Holy Chamber, and the other at the entrance to the Holy of Holies. Thus did Titus not only commit the sacrilege of a Gentile entering the Temple, but he also violated the sanctity of the Holy of Holies, which could only be entered by the High Priest on Yom Kippur.

[45] The challenge of cultural pluralism is most keenly felt in the hour of defeat. How strong must the temptation have been at that moment to adopt the oppressor's point of view and deny utterly the value of one's own religious tradition! Yet it is precisely at that historical moment that Rabbinic Judaism was able to assert itself and achieve its classical definition, in the generation that produced Rabbi Ishmael and Rabbi Akiva.

God'"[46] (Psalm 14:1; 53:2). Of the wicked it is said, "In all his scheming he thinks, 'there is no God'" (Psalm 10:4). The literature of the talmudic period makes frequent mention of people who did not believe in God: "Adam denied the First Principle";[68] "Ahab renounced the God of Israel";[69] Cain said, "there is no judgment and no judge; there is no world to come, nor is there reward and punishment."[70] The sectarians would say, "The world is an automaton"; that is, it moves itself without an external mover.[71] [47] Others said, "There is no sovereignty in heaven";[72] "there is no power in heaven"; "if there is a power in heaven, it is not able to bring death or life, to effect evil or good."[73] We know that the Sadducees did not believe in the resurrection of the dead; the Sages said that Esau, Job, and those whom Ezekiel resurrected did not believe in it either.[74]

To these categories of deniers, we must add those who denied the Torah utterly and completely (just as one must deny the power of idolatry utterly and completely to be a Jew in good standing).[75] The Tosefta says: "Sectarians, apostates, informers, Epicureans, *those who deny the Torah,* those who separate from the ways of the community, and those who deny the resurrection . . . Gehinnom locks them in, and they are punished there for all generations."[76]

This lack of faith is attributed to the Israelites who were uncertain about the Promised Land. It was not originally God's intention to send spies to report on the land. Moses told the Israelites, "See, the Lord your God has placed the land at your disposal. Go up and take possession!" (Deuteronomy 1:21). Only then did the Israelites approach Moses and say, "Let us send men ahead to reconnoiter the land for us!" (Deuteronomy 1:22). Moses replied, "The Ark of the Covenant of the Lord will travel in front of you to seek out a resting place" (Numbers 10:33). Still, they insisted, "Let us send men ahead!" The reason for their lack of trust is that *they did not believe in God's Torah.*[77] Another version says, *they did not believe in the Holy Spirit,* which had told them, "the land is an exceedingly good land" (Numbers 14:7).[78]

In rabbinic times, there dwelt in Israel an early Christian sect whose adherents had come from the Jewish people, who said that the Torah was not written by Moses. They

---

[68] BT Sanhedrin 38b.   [69] BT Sanhedrin 102b.

[70] Jerusalem Targum on Genesis 4:7. See also Leviticus Rabbah 28:1, on the heretical implications of Ecclesiastes.

[71] Midrash on Psalms 1:21, ed. Buber, according to the reading of Musafia.

[72] Midrash Tannaim, p. 202.   [73] Sifre Ha'azinu 329.

[74] BT Bava Batra 16a; and Jerusalem Targum on Genesis 25:19.

[75] BT Megillah 13a; Kiddushin 40a.

[76] Tosefta Sanhedrin 13:5. BT Rosh Hashanah 17a has the variant: ". . . Epicureans who deny the Torah," conflating two categories into one.

[77] TB Shelah 7.   [78] YS Psalms 819.

---

[46] NJV: "The benighted man thinks, 'God does not care'" (literally, "there is no God").

[47] Since one of the conceptions of God (e.g., Aristotle's) was that of the Unmoved Mover, a world that moved itself (auto-matos) had no need of God.

claimed that Moses transmitted the Torah orally with its interpretations to the seventy elders, and it was written only after his death by men who were not themselves prophets.[79] Celsus, writing around 170–180 C.E., also said that the Pentateuch was not written solely by Moses but by other authors as well.[80]

Many heretics challenged the Sages of Israel with their disparaging remarks against Moses. A Roman general found an inaccuracy in the enumeration of the Levites in the second chapter of Numbers and said to Rabban Johanan ben Zakkai in another connection, "Your master Moses was either a thief or a swindler or poor in arithmetic!"[81] Such allegations surely cast doubt on the truth of his prophecy. And the Samaritan who challenged Rabbi Meir, How could the God who filled heaven and earth be compressed between the poles of the Ark,[82] surely did so "in order to question the reality of prophecy."[83]

"It Seems to Us That Moses Forged the Torah"

The Tannaim surely knew of the Ebionites, the early Christian sect that included Jewish followers of Jesus, who held fast to the Mosaic Torah and observed many of its commandments such as circumcision and the Sabbath, but who rejected other mitzvot such as the sacrifices. The majority of this sect lived by the Dead Sea and in eastern Syria. They considered Jesus a true prophet who purified the Mosaic cult of its imperfections, but they regarded the apostle Paul as a heretic.

Jesus said, "Do not suppose that I have come to abolish the Torah and the prophets" (Matthew 5:17). Since he did in fact abrogate several laws of the Torah, the Ebionites concluded that he did not regard them as truly a part of the Torah.

From the sermons attributed to Clement of Rome, we learn of a heretical sect who accepted the Mosaic Torah but said that it contained chapters that were not authored by Moses but were interpolated by others.[84] They distinguished between "true utterances" and "false utterances," between those matters that came from Moses and "forged passages" that were introduced into the Torah by Satan.[85]

In order to counter the claims that Moses forged the Torah or gave laws that he

---

[79] Sermons of Clement of Rome, II, 38; III, 47. See also Epiphanius, *Anakephalaiosis* 18, 19; and A. Schmidtke, *Neue Fragmente und Untersuchungen zu den judenchristlichen Evangelien: Ein Beitrag zur Literatur und Geschichte der Judenchristen* (Leipzig: Hinrichs, 1911), 200ff.

[80] Origen, *Contra Celsum* 4.42.

[81] BT Bekhorot 5a.

[82] Genesis Rabbah 4:4, cited in chapter 5 above, p. 99.

[83] Albo, *Ikkarim*, III, 9.

[84] "*Falsa capitula legis (pseudeis perikopai)*" (Sermons of Clement of Rome, II, 38, 51; III, 50; XVIII, 20). See Hans Waitz, *Die Pseudoklementinen, Homilien und Rekognitionen* (Leipzig: Hinrichs, 1904), 94ff.; and Carl Schmidt, *Studien zu den Pseudo-Clementinen* (Leipzig: Hinrichs, 1929), 200ff.

[85] Sermons of Clement of Rome, II, 38; III, 48. M. Joël thought the expression "Moses spoke the whole Torah at the divine behest, except for this one matter which he spoke on his own," was directed at the Ebionites. See *Blicke in die Religionsgeschichte zu Anfang des II Jahrhunderts* (Breslau, 1883), 2:177.

was not commanded to give, the Tannaim emphasized that Moses did not shrink from including passages in the Torah even to his own detriment.

> There were two outstanding leaders of Israel. One said, "Let my shame not be recorded," while the other said, "Let my shame be recorded." The first was David, as it says, "Of David. A *maskil*. Happy is he whose transgression is forgiven, whose sin is covered over" (Psalm 32:1). The second was Moses, as it is written, "For in the wilderness of Zin, when the community was contentious, you disobeyed My command to uphold My sanctity in their sight by means of the water" (Numbers 27:14). It is like two women who were brought before the court, one for adultery and the other for taking figs of the sabbatical year. The second said, "If it please the court, announce what I am here for, so the public shall not think that I also committed adultery." They tied the figs around her neck and announced, "For these figs she is punished." What crimes might we have suspected Moses guilty of, had his real sin not been made explicit![86]

The deeper meaning of this story is spelled out by Rabbi Judah in another version: "Moses pleaded with the Holy and Blessed One, 'Master of the Universe! Write in Your Torah the real reason why I may not enter the Land of Israel, so that Israel should not say, "Such a scoundrel! *He probably forged the Torah,* or included in it things he was not commanded."' The Holy One replied, 'By your life, I will write that it was only on account of the water episode.'"[87]

The concern that the Torah might be considered a fraud was expressed in another sense.[48] When David handed over the sons of Saul to be impaled by the Gibeonites (2 Samuel 21), the nations of the world objected: "These people's Torah is a fraud![49] It is written in their Torah, 'You must not let [the condemned man's] corpse remain on the stake overnight' (Deuteronomy 21:23), yet these have remained for seven months! It is written in their Torah, 'Two shall not be condemned on the same day,'[50] [88] yet here are seven who were tried together! It is written, 'children shall not

---

[86] Sifre Shalah 137; YS Va'ethanan 810; BT Yoma 86b and Rashi ad loc.
[87] Leviticus Rabbah 31:4. This reason is also given in Sifre Va'ethanan 26.
[88] Mishnah Sanhedrin 6:4.

---

[48] The stories that follow all express the idea that the Torah is vulnerable to falsification after the fact, if people's actions or history ignore it. The underlying idea is expressed most vividly in the following story: "The Book of Deuteronomy pleaded before the Holy One: 'Solomon has made me a fraud, for *any legal document of which two or three particulars have been voided, is rendered completely void.* I contain the laws that a king shall not have many wives, horses, or silver and gold, yet he has all three'" (Leviticus Rabbah 19:2).
Does such a story have bearing on the question of divine authorship? Possibly. A God who authored such laws would not allow them to be ignored with impunity. If the laws fall into disuse, they will no longer be regarded (or already are not regarded) as expressing the divine will.
See Heschel's discussion of this story in chapter 25.
[49] The (corrupted) "Greek" words *plaster* ("forger") and *plaston* ("forgery") are used by the midrash in this context (*plastos* = counterfeit).
[50] It is significant that in these stories, pronouncements from the written Torah, the rabbinic law, and the prophets (see next story) are all given the same weight of divine authority and the same presumption of infallibility.

be put to death for parents' (Deuteronomy 24:16), yet these were put to death for their father's crime!"[51] [89]

Rabbi Luliana said, "A Cretan challenged Rabbi Yose, 'From what I see, your Torah is a fraud! There is written in it, "Nor shall there ever be an end to the line of the levitical priests before Me, of those who present burnt offerings and turn the meal offering to smoke and perform sacrifices" (Jeremiah 33:18). But the Temple is in ruins, and the sacrifices are no more.' Rabbi Yose replied, 'God forbid! There is no fraud or falsehood in the Torah, but it is all true. The Holy and Blessed One said to the priests and Levites, "If you study the laws of sacrifices, I count it as if you were offering them every day."'"[90]

Moses pleaded before God, "Master of the Universe! Allow me to remain alive and dwell east of the Jordan, but not to enter the land of Canaan." The Holy One replied, "Do you seek to make My Torah a fraud? I wrote in it, by your hand, 'Three times a year all your males shall appear before the Lord your God in the place that He will choose' (Deuteronomy 16:16). If all of Israel go up on pilgrimage but you are not with them, they will ask: 'Who wrote this? Moses wrote it. In that case, why doesn't he go up on pilgrimage? If he doesn't go up, we won't go up either.' And My Torah will be null and void."[91]

---

[89] Numbers Rabbah 8:4.

[90] YS Jeremiah 321, citing Yelammedenu. See also *Geniza Studies in Memory of Dr. Solomon Schechter*, vol. 1, *Midrash and Haggadah*, ed. Louis Ginzberg (New York: Jewish Theological Seminary, 1928), 220.

[91] MTD 31:14, p. 179. Found also in the Midrash of Moses' Death, Beit Hamidrash I,125.

The allegation of the Torah's forgery was repeated often among the ancient enemies of Judaism. In the pseudo-Clementine sermons (III, 47), it was alleged that the Torah was written many centuries after Moses' death, then recovered in the Temple, then burned by Nebuchadnezzar five hundred years later and written afresh. Each time, the Jews introduced new fabrications into it. The philosopher Porphyry claimed (in his anti-Christian polemic) that the Torah was written not by Moses but by Ezra 1,180 (!) years later, for according to IV Esdras (26:21), the Mosaic writings were burned together with the Temple.

---

[51] That this last is indeed a problem is made clear in Scripture itself, in the story of King Amaziah, who refused to take vengeance on the sons of his father's assassins, in compliance with the Deuteronomic law cited here. See 2 Kings 14:1–6.

MOSES DID THINGS
ON HIS OWN AUTHORITY

Translator's Introduction

As we noted, chapter 21 was a step outside the line of Heschel's emerging argument, though for the author's purposes, it was a vital one. Going back now to chapter 20, we saw that there were parts of the narrative of the Torah that raised immediate and pointed questions about the notion that every word of the Pentateuch (at least) was given by God to Moses at Sinai. A Sage as important and as noted as Moses of Trani, in the sixteenth century, suggested that it is really impossible to consider dialogue in the Torah (and this is especially so of dialogue subsequent to the events at Sinai) to be divine revelation. At least, it seems impossible to do so without making Moses' later activities seem predetermined and thus meaningless, and/or without undermining the equally fundamental Jewish principle of free will.

In this chapter, this line of argument is picked up. Not only is *dialogue* hard to assimilate into the maximalist position that every word and letter were given at Sinai; any number of places where Moses does something surprising or impulsive, or apparently acts on his own without divine instruction, would also raise the objection to the maximalist view. The former category includes Moses' smashing of the tablets upon seeing the golden calf. The latter would include setting up his tent of communion with God outside the camp after the same episode. Could these things have been told to Moses at the mountain without making a joke of the Torah's narratives?

Methodically, Heschel begins to make the case against the maximalist view by delineating those instances in which there is textual evidence that Moses acted on his own, and he finds that the affirmation that Moses did indeed appeal on occasion to his own authority is consistently associated with the school of Rabbi Ishmael. It is, indeed, an Ishmaelian-type view, and it reaches its apogee in a late midrashic text that Heschel will quote, in which the author swears that Moses had people killed extrajudicially after the golden calf without divine instruction and nevertheless took it upon himself to announce that it was a divine command ("Thus said the Lord God of Israel . . ."). This last, striking phenomenon sets the stage for the subsequent chapter's subject matter.

Sources of the Statement

HE POSITION OF THE "ALTERNATE TRADITION"—that whoever claims of a single verse that the Holy and Blessed One did not say it, but rather that it was Moses on his own authority, is included in the category of "spurning the word of the Lord"—does not express a unanimous view of the Sages. It is a matter of controversy. According to a Baraita that appears under the heading "our Masters stated":[1] "Moses did three things on his own authority, but he was consistent with God's intent:[2] (1) he separated himself from his wife,[[1]] (2) he shattered the tablets, and (3) he added an additional day on his own authority."[3] [[2]] Another source counts a fourth thing that Moses did on his own authority but that was consistent with God's intent: (4) he separated himself from the Tent of Meeting. . . ."[4] [[3]] "On his own authority" means that he did not receive instruction from on high but rather acted "from his own intent and reason," interpreting the words of the Holy and Blessed One.[5] Now on the basis of the analysis of sources it is possible to demonstrate that this entire approach that Moses did things on his own authority stems from the view of Rabbi Ishmael, whose inclination was to interpret the Torah according to the

---

[1] Exodus Rabbah 19:3, and Midrash Haggadol on Leviticus 1:1, in the name of R. Samuel bar Nahmani.

[2] So the language in BT Yevamot 62a; Exodus Rabbah 19:3 and 46:3; and ARN A 2. But BT Shabbat 87a has "And the Holy and Blessed One agreed with him" (i.e., after the fact).

[3] BT Shabbat 87a and Yevamot 62a.

[4] ARN A 2. On the basis of this, Yalkut Shim'oni (Tissa 393) counts four things that Moses did on his own authority. See also *Huppat Eliyahu* in *Otzar Midrashim*, p. 171.

[5] So does R. Judah Loew of Prague (Maharal) interpret "from his intent and reason," in *Gur Aryeh* (to Exodus 19:15): "[Moses] derived it through exegesis . . . for every inference that the Rabbis derived from superfluities in the text is referred to as coming 'from the Scribes' [i.e., is rabbinic in origin], for it is, after all, not written explicitly in the biblical text . . . and every matter deduced through exegesis is not like those in the Torah . . . now since Moses our Master, peace be with him, derived this rule via his reason from the text, it is said that he added the additional day on his own authority." Compare Tosafot Shabbat 87a (s.v. *ve'atah*).

---

[1] This refers to the tradition according to which Moses, after Mount Sinai, did not resume sexual relations with his wife. The source for this tradition is discussed below.

[2] This refers to what was considered to be an additional day of preparation for the revelation at Mount Sinai, ordained by Moses. The source for this tradition also appears below.

[3] This refers to a tradition according to which Moses gave up his free access to the Sanctuary. Actually, the identity of the Tent of Meeting is a complicated issue in the Bible, and there is a great deal of confusion concerning what seems to be Moses' access to the Sanctuary, although he is manifestly not a priest (being a brother, and not a descendant, of Aaron) and thus theoretically unauthorized to enter. It is sometimes theorized that the Tent of Meeting refers to another sacred place, outside the camp, where Moses went to commune with God and receive revelations. But for the purposes of Heschel's exposition here, the Tent of Meeting means the same Sanctuary that Aaron was in charge of, in the center of the camp.

plain meaning of the text. As we shall see, Rabbi Akiva disputed this approach, and said that Moses received instructions concerning all of these things from on high.[4]

He Separated Himself from His Wife

"He separated himself from his wife, but he was consistent with God's intent. How so? He said: If Israel, which was sanctified for but a moment, for the purpose of receiving the ten utterances at Mount Sinai, were told by the Holy and Blessed One: 'Go to the people and warn them to stay pure today and tomorrow' (Exodus 19:10), I, who am on call every single day, at every single hour, not knowing when God may speak with me, day or night,[6] how much more so must I separate from my wife. And his reasoning was consistent with God's intent."[7] This idea flowed, apparently, from the school of Rabbi Ishmael, or from Sages close to his way of thinking, and was disputed by Rabbi Akiva.

The Torah relates: "Miriam and Aaron spoke against Moses because of the Cushite woman he had married: 'He married a Cushite woman!'" (Numbers 12:1). What were the things that they spoke against Moses? Several midrashim relate:[8] "When the elders were appointed, all Israel lit candles and rejoiced over the elders who attained high station. When Miriam saw the candles, she said: 'Happy are these men, and happy are their wives.' But Tzipporah[5] said to her: 'Don't say "happy are their wives," but rather "woe to their wives"; for from the day that the Holy and Blessed One spoke with your brother Moses, he has ceased his relations with me.'"[9]

This interpretation is astonishing, for there is no hint in the text of Moses separat-

---

[6] The question of whether God spoke to Moses at night or only in the daytime was a matter of dispute among the Tannaim and their later interpreters. See the Midrashim on Exodus 12:2 cited in chapter 15, "God Showed Them with a Finger."

[7] ARN A 2. According to Saadia, the Karaites deduced from this reasoning that the Sabbath, which is also a "sanctified" day, should be marked likewise by sexual abstinence—the opposite of the practice of Rabbinic Judaism. See his commentary on Exodus 19:15, copied and translated by Moses Zucker from a genizah manuscript.

[8] Sifre Zuta, p. 274; Sifre Beha'alotekha 99. According to TB Metzora 4, it was Miriam's intention to induce Moses to resume relations with his wife.

[9] According to Tosafot on BT Yevamot 62a (s.v. dikhetiv), quoting the Sifre. See also Tosafot on BT Shabbat 87a (s.v. ve'atah). If we are to take Tzipporah's remarks literally, Moses ceased relations with her from the time of the revelation at the burning bush!

---

[4] And thus continues what is by now the very familiar pattern of the school of Ishmael admitting human innovation and invention to the universe of religious truth, and the school of Akiva insisting that all religious truth was revealed, in toto, from on high, even if in esoteric form. Here we encounter this difference in approach with respect to the degrees of freedom that even the greatest of the prophets could be allowed.

[5] She is the only wife of Moses referred to by name in the Torah. Thus, although this name is not mentioned in Numbers 12—and thus it is possible that this Cushite wife is in fact someone else—the midrashim cited here assume that it is Tzipporah who is intended.

ing from his wife.[6] The plain meaning has it that Miriam and Aaron simply spoke "about the Cushite woman he had married." Furthermore, why was this gossip—about Moses separating from his wife—so important as to require the Holy and Blessed One to testify to Moses' greatness as a prophet?[7] And what is the relevance of the phrase "with him I speak mouth to mouth" in connection with separating from one's wife? The answer to this puzzle lies, I believe, in the standpoint of Rabbi Akiva. For here he attempted to rein in potential chaos. Rabbi Akiva disputed the idea that Moses separated from his wife on his own authority, for he believed that it is a mistake to say that Moses did anything at all on his own authority. But just such an idea was expressed by Aaron and Miriam: they claimed that Moses separated from his wife on his own authority, that is, that he did something he was not commanded to do. And this idea, according to Rabbi Akiva, creates a bad impression[8] about Moses' prophecy. Therefore, the Holy and Blessed One called Aaron and Miriam and said to them: "with him I speak mouth to mouth," that is, "he was told to separate from his wife directly from My mouth."[10] And although this interpretation appears in the Sifre anonymously,[9] in another place we find Rabbi Akiva explicitly disagreeing with those who say that Moses did this on his own authority.[11]

In other parts of the Sifre,[10] Miriam's and Aaron's gossip is also interpreted as referring to Moses' neglecting the imperative to have children (by separating from his wife), but the verse "with him I speak mouth to mouth" is interpreted in accord with its plain meaning as simply one of the ways in which Moses' mode of prophecy was distinguished and unique. According to this interpretation, the Holy and Blessed One did not address Miriam and Aaron concerning the substance of Moses' separation from his wife.

And Rabbi Meir ibn Gabbai[11] held that the Sifre's understanding is that Aaron's

---

[10] Sifre Beha'alotekha 23. See also Midrash Haggadol ad loc.; YS 815.
[11] Exodus Rabbah 46:3.

---

[6] That is, there is no mention of this separation in the story of Aaron's and Miriam's gossiping about Moses in Numbers 12. There is, however, a hint of something of this nature in Deuteronomy 5:27–28, where God, at Mount Sinai, tells Moses to instruct the people to return to their tents, that is, to their normal family routine, but then says to Moses, "But you remain here with Me." Although the plain meaning seems to be that this is intended for a limited time, it was the source of the position that it was at God's instruction that he ceased relations with his wife (see ARN A 2).

[7] See Numbers 12:5–8.

[8] Literally, "imparts a defective taste"—a legal term that describes, for example, residues of forbidden foods that do not contaminate permitted foods because they do not add any positive taste. This is one of many examples of Heschel's appropriation of legal terminology for aggadic purposes.

[9] And thus would, according to the scholarly theory that Heschel accepts, seem to be from the school of Rabbi Ishmael. However, Heschel here cites J. N. Epstein's assertion (in *Mevo'ot le-Sifrut ha-Tannaim* [Jerusalem: Magnes Press, 1957]) that the aggadic sections of the Sifre on Numbers 12 constitute a separate section and cannot be assumed to stem from the Ishmaelian school.

[10] That is, those parts that Heschel's sources consider clearly Ishmaelian.

[11] A kabbalist of the early sixteenth century.

and Miriam's gossip was not about separation from his wife, but was rather a complaint that Moses married a daughter of the pagan priest Jethro: "Was there then no daughter of the descendants of Father Abraham fitting for him that he had to take a foreign wife? . . . this must have been done out of lust for her beauty!"[12]

He Shattered the Tablets

The Torah states: "As soon as Moses came near the camp and saw the calf and the dancing, he became enraged; and he hurled the tablets from his hands and shattered them at the foot of the mountain" (Exodus 32:19). According to the aforementioned Baraita, Moses shattered the tablets on his own authority. Yet according to Rabbi Akiva (and Rabbis Yehudah ben Beteira, Eleazar ben Azariah, and Meir): "Moses did not shatter the tablets until he was so instructed from on high, as it says: 'I gripped the two tablets and flung them away with both my hands' (Deuteronomy 9:17)."[13]

What was Rabbi Ishmael's point of view? Here, truly, was a matter on which Rabbis Ishmael and Akiva diverged. "Rabbi Ishmael said: Moses drew an inference, and said: If the Paschal sacrifice, a single mitzvah, was not to be given to idolators, how much more so the entire Torah! And thus he shattered them. Rabbi Akiva said: The Holy and Blessed One instructed him to shatter them."[14]

He Added an Additional Day

The Holy and Blessed One had said to Moses: "Let them be ready for the third day" (Exodus 19:11). Moses, however, went to the people and said: "Be ready for three days" (Exodus 19:15). From this change of language, the Baraita inferred that Moses added a day on his own authority, taking "three days" literally to mean at the end of three days.[15] "And the Holy and Blessed One agreed with him."[16]

Now in exegesis that apparently stemmed from the school of Rabbi Akiva, this idea was disputed: "'Be ready for three days'—is it possible that Moses said this on his own? The text therefore says both 'let them be ready for the third day,' and 'be ready

---

[12] This interpretation is found in *Avodat Hakodesh,* Siterei Hatorah, 22. See also Naftali Zvi Yehudah Berlin's commentary on Sifre Beha'alotekha, p. 306. See Louis Ginzberg's *Legends of the Jews,* 7 volumes (Philadelphia: Jewish Publication Society, 1909–38), 6:90, n. 488.

[13] ARN A 2; see Schechter's edition of ARN, n. 55 ad loc.

[14] See Tanhuma Tissa 30; Tanhuma Ekev 11; YS 393; PR 20:2 (96b). PT Ta'anit 4:8 (68c) seems to conflate the two views in one tradition; see *Yefei Mar'eh* ad loc.

[15] See Rashi on Exodus 19:15; BT Shabbat 87a, Rabbi Yose's view.

[16] Pesikta Hadetha, Beit Hamidrash VI, 41. In YS Yitro 279 (citing PRE 41): "Moses added a day on his own authority. Said to him the Holy and Blessed One: 'Moses! How many souls could have been created on that night [when all Israelites separated once more from their spouses]!' But I accept that what you have done is done."

for three days,' so that 'ready' and 'ready' create a *gezerah shavah*."[12] That is, just as the former "ready" was the word of the Holy come to Moses, so was the latter "ready."[17] [13]

He Separated Himself from the Tent of Meeting

One other thing "Moses did on his own authority, drawing a logical inference, and he was consistent with God's intent—he separated himself from the Tent of Meeting." How so? He said: "If of my brother Aaron, anointed as he is with the anointing oil, and dressed as he is in the sacred vestments in which he serves in sanctity, the Holy and Blessed One said, 'he is not to come at will into the holy place' (Leviticus 16:2), I who am not similarly primed, how much more so should I separate myself from the Tent of Meeting."[14] He did so, and he was consistent with God's intent.[18]

This point, that Moses did not enter the Tent of Meeting at will, is taught in the Baraita of Rabbi Ishmael:[15] "One verse says, 'When Moses went into the Tent of Meeting to speak with Him' (Numbers 7:89), and another verse says, 'Moses could not enter the Tent of Meeting because the cloud had settled upon it' (Exodus 40:35). Conclude, therefore, that as long as the cloud was there, Moses did not enter; when the cloud departed, he would enter and speak with Him."[16] [19]

[17] MSY, p. 142. In BT Shabbat 86a the debate focused on the issue of for how many days a woman may be rendered unclean by a discharge from recent marital relations. Rabbi Ishmael held that this can extend for three days, while Rabbi Akiva limited the period to two and a half days. In the Middle Ages, the commentators were still debating the implications of these opinions for the length of the period of abstinence before the Sinai revelation.

[18] ARN A 2. According to ARN B 2 and Exodus Rabbah 19:3, he said: "If in the case of Mount Sinai, whose sanctity was merely temporary, I could only go up when called, how much more so in the case of the Tent of Meeting, whose sanctity is eternal! And how do we know that God conceded the point? For it says (Leviticus 1:1), 'The Lord called to Moses' [from the Tent of Meeting]." This a fortiori argument appears also in Targum Pseudo-Jonathan to Leviticus 1:1.

[19] Sifra 3b, and Sifre Zuta 89. Another tradition, attributed to the school of Rabbi Ishmael, suggested

---

[12] One of the accepted means of expounding the text of the Torah, a *gezerah shavah* is based on the appearance of the same word or phrase in two different contexts. When this principle is invoked, it allows for a thoroughgoing analogizing, even identification, of the two contexts. Thus here the use of the word "ready" in both verses is taken to mean that just as one has divine sanction, so does the other. A *gezerah shavah* is generally considered to require a trustworthy tradition and is not, unlike a logical inference, to be invoked on one's own authority.

[13] Which would, presumably, mean that in the interim God decided that an additional day of preparation would be appropriate.

[14] Aaron's restriction applied only to the so-called Holy of Holies, the innermost chamber of the Sanctuary where the Ark stood. But here Moses seems to be inferring that he should in fact give up the free access that he formerly had to the Tent itself, even the less sacred parts.

[15] "The Baraita of Rabbi Ishmael" is the name given to the passage that begins the Sifra (Tannaitic midrash on Leviticus). This passage presents the Thirteen Canons of Interpretation attributed to Rabbi Ishmael, together with examples of how each is used in midrashic practice.

[16] This is an application of Rabbi Ishmael's Thirteenth Canon of Interpretation. We saw another

But against this idea—that Moses separated himself from the Tent of Meeting on the basis of a logical inference and in so doing was consistent with God's intent—the school of Rabbi Akiva offered their own exegesis: "'he [Aaron] is not to come at will into the holy place'—your brother [Aaron] is commanded not to enter at will, but you, Moses, are not so commanded."[20] And in another place, this is added: "Rather, whenever he [Moses] wished, he would enter and stand between the Cherubim and be seized by the Holy Spirit, and inspired by prophecy."[21] [17]

This idea was that of Rabbi Simeon, the student of Rabbi Akiva, and it is the subject of controversy among the Sages: "Balaam would speak to Him whenever he wished, as it is said, 'prostrate, but with eyes unveiled' (Numbers 24:4)—that is, he would simply prostrate himself, and his eyes would behold what he wished to see—but Moses could not speak with Him whenever he wished. Rabbi Simeon said: Moses also spoke with Him whenever he wished, as it is said, 'When Moses went into the Tent of Meeting to speak with Him' (Numbers 7:89)—whenever he wished he would enter and speak with Him."[22]

Other Versions

The tradition about Moses doing things on his own authority is an ancient one. Yet we find many different opinions on what these things were.

that Moses' encounter with the Cloud of Glory was analogous to Israel's passing through the Sea of Reeds. Just as the Israelites entered the sea only part way, so Moses had contact with the periphery of the cloud but did not penetrate to the center of it (BT Yoma 4b; Ein Ya'akov ad loc.; Lekah Tov on Exodus 14:17).

[20] Sifra Aharei Mot 80a. This exegesis serves as a foundation for Maimonides' opinion that Moses our Master "could say anytime he wished: 'Stand by, and let me hear what instructions the Lord gives . . .' (Numbers 9:8)" (see Maimonides, preface to commentary on Mishnah Sanhedrin ch. 10, seventh fundamental principle, and Mishneh Torah I, *Hilkhot Yesodei Hatorah* [Foundational Principles of the Torah] 7:6).

[21] Midrash Haggadol on Leviticus, ed. Rabinowitz, p. 492; RaABaD ad loc. See also Sifre Beha'alotekha 68. J. N. Epstein points out that this aggadic passage in the Sifre is an Akivan interpolation in what is otherwise primarily a midrashic work of the school of Rabbi Ishmael (*Mevo'ot le-Sifrut ha-Tannaim: Introduction to Tannaitic Literature: Mishna, Tosephta and Halakhic Midrashim* [in Hebrew] [Jerusalem: Magnes, 1957], p. 597).

[22] Sifre Zuta on Numbers 9:7; Numbers Rabbah 14:20. Rabbi Simeon's view, that only Moses enjoyed prophetic powers throughout his lifetime, won general acceptance. See Exodus Rabbah 2:6; BT Shabbat 87a.

instance at the start of chapter 19: Verse A and Verse B contradicted each other, and Verse C was brought in as a tie-breaker. In the current case, there is no third verse, so the Sage must arrive at a reconciliation based on his own analysis of the problem.

[17] Note that in this case, unlike the others, the dispute is not over whether Moses' action had the divine sanction, but rather whether Moses in fact took the action at all. Here the school of Akiva is portrayed as denying that Moses ever in fact gave up his access to the Tent of Meeting. We recall that in chapter 16, Heschel showed that Rabbi Akiva affirmed Moses' mystical attainments much more emphatically than did Rabbi Ishmael.

According to Rabbi Levi:

Moses did three things, on which the Holy and Blessed One agreed with him, and they are these: (1) it was said "visiting the guilt of the fathers upon the children" (Exodus 20:5), and Moses nevertheless said, "parents shall not be put to death for children, nor children be put to death for parents" (Deuteronomy 24:16). And how do we know that the Holy and Blessed One agreed with him? Because it says, "but he did not put to death the children of the assassins, in accordance with what is written in the Book of the Teaching of Moses, where the Lord commanded, 'Parents shall not be put to death for children, etc.'" (2 Kings 14:6);[18] (2) when he shattered the tablets; and (3) in the days of Sihon and Og, the Holy and Blessed One said to Moses, "Go out and fight him [Sihon]—seal up his water supply," but Moses did not do so, as it is said, "Then I sent messengers . . . to Sihon" (Deuteronomy 2:26). And the Holy and Blessed One said to him, "As you live, you have done the right thing—I agree with you!"[23]

The Karaite Kirkisani[19] quotes from the aggadic book "The Talmud of Rabbi's Children":

Three things did the Holy and Blessed One learn from Moses. One was during the making of the golden calf, when He wanted to destroy Israel . . . Moses spoke to God [appeasing words] . . . and the Holy and Blessed One said, "You have revived Me with your words, as it is said, 'Nevertheless, as I live . . .' (Numbers 14:21);[20] a second was in the actions relating to Sihon . . . where what Moses did seemed right to the Holy and Blessed One, and He said to him: "Moses, I nullify my own words and affirm yours," which is why it subsequently says: "When you approach a town to attack it, you shall offer it terms of peace" (Deuteronomy 20:10).[24] [21]

With respect to the shattering of the tablets, there were in fact several points of view among the Sages. Most of them felt that Moses shattered them on his own

---

[23] Tanhuma Shofetim 19; in Deuteronomy Rabbah 5:13, only the second and third are mentioned.

[24] *Kitab Al-Anwar Wal-Mara Qib*, ed. L. Nemoy, pp. 33–34; compare Bacher, "Qirqisani, the Karaite, and his Work on Jewish Sects," *Jewish Quarterly Review 7*, original series (1894): 689.

---

[18] The important phrase in the story of Amaziah is "where the Lord commanded"; that is, although Moses had established this unprecedented principle of individual responsibility in his Deuteronomic valedictory, God accepted this principle and it became, after the fact, as if it were God's command.

[19] Joseph ben Jacob Kirkisani, a tenth-century Karaite.

[20] An obvious difficulty here is that the proof text about God's being revivied comes from Numbers 14, in the story of the spies, and not from the story of the golden calf in Exodus! However, it is not unheard of, given the many similarities between the two tales, for there to be a partial identifying of the narratives. Thus, God's speaking about being "alive" in the story of the spies could also be taken as an indication of a similar reaction after Moses' almost identical intercession after the sin of the calf.

[21] In this case, there is actually a general divine command (about suing for peace before going to war) that is understood to have been induced by Moses' unilateral action. The third instance is not mentioned by Kirkisani.

authority and he was consistent with God's intent.[25] Rabbi Akiva and his colleagues believed that he did not shatter them but by the divine command. There were also those who held that after the Israelites made the calf, the Holy and Blessed One attempted to take the tablets back from Moses, for He well knew that they would not repent of that act. Thus did Rabbi Shmuel ben Nahman say in the name of Rabbi Yonatan: "The tablets were six handbreadths long and three handbreadths wide. Moses took hold of two handbreadths, and the Holy and Blessed One took hold of two handbreadths, leaving two handbreadths in the middle. After the Israelites committed this act, the Holy and Blessed One attempted to wrest them from Moses, but Moses prevailed and wrested them from Him. Thus Scripture eulogizes him at the end [of the Torah], saying: 'for all of the strength of hand . . .'" (Deuteronomy 34:12).[26]

There is even a fourth opinion[22] that says: "The will of the Holy and Blessed One was that he not shatter them."[27] According to this opinion, not only did the Holy and Blessed One not agree, but actually chided Moses for shattering the tablets. "Thus does Scripture say: 'Don't let your spirit be quickly vexed' (Ecclesiastes 7:9). Who was it who was vexed? It was Moses, as it is said, 'Moses became enraged and he hurled the tablets from his hands' (Exodus 32:9). Said to him the Holy and Blessed One: 'Whoa, Moses! You let out your anger on the tablets of the covenant! Do you want Me to let out My anger, and show you that the world would not be able to withstand it for a single moment?'" And Rabbi Isaac offered this exegesis: "'When one has thus sinned, and realizing his guilt, restores that which . . . was entrusted to him' (Leviticus 5:23). Said to him the Holy and Blessed One: Were not the tablets entrusted to you?![23] You shattered them, and you shall have to make good on them." That is why Moses was told, "Carve two tablets of stone like the first . . ." (Exodus 34:1).[28] Thus, despite all of the greatness of Moses, master of all the prophets, there were Sages who

[25] Rabbi Simeon ben Lakish commented: "'Which you shattered' (Exodus 34:2; Deuteronomy 10:2)—more power to you that you shattered them!" This midrash (found in BT Shabbat 87a and Menahot 99a) plays on the phonetic similarity of *asher* ("which") and *yishar* (from the phrase *yishar kohakha*—"more power to you"). Ibn Shu'ib rejected this midrash, but deduced the same idea from Deuteronomy 10:2: "'. . . which you smashed, and you shall deposit them in the Ark' [from which we learn that even the broken tablets were put in the Ark together with the unbroken second set]—had the Holy One not approved, how would He tell Moses to put them in the Ark?" (Ibn Shu'ib on Exodus 34:1, citing the midrash of R. Joseph in BT Menahot 99a. See also the Novellae of Nahmanides on BT Shabbat 87a).

[26] PT Ta'anit 4:8 (68c); see similar exegeses in Exodus Rabbah 28:1 and Tanhuma Ekev 11.

[27] See Midrash Haggadol, ed. Margaliot, p. 689.

[28] Deuteronomy Rabbah 3:12, 14–15; Tanhuma Tissa 28; Yelammedenu Ekev; Batei Midrashot I,173.

---

[22] We may summarize the four opinions as follows: (1) Moses shattered the tablets on his own, and God commended him (Ishmaelian); (2) Moses shattered them only because God told him to do so (Akivan); (3) Moses and God fought for control of the tablets, and they fell; (4) Moses shattered them, and God reprimanded him. Of these four positions, only the Akivan position has Moses faithfully following God's commands at every point.

[23] The reference here is to the laws concerning bailments, that is, when an article of value is entrusted to someone else for safekeeping. That object's safety is the responsibility of the bailee. And so Moses is, in this midrash, considered to be a bailee of the tablets.

did not hesitate to say that not always were his opinions correct, and not always was he consistent with the divine intent.[29]

"Thus Says the Lord: Toward Midnight . . ."

Rabbi Johanan counted a [slightly] different list of three things that Moses did on his own authority: separation from his wife, the statement of "toward midnight,"[24] and the addition of one day.[30]

Moses said to Pharaoh: "Thus says the Lord: 'Toward midnight I will go forth among the Egyptians, and every firstborn in the land of Egypt shall die'" (Exodus 11:4–5). But when the actual incident is described, it says: "In the middle of the night the Lord struck down all the firstborn" (Exodus 12:29). In the Tannaitic midrashim close attention was paid to the difference between the words "toward midnight" and "in the middle of the night." Concerning the Holy and Blessed One it is written: "in the middle of the night"—exactly—but Moses said "toward midnight," that is: approximately. And they gave reasons for this distinction—that "it is impossible for a mortal to determine midnight exactly."[31] Thus, Moses changed God's language, and nevertheless he said, 'Thus says the Lord.'"[25]

This point of view was accepted in the Babylonian Talmud: "'Toward midnight I will go forth among the Egyptians.' Why 'toward midnight'? Can we say that the Holy and Blessed One said to Moses 'toward midnight'? Can there then be any uncertainty in heaven? We must therefore admit that God said to him 'at midnight,' and then Moses said 'toward midnight.'"[32] Here it is said explicitly that Moses our master altered the words of the Blessed Name.

Still other Sages found that Moses our Master not only altered the words of the Holy and Blessed One, but actually added something substantive on his own author-

[29] Similarly, God is reported as having said to Moses, "Do not harass the Moabites or provoke them to war" (Deuteronomy 2:9). This implies that Moses intended to wage war against them for the role that they took in the episode of Balaam and Ba'al Pe'or. But God corrected him, pointing out that Ruth the Moabitess and Naamah the Ammonite were destined to be born of them (BT Bava Kamma 38a–b, Tosafot s.v. *nasa*).

[30] Pesikta Hadetha, Beit Hamidrash, VI 41.

[31] MI Pisha 13, and Horowitz's note ad loc. See Responsa of RaDBaZ [Rabbi David ben Abi Zimra, Safed, 1479–1573] 814. Rabbi Simeon bar Yohai elaborated: "Moses could not estimate the subdivisions of time within the night, so he said 'toward midnight.' But the Holy and Blessed One knows every hour, minute, and second, and was able to determine the middle of the night with hairline precision" (PR 17:4 [86b]).

[32] BT Berakhot 3b; YS Psalms 876. Of course, nowhere in the Torah does it say that God said "at midnight"; it was only at the time of the event's occurrence that it says "at midnight," not at the time of the event's announcement.

[24] This is Moses' announcement to Pharaoh of the tenth plague, the plague of the firstborn.

[25] In the remainder of this chapter, and in the next chapter, Heschel deals specifically with the question whether "Thus says the Lord" is to be understood literally or flexibly.

ity: "The Holy and Blessed One only said: 'For that night I will go through the Land of Egypt' (Exodus 12:12)," and he [Moses] "shouted publicly: 'Thus says the Lord, toward midnight. . . .'"[33] [26]

In explanation of this, the Sages did not hesitate to say that even though Moses here said "Thus says the Lord," he did not say these words on the basis of prophecy but rather on his own authority, and the Holy and Blessed One "acted to confirm the decrees of Moses."[34] "Said Rabbi Abin Halevi Be-Rabbi: The Holy and Blessed One said to him: I did not specify [a time], and you said: 'toward midnight'! By your life, I shall confirm your decree [as it is written]: 'in the middle of the night the Lord struck down all the first-born' (Exodus 12:29)."[35] This idea was taught often in the midrashim: Rabbi Berechiah [said] in the name of Rabbi Levi: "'He confirms the word of His servant' (Isaiah 44:26)—this is Moses. . . . Said the Holy and Blessed One: I have already made a promise to Moses when I said: 'he is trusted throughout My household' (Numbers 12:7); shall my servant Moses then be a liar?! Rather, if Moses said 'toward midnight,' I, too, shall act 'in the middle of the night.'"[36]

Note that in the Mekhilta of Rabbi Simeon bar Yohai,[27] close attention was not paid to this difference [between "toward midnight" and "at midnight"]. Perhaps this is because they felt that there was no real difference between *kahatzot* with a *kaf* and *bahatzi* with a *bet*.[37] Or perhaps it is because they disputed the idea that Moses said anything on his own authority or altered the language of the Holy and Blessed One.

In truth, there was preserved another opinion, according to which Moses altered nothing. He heard "toward midnight" from on high, and he announced God's word verbatim. According to this opinion, God's word reached Moses twice. One utterance told him "toward midnight," and the second utterance told him, "For that night I will go through the land of Egypt."[38] And thus Moses neither altered nor added anything.

This opinion is apparently hinted at in the Mekhilta of Rabbi Simeon bar Yohai, which comes from the school of Rabbi Akiva. In the Torah, it simply says, "Moses said: Thus says the Lord, toward midnight . . . ," but it does not say to whom he said

---

[33] PRK 7 (62b); YS I 729 and II 461; Exodus Rabbah 18:1.
[34] YS II 461, quoting Yelammedenu.
[35] PR 49:11 (197b).
[36] PR 17:2 (85b).
[37] So the opinion of E. Z. Melamed in his introduction to MSY, p. 31. See also Rashi on Exodus 11:4.
[38] Lekah Tov to Exodus 11:4.

---

[26] Two different alterations are thus considered here and are somewhat conflated in the texts to be cited presently by Heschel: the first is the idea that Moses altered God's "at midnight" (exact) to "toward midnight" (approximate); the second alteration is that Moses may have taken a simple statement of God's intent to do something dramatic during that night and set on his own a time for the event (i.e., around midnight). Although these are different matters, they are similar in that in both cases Moses alters the divine word.

[27] A work from the school of Rabbi Akiva.

it. According to some midrashim, he said this to Israel. But we find a different idea in the Mekhilta of Rabbi Simeon bar Yohai: "Moses said to Israel 'that night I will go through the Land of Egypt' [i.e., in the same language he heard from the Holy and Blessed One], and he gave no specific time, so that they should not sit and think dark thoughts, such as 'the hour has come and we have not yet been redeemed.' But when Moses spoke to Pharaoh, what did he say? 'Thus says the Lord, toward midnight. . . .' That is, he told him that it would be at the halfway mark of the night."[39] From these lines we can infer two things: (1) "toward midnight" was said to Pharaoh and not to Israel; and (2) Moses heard the words "toward midnight" from the Holy and Blessed One as well.

Some later authorities also objected to the idea that Moses altered the language of the Holy and Blessed One. Rabbi Mordecai Jaffe,[28] the author of the "Levushim," wrote as follows about the words of Rabbi Elijah Mizrahi:

> It seems from his words that he believes that Moses altered the words of the prophecy that came to him from God, so that they should not say that Moses was a liar.[29] But I say that God should forgive him,[30] for how can one say that Moses altered the words of God even while saying, "Thus says the Lord" . . . rather, it is certain that God Himself said so to Moses in his prophecy, the reason being concern that Pharaoh's astrologers would themselves mistake the true hour and accuse God of being a liar, as it were. Our Sages, and Rashi among them, merely ascribed these words to Moses.[40]

"The Holy and Blessed One Never Told Him"

All the statements we have so far cited about things that Moses did on his own are only part of the story. There are yet other verses that begin "Thus says the Lord," which some Sages say Moses said on his own.[31]

---

[39] MSY, pp. 27ff. Midrash Haggadol on Exodus, ed. Margaliot, p. 207.
[40] Mordecai Jaffe, *Tzedah La-Derekh* (Prague, 1623), Bo 46d.

---

[28] Sixteenth century, Poland.

[29] The point here is that if Moses pinpointed the time at exactly midnight, then because human time reckoning is very approximate, the Egyptians might erroneously conclude that he had predicted the wrong time and blame the discrepancy on him. Therefore Moses hedged by saying, "toward midnight," to prevent this misunderstanding.

[30] That is, Elijah Mizrahi (fifteenth–sixteenth century, Turkey).

[31] The following progression may be noted among the things attributed to Moses' initiative in this chapter: (1) He takes on a personal obligation binding only on himself (separating from his wife, or from the Tent of Meeting). (2) He makes slight modifications in commands from God (adding one day, changing "at midnight" to "towards midnight"). (3) He takes drastic action on his own (shattering the tablets); whether he attributes it to God or not is not clear. (4) He conceives matters entirely of his own reason, but attributes them to God (the warnings for the eighth and tenth plagues). (5) He orders capital punishment on a grand scale, and attributes the authority of the action to God. The deviation from the maximal position (every matter, every verse, every word is from God) starts with

On the verse "Moses said, 'Thus says the Lord: Toward midnight I will go forth among the Egyptians . . .'" (Exodus 11:4), Rashi wrote: "This passage was said to him as he stood before Pharaoh." But the author of the Hizkuni[32] commented: "It was said to Pharaoh by Moses [without prior dictation by God]! For if it had been dictated to Moses by the Holy and Blessed One, why did Rashi not comment on this fact apropos of the first verse of the chapter ('And the Lord said to Moses')? But we must deduce that Moses spoke the whole of the warning of the tenth plague to Pharaoh on his own, as similarly the warning of the plague of locusts."[33] [41]

Hizkuni and his sources seemed to have arrived at the view that Moses spoke the words of warning about the plague of locusts on his own, despite his use of the formula, "thus says the Lord," because the text explicitly tells of God's telling Moses about each of the other plagues before Moses tells Pharaoh, but there is no such report in the case of the plague of locusts. The Torah commentary of the Tosafists agrees: "The Holy and Blessed One never told him about the plague of locusts, but Moses deduced it from God's telling him, 'that you may recount it to your sons,' for the plague of locusts is one uniquely deserving of telling, as we find in Joel (1:3): 'Tell your children about it.'"

Similarly, by a literal reading of Exodus 11, we find that the Lord said to Moses, "I will bring but one more plague upon Pharaoh and upon Egypt" (11:1), without specifying what this plague was, yet Moses fills in the blank: "Thus says the Lord . . . every firstborn in the land of Egypt shall die" (11:4–5). The midrashists struggled with this. According to one view, when Moses was told,[34] "Say to Pharaoh . . . now I will slay your firstborn son" (Exodus 4:22–23), the Holy and Blessed One revealed to him that Pharaoh would not let Israel go until after the slaying of the firstborn, and so it was not necessary to specify this at the end."[42] According to another midrash, "The Holy and Blessed One communicated a sign to Abraham, hinting that He would punish the Egyptians by slaying the firstborn, and this was passed down through the family line, Abraham to Isaac to Jacob, to Levi, to Kohath, to Amram, to Moses, who recog-

---

[41] Hizkuni on Exodus 11:4. Hizkuni cites other authorities "in Tractate Pesahim and Midrash Yelammedenu [a lost cousin-work to Tanhuma]" in support of the view that the warning of the plague of locusts was said by Moses on his own.

[42] Exodus Rabbah 5:7; see PR 49:11 (197b), and Saadia's commentary on Exodus 12:5.

---

small things, but builds gradually in scope and severity, until the two positions are clearly demarcated as night and day.

[32] Hezekiah ben Manoah, thirteenth-century French biblical commentator.

[33] Indeed, a close reading of Exodus 10 and 11 will show that Moses makes speeches starting "Thus says the Lord," which go well beyond what the text explicitly reports as God's words to Moses. But there is another possible explanation, that the text condensed the narration of the revelation and speeches to avoid redundancy. (See Nahmanides on Exodus 11:1, cited by Heschel.) Hizkuni seems to ignore this possibility on purpose, in order to stretch the doctrine of Moses' innovation to the maximum possible extreme consistent with a literal interpretation of the text.

[34] In his second prophetic revelation, on the way back to Egypt from Midian.

nized it and acted on it. To Abraham, the Holy and Blessed One said, 'I will execute judgment on the nation they shall serve' (Genesis 15:14). What does 'execute judgment' mean? When the Holy and Blessed One said, 'now I will slay your firstborn son,' it was clear to Moses that it referred to the plague of the firstborn. And when the Holy and Blessed One said, 'I will bring but one more plague upon Pharaoh and upon Egypt,' Moses reasoned, 'Now the sign has come to pass.'"[43] Even though Moses deduced the plague of the firstborn from family tradition and the sign, he announced it with the words, "Thus says the Lord."[44]

"I Call Heaven and Earth to Witness for Me That the Holy and Blessed One Did Not Speak to Him So"

"Moses stood up in the gate of the camp and said 'Whoever is for the Lord, come here!' . . . He said to them, 'Thus says the Lord, the God of Israel . . . go back and forth from gate to gate throughout the camp, and slay brother, neighbor, and kin'" (Exodus 32:26–27). The earliest commentators already exerted much energy on this verse: "'He said to them, "Thus says the Lord, the God of Israel"'—but where do you find that God said this to him? "Hurry down" (Exodus 32:7)—what is the meaning of "down" [Heb.: red]? They require chastisement (mardut).'"[45] The author of the "Lekah Tov" noted: "It was spoken to Moses on the spot, just as in 'Thus says the Lord, "toward midnight"'; where did God say it? [You must say] that God said it to him on the spot."[46] So held Nahmanides: "This was a 'timely teaching' . . . and 'Thus says the Lord, the God of Israel' was not derived from the commandment 'whoever sacrifices to a god . . . shall be proscribed' (Exodus 22:19), for these [worshipers of the calf] could not be held legally liable for the death penalty.[35] Rather, it was a commandment given to Moses from on high, which he did not write down."[47] [36]

---

[43] Exodus Rabbah 15:27.

[44] According to another view, God did indeed instruct Moses concerning the tenth plague, but was induced to do so because of another initiative on Moses' part. Pharaoh said to Moses, "Take care not to see me again!" (Exodus 10:28). Moses replied (without prompting from God), "You have spoken rightly. I shall not see your face again!" God now still had to inform Pharaoh of the tenth plague, but was constrained by Moses' words to Pharaoh and did not want to make Moses look like a liar before Pharaoh. Overriding all precedent, God instructed Moses about the tenth plague on the spot, in Pharaoh's palace. Moses received the colloquy with God in private, then turned to Pharaoh and communicated it publicly (Exodus Rabbah 18:1; Midrash of the 32 Canons, 19, ed. Enelow, p. 358).

[45] Exodus Rabbah 42:5.   [46] Lekah Tov, ad loc.

[47] Nahmanides on Exodus 32:27. Philo thought that Moses arrived at this command through the influence of the holy spirit, though it was not verbally dictated by God (On the Life of Moses 49, 272; see chapter 23 below, section entitled "Philo's Approach," for a discussion of these distinctions in Philo's thought).

---

[35] For such liability requires, according to rabbinic law, very specific conditions concerning witnesses to the act, advance warning of the consequences of the act, and many other details, most or all of which were not present here.

[36] This instance is so grave, since it has Moses ordering a certain amount of indiscriminate killing,

There is yet another difficulty in the biblical text. It is written: "The Levites did as Moses had bidden" (Exodus 32:28). Why did it not say: "The Levites did as God had bidden," since Moses had said to them "Thus says the Lord"? From the "Midrash Yelammedenu" it appears that the killing of those who worshiped the calf was ordered by Moses on his own authority. Once the Levites had done Moses' bidding, Moses appeared before the Holy and Blessed One and said: "Master of the Universe: What should You have done to them—mete out justice? I have already meted out justice for You. Now forgive them."[48] And what is given here in a hint is written explicitly and in a bold spirit in the book "Tanna de-be Eliyahu": "I call heaven and earth to witness for me that the Holy and Blessed One did not tell Moses so, that is, to stand up in the gate of the camp and to say: 'Whoever is for the Lord, come here!' or to say: 'Thus says the Lord, the God of Israel. . . .' But the righteous Moses reasoned for himself by a fortiori. He said: if I tell Israel 'slay brother, neighbor, and kin,' Israel will say: didn't you teach us that a Sanhedrin that executes a person once in seven years is called a 'terrorist court'?[37] Therefore, he appealed to the prestige of heaven."[49]

These matters are quite astonishing, and one of the commentators recounts that scholars appeared before one righteous man [apparently Eliakum Goetzel of Posen— early eighteenth century] and said: "If so, the Torah has been shown to be fraudulent—Elijah has testified that what is written in the Torah is not truthful, and if so, [apply the principle that] a testament that is partially null and void is completely null and void!"[50] And thus, another prophet can also come and nullify other parts of the Torah!"[51] Rabbi David Luria[38] attempted to explain "that the intention [was] . . . that the Holy and Blessed One told him this implicitly, rather than explicitly, and Moses deduced for himself how the chastisement should be accomplished through him."[52] Rabbi Barukh Fraenkel Teomim, author of "Barukh Ta'am," attempted to explain the matter according to the words of Rabbi Akiva: "If you wish to be strangled, hang yourself on a big tree."[53] [If you wish to say something that will be accepted by people, say it in the name of an important person.] For Rabbah said

[48] YS Shelah 744, quoting Yelammedenu.

[49] SER, 4, p. 17.

[50] PT Sanhedrin 2:6 (20c). See also Leviticus Rabbah 19:2 (cited in chapter 21 above, n. [48]), and BT Bava Batra 148b.

[51] Tosafot ben Jehiel on SER, (Jerusalem 1906), loc. cit.

[52] David Luria, glosses to Exodus Rabbah 42.

[53] Barukh Teomim, *Ateret Hakhamim* (Josefow, 1866), Even Ha-Ezer 29, citing Rabbi Akiva's maxim in BT Pesahim 112a.

---

which ultimately totalled three thousand people, that it must, on this view, have come from an explicit divine command rather than from an inference.

[37] This expression is used in Mishnah Makkot 1:11, where some authorities are cited as opposing even infrequent use of the death penalty. If that is the case, then Moses needs extraordinary authority in order to take the action he deems necessary, and thus he invokes God's name, even though God did not so command him.

[38] Eighteenth century, Lithuania.

something in the name of Rabbi Yosi even though he was taught it anonymously, "in order that others would accept it."[54] From this, he found that "if one heard a legal teaching, and he was convinced that it was normative *halakhah,* he is permitted to transmit it in the name of an important person, in order that it be accepted from him." But the author of "Magen Avraham"[55] [39] was not comfortable with this and objected from what the Rabbis, of blessed memory, had said: "One who says something in the name of a Sage from whom he did not learn it causes the Shekhinah to depart from Israel."[56] And he left the matter with the words "needs clarification."

In truth, the approach of the author of "Tanna de-be Eliyahu" is close to the words of the Mekhilta of Rabbi Ishmael, in which are cited many occasions on which we find phrases such as "thus says the Lord," and the question "Where did God say it?"[57] is then raised and answered. In our texts, some of these citations are missing, but they are preserved in the "Yalkut Shimoni."[40] There we find: "'Thus says the Lord . . . each of you put sword [on thigh]' (Exodus 32:27). Where did God say it? 'Whoever sacrifices to a god . . . shall be proscribed' (Exodus 22:19)."[58] Rashi also testifies that "it is thus taught in the Mekhilta."[59] According to this view, Moses was not told explicitly to kill those who worshiped the calf, but Moses arrived at the action through deduction.

It seems also from the Targum Pseudo-Jonathan that it did not interpret "Thus says the Lord" as an explicit command designated for that moment, but rather a deduction from a more general command: "and he said to them, thus did the Lord God of Israel say: 'whoever sacrifices to the idols of the nations shall be killed by the sword.'" And yet the question remains: How could Moses say "Thus says the Lord," when what followed was not said to him explicitly from on high?[41]

---

[54] BT Eruvin 51a. According to Paltoi Gaon, "if you recognize that a certain tradition is authoritative and it is not accepted from you, you may give it in your teacher's name so that it will be accepted" (*Hemdah Genuzah* 102).

[55] Magen Avraham on SA Orah Hayyim 156.

[56] Tractate Kallah 24; BT Berakhot 27b. See also Exodus Rabbah 28:8.

[57] See chapter 23, under "And Where Did He So Speak?"

[58] YS Judges 43. Barukh Teomim's own resolution is based also on a tradition from the school of Rabbi Ishmael in BT Yevamot 65b.

[59] Rashi on Exodus 32:27. See also *Genizah Studies in Memory of Dr. Solomon Schechter,* volume 1, *Midrash and Haggadah,* ed. Louis Ginzberg (New York: Jewish Theological Seminary, 1928), 75 and Ginzberg's notes ad loc.

---

[39] Rabbi Abraham Gombiner, seventeenth century, Poland.

[40] Thirteenth-century German midrashic collection.

[41] Not that Heschel intends to leave it as a question. Rather, he wants to emphasize that it is not a simple matter to conclude that Moses used the words "Thus says the Lord" even when what followed was not a direct quotation. Rabbi Ishmael's school was apparently able to assimilate this into their conceptual scheme, but Heschel's last words in this chapter remind us of how extraordinary a position it is.

Two Methods of Understanding "Thus Says the Lord"

Translator's Introduction

"Thus said the Lord: 'About midnight I will go out in the midst of Egypt . . . .'" So Moses spoke to Pharaoh. But the speech raises several questions: (1) Did God really speak so imprecisely ("about midnight")? And if so, why? (2) Why are we not told, as we are with the other plagues, of God's actually saying this to Moses, before he transmitted the message to Pharaoh? And (3) since Moses had just been rebuffed by Pharaoh and was ordered never to enter his presence again, when had there been time for God to speak to Moses of the execution of the tenth plague?

This is just one example of many problematic cases, in which it is hard to take "Thus said the Lord" literally. Heschel will catalogue many of these for us in the present chapter and will point out that the Ishmaelians made a distinction between two languages of prophecy, one of which is used to indicate a direct transmission of the divine word and the other of which ("Thus said the Lord") indicates that the prophet has set a divine inspiration to his own words, or has even made an *inference* from a divine inspiration.

This is a very far-reaching assertion. It gives Moses, and subsequent prophets as well, considerable degrees of freedom. Indeed, the end result (as in the case of the tenth plague) is that the prophet "forces God's hand," in that the prophecy, now given in God's name, had better come true.

So does the challenge to the maximalist view continue here. Not only did Moses do things on his own authority, but Scripture itself cannot be taken at face value when it seems to say that the prophet is simply serving as God's mouthpiece. Human initiative and freedom are irreducible and cannot be removed from religion, or from Scripture itself.

This line of argument anticipates what will come later (in chapter 26), namely, an examination of different views of prophecy, according to one of which the prophet is no mere vessel but actually God's partner in the mission to the people.

The Meaning of the Phrase "Thus Says the Lord"

THIS DIFFICULT RIDDLE[1] will be answered for us as soon as we see that the entire matter hinges on a disagreement among Tannaim.[2] According to the understanding of the school of Rabbi Ishmael, wherever Moses used the expression "This is what the Lord has (said, commanded) . . . ," he was conveying the words of God without addition or subtraction, or even stylistic change. However, when he used the phrasing "Thus says the Lord . . . ,"[3] he did not intend to convey God's words exactly, but rather intended to say: this is God's will. According to this understanding, Moses was able to alter God's language and to convey the intent alone.

In the Sifre to Numbers, which stems from the school of Rabbi Ishmael, it is said: "'Moses spoke . . . This is what the Lord has commanded' (Numbers 30:2)—this teaches that just as Moses prophesied with the words 'Thus says,' so did the other prophets prophesy with the words 'Thus says'; but Moses outdid them in that it is also said in his case, 'This is what the Lord has said. . . .'"[1] According to this understanding, "the word 'thus' imparts to us the gist of the matter, while the word 'this' imparts to us the intended matter itself. Now since all the other prophets had visions through an unclear lens only,[4] and thus were unable to get the entire substance of the matter shown to them, they had to include in their statements the words 'Thus

---

[1] Sifre Mattot 153; Lekah Tov Mattot 137b. "The question was raised: Didn't Isaiah also use the term 'That is the word [that the Lord spoke concerning Moab long ago]'? The answer is that this prophecy dated from 'long ago'—in the days of Moses, when Balak hired Balaam, 'and now the Lord has spoken'" (Memorial Book of R. Abraham Bacrat (Livorno 5605/1845), p. 81c, citing Rashi on Isaiah 16:13–14).

---

[1] The riddle that Heschel refers to here is the one posed at the end of the previous chapter. How can one sustain the seemingly audacious, even outrageous, position that Moses said "Thus says the Lord" as a preface to things he did not hear from God! Heschel will in this chapter show that, for some early authorities, the multitude of languages used by Moses to convey God's word "forced" them into interpreting each of them a little differently, and thus some of them as denoting cases where the words were not a direct quotation. More likely, however, is the possibility that the multitude of languages was a convenient pretext for a position to which those early authorities were already leaning for philosophical and theological reasons.

[2] This is a fairly typical move in talmudic discussions; when there is a noteworthy disagreement, the Talmud will often attempt to demonstrate that it has more ancient roots, especially in the Tannaitic period. Heschel simply echoes that language here, and in fact he will, in a later part of this chapter, attempt to take this divergence of views back another generation, to that of Rabbi Joshua and Rabbi Eleazar the Modaite.

[3] The seemingly trivial one-letter difference between "this" and "thus" (the former being exact quotation, and the latter being a spokesperson's transmittal of the gist) actually is reflected in the Hebrew as well, where the operative words are zeh and ko, both two-letter Hebrew words in which the second letters are identical. That is, one letter separates the two very different prefaces to prophetic pronouncement in Hebrew.

[4] Or, we might say, "through a glass darkly."

says the Lord . . . ,' which we interpret as introducing the gist of God's words, and not the words themselves. But Moses our Master, peace be with him, whose visions were through a clear lens, and who thus had the power to get in substance exactly what was given him, used the language 'This is what the Lord has said . . . ,' which we interpret as introducing the words themselves without any alteration at all. And since Moses our Master did not, at the beginning of his prophesying, yet attain the level that he merited at the end, he too included in his statements the words 'Thus says the Lord' on many occasions. Once he merited the clear lens, however, he no longer used any language but 'This is what the Lord has said . . . .'[2]

It is in the light of this understanding in the school of Rabbi Ishmael that we will fully comprehend the opinions given above that Moses our Master did things on his own authority even when he said "Thus says the Lord."

But "Thus says the Lord" was not interpreted in this way in the school of Rabbi Akiva. "The Lord spoke to Moses saying: Speak to Aaron and his sons and to all the Israelite people and say to them: This is what the Lord has commanded . . .' (Leviticus 17:1-2). In the Sifra, which comes from the school of Rabbi Akiva, the following is said of this verse: "This is what the Lord has commanded"—this teaches that this ordinance was spoken with the words "Thus says." But this is not only the case here. How do we know that every ordinance was spoken with the words "Thus says"? Because the text says: "This is what the Lord has commanded"—and this serves as a paradigmatic case for all ordinances, all of which were accompanied by "Thus says.'"[3][5]

It is clear that the opinion of the Sifra, which stems from the school of Rabbi Akiva, and the opinion of the Sifre, which stems from the school of Rabbi Ishmael, lie at great distance from one another.[4] According to the Sifra, the expression "Thus says the Lord" and "This is what the Lord has said" are equivalent, and they both signify that "he spoke in the very style that he heard, and it was not that he was given a generality and he invented a verbal style; rather, he spoke every word exactly as he heard them."[5] And every commandment that Moses spoke in the name of the Holy and

---

[2] Elijah Mizrahi, beginning of commentary to Mattot. See also Isaac Profiat Duran, *Ma'asei Ephod* (Vienna, 5625/1865), p. 170, and commentary of David Prado on Numbers 30:2.

[3] Sifra Aharei 83c. RaABaD also cites Exodus 19:3 and 20:19 as paradigmatic instances of "thus" ("Thus shall you say to the Israelites . . .") (commentary to Sifra, ad loc.).

[4] See Louis Finkelstein's notes in his edition of the Sifre to Deuteronomy, paragraph 83. See also R. Menahem Azariah Castelnuovo's Responsa *Emek Hamelekh* 72, and RSY, ed. Hoffmann, p. 6 n. 3.

[5] Korban Aharon ad loc. See also Zohar Balak 198a, expressing the view of the Sifre.

---

[5] The import of this text, attributed according to tradition to the school of Rabbi Akiva, is that there is no meaningful distinction between "This is what the Lord has commanded . . ." and "Thus says the Lord . . . ." In each case, God said to Moses, "tell the Israelites, 'this is what the Lord has commanded . . . ,'" and then Moses went to the people and began his speech with "Thus says the Lord." The distinction noted above between "this" and "thus"—or between *zeh* and *ko*—collapses on this view.

Blessed One, he spoke in the language of the Holy and Blessed One. But according to the Sifre, "Thus says the Lord" imparts to us the gist of the matter, and "This is what the Lord has said" means to impart the words themselves with no alteration at all.

The higher status of the word "this" is emphasized as well in an exegesis of the verse "This is My God and I will enshrine Him" (Exodus 15:2). "Rabbi Eliezer said: How do we know that a maidservant saw at the sea visions that Isaiah and Ezekiel did not see? For it says, '. . . and spoke parables through the prophets' (Hosea 12:11), and also, 'the heavens opened and I saw visions of God' (Ezekiel 1:1)."[6] In other words, the other prophets prophesied through parable and vision, whereas here it says "This is My God," as if one were pointing with one's finger and seeing with perfect clarity.

According to the commentaries, the distinction that Rabbi Ishmael drew between the two languages is based on the difference between "thus" and "this." It would seem possible to argue that the basis of the distinction is in the different meanings of "saying" (amirah) and "speaking" (dibbur). Perhaps Rabbi Ishmael interpreted "Thus says the Lord"[7] to have this meaning: "Thus does the Lord intend" or "Thus does the Lord think." For in biblical Hebrew,[7] and in Rabbinic Hebrew as well, "saying" (amor) can mean either speaking or thinking (as in: "One who says [omer] 'I shall sin and repent, and then sin and repent again,'"[8] or the depiction of Abraham as having "said [amar]: Is it possible that the fortress has no chief?")[9] [8]

According to the author of "Korban Aharon,"[9] speaking (dibbur) denotes the actual formation and articulation of letters, whereas saying (amirah) denotes the conveyance of a subject but not the articulation of the letters that convey it. When we say that a certain person has spoken, we are referring to the words that he uttered in order to talk about his subject. But when we say that a certain person said something, we are referring to the subject spoken of, but not the specific words that were used to do so. And so, speaking is face to face, since it refers to the actual words that are uttered; when we say that a certain person spoke to another person, it means he spoke to him directly.[10] However, we shall see in the coming chapter that the main

[6] MI Shirata 3; MSY, ad loc.
[7] See Genesis 44:28; Exodus 2:14; 1 Samuel 2:30; Psalm 10:6.
[8] Mishnah Yoma 8:9. [9] Genesis Rabbah 39:1.
[10] Korban Aharon on Leviticus, 42b–c.

[6] The deduction here is based on the fact that Hosea and Ezekiel (particularly the latter, for he is often assumed to have had the most vivid visions) use words for prophecy such as demut and mar'ot —"image" and "appearances." But at the sea, the word zeh ("this") is used, not a mental construct but rather a present sight to which one could physically point and, perhaps, share with others.

[7] The Hebrew is ko amar—the verbal root that, it is here conjectured, means something like conveyance of a subject rather than explicit articulation of an exact formula.

[8] In both of these texts, the verb amor is used to describe not an exact articulation of words and letters, but rather a thought process.

[9] Aaron ben Abraham ibn Hayyim, Morocco, sixteenth–seventeenth centuries.

difference is not that between saying and speaking, but rather between "thus" and "this" themselves.

On the verse "The Lord said to Moses, Come up to Me on the mountain" (Exodus 24:12), Rabbi Menahem Recanati[10] says in his commentary: "I have already hinted to you about the difference that exists between 'God said' [vayyomer adonai] and 'God spoke' [vayyedaber adonai]. For 'God said' is of the matters of the Oral Torah, just as is the word 'saying' [lemor]. But 'God spoke' is of the Written Torah."[11] [11]

What brought Rabbi Ishmael to the point of view that not always did Moses convey God's words exactly? I believe that this standpoint was born not of abstract consideration on the nature of prophecy, but rather of an effort to grasp the plain meaning of Scripture.

"The Lord said to Moses and Aaron in the Land of Egypt: This month shall mark for you the beginning of the months" (Exodus 12:1–2). There was a principle that all of the utterances that the Holy and Blessed One spoke to Moses were "only spoken to him during the day."[12] And yet the word "this" seems to describe the moon in its new crescent shape before Moses' eyes, and how is that possible if the utterance came during the day? Rabbi Akiva resolves the problem by this exegesis: "The Holy and Blessed One showed him the shape of a moon with His finger, and He said: 'when you see this, sanctify it.'"[13] In other words, there was a miraculous occurrence here.[12] In contrast to this, Rabbi Ishmael suggests that the word "this" was not uttered by the Holy and Blessed One; rather, Moses added that word when he conveyed the speech to Israel at night. "Moses showed the Israelites the new lunar crescent, and said to them: 'see this, and fix the new month, throughout the generations.'"[14]

The author of "Hizkuni"[13] apparently believed that even in a case where it is written "this is what the Lord has said," it is possible that Moses said the words on his own authority. It is written in the Torah: "Moses spoke to the heads of the Israelite tribes, saying: This is what the Lord has commanded . . ." (Numbers 30:2). And RaSHBaM[14] relates: "I was once asked in Anjou, in the town of Loudun, about the

---

[11] Recanati on Exodus 24:12.   [12] Tanhuma, ed. Buber, Bo 10.
[13] MSY, p. 8.   [14] MI Bo 1.

---

[10] Italian kabbalist, thirteenth–fourteenth century.

[11] It is in the Written Torah, of course, that linguistic exactitude is critical. A single letter misplaced in a Torah scroll renders it unfit for use until it is repaired, whereas an exact text of the Talmud has never been standardized, and variant readings abound among commentators to the present day. Thus, Recanati's suggestion about the respective imports of amor and dabber does seem to fit the distinction we have been treating here.

[12] The miraculous occurrence may not be obvious here, until one realizes that at the beginning of the month, when the very first crescent of the New Moon appears, the moon is visible only for a very brief and fleeting time after sunset. This was the beginning of the month of Aviv, and Moses was spoken to during the day, and yet he was able to see the crescent clearly. This is a miracle on the order of Joshua's making the sun stand still.

[13] Hezekiah ben Manoah, thirteenth-century French biblical commentator.

[14] Samuel ben Meir, a commentator of the school of Rashi, twelfth century.

plain meaning here: where have we ever seen a section of the Torah begin this way? For it does not say earlier 'The Lord spoke to Moses, saying, if a man makes a vow to the Lord . . . .' How then can this section begin with a statement of Moses that was not explicitly given to him from on high?"[15] On this verse, the Hizkuni writes: "It is not here explained where or when this matter was said to Moses. And there are several similar prophecies, such as, 'Thus says the Lord' in connection with the plague of locusts, or 'Thus says the Lord, toward midnight . . . ,' or 'Each of you put sword on thigh,' in the matter of the calf. And many other prophets prophesied with the words 'Thus says the Lord,' although we do not know where and when they were spoken. About this, it is written: '[I] confirm the word of My servant' (Isaiah 44:26)."[16] It is clear that he is referring to the aforementioned opinion of Rabbi Johanan:[15] "Moses said it on his own authority, and the Holy and Blessed One agreed with him, even though He did not say so."[17] Thus, according to the position of the Hizkuni, Moses said things on his own authority even when he announced "This is what the Lord has said . . . ."

A Baraita on another matter illustrates Rabbi Ishmael's usage of "Thus says the Lord": "Our rabbis taught: How did they inquire of the Urim and Thummim? The person making the request faced the High Priest, who faced the Shekhinah [i.e., the Ark]. The requestor would ask, 'Shall I pursue such-and-such a battalion?' The High Priest would respond, 'Thus says the Lord: Go up and be successful!' Rabbi Judah said, 'He should say simply, "Go up and be successful," without saying "Thus says the Lord."'"[18] Now, it is significant that the High Priest, when answering a request through the Urim and Thummim, spoke with divine inspiration, but he was not a prophet,[19] yet the first opinion holds that he could use the formula "Thus says the Lord." Rabbi Judah, who eschewed the formula in such a case, may have been following the view of Rabbi Akiva.

"Thus"—In the Holy Tongue

In the Sifre on Parashat Naso they expounded: "'Thus shall you bless the people of Israel' (Numbers 6:23)—in the holy tongue, for wherever it says 'thus,' it means the

[15] RaSHBaM on Numbers 30:2.

[16] Hizkuni on Numbers 30:2. On Exodus 10:3 he adds: "There are several prophecies *and mitzvot* where it is not explained where the Holy One said them."

[17] Pesikta Hadetha, Beit Hamidrash VI,41.

[18] BT Yoma 73a. The example "go up and be successful" is an allusion to 1 Kings 22:12–15.

[19] The distinctions and levels of prophetic inspiration are detailed by Maimonides in *Guide of the Perplexed* II:45. The High Priest speaking with the Urim and Thummim was the next-to-lowest of the eleven levels. Maimonides discusses the ritual of Urim and Thummim in *Hilkhot Kelei Hamikdash* 10:11–13, based on the talmudic description. See BT Bava Batra 122a; Yoma 73a–b.

[15] In the previous chapter, where Rabbi Johanan is quoted as having his own list of three things that Moses did on his own authority.

holy tongue."[20] In the school of Rabbi Ishmael they grasped the meaning of "thus" as nothing more than "in the holy tongue."[21]

Note that in the Mekhilta of Rabbi Simeon ben Yohai they greatly expanded the meaning of the word "thus." The Holy and Blessed One had said to Moses, "Thus shall you say to the house of Jacob" (Exodus 19:3). And so the Mekhilta of Rabbi Simeon ben Yohai: "'thus'—in the holy tongue; 'thus'—in this style; 'thus'—in this order; 'thus'—punctuated in this way; 'thus'—in these paragraphs; 'thus'—neither subtracting nor adding anything."[22]

The idea embedded in the above, that Moses was commanded to observe the exact order of the verses and paragraphs and not to convey the earlier later, and vice versa, fits the position of Rabbi Akiva but contradicts that of Rabbi Ishmael. In the school of Rabbi Ishmael they fixed this principle: "there is no strict chronological order in the Torah": "The Torah was not particular on the order of earlier and later, and many sections that were spoken earlier were preceded by those spoken later."[23] This principle, which is also hinted at in the words of Rabbi Joshua ben Hananiah,[24] is taught anonymously in the Mekhilta of Rabbi Ishmael[25] and is also given in another place in the name of "a tanna of the school of Rabbi Ishmael."[26]

In the light of this, let us consider the words of the Mekhilta of Rabbi Ishmael:[16] "'thus shall you say': 'thus'—in the holy tongue; 'thus'—in this order; 'thus'—in this style; 'thus'—neither subtracting nor adding anything."[27] Now the first part of this exegesis ["'thus'—in the holy tongue"] fits the exegesis in the Sifre that "wherever it says 'thus,' it means the holy tongue." However, the rest of the exegesis seems as if it is an interweaving from the school of Rabbi Akiva.[28]

It seems that the exegesis in its original formation in the school of Rabbi Ishmael was: "'thus shall you say'—in the holy tongue." And thus is the exegesis preserved in

[20] Sifre Naso 39. See also MI Bahodesh 9 (on Exodus 20:22).

[21] In Sifre Shofetim 210 and Sifre Tetzei 291, a similar interpretation is made of the formula, "They/she shall answer and say . . ." (NJV: "shall make this declaration" in Deuteronomy 21:7; 25:9).

[22] MSY, p. 138, on Exodus 19:3. So also MSY, p. 138, interpreting "these are the words. . . ."

[23] BT Pesahim 6b; Rashi s.v. *ein mukdam*.

[24] MI Amalek 2.   [25] MI Shirata 7.

[26] Ecclesiastes Rabbah 1:12.

[27] MI Bahodesh 2; YS 276.

[28] So says L. Finkelstein (*Akiba*, 310).

[16] In this paragraph, Heschel is anticipating, and warding off, a possible objection. That objection is that a text from the Mekhilta of Rabbi Ishmael seems to support some of Rabbi Akiva's point of view about the exactitude of Mosaic pronouncements. Heschel is forced to conjecture that the Mekhilta text was expanded with non-Ishmaelian elements here. This is not a baseless conjecture, for he does produce a parallel text that does not have the alleged additions. But it is worth reminding the reader that Heschel's argument, though it is often framed as a tight historical one, is more of a phenomenological one—and he has shown that there were two different approaches to the extent to which Mosaic pronouncements tracked the divine utterances, even if on occasion the same person or the same text wavered between one view and the other!

the Mekhilta of Rabbi Ishmael on Exodus 20:22: "'thus shall you say'—in the holy tongue."[29] Consider by contrast how the verse was apprehended in the school of Rabbi Akiva: "'thus'—in the holy tongue; 'thus'—in this style; 'thus'—in this order; 'thus'—punctuated in this way; 'thus'—in these paragraphs; 'thus'—exactly as God commanded, neither subtracting nor adding anything."[30]

In the school of Rabbi Akiva they saw in the word "thus" a warning to convey the words with exactitude. And just as they expounded "thus," so did they expound the word "these" (*eleh*): "'These are the words that you shall speak to the children of Israel' (Exodus 19:6)—'these'—in the holy tongue; 'these'—in this style; 'these'—in this order; 'these'—punctuated in this way; 'these'—neither subtracting nor adding anything."[31]

"And Where Did He So Speak?"

In Moses' speeches to the Israelites we sometimes find language such as "as the Lord has spoken," "this is what the Lord has spoken . . . ," or "Thus says the Lord," and there is no mention in the Torah of when those things were spoken to Moses from on high. The Mekhilta of Rabbi Ishmael brings more than ten such places, and each time they ask and answer the question: "And where did He so speak?"[32] One who compares the words of God with the words of Moses will find that in the opinion of the Mekhilta, in most places Moses was not inhibited about altering the language of the Holy and Blessed One and conveying the intent alone.

"'He said to them, "This is what the Lord meant when He said: Tomorrow is a day of rest, a holy sabbath of the Lord. Bake what you would bake and boil what you would boil"' (Exodus 16:23)—and where did He so speak? 'But on the sixth day, when they prepare what they have brought in' (Exodus 16:4–5)."

Similarly, you see: "This is what the Lord meant when He said: Through those near to Me I show Myself holy" (Leviticus 10:3)—and where did He so speak? "There I will meet with the Israelites, and it shall be sanctified by My Presence" (Exodus 29:43).[33][17]

Similarly: "Thus says the Lord, the God of Israel: Each of you put sword on thigh"

[29] MI Bahodesh 9.

[30] Midrash Haggadol, ed. Margaliot, p. 440; MSY, ed. Hoffmann, p. 114.

[31] MSY, p. 139. Similarly MI Bahodesh 2, where Akivan ideas seem to have been accepted in a work of the Ishmaelian school.

[32] MI Pisha 12.

[33] This is found also in the *mekhilta de-millu'im* (Sifra Shemini 45d), an Ishmaelian addition to the otherwise Akivan work Sifra.

---

[17] The exegesis here is not very transparent. Both texts use the words *kadesh* and *kavod*, referring, respectively, to sanctity and the Divine Presence or Glory. Perhaps it is that Aaron's sons are specifically mentioned (though along with Aaron himself) in Exodus 29:44, and/or it may be a reaction to the context in Exodus 29, to wit a paragraph dealing with the *olah*, the burnt offering.

(Exodus 32:27)—and where did He so speak? "Whoever sacrifices to a god other than the Lord alone shall be proscribed" (Exodus 22:19).[34]

This entire approach fits that of Rabbi Ishmael, for whom the expression "Thus says the Lord" denotes the gist of the matter and not the actual language, as Rabbi Elijah Mizrahi[18] has explained. And as I have demonstrated, Rabbi Ishmael holds that the meaning of the expressions "as the Lord has spoken" and "that is what the Lord has spoken" is just that of the expression "thus says the Lord." The exceptional cases are those in which it says "this [zeh] is what God has commanded."

There is more. In the very same chapter[19] that deals with the problem of "and where did He so speak?" there are brought in one fell swoop numerous examples from the Torah and the Prophets [expressions such as "for the Lord has spoken," "for it was the Lord who spoke," "declares the Lord" . . . "that I have spoken," "for it was the Lord of Hosts who spoke"], without differentiating at all between Moses' prophecy and that of the other prophets. But this difficulty is well resolved in the light of what is said in the Sifre: "Just as Moses prophesied with 'thus says the Lord,' so did the other prophets prophesy with 'thus says the Lord.'" In other words, on a certain level, there is no difference between Moses and the other prophets.

According to these things, it is clear that the idea suggested by Rabbi Elijah Mizrahi that only at the outset of Moses' prophetic career was he forced to use the language "thus says the Lord," and to convey the intent alone, does not really fit the approach of Rabbi Ishmael. For the examples given in the Mekhilta of Rabbi Ishmael are taken from all the periods of Moses our Master's prophecy.

Not only does the answer given by Rabbi Ishmael contradict the approach of Rabbi Akiva; the question itself divides them: "and where did He so speak?" is a question that does not even appear in the midrashim from the school of Rabbi Akiva.[35] The answer that was suggested in the commentary attributed to Saadia Gaon fits this approach of Rabbi Akiva: "'this is what the Lord has spoken.' Now we have not seen this in Scripture explicitly, but the messenger surely heard this previously from the Sender, may He be blessed, though he did not so inform them [his listeners] prior to this."[36]

Two sections are given in the Torah concerning the Paschal sacrifice. The first contains God's words to Moses (Exodus 12:1-20), and the second contains Moses' words to the elders of Israel (Exodus 12:21-27). There are differences between these

---

[34] See also Rashi on Exodus 32:27, and last section of previous chapter.

[35] But see J. N. Epstein, Mevo'ot le-sifrut ha-tannaim [Introduction to Tannaitic Literature], 637.

[36] Manuscript in Bodleian Library, attributed to R. Saadia Gaon by Moses Zucker, cited in Torah Shelemah on Exodus 16:23, n. 123. "This proves that there are many mitzvot which Moses heard but did not proclaim until later . . . such as most of the laws of Deuteronomy."

---

[18] Fifteenth–sixteenth century, Turkey.

[19] In the Mekhilta, that is (Pisha, chapter 12).

two sections. Now in the Mekhilta of Rabbi Ishmael they paid little attention to these differences.[37] However, in the school of Rabbi Akiva they were sensitive to this, and since according to their approach Moses never changed the words of the Holy and Blessed One, they declared that Moses was spoken to twice and that in addition to the words he received in the first section, he also received the words of the second section; and thus Moses changed nothing. Thus it was taught in the Mekhilta of Rabbi Simeon bar Yohai: "Since we have seen that in the first section (12:2-20), God spoke to Moses, and in the second (12:21-27) Moses spoke to Israel, how do we know that both were heard from the Holy One, and then rehearsed to Israel? For Scripture says: 'just as the Lord had commanded Moses' (12:28)."[38] By contrast, they expounded thus in the Mekhilta of Rabbi Ishmael: "'just as the Lord had commanded'—to praise the Israelites, in that they did exactly as Moses and Aaron instructed them."[39]

Rabbi Joshua ben Hananiah and Rabbi Eleazar the Modaite

Most of the halakhic exegeses that have reached us are from the third generation of Tannaim, the generation of Rabbi Ishmael and Rabbi Akiva, and from the fourth generation, that of their disciples. As scholars of midrash have demonstrated, there were fundamental differences in midrashic method between the school of Rabbi Ishmael and the school of Rabbi Akiva. We are attempting to prove that in religious thought processes, and in principles of the faith, there were also differences between Rabbi Ishmael and Rabbi Akiva.

It seems to me that such differences appear already in the second generation of Tannaim (80–120 C.E.). In the words of Rabbi Joshua ben Hananiah we find an approach to biblical exegesis marked by an exotericism that reached full expression later on in the teachings of Rabbi Ishmael. Rabbi Ishmael was close to Rabbi Joshua and transmitted certain things in his name,[40] and Rabbi Joshua affectionately called him "my brother."[41] According to a story told in the Talmud, Rabbi Joshua saved his life.[42]

A signal difference in thought processes emerges from the differences between Rabbi Joshua's explanations of biblical verses and those of Rabbi Eleazar the Modaite. Rabbi Joshua always attempts to explain biblical verses according to their plain logical content and to understand matters historically. Against this, Rabbi Eleazar interprets verses not according to their plain meaning but rather following aggadic exegesis,

---

[37] Indeed, the Mekhilta (Pisha 12) asks: "'When you enter the land that the Lord will give you, as He has spoken'—where did He so speak?" But this relates not to the differences in the Paschal laws between the two sections but to introduction of the extraneous theme of the promise of the land.

[38] MSY, p. 27; see also p. 231.

[39] MI Pisha 12 (end).

[40] PT Pesahim 34c.

[41] Mishnah Avodah Zarah 2:5.

[42] By redeeming him from slavery (BT Gittin 55a; PT Horayot 48b, cited in chapter 1).

expanding and augmenting the verses' meaning and revealing in them allusions and ideas that are not apparent to the reader's eye. Moreover, Rabbi Joshua attempts to interpret biblical narratives naturalistically, while Rabbi Eleazar finds miraculous occurrences even in places where there is no hint of them in the plain meaning of the text, and within the accounts of miracles he tries to magnify the miracle as much as possible.[43] The practice of Rabbi Eleazar the Modaite to find the miraculous in all narratives, as if the world cannot exist without miracles and wonders, did not always please the Sages.[44]

We find that Rabbi Joshua and Rabbi Eleazar the Modaite differed on the matter of whether Moses did anything on his own. It is said in the Torah: "Moses said to Joshua, 'Pick some men for us, and go out and do battle with Amalek' (Exodus 17:9)." The verses do not mention that Moses did this on God's command. Thus Rabbi Joshua ben Hananiah interprets according to the plain meaning of the text: "Said Moses to Joshua: 'Go out from under the [protective] cloud and do battle with Amalek.'" But Rabbi Eleazar the Modaite differs with him and has this picture of the event: "Said the Holy and Blessed One to Moses: Say to Joshua, 'Why are you protecting your own scalp? Is it not in order one day to put a crown on it? Go and do battle with Amalek!'"[45][20]

The Tannaim expound a subsequent verse, each according to his method: "'And Joshua overwhelmed [literally, 'weakened'] the people of Amalek with the sword' (Exodus 17:13). Rabbi Joshua says: He did not disgrace them, but rather judged them mercifully [that is, he weakened them, and did not kill the entire nation]. Rabbi Eleazar the Modaite said: why does it say 'with the sword' [literally, 'by the mouth of the sword']? We learn from this that this war took place only by the mouth of the Most High."[46] Similarly, they differed on another subsequent verse: "'Moses built an

---

[43] MI Shirata 4.

[44] MI Vayyassa' 3, cited above, pp. 68–70. Heschel supplies another example here: "Moses named his second son Eliezer, meaning 'The God of my father was my help, and He delivered me from the sword of Pharaoh' (Exodus 18:3). How did he deliver him? Rabbi Joshua said, 'By arranging for the second Hebrew [Dathan] to retort, "Who made you chief and ruler over us? Do you mean to kill me as you killed the Egyptian?" [whereupon Moses fled to Midian].' Rabbi Eliezer the Modaite said, 'The Egyptians captured Moses and brought him up on the scaffold. They bound him and laid a sword to his neck. An angel came down from heaven, in Moses' identical image. They captured the angel and let Moses go. God thereupon rendered Moses' captors mute, deaf, and blind. When the investigators asked them, "Where is Moses?" the mute could not speak; the deaf could not hear the question; and the blind could not see Moses'" (Midrash Haggadol on Exodus 18:4; MI Amalek 1 conflates the two answers).

[45] MI Amalek 1; MSY, ad loc. Rabbi Eleazar's view became standard in the Amoraic period; see PR 54a, exegesis of Judges 5:14.

[46] MI Amalek 1; MSY, ad loc. (but see note).

---

[20] The difference, in other words, is that Rabbi Joshua sees Moses' exhortation to Joshua in the text as nothing more than a master telling a disciple to get out in the world and do something; this required no instruction from God. But Rabbi Eleazar the Modaite insists that if Moses told Joshua to go out and fight, it was at God's insistence that Joshua submit to God's will and not protect his own safety.

altar and named it Adonai-nissi [the Lord is my banner]' (Exodus 17:15). Rabbi Joshua says that Moses called it 'Nissi,' while Rabbi Eleazar the Modaite says that God called it 'Nissi.'"[47] [21]

Rabbi Joshua disagreed as well with Rabbi Eliezer ben Hyrcanus on the problem of whether Moses did things on his own. "Then Moses caused Israel to set out from the Sea of Reeds. They went into the wilderness of Shur" (Exodus 15:22). The Sages disagreed on this: "Rabbi Joshua says: this journey was undertaken by the Israelites on Moses' instructions, while all other journeys were on instructions from on high, as it says: 'On a sign from the Lord they made camp and on a sign from the Lord they broke camp' (Numbers 9:23) . . . but this journey was undertaken only by Moses' instructions, and thus it says: 'Then Moses caused Israel to set out from the Sea of Reeds.' Rabbi Eliezer ben Hyrcanus said: They journeyed on instructions from on high."[48]

A similar disagreement, on whether all mitzvot in the Torah were spoken from on high, is evident in the matter of the appointment of judges. According to one opinion, "Moses was not commanded concerning judges, but rather proceeded on the basis of what Jethro told him."[49] According to another opinion, he heard this matter from Jethro and afterwards "consulted with God." According to a third opinion, the matter "was already in Moses' hand at Sinai."

Jethro had said to Moses: "You shall also seek out from among all the people capable men who fear God, trustworthy men who spurn ill-gotten gain. . . . let them judge the people at all times" (Exodus 18:21–22), and the Torah testifies, "Moses heeded his father-in-law, and did just as he had said" (Exodus 18:24). Now the Sages differed on the interpretation of this verse: "'Moses heeded his father-in-law'—as the verse says—'and did just as he said'—that is, just as his father-in-law said—so Rabbi Joshua." In other words: Moses appointed the judges according to Jethro's advice and did not consult God. This view, which follows the plain meaning of Scripture, was known as well to Josephus.[50]

By contrast, Rabbi Eleazar the Modaite holds as follows: "'Moses heeded his father-

---

[47] MSY, p. 126. In a similar vein, they disagreed whether Moses or God assigned the place-names of Massah and Meribah (MI Vayyassa' 6).

[48] MI Vayyassa' 1; MSY, ad loc. In Tanhuma, ed. Buber, Beshalah 16, the same dispute is elaborated, with Rabbi Eleazar the Modaite named in place of Rabbi Eliezer ben Hyrcanus.

The Sages differed also on whether Jethro announced his arrival to Moses through a letter, or whether God told Moses of Jethro's arrival (SER, p. 30; MSY, p. 130; MI Yitro 1).

[49] Tanhuma Shofetim 1.

[50] Josephus, *Antiquities* 3.4.1. *Tzeror Hamor* (Abraham Saba, Spain, d. 1508) on Exodus 18:23 says that Moses followed Jethro scrupulously, because Jethro was divinely inspired.

---

[21] The ambiguity is not forced at all in the Hebrew: the pronoun "he" in "and He called it Adonai-nissi" could just as easily refer to God as to Moses (grammatically, that is; the context certainly supports the referent being Moses). Rabbi Eleazar again seems to be reluctant to ascribe any significant act to Moses alone, in the absence of God's instructions.

in-law'—as the verse says—'and did just as he said'—that is, as God said."[51] He interprets the first half of the verse according to its plain meaning, but interprets the second half as if the word "God" were written there and holds that he did not appoint any judges until God told him to.

This matter will explain to us the nature of the disagreement over the matter of when Jethro arrived at the Israelite camp. "Jethro heard": "What news did he hear that made him come? He heard about the Amalekite war and came . . . so says Rabbi Joshua. Rabbi Eleazar the Modaite says: he heard about the giving of the Torah and came."[52] According to Rabbi Eleazar, Jethro arrived after Moses had already received instructions concerning the judges at Sinai.[22]

Philo's Approach

The approach of Rabbi Joshua and Rabbi Ishmael—that not all of Moses' acts were on divine instruction but rather that Moses said things on his own and on his own conformed to the divine intent—was apparently even older. It is found in the writings of Philo of Alexandria (first century C.E.).[23]

In several different places Philo emphasizes the belief that the laws of the Torah are God's words, not simply a human creation. That was why they were given in the desert, to indicate that these laws were not made up by people but were God's words.[53] He even brings in the view of the Essenes—that it would be impossible for mortals to arrive at such laws without inspiration from on high.[54]

Philo believed that all that is written in the Torah is the word of the living God, and he taught that there are three levels in the Torah: (1) things that "were spoken from the mouth of God Himself" for which the prophet played the role of go-between or mouthpiece; (2) things that were spoken in answer to questions from the prophet; and (3) things that "Moses said on his own authority during times in which the Spirit of God addressed him and began to move him," that is, when he was in a state of ecstasy.[55] Those utterances of the first level are from God alone. Those of the

---

[51] MI Amalek 2. See also Exodus Rabbah 27:6, where Jethro is said to have told Moses: "Don't do this on my say-so, but consult with the Holy and Blessed One on this matter!"

[52] MI Yitro 1.

[53] Philo, *De Decalogo* 4.15.

[54] I. Heinemann, *Philons Griechische und jüdische Bildung: Kulturvergleichende Untersuchungen zu Philons Darstellung der jüdischen Gesetze* (Breslau, 1932; reprint, Hildesheim: G. Olms, 1962), 476. Compare Philo, *Quod omnis probus liber sit* 80.

[55] Philo, *De Vita Mosis* 2.35, 188.

---

[22] That Jethro came after Sinai does require an alteration of the chronological order of the text (chapter 18 postdating chapters 19 and 20), and that sort of move actually typifies the school of Rabbi Ishmael! However, this is a bit of a special case, because if there is no such move to postdate Jethro's arrival after the Sinai revelation, just what law was Moses adjudicating before the people that made the new judicial system so imperative?

[23] First century C.E.

second level have some prophetic input, for it is the prophet's questions that are being answered by God. The utterances of the third level are those that Moses said on his own.[56]

Philo believes that Moses spoke as a prophet only when he delivered utterances of the third type. But utterances of the first type, that is, conveying God's words to the people, are not prophecy. In this respect, Moses was a go-between (*hermeneus*) and not a prophet.

Philo found eight places in the Torah where Moses spoke on his own, as a divine strength ("enthusiasm") took hold of him. He devoted the last part of his treatise "The Life of Moses" to explicating these eight.[57] In most of these cases, midrashim, without explicitly following Philo, also held that it was in an ecstatic state transcending physicality that Moses spoke on his own:

(1) In Exodus 14:11–13: "They said to Moses, 'Was it for want of graves in Egypt that you brought us to die in the wilderness?' . . . But Moses said to the people, 'Have no fear! Stand by and witness the deliverance which the Lord will work for you today.'" These words were not said to Moses from on high. They came from his mouth in a state of being "gripped by God," and transcending physicality.[58] The Mekhilta of Rabbi Ishmael also said: "Moses was urging them to have courage, and this indicates the wisdom of Moses, in that he was able to stand and calm down all those thousands and myriads. Of him, Scripture says: 'Wisdom is a stronghold to the wise man' (Ecclesiastes 7:19)."[59] Here it is not Moses' prophecy that is praised, but rather his wisdom. According to this, Moses did not say what is in this verse on instructions from on high.[60]

(2) When the manna descended, Moses said to the Israelites: 'Let no one leave any of it over until morning' (Exodus 16:19). This command, thinks Philo, Moses spoke as the spirit [*enthousiasmos*] imbued him, not on instructions from above. There were people of scant faith, who perhaps reasoned that this command was not spoken from on high and was therefore merely a "king's decree"—and thus "They paid no attention to Moses; some of them left of it until morning" (Exodus 16:20).[61]

(3) According to Exodus 16:5, God said to Moses that on the sixth day the people will gather from the manna "double the amount they gather each day." Now in verse

---

[56] Philo, *De Vita Moses* 2.35, 191. The laws of the blasphemer, the stick-gatherer, the Second Passover, and the daughters of Zelophehad are examples of utterances that fall into the second category.

[57] Philo, *De Vita Mosis* 2.35, 191.

[58] The term is *Theophoretos*. See H. A. Wolfson, *Philo: Foundations of Religious Philosophy in Judaism, Christianity, and Islam*, 2 vols. (Cambridge, Mass.: Harvard University Press, 1947), 2:25, 49.

[59] MI Beshalah 2.

[60] According to another source, "Moses was focused by the Holy Spirit [*mitkavven beruah hakodesh*] and knew that the Holy and Blessed One would bring retribution on the Egyptians in that day, but he did not know what form the retribution would take" (Lekah Tov ad loc.).

[61] Philo, *De Vita Mosis*, 2.47, 258. Compare Midrash Haggadol on Exodus, ad loc., where it is Moses who says, "It is the king's decree, and whoever leaves it until morning transgresses a negative command." Rabbi Nehemiah says elsewhere: "By 'king' is meant Moses himself" (Song of Songs Rabbah 7:11). MI Vayyassa' 4 likewise refers to "Moses' decree." However, in Tosefta Negaim 3:7, Rabbi Meir speaks of "the king's decree" referring to God.

23, we find Moses saying: "He said to them, 'This is what the Lord meant when He said: Tomorrow is a day of rest, a holy Sabbath of the Lord.'" In the commentary on the Torah attributed to Rav Saadia Gaon, he notes as follows: "we have not found such a thing written explicitly in the verses," that God told Moses that the following day would be a Sabbath day.[62] Philo explains that the people knew that the seventh day of creation was a Sabbath, but until Moses informed them, they did not know which was the seventh day. But Moses learned of this not by direct communication but rather by being imbued with the Holy Spirit.[63]

(4) "Then Moses said, 'Eat it today, for today is a Sabbath of the Lord, you will not find it today on the plain' (Exodus 16:25)." Now Philo notes that God did not say to Moses that manna would not fall on the Sabbath, but Moses knew this through the Holy Spirit, and not by direct communication from on high.[64]

(5) Also, with respect to this verse: "Thus says the Lord, the God of Israel: Each of you put sword on thigh" (Exodus 32:27)—Philo writes that it was not from on high that Moses said this, but rather out of the Holy Spirit that imbued him (*katechomenos*),[65] and by the power by which he was transformed.

(6) In the Korah incident, it is written: "By this you shall know that it was the Lord who sent me to do all these things . . . if these men die as all men do . . . it was not the Lord who sent me. But if the Lord brings about something unheard of, so that the ground opens its mouth wide . . . you shall know that these men have spurned the Lord" (Numbers 16:28–30). On these verses as well Philo writes that Moses did not receive them from on high, but rather said them under the influence of the Holy Spirit.[66] In truth, the Sages later said similarly that in the Korah incident, Moses virtually decreed things for the Holy and Blessed One, and He fulfilled them. So did they expound the verse: "But if the Lord brings about something unheard of, so that the ground opens its mouth wide" (Numbers 16:30): "Said the Holy and Blessed One to Moses: What are you seeking? He said to Him: Master of the Universe, 'if a creation,' that is, if there has already been created a mouth for the earth, fine. But if not, then 'God will create,' that is, God should now create such a mouth for it. Said to him the Holy and Blessed One: 'You shall decree a thing, and it shall be established for you, and light shall shine upon your paths' (Job 22:28).[67]

---

[62] Cited in *Torah Shelemah* on Exodus 16:23 (see n. 36 above).

[63] Philo, *De Vita Mosis* 2.48, 263–65.

[64] Philo, *De Vita Mosis,* 2.48, 268. Compare Midrash Haggadol on Leviticus 10:18: "Whenever the leader gets angry, his mind goes blank. Moses got angry (16:20); thus when the people came and said they had gathered double the normal amount, the reason escaped him, until he regained his composure, whereupon he said, 'This is what the Lord meant: Tomorrow is a day of rest, a holy Sabbath' (16:23)."

[65] Philo, *De Vita Mosis* 2.49, 270–72. The rabbinic treatment of this episode was discussed above, pp. 420–22.

[66] Philo, *De Vita Mosis* 2.50, 280.

[67] Numbers Rabbah 18:12; Deuteronomy Rabbah 2:3. Nahmanides cites Moses' recommendation of the contest of the fire-pans in this episode, as an example of "inspiration by the Holy Spirit," which falls short of prophecy in the full sense. See Nahmanides on Numbers 16:5, and supercommentary of R. Meir ben Solomon Abusaula on Nahmanides ad loc.

(7) In Parashat "Vezot Haberakhah" as well, the blessings that Moses gave before his death, and the futures that he foretold for the tribes of Israel, were said by Moses under the influence of the Holy Spirit and were not received directly from on high.[68] This idea is similar to the approach according to which the book of Deuteronomy was spoken by Moses on his own, and we shall treat this in a subsequent chapter.

(8) The verses in which Moses our Master narrated his own death and burial he spoke at a time when the Holy Spirit imbued him.[69] On these verses we shall speak in the chapter entitled "The Eight Final Verses."

What insight got Philo to say that these eight passages were spoken by Moses on his authority? The usual explanation—that in these eight places there is no mention in the text that Moses received the divine words before he spoke to the people—does not seem right, for in the third and fifth examples, we have such phrases as "this is what the Lord meant [*dibber*, literally 'said']," and (in the fifth example) "Thus says the Lord."[70] I am doubtful whether Philo himself created this approach and himself gathered together the places in the Torah where Moses said things on his own. It seems more likely that Philo got this approach from others, perhaps from preachers who came from the Land of Israel to preach in Alexandria. "Every river follows its own course."[24] In the Land of Israel, they interpreted "on his own" to mean that he either inferred from a *gezerah shavah* or from a fortiori reasoning. But Philo interpreted "on his own" to mean "with the Holy Spirit,"[25] that which distinguishes the prophet. As we shall see later on, Philo's understanding of "on his own" to refer to the Holy Spirit, appears as well in the Zohar and in the Tosafot.

[68] Philo, *De Vita Mosis* 2.51, 288.
[69] Philo, *De Vita Mosis,* end of book.
[70] See Wolfson, *Philo,* nn. 76–77, citing the Septuagint on Exodus 16:23.

---

[24] This proverb was used by the rabbis (BT Hullin 18b, 57a) to legitimate different halakhic practices in different localities. Here Heschel comments on the variant aggadic views prevalent in the proto-rabbinic community of Israel as compared with the hellenized community of Alexandria.

[25] Thus, we must be careful on this reading of Philo not to understand the "Holy Spirit" as meaning being taken over by a divine force and forced to speak the divine words (a model that often seems to fit biblical prophecy), but rather a more general inspiration that is then given form in the prophet's own words.

24

IS IT POSSIBLE THAT IT WAS
ON HIS OWN SAY-SO

Translator's Introduction

Having studied the differences of opinion on the exact meanings of the various phrases that prophets used to preface their messages, Heschel now returns to complete the subject begun in chapter 22. The phenomenon of prophets speaking or even acting on their own authority is given further treatment in two ways: (1) Heschel sets forth several additional instances in which Moses took it upon himself to take certain actions. The new element here is the presence in the list of cases where he did *not* get an eventual endorsement from God. The significance of this is that, even though prophets are usually understood to be under an oath to follow divine instructions precisely under pain of death (see Mishnah Sanhedrin 11:5), Moses already had achieved enough status that he could survive several "lapses." (2) Other prophets, subsequent to Moses, are claimed, by certain Sages, to have enjoyed the authority to make logical inferences from divine instructions, inferences that could have significant practical consequences.

All of this, the reader is reminded, is to establish that there was a view in Rabbinic Judaism—far from unanimous, to be sure, but still quite significant—that there is a human element to God's revelatory purpose that cannot simply be reduced to carrying out divine wishes.

Moses Acted on His Own Authority

THE PROBLEM OF WHETHER MOSES OUR MASTER either did or commanded things on his own authority was a very important one in the eyes of the Sages. If you would trouble yourself, you would see that this issue produced differences of opinion between the disciples of Rabbis Ishmael and Akiva concerning many incidents in the Torah, such as Moses' ascent to Mount Sinai, his reporting the people's reactions back to God, the setting aside of the cities of refuge,[1] the rules about guarding the Sanctuary and carrying the Ark, the judgment on those who worshiped Ba'al Pe'or, and the war against Midian.[2]

Consider, for example, Moses' ascent to Mount Sinai: They arrived in the wilderness of Sinai at the beginning of the third month.[3] "Israel encamped there in front of the mountain, and Moses went up to God" (Exodus 19:2–3). Now it is not mentioned here that the Holy and Blessed One told Moses to ascend. According to the Zohar,[4] Moses ascended on his own authority: "Rabbi Jose said, 'from here the Sages derived the principle "one who comes to purify himself is given assistance,"[1] for it is said "and Moses went up to God" and immediately afterwards "The Lord called to him."'"[2] According to this, Moses' ascent preceded the divine speech. Hizkuni[5] also brings the following interpretation: "and some explain that he went up on his own to inquire of the Holy and Blessed One how they should worship Him, so as to fulfill what God had said to him: 'when you have freed the people from Egypt, you shall worship God at this mountain' (Exodus 3:12).[3][6]"

This point of view, which was apparently known to Rabbi Abraham ibn Ezra, was also accepted by Nahmanides,[4] and by Rabbi Isaac Abravanel.[5]

In the Mekhilta of Rabbi Simeon bar Yohai, however, this idea was rebuffed: "Is it possible that he ascended without instructions from on high?[7] The text tells you: 'Then He said to Moses, "come up to the Lord"' (Exodus 24:1), and it further says:

---

[1] BT Shabbat 104a.

[2] Zohar Yitro 79b.

[3] Hizkuni to Exodus 19:3.

[4] Ibn Ezra: "The meaning of 'The Lord called to him' is actually 'The Lord had called to him,' because Moses did not ascend the mountain without permission." Of this explanation, Nahmanides wrote: "This is not apparent to me . . . and it is not correct."

[5] Abravanel to Exodus 19:3.

---

[1] For the purpose of protecting accidental homicides (as described in Exodus 12:13; Numbers 35:9–34; and Deuteronomy 19:1–10).

[2] We will here reproduce Heschel's detailed discussion of only two of these, namely, Moses' ascent to the mountain, and the setting aside of the cities of refuge. These are sufficiently illustrative, and the others will be briefly summarized in a note below.

[3] So do most contemporary translations render (correctly) the Hebrew Ba-hodesh Ha-shelishi—not as "in the third month" but rather "on the third new moon."

[4] The thirteenth-century mystical work that is the premier work of Kabbalah. Heschel is here describing a view that is Ishmaelian, according to his well-established criteria, but he brings no attestations of this view from early works. His sources for this "Ishmaelian" view in this section are all medieval. But the idea that Moses went up the mountain on his own initiative stands as a consistent formulation in what Heschel has identified as the Ishamelian mode, and it also stands in contrast to that which does appear in an early work, the Mekhilta of Rabbi Simeon bar Yohai (see text below), a work from the school of Rabbi Akiva.

[5] Hezekiah ben Manoah, thirteenth century, France.

[6] Moses had been told this when he beheld the burning bush, which was, of course, at the very mountain at which he was now (Sinai-Horeb).

[7] The words "is it possible" may well give support to the idea that the view being refuted in this

'The Lord said to Moses, "come up to Me on the mountain"' (Exodus 24:12)."[6] By contrast, no similar exegesis is to be found in the Mekhilta of Rabbi Ishmael.[7]

Consider also the setting aside of the cities of refuge: According to the Book of Numbers (35:9ff.), God commanded Moses to tell the Israelites that after they cross the Jordan and enter the Land they are to set aside six cities of refuge, to which accidental homicides would be able to flee: three cities in the Transjordan and three cities in the Land of Canaan. Now both the school of Rabbi Ishmael and the school of Rabbi Akiva emphasized that the three cities in the Transjordan did not become effective sanctuaries until the three in the Land of Canaan had been set aside.[8] According to this, there was no need to set aside the cities in the Transjordan until after the possession and the settlement of the Land happened in the days of Joshua. Yet in Deuteronomy 4:41 we are told, "Then Moses set aside three cities on the east side of the Jordan." According to the plain reading of the text, Moses set aside these cities on his own authority.

This idea, that Moses our Master set aside the three cities on his own, was expressed by Rabbi Isaac, who expounded this verse: "a lover of silver never has his fill of silver" (Ecclesiastes 5:9). He said: "How much Torah and how many commandments did Moses transmit to Israel until the day of his death, and yet even this was not enough for him: as he faced death, he grabbed yet another mitzvah, as it says: 'Then Moses set aside . . . .'"[9] [8]

There is preserved a narrative legend based on the assumption that Moses was not told by a divine voice to set aside the cities. Rather, he set them aside because he thought "as long as you can grab a mitzvah, do it while you are alive."[10] How did this happen? "Once Israel reached the Transjordan and were ready to enter the Land of Israel, Moses stood and asked for mercy from the Holy and Blessed One, so that he too could enter the land, but his request was not accepted . . . now as soon as Moses saw that he would not enter the land, he said: 'the Holy and Blessed One commanded that Israel should set up six cities of refuge, and I had assumed that I would set aside

---

[6] MSY, p. 137.

[7] MI Bahodesh 2 (beginning).

[8] Sifre Numbers Masei 159, 160; see also Sifre Zuta, p. 332.

[9] Deuteronomy Rabbah (ed. Lieberman), p. 58. Rabbi Isaac is here brought together with Rabbi Judah and Rabbi Nehemiah, and it is thus logical that he is the Tanna (and not the Amora) by that name. The name of the Tanna Rabbi Isaac is found in halakhic midrashim from the school of Rabbi Ishmael.

[10] *Menorat Ha-Maor* of Rabbi Israel Al-Nakawa (Spain, fourteenth century), III, p. 390.

---

text was a known view, not simply a theoretical one. This makes the absence of early attestations of the "Ishmaelian" view put forth here (that Moses went up on his own) a bit less problematic. It also makes the "argument from silence" that Heschel presently brings—that is, the absence of any parallel treatment in the Mekhilta of Rabbi Ishmael—more interesting than it ordinarily would be.

[8] Rabbi Isaac may have had Psalm 119:72 in mind when he made the connection between love of silver and Moses' love of Torah and commandments: "I prefer the teaching You proclaimed to thousands of gold and silver pieces."

all six. But now that the Holy and Blessed One has decreed that I shall not enter the land, I shall now set aside the three in the Transjordan as long as I am alive. Then, when Joshua enters the Land, he shall set aside the other three.' So Moses got up and set aside the three in the Transjordan . . . and thus Scripture says: 'Whatever is in your power to do, do with all your might' (Ecclesiastes 9:10)."[11]

In the school of Rabbi Akiva they objected to this idea. And thus did they expound the verse: "Then Moses set aside . . .": "Is it possible that it was on his own say-so? The text tells you, 'there [shamma].' Now this word appears here [in Deuteronomy 4:41] and also in Exodus 21:13. Just as the shamma there was on divine authority, so the shamma here was on divine authority."[12] [9]

This difference of opinion continued throughout the period of the Amoraim, and the Babylonian Talmud brings both opinions. According to Rabbi Simlai, a Sage of the transitional generation between the Tannaim and Amoraim: "'a lover of silver never has his fill of silver'—this refers to Moses our Master, who knew that the three cities in the Transjordan would not effectively provide Sanctuary until the three in the Land of Canaan were chosen, and yet said: 'I shall fulfill whatever mitzvah comes my way.'"[13]

On the other hand, Rabbi Simlai, who followed the methodology of Rabbi Akiva, apparently suggested that Moses did not act on his own say-so: "Rabbi Simlai expounded: What means the verse 'Then Moses set aside three cities on the east side of the Jordan'?[10] Said the Holy and Blessed One to Moses: 'Cause a sun to rise for the accidental homicides.'"[11]

---

[11] Deuteronomy Rabbah (ed. Lieberman), p. 57.
[12] Sifre Zuta on Numbers 35:11 (using the reading of the Yalkut).
[13] BT Makkot 10a.

---

[9] The reference is to Exodus 21:13, the first reference to a city of refuge in the Torah. There it is unmistakable that God is speaking. The correspondence of the fairly common word shamma (meaning "there" or "to that place") is a very good example of a gezerah shavah—exegesis based not on logic but on a tradition about the connective significance of a single word or phrase appearing in two different biblical verses.

[10] "The east side of the Jordan" is a rendering of the Hebrew, which literally says, "beyond the Jordan, at the rising of the sun." Hence the opening for this exegesis, in which the rising sun serves as a symbol of hope—in this case, the hope that the city of refuge will give the accidental homicide protection from the hot pursuit of the dead man's relatives hell-bent on revenge.

[11] The other examples of Moses acting on his own that have not been translated here are these: (1) Moses brought the people's answer to the offer of revelation back to God, even though God would, of course, know what was in the people's minds and hearts. (2) Moses, on his own, told Aaron and his sons to sit in a vigil outside the Tent of Meeting for the seven days of their inauguration, even though there is no record that God so instructed them. (3) Moses exercised his discretion in deciding that the Levite clan of Kehat, who were charged with carrying the most sacred objects, would not get any of the wagons that had been donated to the Sanctuary, since he was of the opinion that the holy objects would have to be carried on the shoulder, without additional aids. God had not commanded this either. (4) Moses was apparently told by God, at the time of the apostasy to the

Moses Acted on His Own,
and the Holy and Blessed One Did Not Agree with Him

There is more to this subject, however, for there were times when Moses acted on his own and the Holy and Blessed One did not agree with him.[12] After the making of the golden calf, Moses "would take the Tent and pitch it outside the camp, at some distance from the camp" (Exodus 33:7). But God had not commanded him to distance himself from the camp; Moses did it on his own authority. According to Rabbi Johanan and Rabbi Simeon ben Lakish, "Moses argued: 'if one is excommunicated from the Master, he is certainly excommunicated from the Master's disciples'" [and thus, Israel, which was now cut off from the Master—that is, the Holy and Blessed One—were also to be cut off from the disciple—that is, me—for I am the disciple of the Holy and Blessed One].[14] [13]

This act, which Moses did on his own, did not have the agreement of the Holy and Blessed One:

> God said to him, "Moses, return to the camp." But Moses said, "I will not return." Said to him the Holy and Blessed One: "Know that Joshua is in the Sanctuary"—To what is this analogous? To a woman of the royal family who, angry at the king, left the palace. Now she had been raising a young orphan girl in the palace. Thus, when the king sent a message to her that she should return to the palace, and she did not agree to go, he said to her, since I have asked you to return and you have refused, you should know that the orphan girl is in the palace—so the text says here: "The Lord spoke to Moses face to face"

[14] Exodus Rabbah 45:3.

Moabite God Ba'al Pe'or, to impale all of the tribal leaders, but Moses instead put to death only those people who had actually engaged in idolatrous worship. (5) Moses changed God's command about avenging Israel by attacking the Midianites, for he told Israel that they were to avenge God by this war. In addition, Moses, having been told to prosecute the war himself, chose surrogates to do so, since he had been given refuge from Pharaoh in Midian long ago. In all of these cases, of course, Heschel brings us opposing views (the "Akivan" views) that Moses was actually acting all along on divine authority.

[12] This is a new phenomenon in the context of the last two chapters. Here Heschel will give us an example of a case in which Moses did not enjoy God's retroactive endorsement. Thus, more is added to the picture of Mosaic autonomy that has been emerging here. Moses not only works on his own and comports with the divine will, but acts on his own even when it does not comport with the divine will. The latter fact does not seem to detract from his status as Our Master, the greatest of the prophets, and so on.

[13] "Excommunication" means that no one may have very close contact with you. Rabbi Eliezer, for example, had this done to him by his colleagues after a famously recounted incident in which he refused to bend to the will of the majority. Henceforth, the talmudic stories are clear that his colleagues had to keep a distance of at least four cubits from him. This practice is invoked here not literally, but figuratively, to explain Moses' distancing from the people.

(Exodus 33:11). What did God say to him? "Return to the camp." But Moses did not wish to return. Said to him the Holy and Blessed One: "since I have asked you to return and you have refused, you should know that Joshua is in the Tent of Meeting."[14] Now Moses said to God: Master of the Universe, was it not for Your sake that I got angry with them? But I shall not let You forsake them!"[15]

And a similar exegesis is given in a late source:

Moses said: "if one is excommunicated from the Master, he is certainly excommunicated from the Master's disciples." Said to him the Holy and Blessed One: "Do we need two to be angry? Go back and enter the camp!" For so the text says: "The Lord spoke to Moses face to face"; but it is not clear to what it is referring. But when it continues with the words: "and he then returned to the camp," it teaches us that God nullified Moses' vow[15] and he brought the Tent back into the camp.[16]

Continuation of the Polemics in the Period of the Amoraim

Polemics surrounding this matter continued throughout the generations. Both the Amoraim and Jewish scholars in the Middle Ages deliberated on the matter of whether Moses acted on his own or not.

Moses "saw an Egyptian beating a Hebrew, one of his kinsmen; he turned this way and that, and seeing no person about, he struck down the Egyptian and hid him in the sand" (Exodus 2:11–12). According to the plain meaning of the verses, Moses did

---

15 TB Ki Tissa 15.   16 YS Ki Tissa 393.

---

[14] This text is more than a bit confusing. The meaning most probably intended is that Joshua was at the Sanctuary (Mishkan). In Exodus 33, Moses takes a tent outside the camp and calls it the "Tent of Meeting," which would then contrast with the Sanctuary (Mishkan), which is in the camp. This makes clear the point of the analogy with the woman of the royal family: she is sulking outside the palace, while the king is threatening her with supersession by the young girl she has raised, who is still inside the palace. Thus, this analogy requires that Joshua not be outside the camp, at the "Tent of Meeting," but rather inside. Indeed, the identification of Joshua's position is the very next phrase after the one cited [i.e., "The Lord spoke to Moses face to face"]. But unfortunately, two things make this whole analogy extremely difficult: (1) Even according to those who claim (see chapter 4 above) that the instructions for the Mishkan were given before the sin of the golden calf, at this point in the story, the Mishkan has not yet been built; and (2) the Torah says explicitly that Joshua was in the "Tent," which was, according to Exodus 33, clearly outside the camp!

[15] The text here is imagining that Moses had actually made a vow not to reenter the camp of the faithless Israelites and used that as a way to best God in the argument, since it was, after all, God who had said that vows could never be broken (see Numbers 30:3 or Deuteronomy 23:22–24). The intriguing thing about this text is this: the Rabbis later developed the process of "nullification of vows" a procedure with no biblical precedent at all (indeed, the Rabbis themselves tell us that the "release of vows floats in the air, with nothing to support it"), and God is here depicted as sitting as a Sage to nullify Moses' vow and deprive him of his excuse for not carrying out God's wish that he return to the camp!

not do this by divine command but rather on his own authority. In fact, according to another source, "The Holy and Blessed One said to Moses: 'Did I ever tell you to kill the Egyptian?' And Moses responded, 'You! You killed all the Egyptian firstborn, and I should now stand to die for one single Egyptian!' Said the Holy and Blessed One: 'Are you then like Me? I kill and bring back to life! Are you at all able to give life, as I can?'"[17] [16]

Yet there were other Sages who suggested that it was not on his own authority that Moses killed the Egyptian. "'. . . no person about'—this teaches us that Moses convened courts consisting of ministering angels, and he asked them: 'Shall I kill this one?' and they answered: 'Kill him.'"[18] [17]

According to another Midrash, Moses saw the condition of the Israelites in Egypt: "they had no rest, and he went and said to Pharaoh: 'Whoever has a slave and does not give him a day a week to rest has the slave die on him. These people are your slaves. If you do not give them a day a week to rest, they will all die.' Pharaoh said to him: 'Go and do for them as you say.' And thus Moses went and instituted for them the Sabbath for rest."[19] That is, Moses on his own authority selected the seventh day, that the Israelites not have to work on it. And then, when he stood on Mount Sinai and heard "Remember the Sabbath day and keep it holy" (Exodus 20:8), Moses rejoiced that the Sabbath was now part of his inheritance. That is why we say, "Let Moses rejoice in the gift of his inheritance."[20] [18]

At the time that Pharaoh was pursuing the Israelites, and they complained: "What have you done to us, taking us out of Egypt?" Moses said to them, "Have no fear! Stand by, and witness the deliverance which the Lord will work for you today" (Exodus 14:11, 13). But this utterance did not reach Moses from on high. Rather, "Moses focused by means of the Holy Spirit, and came to know that the Holy and Blessed One would exact retribution from Egypt on that day, but he didn't know the nature of the retribution. That is why he announced it in generalities."[21] Another hint of the idea that Moses said this verse on his own authority is found also in the Mekhilta: "'Moses said to the people, Have no fear!'—here Moses was urging them on; and this demonstrates the prowess of Moses, in how we was able to appease all those thousands and myriads."[22] [19]

---

[17] Midrash Petirat Moshe, *Bet Hamidrash* I, p. 119.   [18] ARN A, ch. 20, p. 72.
[19] Exodus Rabbah 1:28.   [20] *Shibbolei Halleket,* Inyan Shabbat 26.
[21] *Sekhel Tov* (midrashic anthology from the twelfth century) to Exodus 14:13.
[22] MI Beshallah 2; MSBY, p. 54.

---

[16] This scene takes place in a midrash about Moses' last days, and this is part of a longer argument that Moses has with God about the injustice of his having to die before entering the Land.

[17] The exegesis here turns on taking *ein ish*—that there was "no person about"—very literally: no person was there, but supernatural beings were.

[18] This is part of the Sabbath morning liturgy (Amidah for Shaharit), and the emphasis is intended to be on "*his*" in "his inheritance."

[19] That is, Moses was clever enough to come up with a formulation that would calm down these

Another example: After all the good advice that Jethro gave to Moses in the matter of the appointment of judges, we are told, "Then Moses sent his father-in-law away" (Exodus 18:27). Note that it does not say "Jethro went on his way," but rather "Moses sent his father-in-law away." Now the Sages were astonished at this: "Why so?" Why did Moses instruct him to leave the Israelite camp? In this matter, too, we have two points of view. One says that apparently Moses sent him away in obedience to a divine instruction: "The Holy and Blessed One said: 'My children were enslaved, working with mortar and bricks, while Jethro was sitting peacefully in his house, and now he wants to share in the joy of Torah with my children?'[20] And thus, 'Moses sent his father-in-law away.'" But the other point of view says that Moses sent him away on his own: "Moses drew an a fortiori inference: When the Holy and Blessed One gave us a single mitzvah, that of the Paschal sacrifice, the Torah told us, 'No foreigner shall eat of it' (Exodus 12:43); now that God plans to give us 613 commandments, shall Jethro be present and see them[21] as well?" This inference has its source in the school of Rabbi Ishmael.[23]

Rabbi Levi gave this exegesis: "'Confirms the word of His servant' (Isaiah 44:26)—this refers to Moses." And Rabbi Joshua of Sikhnin said in his name: "Whatever Moses decreed, the Holy and Blessed One agreed with him. How so? The Holy and Blessed One did not tell him to shatter the tablets. Moses went and shattered them on his own. And how do we know that the Holy and Blessed One agreed with him? For it is written, 'which you shattered' (Exodus 34:1)—more power to you that you shattered them."[22] Moreover, the Holy and Blessed One told Moses to wage war against Sihon,[23] as it says, "engage him in battle" (Deuteronomy 2:24). But Moses did not do so; rather: "Then I sent messengers . . . to King Sihon of Heshbon with an offer of peace" (Deuteronomy 2:26). The Holy and Blessed One said to him: "So, I told you to engage him in battle, and you offered terms of peace?! By your life, I shall

---

23 TB Yitro 11.

---

masses and buy some time, and it turned out that what he had said on his own authority was fulfilled by God. Considering that what is being discussed here is the premier miracle of the Torah—the splitting of the Sea—this is a very bold statement indeed.

[20] For that was what was going to happen in the next chapter: in Exodus 19, the Israelites arrive at Mount Sinai and ready themselves for the revelation of the Torah.

[21] This is most probably a reference to Exodus 20:15, in which the people were said, at Mount Sinai, to have "seen" the thunder. This midrash conceives of the revelation as the literal meaning of Exodus 20 does, as a visual experience, which Jethro ought not, by rights, enjoy. (It is perhaps worth noting that for Deuteronomy, the revelation at Sinai is consistently described as an auditory, not a visual, experience.)

[22] The play on words here involves the word asher ("that") in the biblical text (in: "that" you shattered), and the word yishar, in the phrase yishar kohakha—a complimentary phrase best translated as "more power to you." This is a good example of a phonetic resemblance serving as a "hook" on which to hang a desired exegesis.

[23] The Transjordanian king of the Emorites.

confirm your decree. For in the case of every war that the Israelites engage in, they will be required first to offer peace, as it says, 'When you approach a town to attack it, you shall offer it terms of peace' (Deuteronomy 20:10)."[24] [24]

In these two instances, Rabbi Levi has been drawn into the approach of Rabbi Ishmael, who holds that Moses on his own shattered the tablets, in contradistinction to the view of Rabbi Akiva, according to which the Holy and Blessed One told him to shatter them. In fact, according to Rabbi Akiva, everything that appears in Deuteronomy was spoken to Moses at Sinai and in the Tent of Meeting, and thus when Moses sent messengers of peace to Sihon—an act that occurred in the fortieth year—Moses already knew the instruction to offer a target city terms of peace. If that is so, how could Rabbi Levi have said that Moses acted without instruction from the Holy and Blessed One? It must be that Rabbi Levi holds the opinion of Rabbi Ishmael that only the generalities of the law were given at Sinai, and the particulars of this law, concerning offering terms of peace, was given only in the steppes of Moab.[25]

Prophets Drawing A Fortiori Inferences

According to Rabbi Ishmael, a prophet is permitted to draw an a fortiori inference from his prophetic vision and to say of the result: "Thus says the Lord." For the Holy and Blessed One did not tell Moses to separate from his wife. "How did he reason? He said: 'If Israel, to which the Presence did not speak but for a moment, and at a pre-announced time, was told by the Torah: "Do not go near a woman" (Exodus 19:15), I, who am on call every single hour, without any prior warning, how much more so. And his reasoning was consistent with God's intent, as it says, "Go say to them, 'return to your tents.'" But you remain here with me'" (Deuteronomy 5:27-28).[25][26]

"He shattered the tablets. How did he reason? He said: If of the Paschal sacrifice, just one of 613 mitzvot, the Torah said, 'No foreigner shall eat of it' (Exodus 12:43), how much more so should the entire Torah not be given to Israel, who are all apos-

---

[24] Pesikta Rabbati 17 (85b); Deuteronomy Rabbah 5:13.

[25] BT Yevamot 62a; Shabbat 87a. According to Nahmanides in his novellae to BT Shabbat 87a, Moses and other prophets as well drew many inferences of this kind.

---

[24] The point here is that this requirement to offer terms of peace appears in the Deuteronomic law code, which, according to the internal reckoning of Deuteronomy, was given by Moses to Israel "after he had defeated Sihon king of the Amorites" (Deuteronomy 1:4). Thus, a surface reading of the text would confirm that Moses offered peace to Sihon before he, or the Israelites, ever heard of any requirement to do so.

[25] Thus, the requirement to offer peace was God's reaction to Moses' initiative. The dispute about whether all the specifics of the law were given at Sinai or whether only general principles were given that were later developed into details is a far-reaching one that we have encountered before in Heschel's exposition.

[26] Presuming "tents" to be a euphemism for normal family life, including sexual relations. Thus, "You remain here with me" would, by contrast, suggest sexual abstinence to Moses.

tates.[27] And his reasoning was consistent with God's intent, as it is written: 'which you shattered' (Exodus 34:1). And Resh Lakish said of this: 'The Holy and Blessed One said to him: More power to you that you shattered them.'"[26]

Moses also added an additional day on his own authority. "How did he reason? God had said, 'Warn them to stay pure today and tomorrow' (Exodus 19:10). Reasoned Moses: 'This means that "today" must be like "tomorrow." Just as tomorrow is a twenty-four-hour period of day following night, so must today be. But last night is already gone. Thus, it must mean two more full days after today.' And his reasoning was consistent with God's intent, for the Presence did not rest on the mountain until the Sabbath."[27] [28]

According to the Mishnah: "One who prophesies that which he didn't hear, or that which was not spoken to him, is subject to the death penalty."[28] About this, the Babylonian Talmud says: "One who prophesies that which was not spoken to him—this refers to Hananiah ben Azzur. For Jeremiah stood in the upper marketplace and announced, 'Thus said the Lord of Hosts: I am going to break the bow of Elam' (Jeremiah 49:35). And thus, Hananiah drew an a fortiori inference on his own: If concerning Elam, which was merely an accomplice of the Babylonians, the Holy and Blessed One said: 'I am going to break the bow of Elam,' how much more so would God say the same of the Chaldeans themselves. So he went to the lower marketplace and said: 'Thus said the Lord . . . I hereby break the yoke of the king of Babylon' (Jeremiah 28:2)."[29] Now according to the Gemara, a prophet may draw an a fortiori inference from that which was spoken to him in prophecy, and to announce "Thus says the Lord" about the results of that inference. [As Abbaye said: "Since it was given to him to draw the a fortiori inference, it is as if it was spoken to him."[30]] The sin of Hananiah was simply that he drew the inference on what was spoken to Jeremiah in prophecy, for "this inference was for Jeremiah, and no one else, to draw."[31] [29]

---

26 BT Yevamot 62a; Menahot 99b; PT Ta'anit 4:8 (68c).
27 BT Yevamot 62a.
28 Mishnah Sanhedrin 11:5.
29 BT Sanhedrin 89a.
30 See Maharsha ad loc.
31 Rabbenu Hananel ad loc.

---

[27] Having made the golden calf.

[28] According to the talmudic account, the revelation took place on a Sabbath, fifty-one days after the Exodus, which took place on a Thursday. This account has an additional interesting twist to it: The festival of Shavuot, the biblical "Day of the First Fruits," occurs fifty days after Passover, but it was also understood in Rabbinic Judaism to be the day of revelation. According to this reconstruction, however, it would have been the day of revelation had God's instructions prevailed, but Moses, by adding an additional day, actually moved the revelation to a day later!

[29] Hananiah, according to the account in the Book of Jeremiah, died before the year was out.

In the Language of Prophecy

There were also those who were not prophets at all but who nonetheless used prophetic language, the import of which must be understood to be referring to a general inspiration or to the intent of Heaven. For example, Laban and Bethuel answered Abraham's servant as follows: "Here is Rebekah before you; take her and go, and let her be a wife to your master's son, as the Lord has spoken" (Genesis 24:51). But we have not found that God spoke at all concerning this. It was rather as a matter of divination[30] that Abraham's servant spoke his words. Seforno[31] explains it as follows: "'As the Lord has spoken'—in that God decrees a mate for each person, and God gave a sign of assent to this match."[32]

In the Book of Isaiah it is written: "Thus said the Lord, where is the bill of divorce of your mother whom I dismissed?" (Isaiah 50:1). "There are those who raise this difficulty: it is written, 'The Lord said to me . . . I cast her off and handed her a bill of divorce' (Jeremiah 3:6,8).[32] And they resolve the difficulty as follows: that the latter were the words of Jeremiah, and not a direct prophecy."[33]

Nahmanides had already noted the fact

> that the Sages are forever bringing words of Torah in order to strengthen matters that they have instituted. For example: "Why did the Torah say that we should pour water libations on the Festival of Sukkot? For the Holy and Blessed One said: 'pour water before Me on the Festival, so that you will be blessed with rain . . . and recite before Me on Rosh Hashanah the verses of Kingship, Remembrance, and Shofar, so that you will cause Me to reign over you, and that your remembrance will come before Me with the sound of the Shofar.'"[34] And yet the Gemara very well knows that these precepts are rabbinic in origin. Indeed, in another discussion there: ". . . [by way of challenging the very nature of a question posed by Rabbi Akiva:] 'If [according to the position of Rabbi Johanan ben Nuri] one doesn't blow the Shofar for Kingships, why do we mention them at all?'[33]

[32] See *Torat Moshe* of Moses Alshekh ad loc.
[33] *Arugat Habosem* (of Abraham ben Azriel, thirteenth century, Germany) I, p. 116.
[34] BT Rosh Hashanah 16a.

---

[30] That is, Abraham's servant had concocted a sign on his own, by which he hoped he would be led to Isaac's intended. It was his chosen sign, not God's instruction to him.

[31] Italy, sixteenth century.

[32] The difficulty seems to be that Second Isaiah (the name given to the anonymous author of the prophecies beginning at Isaiah 40) apparently is asking for what he knows to be a nonexistent bill of divorce, thereby emphasizing to the people that they are still God's beloved, even in exile. But Jeremiah had already stated that the Israelites had in fact been divorced! (Since Isaiah son of Amoz lived and prophesied some one hundred years prior to Jeremiah, this midrash seems to be assuming that the prophecy in Isaiah 50 is post-Jeremian, that is, postexilic).

[33] The issue here concerns a dispute in the Mishnah about when the Kingship (Malkhuyot) verses are said in the Rosh Hashanah Musaf (Additional) service. In the Mishnah near the end of Tractate

Why do we mention them?! The Merciful One *said* to mention them!"[35] And this, even though they [the verses of Kingship] are without a doubt of rabbinic origin![36]

We also read in Tractate Sukkah 53a: "It was taught: they said of Hillel the Elder, that when he would join in the joy of the Drawing of the Water, he would say: 'If I am here, all are here. If I am not here, who can be here?'"[34] Now Rashi explicated this: "He was preaching to the masses, in the name of the Holy and Blessed One, that they not sin: 'If I am here, all are here,' that is, as long as I desire this House and My Presence rests on it, its glory will endure and all will come here; but if you sin, I shall remove My Presence, and then who will come here?" On this, Rabbi Hayyim Joseph David Azulai[35] noted: "This is consistent with that which we read at the end of Tractate Sanhedrin (111b): 'Said Rabbi Simeon: If you carry out the law of the idolatrous city, I will consider it as if you have brought an entirely burnt offering before Me.'"[36] Apparently Rabbi Hayyim Joseph David Azulai found the same difficulty in the words of Hillel the Elder and of Rabbi Simeon, for both of them stood up and virtually said, "Thus says the Lord." And thus, he brought the words of "the great Master Rabbi Joseph Ashkenazi,[37] who said that it was the custom of the Sages to speak words as if they had been spoken by the Holy and Blessed One . . . and thus we can be reconciled to what was said [of Hillel], that when he joined in the joy of the Drawing, that is, the place from which they would draw on the Holy Spirit [he would speak in God's Name]. Hillel, in his greatness, and in the strength of his joy, had the Spirit rest on him, and he spoke as if the Holy and Blessed One were speaking."[37]

---

[35] BT Rosh Hashanah 32a.
[36] Nahmanides, "Critical Glosses to Maimonides' *Sefer Hamitzvot*," principle 1.
[37] *Petah Einayim,* end of Tractate Sukkah.

Rosh Hashanah, Rabbi Johanan ben Nuri says that they are said as part of the third blessing of the Amidah, but that the Shofar is not blown until after the fourth blessing of the Amidah (the one that describes the sanctity of the day). Rabbi Akiva, on the other hand, says that Malkhuyot verses are included in the fourth blessing, with the description of the sanctity of the day, and then the Shofar is blown. The Mishnah then records Akiva's challenge to his colleague: "If one doesn't blow the Shofar for Malkhuyot (according to your position) why recite those verses at all?" The Talmud's surprised reaction to Akiva's question is the basis for Nahmanides' argument here that something which is clearly rabbinic in origin (like the recitation of Malkhuyot) is still spoken of as if it were a divine command.

[34] This may, of course, have been an innocent, and somewhat playful, remark arising out of the intoxicating religious joy of the festival. But it is taken more deeply in the text Heschel cites.

[35] Eighteenth century, Land of Israel.

[36] The exegesis turns on the Torah's use of the word *kalil* ("entirely burnt") to describe how the idolatrous city is to be destroyed. *Kalil* is a word also used in connection with the *olah,* the basic burnt offering that is given to God in its entirety in the altar's fire.

[37] Sixteenth century, Prague and Safed.

THE BOOK OF DEUTERONOMY

Translator's Introduction

In this chapter Heschel takes a new turn in the building of his case that the idea of a human element in Torah is not a modern one that was universally rejected, or perhaps not even considered, in our classical texts. He turns here to a consideration of the status of the fifth book of the Pentateuch, Deuteronomy. He demonstrates to us that the ancients already recognized the significant stylistic and substantive differences between the first four books and the fifth. (The reader need only consider such things as the consistent use of "Horeb" for "Sinai" in Deuteronomy, the fact that only in Deuteronomy are Levites considered to be an impoverished class, and many other unique features.) There were those who were deemed to be sectarians who denied the sanctity of Deuteronomy; but again, Heschel wants us scrupulously to avoid the fallacy of believing that the fact that an idea appeals to sectarians in and of itself disqualifies that view. He suggests strongly that among the Sages, adherents of an Ishmaelian viewpoint on the Torah were ready to believe that Deuteronomy was Moses' creation.

"Moses wrote his own book, and the story of Balaam," says the Talmud. However you read this statement, it is problematic. If "his own book" means the Pentateuch (and "wrote" means "wrote down"), then the mention of the "story of Balaam" (which appears in Numbers 22–24) is superfluous. But if "his own book" means Deuteronomy, then "wrote" must not mean "wrote down" (for what would that then mean about the other four books?). "Wrote" in such a case must mean "composed." And thus, the status of Deuteronomy itself was already recognized (by some!) in ancient times as a significant exception to the view that revelation has no active human element in it.

Moses Delivered the Curses in Deuteronomy[1]
by His Own Mouth

WE READ IN THE MISHNAH: "One does not create a break in the curses."[1] That is, during the reading of the Torah, we do not divide the section known as the Admonition[2] into two sections to which two people would be called to read.[3] About this, the Amora Abbaye[4] said: "The Mishnah refers only to the curses in Leviticus; however, one may divide the curses in Deuteronomy. What is the reason? The former were framed in the plural, and Moses transmitted them from on high, whereas the latter were framed in the singular, and Moses delivered them by his own mouth."[2]

The words of Abbaye, that the curses in Deuteronomy were delivered by Moses on his own, appear also in the commentary of Rabbi Isaac Alfasi,[3] [5] and the distinction that is made here between the curses in Leviticus and those in Deuteronomy is fixed

---

[1] Mishnah Megillah 3:6.

[2] BT Megillah 31b.

[3] BT Megillah 25b reads: "The curses and blessings are read and translated publicly." Alfasi qualifies: "This applies only to the ones in Leviticus."

---

[1] The term used here, and often in the sequel, for Deuteronomy is the classic rabbinic term "Mishneh Torah." This term, which means something like "second Teaching," is actually a translation back into Hebrew of the Greek word Deuteronomy ("second Law"), which was adopted by the ancient composers of the Septuagint. The Hebrew name for this book, which Heschel also uses, is *Devarim*, which, in line with Jewish usage, is the first significant word in the book, which begins *eleh ha-devarim*, "these are the words." The term "Mishneh Torah," however, is the truly significant one in this chapter, because it is the one that points directly to the unusual relationship between Deuteronomy and the rest of the Pentateuch and suggests that it has a special status. It is that status that Heschel wants to highlight here, as part of his treatment of the different views about the divine origin of every word in the Torah.

[2] This term (*tokheha* in Hebrew) refers to the sections of Leviticus 26 and Deuteronomy 28 that specify the calamities that would befall the Israelites should they disobey God's commands. Since they are catalogues of terrible fates and Deuteronomy itself uses the word "curses," they are known also by that word. However, Heschel's argument is going to depend on an ambiguity in the word *tokheha*, or "admonition"—it is sometimes used to refer to these chapters of curses, and sometimes used more generally to refer to chidings and preachings from Moses to the people, such as is characteristic of almost the entire book of Deuteronomy!

[3] The reading of the weekly portion of the Torah each Sabbath is divided into seven parts (Aliyot), each of which a different person is given the honor of reading. There is more than one way to divide each weekly portion into seven, but the Mishnah is telling us that the curses must not be divided up. The accepted way of making the division, as found in standard printed versions of the Pentateuch, follows this rule. But see Abbaye's qualification of this with respect to Deuteronomy (as found in the talmudic discussion), as Heschel immediately reports.

[4] Fourth century, Babylonia.

[5] Eleventh century, North Africa (Al-Fasi = "the one from Fez").

in Jewish practice.[4] Rashi as well, in his commentary on the Torah, accepted Abbaye's point of view, and he wrote the following about the curses in Deuteronomy:

> These curses were delivered by Moses by his own mouth, whereas those given at Mount Sinai were spoken directly by the Holy and Blessed One. So the language itself teaches us. For there [in Leviticus] it says: "But if you do not obey Me," and "if you remain hostile to Me" (Leviticus 26:14, 21), whereas here [in Deuteronomy] he says: "But if you do not obey the Lord your God," "the Lord will make pestilence cling to you," and "the Lord will strike you." (Deuteronomy 28:15, 21, 22)[5]

It is an amazing thing that there is no recorded objection to Abbaye's words in our Gemara. Can it be that Abbaye expressed an outlook that was accepted unanimously by all the Sages? It is, in fact, possible to find a hint of this outlook in the Sifre: "'It was in the fortieth year . . . that Moses addressed the Israelites' (Deuteronomy 1:3): this teaches that he did not admonish[6] them until he was close to death. From whom did he learn this? From Jacob, who did not admonish his sons until he was close to death."[6] Here it appears that it was not by command from on high that Moses admonished the Israelites, but rather by the example he learned from Jacob. Indeed, the Sifre compares Moses' action to those of Joshua, Samuel, and David as well, and thus it appears that the Sifre's intent is that Moses "admonished them by his own mouth, just as all these others did."[7] [7]

The point of view of Abbaye is implied also in the words of Rabbi Levi, from the circle of Rabbi Judah the Patriarch, who served as a master exegete in the Academy of Rabbi Johanan: "Come and see how unlike the divine characteristics are human characteristics: for the Holy and Blessed One blessed Israel with twenty-two letters (Leviticus 26:3–13) and cursed them with eight (Leviticus 26:14–43), whereas Moses

---

[4] Maimonides, *Hilkhot Tefillah*, 13:7: "One may not divide the reading of the curses in Leviticus. As for those in Deuteronomy, if one wishes to divide them, he may, though the general practice is for one person to read them as a unit."

[5] Rashi on Deuteronomy 28:23. But in BT Sanhedrin Rashi refrains from taking this to the ultimate conclusion: "The Deuteronomic review of the Ten Commandments adds the phrase, 'as the Lord your God has commanded you,' in the commandments about the Sabbath and honoring one's parents. Where, then, did He previously command these? We should not infer that Moses added this phrase when reviewing them in the plains of Moab, for *Moses did not formulate Deuteronomy on his own*, but transmitted it exactly as he received it."

[6] Sifre Devarim 2; compare 54.

[7] Elijah Mizrahi on Deuteronomy 1:1.

---

[6] It is beginning here that the words "admonish" and "admonition" are used not just for the curses in Deuteronomy 28 but also for other parts of Moses' speeches (especially the opening speeches) in Deuteronomy. This is important if a bit confusing. The reader is urged to keep this intended ambiguity in mind.

[7] In order to use the last three as models, Moses would have needed to resort to the Holy Spirit, which of course presents no conceptual problem for the Sifre.

our Master blessed them with eight (Deuteronomy 28:1–14) and cursed them with twenty-two (Deuteronomy 28:15–68)."[8] [8]

In yet another source the admonitions in Deuteronomy are called "Moses' words": "'These are the words'—Now what is written just above (at the end of Numbers)? 'These are the commandments.' And then follows 'These are the words.' Said the Holy and Blessed One: Moses' words, by which he admonished Israel, are as dear to Me as all of the commandments that I have given them. Therefore it says: 'These are the commandments,' and immediately 'These are the words.'"[9] The intent here is to teach that not only God's own words, but also Moses' words are Torah and are as dear in the eyes of God as the commandments that God gave to Israel.

Moses Spoke the Book of Deuteronomy by His Own Mouth

Are Abbaye's words that "Moses delivered the curses in Deuteronomy by his own mouth" meant to be taken narrowly, or are they generalizable to the entire Book of Deuteronomy? We read in the Midrash: "'I will now speak my mind to you' (Proverbs 1:23)—[this refers to Moses] at the time when he explicated for them the Book of Deuteronomy."[10] Do we find here a hint of the idea that Moses spoke the entire Book of Deuteronomy on his own? In another source: "'These are the words . . . ,'[9] for Moses gave them Torah, after the Holy and Blessed One gave them the Torah that was delivered by the agency of Moses."[11] Here the author distinguishes between "the Torah that the Holy and Blessed One gave through the agency of Moses" and "the Torah that Moses gave." They said: "The Holy and Blessed One heard Moses' admoni-

---

[8] BT Bava Batra 88b–89a.
[9] YS Deuteronomy 793.
[10] Midrash on Proverbs 31:27; YS II, 932.
[11] *Yalkut Talmud Torah,* JTS microfilm of Leningrad manuscript, beginning of Deuteronomy.

---

[8] The argument here is a curiously clever one. In both Leviticus and Deuteronomy, blessings precede the curses. They describe the bounties that would benefit the Israelites were they to obey God's commands. Now the blessings in Leviticus, given in God's voice, begin at Leviticus 26:3 and end at Leviticus 26:13. Verse 3 begins with the letter *aleph* and v. 13 ends with the letter *tav.* Thus, the entire Hebrew alphabet (twenty-two letters) is in some sense spanned by these blessings. As we would say in English, "God's blessings went from A to Z." By contrast, the curses in Leviticus, also in God's voice, begin in v. 14 and end in v. 43 (from v. 44 on we have some after-the-fact comfort). Verse 14 begins with *vav* (the sixth letter) and v. 43 ends with *mem* (the thirteenth letter). Thus, God's curses spanned only eight letters. Now in Deuteronomy, where the blessings and curses are in Moses' voice, the blessings (from 28:1 to 28:14) begin and end with the letters *vav* and *mem*—amounting to a span of eight letters. But the curses (from 28:15 to 28:68) begin and end with letters *vav* (the sixth letter) and *heh* (the fifth letter), thus once again spanning the entire twenty-two-letter Hebrew alphabet.

[9] The opening words of Deuteronomy.

tions and said to him: 'Giving a straightforward reply is like giving a kiss'" (Proverbs 24:26).[12] Now the expression "Moses' admonitions" is not confined to the curses in Parashat Ki Tavo alone. Here is implied the idea that Moses spoke all of Deuteronomy on his own, for admonitions are the main subject of the entire Book of Deuteronomy: "'These are the words'—this teaches us that they were words of admonition."[13] The Book of Deuteronomy is also called "the Book of Admonitions."[14] And the verses in Deuteronomy 11:16–17 were called the "curses of Moses."[15] [10]

In the Book of the Zohar it says explicitly: "Moses spoke the Book of Deuteronomy by his own mouth."[16] I have not found such a bold formulation in any of the midrashim that are extant, but it is clear that this statement was not made in an unconscious, reflexive way. It comes rather to fix in our minds a fundamental difference between the Book of Deuteronomy and the other books of the Torah. "The Written Torah and the Oral Torah are called, respectively, the Torah and Deuteronomy."[17] That is to say, the Book of Deuteronomy is tantamount to the Oral Torah![18] [11]

---

[12] YS I, 797.

[13] Sifre Devarim 1. The Jerusalem Targum translates Deuteronomy 1:1: "These are the words of admonition. . . ."

[14] SER, p. 19. Compare Lekah Tov, start of Ha'azinu: "'Open reproof is better than concealed love' (Proverbs 27:5)—the reproof is Moses' address to them in Deuteronomy 29:9ff. ('You stand this day . . .'); the love is that which he harbored for them all those years."

[15] BT Sanhedrin 113a.

[16] Zohar Va'ethanan 261a. Elsewhere the Zohar speaks more narrowly of the Deuteronomic curses as Moses' own (Zohar Vayikra 7a, Behukotai 115a).

[17] The Zohar finds in the verse "Jacob left Beer-sheba" (Genesis 28:10) an allusion to Deuteronomy 1:5: "Moses undertook to expound (be'er) this Teaching" and identifies the latter with the Oral Torah, which Israel waited forty years to receive (Megaleh Amukot, Va'ethanan 246). Similarly, Isaiah Horowitz said that the Written Torah is called "the Torah of the Lord," whereas the Oral Torah is called "the Torah of Moses" (Shnei Luhot ha-Brit, 162b–163a, 383a).

[18] This idea is also found in Ma'arekhet ha-Elohut (written in thirteenth century, published in Mantua 5318/1558), p. 129a.

---

[10] The two verses just referred to are part of the second paragraph of the Shema, recited by Jews twice daily. This second paragraph, from Deuteronomy 11, also treats the subject of the rewards and punishments that would follow upon obedience or disobedience, respectively. They are a good example, as Heschel is pointing out, of material in the opening speeches of Deuteronomy that can also well qualify as "admonitions," or even "curses."

[11] The doctrine of the Oral Torah in Rabbinic Judaism is a complicated one, but it certainly was understood to be a necessary companion to the Written Torah; without it, one has an incomplete revelation of the divine will. But since it is oral, it has, ipso facto, a human component to it, since it is at least dependent on human transmission, not being written down. The comparison, nearly an identification, that is made here between Deuteronomy and the Oral Torah is taken by Heschel to suggest that Deuteronomy, too, is a necessary companion to the rest of the Torah (that, incidentally, is another meaning of "Mishneh Torah," one that was later adopted by Moses Maimonides), and that it, too, is dependent on some human input, namely, Moses'. According to this understanding of the Zohar's statement, the Oral Torah already begins (though it does not end) in what we normally call the Written Torah! The suggestion that there is not such a clearly defined line between the Written and Oral Torahs plays well into Heschel's strategy here of getting us to see the complexity of what is often taken to be the doctrinally settled matter of the complete divinity of all of the words of the Torah.

Now it is clear that it did not enter the mind of the author of the Zohar to assert that Moses spoke all of the commandments in Deuteronomy on his own.[19] Second Kings (14:6) refers explicitly, after all, to something that was mentioned "in the Book of the Teaching of Moses (Deuteronomy 24:16), where the Lord commanded . . . .'[12] What is more, it says in Deuteronomy 1:3: "Moses addressed the Israelites in accordance with the instructions that the Lord had given him for them." Now one commentator suggested that Moses accomplished two things on the east bank of the Jordan: he chided the Israelites concerning all that they had done to anger God, and he also explicated the Torah for them. The expression "in accordance with the instructions that the Lord had given him" does not refer to the chidings and admonitions, "but rather to the commandments in Deuteronomy that were not previously written in the Torah." And the explanation of "Moses undertook to expound this Teaching" (Deuteronomy 1:5)? "These are the commandments that they were already commanded, but that Moses now explained and embellished."[20] [13]

The Blessings in Deuteronomy

In the statements of many Amoraim we also find hints that there were things in Deuteronomy that Moses said on his own authority.

> "These are the words": Said Rabbi Tanhuma (an Amora of the fifth generation in the Land of Israel), what is the matter analogous to? To a man who was selling purple cloth, and he would advertise and say: "Purple cloth, here!" Now the king looked out when he heard his voice. He called to him and said: "What are you selling?" He responded: "Nothing." The king said: "I heard your voice advertising 'purple cloth, here!' and now you tell me, 'nothing'?" He said to him: "My master, it is true that it is purple cloth, but by your standards it is nothing at all." So was it with Moses before the Holy and Blessed One, who created all mouths and all speech. He said to God: "I have never been a man of words" (Exodus 4:10). But with respect to Israel, it is written of him: "These are the words."[21] [14]

[19] This may be suggested by the maxim, "Deuteronomy came to add [to the law]" (BT Hullin 63b).

[20] Oholei Yehudah, a commentary on Sifre by Judah Najara (of Constantinople, published in Leghorn 5583/1823), p. 59a.

[21] Deuteronomy Rabbah 1:7.

---

[12] The incident is that of Amaziah, king of Judah, who did not put to death the children of his father's assassins (though he was undoubtedly advised to do exactly that, to secure his reign), because of scruples that stemmed from the verse in Deuteronomy.

[13] Thus, Moses actually did three things in Deuteronomy, according to this reconstruction: (1) he gave new commands of God that had not been heard before; (2) he explicated commandments that had already been heard; and (3) he composed and delivered his own speeches, "speaking his own mind."

[14] The contrast here between Moses' self-presentation before God and his self-presentation before the people turns on the appearance of the identical word devarim ("words") in both contexts. Moses

Now this analogy, which compares Moses to a seller of purple cloth whom a king hears and asks "What are you selling?" flows from the assumption that Moses our Master spoke all of Deuteronomy on his own.[22]

In several places it is said that the blessings in Deuteronomy were also delivered by Moses on his own. This point of view is implied in this exegesis: "with the words that their father Jacob left off with ('and this' [Genesis 49:28]), Moses began.[15] For Moses said: 'I have learned from my elders' (Psalm 119:100). And thus, 'This is the blessing . . .' (Deuteronomy 33:1)."[23] That is, Moses spoke the blessings on his own, and we have, in the name of the Tanna Rabbi Eliezer ben Jacob, the expression "Moses' blessings,"[24] except that the Holy and Blessed One agreed with his formulation.[25]

Whoever Says That Moses Admonished the Israelites on His Own Authority Is But a Sinner

Now even though our Gemara quotes the words of Abbaye that the curses in Deuteronomy were delivered by Moses on his own without dissenting opinion, we do find several Sages objecting to this.

"Moses addressed the Israelites" (Deuteronomy 1:3). Said Rabbi Simeon ben Lakish: Moses was afraid to admonish Israel, for he thought: for a single thing that I said to them, namely, "Listen, you rebels" (Numbers 20:10) I was prevented from entering the

---

[22] This assumption also underlies such a casual statement as: "R. Tanhuma opened his discourse: . . . 'Moses said to them, "You are today as numerous as the stars in the sky"'" (PR 175b, citing Deuteronomy 1:9). Similarly: "Moses, who loved Israel, compared them to the stars, but Balaam, who hated them, compared them to the dust" (Numbers Rabbah 2:17).

The midrashim commonly say of other prophets, "Isaiah said," "Jeremiah said," and so on. They rarely say, "Moses said." When they do so, it is usually in connection with citations from Deuteronomy. See BT Yevamot 49b; YS Yitro 269; Midrash Lekah Tov Va'ethanan 6b; Tanhuma Buber Vayyetzei 20; PR 43b, 132b, 167a; Deuteronomy Rabbah 7:11 and elsewhere.

[23] Genesis Rabbah 100:12.

[24] Deuteronomy Rabbah 1:12; PR 43b.

[25] Rabbi Samuel bar Nahmani said in the name of Rabbi Jonathan ben Eleazar (first-generation Amora of the Land of Israel): "After Moses blessed Israel with the words, 'This is the blessing . . .' (Deuteronomy 33:1), God echoed him by saying, 'This is the Torah which Moses set before the Israelites' (Deuteronomy 4:44)" (Tanhuma Haberakhah 2).

---

denied to God that he could speak "words," and yet the very (Hebrew) title of the book that contains his great speeches to the Israelites is *devarim* ("words").

[15] That is, when Jacob concluded blessing his children on his deathbed, the text says *ve-zot* ("and this is what their father said to them"). When Moses began to bless the Israelite tribes, descendants of Jacob's sons, he began with the word *ve-zot* ("and this is the blessing with which Moses . . . bade the Israelites farewell." The continuity that this implies is one lovely result of this exegesis, but the point here is rather that Moses composed the blessings on his own, using Jacob as a model, as the following understanding of Psalm 119 suggests.

Land. If I now admonish them with all of these words, what might happen to me? And thus he was afraid, until the Holy and Blessed One gave him permission, and said to him: "Speak." Thus, do not read "Moses spoke" (*dibber Moshe*),[16] but rather "Speak, Moses!" (*dabber Moshe*), for the Holy and Blessed One gave him permission to speak. Said Rabbi Johanan: Whoever says that Moses admonished[17] the Israelites on his own authority is but a sinner. And one who says so is told that his refutation is immediately at hand: "in accordance with the instructions that the Lord had given him for them" (Deuteronomy 1:3); that is, he admonished them only with the assent of the Holy and Blessed One."[26] The language of Rabbi Johanan proves that already in his day there were those who said that Moses admonished Israel on his own authority.

Rabbi Johanan ben Nappaha, one of the great Sages of his generation who lived in the Land of Israel, a place where there were many sectarians,[18] felt that the idea that Moses spoke the admonitions in Deuteronomy on his own was a potential stumbling block.[27] Abbaye lived in Babylonia, where there were not many sectarians, and thus he did not hesitate to teach his point of view about Deuteronomy. The Gemara relates that Rabbi Abbahu, a student of Rabbi Johanan, whose home was Caesarea in the Land of Israel, complimented Rav Safra, a Babylonian Amora who often visited the Land of Israel, in the presence of some sectarians. At one point some sectarians asked Rav Safra to explicate a particular verse, and he was unable to answer. They then said to Rabbi Abbahu: "Did you not tell us that he is a great man?" He said to them: "I meant that he was great in Talmud, not in Scripture." They asked him: "Why is it that you have great expertise in Scripture?" He told them: "We [in the Land of Israel] who have many sectarians at hand busy ourselves with Scripture, but the Babylonian scholars who do not have sectarians at hand do not busy themselves with Scripture."[28]

As noted above, the idea that Moses spoke the words of Deuteronomy on his own is a potential stumbling block. In the *Didascalia,* a Christian book written in Syria or in the Land of Israel in the third century, a new form is given to a distinction that had been made by the Ebionites between sections of the Torah that are "true" and those

---

[26] Midrash Haggadol to Deuteronomy, *Ha-segulah,* II,6.

[27] Literally: "that the righteous can walk on them, while sinners [or heretics] stumble on them." The allusion is to Hosea 14:10.

[28] BT Avodah Zarah 4a.

---

[16] In Deuteronomy 1:3, as Rabbi Johanan's comment below makes clear. It is very common for rabbinic exegesis to suggest alternative vocalizations of the consonants in the Hebrew text. They are not meant to be permanent changes, but rather parallel readings that should be "heard" along with the standard vocalization.

[17] That is, spoke this Book of Deuteronomy.

[18] The reference here is perhaps to various Gnostic sects or to those who were making distinctions between the Hebrew Bible and the newer Christian Scriptures, denigrating the eternal status of the former. See below. Thus, the sense that allowing that Deuteronomy had human input could open an unwanted polemical door.

that are "forgeries." Now the distinction was between Torah, or *lex*, and *secundatio legis*, or just *secundatio*. The Ten Commandments and the ordinances following them are Torah, and they will never be nullified, but all the other commandments are *secundatio legis*, and they are no longer in force. "Torah" includes that which was given to Israel before they made the golden calf; after they did that act they were punished with the giving of the additional commandments.[29]

The expression *secundatio legis* is nothing but a translation of the Greek word *deuterōsis*, and this entire matter is discussed as well in the book *Constitutio Apostolorum* in the fourth century. The commandments given to Israel before the making of the golden calf are *lex naturalis*; the rest of the commandments are *deuterōsis*, and only one who knows how to distinguish between Torah and *deuterōsis* is worthy of rising to leadership.[30]

What is the meaning of the word *deuterōsis*? The Church Father Epiphanius, who lived in the fourth century, writes that traditions of the elders that are known among the Jews as *Mishneh*[19] (i.e., *Deuterōsis*) fall into four categories: (1) those that are ascribed to Moses, that is, Deuteronomy; (2) the teachings of the time of the Hasmoneans, that is, the most ancient Halakhah; (3) the teachings of Rabbi Akiva, that is, the renewed Halakhah; and (4) the Mishnah[20] of Rabbi Judah the Patriarch, the culmination that future generations accepted as confirmed law.[31]

In the "Syrian Didascalia," the author admits that Deuteronomy (*Mishneh Torah*) also came from God. But in a Christian book written at approximately 200 C.E. there appears the idea that Deuteronomy did not come from the Most Holy but rather was spoken by Moses, and for that reason was not to be found in the Holy Ark.[32] This point of view aroused astonishment among scholars, and according to one authority it has no parallel in the literature.[33]

---

[29] *Didascalia Apostolorum*, ed. R. Hugh Connolly (Oxford: Clarendon, 1929), chapter 26, pp. 216ff.; see Introduction, pp. vii ff. The positive valuation of the "ordinances" (Exodus 21–23) is mentioned also by Theophilus of Antioch. See R. M. Grant, "The Decalogue in Early Christianity," *Harvard Theological Review* 40 (1947): 13ff.

[30] *Constitutio Apostolorum*, in *Ante-Nicene Fathers*, volume 7 (Edinburgh: T & T Clark, 1965–68); G. Heinrici, *Die Valentinische Gnosis und die Heilige Schrift* (Berlin, 1871), 78ff.

[31] Irenaeus, *Adversus Haereses*, 9.33. The Valentinian Gnostic Ptolemaeus, whom we mentioned in chapter 21 above (p. 402), also used the term *deuterōsis nomou* to refer to the less worthy laws.

[32] *The Dialogues of Athanasius and Zacchaeus and of Timothy and Aquila*, ed. F. C. Conybeare, Anecdota Oxoniensa 8 (Oxford, 1898), p. 66.

[33] A. Lukyn Williams, *Adversus Judaeos* writes: "I can find no parallel to this extraordinary statement and can only conjecture that the similarity of the meaning of the Greek word *deuterōsis* to that of the Hebrew word Mishna . . . is responsible for some confusion of thought" (*Adversus Judaeos* [Cambridge, 1935], p. 72 n. 3).

---

[19] Coming from the Hebrew word for "two" and thus meaning something like "repetition," "companion," or, as used here, "secondary." The biblical term *mishneh la-melekh* means "viceroy," or second in line to the sovereign.

[20] Coming from the Hebrew word meaning "to learn" or "to teach." "Mishnah" (used to refer to Rabbi Judah the Patriarch's compilation of oral "teaching") should not be confused with "Mishneh," used to refer to Deuteronomy in the phrase "Mishneh Torah."

The solution to this riddle, which has vexed many, can be found in a fact that eluded these scholars. In the first centuries of the Common Era many argued about the problem of the Book of Deuteronomy, and among the Christians of the second century there were those who denied the sanctity of the Book of Deuteronomy. *Secundatio legis,* or *deuterōsis* in the "Syrian *Didascalia,*" means simply the Book of Deuteronomy.

He Admonished Them on Instructions from on High

This point of view, that the admonitions in Deuteronomy were spoken by Moses our Master on his own, was objected to as well by Rabbi Simon, a second- to third-generation Amora in the Land of Israel. "Why did he admonish them at the end of forty years? Said Rabbi Simon: For if he had admonished them at the beginning, they would have said: 'What do we need with the son of Amram?' But after he had enriched them with the booty from Sihon and Og, he then admonished them *on instructions from on high.*"[34] The idea that Moses did not want to admonish Israel until the Holy and Blessed One so instructed him, was emphasized in another exegesis. About Moses' admonitions, it was stated: "To what is it analogous? To a disciple who walked with his master and saw a discarded coal. Thinking it was a precious stone, he picked it up and was burned. After many days, he was again walking with his master, and he saw a precious stone but was afraid to touch it. His master said to him: "Pick it up, it is a precious stone!' So did Moses say: Because I said to them, 'Listen, you rebels' (Numbers 20:10), I was punished on their account, and now shall I dare to admonish them?! Said to him the Holy and Blessed One: 'Do not fear.'"[35]

Hints of the idea that even in Deuteronomy Moses said nothing on his own are found in a variety of exegeses. According to Rabbi Simeon ben Lakish, whose opinion on the admonitions we quoted earlier in this chapter, "The Holy and Blessed One said: I told you [Israel] . . . 'The Lord will open for you His bounteous store' (Deuteronomy 28:12).[36] [21] And Rabbi Berekhiah, a fourth-generation Amora, said: "Israel spoke before the Holy and Blessed One, and said, You have told us, 'Remember' (Deuteronomy 25:17); but we ask You to remember, for we are prone to forgetting."[37]

---

[34] Lekah Tov, beginning of Devarim. The expression *mipi hagevurah* (literally, "from the mouth of the Powerful One") is unusual in connection with Moses' admonitions.

[35] Deuteronomy Rabbah 1:6.

[36] Tanhuma Re'eh 18.

[37] Tanhuma Tetzei 9; YS Tetzei 938.

---

[21] That is, God quotes a verse in Deuteronomy as having been spoken by God.

"Not on My Own Do I Tell You This"

The Book of Deuteronomy differs stylistically from the other books of the Torah. "The Lord spoke to Moses, saying"[22] is not found in it; and quite often we find the expression "I said to you." The book is written in Moses' voice, and our Sages of Blessed Memory already expressed astonishment at its beginning: "These are the words that Moses addressed" (Deuteronomy 1:1)—"Did Moses then speak? Didn't the Holy and Blessed One command Moses to speak, as it says: 'in accordance with the instructions that the Lord had given him' (Deuteronomy 1:3)?"[38]

Five times we read in the Sifre to Deuteronomy, that Moses our Master "said to them: Not on my own do I tell you this, but rather from the mouth of the Most Holy do I tell you this."[39] This emphasis is not common in Tannaitic midrashim, and there was justifiable astonishment about this: "From where would it enter the mind that Moses would have said this on his own without instructions from the Holy and Blessed One, so that he would have to say: Not on my own do I tell you this, but rather from the mouth of the Most Holy do I tell you this? Did Moses have to say of every single commandment, 'Not on my own do I tell you this, but rather from the mouth of the Most Holy do I tell you this'?"[40] [23]

This desire to defend the Book of Deuteronomy was perhaps expressed as well by Rabbi Simeon:

It was taught in the school of Rabbi Simeon bar Yohai: The Book of Deuteronomy went up and fell down before the Holy and Blessed One and said: Master of the Universe, Solomon has uprooted me and made me seem a forgery, for any testament in which several items are null and void is null and void in its entirety.[24] Now King Solomon sought to uproot one jot from me, for it is written: "he shall not have many wives" (Deuteronomy 17:17), and he had many wives; "he shall not keep many horses" (Deuteronomy 17:16), and he kept many horses; "nor shall he amass silver and gold to excess" (Deuteronomy 17:17), and he amassed silver and gold to excess. Said the Holy and

---

[38] Midrash Aggadah, ed. Buber, on Deuteronomy 1:1.
[39] Sifre Devarim 5, 9, 12, 19, and 25.
[40] *Tzedah Laderekh* of R. Issachar Baer Eilenburg (Prague, 5383/1623), p. 88c.

---

[22] One of the most common phrases in the other four books of the Pentateuch.
[23] At this point, Heschel goes to some effort, not reproduced here, to explain why passages that seem to be very "Akivan," in that they defend the complete divine origin of Deuteronomy, appear in the parts of the Sifre to Deuteronomy that are usually believed to stem from the school of Rabbi Ishmael. As we have noted before, the exact provenance of each statement in the rabbinic midrashim is less important in this work than the documentation of the different points of view and how they both challenge and interweave with each other.
[24] This seems to have been the rule in Roman Law.

Blessed One: You may go, for Solomon and a hundred of his ilk shall be lost and forgotten and not a single jot of yours shall ever be nullified.[41]

On this passage, the author of Yefei Mar'eh[25] raised this difficulty: Why did the entire Book of Deuteronomy bring charges against Solomon, since he only violated a few of its precepts? If it was because any testament in which several items are null and void is entirely null and void, or because several violations today will lead to more tomorrow, why, then, did not the entire Torah bring charges against Solomon? "In what does the Book of Deuteronomy differ?" He suggests that it was because in the case of Deuteronomy Moses our Master, peace be upon him, "spoke *on instructions from on high* in order to explicate the Torah, and he included in it some mitzvot that were not in the first four books. One who would see Solomon uprooting something from this book, then, would think that Solomon believed that Moses spoke it on his own, and therefore he was not careful about its decrees. This would then lead to a nullification of anything in Deuteronomy that was not in the first four books, as people would say: It is not from God."[42]

"They Were Trebled in the Steppes of Moab from on High"

We have observed that against the opinion of Abbaye, Rabbi Johanan said: "Whoever says that Moses admonished the Israelites on his own authority is but a sinner." And all the more so is it clear that the view of the Zohar that "Moses spoke the Book of Deuteronomy by his own mouth" contradicts the Baraita that says, "Whoever says that the entire Torah was spoken on instruction from the Most Holy, but for this one thing that Moses spoke on his own, is the one referred to in the verse 'because he has spurned the word of the Lord' (Numbers 15:31)."

Common sense dictates that Abbaye did not innovate this idea on his own. As is well known, Amoraim do not generally dispute Tannaim. In many places in the Gemara, Amoraim are challenged in the discussion on the basis of a Mishnah or Baraita, and they always try to reconcile the views of an Amora with those of the Tannaim. "It is possible to say that from the day of the closure of the Mishnah, it was accepted and ratified that future generations would not dispute earlier ones. And so they did with the closure of the Gemara; that is, from the day that it was closed no person had leave to dispute it."[43] Now is there in the literature of the Tannaim any basis for the view of Abbaye and the statement of the Zohar?

It seems to me that this matter hangs on the dispute between Rabbi Ishmael and Rabbi Akiva that we mentioned above. "Rabbi Ishmael says: General principles were spoken at Sinai, and the particulars were given in the Tent of Meeting. Rabbi Akiva

---

[41] Leviticus Rabbah 19:2; PT Sanhedrin 20c; Tanhuma Va'era 5; Tanhuma, ed. Buber, Va'era 2.

[42] *Yefei Mar'eh* on PT Sanhedrin 20c.

[43] *Kesef Mishneh* (commentary of Joseph Caro on Maimonides' Code), on *Hilkhot Mamrim* 2:5.

---

[25] Samuel ben Isaac Yaffe, sixteenth century, Turkey.

says: General principles and particulars were both spoken at Sinai, were repeated in the Tent of Meeting, and were trebled in the Steppes of Moab."[44]

Thus did Rashi explain their statements: "Rabbi Ishmael says: General principles were spoken at Sinai"—"Many matters were given ambiguously at Sinai, for they were not fully explicated, and they were explained fully after the Sanctuary was set up, in the Tent of Meeting. It is evident that the laws of Temple worship were not adequately explicated. There was only the simple statement, 'Make Me an altar of earth and sacrifice on it your burnt offerings and your sacrifices of well-being' (Exodus 20:21),[26] but there was no instruction concerning the sprinkling of the blood, the flaying and dismembering of burnt offerings, or of the smoking of the internal parts of offerings of well-being"—"and the particulars were given in the Tent of Meeting"—"Once the Sanctuary was set up and God spoke to Moses from the Ark covering, Scripture then explicated the commandments, as it is written: 'The Lord called to Moses and spoke to him from the Tent of Meeting' (Leviticus 1:1), and thus in the Book of Leviticus, all of the laws of sacrifices were set forth. And so it was with many things."—"And Rabbi Akiva says: general principles and particulars were both spoken at Sinai, and were repeated in the Tent of Meeting"—"a second time, and whatever was said there was said here, even though it was not written"—"and were trebled in the steppes of Moab"—"from the mouth of Moses to Israel, as it says: 'On the other side of the Jordan, in the Land of Moab, Moses undertook to expound this Teaching' (Deuteronomy 1:5)."[45]

Rabbi Akiva set down two principles: (1) The entire Torah was given at Sinai, and (2) the Torah was spoken three times from the Most Holy to Moses.

Now come and see that Rabbi Ishmael said nothing at all about the steppes of Moab.[46] Perhaps Rabbi Ishmael and Rabbi Akiva disputed this point as well: Rabbi Akiva held that general principles and particulars as well were spoken from on high to Moses in three places, and the Book of Deuteronomy was spoken by Moses on instruction from on high. And Rabbi Ishmael held that the entire Torah was not given to Moses all at once; general principles were spoken to him at Sinai, and the particulars in the Tent of Meeting. And in the steppes of Moab there were no new commandments spoken to him from on high.[27]

Similar to the approach of Rabbi Ishmael was the opinion of Rabbi Yose the Galilean, a regular interlocutor of Rabbi Akiva: "In three places was the Torah spo-

---

[44] BT Sotah 37b, etc. cited above in chapter 20, p. 378.

[45] Rashi on BT Sotah 37b; Hagigah 6b; Zevahim 115b. See also Rashi on BT Berakhot 48b, s.v. *torah nitenah beshalosh beritot*—"the Torah was given to Israel in three places: Sinai, the Tent of Meeting, and Mount Gerizim."

[46] Tosafot remark on this fact (see Tosafot on BT Sotah 37b, s.v. *ve-nishtalshelu*).

---

[26] The point here is that this verse comes at the end of the revelation at Mount Sinai, so it was at Sinai that a very general, undetailed command was given about sacrifices, a command that would obviously need explication later on.

[27] Thus, Deuteronomy, given in the steppes of Moab, was Moses' creation.

ken: In the Land of Egypt, at Mount Sinai, and in the Tent of Meeting."[47] This point of view was explicated by Rabbi Abba bar Kahana: "In three places was the Torah given . . . in the Land of Egypt—the matters of the Paschal sacrifice, the dedication of the firstborn, and the phylacteries.[28] At Mount Sinai the Ten Commandments, the civil law, and the instructions for building the Sanctuary were given.[29] And in the Tent of Meeting the laws of the sacrifices and all other laws were given."[48] [30] Here, too, the steppes of Moab were not mentioned.

"In the Steppes of Moab Nothing New Save the Terms of the Covenant Were Given to Him"

According to the approach of the school of Rabbi Ishmael, that "there is no strict chronological order in the Torah," one can consistently say that there are sections of Deuteronomy that were not spoken in the steppes of Moab, but rather at Sinai, in the Tent of Meeting, or even before the Israelites came to Sinai; and that the commandments that were mentioned in Deuteronomy were spoken to him from on high earlier, except that he spoke them to Israel in the steppes of Moab.[49] [31] But the admonitions and blessings were spoken by Moses on his own. About the section that describes the glories of the Land of Israel (Deuteronomy 11:10–12) they said: "This

---

[47] Sifra 3d; see Rome ms., ed. Finkelstein, p. 7.

[48] Midrash Haggadol on Numbers, ed. Fish, p. 8.

[49] According to Midrash Haggadol on Numbers, Mattot (JTS ms.): "Three portions of law were given to Israel in the steppes of Moab: The portion on inheritance (Numbers 27:1–11 and/or 34:13–18), the portion on the cities of refuge (Numbers 35:9–34), and the portion on vows (Numbers 30:2–17). In case you might say, the portion on sacrifices (Numbers 28:1–30:1) was also given in the steppes of Moab, it was hinted at on Sinai, but was spelled out in the steppes of Moab." At the start of his commentary on Deuteronomy, Nahmanides expresses the opinion that the commandments that appear in Deuteronomy but were not mentioned at all in the previous books, "were all spoken [to Moses] at Sinai or in the Tent of Meeting in the first year, prior to the episode of the Spies. For *in the steppes of Moab, nothing new, except for the terms of the covenant (chapters 27–28), was given to him.* Perhaps they were not written in the earlier books, because they were practiced only in the Land of Israel." Abravanel similarly thought that "these are the words that Moses addressed" applied not to the laws (which were given by God) but only to the narratives, exhortations, and arguments that Moses prefaced to the exposition of the mitzvot (Abravanel on Deuteronomy 1:1).

---

[28] Given in Exodus 12–13, before the arrival at Sinai, reported in chapter 19.

[29] As given in the remainder of the Book of Exodus.

[30] Meaning the Books of Leviticus and Numbers.

[31] Heschel here establishes that the suggestion that there are parts of Deuteronomy that seem to be of divine origin (such as places where Moses says "as God commanded me") is not contrary to what he designates as the "Ishmaelian" view of the Mosaic origin of parts of Deuteronomy. For the Ishmaelian view allows for a chronological rearrangement of sections of the Torah (we saw this many chapters earlier in the Ishmaelian view that the sin of the golden calf preceded the instructions to build the Sanctuary), and those "divine" parts of Deuteronomy can simply be predated.

section was spoken to Israel at the time that they left Egypt."[50] In passing, Rabbi Samson of Chinon[32] suggested that Rabbi Ishmael believed that one should distinguish between the Book of Deuteronomy and the other books of the Torah: In the rest of the Torah, one does not make inferences from juxtapositions in the text, whereas in Deuteronomy one does make such inferences.[51] Perhaps he made the assumption that, according to Rabbi Ishmael, Deuteronomy was spoken by Moses on his own. And a similar position was ascribed to Rabbi Judah ben Ila'i.[33]

Rav Joseph stated this general principle: "Even one who does not make inferences from juxtapositions in the whole Torah, does so in the case of Deuteronomy." And according to the Gemara, Rabbi Judah also "did not interpret juxtapositions in the entire Torah, but did so in Deuteronomy."[52] Why did the Sages see fit to distinguish between Deuteronomy and the other books of the Pentateuch?[53]

Rabbi Eliezer ben Nathan of Mayence (the RaBaN), who lived in the second half of the eleventh century and corresponded with RaSHBaM and Rabbenu Tam,[34] wrote: "even one who does not make inferences from juxtapositions in the whole Torah does so in the case of Deuteronomy. And the reason for that is that the entire Torah was spoken from on high, and thus there is no strict chronological order, but Moses, who composed Deuteronomy section upon section, arranged it in order that it be interpreted."[54] And as we shall see later on, Rabbi Judah believed that the last eight verses of the Torah were written by Joshua.[55]

The Tosafot give a reason, in the name of Rav Hai Gaon[35] and Rav Saadia Gaon,[36] for why it is customary to write twelve lines in a Get (divorce). A Get is called in the Torah "a book of severance,"[37] and "severance" connotes separation and distance. Now the scroll of the Torah has twelve empty lines that separate and distance the four books of the Torah from one another, four lines between each book.

---

[50] Sifre Ekev 37.

[51] *Sefer Keritut, Battei Midot* 2.

[52] BT Berakhot 21b.

[53] One answer is given by Tosafot on Yevamot 4a, s.v. *vekhi mipnei:* A passage is open to extraneous exegesis (such as the significance of juxtapositions) if it is self-evident, or if it is redundant. But the Book of Deuteronomy as a whole is almost entirely redundant (to the laws of the rest of the Torah) or self-evident. Therefore it can all be interpreted by the logic of juxtapositions.

[54] *Even Ha-Ezer* 34. According to Tosafot on BT Berakhot 14b, s.v. *lammah,* the principle "no chronological order" applies especially to Deuteronomy as well.

[55] See below, chapter 32.

---

[32] Thirteenth to fourteenth century, France, author of *Sefer Keritut,* an explication of talmudic principles.

[33] Second-century Tanna.

[34] Both Tosafists of the twelfth century, grandchildren of Rashi.

[35] Eleventh century, Babylonia, the last luminary of the posttalmudic academies in Babylonia.

[36] Tenth century, Babylonia.

[37] Deuteronomy 24:1.

"But the break between Numbers and Deuteronomy does not count because it [Deuteronomy] merely rehearses and repeats what came before."[56]

What of the slight discrepancies in laws common to Deuteronomy and the rest of the Torah? It is written in Leviticus 11:4, "The following, of those that either chew the cud or have true hoofs, you shall not eat . . . ." The corresponding law in Deuteronomy (14:7) reads: "The following, which do bring up the cud or have true hoofs *which are cleft through,* you may not eat . . . ." The Hebrew adds the word *ha-shesu'ah,* "which are cleft through."

Similarly, Leviticus 11:14 enumerates among the unclean fowl that are prohibited for food: "the kite [*da'ah*] and the falcon." In the corresponding verse in Deuteronomy (14:13) is written: "the kite [*ra'ah*], the falcon, and the buzzard [*dayyah*]."[38] In Rabbi Ishmael's school, they taught that *da'ah* and *ra'ah* are different birds. In Leviticus, Moses forgot to mention the *ra'ah* and the word *ha-shesu'ah* ("which are cleft through"), so he went back and mentioned them in Deuteronomy: "Why are the laws of the forbidden animals and fowls taught in Deuteronomy? Because of the *shesu'ah* (in the case of the animals) and the *ra'ah* (in the case of the fowls), to teach you that no one should ever be ashamed to admit, 'I forgot.'"[57] This explanation agrees with the Ishmaelian hermeneutic principle, "When a passage is written in one place with an omission and repeated elsewhere, it is repeated only for the sake of what was omitted."[58] According to this view, Moses added things in Deuteronomy that were not in Leviticus. This agrees with the maxim, "Deuteronomy came to add [to the law]."[59] But Rabbi Akiva argued against this whole approach and taught: "The *da'ah* is one kind of falcon; the *ra'ah* is another kind of falcon."[60] Thus, in Deuteronomy Moses did not add anything that was not already implicitly included in Leviticus.

"For the Lord your God will bless you as He has promised you" (Deuteronomy 15:6). They asked in the school of Rabbi Akiva: "When did God make a promise to

---

[56] Tosafot on BT Gittin 2a, s.v. *hamevi.* Similarly, *Tzeror Hamor* (of Abraham Saba, Spain, d. 1508) comments on Genesis 2:10: "'A river issues from Eden . . . and it then divides and becomes four branches'—this hints at the Torah, which has four books, for Deuteronomy is but a review of the preceding."

[57] Midrash Tannaim to Deuteronomy, ed. Hoffmann, p. 75; BT Hullin 63b, Bekhorot 6b. "If even Moses, the wisest of the wise and the greatest of the great, foremost of the prophets, was not ashamed to admit 'I forgot,' then how much more should a lowly scion, who is only one of the thousands of myriads of his students not be ashamed to admit, 'I forgot'!"

[58] Sifre Naso 2, cited above in chapter 2, p. 48.

[59] BT Hullin 63b, cited above in n. 19.

[60] Sifra 50b–c, RaABaD ad loc., Rome ms. p. 211; Sifre Re'eh 103 (Rabbi Simeon's view); BT Hullin 63b (Rav's view).

---

[38] By the traditional literal reading, it would appear that one bird (*da'ah*) mentioned in Leviticus is absent in Deuteronomy, and in its place are two birds (*ra'ah, dayyah*) that are not mentioned in Leviticus. A modern critical analysis will suggest that the two terms in Deuteronomy are both derived from the one in Leviticus, the one by copyist's error (*da'ah* > *ra'ah,* with *resh* substituting for the look-alike *dalet*), the other by phonetic shift (*da'ah* > *dayyah,* with *aleph* yielding to *yod*). Either way, there is a discrepancy between the two texts which needs to be accounted for.

them? 'Blessed shall you be in the city' (Deuteronomy 28:3),"[61] that is to say, it was a verse in Deuteronomy that God spoke! Against this, it was expounded in the school of Rabbi Ishmael: "'The Lord your God will put the dread and the fear of you . . . as He has promised you' (Deuteronomy 11:28)—and where did God promise it? 'I will send forth My terror before you' (Exodus 23:27)."[62] In the Mekhilta of Rabbi Ishmael, they asked about the verse, "'and that you shall be, as He promised, a holy people to the Lord your God' (Deuteronomy 26:19)—where did God promise this thing?" They answered that it is to be found in Leviticus 20:26: "You shall be holy to Me."[63] Now this verse differs in linguistic style from the verse in Deuteronomy. Why wouldn't they point to verses in Deuteronomy in which the matter is stated in the exact same language: "For you are a holy people to the Lord your God" (Deuteronomy 7:6; 14:2, 21)?[39]

The Book of Deuteronomy—Moses' Words

Now on the view of Abbaye that the curses in Deuteronomy were spoken by Moses by his own mouth, "there are words in the Torah that come from Moses, and not from the Holy and Blessed One,"[64] and this is the opposite of the view of the Baraita, according to which "whoever says that the entire Torah was spoken on instruction from the Most Holy, but for this one thing that Moses spoke on his own, is the one referred to in the verse, 'because he has spurned the word of the Lord.'"[65] The Zohar dealt with this matter: "We have learned that the curses in Leviticus were spoken by Moses by instruction from on high, while those in Deuteronomy were spoken by Moses by his own mouth. What means this 'by his own mouth'? Shall we entertain the notion that even a single letter in the Torah was spoken by Moses on his own authority?"[66] Many Sages struggled with this problem, such as Rabbenu Bahya, Rabbenu Nissim, Rabbi Meir ibn Gabbai, Rabbi Isaac Caro, Rabbi Isaac Abravanel, Maharsha, Rabbi Jacob Emden, Rabbi Elijah of Vilna, and Rabbi Zadok Ha-kohen of Lublin.[40]

---

[61] Sifre Re'eh 116.   [62] Sifre Ekev 52.   [63] MI Pisha 12.
[64] Me'ir ibn Gabbai (sixteenth-century kabbalist), *Avodat ha-kodesh, helek ha-takhlit,* 22.
[65] Sifre Shelah 112, cited above in chapter 20, p. 369.
[66] Zohar Va'ethanan 265a.

---

[39] The implied answer to this rhetorical question is that Rabbi Ishmael's Mekhilta could not quote a verse in Deuteronomy as proof that God had promised that the Israelites would be a holy people. The proof had to come from an earlier biblical book, one which is indisputably divine in origin.
[40] Rabbenu Bahya—thirteenth century, Spain; Rabbenu Nissim—fourteenth century, Spain; Rabbi Meir ibn Gabbai—sixteenth century, Egypt; Rabbi Isaac Caro—fifteenth to sixteenth century, Spain and Turkey (uncle of Joseph Caro of Safed, who was the author of the *Shulhan Arukh*); Rabbi Isaac Abravanel—fifteenth century, Iberia; Maharsha—Samuel Eliezer Edels, sixteenth century, Poland; Rabbi Jacob Emden—eighteenth century, Germany; Rabbi Elijah of Vilna—eighteenth century, Lithuania.

But come and see that many of the greats in Israel believed that Deuteronomy contained the words of Moses, including Rabbi Abraham ibn Ezra, Rashi, Rabbi Eleazar of Worms, Rabbi Eliezer ben Nathan of Mayence, Nahmanides, Rabbi Menahem Ha-Meiri, Hezekiah ben Manoah, Rabbi Isaac Abravanel, Rabbi Joseph of Trani, the Maharal of Prague, Rabbi Yom Tov Lipmann Muelhausen, Rabbi Abraham Azulai, Rabbi David the author of "Turei Zahav," the Maharam Schiff, Rabbi Hayyim ibn Attar, the author of "Sha'agat Aryeh," Rabbi Elijah of Vilna, and Rabbi Zadok Ha-kohen of Lublin.[41]

According to Rabbi Abraham ibn Ezra, the Ten Commandments as written in Parashat Yitro (Exodus) "are God's words without any additions or subtractions . . . but the Ten Commandments as written in Parashat Va'ethanan (Deuteronomy) are Moses' words. The ultimate proof of this is that in Deuteronomy's version it is twice written 'as the Lord your God has commanded you.' . . . Not as R. Saadia Gaon said, that 'remember' was on one tablet and 'observe' was on the other, and both are God's words."[67]

In the curses in Deuteronomy it is said: "The Lord will let loose against you . . . because of your evildoing in forsaking Me" (Deuteronomy 28:20). This expression cries out for interpretation, for it appears as if it were said from on high, and how can we then say that these curses were spoken by Moses? In order to resolve this difficulty, Rabbi Eleazar of Worms explained that the expression "in forsaking me" refers back "to Moses our Master, peace be upon him, who, at the time that Israel is punished, stands up and says of Israel's fate, that it comes upon them because they forsook me and did not heed my warnings."[68]

According to Rabbi Yom Tov Lipmann Muelhausen, whoever says that the Book of Deuteronomy comes from on high is falsifying our Torah, "for this matter cannot be

---

[67] Abraham ibn Ezra, Commentary on Exodus 20:1. It might appear that Abraham ibn Ezra agreed with Rabbi Yose ben Halafta's view (Tanhuma, ed. Buber, Tissa 17) that Moses wrote the version of the Ten Commandments on the second set of tablets. But we see from his (short) commentary on Exodus 34:28 that he agreed with those Amoraim who said that God inscribed the second tablets in accord with the words which Moses verbalized (according to God's command).

[68] Menahem Recanati's commentary on the Torah, Deuteronomy 28.

---

[41] Rabbi Abraham ibn Ezra—twelfth century, Spain; Rashi—eleventh century, Alsace; Rabbi Eleazar of Worms—twelfth to thirteenth century, Germany; Rabbi Eliezer ben Nathan of Mayence—twelfth century, Germany; Nahmanides—thirteenth century, Spain; Rabbi Menahem Ha-Meiri—thirteenth century, Provence; Hezekiah ben Manoah—thirteenth century, France (author of "Hizkuni" on the Torah); Rabbi Isaac Abravanel; Rabbi Joseph of Trani—sixteenth century, Safed; the Maharal of Prague (Judah ben Bezalel Loewe)—sixteenth to seventeenth century, Prague; Rabbi Yom Tov Lipmann Muelhausen—fourteenth to fifteenth century, Prague; Rabbi Abraham Azulai—sixteenth to seventeenth century, Morocco and Land of Israel; Rabbi David the author of "Turei Zahav" (David ben Samuel Halevi)—seventeenth century, Posen; the Maharam Schiff—seventeenth century, Germany; Rabbi Hayyim ibn Attar—eighteenth century, Morocco and Land of Israel; the author of "Sha'agat Aryeh" (Rabbi Aryeh Leib Gunzberg)—eighteenth century, Lithuania; Rabbi Elijah of Vilna—eighteenth century, Lithuania; and Rabbi Zadok Ha-kohen of Lublin—nineteenth century, Poland.

derived from the plain meaning of the text at any point, and, on the contrary, the plain meaning is that Moses our Master, peace be upon him, spoke all of Deuteronomy on his own, as it says: 'Moses undertook to expound.'"[69]

Rabbi Joseph of Trani as well wrote about the Book of Deuteronomy "that the voice in it is Moses' . . . for it appears from the language of the book that it is from the mouth of Moses our Master."[70]

The opinion of Abbaye is followed as well by Rabbi Hayyim ibn Attar in his commentary[42] on Deuteronomy 5:19: "'The Lord spoke these words to your whole congregation'[43]—Now Moses did not say 'all of these words,' for there are some words reported that were not spoken by God, such as the phrase 'as the Lord your God has commanded you' (Deuteronomy 5:16); also, the phrase 'and you shall remember . . .' (Deuteronomy 5:15) is the word of Moses."

"These Are" Excludes What Comes Before

There are places in the Torah in which the words "these are" (*eileh*) appear, and there are places where the words "and these are" (*ve-eileh*) appear. It is common for midrashim to interpret as follows: "these are" implies "just these," whereas "and these are" implies "also these." The father of this interpretation is Rabbi Ishmael.

"'And these are the rules that you shall set before them' (Exodus 21:1)[44]—Rabbi Ishmael says: 'and these are' adds to what came before; just as the former words came from Sinai, so do the latter."[71] But Rabbi Akiva certainly did not expound as Rabbi Ishmael did, for in his view the entire Torah was spoken at Sinai, with its generalities and particulars, and there is no need for any special emphasis to establish its origin at Sinai. Thus, he interpreted the verse as having a different meaning.[72]

Rabbi Joseph ben Zimra (who lived in the time of Rabbi Judah the Patriarch) and Rabbi Abbahu set down this principle: "Wherever it says 'these'—it is meant to push aside what came before (i.e., that the latter are different and distinct from the former), and where it says 'and these'—it is meant to add to the former." So here, "And these are the rules" comes to teach: "just as the former were from Sinai, so are what follows from Sinai."[73] It is possible that this general principle has its basis in the

---

[69] Muelhausen, *Ha-nitzahon* (Koenigsberg, 1847), 123.
[70] Joseph of Trani, *Beit Elohim*, 33.
[71] MI Nezikin 1.
[72] *Be'er Avraham* and *Mirkevet Hamishneh* on MI, loc. cit.
[73] Tanhuma, ed. Buber, Shemot 3. See Wilhelm Bacher, *Aggadot Amorei Eretz Yisrael* (Tel Aviv: Devir, 1924–37), 1/1:110, 2/1:112.

---

[42] Or Ha-Hayyim.
[43] The reference here is to the words of the Ten Commandments, and the question will be why it does not say that God spoke "all" of these words.
[44] This immediately follows the revelation of the Ten Commandments at Sinai.

thought of Rabbi Ishmael. Indeed, in one source this statement in an expanded form is attributed to him: "Rabbi Ishmael says . . . wherever it says 'these'—it means to exclude what came before; and wherever it says 'and these'—it means to add to what came before."[74]

Now from this general explanation, which is found so often in the midrashim, it turns out that the Book of Deuteronomy, which begins with the words "These are the words," and not "And these are the words," must be different and distinct from the earlier books. And in the commentary on the Torah attributed to Rabbenu Asher:[45] "Everyone asks, how we can say that it "pushes aside" what came before? Is it possible that "And these are the words" of the Book of Deuteronomy should be interpreted as pushing aside what came before?! This is impossible!"[75] And Rabbi Mordecai Ha-kohen of Safed, the author of the commentary "Siftei Kohen" on the Torah, concludes from this that the reason that the Book of Deuteronomy begins with "These are the words" and not "And these are the words" is this: "Because the other four books of the Pentateuch were spoken by Moses on instructions from on high, but Deuteronomy was spoken by his own mouth . . . and that is why it was not joined to the others with the phrase 'And these are the words.'" As for the change in language in the Ten Commandments, where in Exodus it says "Remember [the Sabbath Day]" and in Deuteronomy it says "Observe . . . ," the reason is this: "For there [in Exodus] it was the direct speech of the Holy and Blessed One, before whom there is no defect or forgetfulness, whereas here [in Deuteronomy] it is the speech of Moses, who is mortal, and thus forgetful. It was thus inappropriate for him to say 'Remember,' and thus he said 'Observe.'"[76]

Further Reflections on the Subject[46]

A multitude of thoughts have been proposed in order to reconcile the idea that Deuteronomy is fundamentally different from the rest of the Torah. According to one idea, Moses delivered the admonitions on his own, but he was consistent with the divine intent. So the opinion of Rabbenu Bahya:

> Know that the admonitions in Deuteronomy were given in Moses' language; not that Moses spoke them entirely by his own mouth, for we have a tradition that the entire Torah, from "In the beginning" to "before all Israel" was all written by Moses on instruc-

[74] Midrash Haggadol on Exodus, ed. Margaliot, pp. 454–55; *Mishnat Rabbi Eliezer,* chapter 15, ed. Engelow, p. 308.
[75] Manuscript published in *Revue des Études Juives* 54 (1907): 98.
[76] *Siftei Kohen,* Yitro (see also his commentary on Va'ethanan).

---

[45] "The Rosh"—thirteenth century, Germany and Spain.
[46] In this section, the complexity deepens, because we encounter the view here that it was Moses' voice, but with a divine imprimatur.

tion from on high. And what of the rabbinic midrash that the curses in Leviticus were spoken by the Holy and Blessed One and those in Deuteronomy were spoken by Moses by his own mouth? The intention there was to say, "as if by his own mouth," for he was in the end consistent with the intent of the Holy and Blessed One. And why were the curses in Leviticus given in the voice of the Holy and Blessed One and those in Deuteronomy given in the voice of Moses? Because the curses in Leviticus were fulfilled with the destruction of the First Temple, in which there was idolatry . . . and what is more, the Shekhinah dwelled in the First Temple; but the curses in Deuteronomy were all fulfilled with the destruction of the Second Temple, and by the time of the Second Temple, the Shekhinah had already departed. Therefore the voice in Deuteronomy is that of Moses our Master, peace be upon him, and not the voice of the Shekhinah."[77]

Rabbenu Nissim writes in a similar vein.[78] And so does the Maharal of Prague:

One should not interpret this to mean that Moses spoke on his own without the Holy and Blessed One, for Moses did not speak a single thing entirely on his own. Rather, it was either that Moses our Master, peace be upon him, would speak, and the Holy and Blessed One would agree with what he said, or the Holy and Blessed One would tell him: "Speak thus." In the case of the curses in Deuteronomy, the Holy and Blessed One would say to Moses: "Speak thus," and that is how those curses came to be "Moses' own." But both the curses and the blessings in Leviticus were spoken directly by the Holy and Blessed One, and Moses merely repeated to Israel the words that the Holy and Blessed One spoke.[79]

According to Rabbi Isaac Caro and Rabbi Isaac Abravanel, these admonitions [in Deuteronomy] and many other verses as well were spoken by Moses on his own, but after the fact, "the Holy and Blessed One commanded him to write them all down."[80] He "said them on his own" but "their being written in the Torah was a divinely ordained act."[81]

---

[77] *Midrash Rabbenu Bahya* (Naples, 5252/1492), Tavo; Me'iri on BT Megillah 31b.

[78] "Even though the Holy and Blessed One agreed that they be written in the Torah, they are not fully considered divine retribution, and one may say the blessing [of the Torah] over them [if the reader stopped the reading in the middle of them]" (Rabbenu Nissim on Alfasi, pertaining to BT Megillah 31a).

[79] *Gur Aryeh* on Deuteronomy 28:23.

[80] "Our rabbis said that Moses spoke all these admonitions and curses in this book [Deuteronomy]. But this raises problems: (1) Didn't the rabbis also say (in Mishnah Sanhedrin, chapter 10) that whoever says Moses spoke even one verse on his own, has no portion in the world to come? (2) How could they say this in Mishnah Sanhedrin, given that Moses spoke many verses in the Torah, such as: 'Please, Lord, make someone else your agent' (Exodus 4:13), indeed, that whole episode in which he protested to God about his mission to Pharaoh, so much so that God was angry at him? The same applies to the words of the spies, 'We cannot attack that people, for it is stronger than we' (Numbers 13:31). We can solve these difficulties as follows: Many verses contain the words spoken by others, such as Sihon [king of the Amorites], the king of Edom, etc. Afterwards, the Holy and Blessed One said to Moses, 'Write all these verses, from "In the beginning" to "before all Israel."' Thus, Moses did not *write* anything on his own initiative. In the same way, Moses (peace be his) delivered all these admonitions orally [on his own] at the time he lectured the people, but afterwards the Holy and Blessed One commanded him to write them all down" (*Toledot Yitzhak*, beginning of Deuteronomy).

[81] "Even though the saying of these words was of Moses' volition, writing them down was not; for how could he decide independently to write something in God's Torah? But they were right in the eyes of the Faithful Rock, and He agreed to have them written down" (ibid.).

The very expression "Moses said them by his own mouth" can be understood in two different ways: (1) by his own volition, that is, that God did not command him at all to compose the Book of Deuteronomy, or (2) from his mouth, while the command to speak them was given to him by God. Apparently, Nahmanides (and Maharam Schiff and Rabbi David Halevi) understood the expression in the first way; the second meaning was, however, favored by Rabbi Menahem Ha-Meiri and the Maharal of Prague.

Nahmanides, in his commentary on Deuteronomy 1:5, "Moses undertook to expound this Teaching," does not restrict Moses our Master's initiative to the curses alone, but rather believes that the entire Book of Deuteronomy was spoken by Moses on his own: "the reason that the text says 'Moses undertook,' is because Moses wanted to explicate the Torah for them, and the language used informed them that it was on his own that he decided to do this and not on command from God." It is clear that Nahmanides makes a fundamental distinction between the Book of Deuteronomy and the other books of the Torah. According to him, the Book of Deuteronomy is Moses' explication of God's Torah. He emphasizes that in the Ten Commandments as they appear in Deuteronomy Moses our Master

> did not change or gloss anything in "I am the Lord" [the first commandment] or in "You shall have no other gods . . ." [the second commandment], for these were heard by all directly from on high; similarly, with the third commandment . . . but he began to interpret them with "Observe" in place of "Remember" (Deuteronomy 5:12) . . . and he added the gloss "as the Lord your God has commanded you." . . . In all of Deuteronomy Moses speaks as if on instruction from on high. For example, he says: "If, then, you obey the commandments that I enjoin upon you this day, loving the Lord your God and serving Him with all your heart and soul, I will grant the rain for your land in season" (Deuteronomy 11:13–14). It is not, after all, Moses who sends rain to the earth, or makes grass grow in the fields. . . . It is for this reason [because Moses is speaking in his own voice] that in Deuteronomy he always says "the Lord your God," whereas in the rest of the Torah, God's name alone is mentioned . . . but the commandments in Deuteronomy[47] are all from on high."[82]

Rabbi Menahem Ha-Meiri explains: "'Moses spoke them by his own mouth' means in own language."[83] The Maharal of Prague also explains the difference between the other four books and Deuteronomy: "in the entire Torah God would put the words into the mouth of Moses, as it says, 'As Moses spoke God answered him with a voice' (Exodus 19:19), but in Deuteronomy Moses would speak on his own, as a messenger speaks on instruction from the sender, and this is the meaning of . . . 'he

---

[82] Nahmánides, commentary on Deuteronomy 1:1; 5:6; 5:12; 5:14. See Finkelstein's note on Sifre Devarim 4.

[83] Me'iri, *Beit Habehirah* on BT Megillah 31b.

---

[47] As opposed to the "admonitions," that is, Moses' speeches and exhortations.

spoke them by his own mouth,' that is to say, that God did not put the words in his mouth."[84] [48]

There were Sages who expressed astonishment at Abbaye's approach for a different reason, for does it not say explicitly, "Moses addressed the Israelites in accordance with the instructions that the Lord had given him for them" (Deuteronomy 1:3)? Rabbi Elijah Mizrahi suggested: "Perhaps one should answer that although the admonitions were delivered by his own mouth, he did not admonish them without God's permission. And the interpretation of 'in accordance with the instructions that the Lord had given him' is just this: that God *gave him leave* to admonish them. Or perhaps: God literally *commanded* him to admonish them, but did not tell him when to do so. And Moses our Master reasoned on his own, that he should not admonish them until he was about to die, as did Jacob, and as would Joshua, Samuel, and David."[85]

Yet another Sage raised a difficulty about the statement that the curses in Deuteronomy were spoken by Moses by his own mouth:

> Scripture says, "These are the terms of the covenant which the Lord commanded Moses to conclude with the Israelites in the land of Moab" (Deuteronomy 28:69). Do we not see clearly from this verse that these curses were not spoken by Moses on his own, but rather from the command of God? . . . Perhaps we should say that God commanded Moses our Master generally to cut a covenant, and said no more. That is why it does not say, "These are the terms of the covenant which the Lord *spoke* to Moses in order to conclude it with the Israelites," or "that the Lord *established* between Himself and the Israelite people," as it said in the case of the curses in Leviticus.[49] For the particulars did not come from God, and Moses composed the words independently. And since he composed the words, he spoke them in his own voice. And this is why they said that Moses spoke them by his own mouth . . . whereas the other words [in Deuteronomy][50] Moses spoke word for word as he received them from God, with neither addition or subtraction. As he says: "These are the words that Moses addressed to the Israelites," meaning: no more and no less. But the curses were different, for Moses composed their words himself."[86]

The Shekhinah Speaks from within His Voice Box[51]

Another reconciliation was proposed in the Zohar. There they sensed a fine distinction in the very expression "Moses spoke the curses in Deuteronomy by his own

[84] *Tif'eret Yisrael* 43.
[85] Elijah Mizrahi on Deuteronomy 1:1. See Abravanel ad loc.
[86] *Imrei Shafer,* Tavo.

---

[48] But he was expressing the divine intent.
[49] Leviticus 26:46.
[50] That is, besides the curses.
[51] In this section, the complexity further deepens, because we encounter the view here that it was Moses' mouth speaking, but the divine voice was heard through it.

mouth." The expression is not "Moses spoke them on his own." "By his own mouth" conveys the meaning that it was with a voice to which he was connected.[87]

With this approach another difficulty is resolved. One verse says, "God spoke" (Exodus 20:1), and another says, "As Moses spoke God answered him with a voice" (Exodus 19:19)! But here is what happened: the Israelites said to Moses: "You speak to us and we will obey, but let not God speak to us" (Exodus 20:16). And it was that "Moses physically spoke . . . but so that it should not appear that the Torah was being spoken by Moses, it tells us 'God answered him with a voice,' that is, that the Shekhinah actually composed the words, and her voice was heard through the mouth of Moses."[88] "As Moses spoke God answered him with a voice"—"at that moment Moses spoke with the Shekhinah, as it is written: 'With him I speak mouth to mouth' (Numbers 12:8)." "The Shekhinah spoke within Moses . . . for the voice was within him, and his speech was that of the Shekhinah."[89] Or, in other words, "the Holy and Blessed One and His Shekhinah spoke through his mouth."[90]

From the text "The Lord will let loose against you calamity . . . because of your evil-doing in forsaking Me" (Deuteronomy 28:20) Rabbi Menahem Recanati inferred that in the Book of Deuteronomy Moses speaks "by the mouth of the Most High,[52] and it is God who said 'in forsaking Me.' That is why it does not say, 'in forsaking God,' as would have been in keeping with the plain meaning, if these were in fact Moses' words. But rather, Moses spoke as with the mouth of the Shekhinah, and his mouth was hers."[91]

Rabbi Jacob Emden as well wrote: "It is certain that all of the Book of Deuteronomy is Moses' words, as he clearly explained at the beginning of the book. But the Shekhinah spoke from within his voice box, as we shall clearly see from several passages, including even the book's admonitions, such as, 'in forsaking Me' (Deuteronomy 28:20), and many other instances."[92]

The preacher Rabbi Jacob of Dubno[53] relates: "Now I asked my master and teacher, our Holy Rabbi, authority, and saint Rabbi Elijah of Vilna, of blessed memory: What is the difference between the holy Torah and the Book of Deuteronomy? And he replied that the first four books were heard from the mouth of the Holy and Blessed One Himself, through the voice box of Moses. Not so the Book of Deuteronomy; Israel heard the words of this book as they heard the words of prophets who suc-

---

[87] Zohar Va'ethanan 265a.
[88] Zohar Vayikra 7a; Abraham Azulai, Or Ha-hamah ad loc.
[89] Elijah of Vilna, commentary to Tikkunei Ha-zohar, ad loc.
[90] Zohar Pinhas 232b.
[91] Recanati, commentary on Tavo.
[92] Emden, glosses on BT Sanhedrin 99a.

---

[52] Ha-gevurah—an epithet for God (literally: "the Power").
[53] Eighteenth century.

ceeded Moses, with the Holy and Blessed One speaking to the prophet today, and the prophet transmitting the vision to Israel tomorrow. And if it was so, then at the time that the prophet spoke to the people, he was already detached from the divine voice.[54] So was the Book of Deuteronomy heard by Israel from the mouth of Moses our Master, peace be upon him, himself."[93]

The Book of Deuteronomy as "Writings"[55]

A unique point of view was taken by Rabbi Zadok of Lublin. We read in the Babylonian Talmud: "A certain Galilean preached in the presence of Rav Hisda, 'Blessed is the Merciful One who gave a threefold Teaching.'"[94] Both Rashi and Rabbenu Nissim explain that the reference here is to the Torah, Prophets, and Writings.[95] [56] But this explanation was not acceptable to many Sages. For example, Rabbi Eliezer Ashkenazi[57] writes: "One is astonished at this statement . . . and the matter does not sit well, for the Prophets and Writings were not given through Moses!" He therefore explains the intent of the statement as follows: "the Torah itself is threefold, for there is in the first instance the plain meaning that is openly revealed; then there is the latent meaning that is apprehended by the wise; and finally there is the esoteric level that is most deeply hidden. It is about these three levels that it is said in Parashat Mishpatim, 'Moses alone shall come near the Lord, but the others shall not come near, nor shall the people come up with him' (Exodus 24:2). That is, there are three levels here: Moses, the others [the elders], and the people."[96] Now Rabbi Tzadok also disagrees with the explanation of Rashi, and he sees here [in the Galilean's preaching] a suggestion that there was a Torah that was given at Sinai, which was repeated in the Tent of Meeting and trebled in the steppes of Moab.[97] This idea is based on the

---

[93] *Ohel Ya'akov*, Devarim.

[94] BT Shabbat 88a.

[95] Rashi ad loc.; Rabbenu Nissim ad loc. This concept also appears in PRK 105, and Tanhuma, ed. Buber, Yitro 8.

[96] *Ma'asei Ha-shem*, *Ma'asei Avot 9* and *Ma'asei Mitzrayim 2*.

[97] Me'ir Ish Shalom expressed this view earlier in the preface to his edition of the Mekhilta, Section 6, pp. xxxv–xxxvi.

---

[54] That is, Elijah of Vilna disagrees with the view given above and considers the first four books of the Pentateuch to have been transmitted with the divine voice speaking from within Moses, but not Deuteronomy. By waiting a day before transmitting the recollection of the divine revelation, Moses (or any other prophet) would naturally inject more of his own formulation and interpretation into the telling.

[55] In this section, the complexity deepens again, because we encounter the view here that Deuteronomy was delivered by Moses with divine inspiration.

[56] The traditional division of the Hebrew Bible, known by the Hebrew acronym TaNaKh—standing for Torah, Nevi'im (Prophets), and Ketuvim (Writings).

[57] Seventeenth century, Poland.

words of Rabbi Akiva: "general principles and particulars were both spoken at Sinai, were repeated in the Tent of Meeting, and were trebled in the steppes of Moab."[98] From this Rabbi Tzadok concludes that one ought to distinguish three different levels in Torah:

(1) "The Torah that was given at Sinai was the word of God . . . words that emanated from God through the agency of the mouth of Moses our Master." Concerning the word of God, it is written: "So is the word that issues from My mouth: It does not come back to Me unfulfilled, but performs what I purpose, achieves what I sent it to do" (Isaiah 55:11). Similarly, they said that "at the moment that Israel heard 'I am the Lord your God' the study of Torah was implanted in their hearts."[99]

(2) "That which was repeated in the Tent of Meeting was similar to all prophets' uttering 'Thus says the Lord,' that is, that they heard it from God and related it to Israel. Only in specific sections does it say 'This is what God has commanded,' in which Moses went beyond the other prophets by saying 'this is what . . . .'[100] And those utterances in which it is said 'The Lord spoke to Moses' are in the category of 'Prophecy.' Of commandments mentioned in the Prophets it is also written, 'And the Lord spoke'; for example, in the section on homicides in Joshua it says, 'The Lord spoke to Joshua' (Joshua 20:1), because it, too, was Torah,"[101] and this was the category of "Prophecy."

(3) That which was trebled in the steppes of Moab "Moses spoke by his own mouth; even though they were God's instructions, they were nevertheless in the category of 'Writings,' given with the Holy Spirit. This is already the beginning of Oral Torah, which are also words of the Living God and have the Holy Spirit in them, as Nahmanides has written.[102] And when they say that a Sage outweighs a prophet, it means in having the Holy Spirit, for the Holy Spirit means the Spirit from the Most High and Holy.[103] And this was necessitated by their corruption, after which an abundance of wisdom was needed as an antidote to the abundance of anger . . . and this Holy Spirit is considered part of the category of 'Writings.'"[58] According to this idea, "Deuteronomy is the beginning of the Oral Torah, as it is written: 'And on these stones you shall inscribe every word of this Teaching expounding well' (Deuteronomy 27:8)."[104]

---

[98] BT Hagigah 6b (cited earlier).
[99] Song of Songs Rabbah 1:1.
[100] Sifre Mattot 153 (cited above in chapter 23).
[101] BT Makkot 11a.
[102] Nahmanides, glosses on BT Bava Batra 12a.
[103] Zohar Aharei Mot 61a.
[104] Pri Tzaddik, Behar 93–94.

---

[58] Thus, the threefold Torah according to this understanding is that the revelation at Sinai is Torah I, the further instructions to Moses (in the remainder of Exodus, Leviticus, and Numbers) is Torah II (Prophecy), and Deuteronomy is Torah III (Writings).

The Story of Balaam Was Spoken
as from His Own Mouth

We read in a Baraita: "Moses wrote his own book, the story of Balaam, and the Book of Job."[105] It is common to interpret the words "his own book" as a reference to the five books of the Torah. But according to such an interpretation the statement is very puzzling: the story of Balaam is, after all, written in the Book of Numbers, and thus what does "the story of Balaam" add? Perhaps we should understand "Moses wrote his own book" to mean the Book of Deuteronomy, also known as "the book of Moses." And then the intent of the Baraita is to inform us of the special character of the book of Deuteronomy. It seems that this was the view of Rabbi Elijah of Vilna, who held that the story of Balaam in the Book of Numbers was spoken "as from his own mouth."

Note that in Scripture the expression "the book of Moses" refers to the Book of Deuteronomy. So Nehemiah 13:1, which refers to Deuteronomy 23:4; 2 Chronicles 25:4, which refers to Deuteronomy 24:16; and 2 Chronicles 35:12–13, which refers to Deuteronomy 16:7.[106]

In the Zohar, it says that the Exodus from Egypt is mentioned in the Torah fifty times.[107] The commentaries on the Zohar had difficulty with this, because the Exodus is actually mentioned ninety times in the Torah.[108] But Rabbi Elijah of Vilna notes that the Zohar refers only to those times "that the Holy and Blessed One spoke the words, in order that they be recited to Israel." He counted them and demonstrated that it occurs "twenty-five times in the direct speech of God,[59] and twenty-five times in the words of Moses—that is, in the book of Deuteronomy and in the story of Balaam, which itself was spoken as from Moses' own mouth."[109]

[105] BT Bava Batra 14b.
[106] See MI Bo 6.
[107] Zohar Yitro 83b, 85b; Tikkunei Zohar 406, 22a; 432, 76b; 439, 79b.
[108] *Pardes Rimmonim, Sha'ar ha-she'arim* 1; *Shefa' Tal, Sha'ar Shalosh Sha'arei Binah* 1; R. Menahem Azaria of Pano, *Me'ah Kesitah* 7.
[109] Elijah of Vilna's commentary to Tikkunei Zohar, 432, 84b.

[59] That is, in Exodus, Leviticus, and Numbers, excluding the story of Balaam.

ך26ם

IS THE PROPHET A PARTNER
OR A VESSEL?

Translator's Introduction

In this chapter,[1] Heschel returns to treat more fully a matter that arose in chapter 23, in which Moses (and other prophets) were said to have made their own contributions to their prophecies.

Now the question comes in its more general setting: Is the (true) prophet a will-less vessel or an active partner with God in the prophetic mission? As Heschel lays it out in this compelling chapter, the Akivans, who generally rejected the idea of an active human component in prophecy, believed that Moses at Mount Sinai spoke with the voice of the Shekhinah (God's Presence). He was a vessel. The Ishmaelians, on the other hand, stood for the belief that at Mount Sinai, the Shekhinah spoke with Moses' voice; that is, God was given human expression by an extraordinary human being. The Israelites, for their part, were considered by the Akivans to have been overwhelmed by the divine word, their minds taken over and penetrated by God's will. The Ishmaelians, however, maintained that the Israelites never lost their powers of reasoning and in fact processed the divine thoughts coming through Moses' words in a natural, human way.

The different styles of the prophets, not to mention the times when prophets confronted God, must all be dealt with as this controversy develops, and Heschel sets out the texts and the ideas for us.

We thus have two different views of what prophecy actually is. It is a subject that had claimed Heschel's attention ever since he wrote *Die Prophetie* in Germany. Here it serves as another fascinating consequence of the Ishmaelian/Akivan split on revelation.

---

[1] For greater clarity in the flow of the argument, we have transposed the chapter that appeared here in the original, entitled "The Maximalist and Minimalist Approaches," to a position several chapters hence. It is now chapter 30, and the chapters that were originally to be numbered 27–30 are now chapters 26–29.

As Clay in the Hand of the Potter[2]

W E HAVE BEEN GIVEN TWO APPROACHES to prophecy: (1) Moses our Master was merely a vessel that the Holy and Blessed One used, a trumpet that God played; he neither subtracted from, nor added to, what was spoken to him; and (2) Moses our master was a partner in the matter of prophecy.

According to the first approach, the prophet is "as clay in the hand of the potter, who at will lengthens or shortens it." The persona of the prophet is like the appearance of the moon. Just as the moon receives its light from the sun, not having any light of her own, so the prophet receives divine orders or divine inspiration; he is passive, devoid of initiative.[3] This approach is found in Philo, who sees the prophet simply as a vessel, whom God utilizes in order to reveal God's will, and who says not a single thing on his own. At the moment that prophecy comes to him, the prophet is in a state of ecstasy or is "out-of-body." His own vital forces leave him, and the spirit of God enters into him, plucks his vocal chords, and the words emanate from his mouth.[1]

Under Philo's influence this idea entered the Christian literature on prophecy. Athenagoras (ca. 177 C.E.) believed that the holy spirit enters into the prophet just as a flutist blows into the hollow of the flute.[2] Similarly, Justin said that the prophet is like a harp or a lyre, and a divine hammer descends from heaven and plays its strings.[3]

This approach appears also in the thought of the kabbalist Menahem Recanati.[4] "'With him (bo) I speak mouth to mouth' (Numbers 12:8)—it does not say 'to him (lo).' And the reason for this is that the prophet is a vessel for the holy spirit, just as a [normal] vessel receives that which is put into it; just so, when the Word comes to the prophet, he would receive it even against his will, as it is said: 'I thought, "I will not mention Him, no more will I speak in His name."—But [God's word] was like a

---

[1] Philo, *De Specialibus Legibus* 4.8.49; cf. Plato, *Ion* 534.

[2] From Athenagoras, *A Plea Regarding Christians* ch. 9, in *Early Christian Fathers,* ed. C. C. Richardson (Philadelphia: Westminster, 1953), 1:308.

[3] Justin, *Cohortatio ad Graecos* ch. 8; cf. the philosopher's words in *Kuzari* 1:1 [speaking of the perfected human]: "then his vessels [i.e., this person's organs] become . . . entirely vessels for the Active Intellect."

---

[2] The simile here is based on that given by the prophet Jeremiah in chapter 18 of his book. It is also the principal image in a beloved poem, of unknown authorship, recited on Yom Kippur eve. Jeremiah's use of the simile is meant to emphasize that God, like a potter, can start all over again with materials that have not shaped themselves correctly. Here there is a similar purpose: the prophet, according to one approach, is a mere vessel for the deliverance of the divine word and can and will be discarded or remade to suit the divine purpose.

[3] It is noteworthy that in BT Bava Batra 75a Moses is compared to the sun and Joshua is compared to the moon. There the purpose is to downgrade the nature of all post-Mosaic prophecy. See also Albo, *Ikkarim* 3:11. Here the image is used to show that *all* prophecy, even that of Moses, is, according to this first approach, a mere passive reflection of the divine, not an active emanation.

[4] Italy, thirteenth–fourteenth centuries.

raging fire in my heart, shut up in my bones' (Jeremiah 20:9)."[4] According to Shimon ben Tzemah Duran, the prophet "is nothing more than a set of trumpets that produce whatever sounds are blown into them";[5] and he finds a source for this idea in the words of the midrash: "Rabbi Eleazar said in the name of Rabbi Jose ben Zimra: All prophets did not know what they were prophesying even as they prophesied. . . . Rabbi Eleazar said in the name of Rabbi Jose ben Zimra: Samuel, the master of all prophets, prophesied and did not know [what he was prophesying], as it is said: 'And the Lord sent Jerubaal and Bedan and Jephthah and Samuel' (1 Samuel 12:11). It does not say 'and me,' but rather 'and Samuel,' since he did not know what he was prophesying."[6][5]

On the other hand, the verse "You represent the people before God" (Exodus 18:19) was expounded in the school of Rabbi Ishmael as follows: "Be for them as an instrument filled with utterances."[7] Similarly, they expounded: "'The Lord said to Moses and Aaron' (Exodus 12:1)—this teaches that just as Moses was an instrument for utterances, so was Aaron an instrument for utterances."[8]

Now at first glance it would appear that the masters of the midrash and Philo had the very same intent. But it is not so. The meaning of the phrase "instrument of song" is not the same as that of "instrument for utterances." "Instrument of song" means just what it says: it emits only what is played on or through it; its denotation is a will-less vessel, a mere mass devoid of initiative. By contrast, it is clear that the phrase "instrument for utterances" was not intended to express that Moses was a mere will-less vessel, *vasum Dei*. For as we have seen above, it was taught in the school of Rabbi Ishmael that Moses our Master did things on his own authority and that when using the expression "Thus says the Lord," he altered God's language and transmitted only the general intent.[6]

---

[4] Commentary on the Torah of Menahem Recanati, Beha'alotekha.

[5] *Magen Avot* (Leghorn, 1795), 74b.

[6] Midrash Tehillim 90:4. Note that this Midrash considers both Moses and Isaiah to have been exceptions to this rule (and another opinion considers Elihu [one of Job's interlocutors] to have been an exception as well).

[7] MI Amalek (Yitro) 2.

[8] MI Pisha 1, according to the emendation of Israel Levi; see "Ein Wort über die Mechilta des R. Simon" (Breslau, 1889), 38.

---

[5] That is, he was not aware of what he was saying, being in a kind of trance. This classical use of the phrase differs from another, later attested meaning, which is the idea that prophetic utterances sometimes have unexpected meanings. There are examples of the latter in many cultures. One biblical example is that of the prophet Jonah, who foretells the "overturning" of Nineveh. Jonah believes he is foretelling its destruction, when in fact he was foretelling the "turning over" of the city from wickedness to righteousness. But here the idea is that the prophet is in a trance and is speaking without normal, full consciousness.

[6] Here Heschel is relying on the fact that it is also the school of Rabbi Ishmael (in Sifre Numbers) that is the source of the characterization of Moses as an "instrument for utterances."

Each Person Is Addressed as Befits His Ability

Apparently, the two "fathers of the world" dissented from one another on this topic as well. According to Rabbi Akiva, Moses' speaking to Israel was just like the Holy and Blessed One's speaking to Moses.[7] The Holy and Blessed One would give strength and power to Moses, and thus with the same voice that he heard, he would address Israel. Against this, it was taught in the school of Rabbi Ishmael: a person is addressed as befits his ability, and even Moses our master heard only according to his ability. And the Holy and Blessed One spoke to him with Moses' voice, that is, with a voice that he could bear.[8]

Of the assembly at Mount Sinai, it is written, "As Moses spoke, God answered him with a voice" (Exodus 19:19). This verse is astonishing. "It should have said, 'As God spoke, Moses answered Him with a voice.'"9 Now Rabbis Akiva and Ishmael diverged in their explanations of this. According to Rabbi Akiva, the text comes to teach "that with whatever voice, power, and melody that Moses heard, he caused Israel to hear as well."10 [9] At Mount Sinai "the Holy and Blessed One inclined the upper heavens over the top of the mountain and spoke to them from the heavens." Moses "was in the heavens,"11 and the Holy and Blessed One would give "power and strength to Moses . . . while the Holy and Blessed One supported him with the divine voice."12 Thus, "with a voice" in the verse means the voice of the Holy and Blessed One.

Over and against this, Rabbi Luliani said in the name of Rabbi Ishmael (in another version, in the name of Rabbi Isaac13), "in the normal course of events, the master speaks and the disciple answers, but the Holy and Blessed One is not like that, but rather: 'As Moses spoke, God answered him with a voice'—that is, with the voice of Moses."14 [10] Even if this statement did not emanate in this form from the mouth of Rabbi Ishmael, it should have. For in this matter the "fathers of the world" disputed one another. Rabbi Akiva believed that Moses spoke with the voice of the Shekhinah.

---

9 Tanhuma Ki Tissa 15; YS Shofetim 162 (beginning).   10 MSY, p. 144.
11 TB Ha'azinu, p. 51.   12 MI Bahodesh 4.
13 So it appears in YS Psalms 700; TB Bereshit 4; and Midrash on Psalms 24:11.
14 Midrash on Psalms 18:29.

---

[7] This is consistent with the notion (referred to earlier) that Moses was likened to the sun, for the sun's power comes from God. However, Rabbi Akiva's formulation paradoxically turns what had been a compliment into a kind of "demotion," for Moses is here seen as a passive conduit who can only repeat the revelatory experience exactly when transmitting it to Israel.

[8] Thus, even Moses of necessity interpreted and reframed God's message.

[9] That is, when Moses spoke to the people, it was with God's grace, with the voice of God that he himself had heard.

[10] This would imply that Moses' voice had the divine approval, but was not a direct transmission of that which is, after all, infinite.

And Rabbi Ishmael believed that the Shekhinah spoke with Moses' voice. This idea is possibly implied in the well-known principle: "The Torah speaks in human language."

They set forth the following central principle in the school of Rabbi Ishmael: It is written of the assembly at Mount Sinai, "All the people saw the voices and the lightning" (Exodus 20:15). "It doesn't say 'the voice' but rather 'the voices,'"[15] "for each person is addressed as befits his ability, as it is said, 'The voice of the Lord comes with power' (Psalm 29:4)."[11][16] In this they taught that the voice of God contracted itself to fit human abilities. And thus did Rabbi Levi explain: were it written "with His power," the world could not have survived; but it is written, "with power," that is, according to the strength of each individual. Young adults according to their strength, the elderly according to their strength, and children according to their strength. "Many voices" were heard at Sinai.[17]

This approach was taken also by Rabbi Johanan, who believed that "when the Voice came forth, it did not come forth to all Israel, but rather according to the strength of each individual."[18]

Likewise, "Rabbi Levi said: The Holy and Blessed One appeared to them as a portrait whose face looks in every direction, so that a thousand people look at it and it looks at each one of them.[12] So when the Holy and Blessed One spoke, every person in Israel would say, "the Voice is speaking to me." That is why it is not written "I am the Lord your [plural] God," but rather "I am the Lord your [singular] God."[13] Said Rabbi Jose bar Haninah: "According to the strength of each individual did the voice speak. And do not be astonished at this, for the manna would come down for Israel, and each person would taste in it what he or she desired: young children according to their desires, young adults according to their desires, the elderly according to their desires . . . and now, if it was true of the manna that everyone tasted what was appropriate for them, how much more so in the case of the divine voice."[19] [14]

This idea, that "each person is addressed according to his ability," was taught in the Mekhilta of Rabbi Ishmael, and Moses was not excluded from this principle. And in truth, there are preserved some exegeses according to which Moses our Master received only according to *his* own abilities.

"When the Holy and Blessed One was revealed to Moses at the bush, God said to

---

[15] Pesikta Hadeta, Bet Ha-Midrash, part VI, p. 39.
[16] MI Bahodesh 9.   [17] Exodus Rabbah 29:1.
[18] Pesikta Hadeta, Bet Ha-Midrash, part VI, p. 39.
[19] PRK 12.

---

[11] That is, God's voice is commensurate with the power that is there to receive it.

[12] That is, something like what viewers report concerning da Vinci's *Mona Lisa*.

[13] The singular and plural "your" is the same in English but not in Hebrew.

[14] Presumably, this a fortiori reasoning is based on the idea that intellectual capacities vary much more widely across the human race than do physical needs and desires.

him: 'I am the God of your father' (Exodus 3:6). Said Rabbi Joshua the Kohen, son of Nehemiah: when the Holy and Blessed One was revealed to Moses, Moses was still a novice at prophecy. Said the Holy and Blessed One: if I reveal Myself to him with a booming voice, I will terrify him; if with a hushed voice, he will be disrespectful of prophecy. What did God do? God was revealed to him with the voice of his father. Said Moses: 'Here I am, what do you want, father?' Said the Holy and Blessed One: 'I am not your father, but the *God* of your father; I have come to you alluringly, so that you not be afraid.'"[20] [15]

But this principle applies not only to novices at prophecy. "Come see how the voice would go out to Israel: each individual would hear according to his or her ability . . . and even Moses, according to his ability, as it is said, 'As Moses spoke, God answered him with a voice' (Exodus 19:19)—with a voice that Moses could bear."[21] These things were said of Moses our Master at the time of the giving of the Torah; how much more so do they apply to all utterances.[16]

"All things have a measure. Water has its measure, and the heavens have their measure." And the Holy Spirit is no different: a person has measured out to him what he is able to receive. "When He fixed the weight of the winds, set the measure of the waters" (Job 28:25): "Said Rabbi Aha: even the Holy Spirit that rested on the prophets did so only in a measured way."[22] "Every prophet had the Holy Spirit placed in him, each according to his ability."[23]

The idea that a person is addressed according to his ability reached an extreme formulation in exegeses that asserted that the Holy and Blessed One spoke to them in the Egyptian language.

"I [*anokhi*] am the Lord your God"—said Rabbi Nehemiah: What is the meaning of *anokhi*? It is in the Egyptian language. What is this matter like? Like a king whose son was taken captive and spent a long time with his captors, learning their language. When the king was finally avenged on them and brought his son back, he attempted to speak with him in his own language, but he no longer knew it. What did the king do? He began to speak to him in the captors' language. So did the Holy and Blessed One do to Israel. All of those years that Israel was in Egypt, they learned the Egyptian language. And when the Holy and Blessed One redeemed them, God came down to give them the Torah. But they couldn't understand it. So the Holy and Blessed One said: I shall speak with them in the Egyptian language: that is, *anokh* (for when a person wishes to say "I" in Egyptian, he

---

[20] Exodus Rabbah 3:1.   [21] Tanhuma Shemot 25; TB Shemot 22; Exodus Rabbah 5:9.
[22] Leviticus Rabbah 15.   [23] YS Job 916.

---

[15] That is, Exodus Rabbah's interpretation here assumes that we are meant to emphasize the word *elohei* in the phrase *elohei avikha*.

[16] Once again, we have here the foundational Ishmaelian principle of the unbridgeable gulf between the transcendent God and terrestrial humanity.

says "*anokh*"). So did the Holy and Blessed One begin revelation in their language, saying "*anokhi.*"[24]

They taught in the school of Rabbi Ishmael: "A person is addressed according to his ability." Against this, it is implied in the words of Rabbi Akiva that at the assembly at Mount Sinai, Israel was addressed beyond its ability. For that was a time when Israel shed its physicality. At the time "that Israel heard *anokhi* at Sinai, their souls left them. The speech came back to the Holy and Blessed One, and said to God: Master of the universe, You are life, and Your Torah is life, and yet you have sent me to dead people! They are all dead! At that moment the Holy and Blessed One relented and sweetened the speech for them. It was taught by Rabbi Simeon ben Yohai: The Torah restored their souls to them, as it says: 'The teaching of the Lord is perfect, renewing life' (Psalms 19:8)."[25]

A Partner in the Act of Prophecy

Just as Rabbi Ishmael emphasized the role of ordinary reason in interpreting the Torah, so did he assign a role to the power of reason in the prophecy of Moses our Master. The prophet is able, with his internal powers, to hit upon the thoughts of God. Moses did things on his own, and the Holy and Blessed One agreed with his actions. The prophet participates in the act of prophecy, and thus may even alter the language of the Holy and Blessed One.

As we have demonstrated above,[17] the schools of Rabbi Akiva and Rabbi Ishmael differed on the issue of whether Moses always transmitted the words of God without any addition, subtraction, or stylistic change. According to the school of Rabbi Ishmael, when Moses used the expression "Thus says the Lord," he did not intend to transmit the word of God with exactitude. "Thus says the Lord" means: this is God's will. And Moses was at liberty to alter God's language and to transmit the intent alone. But according to the school of Rabbi Akiva, the words "Thus says the Lord" and "This is what the Lord has commanded" are identical, and they indicate that however Moses heard it, so did he speak it.

According to Rabbi Akiva, all is wondrous, all happens according to the Word, all is from on high, and all is according to God's power.[18] At Sinai "they saw what is normally heard and heard what is normally seen." Moses' responsibility was to speak to the House of Jacob in the order he received, with the same punctuation and the same subject headings, without subtracting or adding anything. The Holy and Blessed

---

[24] TB Yitro 16; PDRK 12. In contradistinction to this midrash, other Sages praised Israel for not changing their language in Egypt: see TB Balak 25.

[25] Numbers Rabbah 10.

---

[17] In chapter 23

[18] As opposed, that is, to human power.

One was the one who gave forth, and Moses our Master was the recipient, and no adjustments or compromises were permissible. Moses ascended to Heaven, and at that time his soul was a perfect match to the heavenly thoughts.[19]

In the light of the point of view that the Torah always existed and was written down in heaven even before it was given to Moses, it is certain that Moses could not say even a single thing on his own authority.

In the spirit of Rabbi Akiva's approach it was said: "You find phrases such as 'The Lord spoke to Moses,' and 'The Lord said to Moses'; you also find such phrases as 'Moses said to the Lord' and 'Moses spoke to the Lord.' This is analogous to a cave that faced the sea. When the tides rose, the sea filled the cave. Now the waters did not leave the cave, but from that point on, the sea gave to the cave, and the cave gave to the sea. Similarly, 'The Lord spoke to Moses' and 'The Lord said to Moses.'"[26] That is to say: even Moses' words back to God were spoken with the divine power that suffused him, just as the cave's waters had their source in the sea.[20]

The two approaches to understanding prophecy are hinted at in exegeses of the verse "He engirded him [yesovevenhu], watched over him [yevonenehu]" (Deuteronomy 32:10), which was interpreted as referring to the assembly at Mount Sinai. To "understand" means to apprehend with reason, and to be able to infer one thing from another.[21] At the assembly at Mount Sinai there was a receiving of the Torah. But was there also an "understanding" of the Torah? Following the method of Rabbi Akiva, who taught that the Israelites saw what was normally heard ["saw the voices"], it was expounded: "'yevonenehu'—this refers to the Ten Commandments. This teaches that the speech went forth from the mouth of the Holy and Blessed One, and the Israelites looked at it and immediately knew all of the exegeses it bore, all of the halakhot that it bore, all of the a fortiori inferences in it, and all of the gezerot shavot in it."[27] [22] According to this, all was revealed, all was fixed and clear in the speech

---

[26] Exodus Rabbah 45:3. See the commentary of Maharzo. Perhaps the end of this midrash needs to be emended to "Moses said to the Lord" and "Moses spoke to the Lord."

[27] Sifre Deuteronomy 313; Midrash Tannaim 191a.

---

[19] What is being described in this Akivan view is a kind of merger between the prophet and the divine—consistent with the idea outlined above that the prophet loses his identity in the act of prophecy.

[20] Once again, the idea is that Moses became an extension of God during moments of prophecy.

[21] This exegesis depends on taking the word yevonenehu as coming from the Hebrew root bwn, with the meaning "understanding." Thus, the verse is read as describing God causing Israel to encircle Mount Sinai and then and there imparting the power of understanding to them.

[22] The Akivan view of the "understanding" that Israel received at Mount Sinai was the ability to "see" immediately all that was latent in the words of revelation. Usually, a distinction is drawn between the kal va-homer (a fortiori inference) and the gezerah shavah (exploiting the coincidence of words in different contexts to equate one context to another). For example, in PT Pesahim 33a, we are told that a person may draw an a fortiori inference on his own, but not a gezerah shavah, which must be received by tradition. There is room for both reason and tradition. Here, however, the a fortiori inferences are not drawn by human reason but are, rather, simply apprehended through a supernatural power that descended on the people during revelation.

that could be seen, and there was no need for interpretation or explanation. But in contrast to this, Rabbi [Judah the Patriarch] took a different path in expounding the verse "All the people saw the voices" (Exodus 20:15). "Rabbi said: this informs you of the praiseworthiness of Israel, for when they all stood assembled before Mount Sinai to receive the Torah they would hear God's speech and explicate it, as it says, 'yesovevenhu, yevonenehu'—that as soon as they heard God's speech they would explicate it."[28] Following Rabbi Ishmael, Rabbi believed that the Israelites heard the divine speech, and he took the word "saw" to have the meaning of "understanding; the 'seeing' of reason." According to Rabbi's view, what took place at the assembly at Mount Sinai was not just the receiving of the Torah, but the understanding of the Torah as well. There was a partnership based in reason, for as they heard the words, they would explicate them on their own.[23]

When the Israelites heard the commandments in the assembly at Mount Sinai, which included positive and negative commands, they would answer "'yes' to the positive ones, and 'no' to the negative ones. So said Rabbi Ishmael. But Rabbi Akiva said: they answered 'yes' to the positive ones, and 'yes' to the negative ones."[29] Here as well you find two understandings of the receiving of the Torah. According to Rabbi Akiva, when the Israelites heard the voice of God, they had no capacity to distinguish between positive and negative commands, and they were so profoundly excited that they could only answer "yes" to each utterance. "When the people saw it, they fell back" (Exodus 20:15)—"the language of 'falling back' connotes disorientation."[30] [24] Against this, Rabbi Ishmael believed that even at that moment the Israelites distinguished and differentiated between positive and negative commands, and thus they said "yes" to the former and "no" to the latter. Differentiation in language requires discrimination.[25]

Rabbi Judah also apparently emphasized the thought that Moses was a partner in the act of prophecy: "The Lord said to Moses, 'I will come to you in a thick cloud, in

---

[28] MI Bahodesh 9.   [29] MI Bahodesh 4.
[30] MSY, p. 155.

---

[23] Thus, all hinges on what is taken to be the subject of the verb yevonenehu. If it is God, then God has imparted understanding to Israel through an act of divine grace. However, if it is Israel, then the verse [in Deuteronomy 32] is telling us that God caused Israel to circle Mount Sinai, and then Israel applied its own understanding to the words that it heard.

[24] It is worth noting here that the root of the verb translated here as "fell back" means something like "aimless wandering" and is first used in the Bible of Cain, whose fate was to be an aimless wanderer, that is, to be without orientation.

[25] There is an interesting paradox that dominates this discussion: the Akivan view tends to elevate Israel (in that they are depicted as apprehending the totality of revelation), but only because they are presumed to have lost their (human) abilities to reason, or else they are at that moment prohibited from using them. The Ishmaelian view gives less to the people in terms of how much they get from the initial revelation, but precisely because of that expects more from them!

order that the people may hear when I speak with you and so trust you ever after' (Exodus 19:9)." "Rabbi Judah said: How do we know that the Holy and Blessed One said to Moses: 'If, when I say something to you, you respond to me, I will concede what you say'? For God wanted Israel to say how great Moses was, that God acknowledged his words, as it says, 'and so trust you ever after.' Rabbi [Judah the Patriarch] said: this would not establish Moses' greatness, unless we were to find that the Holy and Blessed One retracted His own words in favor of Moses.'"[31] Rabbi Judah found in this text a great principle: that prophecy was a dialogue between Moses and God. The Holy and Blessed One said something, Moses answered, and the Holy and Blessed One acknowledged the answer. Rabbi [Judah the Patriarch] does not dispute this fundamental idea of Rabbi Judah; he simply restricts it to those cases in which the Holy and Blessed One retracted His own words.[26]

"When He finished speaking with him on Mount Sinai, He gave Moses the two tablets" (Exodus 31:18). "Said Rabbi Judah: This is analogous to a scribe who taught a young child. All week long he would read, and the child would repeat after him. When it came the child's turn to read, he recited together with his master. Thus it was with Moses. At the beginning, 'The Lord spoke to him,' and eventually, 'When He finished speaking with him.'[27] It does not say 'when He finished speaking to him' but rather 'when He finished speaking with him.'"[32] A different formulation of this same idea was taught in the name of Rabbi Simeon ben Lakish: "It is analogous to a student who was taught Torah by his master. Until he learned it, the master would speak and he would simply repeat. After he was taught, his master said to him: "Let us now recite it together." Thus, when Moses ascended to heaven, he began to repeat words of Torah after his Creator. But once he learned it, the Holy and Blessed One said: Let us now recite it together, you and I. That is why it says, 'when He finished speaking with him.'"[33]

It was said that on occasion Moses our Master actually reversed something that the Holy and Blessed One said to him.

Said Rabbi Samuel bar Nahman in the name of Rabbi Jonathan: Bezalel[28] was so called because of his wisdom. When the Holy and Blessed One said to Moses: "Go and tell Bezalel that he should create for me a Tabernacle, an ark, and various vessels," Moses

---

[31] MI Bahodesh 2; and, with some different language, MSY ad loc.
[32] Midrash Haggadol to Exodus 31:18.
[33] Exodus Rabbah 41:5; Tanhuma Ki Tissa 16.

---

[26] For examples of this, see the next section.
[27] Whereas on all previous occasions, when God spoke to Moses, the Book of Exodus used the phrase va-yedabber elav—"God spoke to Moses," here at the conclusion of the revelation, we have for the first time the use of the preposition et, meaning "with." That is, the text, read closely, signals us that at this stage, God was not speaking "to" Moses—that is, in a monologue—but rather "with" Moses, that is, in a dialogue.
[28] The name in Hebrew means "in the shadow of God."

went and reversed the order, saying: "Create an ark, various vessels, and a Tabernacle."
Said Bezalel to him: "Moses our Master, it is the usual practice for a person to build a
house and afterward to bring furniture into it; and you ask me to make an ark, various
vessels, and [only then] a Tabernacle? Where shall I place the vessels that I first make? Is
it possible that the Holy and Blessed One actually told you to create a Sanctuary, an ark,
and various vessels?" Moses said to him: "Were you standing in the shadow of God that
you know this?"[34] [29]

Rabbi Isaac Abravanel distinguishes, as did Maimonides, between the kind of
prophecy that comes to the prophets directly from God and the Holy Spirit with
which the prophets would speak. Direct prophecy is a flow that infuses the intellect
of the prophet, so that he can then tell other human beings what he saw or heard,
without there being any opening for his own will or free choice in what he sees or in
what he prophesies. But when infused with the Holy Spirit, the prophet wills and
chooses what he will speak, and because he is accompanied in this speaking by an
assisting divine spirit, this level of prophecy is called "the Holy Spirit." Now all of the
poetry that you find in the prophetic works are the composition of the prophets
themselves, with the Holy Spirit, but they were not received by direct prophecy.
Prophetic poetry is "the prophet's creation, composed by his will and by his volition."
This is what it means when it says of the Song at the Sea: "Then Moses and the
Israelites sang this song to the Lord" (Exodus 15:1)—"They themselves composed it
and sang it." This principle applied also to the Song of the Well (Numbers
21:17–18). Yet these songs were written in the Torah "because God accepted them,
approved of them, and commanded that they be written down there. If so, then the
composer of these songs was Moses our Master, though their being written in the
Torah was on instruction from on high."[35]

The kabbalists especially stressed the value of the prophet's active role in prophetic
apprehension. Prophecy is proportional to the stature of the receiver, for each
receives according to his power and his rank. "All of the prophets were holy. And yet
the prophecy that is drawn down to them from above is differentiable along different
dimensions because of the different dimensions of the human soul."[36] Thus says the
Zohar: "Even though the prophets taught with God's name and with the power of
prophecy, of which it is said, 'the spirit of the Lord rested on them' (Isaiah 63:14), it

---

[34] BT Berakhot 55b; Ecclesiastes Rabbah 7:11.
[35] Abravanel to Exodus 15:1.
[36] *Or Ha-Hammah* to Zohar Behar 110a.

---

[29] What this midrash is reacting to is the fact that in Exodus 25, Moses gives instructions for the
Ark and other appurtenances first, and then the instructions for creating the structure into which they
will be placed, but Exodus 35 does not follow this order. When Bezalel begins to carry out the
instructions, he creates the structure first, and then the sacred objects that are placed in that structure.
The Midrash cited here assumes that Moses reversed God's instructions, which Bezalel, through incisive
insight, understood correctly. Moses' reversal of God's instructions does not, of course, stand here,
but it is noteworthy that he is depicted as taking such liberties at all.

is nevertheless the case that not all masters of Torah are equal, and not all prophets are equal."[37]

It is a central principle in Kabbalah that the apprehension of the prophets was dependent on the receivers and not on the essence of the Holy and Blessed One. "When the spirit of the king rests on his creatures, that which each of them sees accords with his perception, vision, and imagination, and that is the meaning of 'and spoke imaginatively through the prophets' (Hosea 12:11)."[38]

The kabbalists expounded well when they said that prophecy does not simply float and then cut its way into the empty space of the prophet's soul; rather it is dependent on that soul's composition and its powers. But this idea was in time expanded to the point of making an exclusive claim: that prophecy is not an external act that activates a person internally, but rather reflects a certain intellectual state, a reflective state, an ability to perceive things in the image of the supernal soul, things that then in turn make their impressions on people. Prophecy thus flows from the essence of the soul and has the unique stamp of the prophet himself.

So did the kabbalist Rabbi Azriel explain "the pull of prophecy, which comes in the prophet's solitude, when he focuses his intellect and makes his thoughts adhere to those of Heaven. According to this prophetic adherence would the prophet see in advance and know what the future would bring. And the prophets were distinguishable from one another in their qualities, in their knowledge, and in their adherence to the divine. They would speak their words as if they were receiving them from on high, as if they were stuck to the words as a fish is stuck on a hook . . . and thus there is neither deficiency nor superfluity in their speeches, for all is said of necessity."[39]

"You Have Spoken Well, You Have Taught Me"

Many Sages did not consider Moses our Master to be merely a receiving vessel, without intellectual activity of his own. On the contrary, they saw him as an advisor to the King of Kings of Kings, and the Holy and Blessed One would say to him: "You have spoken well, you have taught Me." Under the influence of Moses, the Holy and Blessed One altered His language in the Torah and nullified both His word concerning punishments, and His decree to wage war against Sihon. And we find this approach in the mouth of Rabbi Ishmael.

After the incident of the spies, when God was ready to destroy the nation in the desert, Moses stood up and argued: "The nations will say, 'It must be because the Lord

---

[37] Zohar Behar 110a.

[38] Zohar Bo 42b. According to the kabbalists, the [lower] Sefirot of "Netzah" and "Hod" were "the places that nurtured the prophets; from them the prophets would draw all of their prophecies, each according to his own power and ability, except for the case of Moses our Master, peace be upon him. He ascended even higher than these Sefirot to receive the Torah" (Shaarei Orah of Joseph Gikatilla).

[39] *Perush Ha-Aggadot*, ed. Isaiah Tishby (Jerusalem, 1945), 41.

was powerless to bring that people into the land He had promised them on oath that He slaughtered them in the wilderness' (Numbers 14:16)." Then the Holy and Blessed One retracted and conceded the validity of Moses' argument, as it says: "I pardon, as you have asked" (Numbers 14:20). "It was taught by Rabbi Ishmael: 'as you have asked'—for the nations of the world will one day say: happy is the disciple whose master concedes his words. 'Nevertheless, as I live' (Numbers 14:21)—said Rava in the name of Rav Isaac: this teaches that the Holy and Blessed One said to Moses: 'Moses, you have revived Me with your words.'"[40] [30]

Thus did our Rabbis teach:

[There were three things] that Moses spoke before the Holy and Blessed One, and the latter said to him: "You have taught me." When the Israelites made the calf, he said before God: "Master of the Universe, how could the Israelites know what they were doing? Were they not raised in Egypt? And the Egyptians are all idolators. And when You gave the Torah, You did not even give it to them, and they weren't even standing there, as it says: 'So the people remained at a distance' (Exodus 20:18); You gave it only to me, as it says, 'Then He said to Moses, "Come up to the Lord"' (Exodus 24:1). And when You gave the Ten Commandments, You also didn't give it to them, for You didn't say, 'I am the Lord your [plural] God' but rather, 'I am the Lord your [singular] God' (Exodus 20:2)— You gave them to me! Now have I sinned?" And the Holy and Blessed One answered him: "By My life, you have spoken well, you have taught Me! From now on, I shall say it as 'I am the Lord your (plural) God.'"

That was the first of the three. The second:

When the Holy and Blessed One said to him, "visits the iniquity of parents upon children" (Exodus 34:7), Moses said: "Master of the Universe, so many wicked people have given birth to righteous ones. Should the latter have to bear the sins of their parent? Terah worshiped images, and Abraham his son was righteous. Similarly, King Hezekiah was righteous, while Ahaz his father was wicked; and likewise, King Josiah was righteous, while Amon his father was wicked. Is it becoming that the righteous should suffer for their parents' sins?" Said to him the Holy and Blessed One: "You have taught Me; I swear by My life that I will nullify My words and confirm yours, as it says: 'Parents shall not be put to death for children, nor children be put to death for parents: a person shall be put to death only for his own crime' (Deuteronomy 24:16). And I swear by My life that I will attribute them in writing to you, as it says, 'in accordance with what is written in the Book of the Teaching of Moses, where the Lord commanded' (2 Kings 14:6)."[31]

[40] BT Berakhot 32a.

---

[30] The phrase translated as "Nevertheless, as I live" is usually taken to mean the following: "Yes, Moses, I will relent now, but eventually I will have satisfaction for the terrible affront of the spies." However, it is in this context detached from what follows and is taken to mean "Nevertheless, I live"; that is, notwithstanding the terrible affront, I, God, have been revived by Moses' argument. God was, as it were, given new life by the principle of forgiveness.

[31] This is one of a handful of very interesting occasions on which the Torah is directly quoted in the prophetic books.

The third:

> When the Holy and Blessed One said to Moses: "Wage war against Sihon, and even if he doesn't seek war with you, you instigate it, as it says, 'Up! Set out across the wadi Arnon! See, I give into your power Sihon the Amorite, king of Heshbon, and his land. Begin the occupation: engage him in battle'" (Deuteronomy 2:24). But Moses did not do so. What does it actually say? "Then I sent messengers . . ." (Deuteronomy 2:26). Said to him the Holy and Blessed One: "I swear by My life that I will nullify My words and confirm yours, as it says: 'When you approach a town to attack it you shall offer it terms of peace' (Deuteronomy 20:10)."[41]

The same idea was taught in a different form:

> "Her ways are pleasant ways, and all her paths, peaceful" (Proverbs 3:17). Everything that was written in the Torah was written in order to establish peace. And even though the Torah contains commands to wage war, those wars, too, were commanded for the sake of peace. You also find that the Holy and Blessed One nullified His decree for the sake of peace. Where? At the time that the Holy and Blessed One said to Moses: "When in your war against a city you have to besiege it a long time in order to capture it . . ." (Deuteronomy 20:19). The Holy and Blessed One told him to destroy them utterly, as it says, "No, you must proscribe them" (Deuteronomy 20:17), but Moses did not do so, but said: Shall I now go and strike down those who sinned along with those who did not sin?! I shall rather offer terms of peace to them, as it says: "Then I sent messengers from the wilderness of Kedemoth to King Sihon of Heshbon with an offer of peace as follows, 'Let me pass through your country'" (Deuteronomy 2:26). Only when he saw that they did not accept the offer did he strike them, as it says: "and we defeated him and his sons and all his men" (Deuteronomy 2:33). Said the Holy and Blessed One: "I said, 'No, you must proscribe them,' and you did not do so. By My life, I shall do just as you said, as it says: 'When you approach a town to attack it you shall offer it terms of peace' (Deuteronomy 20:10)."[42] [32]

"His Thoughts Agreed with God's Thoughts"

Rabbi Ishmael's statement: "Happy is the disciple whose master concedes his words" opens a door to an important approach to the theory of revelation. According to the accepted point of view, revelation only happens through prophecy. And there are two dimensions to prophecy: there is the giving of the Torah from above and the receiving

---

[41] Numbers Rabbah 19:33.
[42] Tanhuma Tzav 3.

---

[32] Tradition always understood the Torah to make a distinction between "obligatory wars" (e.g., the wars of conquest against the indigenous nations of Canaan or the war against Amalek) and "optional (or permitted) wars" (e.g., wars for territorial or economic expansion). This suggests that the distinction between these two was actually *Moses'* innovation.

of the Torah below.[33] Everything is given, everything is spoken, and there is no room for originality. According to the statement of Rabbi Ishmael, Moses had the power to do something below and have the Holy and Blessed One agree from above; that is to say: in addition to revelation through prophecy, which goes from above to below, there is revelation through wisdom, which is a thought revealed below, to which there is then agreement above.

A central principle is embedded in the Sages' words: that knowledge of God's will does not reach human beings only through prophecy. Both prophets and Sages have the great power to do things and have their thoughts agree with the thoughts of the Most High. Yet not all who would like to exploit the Name have permission to do so, and not every person has the merit of having the Holy and Blessed One agreeing with his words. "Happy is the human being whom God acknowledges." The passages about the things that Moses did on his own authority, and "his thoughts agreed with God's thoughts," or "the Holy and Blessed One agreed with him" appear often in Baraitot that emanated from the school of Rabbi Ishmael.[43] And in the exegeses that emanated from the school of Rabbi Ishmael the following assertion is also common: "Happy are those human beings whose words are conceded by God."

This idea was also taught in Amoraic exegeses. According to Rabbi Levi: "All that Moses decreed was agreed to by the Holy and Blessed One."[44] And Rabbi Jonathan said: "How do we know that the Holy and Blessed One retracted and conceded to Moses [who said, according to Rabbi Yannai, 'Master of the Universe, it is only the silver and gold, which you gave the Israelites in such quantity that they had to say "enough,"[34] that caused them to make the calf']? As it says: 'It was . . . I who lavished silver on her, and gold—which they used for Baal'[35] (Hosea 2:10)."[45]

---

[43] See chapter 22 above. Such a concept does appear once in the name of Rabbi Akiva: "The Kohanim bless the Israelites and the Holy and Blessed One ratifies what they say" (BT Hulin 49a).

[44] Deuteronomy Rabbah 5:13.

[45] BT Berakhot 32a.

---

[33] I have translated Heschel's Hebrew phrase *kabbalat ha-torah* as "receiving of the Torah," in order to differentiate it from his translation of the same phrase as "acceptance of the Torah" in *God in Search of Man* (p. 260). Here Heschel intends *kabbalat ha-torah* to denote a passive receipt that he wants to contrast to the Ishmaelian view of the active role of the accepter of the Torah. In *God in Search of Man* he is not describing ancient views but advocating his own (in this case, Ishmaelian) view of revelation.

[34] Rabbi Yannai's exegesis turns on the otherwise obscure reference in Deuteronomy 1:1 to a station in the Israelites' desert travels called *Di Zahav*. He revocalized the word *di* to *dai*, "enough." Since *zahav* means "gold," the unidentified place-name thus was understood as a coded reference to the creation of the golden calf, which was made possible only because God had arranged for the Israelites to get more gold than they could possibly use when they left Egypt. Moses, then, was in this reading accusing God of having supplied the material that made the sin possible, if not inevitable!

[35] Not that the Cannanite deity "Baal" is being identified with the calf made in the desert. It is rather a demonstration that on at least one other occasion, God acknowledged having supplied the Israelites with the instruments of sin.

"See How Great Moses' Power Is"

In contrast to those who said that Moses did not even say a single thing on his own authority, and that even what Moses said to the Holy and Blessed One was said on instruction from the Most Holy, Rabbi Levi emphasized that just as the Holy and Blessed One called to Moses and conversed with him, so did Moses call to God and converse with Him.

> "Then the Lord said to Moses, 'Why do you cry out to Me? Tell the Israelites to go forward'" (Exodus 14:15)—this is what is meant by the verse "You will decree and it will be fulfilled" (Job 22:28). Said Rabbi Levi: Just as the Holy and Blessed One commands Moses and speaks with him, so did Moses command, as it were, the Holy and Blessed One. For so did the men of the tribe of Joseph say to him: "The Lord commanded my lord to assign the land to the Israelites as shares by lot, and my lord was further commanded by the Lord [*tzuvah vadonai*] to assign the share of kinsman Zelophehad to his daughters" (Numbers 36:2). [Do not read "was further commanded by the Lord" (*tzuvah vadonai*), but rather "commanded the Lord" (*tzivah vadonai*).[36]] And just as the Holy and Blessed One calls to Moses and converses with him, so did Moses call to God and converse with Him, as it says: "Moses spoke to the Lord, saying, 'Let the Lord, Source of the breath of all flesh, appoint someone over the community' (Numbers 27:15–16)." See how dominant Moses was! When he saw Pharaoh pursuing the Israelites, he came and cried out, as it says: 'Why do you cry out to Me?' (Exodus 14:15). And God said to him: 'Why are you so agitated?' Said Rabbi Joshua: this is analogous to a good friend of the king who had some troubles, and he came to cry out before the king. Said the king to him: "Why are you crying out? Just issue a decree, and I will do it!" So did the Holy and Blessed One say to Moses: "Why do you cry out to Me?" "Speak, and I will act."[46] [37]

Similarly, Rabbi Abin said that in the incident of Korah "Moses issued decrees to the Holy and Blessed One, and the latter complied." "He said to God: Master of the Universe, 'But if it be a creation that the Lord will create' (Numbers 16:30)—if You have already created a mouth for the earth, well and good; and if not—'the Lord will create'—You must create one now. Said to him the Holy and Blessed One: 'You will decree and it will be fulfilled, and light will shine upon your affairs' (Job 22:28)."[47]

---

[46] Exodus Rabbah 21:2. When Moses besought God to be allowed to enter the Land, he was told: "Don't ask Me about this matter; but about other matters, decree and I shall act" (YS Va-ethanan 820).

[47] Deuteronomy Rabbah 2:3; Numbers Rabbah 18:12.

---

[36] An unusual, but not completely impossible, grammatical construction, requiring no changes of Hebrew consonants whatsoever. The result is a truly audacious reading of Numbers 36:2, in which not only is Moses said to have given God instruction concerning the daughters of Zelophehad and their inheritance, but the tribe of Joseph takes this instruction to God to be common knowledge!

[37] The usual understanding of the story in Exodus 14 is that God told Moses to stop praying and get the Israelites to do something ("speak to the Israelites, and let them go forward"). Here the interpretation is that God told Moses that there was no need for further prayer, since God was prepared

And in another source, it is said: "Moses would issue decrees to God all the time, and God would comply."[48]

A hint of the great power of Moses is also found in the verse, "A righteous man rules, in God's awe" (2 Samuel 23:3). "You find many things that Moses decreed before God, and the latter complied with the decree. For example, it says 'Thus says the Lord: Toward midnight I will go forth among the Egyptians' (Exodus 11:4), whereas the Holy and Blessed One had only said, 'For that night I will go through the land of Egypt' (Exodus 12:12), and yet it says, 'In the middle of the night, the Lord struck down all the firstborn' (Exodus 12:29)—See how great Moses' power is! Of him, Scripture says, 'Mighty creatures, who do his bidding' (Psalm 103:20). To what is this analogous? To a lion that was roaring during the hunt, and the whole world trembled. But one person got near to him, and fed him, gave him drink, and ordered him first to stand up and then to lie down. And as everyone looked at the lion they would say: 'How formidable he is! How magnificent!' But one wise person said to them: 'Don't praise the lion, but say rather how formidable is the power of his attendant, and look how he orders him to stand up and to lie down!' So it is with the Holy and Blessed One, who is called a 'lion,' as it says, 'A lion has roared, who can but fear?' (Amos 3:8). All say: 'See how formidable is His power,' as it says, 'The voice of the Lord is power; the voice of the Lord is mighty' (Psalm 29:4). And all are frightened. But Moses drew near to God, as it says: 'Moses approached the thick cloud where God was' (Exodus 20:18), and even determined when He would stand up and when He would lie down, as it says, 'Advance, O Lord' (Numbers 10:35). This is the meaning of 'A righteous man rules, in God's awe.'"[49] [38]

The Sages of blessed memory reached the summit of boldness in the face of the sacred when they interpreted the expression "Moses, the man of God" to mean that Moses had the kind of relationship to God that a husband has with his wife.[39] "Said Resh Lakish: Had Scripture not said it, we would have been unable to! But just as a man issues decrees to his wife, and she complies, so it was with the Holy and Blessed One—Moses issued decrees, and God complied."[50] This idea was passed on in an even stronger form by Rabbi Judah ben Simon in the name of Rabbi Simeon ben Lakish:

[48] YS Va-ethanan 813.
[49] YS Beha'alotekha 729.
[50] PDRK Ve-zot Ha-Berakhah, Buber ed., p. 198b. TB Berakhah 2 has a different formulation, perhaps out of respect for the divine.

---

to intervene in any way that Moses proposed. He was, in other words, advised to "tell the Israelites to go forward," since God would make that advance possible, in accordance with Moses' wishes.

[38] Yet another stunning analysis of the verses, in which Moses the prophet "civilizes" and "tames" God, and thus brings the ultimate Power safely into the human realm.

[39] The word ish in Hebrew can mean either "man" or "husband," the latter especially when it is conjoined to a proper name or a pronoun following (as in, for example, Genesis 3:6 or 29:32). Thus, ish ha-Elohim can be taken to mean "God's husband."

"Why was Moses named 'the man of God'? Because just as a man has the option of either nullifying his wife's vow or allowing it to stand, as it says: 'Every vow . . . may be upheld by her husband or annulled by her husband' (Numbers 30:14), so did Moses, as it were, say to God: 'Advance, O Lord' (Numbers 10:35), and 'Return, O Lord' (Numbers 10:36)."[51]

In a similar vein did Rava expound the prayer of Moses after the making of the calf: "But Moses implored [vayyehal]" (Exodus 32:11): "Moses released God from the vow. For it is written here vayyehal, and it is written elsewhere, 'He shall not break [yahel] his pledge' (Numbers 30:3)."[52] [40] Again:

> Rabbi Berekhiah said in the name of Rabbi Helbo, who said it in the name of Rabbi Isaac: Moses released the vow of his Creator. How so? For at the time that Israel made the calf, Moses stood to appease God, so that God would forgive them. Said God: Moses, I have already taken an oath: "Whoever sacrifices to a god . . . shall be proscribed" (Exodus 22:19), and an oath, once out of My mouth, cannot be taken back. Said Moses: Master of the World, did You not give me the rules for the nullification of vows? For you said, "He shall not break his pledge" (Numbers 30:3)—which means "he [the one who vows] cannot forgive the oath, but a Sage may forgive it if he is formally asked to do so." And every elder who gives religious instruction and who wishes others to accept his instruction must uphold that instruction himself first. Since You have instructed me about the nullification of vows, it is only right that You get nullification for Your vow, as you instructed me to do for others. Immediately, Moses wrapped himself in his robe and sat as an elder would do,[53] and the Holy and Blessed One stood before him as one who asks release from a vow. And thus does it say: "And I sat on the mountain" (Deuteronomy 9:9) . . . And what did Moses say to God? Stern words. For Rabbi Johanan said: He spoke sternly to God: "Do You then have regrets?!"[41] God said to him: "Yes, I have regrets about the evil that I spoke of doing to my people." At that moment Moses said: "The vow is released, the vow is released! There is no longer a vow or an oath here." That is the meaning of "But Moses implored [vayyehal]"—for Moses nullified the vow of his Creator. . . . Said Rabbi Simeon ben Levi: That is why he is called "the man of God," because he released a vow for God.[54]

---

[51] Midrash on Psalms 90:5.
[52] BT Berakhot 32a.
[53] PT Nedarim 41a stipulates: "One does not ask for nullification of vows while sitting; the one being asked sits and the one asking must stand."
[54] Exodus Rabbah 43:4. In contradistinction to Midrash on Psalms 90:2, the subject here is nullification of a vow by a Sage, not the cancellation of a woman's vow by her husband.

---

[40] The two words vayyehal and yahel have an assonance that is exploited here for the exegetical purpose, even though they are grammatically of different roots.

[41] The expression of regret about a vow taken in the light of unforeseen consequences is a basic requirement in the rabbinic process of nullifying vows. Remember that the idea that a vow may be annulled is entirely a rabbinic—that is, human—construct without any foundation in Scripture, as the Rabbis themselves candidly acknowledged. See chapter 2 above.

No Two Prophets Prophesy
with the Same Symbolism

Said Rabbi Isaac: "A single sign may be given to many prophets, but no two prophets prophesy with the same symbolism." This statement is brought in the midst of a discussion in the Talmud about the scriptural tale (1 Kings 22:6ff.) of how four hundred prophets of Baal all said in the very same words: "March upon Ramoth-Gilead and triumph." The Talmud says that from this King Jehoshaphat understood that their prophecy was not true. He said: "I have a tradition from my grandfather's house, that a single sign may be given to many prophets, but no two prophets prophesy with the same symbolism." That is to say: from the fact that they all prophesied in the identical language, he knew that their words were without substance. It is impossible for two [true] prophets to prophesy with the same symbolism! Each prophet has his own language. And each one transmits his prophecy in his own words.[55] The Maharsha[42][56] explained this along the lines of what is reported about Rav Huna, namely, that when he found witnesses who gave the same testimony in the identical language, he would begin to suspect that they had rehearsed a lie and that it was by mutual agreement that their language matched. He would thus subject them to intense cross-examination. But if they gave the same testimony but the language was not identical, each giving it in his own words, he would not cross-examine them so carefully.[57] [43]

Consider carefully the formulation of the blessing over the Haftarah: "who has appointed good prophets and was pleased with their words, spoken in truth."[58] It does not say "was pleased with His words," but rather "was pleased with their words." The Holy and Blessed One causes the prophets to prophesy, and the prophets then speak their own words in truth. And even that which they speak on their own the Holy and Blessed One agrees with.

In a similar vein did Rava say: "Whatever Ezekiel saw, Isaiah also saw . . . Ezekiel was like a village boy who saw the king . . . while Isaiah was like a city boy who saw the king." And on this Rabbenu Hananel explained: "Ezekiel was like a village boy who saw the king's entourage with its chariots and foot soldiers and he was taken in

---

[55] BT Sanhedrin 89a.   [56] *Hiddushei Aggadot* ad loc.
[57] PT Sanhedrin 21c and 22a.   [58] Tractate Soferim 13.

---

[42] Rabbi Samuel Edels, sixteenth–seventeenth century, Poland.

[43] Maharsha's analogy is an instructive one. The event that the witnesses saw was, after all, a single event. Each witness, however, of necessity sees it and articulates it in a different style. So it is, he says, with the divine word. One is reminded here of Heschel's famous way of expressing, in *God in Search of Man*, chapter 19, the notion that the revelation of the divine word is itself an event requiring interpretation.

amazement, but Isaiah was like a boy from the capital who sees such entourages every day, and he therefore was not amazed by them."[59] [44]

The idea that the prophets from time to time would speak words of their own can be found in a famous passage: "Moses said, 'The great, the mighty, and the awesome God' (Deuteronomy 10:17); came Jeremiah and said: Foreigners are wreaking destruction in God's Sanctuary, so where is God's awesomeness? And so he did not say 'awesome' (see Jeremiah 32:18—'great and mighty God'). Came Daniel and said: Foreigners are enslaving God's children, so where is God's might? So he did not say 'mighty' (see Daniel 9:4—'great and awesome God')." Now the Sages were astonished at this: "How could they have done such a thing, uprooting that which Moses had established?" "Said Rabbi Eleazar: Since they knew that the Holy and Blessed One is all truth, they could not lie about Him."[60]

A Partner in the Writing of the Torah

The issue of whether Moses our Master had a part and a role in the writing of the Torah depends, in my view, on the difference between the schools of Rabbi Ishmael and Rabbi Akiva mentioned above. According to the school of Rabbi Ishmael, Moses our Master did things on his own authority, and when he used the expression "Thus says the Lord,"[45] he occasionally altered God's language and transmitted only the general intent. Yet according to the school of Rabbi Akiva, even in the places where he said "Thus says the Lord," he transmitted God's words without any addition or diminution, and without any stylistic alteration.

According to the approach of Rabbi Akiva, all is in the hands of heaven. The Torah was written and remains in heaven, and Moses our Master had no function but to copy that which was written in Heaven. According to the views of Rabbi Akiva's students, Rabbis Meir and Simeon, the Holy and Blessed One spoke and Moses wrote. Moses' power was just this: that he was the scribe of the Holy and Blessed One. This is how this point of view was explicated: "What is the meaning of 'The Lord spoke to Moses, to say'?—to say to Aaron. From here we learn that Moses spoke only what the Holy and Blessed One had told him. And therefore the Holy and Blessed One said of him: 'Not so with My servant Moses; he is trusted throughout My household.'[46] (Numbers 12:7)."[61]

[59] BT Hagigah 13b; cf. ARN A ch. 47.   [60] BT Yoma 69b.   [61] Tanhuma Tzav 13.

---

[44] That is, Ezekiel's language (in chapter 1 of his book) in describing his vision of God is ebullient, ecstatic, and filled with wondrous imagery. By contrast, Isaiah's language (in chapter 6 of his book) is reverential, to be sure, but comparatively composed and restrained.

[45] As opposed to "This is what the Lord has said . . ."; see chapter 23 above.

[46] That is, trusted to transmit everything with exactitude, unaltered.

Yet we find traces of another standpoint, which understands the word "trusted" differently: "'Write down these commandments' (Exodus 34:27)—the ministering angels began to address the Holy and Blessed One: You are giving Moses permission to write what he pleases! He is liable to tell Israel: 'It is I who gave you the Torah. I wrote it and gave it to you.' Said to them the Holy and Blessed One: heaven forfend that Moses would do such a thing. But even were he to do it, he is still trusted, as it is said: 'Not so with My servant Moses; he is trusted throughout My household'[47] (Numbers 12:7)."[62]

"These very wonderful and astounding words" (so Samuel Jaffe Ashkenazi, the author of Yefe To'ar) are explained in this way by Rabbi David Luria:[48] Moses our Master was the trusted agent of the Holy and Blessed One. And whatever an agent does, he does "by virtue of the power of attorney he has in hand from the One who appoints him." Because of this, it makes no difference whether or not the Holy and Blessed One acts "by Himself or by means of His trustee."[49] This constitutes the high status of Moses. Said the Holy and Blessed One: "Even if Moses does something that I have not instructed him to do explicitly, My presumption is that he does it properly and for My glory. And so I agree to it, for he is wise and can understand much on his own."[63]

It is clear that this explanation does not fit the approach of Rabbi Akiva. An explanation for "he is trusted" in the light of Rabbi Akiva's approach appears in a different source: "'he is trusted'—for he does not subtract anything from my words, and he does not add anything. When he separated himself from his wife, he did not do that on his own authority, but rather by command, and that is why it is written: 'he is trusted throughout My household.'"[64]

Against this, there were Sages who understood the word "trusted" in the sense of a trustee or custodian. At the time that the Israelites stood before the Reed Sea, God said to Moses: "Why do you cry out to Me? Tell the Israelites to go forward" (Exodus 14:15). Said Rabbi Nathan in the name of Abba Jose of Mahoz: "[God said], Haven't I already written: 'He is trusted throughout My household'?[50] You are in My control,

---

62 Exodus Rabbah 47:9.
63 Novellae of David Luria on Exodus Rabbah, ad loc.
64 Midrash Aggadah, p. 104.

---

[47] That is, trusted to act on his own, in God's interests.

[48] Lithuania, nineteenth century.

[49] Here the halakhic principle that "a person's agent is his alter-ego" is applied to Moses as God's agent.

[50] Of course, the verse that God is imagined to be citing here comes from Numbers 12, which is much later in the story than the crisis at the Reed Sea. Yet the chronology is not really important; rather, it is the idea that God conceived of Moses as the divine agent, and that really goes back to the moment of his "call" at the burning bush.

and the sea is in My control, and I have made you a custodian over it."[65] They said: "To what is this analogous? To a king who had many trustees. Each one was in charge of a different piece of property, but one was in charge of them all. So it is here: there is an angel appointed to be in charge of fire, another in charge of the hail, another in charge of the locusts, and Moses had authority over them all. To what else can this be compared? To a wealthy man who bought some land and had the title written in the name of another. They said to him: But he will now claim that the land is his! He said to them: He is trustworthy. So did the Holy and Blessed One create the world from the Torah, and he then called the Torah by the name of Moses, as it says: 'Be mindful of the Torah of My servant Moses' (Malachi 3:22). They said to God: Now Moses will say that he was a partner in the world. Said the Holy and Blessed One: "He is trusted throughout My household.'"[66]

A sign that not all the Sages thought that Moses our Master was, at the time of the writing of the Torah, like a quill in the hands of a scribe, can be seen from the words of "Rabbi Samuel bar Nahman in the name of Rabbi Jonathan: at the time that Moses was writing the Torah, he wrote down the acts of each day [of creation]. But when he reached the verse 'Let us make man' (Genesis 1:26), he said: 'Master of the Universe, why are You giving an opening to the sectarians?'[51] God said to him: 'Write. And those who choose to err, let them err.'"[67]

Three times the Torah mentions the incident at the Waters of Meribah (in Numbers 20:13; 27:14; and Deuteronomy 32:51). In the school of Rabbi Ishmael they said that it was Moses who asked of the Holy and Blessed One: "Let my offense by written in the Torah!" "Write in Your Torah why I am not entering the land." According to this exegesis, Moses our Master had a share in and an influence on the writing of the Torah. However, Rabbi Simeon, the disciple of Rabbi Akiva, disputed this idea and said that the incident was written, repeated, and trebled in the Torah not because of a request by Moses but rather because it is in the nature of the Holy and Blessed One to mention His pain. They analogized this to "a king who was traveling on the road, and his son was with him, riding in one of his carriages. When they reached a narrow pass, the carriage turned over onto his son, and his eye was blinded, his arm was severed, and his leg was broken. And whenever the king would pass by that place, he would say: 'Here is where my son was injured: here is where his eye was blinded, here is where his arm was severed, here is where his leg was broken.' Here too: God men-

---

[65] MI Beshallah 3. In Exodus Rabbah 21:8, it is given in the name of Rabbi Simeon.
[66] YS Beha'alotekha 739.
[67] Genesis Rabbah 8:8; *Menorat Ha-Maor*, 4:408, with minor variations.

---

[51] By saying "us," the Torah would possibly be implying that there is a plurality of divinities—an idea that might have been taken as support for Gnostic ideas of creation. (For other examples of this concern, see BT Sanhedrin 37a and 38a.) Although Moses is ultimately instructed to write down God's intended words, the fact that the colloquy took place at all is apparently enough to suggest to Heschel something other than a straight "dictation model."

tions three times the Waters of Meribah, the Waters of Meribah, the Waters of Meribah. 'Here I killed Miriam, here I killed Aaron, here I killed Moses.'"[68] [52]

At various points in his commentary on the Torah, Rabbi Abraham ibn Ezra writes that "these are Moses's words." For example: "Let us make man in our image, after our likeness" (Genesis 1:26). [That is to say, that this was not God speaking as God was creating humans, but rather this is Moses narrating the story to his contemporaries, telling them that the first human was made "in our image, after our likeness."] Another example: "Abram passed through the land as far as the site of Shechem" (Genesis 12:6). ["This place Shechem was so named by Moses, for Shechem did not yet exist at the time of Abraham."] In these and other examples, could it have been ibn Ezra's intention to tell us that these were words added by Moses on his own authority?[69]

According to the "dictation theory," which we will describe later on, Moses wrote down nothing but that which God spoke to him at the time of the writing. Yet in a late source it is said:

> Why were the marches of the Israelites written? Moses bethought himself: "If I don't write down the various marches from the Exodus from Egypt to the present time, in the future the nations of the world may say that the forty years in the wilderness were without rest, and that they marched constantly, day and night, because they were lost in the desert." So he enumerated all of the marches, so that the nations of the world would know that it is impossible even for a single person to wander aimlessly into all of these places over forty years, let alone 600,000 people, and so that they would know that Israel didn't simply tarry in the wilderness, but that they were there for forty years because of the various things that befell them. That is why Moses wrote down all the marches. But Moses did not know how to enumerate them all, until the Holy and Blessed One hinted to him on the tablets that he brought down from Sinai, for they had forty-two line impressions on them, which suggested to Moses the forty-two marches of the Israelites. And how do we know that the Holy and Blessed One agreed with Moses' plan? Because the text reads: "Moses recorded the starting points of their various marches as directed by the Lord" (Numbers 33:2).[70]

[68] Sifre Pinehas 137; Sifre Va'ethanan 26; Leviticus Rabbah 31:4.

[69] According to Rabbi Moshe Almosnino (Salonika, sixteenth century): "He [ibn Ezra] did not intend, God forbid, to say that Moses our Master, peace be upon him, wrote these things on his own; rather, that God, may He be blessed, would speak and Moses would write. What he meant to say was that God would say the words as if they were from the perspective of the writer. And this seems to me to be the true and correct interpretation of each occasion when ibn Ezra speaks of 'Moses' words.'" See Ben Menahem, "Tosefet Be'ur al Divrei R. Avraham ibn Ezra," *Sinai* 10 (1946): 169.

[70] Midrash Haggadol, beginning of Masei. "Moses recorded the starting points of their various marches as directed by the Lord"—what purpose was there in writing down these marches at the end of Numbers? Each one was already recorded as it happened. Abraham ibn Ezra (according to Abravanel) thought that Moses wrote them down on his own, and that "as directed by the Lord" modified "marches." Nahmanides,

[52] This not only turns its back on the idea that Moses' needs were expressed in the text, but also connects to the strong Akivan idea of God's participation in human pain. See chapters 6 and 7 above.

In a similar vein: "and the tree of knowledge of good and bad" (Genesis 2:9)— "Said Rabbi Pinehas ben Yair: this tree—before the first human ate from it, it was simply called 'a tree'; but after he ate from it, and in so doing violated the decree of the Holy and Blessed One, it became known as 'the tree of knowledge of good and bad.' And Moses in his piety called it 'the tree of knowledge of good and bad' prematurely, because of what would happen to it later."[71]

however, believed that Moses was commanded by God to write them down, and "as directed by the Lord" modified "Moses recorded." See chapter 32 below, "The Torah Given Scroll by Scroll," n. 8.

[71] Genesis Rabbati, 52ff.

פ27

"SEE, HOW GREAT WAS MOSES' POWER!"

Translator's Introduction

This chapter continues the concerns of the previous chapter ("Is the Prophet a Partner or a Vessel?") from another perspective. Though the title specifies Moses, this chapter really deals with the question of all those invested with prophetic charisma and legislative authority in the tradition. What were the personal characteristics that qualified them for such office? And what do these qualifications have to do with whether the prophet (or Sage) merely transmits God's will or has a role in shaping it?

We have two variables here, so there are logically four possible combinations:

(1) Moses (or prophet or Sage) was extraordinary, therefore entitled to add to the Torah or sway God's will. This is the gist of "the righteous decrees, and the Holy and Blessed One fulfills" (see below, pp. 507–9).

(2) Moses is the extraordinary prophet par excellence, yet he is duty-bound to transmit God's will as is, with no alteration. This is apparently the view of Maimonides (see p. 504 below).

(3) Moses is imperfect and all-too-human, yet because God needs a partner in dialogue, God nevertheless selects him and empowers him (and the prophets and Sages after him) to act as God's interlocutor and actually to determine the divine will under certain specified conditions. (See below, pp. 505–7, 509–10, 515–16).

(4) We all (Moses, prophet, Sage, and so on) are imperfect and frail, so we are in need of God to take complete control and provide us with a full, authentic account of the divine will. (See especially chapter 29, pp. 539–42 and 545–48 below, the "dictation theory," "transcription theory," and "divine authorship" theory of the writing of the Torah.)

502

Moses' Stature

O NE WILL NOT UNDERSTAND the talmudic Sages' view of prophecy unless one delves into the hints in their expositions concerning the stature of Moses our Master and his relationship with the Master of the Universe.
The Torah itself stresses Moses' superiority to the other prophets: "Never again did there arise in Israel a prophet like Moses—whom the Lord singled out, face to face" (Deuteronomy 34:10). The Sages said, "All the prophets saw through a dark speculum, but Moses saw through a clear speculum."[1] Moses is called "the Sage of Sages, the greatest of the great, the father of the prophets";[2] "Moses, than whom we have no greater in Israel";[3] "worthy as all Israel";[4] "King of Torah."[5] "No one understood the ways of the Holy and Blessed One as did Moses."[6] He is called an angel,[7] is compared to the ministering angels,[8] and is said to have penetrated to a place in heaven where angels cannot penetrate.[9]

The tradition enumerates eleven persons called "the man of God."[1][10] "When he stood before Pharaoh, he was godlike, but when he fled from Pharaoh, he was only a man. When he was cast into the Nile, he was only mortal, but when he turned the waters to blood, he was godlike. When he ascended to heaven, he was man; when he came back down, he was called godlike. Alternatively, when he ascended to the place where there is no eating or drinking, and he likewise did not eat or drink, he was called godlike, but when he came back down and ate and drank, he was called man. R. Abin said, 'From the middle up he was called godlike; from the middle down he was called man.'"[11]

The Sages sensed the strangeness of this. Rabbi Phinehas said, "It is written, 'You will play the role of God to Aaron' (Exodus 4:16). Was Moses then made Aaron's idol? Rather, this was the Holy and Blessed One's meaning: 'Moses, just as you revere

---

[1] BT Yevamot 49b.
[2] Sifre Pinhas 134–35; Deuteronomy Rabbah 3:10; SER, p. 33; Genesis Rabbah 76:1; YS I,810.
[3] MI Beshalah, introduction.   [4] MI Shirata 1.   [5] Numbers Rabbah 1:3.
[6] Jacob Mann, "Some Midrashic Genizah Fragments," *HUCA* 14 (1939): 317.
[7] YS Va'ethanan 813.   [8] BT Yoma 4b.   [9] Tanhuma Tissa 32.
[10] YS Samuel 91.   [11] Midrash on Psalms 90:5.

---

[1] The others (according to the source in Yalkut Shim'oni) were Elkanah (Samuel's father, from rabbinic interpretation of 1 Samuel 2:27), Samuel (1 Samuel 9:10), David (2 Chronicles 8:14), Shemaiah (1 Kings 12:22), Iddo (identified with the prophet in 1 Kings 13:1–10), Elijah (1 Kings 17:18), Elisha (2 Kings 4–8), Micah (identified with the prophet in 1 Kings 20:13–28 on the basis of 1 Kings 22:9–28), Amoz (father of Isaiah, identified with the prophet in 2 Chronicles 25:7), and Hanan the son of Igdaliah (Jeremiah 35:4).
Scripture does indeed use the phrase "man of God" in all these cases, usually in the sense of "prophet" (i.e., "the man in communication with God"). When the Rabbis apply the term to Moses, they mean something else: "the man with godlike powers."

and obey Me, so shall Aaron revere and obey you.'"[2] 12 Similarly: "Do not get false airs because I called you 'god'; you are only as god to Pharaoh, but don't forget that I am the Lord."13

"'Who is the King of glory?' (Psalm 24:10)—who is the king who imparts glory to His followers? A mortal king does not share his scepter with anyone, but the Holy and Blessed One shared His scepter with Moses, as it says, 'And Moses took the rod of God with him' (Exodus 4:20)."[3] 14

Maimonides accorded extreme praise to Moses our Master: "Moses our Master (peace be his) knew that there was no partition [between himself and God] that he had not removed, and that in him were perfected all ethical and intellectual virtues."15 Inasmuch as "he had completed the ascent from human to angelic status, . . . there remained no curtain which he had not pierced through and penetrated."16 The difference between Moses and the preceding and succeeding prophets was so great, as the Torah testifies (Exodus 6:3; Deuteronomy 34:10) that the very word "prophet" can only be applied to him and to them in a different sense.17 But whereas the Sages went so far as to intimate that by wielding the divine scepter Moses exercised extraordinary *power,* Maimonides spoke only of Moses' extraordinary *intellectual* attainments.[4]

---

12 Song of Songs Rabbah 1:10.   13 TB, Va'era 8.

14 TB, Va'era 7.

15 Eight Chapters (Introduction to Commentary on Mishnah, Avot), chapter 7.

16 Commentary to Mishnah, Sanhedrin, Introduction to chapter 10, Seventh of the Thirteen Principles of Faith.

17 Maimonides, *Guide of the Perplexed,* II:35.

---

[2] Literally, "Just as My reverence is over you, so shall your reverence be over your brother." Compare Avot 4:12 (PB 4:15): "Let the honor of your colleague be as the reverence of your master, and let the reverence of your master be as the reverence of God." Reverence and obedience are intertwined in the relationship of an inferior to a superior.

[3] Of course, by the plain sense, this "rod of God" was an ordinary wooden staff that became temporarily the occasion for displaying God's power. But the midrashist gave it a loftier interpretation.

[4] It is instructive for Heschel's whole Ishmaelian-Akivan schema, that the thought of Maimonides, the greatest Jewish philosopher, does not fit neatly into one or the other side of the polarity. Like Rabbi Ishmael, he denied the preexisting heavenly Torah (chapter 17), denied Moses' ascent to heaven (chapter 18), minimized miracles (chapter 3), and eschewed all concrete essentialist interpretations of the Shekhinah's manifestation (chapter 5). Moreover, in his reinterpretation of the Torah's anthropomorphisms, he took the Ishmaelian method of "the Torah speaks in human language" to unprecedented lengths. Yet he was a maximalist (i.e., an Akivan) in stressing the absolute integrity and authority of the entire written Torah (but not its rabbinic extensions) as both revealed and Mosaic.

We see that here, too, on the question of Moses' personal greatness, Maimonides also took a maximal stance. Why? Perhaps in order adequately to ground his systematic exposition of the Halakhah, given his rationalist method, Maimonides needed *some* strong axioms, and this was a key one for him (in fact, the Seventh of his Thirteen Principles of Faith). He conceived of prophecy as a supremely active process—indeed, the highest achievement of which a human being is capable, requiring perfection of the intellectual, imaginative, and moral faculties. However, philosophically and halakhically, there is

Even Moses Did Not Attain Perfection

The Sages knew and stressed that even Moses' greatness was a gift of grace, and whatever the Holy and Blessed One confers is done out of pure kindness. The Holy and Blessed One said to Moses, "I owe nothing to any creature; by grace do I reward persons who fulfill My commands, as it says, 'I will be gracious to whomever I choose'[5] (Exodus 33:19)." See how even Moses' power is at the whim of the Holy and Blessed One. "Just recently, Moses was giving the orders and the Holy and Blessed One was obeying: 'Advance, O Lord! Return, O Lord!' (Numbers 10:35–36). 'If the Lord brings about something unheard-of . . .' (Numbers 16:30). Now he is begging and pleading to be allowed to enter the land, but is refused. Thus Scripture says, 'The poor man [Moses] speaks beseechingly; the rich man's [God's] answer is harsh' (Proverbs 18:23)."[18]

The notion of human perfection, which made its way into the literature of Israel in the Middle Ages, is an alien growth in the Jewish vineyard, one that bears flowers but no fruit.[6] A person free of any fault, whose life is a luminary without defect,[7] never existed. "For there is not one good man on earth who does only good and does not sin"[8] (Ecclesiastes 7:20).

Even the Prince of the Prophets, whom Maimonides called the most distinguished of mortals, did not achieve either intellectual or ethical perfection. Rav and Samuel said, "Fifty gates of wisdom were created in the world, and all but one were given to Moses, as it says, 'You have made him little less than divine' (Psalm 8:6).[19]

Rabbi Yose ben Halafta already commented that it is not the custom of the Torah to hide the weaknesses and failures of the heroes of the people.[20] In fact, Moses him-

---

[18] YS Va'ethanan 812.   [19] BT Nedarim 38b; Rosh Hashanah 21b.
[20] Genesis Rabbah 7:6.

---

only one right answer on any given issue (another Maimonidean tendency for which he was roundly criticized by RaABaD and others). So the prophet's active participation does not give him carte blanche to arrive at any position he desires, but only to arrive at the predetermined correct position. (This may be why Maimonides did not cite the aggadah of Moses sharing the divine scepter). Objectively, the standard of truth is God's omniscience. Practically, for us, it is the Torah. But for the Torah to have de facto infallible status for us, Moses must have been supremely endowed with moral intellect, in order to be in tune with the dictates of the divine will in all particulars.

[5] NJV: "The grace that I grant," or "I will grant the grace that I will grant" (note).

[6] That is, it is nice to contemplate but provides no useful moral guidance. This is a strong editorial comment by Heschel, interrupting once more the overall objective, evenhanded balancing of opposing points of view. Though he does not mention Maimonides by name, he implicitly condemns here the Maimonidean position cited at the end of the last subsection.

[7] In medieval Ptolemaic-Aristotelian cosmology, the luminaries in the heavens (i.e., sun, moon, planets, stars) were thought to be without defect, unlike material beings in the terrestrial realm. So too is Maimonides' picture of Moses. Likui ("defect") also means "eclipse" (as of the sun or moon).

[8] NJV: "who does what is best and doesn't err."

self requested of the Holy and Blessed One, "Ruler of the Universe! Let the sin that I have committed be recorded!"[21] Similarly, the Sages of the Talmud who were so lavish in their praise of the Prince of the Prophets, did not refrain from relating the improper things that he did.

Jethro's daughters called Moses "an Egyptian" (Exodus 2:19). The Sages took him to task for this and asked, "How did it occur to Jethro's daughters to call him an Egyptian? From this we learn that Moses passed for an Egyptian and hid his Hebrew identity. For this, he was not allowed to enter the promised land." When Moses prayed, "Let me at least be brought into the land after death, like Joseph!" the Holy and Blessed One replied, "When Joseph came to Egypt, he did not hide his origins, but said he was a Hebrew, as it says [the butler reported of Joseph], 'A Hebrew youth was there with us' (Genesis 41:12). Therefore Joseph's remains may be brought into the land [and would be buried at Shechem]. But since you hid your identity in Midian, your bones shall not enter the land."[22] "Whoever acknowledges his land of origin, will be buried in it; whoever denies his land of origin, will not be buried in it."[23]

Rabbi Simeon ben Lakish commented on the maxim "Whoever casts suspicion on honest persons is afflicted in his body" as follows: "Moses complained, 'They will not believe me or listen to me!'[9] (Exodus 4:1). But it was clear to God that the Israelites did in fact believe. The Holy One replied to Moses, 'They are believers, the descendants of believers. They themselves believe, as it is written, "And the people believed"[10] (Exodus 4:31). They are the descendants of believers, as it is written, "[Abraham] put his trust in the Lord" (Genesis 15:6). And as for you, you will one day not believe, as it is written, "Because you did not trust Me . . ." (Numbers 20:12).'[11] How, then, was Moses afflicted in his body? 'The Lord said to him further, "Put your hand into your bosom." He put his hand into his bosom; and when he took it out, his hand was encrusted with snowy scales' (Exodus 4:6)."[24]

When Moses our Master was angry at the Reubenites, he called them "a breed of sinful men" (Numbers 32:14). Therefore his grandson (Jonathan the son of Gershom) became an officiant of Micah's graven image (Judges 18:30). When King David asked him, "How can you, the grandson of such a righteous man, worship an idol?" he responded, "I have a family tradition from my grandfather, 'Sell yourself to strange service [avodah zarah, i.e., idolatry], rather than be dependent on others.' David replied, 'God forbid that he should have said such a thing! Rather, he must

---

[21] YS Va'ethanan 810.   [22] TB, Introduction, p. 134.
[23] Deuteronomy Rabbah 2:8.   [24] BT Shabbat 97a; TB, Metzora 10.

---

[9] NJV: "What if they do not believe in me and do not listen to me?"

[10] NJV: "And the people were convinced."

[11] This refers to the incident at Meribah, where Moses lost his temper with the people, insulting them and striking the rock to produce water. The comment that Moses did not trust the Lord is obscure, but is part of the tradition of Moses' sin for which he was not allowed to enter the Promised Land.

have said, "Sell yourself to service that is strange to you [i.e., ordinary work that you find distasteful], rather than be dependent on others."'"[12] 25

The Righteous Govern God's Actions

The Mishnah tells a story:

> They told Honi the Circle-Drawer, "Pray that it may rain!" He prayed, but it did not rain. What did he do? He drew a circle and stood in the middle of it and declared, "Ruler of the Universe! Your children have turned to me, considering me as a member of Your family. I swear by your great Name, that I will not move from here until You show mercy to Your children!" It started to drizzle. He said, "That's not what I asked for, but for rains such as will fill the cisterns, pits, and caverns!" It started pouring violently. He said, "That's not what I asked for, but friendly rains of blessing and bounty!" The rain fell in proper moderation, until the people left the [lower] city of Jerusalem and went up to the Temple Mount because of the rain. They came and said to him, "Just as you prayed for the rains to come, now pray that they will go away!"[26]

The Patriarch Simeon ben Shetah was irritated at Honi's behavior. He sent word to him: "If you were not Honi, I would put you under the ban. But what can I do to you, seeing how you cozy up to the Almighty, Who then grants your wishes, just as a child cozies up to his father and he grants his wishes! Of you, the verse says, 'Your father and mother will rejoice; she who bore you will exult'!" (Proverbs 23:25).[27]

Despite the Patriarch's criticism, the Sages learned a great lesson from Honi's behavior concerning the divine–human relationship. It is told that the Sanhedrin sent the following message to Honi from the chamber of hewn stones: "'You decree and it is fulfilled; light shines on your path'[13] (Job 22:28)—you decreed from below, and the Holy and Blessed One made it happen from above; through your prayer, you brought bright light to a generation for whom things were dark."[28]

Not only does the Holy and Blessed One bring about fulfillment of the righteous person's decree. The Holy One will even abrogate His own decree in favor of the righteous person's decree.

---

[25] PT Berakhot 13d.   [26] Mishnah Ta'anit 3:8.
[27] Mishnah Ta'anit 3:8.   [28] BT Ta'anit 23a.

---

[12] This midrash plays on two meanings of the word *avodah* ("service")—worship and labor. "Strange worship" is idolatry. "Strange labor" is a distasteful occupation. In typical rabbinic fashion, the Sages interpreted the lapse into idolatry in Moses' family as resulting from an intellectual misunderstanding of a tradition of learning that had been passed down within the family. Because Moses was quick to blame others, he was punished through the disgrace of his progeny.

[13] NJV: "You will decree and it will be fulfilled, and light will shine upon your affairs." The time reference of the Hebrew imperfect tense is flexible to begin with, and all the more so in poetic contexts such as Job.

The Sages established a principle that "the righteous govern the deeds of the Holy and Blessed One," inasmuch as He decreed a decree in the world, and they came and annulled it. Moses made the day night,[14] while Joshua made the night day.[15] Samuel turned the summer to winter,[16] while Elijah turned the winter to summer.[17] Moses turned the sea to dry land,[18] while Elisha turned the dry riverbed into pools of water.[19] Just as the Holy and Blessed One revives the dead, so did Elijah and Elisha.[20] Just as the Holy and Blessed One sweetens the bitter and creates abundance out of scarcity, so did they. The prophets were thus rightly called "men of God"; so too Moses, the father of the prophets, was called "man of God."[29] [21]

It is as if the Ruler of the Universe shared His power with mortals. "The righteous govern, as it were, over that which the Holy and Blessed One governs. The Holy One takes note of barren women, and Elisha took note of barren women."[30]

You will find that not all the Sages accepted this view. In Rabbi Ishmael's school, they established, "'. . . Whose powerful deeds no god in heaven or on earth can equal' (Deuteronomy 3:24)[22]—God's ways are not those of mortals. Among mortals, if one is stronger than another, he overrides his fellow's decree; but who can overturn Yours? Thus it says: 'He is one; who can dissuade Him?' (Job 23:13)."[23] [31]

The view that the Sages could issue a decree and the Holy and Blessed One would carry it out served also as a basis of rabbinic authority. The authority of the Sages is not limited to what they received from the tradition. One is obligated to obey also those decrees which they issued on their own. "A person shall not say, 'I will not obey the injunctions of the elders, for they are not from the Torah.' The Holy and Blessed One says to such a one, 'No, my child, rather obey everything they command you, for

---

[29] Midrash Vezot Ha-berakhah, Batei Midrashot II,120ff.

[30] YS II Samuel 165.

[31] Sifre Pinhas 134.

---

[14] In the ninth plague (darkness), it was dark in daytime (Exodus 10:21–23).

[15] When the sun stood still at Gibeon (Joshua 10:12–13), it was light at a time when it should have been dark.

[16] In Israel, summer is the dry season, and winter the wet season. Samuel called for it to rain in the harvest season, as a warning to the people not to forsake God in pursuit of a monarchy (1 Samuel 12:16–19).

[17] That is, he requested God to withhold rain for three years, including the normally rainy winter season (1 Kings 17:1ff.).

[18] Exodus 14:15ff.

[19] 2 Kings 3:16–20.

[20] 1 Kings 17:17ff.; 2 Kings 4:17ff.

[21] That is, invested with godlike powers. See n. [1] above on the phrase "man of God."

[22] So NJV. The Hebrew is literally a rhetorical question: "What god in heaven or on earth can equal Your powerful deeds?"

[23] The Ishmaelian position in this dispute seems inconsistent with the tendency to favor human initiative in the process of revelation. But two other factors may be taking precedence: the Ishmaelian emphasis on the divine transcendence and the deemphasis of miracles.

it says, "You shall act in accordance with the instructions [Torah] which they give you" (Deuteronomy 17:11). Why? Because the decree is binding on Me as well, as it says, "You will decree and it will be fulfilled" (Job 22:28). For example, when Jacob blessed Joseph's younger son Ephraim before his older brother Manasseh, he reversed their standing. How do we know that Jacob's wish was carried out? When the leaders of the tribes brought their offerings to the Tabernacle, the tribe of Ephraim preceded Manasseh' (Numbers 7:48–59)."[32]

"I Want You to Triumph Over Me!"

R. Kahana said in the name of Rabbi Ishmael according to Rabbi Yose: "Why is it written, 'For the leader,[24] with instrumental music, a psalm of David' (Psalm 4:1)? Sing to the One Who is glad when others are victorious over Him! God's ways are not mortal ways. When a person loses, he is sad. But when the Holy and Blessed One loses, He is glad, as it says, 'He would have destroyed them, had not Moses His chosen one confronted Him in the breach to avert His destructive wrath' (Psalm 106:23)."[33] A similar interpretation: "For the One Who seeks to be bested. The Holy One said, 'When I win, I lose. I won over the generation of the Flood, but I lost. So too with the generation of the Dispersion[25] and the Sodomites—was I not the loser? I won over Jeremiah—did I not lose, that My House was destroyed, and My children exiled? But in the episode of the golden calf, Moses won over Me and I came out ahead. I want you to win over Me!"[34]

It is related that after the Sages decided the halakhah against the view supported by the heavenly voice,[26] the Tanna Rabbi Nathan encountered the prophet Elijah and asked him, "What was the Holy and Blessed One doing at that hour?" Elijah replied, "He was laughing and saying, 'My children have won over Me, my children have won over Me!'"[35]

32 PR 7b; TB, Naso 29.
33 BT Pesahim 119a.
34 PR 168b, 32b. See Deuteronomy Rabbah 5:13.
35 BT Bava Metzi'a 59b. BT Gittin 6b tells of R. Abiathar, of whom it was said that "his Master agreed with him." Why did the concubine in the hill country of Ephraim desert her husband? (Judges 19:2). R. Abiathar said it was because he found a fly in her soup. R. Jonathan said it was because he found another man's hair on her body.
When R. Abiathar met Elijah, he asked, "What was the Holy and Blessed One doing?" Elijah said, "He was studying about the concubine in the hill country of Ephraim."

[24] Hebrew: La-menatzeah. The root n-tz-h has the basic meaning "win, surpass." Hence, it came to be applied to the leader of the Temple choir. The midrashist reverts from this secondary meaning of the word back to the original, taking the pi'el to signify causation, that is, "one who allows others to win."
[25] That is, of the Tower of Babel.
[26] The incident of the Oven of Akhnai (BT Bava Metzi'a 59b), cited at the beginning of chapter 34.

According to the midrash,

> The Holy and Blessed One said, "People should not think they can talk back to Me as Abraham did, and that I should acquiesce.[27] I only acquiesced to Abraham. Why? Because he acquiesced to me. When[28] did he acquiesce to me? When I had promised him, 'It is through Isaac that offspring shall be continued for you' (Genesis 21:12), and then I commanded him, 'Offer him there as a burnt offering' (Genesis 22:2). He was silent for me. So I will be silent for him, even though he directed harsh words at Me: 'Will you sweep away the innocent along with the guilty?' (Genesis 18:23)." Rabbi Judah said, "Vayyiggash indicates that Abraham attacked God as if in war, saying, 'People will say, "This is the Holy One's style, to wreak cruel judgment on people. Just look at the generations—Enosh, the Flood, the Dispersion [and now Sodom]. Will He never abandon this style?" Don't let them talk that way about you!' The Holy One replied, 'What would you have Me do? Let Me show you all the generations that I punished, and I will demonstrate that I did not exact full recompense for their sins, but less. If you think that I acted improperly, teach Me, and I will do as you say from now on.'"[29]36

Elijah on Mount Carmel

Great is the power of the prophets, who can direct their own mind to be in tune with the Divine Mind.[30] This power is given not just to Moses, but to other prophets as well. We find this with Elijah. It is written in the Torah, "If anyone slaughters an ox or sheep or goat . . . and does not bring it to the entrance of the Tent of Meeting to

"So what did He say?"
"He said, 'My son Abiathar says this, My son Jonathan says that.'"
"But is there any doubt in the Divine Mind [what really happened]?"
"The one and the other are the words of the Living God!"
36 Aggadat Bereshit, ed. Buber, 22; TB, Vayera 10; Genesis Rabbah 49:10.

---

[27] Literally, "be silent."

[28] The question "When?" prompts an observation. Abraham acquiesced in the binding of Isaac *after* God acquiesced to Abraham in the matter of Sodom, yet the later event is cited as the motive for the earlier! This midrash implicitly assumes that "there is no chronological order in the Torah." God's acquiescence and Abraham's are timeless archetypes that balance each other and deserve each other.

[29] We skip but summarize briefly Heschel's next subsection. In the battle for Jericho, Joshua commanded the people on the seventh day (presumably the Sabbath): "Do not shout . . . and do not let a sound issue from your lips" (Joshua 6:10). Rav Huna said that they did not even recite the Shema on that day. The Holy One ratified Joshua's decision, by the logic: "My children are in danger, and should I demand that they proclaim My kingship right now?" Here is another case of a divine decree (to recite Shema daily) abrogated by a human (Joshua), and God acquiesces.

[30] Note the reciprocal and paradoxical relationship here. God heeds the decree of the prophet in the exceptional case, because the prophet heeds God's decree as a general rule. Thus the prophet can intuit when an exception is in order to bring about the larger fulfillment of God's will.

present it as an offering to the Lord, bloodguilt shall be imputed to that man" (Leviticus 17:3–4). We learn elsewhere that in the time of the Temple, it was forbidden to offer sacrifices in any other place: "Take care not to sacrifice your burnt offerings in any place you like, but only in the place that the Lord will choose in one of your tribal territories. There you shall sacrifice your burnt offerings" (Deuteronomy 12:13–14). And now Elijah comes and builds an altar on Mount Carmel and sacrifices an offering on it, at the time that the Temple was standing! The Sages expressed astonishment, that Elijah "sacrificed at the time of the prohibition of the shrines!"[31] They saw in this action an example of the principle that "when a prophet tells you to violate one of the mitzvot of the Torah, heed him for the time being," for we are told, concerning a prophet, "him shall you heed" (Deuteronomy 18:15). But the question arises, On what basis did Elijah abrogate a command of the Torah?[32] Was he instructed to do so by the divine word? Or did he issue a temporary decree on the basis of his own reason?

According to one view, Elijah was told in a prophetic communication to build an altar and offer a sacrifice. Thus we read in the midrash, "The Holy and Blessed One said, 'It is I who told him to do it.'" The midrashist brings proof from Elijah's words, "I have done all these things at Your bidding" (1 Kings 18:36). This proves that he acted on the divine word.[37] Maimonides accepted this view.[38]

But we also find another view in this matter. "From where did Elijah learn to act thus in Mount Carmel? From what the Holy and Blessed One said to Jacob: 'A nation, yea an assembly of nations, shall descend from you' (Genesis 35:11)—a descendant of Benjamin is destined to perform an act at the gathering of nations, building an altar at the time when the high places are prohibited, and I [God] accept it. And Elijah was of the tribe of Benjamin."[39] In this utterance, the Holy and Blessed One revealed to Jacob that Elijah was destined to build an altar at a "gathering" when the Israelites were sinning like the "nations."

According to the view that Elijah acted on his own, basing himself on a midrash of

---

[37] Numbers Rabbah 14:1; PT Ta'anit 65d.

[38] Maimonides, Mishnei Torah, *Hilkhot Yesodei Ha-torah* 9:3; *Avodat Ha-melekh* ad loc.

[39] *Midrash Aggadah*, ed. Buber, on Deuteronomy 12:13. See Louis Ginzberg, *Legends of the Jews*, 7 volumes (Philadelphia: Jewish Publication Society, 1909–38), 6:319.

---

[31] *Bamot*—NJV "shrines," NEB "hill-shrines," AV "high places." Throughout the Books of Kings, the kings of Israel and Judah were judged as to whether they allowed worship at shrines other than the Temple at Jerusalem, e.g., 2 Kings 15:4 on Azariah (Uzziah): "However, the shrines were not removed; the people continued to sacrifice and make offerings at the shrines."

[32] This was a real question for the rabbis, since they took the Book of Deuteronomy (which prohibits local sacrifices outside "the place which the Lord will choose") to be of Mosaic origin. However, according to the view of most modern scholars, that Deuteronomy was written in the late monarchic period, Elijah would not have been in violation of this law. Still, regardless of how one views the historicity of this question, the rabbinic midrash on this issue is an important source for their view of the scope of a prophet's authority with respect to Torahitic laws.

a scriptural verse, how could he say, "I acted *according to your word*"?[33] The Tosafists resolved this by saying that Elijah "prophesied to override the ban in the *name* of the Holy and Blessed One, *not* by the Divine Word. . . . He was a prophet who acted on his own, because of the urgency of the occasion. . . . When he said, 'I have acted according to Your word,' he did not mean that the Holy and Blessed One told him to do this, but he was interpreting the verse 'A nation, yea an assembly of nations will proceed from you' to mean [God said to Jacob], 'In time to come, one of your children [i.e., Elijah] will act like the gentiles, that is, sacrifice outside the Temple, and I approve his action.' And since he was a prophet invested with authority, they relied on him, that this verse was speaking of him."[40]

In his commentary on Kings, Gersonides wrote that Elijah did this "on his own, in his confidence that the Lord would perform a miracle by his hand as He did in the case of the lad of Zarephath, as it says, 'But confirm the word of My servant and fulfill the prediction of My messengers' (Isaiah 44:26). Or perhaps the Lord commanded this in order to divert Israel from the great sin in which they were sunk."

R. Isaac Abravanel asked, in his commentary on Kings: If the command to sacrifice in Mount Carmel came from the Lord, why would Elijah have had to approach God in prayer and supplication that He answer him? Abravanel was of the view that the phrase, "I have done according to your word" did not mean that "he did this by divine command, but rather that he did it for the sake of the Divine Name, and for the sake of the Torah, which was God's Word." He based this on Tanhuma Naso 28: "If anyone asks you why Elijah built an altar on Mount Carmel and offered sacrifices there, when the Temple was in existence, tell him that whatever Elijah did, he did *for the sake of* the Holy and Blessed One."[41] In other words: *not* at the divine behest.

Prophecy of the Sages

In the Amoraic period, they distinguished between two kinds of prophecy: prophecy of the prophets, and prophecy of the Sages. Thus said Rabbi Abdimi of Haifa: "From

---

[40] Tosafot on BT Sanhedrin 89b, s.v. *eliyahu*.

[41] Our editions of the Tanhuma (including Solomon Buber's) add the phrase, *u-mippi ha-gevurah* ("and by the divine word"), which evidently was not in Abravanel's version.

---

[33] *Ki-devarekha* (NJV: "at your bidding"). Heschel's question assumes that bringing an original midrashic exegesis of a scriptural verse to support one's innovation does not alter the fact that one did indeed innovate. In n. 2 of the Hebrew edition, Heschel cites the commentators on PT Megillah 72c. *Pnei Moshe* interprets "I acted according to Your word" in the strict sense: the divine word told Elijah there and then, specifically to act as he did. *Korban Ha'edah* interprets the same phrase to mean, Elijah acted according to the midrashic interpretation of Genesis 35:11, which was the divine "word" in question.

Either way, the case of Elijah (as understood by the midrash and commentators) is an important paradigm for rabbinic legal initiative and the use of scriptural verses to support rabbinic innovations.

the day that the Temple was destroyed, prophecy was taken from the prophets and given to the Sages." What was the difference between the prophecy of the prophets and that of the Sages? According to Rashi, the prophecy of the Sages is "the reasoning of the heart which comes to the Sage in prophecy and which is privileged to agree with the Halakhah from Moses at Sinai." Evidence for this was found in respect of Abbaye, Rava, and Rav Ashi, "that each one said his own thing, and it turned out to be identical to what was said in the name of another great authority, or in the name of Rabbi Akiva, or to what was received as a traditional *halakhah* from Moses at Sinai."[42]

How important this kind of prophecy was considered we may see from the words of Amemar: "A Sage is preferred [in authority] to a prophet."

According to one view, the Holy and Blessed One did not command Noah to offer sacrifices, but he did so on his own. The Sages expounded, "Noah built [*vayyiven*] an altar to the Lord" (Genesis 8:20)—What is the meaning of *vayyiven*? [It comes from *binah*, "understanding"]—Noah considered the situation, and thought: Why did the Holy One tell him to bring more of each clean animal into the ark than of the unclean animals?[34] Must it not be for the purpose of offering sacrifices? Immediately, "he took from all the clean animals." This is a case of "instruct a wise man, and he will grow [even] wiser" (Proverbs 9:9)—for a wise person hears a matter, performs it *and adds to it*. Another interpretation: "Instruct a wise man, and he will grow wiser" —*this is Moses*, as it says, "One wise man prevailed over a city of warriors" (Proverbs 21:22)[35]—he learned Torah from the divine mouth, then came and told it to Israel for their benefit and added life for them.[43]

We cited Bezalel as an example of how humans are partners with God in the act of prophecy.[36] Another variant of the story presents it as a debate between Moses, speaking in the name of the Lord, and Bezalel, speaking from the voice of reason.[44]

---

[42] BT Bava Batra 12a-b; Rashi ad loc. "All acknowledge that the Holy Spirit never departed from the Sages. As for the tradition that since the time of the prophets the Holy Spirit has been taken away, this refers to the spirit of prophecy; but the Holy Spirit of wisdom—that a Sage's reason should agree with the Halakhah from Moses at Sinai, or R. Abiathar should agree [with the Holy One]—this has not ceased, and only an Epicurean would deny this" (R. Hayyim Halberstam, Responsa *Divrei Hayyim*, YD 104; see A. J. Heschel, "On the Holy Spirit in the Middle Ages," in *Alexander Marx Jubilee Volume*, ed. Saul Lieberman (New York: Jewish Theological Seminary, 1950), Hebrew section, pp. 179ff.

[43] Exodus Rabbah 50:2, Tanhuma Vayakhel 6.

[44] "'Instruct a wise man, and he will be wiser'—this is Bezalel, when the Holy and Blessed One told Moses to construct the Tabernacle. Bezalel asked, 'What is the purpose of this Tabernacle?' Moses replied, 'To house the Torah and teach it to Israel.' Bezalel asked further, 'Where will the Torah be placed?' Moses replied, 'Once we make the Tabernacle, we will make the ark.' Bezalel said, 'Not so! We should first make the ark, and then the Tabernacle'" (Tanhuma Vayakhel 6; Exodus Rabbah 50:2).

---

[34] Seven pairs of each clean species, as opposed to one pair of each unclean species (Genesis 7:2).

[35] See the rabbinic use of this verse in connection with Moses' ascent to heaven to receive Torah, cited above, p. 346.

[36] See chapter 26, "A Partner in the Act of Prophecy."

The idea that through reason a person could reconstruct what the Holy One said to Moses at Sinai was suggested to Rav Huna by the verse "Bezalel . . . did all that the Lord had commanded Moses" (Exodus 38:22). "It does not say, 'that which Moses commanded Bezalel,' but rather 'that which the Lord commanded Moses.' Even those things which Bezalel did not hear from his master, his reason agreed with what was said to Moses at Sinai."[45] Rabbi Johanan, in the name of Rabbi Benayah, applied the same reasoning to Joshua (based on Joshua 11:15: "he left nothing undone of all *that the Lord had commanded Moses*"). He then added: "'The Torah of truth was in his mouth . . .'[37]—referring to those things he heard from his master's mouth; 'and nothing mistaken was on his lips' (Malachi 2:6)—even those things which he did *not* hear from his master were correct." The Sages added, "'For the Lord will be your trust' (*be-kislekha*)—even matters in which you are ignorant (*kesil*)"[38][46] (Proverbs 3:26).

When the Sages struggle to analyze a matter, in order to lay it out with perfect clarity, the result is that they understand it as it was told to Moses at Sinai. "Every matter that the members of a court give their whole soul to, is established as it was said to Moses at Sinai."[47]

When Rabbi Tarfon heard Rabbi Akiva expound a halakhic matter, he said, "Even though I heard this tradition, I could not explain it. You deduced it through exegesis, and it agrees with what I heard!"[39][48] And on another occasion he said, "By the Temple service! You did not prove false. Happy are you, Abraham, that your line has produced an Akiva. Tarfon saw it and forgot; Akiva deduced it exegetically, and it agrees with the *halakhah*. Whoever parts from you, parts from his life!"[40][49]

---

[45] PT Peah 15b, Shabbat 3d.   [46] PT Peah 15b, Shabbat 3d.
[47] PT Peah 15b.   [48] Sifra Vayikra 6b; BT Zevahim 13a.   [49] Sifre Beha'alotekha 75.

---

[37] NJV: "Proper rulings were in his mouth, and nothing perverse was on his lips."

[38] The last remark is puzzling. It plays on the variant meanings of the word *kesel:* "confidence [in the good sense], false confidence, stupidity." If it were understood to mean that the Sage's authority is to be heeded because of his charisma, even when he is wrong, it would undercut the whole thesis that right is on the side of reason, which agrees with God's word. It probably means rather that one possessed of a powerful enough reason can arrive theoretically at the right conclusion, even when he is not privy to all the relevant facts.

[39] Rabbi Tarfon had learned that the requirements of sprinkling the blood of the sacrifices were somehow more stringent than those of receiving the blood. Akiva deduced on his own exactly what those stringencies ought to be, whereupon Rabbi Tarfon remembered that these were what he had learned.

[40] Akiva said a blemished priest could not blow the trumpet as part of the Temple sacrificial service. Tarfon countered that his own brother had done exactly that. Akiva suggested that maybe Tarfon's brother had blown the trumpets on nonsacral occasions, such as calling the people together on the holy days. Tarfon searched his memory, and indeed, Akiva, who had not been there, had deduced the correct nuances of Temple etiquette from a close reading of the Torah law.

The point of these observations is that truth is one, whether one gets it from reliable tradition or the power of human reason analyzing God's law. Thus, a brilliant reasoner like Bezalel or Rabbi Akiva is able to arrive at the truth by power of analysis. The proof is that when Akiva's conclusions are tested by comparison with tradition, they agree.

The Power of the Court

The words that the Sages utter are spoken also on high; that is, "prophecy" refers equally to the giving of Torah on high and the reception of Torah below. The "wisdom of the Sages"[41] refers to the revelation of truth below and assent on high. "Arousal of the upper realms depends on initiation from below."[50]

The Sages emphasized the great power of the court. According to Rabbi Joshua Deromaya, "Three things were enacted by the terrestrial court and ratified by the heavenly court: reading the scroll of Esther, using the Divine Name in greeting, and bringing tithes [to the Temple]."[42] [51] Proclaiming the new month is entrusted to the terrestrial court, and Heaven follows what is decided on earth.[43] The ministering angels asked the Holy and Blessed One, "When do You make the holidays? It is written, 'This sentence is decreed by the Watchers [i.e., us]'!" (Daniel 4:14). God replied, "You and I will assent to Israel's decision to declare a leap year." The Holy and Blessed One said to Israel, "In the past, it was in My hands, as it says, '[God] made the moon to mark the seasons' (Psalm 104:19). But from now on, it is entrusted to your authority to declare yes or no, as it is written, 'Ha-hodesh ha-zeh lakhem—this new moon is [entrusted] to you'[44] (Exodus 12:1)."[52]

The Holy and Blessed One descends from the heights to imbue the lower realm with the Shekhinah, in order to enlighten them in their halakhic deliberations.

"Happy is the people who know the joyful shout"[45] (Psalm 89:16). Rabbi Abbahu interpreted this scripture as referring to the five elders at the time they meet to deliberate the declaration of a leap year. What does the Holy and Blessed One do? He leaves His heavenly Senate and makes the Divine Presence rest among them. At that moment, the ministering angels proclaim, "Hail, O Divine! Hail, O Mighty! Hail, O

---

[50] Zohar I, 86b (see also I, 77b). The Zohar gives examples of God responding supportively when Abraham took the first move, either in leaving Ur or starting out to rescue his nephew Lot.

[51] PT Berakhot 14c; BT Makkot 23b in the name of Rabbi Joshua ben Levi.

[52] Exodus Rabbah 15:2.

---

[41] *Hokhmah* ("wisdom") in Hebrew is etymologically related to *hakhamim* ("the Sages"), a relation that does not exist in English. Here Heschel uses the single word *hokhmah* to refer to the Oral Torah, which is foreshadowed in the ode to Wisdom in Proverbs 8 (see chapter 17) but is instantiated in the traditions of the Rabbis.

[42] Instead of distributing the levitical tithe directly to the Levites in the provinces.

[43] For instance, Heaven holds one responsible to observe the holidays as they fall out, based on the court's determination of the calendar. Or, once the rabbinic court sets the New Year, God judges the world on that day (see below).

[44] NJV: "This month shall mark for you [the beginning of the months]."

[45] *Teru'ah* generally means "shouting" in Scripture, but in rabbinic Hebrew it came to mean "blowing the shofar (ram's horn)." The midrashist here understands it either as the shouting of the angels, or the blowing of the shofar on the New Year as correctly dated by the rabbinical court.

Truthful One!" Of Him is written, "God revered in the council of the holy, great and feared among all His attendants" (Psalm 89:8)—He leaves His senate and descends to make the Divine Presence rest on the lower realm. Why go to such lengths? So that if the Sages err, the Holy and Blessed One will enlighten them in their deliberations.[53]

According to one view, a miraculous light would appear in the dark of night, by which they would know that the Holy One agreed with them, as it says, "A light shone in the darkness for the upright" (Psalm 112:4) and "I call to God Most High, to the God who decides[46] with me"[54] (Psalm 57:3).

R. Hoshaya said,

> According to the custom of the world, when a mortal king enacts a decree and his senate seeks to annul it, they cannot. They must carry out the king's decree whether they wish it or not, while the king may carry it out or annul it as he sees fit. But the Holy and Blessed One carries out whatever the terrestrial court decrees. When? On Rosh Hashanah. When the Sanhedrin sits in session and decides, "We shall proclaim Rosh Hashanah on the second day of the week," the Holy One immediately convokes the angelic Sanhedrin and instructs them, "See what they have enacted down there!" They reply, "Ruler of the Universe! They have decided that the New Year shall be on Day X." Then the Holy One sits in session on that day and judges the world, as it says, "God ascends amid acclamation, the Lord, to the blasts of the horn" (Psalm 47:6). The thrones are set out, the books are opened, and the Sanhedrin sits with him, as it says, "Thrones were set in place, and the Ancient of Days took His seat" (Daniel 7:9). Some argue for innocence, some argue for guilt—why? Because "it is a law for Israel, a ruling of the God of Jacob" (Psalm 81:5)— that is, that day which Israel legally declares to be the New Year is binding also on the God of Jacob, who abides by their decree. Thus, "I call to God Most High, to the God who decides with me" (Psalm 57:3) who ratifies the decision of Israel.[55]

---

[53] Leviticus Rabbah 29:4.
[54] Exodus Rabbah 15:20.
[55] Midrash on Psalms 84:4. The same thought is expressed in Mishnah Rosh Hashanah 2:9: "'These are the set times of the Lord' (Leviticus 23:4)—whether you proclaim them in the right or the wrong time, I have no other festivals but these."

---

[46] NJV: "to God who is good to me." The traditional Hebrew reading gomer ("finish, decide") is puzzling; the variant reading gomel ("do good") is preferred by modern scholars. But the midrashist put the traditional Hebrew version to good use.

28

MOSES' PROPHECY

Translator's Introduction

The current chapter again presents what may seem at first reading to be a series of miscellaneous observations on Moses' prophecy, and prophecy in general. They are best considered in light of the transcendent/immanent dichotomy that Heschel described in chapter 1–16. Given that prophecy is a process transacted between the divine and the human, one asks, Which prophetic traits bespeak its divine nature, and which bespeak its human nature? In what respects does it appear perfect, transcendent, necessary, and immutable? In what respects does it appear imperfect, all-too-human, contingent, and variable?

"Mouth to Mouth"

THE TORAH SAYS, "With him I speak mouth to mouth" (Numbers 12:8). The divine utterance is described thus in the Tannaitic literature: "From the mouth of the Holy and Blessed One to Moses' mouth."[1] Similarly: "'If you will listen to the *voice*[1] of the Lord your God diligently' (Exodus 15:26)—this refers to the Ten Commandments which were given mouth to mouth in ten utterances (voices)."[2] The Amora Rabbi Abbahu pondered this matter. Moses had said, "I have never been a man of words . . . for I am slow of mouth[2] . . ." whereupon "the Lord said to him, 'Now go, and I will be with your mouth[3] and will instruct you [*ve-horeitikha*] what

---

[1] Genesis Rabbah 1:11.   [2] MI Vayyassa 1.

---

[1] So literally in the Hebrew. NJV translates more in accordance with English idiom: "If you will *heed* the Lord your God diligently. . . ."

[2] So literally. NJV: "slow of speech."

[3] So literally. NJV: "I will be with you as you speak."

to say" (Exodus 4:10–12). Rabbi Abbahu understood *ve-horeitikha* from the root *yarah* ("to shoot"): "I will shoot My words into your mouth like an arrow."[3] By this view, the divine utterance went into Moses' mouth and directly out again.

Moses' prophecy is distinguished by two attributes: "With him I speak *mouth to mouth*" (Numbers 12:8) and "The Lord would speak to Moses face to face" (Exodus 33:11). The Sages saw a difference between these two attributes and said that the divine word came to later prophets "mouth to mouth," but God spoke "face to face" only to Moses. "I will raise up a prophet for them from among their own people, like yourself: I will put My words in his mouth and he will speak to them all that I command him" (Deuteronomy 18:18)—I put My words in the prophet's mouth, but I do not speak with him face to face."[4]

The Amoraic midrashim describe how the divine word came to Moses' ear. According to R. Judah bar Simon, "he was standing, and the Word came to his ear as through a pipeline, while the other Israelites heard nothing. But when Moses' face would redden, they would know that the Word was coming to him."[5] According to the school of Rabbi Akiva, Moses would enter the Tent of Meeting, and "a kind of jet of fire would descend from heaven to between the cherubim, and he would hear the voice speak to him within."[6] These midrashim depict Moses' hearing God's voice as a sensory, auditory perception.[4] For example, this exegesis: "'To speak with you' (Exodus 29:42)—the Word will come to you but not to the people generally. One might think that even though the people did not hear the words, they at least heard a sound? No; it says, *kolo* (= *kol lo*).[5] The sound came to him alone; Moses and no one else heard the sound."[7]

Not only did the holy spirit rest on them while receiving the divine word, but "when the prophets went about on mission from the Holy and Blessed One, the holy

---

[3] Exodus Rabbah 3:15, citing Exodus 19:13 as an example where *yarah* has this meaning.

[4] Sifre Shofetim 176; Midrash Tannaim p. 122.

[5] PR 22a; Numbers Rabbah 12:1. According to Numbers Rabbah 14:21, not even the angels heard God's utterance to Moses.

[6] Sifre Zuta p. 254 (end Naso); Numbers Rabbah 14:19.

[7] Sifra 4a.

---

[4] Apart from the issue of whether Moses' hearing God's voice was a sensory-auditory phenomenon (according to R. Judah bar Simon and Sifre Zuta) or a mental intuition (according to Maimonides), there is the question of the prophet being singled out to hear the divine word. Even if we dismiss the picture of a fiery pipeline from heaven to Moses' ear as fanciful, R. Judah bar Simon invites us to ponder the fact that some people, more than others, seem radically in tune with a transcendent message, while their fellows around them hear nothing.

[5] A play on *kolo* ("His [i.e., God's] voice"), which sounds like *kol lo* ("a voice to him [i.e., to Moses]"). The reference seems to be to Deuteronomy 4:36—an audacious interpretation, since the plain sense of that context seems to be that all Israel heard the voice at the Sinai theophany. Moses heard the voice, but no one else heard the voice.

spirit would rest on them, giving them a fearful aspect; whoever saw them would be in awe of them, for they were like angels."[8] [6]

According to another source, "when the Holy and Blessed One taught him Torah, Moses got his radiant aura from the sparks projected by the Shekhinah."[9]

From the Divine Mouth

Many terms were used to describe the act of prophecy: "from the mouth of the Power," "from the mouth of the Holiness,"[7] "from the Mouth of the Holy and Blessed One," "from the mouth of the Shekhinah,"[8] "from the mouth of his Creator." But these do not always imply verbal communication. Sometimes they connote divine love. "Moses died there by the mouth of the Lord"[9] (Deuteronomy 34:5)—by a divine kiss. This teaches that the death of Moses was from the Holy Mouth.[10] . . . The death of Aaron was similarly by the Holy Mouth."[10] "Because the Holy One loved him, He gave him knowledge and understanding from the Divine Mouth."[11]

Other expressions were also used to refer to revelation. "The Holy and Blessed One *taught* Torah to Moses."[12] "Who knows the *meaning* of a thing—this refers to the Holy and Blessed One who *expounded* Torah to Moses.[13] "Moses *received* Torah at Sinai."[14]

---

[8] Numbers Rabbah 10:5.   [9] Tanhuma Tissa 37.   [10] Midrash Tannaim, p. 225.
[11] TB, Tissa 10.   [12] Midrash on Psalms 18:29.   [13] Ecclesiastes Rabbah on 8:1.
[14] Avot 1:1.

---

[6] Indeed, the Greek *angelos*—like the Hebrew *mal'akh*—means "messenger." The term is occasionally used in the Bible in a context in which it appears to refer to human beings on mission from God. See, for instance, Judges 2:1–3, which the Targum, Rashi, and Gersonides interpret as referring to a prophet.

Heschel describes here the sense of charismatic presence projected by the prophet, whether because of the divine word he received or because people respect the special role he has in carrying out the divine plan.

[7] *Ha-gevurah* ("the Power") and *Ha-kodesh* ("the Holiness") are (like "the Divinity" in English, or "*die Gottheit*" ["the Godhead"] in German) examples of abstract nouns used to denote God. Indeed, the commonest rabbinic term for God is derived from one of these. *Ha-kadosh barukh hu* (which we have generally translated "the Holy and Blessed One") was probably originally *ha-kodesh barukh hu*, "the blessed Holiness." The Aramaic equivalent *kudsha berikh hu* is familiar to traditional Jews from the daily Kaddish prayer. This is but one more indication that already in the rabbinic period, before medieval philosophy, the Sages intuited behind the homey persona of God in the midrashim an ineffable, indescribable, supernal reality.

[8] Literally, "the Indwelling"—another abstract term in the lexicon of divinity. See chapters 5–6, above.

[9] So literally. NJV: "at the command of the Lord." But the midrash picks up on the Hebrew word *pi* ("mouth") and learns from this that Moses died by a divine kiss.

[10] *Mipi ha-kodesh*, literally "from the mouth of the Holiness." It is nearly universal practice to translate such Hebrew phrases into the more idiomatic English adjectival phrase pattern, e.g., "the holy Mouth."

"Moses ascended heaven and approached the dark cloud. He became as the angels and spoke with God face to face, and *received* Torah *from the hand* of the Holy and Blessed One."[15]

This saying was cited in derivative form by the Amora R. Menahem ("son of the saints"), son of Rabbi Simlai: "There were two things, which when the kings of the nations heard them from the mouth of the Holy and Blessed One,[11] they stood up from their thrones and praised Him—"whoever misappropriates the sacred things, shall make restitution" (Leviticus 5:16), and "Honor your father and your mother" (Exodus 20:12).

Once, on a rainy day, the Sages did not come to the meeting house. There were children there who said, "Let us make up the council.[12] What is the meaning of the two forms of the letters *mem, nun, tzadei, peh, kaf?* It means, from speech to speech, from faithful to faithful, from righteous to righteous, from mouth to mouth, from hand to hand.[13] 'From speech to speech'—from the speech of the Holy and Blessed One to the speech of Moses. 'From faithful to faithful'—from the Holy and Blessed One (who is called 'God, Faithful King') to Moses (of whom it is said, 'he is faithful in all My household' [Numbers 12:7]). 'From righteous to righteous'—it is said, 'the Lord is righteous in all His ways' (Psalms 145:17), and of Moses it is said, 'He performed the Lord's righteous works' (Deuteronomy 33:21). 'From mouth to mouth'—from the Holy One's mouth to Moses' mouth. 'From hand to hand'—from the Holy One's hand to Moses' hand." These students graduated, and became great Sages in Israel.[16]

Not through an Angel(?)[14]

First and always, the Sages taught, "Moses received Torah at Sinai not from an angel, nor from a seraph, but from the Supreme King of Kings, the Holy and Blessed One."[17]

---

[15] Tanhuma Va'ethanan 6.   [16] Genesis Rabbah 1:11; PT Megillah 71d.   [17] ARN B 1.

[11] The midrash comments on Psalm 138:4: "All the kings of the earth shall praise You, O Lord, for they have heard the words You spoke" (literally, "the words of Your mouth"). The implication is that even though the communication was indirect—the gentiles hearing only second hand the revelation given to Israel—it is still referred to as being "from the mouth of the Holy One."

[12] So the sources read. Heschel's text reads: "Let us deal with *tzofim.*" This is the word suggested to the Sages by the acronym *MNTzPK,* and means "prophets." The correspondence between form and content is characteristic of the play of midrash.

[13] These five letters are written in one form in the middle of a word and in another form at the end of the word. The duplication is explained that they stand for five correspondences between God and Moses in the act of revelation. The Hebrew words suggested by the letters are *ma'amar* ("speech"), *ne'eman* ("faithful"), *tzaddik* ("righteous"), *peh* ("mouth"), *kaf* ("hand"). The last three are the words approximating the names of the letters themselves.

[14] Though Heschel added no question mark in the Hebrew title, he well might have, for the majority of this chapter cites views that Moses indeed received revelation at times through angelic interme-

"'The Lord spoke to Moses, saying [*lemor*]':[15] (Exodus 31:12)—not through an angel or a messenger."[18] "'With him I speak mouth to mouth' (Numbers 12:10)—this teaches that Moses' prophecy was not through an angel."[19] Not only Moses our Master but the following prophets as well received their words from the divine mouth, not from an intermediary.

Ezekiel was the first in whose prophecy there participates "a man who shone like copper" (Ezekiel 40:3). Zechariah, who came after him, would receive his visionary words from "the angel who talked with me" (Zechariah 1:9). Still, neither Ezekiel's "man" nor Zechariah's "angel" appeared in the place of God or next to God. It is a distinguishing mark of apocalyptic literature that the visionary hears words not from God but from an angel. The angel mediates between God and mortals. Moreover, the notion was conceived that even the prince of the prophets received Torah from an angel. The Book of Jubilees portrays the revelation that Moses our Master received from the Angel of the Presence.[16]

This idea, which has no basis in the Torah, became an obstacle and stumbling block over the generations. The sectarians plagued Israel with the taunt, "You received the Torah through the mediation of angels; it was an angel who spoke to Moses on Mount Sinai; the Torah was composed by angels and go-betweens."[20] [17]

But despite the strangeness of this approach and its vulnerability to distortion, the later Sages were not loath to teach, "From the day that the Holy and Blessed One appeared to Moses, He appeared through an angel, as it says, 'An angel of the Lord appeared to him in a blazing fire out of a bush' (Exodus 3:2)—this is Michael."[18] 21

"When Moses stood in heaven, Yefefiah, Angel of the Torah, handed him the Torah, fully prepared and wrapped."[22] The same idea is found in a later source: "Yofiel, Angel of the Torah, was Moses' teacher. This is the meaning of '[he] would

---

[18] MI Shabbeta 1.

[19] Sifre Zuta p. 276.

[20] See Acts 7:38, 53; Galatians 3:19. See also Louis Ginzberg, *Eine unbekannte jüdische Sekte* (New York/Hildesheim: G. Olms, 1972), 246–49.

[21] *Aggadat Bereshit*, 32.

[22] *Ma'ayan ha-hokhmah*, Beit Ha-Midrash I, 61; "Book of Enoch," Beit Ha-Midrash II, 166.

---

diaries. The discussion may suggest questions of relevance even for disbelievers in traditional angelology: Is all revelation of divine truth direct from the Source, or may it come at times from hidden and unexpected out-of-the-way sources?

[15] The Hebrew *lemor* is used always in Scripture to introduce the actual words spoken, whether by God or by an ordinary person.

[16] Who was identified with Enoch. See above, chapter 18, pp. 347–50, and Hayyim Vital's identification of Enoch with the angel Zagzagel below.

[17] This idea is reflected, though without a hint of disparagement, in Acts 7:38, 53. In Galatians 3:19, Paul cites the angelic promulgation of the law to question its complete validity.

[18] The term "angel" in the narrative of the burning bush is curious. It may refer to the flame itself, as a created manifestation of God's presence.

answer him in a voice' (Exodus 19:19)—through him, Moses learned Torah."[23] "Michael said of Moses, 'I was his teacher, and he was my student.'"[24]

The Babylonian Talmud tells, "A certain sectarian asked Rav Idit, 'The Torah says, "*He* said to Moses, 'Ascend to the Lord'"'! (Exodus 24:1). If it was God talking, why didn't it say, 'Ascend to *Me*'? He replied, 'This refers to the Angel Metatron, whose name is like his Master's.' According to the Jerusalem Targum, Michael, the Angel of Wisdom, said to Moses, 'Ascend to the Lord.'"[25]

Nahmanides interpreted R. Idit's remark to mean: "The Lord said to Moses, 'Ascend to Metatron [who is called by My name YHWH].'" R. Idit replied to the sectarian "that the scripture was referring to the angel who showed Israel the way on the earth. But Moses replied that we would not accept him even in the capacity of guide, as it says, 'If Your Presence does not accompany us,[19] do not make us leave this place' (Exodus 33:15)—we accept no emissary except for the Divine Name."

R. Abraham ibn Ezra interpreted Exodus 24:1: "The Lord said to Moses, 'Ascend to the Lord.'" He laid stress on the principle, "The Lord would speak to Moses face to face, as one man speaks to another" (Exodus 33:11)—"not through the agency of an angel, but Moses would speak directly with the Primal Creator."[26] Maimonides thought similarly. "'Face to face' means each one present to the other, without intermediary."[27] "For every prophet would hear the utterance through the mediation of an angel, except Moses."[28]

In later generations, these hesitations ceased. R. David ibn Zimra[20] commented on Maimonides' statement (that the term "seeing" with respect to God refers not to actual seeing, but intellectual apprehension[29]): "Moses would hear the voice proceeding from the Supreme Glory through the Interpreter, and the Interpreter would explain to him the purport of the voice." When Moses requested, "Oh, let me behold Your Presence" (Exodus 33:18), he was asking that he have no need of the Interpreter. This was not impossible, considering Moses' level of attainment. But the answer was, "You cannot see My face, for man may not see Me and live" (Exodus 33:20)—that is, no person can attain this level and remain alive, for at the instant that one attains this level, his soul will become attached there and will not separate, for this love is strong as death (Song of Songs 8:6), and the Israelites were still in need of Moses.[30]

---

[23] *Me'orei Or* of R. M. Papars, entry *kol* (possibly referring to *Me'orei Or* of R. Meir Bikayam [eighteenth century, Smyrna]).

[24] Deuteronomy Rabbah 11:6.

[25] BT Sanhedrin 38b; see also Genesis Rabbati, p. 28.

[26] Abraham ibn Ezra on Exodus 24:1; 33:23.

[27] Maimonides, *Guide of the Perplexed,* 1:37.

[28] Ibid., 2:45.

[29] Ibid., 1:4.

[30] RaDBaZ, Responsa 1615.

---

[19] NJV: "Unless You go in the lead . . . ."

[20] Sixteenth century, Egypt; halakhic authority and kabbalist.

Rabbi Nathan bar Samuel the Physician[31] interpreted, "Then [one] said to Moses, 'Ascend to the Lord'" (Exodus 24:1) as follows: "The Active Intellect said to Moses, 'Ascend through your well-formed thought to the Lord.'"[32] And the author of *Meor Ha-afelah*[21] wrote, "Scripture calls the divine effluence which reaches the prophet's intellect from the Active Intellect directly, without mediation of an angel, 'face to face.'"[22] [33]

R. Hayyim ibn 'Attar[23] interpreted similarly: "'He would hear the Voice addressing him' (Numbers 7:89)—as we wrote elsewhere, from the utterance which proceeded from the Lord was formed an angel, which would speak to the prophet. This is how I have interpreted every occurrence of the word *lemor*[24] in connection with divine communication. Here, too, the 'voice' speaking to him refers to a voice created for the purpose by the Holy and Blessed One."[34]

Views were preserved that Moses received various things from angels. "Moses' prayer was a variant of the Divine Name which he learned from Zagzagel, the rabbi and scribe of the heavenly realm."[35] And R. Hayyim Vital[25] wrote, "Know that when Enoch died [*sic!*], he was at a higher level than Moses, for he was Moses' teacher; he is the angel Zagzagel. He attained the level of *hayyah*, but Moses only attained *neshamah*. But the Messiah will achieve *yehidah*."[26] [36]

"Our Rabbis said that when Moses ascended to heaven, he heard the ministering angels saying to the Holy and Blessed One, 'Blessed be the Name of His glorious kingdom forever,' and he brought this formula down to Israel."[37] He also got from the Angel of Death the secret for offering incense to stop the plague, and to stand between the living and the dead. This idea is very surprising and is apparently based on a difficulty that the Sages sensed in the Torah's narrative of Korah. After the death of Korah and his company, the Israelites railed against Moses and Aaron, saying, "You two have brought death upon the Lord's people!" The Lord announced to Moses, "Remove yourselves from this community, that I may annihilate them in an

---

[31] Fourteenth century, Spain.
[32] Selected sermons (Leghorn, 5590/1830), Mishpatim.
[33] *Meor Ha-afelah* Ki Tissa, p. 286.
[34] *Or Ha-hayyim* on Numbers 7:89.
[35] Deuteronomy Rabbah 11:10; Beit Hamidrash I, 124.
[36] *Likkutei Torah* (Vilna, 5640/1880), 19a. Compare to the passage in the "book of Enoch" (Beit Hamidrash II, 116) about Metatron, "Angel of the Torah," who revealed secrets to Moses.
[37] Deuteronomy Rabbah 2:36; ed. Lieberman, p. 68.

---

[21] Nathanel ben Isaiah, thirteenth century, Yemen.
[22] But the Active Intellect is itself a mediating agent!
[23] Eighteenth century, Morocco, Italy, Israel.
[24] "[The Lord spoke to Moses] saying . . ."
[25] Sixteenth century, Safed; major propagator of Lurianic kabbalism.
[26] Evidently, *neshamah* ("soul"), *hayyah* ("living being," also a species of angel), and *yehidah* ("unique entity") are three successive levels of spiritual attainment in Vital's exposition of the Lurianic kabbalah.

instant." Moses immediately directed Aaron to take a fire pan, with fire from the altar and incense, to take to the community to make expiation for them, "for wrath has gone forth from the Lord; the plague has begun!" Aaron did as Moses had ordered, bringing the incense to the people, where the plague had begun, and "he stood between the dead and the living until the plague was checked" (Numbers 17:6–13). According to the plain sense of scripture, God decreed a plague on Israel; "wrath went forth from the Lord," and Moses stood in the breach to annul the divine decree. Of the decree is written, "The Lord said to Moses," and of the remedy, "Moses said to Aaron." Moses said this on his own, not at the divine behest.

On the other hand, there are those who say that the Holy and Blessed One Himself revealed this secret to Moses.[38] The Israelites were clamoring after the incense, "saying it was the deadly poison by which Nadab and Abihu had died, and by which two hundred fifty of Korah's followers had been burned. The Holy and Blessed One said, 'You shall see that it can stop the plague, and that sin was the real cause of death.'"[39] It is told in the Aggadah that when the angel told Aaron, "Let me perform my mission," he replied, "Moses ordered me to prevent you." The angel retorted, "I am God's emissary, while you are only Moses' emissary." Aaron replied, "Moses says nothing on his own; it is all at the divine behest."[40]

Moses' Prophecy and Balaam's Prophecy

The rabbinic discussion of Balaam in this section is emblematic of the issue, whether there is communication from God to humanity outside the Jewish people. The short answer is yes. God does make His will known to humanity through more than one avenue. Parallel to this is the notion of the "righteous of the Nations"—those gentiles who observe the seven Noahide Laws (refraining from murder, adultery/incest, theft, blasphemy, idolatry, and cruelty to animals, and establishing courts of justice) are assured a portion in the world to come. However, the rest of the rabbinic traditions concerning Balaam make clear that they regarded him as having abused his prophetic gifts, colluding with Balak to try to have God curse Israel, and instigating the plot to seduce the Israelites into sacred prostitution at Ba'al Pe'or.

It is noteworthy that Heschel does not bring up these traditional negative judgments of Balaam in this context, but limits himself to a positive comparison of the manner of Balaam's prophetic powers and Moses'. Did he consider these rabbinic midrashim as having relevance for the relation of Judaism to Christianity? He does not say. It is in line, however, with his positive involvement in the contemporary ecumenical movement. In "No Religion Is an Island," he said: "A Christian ought to realize that a world without Israel would be a world without the God of Israel. A Jew, on the other hand, ought to

---

[38] *Gur Aryeh* on Numbers 17:13; *Levush Ha-orah* ad loc.
[39] Rashi on Numbers 17:13.
[40] Ibid.

acknowledge the eminent role and part of Christianity in God's design for the redemption of all men" (address, 1965, reprinted in *Moral Grandeur and Spiritual Audacity*, ed. Susannah Heschel [New York: Farrar, Straus, Giroux, 1996], 242).

The Sages tried to understand the characteristics of Moses' prophecy by comparing it with Balaam's prophecy. Thus they said:

Moses possessed three traits that Balaam lacked:[41]

Moses would have God speak to him standing, as it says, "But you stand here with Me."[27] But God would speak to Balaam only prostrate, as it says, "Prostrate, but with eyes unveiled" (Numbers 24:4).[28]

Moses would have God speak to him mouth to mouth, while of Balaam it is written, "Word of him who hears God's speech" (Numbers 24:4), indicating that God did not speak to him mouth to mouth.

Moses would have God speak to him face to face, whereas God spoke to Balaam only through parables, as it says, "He took up his parable[29] and said . . ." (Numbers 24:15).[30]

But Balaam possessed three traits that Moses lacked:

Moses did not know who[31] was speaking with him, but Balaam knew who was speaking with him, as it says, "Word of him who hears God's speech, who beholds the vision of[32] the Almighty" (Numbers 24:16).

Moses did not know when the Holy and Blessed One would speak with him, but Balaam knew when the Holy and Blessed One was going to speak with him, as it says, "who knows the mind of the Most High"[33] (Numbers 24:16). They gave the analogy of a king's chef, who knows what the king is going to serve at his table, and how much the king spends for entertaining at his table. Similarly, Balaam knew when the Holy and Blessed One was going to speak with him.

Balaam also would speak with God whenever he wanted, as it says, "Prostrate, but

---

[41] The Midrash Aggadah (Korah, p. 141ff.) phrases it somewhat differently: "Balaam was greater than Moses in three things . . . Moses was greater than Balaam in three things."

---

[27] So literally (*'amod*). NJV: "But you remain here with Me."

[28] In *The Prophets*, Heschel interpets this as the difference between the nonecstatic character of biblical prophecy and the ecstasy experienced by pagan prophets: "Moses received his revelation while retaining his full power of consciousness, whereas Balaam lost his power of consciousness in the moment of revelation" (*The Prophets: Part II* [New York: Harper & Row, 1975], 119).

[29] NJV: "theme."

[30] This is reminiscent of Maimonides' view that the specific difference of Moses' prophecy was that he received God's message directly through the intellectual faculty, not through the imaginative faculty, and not through images or parables (*Guide of the Perplexed*, 2:45; *Hilkhot Yesodei Ha-torah* 7:6).

[31] Variant reading: "what" (Nahmanides on Numbers 24:1, cited in Heschel, subsection "Variant Readings in the Midrash on Moses' and Balaam's Prophecy," omitted from this translation).

[32] So literally. NJV: "visions from."

[33] NJV: "who obtains knowledge from the Most High." *Da'at* in the Bible generally means "knowledge," but in rabbinic Hebrew also means "mind, view, intention."

with eyes unveiled" (Numbers 24:16)—whenever he prostrated himself, his eyes were unveiled concerning what he asked about. But Moses could not speak with God whenever he wanted. Rabbi Simeon disagreed: "Moses could also speak with God whenever he wanted, as it says, 'When Moses went into the Tent of Meeting to speak with Him' (Numbers 7:89)—whenever he wanted, he entered the Tent and God would speak with him."[42]

Let us examine the second half of the midrash. The first trait—that "Moses did not know who was speaking with him"—is astonishing. Is it possible that its meaning lies with R. Hoshaya's interpretation of the verse, "Moses hid his face, for he was afraid to look at God"? (Exodus 3:6). R. Hoshaya the Elder said, "Moses did well to hide his face," so as not to look at God. Thus Moses did not know who was speaking with him, for he did not look at God.[43]

The Midrash Aggadah underlines this last point: "Moses our Master did not look at the Shekhinah, but Balaam did look, as it says, 'Who beholds the vision of the Almighty.' . . . 'Word of the man whose eye is open'[34] (Numbers 24:3)—he saw what all the prophets did not see."[44]

There are two evaluations of Balaam's prophecy, one that exalted him even above Moses' prophecy, the other that relegated him to a low level of prophecy. Rabbi Akiva thought that "his prophecy was contemptible."[45] On the other hand, we have one who expounds, "'There never arose in Israel another prophet like Moses' (Deuteronomy 34:10)—in Israel there never arose another, but among the nations of the world there did arise another [namely Balaam]."[46] "'And the Lord put a word in Balaam's mouth' (Numbers 23:16)—he twisted his mouth and split it open, like one setting a nail in a board. According to Rabbi Eliezer, an angel spoke with him; according to Rabbi Joshua, the Holy and Blessed One spoke with him, as [the verse continues], 'Return to Balak and speak thus' (Numbers 23:16)."[47]

They said, "The Holy and Blessed One left nothing in the world unrevealed to Balaam the son of Beor. Why? Because all the nations of the world would one day say, 'If only You had given us a prophet such as Moses, we would have accepted Your Torah.' Therefore the Holy and Blessed One gave them Balaam the son of Beor, whose wisdom was greater than Moses'. Moses had one thing that Balaam lacked, and Balaam had one thing that Moses lacked. It is written of Moses, 'VaYiKRA—[The Lord] called [to Moses]' (Leviticus 1:1), and it is written of Balaam, 'VaYiKR—[God]

---

[42] Numbers Rabbah 14:20; YS Naso 714, citing Sifre Zuta.

[43] Exodus Rabbah 3:1. See the contrary view of R. Joshua ben Korhah, "Moses did not act properly when he hid his face . . ." (chapter 15 above, pp. 290–91).

[44] Midrash Aggadah, Korah, pp. 141ff.

[45] PT Sotah 20d.

[46] Sifre Habrekhah 357. See Ephraim Urbach, "Homilies of the Sages on the Gentile Prophets and the Portion of Balaam" (in Hebrew), Tarbitz 25 (1956): 272ff.

[47] Tanhuma Balak 12.

---

[34] NJV: "whose eye is true."

manifested [Himself to Balaam]' (Numbers 23:4).[35] It is written of Moses, "Pray let me know Your ways" (Exodus 33:13), and it is written of Balaam, "Who knows the mind of the Most High" (Numbers 24:16).[48] [36] Another interpretation: "Who knows the mind of the Most High"—Balaam knew how to calculate the exact instant when the Holy and Blessed One is angry.[37] [49] He knew it on his own, not from a prophecy.[50]

There was also a controversy concerning the third trait [which Balaam possessed but Moses did not]. The anonymous view in Sifre states, "Moses would not speak with God whenever he wanted." R. Zerikah interpreted this in praise of Moses: "'The Lord called to Moses' (Leviticus 1:1)—this verse comes only to let us know Moses' humility and modesty. It is the custom of the world that a man with whom the king speaks regularly, is free to come and go without permission, because he is on familiar terms[38] with the king. But Moses our Master (peace be his) was not that way. Even though the Holy and Blessed One spoke with him face to face several times, he still stood in trembling and treated the Shekhinah with respect, as if the Holy One had never spoken with him. Because of this, he was granted a privilege that no other person ever merited: whenever he entered [the Tent], the Shekhinah would speak with him immediately."[51]

In this respect, Rabbi Simeon said, "Moses also could speak with God whenever he wanted."[52] Rashi cited this view in commenting on the verse "whom the Lord knew[39] face to face" (Deuteronomy 34:10)—"he was familiar with God, and would speak to Him whenever he wanted, as he said, 'Yet I will now go up to the Lord' (Exodus 32:30), and 'Stand by, and let me hear what instructions the Lord gives about you'" (Numbers 9:8).[40]

In similar vein, the Sages expounded: "Just as [God] appointed kings and prophets for Israel, so He appointed for the nations of the world. . . . He appointed Moses for

---

[48] SEZ, p. 191.
[49] BT Berakhot 7a.
[50] BT Avodah Zarah 4a, Tosafot s.v. ve-yodea' da'at 'elyon.
[51] Midrash Haggadol, beginning of Leviticus.
[52] Numbers Rabbah 14:20.

---

[35] Thus, the thing Moses had that Balaam lacked was that the verb describing God's manifestation to him had an extra letter (the aleph of VaYiKRA).

[36] Thus, the thing Balaam had that Moses lacked was a certain additional aspect of knowledge of God's ways.

[37] According to the Talmud, this occurs for one 58,888th part of an hour each day. Balaam evidently hoped to use this knowledge to turn God against Israel, by approaching God at that instant with his request for permission to curse Israel.

[38] shelibbo gas ba-melekh. This term has the connotation, on the one hand, of extreme intimacy (as between lovers) and, on the other hand, of crudeness and overstepping the limits of propriety.

[39] NJV: "singled out."

[40] In both these cases, Moses spoke with the assurance that as soon as he inquired of God in these matters, God would give a prompt response.

Israel, who could speak with Him whenever he wanted, and he appointed Balaam for the gentiles, who could speak with Him whenever he wanted."[53] [41]

The Supernal Glory Speaks to God's Self

"When Moses went into the Tent of Meeting to speak with Him, he would hear the Voice addressing H/him[42] from above the cover that was on top of the Ark of the Pact between the two cherubim; thus He spoke to H/him" (Numbers 7:89). Rashi comments on the unusual verbal form *middabber*:[43] "This is the reflexive form. The Supernal Glory, as it were, is speaking to Itself, and Moses overhears it."[54] According to this view, Moses did not hear the voice of the Lord addressing him in the second person, but "God was speaking to God's Self, and Moses overheard."[55] "For it would not be proper respect to the Most High to say that the Blessed One speaks with mortals as a master would speak with his students. Rather, the Voice would issue from the divine mouth as if He was not speaking with Moses, and afterwards the Voice was as if soliloquizing of its own accord with Moses."[56]

R. Isaac Abravanel commented on the same verse: "It appears that Rashi tended toward the view of Maimonides that Moses did not hear a sensory voice but had an abstract prophetic intuition; that is, Moses apprehended the divine order within the Blessed One, which is what he refers to when he says, 'speaking to Itself, and Moses overhearing it.'" Nevertheless, on the basis of the midrash which Rashi cites on the

---

[53] Tanhuma Balak 1.

[54] Rashi on Numbers 7:89. See Maharal, *Gur Aryeh,* ad loc, and Rashi on Isaiah 52:5. R. Ezekiel Baneth (*Mar'ei Yehezkel,* nineteenth century, Hungary) gave a similar interpretation on Leviticus 1:1, playing on the lack of explicit subject and object in the phrase, "And H/he called to Moses, and the Lord spoke to H/him."

[55] Moses Alshekh (sixteenth century, Salonika and Israel), *Torat Moshe* ad loc.

[56] R. Moses Alshekh, *Torat Moshe* on Leviticus 9:2.

---

[41] This midrash reflects the Sages' concern for God's justice. In order for God to be just to all humanity, He must give Jews and non-Jews equal access to His truth. Therefore, prophecy cannot by its nature be restricted to Israel alone, but must be available to all the nations of the world. It has unique moments in which it comes about, but it is a universal phenomenon.

This translation omits the next section, "Variant Readings of the Midrash of Moses's and Balaam's Prophecy."

[42] The Hebrew has no capitalization at all, much less a convention whereby a capitalized pronoun refers to the Deity. Thus the Hebrew pronoun *eilav* is ambiguous in reference as between God and Moses, a fact that gives Rashi's comment further point.

[43] The usual form of the word is *medabber* (active intensive mode). The form *middabber* belongs to the *hithpa'el* conjugation, which generally indicates reflexive mode (in which the subject and direct object of the verb are identical).

same verse, Abravanel deduced that Rashi did indeed admit that there was a sensory voice.

We see how important this view was to Rashi from the fact that he repeated it in other places.[57] Rashi generally drew his main points from rabbinic sources. But I cannot find any source from which he derived this view. On the contrary, we find: "The rabbis said: Every thing which the Holy and Blessed One said to Moses He first said one or two times to Himself, and then said them to Moses."[58]

According to the plain sense of Scripture, the divine utterance was indeed addressed to the Faithful Shepherd [Moses] in the second person, yet according to Rashi, Moses only heard the utterance of the Holy and Blessed One to God's Self, not to him. R. Moses Alshekh suggested a way to understand Rashi's interpretation in the light of the ending of the verse, "and He spoke to him": "It comes to tell of Moses' virtue, that when he came to speak to the eternally blessed God, he was ashamed to start, and he needed permission, as when in front of a king, one needs to ask permission before speaking, so too, the Blessed One must start by indicating that He wanted Moses to speak with him. This occurred not through an angel; rather, Moses would hear the voice as if speaking to itself, and afterwards 'He spoke to him'—in the second person, as a man speaks to his friend, but not at first, for the preparation for the utterance was not proper to be done in the second person."

According to Sforno, *middabber* refers to "between God and God's Self, for all that the Lord does is for Himself, to reflect on Himself, that with this knowledge He will then bestow generously on others abundance without end. The reflexive activity (indicated by the *hitpa'el*) should be regarded as preparatory. The same interpretation should be given to every statement in the Torah which begins, 'The Lord spoke.'" This interpretation is based on the doctrine of Aristotle, which Maimonides considered "the cornerstone of our faith." The Holy and Blessed One alone, not conjoined to any other being, "He and His knowledge are unified in every way. . . . . He is the Knower, and He is the Known, and He is the Knowledge itself—all is One."[59]

---

[57] For instance, on Exodus 33:9: "And when Moses entered the Tent, the pillar of cloud would descend and stand at the entrance of the Tent, while he spoke with Moses."

[58] Genesis Rabbah 104:5.

[59] Aristotle, *Metaphysics*, book 12; Maimonides, *Guide of the Perplexed*, 1:68; *Mishneh Torah, Hilkhot Yesodei Ha-torah* 2:10. See also David Kimhi, *Sefer Ha-shorashim* (Berlin, 1846), 133.

The Shekhinah Speaks from within
Moses' Voicebox[44]

In the Zohar, they expounded,

"Moses would speak, and God would answer him with a voice"[45] (Exodus 19:19)—
exalted things are alluded to here! We have established that "God would answer him
with a voice" means Moses' voice—that voice by which Moses was distinguished.[46] One
might mistakenly think the opposite, for it is written, "The Lord spoke" (Exodus 20:1).
But is it not written here, "Moses would speak"? But some say this is because it is written, "'You speak to us,' they said to Moses, 'and we will obey; but let not God speak to us
[lest we die]' (Exodus 20:16). That is why "Moses would speak, and God would answer
him," for there is no word in the Torah which Moses spoke on his own.[60]

This voice, with which Moses "distinguished himself above all the other prophets . . .
it is the level called Shekhinah, which rests upon Israel."[47] [61]

These words served as the source of the expression that became widespread in the
kabbalistic and Hasidic literature: "the Shekhinah speaks through Moses' voicebox."
"Moses' voice had in it, as it were, the voice of the Holy and Blessed One, as it is written, 'Moses would speak, and God would answer him with a voice.'"[62] "When Moses
spoke with Israel, the Shekhinah would speak from within his voicebox. Thus it is
written, 'Mouth to mouth I speak in him,'[48] (Numbers 12:8); that is, the utterance

[60] Zohar Vayikra 7a. Abraham Azulai (seventeenth century, Morocco and Israel) commented in Or Ha-
hamah: "Moses actually spoke, as it says, 'You speak to us, and we will obey,' but so that it would not turn
out that the Torah was authored by Moses, it says, 'God would answer him with a voice,' that is, the
Shekhinah arranged the words, but the voice was heard through Moses' mouth."

[61] Zohar Va'ethanan 265a.

[62] Divrei David (by David ben Samuel Ha-Levi [seventeenth century, Poland], author of Turei Zahav) on
Deuteronomy 5:24.

---

[44] This phrase was encountered once before, in discussing whether Deuteronomy was primarily the
product of Moses' or God's authorship. Here the full implications of the phrase are discussed.

[45] So literally. NJV: "As Moses spoke, God answered him in thunder."

[46] Later interpretations of the Zohar identify this "voice of Moses" with the ze'ir anpin (Short
Countenance, or Impatient One), one of the aspects of God.

[47] The Sullam commentary on the Zohar interprets this abstruse portion in Lurianic terms as follows: the "Voice of Moses" is to be identified with the Ze'ir Anpin to which Moses was uniquely
attached in his prophetic inspiration; this is the middle portion of the Sefirotic tree, extending below
Hokhmah but above Malkhut. The other prophets, however, were inspired by Shekhinah, which is the
same as Malkhut, the very bottom member of the tree. Thus Moses' prophecy was superior to theirs,
deriving from a higher source. This interpretation obscures, however, what seems to be Heschel's
main point: that the real, human, material voice of Moses became the instrument of the Shekhinah's
revelation of the Torah.

[48] NJV: "With him." The Hebrew particle be- has the primary meaning "in." The idiom, "X speaks

that proceeded from the mouth of the Blessed One would speak within Moses himself. This is also the meaning of the reflexive *middabber* (Numbers 7:89), that is, that the voice would receive [its import from God] and issue forth [from within Moses]."[63]

The idea was also common in the Hasidic literature: "The Shekhinah spoke from within Moses' voicebox. Because of Moses' great sanctity and attachment to the Blessed Name, he would actually unite with his Root, and he was like the Holy and Blessed One speaking His utterance."[64]

> Just as the light of the Blessed Ein-Sof[49] fills all this void of the present world before the present world is created, so it is in actuality after it is created. This is the aspect of Moses, when he says, "For what are we?"[50] (Exodus 16:7). And the Shekhinah speaks from within Moses' voicebox, and so is it in every generation. So did Caro's spirit-mentor say to him, "I am the Mishnah, who speaks through your mouth." And in the gemara, [R. Safra would say to Rava,] "Moses, is this such a brilliant statement?"[51] [65] For the great scholar receives from the aspect of the supernal wisdom the power of the divine utterance. The father establishes the daughter, as it is written, "The Lord founded the earth by wisdom"[66] (Proverbs 3:19). So, too, "the 'word of the Lord' refers to the Halakhah"[67] in the mouth of the scholar. The same is meant by "in the voice of Moses."[52] For "voice" refers to the extension from the hidden to the revealed, as from the vapor of the heart to the voicebox by way of analogy, as we know from the interpretation of the verse, "Acquire wisdom" (Proverbs 4:5), that is, in proportion to one's [i.e., Moses'] self-abnegation vis-à-vis the light of the Blessed Ein-Sof, so truly "God would answer him"—by reading [Scripture] and reciting [the Oral Torah] responsively with him.[68]

The view that the divine utterance did not come to the prophet as from mouth to ear, but that the Holy and Blessed One communicated it to the prophet's heart, is suggested in Philo's statement that the prophet is an interpreter of the word that the All-Present utters (or arouses) within him.[69]

---

[63] *Panim Yafot* of R. Phinehas Horowitz (eighteenth century, Germany), Tissa.
[64] *Likkutei Yekarim* (anthology of early Hasidic masters, edited by R. Samuel ben R. Judah Loeb Segal (Lwow, 5552/1792), on Exodus 19:3.
[65] BT Shabbat 101b; Sukkah 39a; Betzah 38b.
[66] Zohar, Ra'aya Mehemna, Pinhas 256b, 258a.
[67] BT Shabbat 138b; Keritot 13b.
[68] *Torah Or* of R. Shneur Zalman of Lyady (eighteenth century, Eastern Europe), Yitro 68c.
[69] Philo, *De Praemiis et Poenis* 55.

---

be- Y" generally has the meaning, "X speaks with Y." But R. Phinehas Horowitz's hyperliteral interpretation of this phrase finds in it the notion of the Shekhinah speaking from within Moses.

[49] "Infinite"—in Zoharic Kabbalah, the aspect of God that is indescribable and unknowable, which precedes the emanation of the Sefirot.

[50] That is, God is everything; we are nothing.

[51] R. Safra actually calls Rava "Moses" by way of ironic compliment: "Genius, is this the best you could come up with?"

[52] R. Shneur Zalman interprets the saying as referring to the abnegation of the speaker (Moses, Caro, Rava), who becomes truly the mouthpiece of the divine process occurring through him. What

Did the Holy Spirit Rest Only on Moses?

According to Rabbi Akiva's view, all the Torah is the word of God which came to Moses, and all its words were prophesied by Moses. In the light of this we can understand Rabbi Akiva's homily, "'Then Moses and the Israelites sang this song to the Lord. They said' (Exodus 15:1)—Israel responded with song to each phrase of Moses.[70] Moses would say, 'I will sing to the Lord,' and the Israelites would respond, 'I will sing to the Lord'; Moses would say, 'The Lord is my strength and might,' and the Israelites would respond, 'The Lord is my strength and might.'"[71] According to this view, Moses recited every word of the song first, and the Israelites said nothing on their own. The heading, "Moses and the Israelites," indicates only that "Moses said it on behalf of all Israel."[72] In contrast to this, Rabbi Nehemiah was of the opinion "that Moses would recite the opening of each verse, and the Israelites would complete it. Moses would say, 'Then Moses . . . sang,' and the Israelites would say, 'I will sing to the Lord'; Moses would say, 'The Lord is my strength and might,' and the Israelites would say, 'This is my God and I will enshrine Him'; Moses would say, 'The Lord, the Warrior,' and the Israelites would say, 'Lord is His name!'"[73] According to Rabbi Nehemiah, the Israelites took part in the composition of the song, "for by virtue of the faith that our ancestors had in God, they were privileged to have the holy spirit rest on them, and they broke out in song." This view is repeated anonymously in the Mekhilta of Rabbi Ishmael, and it apparently originated in the school of Rabbi Ishmael.[74]

This is not all. There are verses in the Song of the Sea that were recited by Pharaoh and the nations of the world. In Rabbi Ishmael's school, they taught that the verses of the Song of the Sea were not written in the order in which they were spoken. "The foe said, 'I will pursue, I will overtake, I will divide the spoil, My desire shall have its fill of them; I will bare my sword—my hand shall subdue them'" (Exodus 15:9)—"this was the first verse to be spoken. Why, then, is it written here? Because there is no chronological order in the Torah." Pharaoh said this verse in Egypt, and the Israelites

---

[70] Mishnah Sotah 5:4.   [71] Tosefta Sotah 6:2; PT Sotah 20c.
[72] MI Shirata 1; MSY, p. 71.   [73] Mishnah and Tosefta Sotah, loc. cit.
[74] MI Beshalah 6, Shirata 1 and 7.

---

appears as Moses speaking is really the Shekhinah. What appears as Joseph Caro speaking (or writing his mystical diary) is really his *maggid* (spiritual mentor) using him as medium or channel. Rava (in R. Safra's eyes) is but another incarnation of Moses. Each is passively receiving the imprint of God, just as in the primal act of creation through wisdom, the daughter (the lower Sefirot, or Malkhut, or the created world) passively receives the creative effluence of the father (God). It is precisely because Moses had achieved *bittul*—the abnegation of his own self—that he could become the recipient of God's word, with God speaking through Moses' voicebox.

repeated it later at the Sea of Reeds when they saw him drowning in the sea. You might ask, "How did the Israelites know what Pharaoh was thinking about them in Egypt? The holy spirit rested on them, and they knew."

In refutation of Pharaoh's words, the holy spirit responded, "You made Your wind blow, the sea covered them; they sank like lead in the majestic waters" (Exodus 15:10).

One verse, too, in the Song of the Sea was first said by the nations of the world, hence, not by the holy spirit. "When the nations of the world heard that Pharaoh and his host had perished in the sea, and that Egypt's supremacy was shattered, and their idols had suffered judgments, they all renounced their own idols and opened up in acknowledgment of the All-Present: "Who is like You, O Lord, among the gods?"[53] (Exodus 15:11).

It is said to Moses regarding the seventy elders, "Let them take their place there with you"[54] (Numbers 11:16). It is said of this in the Sifre, "Bring them with you into the Tent of Meeting, and all Israel should treat them with awe, reverence, and respect as they treat you; they will say, 'Precious are these, who went in with Moses to hear the utterance from the mouth of the Holy and Blessed One.'"[75] Against this, they seem to have interpreted in the school of Rabbi Akiva: "Bring them in with you to the Tent of Meeting, *not* that they should hear the divine utterance, but that people should treat them with respect and reverence, and say, 'Happy are these who entered with Moses to hear the utterance from the divine Mouth.'"[76]

Has the Holy Spirit Left Me?

The chieftains of Israel—they were the leaders of the tribes in Egypt, who were in charge of the enrollment of the census and the banners.[77] Some of them later followed Korah in his rebellion.[78] Originally they did not want to participate with Moses in

[75] Sifre Beha'alotekha 92.
[76] Sifre Zuta, p. 271.
[77] Sifre Naso 45; Sifre Zuta, p. 251.
[78] PR 27b–28a; Exodus Rabbah 13:6; Tanhuma Korah 2.

[53] NJV: ". . . among the celestials?" This midrash resolves a problem that Heschel discussed above in chapter 12, n. [7]: How could the Israelites say something that seems to ascribe reality to the gods of the pagans? The problem is resolved by putting these words in the mouths of the pagans themselves.

[54] Literally: "Let them stand there with you." It says further, "[The Lord said,] 'I will draw upon the spirit that is on you and put it upon them. . . .' Then the Lord came down . . . He drew upon the spirit that was on him and put it upon the seventy elders. And when the spirit rested upon them, they spoke in ecstasy, but did not continue" (Numbers 11:17–25). Heschel saves full treatment of the implications of this passage for chapter 33 ("The Prophecy of Eldad and Medad").

setting up the Tabernacle. Moses was not overly warm toward them either. "At the time that Moses was engaged in erecting the Tabernacle, he did not want to take advice from the chieftains of Israel."[79] "You find that at the time that Moses announced, 'Take from among you gifts' (Exodus 35:5), what did the chieftains do? They said, 'Didn't Moses know to tell us, that we should make the Tabernacle?' So they gave nothing. They said, 'These people are making the Tabernacle, and he asks us to make a contribution!'"[55] [80]

"On the day that Moses finished setting up the Tabernacle, . . . the chieftains brought their offering before the Lord: six draught carts and twelve oxen, a cart for every two chieftains and an ox for each one. When they had brought them before the Tabernacle, the Lord said to Moses [lemor]:[56] 'Accept these from them for use in the service of the Tent of Meeting, and give them to the Levites according to their respective services'" (Numbers 7:1–5).

The Sages had a problem with these verses. "What is lemor?"[57] The Torah mentioned nothing that Moses should pass on to the chieftains. "R. Oshaya said, 'God said to Moses, "Go out and tell them words of praise and consolation."'"[81] [58] "Moses was afraid and said, 'It seems to me that the holy spirit has left me and rested on the chieftains!'"[59] In another source, the reading is, "In that hour, Moses was

[79] ARN A 11.   [80] TB, Naso 29.   [81] PRK 9a; Numbers Rabbah 12:18.

---

[55] Evidently, giving a contribution was a paltry thing to them, not befitting their high status. They wanted to have a high-profile role or none at all.

These homilies are the expression of the eternal rivalry between religious and secular leadership cadres (kings versus prophets, exilarchs versus geonim, communal councils versus rabbis) that has beset Jewish history (and Christian history as well) over the centuries. Each thought itself uniquely qualified to dictate how affairs should be run. More to the point here, the secular leaders even went so far as to challenge the religious leaders on their own turf. What gave the latter the notion that they had a monopoly on God's word? Here the midrashim express Moses' anxiety that maybe the secular challengers were right.

[56] The ubiquitous Hebrew word lemor is untranslated here. This word creates the interpretive problem that provokes the midrash. Grammatically, it is used simply (like a colon) to indicate that a direct quotation follows. However, most of the time in the Torah, lemor precedes a teaching or law that Moses is required to communicate to the Israelites. Here what follows is only God's instructions to Moses how to deploy the animals he has received. Moses noticed the difference and seems to have responded, "You have told me what I am to do, but where's the message that I should pass on to them?" He feared that he had been stripped of his primary function as bearer of God's word to the Israelites.

[57] See previous note.

[58] R. Oshaya filled in the gap, much as midrashists made up one thing or another to explain the elliptical, "Cain said to his brother Abel . . ." (Genesis 4:8).

[59] If the chieftains were not in need of Moses' guidance (for God had told Moses nothing to tell them), Moses surmised, maybe God was providing the necessary guidance to them directly, and thus they were divinely inspired! As in any politically competitive situation, the party with nothing to say is in danger of being washed up, and leadership passes readily to another faction.

afraid. He said to himself, 'Perhaps the holy spirit has forsaken me and rests on the chieftains. Or perhaps another prophet has stood up and issued new *halakhah*?"[82] The Holy and Blessed One then said to Moses, "If I had told them to bring offerings, I would have done so through you; but they decided to do it on their own."[83]

Moses' question is testimony that, according to the Sages, Moses allowed the possibility that his contemporaries might attain to prophecy. On the other hand, they assumed that any divine utterance with commands addressed to Israel would come not through the chieftains but through Moses.

For Thirty-Eight Years the Holy and Blessed One Did Not Speak to Moses

There was a view among the Sages that for the thirty-eight years of the Israelites' wanderings—from the episode of the Spies until the generation of the wilderness died out—the Holy and Blessed One did not speak with Moses.

> Simeon ben Azzai said, "*lemor* means, teach them according to the language that you hear [Me speaking to you now]." Rabbi Akiva said, "It means, go out and tell them that it was for their merit that God spoke with you." For in all the thirty-eight years that God was angry with Israel, He did not speak with Israel, as it says, "When all the warriors among the people had died off, the Lord spoke to me, saying [*lemor*] . . .'[60] (Deuteronomy 2:16–17). Rabbi Simeon ben Azzai said, "I was not disagreeing with my master, but only adding to his words. Indeed, it was not only Moses to whom God spoke by merit of Israel, but God spoke to all the prophets only by the merit of Israel."[61] [84]

The commentators struggled with the proper understanding of this view. After all, hadn't many mitzvot been communicated during those thirty-eight years?

Rashi tried to mediate the difficulty by suggesting that for those thirty-eight years the verb *amar* ("said") rather than *dibber* ("spoke, uttered") was use to describe the divine–human communication. Indeed, Rabbi Akiva's exact words were, "God did not speak [*lo hayah medabber*] to him." Rashi explains: "For those thirty-eight years,

---

[82] Song of Songs Rabbah 6:4; Midrash on Psalms 101:4.
[83] PRK loc. cit.; YS I, 824.
[84] Sifra Vayikra 4b; MI Pisha 1.

---

[60] According to this midrash, the juxtaposition here indicates that only after the generation of the wilderness had died off did God resume speaking to Moses. The word *lemor* indicates that at that point, the people were again worthy enough for God to bestow His word on them through Moses. As the Hebrew text has no punctuation, it is not quite clear how far Rabbi Akiva's remarks extend. Heschel will make a point of this in discussing the passage. See n. 91.

[61] Or "for the sake of Israel." As Heschel makes abundantly clear in his book *The Prophets*, prophecy in Israel was not simply for the benefit of the individual prophet to have a religious experience and close connection with God, but it was for God to communicate His will to the people Israel.

the divine utterance was not characterized by endearment, face-to-face address, and serenity."[85] "The utterance did not come to him mouth-to-mouth, but in a night vision, in a stammering fashion."[86]

RaSHBaM interpreted after the manner of Rabbenu Gershom, the Light of the Exile, that for those years God did not speak to Moses mouth-to-mouth as formerly, but if there was need for communication, as, for instance, in the episode of Korah (which occurred after that of the Spies),[62] God would communicate through an angel or through the Urim and Thummim. Perhaps, too, [it simply meant that] God would communicate only when forced by the pressure of events.[87] [63] According to Rabbenu Bahya, during this period Moses prophesied through a dark speculum, at the same level as the other prophets.[88]

This view, that the Holy and Blessed One did not talk to Moses for thirty-eight years, is consonant with the approach according to which "[the Holy and Blessed One] did not talk to Moses whenever Moses wanted." It is difficult to reconcile it with Rabbi Simeon's view that "Moses would speak with God whenever he wanted." In one place, we find the explicit statement, "God ceased speaking with all other prophets, but He did not cease speaking with Moses all his days."[89] I suggested above[90] that this issue is the subject of dispute between the schools of Rabbi Ishmael and Rabbi Akiva. Perhaps the notion of a thirty-eight year cessation of prophecy is in agreement with Rabbi Ishmael but not Rabbi Akiva.[91] [64]

---

[85] Rashi on Deuteronomy 2:17.

[86] Commentary attributed to Rashi on BT Ta'anit 30b.

[87] RaSHBaM on BT Bava Batra 121b.

[88] Bahya ben Asher on Deuteronomy 2:16.

[89] Exodus Rabbah 2:6.

[90] See above, chapter 22, pp. 412–13.

[91] Whoever reads the Baraita with a discerning eye will see that Rabbi Simeon and Rabbi Akiva are engaged in explaining the word *lemor*. The statement concerning the thirty-eight-year cessation of prophecy interrupts the thought and is apparently not part of Rabbi Akiva's statement, but an addition. Rabbi Johanan and R. Nahman transmit it with the attribution, "A master said" (BT Ta'anit 30b; Bava Batra 121a–b; see also Midrash Haggadol on Genesis 45:27). Had they known that Rabbi Akiva authored it, they surely would have transmitted it in his name.

---

[62] And is therefore to be dated within the thirty-eight-year hiatus.

[63] By this possibility, such communications occurred in the normal manner, but they were rare exceptions to the general rule that prophetic communication was withdrawn for that period insofar as feasible.

[64] Despite Heschel's argument in n. 91 above, the rhetorical connection between the thirty-eight-year hiatus and Rabbi Akiva's main point (that it was for Israel's sake that God spoke to Moses) is so strong that it is hard to imagine the point itself without the proof text. It is surprising that Heschel argues so strongly for separating them. Moreover, it is difficult to classify this tradition as falling unequivocally on either side of the Ishmaelian-Akivan dichotomy. It has Ishmaelian affinities, in that it sees the event of Mosaic prophecy as contingent and historically determined, rather than unchanging and eternal. But it also has affinities with the Akivan paradigm which sees the divine–human relationship as passionate and highly personal, and therefore subject to falling-out and lovers' quarrels.

See what R. Eleazar ben Abbaye said: "One might have thought he did not speak with him for his own need? The verse says, lemor ("to say")—he did not speak with Him [just] to say to Israel, he spoke with Him for his own need."[92] [65]

According to another view, the divine utterance to Moses ceased not because the Holy and Blessed One was angry at Israel but because He was sad for the generation of the wilderness because of the decree that had been laid on them. Therefore He did not resume speaking with Moses until that generation had passed away.[93]

[92] Midrash Haggadol on Deuteronomy 2:17.
[93] Midrash Haggadol on Genesis, p. 767.

[65] This comment is the reverse of Rabbi Akiva's position. It is suspicious, however. The plain sense of lemor means "to say," that is, to transmit God's word to others. Either the original of this midrash may have used eilai ("to me") as the proof text, or the placement of lo ("not") and its lookalike ela ("except for") may have been corrupted in such a way as to reverse the meaning. (Thus, the original might have read: "One might have thought he did not speak with Him except for his own need? The verse says lemor, that is, he spoke with Him to say to Israel, he did not speak with Him for his own need"). As it stands, however, it is an important complement to Rabbi Akiva's position. The prophet does indeed serve as educator of the people, but he is also an individual with his own need for private communication with God. See chapter 33.

29

HOW THE TORAH WAS WRITTEN

Translator's Introduction

In this chapter, which has a parenthetical quality to it, several issues relating to the actual writing of the Torah are explored. It is not in itself part of the emerging argument that Heschel has been building, but the sources he brings are certainly of sufficient interest to warrant presenting them to the reader in translation here.

The Dictation Theory and the Transcription Theory

THE TORAH DECLARES that Moses wrote certain topics in the Torah, such as the episode of Amalek,[1] the Book of the Covenant,[2] the renewal of the covenant after the episode of the golden calf,[3] the journeys of the Israelites,[4] and the song *Ha'azinu*.[5] There is no ground for maintaining that Moses wrote only these topics,[1] for it says explicitly, "Moses wrote down this Torah[2] and gave it to

---

[1] "The Lord said to Moses, 'Inscribe this in a document as a reminder'" (Exodus 17:14).

[2] "Moses then wrote down all the commands of the Lord . . . then he took the book [NJV: "record"] of the covenant and read it aloud to the people" (Exodus 24:4, 7).

[3] "The Lord said to Moses: Write down these commandments . . . and he wrote down on the tablets the terms of the covenant, the Ten Commandments" (Exodus 34:28).

[4] "Moses recorded the starting points of their various marches" (Numbers 33:2).

[5] "That day, Moses wrote down this poem" (Deuteronomy 31:22).

---

[1] However, there is also no unequivocal statement in the Torah itself that Moses wrote the entire Torah. On the ambiguity of the word "Torah" in Deuteronomy, see next note.

[2] NJV: "Teaching." Nahmanides gives the traditional view that this passage in Deuteronomy refers to the entire Torah from Genesis 1:1 to Deuteronomy 34:12. The prevailing modern interpretation suggests that the reference, read in context, applies at most to the Book of Deuteronomy itself (see Jeffrey Tigay, *Deuteronomy [= Devarim]: The Traditional Hebrew Text with the New JPS Translation*, JPS Torah Commentary [Philadelphia: Jewish Publication Society, 1996], on Deuteronomy 1:5, 31:9 and 31:24). This is a crucial difference. According to the traditional interpretation, the Torah itself testifies that it was written wholly by Moses. According to the modern interpretation, the belief in the Mosaic

the priests, sons of Levi, who carried the Ark of the Lord's Covenant" (Deuteronomy 31:9), and it is written, "When Moses had put down in writing the words of this Torah to the very end . . ." (Deuteronomy 31:24). In several places in Scripture there is mention of a "Book of the Torah,"[3][6] "Book of the Torah of Moses,"[7] "Book of the Torah of the Lord,"[8] "scroll of the Lord's Torah given by Moses,"[9] "Book of Moses,"[10] "scroll of the Torah of God,"[11] "scroll of the Torah of the Lord God,"[12] and "scroll of the Lord."[13]

With respect to the process of writing the Torah, we find two theories, the dictation theory and the transcription theory.[4]

The commonest view was expressed by Rabbi Meir: "Moses wrote whatever the Holy and Blessed One told him: 'Write!' in the same way that [the scribe Baruch said of how the prophet Jeremiah dictated to him]: 'He himself recited all those words to me, and I would write them down in the scroll in ink' (Jeremiah 36:18)."[14] Rabbi Simeon concurred: "The Holy and Blessed One spoke, and Moses wrote."[15] A later source says, "From His mouth [the Holy and Blessed One] spoke the Five Books of the Torah to Moses."[16] This theory was emphasized by Maimonides when he articu-

---

[6] Joshua 1:8; 18:34; 2 Kings 22:8; Nehemiah 8:3; 2 Chronicles 34:15.

[7] Joshua 8:31; 23:6; 2 Kings 14:6; Nehemiah 8:1.

[8] 2 Chronicles 17:9.   [9] 2 Chronicles 34:14.

[10] Nehemiah 13:1; 2 Chronicles 25:4; 35:12.

[11] Joshua 24:26; Nehemiah 8:18.   [12] Nehemiah 9:3.   [13] Isaiah 34:16.

[14] Sifre Haberakhah 357.

[15] BT Bava Batra 15a; Menahot 30a. Rashi comments: "Moses would recite the words after Him, so that he would not write in error, and then he would write."

[16] Numbers Rabbah 13:16.

---

authorship of the entire Torah is itself post-Mosaic by centuries, with the earliest definite reference found in Nehemiah.

Heschel is aware that "Torah" here can mean far less than the entire Torah. At the end of this chapter, he cites the fifteenth-century scholar Abravanel's view that it refers just to Deuteronomy. On the larger question, however, Abravanel maintained on other grounds that the Pentateuch (with the possible exception of the last chapter) was all of Mosaic authorship. How much of the Torah did Heschel think was Mosaic? In this passage (taken with chapters 31, 32, and 33), he seems to say: the greater part (we can never know for sure exactly how much), but probably less than all.

[3] NJV: "Teaching." So, too, throughout the rest of this discussion, we prefer to give the Hebrew original "Torah" (where NJV has "Teaching"), for Heschel clearly wants to draw the association with the rabbinic sense of Torah as Pentateuch. "Torah" started as a common noun (meaning "teaching, law"), but eventually was used also as a proper noun, denoting the first five books of the Hebrew Bible. This evolution may be seen in the Bible itself by comparing the usage in the earlier books of Scripture (e.g., Leviticus 6:2; 14:2) with that in the later books (especially Nehemiah and Chronicles). See also chapter 20 above for Heschel's enumeration of the various uses of the word "Torah" in rabbinic literature.

[4] Both the dictation theory and the transcription theory are maximalist in varying degrees and ascribe every word in the Torah to God. There is a third theory in this section, represented by the parable of Samuel bar Nahmani, which gives scope to human initiative, but Heschel gives no name to it.

lated the Thirteen Principles of Faith: Moses "was like a scribe to whom one dictates, and he would write the events of the days, the narratives and the commandments."[17] Nahmanides wrote similarly: "It is true and clear that the whole Torah, from the beginning of Genesis to the end of Deuteronomy, was spoken from the Holy One's mouth to Moses' ears [just as Jeremiah dictated to Baruch]."[18] By this principle, Moses wrote on the scroll what he heard from the divine mouth; he heard it but did not read it.

According to this theory, the divine utterance came to Moses twice, once for him to convey it orally to the Israelites, and a second time for him to write it on the scroll. This idea of Moses' double prophecy, which is implicit in the dictation theory, is similar to Rabbi Akiva's notion, "General principles and particulars were conveyed once at Sinai, a second time in the Tent of Meeting, and a third time at the steppes of Moab."[19] One may surmise that just as Rabbi Ishmael opposed the view that the divine utterance was repeated to Moses in different places, so he opposed the view that it was repeated at the time of writing. The dictation theory, as formulated by Rabbi Meir and Maimonides, seems to require this repetition. By contrast, Rashi thought that in Moses' last years, "after all the portions of the Torah had been spoken to him, they were ordered in his memory until he wrote them down."[20] There is no suggestion here that at the time of the writing of the Torah, those words were spoken from the divine mouth, which had been spoken to him previously.

In the same vein you find the saying of the Amora Rabbi Samuel bar Nahmani, who asked: Why is it written in connection with every item [in the construction of the Tabernacle at the end of Exodus], "as the Lord commanded Moses"? It is like a mortal king who had a viceroy whom he commanded to build him palaces. The viceroy set out and built him a large palace, fixed it up and furnished it lavishly, and wrote on every spot the name of the king. When he had completed it, the king entered and saw it and was extremely pleased. He said, "My viceroy has prepared all this in my honor and has engraved my name all over it. Here am I inside, while he is outside. Call him in!" So, too, was our master Moses. When he completed the construction of the Tabernacle and wrote in every paragraph, "as the Lord commanded Moses," the Holy and Blessed One appeared and imbued it with the Shekhinah; He saw it and was pleased.[21]

Note that it was after Moses wrote "as the Lord commanded Moses" on his own initiative, that the Holy and Blessed One appeared. This parable cannot be reconciled with the dictation theory, which says that Moses wrote nothing in the Torah except what he heard from the divine mouth. It is evident here that Moses honored God

---

[17] Introduction to Mishnah Sanhedrin 10, Eighth Principle. Letter to Yemen, ed. Halkin, p. 28: "The entire book of the Torah, from the beginning of Genesis to the end of Deuteronomy, God spoke to Moses our Master mouth to mouth."

[18] Nahmanides, introduction to Commentary on the Torah.

[19] See above, chapter 20, pp. 378–80; chapter 25, pp. 462–64.

[20] Rashi on BT Gittin 60a, s.v. *Torah hatumah*.

[21] Midrash Haggadol, end of Pekudei; Leviticus Rabbah 1:7.

precisely by ascribing to God those things which he did himself. The king was surprised to see the honor which the servant had prepared for him, and it was on that account that he invited him into the inner sanctum.[5]

Together with the notion of dictation, Nahmanides cites the view that Moses was "like a scribe copying from a primordial book and writing."[22] This view, which we shall dub "the transcription theory," says that Moses our Master saw the written Torah before him and copied it from one scroll to another. From what source did Nahmanides derive this view? Apparently he based himself on the saying of Rabbi Simeon ben Lakish: "The Torah which was given to Moses had parchment of white fire, and the letters were black fire. While writing it, Moses wiped the pen in his hair, from which he got his radiant face."[23] According to this saying, Moses saw a Torah written in front of him, and he copied it. This opinion is based on Rabbi Akiva's outlook that the Torah was written in heaven, and the Holy and Blessed One had the Torah spread out before him as a single document.[6]

The view that Moses our Master received the entire Torah in writing is perhaps suggested by Rabbi Johanan's words, "Originally Moses would learn Torah and forget it, until it was given to him as a gift, as it says, 'He gave Moses the two tablets of the Pact, ... inscribed with the finger of God'" (Exodus 31:18).[24]

These notions—a primordial book apparently from heaven, and Moses our Master looking into it and copying—bear the imprint of the apocalyptic tradition. Most of the Sages accepted the dictation theory of Moses hearing and writing. But Nahmanides' remarks on the transcription theory are cited by a few other authorities.[25]

Nahmanides' core idea may be based on the view of Rabbi Simeon ben Lakish, but its idiom is late. Consider the idiom, "primordial book" (sefer kadmon). What does this mean? There appears in Ezekiel the expression "ancient days" (yamim kadmonim, 38:17) in the sense of previous historical ages. In rabbinic parlance, the "Ancient of the World" (kadmono shel olam) is a title of God, who existed before the world. The first human being is called adam ha-kadmoni ("primordial man"), because he preceded all other humans who followed him. But in the Middle Ages, they used the word kadmon in the sense of eternally preexisting, as opposed to "created." "Whatever has a beginning is not primordial (kadmon), and whatever is not primordial is

---

[22] Nahmanides, introduction to Commentary on the Torah.

[23] Deuteronomy Rabbah 3:12, alluding to Exodus 34:34–35: "The Israelites would see how radiant the skin of Moses' face was."

[24] BT Nedarim 38a; Tanhuma Tissa 16 in the name of Rabbi Abbahu.

[25] See R. Menahem ben Aaron ibn Zerah (fourteenth century, Spain), Tzedah La-derekh 1.1.20; Simeon ben Zemah Duran (fourteenth–fifteenth century, Majorca, Algiers), Magen Avot (Leghorn, 5545/1785), 29b.

---

[5] It is surprising that Heschel does not list this view as a third theory of the writing of the Torah. It alone voices the Ishmaelian point of view, while the "dictation" and "transcription" theories are both Akivan in varying degrees.

[6] See above, chapter 17, pp. 331–32.

created."[26] *Kadmon* was also used to mean whatever was created prior to the creation of the world (as in *adam kadmon*, "primordial man"). Clearly, "primorial book" was a medieval expression.

A primordial or eternal book does not exist on the face of the earth. Whoever thinks that Moses copied the Torah from a primordial book believes that he ascended to heaven and copied the Torah there, or brought the primordial book down to earth to copy it.

All the Commandments Written on Tablets

According to Hananiah, the nephew of Rabbi Joshua ben Hananiah, "Between each and every statement [in the first tablets] were its distinctions and fine points, 'studded with beryl [*tarshish*]' (Song of Songs 5:14), like the Great Sea."[27] [7] The point of his saying was apparently to say that in the first tablets, all the mitzvot were written. The word *ba-tarshish* is interpreted as suggesting the number 606, which in addition to the seven commandments of the Noahides, comes to 613.[28] [8]

This view is compatible with the approach of Rabbi Akiva, who thought that Moses our Master was in heaven and that all the general rules and specific details were spoken at Sinai. It stands in opposition to the approach of Rabbi Ishmael, who thought that the Torah was not given at one time, but rather the general rules were given at Sinai and the details in the Tent of Meeting. Like a good pedagogue, the Holy and Blessed One gave it to them a little at a time. "Who turned the rock into a pool of water" (Psalm 114:8)—"Rabbi [Judah the Patriarch] said, When Israel were standing at Mount Sinai, they turned over, like that rock. The Holy and Blessed One said, 'To these I am about to give my Torah? Upon these I am about to extend My holy spirit? But I shall give them just the Ten Commandments, until they can learn more and stand firm like this rock.'"[29]

Why were the tablets given to Israel? You find that when a child first comes to school, they first instruct him to read from a tablet, and afterwards he reads from a

---

[26] Bahya ibn Pakuda (eleventh–twelfth century, Spain), *Duties of the Heart, Sha'ar Ha-yihud* 5.

[27] PT Shekalim 49d; Song of Songs Rabbah 5:12.

[28] Commentary of Rabbenu Meshulam in the name of Rabbana Samuel the Hasid, in the edition of the Jerusalem Talmud, Shekalim, by R. Abraham Sofer, p. 71.

[29] Midrash Hallel, *Beit Ha-midrash* V, 97.

---

[7] The word *tarshish* is a homonym, denoting in one usage a precious stone (beryl) and in another usage a proverbial distant port, for which long-distance sailing ships were called "ships of Tarshish" (Psalm 48:8). The incongruous association of the small and subtle with the immense, suggested to Hananiah the infinity of meaning contained within a single utterance of the Torah.

[8] To get this result, the word is broken up: *tar* consists of the letters *tav, resh* (400 + 200 = 600), while *shish* is equivalent to *shesh* (ordinary Hebrew for the number 6).

scroll. So God first gave Israel the Tablets of the Pact, then later the Torah, as it says [at the end of Deuteromony], "Take this scroll of the Torah" (31:26).

Hananiah's view was dear to the heart of Rabbi Simeon ben Lakish, who adhered to the maximalist view of the giving of the Torah, as we saw earlier. He also held that the Torah was given with a seal, that is, complete, finished, and whole. It is told that when he arrived at this verse,[9] he said, "You have taught us well, Hananiah, nephew of Rabbi Joshua! Just as the ocean has little ripples between its great waves, so does the Torah have fine details which are implied between its great subject headings!"[30]

Hananiah's view[10] does not agree with the plain sense of the scriptural narrative. Note that Hananiah did not bring support for his view from the Torah, but from the Song of Songs. The midrashic work Numbers Rabbah, which was apparently composed in the twelfth century, brings this view and another: "The Ten Commandments have the 613 commandments implicit in them, for you find that the 613 letters between [but not including] 'I' and 'your neighbor' correspond to the 613 commandments."[31] According to this view, the 613 commandments were not explicitly written on the tablets, but only implicit in them, a view shared by Philo and Saadia Gaon.[32]

However, the matter is complicated when we come to the controversies concerning the second set of tablets.[11] Of the first set of tablets, it is said that they were "inscribed with the finger of God" (Exodus 31:18).[12] But who wrote the second tablets? Some say that they were written by the Holy and Blessed One.[33] But Rabbi Yose ben Halafta was of the opinion that Moses wrote them. "The Lord said to Moses, 'Write down these commandments' (Exodus 34:27)—I wrote the first tablets, as it says, 'inscribed with the finger of God.' But you should write the second. . . . Rabbi

---

[30] PT Shekalim, loc. cit., Sotah 22d; YS I, 368. In Song of Songs Rabbah this saying is attributed to Rabbi Johanan, but the Jerusalem Talmud's version is superior.

[31] Numbers Rabbah 13:16.

[32] Philo, beginning of *De Specialibus Legibus;* Saadia, sermons on Shavuot. See also chapter 20, pp. 371–73.

[33] Tosefta Bava Kama 7:4; Deuteronomy Rabbah 17:3; Nahmanides on Exodus 34:28.

---

[9] That is, Song of Songs 5:14, which was the basis of Hananiah's midrash.

[10] That the Ten Commandments contained all the 613 commandments.

[11] Two narrative duplications in connection with the giving of the Ten Commandments are at issue here. One is the second set of tablets, which were produced in the wake of the golden calf (Exodus 34). The other is the second recital of the Ten Commandments by Moses in Deuteronomy 5. In each case, the question arises: What was different about the second occurrence? Could there be a correspondence between the second tablets and the second recital (in other words, does Deuteronomy give the text of the Ten Commandments as it appeared on the second set of tablets)? See above, chapter 25, pp. 467–69, esp. n. 67.

[12] And also the tablets themselves were "God's work" (Exodus 32:16).

Yose ben Halafta said, This is as Moses said to them, 'I will inscribe on the tablets'"[13] (Deuteronomy 10:2).[34]

Note that Rabban Johanan ben Zakkai was of the opinion that Moses only carved the blank tablets themselves, but the writing on them was by the Holy and Blessed One.[14] They asked Rabban Johanan ben Zakkai, "Why were the first tablets of divine workmanship and the second of human workmanship?" He replied, "What can it be compared to? To a king who married a woman and brought his own paper and scribe. He bedecked her with his own finery and brought her into his palace. When he saw her playing with a certain servant, he was angry and cast her out. His companion came to him and said, 'Master, don't you know from what background she came? She grew up among the servants, and therefore she behaves familiarly with them.' The king replied, 'Do you then suggest that I should reconcile with her? You bring your own paper and scribe, and I shall do the writing.' Thus Moses said to the Holy and Blessed One when they had come to do that act: 'Don't you know where you got them from? From Egypt, where idolatry is rampant.' The Holy One replied, 'Do you then suggest that I should reconcile with them? You bring me your own tablets, and I shall do the writing.'"[35] [15]

The Torah Written on Stelas

The Talmudic Sages had a tradition, unknown to their followers, that Moses our Master transmitted the Torah written on *stelas,* that is, on upright stone slabs (like monuments).[16] "Moses and the elders of Israel charged the people, saying: . . . As soon as you have crossed the Jordan . . . you shall set up these stones . . . and coat

---

[34] TB, Tissa 17. In a side issue, Rabbi Yose also maintained (against Rabbi Eleazar the Moda'ite) that the Torah was originally written in Hebrew (i.e., Phoenician) script, before Ezra introduced the current "Assyrian" square calligraphy (Tosefta Sanhedrin 4:5). See N. H. Tur-Sinai, *Ha-lashon veha-sefer* (3 vols.; Jerusalem: Mosad Bialik, 1948–55), 123ff.

[35] Deuteronomy Rabbah 3:17; *Eitz Yosef* ad loc.; YS Tissa 397. See also M. Zucker, *On Sa'adia's Translation of the Torah* (New York: Feldheim, 1959), 243.

---

[13] This is apparently in contradiction to the plain sense of Deuteronomy 10:2, whose context places these words in God's mouth. But the Hebrew *ve-ekhtov* ("I will inscribe") can also be vocalized *va-ekhtov* ("I inscribed"). Rabbi Yose is apparently taking this ambiguity as license for a homiletical reading of the verse.

[14] This does indeed seem to be the plain sense of Exodus 34:1 and Deuteronomy 10:1–4.

[15] This midrash suggests that the difference between the first and second tablets is that the first were given unilaterally by God, while the second were the fruit of a divine–human partnership. When humans "buy into" the venture through participation, they are more likely to remain loyal.

[16] For instance, our knowledge of the Babylonian Code of Hammurabi came about by discovery of a stela which has the laws engraved on the body of it, while the top shows a picture of Hammurabi receiving the commission to write the laws from the god Shamash (*Ancient Near Eastern Texts and Pictures,* ed. James B. Pritchard [Princeton: Princeton University Press, 1969], 163). A contemporary scholar has argued from internal evidence that the law code of Deuteronomy 17–26 may have been

them with plaster. . . . There, too, you shall build an altar . . . and on those stones you shall inscribe every word of this Torah [Teaching] most distinctly" (Deuteronomy 27:1–8).

According to the Tosefta and the Jerusalem Talmud, Moses our Master also wrote the Torah on stones in Transjordanian Moab. "In summary, there were three kinds of stones [as memorial of crossing the Jordan]: one that Moses set up on the east bank of the Jordan in the steppes of Moab, one that marked the place where the priests' feet had stood [in crossing the Jordan under Joshua], and one that they carried with them [across the Jordan, and set up on the west bank]."[36] The Jerusalem Talmud calls the first "the stelas that Moses set up."[37] The Babylonian Talmud noted the parallel use of the word be'er: "It is written in one place, 'On the other side of the Jordan, in the land of Moab, Moses undertook to expound [be'er] this Teaching' (Deuteronomy 1:5), and in another place, 'and on those stones you shall inscribe every word of this Teaching most distinctly [be'er heitev]'"[38](Deuteronomy 27:8). Just as the latter refers to inscribing on stones, so does the former. According to this approach, Moses must have written the entire Torah on stones "most distinctly."[39] The commentators drew the inference that the word be'er in Scripture has a common usage denoting digging, engraving, and glyphic writing, as evidenced by our passage and Habakkuk 2:2: "Inscribe it clearly [ba'er] on tablets."

In another source, the question is raised: "Why was Moses called mehokek ('law-giver,' Deuteronomy 33:21)? Because with the fingers of his hand he engraved (hakak[17]) every letter in the Torah."[40]

The Holy and Blessed One Wrote the Torah

According to Rabbi Meir and Rabbi Simeon, Moses our Master actually *wrote* the Torah down (even if God dictated it). But some say that the Holy and Blessed One Himself wrote the Torah—just as the tablets were inscribed by the finger of God, so the entire Torah was written by the Holy and Blessed One. In the view of R. Moses

[36] Tosefta Sotah 8:5.   [37] PT Sotah 21d.   [38] BT Sotah 35b.
[39] *Korban Ha-edah* on the Jerusalem Talmud, ad loc.
[40] Batei Midrashot II, 385.

originally written in columns on a stela, and the order of the portions transposed when it was transferred to a scroll.

The stela (the size of a roadside monument) is to be distinguished as a medium of writing from ordinary tablets (suitable for holding on one's lap while writing, or transporting in the Ark). The entire Hammurabi law code was written on one stela. The Nuzi archives, by contrast, consisted of over four thousand tablets (EJ, s.v. "Nuzi").

[17] There seems to be an etymological relationship between the words for "law" (hok) and "engrave" (hakak), precisely because of the ancient Near Eastern practice of engraving laws on stelas.

Alshekh, "there is no doubt that, just as with the tablets it appeared that Moses was writing them but the essential agent was God, so too with the writing of the thirteen Torah scrolls[18] it appeared that Moses was writing them but the essential agent was God." If we do not grant this, "what mortal could write even one Torah scroll in a single day?"[41] There was need of this miracle in order not to give the Israelites an excuse to maintain that the Torah was not of the same status as the Ten Commandments.

The view that the Holy and Blessed One wrote the Torah is hinted at in several sayings mentioned earlier: "This portion is written before Me"; the Torah "was written and lay in the lap of the Holy and Blessed One."[19] If the Torah was written and existed in Heaven before it was given to Moses, then who wrote it? Evidently God wrote it.

In fact, what is just hinted at here is said explicitly elsewhere. According to a Baraita, "when Moses ascended to heaven he found the Holy and Blessed One *seated and writing* the words 'slow to anger.' He asked, 'Master of the Universe, this means slow to anger to the righteous?' God replied, 'Even to the wicked.' Moses said, 'Let the wicked perish!' God replied, 'You will shortly see what need you have of it.' When Israel sinned [in the episode of the spies], God said to Moses, 'Did you say that "slow to anger" applies only to the righteous?' Moses replied, 'Master of the Universe, You said it applies to the wicked!' Therefore it is written, 'Therefore, I pray, let my Lord's forbearance be great, *as You have declared*'" (Numbers 14:17).[42] Similarly, Rabbi Joshua ben Levi recounted, "When Moses ascended to heaven, he found the Holy and Blessed One sitting and tying crowns on the letters."[43]

We encountered earlier Rabbi Simeon ben Lakish's image of the heavenly Torah as letters of black fire on a parchment of white fire.[44] The *Yefei Mar'eh* commented: "If we take 'parchment' in the plain sense, it cannot apply to the tablets, for they were of stone. But then Moses also wrote the scroll of the Torah himself, at God's dictation. Perhaps God gave Moses the original heavenly Torah, written by God, as was said, 'the sword and the scroll descended together from heaven.'[45] This midrash therefore comes to tell us that this fiery Torah miraculously came into Moses' sole possession,

[41] *Torat Moshe* on Deuteronomy 31:24.
[42] BT Sanhedrin 111a.
[43] BT Menahot 29b. What follows is the story of Moses sitting in Rabbi Akiva's classroom hearing Rabbi Akiva expounding the meaning of the crowns.
[44] See above, chapter 17, pp. 333–34, and pp. 538–42 of the current chapter.
[45] Leviticus Rabbah 35:6; Deuteronomy Rabbah 4:2. Cited above, chapter 17, pp. 324–25.

---

[18] This anticipates the theme of the next section.
[19] These citations are from chapter 17, pp. 331–32, but the entire chapter 17 is relevant to this point.

but the Israelites were not worthy of access to it, so he had to write them a Torah scroll of human workmanship."[20] 46

The Amoraim would frequently say, "the All-Merciful wrote," when citing a verse from the Torah. Was this merely a figure of speech for them?

Let us examine a difference of idiom between the Tannaim and the Amoraim. The Tannaitic literature uses the root *ktv* ("write") in the causative mode, meaning "dictate," as in: "Moses, why do you seek to make My Torah a forgery? I have written through you . . ."[47] "I dictated in the Torah . . ."[48] Moses said, "You have dictated in the Torah through me. . . ."[49] But the Amoraim use "write" in the simple mode. Thus, according to Rabbi Johanan, the Israelites say to the Holy and Blessed One, "Master of the Universe! Were it not for the Torah which You have *written* for us, the nations of the world would have wiped us out."[50] According to R. Isaac Napaha, the Holy and Blessed One says to the soul, "I have written concerning you. . . ."[51] According to Rabbi Levi, the Holy and Blessed One says to Moses, "I am writing concerning you, 'Never again did there arise in Israel a prophet like Moses' (Deuteronomy 34:10)."[52] R. Isaac bar Marion said, "If Reuben had known that the Holy and Blessed One would write concerning him, 'When Reuben heard, he saved [Joseph] from [the brothers'] hand' (Genesis 37:21), he would have carried him on his shoulders and taken him to his father."[21] 53 Rabbi Tanhuma bar Hanilai said, "Be mindful of the two mentions of Amalek which I have recorded for you in the Torah."[54]

A Sage of the thirteenth century took note of this matter: "The Mekhilta employs *hikhtiv* [causative mode] when it says, 'God *had written about Himself* that He created the world in six days and rested on the seventh.' This is because of what we have learned in the Talmud:[55] Up to 'Moses died,' the Holy and Blessed One read

---

[46] *Yefei Mar'eh* on PT Shekalim 49d.
[47] Midrash Tannaim to Deuteronomy 31:14, p. 179.
[48] Midrash Tannaim to Deuteronomy 17:21, p. 112.
[49] Midrash Tannaim to Deuteronomy 3:24, p. 15; MSY, p. 58.
[50] PRK 139b.   [51] Leviticus Rabbah 4:1.   [52] Midrash on Samuel 9.
[53] Leviticus Rabbah (ed. Margoliot) 34:8.   [54] Tanhuma Tetzei 5.
[55] BT Bava Batra 15a, Menahot 30a.

---

[20] This is a marvelous example of the harmonizing tendency of later commentators. Faced with several conflicting alternatives, they find ingenious ways to show that they are all right. Thus, the dictation theory, the transcription theory, and the divine inscribing theory all find their way into Samuel Jaffe Ashkenazi's synthesis.

[21] Here there is no implication that God's writing the episode predated creation and predetermined the action (as we found in chapter 17, pp. 330–32). On the contrary, it is possible that God writes the actions of events as they occur. If Reuben had known it would be recorded for posterity, he might have acted more effectively and changed the outcome of the story (and of subsequent history).

aloud[!][22] and Moses wrote. Thus the Torah was written through divine dictation."[56]

The basic idea that an actual book was handed to Moses by the Holy and Blessed One, is found also in the tradition of the "scroll of the Temple" (which we have in the name of R. Jeremiah in the name of R. Samuel bar Isaac, a third-generation Amora renowned for his piety): "The scroll of the Temple, which the Holy and Blessed One handed to Moses while standing, Moses handed it to Joshua while standing," and Joshua to the elders, the elders to the prophets, the prophets to David, and David to Solomon. When David became ill, he sought mercy from the Holy and Blessed One and said to him, "Master of the Universe! Restore me to health on account of the scroll of the Temple which Samuel passed on to me. Grant that I may stand up from this sickbed, and hand over the scroll to the Temple when it is built."[57] The same Amora also said, "The scroll that Samuel passed on to David was meant to be read exegetically [i.e., according to the standard rabbinic rules of exegesis]. How do we know this? It says, 'All this in writing from the hand of the Lord, for understanding'[23] (1 Chronicles 28:19)—'all this in writing'—this is the traditional text, 'from the hand of the Lord'—this is the holy spirit, 'for understanding'—to be read exegetically."[58]

R. Mana said, "Had not the Holy and Blessed One foreseen that Israel were destined to receive the Torah twenty-six generations hence, He would not have written in the Torah, 'Command the Israelites . . . .'"[59]

How Many Torah Scrolls Did Moses Write?

"Moses and the levitical priests spoke to all Israel . . ." (Deuteronomy 27:9). "What did they talk about? The Israelites came to Moses and complained, 'You have taken the Torah and given it to the priests!' (For it says, 'Moses wrote down this Torah and gave it to the priests, sons of Levi' [Deuteronomy 31:9].) Moses suggested, 'Would you like to enter into a compact, that whoever seeks to learn Torah shall not be prevented?' They said, 'Yes.' They stood and swore that no one should be prevented from

---

[56] *Arugat Ha-bosem* of R. Abraham ben Azriel, ed. Urbach, p. 187.
[57] *Aggadat Bereshit* 38:1.
[58] PT Megillah 70a.
[59] Genesis Rabbah 11:4.

---

[22] Heschel calls attention to this word by an exclamation point. Apparently, by this view God *dictated* to Moses from the primordial heavenly Torah—another combination of the dictation and divine-inscription theories.

[23] NJV: "All this [the plan of the Temple] the Lord made me understand by His hand on me, I give you in writing." The notion that this verse was talking about a scroll of the Torah, required exercise of broad midrashic license.

reading the Torah, as it says, 'to all Israel *lemor*'[24] (Deuteronomy 27:9). Moses said to them, 'Today you have become a people'(Deuteronomy 27:9)"[60]

From this account, it follows that Moses wrote only one scroll of the Torah, and handed it to the levitical priests. So says Rashi: "When the Torah was completed, he gave it to the members of his own tribe."[61] And R. Abraham ibn Ezra writes explicitly: "Moses wrote one scroll of the Torah and gave it to the levitical priests, as it is written, for they were the judges." He elaborates on the commandment that the king shall "have a copy of this Teaching written for him" (Deuteronomy 17:18): "Moses commanded that he should write a second scroll like the first, and that it be given to the king, for he is also a judge."[62]

But in the Amoraic period, the view was expressed that Moses our Master wrote more than one Torah scroll. This view was transmitted in the name of R. Huna: "Moses wrote thirteen Torah scrolls on the day that he died, twelve for the twelve tribes, and one which he placed in the Ark, so that if anyone tried to falsify the text, he could not do so."[63] This view was accepted by Maimonides,[64] the author[25] of *Or Zaru'a,*[65] the Mordecai,[26] and others.[66]

This midrash says that Moses wrote thirteen Torah scrolls on the day that he died. This view requires critical examination: "Why do the Sages need all this, that he wrote thirteen Torah scrolls in a single day within a span of hours—something that takes several years? Why twelve Torahs for the tribes and one for the Ark?"[67]

Some say that Moses started writing on the New Moon of Shevat, a month and six days before his death, "and he wrote thirteen scrolls in his own hand, complete from the beginning of Genesis through the end of Deuteronomy, from the first of Shevat to the seventh of Adar. This could have happened only by a miracle [for no human being can write thirteen scrolls of the Torah within thirty-seven days]. Providence was with him. He served as copyist, therefore he is called *mehokek.*[68] [27]

Then another miracle took place. Some say that "the archangel Gabriel descended and took the Torah from Moses' hand, and brought it up to the High Court in

---

[60] YS Tavo 938, citing Deuteronomy Zuta.

[61] Rashi on Deuteronomy 31:9.

[62] *Sefer Tzahot,* ed. Lippman (Fiorda, 5587/1827), 40a–b.

[63] Midrash on Psalms 3; PRK 197a; Deuteronomy Rabbah 9:9; addenda to Midrash Tanhuma, p. 258; Midrash of Moses' Death, *Beit Ha-midrash* I, 122.

[64] Maimonides, Introduction to Commentary on the Mishnah.

[65] *Or Zaru'a* II, *Hilkhot Motza'ei Shabbat* 89, 24a, in the name of R. Yannai.

[66] Mordecai on *Arvei Pesahim;* commentary of the Tosafists on Vayelekh.

[67] Commentary of Maharzu (Ze'ev Wolf Einhorn) on Deuteronomy Rabbah 9:9.

[68] *Me'or Ha-afelah* p. 464.

---

[24] Here the ubiquitous *lemor* is given yet another sense: "[that they should be allowed] to say [i.e., to read it aloud on their own]."

[25] Hayyim ben Isaac, *Or Zaru'a,* late thirteenth century, Germany.

[26] Mordecai ben Hillel Ha-Kohen, thirteenth-century German halakhic authority.

[27] *Mehokek:* Homonym meaning legislator or engraver; see n. [17] above.

heaven, to proclaim Moses' righteousness to the heavenly host, as it says, 'He performed the Lord's righteousness'[28] (Deuteronomy 33:21). Moreover, the righteous
in heaven read from it on Mondays, Thursdays, Sabbaths, New Moons, and festivals."[69]

The two Tannaim who taught that it was impossible that the Torah that Moses
delivered should be missing a single letter used different proof texts. Rabbi Meir cited
Deuteronomy 31:9, while Rabbi Simeon cited Deuteronomy 31:27. The former verse
reads, "Moses wrote down this Teaching [Torah] and gave it to the priests, sons of
Levi." It is possible to understand "this Torah" in the plain sense as referring simply
to Deuteronomy. The following verses enjoin that "you shall read this Teaching
[Torah] aloud in the presence of all Israel," and according to the Sages it was indeed
customary to read the Book of Deuteronomy in the *Hakhel* ceremony. R. Obadiah
Sforno interpreted similarly.[70] But Nahmanides supported the view that "this Teaching" referred to the entire Torah, from Genesis through Deuteronomy. Even though
he agrees that v. 11 ("you shall read this Teaching aloud in the presence of all Israel")
refers just to Deuteronomy, he maintains that the surrounding verses have broader
application ("when Moses had put down in writing the words of this Teaching to the
very end" [v. 24]).[71]

R. Isaac Abravanel rejected Nahmanides' view:

> Moses did not just now write Genesis through Numbers, nor did he now write the last
> verses of Deuteronomy 34 (describing his death). . . . After explaining the laws and seal-
> ing the covenant for their observance, he thought the Torah had been completed and
> that nothing would be added to it. He then committed Deuteronomy to writing, for he
> had written Genesis through Leviticus at Mount Sinai. When he wrote, "Moses wrote
> down this Teaching"[29] (31:9), he had in mind Deuteronomy, for that was the book to
> be read before all Israel (according to the contiguous passage). Moses wrote this book of
> the Torah, as it then stood, and placed it with the other books, then "gave it to the
> priests, sons of Levi, who carried the Ark of the Lord's covenant, and to all the elders of
> Israel' (31:9). But the Blessed God wanted to add the song *Ha'azinu,* as He commanded
> him, "Write down this poem" (31:19). Therefore Moses now needed to commit the
> poem to writing. After this addition, he gave it to the Levites to place by the side of the
> Ark of the Covenant, because of the song that had just been composed, which was a
> "witness." That is why it says there, "When Moses completed writing the words of this
> Torah on a scroll, to the very end"[30] (31:24).[72]

---

[69] Commentary of the Tosafists, end of Vayelekh.
[70] However, Sforno thought that only the passage of the Law of the King would be read in public.
[71] Nahmanides, commentary on Deuteronomy 31:9.
[72] Abravanel ad loc.

---

[28] NJV: "He executed the Lord's judgments."

[29] Deuteronomy 31 has a great many redundant references to Moses writing the "Teaching" or
the "poem" "to the very end," etc. Abravanel skillfully interprets these as referring to the various
addenda that Moses had to add to the Torah after he thought he had finished it.

[30] NJV: "When Moses had put down in writing the words of this Teaching to the very end."

The common Amoraic view that at the end of the fortieth year Moses wrote the entire Torah by divine dictation, is not taught in the Tannaitic midrashim that we have. The Tanna Rabbi Banai, who said, "The Torah was given scroll by scroll," probably did not teach this. Even from Rabbi Meir's and Rabbi Simeon's words, we cannot prove that the writing of the Torah took place at the end of the fortieth year. The Babylonian Talmud does not cite their statements as counterarguments against the view that the Torah was given scroll by scroll.

30

THE MAXIMALIST
AND MINIMALIST APPROACHES

Translator's Introduction

Although Heschel has, since chapter 20, been building his case that admitting a human element in Torah (i.e., the Ishmaelian view) is compatible with (and even *present* in) rabbinic tradition, it has been at least implicit all along that adherents of the more maximalist (Akivan) view had their own ways of understanding the textual difficulties that animated the Ishmaelian exegeses and understandings. In this chapter, Heschel sets out more fully what the maximalist and minimalist views are and especially to what lengths the maximalists were inclined to go to promote and defend their view.

An example of this is the set of four instances in the Torah in which Moses simply did not know how to deal with a legal situation and sought divine guidance. These passages are all highly problematic for the maximalist view. For if Moses had been given all of the Torah as we have it on the mountain at Sinai, how could he have forgotten the outcome of each of these four circumstances, and how could it have been written of him that he was "stumped" in the first place? (One can perhaps imagine that thirty-nine years later, he had forgotten the rules about daughters inheriting [Numbers 27], but how can one suppose that Moses simply forgot something as central as the punishment for Shabbat violation, or [a mere ten months after Sinai] what to do when impurity conflicts with the most central ritual of the Passover [Numbers 9]?) Even here, however, adherents of the Akivan view had their answers, and Heschel brings them to us. His purpose is not only to fill in the rest of the story of ancient interpretation, but apparently also this: to demonstrate, via the obviously strained and forced nature of the replies that the maximalists were constrained to give, just how powerful and alluring was the idea that all was given from the mouth of God.

Some maximalists even went beyond the Pentateuch itself in asserting what it was that Moses received in toto. Here Heschel establishes again the apparent allure of the position, by commending to our attention the implausible ways in which even the Book of Esther was defended by some as a revelation from God to Moses in his own day!

The positions are now fully stated. For those who take the more minimalist view, Moses became a paradigm for future generations. If he could assert his human input and innovate, then so could religious men and women of every generation. For the maximalists, Moses was pinnacle rather than paradigm. For them, human fulfillment comes from recognizing the divine hand that wrote through him and from using powers of interpretation not to innovate but rather to maintain and defend the Torah's supernatural character and power.

In this and the subsequent two chapters, Heschel will lay out in great detail all of the relevant aspects and ramifications of these two views.

Halakhot That Eluded Moses

IT IS RELATED IN THE TORAH that four *halakhot* eluded Moses our Master: (1) the law of the Second Passover, (2) the law concerning the daughters of Zelophehad, (3) the law concerning the wood gatherer, and (4) the law concerning the blasphemer.[1] From these incidents, one could bring evidence to contradict the approach of Rabbi Akiva. For if Moses our Master received the entire Torah, "general principles along with the particulars," at Mount Sinai, how is it that some of the things written in the Torah afterwards eluded him?[2] In truth, we find that Sages of the school of Rabbi Akiva attempted to prove that these things did not elude Moses.

Perhaps from a desire to reconcile this quandary, they set forth that the incident of the wood gatherer occurred on the second Sabbath, before the giving of the Torah, that is, after they were commanded about the Sabbath at Marah[1] [3]; and that both incidents, that is, that of the wood gatherer and that of the blasphemer, "happened at the same time."[2] However, the law of the Second Passover was given "on the first New Moon of the second year following the Exodus from the land of Egypt" (Num-

---

[1] Sifre Shelah 113. [2] Sifra Emor 104c.

---

[1] All of these laws will be described in detail below.

[2] That is, if in fact the entire Torah, every letter, was received by Moses at Mount Sinai, then he already received not just laws but also the *stories* about the laws. Thus, there would be an almost absurd paradox here. For on this view Moses would have been told at Mount Sinai that, for example, the daughters of Zelophehad (see below) would present a case to him, Moses would not know the answer to the problem, and God would then enlighten him. It would then mean that, when the time came that the case was actually presented, Moses not only would have forgotten the law, but would be forced to relive the ignorance that he had already been told about! The whole thing has the aroma of the paradoxes of time travel to it, which is, indeed, one of the persistent problems with what Heschel will presently call the "maximalist view."

[3] Heschel here alludes to the prevalent tradition that at Marah (end Exodus 15), the Israelites were given the rules of the Sabbath. Among other things that prompt this view is that it explains how, in the next chapter, the falling of the manna seems to presuppose some rudimentary knowledge that the seventh day has some special quality to it.

bers 9:1), that is, after the giving of the Torah. And likewise, the matter of the daughters of Zelophehad occurred in the steppes of Moab at the end of the forty years. Since the civil law was also given to Israel before the giving of the Torah, at Marah,[3] [4] how is it possible that Moses did not know how to answer the daughters of Zelophehad?[4][5] To reconcile this quandary one of the disciples of Rabbi Akiva sought to defend the honor of Moses' wisdom and to restrict his ignorance to a single detail. He said that Moses knew the basic law but had difficulty with just one particular; each of these sections could well have been given directly by Moses, but there were reasons for which others had the merit to prompt them.[6] However, this suggestion was not acceptable to all of the Sages. There were those who did not hesitate to say that in the case of the Second Passover, Moses said: "I have no instructions," or that in the case of the daughters of Zelophehad, he was punished, "and the Holy and Blessed One diminished his strength," or that in the case of the wood gatherer, he did not know "what method of execution was to be applied," or that in the case of the blasphemer, he did not know "whether he had committed a capital crime at all."[7]

What was the law of the Second Passover? In the second year of the Exodus from Egypt, they observed the Passover at its time, on the fourteenth day of the first month. "But there were some men who were unclean by reason of a corpse and could not offer the Passover sacrifice on that day. Appearing that same day before Moses and Aaron, those men said to them, 'Unclean though we are by reason of a corpse, why must we be debarred from presenting the Lord's offering at its set time with the rest of the Israelites?' Moses said to them, 'Stand by, and let me hear what instructions the Lord gives about you'" (Numbers 9:6-8). According to the Sifre, Moses

---

[3] See MI Vayyassa' 1; Seder Olam Rabbah 1; BT Sanhedrin 56b. Interestingly, the Sifre Zuta (p. 316) comments: "When did [the daughters of Zelophehad] come before Moses? When the rest of the Israelites were saying to Moses, 'Let us head back to Egypt!' (Numbers 14:4) [i.e., in the summer of the second year]."

[4] Rashbam on BT Bava Batra 119a, s.v. yodea'. Philo also mentioned these four matters as examples of things that were revealed to Moses in response to his queries.

---

[4] Since the text there says that God there gave them hukkim and mishpatim, and the latter term generally is taken in rabbinic literature to mean the civil law, since that is the very word that introduces the civil code in Exodus 21.

[5] Of course, since the incident with the daughters of Zelophehad happened in the fortieth year, just the fact that the civil law had been given in Exodus, after Mount Sinai, but still in year 1, would have sufficed to raise the question. The idea that the civil law even predated Mount Sinai—to Marah—just sharpens and intensifies the question.

[6] And, literally, to have the section named for them. Thus, the section in Numbers 27 dealing with inheritance laws is often just called "the Parashah of the daughters of Zelophehad."

[7] That is, the difference of opinion documented here is over the question of whether Moses had access to the necessary information before the need for it arose. In the former (Akivan) point of view, Moses did have access to all the information, but he, being human, just forgot a single detail, and had to turn to God to be sure everything was being done with exactitude. According to the second point of view, Moses simply didn't know, because he had never been told.

began debating with these men, but in the end admitted, "I have no instructions."[5] However, "Rabbi Hidka said: Simeon of Shikmona was my colleague, from the disciples of Rabbi Akiva, and he said, 'Moses knew that persons in a state of impurity may not eat of the Paschal sacrifice. What were they debating about? Whether the blood of the sacrifice could be sprinkled on their behalf or not.'[8] This section of the Torah could well have been given directly by Moses, but these men received the merit of having prompted it. For meritorious things come from meritorious people, and liabilities come from guilty people."[6] [9]

What was the law concerning the daughters of Zelophehad? Since Moses our Master had said, "And any matter that is too difficult for you, you shall bring to me and I will hear it" (Deuteronomy 1:17), the Holy and Blessed One diminished his strength. Thus, when the daughters of Zelophehad came before him querying about inheritance law, "he began to struggle with it and did not know what to say." And this was a law "that even little schoolchildren ought to know." Moses was forced to bring their case before God (Numbers 27:5).[7] So retribution was exacted from Moses because he had taken the entire crown for himself, in saying "And any matter that is too difficult for you, you shall bring to me" (Deuteronomy 1:17), whereas he should have said, "you shall bring it to the Shekhinah."[8] Here as well, Rabbi Hidka said: "Simeon of Shikmona was my colleague, from the disciples of Rabbi Akiva, and he said, 'Moses our Master knew that the daughters of Zelophehad would inherit land, but he did not know whether the law of the firstborn would also apply to them.'"[10] And it was further said, "the section concerning inheritance could well have been given directly by Moses, but the daughters of Zelophehad received the merit of having prompted it."[9]

---

[5] Sifre Beha'alotekha 68.

[6] Sifra Emor 104c; BT Sanhedrin 78b. The remark, "this section of the Torah could well have been given by Moses, etc." is reminiscent of other sayings of Rabbi Akiva. See Tractate Semahot 8.

[7] Sifre Devarim 17; Numbers Rabbah 21:11; Tanhuma Pinhas 8; TB, Mikketz 6. Batei Midrashot II, 486 has: "I withhold from you a matter that the women know, as it says, 'The daughters of Zelophehad speak rightly' (Numbers 27:6)."

[8] BT Sanhedrin 8a; Rashi s.v. *al davar zeh*.

[9] BT Bava Batra 119a, Sanhedrin 8a; Sifre Pinhas 133.

---

[8] The Paschal sacrifice had to be eaten, at least according to rabbinic law (in a fairly straightforward extrapolation from the biblical material), in preassigned groups. Given that those with corpse impurity could not eat of the sacred flesh of the animal, could they nevertheless be part of a "Paschal fellowship" and have the blood of the sacrifice sprinkled on the altar with them also in mind (and with the attendant expiation of sin accomplished)?

[9] The idea, then, is that Moses could forget a small detail—any person could. But he could not forget the entire law. So, according to Rabbi Akiva's disciple quoted here, since it is a given that Moses got all laws, it must only have been a small detail that he forgot.

[10] That is, the law of primogeniture set forth in Deuteronomy 21, according to which the firstborn son acquires twice as much of the inheritance as each of his brothers. In the case of daughters inheriting in the absence of sons, would this also apply to the firstborn, that is, would Mahlah, the oldest of Zelophehad's daughters, receive a double portion of the father's share in the land?

What was the law of the wood gatherer? "Once, when the Israelites were in the wilderness, they came upon a man gathering wood on the Sabbath day. Those who found him as he was gathering wood brought him before Moses, Aaron, and the whole community. He was placed in custody, for it had not been specified what should be done to him" (Numbers 15:32–34). Now the Sages were puzzled: "It says, after all, 'He who profanes it shall be put to death' (Exodus 31:14), and thus what is the meaning of the phrase 'for it had not been specified'?" "Said Rabbi Hidka: Simeon of Shikmona was my colleague, from the disciples of Rabbi Akiva, and he said, 'Moses knew that the wood gatherer should be put to death, but he did not know which method of execution was to be applied,'"[10] until he received instructions from the Most Holy. However, "Rabbi Eliezer ben Simeon said: 'Moses knew neither which method or execution to apply, nor even that he was subject to the death penalty. The response he got proves this: "Then the Lord said to Moses, 'The man shall be put to death . . . pelt him with stones'" (Numbers 15:35)—that is, (1) he is liable to the death penalty, and (2) execute him by stoning.'"[11]

What was the law of the blasphemer? When the Israelites were in the desert, and the son of an Israelite woman and an Egyptian man cursed God by name, they brought him to Moses, "and he was placed in custody, until the decision of the Lord should be made clear to them" (Leviticus 24:12). The Sages said in this case: "Moses our Master knew that the wood gatherer should be put to death, for it was said, 'He who profanes it shall be put to death' (Exodus 31:14), but he did not know which method of execution to apply, as it says: 'for it had not been specified what should be done to him' (Numbers 15:34). But in the case of the blasphemer, it says merely 'until the decision of the Lord should be made clear to them' (Leviticus 24:12), for Moses did not know whether he had committed a capital crime at all."[12] And yet, there were those who attempted to reconcile matters according to the approach of Rabbi Akiva, and said, "'for a bird of the air may carry the utterance, and a winged creature may report the word' (Ecclesiastes 10:20)—this tells us that Moses was told at Sinai: 'Take the blasphemer outside the camp . . . and let the whole community stone him' (Leviticus 24:14)."[13] [11]

---

[10] Sifre Shalah 114; Sifra Emor 104c; PT Sanhedrin 22d. So too Philo, *De Vita Mosis* II, 217.

[11] Sifre Zuta, p. 288. The Baraita in BT Bava Batra 119a concludes: "The passage of the wood gatherer could have been written by Moses, but the wood gatherer came and it was written on his account. This is another example of 'meritorious things are brought about by meritorious people, and liabilities by guilty people.'"

[12] BT Sanhedrin 78b; Sifra 104c.

[13] TB, Balak 29.

---

[11] The reader will have noticed an asymmetry here. Of the four cases cited, this one has a noticeable difference. That is, whereas in the other three cases, the Akivan point of view was expressed in the idea that one detail was forgotten, here that was impossible, because it seems that Moses knew nothing about this case at all ("until the decision of the Lord should be made clear"). There was no detail of which to claim that Moses forgot it, so the Akivan response here had to be that Moses in fact

A different resolution was suggested in the Jerusalem Targum, attributed in printed editions to Jonathan ben Uzziel. In this text, it is said of these four cases—of which two were "monetary,"[12] and two were capital cases—that Moses did not want to adjudicate them on his own, in order to teach the leaders of the Sanhedrin in future generations to be scrupulous in monetary cases, and moderate in capital cases, and that they should not be embarrassed to say that they have not yet learned the law.[14] A similar exegesis is brought in the name of Rabbi Simeon ben Lakish: "Moses knew this law, but the daughters of Zelophehad had first come to the chiefs of tens,[13] who had told them: 'this is an inheritance case, and it is not for us, but rather for our superiors.' They then went to the chiefs of fifties, who saw that the chiefs of tens had deferred to them, and they in turn said: 'we also have superiors.' The same happened with the chiefs of hundreds and the chiefs of thousands, and with the tribal chieftains as well. Each group answered them similarly, for none of them wished to speak before their superiors. Said Moses: 'If I tell them the law, I will take all the glory on myself.' So he said to them: 'Even I have a Superior,' and thus, 'Moses brought their case before the Lord' (Numbers 27:5)."[15]

According to Rabbi Isaiah de-Trani,[14] Moses knew the laws of inheritance, but "he was not instructed to transmit them to Israel until the daughters of Zelophehad came."[16] And this is what they meant when they said, "the laws of inheritance could well have been given directly by Moses, but the daughters of Zelophehad received the merit of having prompted it." And the Sages said something similar about the wood gatherer.[17]

Rabbi Simeon ben Yohai, in holding fast to Rabbi Akiva's approach that each and every commandment was given three times: at Sinai, in the Tent of Meeting, and in the steppes of Moab, disagreed with the Sages on this matter: Moses our Master said to his father-in-law: "We are setting out for the place of which the Lord has said, 'I will give it to you'" (Numbers 10:29). The Sages said: "Why did Moses include himself in this declaration? Because the truth eluded him, and he believed that he would

---

[14] Jerusalem Targum on Numbers 9:8; 15:34; 27:5; and Leviticus 24:12.
[15] Tanhuma (standard and Buber editions) Pinhas 9; Numbers Rabbah 21:12.
[16] Tosafot of RID to Bava Batra 119b.
[17] See n. 11 above.

---

knew what to do all along, since he had so been told at Sinai, and for reasons unknown to the readers of Scripture Moses did not want to divulge it on his own.

[12] The term is used loosely here, simply to distinguish it from "capital." The law of the daughters of Zelophehad was certainly a monetary matter—about inheritance—but the law of the Second Passover was not, strictly speaking, monetary (except in the sense that the impure persons did not get an exemption, but were required to provide their own lamb for a Passover "make-up" in the next month).

[13] The reference here is to the system of delegated authority that had been set up by Jethro. See Exodus 18:25.

[14] Thirteenth century, Italy.

join them in entering the Land of Israel." Rabbi Simeon ben Yohai said: "Not so, for it was already said, 'For I must die in this land' (Deuteronomy 4:22), and what is more, it was not necessary to say 'I shall not cross the Jordan' (Deuteronomy 4:22)[15] except that Moses said so to indicate that even his bones would not cross the Jordan. Why then did Moses include himself with the nation in this declaration? So that Israel would not be led to say: 'If the one who took us out of Egypt and did all these miracles and wonders for us is not entering the Land, we must also not be entering!'"[18]

A *Halakhah* Given to Moses from Sinai

Among the fundamentals of the faith is that two Torahs were given to Israel, one written and one oral. But with regard to the meaning of this fundamental, there have also been two approaches: the maximalist and the minimalist approach. According to the maximalist approach, Moses received the Torah at Sinai with all of its explanations, general rules, detailed minutiae, including even those things that were to be said by Sages who succeeded him. According to the minimalist approach, the interpretations of laws and how to fulfill them were spoken at Sinai, but many details and minutiae were explicated or instituted by the Sages of the Oral Torah.[16] According to Maimonides, in the introduction to his commentary on the Mishnah, "everything that has no hint in Scripture, is unconnected to the text and is impossible to extract from the text by logical methods—about such things alone is it said that they are *halakhot* given to Moses from Sinai."[17]

In the maximalist mode they taught in the school of Rabbi Akiva: "These are the laws, rules, and instructions that the Lord established, through Moses on Mount Sinai, between Himself and the Israelite people" (Leviticus 26:46)—"'the laws': these are the exegeses; 'the rules': these are the civil laws; 'the instructions': this teaches that two Torahs were given to Israel, one oral and one written . . . 'through Moses on

---

[18] Sifre Beha'alotekha 78; Midrash Haggadol Beha'alotekha, p. 231; Sifre Zuta, p. 264.

---

[15] Because it was, after the previous phrase, redundant. It is always characteristic of the Akivan view that apparent redundancies cannot be dismissed as style and must be expounded, as the phrase is here.

[16] For example, the Sabbath is mentioned briefly in the Torah, but there is a general explanation linking it to the days of creation and specifying that it is a day of cessation from regular work activities. The immense details about what constitutes work, however, were left for later generations to specify.

[17] Maimonides tells us that "a *halakhah* to Moses from Sinai" is a phrase to be used as a "last resort," when there is no other way to explain the appearance of a certain law. However, most laws do have some scriptural connection, and they are understood on this view to have been extracted from what was given to Moses and not to have been given themselves.

Mount Sinai': this teaches that the Torah was given, with its laws, minutiae, and interpretations all through Moses at Sinai."[19] This general principle was repeated and trebled in the Sifra. But against this Rabbi Ishmael expounded: "'These are the rules that you shall set before them' (Exodus 21:1)—these are the thirteen modes of exegesis applicable to the Torah, that were given to Moses at Sinai."[20] Note that according to the first approach even the minutiae and interpretations were given through Moses at Sinai. But Rabbi Ishmael's statement mentioned only the thirteen modes of exegesis.[18]

According to the approach of Rabbi Akiva, who holds that the Torah and all of its laws, minutiae, and interpretations were given through Moses at Sinai, it is not possible to say of anything that it is a *halakhah* given to Moses from Sinai, as if this distinguishes it. Rabbi Akiva holds that "the entire Torah are *halakhot* given to Moses from Sinai."[21] That is to say: All of the rules and their minutiae are *halakhot* given to Moses from Sinai. Rabbi Akiva took matters that were, according to other Sages, "*halakhot* given to Moses from Sinai," and found scriptural sources for them.[22] "The following, however, of those that either chew the cud or have true hoofs, you shall not eat: the camel—although it chews the cud, it has no true hoofs" (Leviticus 11:4). In the school of Rabbi Akiva they determined that there was superfluous text here. For it could have said, "The following, however, you shall not eat: the camel—although it chews the cud . . ."; but the text intended to add the following: "There are among those animals that chew the cud and have true hoofs that you may not eat, and those are the animals that have been torn."[23] [19]

---

[19] Sifra Behukotai 112c, according to the formulation in YS. Other similar enumerations are found in Sifra Aharei 85d, Sifre Re'eh 58, MI Amalek 2, and MI Vayyassa' 1. The most inclusive is given in the next subsection.

[20] Midrash Haggadol to Exodus, p. 459; Midrash of the Thirteen Hermeneutic Principles in *Birkat Abraham* (Hebrew volume of Festschrift for Abraham Berliner [Frankfurt, 1903], 16); Rashi on BT Hullin 116a and Pesahim 24a.

[21] BT Niddah 45a.

[22] Sifra Tzav 34d–35a. "They said in the name of Rabbi Johanan that the procession of the willow and the water libation were *halakhot* given to Moses from Sinai, whereas Rabbi Akiva said the water libation is taught in the Torah" (PT Shevi'it 33b).

[23] Sifra Shemini 48c. The RaABaD, in his comment on this passage, took the Ishmaelian position: "It seems to me that this is only a rabbinic *asmakhta* [casual textual support], for the eighteen *terefot* are actually a *halakhah* given to Moses from Sinai."

---

[18] That is, the maximalist approach is about discovery of religious laws and truths already given; the minimalist approach is about construction, or even invention, of religious laws and truths out of basic materials previously given. We have already seen this distinction between discovery and construction at the very beginning of this work, when Heschel introduced us to the basic Akivan-Ishmaelian split on the matter of scriptural exegesis.

[19] This is the literal meaning of *terefot*, which came, by derivation, to mean an animal, otherwise fit for eating, that has a serious organic disease. There are, by one tradition, eighteen of these (see next paragraph) that Moses learned. In modern usage, *treif*, a derivative of this word, often is used to mean "unfit for eating" for whatever reason.

But in the school of Rabbi Ishmael they gave the following enumeration: "The laws of the eighteen organic diseases were spoken to Moses at Sinai."[24] "The eleven spices of the incense were spoken to Moses at Sinai."[25] [20] And the laws of the ten saplings,[21] the willow,[22] the water libations,[23] and of the tomb covering and supporting walls[24]—were all *halakhot* given to Moses from Sinai, according to Rabbi Ishmael. And by contrast, Rabbi Akiva derived all of these from Scripture.[26]

It stands to reason that the school of Rabbi Ishmael did not accept the maximalist view. For if they were prepared to say that the entire Torah, with all of its general principles, particulars, and minutiae was given at Sinai, what news would they be imparting in saying that the thirteen modes of exegesis, the eighteen organic diseases, and the eleven spices were spoken to Moses at Sinai? Apparently they believed in the school of Rabbi Ishmael that the modes of exegesis by which the Sages extracted various matters from the text were revealed to Moses at Sinai, but not those matters themselves. That is to say: general principles—that is, explanations of commandments and the thirteen modes of exegesis—were taught by the Holy and Blessed One to Moses, but not the particulars, as was Rabbi Abbahu's opinion,[25] to be discussed below.

In the school of Rabbi Ishmael they believed that many laws and rules were not given to Moses by the Holy and Blessed One, but rather the Sages themselves extracted them from the text by means of the modes of exegesis applicable to the Torah. "The Torah granted wisdom to the Sages to expound and to proclaim."[27] In the case of the prohibition on work on the Intermediate Days of the Festival[26]: Rabbi Akiva derived it from Scripture, while Rabbi Ishmael held that "we do not learn from

[24] BT Hullin 42a.

[25] BT Keritot 6b in the name of Rabbi Johanan; YS Tissa 389 in the name of Rabbi Jonathan, a disciple of Rabbi Ishmael.

[26] BT Moed Katan 3b-4a; PT Shevi'it 33b; BT Hullin 72a.

[27] Sifre Pinhas 134.

---

[20] The Torah, in Exodus 30, had listed only four of these.

[21] Normally there was a prohibition on plowing fields in the months leading up to the Sabbatical (seventh) Year. This special *halakhah,* however, sets forth that a field of a certain size that has at least ten saplings in it may be plowed, for the sake of those young trees, all the way up to Rosh Hashanah of the Sabbatical Year.

[22] I.e., that the altar in the Temple was walked around in procession with the willow branches on the seven days of the festival of Sukkot.

[23] Which were also done on the altar on the seven days of Sukkot. Normally, only wine was poured on the altar.

[24] *Golel* and *Dofek,* the covering placed on a tomb and the walls that support the covering, while not part of the tomb itself, still impart corpse impurity when walked over.

[25] To be presented below, in the section entitled "Things not Revealed to Moses."

[26] Biblically speaking, the five days between the first and last days of Passover, both of which are holy days when work is forbidden, and the six days between the first and eighth days of Sukkot. Of these intermediate days, the Torah does not forbid work, but rabbinic law did place some significant restrictions on activities then.

Scripture that work is prohibited on the intermediate days of the festival . . . Scripture left that in the hands of the Sages, to declare on which day work is prohibited and on which day it is permitted, and which kind of work is prohibited and which is permitted."[28]

Adopting the minimalist approach, Maimonides holds that "every commandment that the Holy and Blessed One gave to Moses our Master, peace be upon him, was given with an explanation: God would tell him the commandment, and then give its explanation and context . . . and here is an example: the Holy and Blessed One said to Moses: 'You shall live in booths seven days' (Leviticus 23:42), and then informed him that this Sukkah (booth) is incumbent on males but not on females, that the infirm are exempt from it, as are travelers . . . and so it was with all 613 commandments, them and their explanations: the commandment was given in writing, and the explanation was given orally." And whatever was given to Moses gave rise to no divergence of opinion. "But that which was not heard explicitly from the prophet, peace be upon him, among the many matters that branch off from those original commandments, were derived by logic and by the thirteen modes of reasoning that were given at Mount Sinai and are applicable to the Torah. And among those derived laws, there are those that did not give rise to controversy, and all accepted them unanimously; and then there are those that did give rise to controversy: one says this, and another says that, each giving some reason that strengthens his case . . . and when such controversy arose, they would side with the majority, as it says: 'to incline in favor of the majority' (Exodus 23:2)."[29] And this is how Maimonides opens the preface to the *Mishneh Torah*: "All of the commandments that were given to Moses at Sinai were given with their explanations, as it says: 'I will give you the stone tablets with the teachings and commandments' (Exodus 24:12): 'the teachings'—this is the Written Torah, 'and commandments'—this is its explanation." Here Maimonides relies on the exegesis of Rabbi Simeon ben Lakish, without accepting literally his declaration that even Mishnah, prophetic works, writings, and Gemara were given to Moses at Sinai. Likewise, Maimonides deviates from the approaches of Rabbi Simeon ben Lakish and Rabbi Joshua ben Levi in that he says that Rav Ashi compiled in the Gemara, "statutes and latent rules that were not received from Moses and that contemporary courts derived." For Maimonides held that "in every generation new matters of law were added" that were not learned from the chain of tradition but rather from one of the thirteen modes of exegesis.[30]

It is reasonable that Maimonides did not accept the maximalist approach. For if he were prepared to say that Moses received at Sinai the entire Torah, with all of its general principles, particulars, and minutiae, how could he have written about "matters

---

[28] Sifra Emor 102b; Sifre Re'eh 135. See BT Bekhorot 26b, Hagigah 18a.

[29] Maimonides, Introduction to the Commentary on the Mishnah.

[30] Maimonides distinguishes between three categories of rabbinic Halakhah: (1) those things passed down by tradition (Oral Law in the proper sense); (2) those things derived by the Sages from the thirteen modes of exegesis; (3) preventive enactments, the "fence around the law," required by the exigencies of the hour—*gezerot* (decrees), *takkanot* (enactments), and *minhagim* (customs).

that were added in every generation"? "What purpose would there have been in inno-vation?"[31]

Maimonides set down this principle: "We do not say of everything that the Sages derived by use of the thirteen modes of exegesis that it was spoken to Moses at Sinai."[32] [27] According to this approach, Moses received only "explanations of the scriptural verses and certain things derivable by exegesis that amount to less than one percent of the laws that are mentioned in the Mishnah and Gemara."[33] Similarly, the Tosafot say that there are rabbinic laws "that were not given as *halakhah* to Moses from Sinai."[34] The Holy and Blessed One "granted to the Sages of each generation, that even if they say of something truly impure that it is pure, or vice versa, there will be no other authority for each generation.[28] And the Holy and Blessed One agrees that each generation's adjudication must follow the best judgment of the Sages who interpret the scriptural verses, whether or not they hit upon the truth. For so did the Divine Wisdom decree, that each matter should be decided by a majority of the Sages in each generation, as their judgment dictates."[35]

Other Sages as well suggested that Moses received only general principles of *halakhah* at Sinai, but not particulars. An example of this is the matter of minimal quantities,[29] which are said to be *halakhot* given to Moses from Sinai.[36] The Holy and Blessed One did not specify to Moses the minimal quantity of each and every individual item, but rather the idea of minimal quantities was given to Moses gener-ally, and the Sages "by the power of their own reasoning set up the exact minimal quantities for each appropriate context."[37] According to the view of Rabbi Jonathan Eibeschutz,[30] "Moses received only generalities: for example, that there are eighteen kinds of organic diseases, and the Sages, of blessed memory, brought all the details of

---

[31] See David Nito, *Mateh Dan,* Third Dialogue, 5.

[32] *Sefer Ha-mitzvot,* Second Principle.

[33] *Responsa Havvot Ya'ir* (of Jair Hayyim Bacharach; seventeenth century, Germany) 192 (Frankfurt am Main, 5459/1699), 183b.

[34] BT Eruvin 21b, Tosafot s.v. *mipnei mah.*

[35] *Responsa Hut Ha-shani* (of Abraham Samuel Bacharach and his son Moses Samson Bacharach; seven-teenth century, Moravia and Germany) 53.

[36] BT Yoma 40a.

[37] Tractate on *Halakhah le-Moshe mi-Sinai* of R. Solomon Raphael Judah Leao Templo (seventeenth-eighteenth century, Netherlands) (Amsterdam, 5495/1735), 3b, 8b.

---

[27] This is like the Ishmaelian position.

[28] That is, there might in fact be a "Platonic" *halakhah,* that is, a real answer as to what the law really is, but it is not directly accessible to us and is thus irrelevant. The only thing that matters, in this view, is the process that the Sages are authorized to use to make legal decisions. They are, by defini-tion, valid.

[29] Examples of these are: the amount of water that an immersion pool (*mikveh*) must contain, the amount of *matzah* that one must eat on the first night of Passover to fulfill the religious obligation, and the amount of wine over which the Sabbath should be sanctified at the Friday night meal.

[30] Eighteenth century, Poland.

organic diseases to light."[38] In a similar vein, Rabbi Zevi Hirsch Chajes[31] explained the following statement of Rabbi Johanan: "The Holy and Blessed One showed Moses the minutiae of the Torah and the minutiae of the Scribes." He said that the intent of this was "that once Moses received the ways of exegeting the text, anything that would be derived through them in a future generation is latent in the Torah through the agency of these principles and modes of exegesis."[39] Even the statement, "Whatever a diligent student will in the future innovate . . ." he restricts and says: "The Holy and Blessed One gave to Moses the modes of exegesis, and the Sages extract from these principles derivatives and branches, learning the obscure from that which is explicit. All of these particulars are latent in the general principle."[40] [32]

Even What a Diligent Student Will Teach in the Future

Rabbi Akiva's approach was greatly expanded in the period of the Amoraim. This approach says that not only the commandments but also how they are to be observed, their derivative rules, minutiae, and interpretations were all given to Moses at Sinai. And now Rabbi Simeon ben Lakish comes and teaches that not only did Moses receive all the commandments and their interpretations, but also all words of prophecy, as well as Mishnah and Talmud. "The Lord said to Moses, 'Come up to Me on the mountain and wait there, and I will give you the stone tablets with the teachings and commandments which I have inscribed to instruct them'" (Exodus 24:12). Rabbi Simeon ben Lakish expounded on this: "'The stone tablets'—this is Scripture; 'the teachings'—this is Mishnah; 'the commandments'—has its usual meaning; 'which I have inscribed'—these are the words of Prophecy, 'to instruct them'—this is the Talmud. This teaches that they were all given to Moses at Sinai."[41]

Evidence for the fact that Rabbi Simeon ben Lakish expanded the Akivan concept emerges from a comparison of his words to that of an exegesis of Leviticus 10:10-11:

"you must distinguish between the sacred and the profane"—these are the laws of Temple dedications,[33] "and between the unclean and the clean"—these are the purities and

---

[38] *Kereti u-feleti* 29.
[39] "Introduction to the Talmud," 3.
[40] Chajes, glosses to BT Berakhot 5a.
[41] BT Berakhot 5a, according to Nahmanides' reading (see his glosses to Maimonides' *Sefer Ha-mitzvot* Principle 1, and the Geonic work *Halakhot Gedolot*, ed. Hildesheimer, p. 222).

---

[31] Chajes, 1805–1855, Austria and Poland.
[32] But not all were given at Sinai.
[33] That is, when a person dedicates the value of another person, or other creatures or objects, to the Temple. These laws derive from Leviticus 27 and are detailed in several talmudic tractates, such as Arakhin.

impurities,[34] "and you must teach the Israelites"—these are the laws of erroneous decisions,[35] "all the laws"—these are the exegeses, "which the Lord has imparted to them"—these are the *halakhot,* "through Moses"—this is Scripture. Shall we think to include Talmud as well? [No,] the text tells you: "you must teach."[36] Said Rabbi Yose ben Judah: How do we know that we should include also Targum? The text tells you: "you must teach."[42] [37] Here "the Talmud" is explicitly excluded from what God spoke through Moses.

According to Rabbi Abraham ben David,[38] the intent here is that the *halakhot* are "from the mouth of God" and the Talmud is "from the minds of the Sages themselves."[43]

The maximalist approach to the giving of the Torah is taught often in rabbinic literature.[44] In the Midrash Numbers Rabbah it is said that six verses in Psalm 19 (beginning with v. 8) correspond to the six orders of the Mishnah. In each of these verses the name of God appears. And they ask: "Why is the Name of the Holy and Blessed One mentioned in connection with each of the six orders? In order to testify that it was from God's mouth that they were spoken to Moses, just as God spoke the Five Books of the Torah."[45] In a similar vein they expounded in Midrash Haggadol: "When He finished speaking with him on Mount Sinai, He gave Moses . . .' (Exodus

[42] Sifra Shemini 46d, which, however, is missing an entire line, restored by L. Finkelstein in his edition of the Rome MS, p. 200. See Finkelstein's article in *Louis Ginzberg Jubilee Volume* (New York: American Academy for Jewish Research, 1945), Hebrew section, p. 312.

[43] Commentary to Sifra, ad loc.

[44] "'Indeed, I wrote down for you a threefold lore' (Proverbs 22:20)—lest one say that the Holy One gave us only Scripture, but not *halakhot,* midrash, and *aggadot,* here Solomon tells us, the Holy One says, 'I gave it all to you'" (A. Marmorstein, "Ein Fragment einer neuen Piska zum Wochenfest und der Kampf gegen das muendlichen Gesetz," *Jeshurun* 12 (1925): 33. "Fifty gates of understanding were created in the world, and all but one were given to Moses" (BT Rosh Hashanah 21b). According to the kabbalists, even the mysteries and supernal wisdom were revealed to Moses. "How is it that Ezekiel could reveal the secrets of the chariot? 'The King has brought me to his chambers' (Song of Songs 1:4)—at the time when the Torah was given at Sinai" (Song of Songs Rabbah 1:4; *Yefei Kol* ad loc.).

[45] Numbers Rabbah 13:16.

[34] That is, the laws concerning how different vessels and articles of clothing can receive impurity, laws that are detailed in the sixth order of the Mishnah, "Purities."

[35] What to do when the religious court gives an erroneous decision that people then follow, relying on their authority. These laws are given in the Tractate Horayot.

[36] The exegesis here seems to turn on the word "you." That is, if the Talmud had also been given, "you" would not be teaching. There has to be a "you" in the teaching of religious law, and the Talmud's independence from Sinai provides that. That is what distinguishes this more "minimalist" exegesis from the "maximalist" view of Rabbi Simeon ben Lakish.

[37] Presumably, what Yose ben Judah had in mind here was that in order to teach, one must have the text in the language that the people being taught will understand. Thus, the Targum in Aramaic must also have been given at Sinai!

[38] Twelfth century, Provence, preeminent commentator on the Sifra (as well as on the codes of Maimonides and Alfasi).

31:18)—"this teaches that the entire Torah, plus Mishnah, Tosefta, and Aggadot, were all from Sinai."[46]

They said: "'And he was there with the Lord forty days and forty nights' (Exodus 34:28). How did Moses know when it was day? When the Holy and Blessed One taught him the Written Torah he knew that it was day. And when God taught him orally the Mishnah and Talmud, he knew that it was night."[47] [39] It was further said: "When the Holy and Blessed One came to teach Moses Torah, it was taught in order: Scripture, Mishnah, Aggadah, and Talmud."[48]

The opinion of Rabbi Simeon ben Lakish was not accepted by biblical commentators as the plain meaning of the verse.[40] Rabbi Abraham ibn Ezra hints at this: "'the teachings and the commandments'—some say that this means the Written Torah and the Oral Torah. But truly, it speaks only of the tablets. And the ultimate proof is in the words themselves: 'which I have inscribed,' which clearly refers back to the tablets, and God wrote no teaching but the Ten Commandments; the rest was written by Moses at God's behest." Rashi also did not accept the approach of Rabbi Simeon ben Lakish. He explains that the referent of this verse is the Ten Commandments alone, but that "all 613 commandments are included in the Ten Commandments. And Rabbenu Saadia explicated in the admonitions that he composed for each of the Ten Commandments all of the commandments that are dependent on them." Such also was the opinion of RaSHBaM. Nahmanides, however, attempted to strengthen Rabbi Simeon ben Lakish's opinion on the basis of the belief in the pre-existence of the Torah: "according to the views of our Masters, there is possibly a hint that the entire Torah was written in God's presence before the world was created." According to this, the expression "which I have inscribed" could refer to the entire Torah.

Rabbi Johanan, according to whom the Torah was not given all at once, but rather "scroll by scroll," did not accept the view of his colleague Rabbi Simeon ben Lakish. It is written: "And the Lord gave me the two tablets of stone inscribed by the finger of God, and on them the exact words that the Lord had addressed to you out of the fire on the day of the Assembly" (Deuteronomy 9:10); and Rabbi Johanan said: "this teaches that the Holy and Blessed One showed Moses the minutiae of Torah and the minutiae of the Scribes, and what the Scribes would one day innovate. And what was that? The law of the reading of the Scroll of Esther."[49]

[46] Midrash Haggadol on Exodus 31:18, Margoliot edition p. 675. Similarly Ecclesiastes Zuta, p. 104.
[47] Tanhuma Tissa 36; Midrash on Psalms 19:7; Midrash Haggadol on Exodus, loc. cit.
[48] TB, Tissa p. 116.
[49] BT Megillah 19b.

[39] The intent here is not entirely clear. Most probably it is referring to the complexity, and sometimes obscurity, of talmudic discussions, certainly as compared to the relatively straightforward clarity of Scripture. The rabbis often described the Talmud in such terms, such as a "sea" that is difficult to navigate.
[40] That is, Exodus 24:12.

Come see what separates the views of Rabbi Simeon ben Lakish and Rabbi Johanan. Rabbi Simeon ben Lakish believes that the prophets, the Mishnah, and the Talmud were given to Moses at Sinai, while Rabbi Johanan exploits the style of the Sifra and speaks only about "minutiae of Torah and minutiae of the Scribes." Rabbi Simeon ben Lakish says: "they were given to Moses," while Rabbi Johanan says: "the Holy and Blessed One showed Moses," "that is to say: Moses received them only as one sees, but not as one has transferred to him, as when a person shows his neighbor something but does not give it to him."[50] Rabbi Johanan also added: "and what the Scribes would one day innovate." Analyze his language carefully. He did not say: all that the Scribes would one day innovate, or all that any wise person would one day innovate. As an example of what he speaks of, he cites the reading of the Scroll of Esther. He gives us a general statement followed by a particular one, and the rule is that the general is thus restricted to the particular—in this case, the reading of the Scroll of Esther.[41]

Rabbi Joshua ben Levi's words had an especially large influence on the development of these thoughts in subsequent generations. Similarly to Rabbi Johanan, he expounded the verse:

> "And the Lord gave to me the two tablets of stone inscribed by the finger of God, and on them the exact words that the Lord had addressed . . ." (Deuteronomy 9:10). The text could have been written: "on them." Why was it written "and on them"? It could have been written: "the words." Why was it written "the exact words"? It could have been written "words." Why was it written "the words"? From the additional letters here Rabbi Joshua ben Levi would expound: "Scripture, Mishnah, Talmud, Aggadah, and even what a diligent student will teach in the future before his Master was already spoken to Moses at Sinai. What is the reason for saying this? "Sometimes there is a phenomenon of which they say, 'Look, this one is new!'" (Ecclesiastes 1:10), and the companion phrase answers it: "it occurred long since" (Ecclesiastes 1:10).[51]

Many Sages accepted the maximalist approach and believed that Moses our Master received at Sinai all of the rules, the innovative interpretations, the logical reasonings, and the dialectic that were produced from his time through the end of time. They saw in the statement of Rabbi Joshua ben Levi a set *halakhah* that may not be challenged, a root principle of the faith.

[50] R. Yom Tov Lipmann Heller (seventeenth century, central and Eastern Europe), introduction to his classic commentary on the Mishnah, *Tosefot Yom Tov*.

[51] PT Pe'ah 17a; Megillah 74d; Hagigah 76d; Ecclesiastes Rabbah 1:9. Variants are found in Leviticus Rabbah 22:1; TB, Tissa 17; Exodus Rabbah 47:1. In the Halakhot Gedolot (p. 223, influenced by the end of Tosefta Kiddushin), it is Abraham to whom all was revealed in advance.

---

[41] This is a playful case of Heschel applying to the Rabbis the exegetical principles that they applied to Scripture. In this case, it is the rule (according to the Fourth Hermeneutic Principle of Rabbi Ishmael) that when the Torah gives a general category and then lists one of the members of that class, the Torah means to restrict the rule in question to that particular only. Heschel here applies this to the words of Rabbi Johanan. It may not be valid to do so, but Heschel may be forgiven for indulging in this playfulness in a matter relating to the Scroll of Esther!

So does Rabbi Moses of Coucy[42] write: "that is why Moses lingered on the mountain for forty days and forty nights: in order to learn all of the explanations and minutiae. For if he were to be given only the tablets, that could have been done in a brief moment. He did not tarry for forty days but for the purpose of explicating the interpretation of the commandments and their minutiae well."[52]

Rabbenu Nissim[43] also interpreted Rabbi Johanan's statement in accordance with the maximalist approach. According to his opinion, "the minutiae of the Scribes are the differences of opinion and the arguments of logic between the Sages of Israel, and all of these were taught to Moses by the Most High."[53] [44]

Rabbi Obadiah of Bertinoro[45] went even farther and said: "The Sages of the Gentiles also composed books of ethics, which they made up themselves, and which advise how a person should behave with other people. Therefore, the Tanna began this tractate [Avot]: Moses received instruction from Sinai, in order to teach you that the moral and ethical principles in this tractate were not made up by the Sages of the Mishnah, but rather these too were spoken at Sinai."[54]

However, this outlook is not uncontroversial, and many of the great Sages of Israel did not go with Rabbi Joshua ben Levi's approach. Concerning the statement of Rabbi Simeon ben Lakish, with which we began this chapter, one Sage explained as follows: that his intention was not "that all of these things were given to Moses to give to us

[52] Moses of Coucy, Introduction to *Sefer Ha-mitzvot Gadol*.
Similarly, Hillel "of Verona" (actually, of Naples and Capua, thirteenth-century philosopher and defender of Maimonides) wrote: "Everything that we learn in the Mishnah, Talmud, and halakhic midrashim (Sifra, Sifre), of the mitzvot and their elaboration, of the rules for interpreting the Torah, instances of *kal va-homer* and *gezerah shavah*, etc., should all be taken at face value. It is incumbent on every Jew to accept them exactly as they were said, without addition or omission, not to question or doubt them or interpret them allegorically or otherwise than as they were intended. For they were all said from the mouth of Moses our Master, peace be his, for the Torah is acquired through faith in the Sages. Whoever questions them or understands them contrary to their plain sense or to the rabbinic interpretation, is a complete heretic and Epicurean, who cuts down the shoots and has no portion in the world to come" (*Tagmulei Ha-nefesh* 25a).
According to the older *Sefer Hasidim* (302), the melodic tropes for public chanting of the Torah and other scriptures were given as halakhah to Moses from Sinai. The HIDA (Rabbi Hayyim Joseph David Azulai) expressed amazement at this: "But there is a variety of practice in the melodic tropes (nay, even in the pronunciation of Hebrew) among Jews in different lands! But the expression 'halakhah to Moses from Sinai' may be meant figuratively, not literally" (*Berit Olam* [commentary to *Sefer Hasidim*], ad loc.).
[53] *Homilies of Rabbenu Nissim*, seventh homily.
[54] Obadiah of Bertinoro, Commentary on Avot 1:1.

[42] The author of *Sefer Mitzvot Gadol*, thirteenth century, France.
[43] Fourteenth century, Spain.
[44] This is the first time that we have encountered here the problem of how to deal with the many differences of opinion recorded in Mishnah and Talmud, if one adopts the maximalist view that all of these, too, were given to Moses at Sinai. This is a major crux and will be returned to several times below. Here Heschel simply gives, without further rationalization, the maximalist view that even the controversies were given to Moses!
[45] Fifteenth century, Italy, a famous commentator on the Mishnah.

... but rather the plain meaning of the statement is that all these things were given to Moses, and he had revealed to him all that would be innovated in the fullness of time; God also showed him all these things in writing, but not so that he would reveal them and speak them to Israel. The Pentateuch alone, with its explanations, God gave him to give to the Israelites of his generation."[55] [46]

The Scroll of Esther

The Sages were agreed that after Haggai, Zechariah, and Malachi died, revelation ceased from Israel.[56] "Since the decease of the last prophets, neither the angels nor humans were permitted to add a single verse."[57] Therefore the Masoretes[47] were able to specify how often a word occurred in the twenty-four books of the canon,[48] for they knew that not a single letter would henceforth be added. From now on, no prophet, no angel, not even Elijah could add anything to the canon of twenty-four books. In Paradise, the angels and the righteous occupy themselves only with those twenty-four books, and with the Oral Torah.

We see that the Sages were amazed that permission was given to write the Scroll of Esther after revelation had ceased. According to the Babylonian Talmud, "Esther wrote to the Sages, 'Write my story for posterity!' They replied, 'We have a tradition, "Have I not written this for you threefold?" (Proverbs 22:20)—The war of Amalek has

---

[55] *Megillat Esther,* a commentary on Maimonides' *Sefer Ha-mitzvot* by R. Isaac Leon ibn Zur (Venice, 5352/1592), Principle 1.

[56] Tosefta Sotah 13:2.   [57] BT Bava Batra 75a.

---

[46] This position seems to be an interesting compromise; that is, Moses saw it all, but it was not revealed to anyone. Thus, it is a matter of discovery, in some sense, as per the maximalist view, but it is definitely not "recollection," a feature of some maximalists that we will also encounter presently.

[47] The Masoretes (seventh–ninth century C.E., Israel) added the current signs of the Hebrew vowels, punctuation, and cantillation signals that have been a part of the standard Jewish biblical text ever since. They also added marginal notes, drawing attention to many external features of the text, such as the frequency of occurrence of certain words in the entire Hebrew Bible.

[48] The count of twenty-four books in the Hebrew canon is arrived at as follows: (1) Genesis, (2) Exodus, (3) Leviticus, (4) Numbers, (5) Deuteronomy, (6) Joshua, (7) Judges, (8) Samuel, (9) Kings, (10) Isaiah, (11) Jeremiah, (12) Ezekiel, (13) the Twelve Minor Prophets, (14) Psalms, (15) Proverbs, (16) Job, (17) Song of Songs, (18) Ruth, (19) Lamentations, (20) Ecclesiastes, (21) Esther, (22) Daniel, (23) Ezra-Nehemiah, (24) Chronicles.

The reader will note that the Book of Esther is included in the traditional enumeration. However, the concern that this tradition expresses is timeless and independent of a particular recension of the canon: How could Esther and Mordecai have added something of sufficient value to be included in the canon, if revelation had presumably ceased? If it was possible for them, would it still be possible after them? What is the meaning of the line that is drawn here? Is privileged access to God's truth to be found only on one side of such a line? Where do the Sages and the rest of Jewish tradition stand with respect to that line? Where do we stand?

been written three times in Scripture,[49] and it may not be written a fourth time!'"[58] In another version R. Jeremiah said in the name of Rabbi Samuel bar R. Isaac: "What did Mordecai and Esther do? They wrote a letter and sent it to our Rabbis, asking that these two days be instituted for observance every year. The Rabbis replied, 'Don't we have enough troubles, that you want to add the trouble of Haman as well?' They wrote back a second letter, as it says, 'Then Queen Esther wrote to confirm this second letter of Purim' (Esther 9:29)." Rabbi Samuel bar Nahman said in the name of Rabbi Jonathan: "Eighty-five Sages, including thirty-some prophets,[50] were vexed by this. They said, 'It is written: "These are the commandments that the Lord gave Moses" (Leviticus 27:34)—these are the commandments that we were commanded by Moses. Moses told us that a later prophet would never come to issue more commands. But Mordecai and Esther are seeking to do exactly that!'"[59]

All the Sages admitted that the reading of the Scroll of Esther is obligatory,[51] and the rules connected with it are taught in many Baraitot and in a dedicated tractate.[52] On what was there controversy? On whether the Scroll itself has sanctity like that of the rest of the Holy Scriptures. According to the Talmud of the Land of Israel, they debated the matter back and forth "until the Holy and Blessed One enlightened them, and they found that it was mentioned in the Torah, in the Prophets, and in the Writings." That is to say: they found support for the remembrance of Amalek[53] in the Torah, the Prophets, and the Writings.[60] This support is built on an exegesis of Rabbi Eleazar the Modaʿite.[61] But according to the Babylonian Talmud, Rabbi Joshua ben Hananiah disputed this.[62]

---

[58] BT Megillah 7a; Rashi ad loc.

[59] PT Megillah 70d.

[60] PT Megillah 70d.

[61] "Inscribe this as a reminder in a document" (Exodus 17:14)—this refers to what is written in the Torah; a reminder refers to the mention in the Prophets (1 Samuel 15:2); in a document refers to the Scroll of Esther (BT Megillah 7a). See also PT loc. cit.: "This refers to the Torah, as in: 'This is the Torah which Moses set before the Israelites' (Deuteronomy 4:24); reminder refers to the Prophets, as it says: 'A scroll of remembrance was written' (Malachi 3:16); document refers to the Scroll of Esther, as it says, 'And Esther's ordinance was recorded in a document' (Esther 9:32)."

[62] Rabbi Joshua argued: "This refers to the mention in Exodus; remembrance to the mention in Deuteronomy; document to the mention in 1 Samuel" (BT loc. cit.).

---

[49] Exodus 17:14; Deuteronomy 25:17; and I Samuel 15:2.

[50] This version is not consistent with Heschel's first premise, that the events in Esther occurred after the end of prophecy. Still, this version raises the same basic problem in another form: Where does one draw the line after which binding commandments may no longer be issued? Are the later generations impotent to innovate in the field of religious practice?

[51] What was vexing to the eighty-five Sages of Esther's generation became accepted as normative in later generations—an instructive lesson in historical perspective.

[52] The Tractate Megillah.

[53] Who was, by tradition, the ancestor of Haman (Haman is referred to in the Scroll of Esther as "the Agagite," and Agag was the king of Amalek in the time of King Saul of Israel).

In line with the view of Rabbi Joshua, the Amora Samuel held that "the Scroll of Esther does not impart impurity to the hands." That is to say: The Scroll of Esther is not in the same category as the rest of the Holy Scriptures, on which they decreed impurity so that they would not be handled too often.[54] Samuel also saw the reading of the Scroll as an obligation;[63] he believes that "the Holy Spirit directed that it be read, but not that it be written." That is to say: "They ratified above that which they accepted below." The reading of the Scroll of Esther was among the things that the earthly court decreed, and the Holy and Blessed One agreed above. But "the Holy Spirit did not dictate that it be written." It happened that two Sages—Levi ben Samuel and Rav Huna bar Hiyya—were busy making coverings for the holy scrolls, and when they reached the Scroll of Esther, they said: "this one needs no covering."[64]

In the midst of this important controversy Rabbi Eliezer and Rabbi Akiva set this down: "The Book of Esther was spoken with the Holy Spirit."[65] In the language of Rabbi Simeon, the disciple of Rabbi Akiva, the Book of Esther also imparts impurity to the hands. And in the period of the Amoraim, they expanded this approach. Rav, Rabbi Hanina, Rabbi Jonathan, Bar Kappara, and Rabbi Joshua ben Levi all said: "This scroll was spoken to Moses from Sinai, but there is no strict chronological order in the Torah."[66] [55] Or, in another formulation: "this scroll was not spoken by any earthly court; it was spoken from Sinai."[67]

This idea conforms perfectly to the maximalist approach, that everything was spoken to Moses from Sinai—and, according to the words of Rabbi Joshua ben Levi, even that which a diligent student would one day teach.

Expressing a different view, however, the Tanna Rabbi Joshua ben Korha said:

---

[63] According to BT Arakhin 4a, Samuel reasoned that priests, Levites, and Israelites alike should take leave of their sacred duties in order to hear the reading of the Scroll of Esther.

[64] BT Sanhedrin 100a.

[65] "Therefore, it has sanctity" (Rabbenu Hananel on BT Megillah 7a). "Therefore it is written together with the other scriptures" (Zohar Hukkat 183b). Note that in the time of the Zohar (thirteenth century), as opposed to rabbinic times, it had become customary to include Esther in a bound volume of the Hebrew Bible, as well as writing it as a separate scroll.

[66] PT Megillah 70d.

[67] Ruth Rabbah 4:4. But note the view, cited in the name of Rabbi Joshua ben Levi, that the reading of the Scroll is among those things which the earthly court decreed, whereupon the Holy and Blessed One agreed with them (Midrash on Psalms 57:2).

---

[54] The Rabbis, odd as it may seem, decreed that the most holy scrolls would be a source of impurity. In some sources, we are told that they did this so that people would not put consecrated food next to the scrolls, which would then put the scrolls in danger of damage from the vermin that the food would attract.

[55] This, of course, is usually an Ishmaelian principle, but it is not unheard of in other circles at all. This is yet another example of how it is rare that any principle can be unequivocally associated with a particular school to the exclusion of all others. It is also why we must be wary of taking Heschel's distinctions among the schools as historical assertions rather than as phenomenological ones.

"After the time of Moses no prophet innovated a mitzvah, except for those connected with Purim."[68] [56]

According to the author of *Yefei Mar'eh*,[57] it seems "that Moses our Master, peace be upon him, did not inform future generations [of the contents of the Scroll of Esther]. For if he had, and they knew the Scroll and the events related in it, all their anxiety, and sackcloth, and fasting would appear to be a joke. He did not pass it on . . . though it is possible that he transmitted it to select individuals in his generation, and that Mordekhai, Esther, and their cohorts did not know it."[58]

More Than What Was Spoken to Moses at Sinai

According to the maximalist approach, everything was given to Moses and there is no real room for innovation; all that remains is to transmit what was already spoken. To what should a Sage be compared? To a limed cistern. However, according to the minimalist approach, not all things were given to Moses, and there remains to expound things that go beyond what was spoken to Moses at Sinai. To what should a Sage be compared? To an ever-flowing spring, or to a cistern that can give out more water than it takes in.

Rabban Johanan ben Zakkai enumerated the good qualities of his disciples. Of Rabbi Eliezer ben Hyrcanus he said: "A limed cistern that does not lose a drop."[69] [59] And Rabbi Eliezer said of himself: "I never said anything that I did not receive from my Master."[70] And thus he taught: "One who says that which he did not receive from his Master causes the Shekhinah to depart from Israel."[71] When he was asked about

---

[68] Megillat Ta'anit, Adar 14, *HUCA* VIII–IX p. 347.

[69] Avot 2:8 (PB 2:11); ARN A 14, B 29.

[70] BT Berakhot 27b. The MaHaRShA (R. Samuel Edels, sixteenth–seventeenth century, Poland) objected: "We have found in many places that the Sages said things that they had not heard from their masters, of their own reason."

[71] BT Sukkah 27b (see also 28a). The same sentiment is expressed in PT Shevi'it 6:1, and in the introduction to the Zohar (I, 5a): "Rabbi Simeon said to his colleagues, 'Please, do not let escape your lips a word of Torah that you do not know, and that you have not heard from our masters!'" (See also Zohar Yitro 87a, that whoever does so, violates the command against a graven image.)

---

[56] That is, Purim and its laws were not given earlier than the time that the events occurred.

[57] Samuel ben Isaac Yaffe Ashkenazi, sixteenth century, Turkey. The work in question is a commentary on the *aggadot* in the Talmud of the Land of Israel.

[58] That is, his view is that, although some people may have known some of these things revealed to Moses, the major characters did not. There was never full and widespread knowledge of what Moses learned.

[59] The Mishnah Tractate Avot preserves two traditions as to who Rabban Johanan ben Zakkai's favorite disciple was. According to the majority opinion, he preferred Rabbi Eliezer ben Hyrcanus, the cistern that does not lose a drop. But according to Abba Shaul (and the evidence of the five disciples' answers to his questions, "What is the best way? What is the worst way?"), he preferred Eleazar ben Arakh, the "ever-flowing spring" (see Avot 2:8–9 [2:12–14 in the Prayer Book]).

something about which he had no tradition from his Master, he would respond, "I have not heard,"[72] or would decline to respond at all.[73]

In subsequent generations they greatly praised this quality and saw in it a path that the wise should take, for it is becoming to him and becoming to Torah. They said in the name of Rabbi Johanan: "If you are able to trace a tradition all the way back to Moses, do so, but if not, at least preserve the order of the chain from beginning to end."[74] In the Middle Ages, the idea was accepted that all of the talmudic Sages followed the model of Rabbi Eliezer: "All of the words of the Sages, of blessed memory, those of the Mishnah and the Gemara, were received by them, great and righteous Sage from great and righteous Sage, head of academy and his cohorts from another head of academy and his cohorts, from the Men of the Great Assembly, who in turn received them from the Prophets, of blessed memory. And it never happened that the Sages of the Gemara (and a fortiori the Sages of the Mishnah) said even a small thing on their own, with the exception of the enactments that they all agreed to institute so as to protect the Torah."[75] However, we find that Rabban Johanan ben Zakkai was not pleased with this model, which sees the Sage as merely a receiving vessel.

It is told that Rabban Johanan ben Zakkai said to Rabbi Eliezer ben Hyrcanus:

"Tell us something from the Torah." He said to him: "My Master, I shall give you an analogy. To what can I be compared? To a cistern that cannot give out more water than it takes in. Similarly, I cannot speak words of Torah beyond what I have gotten from you." He said to him: "I, too, will give you an analogy. What should you be comparing yourself to? To the kind of cistern that has water spontaneously flowing from it [and which can thus give out more water than it takes in]. Similarly, you can speak words of Torah beyond that which was spoken to Moses at Sinai." He said this to him two or three times, but he could not accept it. Rabban Johanan ben Zakkai then left and went his way. Then Rabbi Eliezer sat and expounded things beyond that which was spoken to Moses at Sinai, and his face glowed as with the light of the sun, the rays going forth as did the rays from Moses' face. You could not tell whether it was day or night. Rabbi Joshua and Rabbi Simeon ben Netanel went and told Rabban Johanan ben Zakkai: "Come and see how Rabbi Eliezer sits and expounds things beyond that which was spoken to Moses at Sinai" ... Rabban Johanan ben Zakkai came from behind him and kissed him on his head, and said: Happy are you, Abraham, Isaac, and Jacob, that this one descended from you.[76]

Other Sages as well inclined toward Rabban Johanan ben Zakkai's model, and they expounded: "'Proper rulings were in his mouth, and nothing perverse was on his lips' (Malachi 2:6): 'Proper rulings were in his mouth'—those things that he heard from his Master; 'nothing perverse was on his lips'—even things that he did not hear from his Master."[77] They also said: "Those things concerning ritual law that the schools of

---

[72] Mishnah Nega'im 9:3, 11:7.   [73] Tosefta Yevamot 3:3; BT Yevamot 66b.

[74] PT Shabbat 3a.

[75] Rabbi Abraham ibn David, *Sefer Ha-kabbalah,* Introduction.

[76] ARN B 13. ARN A 6 has the variant: "He expounded things that no ear had ever heard before." See PRE 2 and notes of R. David Luria (nineteenth century, Lithuania); Batei Midrashot II, 248.

[77] PT Pe'ah 15b.

Shammai and Hillel could not resolve were explicated by ben Azzai . . . and those things that had always been obscured were explicated by Rabbi Akiva."[78]

The minimalist approach, the idea that the Sages have the power to permit what had been forbidden by the ancestors, is hinted at in the words of Rabbi [Judah the Patriarch]:

> Rabbi Joshua ben Zeruz, Rabbi Meir's brother-in-law, testified before Rabbi concerning Rabbi Meir—that he ate a vegetable leaf in Bet-Shean.[60] And on the basis of his words, Rabbi permitted all of Bet-Shean [i.e., that it was considered outside the Land of Israel, and its produce did not need to be tithed]. Rabbi's brothers and family got together and challenged him: "Are you going to permit that which your ancestors and ancestors' ancestors forbade?!" He then expounded for them this verse: "He also broke into pieces the bronze serpent that Moses had made, for until that time the Israelites had been offering sacrifices to it; it was called Nehushtan" (2 Kings 18:4). Is it possible that Asa did not destroy it, and Jehosaphat did not destroy it, although they destroyed all the idolatrous objects in the world? We must say that [Hezekiah's] ancestors left him room to make his own mark, and so it is with me: *my ancestors left me room to make my own mark.* We learn from this that a disciple of the Sages who teaches an innovative *halakhah* should not be rejected.[79]

In yet another formulation: "Rabbi permitted buying vegetables immediately after the Sabbatical Year,[61] and all denigrated his decision. But he said to them . . . "the Holy and Blessed One left us this crown to put on our own heads."[80]

These two views are parallel to the two approaches to the question of whether Moses our Master spoke things on his own. The idea that a person should not say anything that he has not received from his Master parallels the view of Rabbi Akiva that Moses said nothing that he did not hear from the mouth of the Most High. And the idea that a Sage "may speak words of Torah beyond that which was spoken to Moses at Sinai" parallels the view of Rabbi Ishmael that Moses spoke things on his own and the Holy and Blessed One agreed with him.

They Did Not Say Even a Small Thing on Their Own

The maximalist approach itself can be analyzed into a good number of ideas and principles. It treats of the giving of the Torah to Moses and also the transmission of those

---

[78] *Midrash Hillel, Beit Hamidrash* V, 97.   [79] BT Hullin 6b–7a.
[80] PT Demai 22c. See Lekah Tov on Genesis 17:13, directed against the Karaites.

---

[60] That is, an untithed vegetable leaf. The question here is whether Bet-Shean, close to the border of the Land of Israel, is subject to all of the laws of tithing that apply to the Land. As we shall see, it had, before this time, been assumed that these laws did apply to Bet-Shean.
[61] Though they might have been grown illegally during the Sabbatical Year.

words of Torah to the Israelites. How was the Torah given to Moses? There was nothing that was not given to Moses. "No Sage can know anything beyond what Moses knew, and even if you were to combine all of the generations of Israel from the day of the giving of the Torah, so that the earth is full of ideas, there would still be nothing new that Moses did not already know."[81] However, in the matter of the transmission of the Torah to Israel the ideas begin to diverge. There are those who say that the Sages of the Gemara did not say even a small thing on their own, and all that they spoke came to them in an unbroken tradition from Moses. But according to another view Moses did not transmit all of the matters of Torah to Israel, and he left them the room necessary in order to acquire on their own those things that were not made explicit to them. There are still others who say that many of the things that Moses transmitted to them were forgotten and that future generations managed to reconstruct them through dialectic, using the modes of exegesis applicable to the Torah, or through the Holy Spirit.[62]

The maximalist approach says that whatever a diligent student will one day innovate was not only spoken to Moses at Sinai but also reached him in an unbroken chain of tradition. The Oral Torah is entirely based in tradition. "It never happened that the Sages of the Gemara (and a fortiori the Sages of the Mishnah) said even a small thing on their own."[82] Rabbenu Hananel also believed "that all that which is set forth in the Mishnah is *halakhah* given to Moses from Sinai, even though they are often taught anonymously."[83] He notes: "Abbaye and Rava lived long after Rabbi Simeon ben Yohai; so how is it that the Gemara will sometimes challenge the latter on the basis of their words?[63] It is in order to teach you that the tradition that Abbaye and Rava had in hand, which is evident in their words, was already in the hands of former generations, by tradition stemming back to Moses at Sinai. They are thus not their words, for such things cannot be spoken except on tradition from the

---

[81] *Or Ha-hayyim* (of Hayyim ibn Attar, eighteenth century, Morocco, Italy, and Jerusalem) on Leviticus 13:37.

[82] Ibn David, *Sefer Ha-kabbalah* (cited in previous section).

[83] Rabbenu Hananel on BT Pesahim 38b.

---

[62] Thus, there are three versions of the maximalist approach that Heschel offers us here: (1) the view that Moses received and passed on absolutely everything, (2) the view that Moses received everything but did not pass it on, leaving others to "discover" that which already existed and was revealed to him alone, and (3) the view that Moses received and passed everything on, but that some things were forgotten and needed to be reconstructed.

[63] This often seems to happen in talmudic discussions, where the position of a particular Sage is challenged on the basis of something that would be said only later on, in a subsequent generation. It is usually interpreted as an editorial style, in which a later position is assumed to be logical enough to have been known or foreseen, and which the Sage under attack should have been able to deal with. Here, however, a more literal view is taken of such passages, as if matters first discussed in the fourth century were, of course, known to the Sage of the second century, since his masters, all the way back to Moses, would have transmitted them to him.

Prophets; and they always spoke only those words that they received from their Masters."[84]

But if it is so, that all laws and rules were transmitted to the Sages, how can we explain the fact that so many doubts and controversies arose in the course of the generations?[64] There is one view, that Moses our Master did not transmit to Israel all that he received at Sinai.[85] But this view was not widespread among the Sages. In its place, they preferred this explanation: that all of the laws and rules were known throughout the nation, but there were those that were forgotten. That is to say: it was not that they were not originally known to the Sages, but that "they forgot them and thus did not know." For example, it once happened that the Eve of Passover[65] fell on the Sabbath, and it eluded B'nai Beteira whether the Paschal sacrifice would override the Sabbath or not: "They forgot and thus did not know."[86]

The matters that were forgotten can be reconstructed by the Sages using the modes of exegesis applicable to the Torah,[87] or through dialectic: "The first time that the Torah was forgotten in Israel, Ezra came up from Babylonia and restored it. It was then forgotten again, and Hillel came up from Babylonia and restored it."[88]

Another view, expressed by Rabbi Yose, served in the Middle Ages as an explanation for the fact that in many places the Sages disputed about the fine points of the law. Here are the words of Rabbi Yose: "At first, there were not many differences of opinion in Israel . . . but when the disciples of Shammai and Hillel grew numerous, and they did not apprentice as fully as they should have, the controversies increased, and the Torah became as if it were two Torahs."[89]

In a challenge to those disciples who would differ with the Geonim and say: "From where do you know this?" Rav Sherira Gaon wrote that the Geonim "are the embodiment of the words of the living God, and they would hold their own even in the Academy of Moses, the Master of all the prophets. Their wisdom and their powers of

---

[84] Rabbenu Hananel on BT Sukkah 45b.

Mahzor Vitri (of Simhah ben Samuel of Vitri, eleventh century, France, disciple of Rashi) records the tradition: "From Moses to Hillel, there were not just six but 600 orders of the Mishnah, all given by the Holy One to Moses at Sinai!" (p. 484).

The *Megaleh Amukot* (classic of gematria, by Nathan Nata ben Solomon Spira, seventeenth century, Poland) gives the following palindromic acronym on the Hebrew name of Moses: *Mahloket SHammai Hillel / Ha-kol SHama' Mi-sinai*—"The controversy of Shammai and Hillel—all was heard at Sinai" (74).

[85] See chapter 33.   [86] BT Pesahim 66a.

[87] As Hillel did in the case of the Paschal sacrifice, just mentioned (ibid.)

[88] BT Sukkah 20a.

[89] Tosefta Hagigah 2:9, presented here as cited in BT Sanhedrin 88b. According to the Letter of R. Sherira Gaon (ed. B. M. Levin, p. 11), the negligent apprenticeship was in turn caused by the dislocation and calamities following the destruction of the Second Temple.

---

[64] Here, now, the critical question of how the maximalists deal with all the divergences of views in the Talmud is dealt with by Heschel.

[65] That is, the fourteenth of Nisan, the day on which the Paschal lamb was to be sacrificed in the afternoon. Would this sacrifical rite override the Sabbath or not?

dialectic are among God's instructions to Moses . . . so that whoever disputes anything that they say is disputing God and God's Torah."[90]

Rabbi Schneur Zalman explained the meaning of the phrase "these and these are the words of the Living God" as follows: "Whatever the school of Shammai said, and whatever the school of Hillel said, and so with the words of Abbaye and Rava,[66] are not, strictly speaking, their words but rather the words of God in their mouths. It is just as the 'Maggid' said to Rabbi Joseph Karo:[67] 'I am the Mishnah, speaking through your mouth.'"[91]

But Maimonides held the following opinion: "Whoever thinks that the laws about which the Sages disputed were also received from Moses, and who further thinks that the disputes arose because of mistakes or forgetfulness . . . such a person's words are, by my life, despicable and very ugly; they are the words of one who simply does not know, and does not grasp basic principles . . . and it is only a deficiency in understanding the words of the Sages in the Talmud that brings one to such inferior beliefs."[92]

Things Not Revealed to Moses

There is a dialectic at work in all systems of thought. In this case, it was the deep veneration that was felt for the person of Rabbi Akiva, the father of the maximalist approach, that itself moved Amoraim to articulate the minimalist approach to the prophecy of Moses our Master. For they took Rabban Johanan ben Zakkai's idea that the Sages can know and expound things "beyond what was spoken to Moses at Sinai" and went one better by saying: "Things not revealed to Moses were revealed to Rabbi Akiva."[68]

Said Rav Judah in the name of Rav: At the time that Moses ascended to Heaven he found the Holy and Blessed One sitting and affixing crowns to the letters. He said to him: "Master of the Universe, who is forcing your hand [in that you must add crowns to what you have written]?" God said to him: "there is a certain man who will live after many

[90] Sha'arei Tzedek (a collection of Geonic responsa edited by Hayyim Modai [eighteenth century, Safed]), introduction.

[91] Schneur Zalman of Lyady (eighteenth century, Russia, founder of Habad Hasidism), Likkutei Torah, Aharei 27b.

[92] Maimonides, Introduction to the Mishnah, ed. Mossad Ha-rav Kuk, Rambam La-am (1961), XVIII, 38.

[66] And, of course, others as well; these examples are merely illustrative.

[67] Karo, a sixteenth-century legalist who was also a noted kabbalist, had a "spirit" of sorts with whom he said that he communed and whom he called his "Maggid," or preacher.

[68] The paradox here is noteworthy. Akiva, who championed the view that Moses knew everything, might not have been pleased with the hagiographic story extolling his virtues that now follows in the text, because it suggests that Moses did not receive all that Akiva later taught.

generations, by the name of Akiva ben Joseph, who will one day extract piles and piles of *halakhot* from each and every jot." He said to God: "Master of the Universe, show him to me." God said: "Turn around." Moses then went and sat at the back of eight rows [in Akiva's academy], and he could not grasp what they were saying. At this, he began to feel powerless. But when they reached one particular matter, the disciples said to Akiva: "Master, where do you know this from?" He said to them, "it is a *halakhah* given to Moses from Sinai."[69] At that, Moses felt better. So he turned back around, to the presence of the Holy and Blessed One, and said to God: "Master of the Universe, you have such a person, and you give the Torah through me?" God said to him: "Silence! So I have decided." He said to God: "Master of the Universe, you have shown me his Torah, now show me his reward." God said to him: "Turn around." So he turned around, and he saw that they were weighing out his flesh in the meat market. He said to God: "Master of the Universe, is this Torah, and is this its reward?!" God said to him: "Silence! So I have decided."[93]

Many Sages were astonished at this passage: "Shall we say, God forbid, that Rabbi Akiva stands on a higher rung than Moses our Master, peace be upon him?!"[94] Still, from these words of Rav we can learn that not all of the Oral Torah was given to Moses. And this approach was also taken by Rav Aha, who said: "Things not revealed to Moses were revealed to Rabbi Akiva. 'His eyes behold every precious thing' (Job 28:10)—this refers to Rabbi Akiva."[95]

The idea that the Torah "with all its *halakhot,* minutiae, and interpretations" was spoken to Moses at Sinai did not put many Sages at ease. For how then can we explain the fact that there is difference of opinion among the Sages, with one declaring liable what another declares exempt, and one declaring fit what another disqualifies?[70]

"It was taught in the school of Rabbi Ishmael: 'like a hammer that shatters rock' (Jeremiah 23:29)—just as a hammer throws off many sparks, so does a single verse

---

[93] BT Menahot 29b. In the kabbalistic midrash *Letters of Rabbi Akiva* (Letter Nun), Rabbi Akiva produces 365 interpretations on each crown. Moses is seized with such dread that he utters the plea, "Please, Lord, send anyone else but me!" (Exodus 4:13) (cited in YS 175, in the name of Midrash Avkir).

[94] MaHaRaL (Judah Loew of Prague, sixteenth century), *Tif'eret Yisrael* 63.

[95] PR 64b; TB, Hukkat p. 117. See above, chapter 15, pp. 280–85.
According to Hayyim Vital (sixteenth century, Safed), in *Pri 'Etz Ha-hayyim, Sha'ar hanhagat ha-limmud, 'inyan Rabbi Akiva,* Moses knew the content of the laws that Akiva cited, but not how they were derived from the written Torah. This view is also found in *Or Ha-hayyim* on Leviticus 13:37. See also *'Emek Ha-melekh* (of Naphtali Bacharach, seventeenth century, Germany) 71, 41d; HIDA's *Me'irat Ha-'ayin* on BT Menahot 29b; and *Petah Einayim* ad loc. Schneur Zalman's *Likkutei Amarim, Iggeret Ha-kodesh 19,* presents the kabbalists' view that R. Isaac Luria understood more than Moses.

---

[69] This phrase did not, as Heschel stated much earlier in this chapter, *distinguish* this from other laws taught by Akiva, since they were all considered to be "to Moses from Sinai." The phrase here is used only to say that there is no scriptural exegesis that produces this, but simply the direct transmission from Moses on.

[70] Here again is the critical problem of the divergences among the Sages and the obvious fact that the minimalists have the easiest way of explaining it. Indeed, the minimalist approach does not even need to explain it.

branch off into many meanings."[96] That is to say: the plain meaning of a verse sometimes includes more than a single message; words have many facets. This passage, which Rashi often used in commenting on verses with halakhic import,[97] connects well with another principle articulated in the school of Rabbi Ishmael: "the Torah granted wisdom to the Sages to expound and to proclaim."[98] The Sages have the power to determine what meaning to ascribe to scriptural verses. This path was also traveled by Rabbi Yannai, a disciple of Rabbi Judah the Patriarch, the founder of the famous "Academy of Rabbi Yannai." He suggested that at Mount Sinai Moses did not receive the Torah "cut and dried," that is to say, finished off; many determinations were given over to the Sages of each and every generation. Here are his words: "Said Rabbi Yannai: Had the Torah been given cut and dried, we would have no leg to stand on. For what is the meaning of 'The Lord spoke to Moses . . . ?'[71] Moses said to God: 'Master of the Universe, inform me what the halakhah is.' God said to him: 'to incline in favor of the majority'[72] (Exodus 23:2)—that is, if the majority says to acquit, acquit, and if the majority says to hold liable, hold liable. All this in order that the Torah be expounded along forty-nine facets toward impurity and along forty-nine facets toward purity. And thus it is said, 'The words of the Lord are pure words, silver purged in an earthen crucible, refined sevenfold' (Psalms 12:7)."[99] This statement argues for the rights of the Sages and asserts their power to determine halakhah according to the majority opinion.

Well did the work "Seder Eliyahu Zuta" explain the minimalist approach and the opinion of Rabbi Abbahu[73] that the Holy and Blessed One gave Israel at Sinai only general principles and that it falls to the Sages to develop those generalities:

> Once I was walking on the road and a certain man accosted me. He began to speak to me in a sectarian sort of way, for he believed in Scripture but not in Mishnah.[74] He said to

[96] BT Sanhedrin 34a.   [97] See *Torah Shelemah* XVII, 287.
[98] Sifre Pinhas 134.   [99] PT Sanhedrin 22a.

[71] The exegetical springboard here is not very clear. Perhaps it is that the oft-recurring phrase "The Lord spoke to Moses . . ." suggests that there was some conversation that this text now reconstructs.

[72] Here is a dramatic instance of a phrase quoted out of context, with fateful (though wholesome) consequences. It comes at the end of the verse: "You shall neither side with the mighty to do wrong —you shall not give perverse testimony in a dispute so as to pervert it in favor of the *rabbim* (mighty or multitude)." The scriptural verse is an injunction not to follow a lynch mob. But the rabbis needed a proof text to legitimate the wholly reasonable principle of majority decision making, so they took the last phrase as a positive command, instead of an addendum to a prohibition. Were they aware of the violence they were doing to the text? In any case, it stands as a prime case of human participation in the construction of the meaning of Torah—Akivan exegesis in the service of an Ishmaelian goal.

[73] Which will be given two paragraphs hence in the text.

[74] There were sectarians of this kind often, even into the Middle Ages. It is noteworthy that as Seder Eliyahu Zuta tells this story (in the voice of the narrator of this late midrashic work) the "sectarian" can nevertheless be relied on to be observing all of the normative laws that the narrator takes for granted. The story makes no sense without that assumption.

me: "Scripture was given to us at Mount Sinai, but Mishnah was not given to us at Mount Sinai." I said to him: "But, my son, both Scripture and Mishnah were given to us from on high. And what difference is there between Scripture and Mishnah? They gave this analogy: To what can it be compared? To a mortal king who had two servants, both of whom he loved unconditionally. He gave each of them a small measure of wheat, and a small bunch of flax. What did the clever one of the two do? He took the flax and weaved a cloth, and he took the wheat and made flour, which he then sifted, ground finely, kneaded, and baked into bread, placed on the table, and spread the cloth over it. He left it in anticipation of the king's arrival. The foolish one of the two did nothing with what he was given. After some days, the king arrived, and said to them: 'My children, bring me that which I gave to you.' One of them displayed the fine loaf on the table, with the cloth spread over it. The other brought out a box with the wheat inside, covered by the bunch of flax. Woe to him for his embarrassment! Woe to him for his humiliation! Now consider: which of these was most dear to the king? You must say that it was the one who displayed the table with the fine loaf on it." So I said to him, "Do you agree, my son, that if I find some of your own practices in the words of the Sages, that your words will be refuted?" He said to me: "Yes." "But," I said to him, "when you lead the congregation in prayer on the Sabbath, how many blessings are there in your prayer?" He said to me: "Seven." I then said to him, "And on other days?" He said to me, "The entire Amidah."[75] "And how many people read from the Torah on the Sabbath?" He said to me: "Seven." "And at Minhah on the Sabbath, or on Monday and Thursday?" He said to me, "Three each time." "And how many blessings do you say when eating of the seven species?"[76] "Two: one before and one after." "And on other foods?" "One blessing."[77] "And the Grace after Meals?" "Three blessings, though the blessing 'who is good and who creates good' makes four."[78] So I said to him, "My son, did we receive any of these from Mount Sinai? Aren't they all from the teachings of the Sages? It is thus the case that when the Holy and Blessed One gave the Torah to Israel, it was given to them as wheat with which to produce flour, and as flax with which to produce a garment."[100]

According to the statement of Rabbi Yannai, space was given to the Sages of each generation to expound in various directions. Moses did not receive the forty-nine facets of interpretation for every thing. The Holy and Blessed One simply said to him: "'to incline in favor of the majority' . . . in order that the Torah be expounded along forty-nine facets." But this very statement was preserved in a form that conforms to the maximalist approach as well: "The Torah that the Holy and Blessed One gave to Moses was given to him with forty-nine facets." "Said Rabbi Yannai: The Torah that

[100] Seder Eliyahu Zuta, p. 171.

---

[75] That is, eighteen blessings (or nineteen in the Babylonian rite).

[76] The seven species associated with the Land of Israel in Deuteronomy 8:8. These foods required, in rabbinic law, both a blessing before and a blessing after.

[77] That is, a blessing before. Ultimately, a final blessing was required for these as well, but that was not apparently the case in the time of the Mishnah and is not assumed in this Midrash.

[78] As rabbinic law specified, the basic Grace was three blessings, but a fourth was later added.

the Holy and Blessed One gave to Moses was given to him with forty-nine facets of purity and forty-nine facets of impurity, as it says, 'and his banner [*ve-diglo*] of love was over me'[79] (Song of Songs 2:4); Moses said to God: 'How shall we proceed?' God said to him: 'If the majority says it is impure, declare it impure; if the majority says it is pure, declare it pure.'"[101] According to this version, all of the interpretations that the Sages would ever give were spoken to Moses.[80]

What does the maximalist approach assert? That the Holy and Blessed One has no limits on His action, and thus one ought not assess prophetic acts by the standards of natural acts and human thoughts. Rabbi Abbahu[81] said: "Did Moses then learn the entire Torah? It is written in Scripture, 'Its measure is longer than the earth and broader than the sea' (Job 11:9). And Moses learned this in forty days?! Rather, the Holy and Blessed One taught him only general principles."[102] With justice did the author of *Leshem, Shevo, ve-Ahlamah*[82] express astonishment at the words of Rabbi Abbahu:

> It is, after all, a simple matter that this presents no difficulty and offers no demonstration, for the teacher was the Holy and Blessed One Himself, and "is anything too wondrous for the Lord"? Why, the righteous Joseph was taught all seventy languages by Gabriel in one night by the addition to his name of one letter from the Name of the Holy and Blessed One.[83] [103] Similarly, it is said of Samuel and David, that "on the night that David fled from Saul he learned from Samuel the prophet that which a diligent student could not learn in a hundred years."[104] And if this is so, what kind of difficulty does it raise about Moses our Master, peace be upon him, that he could learn the entire Torah from the mouth of the Holy and Blessed One in forty days? It is all irrelevant when it comes to assessing miraculous acts.

For this reasoning, the author of *Leshem, Shevo, ve-Ahlamah* suggested that Rabbi Abbahu's statement was made only for the benefit of the sectarians with whom he had regular debates. "In order not to provide an opening to the sectarians brazenly to

---

[101] PR 101a; Tractate Soferim 16, ed. Higger, p. 289; Midrash on Psalms 12:4.
[102] Exodus Rabbah 41:6.   [103] BT Sotah 36a.   [104] YS on I Samuel, 129.

---

[79] The exegesis here turns on the fact that the numerical value of the Hebrew word *ve-diglo* is 49.
[80] And this, therefore, shows how even the apparently "minimalist" view of Rabbi Yannai can itself be interpreted to suit a maximalist, thus keeping the controversy alive, to this day. It is, let us recall, one of Heschel's chief objectives in this work to reveal to us how many ongoing controversies in Jewish thought and interpretation have ancient roots.
[81] A "minimalist."
[82] R. Solomon ben Hayyim Haikel Elyashuv, early-twentieth-century kabbalist, Ukraine and Jerusalem.
[83] See Psalms 81:6, where Joseph is spelled "Jehoseph." The extra *heh* is taken to be a letter of the Divine Name, which thus helped miraculous things happen to Joseph when he "went out into the Land of Egypt." The relevant Midrash here has Pharaoh's courtiers complaining that this unknown now appointed viceroy has no bearing of royalty, for he doesn't even know all the world's languages (taken conventionally to be seventy). God's miraculous intervention thus fixed that.

dismiss the traditions of the Sages, he said various things that were against his own opinions." But he himself believed and knew that everything was given to Moses our Master.[105] [84]

Not All of the Torah Was Given to Him

Rav's approach,[85] that not all of the Torah was given to Moses, was accepted by many Sages. We can, for example, mention the works of Rabbi Moses Alshikh, Rabbi Samuel de Uceda, Rabbi Joseph Albo, Rabbi Abraham Azulai, and Rabbi Isaiah Horowitz, the author of *Shenei Luhot Ha-Berit*.[86]

Rabbi Moses Alshekh notes, with respect to the statement that "Moses received Torah from Sinai and passed it on to Joshua," that it should have said: "The Holy and Blessed One gave Torah to Moses and he gave it to Joshua." Why did it say "from Sinai" and not "from the Holy and Blessed One," since he did not receive it from the mountain! Because even though God placed everything before Moses and Israel, it is still the case that every one receives as much as he is prepared to receive. Thus it is that even in the case of Moses it does not say that Torah was passed to him by the Holy and Blessed One.[87] For it goes without saying that it is unjustifiable to use the term "pass on" when speaking of God to Moses, since the latter was mortal. . . . "Passing on" applies when that which is in the hands of the one who transmits is exactly what gets passed on. But it is an impossible thing that Moses would receive Torah exactly as it was in the mind of God. But the word "receive" may be used even in cases when what is received is not identical with what was in the possession of the giver.[106]

With even greater clarity did Rabbi Samuel de Uceda emphasize that the Holy and Blessed One did not give to Moses "the entire, complete Torah, since he was not prepared to receive all of it, as Scripture said, 'You have made him little less than divine' (Psalm 8:6)." Therefore it did not say, at the beginning of the "chapters of the Fathers" that the Holy and Blessed One gave Torah to Moses, but rather "Moses received Torah from Sinai." "The matter was phrased from the perspective of the

---

[105] *Leshem Shevo ve-Ahlamah*, II, 4.21.4, pp. 170ff.
[106] Moses Alshekh, *Torat Mosheh*, Shemini, on Leviticus 9:2.

---

[84] That is, he elevated the status of Mishnah, as if it went beyond what Moses taught, only in order to defend its honor against Mishnah's detractors among the "sectarians."

[85] As given in the story cited earlier from Tractate Menahot about Moses visiting Akiva's Academy.

[86] Rabbi Moses Alshikh—sixteenth century, Safed; Rabbi Samuel de Uceda—sixteenth century, Safed; Rabbi Joseph Albo—fourteenth–fifteenth century, Spain; Rabbi Abraham Azulai—sixteenth–seventeenth century, Morocco and Land of Israel; Rabbi Isaiah Horowitz, sixteenth–seventeenth century, various parts of Eastern Europe and the Land of Israel.

[87] The Hebrew verb *masar* ("passed on"), which describes all of the transmissions in the beginning of Tractate Avot, pointedly does not appear in the first transmission, from God to Moses.

receiver in order to tell us that what is received depends on the degree of preparation of the receiving vessel. That is also why it did not say that Moses received 'the Torah,' with the definite article, because 'the Torah' would have suggested that Moses received the entire Torah, in its completeness, but that, as we have said, was not so. Therefore, it said: 'Moses received Torah,' that is to say: what he received was Torah, but he received only part of it, and not its entirety."[107] According to the MaHaRaL as well, "it is inappropriate to say that Moses received Torah from the mouth of the Holy and Blessed One . . . for Moses was not the exclusive recipient of Torah from God. And furthermore, it would not have been respectful of Heaven to phrase it so."[108]

Rabbi Joseph Albo explains the minimalist approach thus: "It is impossible that God's Torah should be complete in such a way as to suffice for all ages, since new particulars are always arising in human affairs, and the results of these actions are too numerous all to be included in a single book. That is why these things were given to Moses orally. General principles are implied in the Torah in brief, so that using them the Sages of every generation would be able to derive from them the new particulars. And these[88] are the thirteen modes of reasoning that are mentioned in the Baraita of Rabbi Ishmael in the Sifra."[109] [89]

Rabbi Abraham Azulai makes the following distinction: that the compiler of the Mishnah did not say that the Holy and Blessed One passed on Torah to Moses, "For the wisdom and esoteric knowledge in the Torah are infinite, and it is impossible that they should all be passed on to a human being who is finite."[110]

On the verse: "The Lord spoke those words—those and no more [ve-lo yasaf]—to your whole congregation at the mountain, with a mighty voice out of the fire and the dense clouds" (Deuteronomy 5:19), Rashi brings two interpretations: "ve-lo yasaf is rendered by the Targum as 'it did not cease,' for its sound endures, unabated forever. Another interpretation: ve-lo yasaf means that 'no more' was God shown publicly in that way."[111] On this Rabbi Isaiah Halevi Horowitz wrote:

> There is in this a deep esoteric truth, and the two interpretations are both completely true. Ve-lo yasaf has the meaning "no more" in referring to the rabbinic commands and stringencies, for they and their various "fences" were not commanded from on high. And ve-lo yasaf has the meaning "it did not cease" in that even these things—the rabbinic commands—did not cease from that sound, for they were all included in that powerful, commanding Voice. But there is a time for everything, and the time had not yet come for those commands to move from potentiality to actuality. For such matters are aroused by

[107] Samuel de Uceda, *Midrash Shmuel* on Avot 1:1.
[108] MaHaRaL, *Derekh Hayyim* on Avot 1:1.
[109] Albo, *Ikkarim*, III, 23.
[110] Abraham Azulai, Introduction to Commentary on Avot.
[111] Rashi on Deuteronomy 5:19.

---

[88] That is, the general principles referred to.
[89] The Baraita of Rabbi Ishmael is a kind of prologue to the Sifra, the major work of halakhic exegesis on the Book of Leviticus.

actions below and are dependent on the essence and quality of earthly affairs, and the status of souls in each generation. Then the Sages were able to arouse the power above so as to actualize these potentialities in their time . . . not, God forbid, that the Sages innovated things on their own authority. They simply focused on the divine mind with their souls that stood at Mount Sinai, for at that event all souls stood. They received what they received because of what their souls were, and what their generations needed. Thus, their words were well-ordered and well-received, and in this sense were from on high. A hint of this is to be found in the fact that the numerical value of *mi-de-rabbanan* ("of rabbinic origin") is equal to that of *mi-pi ha-gevurah* ("from the mouth of the most High").[112] [90]

According to the author of *Nezer Ha-kodesh*:[91]

"Mishneh Torah," that is, the Book of Deuteronomy, is parallel to the Oral Torah, which is called "Mishnah."[92] For in the Book of Deuteronomy there are included the roots of the hidden and esoteric wisdom of the Oral Torah. Now Deuteronomy was spoken by Moses on his own, as it is written: "these are the words that Moses addressed" (Deuteronomy 1:1)—which teaches that he apprehended by his reason the deep esoteric wisdom of the Oral Torah, and afterward God agreed with what he did by the Holy Spirit. Thus it is written, "As Moses spoke, God answered him in thunder" (Exodus 19:19) . . . and should your mouth be so bold as to ask whether God's power was insufficient to reveal to Moses the entire Oral Torah fully explained, it would not be wise to do so. For God desired, in God's righteousness, to give Moses merit in that he would apprehend things on his own after exerting effort and laboring to reach the depth of the matter. For the reward is proportional to the effort.[93] This is always how the Oral Torah works, as is written in the Tanhuma in Parashat Noah: "This is the instruction (Torah): When a person dies . . .' (Numbers 19:14)—this is the Oral Torah, that cannot be acquired except by one who gives one's life for it. Furthermore, the Holy and Blessed One did not enter into a covenant with Israel but for the sake of the Oral Torah, as it says: "for in accordance with these commandments I make a covenant with you" (Exodus 34:27)—this refers to the Oral Torah, which is difficult to learn, and which produces great pain, since it is as obscure as darkness. And so it says, "The people that walked in darkness have seen a brilliant light" (Isaiah 9:1)—this refers to the masters of Talmud, who see a great light when the Holy and Blessed One enlightens them about matters of ritual and purity law. And as for the future: "But may His friends be as the sun rising in might" (Judges 5:31); what the verse means to say is that the Oral Torah cannot be acquired by a person except through pain and effort, and that is why its reward is very great. That is why the Holy and

---

[112] Isaiah Horowitz, *Shnei Luhot Ha-brit* (Amsterdam, 5408/1648), p. 25a–b.

---

[90] And thus, this innovative "compromise" between the approaches detailed here has it that all was revealed in the sense that it existed in potentiality, but that historically conditioned events and human initiative are needed to bring all of the Torah into actuality.

[91] R. Jehiel Michael ben Uzziel, early eighteenth century, Germany.

[92] This is a play on the words *Mishneh* and *Mishnah*, which are unrelated semantically, but very similar phonetically.

[93] This is the aphorism of Ben Heh Heh, given at the very end of chapter 5 of Tractate Avot.

Blessed One did not cut a covenant with Israel but for the sake of the Oral Torah, as it says: "for in accordance with these commandments I make a covenant with you and with Israel" (Exodus 34:27). And since it says there "and with Israel," we immediately infer that it was also with Moses that God cut the covenant only for the sake of the Oral Torah, because Moses, too, acquired it only through pain and effort. . . . This is why it [the Oral Torah] is called by his name, as it is written, "Be mindful of the Teaching of My servant Moses" (Malachi 3:22), referring to the Oral Torah, which is what needs remembering in the heart and mouth, since it was not committed to writing. And yet, even though it was not given explicitly in writing, it is nevertheless certain that it is implicitly included in the Written Torah, as we say: "there is nothing that is not implied in the Torah." This also resolves the difficulty with what is said in the first chapter of Tractate Bava Batra, that at the time that Moses wrote down the Torah, the Holy and Blessed One spoke, and Moses also spoke and wrote. It is, at first glance, difficult: Why were both of them, the Holy and Blessed One and Moses, speaking at the time of the writing down of the Torah? But the Holy and Blessed One was speaking the Written Torah, and Moses began to speak the Oral Torah, which was founded by him; and only then did he write, including allusions in his writing to that Oral Torah that he had grasped on his own. If so, it seems that this is why the text says, "Write down for yourself these commandments" (Exodus 34:27), rather than more simply, "write down these commandments." It said what it said—"write down for yourself"—so as to say, "write in allusions that which is yours," that Oral Torah which you apprehended on your own.[113]

All of Them Received Their Share from Sinai

"God spoke all of these words" (Exodus 20:1)—Said Rabbi Isaac: Whatever the prophets were destined to prophesy in every generation was received by them from Mount Sinai. For so did Moses say to Israel: "but both with those who are standing here with us this day . . . and with those who are not with us here this day" (Deuteronomy 29:14). It is not written "with those who are not here standing here with us here this day," but rather "with those who are not with us here this day"; these are the souls that were destined to be created and are without substance, so that they could not be said to be standing. Even though they were not yet created at that moment, each of them received its share of the revelation. Similarly, it says, "A pronouncement: The word of the Lord to Israel by the hand of Malachi" (Malachi 1:1). It does not say "in the days of Malachi," but rather "by the hand of Malachi," for the prophecy was already "in his hand" from Mount Sinai on, but until that moment he did not have permission to prophesy. Likewise, [Second][94]

---

[113] *Nezer Ha-kodesh* of R. Jehiel Michael ben Uzziel (Jessnitz, 5479/1719), on Genesis Rabbah, chapter 1:15, pp. 11d ff.

---

[94] The propehcies in the Book of Isaiah from chapter 40 on are not those of the historical Isaiah (eighth century B.C.E.) but those of an anonymous sixth-century B.C.E. prophet of the Babylonian exile, usually called Second Isaiah or Deutero-Isaiah. However, prior to the advent of modern biblical scholarship, nearly all Jewish and Christian thinkers regarded all the prophecies in this book as the work of

Isaiah said: "From the time anything existed I was there" (Isaiah 48:16). Said Isaiah: I was there on the day that the Torah was given at Sinai, and I received this prophecy there, but "And now the Lord God has sent me, endowed with His spirit" (Isaiah 48:16). Until now I did not have permission to prophesy. And it was not just all the prophets who received their prophecy at Sinai, but even the Sages who arise in every generation—all of them received their share from Sinai. And thus it says, "The Lord spoke these words— these and no more—to your whole congregation at the mountain" (Deuteronomy 5:19).[114]

These words are stunning, and they have within them not only extreme abstraction, but also the air of paradox. Souls that "have no substance" and that have not yet been created are said to have received Torah from Mount Sinai![115] How can the "nothing" receive the "something"?

This homily of Rabbi Isaac was not said simply for rhetorical loveliness; rather, it rendered a decision in a matter of supreme importance. It is an expression of the desire to understand the secrets of cognitive apprehension, to understand the source of all knowledge, and knowledge of Torah in particular. There is an inherent and essential weakness in human reason. The proverb of the wise one says: "Do not rely on your own understanding" (Proverbs 3:5). And we see that thought expands continually, daily, from generation to generation. Sages say things that they did not hear from their masters; they construct narratives, and they innovate halakhot.[95] Is all of this richness simply the fruit of human reason? Rabbi Isaac came and set forth this idea: the source of all new ideas is in the revelation of God's Presence, in a prophetic event at Mount Sinai.

To the untrained eye, which sees externals and surfaces only, this idea is bizarre and internally incoherent. But the heart that knows that the human world contains more than just what the eye sees, the heart that rebels against the idea that what was is what will be, and that there is nothing new under the sun,[96] and that protests against those who see the secret of existence through a routine lens that distorts and edits the heart's vision—such a heart can grasp the concept that just as the Creator created the world in a single utterance and in one event, so did the Creator reveal the Torah in a single utterance to a single assemblage.[97]

---

[114] Exodus Rabbah 25:4; Tanhuma Yitro 11. See BT Shabbat 146a; Sanhedrin 59a.

[115] But consider also Rabbi Johanan's view: "All souls, from Adam to the end of time, were created in the first six days; all were in the Garden of Eden; and all were present at the giving of the Torah" (Tanhuma Pekudei 3; see also Tanhuma Nitzavim 3).

---

the same prophet, some referring to events of his own generation, some speaking of events to occur centuries later.

[95] Or so the plain meanings of their words would suggest.

[96] And therefore, nothing singular and all-inclusive such as the revelation at Sinai could possibly happen.

[97] It seems that Heschel finds a suitable compromise in the words of Rabbi Isaac, which is appealing to him because it cuts the Gordian knot between the maximalist view that denies the human ele-

Plato taught that the soul preexists its physical birth and embodiment in the terrestrial world. Prior to its acquiring physical form it was in the highest heaven, in the footsteps of the gods, and it was then able to understand the Ideas. It learned to recognize them, and in so doing it acquired true apprehension. With the soul's fall to earth and its acquiring physical form, it still retains this acquired apprehension, but it forgets it in the course of time. It then happens that a sensory experience serves as an opportunity to revive apprehension in the soul; and thus human beings, according to Plato, renew their acquisition of this apprehension through a process of recollection. All apprehension is a case of restoring lost property.[116]

Now consider the difference between the Platonic solution and that of Rabbi Isaac. Plato assumed that souls acquired their true apprehension of the Ideas in a world that transcends the physical world, and thus time and history as well. Rabbi Isaac assumed that souls acquired their apprehension in an event, at a point in time, at the moment of the giving of Torah, an occurrence within the frame of history. Plato looked to the spheres and beyond; Rabbi Isaac cast his lot with God and prophecy.

Plato was tripped up[98] on this path by the need to satisfy the claims of the a priori, which commands recognition only of what is already known. Human reason cannot create something *ex nihilo*; it discovers, but does not invent.[99]

It is recognized that the approach of Rabbi Isaac, like that of Plato, is built on a religious determinism. "All is in the hands of Heaven." The Sages do not create anything new on their own, for they once received everything. This approach has its source in the teachings of Rabbi Akiva.[100] But Rabbi Isaac expanded this teaching further and taught that, just as Moses our Master did not say anything on his own authority, so did all the Sages receive all of their teachings at Sinai. And there is yet more. For ancient ideas take on new forms. The ancients taught that Moses received the Torah from Sinai and passed it on to the Israelites. Along came Rabbi Isaac and taught that each and every one of us receives his/her Torah from Sinai. At that one hour, Moses our Master's prayer was answered: "Would that all the Lord's people were prophets, that the Lord put His spirit upon them!" (Numbers 11:29).

---

[116] Similarly, according to R. Simlai, the embryo in its mother's womb is taught the entire Torah, "and when it comes into the light of day, an angel strikes it across the mouth and makes it forget everything" (BT Niddah 30b).

---

ment in revelation, and the minimalist view which seems to ignore the importance, or even the possibility, of an ongoing transcendence in religious thought. In this interpretation, all souls, who were in a timeless state at Sinai, then reenter the stage of history and play out the transcendence they have been endowed with, according to the laws of human thought. No wonder Heschel finds it appealing and chooses to dwell on it at the conclusion of this critical chapter.

[98] From Heschel's vantage point, of course.

[99] That is, the Akivan point of view.

[100] But as noted above, it is taken, according to Heschel, in a new direction, with a new "compromise" twist.

To sum up, the Torah is acquired not only by actual transmission from mouth to ear. Just as there is an Oral Torah, so is there a Torah seated in the soul, in the source of reason. All received their share according to their ability to apprehend it and according to the soul's ability to give it roots. And everyone adds to it, according to what heaven displays to them.

Moses Uttered All of the Prophets' Words as well as His Own

Moses' prestige grew as a result of the diminution of the image of his successors. It is not only that whatever a diligent student would one day teach before his Master was spoken to Moses at Sinai, but also whatever a prophet was destined to prophesy was already uttered by Moses. The prophets were nothing but attendants to Moses, and they said nothing that they did not hear from others, in the name of Moses. It is as if inspiration is not the root of the prophetic utterance, but rather immersion in the Teaching of Moses.[101] It is as if the prophets did not prophesy from the mouth of the Most High, but rather received their prophecy from a succession of prophets.

Rabbi Jonah said in the name of Rabbi Samuel bar Nahman: "Any prophet that arose spoke another prophet's prophecy. And why? In order to confirm the earlier prophecy." And Rabbi Joshua ben Levi said: "Because each was dependent on others' prophecies, except for Moses, *who uttered all of the prophets' words, as well as his own.* And every prophet who prophesied did so in imitation of Moses."[117] "All of the prophets prophesied one from the other; for example, the spirit of Elijah rested on Elisha . . . just as the spirit of Moses rested on the seventy elders."[118]

Some excepted Isaiah, who prophesied "from the mouth of the Most High."[119] But another source refuses even to except Isaiah. Isaiah said: "For the Lord has spoken" (Isaiah 1:2). "They said to him: Isaiah our Master, could the Holy and Blessed One have spoken and the earth not tremble? Why, it has been said: "the earth trembled, the sky rained because of God, yon Sinai, because of God, the God of Israel" (Psalm 68:9). Moreover, the waters shuddered, as it says: "above the thunder of the mighty waters" (Psalm 93:4). And when was that? At the time that "God spoke all these words" (Exodus 20:1). Now if God had spoken to you, would you still be alive?"[120]

But against the maximalist approach, Rabbi Yose bar Haninah said:

[117] Exodus Rabbah 42:8, in the name of Rabbi Simeon ben Nahman.
[118] PRK 125b.
[119] PRK 125b.
[120] Tanhuma Ha'azinu 2.

[101] That is, the prophets are herein made not into people of inspiration, but rather people of learning.

Moses made four evil pronouncements concerning Israel, but four prophets came and nullified them. Moses said, "Thus Israel dwells in solitude"[102] (Deuteronomy 33:28), and Amos came and nullified it, as it says: "O Lord God, refrain! How will Jacob survive? He is so small" (Amos 7:5), and immediately afterward: "The Lord relented concerning this" (Amos 7:6); Moses said, "Yet even among those nations you shall find no peace" (Deuteronomy 28:65), and Jeremiah came and nullified it, saying: "When Israel was marching to quietude" (Jeremiah 31:1); Moses said: "visits the iniquity of parents upon children" (Exodus 34:7), and Ezekiel came and nullified it: "The person who sins, only he shall die" (Ezekiel 18:4); Moses said, "[you] shall perish among the nations" (Leviticus 26:38), and Isaiah came and said: "And in that day a great ram's horn shall be sounded; and the strayed who are in the land of Assyria . . . shall come" (Isaiah 27:13).[121]

About King Solomon it is said, "He was the wisest of all men, [wiser] than Ethan the Ezrahite, and Heman . . ." (1 Kings 5:11). And they expounded this as follows: "'of all men'—this refers to Adam; 'than Ethan the Ezrahite'—this refers to Abraham; 'and Heman'—this refers to Moses, of whom it says 'he is trusted [ne'eman] throughout my household'"[103] (Numbers 12:7). Now according to this idea, Solomon's wisdom exceeded that of Moses our Master.[122]

---

[121] BT Makkot 24a.
[122] PR 60a.

---

[102] This verse, in its original context, is meant to be positive, but badad ("in solitude") is here taken as negative, perhaps in line with the first line of the Book of Lamentations, where Jerusalem is said, in the aftermath of the destruction, to be sitting in solitude.

[103] Thus, we have here a play on words flowing from the phonetic similarity of the proper name Heman and the adjective ne'eman.

The Maximalist Approach to the Principle "Torah from Heaven"

[For an introduction, see the beginning of chapter 30.]

Even One Word, Even One Letter

IN THE COURSE OF THE GENERATIONS, the tendency to broaden the concept of "Torah from heaven" prevailed. According to the Baraita of the "Alternate Tradition," whoever says that the whole Torah is from heaven except for *one verse* which Moses spoke on his own, has "spurned the word of the Lord."[1] Maimonides took it a step further, saying that whoever says that Moses spoke even *one word* on his own, denies the Torah.[2] The Zohar says similarly that "there is not one word in the Torah that Moses said on his own."[3]

The basic idea of the sanctity of the letters in the Torah is found already in the sayings of Rabbi Meir and Rabbi Simeon: "Is it possible that Moses gave the Torah when it was missing a single letter?" In the first Amoraic generation, we find the *aggadah* of Rav and Rabbi Joshua ben Levi, "When Moses ascended to heaven, he found the Holy and Blessed One sitting and tying crowns on the letters."[4] In another source we read that Moses spent "forty days in the mountain, sitting before the Holy and Blessed One like a student before his master, studying scripture during the day and Mishnah at night. . . . Ben Bathyra said, he spent forty days expounding words of Torah and exploring its letters."[5]

It is well known how careful the scribes were in writing not only the words of the Torah, but also its letters. They said, "That is why they were called *soferim*,[1] for they counted all the letters in the Torah." [6] Rabbi Meir, who engaged in the scribal craft,

---

[1] BT Sanhedrin 99a.   [2] Maimonides, *Hilkhot Teshuvah* 3:8.
[3] Zohar Vayyikra 7a.   [4] BT Menahot 29b; Shabbat 89a.   [5] PRE 46.
[6] BT Kiddushin 30a.

---

[1] *Soferim* is a homonym meaning "scribes" or "counters." The point is that the Torah had to be copied letter for letter or the count of the letters would be in error.

heard from his master, "My son, be careful in your work, for it is a sacred task. If you should omit or add a single letter, you might destroy the whole world."[7] According to Rabbi Simeon ben Yohai, the book of Deuteronomy complained to the Holy and Blessed One, that King Solomon sought to uproot a single *yod* from it.[2] The Sages said, "If all the nations of the world come together to uproot a single word from the Torah, they will not be able."[8]

In Rabbi Akiva's teaching, the Torah was the precious instrument with which the world was created. Rabbi Johanan came and taught, "*Be-hibare'am*[3]—with a *hei* He created them"; that is, God created the world with but a single letter. Rabbi Eleazar ben Pedat interpreted the verse "'For in *YH* the Lord is the Rock of worlds'[4] (Isaiah 26:4)—with the letters *yod* and *hei*, the Holy and Blessed One created His world."[9] The letters are the essence of the Torah, the secret of existence. Whoever knows how to combine the letters properly can perform miracles.[5]

Just as Rav's aggadic statements valued the crowns of the letters, so did his halakhic decisions. The Mishnah states, "The four portions written in the Tefillin—if one is absent, it invalidates the others." (Rabbi Ishmael says they are four separate mitzvot—if one is absent, it does not invalidate the others.) The Gemara asks: Is it not obvious (that if one is absent, it invalidates the others)? R. Judah said in the name of Rav: This comes to teach that even the tip of the letter *yod* [if absent, invalidates all].[10]

A late midrash develops this point further: "See how by switching the tips of the letters you can destroy the world. By turning a *het* into *hei*, you change 'we set our hope on the Lord' [to 'we smite (the Lord)'] (Psalm 33:20); by turning a *hei* into *het*, you change 'Let all that breathes praise the Lord' [to 'desecrate (the Lord)']" (Psalm 150:6).[6]

Also in the Akivan vein writes Rabbenu Nissim son of R. Jacob from Kairowan, who lived in the eleventh century:

[7] BT Eruvin 13a; Sotah 20a. The variants of this tradition will be discussed below.

[8] Leviticus Rabbah 19:2.

[9] Genesis Rabbah 12:10. Later commentators interpreted the plural "worlds" to mean this world and the world to come.

[10] BT Menahot 34a.

---

[2] The significance of this remark is spelled out in the next section.

[3] The letter *hei* in this word is written small in the Torah scroll, suggesting that the word be broken up: *be-hei bera'am*. This is one of the cases in which the scribal tradition of writing some letters smaller than normal and others larger than normal gave rise to special midrashic interpretation—which in turn reinforced the tendency to regard these variants as sacred.

[4] NJV: "For in Yah the Lord you have an everlasting Rock."

[5] See also the view of Eleazar ben Pedat that whoever could restore the portions of the Torah to their correct order could raise the dead (see chapter 13, n. [4]).

[6] In the first example, *chiketah* ("hoped") becomes *hiketah* ("smote"); in the second example, *tehallel* ("praise") becomes *techallel* ("desecrate"). Out of delicacy, the midrashist does not spell out the blasphemous results, but leaves it for the astute listener to fill in.

A person should not be careless with even a single letter of the Torah, for every letter contains numerous allusions. Have you not seen the midrashim which our blessed Sages expounded in the Talmud, based on a single extra letter in the text? Thus they said, "The Torah could have written *u-va'al*. Why does it write *u-va'alah*? So that you may learn an extra law from it."[7] Similarly, the Torah could have written *lo takel*. Why does it write *lo tekallel*? So that you may learn an extra law from it.[8] It will be clear to the believer that there is no superfluous letter in the Torah that does not contain some allusion, all the more so a word or verse. Let no one err as King Manasseh erred, who asked, "Why did Moses need to write, 'The sister of Lotan was Timna'?"[9] . . . To him tradition applies the verse "Ah, those who haul sin with cords of falsehood and iniquity as with cart ropes!" (Isaiah 5:18)[11]

Nahmanides wrote:

If you were to say that the language of the Torah is merely conventional[10] like other languages, we would be denying the divine revelation of the Torah from God's mouth. If you say that even one word is merely conventional, this falls into the category of what the Sages condemned: Whoever says the whole Torah is from heaven except one word, spurns the word of the Lord. For if the Torah's language were conventional like other languages (of which the Torah says, "[at Babel] the Lord confounded the speech of the whole earth" [Genesis 11:9]), then its letters, which are like sacred stones, would be scattered like pebbles in the marketplace; the Torah would be emptied of its soul. We would not then need to pay attention to words of full and defective spelling, or open and closed paragraph divisions,[11] much less letters of various shapes and convolutions,[12] or with crowns on them, for all this would be empty vanity. What would we then make

---

[11] *Hibbur Yafeh Meha-yeshu'ah*, p. 89.

---

[7] *U-va'al* ("and he cohabits"), *u-va'alah* ("and he cohabits with her"). The simple law is that cohabitation with intent to marry is enough to make a free woman his wife. The extra law is that the same does not apply to a slave woman.

[8] *Elohim lo takel/tekallel* ("you shall not curse God [or judges]"). Rabbi Ishmael says *elohim* means "judges." Rabbi Akiva says it means "God." Because of the extra *lamed* in *tekallel*, we can make the verse do double duty and say it means both. These are representative of many other legal exegeses of the same type.

[9] See discussion of this example in chapter 21, pp. 396–99.

[10] That is, that each word arbitrarily means what the human creators of language decide it means, and another word could just as easily mean the same thing. Nahmanides is arguing against the doctrine, which Rabbi Ishmael affirmed, that "the Torah speaks human language."

[11] The paragraph divisions in the Torah scroll are of two types. In an "open" paragraph division, the rest of the line is left blank and the next paragraph starts on a fresh line. In a "closed" paragraph division, the new paragraph starts at the end of the same line, after leaving a considerable blank space. Like other typographical features of the Torah scroll, these are fixed by tradition and may not be changed.

[12] There are traditions that certain letters should be written isolated, curled, twisted, broken, and so on. Despite Nahmanides' desire to see these as special marks of the divine quality of the text, there is in fact no uniform tradition as to these variants. See EJ, s.v. "Masorah," 1.2.2, in "Supplementary Entries."

of the tradition, that a Torah scroll missing even one letter is disqualified, if the letters were given only for their mere content and not for their arrangement? Why is the word *toledot* ("generations") spelled in all its fullness in the phrase "generations of the heavens and earth when they were created," in its most defective spelling in "generations of Ishmael," and of intermediate form in "generations of Isaac" and "generations of Esau"?[13] What is the point of all these (and many similar cases)? Why should a Torah scroll be disqualified for an error in one of these variants? But know that every letter in the Torah has heaps of meaning in its component parts, as the rabbis interpreted from the verse *kevutzotav taltalim*[14] (Song of Songs 5:11). So said David, "Open my eyes, that I may perceive the wonders of Your Torah" (Psalm 119:18). If its secrets were hidden even from David, so that he prayed that they be revealed to him, how much more so we, who are lowly and unworthy.[12]

Could the Torah Be Missing a Single Letter?

When Rabbi Meir and Rabbi Simeon exclaimed, "Could the Torah be missing a single letter?" their point was to argue that Moses wrote even the last verses of Deuteronomy describing his own death. It should follow that according to the anonymous Tanna who thought that Joshua wrote these verses, Moses' Torah scroll lacked these verses, yet he did not consider it blemished on that account. On this important issue, the schools of Rabbi Akiva and Rabbi Ishmael were again divided.

The Babylonian Talmud cites differing traditions of Rabbi Meir's apprenticeship. According to a Baraita, Rabbi Meir said, "When I was with Rabbi Ishmael, I would put calcanthum in the ink, and he did not object. When I came to Rabbi Akiva, he forbade me to do this." A second tradition, in the name of R. Judah in the name of Samuel, reverses the positions: "When I was learning with Rabbi Akiva, I would put calcanthum in the ink, and he did not object. When I came to Rabbi Ishmael, he said to me, 'What is your craft?' I said, 'I am a scribe.' He said to me, 'My son, be careful in your work, for it is a sacred task. If you should omit or add a single letter, you might destroy the whole world.' I said to him, 'There is something called calcanthum which I put into the ink.' He replied, 'Does one indeed put calcanthum into the ink? Does not the Torah say, "The priest shall write . . . and rub it off" (Numbers 5:23)— hence, one should write with something that can be rubbed off.'"[15] [13]

---

12 *Ramban vi-Yerushalayim*, II, 30ff.
13 BT Eruvin 13a; see also BT Sotah 20a.

---

[13] The traditional answer is that the fuller the spelling, the more perfect the thing described. Heaven and earth were perfect in their first bloom after creation; the descendants of Ishmael were wicked; the descendants of Isaac were partly good and partly wicked; and so on. See Rashi's comment on the defective spelling of *tomim* ("twins") in Genesis 25:24.

[14] NJV: "His locks are curled." The untranslatable pun yields: "its jots are heaps"; that is, the jots (tiny strokes) of the letters yield heaps of meaning.

[15] The context of Numbers is the law of the ordeal of the suspected adulteress. The priest wrote

Although we cannot settle the matter with certainty, it is reasonable to suppose that the first tradition is correct and that the extended comment that follows was really spoken by Rabbi Akiva. This comment fits best with Rabbi Akiva's teaching, that the Torah was written in heaven, that Moses never said anything on his own, and that he did not change the words of the Holy and Blessed One even in places where the imprecise phrase "Thus says the Lord" is used.[14]

Rabbi Akiva taught, "The tradition [*massoret*] is a fence for the Torah."[15] He evidently meant that the tradition that the Sages gave us concerning the full and defective spellings of various words protects the integrity of the Torah text. Rabbi Simeon tells how the Book of Deuteronomy complained before the Holy and Blessed One: "Master of the Universe! Solomon has made me a fraud! Any document of which two or three particulars have been voided is rendered completely void. Solomon seeks to uproot one *yod* from me—my law prohibits a king from having many horses, wives, or gold, yet he has all three![16]" The Holy and Blessed One replied, "Go in peace. Solomon will be annulled, and a hundred like him, but a *yod* of yours will never be annulled!"[16]

See how Rabbi Ishmael taught: "Great is peace, for the Holy and Blessed One allowed His name, written in sanctity, to be rubbed out in water in order to make peace between a man and his wife."[17] [17] In other words, the value of peace outweighs the sanctity of the letters. Similarly Rabbi Johanan taught: "It is better that one letter be uprooted from the Torah than that the name of Heaven be desecrated in public." Rabbi Simeon ben Jehozadak cites his teaching differently: "It is better that one letter be uprooted from the Torah, in order that the name of Heaven be sanctified in pub-

---

[14] In Tractate Soferim (1:6), Rabbi Simeon ben Eleazar cites Rabbi Meir citing Rabbi Ishmael that calcanthum is permitted (similarly Tractate Sefer Torah 1:7 in the name of Rabbi Simeon ben Lakish). The RITBA attributes the comment "be careful in your task" to Rabbi Akiva. Both are in support of the view argued here.

[15] Avot 3:17. See *Magen Avot* of R. Simeon ben Zemah Duran, and Mahzor Vitri on this saying.

[16] Leviticus Rabbah 19:2.

[17] Leviticus Rabbah 9:9; Sifre Naso 16.

---

curses on parchment, then rubbed the ink off into water, which the woman drank. Hence, in that ritual, it was necessary to use ink that could be rubbed off. This requirement was not universally extended to the ink for writing Torah scrolls; on the contrary, Tractate Soferim cites this Baraita as evidence that calcanthum is permitted in the ink. Apparently, calcanthum (vitriol) made the ink indelible, and whichever of Rabbi Meir's teachers forbade it wanted mistakes to be readily correctable, so that the final result would be perfect.

[16] The rules of royal conduct referred to here are in Deuteronomy 17:16–17. What is the connection of this with uprooting a single *yod*? According to the commentary of the MaHaRZU (Ze'ev Wolf Einhorn), he ignored the letter *yod* of *yarbeh*, thus transforming it from an imperative ("he shall not multiply") to a simple past ("he did not multiply"). Thus removing one letter subverts the entire sense of the passage, and of the book!

[17] This refers again to the ordeal of the suspected adulteress (Numbers 5); see n. [15] above.

lic."[18] [18] If you say that a Torah scroll that is missing one letter is disqualified, how shall these sayings be fulfilled?

It is clear that this saying is meant figuratively, and its meaning is similar to that of Rabbi Simeon ben Lakish: "Sometimes the annulment of the Torah is its foundation."[19] [19] "'It is a time to act for the Lord, they have violated Your teaching' (Psalm 119:126)—such as Elijah on Mount Carmel, who offered a sacrifice at a provincial shrine ["high place"], when such was forbidden.'"[20][20] Note that Rabbi Ishmael himself would sometimes interpret laws on the basis of the full and defective spelling of words in the Torah.[21]

On the other hand, we have the tradition of the "scribal emendations," of which we shall speak below.

The Sages were divided on the law of whether it was permitted to read from a Torah scroll that was found to be missing a letter or word, once it had already been taken out for reading. Rabbi Johanan (who agreed with Rabbi Banai's dictum, "the Torah was given scroll by scroll") taught that "one should not read from a scroll of the Torah which is missing an entire parchment."[22] The Tosafot commented on this statement: "Since he specifies an entire parchment, we may be deduce that if a single verse is missing, this does not apply."[23] Nahmanides interprets differently: "The law of a missing parchment or verse applies when this is missing at the end of the scroll; but if the scribe omitted a single verse or even a single letter in the middle, we do not read from it."[24]

Maimonides laid down the rule that if "the scribe erred in a case of full or defective spelling, or substituted the keri for the ketiv,[21] it is disqualified and does not have the

---

[18] BT Yevamot 79a.   [19] BT Menahot 99a.
[20] BT Berakhot 63a; Rashi, s.v. mi-seifa le-reisha.
[21] BT Sanhedrin 9b.   [22] BT Gittin 60a.
[23] BT Megillah 9a, s.v. bishelama.
[24] Rabbenu Nissim on BT Megillah, chapter 3. Compare Nahmanides' Introduction to his Commentary on the Torah.

---

[18] The context of this remark is instructive. It is cited in connection with the story in 2 Samuel 21, in which David acceded to the request of the Gibeonites to have seven of Saul's line executed and their corpses exposed to public view. Leaving aside the question whether the executions were justified, exposing the corpses was clearly a violation of Deuteronomy 21:22–23. Rabbi Johanan's remark is cited to argue that departing from one "letter" of the Torah was justified, in order to satisfy the non-Jews that justice had been done in accordance with their code of honor.

[19] The context of this remark is Moses' smashing the first set of tablets in response to seeing the golden calf.

[20] This is in accordance with Rava's reversal of the verse: it is sometimes necessary "to violate Your teaching"—when "it is a time to act for the Lord" (BT Berakhot 63a).

[21] In some passages, a word was written one way and traditionally pronounced another. Ketiv is the variant to be committed to writing, and keri is the variant to be recited. For instance, the word for "they grumbled" in Exodus 16:2 is written va-yalinu but read va-yilonu; in Numbers 14:36, where the causative ("they caused the whole community to mutter") is required, the variant is the reverse. Writing the keri in place of the ketiv was another possible scribal error.

sanctity of a Torah scroll at all." The commentary *Migdal Oz* says that this rule is based on Rabbi Simeon's view. Therefore [writes Caro], it was the custom in medieval Spain that if an error was found in a Torah scroll during the reading, they would take out another scroll, even at the end of the portion.[25] The same rule is found in the Tikkunei Zohar.[26]

However, Moses Isserles differed with Maimonides and Caro and wrote: "This rule [to bring out another scroll] applies when there is a flagrant error, but an error in full or defective spelling is not reason enough, for the Torah scrolls are not written so perfectly that we should think that the second scroll will be more kosher than the first."[27] "Know that the Maharal of Prague's custom was never to bring out a replacement scroll even if an entire word was missing."[28]

Changes in the Text of Scripture[22]

Despite the care that Israelites exercised in the writing of the Torah, variants in the scriptural text developed in the course of time. Some say that already the scribe Ezra was uncertain of the correct reading of certain words in Scripture and that he therefore put dots over ten words in the Torah. "Ezra reasoned thus: If Elijah comes and asks me, 'Why did you write this?' I will say, 'I have already marked them with dots.' And if he says, 'You have written well!' I will remove the dots."[29] In other words, these dots "half-deny the text . . . they render the text doubtful."[30]

This statement seems to have come from the school of Rabbi Yose ben Halafta, who in many of his opinions was close to the way of thinking of Rabbi Ishmael, and in halakhic matters as well.[31]

"When any of you or of your posterity who are defiled by a corpse or are on a long journey would offer a passover sacrifice to the Lord, they shall offer it in the second month" (Numbers 9:10–11)—"What is 'a long journey'? Modiin [about fifteen miles

---

[25] Maimonides, *Hilkhot Sefer Torah* 7:11; *Beit Yosef* OH 143.

[26] Tikkunei Zohar 25. Compare Zohar Aharei Mot 70a.

[27] Glosses on Shulhan Arukh, OH 143:4.

[28] *Be'er Heitev* ad loc., n. 9; MaHaRaL, *Tif'eret Yisrael* 63.

[29] ARN A 34, B 37.

[30] Commentary of Jacob ben Asher on Numbers (beginning).

[31] S. Lieberman, *Hellenism in Jewish Palestine*, Texts and Studies of the Jewish Theological Seminary of America 18 (New York: Jewish Theological Seminary, 1950), 44.

---

[22] At the risk of belaboring the obvious, we stress that Heschel's main purpose here (as throughout the book) is to give not his own views of the changes that occurred in the text of Scripture but the views of mainstream Jewish thinkers from the rabbinic through the medieval period. It is commonplace in modern biblical scholarship that many more radical changes probably took place in the scriptural text than Heschel describes here. What is surprising is how aware many traditional Jewish thinkers were of the possibility that even moderate changes could have taken place, and how they integrated this fact into their view of the revealed text of Scripture.

to the west] or further, and the same distance in every direction. Rabbi Yose said, 'Why is there is a dot over the *hei*? To say it not need be truly far, but only from the threshold of the Temple court and further.'"[32] Here is how Rabbi Yose's view is explained in the Jerusalem Talmud: "When the written portion is greater than the dotted, you should interpret the written portion and ignore the dotted; when the dotted portion is greater than the written, you should interpret the dotted portion and ignore the written. But Rabbi Yose did differently: even though there was a dot on only one letter, he interpreted the dot and ignored the written portion. The *hei* of *rehokah* was dotted, so he ignored it, leaving only the word *rahok*. Not the way was remote, but the man was remote."[23] [33]

We shall see that some other Sages disagreed with the assumption that dots over the letters must necessarily indicate doubtful readings. In the verse "Esau ran to greet Jacob . . ." (Genesis 33:4), there are dots on the word *vayyishakehu,* "and he embraced him." Rabbi Jannai followed Rabbi Yose's approach that the dots cancel the plain sense, and interpreted *nashak* after the sense of *nashakh*—"and he bit him." But a second approach accepted the kissing as real and questioned just the intent: "he did not kiss him with all his heart." Yet a third approach said "his emotions were aroused at that moment, and he kissed him with all his heart."[34]

As the copyists increased, so the errors increased.[24] It appears that inaccurate copies of the Torah were prevalent during the Second Temple period. Mention of these is preserved in a Baraita that tells: "Three scrolls were kept in the Temple courtyard, called Meonim, Hei Hei, and Za'atutim. One read *ma'on elohei kedem,* and the other two read *me'onah elohei kedem*[25] (Deuteronomy 33:27). The Sages rejected the one and adopted [the reading of] the other two.[35] [26]

---

[32] Mishnah Pesahim 9:2.   [33] PT Pesahim 36d.   [34] Sifre Beha'alotekha 79.
[35] Sifre Vezot Haberakhah 356; ARN B 46; PT Ta'anit 68d; Tractate Soferim 6:4.

---

[23] The difference between *rehokah* and *rahok* is gender, but the gender of the adjective must agree with the noun. Feminine *rehokah* agrees with *derekh* ("journey, way"); masculine *rahok* agrees with *ish* ("man"). A man can be "remote" even if he is just outside the threshold of the Temple, if he is unavailable for whatever reason.

[24] Stylistically, this statement of Heschel's is in the spirit of the grand historical-theological pronouncements at the end of Mishnah Sotah. ("As the murderers increased, they abolished the ceremony of the heifer . . . as the adulterers increased, they abolished the bitter waters.") In outlook, Heschel subscribes here to the fundamental axiom of the modern historical-critical approach to biblical studies. Anyone who has worked with medieval manuscripts of religious texts knows that there are no two identical handwritten copies of the same text and that variations start with spelling differences and progress inexorably to crucial matters of content. This also, say the modern scholars, was the case with the text of the Bible before printing.

[25] "The ancient God is a refuge." The difference is small (the spelling of the word for 'refuge') but of possible significance, and characteristic of textual variants in every kind of copied manuscript. A full comparative-critical edition of the three Torah scrolls would no doubt have revealed many other differences.

[26] It is not clear from this formulation whether they disqualified the odd scroll entirely on the basis

Textual variants have been preserved from the Torah scroll which was brought in the exile from Jerusalem to Rome, and which was stored in the synagogue of Severus. Here are some sample verses: "The Lord who took me from my house and from my land" (Genesis 24:7), where we have: "The Lord, *the God of heaven,* who took me from my *father's* house and from my *native* land"; "He sold his *sale*" (Genesis 25:33), where we have "he sold his *birthright*"; "Thus shall you say to the *sons* of Jacob" (Exodus 19:3) where we have: "Thus shall you say to the *house* of Jacob"; "Do not take the mother-bird *while she is in labor*" (Deuteronomy 22:6), where we have "[do not take her] *together with her young.*"[36]

David Kimhi[27] reports a variant from the Severus Torah: instead of *vehinei tov me'od* ("and behold it was very good") (Genesis 1:31), it reads *vehinei tov mavet* ("and behold it was good—death"). Midrash Genesis Rabbah reports the same variant in the Torah of Rabbi Meir. It is very likely just such a case that led Rabbi Meir's teacher to warn him that the change of a single letter could destroy the world. It is strange that Rabbi Meir, of all people, would have introduced a change in the text of the Torah![28] Nahmanides writes that "Rabbi Meir was a scribe, and while writing a Torah scroll he was considering how the phrase 'it was very good' must encompass even death and nothingness. His hand followed his thought; thus he erred and wrote in the Torah scroll, 'behold it was good—death.'"[37]

Early on, there started the activity of the propagators of the *massoret*,[29] who tried

---

[36] Genesis Rabbati of Moses the Darshan, ed. Albeck, pp. 209ff. See Lieberman, *Hellenism in Jewish Palestine,* 23ff. Albeck (loc. cit.) discusses the relation of this to Rabbi Meir's Torah. See A. M. Haberman, "Iyyonim bi-Megillot Midbar Yehudah," *Sinai* 32 (1953): 161-64.

[37] Nahmanides, "Sermon on Ecclesiastes," ed. Schwartz, p. 10.

---

of this one passage, or (as Kimhi suggests in a passage cited below) merely used the two-out-of-three rule for any passages where there were discrepancies (as Joseph Caro was later to rule halakhically issue by issue from comparing the positions of Alfasi, Maimonides, and Rabbenu Asher).

[27] Kimhi (twelfth–thirteenth century, Provence) was one of the great medieval Jewish exegetes of the Bible; he followed a moderately rationalistic approach.

[28] Lieberman suggests that Rabbi Meir "copied the *vulgata,* the text to which the public was accustomed. . . . The *koina,* the common texts, of the Bible were not simply erroneous texts. They represented a variant text which perhaps did not contain some of the emendations of the Soferim and corrections of the sages, for it is unlikely that all those alterations were immediately introduced into the popular texts" (*Hellenism in Jewish Palestine,* 25–26). It is at any rate unsettling to us to learn that such a familiar expression as "it was very good" was not the universally accepted text in the second century C.E. Again, the relevant question for this chapter is, how aware were the rabbis of such variations, and how did they try to account for them in the light of their theories of the literal inerrancy of Torah?

[29] *Massoret*—"traditions [of the text]." Heschel deliberately uses a term that recalls Rabbi Akiva's statement "The *massoret* is a fence for the Torah," and is a precursor of the term *Masorah* (which refers to the writing down of the pointings and marginalia of the text in the seventh to ninth centuries). The picture he draws of gradual development from the one to the other is in agreement with the standard scholarly interpretation. See C. D. Ginsburg, *Introduction to the Masoretico-Critical Edition of the Hebrew Bible* (1897; reprint, New York: Ktav, 1966); and EJ, s.v. "Masorah."

to preserve the sacred writings from any change. Their tradition was originally oral, but at some time after the redaction of the Babylonian Talmud it was committed to writing. They would record in the margins of the books those notes which they had previously kept in memory, as to the manner of writing each word—the verse divisions, cantillation tropes, departures from standard spelling, keri and ketiv. This is alluded to in the talmudic statement: "The scribes were called soferim because they counted all the letters in the Torah."[38]

When Rabbi Akiva was imprisoned, he gave Rabbi Simeon ben Yohai five instructions. Among them was: "When you teach your son, teach him from a scroll that has been proof-read."[39] This was said of an individual's scroll, used for study, of which people were less scrupulous. In connection with a Torah scroll from which they would read in public, it says in the Babylonian Talmud: "An unproofed Torah may be kept for up to thirty days. Beyond that point, it must either be corrected or stored away, for it says, 'Let no falseness reside in your tents'[30] (Job 11:14)."[40] It was established in a Baraita: A Torah scroll that has three errors per page shall be corrected; if four [or more], it shall be stored away.[31] [41]

The Masoretic Sages made every effort to purify and refine a true and correct edition of the scriptural text. Nevertheless, we find in several places in the Talmud and midrashim verse citations that deviate from the Masoretic text.[32] The Tosafists concluded that our talmudic sources differ from our scriptural books.[42] On the other hand, R. Hai Gaon writes on verses "which we find in the Talmud but are not in Scripture, and the like. God forbid that they should contradict each other! . . . Know that the Sages would not err in citing a verse, for they labored long and hard to preserve their oral traditions without change, and everyone was careful to transmit his master's words exactly, all the more so Torah and Scripture. But you should examine each doubtful case to determine the correct cause, whether it was a scribal error, or

[38] BT Kiddushin 30a.
[39] BT Pesahim 112a.
[40] BT Ketubot 19b.
[41] BT Menahot 29b. See Tractate Soferim 3.
[42] Tosafot on BT Shabbat 55b, s.v. ma'avirim; ibid. 128a, s.v. ve-natan (see MaHaRSHaL and MaHaRSHa on Berakhot 61a); Megillah 3a s.v. va-yalen.

---

[30] NJV: "Do not let injustice reside in your tent."

[31] Though three errors per page does not sound like a lot, it adds up over time. If ten scrolls were copied from one original, and ten from each of those, then within a few copy-generations, hundreds of variants could theoretically result. That there were relatively few variants in the Torah text (as compared with rabbinic writings, for instance) is a tribute to the scribes' scrupulousness and their thorough familiarity with the text.

[32] Recently, Sid Z. Leiman has taken inventory of these, especially those where the superseded talmudic text was the basis of halakhic conclusions. See "Masorah and Halakhah: A Study in Conflict," in Tehillah le-Moshe: Biblical and Judaic Studies in Honor of Moshe Greenberg (Winona Lake, Ind.: Eisenbrauns, 1997), 291–306.

the careless recall of sophomoric students, or something that was originally said not as a scriptural citation."[43]

According to Rabbi Isaac, "scribal readings and omissions, *keri* and *ketiv* are *halakhah* to Moses from Sinai." R. Nissim commented: "Thus Moses received at Sinai and transmitted to Israel."[44] R. David Kimhi was of a different opinion: "The books were lost in the first Exile and scattered, and the Sages knowledgeable in Scripture died. The Men of the Great Assembly, who restored the Torah to its former estate, found differences among the scrolls,[33] and followed the version of the majority according to their judgment, and where they were not able to achieve full clarity, they wrote one version and did not dot it, or they wrote one version outside and did not write it inside, or they wrote one meaning inside and another outside."[34] [45]

R. Isaac Abravanel objected to Kimhi's statements: "How can I myself believe, and voice the possibility that Ezra the Scribe found doubtful books of God's Torah in a state of neglect and confusion? Is not a Torah scroll that is missing one letter disqualified? How much more so if the *keri* and the *ketiv* came together in the Torah, for on account of the *keri* the Torah would be missing several letters." According to his view, Ezra and the Men of the Great Assembly "found scrolls of the Torah in complete and perfect condition." He thinks there are two kinds of *keri* and *ketiv*. Sometimes the prophet himself[35] wrote an unusual form and intended thereby to allude to "one of the secret mysteries of Torah, depending on his level of prophecy." Therefore Ezra did not presume "to come near and erase a word from the divine books, for he understood that they were written out of profound wisdom, and that a reason underlay every missing or added letter or strange idiom." Ezra wrote in the margins "the *keri*, which is the simple meaning of the unusual form according to linguistic sense and context. You will find every *keri* and *ketiv* in the Torah to be of this sort. . . . It is also possible that Ezra thought there were words that were only written in such a strange fashion because whoever spoke [or wrote] them had insufficient knowledge of the Hebrew language or the rules of proper writing and spelling. Such instances, in the prophetic books or inspired writings,[36] are as 'an error committed by a ruler' (Ecclesiastes 10:5), and you will find that most of the *keri* and *ketiv* in Jeremiah is of this kind."[46]

---

[43] *Otzar Ha-geonim, Teshuvot* on Berakhot 48a.
[44] BT Nedarim 37b.
[45] Kimhi on Early Prophets (Introduction) and 2 Samuel 15:21.
[46] Abravanel, Introduction to Commentary on Jeremiah.

---

[33] See the Sifre reference to the three scrolls in the Temple courtyard, cited above.
[34] That is, one as the *keri* and the other as the *ketiv* (or in the Masoretic edition, one in the body of the text and the other in the margin).
[35] That is, Moses (for he speaks here of *keri* and *ketiv* in the Torah, which had a higher level of sanctity and inerrancy than in the rest of scripture).
[36] "Inspired writings"—that is, the Hagiographa, the third section of Hebrew Scripture (Psalms, etc.).

R. Jacob ben Hayyim ibn Adonijah[37] objected to Abravanel's statement: "I am amazed that words such as these proceeded from such a man as the late gentleman! Would anyone imagine that the prophets were deficient in such a respect? In that case, the late gentleman was a greater master of Hebrew grammar than they! By my life, I shall not believe such a thing. If there was an error, as he wrote, why did not the prophet or inspired writer correct it?" He based himself on the Gemara, "All words which are recited but not written, or written and not recited, are according to the tradition [*masorah*], a *halakhah* to Moses from Sinai."[47]

We learn in the Mishnah:

Rabbi Ishmael asked Rabbi Joshua when they were on a journey, "Why did they forbid idolators' cheese?" He replied, "Because they curdle it in the rennet of idolators' calves." . . . He asked, "In that case, why do they not forbid having any benefit from it?" He changed the subject, and asked him: "Ishmael, my brother! Do you read *ki tovim dodekha* —'for your love [masculine] is better than wine' (Song of Songs 1:2), or *ki tovim dodayikh* —'your love [feminine]'?"[48] Someone asked the RIBaSH:[38] "How is it possible that a great Sage like Rabbi Akiva (*sic!*) should err in pronunciation of a verse that even school-children know?" The RIBaSH answered: "Even if their books were provided with vowel-points, it is not that far-fetched that Rabbi Akiva might err in the pronunciation of a verse, for it is possible that there was a difference of opinion in their books on this word, as there is today in many words between the 'Western' and 'Eastern' versions, or between that of Ben Asher and Ben Naftali.[39] Was there not a difference even in word division between one scroll and another, so that they had to go after the majority, as we learned in Tractate Soferim about the three scrolls in the Temple courtyard?"[49]

And in the responsa of RaSHBA (attributed to Nahmanides) it says:

Ought we to disqualify a Torah scroll on account of full and defective spellings counter to the Masorah? I say that the readings authorized by the Masorah are not superior to those of the Talmud, which has defective spellings of *pilagshim* ("concubines," 2 Samuel 5:13), *asimem* ("I will place them," Deuteronomy 1:13), *kalot* ("completion," Numbers 7:1), and *karnot* ("horns," Leviticus 4:7), while our books have full spellings of all these words. Yet we do not feel obligated by the talmudic reading that we should correct our

---

[47] C. D. Ginsburg, ed., *Jacob ben Chajim Ibn Adonijah's Introduction to the Rabbinic Bible* (New York: Ktav, 1968).

[48] Mishnah Avodah Zarah 2:5.

[49] RIBaSH, Responsum 284.

<hr />

[37] Sixteenth century, Italy. He edited the Masorah in the second printed edition of Bomberg's Rabbinic Bible.

[38] Rabbi Isaac ben Sheshet, fourteenth century, Spain and northern Africa.

[39] In the period of crystallization of the Masorah (seventh–tenth centuries), the Western (Tiberian, Israel) and Eastern (Babylonian) traditions constituted the two main streams. Aaron ben Asher and Moses ben David Ben-Naftali are two classic Masoretic authorities, whose differences were summarized in an eleventh- to twelfth-century work, *Kitab al-Hulaf*—"The Book of Differences between the Two Masters, Ben-Asher and Ben-Naftali."

books to conform to it, as you would hold we ought to. Why, then, should we feel obligated to conform to the Masorah, which is a recent arrival? I have support for my view from chapter 1 of Tractate Kiddushin, which says that in the generation of R. Judah and R. Joseph they were not expert in full and defective spellings—all the less so, then, are we.

And Jedidiah Solomon Raphael Norzi[40] put it well:

Were it not for the propagators of the Masorah, who set the Torah and the tradition[41] on a firm footing, no one could find his hands or feet amid all the controversy, and Torah would be forgotten from Israel or be made into many Torahs, God forbid; we would then not find two scrolls of scripture that agreed, the same as has happened with the books of other authors. See the superiority of the Masorah, that there are several places where the Talmud differs from it, yet we hold the reading of the Masorah to be the correct one. It is the standard for all our books and for correcting Torah scrolls, and we hew to it, for the Men of the Great Assembly established it, and we follow them.[50]

And R. Abraham ibn Ezra wrote: "The guardians of the fortified sanctuary, the foundation of the hands of our God, which no foreigner can destroy. The sanctuary is Scripture, and the men of Torah are the propagators of the Masorah, who separated the alien admixture from the sacred."[51]

Variants in "Ptolemy's Torah"

We find that the elders who translated the Torah into Greek changed the wording of the Torah. "It is taught: Ptolemy the King assembled seventy-two elders and put them in seventy-two separate houses, without telling them for what purpose. He then came in to teach each separately and said, 'Write for me the Torah of Moses your master!' The Holy and Blessed One gave counsel to each of them, and they all arrived at the same result. They made thirteen changes in the text."[42]

This matter is elaborated in the Mekhilta of Rabbi Ishmael:

[50] *Mikdash Yah*, ed. Jellinek (Vienna, 5636/1876).
[51] *Reish Moznayim*. The final phrase is an allusion to Nehemiah 13:3.

---

[40] Italy, seventeenth century.
[41] Kabbalah. Here the term probably refers to the post-Torahitic books of Scripture—the Prophets and Hagiographa.
[42] This tradition of the writing of the Septuagint (recorded centuries after the event) is important especially as it reflects the rabbis' perceptions and attitudes concerning the whole enterprise of translating the Torah into Greek. By giving the story a miraculous embellishment, they indicate that they approved of it and even attached to the Greek text a measure of sanctity and revealed status. They recognized that there were departures from the Hebrew text, but even these were at least tolerated, and possibly included in that divine sanction.

"The length of time that the Israelites lived in Egypt and in the land of Canaan *and in the land of Goshen* was four hundred and thirty years" (Exodus 12:40)—this is one of the things that they changed for Ptolemy. Similarly they wrote:[43] (2) "God created in the beginning" (instead of 'In the beginning created God,' Genesis 1:1); (3) "Let Me make man in My image and likeness" (instead of 'Let us make man in our image, after our likeness,' Genesis 1:26); (4) "Male and his females He created them" (instead of 'Male and female He created them,' Genesis 5:2); (5) "God finished his work on the sixth day, and ceased on the seventh day" (instead of 'finished his work on the seventh day,' Genesis 2:2); (6) "Let Me go down and confound their speech" (instead of 'Let us go down . . . ,' Genesis 11:7); (7) "And Sarah laughed to her relatives" (instead of 'and Sarah laughed to herself,' Genesis 18:12); (8) "In their anger they slew oxen, and when pleased they uprooted stables" (instead of 'they slew men . . . they maimed oxen,' Genesis 49:6); (9) "Moses took his wife and sons and seated them on a *conveyance*"[44] (instead of 'on an ass,' Exodus 4:20); (10) "I have not taken the *desire*[45] of any one of them" (instead of 'the ass of any one of them,' Numbers 16:15); (11) "These [i.e., the sun, moon, and stars] the Lord your God allotted *to give light* to other peoples" ('to give light' has been added, Deuteronomy 4:19); (12) "turning to the worship of other gods . . . to the sun or the moon or any of the heavenly host, something I never commanded *to the nations for worship*" (the last words have been added, Deuteronomy 17:3); (13) "The following you shall not eat: . . . the hairy-footed" (Leviticus 11:5 or 11:6), instead of "hare," because Ptolemy's wife was named Hare,[46] so that he should not say, "The Jews have made fun of me, by putting my wife's name in the Torah."[52]

Note that this matter is recounted in the Mekhilta of Rabbi Ishmael, but is missing from the Mekhilta of Rabbi Simeon ben Yohai.[47] And according to Tractate Soferim, the elders wrote the Torah for Ptolemy "as it is."[53] The later Sages were amazed at this episode. How did the elders dare to change the words of the Torah?

[52] MI Pisha 14; BT Megillah 9b.
[53] Tractate Soferim 1, p. 103.

---

[43] The changes mentioned in this rabbinic tradition are not all found in the current standard Septuagint (ed. Brenton). Only examples 1, 5, 9, 10 and 13 are attested in our current Septuagint text. However, there was at least as much variation in the ancient Greek manuscripts as in the Hebrew texts, and there was a tendency over the centuries to "correct" the Septuagint versions, so as to bring them closer to the standard Hebrew text. It is likely, therefore, that the rabbinic tradition is based on early versions of the Septuagint before those corrections were applied—or even to other independent Greek translations of the Torah!

[44] Hebrew *nosei adam* (a "person-carrier"), Greek *hypozygia* (one that goes "under the yoke"). In each case, a functional word was substituted euphemistically for the lowly "ass."

[45] *Hemed,* a word easily transposed in writing with *hamor* ("donkey").

[46] Actually, Ptolemy's father's name was Lagos (*hare*—see Soncino Talmud on BT Megillah 9a, p. 50, n. 9). The current Septuagint has *dasypod* ("hairy-footed," an appellation for rabbit) for Leviticus 11:5, not 11:6. In the Hebrew to the Mekhilta, *se'irat ha-raglayim* ("hairy-footed") has been changed to *tze'irat ha-raglayim* ("small-footed").

[47] Heschel seems to suggest that the flexibility of translation depicted in this *aggadah* is characteristic of the Ishmaelian school. He could argue as follows: The Ishmaelian school taught elsewhere that the prophet could sometimes convey the gist of the divine mandate, with words filled in by the human

According to R. Solomon Luria: "It was Heaven's doing that [the seventy-two elders' versions] agreed, amounting to a kind of divine inspiration." It even says explicitly that the Holy and Blessed One gave counsel to each of them, "which amounts to divine revelation. Moreover, they did not change the meaning of anything, but only the language, so that one should not be misled into heresy; and as they changed it, so is the plain sense of Scripture."[54] [48]

One of the commentators on the Torah noted that even though it says, "Then Moses recited the words of this poem . . . in the ears of *the whole congregation of Israel*" (Deuteronomy 31:30), we also find, "Gather to me all *the elders of your tribes* and your officials, that I may speak these words in their ears" (Deuteronomy 31:28) The elders seem to have received a "mouth to ear" communication that was not revealed to all the people. What was this? It refers to the divine guidance in translating the Torah. After recounting the basic story from the Talmud, R. Mordecai Ha-Kohen concludes: "They made all these changes so as not to cause denigration of the Torah. But in order that one might not say, 'You have committed a fraud, for that is not how it is written in the Torah,' Moses stood and communicated these changes in the ears of the elders whom Ptolemy had assembled. That is the meaning of 'these words.'"[55]

The Text Euphemized—"Scribal Emendations"

In the midrashim from the school of Rabbi Ishmael, we find the view that sometimes the text tells things not as they really were but with a modification, in order to disguise and veil the true meaning out of respect for the divinity. The Mekhilta of Rabbi Ishmael brings eleven scriptures, and the Sifre seven, in which the Torah speaks euphemistically for the honor of the All-Present and replaces a more literal designation[49] with a more honorific one. The text uses an unusual expression to avoid one that does not befit the divine honor. This notion, in turn, is found regularly in the teaching of Rabbi Ishmael, who would respond to such verses, "Is it possible to say this?" and try to explain them in a more rational way. On the other hand, we saw that in Rabbi Akiva's school they did not hesitate to underscore such expressions and

---

[54] *Yam shel Shelomo* on Bava Kama, 4:9.
[55] R. Mordecai Ha-Kohen, *Siftei Kohen,* end of Vayelekh.

---

speaker. (See chapter 23 above, pp. 424–28). The Akivan approach, on the other hand, demands that not a word or letter be changed in the divine command; hence even translations of the Torah should be as exact as possible.

[48] This is an astute and accurate observation. Especially the changes of the divine self-address from "we" to "I" can be seen as emphasizing the monotheistic "plain sense" of the Torah and avoiding misunderstanding, when writing for an audience that included polytheists.

[49] Heschel seeks here to give an etymological explanation of the phrase *kinnah ha-katuv*. The basic meaning of *kinnah* is "to name," especially to assign a nickname (*kinnui*). A euphemism is essentially an alternate way of naming the same reality.

even to invent new ones in their homilies.[50] Note how the explanation "the text speaks euphemistically" is found in the Mekhilta of Rabbi Ishmael and the Sifre to Numbers, and is absent from the Mekhilta of Rabbi Simeon ben Yohai.

"In Your great triumph You break Your opponents" (Exodus 15:7)—"You triumph over those who attack you. And who are those who attack You? Those who attack Your children. The text does not say, 'You break *our* opponents,' but 'You break *Your* opponents.' This tells us that if someone attacks Israel, it is as if he attacked the Holy and Blessed One. Thus it says, 'Do not ignore the shouts of Your foes, the din of Your adversaries that ascends all the time' (Psalm 74:23)." Here the midrash cites four more verses which speak of the enemies of God, where the implied reference in each case is to the enemies of Israel. It then continues: "And thus it says, 'Whoever touches you touches the pupil of his own eye' (Zechariah 2:12). Rabbi Judah says, '"The pupil of the eye"—not so, but it is written "the pupil of his eye," referring as it were to God, but *kinnah ha-katuv*.'"[51] [56]

What is the exact meaning of the statement, *kinnah ha-katuv?* Apparently the meaning is similar to that of the saying, "the Torah spoke in human language"—the text itself spoke thus. It should have written, "the pupil of My eye," but wrote "the pupil of his [own] eye" for the sake of the divine honor. But we find that in the Midrash Yelammedenu[52] (and in our current Midrash Tanhuma) they interpreted this phrase in the sense of *scribal emendation*. This interpretation (which was accepted by the author of the *Arukh* and Rashi) may have originated with Rabbi Joshua ben Levi.

It is well known that the chapters in Midrash Tanhuma from Bo 5 through the end of Beshalah, derive from the Mekhilta of Rabbi Ishmael. This section includes the whole exposition on the verses that are "euphemized," with an important addition: "Thus it says, 'Whoever touches you touches the pupil of his own eye'—it should have said 'My eye,' but the text euphemized it, that is, referring as it were to God, but the text euphemized it, *that it is a scribal emendation of the Men of the Great Assembly* . . . the Men of the Great Assembly euphemized these verses, and that is why they were called Soferim, for they counted all the letters in the Torah, and interpreted them."[57]

According to this source, the meaning of *kinnah ha-katuv* is that the Men of the

---

[56] MI Shirata 6, cited with variants in Sifre Beha'alotekha 84. See ARN B 44.
[57] Tanhuma Beshalah 16.

---

[50] See chapter 12 above.

[51] Heschel will now entertain two possible understandings of this phrase: (1) "The text euphemized" (taking the subject of *kinnah* to be "the text"); or (2) "[One] euphemized the text" (taking "the text" to be the object of the verb, with subject unspecified). For shorthand, we shall represent both these possibilities with the ambiguous: "the text [was] euphemized," which can be read either with or without the word "was."

[52] A midrash, no longer extant, known from citations in other sources and thought to be a source for Midrash Tanhuma.

Great Assembly emended and corrected the wording from what was originally written.

In the same vein the author of the *Arukh*[53] writes: "There are eighteen scribal emendations, as specified in Midrash Yelammedenu . . . 'whoever touches you touches the pupil of his own eye'—*in the earlier scrolls was written 'the pupil of My eye.'*"[58] Similarly it is written in Exodus Rabbah: "For Israel are dear as the pupil of the divine eye, as it says, 'Whoever touches you touches the pupil of his own eye'—these are the scribes and Sages who established this hedge."[54][59]

Rashi also interpreted the expression *kinnah ha-katuv* in the sense of scribal emendation.

> "They condemned Job" (Job 32:3)—this is one of those scriptures in which the scribes emended the wording of the text. It ought to have written that they condemned God through their silence, but the text [was] euphemized. Similarly, "they exchanged *their* glory for the image of a bull" (Psalm 106:20), where it ought to have written "*My* glory," but the text [was] euphemized. And similarly: "Let me suffer no more of my evil" (Numbers 11:15), where it ought to have written, "of Your evil," but the text [was] euphemized. There are many similar passages in the Sifre and in the Greater Masorah.[60]

Though this topic is presented anonymously in the Tanhuma, we find it elsewhere in the name of its author: "'Whoever touches you touches the pupil of his own eye'—Rabbi Joshua ben Levi said, 'It is a scribal emendation; it ought to have written "My eye."'"[61] Rabbi Joshua ben Levi's student, Rabbi Simon, adduced another example not mentioned in the Mekhilta: "'Abraham remained standing before the Lord' (Genesis 18:22)—this is a scribal emendation, for actually the Shekhinah was waiting for Abraham."[62] Rashi paraphrases: "It ought to have read, 'The Lord[55] remained standing before Abraham,' but it is a scribal emendation, for our rabbis reversed the text."[63]

In contrast to the view that *kinnah ha-katuv* refers to scribal emendation, which was an action carried out by the Men of the Great Assembly, other Sages said in the Middle Ages that "scribal emendation" means "that is how the prophets wrote." R.

---

[58] *Sefer He-arukh* entry *kabbed*, 1.
[59] Exodus Rabbah 30:15.
[60] Rashi on Job 32:3.
[61] Exodus Rabbah 13:1. See Lieberman, *Hellenism in Jewish Palestine*, 28.
[62] Genesis Rabbah 49:7.
[63] Rashi on Genesis 18:22, Berliner edition.

---

[53] Nathan ben Jehiel of Rome, eleventh century.
[54] *shetikkenu ha-seyag ha-zeh*—that is, who emended the text in this fashion as a hedge (protection) to protect the divine honor from blasphemy.
[55] That is, one of the three angels mentioned at the beginning of chapter 18. The terms "the Lord," "the men," "the angels"—"they" are interchanged throughout Genesis 18–19.

Abraham ibn Ezra expressed amazement at this view: "In that case, why is it called 'scribal emendation'?"[64]

The RaSHBA also was of the opinion,

> God forbid that they added or subtracted even one letter from what was written in the Torah! It means rather that they analyzed each of these scriptures carefully, and found that the true meaning is not what we find on the surface of the text, but otherwise, still, it was not proper to write other than they did. In the case, "Abraham remained standing," it really means "the Lord remained standing," but the text departed from the true meaning. They are not scribal emendations[56] in the proper sense, except that the scribes analyzed them and found that they are euphemisms."[65]

According to Joseph Albo, "what our rabbis said of some words in the Torah, that they are tikkunei soferim—'fixings of the scribes'—this does not mean that they changed what was in the Torah, God forbid, but rather that Moses fixed the language at the divine behest."[66] R. Azariah "of the Edomites" protested against the understanding of "scribal emendation" in the Tanhuma: "Is this not contrary to what our rabbis inculcated in the chapter on the World to Come, that whoever says that even one letter [sic!] of Torah is not from heaven, despises the word of the Lord?"[67] And in Tractate Megillah, they said, "Any verse-divisions that Moses did not make, we do not make."[57] [68] And the author of the Arukh gave the following interpretation of the injunction, "He who euphemizes the passage of the illicit relations, is to be silenced":[69] "If he reads [from the Torah] 'his father . . . his mother' instead of 'your father . . . your mother,' we tell him, 'read the verse as it is written! Do you think it is up to you to make these words more elegant than Moses our Master made them?'"[70] Similarly, in all the rest of the Scriptures, "who shall lay hands on them and be blameless?[58] . . . Was Ezra so great and powerful that he could add or subtract anything from God's writing? Far be it from him, and from us!"[71]

---

[64] Tzahut, end.
[65] Halikhot 'Olam 2:1. This is cited in Elijah Mizrahi on Genesis 18:22.
[66] Albo, Ikkarim, 3:22.
[67] Commentary on Sanhedrin 99a.
[68] BT Megillah 22a.
[69] BT Megillah 25a.
[70] Arukh, article ken.
[71] Imrei Binah 19.

---

[56] We have generally translated the term tikkun soferim as "scribal emendations" (which was the standard understanding of it from the Tanhuma on). RaSHBA would not necessarily reject the term, except to reinterpret tikkun ("fixing, straightening") to mean fixing not the text itself but our understanding of the text.

[57] This was said in response to the question, whether additional verse divisions can be inserted in the text to facilitate the requirement of reading three verses for each person called to the Torah. This was not allowed, for even the verse divisions are sacred and cannot be changed.

[58] Allusion to 1 Samuel 26:9.

Also in recent generations, many scholars have grappled with this problem. Some think that the midrashim differ on the issue.[72] It is likely that this is another issue of dispute between the schools of Rabbi Akiva and Rabbi Ishmael.

The King's Scroll, and the Words on the Stones

According to Deuteronomy 17:18–19, it is incumbent on the king of Israel to have written "a copy of this Teaching . . . let it remain with him and let him read in it all his life." Similarly it is written in the Mishnah: "He shall write a scroll of the Torah in his name."[73] Maimonides says this means the entire Torah.[74] Midrash Tannaim gives the following exegesis: "'A copy of this Teaching' means the whole Torah. Or might it refer to some teachings of Torah? When Scripture states, 'to observe faithfully every word of this Teaching,' this refers to teachings of Torah. What, then, does 'a copy of this Teaching' come to tell us? The whole Torah."[75] The Tosefta agrees.[76] Maimonides lays down the law: "It shall never leave his presence, except when he goes to the toilet or the bath, or to any place unfit for reading scripture."[77] According to the Gemara, "He shall make it a kind of amulet and tie it on his arm."[78] But "it is hard to believe that an entire Torah scroll, which must be no less than six hand-breadths long and in girth, should be carried on the king's arm always?"

R. Isaac Abravanel sensed the difficulty in this and suggested, "It would seem that this refers to the Book of Deuteronomy, which contains most of the essential laws of Torah but is smaller and could be carried as an amulet. But the Sages accepted that it refers to the entire Torah."[79]

R. Samuel Strashun[59] writes: "If I did not shrink from it, I would say that the second scroll of the Torah was not a complete Torah but a short enumeration of the mitzvot."[80] The Tosafists wrote: "I heard that this Scroll of Instruction attached to his arm had written on it only the Ten Commandments. However this excerpt is called 'the Torah Scroll' because it contains 613 letters, corresponding to the 613 commandments."[81]

---

[72] Meir Friedman's commentary on Mekhilta Shirata 6; Lieberman, *Hellenism in Jewish Palestine*, 28–37.

[73] Mishnah Sanhedrin 2:4.

[74] Tosefta Sanhedrin 4:7; Maimonides' commentary on Mishnah ad loc.

[75] Midrash Tannaim, p. 105.

[76] Tosefta Sanhedrin 2:5.

[77] Maimonides, *Mishneh Torah, Hilkhot Melakhim* 3:5.

[78] BT Sanhedrin 21b, but the MaHaRSHaL rejects this phrase as spurious.

[79] Abravanel, ad loc.

[80] "Glosses and Novellae" of R. Samuel Strashun to Sanhedrin 21b.

[81] Raboteinu Ba'alei Hatosafot on Deuteronomy 17:20.

---

[59] Nineteenth-century Lithuanian Talmudist.

Moses our Master commanded the people that when they crossed the Jordan, they should write on large stones "all the words[60] of this Teaching most distinctly" (Deuteronomy 27:8). And in the Book of Joshua (8:32) it says that Joshua wrote on the stones "a copy of the Teaching of Moses." In the *Sefer Tagin*[61] is written: "the whole Torah from Genesis to Deuteronomy was written with its crowns and ornaments, and from it were copied all the crowns and ornaments, the twisted and curly letters, that have remained in our ancestors' and our possession, in the entire Torah. And it is likely that the stones, even being precious stones,[62] were large enough to suffice, or else it was a miracle that the small contained the immense, as we have found many times. For they were a generation of knowledge, more experienced in miracles than other generations. These things are not at all improbable."[82] This view is mentioned also by Nahmanides and Bahya.[83] "Some of the kabbalists wrote that the Ten Commandments were written on them, and these include the 613 commandments, as we explained, which is the entire Torah."[84] But Saadia Gaon wrote: "There was written on them a summary enumeration of the commandments, as these are written in legal compendia, as injunctions."[85]

Now the Tannaim were divided on this issue: according to Rabbi Simeon ben Yohai, only Deuteronomy was written on the stones, as it says, "He inscribed a copy of the Teaching of Moses" (Joshua 8:32). Rabbi Yosah ben Yose said in the name of Rabbi Eleazar ben Simeon: "They only wrote on the stones what the nations of the world would want, such as: 'When you approach a town to attack it, you shall offer it terms of peace; . . . when you have to besiege a city a long time, . . . you must not destroy its trees' (Deuteronomy 20:10, 19)."[86] But in Mishnah Sotah, it says: "They wrote on them all the words of the Torah in seventy languages."[87]

In one respect, too, the Geonim thought that the Ten Commandments by themselves constituted a "scroll of the Torah." R. Hai Gaon wrote, "Concerning that which you asked, about what the Rabbis said, 'A man should not wear tefillin on his head and hold a Torah scroll in his arm and pray,'[88] this is a Torah scroll on which is written from 'I the Lord am your God' to 'anything that is your neighbor's,' which contains 613 letters corresponding to the 613 commandments in the Torah."[89]

---

[82] Tzioni, Tavo (Cremona, 5319/1559), 108b.

[83] Nahmanides and Bahya on Deuteronomy 27:3.

[84] Tzioni, Tavo.   [85] Rabbenu Bahya on Deuteronomy 27:3. See also Meiri on Sotah 33b.

[86] S. Schechter, "Mekhilta to Deuteronomy (Re'eh)," *Tif'eret Israel*, Jubilee Volume for R. Israel Levy (Breslau: M. & M. Marcus, 1911), Hebrew section, p. 169.

[87] Mishnah Sotah 7:5.   [88] BT Berakhot 23b.

[89] *Otzar Ha-geonim* on BT Berakhot 23b. The *Arukh* (entry *tafel*) cites Rabbenu Hananel who wrote similarly in the name of Rabbenu Nahshon Gaon.

---

[60] "Words"—the Hebrew *devarim* here is actually ambiguous between "words" and "topics."

[61] *Sefer Tagin:* "Book of Crowns," a kabbalistic work by Shem Tov ben Abraham ibn Gaon (thirteenth–fourteenth centuries, Spain and Safed), edited with commentary by Shneur Sachs, 1866.

[62] Apparently Ibn Gaon understood "stones" to mean precious stones [rather than stelas], which raised the problem, how such a long text as the Torah could be copied on them.

R. Samuel Strashun points out that one verse was considered by itself a "scroll of the Torah": "The Rabbis said to Rav Hamnuna, 'R. Ammi wrote 400 Torah scrolls.' He replied, 'Maybe he wrote "Moses charged us with a Torah" (Deuteronomy 33:4) 400 times.'"[90]

It is a positive command to gather all of Israel at the end of the Year of Remission, and to read the Torah aloud to them: "Read this Teaching aloud in the presence of all Israel . . . that they may hear and so learn . . . to observe faithfully every word of this Teaching" (Deuteronomy 31:10–12). The Sages interpreted: "On the Day of Gathering, they only read the Book of Deuteronomy."[91]

---

[90] BT Bava Batra 14a. Rashi comments: "But he did not write 400 Torah scrolls, for no one has the time to do all that."

[91] Sifre Shofetim 160.

32

The Minimalist Approach to the Principle "Torah from Heaven"

[For an introduction, see the beginning of chapter 30.]

The Last Eight Verses

THE DOCTRINE OF TORAH FROM HEAVEN consists of two assertions: (1) Moses did not say the words of Torah on his own, and (2) Moses did write the Torah. We saw above that the schools of Rabbi Ishmael and Rabbi Akiva differed on the sense of the first assertion. In this chapter, we shall see that they differed also on the scope of the second.

This difference is articulated in the Tannaitic discussion of the status of the last eight verses of the Torah.

There was an old view prevalent in Israel that even the last section of the book of Deuteronomy, beginning "So Moses the servant of the Lord died there" (34:5), was written by Moses. Some expressed surprise at this already in the first century, and Josephus tried to solve the riddle: "Moses wrote of his own death in Scripture, out of fear that someone would dare to claim that on account of his great righteous deeds he went up alive to heaven."[1] But in the school of Rabbi Ishmael, they suggested a bold solution to this problem. The anonymous voice of the Sifre says: "'So Moses died there'—is it possible that Moses died and then wrote, 'Moses died there'? Rather, Moses wrote up to that point, and from there onward Joshua wrote."[2] Whoever reads these words with a perceptive eye will see that the Tanna formulates his question according to the plain sense of scripture. "Moses died"—the verse does not speak of a future event, but an event that had occurred: Moses' death. How, then, shall we say that Moses wrote this verse after his death?

---

[1] Josephus, *Antiquities of the Jews,* book 4; see also end of Philo's *De Vita Mosis.*

[2] Sifre, Vezot Ha-berakhah 357. This portion of the Sifre comes from the school of Rabbi Ishmael. See J. N. Epstein, *Mevo'ot le-Sifrut ha-Tannaim: Introduction to Tannaitic Literature: Mishna, Tosephta and Halakhic Midrashim* (in Hebrew) (Jerusalem: Magnes, 1957), 628. But the beginning of the Sifre to Deuteronomy declares, "Moses wrote the entire Torah, as it says, 'Moses wrote this entire Torah.'" There, the Sifre holds by the view of Rabbi Meir. Clearly, these two passages were written by different hands.

The "Midrash Tannaim" presents the same Baraita but draws a slightly different lesson from it. "'So Moses died there'—Is it possible that Moses *was alive* and wrote 'Moses died'? Rather, Moses wrote up to that point, and from there onward Joshua wrote." According to the Sifre's version, the Tanna argues that Moses' writing these verses runs counter to reality. According to the Midrash Tannaim, it runs counter to the principle of Moses' veracity. In other words, if you say Moses wrote "Moses died" when he was dead, can a dead man write? But if he wrote it when alive, was he then a liar?

The plain sense of the text also guided the author of the famous Baraita who put aside all previous claims and sought to establish once and for all the order of the canonical books and their authors, and whose classical formulation served as the starting point for all future discussions: "Our Rabbis taught: Moses wrote his book, the episodes of Balaam, and the book of Job. Joshua wrote his book and eight verses of the Torah."[3] This Baraita speaks in the language of certainty, as if there were no dispute over it.

But Rabbi Meir did dispute this view. According to the Sifre: "Rabbi Meir said, 'Moses wrote down this Torah' (Deuteronomy 31:9). Is it possible that he would write it if it were missing a single letter? Rather, he wrote whatever the Holy and Blessed One told him, 'Write!'"[1]

We have two approaches here. The plain-sense approach argues that Moses could not have written about his own death. Since these verses indicate that they were "after Moses' death,"[4] the Tanna of the Sifre said that Joshua wrote them. But Rabbi Meir, whom all acknowledged was a disciple of Rabbi Akiva[5] and was ordained by Rabbi Akiva,[6] perhaps did not mean to contradict Scripture, but adhered consistently to Halakhah on principle.[2] Plain sense leads one way, Halakhah another way. Logic uproots Scripture. But the Tanna of the Sifre might respond to Rabbi Meir in the fashion that Rabbi Johanan ben Nuri responded to Rabbi Akiva: "You have responded according to logic; what do you respond to Scripture?"

Perhaps Rabbi Meir availed himself of the principle that appears in the midrashim: "He foretells the end from the beginning" (Isaiah 46:10); that is, "he tells at the beginning what will be at the end,"[7] "all is foreseen by the Holy and Blessed One,"[8] "and he anticipates things that have not yet occurred."[9] The Midrash uses this principle to explain the verse "The name of the second river [flowing from Eden] is Gihon, the one that winds through the whole land of Cush" (Genesis 2:13)—"the land of

---

[3] BT Bava Batra 14b.   [4] Maimonides, Mishneh Torah, *Hilkhot Tefillah* 13:6.
[5] PT Berakhot 2:1, 4b.   [6] BT Sanhedrin 14a.
[7] Tanhuma Va'era 11; Exodus Rabbah 9:1.
[8] Tanhuma Shelah 9.   [9] Numbers Rabbah 5:5.

---

[1] See above, chapter 31, pp. 592–95, on how Rabbi Meir's scribal profession encouraged him to take a scrupulous view of the integrity of the Torah text.

[2] From a halakhic standpoint, Moses' nearly complete scroll could not be called "this Torah" as long as it was missing a single letter.

Cush was not yet in existence, and you say that this river wound through the land of Cush? But 'he foretells the end from the beginning.'"[10] Similarly: "[Chedorlaomer, a contemporary of Abraham] subdued all the territory of the Amalekites" (Genesis 14:7) "but the Amalekites did not yet exist,[3] and you say that he subdued all the territory of the Amalekites? But 'he foretells the end from the beginning.'"[4][11]

The dispute concerning the last eight verses of the Torah is recounted also in the Babylonian Talmud. There Rabbi Judah (and some say, Rabbi Nehemiah) holds that Joshua wrote the last eight verses. Rabbi Simeon, another accomplished disciple of Rabbi Akiva, says that up to "Moses died," Moses recited and wrote, from that point on he wrote in tears.[5][12]

The controversy between the Tanna of the Sifre and Rabbi Meir, or between Rabbi Judah and Rabbi Simeon, was not resolved explicitly. But the redactors of the Talmud tried to prove that halakhic practice follows the opinion of Rabbi Judah: "According to which Tanna's view is the dictum of R. Joshua bar Abba in the name of R. Gidel in the name of Rav, that the last eight verses of the Torah may be read by an individual[6] in the synagogue? Shall we say that this agrees with Rabbi Judah and not with Rabbi Simeon? Even if you say it is consistent with Rabbi Simeon's view, since they are different [in some respect], they are different [altogether]."[7][13] But Rabbi Johanan

---

[10] Genesis Rabbah 16:2.   [11] Genesis Rabbah 42:7.
[12] BT Bava Batra 15a; Menahot 30a. The RITBA (on the *Ein Ya'akov* ad loc.) interprets this to mean that Moses wrote the last eight verses with tears instead of with ink. But Elijah Mizrahi and the Maharal (in *Gur Aryeh*) to Deuteronomy 32:5 say it means Moses was weeping as he wrote these verses.
[13] BT Bava Batra 15a.

---

[3] According to Genesis 36:12, Amalek was a grandson of Esau, and therefore of the fourth generation after Abraham.

[4] In the last two instances, "he foretells the end from the beginning" is reminiscent of the literary convention of the omniscient narrator. The author of a narrative knows things that will occur later, that will put the earlier events he is narrating into perspective, so he brings this knowledge to the reader's attention when relating the earlier events. The difference is that Moses was living the narrative himself and was not privy to later events. However, God, whose knowledge (according to the medieval philosophers) is timeless, did know the future, and therefore dictated to Moses the events of his death before they occurred.

[5] The plain sense of this is that Moses wrote the last eight verses while weeping. But "wrote in tears" was also taken to mean that the letters on the scroll contained his tears. See R. Menahem Azariah of Fano's opinion below.

[6] This is a departure from the general rule that any reading from the Torah in the synagogue must be done in the presence of a quorum of ten. The implication is that if an individual may read them without such a quorum, these verses must be of lesser sanctity. But the phrase "read by an individual" is subject to various interpretations, as we shall see.

[7] Since even Rabbi Simeon allows that the last verses differ in some respect (in that they were written in tears), this may be grounds enough for him to concede that they may be read by an individual. This argument is a stretch, but is characteristic of the method of the Talmud not to overlook any relevant possibility.

established the principle that Rabbi Judah's opinion is accepted in preference to Rabbi Meir's or Rabbi Simeon's when they disagree with him.[14]

In what respect are the last eight verses different? According to Rashi, since the last verses differ from the rest of the Torah in that they were written in tears, so they should be read differently also. But another explanation is found in Maimonides' words. He seems to have sensed the difference we mentioned above between the halakhic requirement and the sense of Scripture, and decides halakhically according to Rabbi Simeon and not according to Rabbi Judah: "The last eight verses at the end of the Torah may be read in the synagogue with less than ten present. Even though all the Torah was spoken by Moses at the divine dictate, still they are different since their sense relates to what happened after Moses died. Therefore it is permissible for an individual to read them."[15] Maimonides, who decided halakhically according to Abbaye with reference to the curses in Deuteronomy,[8] says here of the last eight verses of Deuteronomy, "Moses said them at the divine dictate." And in his preface to the Mishnah, Maimonides writes: "When he was about to die, he decided to commit the Torah to writing, and wrote thirteen scrolls of the Torah, all of them from 'In the beginning' to 'before all Israel.'"

However, R. Zevi Hirsch Ashkenazi,[9] the "Hakham Zevi," decides with Rabbi Judah, and emphasizes that, according to Rabbi Judah, "these eight verses are of lesser status than the rest of the Torah, since Moses wrote the rest of the Torah at the divine dictate, whereas these verses were written by Joshua." That is why the Gemara sets forth that an individual may read these verses, "to show that they have a different status than the rest of the Torah." Therefore the Hakham Zevi rejects the Mordecai's[10] interpretation that "an individual reads them" means they should be read by a distinguished scholar. Even from Maimonides' statements it appears that "he depreciated their status and did not elevate them, and we see that it is common practice to call as a 'Hatan Torah' whomever it pleases the congregation, whether he be learned or ignorant, poor or rich, so long as he pledges a fitting contribution."[16]

Indeed, one of the greatest scholars of all time, R. Joseph ibn Migash, the teacher of R. Maimon the Judge[11] and perhaps the teacher of Maimonides in his youth,[17] accepted the view that the last eight verses of the Torah were written by Joshua.

---

[14] BT Eruvin 46b.

[15] Maimonides, *Hilkhot Tefillah* 13:6. RaABaD disagrees: "We never heard of such a thing. . . . This is very strange. Where did the congregation disappear to?" The *Kesef Mishneh* (Karo) explains: "It might happen that there were ten in the synagogue but one of them left, or there were only nine to begin with."

[16] *Hakham Zevi* 13.

[17] See Maimonides, *Hilkhot She'elah u-fikkadon* 5:6, and the opening to R. Menahem Ha-me'iri's com-

---

[8] That Moses said them on his own, and it is permissible to break up the reading of them. See above, chapter 25.

[9] Seventeenth–eighteenth centuries, Sarajevo, Germany, and Poland.

[10] Mordecai ben Hillel Ha-kohen, thirteenth century, Germany.

[11] R. Maimon, father of Maimonides.

The last eight verses of the Torah should be read "by an individual," that is, whoever reads the verses before them may not complete to the end of the Torah, for he would then be reading what Moses wrote together with what Joshua wrote. Rather, the one should stop and another should come up and read the last verses by themselves, so that it will be clear that Moses did not write them, but Joshua. Another explanation: "an individual shall read them"; that is, he is not permitted to stop in the middle of them, so it will be clear that Joshua wrote them."[18]

Also R. David ben Levi, one of the great scholars of Provence, whose life bridged the generations of Nahmanides and RaSHBA,[12] [19] wrote: "The 'ten [sic] verses of the Torah, an individual reads them' means: The last eight verses of the Torah (from 'Moses died') should be read by a separate individual and not be combined with the preceding verses, *for they are practically not a part of the Torah at all, since Joshua wrote them.*"[20]

R. Jacob of Vienna[13] also denied that Moses wrote the last eight verses,[21] as did Nethanel ben Isaiah of Yemen.[22] [14] But even though this view was rooted in ancient traditions, there were those who vociferously opposed it. Rabbenu Bahya came out vehemently against R. Abraham ibn Ezra, who accepted this view in his commentary: "It is not true, and his interpretation is not correct, but the correct doctrine and true tradition that we have is that Moses wrote the whole Torah from 'In the beginning' to 'before all Israel,' all by divine dictate, and indeed Moses was as a copyist from a primordial book from the beginning to the end, letter by letter."[23] Similarly R. David Messer Leon[15] held: "It is not proper to believe that another prophet [than Moses] wrote even a single letter of the Torah of Moses; to such a one our rabbis applied the saying, 'He has spurned the word of the Lord.'"[24] And R. David Pardo[16] held that Rabbi Simeon was correct, "otherwise why would these eight verses be written in the Torah? Joshua should have written them at the start of his own book."[25]

mentary to *Avot* (New York, 5704/1944), 68. Maimonides wrote of him: "That man's understanding in Talmud was overpowering to whoever would look into his words and the depth of his analytical mind, so that one would almost say of him, that there was no one like him previously, a king in bearing and manner; and I gathered what I could of halakhic knowledge from his own commentary" (Introduction to the Mishnah, *Sefer Ha-Ma'or, Otzar Ha-hakdamot,* ed. Rabinowitz, p. 83).

[18] *Shittah Mekubetzet* to Bava Batra 15a.

[19] According to *Or Ha-hayyim* of R. Hayyim Mikhal, 742.

[20] *Ha-mikhtam* on Tractate Megillah, p. 9.   [21] *Peshatim u-ferushim,* Berakhah p. 233.

[22] *Me'or ha-afelah,* end.   [23] Rabbenu Bahya, *Commentary on the Torah,* end.

[24] *Tehillah le-David* 1:46.

[25] *Sifre de-vei Rav* with commentary of R. David Pardo, end.

[12] The dates of these authorities are: Nahmanides (1194–1270) and RaSHBA (R. Solomon ben Abraham Adret, 1235[?]–1310).

[13] Fourteenth–fifteenth centuries.

[14] Fourteenth century.

[15] Ca. 1470–1526, Italy, Salonika.

[16] Eighteenth century, Italy, Sarajevo, Jerusalem.

Also Hayyim ibn Attar writes at the end of his *Or Ha-hayyim* that the last eight verses "are the words of the Lord, which He spoke and Moses wrote. . . . I saw how Ibn Ezra wrote that Joshua wrote these words. But it is improper to write plainly that Moses did not complete the scroll of the Torah which he passed on to the Levites. For I have heard how our fellow Jews become embroiled in this matter, and are thereby thrown into doubt concerning the Torah. For it is the contention of the heretics that the Israelites amended the Torah, so that it now contains what was *not* there originally, and lacks what *was* there originally, and such ideas have taken root. Turn your eyes from them.[17] The correct view is that Moses wrote the entire Torah, and completed it in tears, as the Rabbis said." But it is possible to direct such criticisms against Rabbi Judah and the first Tanna in the Baraita of Sifre. The truth will find its way.

Some Sages felt that Rabbi Simeon's interpretation was forced and tried to explain it. In R. Hayyim Vital's *Sefer Ha-likkutim* we read: "It is actually not so farfetched that Moses wrote [the last eight verses] in tears, for he saw that his aura was departing, so that he was like someone who was not there."[26] Others cite the Ari's[18] view that the Holy and Blessed One restored Moses' soul after he died so that he could write the final eight verses of the Torah.[19] [27]

According to R. Menaham Azariah of Fano,[20] the last eight verses are of greater value than all the rest of the Torah, "for Moses our Master did not delegate them to Joshua, nor give any of them over to him or anyone else." He bases his interpretation on Rashi's interpretation of the Gemara "wrote them in tears," that Moses did not recite these verses as he wrote them (as he had the rest of the Torah), because of his great anguish. "He was shedding tears not at his own death, but at the suffering of Israel, that they would have to go into exile. The tears mixed with the ink, which had originally been black as the pupil of the eye, and dripped into every letter so that they shone as the very heavens. Indeed the whole Torah ought rightly to have been written with those tears, except that we would have been unworthy of using it." In fact, Moses wrote the final eight verses only of the scroll that was placed in the Ark, but Joshua added them to the twelve scrolls which Moses had written that day for the twelve tribes. Thus the views of Rabbi Simeon and Rabbi Judah are both correct.

How does R. Menaham Azariah reconcile the difficulty that Moses wrote of his death and burial? He suggests that the Holy and Blessed One dictated, "Moses died,"

---

[26] *Sefer Ha-likkutim* (Jerusalem, 5673/1913), *Sha'ar Ha-pesukim* (Gate IV, Part 2), 69b. See *Zohar Vayehi* 217b and *Or Ha-hayyim* beginning of Vayehi.

[27] *Sefer Keneset Israel* on Psalm 19:8: "The Torah of the Lord is whole, restoring the soul."

---

[17] Allusion to Song of Songs 6:5.

[18] Isaac Luria (sixteenth century, Safed), author of a revolutionary new method in Kabbalah, and teacher of Vital.

[19] Whether Simeon's original view was more farfetched, or Hayyim Vital's attempt to rescue it, Heschel lets the reader decide.

[20] Sixteenth–seventeenth century, Italy.

whereupon Moses started dying and writing in tears. He wrote *mehokkek safun* (lawgiver, hidden) referring to himself when he was in the process of being buried, for when he wrote "He died . . . He buried him," he was being buried, for the Holy One dictated "He buried him" and Moses wrote it.[28]

Another difficulty is presented in the name of the Rosh:[21] How can we reconcile Rabbi Simeon's view that Moses wrote the last eight verses with the tradition that Moses our Master died on the Sabbath day?[29] R. Menaham Azariah of Fano suggests that "on the eve of the Sabbath he was writing and dying, but he did not pass away finally until Sabbath afternoon at the time of the Minhah prayer."[30] R. Isaiah Horowitz, author of *Shnei Luhot Ha-berit,* writes that Moses indeed died on the Sabbath, but what he wrote that day was by conjuration of the pen, which does not count under the Sabbath-work definition of "writing."[31]

On the festival of Simhat Torah, we read the portion *Ve-zot Ha-berakhah.*[22] According to the Babylonian Talmud, the accompanying Haftarah for this portion is from 1 Kings 8:22ff.[23] In the Tosafot, it is mentioned that there were places where it was customary to select the Haftarah from the beginning of the book of Joshua: "This is in error, for the Talmud does not say to do so. However, some say that R. Hai Gaon enacted that one should read the beginning of Joshua, but they do not know what was his reason for departing from the Talmudic rite."[32] The *Or Zaru'a*[24] offers a rationale: "On all the days of the festival, the Haftarah is topically related to the theme of the day. On Simhat Torah we complete the reading of the Pentateuch, and read of the death of Moses our Master. Therefore we start the reading of the Prophets [which follows immediately after the Pentateuch in the order of scripture], which contains further reference to the death of Moses and the installation of Joshua in his place. They also asked the same question of R. Isaac ben Judah, and he responded that such is the custom, and custom overrides *halakhah.*"[33]

[28] Fano, *Imerot Tehorot, Hikkur Ha-din* 2:13.

[29] Responsa of the *Hatam Sofer* VI, 29: "Moses passed from this world at the time of the Minha prayer on the Sabbath" (Zohar Terumah 156a).

[30] Fano, loc. cit.

[31] See *Bayit Hadash* OH 292 and *Hatam Sofer* loc. cit. According to *Ma'aseh Rokeah* on Vayelekh, since Moses wrote the last eight verses in tears and not ink, it was an impermanent kind of writing and therefore permissible on the Sabbath.

[32] BT Megillah 31a, Tosafot s.v. *le-mahar.* So also *Mahzor Vitri* p. 447.

[33] *Or Zaru'a,* "Readings on the Festivals," 393.

---

[21] Rabbenu Asher ben Jehiel, thirteenth–fourteenth century, Germany and Spain. His halakhic digest of the Talmud (emulating Alfasi's) was a major step toward the late-medieval codification of Jewish law.

[22] Deuteronomy 33:1–34:12.

[23] The prayer of Solomon at the dedication of the Temple. This was considered appropriate because of its connection with the sequel, "On the eighth day he let the people go," which is read on Shemini Atzeret, the calendar-twin of Simhat Torah.

[24] Isaac ben Moses of Vienna (thirteenth century, France and Germany).

Another of the later authorities[25] wrote that R. Hai Gaon

> enacted that we should select the Haftarah from Joshua, so that one may recognize its resemblance to the Torah reading and realize that the end of the Torah reading was written by Joshua after the death of Moses. . . . This is an allusion that Moses received Torah from Sinai and passed it on to Joshua to complete it, inasmuch as Joshua wrote the last eight verses. Similarly, in every generation one completes it. And it is not thereby considered a defective scroll of the Torah, as Rabbi Simeon objected, for thus the Giver of Torah desired, that it should not be complete until the coming of the Messiah, but it is complete in part.[34]

It is interesting that no one tried to solve the problem of the eight verses according to the view in the Gemara that Moses never died. This view was transmitted in the Zohar in Rabbi Simeon's name.[35] It is possible that Maimonides had this view in sight when he emphasized that Moses wrote the entire Torah "from 'In the beginning' to 'before all Israel,'" for immediately after this he says, "Moses did not die."[26] [36]

It is in accordance with the Sifre Tanna's view that R. Nahman puts the verse "So Moses the servant of the Lord died there" in the mouth of the angel Semilion and interprets it as an elegy: "Moses died there, the great scribe of Israel."[37] [27]

In Moses' blessings is written, "He chose for himself the best, / For there is the portion of the revered chieftain, / Where the heads of the people come, / He executed the Lord's righteousness / And His judgments for Israel" (Deuteronomy 20:21). The rabbis held that this verse referred to Moses our Master. Now, Rabbi

---

[34] *Si'ah Yitzhak* of R. Hayyim Isaac Justman, accomplished disciple of the *"Hiddushei ha-RIM"* (Isaac Meir Rothenberg Alter, nineteenth-century founder of the Hasidic Gur [Ger] dynasty), first edition (Warsaw, 5688/1928), p. 66b.

[35] Zohar Terumah 174a, Bereshit 37b.

[36] Introduction to Commentary on the Mishnah.

[37] BT Sotah 13b; *Ein Ya'akov* ad loc.

---

[25] From the date and place of publication (Warsaw, 1928), it is possible that this "later authority" (R. Hayyim Justman) was known personally by Heschel. Heschel must have found his notion of continuing revelation dear to his own heart.

[26] We have seen before how Maimonides may have understood this statement philosophically. See above, chapter 18, pp. 353–54, and our editorial note there.

[27] The passage in Sotah 13b is puzzling and has given rise to many interpretations. The passage is an extended midrashic rhapsody on the death of Moses. Various voices suggest verses that are apropos of Moses' death. In this context, we read: "R. Nahman said, So Moses the servant of the Lord died there. Semilion said, Moses died there, the great scribe of Israel." The Talmudic text lacks quotation marks, so it is not clear where each utterance begins and ends. Perhaps R. Nahman suggests that God mourned Moses with the verse "So Moses the servant of the Lord died there," and another rabbinic Sage named Semilion gave as an alternative, "Moses died there, the great scribe of Israel." Others, such as the MaHaRShA, interpreted the unusual name "Semilion" as referring to an angel and put the whole sequence (including Semilion's comment) in R. Nahman's mouth; Heschel adopted this reading. Either way, the voice that said the verse is external to Moses and after his death, reflecting the commonsense understanding of the last eight verses of Deuteronomy.

Judah, who held the view that the last eight verses were written by Joshua, was of the opinion that this verse was spoken by the ministering angels:[28] "The ministering angels were mourning before him: 'He executed the Lord's righteousness and His judgments for Israel.'"[38] "No one would think that Moses would say this about himself."[29] [39]

The Last Twelve Verses

It is written in the Torah, "That very day the Lord spoke to Moses: 'Ascend these heights of Abarim to Mount Nebo . . . you shall die on the mountain that you are about to ascend" (Deuteronomy 32:48–50). Immediately afterwards it says, "Moses went up from the steppes of Moab to Mount Nebo" (34:1). The Midrash asks, "Why does it say, 'that very day'? Because the Israelites were saying, 'if we sense he is going, we will not let him. The man who took us out from Egypt, and split the sea for us, and brought down the Torah for us, and arranged for the quail to come, and brought down manna for us, and performed so many miracles for us, we will not let him go.' The Ever-Present said, 'I will have him in the burial-cave by midday, and then if anyone thinks he can undo it, let him.' Therefore it says, 'that very day.'"[40] Also it appears from the plain sense of Scripture that once Moses ascended Mount Nebo, he never came back. R. Phinehas Horowitz, the author of *Sefer Hafla'ah*,[30] asked, if it was problematic for Moses to have written the last eight verses because he would have had to write of future events in the past tense, "then 'Moses went up' is equally problematic. How could he have written this in the past tense, prior to his ascent?" Horowitz suggests that Moses went up twice, and wrote 'Moses went up' after his first ascent.[41] But this interpretation does not agree with the midrash we just cited.

---

[38] Tosefta Sotah 2:9 (in Vilna Talmud); Sifre Beha'alotekha 106.
[39] MaHaRShA on BT Sotah 13b.
[40] YS I, 948.
[41] *Panim Yafot* ad loc.

---

[28] This view is attributed to Rabbi Judah in the same midrashic-rhapsodic passage in Sotah 13b. His argument is as follows: (1) Moses died in the territory of Reuben; (2) he was buried in the territory of Gad, many miles distant; (3) therefore, he must have been carried on the wings of the Shekhinah all the way in a vast funeral procession, with the angels murmuring eulogies. It is hard to tell how seriously to take such an imaginative scenario as implying a point of doctrine.

[29] By implication, then, this verse (if referring to Moses) would have to have been said by someone else, and at least part of the end of Deuteronomy is non-Mosaic in authorship! This is presented playfully by Heschel. He is fully aware that in the plain sense of the verse, read in context, it refers not to Moses, but to the tribe of Gad, as part of the blessing of the tribes explicitly ascribed to Moses. But the midrash has so thoroughly identified this verse as a paean to Moses that it becomes possible to take the next step: if modesty would forbid Moses' saying this about himself, then who said it?

[30] Eighteenth-century, Germany. He is not to be confused with an earlier Phinehas Horowitz of sixteenth-century Poland.

R. Moses Sofer, who studied Torah from Horowitz, asked, "Who wrote the passage from 'Moses went up' to 'Moses died'? It is farfetched to say that he brought a scroll of the Torah up with him to the mountain, then after the Lord showed him the land of Israel he wrote 'Moses died,' and only after that the Israelites ascended the mountain and found the Torah scroll resting there. The text implies that he handed the scroll from his hand directly to the tribe of Levi, as it says, 'Take this book of the Torah and place it beside the Ark of the Covenant of the Lord your God' (Deuteronomy 31:26)."[42] Truly, R. Abraham ibn Ezra was suggesting that Joshua wrote the last twelve verses.[43]

Also from the words of the Tosafot it appears that they used the phrase "eight verses" to designate the whole last chapter, starting "Moses went up." They say: "An individual reads them himself; that is, there should not be two readers breaking up the eight verses which start 'Moses went up,' for that is the beginning of the section (parashah)."[44] [31] Rabbenu Asher paraphrased: "It is the beginning of the section which Joshua said. And even according to the view that Moses said it, it is still of different status, for he wrote it in tears."[45]

According to R. Simeon ben Zemah Duran,[32] there was one who argued that the verse "Abraham . . . went in pursuit as far as Dan" (Genesis 14:14) was among the verses added later to the Torah.[46] The Tannaim already raised this problem. "'The Lord showed him the whole land: Gilead as far as Dan' (Deuteronomy 34:1)—the tribes had not yet come into the land, nor had the land been assigned to them, so how can the text refer to 'as far as Dan'? Similarly, it says, 'Abraham . . . went in pursuit as far as Dan'—if the land had not been assigned to the tribes, how can the text refer to 'as far as Dan'?"[33] [47]

It says in Genesis 10 concerning Nimrod: "The mainstays of his kingdom were Babylon, Erech, etc." (10:10). R. David Gans[34] commented: "The text calls the city

---

[42] Torat Moshe Ve-zot Ha-berakhah, ad loc.

[43] See below, pp. 633–38, concerning Ibn Ezra's views on the Mosaic authorship.

[44] BT Megillah 21b, Tosafot s.v. tena.

[45] Cited by MaHaRShA ad loc. See also Rabbenu Asher's commentary on the Torah and the commentary of the Tosafists: "an individual reads these eleven verses."

[46] Magen Avot (Leghorn, 5545/1785), 29b.

[47] MI, Amalek 2.

---

[31] Parashah (which we commonly translate "portion" or "section") has the technical sense of a section of the Torah written from one paragraph spacing to another. In this case, there is a spacing before Deuteronomy 34:1, and no more spacings for the rest of the book, so 34:1–12 is one parashah.

[32] Fourteenth–fifteenth century, Majorca and North Africa.

[33] This argument starts to raise wider doubts concerning the full Mosaic authorship which anticipate the rest of this chapter (especially pp. 633–38 on Ibn Ezra's more far-reaching views). It is relevant here insofar as it offers additional reasons for doubting whether Moses authored Deuteronomy 34.

[34] Sixteenth–seventeenth century, central Europe, chronicler and astronomer.

Babylon, even though it was not given that name until the confounding of languages, as it says [in the next chapter]: 'That is why it was called Babel [= Babylon], because there the Lord confounded [*balal*] the speech of the whole earth' (11:9), for when the Torah was given, Moses wrote the name of the city as it was commonly known in his day."[35] 48

The Pericope of the "Cities of Refuge"

It is written in the book of Joshua, "On that day at Shechem, Joshua made a covenant for the people and he made a fixed rule for them. Joshua recorded all this in [a/the] book of God's Torah" (Joshua 24:25–26).[36] If we assume that the two verses were speaking of the same matter, it would then appear according to the plain sense of the text that it was the covenant that he made with Israel that was being recorded in this "book of God's Torah." It would then agree with the sense of the Jerusalem Targum: "Joshua wrote these words in a book and placed them in the book of God's Torah." R. David Kimhi[37] cites the views of Rabbi Judah and Rabbi Nehemiah (cited below) and writes, "Neither agrees with the plain sense; the truth is according to the Jerusalem Targum."49 According to this view, Joshua wrote in the "book of God's Torah" the words of the covenant that he made with Israel in Shechem. This view is very strange, for the words of that covenant are not found in our Torah at all!50 If we say that according to this view, Joshua placed these words "in the same place where the Torah was placed,"51 how can Kimhi say that this agrees with the "plain sense"? The text does not say "beside" or "next to God's Torah," but "in the book of God's Torah."52

In the Babylonian Talmud, Rabbi Judah and Rabbi Nehemiah debated the meaning of this verse. The first says it refers to the last eight verses of the Torah, while the sec-

---

48 David Gans, *Zemah David*, "Second Millennium."
49 Kimhi on Joshua 24:25.
50 *Arukh La-ner* on BT Makkot 11b.
51 *Metzudat David* on Joshua 24:25.
52 See the commentary on Joshua by Joseph Kara (eleventh–twelfth century, France, of the school of

---

[35] The case of Babylon is similar to Dan in that both were referred to by their later names at an earlier part of the narrative. The argument from the case of Dan is stronger, however, because the assignment of the name "Dan" to that territory presumably did not occur until after Moses' death. Yet according to the maximalist view, both Genesis 14:14 and Deuteronomy 34:1 were written by Moses.

[36] *Be-sefer torat elohim*—NJV: "in a book of divine instruction." The Hebrew is ambiguous in two respects: (1) it is unclear from this use of the "construct" (*semikhut*) form whether it should be rendered with the definite or indefinite article ("a book" or "the book"), and (2) it is unclear whether Torah is a common noun ("instruction") or a proper noun ("the Torah"). On this ambiguity hangs the whole issue, whether Joshua was making a separate record of the covenant at Shechem or including it in the Mosaic Torah. As Heschel makes clear, the rabbis as well as the moderns were of divided opinions on this question.

[37] Twelfth–thirteenth centuries, Provence.

ond says it refers to the "cities of refuge."[38] The Gemara comments: "The first view is consistent with the text, for it says, 'in the book of God's Torah.' But according to the view 'cities of refuge,' what is the meaning of 'in the book of God's Torah'? Read the verse as follows: 'Joshua wrote *in his book* these things written in a book of God's Torah.'"[53] In other words, it refers to the passage on the cities of refuge in Joshua 20.

The Gemara's interpretation of the second view is problematic, however. "What is the point? It is obvious, for Joshua wrote his whole book, as we have learned (in Bava Batra 14b), and the portion of cities of refuge is included in it, so he obviously must have written it! And if it means to tell us that Joshua wrote his book, why does it only mention the portion of the cities of refuge?"[54] Rashi therefore interprets the controversy as focusing on the question: What did Joshua write *in the book of the Torah?*" Rabbi Judah says, the last eight verses of the Torah; Rabbi Nehemiah says, the portion of the cities of refuge.

It is likely that the meaning of the assertion that Joshua wrote the portion of the "cities of refuge" in the book of God's Torah is that originally Joshua wrote his own portion of the cities of refuge into the scroll of the Torah, but later it was transferred to the book of Joshua. Note that this section (i.e., Joshua 20) starts with language that is used for no prophet except Moses: "The Lord spoke to Joshua, saying . . . Designate the cities of refuge—about which I commanded you through Moses. . . ." R. Hama bar Hanina expressed amazement about this: "Why was the portion of manslaughterers spoken in firm language?[39] . . . Because it is part of the Torah."[55]

R. Isaac Abravanel writes of the opinions of Rabbi Judah and Rabbi Nehemiah: "Both of these views are very strange."[56] Why did he reject the views of these Tannaim? Perhaps he thought that the second view referred to the passage of the cities of refuge in Deuteronomy, and he rejected even the view that Joshua wrote the last eight verses.

Rashi), *Jahrbuch der Jüdisch-Literarischen Gesellschaft* (Frankfurt am Main: J. Kaufmann, 1903–31), 5:59. In the opinion of Yehezkel Kaufmann (his commentary on Joshua, *Sefer Yehoshua* [Jerusalem: Kiryat Sefer, 1959], 254), the meaning is not that Joshua wrote entries in Moses' book of the Torah. Rather, the phrase *sefer torat elohim,* which later came to designate the Mosaic Torah, here means simply "a book of divine laws," laws that were given through Joshua.

[53] BT Makkot 11b; see MaHaRShA ad loc.
[54] *Arukh La-ner* on Makkot 10a.
[55] BT Makkot 10b–11a.
[56] Abravanel on Joshua 24:19.

---

[38] "Cities of refuge" is also ambiguous. There are passages on this topic in Deuteronomy 4:41–43, and in Joshua 20. Which did Rabbi Nehemiah mean?

[39] The verb *dabber* ("speak") was thought to designate firm or hard speech, as opposed to the verb *amar* ("say") connoting gentle speech. More to the point, the Torah's regular formula introducing God's communications to Moses uses *dabber*. Most of God's communications to Joshua use the verb *amar*. Since 20:1 uses *dabber*, it is strongly reminiscent of the style of the Torah, suggesting that this passage belongs in the Torah.

R. Obadiah Sforno suggested another solution. It is written in 2 Kings 22:8 that Hilkiah the High Priest found a "scroll of the Torah" in the temple. Sforno thinks this is the same scroll that is mentioned in Deuteronomy 31:9 ("Moses wrote down this Teaching and gave it to the priests, sons of Levi, who carried the Ark of the Lord's Covenant, and to all the elders of Israel"), "which was only the portion of the rules of kingship, and on it Joshua wrote the covenant that he made with Israel."[57]

It is possible that the matter of "cities of refuge" is similar to that of the "eight verses." That is, Joshua wrote them in Deuteronomy. It must then refer to Deuteronomy 4:41–43: "Then Moses set aside three cities, etc." These verses speak of Moses in the third person, not in the first person, as is customary in the rest of Deuteronomy. The midrashim were amazed at the language: "It does not use the normal past tense *vayyavdel*, but rather *az yavdil* ('then he will set aside'). *Az* is poetic, like the Song of the Sea *az yashir* ('then Moses and the Israelites sang . . .'). The future tense indicates that it was up to Joshua to set them aside."[58] It was said in the midrash that Joshua received a legacy of honor from Moses. "Moses wrote the Torah, as it says, 'Moses wrote down this Teaching (Torah)' (Deuteronomy 31:9). Similarly Joshua: 'Joshua recorded all this in a book of divine instruction (Torah)' (Joshua 24:26)."[59]

The Portion *Ha'azinu*[40]

A story related in late midrashim tells how before Moses' death the Israelites came to the door of Joshua's tent and found Joshua sitting and expounding before Moses. "R. Samuel bar Nahmani said in the name of Rabbi Jonathan ben Eleazar: At the moment that Joshua opened with the words, 'Blessed is He Who has chosen the righteous and their teaching,' the traditions of wisdom were taken from Moses and given to Joshua. Moses could not understand what Joshua was expounding. After the Israelites stood up, they said to Moses, 'Seal[41] the Torah for us.' Moses said, 'I do not know what to answer them.' He stumbled and fell. At that moment, he said, 'Master of the Universe! Until now, I sought life, but as of now I return my soul to you.'"[60]

What is the meaning of this story? The expression "seal the Torah for us" demands to be explained. *Satam* means to close up, to hide something. The sealed is the opposite of the explicit and revealed. We have the expression *yilmad satum min ha-meforash* (an enigmatic passage may be explained on the basis of an explicit one).

[57] Sforno on Deuteronomy 31:6.

[58] YS I, 829; *Ginzei Schechter* (New York, 1928), 1:167.

[59] *Yalkut Ha-makhiri* to Isaiah 9:7; Louis Ginzberg, *The Legends of the Jews,* 7 volumes (Philadelphia: Jewish Publication Society, 1909–38), 6:146.

[60] Tanhuma (Warsaw and Buber editions) Va'ethanan 6; Deuteronomy Rabbah (ed. Lieberman) p. 41; YS I, 821.

[40] Moses' valedictory song, Deuteronomy 32:1–43.

[41] Using the unusual verb *satam*, which Heschel will explain shortly.

God orders Daniel, *setom he-hazon*—"keep the vision a secret," that is, make it enigmatic. Surely the Israelites did not request Moses to keep the Torah hidden! But what is enigmatic here is made explicit elsewhere.

In two other places, we find the variant expression: "The Israelites said to Moses, 'Complete the Torah for us!'"[61] The upshot of all these midrashim is that the Israelites asked Moses to "complete" or to "seal" the Torah, but Moses did not succeed in doing so.

The same idea is found in another ancient source (the *Midrash Haserot viyeterot*[42]): "The name 'Moses' is always spelled without a *vav*.[43] Why? Because he was missing one of the gates of wisdom, as it says, 'You have made him little less than divine' (Psalm 8:6). There are fifty gates of wisdom. Forty-nine were given to Moses at Sinai, but one was not given to him. And which is that? The gate of completing the book."[44] This source, too, is unclear.

In another midrash, depicting Moses' last hour, we read: "When Moses saw that no one could save him from death, he said, 'The Rock!—His deeds are perfect, / Yea, all His ways are just; / A faithful God, never false, / True and upright is He' (Deuteronomy 32:4).[45] What did Moses do? He took the scroll and wrote on it the Ineffable Name, but did not finish writing the Scroll of the Song at the moment of his death."[62] Here is suggested that Moses did not finish the "Scroll of the Song" before he passed away.

The solution to this riddle is found in yet another midrash, from which it appears that Moses failed to complete the song *Ha'azinu* (Deuteronomy 32). This seems to be the basis of all the *aggadot* we have mentioned here.

It is an ancient tradition that in the scribal writing of *Ha'azinu*, the first letter of v. 6[46] is written large and separated from the rest of the word, as a separate word unto itself.[63] Nowhere else in scripture is a letter written as a separate word.[47]

---

[61] Midrash on Proverbs, ed. Buber, 14; Midrash of Moses' Death, *Beit Ha-Midrash* I, 127. Buber cites *setom* as an alternate reading in his note. Another version has: "Explain the Torah for us, seal (*hatom*) the Torah for us!" ("Chronicles of Moses," *Otzar Ha-midrashim*, 376).

[62] Deuteronomy Rabbah 11:9; YS Vayelekh 940; Ginzberg, *Legends of the Jews*, 6:58 n. 943; Deuteronomy Rabbah, ed. Lieberman, p. 134 n. 2.

[63] Tractate Soferim 9:5; PT Megillah 71c; Exodus Rabbah 24:1.

---

[42] "Midrash on defective and full spellings" (words in the Torah missing a letter or having an extra letter).

[43] The vowel o (*holam*), which may be represented with or without a *vav*, is always without a *vav* in the spelling of *Moshe* (Moses).

[44] Wertheimer, *Batei Midrashot* II, 249.

[45] This verse is from the song *Ha'azinu*, prior to the fateful *hei*, which some of the midrashim take to be the end of Moses' composition.

[46] The *hei* of *Ha-ladonai tigmelu zot* ("Do you thus requite the Lord?").

[47] Though there are many instances of supersized letters, they are generally written connected to the words of which they are a part.

R. Samuel Ha-nagid noted that it is a "strange word."[64] R. David Kimhi noted, "The vowels of this word are unusual. . . . This word comes to impart a secret."[65] R. Menahem de Lonzano found that there is a scribal difference here between the eastern and western traditions: the western tradition writes it as one word and the eastern as two words, and even though we normally follow the western tradition, here the eastern tradition prevails.[66]

Now the secret of the large *hei* is explained in Midrash Tanhuma: "Why is the *hei* written apart from the word? Because it is Moses' farewell signature. Take the initial letters of the verses up to and including this one, and you will find that their combined numerical equivalent is equal to that of the name *Moshe* (Moses). It is like a man who completes a book and signs his name at the end."[67]

But if Moses did not complete the song *Ha'azinu*, who completed it?

The song *Ha'azinu* was sung by the Levites at the additional service on Shabbat.[68] It was called "the song of the Levites."[69] They divided it into six sections whose initial letters spelled the mnemonic acronym *HaZIV LaKh*.[48] They would read one section each Sabbath and return to the beginning after completion.[70] The practice of reading *Ha'azinu* in the synagogue follows a similar pattern of demarcation.

Abudarham[49] expressed surprise that the Sages singled out this portion for such a mnemonic of the divisions. A solution to this riddle is offered in the responsa of R. Nissim ben Jacob:[50] "What is the reason that the sections of *Ha'azinu* are demarcated by *HaZIV LaKh*? Because their numerical equivalent is 78, representing the seventy-eight righteous by whose hand *Ha'azinu* was written."[71]

R. Isaac Abravanel held that all poetry in the prophetic writings was verbally com-

---

[64] *Moznaim* of R. Abraham ibn Ezra.

[65] *Mikhlol*, ed. Rittenberg (5622/1862), 40b.

[66] *Shetei yadot, Or Ha-torah* (Venice, 5375/1615), 25b–26a; *Minhat Shai* ad loc.

[67] Tanhuma Ha'azinu 5. The Rosh suggests that it is for this reason that the text does not explicitly say, "Thus sang Moses, etc." (*Imrei No'am*, Ha'azinu; so too R. Isaac bar Juda Ha-levi in *Pa'aneah Raza*, Ha'azinu).

[68] BT Rosh Hashanah 31a; Maimonides, Mishneh Torah *Hilkhot Temidin u-musafin* 6:9.

[69] Tractate Soferim, ed. Higger, 12:7; PT Megillah 74b.

[70] The medieval commentators had different interpretations of exactly which stopping points were indicated by these letters.

[71] *Mahzor Vitri* p. 388. Midrash *Osfah* (on Numbers 11:16, in Albeck's edition of Zunz's *Preaching in Israel* [Jerusalem: Mosad Bialik, 1954], 141) lists seventy-two elders of ancient Israel of that generation. Apparently R. Nissim arrived at seventy-eight by adding Moses, Joshua, Caleb, Eleazar, Ithamar, and Phinehas. R. Jacob of Vienna adds that *HaZIV LaKh* was one of God's names (*Peshatim u-ferushim*, p. 230).

Nahmanides cites the plural verb, "Therefore, *write down* this poem" (Deuteronomy 31:19), as evidence that Moses and Joshua wrote *Ha'azinu*. Abravanel qualifies this by saying, "God forbid that Joshua authored even a single letter, but God commanded that they write many copies of this song to give it to everyone."

---

[48] A good Hebrew phrase meaning, "The splendor is yours."

[49] R. David ben Joseph Abudarham, fourteenth-century Spanish liturgical commentator, author of *Sefer Abudarham*.

[50] Eleventh century, Kairouan (North Africa).

posed by the prophets themselves under divine inspiration, but was not verbally dictated by God. Similarly the song *Ha'azinu,* "God commanded that Moses should compose the language; the words were Moses', not God's. The language indicates this very fact: 'Give ear, O heavens, let *me* speak. . . . For the name of the Lord I proclaim,' etc. . . . Therefore it does not say, 'The Lord spoke to Moses saying.'"[51] [72]

According to another view, "Moses wrote his book" refers to *Ha'azinu,* which is called Moses' book. Evidence for this is found in the additional command which the Holy and Blessed One issued to Moses, to "write down this poem" (Deuteronomy 31:19), and it says further, "Moses wrote down this poem" (31:22). But surely *Ha'azinu* would have had to have been written down, like all the rest of the Torah; what need, then, for this additional command? R. Eliezer Ashkenazi[52] suggested that the bulk of the Torah "was not given out to any of the Israelites, but was kept beside the Ark, as it says, 'Take this book of Torah and place it beside the Ark of the Covenant, and let it remain there as a witness against you' (31:26). But the song was written and given to all of them, in addition to being written in the Torah scroll. Therefore the song was called 'Moses' book.'" According to Ashkenazi, in *Ha'azinu* Moses resolved the three questions around which the book of Job revolves, and also wrote of the final end of Israelite history as did Balaam; therefore the rabbis said that Moses wrote "his own book" (referring to *Ha'azinu*) as well as the book of Job and portion of Balaam.[73]

R. Levi Isaac of Berditchev pointed out "a marvelous thing."

> Why in the song of *Ha'azinu* is Moses' prophecy very enigmatic, unlike anything else that we find in the Torah? We say that Moses' prophecy is through a clear lens, but that of the other prophets is through a dim lens. Since Moses' prophecy is through a clear lens, he had the power to articulate the matters as he received them from the blessed God, without cloaking them in parables and riddles. But the other prophets did not have this power, and therefore had to embellish their prophecy through parables and riddles, such as the prophecies of Zechariah and others which are very enigmatic; that is called "through a dim lens." But before Moses' death, the tradition of wisdom was taken from him and given to Joshua, and therefore the song *Ha'azinu* is cloaked in enigmatic imagery.[74]

[72] Abravanel on Deuteronomy 31:19.
[73] Ashkenazi, *Ma'asei Hashem, Ma'aseh Torah,* 40.
[74] *Kedushat Levi,* Vayelekh.

---

[51] Heschel is now done with presenting the theory that *Ha'azinu* was written in part by other hands than Moses. He presents other views, however, which find some difference between *Ha'azinu* and the rest of the Torah. Abravanel holds, for instance, that *Ha'azinu* resembles later prophetic writings, in that the thoughts are divinely inspired, but the language is of human composition. R. Joseph Ashkenazi and R. Levi Isaac of Berditchev find other marks of difference.

[52] Sixteenth century, Levant and central-eastern Europe.

The Torah Given Scroll by Scroll

The Tannaitic controversy over who wrote the last eight verses of the Torah is bound up with the Sages' respective notions of the general principle of Moses' writing of the Torah. We have two views of this principle before us. One says that it is a comprehensive rule.[53] Moses our Master wrote the entire Torah from the first verse of Genesis to the last verse of Deuteronomy; the Torah book that he handed over to Israel before his death was not missing a single letter. The second view says that it is a general rule of thumb. Moses our Master wrote the Torah, but various verses were written by Joshua.

These two views of the writing of the Torah are parallel to the two views of Moses' prophecy. Rabbi Akiva thought that every matter came to Moses from divine dictate and that he did not say a single thing on his own; Rabbi Ishmael thought that, as a general rule, Moses received the Torah from divine dictate but that there are various exceptions to the rule of things that Moses said on his own and the Holy and Blessed One agreed with him.

R. Jacob Emden[54] suggested that the controversy over the last eight verses is related to the controversy whether the Torah was given scroll by scroll, or "signed and sealed."[55] Rabbi Judah thought it was given scroll by scroll, and therefore one need not scruple over the last eight verses; "one may well call it a complete Torah scroll, since the lack of those verses does not disqualify it. Originally each section was written by itself [and the last eight verses also constitute a separate portion by itself]. Each individually was called a 'scroll of the Torah.'" But Rabbi Simeon held that it was given signed and sealed; therefore we need all of it [to be valid].[75]

Note that Rabbi Bana'ah, a Sage of the Tannaitic generations,[56] whose words are cited in teachings of the Ishmaelian school, taught that "the Torah was given scroll by scroll" (i.e., when a section was told to Moses, he would write it, and at the end of the forty years, when all the sections had been completed, he sewed them together with thread[57]), as it says, "Then I said, 'See, I will bring a scroll written by me'[58] (Psalm

---

[75] *She'elat Ya'abetz* 33.

[53] Heschel uses the terms *klal she-ein bo hutz* (generality without exception), and *klal she-eino malei* (generality that is not full [complete]), that is, "perfect generalization" and "imperfect generalization," or "universal rule" and "non-universal rule."

[54] Eighteenth century, Germany.

[55] That is, whether it was given in installments at various times, or in its entirety at one time.

[56] He was a teacher of the first-generation Palestinian Amora Rabbi Johanan ben Nappaha (EJ ad loc.). This would seem to place him in the last generation of Tannaim.

[57] *Giddin*—a special thread from kosher tendons, used in Torah scrolls to this day. There was no doubt in the Rabbis' minds that Moses put together the physical scroll observing all the rules and customs of the scribal arts that have come down to us from time immemorial.

[58] NJV: "See, I will bring a scroll recounting what befell me" [meaning of Heb. uncertain]. *Katuv alai* can also mean, "written for me," "written about me," or "written on my account." The context of the psalm suggests that it refers to one who brings a celebratory scroll in place of a sacrifice to give

40:8).[76] This Tanna thought that each topic was communicated to Moses by God at the proper occasion or circumstance, and he wrote down each topic on a separate scroll. Thus the "scroll of Genesis" was written first, then the "scroll of Noah," the "scroll of Abraham," etc.[77]

In contrast to Rabbi Bana'ah's view (transmitted by Rabbi Johanan), Rabbi Simeon ben Lakish (who followed Rabbi Akiva's views on the issue of giving the Torah) taught: "The Torah was given signed and sealed."[59] (That is to say, it was finished, complete, and whole. It was written only at the end of the forty years, after all the portions had been communicated orally. Whatever was communicated in the first and second year was fixed in formula until he wrote them.) "For it is said: 'Take *this* book of the Torah' (Deuteronomy 31:26)."[78]

In Rabbi Bana'ah's view you find a rational and historical conception of the exalted and sacred act of writing the Torah by the hand of Moses our Master. He sees the act of writing in a temporal aspect and says, the Torah was not written at one instant, but scroll by scroll; that is, it was written over the course of various times. There is another approach in the view of Rabbi Simeon ben Lakish, who thinks that the writing of the Torah is not a tangible, measurable thing, given to quantification. The Torah was given signed and sealed; that is, it was written at an instant, and given to Israel in one fell swoop.

How are these views parallel to the views of Moses' receiving the Torah? As we saw earlier, Rabbi Akiva taught that all the Torah was given in one fell swoop, in one delivery, general rules and details together, at Sinai. From that point on, they could only be repeated. In this doctrine of revelation, there is no place for historical distinctions, what came earlier or later. The revelation of Torah transcends time. As opposed to this, Rabbi Ishmael struggled to grasp the Torah with the tongs of reason. In his view, the Torah was not given to Moses at an instant; the general rules were given at Sinai, but the details only in the Tent of Meeting.[79]

---

[76] BT Gittin 60a. RaSHBA (ad loc.) comments: "He would write down portions of which they had immediate need, so they could see and learn from the written text."

[77] Rashi ad loc., s.v. *katuv alai*.

[78] Midrash Haggadol, Pekudei, p. 796. Note the use of the proof text. Moses told the Levites to take *this* book of the Torah and to place it beside the Ark of the Covenant. It must therefore have been in a complete form when he gave it to them.

[79] Similarly, R. Samuel bar Nahmani thought that the portion of the design of the Tabernacle was written when the Tabernacle was completed and not at the end of the forty years (Midrash Haggadol, Pekudei p. 796).

---

thanks for God's deliverance. The traditional commentators interpret the verse as referring to the Torah in one guise or another.

[59] *Torah hatumah nittenah*. The word *hatumah* means "sealed." In ancient times, it referred to the wax seal on the outside of a rolled document, imprinted with the sender's signet ring. It could be sealed in this manner only after it had been completed; and, once sealed, it could not be revised without the seal being broken. The implication is clear: the Torah was complete when given, and not subject to any further alteration or amendment.

The view that the Torah was given scroll by scroll, may be alluded to in the words of Rabbi Abba bar Aivu[60] on Numbers 4:18:[61] "When this portion was written, the Holy and Blessed One foresaw that Korah, who came from the Kohathite clan, would rebel against Moses, . . . and that Moses would ask God to make the earth swallow them."[80] According to this homily, this portion was written before the episode of Korah.[62] Rashi, Maimonides, and Meiri all accepted the view that the Torah was given scroll by scroll.[81]

Support for the scroll-by-scroll view was adduced from the verse "Moses recorded the starting points of their various marches as directed by the Lord" (Numbers 33:2). "Let us read closely: What does this verse tell us by saying so? If you say it tells us that Moses wrote them down, didn't he write the whole Torah, and aren't these marches included in the Torah? But it would seem that this verse intended to tell us the procedure by which the marches were written, that they were not written in one day, but in the following fashion: Moses started writing his log of the King's commands from the day that they left Egypt" . . . and he would then write each march at the proper time, "and afterwards the Lord told him to arrange them in the Torah in the order that he had them written down."[82]

Note that the scroll-by-scroll approach is the guiding assumption of Rabbi Ishmael's interpretation of the ceremony described in Exodus 24. After the Sinaitic theophany, "Moses went and repeated to the people all the commands of the Lord. . . .

---

[80] Numbers Rabbah 5:5.

[81] Rashi comments on Exodus 24:4: "'Moses then wrote . . .'—he wrote from 'In the beginning' to the giving of the Torah, including the commands that had been given at Marah (15:23-26)." According to Maimonides, after the Israelites heard the commandments from Moses, they wrote "those commands on scrolls" (Introduction to the Mishnah). R. Menahem Ha-meiri on BT Gittin 60a takes the position that "the Torah was not given signed and sealed (i.e., all communicated orally and set in formula until he wrote them down together at the end of the forty years), but rather scroll by scroll (i.e., when each portion was communicated to Moses, he would write it down and give it out, and similarly the rest of them, one by one)." See also Nahmanides' introduction to the Torah. According to the opinion of the Rosh, expressed at the end of chapter 5 of Gittin, it is possible that R. Alfasi thought the *halakhah* was according to Rabbi Johahan [i.e., scroll by scroll].

[82] *Or Ha-hayyim* (R. Hayyim ibn Attar) on Numbers 33:2. TB, Mas'ei 1 holds a different view: "The Holy and Blessed One said to Moses: 'Write down the marches that the Israelites marched in the wilderness, so that they should know how many miracles I performed for them in each march." The notion that Moses wrote the various portions in a log is suggested also in Midrash Haggadol on Exodus 19:10: "'Moses wrote down all the commands of the Lord' (24:4)—like a man writing down in codicils."

---

[60] Commonly called "Rav," leading Babylonian Amora of the first generation.

[61] "Do not let the group of Kohathite clans be cut off from the Levites." This is said at the beginning of the second year, during the census, well before the Korahite rebellion (which comes in Numbers 16).

[62] Therefore, Rav must have held that portions of the Torah were written down at various times during the forty years, as events occurred.

Then he took the Book[63] of the Covenant and read it aloud to the people. And they said, 'All that the Lord has spoken we will faithfully do!'" (Exodus 24:3–7). The Sages asked: "From what did he read aloud?" In other words, what was written in this "Book of the Covenant" that Moses wrote on Mount Sinai before the tablets were given? Rabbi Yose ben Rabbi Assi said: "From the beginning of Genesis to this point." Rabbi [Judah the Patriarch] said: "The commandments that were given to Adam, to the Noahides, and to Israel in Egypt and Marah."[83] According to the latter view, the Book of the Covenant was a separate book, in which were written only laws, but no narratives of the patriarchs and the Exodus.

Rabbi Judah the Patriarch's view on this question is similar to Rabbi Ishmael's, who held that the Book of the Covenant was a separate book, in which were written the portions "Behar" and "Be-hukkotai," which were later incorporated into the end of Leviticus.[64] Rabbi Ishmael said, "At the beginning of this passage, what does it say? 'The Lord spoke to Moses on Mount Sinai. . . . Six years you may sow your field. . . . But in the seventh year the land shall have a sabbath of complete rest' (Leviticus 25:1–3). It goes on to give the laws of Sabbatical and Jubilee years, followed by blessings and curses. At the end, what does it say? 'These are the laws, rules, and instructions that the Lord established, through Moses on Mount Sinai, between Himself and the Israelite people' (26:46)."[84] In other words, the Torah does not observe chronological order. Leviticus 25–26 rightly belong with Exodus 24. The superscription tells us they were given on Mount Sinai, but once the Tabernacle was constructed, the divine utterance came through the Tent of Meeting, not on Mount Sinai. Furthermore, the covenant whose terms are elaborated in Leviticus 26 is the very covenant alluded to in Exodus Chapter 24.[85]

It is clear that this view assumes that the Torah was given not in one fell swoop, but scroll by scroll. For if you say that the Torah was given signed and sealed, how can you say that the Book of the Covenant, which contains a portion of the Torah, was written on Mount Sinai many years before other portions of the Torah were written? Correspondingly, it would make sense that Rabbi Akiva, who thought that general rules and details were all communicated together at Sinai, would not have subscribed to the view that the Book of the Covenant contained a *portion* of the Torah.[65]

But from Rav Ashi's rhetorical question, "Was the Torah then given multiple times?" (BT Eruvin 21b, Ein Ya'akov ad loc.), it appears that he subscribed to the view that the Torah was given signed and sealed.

[83] MI, Bahodesh 3.
[84] MI, Bahodesh 3; Midrash Tannaim p. 56.
[85] Abraham ibn Ezra on Leviticus 25:1.

---

[63] NJV: "record."

[64] Leviticus 25:1–26:2 and 26:3–27:34, respectively.

[65] What, then, would Rabbi Akiva have thought was contained in the Book of the Covenant? Heschel does not say here, but the view of Rabbi Yose ben Rabbi Judah (in the next subsection) spells it out: the Book of the Covenant comprised the *whole* Torah.

R. Zevi Hirsch Chajes[66] suggested that this controversy is connected with another, namely, whether one can find significance in the juxtaposition of one Torah portion to another. For if the Torah was given scroll by scroll, then it was not given all together at one time. How, then, can one find significance in the juxtaposition of one portion to another, if they were presumably given at different times during the forty years? On the other hand, Deuteronomy is different; since even the scroll-by-scroll view concedes that it was given at one time, juxtapositions within it can have significance.[86]

This reasoning strengthens the argument that Rabbi Ishmael, who did not interpret juxtapositions outside of Deuteronomy, subscribed to the scroll-by-scroll view. On the other hand, Rabbi Akiva, who said, "Every portion that is next to another, comes to teach a lesson,"[87] and interpreted juxtapositions throughout the Torah,[88] also held that the Torah was given signed and sealed.

The approach, that "the Torah was given scroll by scroll," also goes hand in hand with the principle taught in Rabbi Ishmael's school, that *there is no chronological order in the Torah*. For the chapters of the Torah were not always composed at the time that they were communicated, or in the order that the events occurred. The Torah was not exact about telling first things first and last things last. Moses wrote down each topic on a separate scroll, and before his death he wrote everything down in another order, not in the order of the scrolls.[89]

When death was decreed for Aaron the High Priest, the Holy and Blessed One said to Moses: "Do me the favor of telling Aaron about his death, for I am ashamed to tell him." R. Huna said in the name of Rabbi Tanhum bar Hiyya: What did Moses do? He got up early in the morning and went to Aaron's tent. He called out, "Brother Aaron!" Aaron went down to him. He said, "What brings you to me so early today?" Moses said, "I was puzzling over a certain matter in the Torah last night, and found it very difficult, so I got up early and came to you." Aaron asked, "What is it?" Moses

---

[86] Chajes, glosses on BT Berakhot 21b. Leiter (*Mi-toratan shel Rishonim* on Gittin 60a) rebuts this, arguing that according to BT Sukkah 40b, Rabbi Johanan (who subscribes to the scroll-by-scroll view) also held that juxtapositions are significant.

[87] Sifre Balak 131.

[88] BT Yevamot 4a, Tosafot s.v. *ve-khi*.

[89] But see MaHaRaM Schiff (Meir ben Jacob Ha-kohen Schiff, seventeenth century, Germany) on BT Gittin 60a.

Additional support for this correlation may be found from Rabbi Yannai's homily: "The Torah ought to have started from 'This month shall mark for you the beginning of the months' (Exodus 12:2). Why, then, did the Holy and Blessed One reveal to Israel what was on the six days of creation? Because they said, 'All that the Lord has spoken we will faithfully do!' (Exodus 24:7). Immediately, He revealed it to them." Rabbi Berekhiah may have had something similar in mind when he interpreted: "'He declared to you the covenant that He commanded you to observe' (Deuteronomy 4:13)—'he declared'—referring to the Book of Genesis, telling of the creation of the world; 'that He commanded you to observe'—namely, the Ten Commandments" (Song of Songs Rabbah on 1:4: "the King has brought me into His chambers").

---

[66] Nineteenth century, Poland.

replied, "I don't remember exactly, but I know it was in the Book of Genesis. Bring it out, and let's read it." They took out the Book of Genesis and read it, paragraph by paragraph. After each paragraph, Aaron said, "How well He did! How well the Holy and Blessed One created everything!" When they came to the creation of the human kind, Moses said, "What shall I say about Adam, who brought death into the world?" Aaron replied, "Don't say that in this matter we do not accept the divine decree!"[67]90

R. Levi thought that eight portions were communicated, written, and transmitted on the day that the Tabernacle was erected: those of the Priests, the Levites, the Impurities, the Quarantining of the Impure, the Atonement Ritual, on Inebriation, the Lamp, and the Red Heifer.[68] 91

According to Rashi, at Marah "they were given several portions of Torah to study: the Sabbath, the Red Heifer, and the civil laws."[69] 92

The Book of the Covenant

Two questions were raised about the Book of the Covenant, which Moses read before the people: (1) What was written in it? (2) When did the event occur? Rabbi Ishmael thought that the event occurred on the day before the Torah was given: It was then that "they said, 'We accept it.' When Moses saw that they accepted, he took the blood and sprinkled it on the people, as it says, 'Moses took the blood and dashed it on the people.' (Exodus 24:8). He said, 'Now you are connected, involved, and bound. Tomorrow, come and accept all the commandments.'"93

In contrast to this view, Rabbi Yose ben Rabbi Judah (whose father was a disciple of

90 YS Hukkat 764.
91 BT Gittin 60a; Rashi ad loc. The homily in Leviticus Rabbah 1:7 also supports the scroll-by-scroll view.
92 Rashi on Exodus 15:25. But on BT Yevamot 106b (s.v. ve-hilkheta), Rashi says: "And we hold that the Torah was given signed and sealed."
93 MI, Bahodesh 3.

---

[67] This hauntingly beautiful tale far exceeds Heschel's obvious immediate purpose, to illustrate an occasion where the scroll-by-scroll process can be seen in full-blown description. Maybe he wishes to intimate: Whatever was the process by which the Torah came to be (whether "scroll by scroll" or "signed and sealed") is ultimately beyond our power to determine by argument. Whatever was, was, and God must have wanted it that way. Don't say that in this matter we do not accept the divine decree!

[68] These would seem to be the portions of the Torah that were essential to the functioning of the Tabernacle from its inception.

[69] These represent the three principal categories of laws: edot ("testimonies," or commemorative laws), hukkim (rituals with no discernible rational reason), and mishpatim (rationally based laws). Together, these were integral to the functioning of the community. Le-hit'assek (translated "to study") also means: to practice to achieve familiarity, before one is fully obligated to perform them.

Rabbi Akiva) said, "They did everything on that day."[94] Thus, on the day after the Torah was given, they did everything else associated with the covenant: reciting the words of the Lord, giving the civil laws to the people, writing the Book of the Covenant, building the altar, offering the sacrifices, and concluding the covenant. It is likely that Rabbi Yose ben Rabbi Judah transmitted the approach of the Akivan school.[95] Note that on the question of the content of the Book of the Covenant, his view fits well with the Akivan doctrine that general rules and details were all given from Sinai: "What are the 'words of the covenant' that God made with Israel at Horeb, as it says, 'Then [Moses] took the record of the covenant and read it aloud to the people' (Exodus 24:7)? He read to them from the first verse of Genesis to the last verse of Deuteronomy."[96] R. David Zevi Hoffman expressed surprise at this interpretation: "How did he read to them deeds which did not occur until years later?" But as we saw earlier, many Sages taught that everything is foreseen by the Holy and Blessed One, Who tells beforehand what will happen afterwards. Moses showed Israel "that if they sinned, how they would be exiled, how they could repent, and how they could be redeemed."[97] Didn't they say that even the Book of Esther was foretold to Moses at Sinai?[98]

According to another source, on the Day of Atonement Moses descended from the mountain with the second pair of tablets in his hand. According to one view, they read in the Torah that day and found in it, "You shall practice self-denial" (Leviticus 16:29).[70] [99]

On the other hand, we find one who says, "The Ten Commandments were not preceded by any other commandments." The laws associated with Marah, the permanent Passover ritual, and the sanctification of the firstborn (Exodus 12, 13, and 15–16) were actually given after the Sinai theophany.[100] Apparently, according to this

---

[94] MI, Bahodesh 3. Which day? One assumes, the same day the Torah was given. But traditionally, that was the Sabbath. Therefore, Nahmanides and others interpret: All the subsequent actions enumerated by Rabbi Yose took place on the following day.

[95] Yet there is some evidence that on the question of what day the events of Exodus 24 occurred, Rabbi Akiva agreed with Rabbi Ishmael that they occurred the day before the Sinai theophany. See Song of Songs Rabbah 2:14.

[96] Midrash Tannaim, p. 56.

[97] Hoffman on Midrash Tannaim, ad loc. See beginning of this chapter, on the saying "He foretells the end from the beginning."

[98] PT Megillah 70d.

[99] PRE 46.

[100] Sifre, Va'ethanan 34–35; see Finkelstein's notes, p. 60, and Me'ir Ayin on Sifre Pinhas 136.

---

[70] The first mention of the Day of Atonement (in Leviticus 16) occurs after the death of Aaron's sons, presumably during the second year in the wilderness. But the second pair of tablets was brought down (according to tradition) on the Tenth of Tishrei [i.e., what would eventually be the Day of Atonement] of the first year. Here seems to be another case of anticipation of later events at an earlier historical moment.

view, the Book of the Covenant was also concluded after the Ten Commandments were given.

R. Judah the Hasid[71] thought that the covenant was concluded after the Sinai theophany, and that the Book of the Covenant included the Ten Commandments, "for it was now necessary to explain them, for it was written, 'You shall not murder,' but it was not spelled out under what circumstances this applied, or how judgment should be carried out."[101] Some said that the Book of the Covenant contained everything written from Exodus 20:19 to the end of chapter 23, interpreting "Book of the Covenant" to mean "the book in which are written the words of the Lord and the judicial rules."[102] But the author of Midrash Haggadol cites Exodus 29:38 ("Now this is what you shall offer upon the altar: two yearling lambs each day, regularly") and comments: "Thus it is commanded in the Book of the Covenant."[103] [72]

As R. Isaac Abravanel noted, the medieval Sages also debated this issue. "The Sages of Germany said it happened before the giving of the Torah, but the Sages of Spain have an established tradition that it was after the giving of the Torah."[104] According to Lekah Tov,[105] Rashi,[106] and Rabbenu Bahya,[107] the chapters are not in chronological order, and chapter 24 belongs before chapter 20, for it occurred before the Torah was given. Nahmanides differs, and he comments on the view of Rabbi Yose ben Judah, "Listen to this, for what he said is correct."[108] So, too, thought R. Abraham ibn Ezra, RaSHBaM, and R. Isaac Abravanel.

The Beggar's[73] Wisdom

It is well known that Abraham ibn Ezra hinted in many places in his Torah commentary (the "short" commentary) that there are Scriptures that were not written in the days of Moses. Most of his hints are found at the beginning of his commentary on

---

[101] *Pa'aneah Raza,* end of Mishpatim.

[102] Sforno, end of Mishpatim.

[103] Midrash Haggadol on Leviticus, p. 110.

[104] Abravanel on Exodus 24:1.

[105] "Moses wrote the entire Book of the Covenant before the Ten Commandments" (Lekah Tov II, 65a).

[106] "This portion was said before the Ten Commandments" (Rashi on Exodus 24:1).

[107] "According to the plain sense, . . . the entire portion, including 'all the people witnessed the thunder' (20:15) belongs before the Ten Commandments" (Rabbenu Bahya on Exodus 24:1).

[108] Nahmanides on Exodus 24:1.

---

[71] Twelfth century, Germany.

[72] Apparently he took "Book of the Covenant" to include the laws of the construction of the Tabernacle as well—indeed, all the laws of Exodus.

[73] Abraham ibn Ezra (twelfth century, Spain) spent most of his productive career as a poor wandering scholar, tossing off scholarly works for one patron after another. This chapter deals with his most radical ideas about the non-Mosaic authorship of parts of the Torah.

Deuteronomy, where he writes: "If you understand the secret of the 'twelve,' and 'Moses wrote,' 'the Canaanites were then in the land,' 'on the mount of the Lord there is vision,' and 'his bedstead is an iron bedstead,' you will recognize the truth." These hints were explained by R. Joseph ben Eliezer ben Joseph Bonfils the Sephardi[74] in his book *Tzafenat Pa'aneah*.[109] The "twelve" are the twelve verses at the end of Deuteronomy; "Moses wrote" is from Deuteronomy 31:9; "the Canaanites were then in the land"—Genesis 12:6; "on the mount of the Lord there is vision"—Genesis 22:14; "his bedstead is an iron bedstead"—Deuteronomy 3:11.

At the beginning of the last chapter of Deuteronomy, Ibn Ezra says: "In my opinion, Joshua wrote from this verse on, for after Moses ascended [Mount Nebo], he no longer wrote. Joshua wrote it by way of prophecy, as we see from 'the Lord showed him, . . .' 'the Lord said to him, . . .' and 'He buried him." Here Ibn Ezra contends that Joshua wrote the last twelve verses, and not just the last eight.

"Moses wrote down this Torah and gave it to the priests, sons of Levi" (Deuteronomy 31:9). How could Moses write this? Surely when he was writing, he had not yet given the book to the Levites? The words "wrote down" and "gave" testify that the Torah had already been given before this verse was written.[110]

On the verse "the Canaanites were then in the land," Ibn Ezra writes, "It has a secret, and the enlightened will be silent."[111] The *Tzafenat Pa'aneah* explains:

How can he say "then," implying that they were in the land then but are now there no longer? When Moses wrote the Torah, were not the Canaanites still in the land? So it is unlikely that Moses wrote "then," for reason dictates that the word "then" was written at a time when the Canaanites were not in the land. We know that the Canaanites did not leave until after Moses' death, when Joshua conquered the land. Therefore it appears that Moses did not write this word here, but rather Joshua or another of the prophets. We find similarly in Proverbs: "These too are proverbs of Solomon, which the men of King Hezekiah of Judah copied" (Proverbs 25:1). For if Solomon indeed composed the whole book, why is there mentioned the name of Hezekiah, who was born several generations later? But it was a tradition in their land, from one man to the next, going back to Solomon, therefore they wrote it and it was considered as if Solomon had written it. So too here, it was a tradition in Israel that in the days of Abraham the Canaanites were in the land, and one of the prophets wrote it here. Since it is incumbent on us to believe the

---

[109] *Tzafenat Pa'aneah*, II, ed. Herzog (Berlin, 5690/1930), p. 65.

[110] Ibid.

[111] One of the commentators on Ibn Ezra, R. Eleazar ben He-hasid Ha-gaon Mattathias, points out: "He did not say, 'the enlightened will understand,' but 'will be silent.' He was very unwilling to reveal it, but in his commentary on Deuteronomy he did reveal his secret" (Naftali ben Menahem, Vatican Jewish Archives, p. 128).

---

[74] Fourteenth century, Spain and Levant. The title of his work is the Egyptian name bestowed on Joseph the interpreter of dreams and riddles (Genesis 41:45).

words of tradition and prophecy, what difference does it make to me whether Moses or another prophet wrote it? All their words are true and prophetic.[75]

If you object, "Is it not written, 'Do not add to it' (Deuteronomy 13:1)?" The answer . . . in Ibn Ezra's first commentary to the portion *Lekh Lekha* (12:4) he said this only prohibits adding to the number and substance of the commandments, not to words. Therefore, if a prophet added a word or a few words to explain something in the light of what he heard from tradition, this is not really an addition . . . for they had the power to add words by way of explanation, and all the more so a prophet was allowed to add words to those of another prophet to make them clearer. However, this was just in matters that did not involve commandments, but only recounting events that happened, so it is not truly called an addition.

If you object further, that our Rabbis said[112] that whoever said, "All the Torah is divine except for one verse which the Holy and Blessed One did not say, but Moses said it on his own, to such a one the verse applies, 'he has spurned the word of the Lord' (Numbers 15:31)" the answer is that this too applies only to the commandments, and not to narratives.[113]

R. Moses ben Judah, in his supercommentary *Tappuhei Zahav*, commented on Ibn Ezra's view that Moses did not write this verse: "Even though we do not agree with him, since it is incumbent on us to believe that Moses our Master wrote from the first verse of Genesis to the last verse of Deuteronomy, without missing a single letter, I have thought to write in his defense. For he points out that simply because a future or present sensory fact has escaped a prophet's attention, this does not detract from his perfection as a prophet."[76] [114]

R. Moses Almosnino also solved Ibn Ezra's riddle, pointing out that in Moses' day the land "was still in the hands of the Canaanites, but this verse was presumably written by Joshua or Ezra. This is the secret, that Moses our Master did not write this."[115]

In his commentary on Genesis 22:14, Ibn Ezra writes: "The meaning of 'in the mount of the Lord there is vision'[77] is in [my commentary on] Deuteronomy." R. Joseph Bonfils interprets his meaning as follows:

---

[112] BT Sanhedrin 99a.

[113] *Tzafenat Pa'aneah* I, 91–93.

[114] M. Friedlaender, *Essays on the Writings of Abraham Ibn Ezra* (Jerusalem, 1963), 239.

[115] R. N. Ben Menahem, "An Addition to R. Moses Almosnino's Commentary on Ibn Ezra" (in Hebrew) *Sinai* 10 (5706/1946): 153.

---

[75] This is a very early anticipation of Franz Rosenzweig's response to the higher criticism: "For the Higher Critic, 'R' is 'Redactor,' for us it is 'Rabbenu.'"

[76] In other words, the fact that the Canaanites disappeared from the land at a later time is a mere sensory fact, not a spiritual truth. It is no reflection on Moses to say that he was unaware of this (since it happened after his death), and that some later prophet may have filled in the gap. Nor does it reflect on the deeper truth of the Torah.

[77] Implicit in the discussion of this verse is the understanding that by "vision" is meant the appearance of people to God (or in the earliest version, of God to the people) when the Israelites came three times annually to the Sanctuary for communion with the Divine Presence at the pilgrimage festivals. Thus: "Three times a year all your males shall appear before the Sovereign, the Lord" (Exodus

For the "mount of the Lord" is Mount Moriah, on which the Temple was built, as is written in 2 Chronicles (3:1). Moses did not write in the Torah what mountain it was, but
referred to it as "the place that the Lord will choose" (Deuteronomy 12:11). This indicates that he did not know what mountain it was, for God did not reveal it until the days
of David. How, then, can he say here, "in the mount of the Lord there is vision," which
implies that Moses did know it? Furthermore, the verse says, "of which it is said
today,"[78] which implies, "this is what they say now in our generation when they go up
on pilgrimage, 'on the mount of the Lord is vision'"; that is, one goes up to celebrate the
holiday in Jerusalem and to worship in the mount of the Lord. It is not likely that they
said that in the days of Moses. Therefore Moses did not write this verse, but the later
prophets wrote it, in the same way as I explained on the verse, "the Canaanites were then
in the land."[116]

On the verse "his bedstead is an iron bedstead" (Deuteronomy 3:11), R. Joseph
Bonfils writes that the purpose of the verse is to point out that it is in Rabbah of the
Ammonites.

> But it is known that Moses did not enter the territory of the Ammonites, as it says, "But
> you did not encroach on the land of the Ammonites" (Deuteronomy 2:37). If he did not
> set foot there, how did he know that Og's bedstead was there? It is known that the
> Israelites did not come into Rabbah until the days of David, who sent Joab to conquer the
> land of the Ammonites, and then they knew that the bedstead of Og was in Rabbah. This
> is the evidence that the verse was added to the Torah later, that Moses did not write it,
> but one of the later prophets wrote it.[117]

According to R. Joseph Bonfils, R. Abraham Ibn Ezra thought that the first five
verses of Deuteronomy "were not written by Moses, but by one of the later prophets,
and the verse, 'the Lord our God spoke to us at Horeb' (1:6) follows from the verse
'These are the commandments and regulations,' which is the last verse of Numbers.
Whoever looks closely at the content of these verses will perceive the truth and will
recognize that the first five verses of Deuteronomy are spoken in a foreign voice, as if
someone else is speaking them. Might you say that the whole Torah speaks in the
voice of an outside narrator?[79] Know that there is a difference here, for [the narrator

---

[116] *Tzafenat Pa'aneah* I, 112.
[117] *Tzafenat Pa'aneah* II, 65.

23:17; similarly Exodus 34:23 and Deuteronomy 16:16). Genesis 22:14 thus identifies Mount Moriah
as the place where this thrice-annual communion would take place, once the Temple was built there.
Either Moses knew prophetically that the Temple would be built there (which Bonfils, following Ibn
Ezra, doubts, but Rashi maintains), or else the verse was written after the Temple was built.

[78] NJV: "whence the present saying."

[79] There are certainly grounds for claiming this. The fact that Moses is referred to always (except
in Deuteronomy) in the third person, would be one kind of prima facie evidence that someone besides
Moses wrote it. From a traditional point of view, however, this could easily be defended by saying that
this was meant for the reader to be able to tell the story while referring to Moses in the third person.

of Deuteronomy 1:1–5] takes note of the places where the commandments were given (as when he says, 'Through the wilderness, in the Arabah . . .'), and if Moses had written this there would have been no need of this, for all of Israel knew those places, so why would he have had to mention the places, since they knew them?"[80]

On the verse "These are the kings who reigned in the land of Edom before any king reigned over the Israelites" (Genesis 36:31), Ibn Ezra writes; "Itzhaki wrote in his book that this portion was written in the days of Jehoshaphat, and he interpreted the generations as he wished. Rightly is his name called Itzhaki, for whoever hears will laugh at him. . . . God forbid that this be from the days of Jehoshaphat as he said! His book ought to be burned."[81]

R. Joseph Bonfils explains:

His reason for saying this was that if it was written in the days of Jehoshaphat, they would have added to the Torah an entire section, and the Torah said, "Do not add to it" (Deuteronomy 13:1). If someone should argue, did not R. Abraham himself hint at the beginning of Deuteronomy that the later prophets added words and verses to the Torah? —the answer is that adding a word or verse by way of explanation of what Moses wrote, is very different from one who adds an entire section. A word or verse can count as an explanation; an entire section is truly an addition.[118]

R. Abraham ibn Ezra's views aroused considerable opposition. R. Ezra[82] said, "Keep yourself from heresy, saying that Ezra added words as he copied the Torah, such as 'the Canaanites were then in the land,' or 'his bedstead is a bedstead of iron,' for this is complete apostasy, and of this the Sages said, 'he spurns the word of the Lord.' This is the one who denies that Torah is from heaven, for whoever says that the entire Torah is from heaven except for one verse which was not dictated by God, or which Moses said on his own, has spurned the word of the Lord."[119]

Already in the Middle Ages, some Sages sought to defend Ibn Ezra by saying that he

---

[118] *Tzafenat Pa'aneah* I, 149.

[119] End of commentary on Song of Songs attributed to Nahmanides (actually by R. Ezra). See *Emunat Hakhamim* of R. Aviad Sar Shalom, chapter 2.

---

[80] To put the matter more forcefully (and perhaps a bit more clearly): Moses did not have to introduce his speech by saying: "I am now speaking to you from the wilderness, between Paran and Tophel, etc." (unless he were broadcasting it to an overseas audience)! Hence, this framing introduction was probably added by someone who, at the time he was writing it, was at a different geographic location (and—extending the argument to "it was in the fortieth year . . ."—at a different time).

[81] This vitriolic attack on Itzhaki is an indication of how firmly Ibn Ezra drew the limits beyond which he would not question the Mosaic authorship of the body of the Torah. Actually, the reference "before any king reigned over the Israelites" would seem grist to a skeptic's mill, as it alludes to a period when there were kings in Israel. Uriel Simon has argued that certain of Ibn Ezra's antagonists, such as Itzhaki, were Karaites, who had a very different conception of the definition of Mosaic authorship from Jews of the rabbinic tradition.

[82] Ezra ben Solomon, thirteenth-century Spanish kabbalist.

never intended to claim that there were verses in the Torah of non-Mosaic authorship. "The Epicureans have spread slander against this author, attributing to him the view that there were thirty-three verses that were not written by Moses, but they have been roundly refuted; may they be rubbed out from the Book of Life."[120] "God forbid such a holy man be called wicked!" wrote R. Shemtov bar Isaac ibn Shaprut from Toledo in his manuscript (also entitled *Tzafenat Pa'aneah*). In his view, Ibn Ezra never dissented from rabbinic views, but believed that all the Torah "was said by divine dictate." The verses he mentioned in the beginning of his commentary to Deuteronomy were written by Joshua not to tell a story "but as commentary, by divine dictate."[121]

Also R. Samuel Zarza[83] wrote on Ibn Ezra in his commentary on Deuteronomy: "Our Rabbis said that even if one says all the Torah is from heaven except for one verse which was not said by the Holy and Blessed One, but Moses wrote it on his own, he has no portion in the world to come. In that case, shall we say that the gentleman Ibn Ezra is of that opinion! God forbid that he be of that opinion!"[122] Some even thought that these words never came from Ibn Ezra's pen but were added later by his students to his book.

Individual Views

Come and see how R. Moses ben Nahman (Nahmanides), one of the greatest Torah scholars of all generations, on whose decisions "all the provinces of Catalonia relied as on Moses by God's word,"[123] did not hesitate, in the opinion of R. Isaac Abravanel, to drop a hint in his commentary that there is something in the Torah which Moses did not write. This will solve another riddle for us. In the introduction to his commentary he writes, "With R. Abraham ibn Ezra we will show outward criticism and secret affection." In many places he criticizes him and rejects his opinions. But he never saw it necessary to criticize the views of Ibn Ezra that we have just mentioned, as we saw Rabbenu Bahya did.[84]

Numbers 21:1–3 says: "When the Canaanite, king of Arad, who dwelt in the Negeb, learned that Israel was coming by the way of Atharim, he engaged Israel in battle and took some of them captive. Then Israel made a vow to the Lord and said, 'If you deliver this people into our hand, we will proscribe their towns.' The Lord heeded Israel's plea and delivered up the Canaanites; and they and their cities were proscribed. So that place was named Hormah."

---

[120] Manuscript cited by Friedlaender, *Essays on the Writings of Abraham Ibn Ezra*, 226.
[121] Friedlaender, *Essays on the Writings of Abraham Ibn Ezra*, 223.
[122] *Mekor Hayyim* on Deuteronomy, beginning.
[123] Responsa of RIBaSH, 415.

---

[83] Fourteenth century, Spain.
[84] See above, pp. 610–18.

Who was the king of Arad, and when did this battle take place? Nahmanides explained that the king of Arad was mentioned among the conquests of Joshua (Joshua 12:14) and that the king of Arad is mentioned in the passage of the Israelites' journeys, "the Canaanite, king of Arad, who dwelt in the Negeb, in the land of Canaan" (Numbers 33:40). "But the text does not simply call 'land of Canaan' what is east of the Jordan." It appears that this text speaks not of a battle in the time of Moses but of a battle that took place after Moses' death. The question arises: When were these verses written?

R. Abraham ibn Ezra writes in his commentary: "Many said that this portion was written by Joshua. They cite the entry: 'The king of Arad—one'[85] (Joshua 12:14). They also found that the tribe of Judah called the place Hormah." Ibn Ezra rejects this view and explains that there are two places with the same name, and that this king of Arad was from Transjordan.[124]

But Nahmanides disagrees and says:

> It seems to me that this king of Arad dwelt on the west side of the Jordan in the land of Canaan, near the Jordan in the territory of the tribe of Judah, near Hebron, which is in the Negeb. He heard from afar of the approach of the Israelites, and he came by way of Atharim to fight them. Israel vowed a vow to the Lord that if He deliver them into their hand, they will devote all of their possessions to the Lord. The text tells that God heard their prayer, *and completed the story, telling that Israel also proscribed their towns after they came into the land of Canaan, and after the death of Joshua.* That is what it tells in the Book of Judges: "The descendants of the Kenite, the father-in-law of Moses, went up from the City of Palms to the wilderness of Judah; and they went and settled among the people in the Negeb of Arad" (Judges 1:16). It further says: "Judah with its brother-tribe Simeon went on and defeated the Canaanites who dwelt in Zephath. They proscribed it, and so the town was named Hormah." That is the final fulfillment of the vow. But the text in Numbers completes the story by mentioning it there.

It appears that Nahmanides meant to say that the text projected all this into the future, after the pattern of "he foretells the end from the beginning." However, R. Isaac Abravanel responded to him:

> It was too shameful for him to say outright that Joshua wrote this, and he left it vague, saying "the text completed the story," without mentioning who wrote it, since it could not have been Moses. This whole approach was taken by Ibn Ezra from the Karaites, who in their commentaries on the Torah decided summarily that Moses did not write this part. Nahmanides here followed Ibn Ezra's lead. It is amazing that this paragon of learning and sanctity let drop a word that there is something in the Torah that was not written by Moses—which falls in the category of "spurning the word of the Lord." I have explained in my commentary on "the Israelites ate manna forty years . . ." (Exodus

---

[124] We shall see that Abravanel intimates that Ibn Ezra attributed this passage to Joshua. But we see here that Ibn Ezra explicitly rejected this attribution.

---

[85] This occurs in the list of kings defeated by Joshua.

16:35) that Moses wrote the Torah as God commanded him, word by word, so it is not absurd that he would write of things that would happen after his death, such as "These are the names of the men through whom the land shall be apportioned for you" (Numbers 34:17). For Moses our Master (peace be his) wrote everything by his hand, everything by divine dictate, as things were destined to be. Therefore he wrote how long the Israelites would eat the manna, as God told him.[125]

Here is the text in Exodus that Abravanel cited: "The Israelites ate manna forty years, until they came to a settled land; they ate the manna until they came to the border of the land of Canaan" (Exodus 16:35). The verse comes to tell us that the Israelites ate the manna also "after they crossed the Jordan"—that is, after Moses' death. This fits with what it says in the Book of Joshua, that the manna fell until after the first Passover which the Israelites celebrated in the land of Canaan in Joshua's days.

The difficulty, that Moses would write about an event that occurred after his death, was felt in the Sifre: "But at the time of writing, were they not still eating manna?[86] This teaches you that there is no chronological order in the Torah."[126] The meaning here is that the Torah can speak of something which is still in the future. But in ordinary language, "they ate" refers to the past, not the future.

Nahmanides also explained that this portion speaks of what happened "after Moses' death, until after the Passover. Similarly, 'These are the names of the men through whom the land shall be apportioned for you' (Numbers 34:17) was by way of prophecy, that they would still be living, for it is not probable that God would appoint people of whom this was doubtful. Nevertheless, it would have been proper to appoint them through Joshua at the time of the apportioning."[127]

R. Isaac Abravanel mentioned the view, "that Joshua wrote this verse in the Torah, but it is not so. Moses wrote all this, though it was still yet to be, by divine dictate, for God commanded him to write so, the same as he wrote "Moses ascended Mount Nebo," "and Moses died there" (Deuteronomy 34:1, 5).[128]

---

[125] Abravanel ad loc.

R. Eliezer Ashkenazi (sixteenth century, Levant and Europe) followed Nahmanides in postdating the battle, but did not assign authorship to this passage. Ibn Ezra and MaHaRShA showed how the talmudic Sages wrestled with the problems of this passage. Some of them equated the king of Arad with Sihon, or Arad with Amalek (BT Rosh Hashana 3a, Tosafot s.v. *va-yishma'*; MaHaRShA ad loc., Tanhuma Hukkat 18, Numbers Rabbah 19:20).

[126] Sifre Beha'alotekha 64.

[127] Nahmanides on Numbers 21:1.

[128] Abravanel on Exodus 16:35.

---

[86] So it would not make sense to tell Moses' contemporaries of a time when the eating of manna stopped.

LOST BOOKS

Translator's Introduction

The notion that some books of the original revelation were lost poses a special challenge to the maximalist view. "The Torah of the Lord is perfect" (Psalm 19:8)—but is the Torah that is in *our* possession the perfect exemplar of that Torah? Or is the earthly Torah but a "fallen, unripe fruit" (novelet) of the Supernal Wisdom (see above, chapter 14, and below, chapter 35)?

The best way to summarize what Heschel's aim is in this chapter is this: in addition to all the issues that he has brought to our attention until now, with respect to the authorship of those books, chapters, and verses that are part of our scriptural canon, there is still one additional matter, and that is how the canon itself came to be. Even if one were to be utterly convinced that there is no human element in the Scripture that sits before us, one cannot be oblivious to the fact that the creation of an official list of scriptural books is itself a product of human decision, and that the survival of certain books is at the mercy of the contingencies of history. In this respect, all of the interesting material that he collects for us here on the subject of the existence of sacred but noncanonical books, or on the subject of the transferring of texts from one book to another, points once more in the direction of a significant and irreducible human element in the sacred texts. And thus it is with this postscript that Heschel's long argument concerning that human element, which has taken up so many chapters in the second Hebrew volume of *TMH*, finally comes to an end.

The reader should note also that in the very last section of this chapter, which brings us to the beginning of the Hebrew volume 3, Heschel performs a dramatic reversal. All the previous parts of the present chapter seek to demonstrate the historical limitations and contingency of the actual written Torah that is in our possession. If (as according to Rabbi Ishmael) the Torah speaks in human language, then it should not surprise us either that it evolved like a human document, losing valuable parts and gaining accretions from all manner of sources. "Everything is subject to luck, even the Scroll of the Torah in the Temple." But in the conclusion to the chapter, Heschel will remind us once more of the infinite, absolute divine Torah that our finite, human-couched Torah points to, and that it seeks to express the best it can. The greatness of Moses is that he reached out to that absolute truth and made contact with it. One dimension of that truth he committed to writing in the Written Torah (this is the "remembrance," or the hint that we are given in the written texts), and the original intensity of the message may have been moderated in translation to that public, universal medium. ("The text adjusts to what the ear can hear.") Another dimension he imparted directly through personal contact to Joshua, inaugurating the chain of person-to-person transmission which is the Oral Torah.

In other words, while invoking again the Akivan theme of the divine Torah, Heschel reconnects with other Akivan ideas that were developed in earlier chapters: the correspondence of heavenly prototypes with their earthly realizations (chapter 14); the notion of the heavenly Torah itself (chapters 17–20); and the reality of the mystical experience (chapters 15–16). Heschel's final message to us may be to beware of reductionist criticism in every form. As moderns, we may see more clearly than ever before the human side of Torah: its historical development, contingency and finitude. But we must never lose sight of the ineffable reality of the living God to which our Torah bears testimony.

The Prophecy of Eldad and Medad

HARD WAS THE DAY FOR ISRAEL, when the mixed multitude in their midst felt a gluttonous craving, and the Israelites wept and said, "If only we had meat to eat!" On that day Moses called out to God for help, and the Lord responded, "Gather for me seventy of Israel's elders, and I will pour out My spirit on them. . . . The spirit rested on them and they prophesied but did not continue.[1] Two men, however, remained in the camp—Eldad and Medad —and carried on like prophets in the camp" (Numbers 11).

Who were Eldad and Medad, and what was their prophecy?

Some said Eldad and Medad were Moses' paternal half-brothers,[2] for Amram had married his aunt Jochebed (Exodus 6:20),[1] and when the Torah was given and this degree of sanguinity was prohibited, he divorced her, married another woman, and begat Eldad and Medad.[2] According to another view, Eldad and Medad were Moses'

---

[1] *Toledot Yitzhak* of R. Isaac Karo, Beha'alotekha.
[2] *Sermons on the Torah* of Joshua ben Shu'eb (Costa, 5283/1523), Beha'alotekha; commentary of the Tosafists on Numbers 11:27.

---

[1] Hebrew: *velo yasafu*. Some of the commentators interpret: "they did not stop" (from *sof* ["end"]) —an interpretation especially apt as applied to Eldad and Medad.
[2] The legend of their biological kinship to Moses is symbolic of their deeper spiritual relationship— the common vocation of prophecy. Moses may have been foremost among prophets, but by attending exclusively to him we risk ignoring the many other spiritual geniuses, many anonymous, and the inimitable expressions of divine wisdom they have to offer us.

maternal half-brothers, from the time in Egypt, when Amram divorced Jochebed out of fear of the Pharaonic decrees.[3]

Eldad and Medad's prophecy was of a high order, for God said of the elders, "I will draw upon the spirit that is on you [Moses] and put it upon them"(11:17), but Eldad and Medad had their inspiration directly from God, as it says, "the spirit rested upon them" (11:26). Furthermore, the elders prophesied only for an hour, but Eldad and Medad continued until the day of their death.[4]

In addition, the content of the elders' prophecy is not preserved. Some say they prophesied that Moses would die and Joshua would lead them to the Promised Land.[5] Some said they anticipated Ezekiel in prophesying about Gog and Magog.[6] Some say they prophesied about the quail that were to come and satisfy the people's hunger.[7]

Now, two verses in Numbers (10:35–36) are written as a separate unit, bracketed by inverted nuns. Rabbi [Judah the Patriarch] said, "They are a book unto themselves." Rabbi Ishmael said, "This is to indicate that this is not their proper place."[8] Rabbi Simeon ben Gamaliel said, "This section is destined someday to be uprooted from here and written in the proper place."[9] A midrash dwelt on the puzzling tradition: "'Wisdom has hewn her seven pillars'—these are the seven books of the Torah" —but is not the Torah composed of *five* books!? It is seven if you count the book of Numbers as three: the portion of the book before the inverted nuns, the two verses in between, and the remainder of the book after this anomaly![10]

A source from the eleventh century comments: "Some midrashim explained the reason for the inverted nuns as follows: The whole Torah is devoted to the prophecy of Moses, except for these two verses, which are of the prophecy of Eldad and Medad."[11] And Midrash Proverbs repeats the "separate book" view with a twist: "Rabbi says, 'It was a separate book that was suppressed.'"[12] This hints that the two verses are the remnant of a larger work of prophecy of Eldad and Medad, that was suppressed.[3]

This view, that the prophecy of Eldad and Medad was written in a separate book, will explain the mysterious phrase in the Torah: "The spirit rested upon them, and they were among those that were written" (Numbers 11:26). The passage itself is

[3] Jerusalem Targum on Numbers 11:26.
[4] BT Sanhedrin 17a; Numbers Rabbah 14:19; TB, Sifre, Sifre Zuta and YS ad loc.
[5] Sifre Beha'alotekha 95.
[6] Numbers Rabbah 15:9.
[7] BT Sanhedrin 19a.
[8] Sifre Beha'alotekha 84 (see Horowitz's note).
[9] BT Shabbat 115b–116a.
[10] BT Shabbat 116a; Leviticus Rabbah 11:3; Midrash Lekah Tov on Beha'alotekha, 100a.
[11] E. N. Adler, ed., *Ginze Mitzrayim* (Jerusalem: Makor, 1969), 11; S. Lieberman, *Hellenism in Jewish Palestine*, Texts and Studies of the Jewish Theological Seminary of America 18 (New York: Jewish Theological Seminary, 1950), 41.
[12] Midrash on Proverbs 26:4; ed. Buber, 50b; *Yalkut Hamakhiri* ad loc.

---

[3] *Suppressed: nignaz.* On *genizah*, see n. [16] below.

opaque, for the main point is not made explicit: What was the prophecy of Eldad and Medad, which motivated the youth to request, "My lord Moses, restrain[4] them!" (11:28)? The word ketuvim[5] ("written") is also unclear. [6]

In Scripture, the word ketuvim refers to matters that are written in some official journal: "All [Ahashuerus's] mighty and powerful acts . . . are written in the Annals of the Kings of Media and Persia" (Esther 10:2); "these [genealogies] are written in the book of the kings of Israel" (1 Chronicles 9:1). But in rabbinic Hebrew, ketuvim refers to the Hagiographa, the third division of scriptural writings after the Torah and prophets.[13] Perhaps in the Torah, ketuvim is synonymous with "books," so our enigmatic passage would mean: "their words of prophecy are in the books of Eldad and Medad." It is of interest that one passage uses the term ketuvim in reference to prophetic books.[14] Moreover, a proof text from the apocryphal Ecclesiasticus of Ben Sira is cited by the third-generation Babylonian Amora Rava bar Mari with the prefatory formula: "And we find a third proof in the ketuvim . . . ."[15][7]

In similar fashion, the Sages speculated about the prophecy of Miriam and Aaron. When they were in Hazeroth, Miriam and Aaron spoke: "Has the Lord spoken only through Moses? Has He not spoken through us as well?" (Numbers 12:1-2). The Sages inferred that Miriam received the prophetic word before Moses was born, for Scripture in one place refers to her as the sister of Aaron, as if Moses did not exist (Exodus 15:20).[8] Furthermore, they learned from the prophetic diatribe against Eli ("Thus said the Lord: Lo, I revealed Myself to your father's house in Egypt when they were subject to the House of Pharaoh" [1 Samuel 2:27]) that Aaron also received the prophetic word before Moses. Yet neither in the Pentateuch nor in 1 Samuel is the content of Aaron's prophecy explicated. "This prophecy was suppressed for over 886 years, until Ezekiel came and proclaimed it, as he said, 'When I made Myself known to them in the land of Egypt, . . . I said to them, "Cast away, every one of you, the

---

[13] BT Bava Batra 14b; Megillah 31a; ARN B 1.

[14] "Here are the forty-eight prophets and seven prophetesses who prophesied for Israel and were written in the ketuvim" (SER 21, ed. Rottner, p. 90).

[15] BT Bava Kama 92b. See M. H. Segal's introduction to his edition of the Hebrew *Ecclesiasticus* (Jerusalem: Mosad Bialik, 1958), 138.

---

[4] Hebrew *kela'em* is taken by the commentators in an even stronger sense: "annihilate them from the world!" (Rashi).

[5] Passive plural participle of *katav* ("to write"). NJV: "among those recorded."

[6] Rashi says that Eldad and Medad were among the seventy-two elders whose names were written on parchment.

[7] Of course, Heschel would like to classify the books of Eldad and Medad in the same category: as apocryphal books that, if they only would have been preserved, would have been candidates for the Hagiographa, the third section of the Hebrew Bible.

[8] Miriam in that passage is referred to as "Miriam the prophetess, the sister of Aaron." Thus, the inference that she was a prophet when she was only the sister of Aaron, that is, before Moses was born. According to one midrashic tradition, the prophecy was precisely about the birth of Moses, who would be the deliverer.

detestable things that you are drawn to, and do not defile yourselves with the fetishes of Egypt"' (Ezekiel 20:5–7)."[16]

And now we find a mention of the "book of Eldad and Medad" preserved in early Christian literature, telling us that it comprised four hundred verses. One source cites from it the verse "The Lord is near to those who return."[17] Would that he had copied out for us the entire book![9] *Habent sua fata libelli!*[10]

In my humble opinion, there are grounds for surmising that another fragment of the "book of Eldad and Medad" is preserved in the Babylonian Talmud and Genesis Rabbah. According to one of the great masters of Aggadah, Rabbi Isaac Nappaha, a second-generation Amora of the Land of Israel, at the time of breaking camp, when Moses would say, "Arise, O Lord" (Numbers 10:35), the Israelites would respond as follows:[11]

> Raise yourself up, O acacia wood,
> Carry your splendor like a banner,
> You who are decorated with gold,
> And are enshrined in the royal palace,
> (Shrouded between the cherubim,)
> And adorned with the most precious of ornaments.[18] [12]

---

[16] *Midrash of the 32 Principles,* Principle 4, p. 17. See also Exodus Rabbah 28:6, Midrash Haggadol on Exodus, p. 67.

[17] "The Book of Eldad and Medad," and the verse I have cited in the text, are mentioned in *The Pastor* of Hermas, Vision II, chapter 3. *The Pastor* was composed in the first half of the second century C.E. See also Emil Schürer, *Geschichte des jüdischen Volkes im Zeitalter Jesu Christi,* 4th ed. (Leipzig: Hinrichs, 1909), 3:361, and Louis Ginzberg, *Legends of the Jews,* 7 volumes (Philadelphia: Jewish Publication Society, 1909–38), 6:89 n. 482.

[18] BT Avodah Zarah 24b; Genesis Rabbah 54:4. The latter source has the fifth line, and lacks the last line.

---

[9] There are surely a number of ways of translating the Hebrew phrase that Heschel uses here, which is a direct quotation from Job 19:23—"would that my words were inscribed in a book." It could mean to say "would that Eldad and Medad's words were all written down. But since Heschel here is speculating that there may indeed have been such a book (see the subsequent note), this translation seems closer to Heschel's intent.

[10] "Books have their own destinies!"

[11] In the parallel sources in Genesis Rabbah, Midrash Samuel, and *Seder Eliyahu Rabbah,* the ensuing poem is presented as the song that the oxen carrying the Ark back from Philistine captivity sang, in the time of the prophet Samuel. Only the version that has the Israelites singing this song during the desert travels would seem to fit Heschel's conjecture here that the poem comes from a lost book of Eldad and Medad.

[12] This poem uses imagery from the Torah to describe the Ark. The body of the Ark was made from acacia wood. It was overlaid with gold both inside and out. It was housed in the innermost part of God's sanctuary and was covered on top by the Cherubim. The "most precious of ornaments" with which it was adorned was, of course, God's Teaching that was laid within it.

This poem is a pearl without price. It bears the stamp of antiquity. "Without a doubt, Rabbi Isaac Nappaha did not say this out of his own head, but on the basis of tradition."[19] But from what source did he get it?

Perhaps the editor of Genesis Rabbah had the "Book of Eldad and Medad" before him. And perhaps the original text had the words *teni el'* (an abbreviation for "Eldad taught"), which a copyist later misinterpreted as *teni eliyahu* (Elijah taught).[20] [13]

Apocryphal Books

We find the following reference in Numbers 21:14: "Therefore the Book of the Wars of the Lord speaks of '. . . Waheb in Suphah, and the wadis: the Arnon . . . .'" What is the "Book of the Wars of the Lord"? According to the Jerusalem (Pseudo-Jonathan) Targum, this is simply the Torah. According to another view, this is the Book of Exodus, which records the wars that the Holy and Blessed One waged against Egypt, and most notably the battle at the Sea of Reeds.[21] The Sages also interpreted "trained in warfare" (Song of Songs 3:8) to refer to the war of Torah, as evidenced by this verse.[22] But according to Abraham ibn Ezra,[23] "there was an independent book, in which the wars of the Lord were written for His followers. It is likely that it existed from the time of Abraham. Indeed, many books were lost and are no longer in our possession, such as the words of Nathan[24] and Iddo,[25] the Annals of the Kings of Israel,[26] and the

---

[19] R. Meir Friedmann, Introduction to *Seder Eliyahu Rabbah*, p. 77. See Zunz, *Preaching in Israel* (Jerusalem: Mosad Bialik, 1954), 44.

[20] *Teni eliyahu* is the introductory formula of this poem in Genesis Rabbah and Midrash on Samuel. Since this poem is also found in *Seder Eliyahu Rabbah*, it was thought that the redactor of Genesis Rabbah drew this passage from *Seder Eliyahu Rabbah*. On this basis, some were inclined to date the latter work as early as Genesis Rabbah. See M. Zucker, *The Targum of Saadiah Gaon on the Torah* (in Hebrew) (New York, 1959), 116ff.

[21] Midrash Aggadah, ed. Buber, ad loc.

[22] Numbers Rabbah 11:13. See also PT Ta'anit 69b; Tanhuma Noah 3; Seder Olam Rabbah 25.

[23] Abraham ibn Ezra, commentary on Numbers 21:14. Bahya ben Asher (thirteenth century, Spain) seems to accept this view as well; so too Joseph Bekhor Shor (twelfth century, France).

[24] "The other events of Solomon's reign, early and late, are recorded in the chronicle of the prophet Nathan and in the prophecies of Ahijah the Shilonite and in the visions of Jedo the seer concerning Jeroboam son of Nebat" (2 Chronicles 9:29).

[25] "The other events of Abijah's reign, his conduct and his acts, are recorded in the story of the prophet Iddo" (2 Chronicles 13:22).

[26] The "Annals of the Kings of Israel" and the "Annals of the Kings of Judah" are mentioned frequently throughout the Second Book of Kings.

---

[13] We need not be overly credulous about the slim and shaky (though surely interesting) evidence Heschel brings about an actual Book of Eldad and Medad. After all, the Pseudepigrapha are filled with documents of the Hellenistic period pretending to origins of hoary antiquity. Nevertheless, the point he raises is still theologically crucial, that it is presumptuous of us to claim that the well of prophecy is exhausted with those books that have survived the whims of chance and fortune and come down to us. The names Eldad and Medad are emblematic of all those divinely inspired visionaries whose words are forever lost. Whether the specifics that Heschel brings are verifiable or not, his general proposition still stands.

Songs and Proverbs of Solomon.[27] Nahmanides also thought: "The plain sense of 'Book of the Wars of the Lord' is that in those generations there were people of sound understanding who wrote an account of the great wars, for so it is in all generations. The authors of these books were called *moshelim* ("bards"),[14] for they expressed themselves in parables (*meshalim*) and figures of speech. As for the victories which they regarded as marvelous, they ascribed them to the Lord, for they were indeed His."[28]

In RaSHBaM's view, the talmudic Sages already sensed that this was a "passage that did not belong." In the Gemara in question, we read that R. Samuel bar Nahmani said in the name of Rabbi Johanan: "'Therefore the *moshelim* say, Come to Heshbon'—*moshelim* are those who prevail over their urges; 'Come to Heshbon' means, come let us take an accounting (*heshbon*) of the world."[29] The MaHaRaL was astonished at this interpretation: "This interpretation and exegesis seem very strange, uncharacteristic of the Sages. It bears no relation at all to the context of Sihon's conquest of the city Heshbon and stretches the meaning of the words extremely far from the plain sense."[30] The commentary "*Siftei Kohen*" suggests: "They interpreted thus, because the plain sense itself is so difficult. To interpret *moshelim* as "rulers" (i.e., Balaam and his father, hired by Balak, as Rashi wrote, following Tanhuma) is problematic. In 'come [to] Heshbon,' the Hebrew text drops the particle 'to.' *Vaniram* is another strange word. The rabbis finally decided that the whole passage is here solely for the purpose of exegesis."[31]

We may suppose that this debate is connected with the earlier discussion of the place of this passage in the Torah. Rashi paraphrased the view of some rabbis, "that there was no need to write these verses, that they have no proper place in the Torah, and it is demeaning to combine them with what is sacred."[32] Rabbi Simeon ben

---

[27] "[Solomon] composed three thousand proverbs, and his songs numbered one thousand and five" (1 Kings 5:12).

[28] Nahmanides, commentary on Numbers 21:13. So far, we have the view of those who considered the Book of the Wars of the Lord an extraneous Israelite source that Moses used. But R. Isaac Abravanel and Hizkuni express the view that it was "a book of the gentiles, in which they recorded the wars that occurred in the whole world, and attributed it to the Lord, for they were indeed His." R. Samuel Sarsa attributes to R. David ibn Bilya the view: "The 'Book of the Wars of the Lord' is a name for the 'Book of the Courses of the Stars'" (*Mekor Hayyim* to Numbers 21:14).

[29] BT Bava Batra 78b; RaSHBaM ad loc.

[30] *Be'er Hagolah* (Warsaw, 5633/1873), p. 14d.

[31] *Siftei Kohen* ad loc.

[32] Rashi on BT Hullin 60b. See chapter 21 above, pp. 396–99.

---

[14] These are referred to in the continuation of the passage, Numbers 21:27: "Therefore the bards would recite: 'Come to Heshbon; firmly built and well founded is Sihon's city. . .'"—another apparent citation from an extrabiblical source. Heschel also cites other interpretations of *moshelim*: "Balaam and his father" (Exodus Rabbah 19:30); "those who invent parables out of their imagination" (Abraham ibn Ezra, ad loc.) Nahmanides suggests that they may have been bards of Sihon's own circle (loc. cit.)

Lakish cited them as an example of "scriptural passages which on the face of it seem worthy of being burned like the books of Homer, nevertheless they are essential words of Torah."[33]

It says in the Book of Joshua: "'And the sun stood still, and the moon halted, while a nation wreaked judgment on its foes'—as is written in the Book of Jashar" (Joshua 10:13). Again, the Amoraim asked: "What is the Book of Jashar? R. Hiyya bar Abba said in the name of Rabbi Johanan: This is the book of Abraham, Isaac, and Jacob who were called upright (yesharim) [i.e., Genesis]. R. Samuel bar Nahmani said: This is the Book of Judges."[34] In the Talmud of the Land of Israel, they debated the same issue. One said it was Genesis, the other said the Book of the Census (i.e., Numbers).[35]

Other Sages interpreted "Book of Jashar" allegorically, as referring to those portions of Scripture which spoke to the question of God's justice.[15] [36] But according to R. Abraham ibn Ezra, the Book of Jashar was an independent book that had existed in biblical times but was lost.[37]

We know that there were many books and scrolls in ancient Israel that the Sages consigned to the genizah.[16] "And more than these, my son, beware of making many books"[17] (Ecclesiastes 12:12)—read not mehemah ("than these") but mehumah ("confusion"), for whoever brings more than the Twenty-Four canonical books[18] into his house, brings confusion."[38] A remark is preserved in the apocryphal 2 Esdras (14:44–46),[39] that ninety-four books were written, of which twenty-four entered the canon, while seventy were excluded.

---

[33] BT Hullin 60b; Midrash Haggadol, Hukkat, manuscript at JTS. This reading should be added to those cited by Lieberman in Hellenism in Jewish Palestine, 110.

[34] BT Avodah Zarah 25a. See Genesis Rabbah 6:9.

[35] PT Sotah 17c.

[36] See Midrash on Psalms 9:2.

[37] Abraham ibn Ezra, Commentary on Exodus 17:14. See also his commentary on Esther 9:12.

[38] Ecclesiastes Rabbah ad loc.

[39] Probably written in Jerusalem in the first century C.E.

---

[15] Jashar is connected with yosher ("uprightness, justice").

[16] Genizah: A storeroom in which extracanonical books (and old, worn sacred books) were physically preserved but not to be read. In the long run, most of these books were simply lost. However, those books classed as the Apocrypha (from Greek apo + kryptein, "to hide away") were kept by the Christian church in Greek translation. In modern times, some genizot were rediscovered, especially the Cairo Genizah, from which Solomon Schechter recovered a treasure trove of ancient and medieval manuscripts. The verb ganaz (used by the Rabbis and by Heschel) means "to hide away, to place in the genizah." We have generally translated it, "excluded [from the canon]," "suppressed."

[17] NJV: "A further word: Against them, my son, be warned! The making of many books is without limit. . . ."

[18] See chapter 30, pp. 568–71, and the editorial notes there.

The "extracanonical books" were ancient books and may have been in the people's possession since the early prophets, but they were not included in Sacred Scripture. There is support for this in the words of the Talmud of the Land of Israel: "Rabbi Akiva says, 'Also one who reads in the extracanonical books [has no portion in the World to Come].' Such, for instance, are the books of Ben Sirah and Ben La'anah. But as for the books of Homer, *and all books written from this point onward,* whoever reads them is as one reading a letter. They were given for casual reflection, not for exhaustive study."[40][19]

On the other hand, some Sages raised objections to books that were eventually accepted in Scripture. They sought to exclude three books. "But one man will be remembered for good—his name is Hananiah ben Hezekiah—for were it not for him, the book of Ezekiel would have been consigned to the *genizah,* for its words [in the later chapters, dealing with the sacrifices] contradicted the Torah."[41] Similarly, they sought to exclude Proverbs, for its words were mutually inconsistent. As for Ecclesiastes, not only were its words mutually inconsistent, but they tended toward heresy.[42]

King Hezekiah suppressed the "Book of Healings," and the Sages approved his action.[43] On the other hand, they said, "From the day that the Book of Genealogies was suppressed, the strength of the Sages has failed, and the sight of their eyes has gone dim."[44] R. Simeon ben Lakish lamented this, and said, "If someone told me that the Book of Annals existed in Babylonia, I would go there and bring it here. But now, even if all our Rabbis gathered there, they could not recover it."[45]

---

[40] PT Sanhedrin 28a.
[41] BT Shabbat 13b, Hagigah 13a.
[42] BT Shabbat 30b; Leviticus Rabbah 28:1; PRK 68b.
[43] Mishnah Pesahim 4:9.
[44] BT Pesahim 62b. Rashi comments: "Because with it were lost the meanings of Torah that it contained."
[45] PT Sanhedrin 28a.

---

[19] Heschel argues here, against the accepted wisdom of biblical scholars, that instead of postdating the main books of Hebrew Scripture, the extracanonical books may have been contemporaneous with them. The evidence he gives here is weak; Ben Sirah (Ecclesiasticus) is clearly from the second century B.C.E., and we cannot identify "Ben La'anah." But by combining the standard apocryphal works (Ecclesiasticus, etc.) and the "lost books" of ancient Israel (the Book of the Wars of the Lord, etc.) under a single rubric, Heschel underlines the fact that there was a selective process of one kind or another at work in the development of the scriptural canon for approximately one thousand years. There are two points of view as to the value of the excluded works. According to Rabbi Akiva, they are false and dangerous. But according to the last views cited in this subsection (Rabbi Simeon ben Lakish, etc.), at least some of them would have rewarded great effort spent for their recovery. Again, Heschel demonstrates just how problematic is a simple-minded identification of the "divine word" with only those books that made it into the final canon.

The Book of Genesis Prior to Moses[20]

The view that Moses had recourse to books that were in the possession of the people's Sages is found in the Chronicles of Jerahmeel:[21]

> In the days of Moses our Master, there existed books in which were written the events of times gone by, from the first generations, all the way back to Adam, as we find in the Aggadah. The Book of Adam had written in it the Works of Creation and the Workings of the Chariot, in hints similar to the Amora Samuel's astronomical treatise. Adam passed it on to Seth, who passed it on to Methuselah, who passed it on to Noah, and so on through Shem, Eber, Isaac, and Jacob, who finally passed it on to Joseph and his brothers. Even in Egypt, our ancestors continued to study the traditions. When Moses wrote the commandments, he saw fit to write about how Israel received the Torah. In order to explain the events of his own time, he described the whole chain of circumstances by which the Israelites came down to Egypt, starting with the first patriarchal narratives. He looked at the books and wrote the events from the beginning according to their account. He was inspired to do this by the Holy Spirit, and thus "the power of His deeds he told to his people"[22] (Psalm 111:6).[46]

We find mention in the midrashim that the "Book of Genesis" was written before Moses' time, and he read it. "Moses returned to the Lord and said, 'O Lord, why did You bring harm upon this people?' (Exodus 5:22). It is customary among mortals, when one condemns one's fellow's action, that he address him angrily, yet Moses

---

[46] A. Neubauer, *Seder Ha-hakhamaim ve-korot ha-yamim* (Oxford, 1887), 1:163. See also M. Gaster, trans., *The Chronicles of Jerahmeel: or, The Hebrew Bible Historiale . . .* (New York, 1899).

---

[20] Up to this point, Heschel has been questioning, from a number of standpoints, the equation "Torah = God's revelation to Moses" (or "True Scripture = the twenty-four Books of the Hebrew canon"). First, there may have been true prophets (Eldad and Medad) contemporaneous with Moses, whose prophecies were not preserved. Second, there may have been chance and luck at work in the selection of the canon, and some books that were excluded may have been worthy of inclusion. He goes a step farther now and suggests that there may have been revelations of truth *prior* to Moses, and Moses may have used these early revelations as sources in composing the Torah. There is support for this in the main narrative thrust of the Bible. God created human beings in order to be known by them. Adam, Noah, and the Patriarchs were the most prominent among those to whom God gave revelations, but not the only ones. Why, then, restrict the true Torah to what began with Moses?

The question is a commonplace for moderns. But Heschel shows here that it was the subject of lively debate in the mainstream of medieval Jewish thought as well.

[21] Jerahmeel ben Solomon, twelfth century, Italy.

[22] NJV: "He revealed to His people His powerful works." The implied subject in the psalm so translated (as generally understood) is God. See, e.g., Rashi's very first comment on Genesis 1:1. But Jerahmeel understands the subject of the verse to be *Moses* (and thus the lower case "he" and "his" in the translation given here). That is, Moses informed the Israelites of the power of God's deeds, and he did so by citing earlier works that he neither authored nor had dictated to him (though Jerahmeel is careful to add that in this project, he was at least inspired by the Holy Spirit).

addressed the Holy and Blessed One reverently—'O Lord, why did You bring harm . . .'!
This is what Moses said: *'I took the Book of Genesis and read it,* and I saw how the generation of the Flood was punished, and how the generation of Babel and the
Sodomites were punished. But what has this people done, that they have been
enslaved more than the other generations?'"[47][23] And other midrashim attest that
while the Israelites were slaves in Egypt, "they possessed scrolls with which they
would delight themselves on the Sabbaths, to remind them that the Holy and Blessed
One was going to redeem them."[48]

Maimonides was familiar with this view.[24] The Sages said that thirteen covenants
were established concerning circumcision.[49] Some said that "these thirteen
covenants are all implicit in the Torah's account of circumcision,[25] that they were
spoken to Abraham, who remembered them and wrote them down. When Moses our
Master came, he copied into the Torah those sentences that Abraham had written,
just as ordinary people cite the words and verses of others into their own writings."
Maimonides disparaged the holders of this view as "the blind who want to be considered as among the seeing. . . . Whoever does not believe that these verses were spoken
together with all the rest of the Torah by the Divine Power, is to be classed with those
who say that the Torah is not from heaven. . . . We make no distinctions in the Torah.
'Torah, which Moses commanded us'[26] (Deuteronomy 33:4)—it is all from Moses,
from the Blessed Lord. Whatever it may contain from previous times, such as the
Seven Commandments of Noah, or circumcision from Abraham, we accept and
believe not because of the earlier command but because of the latest command
addressed to us, the congregation of Jacob.[27] To elaborate on this further would be a
waste of time."[50]

[47] Exodus Rabbah 5:22.
[48] Exodus Rabbah 5:18; Tanhuma Va'era 6; YS I,176.
[49] BT Shabbat 132a.
[50] Maimonides, responsum to Joseph ben Gabir of Baghdad, in *Ta'am Zekenim,* p. 74; *Letters and
Responsa of Rambam,* II, 16a. Maimonides follows the same principle in the Mishnei Torah, *Hilkhot
Melakhim* 8:11: "Whoever accepts the seven Noahide commands and performs them scrupulously is
counted among the righteous of the gentiles, and has a portion in the world to come—that is, providing
that he accepts and performs them because the Holy and Blessed One commanded them in the Torah, and
because He made known through Moses our Master that the Noahides in antiquity were charged with

---

[23] The point of the midrash is that Moses spoke not to condemn God's action but to request an
explanation of the people's suffering. Heschel's point is that, according to the midrashist, Genesis was
already in existence early in Moses' career, before the revelation at Sinai, and was apparently written
before Moses was born.
[24] But he rejected it, as the sequel makes clear.
[25] Because the word *berit* ("covenant") occurs thirteen times in the passage.
[26] NJV: "When Moses charged us with the Teaching . . . ."
[27] Another way of expressing this idea would be to say that the recorded events may have happened, and certain practices may have been adopted in the past, but any pre-Sinai record of those
events or practices is history, but not yet Torah. Torah comes only with God's spoken word at Sinai.

When Moses our Master was selected at the burning bush to be the emissary of the Holy and Blessed One in the redemption of Israel, he said, "When I come to the Israelites and say to them, 'The God of your fathers has sent me to you,' and they ask me, 'What is his name?' what shall I say to them?" (Exodus 3:13). Moses was sure that the Israelites would know the name of the Holy and Blessed One, "for it was a tradition that their elders had from previous generations, as it is written, 'I am the Lord who brought you out from Ur of the Chaldeans' (Genesis 15:7). But Moses himself did not know the Divine Name, for he was not privy to the traditions of the elders. Therefore he asked, 'What shall I tell them is His name?'"[51]

But why did it occur to Moses to ask this? He reasoned: "The angel wrestled with Jacob, and when it came time to part, he asked him, 'What is your name?'[28] I, who am speaking with the Shekhinah, how much more so!"[52] This midrash is based on the assumption that this story was familiar to Moses when the Holy and Blessed One revealed Himself to him at the burning bush.[29]

Also, "the secret of intercalating the year was passed from Adam to Noah, who passed it to Shem, who passed it to Jacob, and so on to Kohath and Amram, from whom Moses received it."[30] [53]

According to R. Hama bar Hanina, "there was never a time that our ancestors did not engage in study. When they were in Egypt, they engaged in study." Abraham,

---

them. But if one performs them because of the dictates of reason, such a one is not a 'resident alien,' and is not included among the righteous of the gentiles, but among their Sages." Similarly, in his Commentary on the Mishnah, Hullin chapter 7, Maimonides wrote that Jews do not observe the prohibition of the "limb of the living animal" because of Noah, nor circumcision because of Abraham, nor the prohibition of the sciatic nerve because of Jacob, but all of them solely because they were commanded by Moses. BT Hullin 101b corroborates his view: "The sciatic nerve was communicated at Sinai, but written in the relevant place." Rashi comments: "This Scripture ('That is why the children of Israel to this day do not eat the thigh muscle that is on the socket of the hip' [Genesis 32:33]) was not spoken at Sinai, but after Moses received it at Sinai and came to write the Torah, he wrote this prohibition in the context of the narrative [of Jacob's wrestling with the angel], so one might know the reason why it was prohibited." According to the Gemara, the sons of Jacob themselves were permitted to eat the sciatic nerve. "Would the Torah have been given multiple times?"

[51] Midrash Sekhel Tov on Exodus 3:13.
[52] Sekhel Tov, loc. cit.; Lekah Tov ad loc.
[53] Sekhel Tov and Lekah Tov on Exodus 3:13–15 (based on PRE 7:1).

---

[28] In the verse with this wording (Genesis 32:28), it is the angel who asks for Jacob's name. But later on, in slightly different words, Jacob asks the angel the same thing—which is a better parallel to the case of Moses asking God's name.

[29] This is one of many midrashim in which later biblical characters cite the precedents of earlier characters as a context for their actions or as evidence of the right thing to do in respect of God's will. Heschel is drawing on the deep structure of the biblical narrative itself, as elucidated by the midrash, to support the view of revelation as an ongoing process, not a once-and-finished event.

[30] As the Hebrew lunar calendar was 354 days long, an extra month had to be added approximately once in three years to keep it roughly in synchronization with the solar year. This was done by a rabbinic court. It was thus a legal (halakhic) procedure, based on expert knowledge, a part of Oral Torah revealed ultimately by God. According to this statement, this revelation occurred not at Sinai but at the beginning of human history. Again, divine revelation is not coextensive with Sinaitic Torah.

Isaac, Jacob, Eliezer the servant of Abraham—every one of them was "an elder [teacher] and resident [studying] at a yeshivah."[54] [31] When Joseph parted from his father Jacob, he knew what chapter they were studying; indeed, Jacob was teaching him the chapter of the broken-necked heifer.[55] [32] Jacob studied Torah all his life.[56] He studied in the academy of Shem and Eber, and all the *halakhot* that Shem and Eber transmitted to Jacob he passed on to Joseph.[57] The Torah of the patriarchs was preserved until Moses' generation. It was a tradition in Israel that whoever would proclaim, "I have taken note of you" (Exodus 3:16) would be the one to redeem them.[58] It is said of those who left Egypt, that they possessed Torah and the prophetic books.[59] Before Moses took charge, Aaron prophesied in Egypt for eighty years.[60] Therefore Moses initially refused, at the burning bush, to accept God's mission: "I shall enter my brother's domain, and he will be vexed."[61] According to Maimonides, thousands and myriads flocked to Abraham, and they are referred to as "the men of Abraham's household." He planted the faith in God in their hearts and composed books for them.[62]

The Great Hallel (Psalm 136)

An ancient Baraita in Tractate Bava Batra states: "David wrote the Book of Psalms, with the aid of ten elders."[63] One of these was Moses. Another source declares that

---

[54] BT Yoma 28b.   [55] Genesis Rabbah 95:3; 43:1.

[56] YS Psalms 874.   [57] Genesis Rabbah 68:5; 84:8.

[58] Exodus Rabbah 3:8; Midrash Haggadol to Genesis 50:24 ("God will surely take notice of you and bring you up from this land . . .").

[59] SER 21, p. 124.   [60] Exodus Rabbah 3:19.

[61] Exodus Rabbah 3:21.   [62] Mishneh Torah, *Hilkhot Avodah Zarah* 1:3.

[63] BT Bava Batra 14b. These are enumerated: Adam (Psalm 139), Melchizedek (Psalm 110), Abraham (identified with "Ethan," Psalm 89), Moses (Psalm 90 etc.), the three sons of Korah (Psalms 42–49, 84–88), Asaf (Psalms 50, 73–83), Heman (Psalm 88), and Jeduthun (Psalms 39, 62, and 77) (Rashi ad loc.).

---

[31] The word *yeshivah* comes from the verb *yashav* ("to sit, reside"). *Avot* records the proverb, "Who increases *yeshivah*, increases wisdom." Thus, the tradition says that the patriarchs were resident at a place of study, where they sat and engaged in study. The Sages of the rabbinic period (and later) portrayed the patriarchs as maintaining the classic institutions of later Jewish learning.

[32] Deuteronomy 21:1–9 tells of the ritual breaking of a heifer's neck when an unidentified corpse was found. This was a significant omen of the next event in the Joseph story (when the brothers delivered the blood-stained coat, and Jacob gave up Joseph for dead). It was also, in rabbinic midrash, considered to be the key to understanding why Jacob believed the brothers' later report that they had seen Joseph alive in Egypt (as reported in Genesis 45:27) only when he caught sight of the wagons that Joseph had sent to move the family down. For "wagons" in Hebrew are 'agalot, a word that has a direct orthographic and phonetic connection to 'eglah, a heifer. More to Heschel's purpose, we have here yet another reference to the Torah as a literary document that was studied prior to the Sinai revelation. From the Akivan viewpoint (the only one that can make sense of this point of view), this means that although the preexisting Torah was revealed to the entire people after the Exodus, it was nevertheless available to the elect long before the Israelites entered the Sinai peninsula.

Moses wrote eleven psalms, corresponding to the eleven tribes that he blessed.[64] [33] Rashi ascribes Psalms 90 through 100 to Moses.[65] But they are not of the same sanctity as the Torah. Rabbi Levi said in the name of Rabbi Hanina, "The eleven psalms that Moses said, he said in the capacity of a prophet. Why are they not written in the Torah? Because words of Torah and words of prophecy must be kept separate." Yet there is a view that one psalm that Moses authored—Psalm 136—was once part of the Pentateuch.

R. Menahem Ziyyoni[34] wrote: "According to R. Judah the Hasid, the Great Hallel (Psalm 136) was written after Israel was rescued from Sihon and Og, and crossed the wadi Arnon. It was written in the Pentateuch, until King David (peace be his) came and removed the Psalms of Moses, and included them in the Book of Psalms. The last two verses ("Who gives food to all flesh . . . Praise the God of heaven . . .") allude to the manna, which was food from heaven. Joshua wrote Psalm 135 on the model of Psalm 136, adding only the detail that God struck down (in addition to Sihon and Og) "all the royalty of Canaan" (135:11), as if to say, "This miracle occurred through me." When David conquered Jerusalem, he added the last verse to Psalm 135: "Blessed is the Lord from Zion, He who dwells in Jerusalem. Hallelujah." This was their habit in those days, that when they wished to establish a song for a miracle, they would search for a good source, as it says, "In assemblies bless God" (Psalm 68:27)."[35] [66]

The Books of Balaam and Job

Do not be astonished that there are verses in the Torah that are not part of Moses' prophecy, for we find entire chapters that are from the prophecy of Balaam the son of Beor.[36]

[64] PRK 198a.
[65] Rashi on BT Bava Batra 14b.
[66] Menaham Ziyyoni, commentary on Hukkat, according to Adler MS 528 in JTS library.

---

[33] In Deuteronomy 33, we find Moses' blessings of the tribes. There is no mention there of the tribe of Simeon.

[34] Menahem Ziyyoni: kabbalist, fourteenth–fifteenth centuries, Cologne.

[35] The view that Heschel cites is interesting in one respect and astonishing in another. It is interesting inasmuch as it portrays the gradual evolution of the Psalms as embodying the experiences of individuals (Joshua, David) who wished to find a suitable medium for praising God, and who adapted existing models to express their unique circumstances. It is astonishing, inasmuch as it suggests that David (who lived generations after the Sinai revelation) did not consider the text of the Torah sacrosanct but saw fit to remove what he considered extraneous portions (Psalms 90–101 and 136) and to transfer them into the new Book of Psalms that he was composing. Was this, too, the working of the Holy Spirit?

[36] In the Hebrew edition, this paragraph and the following are found at the start of the subsection "Apocryphal Books."

It is taught in a Baraita, "Moses wrote his book and the episode of Balaam [and Job]."[67] The Sages expressed astonishment: What are we to infer from this? "Is there a single letter in the Torah that was not written by Moses? Isn't the episode of Balaam in the Torah?"[68] In our view, this Baraita means to tell us, that not everything a prophet wrote in his book was received by him from the divine source. Sometimes he would include in his book the prophecies of other prophets, just as David included the work of ten of his predecessors in the Book of Psalms.[69]

Some did indeed think that Moses wrote a separate book called "the Book of Balaam." R. Joshua ibn Shuaib[37] suggested: "It appears, from the statement of our Rabbis, that Moses composed another book in addition to what he wrote in the Torah. This included the narratives of Balaam and Job. It was a separate book, and was lost, just as other books were lost from the present collection of twenty-four sacred scriptures.[70]

RITBA[38] espoused this view,[71] as did Menahem Ziyyoni.[72] We find it in the Talmud of the Land of Israel: "Moses wrote five books of the Torah, then went back and wrote the episodes of Balak and Balaam, and the book of Job."[73]

According to R. Menahem Azariah of Fano,[39] the "Book of Balaam" refers to a number of verses that Moses wrote, which were later included in the Book of Joshua. "This is the scroll which Moses passed to Joshua, starting 'And so Moses assigned [the following] to the tribe of the Reubenites' (Joshua 13:15), to the end of the chapter, and including the verse 'The Israelites put Balaam son of Beor, the augur, to the

---

[67] BT Bava Batra 14b.

[68] R. Isaiah Horowitz, *Shnei Luhot Ha-berit* (Frankfurt-on-Oder, 5477/1717), 362b.

[69] See preceding section.

[70] Sermons of Joshua ibn Shuaib, Pinhas.

[71] Novellae of Ritba on Bava Batra 15a.

[72] Ziyyoni, Sermons, on Balak.

[73] PT Sotah 20d. R. Louis Ginzberg wrote (in *Perushim ve-hidushim ba-Yerushalmi* [New York: Ktav, 1971], 1:167): "Some heretics would challenge Israel and say that not all the Torah was from Moses, but it included additions from later generations. They especially disputed the truth of such narratives as the episode of Balak and Balaam. Since Moses was not present with Balak and Balaam, how would he know the discussions that took place between them? . . . To refute these heretical views, the rabbis especially emphasized that Moses wrote his book as well as the episode of Balaam. . . . Thus the Talmud of the Land of Israel states (Berakhot 3b) that it would have been proper even to read the portions of Balak and Balaam publicly every day in the synagogue, as a public statement that the whole Torah was written by Moses, only they did not want to burden the community. This tradition is cited immediately after the statement that they abolished the recitation of the Ten Commandments on account of the heretics [who would argue that *only* the Ten Commandments were revealed], and for the same reason, they were prepared to institute the reading of these two portions."

---

[37] Kabbalist and preacher, fourteenth century, Spain.

[38] R. Yom Tov ben Abraham Ishbili, thirteenth–fourteenth century, Spain, talmudic commentator.

[39] Sixteenth- to seventeenth-century Italian kabbalist.

sword' (13:22). Since it was so short, Joshua combined it with his book, just as Isaiah included the two verses of Beeri, the father of Hosea."[74] [40]

Moses Did Not Transmit Everything

Moses our Master did not transmit to Israel everything that he received. Thus Rabbi Isaac interpreted, "And *me* did the Lord command" (Deuteronomy 4:14)—"The word 'me' is superfluous. Don't we know, that Moses spoke and taught the entire Torah? But it intimates that 'God told me certain things to impart to you, and other things that were meant for my ears only.'"[75] In connection with the red heifer, Rabbi Yose said in the name of Rabbi Hanina, "The Holy and Blessed One said to Moses, 'I will reveal the purpose of this ordinance to you, but to others it will seem an arbitrary fiat.'"[76] The purposes of the mitzvot are among those things of which it was said, "Those things which are hidden from you in this world, will be clear in the world to come." R. Menahem Ziyyoni also wrote, "Whatever Moses our Master (peace be his) saw in all the chambers of heaven, in the innermost houses and also the outer houses, he did not reveal in the manner of the other prophets. Should you think he did not see them, it is written: 'He is trusted throughout My household' (Numbers 12:7). He has seen everything in My house, and He knows all the staircases and levels, all the ways and paths and dimensions. For above is the Holy Spirit, with open eyes.[41]"[77]

R. Menahem Azariah of Fano comments on the nuance of the Mishnah's language,[42] "Moses received *Torah* from Sinai and passed it on to Joshua": "Not *the* Torah, for we are not speaking here of the hidden essence of Torah, which is not

---

[74] *Imerot Tehorot,* "Ma'amar Hikkur Ha-Din" 5:8.
[75] PT Avodah Zarah 41d; Song of Songs Rabbah on 1:2b.
[76] Numbers Rabbah 19:6.
[77] Menahem Ziyyoni on Beha'alotekha.

---

[40] The verses in question are Isaiah 8:19–20. On the intriguing matter of this brief prophecy of Beeri, see Leviticus Rabbah 6.

To sum up this section, it appears that the episode of Balaam is another "boundary question" with respect to the extent to which the Torah is the total embodiment of Mosaic authorship and divine revelation. Again, the possibilities that Heschel entertains question this identity, but in different ways. On the one hand, he points out the possibility that the Torah's episode of Balaam may be divinely inspired but non-Mosaic (on the view that Moses included Balaam's genuine prophecies in his own book). On the other hand, the Baraita may be referring to another Book of Balaam, authored by Moses but now lost. Either way, the simple equation "Torah = God's revelation = Moses' *oeuvre*" is challenged.

[41] And since the Holy Spirit would inspire Moses when he ascended heaven, then Moses too would have clear vision of all that was in the supernal realm.

[42] In Avot 1:1.

susceptible to receiving and transmission, but only to intellectual apprehension. Indeed, at Sinai Moses had dealings with the very Delight[43] itself, but he was not permitted to pass it on to others." He distinguishes between "the very Delight itself" with which Moses had dealings, and the *"vessel* of delight,"[44] which he received for the need of others, so that they should know what to do, for Moses was not himself in need of raising his soul to a higher level through deeds. This is the meaning of 'The Lord spoke to Moses *lemor*' ('to say')—that is, to say to Israel. For Moses and Israel were not equal, but each received from God's word what was fitting for him: the esoteric meaning for Moses, the exoteric for Israel."[78]

R. Phinehas Horowitz,[45] author of *Hafla'ah,* commented on the verse, "Then the Lord said to Moses, 'Inscribe this in a document as a reminder, and speak it in Joshua's ears'"[46] (Exodus 17:14):

> One may interpret this . . . that the Lord did not want to proclaim this among all of Israel, as we find in the midrash of "I Am Who I Am" (Exodus 3:14), that God did not want to make the exile known to anyone but Moses.[47] So too here. Therefore the text says, "Speak it in Joshua's ears," i.e., whisper it to him privately. . . . It says, "Inscribe this in a document"—referring to the message whose totality was shown to Moses (in his prayer), with the full forms of the letters. The Zohar explains that the word *zot* ("this") refers often to this aspect, as here: "Inscribe this in a document as a reminder." Our Sages said that the Sages impart these things to their students privately, as it says, "Speak it in Joshua's ears." Israel was given a remembrance of it in writing, but did not hear it directly; but God gave Moses permission to impart it privately to his student Joshua, as our rabbis (of blessed memory) said, "Moses received Torah . . . and imparted it to Joshua."[79] [48]

[78] *Imerot Tehorot,* "Ma'amar Hikkur Ha-Din" 2:6; *Yad Yehudah* ad loc.
[79] *Panim Yafot* on Beshalah.

---

[43] This word (*hemdah* in Hebrew) seems to be something of a synonym for *kavod,* or Glory—a word that is meant to denote something like the luminous Presence of God.

[44] Rabbi Akiva calls the Torah "vessel of delight" in Avot 3:14. Needless to say, a "vessel" of X is never quite X itself.

[45] Eighteenth century, Poland and Germany.

[46] NJV: ". . . read it aloud to Joshua."

[47] According to Exodus Rabbah 3:6, the meaning of the duplication of "I am" was that God promised: "As I am with you in the current troubles, so will I be with you in future troubles." Moses objected: "It is enough that they worry themselves about the current trouble alone!" God relented: "Say, '"I am" sent me to you'—I will tell you about the future troubles, but I will not tell them."

[48] We have here the interesting notion, found elsewhere in Heschel's writings as well, that there is an important difference between what is the content of revelation, and what can be captured in a text. This is an excellent way of understanding the concept that Moses did not transmit everything, since he simply couldn't.

34

IT IS NOT IN THE HEAVENS

Translator's Introduction

With this chapter, the third Hebrew volume of *TMH* begins. This is the first chapter that was not published in Heschel's lifetime. Indeed, it was first published in 1990, some eighteen years after his death. More will be said about the redaction of this third volume in the introduction to chapter 37. For now, it should be noted that this third volume was given, at publication, a Hebrew subtitle meaning "both these and these are words of the living God." Coming as a continuation of volume 2, which was subtitled "Torah from Sinai and Torah from Heaven," the present subtitle indicates, accurately, that Heschel's ultimate goal in this work is to argue for the inevitability of some kind of synthesis between the views that he has been explicating. In fact, "both these and these . . ." has a double meaning in these closing chapters of the work. On the one hand, it refers to the plurality of voices that are made inevitable by the fact that God's word is mediated through human agency, and with human partnership. In this sense, the phrase mirrors much of what has been established as an Ishmaelian approach to revealed religion. As the title of chapter 36, the phrase is used in this sense. But as the subtitle of the entire volume, "both these and these . . ." is referring to something that looms even larger in Heschel's mind. It is the necessity of incorporating both the Ishmaelian and the Akivan, the human, rationalistic, history-bound understanding of revealed religion, and the supernatural, spiritual, and timeless understanding. As Heschel will tell us later on, failure to incorporate both of these yields a religious worldview that is flat and lacking in depth of field.

And so, in this chapter, Heschel will, on the one hand, bring to our attention many interesting rabbinic and medieval insights into the inescapable human element of revelation. He will even (and this is somewhat ironic, given his own history at Jewish Theological Seminary) present us with an analysis from the Geonic period of the real source of the Torah's sanctity that could have been written by Mordecai Kaplan in the twentieth century. But in a later subsection, he will argue that too much attention to the historical when it comes to revelation is to "ask time-bound questions in the face of the eternal." He is also arguing for "both . . . and . . ." when it comes to the legacy of the "fathers of the world," or (as we have called them) the "eternal paradigms." At the end of the present chapter, he reminds us that the Torah's unity is not destroyed by historical analysis, nor does its reclaiming depend on reconstructing a redactional process, but rather on the conviction (as always, a matter of faith) that the Torah reflects the divine will, which is perforce unitary.

It Is Not in the Heavens

AS IT IS USUALLY UNDERSTOOD, there are two mutually exclusive elaborations of the fundamental of the faith which we shall call: "Torah from Heaven" and "It is not in the heavens." With respect to the latter, the greatest of the Sages struggled mightily; and some of their dealings with it can be overheard in their disagreement over a matter of purity and impurity (the so-called "Akhnai Oven"[1]).

Rabbi Eliezer ben Hyrcanus, always stalwart in his positions and unswerving in following his received traditions, refused in the course of this disputation to submit to the view of the majority of the Sages, even though they pressured him with arguments and legalisms:

> On that day Rabbi Eliezer advanced every possible logical argument, but they did not accept them. He then said: "If the law is with me, this carob tree will prove it!" The tree then uprooted itself and moved one hundred cubits (some say four hundred cubits). They said to him: "Proof cannot be brought from a carob tree!" Again, he said to them: "If the law is with me, this stream of water will prove it!" The stream then began to flow backwards. They said to him: "Proof cannot be brought from a water stream!" Again, he said to them: "If the law is with me, the walls of the house of study will prove it!" The walls of the house of study tilted as if to fall. Rabbi Yehoshua (ben Hanania) scolded them, saying: "If scholars are attempting to best one another in Halakhah, what is it your business?" The walls did not fall out of respect to Rabbi Yehoshua, yet they did not stand upright out of respect for Rabbi Eliezer; they remain tilted still. Again, he said to them: "If the law is with me, proof shall be brought from Heaven!" An echoing voice rang out and said: "Why bother Rabbi Eliezer, seeing as the law is *always* with him!"[2] Rabbi Yehoshua stood up and declared: "It is not in the heavens!"[3] [1]

---

[1] BT Bava Metzia 59b.

---

[1] What this phrase means is not entirely clear. Since *akhna* in Aramaic denotes a snake, the Talmud understands the import to be that the issue surrounding this oven and its purity status was the occasion for the Rabbis to assert their authority and power as does a snake that has encircled its victim. This striking image will be borne out below. It is also possible that it simply refers to a serpentine construction of the oven chambers, or that it has nothing to do with snakes at all.

[2] Thus, there is a progression in this text: Rabbi Eliezer first appeals to the realm of logic in order to win others over to the validity of his point. Failing at that, he then appeals to the forces of nature —first a one-time occurrence (the uprooting of the tree), then a continuous occurrence (the stream flowing backwards), and finally a potentially fatal collapse that threatens the Sages directly. At last, he must appeal to the supernatural realm.

[3] This is a quotation from Deuteronomy 30:12.

What meaning did Rabbi Yehoshua intend in his use of the phrase "It is not in the heavens"? According to Rabbi Jeremiah, a third- to fourth-generation Amora, it was: "We pay no heed to an echoing voice, because You have already written in the Torah given at Sinai: 'to tilt in favor of the multitude' (Exodus 23:2)."[4] It was told of the Tanna Rabbi Nathan: "Rabbi Nathan encountered Elijah, and said to him: 'What did God do at that hour?' Elijah said to him: 'He smiled and said: "My children have defeated Me, My children have defeated Me."'" In other words: all of the wonders performed that day demonstrated that the Holy and Blessed One said that the law was with Rabbi Eliezer, and the echoing voice had declared: "Why bother Rabbi Eliezer, seeing as the law is *always* with him!" And nevertheless, Rabbi Yehoshua stuck to his conviction that the Torah is entrusted to the Sages, who have the authority to determine the *halakhah* as they see it.[2]

Rabbi Yehoshua's words are bold, and were they not in the text before us we could not say them. Is it possible that a declaration destined for mortals through miraculous means, in accordance with the will of God, should be ignored? What hubris! It is clear that the intention was to determine that the *understanding* of Torah was entrusted to the Sages; that is, the Torah was not given exclusively from the mind of God; it is refracted also through the interpretation of the Sages.

The principle "It is not in the heavens" constitutes a turning point in the history of the religion of Israel. Many generations had passed from the cessation of prophecy, and many lamented that cessation. But what was the antidote, the consolation? In the polemics surrounding the Akhnai Oven was born the idea that the Sages are the

---

[2] BT Bava Metzia 59b; BT Berakhot 52a, and other places.

---

[4] The use of the verse from Exodus 23 serves at least two purposes here. On the literary level, it ties the story together, for the word translated here as "to tilt" is the same word that is used to describe the tilting of the walls of the house of study at Rabbi Eliezer's command. But more important, there is a profound irony in the use of this verse. For the Torah does not apparently intend to instruct us that the majority should always be followed. On the contrary, the simple meaning of the verse seems to be quite the opposite: that majorities can be wrong, and contrary to the will of God, and that we must take care not to follow a multitude blindly. That is why the NJV translation renders these words not as "to tilt in favor ..." but rather as "to pervert in favor ...." It is only by taking the last three words of the verse (*aharei rabim le-hattot*) out of the larger context that Rabbi Jeremiah can claim that it means that we should always "tilt" in favor of a majority! Indeed, Rabbi Yehoshua's verse "it is not in the heavens" is *itself* quoted out of context. For in Deuteronomy, its intent is to reassure Israel that it has access to the teachings of God and that they do not need another Moses to ascend to heaven. It does not, however, seem to suggest that God has no part or say in how the Torah's words are to be understood or used. Thus, the medium and the message here converge. The story is here to tell us something about the ways in which the Rabbis claimed the authority to interpret the word of God autonomously, and the proof texts brought are proof texts only because they are being construed in a very nonstandard way, suited specifically to the rabbinic purposes here. Heschel does not intend this to be a cynical representation of rabbinic power games, but rather an emphatic statement of the intimacy the Rabbis had with the text of the Torah, and thus the ease with which they asserted their custodianship over it.

inheritors of the prophets, and that the voice of the Sages outweighs an echoing voice from Heaven.

There crystallized the idea that the Torah flows from two sources: the wellspring of prophecy and the wellspring of human wisdom. Just as Moses took certain actions on his own initiative, so did the Sages claim to know many things from their own reasoning. The Torah itself said: "Should a legal matter elude you . . . go to the levitical priests and to the judge . . . they shall inform you of the law . . . do not swerve from their teaching right or left" (Deuteronomy 17:8–11). And the Sifre contains this exegesis: "even if they represent to you that right is left and left is right, obey them."[3] [5]

Moreover, the Sages were so bold as to (anachronistically) subordinate prophets to *their* contemporary Sages, and they stated that they could not speak without leave from the Sanhedrin! Ovadiah, for example, prophesied only by leave of the Sanhedrin. Even Isaiah prophesied only by leave of the Sanhedrin. Even though they prophesied the word of the Holy and Blessed One, were the Sanhedrin to remove its sanction, they would not have had permission to prophesy; that is why they both began with the word *Hazon,* the numerical value of which is 71—for they both prophesied by leave of the Sanhedrin of 71.[4]

Thus, we have the bold statement of Rabbi Avdimi of Haifa (a second to third generation Palestinian Amora): "On the day that the Temple was destroyed, prophecy was taken from the prophets and given over to the Sages."[6] And according to Amemar, one of the greats of the fifth to sixth generations of Amoraim, "A Sage outranks a prophet."[5]

Indeed, Pirkoi ben Baboi[7] polemicized against the Karaites (a medieval sect that denied the authority of the rabbinic exegetical tradition) as follows: "A beautiful

---

[3] Sifre, Shofetim, 154; in contradistinction to this, PT Horayot 1:1 (45d) has the following exegesis: "Might you think that if they tell you that right is left and left is right you should obey them? The verse thus says: 'to go to the right or the left'—that is, when they tell you that right is right and that left is left.'"

[4] Yalkut Shim'oni, Isaiah, 385.

[5] BT Bava Batra 12a.

---

[5] This exegesis in the Sifre indicates quite clearly to what extent this "populist" idea of the Torah not being in heaven, but rather subject to human understanding, can be a prelude to hierarchical and coercive structures. For it may be that a rabbinic elite will claim such mastery over the text that it will literally assert that its courts must be followed, even if they apparently call right left and left right. That is what makes Heschel's footnote to PT Horayot so crucial here, for it shows that even within the rabbinic world, there were different tendencies with respect to how exegetical power was to be used, and whether it was still answerable to some standard. This difference between the Sifre and PT Horayot concerned many later commentators. Of special interest is the treatment given it within the last century by David Tsevi Hoffmann, *The Highest Court* (New York: Maurosho Publications, 1977).

[6] Prophecy was, of course, understood to have ended long before 70 C.E. However, the point being made is that it was in some sense God's will that prophecy be replaced by the activity of the Sages, and that assertion is best made by linking it to a dramatic event in which people were accustomed to see the hand of God. The net effect, it should be noted, is to ameliorate considerably, from the rabbinic point of view, the catastrophe of the Temple's destruction.

[7] A rabbinic figure associated with the Geonic Babylonian academy of Rav Yehudai Gaon.

woman of deviant character (is like a gold ring in a swine's nose)" (Proverbs 11:22)
—"A beautiful woman" means the written Torah, which is as beautiful as gold, and
when a person does not heed the words of the Sages, that person is like a swine, for it
is written: "the scoundrel believes that there is no God" (Psalm 14:1)—the Sages
interpreted: "scoundrel" (*nabal*) can only mean a swine, which filthies (*menabel*)
itself with dung and other filth, and a swine is one who has learned the written Torah
but has denied the Oral Torah, and denied the authority of the Sages—and when a
person has learned the Written Torah but not the Oral Torah, which is the exegesis of
the Written Torah, we have a "beautiful woman of deviant character" who understands nothing.[6]

> Whence do we know that we are to blow the Shofar on Rosh Hashanah [at all]?[8] [Pre-
> sumably, from the explicit command in the written Torah.] And whence do we know
> that the written Torah is in fact the one written by Moses from the words of the All-
> Powerful? Why, it is only on the authority of the people Israel! And the very same who
> testify to the latter also testify that we fulfill our obligation by these acts (the specific
> musical notes under consideration), and indeed that they have been transmitted by tra-
> dition through the prophets, going back to Moses at Sinai. The majority determines each
> Mishnah and Gemara. And quite apart from all such proofs, "go see what the folk does."
> This is the main point and the main authority. Only after that do we look at what has
> been written in the Mishnah or the Gemara on the subject. Whatever can be inferred
> from them is well and good; but whatever is in those texts that appears to contradict our
> experience and does not stand up to scrutiny cannot override the main authority.[7]

"Rabbi Shimon ben Menasia said: The Torah says, 'Keep the Sabbath for it is holy
to you' (Exodus 31:13)—the Sabbath is entrusted to you; you are not given over to
it."[8] [9] Such statements make the rooftops shudder, they make the world of Halakhah
quake. Shall we say that in the relationship between the Sabbath and Israel, *Israel* is
the principal party? That the Sabbath is beholden to humanity, and not vice versa?
We would thereby turn the tables thoroughly: the first would become last, and the
last first!

Truthfully, this mighty statement, reverberating as it does in rabbinic literature,
stands virtually without echo or respondent. And yet it has a companion which is a
keystone in the edifice of the sanctification of festivals:

[6] *Ginzei Schechter*, 2:570ff.
[7] *Otzar Hageonim*, Rosh Hashanah, pp. 62ff.
[8] MI, Shabbata, ch. 1.

---

[8] The text Heschel is quoting from here is a responsum of Rav Hai Gaon, a major figure in the
rabbinic academies of Babylonia in the eleventh century. The responsum is directed to a query concerning how the various sequences of notes sounded on the Shofar on Rosh Hashanah (e.g. Teki'ah,
Shevarim, Teru'ah, Teki'ah) were arrived at.

[9] The similarity to Jesus' statements in the Gospels concerning the relationship between Shabbat
and human authority is noteworthy and is undoubtedly why Heschel proceeds to speak of such texts
as "making the rooftops shudder."

"This month is for you" (Exodus 12:2)—"It is entrusted to you; you are not given over to it."[9] Similarly:

> The ministering angels said in the presence of the Holy and Blessed One: "Master of the Universe, on what days are you fixing the festivals?" . . . God said to them: "You and I will agree to whatever Israel concludes concerning the intercalation of the year. . . . "These are God's festivals, the sacred times, which you shall proclaim in their season" (Leviticus 23:4)—You—whether it be their proper time or not . . . formerly, the festivals were in my hands (as it says: "God made the moon for the festivals" [Psalm 104:19]), but hereafter, they are entrusted to you, they are in your realm. Should you say yes, it will be yes, and if no, no. Whatever the case, this month shall be *yours*. Moreover, should you wish to intercalate[10] the year, I shall agree to it. Thus it says: "This month is for you."[10]

No single generation can make constructions for *all* generations. But in every generation the officers of Israel construct and innovate and thus add to those who preceded them.[11]

Without Sages There Is No Torah

The giving of the written Torah is the beginning, not the end, of Torah. "When the Holy and Blessed One gave the Torah to Israel, it was given as wheat or flax are given to have flour or garments produced from them."[12] "Had the Torah been given cut and dried (as uncontroverted judgments) we would have no leg to stand on."[13][11] "Without Sages there is no Torah."[14]

According to Rabbi Ishmael, there are three places in which the Halakhah circumvents Scripture. Even though the sense of Scripture is otherwise, Halakhah comes and uproots the surface meaning.[15] Rabbi Judah the Patriarch devoted a whole chapter of the Mishnah to the law of the wayward and defiant son. Yet according to Rabbi Shimon, this law is entirely astonishing: "Just because this boy ate a *tartemar*[12] of meat

---

[9] TB, Bo, 8.   [10] Exodus Rabbah 15:2.   [11] *Lekah Tov*, Lekh Lekha, 13:13.
[12] SEZ, chapter 2 (Ish-Shalom edition, p. 171).   [13] PT Sanhedrin 4:2.
[14] Leviticus Rabbah 11:7.   [15] BT Sotah 16a.

---

[10] That is, to add a thirteenth month so as to adjust the lunar to the solar calendar. This is now done according to a fixed cycle of nineteen years, of which seven are of thirteen months. In early rabbinic times, however, the decision to intercalate was made on an annual basis, after a consideration of the climatic conditions and the state of the flora and fauna in the very early spring. It was the court's prerogative.

[11] The text quoted here by Heschel goes on to say that the majoritarian principle was ordained by God, *so that* the Torah would be able to be expounded forty-nine ways in one direction and forty-nine ways in another. It is a striking statement of the conviction that Torah is, in some sense, *made* by its treatment by the Rabbis.

[12] An ancient measure of weight.

and drank a half *log*[13] of Italian wine,[14] shall his parents bring him to be stoned?" This astonishment could certainly be countered by saying that it is a biblical decree, to which we cannot bring rational objections. Yet Rabbi Shimon did consider its rational basis and concluded: "There never was and never will be a case of a wayward and defiant son. Why then did Scripture record it? That you may study it and reap reward."[16] [15]

According to Rabbi Hanina bar Hama, "by biblical law, monetary cases, like capital cases, require examination and interrogation of witnesses, for it is said, 'You shall have one standard' (Leviticus 24:22). Why, then, did they say that monetary cases do not require examination and interrogation? So that borrowers should not find doors shut in their faces."[16] Later authorities stated: "that we do not require professional judges [to try cases involving debts] is also due to Rabbi Hanina." With this enactment, that three lay judges may try certain monetary cases, the Sages uprooted a biblical law.[17] [17]

Even though courts generally lack the power to uproot a biblical law by allowing a forbidden act, they always have the power to declare property ownerless: "What the court declares to be ownerless is ownerless." And by utilizing this power of the court, various prohibitions can be made to disappear, such as those concerning the slaughter of nonsacrificial meat in the Temple, the marriage of a Canaanite slave to a free Israelite, dealing in sabbatical year produce, work on the Sabbath,[18] and others. When the court declares the money with which a man betrothed a woman to be ownerless, the marriage becomes null and void.[18] Concerning such an annulment, even when the marriage originally was validly contracted, the Bavli states: "How can it be

---

[16] Tosefta Sanhedrin 11:1, BT Sanhedrin 71a. See also Tosefta Sanhedrin 14:1 and Tosefta Nega'im 6:1 for similar conclusions about other biblical laws.

[17] BT Sanhedrin 2b–3a; see *Margoliot Hayyam,* ad loc.

[18] See *Talmudic Encyclopedia* (Jerusalem: Mosad ha-Rav Kuk, 1947–), 10:103ff.

---

[13] An ancient measure of volume.

[14] This was the precise definition given by the Rabbis to the general biblical description of the defiant son as "a glutton and a drunkard" (Deuteronomy 21:20).

[15] That is, the Rabbis essentially abolished a biblical rule set forth carefully and precisely in a clear passage.

[16] That is, lenders would be loath to lend money, for if there were to be any dispute concerning repayment, they and their witnesses would have to endure complicated and time-consuming legal proceedings in order for recovery to be made.

[17] The uprooting was explicitly done for a social purpose, that is, to make loans more readily available to the needy. This required the Rabbis to assert, at least implicitly, a knowledge of the underlying *purpose* of the Torah's legislation, which could be deemed to override the normal judicial procedures it ordained. This, too, is a radical claim.

[18] In the cases given, the critical move is the destruction of the link between some property and its owner, by court decree. Thus, for example, a Canaanite slave, normally the property of his owner, could be retroactively "freed" by a court decree that he is ownerless property, and an otherwise illicit marriage thus be legitimated.

that biblically this is no dissolution of the marriage, and yet because of those who are exceedingly modest or excessively promiscuous, a married woman is permitted to remarry? Yes, it is so, because whoever contracts a marriage does so by leave of the Rabbis, and the Rabbis thus may strip him of the property used for the betrothal."[19]

The Sages often add to and detract from the Torah, such as when they added a day to the festivals in the Diaspora, or abolished the blowing of the Shofar and the taking of the Lulav when the holiday coincides with the Sabbath.

See just how great is the power of the Sages: Pinhas, son of Eleazar, so praised in Scripture for having abated God's anger toward Israel by acting out God's jealousy in the matter of Zimri son of Salu, did not enjoy the approval of the Sages. In killing Zimri, he is said to have relied on the law that "one who cohabits with a heathen may be killed by zealots." And yet of this *halakhah,* which according to Rav was personally taught to Pinhas by Moses, it is said: "It was taught: this is contrary to the will of the Sages [i.e., were a zealot to consult a court before taking action, they would not give him leave]." And this: "They wished to anathematize Pinhas, and they were prevented only by the intervention of the Holy Spirit, which declared: 'It shall be for him and his descendants after him a pact of priesthood for all time' (Numbers 25:13)."[20] "Moses was a zealot and Elijah was a zealot."[21] Moses was zealous for God and said: "Thus says the Lord, the God of Israel: Each of you put sword on thigh . . ." (Exodus 32:27). And of this, it was said: "I[19] call heaven and earth to witness that the Holy and Blessed One did not so instruct Moses to stand up in the gate of the camp and say: 'Whoever is for the Lord, come here!' (Exodus 32:26)."[22] And when Elijah said in God's presence: "I am moved by zeal for the Lord, the God of Hosts" (1 Kings 19:10), "At that moment the Holy Spirit informed him: 'Go back by the way you came . . . and anoint Elisha son of Shaphat . . . to succeed you as prophet' (1 Kings 19:15–16)."[23] [20]

[19] BT Ketubot 3a, and variant readings there.
[20] PT Sanhedrin, end of chapter 9.
[21] PR, chapter 4, 13b.
[22] SER, chapter 4.
[23] SEZ, chapter 8; see also Song of Songs Rabbah 1:6.

---

[19] The speaker here is not Moses, but rather the voice of the (relatively late) *midrash,* which is here asserting that what Moses did in commanding in God's name the slaughter of three thousand Israelites who worshiped the golden calf was *not* in fact God's will.

[20] It may be protested that this last reference to Elijah demonstrates that humans can presume too much on the divine will, and that God will successfully intervene in order to restore heaven's intent, as happened with the "recall" of Elijah and the anointing of Elisha. This would seem to undermine Heschel's point here about the power and authority of the Sages. It is thus important to recall that in the rabbinic mind, there was generally an identification (anachronistic as it was) between Pinhas and Elijah. And thus, Heschel brings Elijah here as a reinforcement of what has already been said about Pinhas. That is, God originally like Pinhas's zealotry, but the Rabbis later disregarded that and damned him with faint praise. Elijah's "recall" by God thus serves to bolster the idea that God can be swayed by a negative human verdict on the zealotries of heaven.

The Sages Finish and Complete the Torah

The Maharal of Prague[21] held this opinion: "Consider all of God's creations, and you will see that they are all in need of some finishing act. Wheat must be processed in order to be fit for human consumption; it was not created by God in finished form. Now since the Torah was given by God via a prophet, and the virtue of reason surpasses the virtue of prophecy (as it was said, that a Sage outranks a prophet), it follows that the Sages finish and complete the Torah, even though it was given at Sinai through Moses."[24]

The Heavenly in the Torah[22]

Don't think that the intellect grasps only the enduring, received, given text, but that it cannot grasp the mystery of prophecy, an event that, having occurred, cannot repeat. For the intellect itself rises up in question about the genesis of this book: not concerning the nature of the quill and the ink with which it was penned, nor on the material of its tablets or sheets, but rather concerning the mystery of its inspiration. Was the Holy and Blessed One a partner in the composition of the Torah?

Even those of little faith will acknowledge that whatever hand wrote the Torah included the "finger of God." But of what use is such a formulation if the meaning of "finger of God" is alien to one's understanding? One who has never seen the lights of heaven, one who has never looked and seen in the skies "the work of God's fingers,"[23] one who has not seen the heavenly in the words of Torah—how will such a person understand the meaning of the phrase "Torah from Heaven"? Is it really possible to interpret the phrase "Torah from Heaven" according to the semantic structure of "water from the well" or "dust from the earth"?[24]

The expression "The Holy and Blessed One spoke and Moses wrote" is nothing but a way of giving voice to amazement in the face of the hidden and the wondrous, and

---

[24] *Tiferet Yisrael,* chapter 69.

---

[21] Rabbi Judah Loewe, sixteenth century.

[22] The phrase used here is *shamayim min ha-torah,* an exact reversal of the name of this work, *torah min hashamayim.* Through a typically unexpected inversion of words, Heschel in this chapter makes a powerful statement concerning the relative triviality of determining the Torah's physical and temporal origin (as in: "given by God to Moses in such and such a year after the creation of the world"), as opposed to the more urgent importance of *experiencing* the heavenly qualities of Torah.

[23] The reference is to Psalm 8:4.

[24] That is, the phrases may *look* alike, in that they have the same *syntactic* structure, but Heschel's claim is that we must not be fooled by the syntax. The meaning of the phrase "water from the well" is simply not similar to that of "Torah from Heaven." One denotes a physical extraction, and the other is intended as a metaphor.

it should be treated as is any phrase the role of which is to ease communication and to bring the mysterious into contact with common sense; that is, its value is dissipated as soon as it is taken literally. Literalism with respect to the divine mysteries is a stepping out of bounds, and it obscures more than it explicates. Shall we compare the Holy and Blessed one to Jeremiah and Moses our master to Barukh son of Neriah![25] Metaphor can be mistaken for reality and can obscure the fact that the dissimilarities far outweigh the similarities!

The language "Torah from Heaven" is formulated for the human ear, but it is of no use if the ear is sealed off to its import. The sanctity of the Torah lies in its secrets. And a person cannot recognize that sanctity without first understanding that just as mortals can sink to the lowest depths, so can they rise to sublime heights.

The gift of Torah is a gift of heaven. And the way to faith in the "Torah from Heaven" is the preparation of the heart to perceive the heavenly in the Torah. Such a perception may be momentary; it may happen in a mere blink of the eye. But all of life is scarcely worth that momentary gift of heaven.

The saying "Torah from Heaven" taken as an abstract idea, as a self-contained matter, is like a driven leaf, an herb with volatile aroma that quickly evaporates until no trace is left in the stew. We do not say: "Had God given us the Torah, and not taken us out of Egypt, it would have been enough!"[26] Just as there can be no giving of the Torah without a receiving of the Torah, so there can be no Torah in heaven without the people of Israel on earth. The school of Rabbi Ishmael seems to have sensed this,[27] for they asked: "Why were the Ten Commandments not placed first in the Torah? The answer lies in a parable. To what does this compare? To one who entered a certain land and said: 'I shall be your ruler.' They said to him, 'What good have you done for us that we should make you our ruler?' What did he do? He built them a wall, brought in an aqueduct, and led them in battle. He then asked: 'Shall I be your ruler?', and they answered, 'Yes, yes!' So, too, did God take Israel out of

---

[25] The prophet Jeremiah's scribe.

[26] Heschel's train of thought here is not obvious, but it is most likely this: the true import of the idea of the heavenly Torah can only be grasped in the context of the actual religious life of Israel. As an unconnected, abstract notion, it is without significance. And the true import lies in the way in which we freely and autonomously use the experience of the heavenly in the Torah. That is why Heschel suddenly shifts to a kind of *midrash* on the Seder song *Dayyenu* and notes that it is not accidental that the giving of the Torah does not precede the Exodus in the list. Had God given us the Torah before we were free and autonomous individuals, it would *not* have been enough! Torah's significance, as Heschel goes on to explain, is as much wrapped up in the free *receipt* of the Torah as in its giving. And the subliminal message may be that it is not just Pharaoh from whom we need autonomy in order to feel the living power of Torah, but even, perhaps, from the imposing Voice of God itself. That would certainly connect this chapter both to the Oven of Akhnai story above and to the section below entitled "On This Very Day."

[27] It is not at all surprising that Heschel now proceeds to link these reflections to Rabbi Ishmael, for as we have long seen in this work, it is Rabbi Ishmael's standpoint that upholds the idea of a transcendent God Who grants us much autonomy in how we experience and develop Torah.

Egypt, split the sea for them, provide manna, bring up water springs, produce quails, and battle Amalek. God then asked: 'Shall I be your ruler?' and they answered, 'Yes, yes!'"[25]

You cannot grasp the matter of the "Torah from Heaven" unless you feel the heaven in the Torah. And the question as to whether the Pentateuch was entirely written in forty years or in eighty years is a temporal question asked in the context of the problem of eternity. The scroll of the Torah is the wondrous become fixed, a great event become routine. But whoever denies the wondrous has no share in *this* world; how much more so can such a person have no dealing with heavenly matters.[28] The essence of prophecy is an event between God and the prophet. So have it as you wish: if this event is like an everyday occurrence, given to accurate apprehension and description, then it is no prophecy. And if the prophetic encounter is sublime and awesome, without parallel in the world, then it is clear that no description will do it justice, and silence becomes it.

Would you like to know the real value of the Torah for the world? Consider this. The world is an amalgam of good and evil, of light and darkness. There is no ready way to know whether the evil or the good predominates, whether the darkness or the light is primary. With all the books in the world, with all the cultures human history has produced, there is no answer to the question of whether there is a judgment and a judge. Does the Highest Being seek justice?

"A parable: A person was traveling about, and saw a palace ablaze. He exclaimed: 'Can it be that there is no one in charge of the palace?!'"[26] There is, indeed, someone in charge, but could that One be a misanthrope, a scheming and oppressive God?

The human soul is inundated with temporal concerns, benighted by its drives, and in all of its longings, it vacillates, unable to distinguish between holy and profane, between bondage and freedom, between temporal concerns and that which transcends time. It is the receiving of Torah that enables the soul to overlap two domains: the domain of nature and the domain of Torah, like the spirit of God that hovers just above the deep waters. In the domain of Torah, a person can be seen through a heavenly lens, as God conceives of us.

[25] MI, Bahodesh, beginning of chapter 5, and Vayyasa, beginning of chapter 5.
[26] Genesis Rabbah 39:1.

---

[28] This is an exquisite Heschelian inversion. The reference here is to the Mishnah in Sanhedrin 10:1, which states, among other things, that those who say "the Torah is not from heaven" (literally, who deny the doctrine of *Torah min Hashamayim*) have no share in the future world. This is, apparently, a codified anathema against those who were deemed to hold heterodox and heretical views. Since Heschel in this chapter is taking aim, to some extent, at those fundamentalists who have converted the rich metaphor of *Torah min Hashamayim* into a dry, oppressive dogma, it is beautifully fitting that they be hoist by the petard of this very Mishnah. So Heschel's reading of the Mishnah has it that those who deny [not the doctrine but] the wondrous metaphor of the heavenly in the Torah have no share in God's true world, because they don't even have a proper share in *this* world; that is, they are ill-equipped to experience human religious life to the fullest.

Lest You Forget

In setting down his list of religious principles, Maimonides shifted the bottom line from the giving of Torah to the book itself, that is, from an event in the nation's life to an event in Moses' life.[29]

In truth, the great principle about which we are admonished in Deuteronomy is that we not forget the standing at Sinai. "But take utmost care and watch yourselves scrupulously, so that you do not forget the things that you saw with your own eyes . . . the day you stood before the Lord your God at Horeb" (Deuteronomy 4:9–10). And one of the commandments, according to Nachmanides, is "that we not forget the standing at Mount Sinai . . . and the utility of this commandment is enormous. For suppose Torah had come to us only through Moses. Even though his prophecy was confirmed by signs and miracles, had another prophet arisen, commanded us something contrary, and performed some sign or miracle, people would have entertained doubt. But since Torah reached our ears directly from on high, before our very eyes, with no intermediary, we can refute anyone who deviates or seeks to implant doubt, and no sign will help such a person . . . and when we rehearse this for our children, they will know that it is indubitably true, as if all generations had seen it."[27] [30]

That moment of revelation has great value for the world, for Israel, and, as it were, for the Shekhinah itself. What was its value for the world? "Until Israel received the Torah, the world was as a wasteland. Once they received the Torah, the world became like a walled city.[28] "The world was all night until Israel received the Torah. But once they came before Mount Sinai and received the Torah, the world lit up."[29]

As for Israel and the Shekhinah: according to the Torah, "Face to face the Lord spoke to you on the mountain out of the fire. I stood between the Lord and you at that time to convey the Lord's words to you" (Deuteronomy 5:4–5); according to Judah Halevi, the people at Mount Sinai prepared itself "for the level of prophecy, even to hear God's words directly,"[30] "the words came and penetrated our ears."[31]

But in the *Guide of the Perplexed*, Maimonides suggests that, while standing at Mount Sinai, the words came only to Moses, and the people heard only sounds, "not

[27] Commentary of Nachmanides on Deuteronomy 4:9. In his commentary on Maimonides' *Book of the Commandments,* he enumerates this one among those commandments that eluded Maimonides.

[28] Exodus Rabbah, end of chapter 24.

[29] Tanhuma Numbers 13.

[30] Kuzari 1:87. See also Abraham ibn Ezra and Nachmanides to Exodus 19:10.

[31] Kuzari 1:89. Maimonides, in *Mishneh Torah,* "Laws Concerning the Fundamentals of the Torah" 8:1, says something similar.

[29] This is clearly a criticism of Maimonides.

[30] This is a restatement of Heschel's conviction that it is the *experience* of Torah, and not its objective nature, that confirms its importance.

distinct words . . . it was Moses who heard the words and conveyed them." And as for the statement in Tanna De-be Rabbi Ishmael, that "the first two of the Ten Commandments were heard directly from on high": Maimonides interprets that to mean that these utterances were received by the people just as they had been received by Moses [that is, by reason], for "God's existence and unity can be apprehended by human reason."[32]

On This Very Day

We must distinguish between factual truths and eternal verities. Every fact depends on time, and when its time has passed, the fact disappears. Yet there are moments that are like eternity, and what happens in them transcends time. The passage of time brings forgetfulness; the present moment makes us forget the moment past. Two moments in time cannot coexist. They crowd each other out. But the opposite is the case with eternity, for there is no forgetting at the throne of glory, and for God, past and future come simultaneously. So the giving of Torah is past as a factual truth, but endures as an eternal verity. God's voice, as it emanated from Mount Horeb, was never muted.

"On the third new moon after the Israelites had gone forth from the land of Egypt, on this very day, they entered the wilderness of Sinai" (Exodus 19:1). Said Ben Zoma: It is not written, "on that very day," but rather "on this very day." "Each day that you busy yourself with Torah, you may say 'On this day I received it from Sinai.' Moreover, it says: 'The Lord your God commands you this day' (Deuteronomy 26:16)."[33] Similarly, it was said: "Year in and year out, a person must see himself as if he stood at Mount Sinai. That is why, in the account of the giving of Torah, it is written 'on this very day.'"[34] Rabbi Judah ben El'ai, the Rabbis' "chief spokesman," expounded on the glories of Torah as follows: "Silence! Hear, O Israel! Today you have become the people of the Lord your God" (Deuteronomy 27:9)—"was it then on that day that the Torah was given to Israel? Why, this was forty years later?! This thus comes to teach you that the Torah is as beloved to those who study it as it was on the day it was given at Mount Sinai."[35]

And it is said in the Zohar: "If one grapples with Torah, it is as if he stands each day at Mount Sinai and receives the Torah."[36]

[32] Maimonides, *Guide of the Perplexed*, 2:33.
[33] TB, Yitro, 7.
[34] Pesikta Hadeta, Bet Midrash, Part 6, p. 40.
[35] BT Berakhot 63b.
[36] Zohar, beginning of Hukkat, 179b.

A Mighty Voice, and No More//A Mighty Voice without End[31]

Some say that the standing at Sinai was the end of revelation and that there can be no innovation after the giving of Torah at Sinai; whatever a diligent student will teach in the future was already spoken to Moses. And there are those who say that the standing at Sinai was not the end of the giving of Torah, nor was it a total revelation. The Holy and Blessed One renews Halakhah each day and gives Torah at many times.

"The Lord spoke these words to your whole congregation at the mountain out of the fire and the dense clouds, with a mighty voice, and no more [*velo yasaf*]" (Deuteronomy 5:19). This verse was interpreted in two ways. The first: "*velo yasaf*" means "without end" (so Onkelos and Targum Yerushalmi), "for God's voice is mighty and eternally enduring" (Rashi).[37] The second: "*velo yasaf*" means "God never again appeared so publicly" (the alternative understanding quoted in Rashi).

"'Moses received Torah from Sinai'; now had it said 'Moses received Torah from the Holy and Blessed One' we might have inferred that Moses was singled out particularly to receive it from God. But this is not so . . . for wisdom flows from God to all creatures, and each day we say 'enlighten our eyes with Your Torah,' and thus the flow of Torah is not confined simply to God and Moses . . . had Moses not received the Torah, someone else would have received it, as the Sages of blessed memory said: 'Ezra was worthy to have the Torah given through him, but Moses preceded him.'"[38]

In the blessing over the Torah, we say "'who gives the Torah.' In truth, God already gave it, but God still is giving it, with no cessation."[39]

There are secrets in the Torah "which are still hidden, for they have not yet been revealed to the world. Thus part of the Torah is hidden, and its light does not radiate. Now when people discover these secrets in this world for the first time, they cause those implied secrets to be revealed and to spread out, for the supernal Torah to be enlarged, and for all of Torah to be renewed . . . it causes greater unity above and a sowing of light for the righteous."[40]

There is no generation without its Moses.[41] "After he left this world, the faithful shepherd shone through the 600,000 souls of Israel."[42] "Moses' influence extends

[37] This interpretation is also found in BT Sotah 10b, in the name of Rabbi Samuel bar Ami (who also understands Genesis 38:26 to be saying that Judah continued to cohabit with Tamar—see Rashi on the biblical verse). See also Zohar, Va'ethanan, 261a.

[38] Maharal of Prague, *Derekh Hayyim,* beginning of Tractate Avot.

[39] *Shenei Luhot Heberit,* 25a.

[40] Rabbi Abraham Azulai, *Hesed Le-Avraham,* Fountain #2, River #3.

[41] Genesis Rabbah 56:9.

[42] Zohar, Ra'ya Mehemna, Pinhas, 216b.

[31] The translation of the biblical phrase from Deuteronomy 5:19 is deliberately given in dual, ambiguous form here, for it is precisely that ambiguity that concerns Heschel in this chapter.

through all generations, to every righteous person."[43] "Moses' light sparkles in the Sages of every generation to assist them in the direction of truth." And when the Talmud records the question [in a conversation between the Amoraim Rav Safra and Rava]: "Moses, have you spoken well?"[44] the meaning is that every Sage may be called "Moses" and "the spark of Moses' soul is now in you, to direct you to the truth."[45]

The soul of Moses our Master expands out to all other souls. "And just as the light of the moon is really the light of the sun, so is the light of Torah that shines from the Sages even in these days really the light of the Torah of Moses our Master, may he rest in peace. That is why we call him "our Master."[46]

A person must "always see himself, at every moment, as if he is standing at Mount Sinai to receive the Torah. For humans are subject to past and future, but God is not, and each and every day God gives the Torah to the people Israel. Therefore, when a person opens any book in order to learn, he should remember at that time the standing at Sinai, as if he received the Torah directly from on high. Thus will he achieve a measure of reverence and awe, just as was the case when the Torah was given in fear and in trembling: 'and all the people who were in the camp trembled' (Exodus 19:16)."[47]

What are the fundamentals of Torah? They are creeds and remembrances. Maimonides defined the creeds, and the disciples of Isaac Luria instituted the remembrances.[32] Creeds define ideas, while remembrances revive them, and resurrect experiences.[48] [33]

Timna Was a Concubine

Maimonides, in formulating his creedal principles, established that "this entire Torah, given via Moses our Master, may he rest in peace, is from on high in its

---

[43] Tikkunei Zohar, 469, 112a.

[44] BT Shabbat 101b (the question is addressed to Rava by Rav Safra).

[45] *Kissei Melekh*, on Tikkunei Zohar (Lemberg, 1864), 2a.

[46] Abraham Azulai, *Hesed Le-Avraham*, Fountain #2, River #37.

[47] Rabbi Abraham Joshua Heschel of Apt, *Ohev Yisrael*, Ki Tetze.

[48] See Heschel, *Man Is Not Alone* (New York: Harper & Row, 1966), 162ff. Also *Siddur Tselota De-Avraham*, part I, p. 420.

---

[32] Heschel is referring to two texts that appear in many traditional prayer books, at the conclusion of daily services. The first is called "The Thirteen Principles of Faith," a collection of creedal statements based on Maimonides' list of fundamentals of Judaism in his *Commentary on the Mishnah*, Sanhedrin ch. 10. The second is called "The Six Remembrances" [there are other lists of "remembrances" with different numbers of entries].

[33] Once again, we have Heschel emphasizing the phenomenology of a life with Torah and denigrating the Maimonidean program of formulating cognitive doctrine with respect to the Torah. The very next chapter, predictably, explores some of the inevitable consequences of the Maimonidean approach.

entirety . . . and there is no distinction to be made between the verses 'The descendants of Ham: Cush, Mizraim, Put, and Canaan' (Genesis 10:6), 'his wife's name was Mehetabel daughter of Matred' (Genesis 36:39), 'and Timna was a concubine' (Genesis 36:12), and 'I the Lord am your God' (Exodus 20:2). For all comes from on high, all is God's perfect Torah, pure, holy, and true."[49]

Concerning the custom to stand in the synagogue during the reading of the Ten Commandments, Maimonides ruled in accordance with those who called it a sectarian practice, for it leads to a diminution of faith: "for they will be led to think that some parts of the Torah are superior to other parts, and that is serious indeed; all paths leading to such a sinful belief should be blocked."[50]

This point of view is rooted in the apprehension of the Torah according to the approach of Rabbi Akiva, who viewed the Torah through a heavenly lens and expounded on every single tittle piles and piles of *halakhot*. The Torah, in this view, was written in and resided in the heavens, and Moses went up and brought it down to earth. One who allows that the Torah has a heavenly existence, that is, an autonomous, transcendent existence, and who believes that the Torah is studied in the heavenly academy just as it is studied on earth, will certainly hold that human reason has no sovereignty over it and cannot be trusted to distinguish among its parts, to measure them by the intellect's yardsticks and say, "this verse is of a different nature from this one; this one pleases me, and that one does not." The sanctity of Torah is beyond measure, and you come to gauge it with a plumb line?!

Scholars and exegetes are forever offering rationales for biblical verses, be they flattering or unflattering ones, but all their words are fleeting. For rationales are beside the point. Rationales come and go, while the words of Torah endure forever. "Many calves have died, and their hides have become spreads on their mothers' backs."[34]

---

[49] Preface to commentary on Mishnah Sanhedrin, chapter 10, principle #8. In SEZ, chapter 2: "From this they derived that if a person has proficiency neither in Scripture nor in the Oral teachings, but sits all day and recites 'and Lotan's sister was Timna' (Genesis 36:22), he merits the reward of studying Torah."
[50] Responsa of Maimonides, Blau edition, #263.

---

[34] This is a prevalent rabbinic proverb used to point out that that which seems new and stylish may be long outlived by the old and the enduring. The text itself, without rationales supporting it, is here taken to be the enduring substance, and those stylish attempts to give it some rational basis may turn out to be fleeting and transitory. This, of course, is what Heschel understands to be the Akivan view, one that does not allow for the human autonomy represented by the drive to discern rationales for the Torah's commands, and for which Heschel has been arguing throughout this section. This is one of many examples of a noticeable preference for the Ishmaelian view in the latter part of this work. Maimonides, it should be noted, is no pure Ishmaelian or Akivan. Here, his logical insistence on the homogeneity of Torah leads him to what Heschel understands to be an Akivan totalism with respect to the text. In earlier chapters, we have seen Maimonides' rationalism more closely approximating an Ishmaelian point of view. This is no refutation of Heschel's scheme; rather, it is a reminder that there are, in Jewish religious life, no pure Akivans or Ishmaelians. Heschel will yet make that repeatedly clear about himself!

Should you ask: Why were the rationales for the Torah's words not revealed? "It is because the rationales were revealed in two cases, and the wisest man in history stumbled on them."[51] [35] Silence protects wisdom, and caution protects Torah. "It is written: 'Make them known to your children and to your children's children' (Deuteronomy 4:9), and immediately thereafter, 'the day you stood before the Lord your God at Horeb' (Deuteronomy 4:10)—just as the latter was with reverence and awe, with fear and trembling, so must the former be."[52] One who weds himself to Torah because of its beauty detracts from its honor.

"Why was the Torah compared to a fig?[36] Because all fruits have waste: dates have pits, grapes have seeds, pomegranates have peels, but the entire fig is fit to be eaten. Similarly, there is no waste in the words of Torah, as it is said: 'it is not an empty matter for you' (Deuteronomy 32:47)."[53]

In contradistinction to this, Rabbi Ishmael—who viewed the Torah through its surface meaning—measured its words and set limits and boundaries to them. His outstanding characteristic was his discrimination—this word is a proper subject for exegesis, and this one is not, for it is simply a convention of human language. Or: this section is not in proper sequence, because there is no exact chronological order in the Torah. He drew distinctions between those occasions on which Moses said "this is what the Lord has commanded" and those on which he said "thus says the Lord," between the last eight verses and the remainder of the Torah, between "I the Lord am your God" and "You shall have no other gods" and the rest of the Ten Commandments. And should you say that there is no distinction between "Timna was a concubine" and "I the Lord am your God," then there could be no room for the question that arose in Rabbi Ishmael's academy: "Why were the Ten Commandments not placed first in the Torah?"[54] [37]

There is a hint of the idea that the Ten Commandments have a greater significance in the question that King Agrippa asked Rabbi Eliezer the Great. He asked: "if circumcision is such a beloved mitzvah, why was it not included in the Ten Commandments at the giving of the Torah?"[55]

[51] BT Sanhedrin 21b.
[52] BT Berakhot 22a.
[53] YS, Joshua, 2, quoting Yelamedenu.
[54] MI, Bahodesh, beginning of chapter 5.
[55] Aggadat Bereshit, chapter 16.

---

[35] The reference is to Solomon, and the commands to the king not to have too many horses or too many wives. Rationales were given for each of these (so that there not be entangling alliances with Egypt, and so that the king not be led away from the worship of God by foreign wives), and Solomon was sure he could avoid the predicted pitfalls. But he failed.

[36] This midrash assumes that Proverbs 27:18 is referring to Torah when it says "the one who guards the fig tree shall eat of its fruit."

[37] That is, the question presumes that the Ten Commandments are the most important part of the Torah, and thus should have pride of place. This presumption thus contradicts the idea of absolute parity among all words and letters of the Torah.

Where there is smoke there is also fire. The very warnings issued against distinguishing between passages that are more consequential and those that are less so are testimony to the human tendency to make such distinctions. "His locks are curled, and black as a raven" (Song of Songs 5:11)—"Rabbi Samuel bar Isaac applied the verse to passages in the Torah. "Black like the raven" refers to those teachings of the Torah which appear dark and unseemly, unfit for public recitation. The Holy and Blessed One says of them, "they are pleasing to me" . . . know that this is so, for the passages dealing with male and female genital flows were not combined into one passage, but were given each its own formulation."[56][38]

The Entire Torah Has a Single Subject

The point of view that there is no distinction to be made in Torah between primary and secondary, central and peripheral, essential and derivative, important and unimportant, ultimately gained ascendancy.[39] "Even if a person has proficiency neither in Scripture nor in the Oral teachings, but sits all day and recites 'and Lotan's sister was Timna' (Genesis 36:22), he merits the reward of studying Torah."[57][40] This assertion was explicated as follows: "The entire Torah is such that it speaks of the mundane, but hints at the sublime. And thus there is no difference between the verse 'Timna was a concubine' and the verse 'Hear, O Israel!', for they all hint at matters the significance of which reach higher and higher, without end. And the reason the Rabbis of blessed memory focused on this particular verse ['Timna was a concubine'] is to be found in this verse in Psalm 19: 'The teaching of the Lord is *perfect, renewing life;* [the] *decrees . . . .'* The four adjacent Hebrew words for 'perfect, renewing, life, decrees' form an acronym for 'Timna.' And the verse states that the Torah of the Lord is perfect, that is, in its entirety from beginning to end."[58]

For this reason several Sages opposed efforts to establish core principles of the faith, as if some matters have greater value than others also found in the Torah: "You

---

[56] Song of Songs Rabbah 5:11; see *Yefei Kol* ad loc.
[57] SEZ, end of chapter 2.
[58] *Shenei Luhot Haberit,* 264b, s.v. *ki ner mitzvah.*

---

[38] The reference is to Leviticus 15, which actually has *four* sections: one for abnormal male genital flows, one for normal (i.e. seminal) male flows, one for normal (menstrual) female flows, and one for abnormal female flows. The care taken with these "indelicate" subjects reflects God's loving attention to all human obligations. On the other hand, Heschel's point is that the very need to explain the verbosity and expansiveness of Leviticus 15 reflects the natural presumption that its contents could not possibly be "as divine" as say, "love your neighbor as yourself."

[39] Once again, we have Heschel's insistence that the balance has historically swung against the Ishmaelian view. See the end of chapter 1 above.

[40] Thus, the words of Torah have an *inherent* value, not just an informational value. It is what the words *are,* not just what they denote, that entitles and requires us to say a blessing before studying them. This is a classic formulation of the Akivan view on the words of Torah.

have asked me about principles of the faith and about which enumeration I endorse—that of Maimonides, or of Crescas, or of Albo. My answer: I don't endorse identifying any core principle to our Torah, since it stems in its entirety from on high. The Rabbis of blessed memory said that whoever says that the entire Torah is from heaven save one single verse is a heretic, and if so then each and every *mitzvah* is a cornerstone of the faith."[59] [41]

Yet other approaches and opposing views were also heard. According to Rabbi Abraham ibn Daud, philosopher and historiographer,[42] "the Torah is a book of instruction composed of many parts. One part deals with religious faith and its ideas; a second deals with ethical values; a third is a manual of daily religious practice; a fourth is a manual of political practice; and a fifth is that which we have termed wisely framed commandments.'"[60] According to ibn Daud, one must distinguish between the various components of the Torah, and he believed that the cultic rules have far less significance than the ethical rules; that is, the cultic rules are means toward the Torah's ethical demands: "the components of the Torah are not all equal . . . rather, the essence and pillar of Torah is the faith, and next in importance come ethical instruction and the behavioral norms. But for these civilization would be impossible. For this reason, the practices of all the nations agree, or nearly agree, with the Torah's political teachings. . . . But as for those commandments that are poor in reason (that is, their motives are not known to us), their relative status is quite weak."[43] Ibn Daud gives as evidence of this the prophetic polemic concerning the sacrificial cult.[61] [44]

And concerning the biblical portion "Vayyikra," which deals entirely with the details of the sacrifices, Rabbi Joseph ibn Kaspi[45] writes as follows:

> . . . my nature is strongly to prefer brevity whenever possible. Therefore, when I considered this portion and the many that follow it, I saw that they all revolve around the sacri-

---

[59] Responsa of Rabbi David ibn Zimra, Part I, #344.

[60] *The Exalted Faith,* Treatise III, pp. 75–76.

[61] Ibid.

---

[41] That which is being opposed here would include such things as Maimonides' Thirteen Principles, the kabbalists' "Remembrances," and the identification of the "Ten Commandments" themselves as a religiously significant category.

[42] Spain, twelfth century.

[43] That is, ibn Daud creates a hierarchy in which rational principles of faith rank highest, then rational principles of ethics, then norms of practice (which may or may not be rational), and finally principles of political organization. This lowest rung unites many nations, because of the sheer pragmatism inherent in it, but as you go up the hierarchy, specifically Jewish thought distinguishes itself from the rest of humanity. What is striking is how low on this scale the practical, performative commandments are.

[44] Maimonides himself would just decades later promote an instrumental and utilitarian view of the sacrifices. See chapter 4 above.

[45] Spain and North Africa, fourteenth century.

ficial practices. Those practices, as is known, were written down by Moses our Master by a kind of compulsion; for while God has no desire for burnt offerings, they were necessitated by the universal practice among the nations at that time. Therefore, these few words of mine will suffice; indeed, even if they are not known, no harm will be done; what Rashi has already written, not to mention the commentary of ibn Ezra, will be more than enough. So I will let this portion be, and the portions of "Tzav" and "Shemini" as well. Moreover, I will be content with the ancient commentaries on "Tazria" and "Metzora," which deal with purity laws no longer practiced. As for "Aharei Mot," I shall also neglect those parts that treat sacrificial laws, and write only concerning the laws regulating sexual relations."[62]

The Unity of the Torah

Rabbi Eleazar ben Azariah's statement that even the disagreements among the Sages "were given by the one God," and the saying "these and these are the words of the living God" both come to teach a great fundamental: the unity of Torah. Just as the Giver of the Torah is One, so is the Torah. From a late Midrash:

> When the Holy and Blessed One came to create the world, the twenty-two letters came and each pleaded: "Create the world through me." When the *aleph* saw that the Holy and Blessed One began creation with the *bet,*[46] it stepped to the side silently. The Holy and Blessed One called to it, saying, "*Aleph, aleph,* why are you silent?" The *aleph* responded by saying that "letters are ranked according to their numerical value, and my value is so small. Even *bet* represents 2, and I only represent 1." The Holy and Blessed One responded: "Do not fear. You are a virtual king over the others. For you are 1 and I am One; and the Torah 'is entirely a single matter.'"[63]

How mightily did the Sages labor to preserve the unity of the Torah! Wherever they turned they found that when the language of the Torah is poor in one place, it is rich in another. There are commandments in the Torah whose intents are explicit and others whose intents are partially obscure; in such cases, the Sages exploited the appearance of similar language in order to set up analogies and make mutual derivations. Similar words written in two different places would, for example, allow for such mutual derivation, so that details explicit in only one of the texts would apply as well to the other.[47]

Yet the concept of the unity of Torah can be understood in two ways. Some understand it to mean that the Torah is a simple monolith, not a composite, without a

---

62 *Mishneh Keseph,* of Joseph ibn Kaspi, volume 2 (Cracow, 1906), p. 229.
63 "Alphabet of Rabbi Akiva," *Otzar Midrashim,* p. 426.

---

[46] That is, *bet* is the first letter of the Torah, which begins with the story of creation.
[47] This is describing the *gezerah shavah,* the second of the thirteen hermeneutical rules by which the Torah is expounded.

multiplicity of subjects. From whatever angle it is viewed and by whatever standard it is assessed, it will always be found to be a unitary whole. Others, however, assert that the Torah is one, but not in the same sense that God is One. It displays multiplicity, just as a single genus includes many species, and a single species includes many individuals.

The first understanding is reflected in a teaching from the school of Rabbi Akiva: Just as the Giver is One, so is the receiver one. The divine presence imbued none but Moses our Master; the entire Torah is the word of God as it reached Moses, and all of its words were Moses' prophecy, including even the Song of the Sea, for the Israelites spoke nothing on their own.[48] The seventy elders were brought by Moses into the Tent of Meeting "not so they would hear the Voice, but rather that others would treat them with respect."[64] [49]

In conformity with the second understanding, Rabbi Ishmael strove to grasp the Torah with the tongs of reason. According to him, Moses did not receive the Torah in one fell swoop. General principles were given at Sinai, and details were provided in the Tent of Meeting. But even though the Torah was not given at one time, in one revelation, God remains immutable.[50]

According to this understanding, the Sages were empowered to distinguish between those things that were spoken to Moses by the Most Holy, and those that Moses spoke on his own authority. His words matched the divine intent, and the Holy and Blessed One confirmed them. Such distinctions do not diminish the image of the Torah, nor do they attack its unity. The prophet is simply a partner in the enterprise of prophecy. Since everything was spoken and written according to the divine will, of what moment is it if Moses wrote it all or if Joshua added to it?[51]

The unity of the Torah has its root in the unity of the Will revealed in it. That is why the Sages believed that the *Tanakh* was a unit, and that the written and oral Torahs were one Torah. Note what was said about a student sitting before his master who asks a question off the subject at hand. Rabbi Meir says: "He must say that he is asking off the subject. But the Sages say: he need not, since the entire Torah has a single subject."[65]

Woe to the heretics who deny the authority of Halakhah and say: Moses received naught but the Ten Commandments. They do not realize that the Torah, the Prophets, the Writ-

[64] Sifre Zuta, Beha'alotekha, 11, 16.
[65] Tosefta Sanhedrin, 7:7.

[48] That is, even though the Torah says "Moses and the children of Israel sang . . . ," they were really just repeating the words that reached Moses through prophecy.

[49] Again, Moses was, according to this view, the only prophet in that generation. Apparently, this (Akivan) view could not consider the idea of multiple human recipients of the divine word, since that would open up the possibility of diverse formulations of what is, inherently, unitary.

[50] And, according to this view, that the Torah is "unitary" means not that it is "indivisible" but rather that it is all directed to a common, godly goal.

[51] For example, the last eight verses of Deuteronomy, which presuppose the death of Moses.

ings, the Mishnah, Halakhah, Aggadah, and the details of law are all of the Ten Commandments. Know that just as the Tabernacle was composed of pieces . . . all of which were joined into one whole . . . so are the Torah, Prophets, Writings, and Mishnah all one. We find it thus in the text: "As for the tabernacle, make it of ten strips of cloth" (Exodus 26:1)—these are the Ten Commandments;[52] it also says: "join five of the cloths" (Exodus 26:9)—these are the five books of the Pentateuch, "and the other six cloths" (ibid.)—these are the six orders of the Mishnah,[53] "and fold over the sixth cloth"—(ibid.)—this is the Talmud, which doubles and redoubles its inferences from Torah. And all were given by One Shepherd.[66] [54]

[66] Midrash Haggadol, Exodus, 26:7.

---

[52] The verses here refer to the innermost cloth coverings of the Tabernacle.
[53] The verses here refer to the goatskin hangings that overlay the innermost cloth ones.
[54] This is, of course, the Akivan view that everything was given by God.

RENEWAL OF TORAH

Translator's Introduction

Having brought up the issue of the unity of God's will at the end of the previous chapter, Heschel now proceeds to the next, natural question. Is the Torah that we have in our possession—whose unity we associate with the unity of God's will—an adequate expression of that divine will? In particular, is this true of the laws that are embodied in the Torah? Those who believed steadfastly in the absolute transcendence of God were caught in this respect on the horns of a dilemma. In the face of a Christian challenge to the eternal validity of the Sinai covenant, it was clearly important to maintain the immutability of the Torah and its laws. On the other hand, how could a document written in human language possibly capture the fullness of an infinite will? Indeed, as Heschel demonstrates at the very beginning of this chapter, there arose a notion that the Torah itself, for all its sanctity, was a mere surrogate for Wisdom itself—the mind of God, as it were. Although Ishmael and Akiva no longer enjoy very prominent mention in the chapters from here to the end of the work, the signatures of the schools of thought that they represented are very much present. For the idea that the Torah is an incomplete expression of God's wisdom flows from an Ishmaelian insistence on God's transcendence. Hints of this were already present at the outset of Heschel's exposition of the two paradigmatic views in his earliest chapters.

Now one consequence of concluding that the Torah is an incomplete expression of God's will is the idea that the Torah and its laws may change at some point. And although Judaism could not—for reasons given above—incorporate the idea that the commandments could change in normal time, it was able to articulate the notion that the commandments might be modified or even abrogated in a future world. This idea was not, of course, universally held. It could not be by those who believed that the Torah in our possession was the primordial Torah that was "Heaven's Daughter." But Heschel does document in this chapter what might otherwise be a startling Jewish view that prohibitions taken for granted in Judaism might lapse in messianic times. More than that, he gives us a good sense of why and how this strange view arose.

Just to look ahead chronologically, in a final introductory note: The idea that our Torah has imperfections, and that a more perfect Torah awaits revelation in a more perfect time became prominent centuries later, among certain kabbalists. For more on this, see Gershom Scholem, "The Meaning of the Torah in Jewish Mysticism," in *On the Kabbalah and Its Symbolism* (New York: Schocken Books, 1965).

Wisdom's Surrogate[1]

THE TORAH IS "AN ETERNAL LEGACY TO ISRAEL."[1] "Though our Temple, our City, and all our precious things be taken from us, the Torah will remain with us forever. And wherever a Jew may be, though he be exiled from his homeland to faraway lands, he will not fear the wrath of harsh rulers as much as he fears the Torah's laws."[2] This point was emphasized repeatedly in rabbinic literature and in the Apocrypha.

Against the Christians, who would taunt Israel and say, "Since you were exiled from your land Moses' Torah has been superseded by another Teaching,"[3] Rabbi Simeon bar Yohai said this: The Holy and Blessed One said to the Book of Deuteronomy, "Solomon and a thousand like him shall pass away, but not a word of yours will ever be voided."[4] [2] "These are the commandments that God commanded Moses, and one may not introduce into them anything new."[5] The Torah is perfect and complete as we have it. This principle was established by Maimonides in his creed: "this Torah shall not be changed, and there shall not be another Torah from God."[3]

But in the very shadow of the principle that there will be no modification of the Torah there arose the question of whether there will be an expansion of the Torah in

---

[1] Exodus Rabbah 33:7.
[2] Josephus, *Against Apion* 2.38.
[3] BT Shabbat 116b.
[4] PT Sanhedrin 2:6 (20c).
[5] Targum Yerushalmi to Leviticus 27:34.

---

[1] There is no clear English equivalent of the Hebrew term here, *novelet*. It comes from a root that refers to unripeness (in fruits), and thus it denotes something that is a substitute or stand-in for something else, but generally of poorer quality, a pale facsimile. That Torah is described in this way vis-à-vis the Divine Wisdom (e.g., in Genesis Rabbah 44) is noteworthy if not startling. It suggests that Torah is merely a projection in a finite dimension of what is, in essence, infinite. It is clearly a view of Torah that has been identified throughout this work with the approach of Rabbi Ishmael.

[2] The impetus for this statement is the fact that King Solomon, as great as he was, was reported (by the Book of Kings) to have violated the three major restrictions imposed by the Book of Deuteronomy on the monarch: not to have too many horses, not to have too many wives, and not to have too great a treasury. Solomon, who built what was to be the eternal House of God, would, according to this, fade from memory before the Torah that he had violated would ever fade.

[3] The formulation is not that of Maimonides but rather of an unknown epitomizer of the Thirteen Principles that he set down in his commentary on Mishnah Sanhedrin 10:1. The epitome is known as "Ani Ma'amin," and this is the formulation of the ninth article of faith.

times to come. Will the Torah remain unchanged forever, or will its boundaries be widened and its secrets revealed in messianic times? Some held that the Torah will endure undivided for all eternity, and that even Elijah and the Messiah will neither detract from nor add to Moses' Torah. Others believed in a "renewal of Torah," and even in the revelation of a "new Torah."[4]

There are two ways of apprehending the Torah's existence. One way says that the Torah in our possession is just "a surrogate for the Divine Wisdom."[6] Moses received Torah at Sinai, but not the entire Torah. It is impossible for all of God's wisdom to be transmitted to mortals. Many things were not revealed to Moses, nor did Moses transmit all that he received to Israel. The giving of the Torah was, as it is conventionally understood, a one-time event. With the completion of that revelation, a door closed. Yet in addition to the memory of that past event, we were inspired with the vision of "in that day."[5] Memory says: the most exalted event, the standing at Sinai, is past. Whatever a diligent student will teach was already spoken, and no prophet may innovate anything from this time forth. But future vision says: The most exalted event, "the end of the awesome things," will yet be. The Torah that a person learns in this world is vacuous compared to the Torah of the Messiah.

The second understanding of Torah says: "Concealed acts concern the Lord our God; but with overt acts, it is for us and our children ever to apply all the provisions of this Teaching" (Deuteronomy 29:28). "It is not in the heavens, that you should say, 'Who among us can go up to the heavens and get it for us?'" (Deuteronomy 30:12)—"Said Moses to them: So that you should never say that another Moses will come along and bring us another Torah from heaven, I now tell you 'It is not in the heavens'—nothing of it is left in the heavens."[7] "The Torah has already been given at Mount Sinai."[8]

According to this second understanding, there is no difference between the Torah of premessianic days and that of messianic days. The Torah is complete as we have it, and just as a prophet may not any longer innovate,[9] so the Son of David has no power to add to or detract from the Torah. By this understanding, according to Rav Hanin, an Amora of the Land of Israel: "Israel requires no teaching of the messianic king in

---

[6] Genesis Rabbah 17:7.

[7] Deuteronomy Rabbah 8:6.

[8] Rabbi Jeremiah's words in BT Bava Metzi'a 59a, expressing the idea that no new revelation, even by God, could alter what was given on Mount Sinai, for that was all that God had to reveal.

[9] BT Shabbat 104a.

---

[4] As should be clear, Heschel means to associate the view that the Torah is eternal and complete with the Akivan approach, and the idea that a renewal of Torah, or even a new Torah, is possible with the Ishmaelian approach.

[5] Hebrew: ve-haya bayyom ha-hu, a prophetic phrase that appears a few dozen times in the Bible. Often, as in Isaiah 11:10–11 and 27:13, it looks forward to a redemption in future times, and an escape from the travails of the present.

the hereafter, for it is written, 'nations shall seek his counsel (Isaiah 11:10)'—not Israel! Why then does the Messiah need to come, and what is he to do? To gather in the exiled of Israel and to give (the gentiles) thirty commandments."[6] 10 The only difference between the Torah studied now and that which will be studied in the hereafter is this: now we study and forget; in the hereafter, Torah will become embedded in the heart.11

Rabbi Phinehas delivered himself of a statement so forceful as to have given rise to great consternation: "'I said to myself, "Come, I will treat you [anasekhah] to merriment. Taste goodness!" That, too, I found, was vacuous' (Ecclesiastes 2:1)—Rav Phinehas and Rav Hezekiah in the name of Rav Simeon bar Zavdi both expounded this verse. Rav Phinehas said: anasekhah—I shall try out [anaseh] Torah and I shall try out [anaseh] heresy, and then flee [anusah] from heresy to Torah. 'Taste goodness' means the goodness of Torah—and 'that, too, I found, was vacuous.'" Those who heard this were rendered speechless: "'That, too, I found, was vacuous'!?" Thus, they immediately appended Rav Hezekiah's version of Rav Simeon bar Zavdi's words: "All the Torah that you learn in this world is vacuous compared to that of the Torah of the world to come. For in this world a person learns Torah and forgets it, but in the hereafter: 'I will put My Teaching into their inmost being' (Jeremiah 31:33)."12

According to Rabbi Abba bar Kahana, a third-generation Amora of the Land of Israel, "The Holy and Blessed One said: 'Torah shall go forth from Me' (Isaiah 51:4)—that is, a renewal of Torah shall go forth from Me."[7] 13 The language in Isaiah is here quite interesting, for in two early printed editions (and in two manuscripts) of Leviticus Rabbah, the verse is quoted as follows: "a new Torah shall go forth from Me." And there are other sources which speak of a new Torah that the Holy and Blessed One will give via the Messiah.

The anticipation that God will in the future reveal to Israel the explanations of the esoterics of Torah was already expressed in Tannaitic literature. Of Balaam ben Be'or they said: "His eyes saw Israel sitting before the Holy and Blessed One in the hereafter, as a student sits before his master, and inquiring why each portion of Torah was written. Indeed, it is said: 'Her profits go to those who sit before the Lord, that they may eat their fill and clothe themselves elegantly' (Isaiah 23:18). . . . The ministering

10 Genesis Rabbah 98:9.
11 So the view of Rabbi Yehudah, Song of Songs Rabbah 1:2.
12 Ecclesiastes Rabbah, beginning of chapter 2.
13 Leviticus Rabbah 13:3.

[6] This refers to a tradition, recorded in BT Hullin 92a and elsewhere, that the gentiles received thirty commandments, but that they generally only observe three of them. The whole exegesis is based on Zechariah 11:12, an apocalyptic prophecy that speaks of thirty shekels of wages that the prophet receives. In the messianic era, the thirty commandments are to be renewed (repromulgated).

[7] It must be a renewal, that is, a new form of Torah, else how could the verse be speaking in the future tense? The Torah we have now was already given at Mount Sinai. This must be speaking of a new Torah.

angels then see them and ask them: "What did the Holy and Blessed One teach you?" —for they (the angels) could not join with them, as it is said: 'Jacob is told at once, Yea Israel, what God has planned' (Numbers 23:23)."[14]

And this: "In that day, there shall be neither sunlight nor cold moonlight [*ve-qippa'on*]" (Zechariah 14:6)—"But it is written *ye-qippa'on* [an apparently future form]. For those things that are hidden from you in this world will in the future be as clear as crystal to you."[15]

As we have stated, the desire for a renewal of Torah in messianic days was nourished by the sense that not all was revealed, and that not all that was revealed was sufficiently clear: "Do not say that the book is before you and that you need only read the book to find all knowledge, for it says: 'If the document is handed to one who cannot read and he is asked to read it, he will say, "I cannot read"' (Isaiah 29:12). Thus, David said: 'I am Your servant; give me understanding' (Psalm 119:125)."[16]

"I am only a sojourner [*ger*] in the land; do not hide Your commandments from me" (Psalm 119:19)—"But was David a sojourner!? Rather, David said to God: Just as one who becomes a proselyte[8] [*ger*] knows nothing of Torah on that day, so every person, though his eyes be open, barely knows his right from his left in Torah. Now if David, who composed all these songs and psalms, said 'I am only a *ger* in the land,' knowing nothing, how much more so do we know nothing of Torah."[17] "Now when the Holy and Blessed One comes to heal the world, the healing will begin with the blind, as it is written: 'The Lord restores sight to the blind' (Psalm 146:8). And who are the blind? These generations, which stumble blindly through Torah. They all read, but know not what they read; they learn, but know not what they learn. Yet in the hereafter: 'Then the eyes of the blind shall be opened' (Isaiah 35:8)."[18]

Renewal of Torah

Will there be any changes in the observance of the commandments in the hereafter? Many Sages believed that in messianic days, when the earth will be filled with knowledge of God, humankind will merit hearing "the Messiah's Torah," "the Messiah's Teaching," even "Renewal of Torah." Is it plausible that they meant only that theoretical matters that eluded the ancestors would be apprehended and grasped, but that nothing would change with respect to practical Halakhah, that the descendant of David would come and the world would remain just the way it always was? This ques-

---

[14] TB, Balak, 23.   [15] PRK, Parah 39a.
[16] Midrash Tehillim 119:56.   [17] Midrash Tehillim 119:10.
[18] Midrash Tehillim 146:10.

---

[8] *Ger*, which meant "sojourner" in the Bible, came to mean "proselyte" in the postbiblical period. Indeed, the question in Midrash Tehillim here is probably "was David a proselyte?"

tion was a critical one to the Sages, and many dealt with it in disparate ways. The give and take began in the generation of Rabbis Ishmael and Akiva and continued through the period of the Amoraim, up to the most recent generations.

It is written: "I will make the unclean spirit vanish from the land" (Zechariah 13:2), and "I will sprinkle clean water upon you, and you shall be clean" (Ezekiel 36:25). So how can it be imagined that in messianic days there will still be laws of uncleanness and an abhorrence of unclean animals? It is written: "I will remove the heart of stone from your body and give you a heart of flesh" (Ezekiel 36:26), and from this Rabbi Simeon bar Yohai learned that in the hereafter the Holy and Blessed One will uproot the evil constitution of human beings and they will no longer be drawn to idol worship.[19] And if so, what will be the point of observing those commandments that were given in order to keep people away from idolatry?[9]

When Moses went up to heaven to receive the Torah, the ministering angels said: "Cover the heavens with Your splendor" (Psalm 8:2).[10] [20] Said the Holy and Blessed One to Moses: "Answer them." Moses then said to them: "What does the Torah contain? 'You shall not murder. You shall not commit adultery. You shall not steal.' Do you angels know envy? Do you have sexual lust among you?" Immediately, they conceded to the Holy and Blessed One that they had no need of Torah and commandments.

Now "In the hereafter, the Holy and Blessed One will take hold of the evil constitution and slaughter it in the presence of the righteous";[21] "in the world to come, I will uproot the evil constitution from you."[22] So the question must be raised: If there is to be no evil constitution, won't some of the commandments become null and void? According to Rabbi Hananiah ben Akashia, "the Holy and Blessed One wished to grant Israel merit, and thus gave them a multitude of teachings and commandments."[23] But if in messianic days "there will be neither merit nor liability,"[24] [11] then it is clear that there is no point to the observance of the commandments.

---

[19] Exodus Rabbah 41:7.   [20] Exodus Rabbah, end of chapter 41.
[21] BT Sukkah 52a.   [22] Tanhuma Ekev, 11.
[23] Mishnah, end of Tractate Makkot.   [24] BT Shabbat 151b.

---

[9] Maimonides, for example, draws our attention to several commandments whose sole purpose, he claims, is to keep us away from idolatrous practices. These include not shaving the head in a circular fashion, not wearing wool and linen combined, not sowing with diverse seeds, and not using the fruit of trees for its first three years (Guide of the Perplexed 3:37). On such an account (and it is not the only one of its kind), the absence of any threat from idolatry would obviate the need for such commandments.

[10] The meaning of the angels' statement is, roughly, "leave the Torah here for us."

[11] The apparent meaning of this phrase in the talmudic source is not what Heschel attributes to it here (see Rashi to BT Shabbat 151b). We must assume that Heschel meant simply to appropriate the Hebrew phrase, which can mean what Heschel intends here, and to use it to describe the views of those who see the messianic age as different from ours with respect to the commandments.

In addition, we have preserved for us the idea that "at the beginning of Creation, all was permitted."[25] This idea is hinted at in the Sifra. For it is written in the Torah: "Cain knew his wife, and she conceived and bore Enoch" (Genesis 4:17). Who was this wife? Our Rabbis expounded and said that a twin sister was born with Cain, and he married his sister.[26] Now according to the belief that the Torah preceded Creation, how could Cain have married his sister, since it is written "If a man marries his sister, the daughter of either his father or his mother, . . . it is a disgrace [*hesed*]; they shall be excommunicated" (Leviticus 20:17)? They thus expounded: "Should you wonder at the fact that Cain married his sister, the Torah says it is a *hesed* [which can also mean an act of kindness]. From its inception, the world was created through *hesed*, as it is written, 'I declare, the world is built through *hesed*' (Psalm 89:3)."[27]

"You shall add three more towns to those three" (Deuteronomy 19:9): "The text speaks of messianic days. But perhaps it is speaking not of messianic days but rather of the hereafter?[12] Therefore, the text says: "if you faithfully observe all this Instruction" (Deuteronomy 19:9). Are there to be commandments in the hereafter!?"[28] Here we find a distinction between messianic days, in which commandments still apply, and the hereafter, when commandments no longer all apply.[29]

The Lord Releases Prohibitions

"'The Lord releases the bound' (Psalm 146:7)—what does it mean to release the bound? There are those who say: All animals that were prohibited in this world, the Holy and Blessed One will purify in the hereafter. Similarly, it is said: "That which has happened will yet happen, and that which has occurred will yet occur" (Ecclesiastes 1:9)—"which has occurred" refers to the fact that all animals were once pure for all humanity, as it is said: "as with the green grasses, I give you all these [creatures]" (Genesis 9:3). Why then were they prohibited? So that God could determine who would accept God's command, and who would not.[13] But in the hereafter, God will

[25] Tanhuma Shemini, 8.

[26] Tosefta Yevamot, chapter 8; BT Yevamot 62a; BT Sanhedrin 58b.

[27] Sifra Kedoshim 92:4.

[28] Midrash Tannaim, Deuteronomy 19:9.

[29] Compare this with the formulation in a Baraita found in BT Sanhedrin 97a and Avodah Zarah 9a: "It was taught in the School of Elijah that the world endures for 6000 years; 2000 years of chaos, 2000 years with Torah, and 2000 years of messianic days.

[12] Note carefully the difference between the two: the messianic era is simply an extension of present history into an era of peace and plenty. "The hereafter" is a more ambiguous phrase that suggests a new era that is not continuous with this world and its history. Thus, the Torah and its commandments could conceivably change there.

[13] This has the sound and feel of a polemic against Paul's vision of the now-permitted animals reported in Acts.

release that which was prohibited."[30] The above comes from a relatively late midrash. Yet an earlier text contains a similar idea: "How will Behemoth and Leviathan be slaughtered in the hereafter? Behemoth will stab Leviathan with its horns, and Leviathan will tear Behemoth with its fins. And will the righteous consider this to be a proper slaughtering? Have we not learned, 'All may slaughter, and at any time, and with every implement, except for a sickle, a saw, teeth, or a fingernail, for these strangulate the animal'? Said Rabbi Abba bar Kahana: The Holy and Blessed One said 'Torah shall go forth from Me' (Isaiah 51:4)—that is, a renewal of Torah shall go forth from Me."[31] That is: The Holy and Blessed One will create a new teaching, which will release the prohibition on animals not slaughtered in accordance with *halakhah*.[32]

It is commonly assumed that this idea concerning the voiding of mitzvot in the hereafter is an alien growth in the field of Jewish thought, a foundling of dubious parentage. All the more so is the reading of the verse "The Lord releases the bound" as referring to permissions and prohibitions considered to be an unworthy exegesis, from which exudes an odor of heresy[14] and frivolity. But note that already in the period of the Tannaim there was discussion concerning the continuation of certain mitzvot in the hereafter. Indeed, Rabbi Ishmael and Rabbi Akiva themselves differed on the import of one explicit biblical text,[15] which had the potential to support the idea of the voiding of certain mitzvot in the hereafter. For whoever argued that things currently forbidden are destined to be permitted by the Holy and Blessed One in the age to come would seek to demonstrate from a biblical verse that this permissiveness was from hoary antiquity; it was simply that something that the Holy and Blessed One forbade in a particular era He would once again permit in a subsequent era.

"When the Lord enlarges your territory . . . you may eat meat whenever you wish" (Deuteronomy 12:20)—"Rabbi Ishmael said: This indicates that meat on demand was forbidden to the Israelites in the desert, but permitted to them when they entered the Land. Rabbi Akiva said: This verse comes only to teach you the regulations associated with it."[33] That is, according to Rabbi Ishmael, the verse in Deuteronomy that seems to be the issuance of a dispensation to eat nonsacrificial meat is just that—it permitted something that was previously forbidden. This, of course, is in keeping with the general Ishmaelian trend to read verses in their most natural way. Rabbi

---

[30] Midrash Tehillim 146:4. See also Y. Baer, "Hamidrashim Hamezuyafim shel Raimondos Martini," in *Studies in Memory of Asher Gulak and Samuel Klein*, ed. S. Assaf (Jerusalem: Hebrew University Press, 1942), 28–49, concerning the spurious text which interprets the word *hazir* ("swine") to signify that God will one day return (*hahazir*) it to Israel as a permitted animal.

[31] Leviticus Rabbah 13:3.

[32] See also Tanhuma Shemini 7 and Tanhuma Re'eh 6.

[33] Sifre, Re'eh 75.

---

[14] It definitely has an "aroma" of antinomianism. But the point here is that while (at least part of) Jewish thought was prepared to consider the idea of amendment or abrogation of certain prohibitions, it was, unlike the Pauline arguments, not directed at life in our own (premessianic) times.

[15] To be presented in the next paragraph.

Akiva, however, reads Deuteronomy 12:20 not as permitting something that is forbidden but rather as adding restrictive regulations with respect to how to eat meat on demand. Rabbi Ishmael held that during the time that the Israelites were in the desert (that is, from the time that the Tabernacle was erected) they were forbidden to slaughter animals outside the Tabernacle, and were required to bring all meat to be slaughtered to the Tent of Meeting. In other words: they were forbidden to eat "meat of desire," that is, secular slaughter that was done only to satisfy a desire for meat. According to this view, they ate only "sacrifices of well-being," that is, the flesh of animals that had been offered sacrificially. Only after they entered the Land were they permitted meat on demand. Over and against this, Rabbi Akiva held that the Israelites were never forbidden to eat meat on demand and that the purpose of Deuteronomy 12:20 was to add a restriction that they never had. For in the desert they were in the habit of piercing the animal (that is, they would kill the animal with a thrust to the neck with a knife or sharp rod), but when they entered the Land, pierced meat was forbidden to them, and they were given the regulations for slaughter that are referred to in the next verse (Deuteronomy 12:21).[16]

Pay close attention to the fact that those who held the position that certain stringencies might be nullified in the age to come associated themselves with the view of Rabbi Ishmael. "The Sages said: The Holy and Blessed One forbade many things that He then permitted again at another time. The proof? The Holy and Blessed One forbade the Israelites from slaughtering and eating meat unless it was brought to the Tent of Meeting (so Leviticus 17:4), and then He once again permitted them to do so (so Deuteronomy 12:15, 20)."[34] The author of this midrash apparently left something out, for he announces that "many things" were forbidden and then permitted again, but he gives but a single example. It is possible that he intended us to think also of a matter that appears in the Babylonian Talmud in the name of Rav: "The first man was not permitted to eat meat at all, for it is written: 'I give you every seed-bearing plant that is upon all the earth, and every tree that has seed-bearing fruit; they shall be yours for food, and for all the animals on land (Genesis 1:29)—but the beasts of the field are not for you to eat. But along came the sons of Noah, and God permitted it to them, as it says: 'as with the green grasses, I give you all these' (Genesis 9:3)."[35]

Even more impressive than this is what is said in the Sifre on the verse "[You shall not] erect a stone pillar; for such the Lord your God detests" (Deuteronomy 16:22): "The pillar, which was beloved in the case of the ancestors, was hated in the case of

[34] Deuteronomy Rabbah 4:6.
[35] BT Sanhedrin 59b.

---

[16] Heschel here makes the observation that, since the Akivan view was that the entire Torah was given in one fell swoop, it was not possible to say that originally meat on demand was forbidden but then later was permitted (out of practicality, when they entered the Land of Israel, and the central Sanctuary was too distant to be visited whenever meat was desired). It is, however, compatible with this view (though Heschel does not explicitly say this) that additional restrictive regulations might have been added later.

the descendants."[36] Note also that at Sinai, Moses or Master erected "twelve pillars for the twelve tribes of Israel" (Exodus 24:4) and that in the steppes of Moab, the pillars were forbidden.

Moreover, one should note yet another matter in which there was a disagreement over whether changes could happen in God's commandments, that is, whether something that was forbidden by God at one time was later permitted again. In the school of Rabbi Ishmael, they expounded as follows: "These are the animals that you may eat" (Deuteronomy 14:4)—"Why was this said? For since God had said, 'as with the green grasses, I give you all these' (Genesis 9:3), I might have thought that 'all these' meant to include all animals. Thus the text says: 'These are the animals'—to tell us that everything had been permitted until the Torah was given, but that once the Torah was given, it was said: 'So you shall set apart the clean beast from the unclean' (Leviticus 20:25)." Over and against this, it was expounded in the school of Rabbi Akiva: "These are the creatures that you may eat" (Leviticus 11:2)—"This clarifies something that came before. For since it had been said 'As with the green grasses, I give you all these' (Genesis 9:3), I might have thought that all animals were included. Thus the text says: 'These are the creatures that you may eat.'" According to this point of view, the descendants of Noah as well were not permitted to eat all animals, and thus that the prohibition on impure animals given to the Israelites contained no change in God's commands.

Changes in Halakhah

The law concerning the offering of a sacrifice at a "shrine"—that is, a place, other than the Tabernacle or the Temple, at which an altar was raised for the offering of sacrifices—changed several times, sometimes permissively and sometimes restrictively. Until the Tabernacle was erected [in the desert], the Israelites would offer their sacrifices at shrines created wherever they wished, as had been done from the time of Adam through the time of Moses our Master. Once the Tabernacle was erected, the shrines were forbidden, and sacrifices could be offered only in the desert at the Tent of Meeting (Leviticus 17:9). After the Israelites had crossed the Jordan and come to Gilgal, where the Tabernacle stood for the seven years of conquest and the seven years of land distribution and settlement, the shrines were permitted, "for they no longer camped around the Tabernacle and thus the sanctity of the Israelite camp was nullified."[37] When the Tabernacle had come to Shiloh (Joshua 18:1), the shrines were once again forbidden. After the destruction of Shiloh, when the Tabernacle moved first to Nob, and then to Gibeon, the shrines were once again permitted. But once

---

[36] Sifre Shofetim 146; see also Joseph Albo, Ikkarim, Part III, chapter 16. This matter is very difficult to reconcile with Rabbi Akiva's view that the entire Torah was given at Mount Sinai, unless one is to say that since the ancestors predated Sinai, the problem never arises.

[37] Rashi, BT Zevahim 112b.

King Solomon built the Temple in Jerusalem, the shrines were forbidden and never again permitted.[38]

The Torah decreed that daughters [who have inherited land from their fathers] should not marry men from another tribe: "This is what the Lord has commanded concerning the daughters of Zelophehad: They may marry anyone they wish, provided they marry into a clan of their father's tribe. No inheritance of the Israelites may pass over from one tribe to another, but the Israelites must remain bound each to the ancestral portion of his tribe. Every daughter among the Israelite tribes who inherits a share must marry someone from a clan of her father's tribe" (Numbers 36:6–8). Thus was some intermarriage among tribes forbidden.

According to the school of Rabbi Akiva, this prohibition applied only to that generation, the generation "that stood before Mount Sinai," but not for all subsequent generations.[39] This matter was inferred from the phrase "This is what the Lord has commanded" (Numbers 36:6)—"This matter shall not apply except in the current generation."[40] In other words, this prohibition was limited from the outset to a single generation, and thus there was never any reason to release it.

However, according to the plain meaning of the Gemara, this prohibition was in force in Israel until they arose and released it: "Rabban Simeon ben Gamaliel said: There were no days as good for Israel as the 15th of Av and the Day of Atonement. . . . What was the 15th of Av? Said Rav Judah in the name of Samuel: It was the day on which the tribes were permitted to intermarry freely."[41] "Were permitted" implies that they were originally forbidden to each other.[42]

A change occurred also in the law of the authorized officiants in the Temple: "At first, the Service was performed by the firstborn, but since they sinned in making the calf, the Levites earned the right to succeed them."[17] [43] In other words: "Until the Tabernacle was erected, the shrines were permitted, and the Service was performed by the firstborn. Once the Tabernacle was erected, the shrines were prohibited, and the Service was performed by the Priests."[44]

[38] Mishnah Zevahim 14:4–8; Sifre Re'eh 65.

[39] Sifra Emor 100a; see also BT Bava Batra 120a.

[40] BT Bava Batra 120a; see Rava's statement in BT Bava Batra 121a and Samuel's statement in BT Ta'anit 30b. It is clear that this exegesis has its source in Tannaitic midrashim. Perhaps its original setting was the Sifra, for as it stands, the Sifra's source for its conclusion is absent.

[41] BT Ta'anit 30b, and the commentary attributed to Rashi there: "For God had commanded . . . 'but the Israelite tribes shall remain bound each to its portion' . . . and they arose and released this restriction on the 15th of Av."

[42] The view that inheriting daughters were obligated to marry within their tribe well beyond the first generation is preserved also in the "Tosefta of the Targum" (as quoted in Kimchi on Judges 11:1), in Saadia Gaon, *Sefer ha-Mitsvot* [*The Book of the Commandments*], ed. Yeroham Fishel Perla (New York: Y. A. Grosman, 1961), 3:321ff.), Abraham ibn Ezra (to Numbers 36:8), and Bahya ben Asher (Numbers 36, where he also quotes Targum Jonathan).

[43] Numbers Rabbah, chapter 3.

[44] BT Zevahim 112b, Bekhorot 4b.

[17] That the Levites were innocent in the matter of the calf is implied by Exodus 32:26.

It is written in the Torah: "No Ammonite or Moabite shall be admitted into the congregation of the Lord; none of their descendants, even in the tenth generation, shall ever be admitted into the congregation of the Lord" (Deuteronomy 23:4). Now since it is the Torah's style to speak in the masculine gender,[18] it would seem that the plain meaning of this verse is that an Ammonitess or a Moabitess is also forbidden to enter the congregation of Israel.[19] Now Boaz is said to have spoken as follows to Ruth the Moabitess: "[you] came to a people you had not known yesterday or the day before" (Ruth 2:11). A midrash reads it as follows: "He said to her that had she come yesterday or the day before, she would not have been accepted, for as of then there had not yet been the halakhic innovation, according to which the verse meant "an Ammonite and not an Ammonitess; a Moabite and not a Moabitess."[45]

This last innovation, according to the Talmud came from the court of Samuel the Ramatite.[46] Yet there were those of that generation who objected to this new ruling, and thus ridiculed David.[20] [47] Rabbi Abba bar Kahana gave this exegesis: "So tremble, and sin no more" (Psalm 4:5—the Hebrew consists of three words, which, as an acronym form the name "Ruth")—"Said David before the Holy and Blessed One: How long will they agitate[21] against me, saying that I am of unqualified lineage, descending as I do from Ruth the Moabitess?"[48] And it is possible that not all of the Sages agreed that it is proper to restrict this prohibition to males alone.[49]

The Babylonian Talmud states that they wanted to suppress the Book of Ezekiel, because it contains passages that flatly contradict the Torah, such as: "Priests shall not eat anything, whether bird or animal, that died or was torn by beasts" (Ezekiel 44:31), which implies that Israelites[22] may do so. Or this: "You shall do the same on the seventh day of the month . . ." (Ezekiel 45:20), a sacrificial rite that is nowhere

---

45 PRK 16.
46 BT Yevamot 77a; Samuel the Ramatite is Samuel the Prophet.
47 BT Yevamot 76b; PT Sanhedrin 2:3; Midrash Samuel chapter 22.
48 Ruth Rabbah, beginning of chapter 8.
49 Sifre Deuteronomy 249, giving a difference of opinion between R. Judah and the Sages. See Finkelstein's note there.

---

[18] That is, even when not intending to restrict the matter at hand to males; this is a common feature of the Hebrew language, which has no ready method of speaking in gender-neutral terms, and in which mixed male and females groups (even one thousand females and one male) are always, by grammatical rule, spoken of in the masculine.

[19] "Entering the congregation" had, from earliest times, been understood as synonymous with "marrying an Israelite man or woman." It is by no means certain that this is the plain meaning of the verse in the Torah, but that is its normative assigned meaning from earliest rabbinic (and perhaps pre-rabbinic) times.

[20] The reason for the ridicule is that David was a third-generation descendant of Ruth the Moabitess, and if the Torah meant to exclude Moabite women as well, then David was not only not fit to be king, but he was not even fit to marry an Israelite woman!

[21] The Hebrew word comes from the same root as the word for "tremble" in the verse being expounded.

[22] That is, non-priests.

mentioned in the Torah! And by the same token, "the flour offering is not the same as the one described in the Torah; there is thus here an innovation for the future. Moreover, he has not mentioned at all the daily evening offering, and thus it seems that in the future, there is to be only a morning offering."[50] The Babylonian Talmud made much of this difficulty, and said of these verses that "Elijah will someday interpret this section for us."[51] According to Maimonides, the sacrifices and the order of the service given in the Book of Ezekiel will apply in the days of the messianic king, when the Third Temple is built.[52]

Rabbi Abraham ibn Ezra quotes those who say that when Abraham was told "bring him [Isaac] up as a burnt offering" (Genesis 22:2), what God intended was that Abraham would simply "bring Isaac up" to the mountaintop, and that would be considered as if he had brought a burnt offering. But Abraham, according to this view, did not have this prophetic insight, and rushed actually to slaughter him. God then told him, "this is not what I wanted. . . ." Now, says ibn Ezra, "these Sages were forced to offer this interpretation because on their view it is impossible that once God has issued a command it could be rescinded. But what escaped their attention was the elevation of the firstborn, who were then replaced by the Levites after a year."[53]

Rabbi Moses Isserles was astonished at Gersonides' view that such things represent "a change in the will of the Creator, may He be blessed, and not a change brought about by the recipients of the command." Isserles believes that "primeval human beings would worship oxen, lambs, and other animals . . . and this mistake came upon them when they inferred from the prohibition on eating meat not that it was God's will, but rather that the animals had a godly quality to them. They thus erred, and this continued until they were wiped out in the generation of the Flood. Then, in order to remove all confusion, since the Holy and Blessed One wished to make the world righteous after the Flood, God permitted the eating of meat, and thus the killing of animals, so that people would know that there is no godliness in them."[54] There was no change in God's will here, says Isserles; the change was generated by those subject to the command. In Isserles' view, this reasoning resolves a question posed by Nahmanides: According to the midrash that Father Abraham fulfilled the entire Torah and taught it to his children even before it was given, how is it possible that Jacob set up a pillar and married two sisters . . . how could Jacob have permitted to himself things that were forbidden by the Torah to Abraham? "However, according to what we have written in the matter of changes in the commandments . . . it is possible that the marrying of two sisters was not a transgression at all in patriarchal times, but was rather instituted later on."[55]

---

[50] David Kimchi to Ezekiel 46:13, and also to 45:22 and 46:4.

[51] BT Menahot 45a.

[52] Maimonides, *Mishneh Torah*, "Laws Concerning the Offering of Sacrifices," 2:14 (and see *Lehem Mishneh* there).

[53] Ibn Ezra to Genesis 22:1.

[54] Torat Ha-Olah II, chapter 44.

[55] Ibid.

Will the Commandments Be Nullified in the Age to Come?

The most extreme statement on this subject is preserved in the Babylonian Talmud in the name of Rav Joseph: "The commandments will be nullified in the age to come."[56] Certainly, this statement is no inadvertence.[23] The Sages were careful with their pronouncements, and the inadvertence of a Sage amounts to a willful act.[24] The author of this particular statement was praised by his contemporaries as "Sinai,"[25] because of his fluency in all oral tradition, and they said of him that "everyone needs a grain merchant"; that is, the *halakhot* that are the Jewish staples were well ordered in his mind "as on the day they were given at Sinai."[57]

Many Sages dealt with the matter of laws that do not apply in contemporary times; for example, they studied Mishnayot and even differences of opinion concerning the Temple service, assuming as they did that these were "*halakhot* that would be necessary in messianic times, when the Temple is rebuilt." Rav Joseph was the only one who, when determinations were made in such areas of law, raised the question: "Are you deciding law for messianic times?" That is, he believed that the commandments would be nullified in the age to come, and thus "there is no need to treat matters of Halakhah for the messianic age."[58]

Yet Rav Joseph did not invent this idea by himself. It preceded him and is taught already in Tannaitic literature. The fulfillment of commandments in messianic times was a matter that many Sages struggled with. Ben Zoma is the first Sage known to us who broached the matter of the nullification of the commandments in messianic times. Ben Zoma was a colleague of Rabbi Akiva and was among those who entered the *Pardes*. The Sages interpreted the verse "so that you may remember the day of your departure from the land of Egypt all the days of your life" (Deuteronomy 16:3) as follows: "'the days of your life' would already denote this world; 'all the days of your life' thus comes to add messianic days."[26] But Ben Zoma said to the Sages: "Are we really going to recall the Exodus from Egypt in messianic days? Was it not already said,

---

[56] BT Niddah 61b. See Tosafot s.v. *amar Rav Yosef,* and also BT Ketubot 111b and the Tosafot there.
[57] See Rashi on BT Horayot 14a.
[58] Reuven Margoliot, *Margoliot Hayyam,* Sanhedrin 51d; see also Tosafot Yeshanim, Yoma 13a.

---

[23] Literally, "an error issuing from the mouth of a ruler"; the reference is to Ecclesiastes 10:5, a phrase used in rabbinic usage to refer to an utterance (esp. a vow) that has power greater than that imagined by the one who utters it.

[24] Here the reference is to Rabbi Judah's statement in Mishnah Avot 4:13.

[25] This nickname for Rav Joseph was intended to express his embodiment of Torah. See BT Berakhot 64a and Horayot 14a.

[26] This much of the colloquy is familiar from the standard text of the Passover Haggadah.

'Assuredly, a time is coming—declares the Lord—when it shall no more be said, "As the Lord lives, who has brought the Israelites out of the land of Egypt," but rather, "As the Lord lives, who brought out and led the offspring of the House of Israel from the northland and from all the lands to which I have banished them." And they shall dwell upon their own soil' (Jeremiah 23:7–8)." But the Sages retorted: "It is not that the Exodus from Egypt will be forgotten, but rather that it will remembered in addition to the Exodus from all of the oppressive kingdoms; they will be primary, and the Exodus from Egypt secondary."[59]

Embedded in Ben Zoma's words is the idea that many commandments will be nullified in the age to come, for all of the festivals, the eating of Matzah, the prohibition on Hametz, the Paschal sacrifice, the recitation of the Shema, and many other commandments as well, are remembrances of the Exodus. And if the Exodus is not to be recalled in messianic times, then these commandments will become null and void.[60]

"A mamzer shall not be admitted into the congregation of the Lord; none of his descendants, even in the tenth generation, shall be admitted into the congregation of the Lord" (Deuteronomy 23:3). This was interpreted to mean that a mamzer may not marry into an Israelite family; a male mamzer may not marry an Israelite woman, and a female mamzer may not marry an Israelite man, forever. For immediately adjacent in the text is the verse: "No Ammonite or Moabite shall be admitted into the congregation of the Lord"—for they too are children of incest, from the daughters of Lot—and in that verse it says, "None of their descendants, even in the tenth generation, shall *ever* be admitted into the congregation of the Lord" (Deuteronomy 23:4). Just as the tenth generation mentioned below means "forever," so does the tenth generation listed above mean "forever."[61]

There were Sages who were sensitive to the "tears of the oppressed" who poured out their hearts to the Holy and Blessed One and argued before God: "Master of the Universe: even if my ancestors sinned, what have I done? My own actions have been proper before You."[27] And along came masters of the Aggadah and said that their remedy would come in the age to come. This matter was in fact a subject of controversy among the Tannaim.

Mamzerim and Netinim "will be purified in the age to come, according to Rabbi Yosi. Rabbi Meir said: they will not be purified. Rabbi Yosi responded: Was it not said, 'I will sprinkle clean water upon you, and you shall be clean' (Ezekiel 36:25). Said to him Rabbi Meir: when it says there 'from all your uncleanness and from all your fetishes' (ibid.), it means to exclude mamzerut. Rabbi Yosi responded to him: When it says 'I will cleanse you' (ibid.), you must say that it includes even *mamzerut*."[62]

---

[59] Tosefta Berakhot 1:10; see also the formulation in MI, Pisha Bo 16.

[60] See RaSHBA (Solomon ben Adret, thirteenth century, Spain), in his "Perush Aggadot" on *Ein Ya'akov*, Berakhot 12, where he cites a debate on this subject in his own generation.

[61] Sifre Deuteronomy 248.

[62] Tosefta Kiddushin 5:2; BT Kiddushin 72b; PT Kiddushin, end of chapter 3.

---

[27] This complaint expresses the apparent injustice of stigmatizing mamzerim for the misdeeds of their parents.

"Rav Huna said: if the *halakhah* is not according to Rabbi Yosi, then future genera-tions are unfortunate indeed."[63] In the Babylonian Talmud the law was decided in accordance with Rabbi Yosi. And Rav Joseph said: "Had Rav Judah not said in the name of Samuel that the law agrees with Rabbi Yosi, Elijah would have to remove whole groups from our midst forcibly."[64]

Note that Rabbi Johanan, Rabbi Phinehas, and Rabbi Levi all transmitted a bold saying in the name of the Tanna Rabbi Menahem of Galatia: "In the age to come, all of the sacrifices will be null and void," and only the Thanksgiving Offering will not be nullified.[65] Similarly, they said: "The sacrifices apply only in this world, but the prac-tices of charity and civil justice apply both in this world and the next."[66]

On the other hand, most of the Sages anticipated and hoped for the renewal of the sacrificial service. From the time the Temple was destroyed, Rabban Johanan ben Zakkai instituted a rule that on the entire day on which the Omer used to be waved, the 16th of Nisan, it would be prohibited to eat of the new grain. This, even though when the Temple was standing the offering of the Omer would immediately permit the eating of new grain.[67] [28] The Babylonian Talmud says: "What is the reason for this decree [that the new grain would be forbidden all day]? When the Temple is speedily rebuilt, they might say: 'Last year we ate the new grain as soon as the day dawned. We will do so again this year'; they would do this out of ignorance of the fact that last year, when there was no Omer, the dawn permitted it, but now that there is an Omer offering, it is only the offering that permits it.[68]

In a late midrash, it is said: "All of the festivals will one day be nullified, but the days of Purim will never be nullified . . . . Rabbi Eleazar said that even the Day of Atonement will never be nullified."[69] Compare with this: It once happened that a cer-tain Gentile asked Rabbi Akiva: "Why do you observe festivals? Did not the Holy and Blessed One say to you, 'Your New Moon and fixed seasons fill Me with loathing' (Isaiah 1:14)?" Rabbi Akiva answered him: "Had it said, 'My new moon and fixed seasons fill Me with loathing,' I would agree. But it says, 'Your new moon and fixed seasons,' for it was because of the festivals that were instituted by Jeroboam son of Nebat, as it is said: 'And Jeroboam established a festival on the fifteenth day of the eighth month; in imitation of the one in Judah, he established one at Bethel, and he ascended the altar to sacrifice to the calves that he had made, and he stationed at

[63] Leviticus Rabbah 32:7 (Margoliot ed., p. 754).
[64] BT Kiddushin 72b.
[65] Leviticus Rabbah 9 and 27: see also chapter 4 above, pp. 85–87.
[66] Deuteronomy Rabbah 5:3.
[67] Mishnah Rosh Hashanah 4:3.
[68] BT Rosh Hashanah 30a, and see the comments of Jacob Emden on that passage.
[69] Midrash Mishlei 9:2; PRE 46; YS Mishlei 944.

[28] That is, the grain that had matured subsequent to the offering brought in the previous year on 16 Nisan.

Bethel the priests of the shrines that he had appointed' (1 Kings 12:32). Our festivals, however, will never be nullified, and neither will the New Moons. Why? Because they belong to the Holy and Blessed One, as it is said: 'These are My fixed times, the fixed times of the Lord' (Leviticus 23:2), and it is written: 'So Moses declared to the Israelites the set times of the Lord' (Leviticus 23:44), and that is why they can never be nullified."[70]

An even bolder statement was made: "There is no prohibition more stringent than that of the menstruant, for when a woman sees blood, the Holy and Blessed One forbids her to her husband. But in the age to come, she will be permitted: 'In that day . . . I will also make the "prophets" and the unclean spirit vanish from the land' (Zechariah 13:2)."[71] But against this Rabbi Simeon put forth this idea in the name of Rabbi Simon Hasida: "In this world, if a man goes to harvest figs on the Sabbath, the fig tree is silent; but in the future world, if a man goes to harvest figs on the Sabbath, the tree will shout out: 'It is Shabbat!' Similarly, in this world, if a man intends to have relations with his menstruating wife, his bed will not impede him. But in the future world, should he set out to do so, his very genitals[29] will shriek, 'she is a menstruant!'"[72] And even in the matter of forbidden foods, others say, "they will not be permitted in the age to come, for so it says: 'those who eat the flesh of the swine, the reptile, and the mouse, shall one and all come to an end, declares the Lord' (Isaiah 66:17). . . and some say that *all* sexual intercourse will be forbidden in the age to come."[73]

Medieval (and Hasidic) Echoes of the Debate on the Renewal of Torah

Most Sages in the Middle Ages taught "that the commandments will never be nullified, not in this world, not in the messianic age, nor at any other time, save for the resurrection of the dead, for those who have died will have already been freed from them."[74] They were opposed to any suggestion that the commandments of the Torah were temporary, and they did this in order to distinguish themselves sharply from the Christians, who maintained that point in disputations with Jewish Sages.[75]

In the matter of the Temple and sacrifices, Maimonides set forth: "The messianic king will in the future come and reestablish the Davidic monarchy . . . and will build the Temple . . . and all laws will return to how they were when the Temple existed:

[70] Numbers Rabbah, end of Phinehas; see also Tanhuma and TB there, and Lamentations Rabbah 2:6.
[71] Midrash on Psalms 146:4.
[72] Midrash on Psalm 73 (end).
[73] Midrash on Psalms 146:4.
[74] See Leviticus Rabbah 13:3 and textual variants, Margoliot ed. p. 278; Yefe To'ar, ad loc.
[75] Compare R. Solomon Adret on Ein Ya'akov, Berakhot, end of chapter 1; and Isaac Abravanel, *Rosh Amana*, chapter 13.

---

[29] Reading *ha-even tzo'ek* (a grammatical impossibility) as *ha-ever tzo'ek*.

they will bring sacrifices . . . and whoever does not believe in this . . . denies the Torah and Moses our Master."[76] In this, other Sages disagreed with him;[77] this includes Nahmanides, who evidently interpreted literally the saying that "all sacrifices would be nullified in the age to come."[78] However, in the matter of the Scroll of Esther and the festivals, Maimonides wrote otherwise: "All of the prophetic books and all of the Hagiographa will be nullified in the messianic age, except for the Scroll of Esther, which will endure just as the Pentateuch will, and just as the *halakhot* of the Oral Torah, which will never be nullified."[79] RaABaD at this point disputed Maimonides: "None of the sacred Scriptures will ever be nullified, for none of them are devoid of teaching; rather, this is what was meant: even if we were no longer to read from the other books of Scripture, the Scroll of Esther will never cease to be read in public."[80]

In contrast to this, Joseph Albo wrote: "We can surely say that there is nothing to prevent a divine command from releasing some prohibitions. For example, the prohibition on eating suet, or blood, or sacrifices slaughtered outside the Temple—these were originally prohibited when they left Egypt because the Israelites had been steeped in a culture that worshiped demons, and in doing so they ate suet and blood. Moreover, with respect to sacrifices slaughtered in any place, it was written: 'that they may offer their sacrifices no more to the goat-demons after whom they stray' (Leviticus 17:7). But once these cultic practices have been long forgotten, and all will come back to the worship of God, the reason for these prohibitions will be null and void, and it is possible to say that they will be permitted."[81]

According to the Zohar, the Torah exits in two degrees, in *beri'ah* and in *azilut*.[82][30] The Torah of Beri'ah is what is represented by the Tree of Knowledge, and the Torah of

---

[76] Maimonides, *Mishneh Torah,* "Laws Concerning Kings," 11:1.

[77] See, e.g., Meir ibn Gabbai, *Avodat Hakodesh,* "Ha'avodah," chapter 43, where he states his belief that after the resurrection, "there will be neither sin nor death. And thus there will be no purification offerings, no guilt offerings, indeed no sacrifices at all in the age to come, save the daily and additional offerings and the thanksgiving offering, all of which will never be nullified."

[78] See his commentary on the Torah, Leviticus 23:17. According to Meir ibn Sahula (who wrote a kabbalistic supercommentary on Nahmanides), the reason for this is that in messianic times there will be no need for the effluences of holiness that the sacrifices generate.

[79] Maimonides, *Mishneh Torah,* end of "Laws Concerning the Scroll [of Esther]."

[80] For similar views, see Meiri, end of Makkot, Responsa of Rashba, Part I #93, and Responsa of Radbaz, Part II, #666 and #828.

[81] *Ikkarim,* Part III, chapter 16.

[82] Preface to Tikkunei Ha-Zohar 4b; Zohar Bereshit 23a. See also Gershom Scholem, *Major Trends in Jewish Mysticism,* pp. 76ff, and Y. Tishbi, *Mishnat Hazohar* (Jerusalem: Mosad Bialik, 1949-61), 2:387ff.

---

[30] The worlds of *azilut* and *beri'ah* are, respectively, the realm of the emanations from the Godhead and the realm that connects that upper realm to the world of creation. Thus, the idea arose that the Torah had a pure, abstract form suitable for the realm of emanation, and necessarily had to take on a more worldly form, appropriate to the realm of creation. The latter, however, can be seen as a masquerade that will be removed when the realm of creation (i.e., the physical world) has had its day in times to come. This idea that the physical commands of the Torah are not the true Torah was, as might be imagined, an important tool in the hands of antinomians, who could claim that the world of Halakhah was not the "true" world.

Azilut is represented by the Tree of Life.[83] At the final redemption, according to Raya Mehemna, "Israel will taste of the Tree of Life, that is this book of the Zohar, and they will thus be released from exile in mercy . . . and the Tree of Knowledge of good and evil, that is the categories of permitted and forbidden, impure and pure, will no longer hold sway over Israel."[84]

"The first human being served God by contemplation, directed study and apprehension of the esoteric secrets of the supernal existences . . . he did not need the garments of the world of creation . . . now our Sages of blessed memory said: 'to till and tend it' (Genesis 2:15) means this—'to till it' refers to the positive commandments, and 'tend it' refers to the negative commandments[31] . . . and now it is legitimate to inquire: Would Adam need to plow in the Garden of Eden, so that he had to be commanded not to 'plow with an ox and an ass together'? (Deuteronomy 22:10) . . . would there be any strangers, orphans, or widows there? . . . rather, the intent [of the verse in Genesis 2:15] is the contemplative commandments . . . and there is no connection at all with the performative commandments . . . and just as the soul takes on a physical attire, so did the Torah take on a physical attire. And just as when the soul returns to its inner state, it takes off its physical garb, so will the Torah take off its physical garb, and then its generalities, particularities, and all of its teachings be known in their inner meaning. And this is the work of the righteous in the Garden of Eden.[85]

The Baal Shem Tov explained the saying "the commandments will be nullified in the future age" to mean that then "they will apprehend all aspects of the commandment and the root of the vitality of the commandment, and how it is identical with the vitality of one's own soul and that of the entire world . . . and how its secret essences illuminate the life of human beings and give life to all the worlds, and how it is impossible to achieve completeness in any other way."[86]

Rabbi Jacob Joseph of Polonnoye[32] writes: "In the future . . . the commandments will reside in spirituality . . . and it is to this that the Talmud referred when it said that they would be nullified in the future . . . that commandments will no longer have a

---

[83] Zohar Hadash, Tikkunim, 106d; Zohar Noah 63b.

[84] Raya Mehemna, Naso, 124b; see also Tishby, *Mishnat Hazohar*, 2:397.

[85] Moses Cordovero, *Pardes Rimmonim*, "The Gate of the Soul," chapter 6; see also R. Abraham Azulai, *Hesed Le-Avraham*, Ma'ayan II, Nahar 12.

[86] *Degel Mahanei Ephraim*, Tzav; see also *Shenei Luhot Haberit*, "The Gate of the Letters," 59a.

---

[31] The Hebrew supports this identification more than the English does. "To till it" is in Hebrew *le-ovdah*—which comes from the root meaning "to serve" or "to worship," and thus could be taken to mean positive acts of service to God, that is, positive, performative commandments ("thou shalts"). By contrast, "to tend" in Hebrew is *le-shomrah*, coming from the root that means "to guard," a root often used in rabbinic literature to refer to prohibitions (which guard against improper behavior), and which thus could be taken to refer to negative commandments ("thou shalt nots").

[32] Eighteenth century, Ukraine.

physical form, but rather a spiritual one."[87] According to Rabbi Menahem Mendel of Vitebsk,[33]

> this is what our Masters of blessed memory meant when they said that the commandments would be nullified in messianic times, for the earth would be full of the knowledge of God. They will then have a different Torah . . . and as they go from strength to strength, ever upward, until they reach the root of all Torah and all commandments, viz., "I am the Lord your God"—a simple and never ending unity—as they stand in that place, the wings of all the commandments and laws will droop, and all will be nullified. For the covenant is about the voiding of the evil inclination, and if one is now standing at a place so high that it precedes Beri'ah, then where can the evil inclination come from?[88]

In other kabbalistic works the following is said: "In this age, the *halakhah* follows the school of Hillel . . . but in the future, it will follow the school of Shammai. Similarly with the teachings of Rabbi Simeon bar Yohai: usually, the *halakhah* does not follow his opinion in the Gemara, for the world is not worthy of his teachings in this world; but in the future, the *halakhah* will follow Rabbi Simeon bar Yohai, when they will be able to uncover these laws from the esoteric secrets of the Torah."[89] "And this is the meaning of their statement: 'every controversy that is for the sake of Heaven will in the end be established'[90]—that in the end the opinion of the school of Shammai will be established, for both these and these are the words of the living God."[91]

According to Rabbi Levi Yitzhak of Berditchev,[34] "the school of Shammai represented the attribute of justice, and the school of Hillel the attribute of mercy. Because of this, the halakhah always followed the school of Hillel, for the Sages of blessed memory saw that the world needed the attribute of mercy. It thus emerges that with the coming of the Redeemer (speedily and in our day) the approach of the school of Shammai will predominate, for the world will no longer need mercy; indeed, justice will become mercy, and the halakhic decisions will follow the school of Shammai. And this is the new Torah that will come from God. It would seem that it is difficult to apply to the Torah the word "new," for is it not the case that Torah does not change? Rather, according to what we have said, there is no actual newness here, for the words of the school of Shammai are written right now in the Oral Torah. It is just that in the future the decision will follow them. For the root principle is that the decision in *halakhah* follows that which the world needs. And thus it all depends on the

---

[87] *Toledot Yaakov Yosef*, Preface.
[88] *Peri Ha'aretz*, Toledot; see also *Maggid Mesharim*, Vayyakhel.
[89] Moshe ben Menahem of Prague (seventeenth century), *Vayyakhel Moshe* (Dessau, 1699), 54a.
[90] Mishnah Avot 5:17.
[91] Hayyim Joseph David Azulai, *Petah Enayyim*, Avot chapter 5.

---

[33] Eighteenth century, Belorussia.
[34] Eighteenth century, Ukraine.

children of Israel; as we decide here, so does the Holy and Blessed One act toward God's creatures."[92]

According to Rabbi Nahman of Bratzlav,[35] "After this final exile will come the true revelation of the Torah."[93] [36]

---

[92] *Kedushat Levi*, Likkutim (Lublin, 1877), 3a; see also Rashi, Yoma 80a, where he speaks of the possibility of new *halakhot* in the future.

[93] *Likkut Etzot Ha-Meshulash*, "Awe and Service," 116.

---

[35] Eighteenth–nineteenth century, Ukraine.

[36] Heschel ends this chapter with a section laying out the differences that are apparent in rabbinic tradition and beyond with respect to the question of continuity of the messianic age with our own world. There were, clearly, two main points of view of this as well: (1) that the messianic age would be a radical departure from the world as we know it, with fundamental discontinuities in nature and in human society; and (2) that the messianic age will evolve continuously out of our own world, that it will feature no fundamental break in the laws of nature, and that its distinctive feature will be greater peace and prosperity. Heschel takes time to map out the various views because they are obviously related to the topic of whether Halakhah as we know it will continue to have the same force in the messianic age. But this section is really tangential here, interrupting as it does what is an unfolding treatment of the role of Halakhah in religious life, continuing into the next chapters. It is thus omitted in this translation.

36

BOTH THESE AND THESE
ARE THE WORDS OF THE LIVING GOD

Translator's Introduction

As noted in an introduction to a previous chapter, the well-known and well-worn phrase "both these and these are the words of the living God" is the subtitle given to the last eight chapters of *TMH*. To the extent that it is possible, Heschel is committed to tackling the problem of how the various theological strands of the rabbinic tradition can be recombined into a unified, though complex, view of revealed religion. This requires him to undertake an explication of how "both these and these . . ." can be understood (where "these and these . . ." is taken to refer to the humanist/rationalist/transcendent stance associated with Ishmael and the supernatural/spiritual/immanent stance associated with Akiva). Can these two perspectives really be merged in any coherent way?

He begins with a recognition that there is a natural tendency among many to reject the idea of a joining of opposites, the concept that two views that exclude each other could both have a divine imprimatur. In what sounds like a bit of condescension—or perhaps exasperation—Heschel begins by referring to "adherents of plain meaning," by which he does not mean Ishmaelians, but rather those who take an overly logical, linear view of religious thought. "How can Torah be learned in this way?" these thinkers ask. And indeed, the Jewish theological circles in which Heschel found himself were often taunted with just that criticism. As Elijah sneered at the Israelites at Mount Carmel: "How long will you continue to hop between two boughs?" Choose your religious stance! If it is a humanist/historical stance, so be it. If it is a belief in the eternally supernatural validity of Torah as God's word, so be it. But you cannot have it both ways.

Heschel's burden in the present, very pivotal, chapter is to answer those who negate the possibility of holding simultaneously noncongruent theological views. His most compelling answer is embodied in the section entitled "One Who Is Blind in One Eye Is Exempt from the Pilgrimage." It is written in signature Heschelian style, using an unexpected halakhic phrase in order to make a profound "aggadic" point about religious thought. Depth of field must not be sacrificed on the altar of consistency. And while inconsistency is not in itself a virtue, its opposite also must not be made into an absolute value. The arguments presented here are designed to provide succor to those

701

who, like the author himself, insist on honoring the ineffable complexity inherent in religious faith.

At the end of this chapter, Heschel turns briefly to the ways in which Halakhah is affected by these considerations, but that line of thought and argument is really taken up in the subsequent chapters.

One Thing God Has Spoken, Two Things Have I Heard

ADHERENTS OF PLAIN MEANING, who look for a clear bottom line in everything, including matters of faith, upon seeing the mighty struggles of opposing views, will ask in agitation: How can Torah be learned in this way? If there are two mutually exclusive ways of interpreting a single statement, and each has its justification, so that each carries its own truth, do we not have dualism?

But the pillars of their faith need not fail. Is it possible to have a living Torah without the struggle of opposites, without disputes, without the many permutations of ideas and outlooks? Thus did the Sages teach: "If one sees a large human population, one should say: 'Blessed is the One who is wise to all secrets.'" For just as the faces of human beings are not alike, so are their minds not alike. Each individual has thoughts of his or her own. And thus it is said, 'He fixed the weight of the spirit'[1] (Job 28:25)—the weight of each and every one."[1] "This teaches the greatness of the Holy and Blessed One. For when a human being mints many coins from a single die, each one is just like every other. But the King of kings of kings, the Holy and Blessed One, minted every person from the die of the first human, and no one is just like his fellow."[2] The human soul oscillates between two worlds; it flitters among opposites and contradictories. If what we are after is clear, unambiguous Halakhah, then we must take issue with every court from the days of Moses to the present.[2] "Do not imagine yourself to be the Chief Judge."[3]

---

[1] TB Pinehas 1; see also Tosefta Berakhot 6:2, and BT Berakhot 58a.   [2] Mishnah Sanhedrin 4:5.

---

[1] JPS renders this "weight of the wind." But the rabbinic homily here takes the Hebrew *ruah* in its other meaning of "spirit." Thus, it extracts from the verse in Job the notion that God is the Master of everyone's spirit and that each person's inner life, that is, thoughts, is individually created and fixed by God.

[2] This is a phrase taken from Mishnah Rosh Hashanah 2:9; a Baraita in BT Rosh Hashanah 25a affirms the legitimacy and authority of the religious leaders of every generation, even when they take issue with their predecessors. Here Heschel gives the argument another twist. He is saying that the halakhic pluralism that is implied by BT Rosh Hashanah is a long-established fact, and thus anyone who is offended by it will have to take issue with every generation of halakhists who have "upset" the (mythic) monolith of Halakhah!

[3] This translation follows Judah Goldin's suggestion for understanding *orkhei ha-dayyanin*—with *orkhei*

On this subject, Rabbi Eleazar ben Azariah, a contemporary of Rabbis Ishmael and Akiva, expounded: "those that are composed in collections" (Ecclesiastes 12:11)—"these are the disciples of the Sages who sit in groups and busy themselves with Torah. There are those who declare things impure, while others declare them pure; this group forbids, and this one permits; these declare 'unfit,' and these 'fit.' Should a person say: 'How can I learn Torah in this way?' the answer comes from Scripture: 'they were given by one Shepherd' (Ecclesiastes 12:11)—one God gave them, one Creator spoke them; they have all come from the blessed Master of all, as it is written: 'God spoke all these words'[4] (Exodus 20:1)."[3] "So should make your heart into many chambers, and acquire the skill to hear the words of those who say 'impure' as well as those who say 'pure,' of those who forbid and those who permit, of those who say 'unfit' and those who say 'fit.'"[4] Similarly, they said: "For three years the schools of Shammai and Hillel disputed each other. One said, 'the Halakhah agrees with us,' and the other said 'the Halakhah agrees with us.' Finally, an echoing voice came out and said: Both these and these are the words of the living God, and the Halakhah agrees with the school of Hillel."[5]

The MaHaRaL of Prague[5] said: "When the blessed God gave the Torah to Israel, every matter in the Torah was given just as it was, meaning that God said that this particular case has within it an aspect of innocence and an aspect of guilt; in matters of ritual prohibition, it was said that a particular case has an aspect of permissiveness and an aspect of prohibition, and similarly in matters relating to family relationships: there were always opposing aspects. Just as in the world generally, everything is composed of opposing elements . . . and you will not find any completely simple substance, so in the Torah there is no such thing as something so completely impure that it has no pure facet to it, though it has a facet of impurity as well. When one examines something from the point of view of purity, and applies his intellect to proving its purity, he has revealed one aspect of it . . . and when another gives reasons for saying "impure" of the same object, he has revealed another aspect of it. And that is

---

[3] BT Hagigah 3b.

[4] Tosefta Sotah 7:12; in Tanhuma Vayyelekh 1, it adds: "all were said through Moses from on high."

[5] BT Eruvin 13b; PT Berakhot 1:4 (3b); see also (for a similar use of the phrase) BT Gittin 6b. In PT Sotah 3:5 (19a): "the Halakhah always agrees with the School of Hillel."

---

understood as a corruption of the Greek *archae*. The more usual translation, which makes no sense here, is "Do not play the role of counsel for the litigants." In the translation given here, Heschel is presumed to be saying that one should not imagine that one could have access to a final, unchallengeable truth.

[4] This is a critical exegesis, in which the words that introduce the Ten Commandments in Exodus 20 are closely read to reveal that God spoke *all* these words. That is, it could have said *va-yedabber elohim et ha-devarim ha-eleh lemor*—"God spoke these words . . . ." But instead, the word *kol* was included, to say that "God spoke all these words. . . ." The inference drawn here is that it is not just the words written down in Exodus 20 that are from God, but all of the diverse and differing interpretations of those words as well.

[5] Rabbi Judah Loewe, seventeenth century.

what it means to say that all were said from the mouth of the Master of all . . . that is, just as the blessed Lord is the Master of all and the source of the complex world that includes combinations of opposites, so is it here. For given that the world is not simple, everything has aspects within it that fluctuate back and forth. . . . It is just that when it comes to practical Halakhah, there can be no doubt that often one of these aspects is more primary than the other . . . and on occasion even here the aspects may be of equal value . . . and then both derive from the blessed Lord equally, and neither can be established over the other, and such are the differences between Hillel and Shammai."[6] 6

"The sayings of the wise are like goads" (Ecclesiastes 12:11)—"Just as the goad directs the cow to plow so that the furrows are even, so do the words of Torah direct those who study them to say of the forbidden that it is forbidden and of the permitted that it is permitted . . . and should you say that there are those who permit and those who forbid, those who say 'unfit' and those who say 'fit,' those who say 'impure' and those who say 'pure,' Rabbi Eliezer imposes liability and Rabbi Joshua does not, the school of Shammai forbids and the school of Hillel permits—whom shall I obey? Even so, know that all were given by one Shepherd."[7] At first glance it is difficult to assimilate this; since the words of the school of Shammai are not the Halakhah, and the school of Shammai has no standing in the face of the school of Hillel, how is it possible to say "both these and these are the words of the living God"? Their statements contradict one another, and if one of them expresses a true opinion, does it not imply that the other is false? How can you then say "both these and these are the words of the living God"? Can two opposites dwell side by side?

Here are various interpretations that have been given to the phrase "both these and these are the words of the living God":

(a) Rashi:

When two Amoraim differ with one another in a matter of civil or ritual law, and each one gives a reasonable argument for his position, there is no falsity present. Each gives his own view; one argues for permissiveness, and the other for restrictiveness . . . and thus it can be said that both these and these are the words of the living God. For at times one argument applies and at other times the other argument applies, for the grounds for a decision shift as the conditions shift, even if slightly.[8] [7]

(b) Rabbi Meir ibn Gabbai:

There is nothing in the Torah on which there is a dispute, with some Sages saying one thing and others another, in which all does not ultimately flow to one place and come

---

6 Be'er Hagolah, Be'er 1.   7 TB Beha'alotekha 25.
8 Rashi on BT Ketubot 57a, s.v. *ha ka-mashma lan*, end.

---

[6] Again, we have the notion that there are no inherent qualities that would help us decide between Bet Hillel and Bet Shammai; it was merely a pragmatic consideration that elevated Bet Hillel to normative status (apart from a few exceptional cases).

[7] In other words, reason itself guarantees that each position will "have its day."

from one source. For it is written: "All streams flow into the sea" (Ecclesiastes 1:7) and "Both go to the same place" (Ecclesiastes 3:20).[9] . . . All flows from the same source, and in it are always opposite facets, and these give rise to the divergences and oppositions that cause fluctuation between impure and pure, forbidden and permitted, unfit and fit, as is known to those of discerning hearts. And the great voice without end draws from and comes forth from that source, and it is composed of all the fluctuating facets, leaving nothing out. With this great power, each thing shares in its opposing aspects, with each prophet and Sage apprehending what he apprehended of it. One would perceive "impure" or "pure" depending on his station and perspective; and yet all comes from one source, and flows to the same place . . . that is the "sea" in which all is united and in which unity is again established. And it is in respect of this that it was said "they were given by one Shepherd." And likewise, the Sages said "one God gave them," in order to assert that these opposites and variations do not flow from a plurality of domains, but rather from one certain place . . . it is in order to underscore this wonderful fundamental that each Sage upholds his own view and supports it with proofs from the Torah . . . and it is of this that it is said "both these and these are the words of the living God." . . . and though these things seem to be divergent from and contradictory to one another, that is just from our perspective, for we haven't the wherewithal to encompass them all. Thus, it seems to be impossible to sustain both sides of a dispute, and the Halakhah must be established according to one of the two opinions . . . though it is all one from God's perspective, from ours there are divergences and thus the Halakhah can only follow the school of Hillel.[10] [8]

(c) Hayyim Joseph David Azulai[9]:

The words of those who forbid and those who permit are all words of the living God given by one Shepherd, since the reasoning behind the position that is not the Halakhah helps us to understand the reasoning behind the position that is. This follows the principle that the true is best known through the false. And thus, the correct reasoning will not be fully and completely known to be true without the presence of the opposing reasoning."[11]

(d) Rabbi Salomon ben Abraham ibn Parhon[10] understands our statement as an elliptical one. It means to say, "both these and these are expounding the words of the living God," for "it is impossible that God's words should suffer any division, but

---

[9] *Avodat Hakodesh,* "Ha-takhlit," chapter 23.
[10] Ibid.
[11] *Devash Le-Fi,* 4:11, quoting *Me-Harerei Nemerim* (of Abraham ben Solomon Akra, sixteenth century).

---

[8] Here we have the mystical idea that the many just hide the essential unity that underlies all. Although such an approach can affirm pluralism as a manifestation of different aspects of an underlying unity, its emphasis on unity necessarily leads to a certain suspicion of pluralistic claims.
[9] Eighteenth century, Israel and Italy.
[10] Twelfth century, Italy.

rather the Halakhah must be like one of them, and the other must be rejected; one who does so[11] receives a reward for his study."12 [12]

(e) Rabbi Solomon Luria[13]:

All are the words of the living God, as if they had all been received from on high and from the mouth of Moses, although it may never have come from Moses' mouth in the form of two opposing views of the same subject. . . . The kabbalists gave a reason for this: it is because all souls were present at Mount Sinai and received the Torah through forty-nine separate channels . . . those being the sounds that they heard and also saw. All Israel "saw the sounds"—these were the interpretations that diverged through each channel, with everyone seeing through his own channel, according to his power . . . so that one perceived complete impurity and another perceived complete purity, and yet a third perceived a middle position between these two. All are true . . . they are all words of the living God."13 [14]

(f) Abraham ben Mordekhai Azulai:[15]

Just as God created one species of grass with many varied uses, or, to take another example, wine—which the physicians have told us has some sixty medicinal uses—and it is impossible to tell for which of those purposes they were created, how much more so is it the case with the divine word that it must bear many interpretations. And we cannot tell for what purpose the divine word was given.14

The problem before us—how it is possible that when some forbid and others permit, they can both be the words of the living God—was explained in a daring way by Rabbi Moses Sofer.[16] According to him, even a halakhic ruling that appears to us to be firm and correct may not be so according to the ultimate truth.

For forty-nine gates were revealed to Moses, and the fiftieth gate was not. And thus, given that in our eyes it seems certain that a certain thing is impure, it is possible that were we able to perceive the fiftieth gate, which represents a higher knowledge, then we would see that it is in fact pure. And thus, one who studies Torah for its own sake and quests for an apprehension of truth, may yet succeed in reaching the truth according to the fiftieth gate. Although it was never revealed, he may yet have the merit of apprehend-

---

12 *Mahberet He-Arukh*, ed. Zalman ben Gotlieb 5d.   13 *Yam shel Shelomo*, preface.
14 *Ba'alei Berit Avram*, preface.

---

[11] That is, studies the other opinion so as to reject it.

[12] The addition of the word "expounding" here makes it possible for ibn Parhon to treat this fundamental phrase as a *rejection* of pluralism.

[13] Sixteenth century, Poland.

[14] The many different points of view still share a common origin because they are projections in (necessarily) finite, human dimensions of an infinite whole. A helpful analogy (not, of course, intended by Luria) might be the various colors into which the continuous spectrum of light may be analyzed, with different observers seeing different colors through different filters.

[15] Seventeenth century, Morocco and Israel.

[16] Nineteenth century, Hungary.

ing just a spark of that fiftieth gate, just as it was said of Joshua son of Nun, that he had an understanding of the fiftieth gate.[17]

What did the echoing voice say? "Both these and these are the words of the living God, and the Halakhah agrees with the school of Hillel." Many students who were not sufficiently attentive used this statement in such a way as to sever its two parts; they focused on the first clause and ignored the second, as if it is fine for a person to "hop between two boughs."[18] As if the statement described a chaotic world in which everyone has the right to build his own shrine. In the Babylonian Talmud, it is asked: "Now since both these and these are the words of the living God, why did the school of Hillel have the merit of having the Halakhah agree with them? Because they were temperate and modest, teaching both their words and those of the school of Shammai, even letting those of the school of Shammai precede their own."[15] [19]

Even though it was determined early on that the Halakhah follows Rabbi Akiva and his disciples, they did not hesitate to preserve the Torah of Rabbi Ishmael. "And why do they mention the position of the individual together with the position of the majority, seeing that the Halakhah follows the majority? It is against the possibility that a court in the future may see matters like that individual and will be able to rely on his stated position."[16] Rabbi Judah said: "They mentioned the words of the individual alongside those of the majority so that if an urgent need were to arise they could rely on them."[17]

There never arose in Israel any Sage who so imprinted his characteristic stamp on Judaism as did Rabbi Akiva. According to an *aggadah,* the very heavens announce: "be scrupulous with respect to Rabbi Akiva and his teachings."[18] And yet it seems to me that the hour demands the teachings of Rabbi Ishmael, the minimalist teaching regarding the principle of "Torah from Heaven."[20]

---

[15] BT Eruvin 13b.   [16] Mishnah Eduyot 1:5.   [17] Tosefta Eduyot 1:4.   [18] BT Kiddushin 81a.

---

[17] This idea is based on a play on words. The Hebrew letter *nun* represents the number 50. And thus, *ben Nun* is not understood here to be Joshua's patronymic but rather a statement that he was familiar with the fiftieth and ultimate gate of understanding. Heschel unfortunately gives here no citation for this remarkable statement of Moses Sofer.

[18] The phrase is the one used by Elijah to deride the syncretism of the citizens of the northern kingdom of Israel in 1 Kings 18. Here it apparently is echoing the admonition in BT Eruvin 6a (and elsewhere) that it is sinful to pick out only the lenient positions of either Bet Hillel or Bet Shammai and follow them.

[19] That is, it is not that one position was inherently better than the other, but rather that practical reasons necessitate a uniform method of determining normative practice. Bet Hillel's reputed humility was a fine criterion for this purpose, since honoring it also tended to promote the value of tolerance.

[20] Having established in the previous paragraph what he believes to be the parallel between the school of Akiva and the school of Hillel, Heschel now drives his point home. Although there was never anything inherently superior about the Akivan school, they prevailed for reasons dependent on the needs of the times. And now, in our (Heschel's) age (which, according to BT Rosh Hashanah, has a standing equal to every other), practical considerations dictate a recapturing of the more humanistic (and pluralistic) exegesis of the Ishmaelian school.

One Who Is Blind in One Eye Is Exempt
from the Pilgrimage

Jewish thought is nourished from two sources, and it follows two parallel paths: the path of vision and the path of reason. With respect to those things that are given to objective measurement, reason is primary. With respect to things of the heart, vision is primary. It was, after all, a violation of the law of noncontradiction when they said of two mutually exclusive ideas: "both these and these are the words of the living God." A great principle was enunciated concerning religious faith: "'Observe' and 'Remember' were said in a single utterance."[21] Observe [guard] the plain meaning, but remember the esoteric meaning.[22] Just as we are obligated to observe, so are we required to remember. The Torah cannot be fulfilled unless one safeguards the plain meaning of the text and also remembers the revelation at Sinai. Torah can only be acquired in two ways: with reason's lens and the heart's lens. One who is blind in one eye is exempt from the pilgrimage.[23]

Here is a rule of thumb: there is no verbalization of wisdom that does not contain within it both give and take, that does not both wax and wane. Negative statements have positive connotations, and vice versa. Thought develops only through dialectic: through the synthesis of concepts that are opposed to one another and complement one another. A knife can only be sharpened by the blade of its counterpart. And here

---

[21] This, of course, was said concerning the two versions of the Fourth Commandment (the Sabbath) that appear in Exodus 20 and Deuteronomy 5, respectively. "Remember" (*Zakhor*) is the word that begins this commandment in Exodus, and "Observe" (*Shamor*) in Deuteronomy. The classical application of this phrase is meant to unite the performative and prohibitive aspects of Sabbath observance into one unitary whole. Here, however, Heschel exploits this common phrase to make a more sweeping statement about the phenomenology of human religiosity—that the religious temperament itself, not just a particular practice, is composed of two elements: the rational and the ineffable.

[22] This takes us back to the distinction Heschel made in the previous chapter between the creeds of Maimonides and the "remembrances" of Isaac Luria.

[23] Here again, Heschel exploits for his own rhetorical purposes a phrase from the halakhic literature. In BT Hagigah 2a, one Tanna makes this assertion quite literally—that one who cannot see out of one of his eyes is already exempt from the three-times-per-year pilgrimage to Jerusalem that was incumbent on all Israelite males. Here, however, Heschel has another kind of pilgrimage in mind, namely, the religious quest itself, the desire to be in the Presence of God. In this paragraph, he has maintained that a true religious vision requires the "depth of field" that can come only from having two eyes that see slightly differently. Just as this "parallax effect" is essential for proper vision, so is its spiritual counterpart essential for a full religious life. One who lacks one of these perspectives—either reason without heart, or heart without reason—is "exempt" from this religious quest, because he is quite literally unable to complete it!

is a precious principle that was articulated by our Rabbis: "A controversy that is for a heavenly purpose will in the end endure."[19] [24]

Thus, whoever says that these two approaches contradict one another is simply mistaken. Both are focused on one reality, and each is subsumed by the other. The hidden essence of reality is that of two natures coming together. They are both embedded in the human mind, competing with one another, struggling to emerge. And just as it is with reality itself, so it is with Torah. It was taught in the school of Rabbi Ishmael: "'Behold, My word is like fire—declares the Lord—and like a hammer that shatters rock' (Jeremiah 23:29)—just as the hammer throws off different sparks, so does a single verse throw off different interpretations."[20] Each interpretation has its own truth, but none can stand all by itself. "Had the Torah been given cut and dried, we would have no leg to stand on."[21]

The source, "the beginning"—this is one; the resultant streams, "heaven and earth"—these are two.[25] The light is one, and the vessels that contain it are two.[26] God created ideas Janus-like, in complements; what is sought is one, but the paths to it are two. Two modes of thought, vision and reason, appear to us as separate and distinct, vying and competing with each other. But in truth they are but two stakes of the same tent that support each other, with each unable to stand firm but for the presence of the other. Both share the same crown. One who stands outside sees an infringement of domains; one who stands within sees a blending of domains.[27]

Thus, it is necessary to shift viewpoints from time to time in order to see the fullness of reality. One must move from domain to domain, not with the purpose of

[19] Mishnah Avot 5:17.   [20] BT Sanhedrin 34a.   [21] PT Sanhedrin 4:2.

---

[24] This assertion in Mishnah Avot probably means something like "a controversy that is for the sake of Heaven will in the end be resolved constructively." Here, however, Heschel takes the phrase more literally, in keeping with his own argument: controversies that are born of sincere religious quests will endure; that is, they will *not* be resolved but will continue as controversies so as to ensure that we see the multidimensionality of religious truth! David Hartman gives a similar interpretation of the phrase in Avot in his book *Conflicting Visions: Spiritual Possibilities of Modern Israel* (New York: Schocken Books, 1990).

[25] That is, from the very beginning of creation, there was a duality in the world.

[26] In keeping with the emphasis on duality (as opposed to pluralism more generally) in this chapter, Heschel here suggests another analogy with respect to light—not the resolution of the continuous spectrum that we suggested in the previous section of this chapter, but rather the familiar wave/particle duality of light. Light is one, but it is contained by two complementary but distinct vessels.

[27] Yet another apt analogue to physical vision. From "inside the head," the two images created by the two eyes blend perfectly. The one who sees is not even aware of the duality/parallax. However, from the "outside," the eyes' two different images seem different, even incompatible. It all depends on vantage point. And the same is true of religion. Viewed from the perspective of one who has successfully "made the pilgrimage," the rational and spiritual components of religion are part of a seamless whole. Conversely, those who see the two as antithetical and in competition have not yet arrived at a religious fulfillment.

estranging oneself from the other, but rather in order to achieve fullness of vision. Neither univocality nor dualism, but rather manifold vision is the characteristic spirit of Aggadah. The nation has two countenances, which reflect two domains that are one. Despite the appearance of contradiction, there is in fact a covenant between opposites,[28] a covenant that unites different modes of apprehension. And there is vision in the seeing of both sides at once. The Torah can be both an elixir of life and a potion of death. The ashes of the cow purify the impure and pollute the pure. The Holy and Blessed One is both gracious and compassionate and jealous and vengeful. God is both immanent and transcendent.[29]

What Is Revealed and What Is Concealed

A person cannot correctly grasp the matter of "Torah from Heaven" unless he is on a ladder standing on earth with its head reaching the sky. But who will ascend a ladder standing straight up?[30] The purist tends to believe that his reason corresponds to reality and forgets that reason is to reality as a dwarf is to a giant. The visionary knows that truth is expressed only in fragments and is revealed only through the lens of metaphors and parables. Is it really possible to see what is concealed without a veil?[31] Or to peek past our bounds without metaphors? What is revealed and what is concealed coexist in admixture, and what is revealed is nothing more than a shroud that the Holy and Blessed One has placed upon that which is concealed.[32]

Take, for example, this disagreement among the Sages: Some say that Moses ascended to the heavens, and others say that Moses never ascended. Some say that the Presence descended on Mount Sinai, and others say that the Shekhinah never so descended. But there is no giving of the Torah without a receiving of the Torah. The giving of the Torah suggests a revelation of the Shekhinah. But what, then, is the receiving of the Torah? Is it possible for a human being to hear Torah from on high while still retaining his status as flesh and blood, unchanged and unelevated? On the

---

[28] The Hebrew term Heschel uses here for "covenant between the opposites" is a slight variation on the "covenant between the pieces," that is, the covenant God made with Abraham, as recounted in Genesis 15, the first covenant made specifically with and for the people Israel. The use of the reminiscent phrase is meant, evidently, to accentuate the centrality of the apprehension of unity amid this apparent duality.

[29] That is, the Ishmaelian and Akivan elements are complementary moments in religious life. But right now, according to Heschel, the Ishmaelian perspective is more needed. See the previous section of this chapter.

[30] The import seems to be that we naturally tend to believe that nothing but reason can support truth. Anything less will seem to be a ladder that is unsupported, and we will be reluctant to step onto it.

[31] That is, some things cannot be seen "straight," in the full light of reason.

[32] Since classically, what is revealed is law—Halakhah—we have here another expression of the idea that Halakhah, while important, is hardly the final articulation of what religion is about.

other hand, if you follow this thought as it presents itself, as if earth and heaven were like a house and a loft, with Moses ascending to the supernal world as a person goes up to a rooftop, you are then profaning the Holy and extinguishing the lights.[33]

At the giving of the Torah, it was written: "On the third day at morning there was thunder and lightning and a heavy cloud upon the mountain" (Exodus 19:16). Now this thunder and lightning: were they actual thunder and lightning or not? This question was much esteemed by devotees of plain meaning, and a matter of complete indifference to other Sages.[34] According to Maimonides, "It is well known . . . and a celebrated fact among our nation that the day of the standing at Sinai was a thickly clouded day, with a bit of rain."[22] Rabbenu Bahya[35] also believed "that the plain meaning is true and firm . . . that the day of the giving of the Torah was a sort of cloudy day with rumblings of thunder, as often happens, and lightning, and a bit of rain . . . and the cloud came first, then the lightning, and then the thunder. That is, the verse gave the phenomena in reverse order, for it is natural to see lightning first, and then to hear thunder."[23] But against this is the opinion of Rabbenu Hananel: "The thunder was the sound of angels who praise the Holy and Blessed One each morning . . . and the lightning was the presence of the angels themselves."[24] According to Abravanel, "The Holy and Blessed One made the thunder and lightning happen in a miraculous way."[25] And in another opinion: "This is the condition of prophets at the time they are prophesying: terrifying things come upon them that present themselves as thunder and lightning."[26]

Disagreements among the Sages

On the other hand, there are times when the talmudic Sages attempt to demonstrate that two apparently distinct opinions are not truly opposed to each other. For example, they say: "One master said one thing, another said another, but they do not really disagree." "This master speaks of the practice in his place, and the other of the practice in his place."

[22] *Guide of the Perplexed* 3:9; see also Midrash Hagadol p. 389.
[23] Rabbenu Bahya, Exodus 19:16.
[24] Cited in Rabbenu Bahya, Exodus 19:16.
[25] Abravanel on Exodus 19:16.
[26] *Me'or Ha'afela* (of Netanel ben Isaiah, thirteenth century, Yemen) on Exodus 19:16.

[33] This paragraph is intended, again, to demonstrate the inadequacy of reason to deal with the ineffable aspects of revelation. Maintaining a "proper" gap between heaven and earth, between God and human beings, makes revelation seem an illusion. On the other hand, making the divine and the human come together threatens to undermine the very majesty of the divine.

[34] That is, some thought it important to explain the meteorological phenomena, and others were content to live with the unexplained but evocative metaphor.

[35] The exegete Bahya ben Asher, thirteenth century, Spain.

In many places they bring a short-lived view, that is, a piece of hypothetical reasoning. For example, "You might think . . . and thus the text comes to set you right." Of this phenomenon, Rabbi Isaiah Halevi Horowitz[36] wrote:

The Talmud is full of such hypotheticals that are at first considered and are then rejected in the conclusion. It is an apparent difficulty concerning the redactor, for why did he edit in . . . what is not in fact true? He should have, in his editing, brought us straight to the conclusion. But know that not a single thing is mentioned in our holy Talmud in vain. All that is there is true. And even though the hypothetical is no longer there at the conclusion of the matter, still it remains true with respect to some other matter . . . for all that is written in the Talmud is the word of the living God. And beyond this, I found written in the book *Asarah Ma'amarot*[37] that on the contrary, the hypothetical is often primary.[27]

In various places I have attempted to demonstrate that one ought not understand the essence of Judaism via one simple category, but rather through a process of polarities. Sometimes this presents itself as a system of tension, as a coincidence of opposites, that in the complementarity between different vectors fashions its product.

The entire history of Jewish thought is a process of fusing together two extremes. And the direction of Jewish thought in this generation must be a fusion of thought and vision, of criticism and imagination. In the wedding of these two proclivities will the polychrome fabric of reason and faith shine forth.

Whoever takes principles of the faith at face value distorts their true meaning. Dogmatism does not do justice to the dual aspects of religious experience. The mind can contain both aspects. Do you think that together they will bring chaos to the world of thought? It is not so. There is a complementarity between them as there is between language and meaning, between expression and concept. In every aspect of existence that human beings can sense, that existence itself is a melding of opposites. Without impurity there is no purity, and without the mundane there is no holy. Without innocence, there is no guilt. "Said the Holy and Blessed One to Israel: My children, all that I have created has been created in pairs. Heaven and earth . . . sun and moon . . . Adam and Eve . . . this world and the world to come . . . only My Presence is one and unique."[28] [38]

Note that in many areas we find that the Sages adopted positions at opposite extremes. Ben Azzai said that a man is obligated to teach his daughter Torah, and Rabbi Eliezer said that whoever teaches his daughter Torah is, as it were, teaching her obscenity.[29] Of the well-known principle that "even if one were to read nothing but

---

[27] *Shenei Luhot Ha-Berit* 407b.   [28] Deuteronomy Rabbah 2:31.
[29] Mishnah Sotah 3:4.

---

[36] Sixteenth–seventeenth century, Poland.

[37] Authored by Menahem Azariah da Fano, sixteenth–seventeenth century, Italy.

[38] This is a clever way of understanding the text from Deuteronomy Rabbah—as an expression of Heschel's sweeping idea of duality's ubiquity in the world.

the Shema morning and evening, he has already fulfilled the command of 'Let not this Book of the Teaching cease from your lips, but recite it day and night' (Joshua 1:8)," it was said by some that "it is forbidden to attest this principle in the presence of the unlearned," and Rava said that "it is a mitzvah to attest it in the presence of the unlearned."[30] [39] Rabbi Johanan said: It is a mitzvah to pray [morning and evening] when the sun is still at the horizon; and on the other hand, we are told that "in the West,[40] they revile those who wait until sunset to recite the afternoon service."[31] Again, one says, "Whoever seeks compromise [in litigation] is a sinner," and another says that "it is a mitzvah to seek compromise."[32]

Even when there were differences of opinion in matters of Halakhah, such as those between the school of Shammai and the school of Hillel, the Torah never became two Torahs, for their intention was for the sake of heaven. Likewise, when there were intellectual differences, such as those of the school of Rabbi Akiva versus the school of Rabbi Ishmael. Rabbi Ishmael's way was that of the contextual meaning, and Rabbi Akiva's way was that of the esoteric meaning. Both of these paths were legitimate expressions of Judaism, and the nation stored up its vital energy in both of these throughout its existence. At times, these two approaches stood parallel to each other, at times one was subsumed by the other, at times one was eclipsed by the other, and at times they were joined together so that it seemed that two apparently rival world-views could coexist in a single arena, in a single heart. For example, Rabbi Akiva's formulation "All is foreseen, and freedom of choice is granted"[41] is nothing but a difficult synthesis between divine foreknowledge and human freedom. There were those who would on occasion emphasize one of these, and on another occasion the other. All depended on changing conditions, sometimes even according to the moods of the Sages. Among the striking expressions of this are the debates concerning the relationship between a perfect Creator and an imperfect world. On the one hand, there was a pure and perfect faith, and on the other there was a sharp and deep critique of the created world.

One should not neglect the fact that the dual aspects of religious thought are liable to strengthen the hands of those of little faith. They may say that lofty matters are ambiguous and thus undecidable.[42] But it has already been said that the Torah was not given for fools.

---

[30] BT Menahot 99b.   [31] BT Berakhot 29b.   [32] BT Sanhedrin 6b.

---

[39] The disagreement turns on this: some thought it was a bad idea to "define Torah study down" to the masses, while Rava thought it was essential to let the unlearned know that the gates of Torah were open to them as well, on their own level.

[40] That is, the Land of Israel.

[41] From Mishnah Avot 3:15. The attribution to Akiva is not made explicitly in that Mishnah but is traditionally inferred from the attributions in the previous Mishnayot.

[42] Something like this was already said, classically, about nonhalakhic—for example, theological—learning. See Rabbi Zeira's admonition to Rabbi Jeremiah in PT Ma'aserot 3:10 (51a).

What is the path of virtue that a person should follow? Sober contemplation is like snow, and esoteric contemplation is like live coals. The world cannot exist without snow, but it also cannot exist without fire. "All is in the hands of heaven except for cold drafts."[33] [43] To what can this be compared? "To a troop that was marching between two paths, one of fire and one of snow. If they march near the fire, they are burned, and if they march near the snow, they will suffer frost. What shall they do? Let them walk in the middle, and take care not to be burnt by the fire nor frostbitten by the snow."[34] [44]

In his commentary on the Mishnah, Maimonides wrote: "I have already noted for you many times that every dispute among the Sages that does not impinge on practice but is just a matter of faith should not be resolved one way or the other."[35] In the beginning, the Holy and Blessed One sought to create the world with the attribute of judgment. But God saw that the world could not thus endure, and thus was a partnership formed with the attribute of mercy.[45] So it is with the two perspectives we have been dealing with: neither one contains the complete truth by itself. The value of each is revealed only in their synthesis. And yet the question arises as to how to create a synthesis between two such different perspectives.

In the course of the generations they have struggled with the problem of discrepancies between religion and science, that is, with the external challenge to religious thought. However, before us now is the conflict between two different conceptions within religious thought itself. And the question concerning the relationship between religious truth and scientific truth must necessarily yield priority to an analysis of religious truth itself.

Ad Hoc Rulings on Biblical Law[46]

In an extreme formulation, they [the Sages] said: "One does not appoint anyone to the Sanhedrin unless he be a Sage who knows how to argue for the purity of an insect on the

---

[33] BT Bava Metzi'a 107b.   [34] ARN A 28.   [35] Commentary on Mishnah Sanhedrin 10.

---

[43] The plain meaning of this passage is practical advice to watch out for dangers in the world and not to expect divine interventions when matters are within our control.

[44] This statement served as an opening quotation for Nahman Krochmal's *Guide for the Perplexed of the Age*, an early-nineteenth-century treatise, also designed to synthesize reason and faith.

[45] For the classical sources of this idea, see Genesis Rabbah 12, and Rashi's commentary on Genesis 1:1.

[46] In this section, Heschel will cite rabbinic passages about the possibility, and even legitimacy, of interpreting biblical commands according to the dictates of ambient conditions. His motive in doing so is this: to highlight the view that Halakhah does not have a fixed, intrinsic substance to it but is rather subject to the contingencies of human life and history. This is, of course, the Ishmaelian view, which Heschel is now promoting quite openly.

basis of the Bible." It seems to me that the meaning of this is that if the members of the Sanhedrin see inequities resulting from one or another biblical law in their own generation, they will be able to go forth and innovate laws, to add or subtract as the moment necessitates, and to support their decision from the Torah. Similarly, the Geonim wrote about talmudic law that the Sages have the power to create new decrees and ordinances, be they general or particular, in order to do away with a matter that seems noxious to them in their time, and this even on a slight pretext. In the same vein the greatest of the commentators wrote: the Talmud was given only to those expert in the tradition, possessed of valid powers of reasoning and precise judgment, so that they can subtract, add, and interpret. This curtain remains closed before most people, and the only ones worthy of penetrating it are those distinguished in their generation for knowledge, sharpness, casuistry, and temperate reasoning.[36]

We have seen that the Holy and Blessed One prized the oil of the olive more than all other oils. "You shall further instruct the Israelites to bring you clear oil of beaten olives for lighting, for kindling lamps regularly" (Exodus 27:20). The Sages of Israel went to great lengths in connection with the commandment of lighting the Shabbat candles, making sure that the oil would be of the highest quality to honor the Sabbath. With which oils may one kindle the Sabbath lamps, and with which oils not? Rabbi Tarfon said: One may only light with olive oil. "Rabbi Johanan ben Nuri stood on his feet and said: 'What shall the people of Babylonia do? They have only sesame oil. What shall the people of Media do? They have only nut oil. What shall the people of Alexandria do? They have only radish oil. And what shall the people of Cappadocia do? They have none of these, but only naphtha.'"[37]

The author of "Maggid Mishneh"[47] notes that

our perfect Torah gave, for the purpose of perfecting us in our ethical behavior, general principles, when it said "You shall be holy"; the intent was what our Masters of blessed memory said: Sanctify yourself within what is permitted to you, so that you not be swept away by desires. Likewise, it said: "Do what is right and good in the sight of the Lord," the intent being that a person behave in a good and right way with other people. It is not appropriate in such areas to give detailed commands, because commands of the Torah are such that they apply at all hours and at all times, in every context, and one necessarily has to obey them. But human character and ethical behavior are relative to the times and to the personalities involved. So the Sages of blessed memory gave us some details that fall under these general principles. Some were given as absolute rules, and some as ideal standards, but all were their creation, may their memory be blessed. And of this, they said that the words of the beloved [Sages] are more cherished than the wine of Torah, as it is said: "for your love is more delightful than wine" (Song of Songs 1:2).[38]

[36] Menahem Ha-Meiri, *Bet Ha-Behirah,* Sanhedrin 17a.
[37] BT Shabbat 26a.
[38] Maggid Mishneh, "Laws Concerning Neighbors" 14:8.

[47] Vidal of Tolosa, fourteenth century, Spain.

Joel ibn Shuaib[48] writes

> that it is inappropriate to judge matters the same way in every time, for it will often happen at a given time that it is appropriate to rule leniently, and at another that stringency is called for; that is why courts have the power of enforcement, whether the law explicitly authorizes it or not, as the hour demands. (The Gemara has already given us many examples of this in the area of practical Halakhah.) This trait is called *hesed* by the Sages, and it operates to rectify inequities in religious law, whenever there is need for such rectification. This does not undermine religious foundations. It is rather a drawing near to God's will, God's intent, if not God's very words.[39]

"Rabbi Simeon ben Nahman began his exposition:[49] 'For I am mindful of the plans I have made concerning you' (Jeremiah 29:11)—the [ancestors of the] tribes were busy with the selling of Joseph, Jacob was busy with his sackcloth and fasting, and Judah was busy with finding himself a wife, and the Holy and Blessed One was creating the light of the Messiah, as it is said, 'About that time Judah left his brothers . . .' (Genesis 38:1)."[50] [40] This Midrash is astonishing to all who read it. But Rabbi Simhah Bunem of Przysucha explained it as follows:

> This midrash comes to teach us an amazing thing. The tribes and Jacob were all busy with fasting and crying out to God. The tribes, on account of the sale of Joseph; Joseph himself, on account of his sale; and Jacob, out of mourning for his son. They all prayed to God with all their hearts and all their souls. And Judah went and took a wife. It would appear to mortals that their actions were more attuned to God, for Judah was merely occupied with marrying a woman. But in spite of this, says the midrash, no human being knows the thoughts that are embedded deep in the human heart. And the Holy and Blessed One paid more attention to Judah's actions, and it was from him that the light of the Messiah was created.[41]

Happy Are Those Who Rule Stringently— Happy Are Those Who Rule Leniently

In these our own days, opinions have diverged concerning the conception of Halakhah. There are those who say, "Happy are those who rule stringently," and

[39] *Olat Shabbat*, Shofetim 149c.   [40] Genesis Rabbah 85.   [41] *Kol Simhah*, Vayyeshev.

---

[48] Fifteenth century, Spain.

[49] Classically, homilies generally began with verses from Psalms or the prophetic books.

[50] This midrashic passage takes as its point of departure the fact that Genesis 38 constitutes an interruption of the narrative of the sale of Joseph. In this chapter, Judah's marriage, his widowerhood, and his unwitting sexual encounter with his widowed daughter-in-law Tamar are recounted. The midrash here highlights the literary contrast between, on the one hand, Joseph's plight, Jacob's mourning, and the brothers' (presumed) guilt feelings as they watch their father mourn, and, on the other hand, Judah's more mundane concerns. The punch line here arises from the fact that King David (ancestor of the Messiah) will eventually descend from the incestuous relationship of Judah and Tamar.

there are those who say, "Happy are those who rule leniently." Some say: "One who relativizes his Torah to the times abrogates the covenant."[42] Rabbi Simeon bar Yohai said: "The Book of Deuteronomy went and prostrated itself before the Holy and Blessed One and said: 'Master of the Universe! Solomon has uprooted me and made me seem a forgery. For any testament in which two or three things are void is entirely void, and Solomon has attempted to remove the letter *yod* from me.' . . . The Holy and Blessed One said, 'Go your way, for Solomon will one day be gone, and a hundred others like him, but a single *yod* of yours will never be annulled."[43]

Others, however, say: All depends on the person, the personality, the time, the hour, the place. And sometimes they even say, "It is time to act for God by annulling the Torah."[44] Rabbi Simeon ben Lakish said: "There are times when the annulment of something in the Torah strengthens its foundation."[45] And the early talmudic commentators had this principle: "The Sages have the power to uproot something from the Torah."[46]

The Mishnah had established that "a court may not abrogate the ruling of another court unless it is greater than the first in both wisdom and numbers."[47] And yet Rabbi Judah the Patriarch released several prohibitions, saying, "My ancestors left me space in which to set my own boundaries."[48] On the one hand, there are those who say that "given a choice between analogizing to a stringent or a lenient case, choose the stringent one."[49] On the other, some said that "the power of leniency is preferred."[50]

There are those who follow the principle "if our predecessors were like human beings, then we are like asses."[51] And then there are those who say: "The law follows the later authorities."[52]

The counsel that one not erect a protective barrier higher than the original prohibition has not been accepted in the designated circles of Halakhah. The deciders do not heed Rav, who said that the commandments were given in order to refine human beings. They rather heed Rabbi Hananiah ben Akashia: "The Holy and Blessed One wished to increase Israel's merit, and therefore God gave them much instruction and many mitzvot." They attempt to increase the number of rules, and they have added protective regulations on top of protective regulations.

Most Sages have made the Halakhah primary and life secondary to it. As for one who says that a certain decree or another cannot be lived with, they coerce him until he says "I am willing." [They say:] "The Halakhah was not given to be marked up and

---

[42] PT Berakhot 9:4 (14d).   [43] Leviticus Rabbah 19:2.

[44] Mishnah Berakhot 9:5; see last section of chapter 37 below.

[45] BT Menahot 99b.

[46] BT Berakhot 16a, Tosafot s.v. *ve-hotem*; see also BT Nazir 43b, Tosafot s.v. *ve-hai*, and BT Yevamot 89b, Tosafot s.v. *ve-khevan*.

[47] Mishnah Eduyot 1:5.   [48] BT Hullin 7a.   [49] BT Yevamot 8a.

[50] BT Betzah 2b; see Rashi there: "He would rather teach us the words of the one who permits, who relies on his learning and is unafraid to rule permissively. But the power of those who forbid demonstrates little, for anyone can rule stringently, even concerning something that is permitted."

[51] BT Shabbat 112b.

[52] *Epistle of Rav Sherirah Gaon*, ed. Levine, p. 38; see also Isaac Alfasi at the end of BT Eruvin.

evaluated. It is absolutely unique. All is contained in it, including its own foundations and boundaries. It is above all critique. And of what is beyond you, you may not ask."

I object to the provinciality of thought, and to the constriction of mind in all of this. There is disregard of the problems that bubble up to the surface each day, of the spiritual struggles and mental anguish of those of our generation who are stumbling. The laws of marriage [ishut] are surely important. But are the laws governing human personality [ishiyut] devoid of value? Do the problems associated with medicine concern only the dissection of the dead, but not how we relate to the living, in our treatment of the sick?

Several great Sages in Israel did not hesitate to demand justice of the Unique One of the Universe. And yet, in our generation, criticism of the halakhists is prohibited even in the minutest measure!

Even though it was said: "Whoever second-guesses his master, it is as if he second-guessed the Shekhinah,"[53] it was never suggested that the teachers of Halakhah are immune to error. It is distant from and alien to the thought of the Torah to establish infallibility as a fundamental of the faith. On the contrary: 'and let this failing be under your hand'[51] (Isaiah 3:6)—"A person cannot learn the ways of Torah until he fails at them"; that is, "A person cannot recognize the truth of words of Torah until he fails in his teaching and is humbled, for then he will pay closer attention and will understand."[54]

Maimonides explains the juxtaposition of Tractate Horayot to Tractate Avot: "Once the Mishnah had completed the exhortations of the judges, it turned to describing their mistakes, for whoever is made of flesh and blood must necessarily err and sin, and that is why Horayot was redacted right after Avot."[55]

Rabbi Nehunia ben Hakkaneh would pray thus when he entered the House of Study: "May no harm come from my teaching, and may I not falter in matters of Halakhah."[56] This shows that failure in Halakhah is a possibility. And have we not failed in judgment? Look at how many great Sages in Israel did not understand the importance of the Zionist movement or the needs of the multitudes who emigrated to the United States. Community leaders two or three generations ago bemoaned, for example, the socialist movement simply because they saw boys and girls walking together.

All paths should be presumed to carry danger. There is no path forward that is without crookedness or ambushes. Some say: What do I need this trouble for? I will watch my step and not sin, and I will have saved my soul. But the Sages have

---

[53] BT Sanhedrin 110a.　　[54] Rashi to BT Gittin 43a.
[55] Commentary on the Mishnah, preface to the Order Zera'im.
[56] BT Berakhot 28b.

---

[51] This is not the NJV translation of the verse, but is rather rendered here to conform to the rabbinic reading of it in the midrash cited.

expounded: "and to him who blazes a path I will show the salvation of God" (Psalm 50:23)—This refers to those who light lamps for the multitude."[57]

One more parable: "It is like two ships on the high seas. Between them they had two captains. One saved himself but did not save his ship, while the other saved both himself and his ship. Who is more deserving of praise? Is it not the one who saved both himself and his ship?"[58] [52]

[57] Leviticus Rabbah 9:2.
[58] Deuteronomy Rabbah 11:3.

---

[52] The midrashic passage here imagines Noah lording it over Moses, that he, who alone (with his immediate family) was saved from a global catastrophe, must have been greater in God's eyes than Moses (who was only one of 600,000 saved from Egypt). Moses' reply centers on this parable, which draws our attention to the fact that Noah did not challenge God's destructive plan, and thus saved no one but himself, while Moses, through his challenge to God, saved an entire people from destruction. The message for Heschel is that inflexible submissiveness to dictates from on high often consign the masses to destruction, whether physical or spiritual.

AGAINST MULTIPLYING RULES

Translator's Introduction

Here begins a cluster of five final chapters in this work, and this introduction will cover them all.

It is worth quoting here some of the words of Rabbi David Feldman, from his foreword to the Hebrew Volume 3 of *TMH,* which he edited and arranged for publication:

> When I was asked . . . to edit these manuscripts for publication, I discovered that there was more there than I had expected. Many chapters are of the nature of a continuation and summation, and yet others have the quality of apologetics.[1] It is as if there were material from two different books here—distinct but interrelated. For there is a natural connection between the early chapters (34–36)—the subject of which is the two approaches to understanding Torah and the concept "Torah from Heaven"—and the later ones (37–41)—the subject of which is the relationship between Aggadah and Halakhah, and the extent to which the latter can/should accommodate the former.

Heschel uses these last five chapters to present material that relates to the most practical and most visible application of the theological underpinnings of Judaism—the attitude toward Halakhah, its authority, and its susceptibility to modification and development. They are perhaps best read as a compilation of sources that give background and backup to his general arguments in *God in Search of Man,* chapters 32–34. In those chapters, Heschel lodges his famous complaint about "religious behaviorism" and the reduction of Judaism to Halakhah. If Judaism stands for the fulfillment of God's will through the observance of *halakhah,* then the "purer" the *halakhah,* the better. And thus arises the notion that "happy are those who rule stringently." If, however, "Judaism is not another word for legalism . . . [if] the rules of observance are law in form and love in substance . . . [if] law is what holds the world together; love is what brings the world forward . . . [if] the law is the means, not the end,"[2] then one might well come to the conclusion that in the realm of Halakhah, "whoever adds, detracts." The coming chap-

---

[1] "Apologetics" here, of course, means a defense of a particular worldview that is of special importance to the author, and not what "apologetic" means in common parlance.

[2] Heschel, *God in Search of Man,* 323.

ters provide a rich companion to this line of argument, by providing the reader with many classical sources on both sides of the divide.

These are hardly matters of mere theoretical interest. To quote Feldman's Hebrew Foreword once more: "In our generation, this question of the source of the Torah is not simply theoretical. . . . Assuming a position on the matter of "Torah from Heaven" . . . is quite fundamental to the formulation of the theologies that characterize the various movements in contemporary Judaism." Reading the following chapters in conjunction with *God in Search of Man* makes it even clearer where Heschel's own sympathies lay in this contemporary dialogue and debate. The reader is particularly referred to the very suggestive metaphor of the ship's captain, with which he ended the previous chapter (36), and which articulates for him the importance of combining fealty to the law with an understanding of human nature and human history.

The last three chapters deal with two separate but related matters. Chapter 39 takes up the question of religious authority, and whether the veneration of generations past entails a preemption of the creativity of later generations. Here, too, there is much source material on both sides, and Heschel's own sympathies seem to be quite apparent. Did he not ask, also in *God in Search of Man*: "Is the archaic a mark of vital preference? Is unconditional respect for the past the essence of Judaism? Did not Judaism begin when Abraham broke with tradition and rejected the past?" And yet, in keeping with the open-ended quality of his inquiry here, he is unwilling even in this case to settle the matter unambiguously. Chapter 39 in fact ends with a nod to the other view, concluding as it does with a note concerning "not second-guessing the lion [i.e., a great Sage] after his death."

Chapters 40 and 41 contain a collection of material that again echoes the chapters referred to above, in *God in Search of Man,* in restoring a sense of the goals that Halakhah seeks to achieve, both in the realm of theology (chapter 40) and in interpersonal ethics (chapter 41). In both chapters, he is adding to his insistence that a one-dimensional view of Halakhah (religious behaviorism) betrays our classical sources and the very essence of Judaism.

As noted in the overall foreword to this translation, there is no natural concluding point for *TMH*. These last few chapters could, indeed, have been arranged in a different order. And there is no grand conclusion, as if working out the implications of the sources marshaled here is left as an exercise to the reader. In part, this is because Heschel did not live to see the entire work through to publication. But Heschel's own proclivities in this area, his insistence that there is no unambiguous bottom line when it comes to religious perspectives, make it likely that even had the master published this work, it would have had an unfinished quality to it. Working out all the implications was a lifelong exercise for the author himself. And it is right, after all, for form to match substance. We consequently let the book end in the absence of any finishing flourish, with the open-ended texture of the original Hebrew, without apology.

Whoever Adds, Detracts

T HE MEN OF THE GREAT ASSEMBLY SAID: "Place a buffer around the law."[1] "A vineyard surrounded by a fence is better than a vineyard not surrounded by a fence."[2] Now there are those who believe that buffers and stringencies are among the things that cannot be overdone—that whoever adds and increases is praiseworthy. In the loft of Hananiah ben Hizkiahu ben Garon "a vote was taken, and the school of Shammai outpolled the school of Hillel. Eighteen matters were decreed that very day, and that day was as bitter for Israel as the day on which the calf was made."[3] Why was the matter bitter? Said Rabbi Joshua: "On that very day they filled the measure to the very top" (Rashi's understanding: "they decreed too much, more than people could tolerate, and thus people were led to violate the laws of the Torah"). "To what can the matter be compared? To a tub filled with honey. If you then place pomegranates and nuts into it, it will disgorge the honey." In contrast to this, Rabbi Eliezer held: "On that very day, they overfilled the measure" (Rashi's understanding: "they increased the number of buffers around the Torah to bursting, and they did well, in order to increase the number of Israel's 'fences.'") "To what can the matter be compared? To a crate filled with gourds and pumpkins. If one places mustard seed into it, it can still contain it."[4] [3]

"Do not add to His words, lest He indict you and you be proved a liar" (Proverbs 30:6). "Rabbi Hiyya taught: Do not make the buffer greater than the core, lest it collapse and lop off the plants. Thus said the Holy and Blessed One [to the first man]: 'but as for the tree of knowledge of good and bad, you must not eat of it; for as soon as you eat of it, you shall die' (Genesis 2:17), but she [the first woman] did not repeat it that way, but rather so: 'God said: "You shall not eat of it or touch it, lest you die"' (Genesis 3:3). As soon as the serpent saw her passing in front of the tree, he

---

[1] Mishnah Avot 1:1.   [2] ARN B, chapter 1.
[3] Tosefta Shabbat 1:16.   [4] BT Shabbat 153b.

---

[3] The import of the statements of Rabbi Joshua and Rabbi Eliezer is far from clear. According to Rashi, as cited by Heschel here, Rabbi Joshua seems to be agreeing with the assessment that the day of the eighteen decrees was a bitter day in Jewish history, and Rabbi Eliezer seems to be disagreeing with that assessment. But their language does not seem to comport with this understanding, since Rabbi Eliezer has the Sages actually *overfilling* the measure with stringencies. An alternative understanding (see Lieberman, *Tosefta Kifeshuta*, Shabbat 1:16) is this: both intend to give their own explanations for the statement that the day of the eighteen decrees was a bitter day in Jewish history. Rabbi Joshua gives the image of a barrel filled to the very brim with a viscous liquid—it is bound to spill its contents, and it would have been better to leave it a bit less full. That is, the Sages should not have created so many stringencies. Rabbi Eliezer's image is of a barrel filled to overfull with solid produce. The overfilling causes spillage, but had it been filled just to the brim, there would have still been interstices to contain additional material. In this way, both can be understood to be criticizing, albeit with different similes, the enterprise of multiplying stringent decrees.

pushed her into it. He then said to her: 'See, you have not died; and just as you have not died by touching it, so will you not die by eating of it.'"[5] [4]

Rabbi Hiyya's son Hezekiah taught in the same vein as his father: "How do we know that whoever adds, detracts? For it is written: 'You shall not eat of it or touch it.'"[6] And further, "Hezekiah taught: Whoever is exempt from doing something and does it anyway is called a simpleton."[7] [5] And Rabbi Eleazar said: "Just as it is forbidden to declare the impure to be pure, so is it forbidden to declare the pure to be impure."[8]

Against those who believed that the number of buffers has no upper limit stood those Sages who said that just as we do not trust one "who places no buffers around his words," so we do not trust one "who overdoes it"[9]

To one who would undertake oaths to add to biblical prohibitions, they [i.e., Rav Dimi in the name of Rabbi Isaac] would say: "Is not what is already prohibited to you enough, that you seek to prohibit more to yourself?"[10] Maimonides wrote concerning this passage: "I have not heard a more wonderful principle than this one. It . . . denigrates those who subject themselves to vows and oaths to the point of their becoming like genuine prohibitions . . . said Rav Idi in the name of Rabbi Isaac: Is not what the Torah prohibited to you enough, that you prohibit more to yourself?"[11]

"A Tanna[6] taught in the presence of Rava bar Rav Huna: One who kills snakes and scorpions on Shabbat displeases the pious ones. Said he to him: And those pious ones displease the Sages."[12] [7]

---

[5] Genesis Rabbah 19:3.
[6] BT Sanhedrin 29a. According to BT Bava Metzi'a 85b, Elijah revealed to Rabbi [Judah the Patriarch] that the patriarchs—Abraham, Isaac, and Jacob—have equivalents in this world, to wit Rabbi Hiyya and his sons.
[7] PT Shabbat 1:1 (3a).   [8] PT Sotah 8:2 (22b).   [9] BT Niddah 4b.
[10] PT Nedarim 9:1.   [11] Maimonides, *Eight Chapters,* chapter 4.   [12] BT Shabbat 121b.

---

[4] The issue being addressed in this midrash is that the first couple got into trouble because Adam had decided to give Eve a more stringent form of God's prohibition of eating from the Tree of Knowledge. He told her not even to touch it. The serpent's ability to reason with the woman in the way he did demonstrates that Adam must have conveyed the prohibition to her in that way; for had she added it on her own accord, she would not have been so impressed by the serpent's ability to touch the tree and not be harmed. Thus, Adam plays the role of the Sages who take it upon themselves to convey God's commands to us (the counterparts of Eve in real life) in a more stringent form than is called for. This very bold midrash thus constitutes a powerful polemic against such pseudo-pious practices.

[5] The Hebrew term is a very derogatory one in the rabbinic lexicon; it denotes one who is untutored and uncultured.

[6] In this case, not a Sage of the period prior to the publication of the Mishnah, but rather "reciter," that is, one who recited from memory old traditions in the House of Study.

[7] The text here is suggesting, through an unexpected twist at the end, that though there are always pietists who will expect heroic standards from people (in this case, refraining from killing dangerous animals on Shabbat, if they are not attacking at that very moment), those pietists' expectations do not sit well with the Sages. Again, we have a clear implication that over-stringency is a sign of ignorance. Those who are worthy of being called Sages have a more moderate view.

"Every excess can be considered a lack."[13] From the story of the Tree of Knowledge they concluded: "Let not a person add to that which he hears. Rabbi Yosi said: Better a standing wall of just ten handbreadths than a collapsed wall of a hundred cubits."[14]

Stringencies are not always constructive, and leniencies are not always destructive. Not every fence protects, and not every breach destroys. There are times when the Torah is preserved by overriding it. "All is determined by the root,"[8] by the time, by the person, by the generation, by the matter at hand.

The Sages are entitled to go beyond the stringencies of the Torah, to prohibit, to declare impure, and to forbid that which is legally permitted, in order that laws not be taken lightly. But there are various limits to this power. See how Rabbi Ishmael, who stayed away from excessive stringencies and said to strict judges "whoever imposes stringencies must prove their validity,"[15] formulated two important principles regarding the minimization of decrees: "Rabbi Ishmael ben Elisha taught: From the destruction of the Temple onward, it would have been proper to decree for ourselves no longer to eat meat or drink wine; but one does not issue a public decree with which a majority of the public cannot live.[16] And from the time that we fell subject to the wicked empire which imposes on us difficult and evil decrees, declares our Torah and commandments to be null, and does not even allow us to circumcise our sons—some say, does not allow us to redeem our sons—it would have been proper to decree for ourselves no longer to marry and to have children, which would have resulted in the passive death of the seed of Abraham our Father. But let Israel be—better that they do the improper unwittingly than wittingly."[17] And this principle applies even to biblical prohibitions.[18]

We have some hint that in ancient times people used to deride those who attempted to proliferate stringencies, even if that person were the leading scholar of

---

[13] BT Hullin 25b.   [14] ARN, chapter 1.

[15] The land of Ammon and Moab, which is adjacent to the Land of Israel, is subject to *terumot* [agricultural gifts to the priests] and tithes by rabbinic enactment, but the law of the sabbatical year does not apply to it. It was thus asked whether the produce of the seventh year is subject to the second tithe [prescribed for years 1, 2, 4 and 5] or the poor tithe [prescribed for years 3 and 6]. Rabbi Eleazar ben Azariah decreed: It is subject to the second tithe. Said Rabbi Ishmael: Eleazar ben Azariah! You must bring proof, for you are ruling strictly [that farmers must give the second tithe, which has sanctity, rather than give the poor tithe, which does not], and whoever imposes stringencies must prove their validity" (Mishnah Yadayim 4:3). See Tosefta Sanhedrin 7:6.

[16] See BT Avodah Zarah 36a–b.   [17] BT Bava Batra 60b.

[18] BT Shabbat 148b. Rabbenu Asher—Beitzah, chapter 4—quotes the *Itur* as saying that this principle, "better that they do the improper unwittingly than wittingly," "applies to rabbinic enactments only, but with a biblical law, we explicitly protest."

---

[8] See Mishnah Parah 2:5 (where it refers to the varying colors of hair at the roots and at the surface). Heschel quotes the phrase here to indicate that while on the surface a leniency may seem a betrayal, it may be closer to the underlying essence of what the purpose of Torah is. Such clever quotation out of original context is a regular practice for Heschel.

the time, such as Joshua ben Perahia (president of the Sanhedrin and chief Sage in Israel at the time of Johanan, the Hasmonean High priest). "Hilfata ben Kavina said: '"Baalbek[9] garlic" is impure.[10] ' Said the Sages: 'Very well. Let it be impure for Hilfata ben Kavina, and pure for the rest of Israel.' Joshua ben Perahia said: 'Alexandrian wheat is impure.'[11] Said the Sages: 'Very well. Let it be impure for Joshua ben Perahia and pure for the rest of Israel.'"[19]

"The Halakhah always follows the school of Hillel. Whoever wishes to follow: (1) the school of Shammai, may do so; (2) the school of Hillel, may do so; (3) all the leniencies of the schools of Shammai and Hillel, is wicked; (4) all the stringencies of the schools of Shammai and Hillel, is spoken of in the verse: 'a fool walks in darkness' (Ecclesiastes 2:14)."[20]

Against Multiplying Rules

In the light of the love of the commandments rooted in the hearts of the Sages, it is both strange and astonishing that the greatest of the fourth generation of Tannaim, "a great, holy, unassuming man,"[21] put in the mouth of the Creator an apologetic justification of the commandments based on the fact that alongside forbidden things there are those that are permitted: prohibitions in one category are permitted in other categories. To what can this be compared? To a king who boastingly says: More even than I have planted gardens and orchards, I have created for you deserts and wastelands. "Could a holy mouth have said such a thing?"[22] For they reported in the name of Rabbi Meir: "More than I have prohibited to you have I permitted to you. I have prohibited menstrual blood, but permitted virginal blood; I have forbidden married women, but permitted captive women; I have forbidden marriage to a sister-in-law, but permitted a levirate marriage; I have forbidden a wife's sister, but permitted her after the wife's death; I have forbidden mixed fibers, but permitted a linen garment with wool *tzitzit;* I have forbidden swine flesh, but permitted fish tongue; I have for-

---

[19] Tosefta Makhshirin 3:4.   [20] BT Rosh Hashanah 14b; Tosefta Sukkah 2:3.
[21] PT Mo'ed Katan 3:5 (13b).
[22] So said Resh Lakish about Rabbi Meir [in a different context]; BT Sanhedrin 23a.

---

[9] A city in Syria.

[10] That is, it is susceptible to contracting ritual impurity upon contact with something already impure. The general rule was that foodstuffs could be so susceptible only if they had already been moistened with some liquid. Hilfata apparently felt that the garlic from Baalbek could be assumed to have been moistened so as to make the braiding of the garlic easier. Just as apparently, the Sages felt that this was an unnecessary and unwarranted assumption.

[11] Here the issue was apparently Joshua ben Perahia's assumption about the ways in which the wheat was harvested and baled in Alexandria—that they would inevitably result in the moistening of the wheat. The Sages render the same sarcastic verdict in his case as in the previous one.

bidden suet, but permitted fat; I have forbidden eating blood, but permitted milt; I have forbidden meat and milk, but permitted the udder."[23]

"A currency exchanger does not normally give up an *isar* until he has gotten his *dinar*."[24] From Rabbi Meir's statement, one can infer to what thoughts of others he was responding. "There is no generation without its scoffers,"[25] no generation in which is not heard the complaint: "What is this ritual of yours?" The multiplicity of rules which swaddled the average Jew right down to the soles of his feet were not always accepted lovingly. Evidence that derision existed among Jews can be found in the statement of Rav Aha bar 'Ula: "Whoever derides the words of the Sages is condemned to boil in excrement."[26]

"Rabbi Hanania ben Akashya said: The Holy and Blessed One wished to give Israel merit. Therefore, He gave them many teachings and commandments, as it is written: 'The Lord desires His [servant's] vindication, that he may magnify and glorify [His] teaching' (Isaiah 42:21)." On this passage, Rabbi Samuel Uceda[12] wrote in his commentary *Midrash Samuel:* "God wished for the human heart to be raised up to God's service through teachings and commandments, and not to respond foolishly to the multiplicity of details and conclude that since there are so many, no one can possibly do them all. Therefore the Tanna taught us that God, who has sanctified us with His commandments and instructed us, does not issue commands as a mortal king does. The latter fixes for his servant the exact amount of work required; and thus, when the servant fails to complete all of it, he is punished for not having fulfilled the entire command of the king. But the Holy and Blessed One is different. By multiplying teachings and commandments for Israel He did not intend to say that they must complete all teachings and fulfill all commandments, and that they would be punished for not doing so, even if they had fulfilled some, or even most, of them. Were that the case, the multiplicity of teachings and commandments would serve primarily to generate punishment. The matter is not so. You are not required to complete the work; one who does less is acceptable along with the one who does more, as long as they intend what they do for the sake of heaven. . . . Thus, the multiplicity is not a reason for punishment; on the contrary, God wanted to provide Israel with merit, for those who cannot fulfill them all. Wondrous reward grows without end as a person grows in learning and in fulfillment of commandments, and that is why God multiplied for us teachings and commandments."[13]

According to the Mishnah, one may tear open the udder and remove the milk in it, and it may then be cooked with other meat and eaten. If one did not tear it open and

---

[23] Leviticus Rabbah, chapter 22 (Margoliot edition, pp. 521ff.); see also BT Hullin 109b.
[24] Mishnah Shevi'it 7:6.   [25] PT Berakhot 2:1 (4d).   [26] BT Eruvin 21b.

---

[12] Sixteenth century, Safed. *Midrash Samuel* is his commentary on Mishnah Avot.

[13] Though perhaps unintended, the answer to the classical Pauline complaint about the Law inherent in Uceda's commentary is notable!

ate it, he is not legally liable for the eating of meat and milk together,[27] since the milk inside the udder is not legally categorized as milk. Came Rav, the founder of the academy in Sura, and forbade the eating of the udder, even after it was torn open. This stringency was accepted in Sura, while in Pumbedita they felt free to eat the udder.[28]

Now Rami bar Tamri of Pumbedita came to Sura on the Eve of Yom Kippur. When he saw the Suraites throwing out the udders, he went and collected them and ate them. This action aroused anger among the Suraites, who detained him and brought him before Rav Hisda, the head of the academy (he was Rav's student and among the greatest of the Babylonian Amoraim of the second–third generation), and bound him to the pillar to be flogged.[29] Rav Hisda asked him: Why have you done this? Rami answered him: I come from Rav Yehuda's place, from Pumbedita, and there the udder is eaten.[14] Said to him Rav Hisda: Are you not mindful of the (Mishnah's) teaching that one should not violate the local custom? That when one travels from city to city he is subject to the stringencies of his home base and those of the place he is in?[30] Rami answered him: I ate them outside of Sura's city limits. Rav Hisda asked him: With what did you roast the udders (where did you find firewood)? He answered him: Grape pulp that I found near the winepresses. Rav Hisda asked him: Isn't it possible that they were grapes used for pagan libations, and they were thus prohibited for all purposes? He answered him: They were at least twelve months old (and after twelve months they lose all scent of wine and become permitted).[31] Rav Hisda asked him: Isn't it possible that it was someone else's, and you should not have benefited from stolen goods? Rami answered: If so, the owners surely had given up on it,[15] because the pulp gets spoiled and rotten in the field, and since it was not removed from there, it is clear that the owners didn't care. Rav Hisda then saw that he was not wearing Tefillin. He asked him: Why are you not wearing Tefillin? He answered him: I have an intestinal illness, and Rav Judah said: One with an intestinal illness is exempt from Tefillin.[32] Rav Hisda then saw that his outer garment had no fringes, and he asked him: Why are there no fringes on your cloak? Rami answered: It is a borrowed cloak, and Rav Judah said: A borrowed garment is exempt from fringes for thirty days.[33] Presently they brought into court a man who had not acted respectfully

---

[27] Mishnah Hullin 8:3.

[28] Several Amoraim followed Rav's practice. Yet Rabbi Eleazar opposed this stringency and told his servant: "Tear it open for me, and I shall eat it" (BT Hullin 109b–110a).

[29] So the text according to Rabinowitz, *Variae Lectiones.*

[30] Mishnah Pesahim 4:1.   [31] BT Avodah Zarah 34a.

[32] "Tefillin require a body as clean as that of 'the winged Elisha'" (BT Shabbat 49a); see also PT Berakhot 2:3 (4c).

[33] BT Hullin 136a.

---

[14] This entire story seems to have the quality of a conventional polemic composed by adherents of the Pumbedita academy against those of the Sura academy. Such polemics are not at all uncommon in talmudic literature.

[15] And consequently, title no longer was theirs, according to rabbinic law.

to his parents, and they bound him to the pillar to be flogged. Rami said to them: Leave him be, for it is taught: Any positive commandment for which a reward is explicitly promised is not subject to penalties by the earthly court.[34] Said to him Rav Hisda: I see that you are very sharp! Rami answered him: Were you in Rav Judah's locale (Pumbedita), I would really be able to show you how sharp I am![35]

The entire narrative is bizarre and unusual from every angle: (A) Was there no other food in Sura that a visitor had to scavenge and eat udders? (B) Rami would eat udders that the Suraites threw out, but with respect to Tefillin he pleaded a weak stomach! (C) Given that he was forced to neglect the commandment of Tefillin, why did he not make every effort at least to fulfill the commandment of tzitzit? The garment was borrowed; why did he not wear his own garment? And should you say that he was forced to borrow someone else's garment, why did he not ask the lender to give him the garment as a "gift conditional on return,"[36] so that it would be subject to the law of tzitzit? (D) And is it not astonishing that a scholar would be naked, with no clothes of his own, so that he would have to borrow a cloak in order to cover his body? And is it plausible that all of these strange occurrences coincided—moreover on the eve of the day of which it was expounded, "For great is the day of the Lord, most terrible—who can endure it?" (Joel 2:11)—"This is Yom Kippur"?[37] Let us not forget that even though it was taught that the imperative to confess on Yom Kippur commences at nightfall,[38] the Sages said: "Let one confess before eating and drinking, lest he get disoriented as a result of the meal."[39] Is it befitting the honor and spirit of a scholar to seek excuses in order to be free of the yoke of the law and to find leniencies on such a day? If this was merely frivolity on his part, why did Rav Hisda not rebuke him? More could be asked. Indeed, his entire behavior contradicts the Baraita that says that things that are permitted, but which others customarily forbid, may not be permitted in their presence.[40]

Note that Rami bar Tamri addressed Rav Hisda, the author of the statement "Who is a scholar? One who can judge terefot for himself."[41]

Rami bar Tamri was certainly a great scholar. Rav Hisda, whose contemporaries marveled at the keenness of his intellect, of whom his colleague Rav Huna said, "His teachings are sharp,"[42] before whose casuistry his colleague Rav Sheshet would tremble,[43] was impressed by Rami and said to his face: "I see that you are very sharp," and he even accepted his instruction in the case of the son who did not respect his parents. It is clear that a sharp Sage such as he must have done what he did intentionally—and deliberately on the eve of the Holy Day—in order to demonstrate examples of "the power of leniency," of leniencies which exist within the bounds of the halakhah.

---

[34] PT Bava Batra 5:8.   [35] BT Hullin 110a–b.
[36] See BT Sukkah 41b. [37] Tanhuma, Vayyishlah, 2.
[38] Tosefta, end of Yoma.   [39] BT Yoma 87b.
[40] BT Pesahim 50b.   [41] BT Hullin 43b.
[42] BT Shabbat 82b.   [43] BT Eruvin 67a.

Is it possible that he also intended a proclamation, a public expression of protest against false piety, and against a multiplication of decrees and stringencies?[16]

Tannaim and Amoraim

Rabbi Joshua ben Zeruz, Rabbi Meir's brother-in-law, testified to Rabbi [Judah the Patriarch] that Rabbi Meir had eaten a vegetable leaf in Bet She'an,[17] and Rabbi [Judah the Patriarch] permitted all of Bet She'an on that basis. His brothers and relatives besieged him, saying: "Shall you permit that which your fathers and fathers' fathers prohibited?" In response, he expounded for them this verse: "He . . . broke into pieces the bronze serpent that Moses had made, for until that time the Israelites had been offering sacrifices to it; it was called Nehushtan" (2 Kings 18:4). How is it that Asa and Yehoshafat both did not get rid of it, for Asa and Yehoshafat got rid of every known idolatry? Rather, his [i.e. Hezekiah's] ancestors left him his own domain of action, and my ancestors have similarly left me my domain.[44] [18]

According to Rabbi Eliezer, reporting the view of Rabbi Hanina, "Rabbi planted a tree on Purim,[19] bathed himself in the market of Sepphoris on the seventeenth of Tammuz[20] (on the market day, publicly), and proposed to abolish Tish'ah B'av, but

[44] BT Hullin 6b–7a.

---

[16] Heschel may perhaps be taking the details of what is a stylized polemic far too literally here. And yet it is possible that, although the setting of the original formulation may have been "Pumbedita vs. Sura," the purpose of its narration in the edited talmudic setting may well have been to make something like the point that Heschel is attributing to it here. That is, the talmudic redactors may have found use for an old piece of propaganda in order to score points not against Sura but rather against those who attempt to make the law as difficult as possible to comply with. The possibility, at least, cannot be dismissed.

[17] The issue here is the requirement for the setting aside of tithes, and that, in turn, hinged on whether Bet She'an was technically part of the Land of Israel. If it were not, then the tithe on vegetables and herbs, which is only rabbinically ordained in the Land of Israel, would not apply at all outside the borders. In this story, Rabbi Judah the Patriarch seized on one piece of anecdotal evidence to release all Bet She'an produce from the requirements of tithing.

[18] That is, either they didn't get around to permitting Bet She'an, or they just didn't realize that Bet She'an was problematic in terms of its location in the border area. In any event, the parallel drawn in this text to the idolatry of the brazen serpent is astonishingly bold. The clear implication is that continuing certain stringencies when they have no good reason is tantamount to a form of idolatry!

[19] It was customary to refrain from forms of work on Purim, though it was not legally required to do so.

[20] A minor fast day, when bathing was, apparently, eschewed by many, even though legally not banned.

they did not agree to it."[21][45] Rabbi Judah Nesi'ah and his court voted to permit the oil of Gentiles.[46] Such things have not been common among Sages from the time of Rabbi to the present.[22]

Rabbi Isaac bar Samuel bar Marta came to Netzivin. He found Rabbi Simlai of the South sitting and expounding: "Rabbi and his court permitted the oil [of Gentiles]. Samuel accepted it and consumed the oil, while Rav did not. Samuel said to Rav: Consume it or I shall declare you a rebellious elder. He pressured him, and he ate it."[47]

Rabbi related: when we used to study with Rabbi Eleazar ben Shamu'a, figs and grapes would be brought to us, and we ate them as a snack outside the Sukkah.[48] Rabbi took a wife for his son Rabbi Simeon, and the guests clapped with the backs of their hands on Shabbat. Rabbi Meir came by and heard the sound of their clapping on Shabbat. He said: Gentlemen! Has Shabbat been undone? Is it then permitted to profane Shabbat?! For Rabbi Meir held that it is forbidden to clap even with the backs of the hands. Rabbi heard his voice and said: Who is this who comes to rule over us in our own house? Rabbi Meir heard Rabbi's voice and fled.[49]

Rabbi Eleazar asked Rabbi Johanan: In those places that are surrounded by mountains, if one threw an object from there to a public domain, or from a public domain into it, has one violated the rule against carrying from domain to domain?[23] Said to him Rabbi Johanan: "Your implication is that there is no such thing as a public domain" (Korban Ha'edah: "for the entire world is surrounded by mountains"). It appears that Resh Lakish also attempted to abolish the rule against carrying from domain to domain by saying: "nothing can be a public domain unless it is open-ended to both ends of the world" (P'nei Moshe: unless you know that it does not end in mountains or hills). In another place, Resh Lakish said: "there is no public domain in this world (because of mountains and hills), but only in the coming age, as it is said: 'Let every valley be raised, every hill and mount made low' (Isaiah 40:4)."[50]

Close to this view are the words of Abbaye, from which "it may perhaps be inferred" that there is no public domain in these days since there are not places with 600,000 people, as there were in the desert.[51]

---

[45] BT Megillah 5a-b. The Gemara expressed astonishment at Rabbi; see also Tosafot, s.v. uvikkesh.
[46] Tosefta Avodah Zarah 5:1; BT Avodah Zarah 38b.
[47] PT Shabbat 1:4. See BT Avodah Zarah 36a, Tosafot s.v. asher, in the name of the Palestinian Talmud.
[48] BT Yoma 79b.   [49] PT Beitzah 5:2.
[50] PT Eruvin 8:8. Abbaye held a similar view—BT Eruvin 22b.
[51] BT Shabbat 6b.

---

[21] Apparently, what they did not agree to was what he is said to have "proposed," that is, the abolition of Tish'ah B'av.

[22] This is a rather amusing deadpan on Heschel's part.

[23] Sabbath law forbids transporting objects, even by throwing, from one domain to another. The principal prohibitions are against transporting from a private to a public domain or vice versa, and against transporting four cubits through a public domain. By the implication (see the sequel) that there may be no such thing as a truly public domain, the applicability of this entire section of Sabbath law is called into question.

Said Rav Judah quoting Rav: "It happened that Rabbi Osha'ia's daughter-in-law went to the bathhouse [on Friday afternoon] and it got dark while she was there, and her father-in-law set an *eruv* [a formalistic extension of the Shabbat boundary] for her. The matter was reported to Rabbi Hiyya, and he prohibited the practice. Rabbi Ishmael be-Rabbi Yosi said to him: You Babylonian! You are so stringent concerning the *eruv*! My father said the following: Whenever you can be lenient with respect to *eruv*, do so!"[52] And thus said Rabbi Joshua ben Levi: "the *halakhah* always follows the lenient ruling in matters of *eruv*."[53] And Samuel determined this rule: "the *halakhah* always follows the lenient ruling in matters of mourning."[54][24]

When Rav bar Shaba visited with Rav Nahman, he was served cooked liver,[25] and he didn't eat it. The servants told Rav Nahman that he follows a stringency and does not eat what he is served. He said to them: "stuff Shaba" [force-feed him].[55]

Against Those Who Are Stringent

The author of the Book of Proverbs wisely warned: "Do not swerve to the right or the left; keep your feet from evil" (Proverbs 4:27). "Every word of God is pure, a shield to those who take refuge in Him. Do not add to His words, lest He indict you and you be proved a liar" (Proverbs 30:5–6). Many Sages warned against excess in stringencies and were wont to be lenient even when giving practical rulings.

"I found that Rabbi Yesha'ia of blessed memory used to travel around Venice on Shabbat by gondola, since neighborhoods were connected only by waterways. And he used to say that the Gentile gondoliers do the work for their own purposes."[26][56]

Rabbi Yesha'ia de-Trani the Elder wrote: "I was much astonished at the holy Rabbis of France, who were wont to rule stringently on the strength of the slightest justification."[57] And Rabbenu Asher: "I am amazed. How could the Geonim originate decrees even after Rav Ashi completed the talmudic canon?"[27][58] And one of the later

---

[52] BT Eruvin 80a; see Rashi, and Tosafot s.v. *ma'aseh*; PT Eruvin, end of chapter 7.
[53] BT Eruvin 46a.   [54] BT Mo'ed Katan 18a.   [55] BT Hullin 111a.
[56] Shibbolei Halleket, section 111 (42a).   [57] Hamakhri'a, 10 (Lublin edition, p. 116).
[58] Rabbenu Asher, BT Shabbat, chapter 2, #15.

---

[24] All of the leniencies just discussed involve laws that are of rabbinic origin.

[25] The issue here is this: liver, if cooked, will give off blood and render the food in the pot forbidden for that reason. However, if the liver were scalded first (one method was to soak it in vinegar), then the blood was deemed to be sealed in, and cooking it would not be a problem. In this story, Rav bar Shaba did not wish to avail himself of that leniency. The end of the story is amazingly harsh, which is why Heschel quotes it here.

[26] That is, they would be driving the boats anyway and are not doing so for the specific benefit of the Jewish passengers, a somewhat debatable proposition if there were no non-Jewish passengers, though still arguable.

[27] For the general talmudic understanding was that Rav Ashi's career brought substantive ruling to a close.

Sages[28] complained: "Slaughterers learn the laws of slaughtering and treat them as if they were given at Sinai, and the present-day Sages do not pay due attention to these Johnny-come-latelies to slaughtering and inspecting, with the result that each one seeks to create a new stringency not found in the classic codes."[29] 59

Rabbi Simeon ben Tzemah Duran was asked whether it was permissible to slaughter an animal on a Festival for use that day (since there were those who ruled stringently lest one be led to *purchase* an animal that day). This was his answer: "We have never heard of such a prohibition . . . and those who rule stringently in this matter have abandoned their usual generosity . . . many leniencies were created . . . for the sake of the joy of the festival. And if they (the talmudic Sages) often permitted the *prohibited* for the sake of the joy of the festival, how shall we forbid that which is permitted. . . . just as it is forbidden to declare the impure pure, so it is forbidden to declare the pure impure."60

One of the greatest of the exegetes[30] writes:

The following sayings always stuck in my craw: "Whoever is exempt from doing something and does it anyway is called a simpleton,"61 and "are you not satisfied with the Torah's prohibitions that you seek to add others on yourself?"62—for how can we justify what we have always done in the House of Study? We do hundreds, if not thousands, of things from which we are legally exempt because of stringency or general abstinence. Indeed, the Sages instructed us: "Sanctify yourself (even) with that which is permitted to you," and they also interpreted the verse "you shall keep my charge"—"you shall stand guard over my commandments." And there are many more such instances. It therefore seemed to me that the resolution was that the statement "one who does something from which he is exempt is a simpleton" applies only to a case where the exemption cannot possibly lead to some violation, for then stringency and pious separatism do not apply. But then I checked the Palestinian Talmud *ad locum* and I found that it was not so . . . for it is presently explained there that even with respect to a matter that *can* lead to a violation they said "whoever is exempt from doing something and does it anyway is called a simpleton."63

Rabbi Moses Schreiber writes in one of his responsa: "It is certain that the rabbinic enactment that one should not learn from 'their' ways had its roots in antiquity when Israel lived in its own land and Gentiles were not common among them. Had they associated with the Gentiles then, they would have learned from their practices,

---

59 Panim Me'irot, Part II, #157.   60 Tashbetz, Part II, #10.
61 PT Shabbat 1:2.   62 PT Nedarim 9:1.
63 Be'er Sheva, Responsa, #21.

---

[28] Heschel is referring here to Meir Eisenstadt, eighteenth century, Poland and Austria.

[29] This statement, in other words, is an indictment of those Sages who passively acquiesce in the accretion of stringencies which are born of ignorance.

[30] Heschel refers here to Issachar Baer Eilenburg, sixteenth–seventeenth centuries, Poland and Italy.

and that's why the rabbis imposed the stringency . . . but today when we perforce associate with them, the protective enactment doesn't apply."[64]

According to the Zohar, there are two parts to the Torah: the part that speaks of the permitted, the pure, and the proper, and the part that speaks of the forbidden, the impure, and the improper. The first part comes from the good side of nature, and the second from the evil side of nature. Were there not an evil side to nature, this part of the Torah would not exist.[65] Prohibitions stem from the Tree of Knowledge of Good and Evil, not from the Tree of Life; that is, they flow from the mysterious conjunction of good and evil, and not from the good and the pure.

Rabbi Moses Cordovero explicated the ongoing dispute between the schools of Shammai and Hillel in a kabbalistic style:

> The dispute between Hillel the kind Patriarch, and Shammai the vigorous Chief Judge can be recognized in their personal qualities: Hillel never lost his temper, so as to avoid hurt, and Shammai had by nature a short fuse. But the root of their controversy was for the sake of Heaven—for they sought a determination of truth—and that is why their dispute endured constructively. In this way one can understand the statement of the Sages of blessed memory, "Why was it given to the School of Hillel to have the *halakhah* fixed in accordance with their position? Because of their humility." The intent here was that since they adhered to the side of kindness humbly and unpretentiously, and since they were irenic, the *halakhah,* which is the Shekhinah, follows their inclination to the side of kindness. Again, one can in this way understand the saying of the rabbis of blessed memory, "these and these are the words of the Living God." The explanation is as follows: The Living God is the pinnacle of Understanding from which the edifice then slopes down. Now both those who declare "impure, improper, guilty" (who incline toward the side of vigor, to stringency, confirming that the husks[31] have reign there) and those who declare "pure, proper, innocent" (who incline toward the side of kindness, to leniency, confirming that the husks have no reign there) have their origin in the Understanding from which both extremes emanate. When the emanation to one of these sides gains power, then the *halakhah* follows that side, whether to forbid or to permit . . . and therefore both the one who declares "pure" and the one who declares "impure" are right; therefore, the *halakhah* sometimes even follows the school of Shammai. The latter, however, happens only with some strain, since the greater inclination is to the side of kindness, and it was to inform us of *that* that they of blessed memory said that the School of Hillel inclined to leniency and the school of Shammai to stringency, each according to its kind or vigorous nature.[66]

It is well known that everything can be judged from opposing sides, from right and from left. These tendencies are what is known to the Gemara and to the Kabbalah as

---

[64] Responsa Hatam Sofer, Orah Hayyim, #92.
[65] Zohar, Genesis, 77b.
[66] Pardes Rimmonim, "The Gate of the Decisors," chapter 2 (end).

---

[31] Hebrew: *kelipot*—in Kabbalah, a term for forces of evil and darkness in the universe.

the disputes of the schools of Shammai and Hillel. In simpler terms they are known as the positive and the negative, the thesis and the antithesis. By way of example: when one comes to assess another person, if he wishes to judge him charitably, he will choose to relate his good deeds and qualities and ignore his bad side. Conversely, if he wishes to judge him harshly, he will find shortcomings galore and virtually no good side. These two tendencies may be called "Bet Shammai" and "Bet Hillel." For the school of Shammai generally deal stringently and judge harshly, while the school of Hillel are permissive—they deal leniently and judge charitably. It is all a matter of will. We have seen a similar phenomenon in the Torah, concerning the creation of the world, where it says: "God saw all that He had made, and found it very good" (Genesis 1:31), and somewhat later: "The devisings of man's mind are evil from his youth" (Genesis 8:21)—that is, absolutely evil, with no good whatsoever. Indeed, every human being has these dual aspects.

In contradistinction to the ways of "the pietists who in their fear would extract from seventy gates of the permitted one gate of the forbidden," Rabbi Israel Baal Shem Tov taught: "A person should not be excessively meticulous in what he does, for the evil inclination works to instill in a person fear that he is not fulfilling his obligations, so that he is brought to moroseness."[67] Also, Rabbi Phinehas of Koretz taught: "It is not fitting for a person to create stringencies and to be excessively anxious, for he might, Heaven forbid, invoke heavenly judgment." He was rigorous "not to be exceedingly stringent, for by doing so people extend for themselves the condition of exile."[68]

> [He himself] was rigorous not to be exceedingly stringent, for by doing so people extend for themselves, Heaven forbid, the condition of exile, since stringencies come from the side of judgment. The proof: Latter authorities tend to rule more stringently than earlier authorities. With each new book there appear several new stringencies, and this is caused by the potency of exile, which is constantly becoming weightier because of our many sins. Therefore, a person should rule no more stringently than the *Shulhan Arukh*, and moreover, even if a stringency appears in the *Shulhan Arukh*, if it is not the final conclusion, one should not act in that way. Only with respect to Passover should one apply all of the stringencies mentioned in the *Shulhan Arukh*, and yet even on Passover, one should not apply a stringency not found in the *Shulhan Arukh*.[69]

In a similar vein, Rabbi Nahman of Bratslav said:

> All of the "wise counsel" in the world which is taken on by those who are beginners in the service of God are not wise counsel at all, but rather fantasies, foolishness, and great confusions; indeed, these "wisdoms," that is, calculating, searching, and nitpicking to excess to determine if one's actions truly fulfill obligations, do much to distance a person from the service of God. For mortals cannot ever fulfill their obligations fully, and the Holy and Blessed One does not treat His creatures despotically. The Torah was not given

---

[67] Tsava'at Harivash, 6a.
[68] Ge'ulat Yisrael, Ostravha (5581/1821), Part II, 11b.
[69] See my article, "On the life of Rabbi Pinehas of Koretz," *Alei Ayyin*, p. 219.

to angels. Concerning those nitpickers and lovers of stringencies it is said: "That he may live by them—and not die by them" . . . and they get no vitality from any mitzvah on account of their nitpicking and morose attitudes.[70]

"In the name of Rabbi Simha Bunim: When a person feels incomplete in reverence for God, it is then that he needs many fences, and that is why certain stringencies and fences have been added; but one who is wholehearted in reverence for God does not need them. And that is why it is written: 'And you who cleave to the Lord' (Deuteronomy 4:4), and earlier in the same section of the Torah, 'Do not add to that which I command you' (Deuteronomy 4:2)—for you will not have need of additional fences. Mark this well."[71] In the Torah it is written: "An Ammonite or Moabite may not enter the congregation of the Lord . . . forever . . . do not seek their peace or welfare for all your days, forever" (Deuteronomy 23:4, 7). Some interpret: "'Do not seek their peace or welfare' — to receive from them converts, 'all your days, forever'—and for all eternity."[72] "Ammonites and Moabites are forbidden, and their ban is eternal."[73] Yet the Tannaim struggled with this matter. "On that day Judah, an Ammonite convert, came and stood before them in the House of Study. He said to them: May I marry within the congregation? Rabban Gamliel said to him: You may not. Rabbi Joshua said to him: You may. Said Rabban Gamliel: the text says 'An Ammonite or Moabite may not enter the congregation of the Lord, even the tenth generation, etc.' Said Rabbi Joshua: Do you think that Ammonites and Moabites still exist as they were? Sennacherib king of Assyria already came and commingled all of the nations."[74] The author of Peri Hadash writes of the law concerning milk milked by a Gentile, that "in a city where there is no milk of unkosher animals, or if it is more expensive than milk of kosher animals, it is permitted to buy milk from a Gentile even without Jewish supervision."[75] Most later authorities came out fighting concerning this leniency.[76] By contrast, however, Rabbi Moshe Alashkar[32] wrote in protest against a Rabbi who ruled stringently concerning an abandoned woman: "one who rules her to be chained and deals stringently with the matter is the subject of the saying 'he is counseled by his ass.'"[77][33]

---

[70] Likkutei Moharan Tanyana, Part II, #44.

[71] Yakar Mipaz, of Rabbi Alexander Zusha of Plutzk (Warsaw, 5692/1932), 102; Siah Sarfei Kodesh, Part V, 70.

[72] Lekah Tov, 491, 39b.

[73] Mishnah Yebamot 8:3.

[74] Mishnah Yadayim 4:4; PT Demai, 2:1 (22c): "Rabbi Yose posed this problem: We should therefore reject anyone who comes to convert, for he may be from Ammon or Moab!" See Tashbetz Katan, #538, concerning one who asked Rabbi Judah the Patriarch whether, since we often take care concerning matters of small probability, we should worry about Ammonite and Moabite ancestry as well.

[75] Yoreh Deah, #115, paragraph 10.

[76] Arukh Hashulhan, paragraphs 5, 6; Darkhei Teshuvah, to Yoreh Deah #115.

[77] Responsa of Maharam Alashkar, #112 (end).

---

[32] Sixteenth century, North Africa.

[33] The phrase is a play on words: hamor means "ass," whereas hamur means "stringency." This is really a wordplay on a wordplay. Hosea 4:12 takes the Israelites to task for being guided by their

Stringencies of Vigor

There are instances in which the tendency of later authorities to add fences and buffers to the rulings of earlier authorities is held up for praise.

Concerning Rabbi Elijah of Vilna it is told:

> From the time that he was thirteen years old . . . he did not look outward from his four cubits for the rest of his life, for he did not want to derive pleasure from this world. He ate meager morsels of bread that were soaked in a small quantity of water; he consumed these twice a day, and did not taste them, but swallowed them whole . . . false fantasies of the pleasures of this world did not succeed in turning him away from a single detail of God's commands, which he was meticulous in fulfilling as given. He did not stumble into iniquity by relying on lenient rulings, but gave himself over to upholding every detail of the words of the Rabbis of blessed memory—even those things not mentioned in the *Shulhan Arukh*.[78]

Such Sages did not pay much attention to the roads they traveled, much as when a person walks his eyes tend to look up, and not generally focus on what lies at his feet.

But it was said in the name of Rabbi Akiva: "The mitzvot were given in order to live by them, as it says: 'which a person shall do to live by them' (Leviticus 18:5)"[79] [34]

It Is Time to Act for the Lord

A single verse in the Book of Psalms served as a firm foundation for a modest measure of flexibility in the legal construction of mitzvot. "It is time to act for the Lord, for they have nullified your teachings" (Psalm 119:126), and it is offered at the end of Mishnah Berakhot as a basis for some ancient enactments. But the plain meaning of the verse is not evident; it can, in fact, be understood in many different ways.

[78] His sons' introduction to the Commentary of the Vilna Gaon on Shulhan Arukh Orah Hayyim.

[79] Tosefta Shabbat, end of chapter 16.

---

makel (understood to be either a kind of divining rod, the use of which was forbidden to God's people, or a more graphic reference to the people's physical passions). But the word for one who rules leniently is *mekil*, which has a strong phonetic assonance with the subject of Hosea's condemnation. Thus, in BT Pesahim 52b (and in many instances in the medieval codes), Hosea's phrase was used to denigrate those who were "guided" by lenient positions, that is, who shopped around for leniencies. Here, *hamoro* is used as a parallel to *maklo*, not in the latter's original meaning, but rather in its word-play meaning. The net result of the secondary wordplay here is the judgment that one who is guided by the tendency toward stringencies is as one who takes counsel with an ass (or is one himself).

[34] The Gaon of Vilna was the symbol of Lithuanian opposition to the nascent Hasidic movement. It is surely not coincidental that Heschel's one example, in this chapter devoted to criticizing stringencies, of one who imposed them routinely, is the Vilna Gaon. It is quite clearly intended to underscore just how much early Hasidism sought to move away from ascetic rabbinism.

(1) There are those who interpreted the verse as applying to God; that is, the time has come for God to act (as if the verse read "It is time to act, i.e., for the Lord to act"), for the wicked have nullified His teachings. Or, alternatively, it is now the moment for God to exact punishment on the wicked.[80] Or, yet another variation: "when the time arrives for God to wreak punishment and vengeance on the wicked, they will coincidentally find many occasions to nullify the Torah so that their punishment will be just."[81]

(2) There are those who interpreted the verse as an explanation of the actions of Gideon (Judges 6:25)[82] and Elijah (1 Kings 18:33), both of whom sacrificed on local altars when that was already prohibited, because of their concern to create a buffer and fence against worship in Israel of anything but God.[83]

(3) According to another interpretation, the intent of the verse is to encourage everyone by saying that the time has come to go out and perform acts that honor God. When people nullify the Torah and do not support it, it is time to add strength to it. Hillel the Elder said: "When others draw in, give forth, and when others give forth, draw in . . . if you see that the Torah is not beloved of your generation, draw it in, for it says: 'It is time to act for the Lord, for they have nullified your teachings.'"[84]

(4) According to another preaching, "One who observes the Torah sporadically nullifies the covenant." Why so? "They have nullified your teachings, for it is *time* to act for the Lord."[85]

(5) There is also an interpretation that takes the intent of the verse to be a major principle for applying the Torah's commands. "There are times when one cancels the words of Torah in order to act for the Lord. So this person who intends to greet his neighbor is doing God's will—as it says: 'Seek peace and pursue it' (Psalm 34:15)—and it is thus permissible to nullify the Torah and do something that would appear to be forbidden."[86] [35] On this interpretation, the verse serves as a support for doing something impermissible when it is necessary to do so for the sake of Heaven, such as greeting a person with God's name, that is, to use God's name for apparently mundane purpose. Similarly, this verse was relied on for the writing down of *halakhah* and *aggadah,* which it is forbidden to write down. For "oral teachings may not be recited from a written text"[87]; and yet in order that Torah not be forgotten in Israel, the Sages agreed to commit the Oral Torah to writing, by this exegesis: "It is time to act for the Lord, for they have nullified your teachings"—"Better to uproot a single precept of

---

[80] Rabbi Abraham ibn Ezra, on Psalm 119:126. See the commentary of David Kimhi, ad loc.

[81] Maimonides, Commentary on the Mishnah, end of Berakhot.

[82] According to Rabbi Aba bar Kahana, "seven sins were permitted when Gideon sacrificed his bull" (PT Megillah 1:14 [72c]; Leviticus Rabbah 22:9).

[83] Rashi, BT Berakhot 63a.

[84] BT Berakhot 63a; see Sifre Zuta, p. 317; also the words of Rabbi Simeon bar Yohai, PT Berakhot 9:5.

[85] Midrash Samuel, chapter 1.   [86] Rashi, BT Berakhot 54a.   [87] BT Gittin 60b.

---

[35] One might put it as follows: to violate the letter of the law in order to uphold its spirit or intent.

Torah than for the Torah to be forgotten in Israel."[88] Again, this verse was relied on for the publication of *haftarot* in a separate volume, even though the prophetic books should not be anthologized.[89] "Books of *Aggadah,* even though they should not be written down, are rescued from fire on Shabbat. Why? 'It is time to act for the Lord, for they have nullified your teachings.'"[90]

According to biblical law, there are circumstances when a woman might be required to bring as many as five pairs of birds (turtle-doves or pigeons) as a sacrifice to the Temple. "It happened that bird-pairs were costing as much as a gold dinar (the price had escalated since the law demanded that so many of them be brought as sacrifices). Rabban Simeon ben Gamliel said: I swear by the Temple that I shall not sleep tonight until the price has lowered to a silver dinar. He entered the court and ruled: a woman in such circumstances need not bring more than a single bird-pair."[91] In this instance, Rabban Simeon ben Gamliel ruled leniently on a matter of biblical law, because of the verse "It is time to act for the Lord. . . ."[92]

This fifth interpretation is audacious, and it should not be entrusted to any but the wisest of Sages, who truly understand contemporary times. "To everything there is a season, and a time is set for every experience" (Ecclesiastes 3:1). "It is time to act for the Lord, for they have nullified your teachings," but it is also written, "That he not enter the Holy at all times" (Leviticus 16:2).[93] The great legal deciders of Israel were not wont to use this principle in their rulings. The RaABaD stated only in general terms that the reason that the court has the power to make enactments that temporarily forbid the permissible or permit the forbidden is the verse "It is time to act for the Lord, for they have nullified your teachings."[94] Yet Maimonides, in his commentary on the Mishnah, embraced this fifth interpretation, and he utilized it as an operative principle, both in *aggadah* and *halakhah.*

Maimonides wrote that even though he remained "very frightened" of writing on esoteric matters, he decided to compose his book *The Guide of the Perplexed,* and he relied on two precedents. The first was that the Sages of blessed memory had said in a similar matter: "It is time to act for the Lord, for they have nullified your teachings," and the second was their statement: "all your actions should be for the sake of Heaven."[95]

Maimonides instituted a rule under which the congregation would not pray silently any of the statutory prayers; rather, the leader would pray out loud, and the congregation would silently listen to his words.

---

[88] BT Temurah 14b; see Sefer Hasidim, Mekitzei Nirdamim edition, p. 419.

[89] BT Gittin 60a.

[90] Tractate Soferim, Higger edition, end of chapter 16.

[91] Mishnah Keritot, end of chapter 1.

[92] Rashi BT Keritot 8a. And according to the RaABaD (on Hilkhot Mehusarei Kapparah 1:10), this ruling was not a one-time ruling. See BT Bava Batra 166a, Tosafot s.v. *nikhnas.*

[93] See Zohar, Mikketz, 194a.

[94] RaABaD, critical comments to *Hilkhot Mamrim,* 2:9.

[95] Maimonides, *Guide of the Perplexed,* Preface to Part I.

What necessitated this system was that during the leader's prayers, the people would not pay attention to him, but would instead talk to one another, or leave the premises, and it would be very nearly a blessing in vain since no one would hear it. And whoever was untutored would observe the learned speaking with one another, blowing their noses, and coughing out phlegm, and he would imitate them and conclude that the silent prayer is the only one that matters. Now we say in respect of biblical prohibitions "It is time to act for the Lord, for they have nullified your teachings"; how much more so should we invoke this in a case which is a rabbinic order of prayer, and where there is the need to avert the desecration of God's name which would result from others thinking that Jewish prayer is a laughing and frivolous matter, or that it is a process designed to fulfill the people's obligation mechanically. If we then pray a bit each weekday together with the other worshipers, then we will restore the original construction and we will once again pray silently and then afterwards pray aloud.[96]

And here are the words of Rabbi Israel Baal Shem Tov: "It is time to act for the Lord, for they have nullified your teachings" (Psalm 119:126). "For occasionally there is a mitzvah that has within it an aroma of transgression; one should not attend to the evil inclination which attempts to dissuade one from doing that mitzvah. He should say to the evil inclination: 'My only intention in doing this mitzvah is to bring some satisfaction to my Creator by my doing it.' That will cause the evil inclination to depart from him, with God's help. But in any event, one must decide using his own reason whether or not to do that mitzvah."[97]

Rabbi Mendel of Kotzk expressed amazement: "Is it possible that the entire Oral Law has been kept alive because of a transgression? Oral teachings may not be recited from a written text. And yet they write it all down because of 'It is time to act for the Lord'!"[36]

[96] Responsa of Maimonides, Blau edition, #256.
[97] Tzava'at Harivash, 6b.

---

[36] This is a verse from Psalms, part of the Hagiographa, and thus it does not have authority on a par with a verse from the Torah. The Kotzker Rebbe's answer to this question is clever and far-reaching. See Heschel, *God in Search of Man*, 276.

ל 38 ל

STRINGENCIES AND LENIENCIES

[For an introduction, see the beginning of Chapter 37.]

Beloved Are Prohibitions

HUMAN BEINGS ARE ADDICTED to the pleasures of this world. A person can barely achieve half of his worldly desires in his lifetime. Give him a hundred, and he wants two hundred. Life is a pursuit of pleasure, and the schemings of the ego know no bounds. Fortunate is the nation that recognized the value of austerity and the subjugation of the ego.

"A slave is happier with a wanton woman"[1]—that is, he prefers being a slave and being permitted the unbridled sexuality of slave girls, to being a free man, permitted to a free Israelite woman, whose sexuality will not be cheap or ever-present for him.[1]

Lust impedes love and creates a barrier between a person and his Creator. This is the source of the desire for "prohibitions of love," which dam up pleasures that constrict the realm of discipline and shrink reality. Beloved are prohibitions.

The inclination to austerity is implanted in the heart of our jurists. In their eyes, whoever proliferates prohibitions and is stringent in rulings is to be praised. Let this be the general rule: Let a person be more satisfied with prohibitions than with all the goods of the world. Do you seek innovation? Look for new prohibitions. Whoever is stringent will be blessed; a person of *halakhah*[2] is especially blessed. A cautious person will rebel against leniencies. And one who seeks leniencies should be suspected of

---

[1] BT Gittin 13a.

---

[1] This talmudic statement, perhaps having as its origin an apologetic for slavery, is apparently intended metaphorically here by Heschel. We are all slaves to our passions, and thus we often prefer to think of ourselves that way in order to absolve ourselves from responsibility. In moments of clarity, however, we recognize the self-destructiveness of this "slavery" and we look for methods of discipline and control—sometimes even going to the other extreme: "beloved are prohibitions." The Freudian influence on Heschel is quite clear.

[2] This phrase echoes the title of a book by Joseph Soloveichik: *Halakhic Man* (Philadelphia: Jewish Publication Society, 1983).

a frivolous nature. Thus did they add decrees to decrees, stringencies to stringencies, to create a buffer around each biblical prohibition, to declare impurity or impose liability, in order to avoid the possibility of leniency. In several places, the rule was determined: "Choose to analogize to a stringent, rather than to a lenient case";[2] "Choose to argue from a stringent, rather than from a lenient case."[3] [3]

The person who was careful to impose stringencies on himself was highly praised. "Whoever imposes stringencies on himself earns longevity."[4] This is, indeed, the characteristic of the pious: "The pious are different, for they impose stringencies on themselves."[5]

Rabbi Zera said: "The daughters of Israel were stringent with themselves in that whenever they saw a blood stain of as little as a mustard seed's diameter, they observed a seven-day bloodless waiting period."[6] "But the Torah had only required seven bloodless days for nonmenstrual flow."[7] [4] The jurists were accustomed to motivating the people to be wary of those things that raised even a slight doubt:[5] "Our Creator will bless the one who is stringent"; "One who is stringent will live long"; "One who is stringent will be graced by God"; "As for one who is stringent . . . may blessing come upon him."[8]

Now they *were* willing to restrict the Sages' power to issue protective decrees by establishing this principle: "One does not issue a decree on a decree." That is if something is itself a protective decree, we do not protect it with another decree; we do not build fences around fences.[9] Other such principles are: "One does not interpret a decree innovatively"; "One does not add to a decree";[10] "One does not add to a

---

[2] BT Yevamot 8a; BT Kiddushin 68a.   [3] BT Avodah Zarah 46b.   [4] BT Menahot 41a.

[5] BT Berakhot 22a.   [6] BT Berakhot 31a.

[7] Rashi, BT Berakhot 31a, s.v. *yoshevet;* BT Megillah 28b, Rashi s.v. *shehehmiru* and Tosafot s.v. *sheafilu.*

[8] A. Aptowitzer, *Sefer Ra'aviah,* Preface, pp. 97ff.

[9] Said Rava: "It itself is a decree. Shall we come and issue a decree on a decree?"—BT Shabbat 11b; similarly, Rav Nahman—BT Yevamot 109a; Abbaye—Betzah 3a. Also, PT Pesahim 1:4: "Is there a fence to be built around a fence?"

[10] PT Shevi'it 2:4. It is sufficient that the Sages ruled that one should not plant a tree even within thirty days prior to Rosh Hashanah of the Sabbatical Year, and that a tree so planted be uprooted. But if one did not uproot it, we should not decree additionally that the fruits are forbidden (P'nai Moshe).

---

[3] These hermeneutical rules suggest, says Heschel, that stringencies are normal and canonical, and thus are the proper bases for inference and analogy.

[4] Leviticus 15 had established ritual impurity for women who experienced blood flows. In the case of normal—that is, regular menstrual—flows, the period of impurity was seven days. In the case of irregular flows—that is, at a time other than the expected menstrual flow, or an unusually extended flow—the impurity lasted for the duration of the bleeding, and then another seven "clean" days. Rabbi Zera reports that, notwithstanding the fact that both biblical and rabbinic law required only seven days of impurity (and sexual abstinence) for the menstruant, Jewish women nevertheless took upon themselves the more stringent rules of the irregular flow even in the case of the regular cycle. That supererogatory stringency remains in force to this day among ritually observant Jews.

[5] That is, resolve all doubts in the favor of stringency. For example, better to abstain from a food about which there is even a 1 percent doubt as to its ritual fitness (*kashrut*).

received law";[11] "We do not add regulations to regulations";[12] "Come, let us at least not add to it";[13] "Innovative decrees do not apply retroactively";[14] "One should not add to the stipulations clearly set forth in a Mishnah."[15]

Yet the jurists did not pay attention to this principle that one does not issue a decree on a decree.[16] Rabbi Jonathan Eibeschutz held the view that in the case of many stringencies there were often decrees on decrees.[17] And once a teaching issues from a jurist it is considered perfect, and it persists in all of its minutiae. That which has been decreed forbidden is as if "a lion crouches on it," saying to us: "Get back!"[18] Each legal buffer is justified by the slogan: "We say to the Nazirite 'Get away! Go around! Do not come near the vineyard.'"[19]

In the Sifre it was expounded: "For you are a people consecrated to the Lord your God" (Deuteronomy 14:21)—"Consecrate yourself."[20] However, Rava added, "Consecrate yourself [even] with that which is permitted to you,"[6] that is, consecrate yourself to stand guard against even that which is permitted, such as [permitted] secondary relationships that were forbidden in addition to the primary biblical sexual taboos.[21][7] In the words of Rav Kahana and Rav Ashi: "you shall keep my charge" (Leviticus 18:30)—"you shall stand guard over my charge."[22][8]

---

[11] Even if it is a received law and not a mere protective decree, we should not add a prohibition on the fruits (P'nai Moshe).

[12] BT Bava Metzi'a 5b.   [13] BT Shevuot 48b, and Rashi ad loc.

[14] BT Bava Kamma 72b.   [15] PT Nazir 1:1.

[16] Despite the opinion of early authorities that decrees should not be issued after the canonization of the Talmud, in each generation Sages came and issued decrees and regulations of stringency and prohibition, creating impurities and liabilities. See Rabbenu Asher, Shabbat, chapter 2, #15: "I am amazed. How did the Geonim permit themselves to innovate a decree after the Talmud was closed by Rav Ashi?" See also Maggid Mishneh, Hilkhot Hametz Umatzah 5:20; Keseph Mishneh, Hilkhot Mamrim 2:6.

[17] Kreti uphleti, #66, in connection with the ruling of Moses Isserles, that if the slightest amount of blood is found on the membrane of the albumin the entire egg is prohibited—a decree intended to prevent eating of blood on the yolk membrane, which is forbidden. The author of Peri Hadash also stated in this connection: "It is astonishing to issue decrees . . . on one's own authority when the Talmud explicitly permits it."

[18] See BT Eruvin 78b.   [19] BT Shabbat 13a.

[20] Sifre Devarim, paragraphs 97, 104.

[21] BT Yevamot 20a, and Rashi ad loc.

[22] BT Mo'ed Katan 5a; BT Yevamot 21a.

---

[6] In the Middle Ages, this principle became a call to the duty to eschew legal behavior that might be considered unethical, even though legal. I am, for example, perfectly permitted, under the law, to refuse use of my land to another even though it may cost me nothing. It is, after all, my property. Doing so, however, was considered to be unethical and was even referred to as "Sodomite behavior."

[7] In Leviticus 18 and 20, the Torah forbids many consanguinous (and some other) sexual relationships. However, the Rabbis added a secondary list that also became forbidden. One example of this is the prohibition on sexual relations with a grandson's wife (even if the marriage is no longer in force). The Torah had forbidden only relations with a woman who had been married to one's son, but the Rabbis added the next generation (and all subsequent generations) to the basic taboo.

[8] This is a play on the Hebrew root sh-m-r, which is repeated in this verse, and which can mean either (the more informal) "to watch" or (the more stringent) "to stand guard over."

"It happened that a snack of some cooked food was brought to Rabban Johanan ben Zakkai, and two dates and a jug of water to Rabban Gamliel, and they said: 'bring them up to the Sukkah.'"[23] In the Bavli, they commented on this: "Not because that was the received law, but rather because they wished to act stringently."[24][9] Legally, one may eat and drink casual snacks outside the Sukkah all festival long, but "if one wants to act stringently he may do so, and it is not considered to be 'holier than thou.'"[25]

Concerning the law of Tzitzit (whether the wearer or the garment worn requires them), the pious of old used to attach the blue-dyed thread to a garment as soon as they had woven three handbreadths of it. They said of this practice: "The pious are different, for they impose stringencies on themselves."[26]

In the matter of one who had a nocturnal emission: does he need to immerse in a *mikveh,* or is it enough for him to be washed with nine *kabs* of water?[10] Said Rabbi Yannai: "I have heard of those who are lenient, and of those who are stringent. Whoever acts stringently in this matter will have length of days and years."[27]

"At first [prior to the confusion caused by the Samaritans, who would light flares on a day which had not been determined to be the New Moon, in order to lead Israel astray], they would light flares (and everyone in the Diaspora, both near and far, would know the exact beginning of the month, and thus they would have only one day of each festival). After the Samaritan confusion, they instituted that messengers would be sent out[11] . . . but today, when we know the exact beginning of each month, why do we observe two days of the festival?[12] Because of this instruction that was received from the Land of Israel: be vigilant concerning ancestral customs!"[28]

It was a principle among jurists that "one should not abolish or denigrate any established custom, for it was not instituted for nothing."[29] "Even in a pressing matter, one should not change such a custom, as was said concerning the inhabitants of Beshan (BT Pesahim 50b: "Your ancestors already took on the obligation").[13] Even

---

23 Mishnah Sukkah 2:5.   24 BT Yoma 79a.   25 BT Sukkah 26a.
26 BT Menahot 41a.   27 BT Berakhot 22a.   28 BT Betzah 4b.
29 Moses Isserles, Orah Hayyim, #690, quoting Bet Yosef, who in turn quoted *Orhot Hayyim.*

---

[9] The expression used is "bring them up," since Sukkot were typically constructed on rooftops. For a biblical precedent, see Nehemiah 8:16.

[10] A *mikveh* requires forty *se'ah* of water, a much greater quantity than nine *kabs.*

[11] This led to the second day of festival observance in the Diaspora, for the speed of a horse is far slower than the speed of light, and outlying Jewish communities would typically not receive word of the determination of the New Moon by the time a full-moon festival was to begin (e.g., Passover). There would thus be a one-day doubt, or margin of error, with respect to which day was actually the holy day.

[12] That is, a fixed calendar already existed from the fourth century on.

[13] The custom here involved abstaining from certain market trips on Fridays, lest there not be enough time to get back home for the Sabbath. See the end of this chapter.

if the custom has a hint of the prohibited,[14] it should not be abolished. Yet if the conditions so changed from what they were originally, the custom may be changed to fit the times."[30] [15]

According to the Bavli, one may eat meat immediately after eating cheese. And Rabbi Meir of Rothenberg wrote: "In my callow days I used to deride those who would take care not to eat meat after cheese. Not only did I not observe that restriction, but, God forgive me, I considered it a kind of sectarianism. Then one day, from one meal to the next, I found cheese between my teeth. I then decreed on myself to refrain from meat after cheese, just as I refrained from cheese after meat. This practice does not constitute dissent from the Talmud, nor a gratuitous increase in restrictions; for Mar Ukva is quoted as follows: 'I am like vinegar born of wine in this matter (for my father used to wait twenty-four hours after meat before eating milk, and I wait merely from one regular meal to the next).'[31] Every individual may self-impose stringencies in order to stand guard."[32]

I Have Imposed Many Decrees on Myself

Beloved is Israel, for they were given Torah and commandments.[16] A great love has been acknowledged to them, for they are "laden with mitzvot,"[33] and daily take upon themselves "the yoke of the mitzvot,"[34] and do not do them "grudgingly, but rather with joy."[35] "It was taught in the name of Rabbi Meir: There is no person in Israel who does not do one hundred mitzvot each day . . . and in the same vein, Rabbi Meir used to say: There is no person in Israel who is not surrounded by mitzvot."[36] The reason for this is given in the words of Rabbi Hananiah ben Akashia: "The Holy and Blessed One wished to make Israel meritorious, and thus He gave them much Torah and many mitzvot."[37] Isi ben Judah said: "When God gives Israel a new mitzvah, He increases their sanctity."[38] Not only that, but "A lover of money never has his fill of money" (Ecclesiastes 5:9), and thus "A lover of mitzvot never has his fill of mitzvot,"

[30] Magen Avraham, Orah Hayyim #690, 22. Responsa of the Remah, #21 (#19 in the Asher Sieff edition).
[31] BT Hullin 105a.   [32] Mordecai, Hullin, #687.   [33] BT Berakhot 17a.
[34] See Mishnah Berakhot 2:2.   [35] Midrash on Psalms 112:2.
[36] PT Berakhot, end of chapter 9.   [37] Mishnah, end of Makkot.
[38] Mekhilta, Mishpatim, 20 (beginning).

---

[14] That is, the custom itself *seems* questionable; and yet the benefit of the doubt still goes to the entrenched custom.

[15] This last comment reestablishes the dialectic between the eternality of stringencies and the needs of the times.

[16] This is Heschel's paraphrase and takeoff on a statement attributed to Akiva in Mishnah Avot 3:14.

says Rabbi Isaac.[39] The children of Israel restrict that which is permitted to them, and add decrees, buffers, and fences.[17]

Rabbi Avira expounded in the name of either Rabbi Ami or Rabbi Asi:

> The ministering angels said to the Holy and Blessed One: Master of the Universe, it is written in your Torah: "who shows no favor" (Deuteronomy 10:17), and yet you show favoritism to Israel, as it is said: "The Lord bestow His favor on you" (Numbers 6:26). He said to them: Shall I not favor them? For I wrote for them in the Torah: "When you have eaten your fill, give thanks" (Deuteronomy 8:10), and they act stringently [so as to say grace even] for so much as the size of an olive or an egg.[40] [18]

And Rabbi Zera said: "The daughters of Israel were stringent with themselves in that whenever they saw a bloodstain of as little as a mustard seed's diameter, they observed a seven-day bloodless waiting period."[41] [19] Rava expounded: "The Assembly of Israel spoke before the Holy and Blessed One: Master of the Universe, I have imposed many decrees on myself, more than You have decreed on me, and I have fulfilled them all."[42]

In the matter of monetary cases, jurists often acknowledged that some things had changed since talmudic times. "According to our local custom, the law may change . . . with the changing of the times." Yet would they ever say in the case of ritual law: "the law changes with the changing of prevailing custom?" Consider the words of the Meiri: "Even though compromise is preferable in the case of monetary disputes, it is not so in the case of ritual prohibitions. A judge should not say: Let us permit him this so that he will not come to eat that, or the like. This is what was meant when they said: This verse—that is, "One who honors compromise blasphemes God" (Psalm 10:3) [a non-standard reading of the verse]—refers only to Aaron [and his agreeing to build the Calf]."[43]

In Derogation of Those Who Are Lenient

Already at an early period, the Sages divided into two schools of thought on Halakhah: the stringent approach and the lenient approach. "In all cases the school of Shammai is stringent and the school of Hillel is lenient."[44] For this reason they

---

[39] Devarim Rabbah, 2:26 ("Then Moses set aside").   [40] BT Berakhot 20b.
[41] BT Berakhot 31a.   [42] BT Eruvin 21b.   [43] Meiri, Sanhedrin 7a.
[44] BT Mo'ed Katan 3b, Tosafot s.v. ad atzeret.

---

[17] This paragraph thus has collected several statements expressing the sentiment that "the more the better" when it comes to ritual restrictions.

[18] The obligation to say Grace after Meals does not require eating to the point of satiation, as the text of the Torah would imply. According to Israel's accepted halakhah, even the size of an egg triggers the obligation to say Grace.

[19] See the previous section.

enumerated those *halakhot* that are exceptions to the rule, in which the school of Shammai is lenient and the school of Hillel stringent: "These are among the leniencies of the school of Shammai and the stringencies of the school of Hillel."[45] "Everywhere Rav Aha rules stringently and Ravina leniently except for these three matters."[46]

The tendency to increase stringencies is very old among the Jews, and it finds expression in the custom of uttering prohibitive vows, that is, when a person would prohibit to himself things that are permitted, such as eating or sleeping, or would take on an obligation to do something that is not incumbent upon him.

The taking of vows was quite common in biblical times; it is found in the lives of the Patriarch Jacob (Genesis 28:20), of Hannah (1 Samuel 1), of Absalom (2 Samuel 15), and others. And the Torah specified the means of releasing or nullifying vows.

Rabbi Meir articulated this principle: "Best of all is that one not vow at all."[47] The following verse in Ecclesiastes was the general rule for the Tannaim: "It is better not to vow at all than to vow and not fulfill." There was fear of laxity in fulfilling vows on the part of one who takes them freely, and it was said "Whoever freely vows is not approved of by the Sages."[48] But they did not object to the taking of vows in principle. On the contrary, "Vows protect abstinence."[49]

"Jacob then made a vow, saying" (Genesis 28:20). What does "saying" mean? To say to the coming generations that they, too, should take vows in times of distress.[50][20] And if a person fears that he will be lax with respect to the mitzvot, he may take a vow in order to bolster his resolve.[51]

"If you see a Sage who enjoys longevity, you can be sure that he has surpassed his colleagues in legal minutiae not biblically ordained. For they explicitly said, 'Why have you lived so long, etc.,' and every cause suggested there is not biblically ordained, but is rather a minutia created by reason, and not by the text."[52]

Many of the righteous were wont to load on themselves stringencies as heavy as olive presses and to subordinate their bodies to their souls. These influenced the course of history; those greats who opposed asceticism and mortification of the flesh were made to defer to them. Evidently, this tendency to abstinence flowed from a strong desire for sanctity. What appeared to others as a bent that could crush a person with burdens was in the eyes of the austere the most sublime desideratum in life, that which can create an inner world unaffected by the accidents of events and by human passions.

Stringencies are a protest by the soul, which is suppressed by its subjugation to the

---

[45] Mishnah Eduyot, chapter 4ff.   [46] BT Pesahim 74b.
[47] BT Nedarim 9a; BT Hullin 2b.   [48] See BT Nedarim 22a; BT Hullin 2a; and other places.
[49] Mishnah Avot 3:13.   [50] Bereshit Rabbah 70:1.
[51] BT Nedarim 8a.   [52] Sefer Hasidim, #210.

---

[20] This was Jacob's first night alone as he was fleeing from the murderous wrath of his brother Esau.

passions, against the relentless pressure exerted by human desires and base traits. Ascetics aspire to independence from that which enslaves the spirit, to detachment from the vanities of this world, to distance from their realm. The tendency to praise the stringent and to derogate the lenient was strong. When in doubt, they said: Whoever is stringent, may blessing come upon him.[21]

Rabbi Simeon bar Kahana and Rabbi Eleazar passed by a certain vineyard, and Rabbi Simeon said to Rabbi Eleazar: Bring me a splinter from the vineyard's fence to clean my teeth with. But he presently changed his mind, and said: Don't bring me anything, for if everyone who passed did likewise, the entire fence would be ruined.[53][22]

"Our Rabbis taught: Produce [of the Sabbatical Year] which is brought out of the Land of Israel must be disposed of (when the time for disposition arrives) wherever they are.[23] Rabbi Simeon ben Eleazar said: They should be brought back to their point of origin and then disposed of." There then is told the story of Rav Safra, who left the Land of Israel with produce of the Sabbatical Year. He was joined by two students of the Sages. When the time for disposition arrived, he asked them whether they knew the law concerning disposition of Sabbatical Year produce that had left the Land of Israel. One said in the name of Rabbi Abbahu, that the law follows the opinion of Rabbi Simeon ben Eleazar (and thus, that he must return the produce to the Land of Israel and to dispose of them there). The other said in the name of Rabbi Abbahu: The law does not follow the opinion of Rabbi Simeon ben Eleazar, and he may dispose of them outside the Land. Rav Safra inclined to the lenient position. "Rav Yosef applied to him the verse: 'My people: It consults its stick, Its rod [*maklo*] directs it' (Hosea 4:12)—He is directed by whoever is lenient with him [*hamekil-lo*]"[54] (that is: he latches on to the lenient opinion, without checking scrupulously to see if the law really is so. Rav Yosef revocalized the consonants of *maklo* to read *mekil-lo*).[24]

Rabbi Tzvi Hirsch Shapira, the head of the rabbinic court of Munkacz, prefaced his book "Darkhei Teshuvah" on the Yoreh De'ah section of *Shulhan Arukh* with the following words:

---

53 PT Demai 3:2.   54 BT Pesahim 52b.

---

[21] The concept of self-denial creating a sense of liberation is masterfully explicated for the early Christian world by Elaine Pagels in *Adam, Eve, and the Serpent* (New York: Random House, 1988).

[22] Rabbi Simeon was, of course, using the fence to make the more general "slippery slope" argument, that is, that even a small incursion into the realm of what is considered prohibited can quickly get out of control.

[23] The basic rule on sabbatical (i.e., seventh-year) produce is that the owner of the field may hold onto reserve quantities of produce of a given species as long as some produce of that species is still available in the fields in that vicinity. Once that availability disappears, the reserve quantities of the produce must be returned to the field. This is the meaning of "disposition" in this context.

[24] See previous chapter, pp. 734–35.

We are in need of guidance here![25] [And thus,] I have not been inhibited in my book "Darkhei Teshuvah" from quoting even rulings of the lenient, such as those in the book "Da'at Torah ve-Gilui Da'at" (which, with all due respect of its very scholarly author, is prone to excessive leniency in his rulings, contrary to the opinions of the greatest of the later authorities who are our source of life and teaching, and contrary to well-accepted prohibitive rulings). And those who read my book in depth will see that where there were excessive leniencies, I have either written that one should not, God forbid, rely on them for practical purposes, or have subsequently quoted stringent rulings which *ipso facto* set them aside. And I have quoted their words only to prevent others from ruling leniently upon seeing such rulings in the aforementioned book, or similar ones.

Those Who Fear to Rule

"Fears to rule" became the accepted epithet for a Rabbi who was frightened of issuing a ruling, prohibitive or permissive, lest he not rule correctly. Those who fear to rule would keep a safe distance from becoming accessories to leniency.

According to the Bavli, Rabbi Judah Nesiah[26] did not want to permit the bread of Gentiles, since he had already permitted two other things, and he did not want his court to become known as "a permissive court."[55] According to the Yerushalmi, his court *was* known as a permissive court, because any court that abrogates three things is so known, and the court of Rabbi Judah the Patriarch ruled permissively with respect to divorces, oil [of Gentiles], and flattened fetuses.[27][56]

One who was stringent took precedence over one who was lenient. Mar Ukva, a first-generation Babylonian Amora, who was not as stringent as his father with respect to the eating of cheese, said: In this matter, I am inferior to my father; I am like vinegar born of wine (like wine that has turned).[28][57]

The author of *Halakhot Gedolot* pronounced: "Whenever we say that an animal requires inspection, as, for example, one that suffered a fall or broke a limb or was

---

[55] BT Avodah Zarah 37a.   [56] PT Shabbat 1:4 (3d).
[57] BT Hullin 105a.

---

[25] The phrase Shapira uses literally means "we are in need of the Moda'ite." This was a talmudic phrase that referred to the dispositive wisdom of Eleazar the Moda'ite, and it became a conventional way of saying that guidance is urgently needed.

[26] The grandson of Rabbi Judah the Patriarch.

[27] Literally "sandals." Talmudic physiology believed that a pregnancy could occur on top of another pregnancy and that the result would be that the first fetus would be flattened into a faceless, fish-like creature. The question of law here is what, if any, impurity rules apply to a woman who has expelled such a defective fetus. Heschel is here assuming that the "Judah the Patriarch" referred to in PT Shabbat is the same as "Judah Nesiah" in BT Avodah Zarah. This is not at all impossible: see Rashi on BT Avodah Zarah 37a. s.v. *Rabbi Yehudah Hanasi*.

[28] This last is an expression commonly used to describe children who are less worthy than their parents.

trampled and inspection renders it kosher, that refers only to earlier generations, when they were expert in inspection. But we who are not expert should not rely on ourselves."[58] This decree engendered several stringencies in matters of ritual law. Now Rashi rejected this decree and said: "It seems to me that a jurist can only judge by what is before him, and he may rely on that judgment, for it is written: 'or to the magistrate in charge at the time' (Deuteronomy 17:9)."[59] But Rabbi Isaac,[29] the author of Or Zaru'a, noted that Rashi wrote for his own generation "and for similar generations [of scholars] whose Torah had abundance and clarity, who had a surfeit of wisdom, who were well qualified to issue rulings, and whose contemporaries could rely on them. But we, in our day, when because of our sins the Torah has diminished and wisdom has been lost, I rather praise the indolent who do not rely on their skill in inspection; they shall reap greater reward from desisting than from expounding."[30][60]

Rabbi Isaac Alfasi ruled "that nowadays no one is expert in soaking (i.e., liver in vinegar, so as to draw out the blood)."[61] But Rabbi Yosef Karo reacted: "In truth it is surprising: what great expertise does such soaking require, that it should be said that no one is expert in it?"[62]

Some issued decrees after noticing that contemporaries were disregarding prohibitions. For example, in the time of Nehemiah ben Hakhalia they decreed that no vessels should be carried on Shabbat, in order to fence off real prohibitions, because people were "belittling the Sabbath."[63] And Rav, when he saw that residents of his city were lax concerning the prohibition of meat and milk became stringent with them and forbade the eating of the udder.[64] Note also that for this reason they were loath to reveal various permissive rulings to the rank and file.[31]

"Said Rabbi Ami: From the words of Rabbi Yosi we may infer that even if a person studies but a single chapter of Mishnah in the morning, and a single chapter in the evening, he has fulfilled the commandment 'Let not this Book of the Teaching cease from your lips' (Joshua 1:8). Rabbi Johanan said in the name of Rabbi Simeon ben Yehotzadak: even just the recitation of the Shema morning and evening fulfills 'not . . . cease from your lips'; but it is forbidden to state this in the presence of the untutored." (Rashi: "So that he not say that the Shema is sufficient, and thus not train his

---

[58] *Halakhot Gedolot,* Laws of Terefot, Warsaw edition, 129a (quoted in Rashi, BT Hullin 52a).
[59] BT Hullin 52a, Rashi s.v. *bitrei gapei.*
[60] *Or Zaru'a,* quoted in Isserles' "Darkhei Moshe," Yoreh De'ah 57:11.
[61] RIF, Hullin 111 (39b in the RIF).
[62] Bet Yosef, Yoreh De'ah 73.
[63] BT Shabbat 123b, and Rashi s.v. *mishnah zo.*
[64] BT Hullin 100a, and Rashi s.v. *biq'ah matza.*

---

[29] Rabbi Isaac ben Moses of Vienna, thirteenth century.
[30] This was originally said of Simeon (or Nehemiah) Ha-Amsoni; see BT Pesahim 22b.
[31] See BT Avodah Zarah 35a.

children in the study of Torah.") In contrast to this, Rava held: "It is essential to state this in the presence of the untutored."65 [32]

In the case of one who inadvertently cooked on the Sabbath, Rabbi Meir permits him to eat the food that day, while Rabbi Judah says: it should be eaten after the Sabbath. Now Rav, when he would expound these laws to his students, ruled like Rabbi Meir, while when he expounded them publicly in the presence of the untutored, he would rule stringently, like Rabbi Judah, so that they would not come to belittle Sabbath laws.66

One who is on the road with money on his person when the Sabbath arrives, should give his purse to a Gentile and retrieve it after the Sabbath. According to Rabbi Isaac, there is another remedy that would protect the money: One could transport the purse oneself in increments of less than four cubits. But the Sages did not want to publicize this lest it lead to laxity concerning carrying on the Sabbath.67

This is how Rashi explained the matter: "It is characteristic of people that when something is permitted in duress, they conclude that it is fundamentally permitted, and thus they are excessively lenient . . . therefore in those cases where the Sages decreed . . . and said: *ab initio* it is forbidden, but *ex post facto,* it is permitted, there are those people who will tend to do it *ab initio* as well; thus, I don't teach these things to them at all, so that they do not transgress."68

Stringencies Proliferate

According to the school of Hillel, "Better to render the hands impure, for this is not rooted in biblical law, than to render foodstuffs impure, for this is rooted in biblical law."69 In a similar vein, they said: "Better to eat [the Paschal offering] when the *meat* is impure, for that is a simple prohibition, than to eat it when *you* are impure, for that is a prohibition that carries the penalty of *Karet* (excision)."70 "Better that Israel should eat slaughtered sickly animals than that they eat sickly animals that have died."71 [33]

---

65 BT Menahot 99b.   66 BT Hullin 15a.
67 BT Shabbat 153b. See *Mishneh Torah, Hilkhot Shabbat,* 6:22.
68 Pardes Haggadol le-Rashi, #246 (Warsaw, 1790). If the lungs are misplaced before they have been checked, the animal may be eaten: "but we do not publicize this" (Rashi, Hullin 12a). Work is permitted on the night of Tish'ah B'av, "but we do not publicize this" (pseudo-Rashi, Ta'anit 13a).
69 BT Berakhot 52b.   70 BT Pesahim 79a.   71 BT Kiddushin 21b.

---

[32] Thus, we have here a debate about how to treat the unlearned. Shall they be made to feel inadequate, so as to spur them on (Rabbi Johanan), or should they be given a sense that they are already accomplishing something, so as to spur them on (Rava)?

[33] All of these cases are brought in order to highlight the view exemplified by the school of Hillel (in the first case) that there are grounds for considering some prohibitions to be more serious than others, and to be somewhat lenient with the latter. This subsection will show how this position was progressively eroded over the generations. *Karet* is a penalty mentioned in the Torah for particularly heinous ritual infractions. It is variously understood to mean anything from excommunication and ostracism to premature death by Heaven's hand.

According to Rabbah bar Abuha, we distinguish between simple prohibitions and prohibitions resulting in *Karet,* for in the latter we are more concerned about doubtful situations and we are more stringent than we are with the former. In contrast to this, Rava held: "Since each of the prohibitions is biblical, what concern is it of mine whether the sanction is *Karet* or flogging?" One should be stringent with both.[72] In another context it was said: "Why should I be concerned with whether it is a great prohibition or a small one?"[73]

It is written and repeated in the Torah: "You shall not add anything to what I command you or take anything away from it" (Deuteronomy 4:2); "neither add to it nor take away from it" (Deuteronomy 13:1). Yet according to Resh Lakish, the righteous are fastidious concerning "nor take away," but do not pay attention to "neither add to it." Said Resh Lakish: "It is written: 'Be careful to observe only that which I enjoin upon you: neither add to it nor take away from it' (Deuteronomy 13:1)—but the righteous add to it, while not subtracting from it."[74]

The author of Hakaneh[34] took note of this in his pungent style: "Master of the Universe: You wrote in your Torah 'do not deviate . . . from any of the commandments,' and we are so cautioned. Now you commanded them 'do not add and do not take away,' and yet they add and subtract: they obligated women to eat Matzah by arguing from analogy, and it is a flawed analogy."[75]

"Your ointments yield a sweet fragrance" (Song of Songs 1:2)—"Said Rabbi Yannai: You gave commandments to those in antiquity: To Adam you gave one commandment, and to Noah and his children you gave seven commandments. But as for us, when we came to Mount Sinai: as a person pours out a barrel, so did you pour out commandments on us, as it was said: 'oil pours out of your skies'[35] (Song of Songs 1:2)."[76]

"At first You approached us with but one demand: 'What does the Lord your God demand of you? Only this: to revere the Lord your God, to walk only in His paths, to love Him, and to serve the Lord your God with all your heart and soul' (Deuteronomy

[72] BT Yevamot 119a, and in *Gilyon Hashas* 82a.

[73] BT Yevamot 7a, and in the *Tosafot Yeshanim.*

[74] Ecclesiastes Rabbah 3:14. According to the Rashba, "the prohibition against adding applies only to that which a person adds on his own authority, but not to that which the Sages have instituted in order to strengthen a commandment or for some other reason, such as the two days of the festival in the Diaspora —even though we now know exactly when the month begins. The same applies to a subtraction for a pressing reason, such as when Rosh Hashanah falls on the Sabbath. Although the Torah commands that the Shofar be blown, they decreed that it not be blown . . . and we are commanded to heed the words of the Sages by the verse "you must not deviate" (Deuteronomy 17:11).

[75] Hakaneh, Poritzk, 1786, 47c.

[76] Tanhuma Yitro, 3.

[34] Anonymous, apparently fourteenth century, Spain.

[35] This translation of the phrase from the Song of Songs (which differs from the Jewish Publication Society translation), results from a rereading of the verse, taking *shemekha* to mean "your skies" (from the same root as *shamayim,* "heaven").

10:12). But afterwards, you broached many mitzvot to us: 'to love the Lord your God and to walk in all His ways, and to keep His commandments and hold fast to him, and to serve Him with all your heart and soul' (Joshua 22:5)."[77] [36]

The author of *Hovot Halevavot*[37] suggests a reason behind the proliferation of commandments and prohibitions:

> The difference between the primevals and us with respect to asceticism is this: Enoch, Noah, Abraham, Isaac, and Jacob had pure reason and faint passions; their souls followed their reason, and thus a minimum of mitzvot sufficed for them . . . when their descendants went down to Egypt and lived there peacefully for some seventy years in the time of Joseph, their desires grew stronger, and their lusts grew; their passions overwhelmed their reason, and they came to require a degree of retreat to that which would negate their desires and stand up to their passions. So their Creator gave them additional nonrational commandments . . . and when they conquered the Land of Canaan, entered it, and did well in it . . . the more the land was settled the more their reason was destroyed . . . and the more their desires increased and gained strength, the weaker became their reason . . . and they required a very strong asceticism."[78]

And the author of *Shenei Luhot Haberit*[38] gives an explanation consistent with his style and approach:

> Let me also explain our experience that in every generation the stringencies proliferate. In the days of Moses our Master, peace be upon him, the only prohibitions were those he had received explicitly at Sinai. Yet he added certain enactments as he considered necessary. The prophets, Tannaim, and every generation's exegetes did likewise. The point is that the more there is a proliferation of the snake's venom, the more fences are required; he who breaches a stone fence will be bitten by a snake. The Holy and Blessed One commanded 365 "thou shalt nots" in order to avoid arousing the snake's venom, and as the generations' infection proliferated, so did the need for prohibitions. Had this been the case at the time of the giving of the Torah, the Torah would have stated these prohibitions. But all of this was implied in the Torah's prohibitions, for they are all of a piece, and that is why God commanded "stand guard over my charge," for all depends on the circumstance. It follows that when it is appropriate in any generation to add stringencies, they are all biblically ordained. For since the snake's venom proliferates and goes from potentiality to actuality, the Holy and Blessed One, who created the evil inclination, also created the antidote. For we require a supreme arousal in order to draw prohi-

[77] Midrash on Psalms 27:5.
[78] *Hovot Halevavot*, Sha'ar Haperishut, chapter 7.

---

[36] This is a very unusual midrash. For one thing, Deuteronomy also sets out many detailed mitzvot, not just one general demand. What is more, the midrash seems to make Joshua out to be the lawgiver! What is behind this midrash? Perhaps it was a protest of sorts against too many restrictive mitzvot.
[37] Bahya ibn Pakuda, eleventh–twelfth century, Spain.
[38] Isaiah Horowitz, sixteenth–seventeenth century, Poland.

bitions from potentiality to actuality so as to hasten the time when we will cleave to the supernal source. This is sufficient for those with reason and understanding.[79]

In this vein, the Gaon of Vilna also wrote: "In every generation, we create new fences. Since the generations continually decline, and the riffraff gain power, a new fence is needed in order to close the breach opened by the riffraff. This is what 'keep my charge' means—standing guard on the charge, a seal within a seal. And thus it is written: 'A garden locked is my own, my bride'—the Oral Torah is a locked garden."[80]

It was said in the Mishnah: "Not all women, trees, or ovens are identical;"[81] "Not all persons, places, or times are identical;"[82] "The times are not all alike."[83] Should one entertain the thought that the Torah's laws change with the times? "Were that so, you would be relativizing everything!"[84]

Concerning the power of licentiousness, it was said: "A slave prefers a wanton woman, who is cheap to him (he views her as cheap, available to be degraded before his lusts) and lewd to him (she behaves lewdly with him)."[85] That is: a slave who has "tasted the illicit" "prefers being a slave, and being permitted the unbridled sexuality of slave girls, to being a free man, permitted to a free Israelite woman, whose sexuality will not be cheap or ever-present for him."[86] [39]

Against Breachers of the Fence

The author of "Peri Hadash" and others objected to latter-day jurists who added stringencies in matters that were not treated in the Talmud. Despite that, you will find throughout Jewish history that those who imposed stringencies enjoyed the upper hand. The voices of those who opposed them remained a still, small voice. Whoever proposes even minor changes is suspected of being a sectarian.

Even concerning those stringencies whose entire substance is rooted in custom it is thought that whoever touches them touches the very essence of Judaism; displace the slightest stone from the wall, and the wall will fall. The Torah is compared to "a stone vault, in which the displacement of one stone makes them all collapse."[87]

[79] *Shenei Luhot Haberit* 25b.
[80] Vilna Gaon's commentary to *Tikkunim Mizohar Hadash* 34a.
[81] Mishnah Pesahim 3:4, in the name of Rabbi Akiva.
[82] Mishnah Yevamot 16:3, in the name of Rabbi Judah ben Baba.
[83] Mishnah Tamid 1:2.
[84] Abbaye to Rav Yosef, BT Megillah 18b; BT Hullin 9a; Abbaye to Rava, BT Bava Batra 29a. Rav Huna son of Rav Nehemiah to Rav Ashi, BT Gittin 14a. See also BT Hullin 32a; BT Shabbat 35b.
[85] BT Gittin 13a.
[86] BT Ketubot 11a, Rashi.
[87] PT Sanhedrin 6:1.

[39] Again, we have here the motif of indulgence being a kind of slavery, and continence being a kind of liberation.

The residents of the city Biscar asked three questions of law, and Rav Menasia rendered a stringent judgment for all three, "since they were not scholars in Torah" "and permission would have become license for them. This is why they received stringent rulings."[88]

Such a question, with respect to burial on the second day of the festival in the Diaspora, was asked many generations later in Melun, France. The Sage who was asked, Rabbi Meshulam of Narbonne, did not follow Rav Menasia's example and ruled leniently, in accordance with the Gemara. But Rabbenu Tam chided him and sent the following message: "The residents of Biscar were not scholars in Torah, and the residents of Melun are?!"[89]

In this spirit, the RaSHBA wrote in a responsum to one of his correspondents: "If you have seen or heard of someone accepting as kosher the lobe of the liver, or anything which the Sages enumerated as being in the category of forbidden foods, neither assent nor give heed to him, that such things not occur in Israel. Whoever declares such things kosher seems to me to defame the teachings of the Sages. . . . let one who so testifies and a thousand others like him waste away, rather than allow the withering of a single jot of what the holy Sages of Israel, the prophets, and their heirs have agreed on, or of what was spoken to Moses at Sinai . . . be very cautious about such things, for there are those who are ever eager to be lenient, and utterly neglect root principles."[90]

A certain Sage tossed a question at the two greatest scholars of the generation, Rabbi Isaac ben Sheshet[40] and Rabbi Simeon ben Tzemah Duran,[41] concerning the prohibition on animals with lung lesions; the question was raised because of those people "who flout and disregard the teachings of the Sages of blessed memory," and say that "they decreed for us decrees that cannot be lived with, for the prohibition on the lesions causes great financial loss to Jews."[91]

The RIBaSH notes that "there is an uproar in some communities at some times, when on a given day, every animal slaughtered is declared unkosher because of the tiniest of tiny lesions; they say publicly very inappropriate things concerning the Rabbis of blessed memory, such as: 'See how they have pressed us in this, our exile, to the point that we can no longer raise our heads because of the multitude of fences they have constructed, and their having trampled us to the ground.' They also say that such punctiliousness with every tiny lesion is the greatest squandering of Jewish money."[92]

---

[88] BT Shabbat 139a and Meiri ad loc.
[89] BT Shabbat 139b, Tosafot s.v. *Yom Tov.*
[90] Responsa of RaSHBA, I:98.
[91] Tashbetz, part I, #67.
[92] Responsa of RIBaSH, #163.

---

[40] Fourteenth century, Spain and North Africa.
[41] Fourteenth–fifteenth century, Spain and North Africa.

One of the Sages of France, Rabbi Hayyim ben Avraham Galipapa (1310–1380), about whom the RIBaSH wrote: "proficient in everything, a pious man, a well-stocked chest, a limed pit that preserves every drop, a complete Sage," planned to permit several things that it was customary to prohibit, such as combing the hair on the Sabbath and eating the cheese of Gentiles. Now the RIBaSH took him to task in a letter and warned him not to permit that which his predecessors had forbidden. This Rabbi Hayyim bought support from Rabbenu Tam, who permitted things "that his predecessors had forbidden." But the RIBaSH scolded him: "Do you account yourself an authority on his level, that you can act with his power?" Why, he said, "all of the contemporary Sages of Israel are as a garlic peel or a sesame seed compared to one of the least of his pupils." The RIBaSH also took him to task for his stated opinion that nowadays "we do not conceal a permissive ruling for fear of the masses, for all are sagacious and wise, knowledgeable in Torah, fluent in the details of mitzvot and full of good deeds as a pomegranate is full of seeds."[93]

In the year 5475 (1715) a pamphlet entitled "Tosafot Bikkurei Katzir" was published, on the subject of the melody customarily used in the city of Ferrara for the priestly blessing. In it, the author sought to prove "that a custom or construction can abrogate a law, even a rabbinic prohibition that has some basis in the Torah." In the course of his argument he critiqued several of the great jurists and wrote (to one who had argued with him): "what makes you think that the ROSH, the RaDBaZ, and the author of the "Peri Ha'aretz" have redder blood? Perhaps Rabbi Yosef Kolon and the authors of "Ba'al Massa Melekh" and "Be'er Sheva" have redder blood!"[42] The author of the pamphlet believed that "veteran jurists in every generation are fully authorized to be permissive and lenient with respect to the decrees and institutions of the Rabbis who preceded them." The Sage Rabbi Aharon Ashkenazi, who had taken issue with the pamphlet, believed that according to this approach "power over the Torah is given to individuals of every generation, and over time it is possible to abrogate all enactments and decrees, until, God forbid, the Torah is left as a breached city with no wall."[94]

The Sages were very careful not only with all mitzvot, large and small, or with *halakhot* that were derived through discussion and debate, by in-depth study and logic. They also were exacting with respect to the immutability of customs. "Since your ancestors were accustomed to prohibit, you must not abrogate the custom of your ancestors, may they rest in peace!"[95] "Be careful concerning an inherited ancestral custom."[96]

---

[93] Responsa of RIBaSH, #394.
[94] *Divrei Yosef,* Rabbi Yosef Ergas [Italy, eighteenth century], #27 (Livorno, 1742).
[95] PT Pesahim 4:1.
[96] BT Betzah 4b.

---

[42] A paraphrase of BT Sanhedrin 74a, dealing with a very different subject.

The market day in Sidon was on Friday, and the residents of Beshan were accustomed not to make the trip from Tyre to Sidon on Friday; they imposed this stringency on themselves so as not to neglect preparations for the Sabbath. Their descendants came to Rabbi Johanan and said to him: Our ancestors could allow themselves to miss the market, since they were wealthy. For us it is not possible. He said to them: Your ancestors have already accepted the stringency on themselves [and therefore you too are bound], as it is said: "My son, heed the discipline of your father, And do not forsake the instruction of your mother" (Proverbs 1:8).[97]

---

[97] BT Pesahim 50a.

39

FORMER AND LATTER AUTHORITIES

[For an introduction, see the beginning of chapter 37.]

If the Former Were as Angels . . .

THE IMAGE THAT THE SAGES HAD of the generations was that of a descending course, of an impoverishment of wisdom, of spiritual deterioration. Moses received the Teaching at Sinai and passed it on to Joshua; "Moses' face was as the face of the sun, while Joshua's face was as the face of the moon."[1] Conceptual power continually declines. And the saying "The best is saved for last"[2] is empty rhetorical comfort.

What sort of spiritual deterioration? "Originally, when intentions were for the sake of the commandment, the command to enter levirate marriage took precedence over the commandment concerning removal of the shoe [to release the levirate bond]. Now, when [the sexual act] is not for the sake of the commandment, they ruled: 'the commandment concerning removal of the shoe takes precedence over the command to enter levirate marriage.' Said Rami bar Hama in the name of Rabbi Isaac: they revisited the issue and ruled that the levirate marriage takes precedence over removal of the shoe. Said Rav Nahman bar Isaac to him: Are you implying that the later generations improved?!"[3] [1] The Mishnah ruled that butchers may not be trusted concerning the removal of the sciatic nerve, because it is so tedious for them to bore in for it. "Said Rabbi Hiyya bar Abba in the name of Rabbi Johanan: they revisited the matter and ruled that they may be trusted. Said Rav Nahman: Are you imply-

---

[1] Sifre Pinehas, 140.   [2] Bereshit Rabbah 78:11.   [3] BT Yevamot 39b.

---

[1] The levirate marriage, which is, in both biblical and rabbinic law, contracted through a sexual act between brother-in-law and sister-in-law is, by its very nature, a complex amalgam of commandment (per Deuteronomy 25) and sexuality. Both pious intent and sexual lust can converge in the act of levirate marriage. According to Rav Nahman bar Isaac, sexual lust must progressively gain the upper hand over the pious desire to fulfill God's will. This process of the carnal overtaking the spiritual is, for him, irreversible.

ing that the later generations improved?!"[4] The contrary is the case. The character of the generations continually declines. Rabbi Johanan said in the name of Rabbi Judah bar El'ai: "Come and see how the latter generations are unlike the former ones. In former generations people made Torah their vocation and their trades their avocations, and they succeeded in both; in latter generations, when people made their trades their vocations and Torah their avocation, they did not succeed in either. . . . In former generations they used to gather in their produce via the main gate, so that they would become liable to the tithe; in latter generations they gather them in via rooftops, courtyards, and terraces, in order that they be exempt from the tithe."[5] [2]

Rabbi Haggai said in the name of Rabbi Samuel bar Nahman: "Those of former generations ploughed, planted, weeded, mowed, hoed, harvested, sheaved, threshed, winnowed, ground, sifted, kneaded, shaped, and baked—and we: why, we have nothing to eat."[6] "That is to say: they expended great energy in matters of Torah, and they set themselves up and prepared themselves to understand all of the generalities and particularities of Torah, just as a person exhausts himself with all that is involved in working grain until he has finally baked the loaf. And despite all that, we haven't the discernment to understand it, just like a person who has no loaf to eat."[7] "If the elders tell you to dismantle, and the youth tell you to build, dismantle rather than building, for the elders' dismantling is constructive."[8] Parents are to be preferred to their children, as they said: "Parents' strictness is better than children's tolerance."[9] "Better the strictness of parents than the forbearance of children."[10]

When Rabbi Judah the Patriarch wished to refute the words of Rabbi Yosi ben Halafta, he would say: How can we unfortunates presume to dispute the words of Rabbi Yosi? The difference between our generation and that of Rabbi Yosi is like the difference between the most secular and the Holy of Holies. And Rabbi Ishmael, Rabbi Yosi's son, said: our generation compared to father's generation is as dust compared to gold.[11]

And Rabbi Zera said in the name of Rava bar Zimona: "If the former were as angels, we are as mortals; and if the former were as mortals, then we are as asses —

---

[4] BT Hullin 93b.   [5] BT Berakhot 35b.   [6] PT Shekalim 5:1 (48c).
[7] Penai Moshe, ad loc.   [8] BT Megillah 31b.   [9] Midrash Samuel, chapter 22.
[10] Tanhuma Vayyetze, 13.   [11] PT Gittin, chapter 6 (end).

---

[2] Tithes became due from one's produce when the produce was brought into one's house. The rule (based on a literal reading of a biblical verse) was that there had to be a "canonical entry" into the house in order for the tithe obligation to be triggered. That is, if it entered through the main gate and main entrance to the house, the owner was now considered to have taken possession of it and thus owed the tithes and other offerings. But if the produce entered the house in a "nonstandard" way, for example, through the roof, through an auxiliary courtyard, or through a backyard, then it was still not considered liable for tithes, at least under biblical law, and the produce could be snacked on. The claim here is that previous generations were anxious to pay the tithes, whereas the passage of time had habituated the farmers to finding loopholes and technicalities that would put off the obligation as much as possible. This, too, is a sign of spiritual degeneration.

and not as the asses of Rabbi Hanina ben Dosa or Rabbi Pinehas ben Yair,[3] but as common asses."12

According to Rabbi Johanan, "The intellect of the ancients was as wide as the entrance to the *ulam*,[4] and that of later generations was as the entrance to the *hekhal*.[5] But ours is as the eye of a mending needle (an exceedingly thin needle used for repairing a slit in a garment). 'The ancients'—refers to Rabbi Akiva, and 'later generations'—refers to Rabbi Eleazar ben Shamu'a; but some say that 'the ancients' refers to Rabbi Eleazar ben Shamu'a, and 'the later generations' refers to Rabbi Osha'ia the great." In the same spirit, Abbaye said: "And we are as a mere piton in a wall," that is, as a pin that is driven into a thin crack in a wall, and which enters only with difficulty; analogously, we can comprehend what we receive only minimally and with difficulty (Rashi). Rava and Rav Ashi spoke similarly.13 And Rabbi Aha: "The idle conversation of the patriarchs' servants was better than the childrens' Torah."14

Using the same approach, they ruled that an Amora may not dispute a Tanna,15 "For from the time of the canonization of the Mishnah, future generations committed themselves not to dispute their predecessors. And they acted likewise at the time of the canonization of the Gemara, inasmuch as from its closure onward no one is authorized to dispute it."16 [6] And the leading Sages of Israel used to refer to the Sages who preceded them thus: "they whose pinkies were thicker than our loins."17[7]

The Dictum of the Master and the Dictum of the Student

An assumption of the Bavli is that the *halakhah* cannot follow the opinion of a student whose teacher explicitly disagrees, for "How can we reject the opinion of the

---

12 BT Shabbat 112b; PT Demai 1:3 (21d); PT Shekalim 5:1 (48d); Bereshit Rabbah 60:32.
13 BT Eruvin 53a.   14 Bereshit Rabbah 60:11.
15 BT Yoma 3b, Tosafot s.v. *De-rabei*.   16 Kesef Mishneh, Hilkhot Mamrim, 2:1.
17 As, for example, in the Responsa of the RIBaSH, #446.

---

[3] They were known to have animals that had uncanny senses of what was required by Halakhah. See, e.g., BT Hullin 7a–b.

[4] The outer porch of the Temple, which had a relatively wide entrance.

[5] The main enclosure of the Temple (outside the *devir*, or Holy of Holies), which had a relatively small entrance way.

[6] Joseph Caro, the author of this commentary on Maimonides, here articulates a theory of strict periodization. That is, the end of a certain era signals an end to the legitimacy of certain kinds of reasoning, legislation, commentary, and so on. The editing of the Talmud is here the watershed; and Maimonides' own introduction to *Mishneh Torah* makes that clear as well. Later generations would latch on to other events, such as the publication of Caro's own *Shulhan Arukh* and claim that they signaled yet other changes in what are legitimate exercises of rabbinic authority.

[7] This phrase was used by the young advisers of Rehoboam, Solomon's son, when they urged him to declare to the "tax revolters" in Judea that he intended his own reign to be even more burdensome on the rank and file than his father's had been. In 1 Kings 12, they advised him to declare "my

master and heed the opinion of the student?"[18] "We have the dictum of the master and the dictum of the student: which shall we consider?"[19] [8] "Have you set aside the words of the greater and followed the words of the lesser?"[20] But latter authorities expressed astonishment at this principle, according to which "no rabbinical student would be allowed to survive [i.e., achieve an authority of his own]."[9][21]

According to Rabbenu Nissim, "the Geonic tradition was that this principle applied when the master and student disagreed in the master's lifetime, since the master's failure to be persuaded by his student's opinion disqualified it. When, however, the student dissented from the master after the latter's death, the principle did not apply."[22] [10] In another formulation: when a student dissents from his master out of the latter's presence, the *halakhah* sometimes follows the student's opinion.[23]

On several occasions Rav Sheshet said of his master's dicta: "Rav gave this ruling after he inclined toward death."[24] Rabbi Israel Isserlin also ruled that a Sage who becomes preeminent in his generation is on a par with his master.[25] The HIDA's[11] opinion was this: "With respect to our principle that a student may not dispute his master: may he do so when he has clear and convincing proof? Answer: in earlier days, students did just that; indeed, in every generation a student may dispute his master during debate with clear and convincing proofs . . . similarly, after the master's death the student may dispute him, rule according to his own lights, and even engage in practices that violate his master's rulings . . . for whoever considers both of their rulings will choose one or the other. So did all the former Sages. All such practices should be just for the sake of heaven."[26] He was commenting on the words of

---

[18] BT Niddah 14b.   [19] BT Sanhedrin 29a.   [20] BT Bava Batra 51b.

[21] *Zekan Aharon*, 3 (Rabbi Elijah Halevi, sixteenth century, Turkey).

[22] Rabbenu Nissim to Rif, beginning of Sukkah.

[23] See Hayyim Joseph David Azulai, *Ya'ir Ozen*, 5:60.

[24] BT Yevamot 24b, and variant readings there.

[25] *Terumat Hadeshen*, #138.   [26] *Birkei Yosef*, Part Ten, 242:3.

---

pinky is thicker than my father's loins." Here the phrase is inverted, to declare that the older generations have greater potency than the younger ones.

[8] This phrase is used in the Talmud in various contexts. One of these is the matter of whether a person who commits an infraction while acting as someone else's agent can pass responsibility for the act on to the one who appointed him. The answer is that the "dictum of the master"—that is, God—has to take precedence over the "dictum of the student"—that is, the human being who instructed him to commit the crime. Similarly, in discussing whether the obligation to obey parents extends to cases in which they instruct a child to commit a sin, the Talmud uses the same phrase to conclude that the child must obey God, not the parent. The fact that the phrase was used in making these fundamental arguments demonstrates that it was well known.

[9] Because he would be confined to repeating his master's teachings. Something like this was reported of Rabbi Eliezer ben Hyrcanus, who is said never to have taught anything that he did not hear from his own teachers.

[10] This principle was, no doubt, very useful to the Geonim, who lived after the death of the talmudic masters.

[11] Hayyim Joseph David Azulai, eighteenth century, Italy/Israel.

Rabbi Simeon bar Yohai: "Four things were subjects of Rabbi Akiva's exegesis, and my own; mine seems more convincing than his."[27] Even Rabbenu Asher expressed the belief that one may dispute the rulings of the Geonim. "The Sages in all the generations after them are not mere reed-cutters at the water's edge.[12] . . . Jephthah in his generation is equivalent to Samuel in his, and you never have any judge but the one who lives in your time. One may even contradict their statements, for all matters that are not commented on in the Talmud edited by Rav Ashi and Ravina are open for people to tear down or to build up, even if it means disputing the Geonim."[28] [13] He wrote similarly in a responsum: "Who was as great as Rashi—may the memory of the righteous be a blessing—who enlightened the entire Jewish world with his commentaries? And yet his own descendants—Rabbenu Tam and Rabbi Isaac (ben Samuel) of blessed memory[14]—differed with him in many places, and contradicted his words. For Torah is concerned with truth, and no one should be lionized."[29]

Later Is Better

It might often seem as if the image of the generations as a descending course was itself given to Moses at Sinai, that it is a structure that mirrors truth and cannot be challenged. Yet the gates of questioning never fully close. Could it be a divine decree that the tide of wisdom flowing from Mount Sinai must always and forever ebb? That the revelation of the Presence is a one-time historical event, and the greater one's distance the more one is benighted?

Some lonely voices were raised to counsel caution with this axiom of the retreating of the generations and the inferiority of later authorities. Note that Rabbi Eleazar was asked: "Which were greater: the former generations or the latter ones?"[30] In another version: "Were the latter generations more fit than the former" or not?[31] He did not repudiate the questioner as one would react to an asinine question; rather, he considered it a proper question deserving of an appropriate answer: "The building of the

[27] Sifre Deuteronomy 31.
[28] Rabbenu Asher, Sanhedrin, chapter 4, #6.
[29] Responsa of Rabbenu Asher, 55:9.   [30] BT Yoma 9b.   [31] PT Yoma 1:1 (38c).

[12] The phrase is a fairly common one, which is intended to describe mindless maintenance work. Repeating teachings without the power of innovation (and, by implication, the power to disagree with predecessors) would be intellectual, mindless custodial work.

[13] Note well how here, again, we have a medieval Sage (Rabbenu Asher) making an exception for the talmudic period. Just as Maimonides argued, Rabbenu Asher says here that the Babylonian Talmud has a privileged position inasmuch as consensus positions articulated in it are no longer challengeable, even though post-talmudic consensuses are.

[14] Rabbenu Tam (Jacob Tam) was Rashi's grandson, and Rabbi Isaac ben Samuel was Rabbenu Tam's nephew.

Temple serves as evidence, for it was rebuilt for the ancients, but not for us. This is emblematic of the superiority of the former generations over the latter."

When Rabbi Johanan said: "The fingernails of the ancients were better than the bellies of their successors" (i.e., the lowliest in earlier generations were greater than the most illustrious in later ones), his colleague Rabbi Simeon ben Lakish responded: "On the contrary, the later ones are to be preferred, for even in the face of political oppression they still busy themselves with Torah."[15]

Occasionally they extolled later generations more than earlier ones. According to Rabbi Eleazar ben Berekhiah, the earlier, that is, the Ten Tribes, divested themselves of the yoke of Torah, whereas the latter generation, that of Hezekiah, tightened that yoke, and thereby made themselves as worthy of miracles as those who walked through the Sea or crossed the Jordan.[16] [32]

Rabbi Abbahu said: "We have seen that the Holy and Blessed One keeps faith with latter generations because of the merit of the former ones; but how do we know that the Holy and Blessed One keeps faith with former generations because of the merit of latter ones? For it says: 'But Noah found favor,' because of the merit of his descendants: 'This is the line of Noah.'"[33] According to Rava, "Greater things are attributed to Samuel than to Moses"[34][17]; "Greater things are attributed to Moses and Aaron than to Abraham."[35][18] According to Rabbi Abba, "Greater things are attributed to Ovadiah than to Abraham."[36][19]

Over and against those who say "that former times were better than these, and

---

[32] BT Sanhedrin 94b.   [33] Bereshit Rabbah 29:5.
[34] BT Nedarim 38a.   [35] BT Hullin 89a.
[36] BT Sanhedrin 39b.

---

[15] That is, even under Roman oppression, during which it was on occasion literally dangerous to teach Torah, the more recent generations persisted in fulfilling this cardinal obligation of studying Torah.

[16] The Talmud is here making the point that the deterioration of the generations is not inevitable, and that it can be reversed, just as Hezekiah represented a dramatic reversal from the last of the Israelite rulers just prior to his reign.

[17] Both Moses (Numbers 16) and Samuel (1 Samuel 12) declared before the people that they had not abused their authority to take any Israelite's property. But the Rabbis' reading of the texts here leads them to conclude that, whereas Moses declared that he didn't even pay someone to rent his property against his will, Samuel was able to declare that he never had use of anyone else's property, with or without payment, even with the other person's consent! Samuel is thus depicted as having a higher degree of sensitivity to the fact that consent to a person with power and authority may never really be free.

[18] Whereas Abraham, in an expression of humility, had described himself as mere "dust and ashes" (Genesis 18), Moses and Aaron later said of themselves that they were of no substance at all (Exodus 16).

[19] Ovadiah was King Ahab's steward. He is said (in 1 Kings 18) to have been "very God-fearing," whereas Abraham, even at the time of the binding of Isaac, was said (in Genesis 22) to be "God-fearing."

therefore one should heed earlier authorities more than later ones,"[37] it was recorded in a Baraita:

> Why were we not given the names of the elders who ascended Mount Sinai with Moses and Aaron (Exodus 24:9)? So that should one ever say of the contemporaneous court: "are so-and-so and his colleagues like Moses and Aaron that I should accept their rulings?" it could be retorted: "he may not be like Moses and Aaron, but he may well be like one of the elders whom you cannot identify." Samuel said to the people: "and the Lord sent Moses and Aaron, who brought your ancestors out of Egypt . . . and the Lord sent Jerubba'al, and Bedan, and Jephthah, and Samuel, and delivered you from your enemies" (1 Samuel 12:8–11). . . . The text has equated three lightweights with three of history's greatest.[20] This is to teach you that the court of Yeruba'al is as illustrious before God as Moses', and the court of Jephthah as illustrious before God as Samuel's. All this is to inform you that when one is appointed to a position of communal authority, even the lightest lightweight must be treated as the mightiest of the mighty. And so it is said: "and appear before the levitical priests, or the magistrate in charge at the time, and present your problem. When they have announced to you the verdict of the case . . ." (Deuteronomy 17:9). You have none but the magistrate in your generation. Moreover, it says: "Don't say, 'How has it happened that former times were better than these?' For it is not wise of you to ask that question" (Ecclesiastes 7:10).[38]

"Jephthah in his generation is equivalent to Samuel in his."[39]

"One generation goes, another comes" (Ecclesiastes 1:4). "The coming generation should be, in your estimation, like the departing one. For you should not say: If only Rabbi Akiva were alive, I would study Scripture with him; if only Rabbi Zera and Rabbi Johanan were alive, I would study Mishnah with them. Rather, your own generation and your contemporary Sage are like the bygone generations and the early Sages who preceded you." Moreover, even had Aaron been alive in the generation of Yehoyada, or Aaron and his sons in the generation of Zadok, Yehoyada and Zadok[21] "would have outranked them in their time."[40] "There is no generation without its equivalent of Abraham, and no generation without its equivalent of Jacob, Moses, or Samuel."[41]

One also finds the opinion that the Sages of the later generations and their wisdom exceed in rank and in honor those of the earlier ones. Rabbi Aha said: "Things

---

[37] BT Rosh Hashanah 25b, Tosafot s.v. *shehayamim*.
[38] Tosefta Rosh Hashanah, end of chapter 1, and, with some variations, in BT Rosh Hashanah 25a-b.
[39] BT Rosh Hashanah 25b.
[40] Ecclesiastes Rabbah 1:4.
[41] Bereshit Rabbah 56:9. "The enduring essence of Moses inheres in every generation, and in every righteous person" (Tikkunei Zohar, 469, 114a [beginning]).

---

[20] Yeruba'al was Gideon, as the Book of Judges itself reports. Bedan was taken by the Rabbis to be Samson, who was of the tribe of Dan. Thus, we have Moses, Aaron, and Samuel, the three greatest of the prophets, equated in the same breath with Gideon, Samson, and Jephthah, all heroes in the Book of Judges, but every one of them a deeply flawed hero (ergo, "lightweights").

[21] Both priests in the time of the monarchy.

not revealed to Moses were revealed to Rabbi Akiva. 'His eyes behold every precious thing' (Job 28:10)—that is Rabbi Akiva."[42]

"At our doors are all choice fruits" (Song of Songs 7:14).

> The school of Rabbi Shila and the Sages [interpreted this]. The school of Rabbi Shila said: It is like a woman of status, whose husband departed, leaving her very few goods and little money. When he returned, she said to him: Remember what you left me, and see what I have saved of it, and even added to it. The Sages said: It is like a king who turned his orchard over to a tenant farmer. What did the farmer do? He filled up fig baskets with the orchard's produce, and placed them at the entrance to the orchard. When the king came by and saw all of this yield at the entrance of the orchard, he concluded that there must be all the more in the orchard itself. Similarly, in earlier generations: there were the Men of the Great Assembly, Hillel, Shammai, and Rabban Gamliel the Elder. And in the later generations: Rabban Johanan ben Zakkai, Rabbi Eliezer, Rabbi Joshua, and Rabbi Akiva. As for *their* students, how much more must they have produced. About them it is said: "Both freshly picked and long-stored have I kept, my beloved, for you." (Song of Songs 7:14).[43]

There were those who said: The ancients had no monopoly on wisdom, nor are all of their successors inept.[22] Some matters were revealed to the latter and were not known to the former. "The latter ones can innovate in ways that the former could not, for the time for such innovations had not yet arrived."[44]

Rabbi Isaac de Leon was apologetic for being so bold as to contradict an earlier opinion, namely, that of Nahmanides in his critique of Maimonides' *Book of the Commandments.* So in the preface to his book, de Leon quotes the physician-scholar Rabbi Shelomo Almoli,[23] who, at the end of his short book *Me'asef Lekhol Hamahanot,* gave a logical explanation for the superiority of later authorities: "It is plausible that the knowledge and understanding of the latter generations should exceed that of the former ones for two reasons. First, it is possible for a later Sage to have so intensely studied a particular interpretation, penetrating it with all of his intellect and energy, that he has comprehended it better than his predecessors did. Second, we today, even studying with less intensity, comprehend much more in less time than the ancients did in considerably more time. This is because in their days many bodies of wisdom were unknown or incomplete, and they had to derive them themselves with enormous effort. But we have everything spread out before us like a fully set table; all of our predecessors' words and demonstrations are well organized, and are there to enlighten us."[45]

---

[42] PR, Pesikta Parah, 64b; see above, chapter 30, pp. 576–81.
[43] Shir Hashirim Rabbah 7:14.   [44] Devash Lefi, 8, letter "Dalet."
[45] Preface to his book "Megillat Esther."

---

[22] This is a Hebrew wordplay by Heschel (based on the assonance of the roots for wisdom and foolishness) that is, unfortunately, not reproduceable in English.
[23] Spain, circa 1400.

One of the kabbalists even suggested that while the middle generations may not have been as wise as the early ones, the later generations were wiser yet: "You shall in this way be able to comprehend and understand the power of your God, and the essence of His might and wonders better than the ancients did with all of their great wisdom. For the truth is that the wisdom of the earliest generations endures, for they are genuinely wise, while the middle generations are not so; but the later generations transcend the wisdom of the ancients. And this is simply the way reality is constructed, just as the way the wheel turns, the first buckets come up full, the middle ones empty themselves, and the last draw more as they come up."[46] In this vein, it was also said of Rabbi Pinehas of Koretz:

> Concerning ibn Ezra, who had sharply disputed Eleazar Kalir, the master said: "I prefer to give ibn Ezra the benefit of the doubt. Indeed, once I dreamt that I was called to the Torah and I was told that it was the scroll of ibn Ezra himself." He further gave a parable demonstrating why one should judge him kindly: "Imagine one is walking in a very dark place and sees from the distance a very bright light or torch. There are those whose eyes are very strong, and who can therefore make use of the light even at a distance. And there are those whose legs are very strong, and who can therefore run closer to the light in order to make use of it. Similarly, the Tannaim and Amoraim were close to the destruction of the Temple, and they could still get illumination from its only recently departed light. And the latter day Tzaddikim, of our own time, are close to the light of the Messiah, and thus it is not surprising that they can also comprehend the truth." (He even said [of these generations]: "One must either be blind or be unwilling to see the light of the Messiah") "But ibn Ezra was in the Middle Ages; he was far from the light of the Temple, and far also from the light of the Messiah, and thus he could not comprehend Kalir's greatness."[47]

Isaac Luria explained the maxim "Moses, you have spoken well," used by Rav Safra in his colloquys with Rava[48] and Rabbi Oshaia,[49] as follows: Every student of Torah who achieves preeminence in his generation has within him a spark of Moses our Master, peace be upon him. And there were those who said that the godly Rabbi Isaac, of blessed memory, comprehended even more than Moses our Master. For Moses our Master's comprehension was of the hindmost parts of wisdom,[24] whereas the godly Rabbi Isaac "uncovered several secrets in the innermost realm, even concerning the Sefirot and that which far transcends the emanations."[50]

[46] *Berit Menuhah* (a kabbalistic work of disputed authorship, from fourteenth-century Spain), Amsterdam edition, 17b.
[47] Midrash Pinehas (Warsaw, 1876), p. 55.
[48] BT Shabbat 101b; BT Sukkah 39a.
[49] BT Betzah 38b. See also BT Hullin 93a.
[50] See Rabbi Shneuer Zalman, *Iggeret Haqodesh*, 19.

---

[24] The phrase here recalls God's statement to Moses that the latter would be able to see only God's "hindmost part" (Exodus 33).

Of Rabbi Israel Ba'al Shem Tov, it is said that he asked: "Why is it that in former days intellectuals believed in the primordial (i.e., that the universe existed from eternity, God forbid), whereas now it is believed that God, blessed be His name, is and was One and unique? And he answered that this was because of the turbidity of the earth's material, which was much greater in those days, and which is not so now."[51][25]

The Law Follows the Later Authority

Over and against the principle according to which the earlier is always greater and the aura of wisdom continually dims, we have a tradition from the Geonim that whenever two Amoraim dispute one another and the Talmud does not fix the law according to either of them, the law follows the later one.[52] Two reasons were given for this. Some say that the advantage enjoyed by the later authorities is "that the later Amoraim pored over the reasoning of the Tannaim and thus clarified the halakhah, whereas the early ones did not probe others' teachings, but simply passed on to their students verbatim what they received from their masters."[53] According to another opinion, "we mainly latch on to the teachings of the later authorities because they knew the thinking of their predecessors as well as their own, and they made a determination among all positions and came to an appropriate conclusion."[54]

This last reason was also given for the established principle that whenever the Babylonian Talmud and the Palestinian Talmud disagree, the law follows the Bavli. For the Bavli came last, and was thus aware of the Yerushalmi and knew that it was unreliable in this matter of law.[55]

In the course of the generations some lonely but venerable voices spoke out against the idea of the absolute superiority of the earlier over the later, an idea that shuts the door in the face of all innovation and robs any Sage of his right to disagree with another who has already passed away.

After the passing of Rabbi Eliezer ben Hyrcanus, four elders, namely, Rabbi Yosi of Galilee, Rabbi Tarfon, Rabbi Eleazar ben Azariah, and Rabbi Akiva, gathered to refute his teachings. After each of them had made known his views, Rabbi Joshua said to them: "One doesn't second-guess the lion after his death" (Rashi: "Were he alive, he

---

[51] Toledot Ya'akov Yosef, end of Vayyeshev.

[52] "When an earlier and a later authority dispute, the law follows the later one" (Introduction to the Talmud by Rabbi Samuel Hanagid).

[53] BT Kiddushin 45b, Tosafot s.v. hava uvda. BT Niddah 7b, Rashi at the end of the page.

[54] Rabbenu Asher, Sanhedrin, chapter 4, #6.

[55] Alfasi, end of Eruvin.

---

[25] This expresses a view about the unworthiness, relatively speaking, of physical matter. The idea that material substance is an impediment to matters of the spirit is one that goes back to Greek times, and that clearly made some inroads into Jewish thought from there.

might have parried your refutation").[56] Concerning this maxim, Rabbi Abraham ibn Ezra had this reaction: "We are all created by the spirit of God, and the ancients were flesh and blood just like us, and their words must convince."[26] Why, we know that Daniel was a prophet, greater in wisdom than all of the wise men and sorcerers of Babylon, and of him it was said by the Sages of Blessed Memory: 'Daniel erred in his calculation,' and calculation is a minor matter."[57] When Rabbi Isaiah of Trani (the elder)[27] was asked: "How could a person think of rebutting the teachings of the early Geonim, of blessed memory, whose intellects were as wide as the entrance to the *ulam?*"[28] he was quoted as answering: "I reason for myself just as the philosophers do. One of the greatest among them was asked: We all agree that the ancients were wiser and more learned than we, and yet we criticize them, often refute their teachings. Truthfully, how can this be justified? The philosopher answered: Who sees for a greater distance, a dwarf or a giant? Evidently, the giant does, since his eyes are much higher than the eyes of the dwarf. But if you were to place the dwarf on the neck of the giant, who would see for a greater distance? Evidently, the dwarf would, since now the eyes of the dwarf are higher than the eyes of the giant. So do we dwarves ride on the necks of the giants, for we are aware of their erudition, and we delve into it and are empowered by their wisdom. We need not be greater than they."[58]

Elsewhere, Rabbi Isaiah of Trani wrote: "I am well aware that the fingernails of those ancient and holy Rabbis were better than our bellies," yet my practice is "that whatever does not convince me in the text, even if it was said by Joshua son of Nun, I shall not obey it and will not shrink from writing what appears correct to me. For this is the whole method of the Talmud: the latest Amoraim did not shrink from criticizing the earliest, and even the Tannaim. Several Mishnayot were radically contradicted, many majority opinions were voided, and halakhic rulings were given following the minority . . . and we should probe and investigate for clear demonstrations in the text, in order to determine to which direction the *halakhah* tends. We have neither the power nor the skill to weigh mountains as on a scale, to determine which is more substantial. Therefore, let us leave the Rabbis . . . peace be upon them, in their luster, and return to the study of the books, to determine in which way the law tends."[59] "The Amoraim contradicted several Mishnayot and claimed that the law was otherwise. For wisdom is greater than the wise, since there is no Sage free

---

[56] BT Gittin 83a. Rabbi Joshua himself did not rule in agreement with Rabbi Eliezer.

[57] Ibn Ezra's Commentary on Ecclesiastes 5:1.

[58] *Shibolei halleket* (of Zedekiah ben Abraham, thirteenth century), preface.

[59] S. Schechter, "Notes on Hebrew Mss. in the University Library at Cambridge," *Jewish Quarterly Review* old series 4 (1892): 93.

---

[26] The last phrase comes from Job 12:11, in which chapter it is used by Job, in response to his third friend, to declare that words spoken will have to be examined and studied in order to test their veracity. The standing of the one who uttered them is irrelevant to this determination of truth.

[27] Thirteenth century, Italy.

[28] See above, pp. 757–59.

from error, and perfect wisdom belongs to God alone."[60] In yet another place, he wrote: "that which the Amoraim answer there . . . should not be relied on. They are simply intellectual games, casuistries to which the Amoraim were prone and are not to be relied on. You find such things in many places in the Talmud."[61]

Even in disputes among post-talmudic jurists, "when you find the words of the early Geonim written down in a well-known book, and later jurists rule in a contrary fashion," Rabbi Yosef Kolon holds that "you should follow the later jurists, for it is obvious that they also knew the words of the early Geonim and even so did not accept them. You certainly must conclude that they had good reason to take issue with their predecessors . . . for they knew the early traditions better than we do, and they simply found these unsupportable."[62]

Over and against this Rabbi Moses Alashkar[29] wrote that the Geonim said that the law follows the later authority "only with respect to prior generations, that is, those of the talmudic Sages, but not with respect to later generations, who neither knew nor understood the ways of the talmudic Sages." Therefore, if there is a dispute among jurists, "we follow only the greatest among them, and certainly so if he came first, for earlier is better. Moreover, how far is his [Rabbi Yosef Kolon's] principle of 'follow the later authority' to extend? If only until a certain generation, you have relativized the principle. And if forever, we cannot allow ourselves such a supposition; we would be laughingstocks, for the relationship of these generations to the ancients is not even that of a monkey to a human. Would that today's generations, not to mention those to come—for the intellect only loses force—understood the simplest of the teachings of the ancients."[63]

Rabbi Simeon ben Tzemah Duran determined a certain law against the opinion of Maimonides and wrote: "Let it not trouble you that I dispute the master, of blessed memory, concerning the obligation for this oath, and do not think that I have overstepped ethical bounds in second guessing the lion after his death, for a judge has only what his eyes see, and we should not show deference in matters of Torah. When a matter hinges on logic, later authorities may have revelations that the earlier never imagined."[64]

In the period of the codifiers we find that Rabbenu Asher sometimes rejected the rulings of the greatest of his predecessors, such as Isaac Alfasi.[65] At one point he wrote concerning Maimonides: "We have no obligation to accept what the RaMBaM wrote here as God-given *halakhah*."[66] And Rabbi Shlomo Luria said: "I have not

[60] Ibid., 95.   [61] *Hamakhri'a,* #67, Lublin edition, p. 136.
[62] Responsa of Rabbi Yosef Kolon, principle 94.
[63] Responsa of Rabbi Moses Alashkar, #53, 54.
[64] Tashbetz, part II, #19.
[65] ROSH, Bava Batra, chapter 9, #26.
[66] Responsa of the ROSH, #100.

[29] Fifteenth–sixteenth centuries, North Africa.

shown deference to any author, even though our present generation, because of its feebleness and impotence, is unable to grasp that one of the great early authors may have made an error of judgment, and may believe that whatever is written in an ancient book is not worth reflecting on."[67]

Rabbi Jacob of Lissa,[30] in his preface to the book *Havvat Da'at,* wrote that the title of the book "demonstrates that I have written merely to express opinions, and not, God forbid, to fix *halakhah.*" Let not one who studies my book suspect me "when he finds in my words a critique of a jurist . . . of an intention to be critical, for I know that beside them I am as nothing." Against those who say that later generations are empowered to critique the earlier, because the later ones are like dwarves riding on the backs of giants, he wrote: "the analogy doesn't fit, for we are weak of vision, like chicks whose eyes have not opened . . . and perhaps what we think we see in their words is, because of our feeble and impoverished intellects, the opposite of what they intended."[68]

A questioner turned to the RaSHBA with a legal question and noted that Nahmanides had ruled prohibitively in the matter. The RaSHBA deliberated on the issue and proved the opposite of what Nahmanides had ruled. Moreover, he demonstrated that Maimonides and the RaABaD had ruled permissively. Nevertheless, he concluded: If you found that Nahmanides ruled thus, I say that the Elder has already ruled, and one does not second-guess the lion after his death.[69] [31]

---

[67] *Yam shel Shlomo,* Gittin, preface.
[68] *Havvat Da'at,* preface.
[69] Responsa of the RaSHBA, Part I, #404.

---

[30] Eighteenth–nineteenth centuries, Poland.

[31] It is noteworthy how open-ended and inconclusive this last paragraph is. Heschel has brought us to the point of accepting the arguments for the right of later generations to assert themselves. But then, at the very end of the chapter, he brings to our attention a responsum that says that, although a previously stated view may seem wrong, if it was indeed stated that way, it was best to let it stand and not try to challenge its author after death. Heschel has brought us to an apparent conclusion (and, apparently, the conclusion he wants to advocate), only to remind us at the end of just how great is the duality of the tradition on these matters. One may incline to one view or another, out of a conviction that the times demand it, yet one may not ever escape the fact that authenticity consists in the complex interweaving of views that Judaism has historically exhibited.

40

THEOLOGY IN THE LEGAL LITERATURE

[For an introduction, see the beginning of chapter 37.]

I T WAS AXIOMATIC IN ISRAEL that the number of mitzvot is 613, no more and no less. This number is mentioned in the Tannaitic literature. Its source is in an aggadic exegesis attributed to Rabbi Simla'i, an aggadist of the second generation of Palestinian Amoraim. "Rabbi Simla'i expounded: 613 commandments were spoken to Moses. The negative ones numbered 365, corresponding to the days of the solar year, and the positive ones numbered 248, corresponding to the organs in the human body.[1] Said Rav Hamnuna: What is the textual source? 'Moses charged us with the teaching (*Torah*) as a heritage' (Deuteronomy 33:4)—'Torah' has the numerical value of 611; and 'I the Lord' and 'You shall have no other gods' were heard directly from God."[1] [2]

Note well, that when Rav Hamnuna felt constrained to find a source in the Torah for the number 613, he had to resort to a numerological hint, a method peculiar to *aggadah*. Indeed, Maimonides, in his *Book of the Commandments*,[2] used this aggadic statement to establish principles concerning the number of the mitzvot, a matter on

---

[1] BT Makkot 23b–24a.
[2] *Sefer Hamitzvot,* Root Principle 1.

---

[1] Physiology among the Jews of late antiquity featured this number repeatedly. It is not clear just how they were counting.

[2] That the first two of the Ten Commandments were heard directly from God is based on two textual elements. First, it is reported in Deuteronomy 5 that the people, once they began hearing the voice of God, became terrified and asked Moses to serve as an intermediary. Second, the first two commandments are indeed phrased in the first person, as if God is speaking, whereas the last eight speak of God in the third person, as if Moses is speaking to the people about God. Note that the whole calculation here is very imprecise, since what we call the "Ten Commandments" do not correspond to ten commandments in the various lists of 613. For example, Maimonides counts seven commandments in what we call the "First and Second Commandments." And thus, by Maimonides' reckoning, if we heard the first two of the Ten Commandments directly from God, Moses would have taught us 606, not 611!

which depend several prohibitions and permissions, leniencies and stringencies.[3] Thus did he build the halakhic edifice on an aggadic foundation.

Several Sages expressed misgivings about the number 613. Judah ibn Bal'am denigrated those who number the mitzvot, and who attempt "to force their count to equal 613." In his opinion, this is impossible, for if we were to count all of the mitzvot, including those that were temporary commandments and those that were intended to endure, the number would be far greater than 613. "And if we confined ourselves only to those that endure, we would find fewer than this number."[3]

Rabbi Abraham ibn Ezra wrote in a similar vein: "Some Sages enumerate 613 mitzvot in many diverse ways . . . but in truth there is no end to the number of mitzvot . . . and if we were to count [only] the root principles[4] . . . the number of mitzvot would not reach 613."[4]

Note that Nahmanides also expressed doubt as to whether this number was fixed as a matter of law. "Perhaps we should say that this statement of Rabbi Simla'i is not unanimously accepted but is the subject of dispute. That is, Rabbi Simla'i enumerated the mitzvot according to his opinion and his reasoning, found them to equal this number, and then founded it on this exegesis." Yet, in the end, Nahmanides allowed that since "this total has proliferated throughout the aggadic literature . . . we ought to say that it was a tradition from Moses at Sinai."[5]

When the Karaites came along, and did not light candles in their houses for the Sabbath because of the verse "You shall kindle no fire throughout your settlements on the Sabbath day" (Exodus 35:3), they were refuted by the Sages of Israel not with halakhic but with aggadic arguments:

> The following refutation was given by Rabbenu Meshullam,[5] may his soul be in Paradise: It is written, "God blessed the seventh day" (Genesis 2:3), but do we know wherein He blessed it? We can learn it from the curse that Job leveled at the day of his birth, for he cursed it with darkness, as it is said: "May obscurity carry off that night"

---

[3] See Rabbi Yehiel Mikhel Gutmann, *Behinat Hamitzvot* (Breslau, 1928), p. 46.

[4] *Yesod Mora*, chapter 2.

[5] Nahmanides, critical comments on Maimonides' *Sefer Hamitzvot*, Root Principle 1. Even Rabbi Simeon ben Tzemah Duran, at the end of his book *Zohar Haraki'a* (Lvov, 1858), p. 99, wrote: "Perhaps the agreement that the number of mitzvot is 613 (248 for the positive ones) is just Rabbi Simla'i's opinion, following his own explication of the mitzvot. And we need not rely on his explication when we come to determine the law, but rather on the [relevant] talmudic discussions." See Rav Saadia's *Book of the Commandments*, with the commentary of Rabbi Jeroham Fischel Perla, introduction, chapter 1.

---

[3] What this means is this: if, when counting up the mitzvot in the Torah, we are constrained by the number 613, then the number of possible prohibitions, for example, cannot be unlimited. Some prohibition that one might be inclined to read out of the text of the Torah will not be able to "make the cut," as it were.

[4] Ibn Ezra here means something like what Maimonides did in organizing his *Book of the Commandments*, namely, the categorization of commandments by major category, e.g., dietary laws, laws concerning festival days, and so on.

[5] Twelfth century, France.

(Job 3:6), "May it hope for light and have none" (Genesis 3:9). We can thus infer that the blessing with which God blessed the Sabbath was light, which is what brings peace to the home. Indeed, whatever Job uttered as a curse can be inverted into a blessing with respect to the Sabbath. It is written in Job: "May no sound of joy be heard in it" (Job 3:7), and from this we learn that one should sing out songs and praises on the Sabbath.[6]

Rashi wrote a responsum on the subject of a woman who developed physical flaws after her marriage, and whose husband now wishes to divorce her:

> He has no claim against her on the basis of physical flaws. He has shown himself to be of evil bent and not to be of the descendants of our father Abraham, whose nature it was to be compassionate to people, and certainly to his closest of kin with whom he has covenanted. Had his zeal to draw her in been as great as his zeal to divorce her, her charms would have endeared her to him, for our Rabbis said: each place endears itself to its inhabitants,[7] even if it is plagued with foul waters . . . and it is likewise with a woman's charms and her husband. He is fortunate if he has the merit to win her over and to acquire with her the life of the world to come . . . but if he will not draw her to him with compassion and with honor, let him divorce her but pay her her entire *ketuba*.[8]

The Mishnah stated: If one says "May You be blessed by the good,"[6] that is a sectarian way of worship. Rashi explained: For he does not include the wicked in the praise of God, and the Sages inferred this from the galbanum,[7] which has a bad odor, but was included by the text among the spices of the incense, for the text wishes them to be a united collective when they seek grace.[9] [8] The source of this matter is to be found in the words of Rabbi Simeon Hasida: "A fast that does not include the

---

[6] *Sefer Hasidim*, 1147a. See *Mekor Hesed*, ad loc., which brings another argument in the name of Rabbenu Meshullam, based on the plain meaning of Scripture. According to *Lekah Tov*, Beshallah, 16:8, "the lighting of candles for the Sabbath is obligatory, so that one may enjoy food and drink on the Sabbath." In BT Shabbat 25b: "The lighting of candles for the Sabbath is mandatory."
[7] BT Sotah 47a.   [8] Responsa of Rashi, Elfenbein edition, #207.   [9] BT Megillah 25a.

---

[6] This is a very ambiguous phrase. It may mean "May You be blessed for the good [that You do] . . . ," and thus it is a liturgical phrase that suggests that God deserves praise only from those who are right now enjoying God's bounty. Or it may refer not to a way of worship [as Heschel assumes here], but rather to a mode of greeting another human being, that is, "May the Good One bless you," thus leaving open the possible inference that the blessing of the God of good [as opposed to the God of evil] is being invoked. In either case, the formula is limiting of God and is thus theologically out of bounds. Rashi, as the sequel shows, had yet a third way of understanding it, not as a theologically heterodox formula, but rather as a limitation on the worshiping community.
[7] Hebrew: *helbenah*; this is one of the spices that is listed in Exodus 30 among the ingredients of the sacred incense. The Sages identified it as a foul fragrance when it stood by itself, but as a positive contribution to the incense, in combination with the other ingredients. Thus arose their analogy between the incense and the diverse, worshiping community.
[8] The seeking of grace enters here because, although incense was burned twice every day in the Temple, the most vivid and dramatic use of incense was on the Day of Atonement, when the High Priest would enter the Holy of Holies three times to seek the divine grace on the nation, and the first of these entries was done with a pan full of smoking incense.

sinners of Israel is no fast, for the galbanum has a bad odor, and the text nevertheless included it among the spices of the incense."[10]

"And she that is sick with her separation" (Leviticus 15:33): "The elders of old said (taking it literally: like something that separates and distances her from her husband): that she [the menstruant] should not use eye makeup, nor rouge, nor doll herself up in gay colors. This stood until Rabbi Akiva taught: 'If so, you will make her repulsive to her husband and he will divorce her.'"[11] [9]

The Mishnah stated: "On Yom Kippur it is forbidden to eat, drink, or bathe . . . but a king or a bride should wash their faces."[12] And in the Bavli: "For what reason? A king, because it is written: 'May your eyes behold the king in his splendor' (Isaiah 33:17). But why a bride? So that she not become repulsive to her husband."[13]

"Shabbat was given to Israel for sanctity, delight, and rest, not for pain. Thus, one prays the first three and last three blessings and the single blessing concerning rest in the middle."[14] [10] "The honor of Shabbat is preferable to a thousand fasts."[15]

In order to rescue Israel, the Sages are authorized to permit to those with connections to the government even that which is biblically forbidden.[16] [11] "And why was he (Nehemiah) called hatirshata?[12] Because they allowed him (hitiru lo) to drink the (king's) wine."[17] [13] "Three things were permitted to the family of Rabbi (i.e., the Patriarch's family): that they use mirrors, that they cut their hair at the front,[14] and that they teach their children Greek."[18] "It was taught that Nahum of Galatia said: A

---

[10] BT Keritot 6b.   [11] BT Shabbat 64b.   [12] Mishnah Yoma 8:1.
[13] BT Yoma 78b.   [14] Tanhuma, Vayyera 1.
[15] Tanhuma, Bereshit 3. Rashi's commentary on BT Yevamot 93a, s.v. kol hayamim, implies that the enjoyment of Shabbat is a biblical obligation.
[16] Kesef Mishneh, Hilkhot Avodah Zarah, 11:3.
[17] PT Kiddushin 4:1. For they had already decreed against Gentile wine in the court of Daniel, BT Avodah Zarah 36a.
[18] PT Shabbat 6:1 (7d).

---

[9] Admittedly, this does not reflect the most enlightened view of relations between the sexes, when evaluated by modern standards. See Akiva's similar view of male prerogatives in Mishnah Gittin 9:10. But still, in the context of ancient standards, this text does reflect some measure of concern to preserve a woman's power of endearment to her husband.

[10] This is referring to the fact that the Amidah, the central text of Jewish worship, takes its shortest form of the week on Shabbat. The thirteen benedictions in the middle, which are all petitions of one sort or another, are all omitted in favor of a single middle blessing that expresses not the distress of need but rather the joy of good fortune and grace.

[11] The ability of Jewish leaders to mingle effectively with the governing Gentile authorities was critical for the survival of the Jewish community.

[12] Nehemiah is given that title in Nehemiah 8:9. It certainly has nothing to do with the "folk etymology" that it is given here; rather, it seems to be a Persian title of some kind.

[13] According to Nehemiah 2:1, Nehemiah was wine steward to Artaxerxes, and in such a position he would be required to taste of the wine, to make sure that it was potable and up to taste standards.

[14] This seems to refer to a stylish Roman hairstyle, in which the hair was cropped closely in the front, and was left full in the back. This would not conform to the Jewish standards based on Leviticus 19, but was necessary for the Patriarch if he was to be accepted in the circles to which he had to have access.

gutter (which channels water from the roof) that has become clogged with straw and grass (and the waters overflow and spread over the roof and leak into the house) may be tamped down with the foot on Shabbat with impunity. Why? He is correcting it in an unconventional manner (by doing it with his foot), and the Rabbis' decree against this was not applied to a case of great monetary loss. Said Rav Joseph: The law follows the opinion of Nahum of Galatia."[19]

"It was taught that Rabbi Marinus said: One who wails from depression may suck milk on Shabbat (goat's milk is a palliative). Why? One who sucks is removing the milk in an unconventional manner (for people do not generally suck, but milk by hand), and the Rabbis' decree against this was not applied to a case of suffering (for he suffers from his depression). Said Rav Joseph: The law follows the opinion of Rabbi Marinus."[20]

According to Rabbi Ishmael, one does not kindle with tar on Shabbat, "because of the honor of Shabbat."[21] And in the Mishnah, it was determined that stores are closed on public fasts except that on Thursdays the stores are kept open all day, "in order to honor Shabbat, so that necessities for Shabbat may be purchased."[22] "The men of the Temple watch may not cut their hair or wash their clothes, but on Thursday they may, because of the honor of Shabbat,"[23] lest they not have time on the eve of Shabbat. . . . Said Rabbi Yohanan: it is so that they not begin their watch in a loathsome state.[24] And the men of the *ma'amad* "did not fast on the eve of Shabbat because of the honor of Shabbat," so that they not enter Shabbat ravenous.[25]

According to both Samuel and Rava, they instituted Eruv Tavshilin on festivals falling on the eve of Shabbat because of the honor of Shabbat, in order that one remember not to finish all of the food on the festival, but to leave a good portion for Shabbat. However, according to Rav Ashi, the point of the institution is "so that it may be inferred: if one may not bake on the festival for Shabbat, one may certainly not do so for a weekday."[26]

"A servant may take of the intestines[15] . . . although there is no textual proof for this, there is a textual intimation, for it says: 'plough your ploughfields, and do not plant among the thorns' (Jeremiah 4:3). Rashi explained: "When you toil, toil in something from which you can derive pleasure. And this servant who is busy in the abattoir preparing the meal will suffer if he cannot derive some pleasure from it."[27]

---

[19] BT Ketubot 60a.   [20] BT Ketubot 60a, see Tosafot s.v. *goneah*.
[21] BT Shabbat 24b.   [22] Mishnah Ta'anit 1:6.   [23] Mishnah Ta'anit 2:7.
[24] BT Ta'anit 17a.
[25] Mishnah Ta'anit 4:3. See Ovadiah of Bertinoro, end of chapter 2, Ta'anit 4:7; Hagigah 3:7.
[26] BT Betzah 15b. Maimonides' ruling, in Hilkhot Yom Tov, 6:1, follows Rav Ashi.
[27] BT Pesahim 107b.

---

[15] The setting here is the eve of Passover. On that afternoon, no eating is to occur after a certain hour, so that the Matzah and the Seder meal are eaten in a state of heightened appetite. However, certain kinds of snacking were permitted, and in the case here, a verse from the prophets is used to create a halakhic exception to the general rule by suggesting that it is too cruel to the person preparing the tasty meal not to allow him at least to taste a bit of it.

The following aggadic principles were relied on in halakhic decisions: "The rem-nant of Israel shall do no wrong"; "The beauty of Japheth shall dwell in the tents of Shem"; those things that were taken to be "wisdom and discernment in the eyes of other peoples"; and the creation of human beings in the image of God:

The Mishnah established this rule: "One who removes rubble (from on top of a person who is not known to be alive or dead), and likewise one who has been promised release from prison, or a sick person . . . can be included in a consortium for which a paschal lamb is slaughtered. But none of these may have a lamb slaugh-tered for him alone (the one who removes rubble, lest the person be found dead;[16] the prisoner, lest he not be released; the sick person, lest his illness worsen and he be unable to eat an olive's size of the lamb)."[28] Concerning this, Rabbi Yohanan said: "The Mishnah ruled (that a prisoner may not have a lamb slaughtered for him alone) only in the case of a Gentile prison, but in the case of a Jewish prison the lamb may be slaughtered only for him. For since they promised him, they will release him, for it is said: 'The remnant of Israel shall do no wrong and speak no falsehood' (Zephaniah 3:13)."[29]

Rabban Shimon ben Gamliel said: "Even concerning the Writings, [if not written in Hebrew], they permitted them to be written only in Greek." And the reason, according to Rav Hiyya bar Abba, was: 'May God enlarge [yaft] Japheth, and let him dwell in the tents of Shem' (Genesis 9:27)—the beauty [yofyuto] of Japheth[17] shall dwell in the tents of Shem.[30]

Said Rabbi Johanan: "Whence do we know that a person is obligated to calculate the equinoxes and the movement of the constellations? For it is said: 'Observe them faithfully, for that will be proof of your discernment and wisdom to other peoples' (Deuteronomy 4:6). What discernment and wisdom are evident to the nations? Say: it is the calculation of equinoxes and of the movement of constellations."[31][18]

"A person should wash his face, his hands, and his feet each day, for the sake of his Creator (Rashi: to honor his Creator, for it is written: 'For in His image did God make

---

[28] Mishnah Pesahim 8:6.   [29] BT Pesahim 91a.
[30] BT Megillah 9b.   [31] BT Shabbat 75a.

---

[16] And the person trying to save him thus turns out to have contracted corpse impurity by virtue of having been directly over the dead body. If impure in this way, he could not participate in the sac-rificial rite.

[17] Japheth was, according to Genesis 10:2, the father of Yavan, which was the name for Greece in ancient (and modern) Hebrew.

[18] The astronomical calculations were important for setting the calendar, upon which depended the sanctity of the festival days. It was thus an important science. But more than that, as Rashi points, out here, proficiency in this science is readily demonstrable, inasmuch as it allows the prediction of various phenomena. Thus, expertise in astronomy is a direct and effective way of proving the superiority of Israel.

man' (Genesis 9:6); and furthermore, when one sees a beautiful creature, one says: Blessed be He who has such things in His world), for it says: 'The Lord made everything for His purpose'" (Proverbs 16:4) (Rashi: He created everything for His glory). In another formulation: A person should wash his face, his hands, and his feet on Shabbat, for the sake of, etc. This *halakhah* as well has an aggadic foundation.[32]

"Whence do we know that a threat to life sets aside Shabbat prohibitions?" When that question was asked, it was answered in both a halakhic and an aggadic mode. What was the halakhic mode? "Rabbi Nathan said: The text after all says "You shall keep the Sabbath . . . observing the Sabbath throughout the ages' (Exodus 31:14,16) —desecrate one Shabbat for him [the person in danger], so that he may observe many Shabbatot."[33] This exegesis begins and ends with a concern for the proper observance of Shabbat. Its intent is the salvation of the Shabbat and not the salvation of human beings. Desecrate one Shabbat so as to rescue many Shabbatot. And Rabbi Hayyim ibn Attar[19] correctly inferred from this that we do not set aside Shabbat prohibitions for a *de minimis* extension of life: "If one will certainly not recover so as to be in a position to observe another Shabbat, then even if various healing remedies will extend his life by hours or days, Shabbat should not be desecrated for him."[34] [20]

By halakhic standards, there is no more serious transgression than adultery.[21] On the other hand, one who embarrasses someone publicly violates no biblical command. But David came and asserted that the sin of public embarrassment is greater than the sin of adultery: "Wretches gather against me, I know not why" (Psalm 35:15)—People of flawed character gather against me and taunt me, and I did not know that a dispensation had been given to embarrass me. "Thus spoke David before the Holy and Blessed One: Master of the Universe! It is well known to you that were my flesh to be torn, no blood would flow.[22] In fact, when they deal with the laws of capital punishment, they interrupt their studies and say to me: David, how is an adulterer to be executed? And I say to them: An adulterer is executed by strangulation, and he has a share in the world to come. But one who embarrasses a person publicly has no share in the world to come."[35]

---

[32] BT Shabbat 50b.   [33] BT Shabbat 151b.   [34] Or Ha-Hayyim, Exodus 31:16.
[35] BT Sanhedrin 107a; see also BT Bava Metzia 59a.

---

[19] Eighteenth century, Morocco and Israel.

[20] The aggadic mode is not spelled out here by Heschel, but it does appear in chapter 1, pp. 4–6. It is, in the context of extinguishing a candle that disturbs a sick person's sleep, a comparison between a human lamp and "God's lamp" (i.e., the human soul). Which is it better to have extinguished?

[21] It carries the ultimate sanction, that is, execution by a human court.

[22] Presumably, because it is all already gone, having been "sucked away" by his tormenters. This exegesis is based on what is supposedly a literal reading of Psalm 35:15, which actually means something like "they tore at me without any letup." *ve-lo domu* ("they were not quieted") is read here as "without blood [*dam*]."

INTERPERSONAL RELATIONSHIPS

[For an introduction, see the beginning of chapter 37.]

Between One Party and Another

IT IS AMONG THE MOST COMMON OF LAMENTS that people who are the most scrupulous concerning obligations to God are liable to be lax concerning obligations to another person, and that duties pertaining to the spirit tend to get trampled underfoot.

According to Rabbi Levi, "retribution for wrongs of character is greater than that for sexual infractions,[1] for one can repent of the latter, but not of the former."[1] In a similar vein he said: "stealing from another person is worse than stealing from the Temple." And Rabbi Johanan said: "See how powerful are the sins of personal violence; for the generation of the Flood committed every transgression possible, but their sentence was not sealed until they got involved in larceny, as it says: 'for the earth is filled with lawlessness[2] because of them: I am about to destroy them with the earth' (Genesis 6:13)."[2]

Adopting this approach, Maimonides ruled as follows: "we are required to be more scrupulous with the commandment of charity than with any other positive commandment, for charity is emblematic of the righteous descendants of Father Abraham, as it says: 'For I have singled him out, that he may instruct his children and his posterity to keep the way of the Lord by doing what is just'[3] (Genesis 18:19). Jewish sovereignty and the true faith itself can only endure through charity, as it says: 'you

---

[1] BT Yevamot 21a; BT Bava Batra 88b.
[2] BT Sanhedrin 108a.

---

[1] Literally: incestuous or adulterous acts. The comparison is here made to these infractions because in the rabbinic mind they were among the most heinous of sins. Indeed, "sin" in the rabbinic lexicon often meant "sexual sins." The comparison thus indicates just how horrible are character defects.
[2] Hebrew: *hamas*, understood by the Rabbis to mean larceny, even petty thievery, which was pervasive.
[3] Hebrew: *tzedakah*, the word that denotes charity in the rabbinic lexicon.

shall be established through righteousness'[4] (Isaiah 54:14). Through charity alone will Israel be redeemed, as it says: 'Zion shall be saved by justice, her repentant ones by righteousness'[5] (Isaiah 1:27)."3

According to Rabbenu Asher,[6] "The Holy and Blessed One values more those commandments through which the needs of people are satisfied than those that are strictly between a person and the Creator."4

Rabbi Hayyim Vital[7] writes: "Character traits are propaedeutic to the 613 commandments, whether in their observance or in their breach . . . therefore, bad character traits are even worse than actual transgressions . . . and one's scrupulousness in avoiding such traits must exceed that in observing positive or negative commandments."5

The pious Abba Tahnah entered his town toward nightfall on Friday, with his pack resting on his shoulder, and encountered a person afflicted with boils lying in the crossroads. The outcast said, "Rabbi, do right by me and carry me into the town." He thought, "If I leave my pack here, how shall my family and I support ourselves? But if I leave this afflicted man here, my life shall be forfeit." What did he do? He had his good inclination subjugate the bad, and he carried the afflicted man into the town. He then returned for his pack and entered the town with the last rays of the sun. Everyone was astonished and said, "Is that the pious Abba Tahnah?" He himself worried silently that others would think he was violating the Sabbath. But just then the Holy and Blessed One caused the sun to shine on, as it is written: "But for you who revere My name a sun of righteousness[8] shall shine" (Malachi 3:20). He further worried that perhaps he had thereby received all his reward. A heavenly voice then echoed out: "Go, eat your bread in gladness, and drink your wine in joy; for your action was long ago approved by God" (Ecclesiastes 9:7)—your reward has not been fully received.6 [9]

In the days of Rabbi Tanhuma, a public fast became necessary because of drought.[10] They came to him and said, "Master, decree a fast." He decreed fasts for

---

3 Maimonides, *Mishneh Torah*, "Laws Concerning Gifts to the Poor," 10:1.
4 Rabbenu Asher's commentary on Mishnah Peah 1:1.
5 Sha'arei Kedushah, Part I, 2.   6 Ecclesiastes Rabbah 9:7.

---

[4] See previous note.

[5] See previous note. The translation given here is the one given in the NJV footnotes.

[6] That is, Rabbenu Asher ben Jehiel, thirteenth–fourteenth century, Germany and Spain.

[7] Sixteenth–seventeenth century, Safed and Damascus.

[8] Again, the Hebrew is *tzedakah*. The translation here departs slightly from the NJV so as to accentuate the basis of the rabbinic reading of the verse.

[9] The text here is somewhat difficult, and in particular, it is not clear exactly how the proof text from Ecclesiastes is meant to allay Abba Tahnah's fears (which was that the miracle of the extended sunshine had, perhaps, "depleted his account," and that he might not have any remaining reward for his life of righteousness. The version of the text given here by Heschel follows the reading attested in "Ot Emet," as reported in "Matenot Kehunah" on Ecclesiastes Rabbah.

[10] See Mishnah Ta'anit 1:4–7, for the rabbinic laws concerning such fasts.

three days,[11] and still no rains came. Rabbi Tanhuma then entered the House of Study and preached to them: "My children, be merciful one to the other, and the Holy and Blessed One will then be merciful to you." As they were distributing charity to the poor, they saw a certain man giving money to his divorced wife, and they suspected him of immorality. Rabbi Tanhuma summoned the man and woman and they appeared before him. He asked the man: "Why were you giving money to your divorcee?" He replied, "I saw her in distress, and I was filled with compassion for her." Rabbi Tanhuma turned toward Heaven and said: "Master of the Universe, this man, who no longer had any obligation to support this woman, was nevertheless filled with compassion for her. Of You it is written: "The Lord is compassionate and gracious" (Psalm 103:8), and we are Your children, the descendants of Abraham, Isaac, and Jacob; how much more so should You be filled with compassion for us!" Immediately, the rains came and watered the earth.[7] [12]

Social Responsibility[13]

There are duties that are not mentioned in the Torah, such as those of social welfare and etiquette, including the duty to work for financial sustenance. Therefore it is stated in the Mishnah: "The study of Torah goes well with a gainful occupation,[14] for when a person toils in both, sin is driven out of mind."[8] The following principle was also established: "Social responsibility takes precedence over everything."[15][9] And Nahmanides especially dwelt on the importance of those obligations not explicitly commanded in the Torah.[10]

According to Rabbi Eleazar ben Azariah, "without social responsibility there is no Torah."[11] And in the Midrash, it is magnified: "The importance of social responsibility is equal to that of the entire Torah; thus did Bar Kappara preach: "on what concise matter does the entire spectrum of Torah depend? It is social responsibility, as it says:

---

[7] Genesis Rabbah 33:3.   [8] Mishnah Avot 2:2.   [9] SER, chapter 1.
[10] In his commentary on the verse "You shall be holy" (Leviticus 19:2).
[11] Mishnah Avot 3:17.

---

[11] The reference here is, apparently, to the first set of three public fasts prescribed in Mishnah Ta'anit 1:5 for times of drought.

[12] The lesson, of course, is the importance of obligations between one human being and another. Their influence extends beyond the individuals directly involved, to implicate the entire society.

[13] In this subchapter, "social responsibility" is the translation generally employed for the Hebrew term derekh eretz. That term can refer to worldly occupations, to social graces, even to conjugal relations. The common denominator of all of these meanings is the quality of engaging in worldly activity or social interaction in a constructive way. Thus, the all-encompassing translation employed here.

[14] This is the specific meaning of derekh eretz in this text. It is quite clearly a subcategory of social responsibility.

[15] In particular, it takes precedence over Torah itself, for the exegesis there reads "Derekh Eretz" out of the verse (Genesis 3:24) before it reads out "Torah."

'In all your ways acknowledge Him' (Proverbs 3:6). . . . Social responsibility is great, for whoever has achieved it has befriended both the Holy and Blessed One and human beings."[12]

Some say: "Rabbi Jacob was wont to say that the study of Torah was secondary to social responsibility, for it was taught: "The study of Torah goes well with a gainful occupation" (Mishnah Avot 2:2), that is, social responsibility is the main matter."[13]

Ways of Peace and Pleasantness

The Sages instituted many things in order to prevent the quarreling and bickering that result from envy and pursuit of honor, from financial affairs, or from neglect of social etiquette. Such institutions were done to promote "ways of peace." They went so far as to say, "the entire Torah exists only to promote ways of peace, for it is written, 'Her ways are pleasant ways, and all her paths, peaceful' (Proverbs 3:17)."[14] "All that is written in the Torah was written for the sake of peace; and although wars are written about in the Torah, even they were written of for the sake of peace."[15]

The institution of the eruv,[16] which appeared to be a great leniency over what seemed to be the plain meaning of the Torah,[17] was understood by Rabbi Joshua ben Levi to have been "to promote ways of peace." It happened that a certain woman who was disliked by her neighbor sent her son with her eruv.[18] The neighbor accepted it, and hugged and kissed the boy. The boy reported to his mother that her neighbor had kissed him. She said: I had no idea that she liked me! Because of this, they ended up making peace with one another. Thus it is written, "Her ways are pleasant ways, and all her paths, peaceful."[16] The saying "to promote ways of peace" was understood here as meaning that the institution of the eruv would require people to communi-

---

[12] Bet Hamidrash, 3, p. 127.   [13] Tosafot Yeshanim, BT Yoma 85b.
[14] BT Gittin 59b.   [15] Tanhuma, Tzav, 3.   [16] PT Eruvin 7:9.

---

[16] The rabbinic institution that allows for the blending of private domains on the Sabbath into one large communal domain. Since transporting objects from one domain into another was forbidden by rabbinic law on the Sabbath, the eruv allowed for the transportation of objects, especially food, between one family's dwelling and another's. Communal life was thus enhanced.

[17] Although the term "plain meaning" has an objective connotation to it, the plain meaning of any text is always a matter of subjective judgment. In this case, the Rabbis read Exodus 16:19 ("let no man leave [yetze] his place on the seventh day") as if it were written "let no man remove [yotzi] anything from his place on the seventh day." So taken for granted was that reading that it became, for all intents and purposes, a "plain meaning" of that text. See Tosafot to BT Eruvin 17b, and Maimonides, Mishneh Torah, "Laws Concerning Unintentional Sins," 14:2. It is this "plain meaning" to which Heschel here refers.

[18] That is, with her contribution to the pooled food required to create the blended domain.

cate with one another. Moreover, the *eruv* makes everyone, as it were, into a single person."[17] [19]

A central principle in the understanding of Torah is that the Torah never intends to do things contrary to ways of pleasantness and peace. This principle was employed in connection with the laws of levirate marriage,[18][20] of the four species included in the Lulav,[19][21] and others. Some latter authorities even used the principle of "ways of pleasantness" to mean that "the laws of our Torah must agree with reason and common sense."[20]

It is said in the Mishnah: "Although the one prohibited and the other permitted, the one delegitimated and the other legitimated,[22] the school of Shammai did not hesitate to marry into families of the school of Hillel, and vice versa. And although there were numerous purity issues on which the one considered vessels pure and the other considered them impure, they did not hesitate to commingle their pure vessels."[23][21] The Tosefta adds: "They acted with one another honestly and peacefully . . . in fulfillment of the verse 'you must love honesty and integrity'[24] (Zechariah 8:19)."[22]

We learn from this that because they loved peace they were willing to be lax with respect to their own stated prohibitions. In the Babylonian Talmud, much amazement was expressed over this, and it was suggested that each school would inform the other concerning their specific practices so that the other would not be misled con-

---

[17] Korban Ha'edah, on PT Eruvin 7:9.　　[18] BT Yevamot 87b.　　[19] BT Sukkah 32a.
[20] Responsa of RaDBaZ (David ibn Zimra, sixteenth century, Egypt), Part III, 624 and 627, also MaHaRShaL (Solomon Luria, sixteenth century, Poland) to BT Yevamot 87b.
[21] Mishnah Yevamot 1:4; Mishnah Eduyot 4:5.　　[22] Tosefta Yevamot, chapter 1.

---

[19] By merging everyone's private domain into a single domain.

[20] That is, the requirement that the brother-in-law of a childless widow either marry her or, refusing to do so, submit to a ceremony of humiliation and separation (*halitzah*)—see Deuteronomy 25:5–10. Heschel here refers to a lenient rabbinic ruling that nullified, in a special circumstance, a doubtful bond between a woman and her brother-in-law so as to exempt her from the requirement of *halitzah* and its attendant humiliation.

[21] That is, the palm, citron, myrtle, and willow that are taken and waved together on the festival of Sukkot. Here Heschel refers to the talmudic statement that the Torah's instruction to take "branches of palm trees" could not possibly refer to the palm spike because it would injure the hands.

[22] The issue here is the status of a levirate marriage between a brother-in-law of a woman whom, for reasons of consanguinity, he could not marry, and one of her co-wives (i.e., the deceased brother had plural wives, which was permitted by biblical and rabbinic law). The school of Shammai permitted such marriages and considered the offspring legitimate, while the school of Hillel forbade such marriages and considered the offspring to be illegitimate (and thus ineligible to marry legitimate members of the community).

[23] That is, the vessels each of them *considered* to be pure.

[24] "Integrity" here translates *shalom*, taken here in the sense of completeness, hence integrity. The Tosefta cited here takes it in the usual sense of "peace," the subject of the reminiscence about the schools of Shammai and Hillel.

cerning things they felt were prohibited.[23] But if that were the case, what would be notable about the Mishnah's statement?[25]

In a similar vein, Rabbi Meir said: "Although I say one thing and my colleagues another, I never presumed to transgress my colleagues' rulings."[24] [26]

A Scoundrel within the Bounds of the Torah[27]

The Halakhah is the lens through which, seeing human life, one distinguishes between the forbidden and the permitted, the suitable and the unsuitable, the liable and the exempt. Its mode of thought is that of rules, justice, legislation. But this raises several questions. Does the Torah contain but one mode of thought, the legal mode? Is there no room for the mode of mercy, that which commands action beyond the legal boundary? Moreover, does the Torah give us no life values other than those of "kosher" and "unkosher"? Do we not need to take account of the values of pleasantness and righteousness? If, according to Nahmanides, a person may be a "scoundrel within the bounds of the Torah," it is implied that there is another path, beyond the line of the Halakhah.

Many Sages have noted that although, in general, laws are not to be derived from the Aggadah, there are some specific *halakhot* that *were* learned from *aggadot*.[28] Most important is the fact that when, in halakhic debate, a doubt or impasse arose concerning any law of the Torah, ideas and postulates flowing from the sources of aggadic thought were used to determine the law. The Sages knew that one could be a "scoundrel within the bounds of the Torah," that is, within the bounds of the

---

[23] BT Yevamot 14a.   [24] BT Shabbat 134a.

---

[25] It is notable here that Heschel is rejecting the explanation of the BT concerning the Mishnah's depiction of the behavior of the schools of Shammai and Hillel. Heschel's claim is that the Mishnah, in its very rhetorical form, is making an important statement, and that the BT's attempt to explain it away vitiates the Mishnah's entire force. It is a legitimate argument. Whether the Mishnah's depiction of the irenic relationship between the schools is historically accurate or not is another matter. Many other passages tend to belie this "recollection," but in any event, the historical record is not of relevance here.

[26] Apparently, he respected the more stringent majority ruling for purposes of his own practice.

[27] The phrase *naval bireshut hatorah* is conventionally translated "scoundrel with the Torah's permission." But *reshut* primarily means "domain," and as this chapter will make clear, the principle behind this phrase is that one does *not* have the "permission" of the Torah to act in the ways that the phrase describes. Rather, the issue is that the Torah's strict legal boundaries would seem to allow certain behavior, at least technically. Thus, the better translation would seem to be "scoundrel within the bounds of the Torah." Heschel actually begins this section with what is a reprise of material from chapter 1, pp. 4–9. That reprise is not given here, but the reader may want to refer back to it as a prelude to what is given here, namely, a critique of the idea that the bounds of Halakhah are the bounds of Judaism.

[28] See chapter 40.

Halakhah, and they therefore declared: "Jerusalem was destroyed only because . . . they judged solely by the Torah's law, and did not act beyond the line of the law."[25]

What is the distinction between those things that are on the line of the law and those that lie beyond the line of the law? We can enforce the line of the law, but not what lies beyond the line of the law. The law is manifest, fixed, and constant, while that which lies beyond the line of the law is not explicit, but rather subjective and given to discretion. Here is an example: the secret of the persistence of the Jewish people throughout the generations lies in its willingness to sacrifice its very existence. But the question must be asked: What is important enough to sacrifice one's life for? Should one treat every commandment as inviolable to the point of death? The masters of Halakhah gave the fixed points: "In the case of all commandments in the Torah, should a person be told to transgress them or be killed, he should transgress and not be killed, with the exception of idolatry, incest/adultery, and murder." Such is the line of the law. But an aggadic text added this statement: "Better for a person to jump into a fiery furnace than to embarrass another person publicly. Whence do we learn this? From the story of Tamar."[29] That is, it is better to be killed and not transgress. This situation was not included in the list of commandments about which they decreed "be killed and do not transgress," and it was not fixed in law. Notice that this statement was not formulated in legislative language, but rather in suggestive language, as if "the text is giving us sound advice": the language is "Better for a person. . . ." And this entire matter is learned from a narrative in the Torah, from the story of Tamar.[30]

The aggadic element of Halakhah brings about a widening of one's field of vision and an expansion of horizons. For halakhic masters are not usually attentive to the depths of life, that is, to the life that plays out within a person's soul, and against those who complain about the tradition's shackles there is no one to explicate its grand vision. Where are those who would broaden the base and thus raise the edifice even higher?

According to Halakhah, the court is positively commanded to execute whoever has been found guilty of a capital crime, and failing to do so, the court is guilty of neglecting a positive commandment.[26] But alongside this, it was established in the Mishnah: "A Sanhedrin that executes once in seven years is called 'destructive.' Rabbi Eleazar

---

[25] BT Bava Metzi'a 30b.
[26] Maimonides, *Mishneh Torah*, "Laws Concerning the Sanhedrin," 14:2–3.

---

[29] In the story told in Genesis 38, Tamar, Judah's daughter-in-law, was being taken to a gruesome death by fire on suspicion of adultery, and only her demonstration that it was Judah who was her consort could have saved her life. But although she had the proof, she did not publicly implicate Judah, but rather left it to him to deduce the truth and to make admission himself. In other words, this Canaanite woman preferred death by fire to the public humiliation of another human being. How much more so, reasoned the Rabbis, should a Jew have the same revulsion to public humiliation.

[30] That is, this is not a halakhic rule, but rather an exhortation that gets to the very heart of what Jewish ethics is about.

ben Azariah said: even if once in seventy years. Rabbi Tarfon and Rabbi Akiva both said: had we been on the Sanhedrin, no one would ever have been executed." (Rashi: for they would have asked the witnesses questions that they could not answer.)[27]

The view of those last two Sages stands in contrast to the plain meaning of biblical verses, and for all practical purposes abrogates the rules pertaining to the four forms of capital punishment. And this is no small matter, for the Rabbis said that "plague is visited on the world because of capital crimes enumerated in the Torah that could not be requited by the earthly court."[28] These Sages thoroughly turn the tables by demanding that members of courts of justice leave the seat of justice and occupy the seat of mercy: as if it is kindness that should split mountains![31] Does not this preaching destroy a major foundation of biblical jurisprudence? Whence came the extreme suggestion that the laws of capital punishment be abrogated? Is it conceivable that just as Abraham begged mercy for Sodom, every judge is to seek acquittal for every outlaw guilty of a capital crime?

"For three years the schools of Shammai and Hillel held to their opinions, and each said: 'the halakhah agrees with our view.' An echoing voice came out and said: 'These and these are words of the living God, and the halakhah follows the view of the school of Hillel.' But if these and these are words of the living God, why did the school of Hillel merit that the halakhah be fixed in agreement with them? Because they were irenic and humble,"[29] even though the school of Shammai was more sharp-witted. It is hard to be reconciled to this rationalization.[30] Have it as you wish: if the opinions of the school of Hillel stand on their own, then the halakhah should be fixed in agreement with them; if they do not, then what does it matter if they were irenic and modest? There have been many Sages who were exceedingly pious, but whose opinions were not for that reason preferred in settling halakhah.[31] Indeed, the accepted principle was that if two Tannaim disagreed, "with one declaring 'impure' and the other declaring 'pure,' the one forbidding and the other permitting, then if one was greater in wisdom and numbers, he is to be followed, and if not, the one who rules stringently should be followed."[32]

Thus, the settling of the halakhah on the side of the school of Hillel, against the school of Shammai, was one of the most critical events in Jewish history. Yet the rationalization for this determination given here, "because they were irenic and humble," is quite surprising. Is it really on the basis of a Sage's pieties that halakhah is settled to agree with his view? What does piety have to do with legal decision?

"Rabbi Meir said: What is the meaning of the verse 'Then you shall know the Lord' (Hosea 2:22)? It comes to teach us that whoever has the enumerated characteristics

[27] Mishnah Makkot 1:10.   [28] Mishnah Avot 5:8.   [29] BT Eruvin 13b.
[30] See BT Eruvin 6b, Tosafot s.v. kan.   [31] See Mekor Barukh, Part I, p. 104.
[32] BT Avodah Zarah 7a.

[31] A play on the phrase, more familiar among the Sages, that "the law must split mountains," that is, that nothing should stand in the way of the fulfillment of the law.

will know God's thoughts."[32] From this statement we learn that it is not only the characteristic of wisdom that prepares a person to apprehend divine thoughts, but also the characteristics of righteousness, justice, goodness, and mercy (Hosea 2:21).[33]

"Once bones were found in the Temple woodshed,[34] and the Sages wanted to decree a state of impurity on all of Jerusalem. Rabbi Joshua then stood up and said: Would it not be a shame and disgrace for us to decree impurity for our ancestral city! Where are the victims of the Flood (they must be all over, and thus here as well), and where are the victims of Nebuchadnezzar?"[35] This rationalization is also quite surprising. Shall shame and disgrace prevent us from acknowledging the truth? Are we to show preferences?[33]

One is forbidden to bring vessels out into a public domain on Shabbat, but those which are ornaments may be carried. It would appear that an ornament is anything that beautifies or otherwise enhances the appearance of the one wearing it. And thus, social convention must determine the halakhic status of the "ornament." Yet along came the Sages and proposed that with respect to one category of ornaments, not social convention but rather prophetic vision would define its status; for in the prophetic view, a certain ornament highly valued among people was nevertheless demeaning. The Mishnah states: "A man may not go into a public domain with a sword, a bow, a shield, a lance, or a spear; if he did so, he must bring a purification sacrifice. Rabbi Eliezer said: They are ornamental for a man.[34] But the Sages said: They are demeaning to him, for it says: 'and they shall beat their swords into plowshares, and their spears into pruning hooks: nation shall not take up sword against nation; they shall never again know war' (Isaiah 2:4)."[36]

According to an anonymous mishnah, royalty may salve wounds with rose oil on Shabbat, for they are accustomed to using it just for pleasure every day. But for the common person, such medicinal use is forbidden on Shabbat.[35] Rabbi Simeon dissented and said: "All Israel are considered to be royalty."[37] That is: even if rose oil is scarce, and therefore expensive, and it would thus be obvious that it is only being used for medicinal purposes, one may still use it, for all Israel are to be considered royalty. Patently, Rabbi Simeon's reasoning is aggadic in nature. And indeed, it was

---

[33] ARN chapter 37.   [34] According to PT Shekalim 6:1, "the Ark had been secreted there."
[35] BT Zevahim 113a; Tosefta Eduyot 3:1.   [36] Mishnah Shabbat 6:4.
[37] Mishnah Shabbat 14:4.

---

[32] The qualities enumerated in Hosea 2:21, the previous verse, are: righteousness, justice, goodness, and mercy.

[33] That is, make an exception to the rule of impurity simply because we deem it unseemly to the dignity of Jerusalem to declare all of it impure? Partiality of this sort (in this case, to Jerusalem and its residents) is supposed to be ruled out by a strict legal approach.

[34] But not for a woman.

[35] Medicines used for nonserious illnesses were generally shunned on the Sabbath, for fear that it would lead to forbidden acts of grinding (for the preparation of the drugs), where no life-threatening (and thus mitigating) circumstances existed. Here, substances that were routinely used were not considered medicines, and could be used on the Sabbath.

established in the Babylonian Talmud that "the *halakhah* agrees with Rabbi Simeon, but not on his grounds."[38]

Rabbi Eleazar ben Azariah said: "Whence do we derive that when a woman has a levirate bond to a brother-in-law who is afflicted with boils,[36] we do not "muzzle" her (i.e., we do not ignore her complaints, and rather than force her to marry, we force him to release her through *halitzah*)? Because the Torah says, 'her husband's brother shall unite with her' (Deuteronomy 25:5), and just adjacent to it, 'You shall not muzzle an ox while it is threshing' (Deuteronomy 25:4)."[39] This exegesis, the effect of which is to nullify (in this case) the commandment to produce children in the deceased husband's name, is also aggadic in nature; it expounds juxtaposed texts, in a metaphoric and poetic way.

If one has been sentenced to death and has fled, we do not nullify his sentence; wherever two witnesses may come forward and say: "we testify that this person was sentenced to death by that court," he may be executed. However, if he fled from the Diaspora to the Land of Israel, we do nullify his sentence, because of the "acquitting power" of the Land of Israel.[40] That is: even though the fugitive may not have a specific argument to offer, but merely wants a court to reconvene so that they might find grounds for acquittal, we nullify the first trial. And "the acquitting power of the Land of Israel" is not a legal but a metaphysical concept.

A certain Boethusian asked Rabbi Joshua Hagarsi: "Whence do we know that one may not write *tefillin* on the hide of an impure animal? Rabbi Joshua responded: 'In order that the Teaching of the Lord may be in your mouth' (Exodus 13:9)—it must be on something permitted to your mouth." The Boethusian then went on to ask: "If so, it should also be forbidden to write it on the hides of torn animals [*terefot*] or of those that have died naturally [*nevelot*]! Said Rabbi Joshua: I shall give you a parable. To what is this comparable? To the case of two persons who were sentenced to death by royal decree. One was executed by the king, and the other by the chief executioner. Which of the two is the superior? Evidently, the one executed by the king himself."[37]

---

[38] BT Shabbat 111b. According to Abbaye, Rabban Simeon ben Gamliel, Rabbi Ishmael and Rabbi Akiva all agree that all Israel are to be considered royalty —BT Shabbat 128a.

[39] BT Yevamot 4a.

[40] BT Makkot 7a; Tosefta Sanhedrin, end of chapter 3.

---

[36] Generally speaking, women were entitled to sue for divorce if their husbands developed physical conditions that were repulsive to them. If he had them prior to the marriage, some argued that she could not do so, since she had patently agreed to marry him under those conditions. But here, in the case of levirate marriage, her consent is not necessary, since it is an obligatory marriage under biblical law (only he can refuse to carry it out), and thus one might have thought that she could be forced to marry the brother-in-law even if he had the repulsive condition of boils.

[37] The status of the executioner, in an odd way, bestows status on the one put to death. The point of the parable here is that slaughtered animals are put to death by human beings, God's servants. If their hides are fit to be used for God's holy scripture, then certainly we ought to be able to use (otherwise kosher) animals that died of their own accord, that is, that were put to death by the Master of the Universe. Note that this logic might also be employed to argue for the acceptability of

And the author of Tractate Soferim adds: "From this we learn that *tefillin* may be written on the hides of *nevelot* or *terefot*."[41] This rationalization also is no logical deduction, and it strays from the usual modes of halakhic discourse.

If someone stole a wooden beam and built it into a mansion, the school of Shammai ruled that the mansion must be dismantled and the beam returned to its owner. The school of Hillel ruled that the owner can only claim the value of the beam, because of the Ordinance for the Penitents.[42] The Mishnah established the law in agreement with the school of Hillel.[43] "According to the letter of the law, whoever steals is required to return the stolen object itself, for it is said, 'he would restore the robbed item which he robbed' (Leviticus 5:23) . . . even if he stole a beam and built it into a large mansion . . . biblical law would require that he destroy the entire building and return the beam to its owner; but the Sages instituted, as an Ordinance for the Penitents, that he should repay the value of the beam and not forfeit the entire building."[44]

Human Dignity

The basis of the claim of human dignity is the divine image. It was asserted in the Aggadah that one should not distinguish between the honor due God and the honor due human beings. Since the Holy and Blessed One cares for human dignity,[45] how much more so should mortals take care. When standing at Mount Sinai, Israel heard God say, "Honor your father and your mother." "The entire world belongs to the Holy and Blessed One, and all the Holy One asks of a person is to honor father and mother!"[46]

Human dignity is one of those concepts that are not classified as positive commandments in themselves, and its content is not explicitly defined in the Torah. Yet the Tannaim employed it for halakhic purposes, and they asserted: "Human dignity is important enough to override a negative commandment in the Torah."[47] The Rabbis in fact presented us with two principles. According to one, "Human dignity is important enough to override a negative commandment in the Torah." According to the second, "No wisdom, no prudence, and no counsel can prevail against the Lord" (Proverbs 21:30)—"wherever there would be a desecration of God's command, no honor is to be shown to a [mortal] master." Following this second principle, Rav Judah asserted in Rav's name: "One who discovers mixed fibers in his garment should remove it, even in a public place."[48] The Babylonian Talmud deals with the

---

[41] BT Shabbat 108a; Soferim 1:2.   [42] BT Gittin 55a.   [43] Mishnah Gittin 5:5.
[44] Shulhan Arukh, Hoshen Mishpat, 360:1.   [45] SER, chapter 11.
[46] SER, chapter 27.   [47] BT Berakhot 19b.   [48] BT Berakhot 19b.

---

eating animals that were not slaughtered, but the logic cannot extend that far, since the Torah itself forbade the eating of such animals.

contradiction between these two principles and suggests that it is only rabbinic ordinances that are overridden by concerns for human dignity, or perhaps biblical laws, when overriding them entails no overt action.[49]

"Rabbi Moses Isserles wrote in a responsum[38] that in a pressing situation . . . where there could be both great financial loss and embarrassment to the bride and groom, it is permitted to officiate at a wedding on Shabbat; and he himself officiated at such a wedding, because of the importance of human dignity."[50]

"Others say: a dung-scraper, a copper smelter, and a tanner are exempt from the pilgrimage, for it says: 'all your males shall appear' (Exodus 23:17)—that is, those who can make the pilgrimage with all the males, as opposed to those who cannot properly do so." For the enumerated people "have a bad odor and cannot go up with their colleagues" (Rashi).[51]

"One cannot actually spit on another person. And thus the Targum rendered 'if her father spat in her face' (Numbers 12:14) as 'if her father rebuked her,' for it is impossible for a father, even in anger, to spit on his daughter."[52] This statement now explains for us the Sages' modification of the procedure for halitzah, a modification that departed from the plain meaning of scripture. For it is written in the Torah: "his brother's widow shall go up to him in the presence of the elders, pull the sandal off his foot, spit in his face . . ." (Deuteronomy 25:9). But the Sifre expounded: "Shall I understand it to mean literally in his face? The text says: 'in the presence of the elders,' that is, spittle that can be seen by the elders."[53] And Rashi commented: "spit in his face"—"on the ground."

Similarly: "and they shall spread out the cloth before the elders of the town" (Deuteronomy 22:17)—"this is one of the texts of the Torah that Rabbi Ishmael used to expound metaphorically . . . 'they shall spread out the cloth'—that the facts be as plain as a spread out cloth."[54]

And concerning the law of the Hebrew slave, it is written: "You shall take an awl and put it through his ear into the door, and he shall become your slave in perpetuity. Do the same with your female slave" (Deuteronomy 15:17). Here too they made the text mean something other than its plain meaning, apparently out of concern for a woman's dignity. "Do the same with your female slave"—"shall we say that that applies to the awl as well? The text says: 'But if the male slave [eved] declares' (Exodus 21:5)—that is, a male slave [eved] and not a female slave [amah]."[55]

---

[49] BT Berakhot 20a.   [50] Hayye Adam, Hilkhot Shabbat, 38:6.
[51] BT Hagigah 4a.   [52] Sefer Hasidim, 636.   [53] Sifre Deuteronomy, 291.
[54] Sifre Deuteronomy, 237.   [55] Sifre Deuteronomy, 122.

---

[38] Responsa of Remah, #125.

Appendixes

1. Abbreviations

For additional bibliographical information, see appendix 4 below.

ARN   *Avot de Rabbi Nathan,* given according to the edition by Solomon Schechter, which presents two versions, "A" and "B."

AV   Authorized Version (King James Bible, 1611)

Avot   *Pirkei Avot* [Ethics of the Fathers]. References are given according to the paragraph divisions of the Mishnah, which differs slightly from the version of Avot found in the Jewish Prayer Book. Apart from this, the texts are nearly identical.

BT   Babylonian Talmud

DER   *Derekh Eretz Rabbah*

DEZ   *Derekh Eretz Zuta*

EJ   *Encyclopedia Judaica* (Jerusalem, 1982)

MI   *Mekhilta de-Rabbi Ishmael*

MSY   *Mekhilta de-Rabbi Simeon ben Yohai*

MTD   *Midrash Tannaim* to Deuteronomy. Edited by David Z. Hoffmann. Berlin, 1908.

NEB   *New English Bible* (Oxford, 1972)

NJV   New Jewish Version of the Bible: *Tanakh: The Holy Scriptures: The New JPS Translation According to the Traditional Hebrew Text* (Philadelphia: Jewish Publication Society, 1985)

OJV   Old Jewish Version of the Bible: *Holy Scriptures* (Philadelphia: Jewish Publication Society, 1917)

PB   Standard Jewish Prayer Book

PR   *Pesikta Rabbati*

PRK   *Pesikta de-Rav Kahana*

PRE   *Pirkei de-Rabbi Eliezer*

PT   "Palestinian Talmud," more properly called "Talmud of the Land of Israel," also called in Hebrew the "Jerusalem Talmud"

SER   *Seder Eliyahu Rabbah*

SEZ   *Seder Eliyahu Zuta*

TB   "Tanhuma Buber," i.e., *Midrash Tanhuma,* edition of Solomon Buber (a significantly different text from the standard *Midrash Tanhuma* of the Warsaw edition).

YS   *Yalkut Shim'oni*

2. Rabbinic Authorities of the Mishnah and Talmud (Tannaim and Amoraim)

The major authorities cited by Heschel for his main argument comprise the teachers of the classic rabbinic period in Jewish thought. These include the Tannaim (teachers of the period of the Mishnah) and Amoraim (teachers of the period of the Talmud). They are conventionally grouped into "generations" of scholars as follows:

Generations of Tannaim
(Period of the Mishnah)

1	40–80 C.E.	Johanan ben Zakkai et al.
2	80–110 C.E.	Gamaliel II, Eliezer ben Hyrcanus, Joshua ben Hananiah, et al.
3	110–135 C.E.	Akiva, Ishmael, et al.
4	135–170 C.E.	Simeon ben Yohai, Judah ben Ilay, Meir, et al.
5	170–200 C.E.	Judah the Patriarch et al.

Generations of Amoraim
(Period of the Talmud)

		LAND OF ISRAEL	BABYLONIA
1	220–250 C.E.	Joshua ben Levi	Rav, Samuel
2	250–290 C.E.	Johanan, Resh Lakish	Huna, Judah
3	290–320 C.E.	Ammi, Assi, Zera	Rabbah, Joseph
4	320–350 C.E.	Hillel II	Abbaye, Rava
5	350–375 C.E.	Tanhuma ben Abba	Pappa
6	375–425 C.E.		Ashi, Ravina I
7	425–460 C.E.		Mar ben Rav Ashi
8	460–500 C.E.		Ravina II

Spelling. In this list, and in the text generally, we have adopted (with some slight simplification) the orthographic conventions of the *Encyclopedia Judaica*. Names occurring in the Bible retain the spelling of standard English Bible translations. Other names are spelled phonetically.

Patronymics. If the patronymic is enclosed in parentheses, then this is the rabbi generally understood when this name is used without patronymic. For example, "Rabbi Judah" without patronymic refers generally to Rabbi Judah (ben Ilay).

Titles. The following titles were in use to designate authorities of varying degree and provenance:

"Rabban" was used to designate the Nasi (Patriarch) of the Sanhedrin or Academy.

"Rabbi" was used to designate those fully ordained in the tradition of the Land of Israel—Tannaim and Amoraim of the Land of Israel.

"Rav" (indicated by "R." in our text) was used to designate the leading teachers of the Babylonian community.

Name	Tanna or Amora	Israel or Babylonia	Generation
Abbahu	Amora	Israel	2nd–3rd
Abbaye (*colleague of Rava*)	Amora	Babylonia	4th
Aha	Amora	Israel	4th
Akiva (ben Joseph)	Tanna		3rd
(*leader of one of the two great schools of thought analyzed in this volume*)			
Alexander (= Alexandri)	Amora	Israel	2nd–3rd
Ammi	Amora	Israel	3rd
Ashi	Amora	Babylonia	6th
(*played major part in redaction of the traditions of the Babylonian Talmud*)			
Avin (two teachers, father and son)	Amoraim	Babylonia	3rd–4th/5th
Bar Kappara (*Transitional*)	Tanna	Israel	5th
(*possibly identified with Eleazar ha-Kappar, or his son*)	Amora		1st
Berechiah (*aggadist*)	Amora	Israel	4th
Bibi	Amora	Israel	3rd
Dimi	Amora	Babylonia	3rd–4th
Eleazar ben Arakh	Tanna		2nd
(*favorite disciple of Johanan ben Zakkai, attracted to mysticism*)			
Eleazar ben Azariah	Tanna		3rd
Eleazar (ben Pedat)	Amora	Babylonia	2nd
		(*moved to Israel*)	
Eleazar ha-Kappar (Kappara)	Tanna		5th
Eleazar the Modaite (*of the town Modi'in*)	Tanna		3rd
Eliezer (ben Hyrcanus)	Tanna		2nd
(*one of Rabbi Akiva's primary teachers*)			
Eliezer ben Jacob (*disciple of Rabbi Akiva*)	Tanna		4th
Eliezer ben Yose the Galilean	Tanna		4th
Eliezer Hisma	Tanna		3rd
Elisha ben Avuyah	Tanna		3rd
(*colleague of Akiva, one of the "four who entered Pardes," later turned apostate*)			
Gamaliel (II)	Tanna (and Patriarch)		2nd
Hanina (bar Hama)	Amora	Israel	1st
Hillel			
(*pre-Tannaitic Pharisaic teacher, first century B.C.E., colleague of Shammai*)			

Name	Tanna or Amora	Israel or Babylonia	Generation
Hiyya (Rava—"the Greater") (*Transitional*)	Tanna		5th
(*student of Rabbi Judah the Patriarch, born in Babylonia but moved to Israel*)	Amora		1st
Hiyya bar Abba	Amora	Babylonia (*moved to Israel*)	3rd
Hoshaiah	Amora	Babylonia (*moved to Israel*)	3rd
Huna	Amora	Babylonia	2nd
Isaac (ben Aha)	Amora	Israel	2nd–3rd
Ishmael (ben Elisha)	Tanna		3rd
(*leader of one of the two great schools of thought analyzed in this volume*)			
Issi ben Judah (= Joseph the Babylonian)	Tanna		5th
Johanan (ben Nappaha)	Amora	Israel	2nd
Johanan ben Zakkai	Tanna		1st
(*established the Academy of Yavneh upon the destruction of Jerusalem in 70 C.E.*)			
Jonathan	Tanna		4th
(*disciple of Rabbi Ishmael; "Rabbi Jonathan" cited in halakhic midrashim refers to this authority*)			
Jonathan (ben Eleazar)	Amora	Israel	1st
(*"Rabbi Jonathan" cited in the aggadic midrashim refers to this authority*)			
Joseph (ben Hiyya)	Amora	Babylonia	3rd
Joshua (ben Hananiah)	Tanna		2nd
Joshua ben Levi	Amora	Israel	1st
Judah (ben Ezekiel)	Amora	Babylonia	2nd
Judah (ben Ilay)	Tanna		4th
(*disciple of Akiva*)			
Judah Nesiya	Amora	Israel	1st–2nd
(*grandson of Judah the Patriarch; served as Patriarch himself*)			
Judah the Patriarch	Tanna		5th
(*Hebrew: Yehudah ha-Nasi, also called "Rabbi; political leader of Jewish community in Israel in late second century; chief compiler of Mishnah*)			
Levi	Amora	Israel	2nd–3rd

Name	Tanna or Amora	Israel or Babylonia	Generation
Meir	Tanna		4th
(disciple of Akiva, major contributor to Mishnah)			
Nahum of Gimzo	Tanna		2nd
(one of Rabbi Akiva's primary teachers)			
Nathan (the Babylonian)	Tanna		4th
(associated with the Avot de-Rabbi Natan)			
Nehemiah	Tanna		4th
(traditional contributor of anonymous views in the Tosefta; student of Rabbi Akiva who often followed Rabbi Ishmael in aggadic matters)			
Phinehas (bar Hama ha-Kohen)	Amora	Israel	4th
Phinehas ben Jair	Tanna		5th
Rabbah (bar Nahmani)	Amora	Babylonia	3rd
Rav (R. Abba bar Aivu)	Amora	Babylonia	1st
(colleague of Samuel)			
Rava *(colleague of Abbaye)*	Amora	Babylonia	4th
Ravina	Amora	Babylonia	6th
(disciple-colleague of R. Ashi)			
Resh Lakish. *See* Simeon ben Lakish			
Samuel *(colleague of Rav)*	Amora	Babylonia	1st
Samuel bar Nahmani	Amora	Israel	2nd–3rd
Shammai *(pre-Tannaitic Pharisaic teacher, 1st century B.C.E., colleague of Hillel)*			
Sheshet	Amora	Babylonia	3rd
Simeon ben Azzai	Tanna		3rd
(collegue of Akiva, one of "four who entered Pardes)			
Simeon ben Gamaliel *(two rabbis of this name, both Patriarchs; most quoted remarks belong to the later rabbi)*			1st; 4th
Simeon (ben Yohai)	Tanna		4th
(disciple of Akiva, associated with the Tannaitic midrash Mekhilta of Rabbi Simeon ben Yohai; depicted in the Zohar [13th century] as the great teacher of mystical doctrine)			

Name	Tanna or Amora	Israel or Babylonia	Generation
Simeon ben Lakish (disciple and colleague of Johanan [ben Nappaha]; also called Resh Lakish, from a corruption of the abbreviation R.Sh.)	Amora	Israel	2nd
Simeon ben Zoma (colleague of Akiva, one of the "four who entered Pardes)	Tanna		3rd
Simlai	Amora	Israel	2nd
Simon	Amora	Israel	2nd–3rd
Tanhuma (bar Abba) (Midrash Tanhuma presumably named after this figure)	Amora	Israel	5th
Tarfon (senior colleague of Akiva)	Tanna		2nd–3rd
Yose (ben Halafta) (disciple of Akiva who generally followed Ishmael in aggadic matters)	Tanna		4th
Yose ben Hanina	Amora	Israel	2nd–3rd
Yose the Gailiean	Tanna		3rd
Zeira	Amora	Babylonia (moved to Israel)	3rd

3. Medieval and Modern Authorities

Heschel's references to medieval and modern authorities in this work are important for seeing how the issues he examines were played out in Jewish thought of different periods and places. This list will assist the reader in placing Heschel's discussion in the context of general Jewish intellectual history. Spellings of names, dates, and biographical data are taken, for the most part, from the *Encyclopedia Judaica*. Names in biblical texts follow the spelling of standard English translations of the Bible. Other names are spelled phonetically.

N.B. Personalities are generally listed by first name if they lived prior to the Renaissance and by surname from the Renaissance onward. However, major medieval thinkers (e.g., Maimonides, Halevi, and others) are listed by their generally known names. Names with Arabic patronymics (Ibn . . .) are generally listed under "Ibn."

AARON BEN ABRAHAM IBN HAYYIM. Morocco. 16th–17th cent. Author of *Korban Aharon,* commentary on Sifra.

ABOAB, ISAAC. Spain (?). Late 14th cent. Author of the moralistic treatise *Menorat ha-Maor* [Candlestick of Light].

ABRAHAM BEN DAVID OF POSQUIERES (RaABaD). Provence. 1125–1198. Commentator on Talmud, Sifra, Maimonides, Alfasi, etc.

ABRAHAM BEN MOSES BEN MAIMON. Egypt. 1186–1237. Son of Maimonides, halakhist and philosopher.

ABRAVANEL, ISAAC. Spain. 1437–1508. Statesman, biblical commentator, and philosopher.

ABUDARHAM, DAVID BEN JOSEPH. Spain. 14th cent. Liturgical commentator.

ADRET, SOLOMON BEN ABRAHAM (RaSHBA). Spain. 1235–1310. Major talmudist, commentator, and halakhist.

AL-NAKAWA, ISRAEL. Spain. d. 1391. Moralist; his *Menorat Ha-Ma'or* served as source for Isaac Aboab's work (1514) of the same name.

ALBO, JOSEPH. Spain. ca. 1365–ca. 1465. Philosopher, author of *Ikkarim* [Principles of Faith].

ALFASI, ISAAC. Morocco. 1013–1103. Major talmudic codifier, author of standard halakhic digest of the Talmud.

ALMOSNINO, MOSES. Salonika. 1515–1580. Commentator on Torah, supercommentator on Ibn Ezra.

ALSHEKH, MOSES. Levant/Safed. d. ca. 1593. Author of Torah commentary *Torat Moshe.*

ANAV, ZEDEKIAH BEN ABRAHAM. Italy. 13th cent. Talmudist, author of *Shibbolei Ha-Leket,* a halakhic compendium on the liturgy.

ARISTOBULUS OF PANEAS. 2nd cent. B.C.E. Hellenistic philosopher.

ASHER BEN JEHIEL (ROSH). Germany, Spain. ca. 1250–1327. Major talmudist and codifier, author of digest of Talmud after Alfasi.

ASHKENAZI, ELIEZER. Levant, Poland. 1513–1586. Author of Tora commentary *Ma'aseh Adonai.*

ASHKENAZI, JOSEPH. Safed, eastern Europe. 1525–1577. Mishnah commentator and antirationalist polemicist.

ASHKENAZI, ZEVI HIRSCH ("Hakkam Zevi"). Germany, Holland. 1660–1718. Halakhist who addressed questions of philosophy and mysticism.

ATTAR, HAYYIM BEN MOSES IBN. Morocco, Italy, Israel. 1696–1743. Author of Torah commentary *Or Ha-Hayyim,* which expresses mystical outlook.

AZRIEL OF GERONA. Spain. Early 13th cent. Kabbalist, sometimes confused with Ezra ben Solomon.

AZULAI, ABRAHAM BEN MORDECAI. Morocco, Israel. 1570–1643. Kabbalist.

AZULAI, HAYYIM JOSEPH DAVID (HIDA). Israel, Italy. 1724–1806. Halakhist and kabbalist

BA'AL SHEM TOV. *See* Israel ben Eliezer Ba'al Shem Tov.

BACHARACH, JAIR HAYYIM. Germany. 1638–1702. Halakhist who combined Kabbalah with general learning

BACHARACH, MOSES SAMSON. Germany. 1607–1670. Halakhist.

BACHARACH, NAPHTALI. Germany. Early 17th cent. Kabbalist of the Lurianic school, author of *Emek Ha-Melekh.*

BAHYA BEN ASHER ("Rabbenu Bahya"). Spain. 13th cent. Author of popular mystically inclined Torah commentary.

BANETH, EZEKIEL BEN JACOB. Hungary. 1773–1854. Preacher and teacher.

BEKHOR SHOR, JOSEPH. France. 12th cent. Biblical "peshat" commentator.

BERECHIAH BERAKH BEN ISAAC EISIK. Poland. d. 1663. Preacher, Torah commentator.

BERLIN, ISAIAH. Germany. 1725–1799. Talmudist, commentator, and bibliographer.

BERTINORO, OBADIAH BEN ABRAHAM YARE. Italy. ca. 1450–ca. 1516. Author of standard commentary on Mishnah.

BONFILS, JOSEPH BEN ELIEZER THE SEPHARDI. Spain, Levant. Late 14th cent. Author of *Tzafnat Pa'neah* (supercommentary on Ibn Ezra).

CARO, ISAAC. Spain, Turkey. 15th–16th cents. Uncle of Joseph Caro, wrote Torah commentary *Toledot Yitzhak.*

CARO, JOSEPH. Spain, Turkey, Safed. 1488–1575. Epochal halakhist and kabbalist, author of *Shulhan Arukh* and *Maggid Mesharim.*

CHAJES, ZEVI HIRSCH. Austria, Poland. 1805–1855. Talmudist, pioneer in talmudic methodology.

CORDOVERO, MOSES (RaMaK). Safed. 1522–1570. Kabbalist, author of *Pardes Rimmonim,* etc.

CRESCAS, HASDAI. Spain. d. ca. 1412. Philosopher, critic of Maimonides.

DAVID BEN LEVI OF NARBONNE. Provence. Late 13th cent. Halakhist, author of *Ha-Mikhtam.*

DAVID BEN SAMUEL HALEVI ("TaZ" < Turei Zahav). Poland. 1586–1667. Halakhist, wrote commentary *Turei Zahav* on the *Shulhan Arukh*.

DAVID BEN SOLOMON IBN ABI ZIMRA (RaDBaZ). Egypt. 1479–1573. Talmudist, halakhist, kabbalist.

DURAN, ISAAC PROFIAT (EPHoD). Spain. d. 1414. Philosopher and polemicist, author of *Ma'asei Ephod*.

DURAN, SIMEON BEN ZEMAH (RaShBaTZ). Majorca, Algiers. 1361–1444. Halakhist and philosopher.

EDELS, SAMUEL ELIEZER BEN JUDAH (MaHaRShA). Poland. 1555–1631. Talmudic commentator with great interest in Aggadah.

EILENBURG, ISSACHAR BAER. Prague. 16th–17th cent. Author of Torah commentary *Tzedah La-Derekh* (1623).

EINHORN, ZE'EV WOLF (MaHaRZU). Commentator on Midrash Rabbah.

ELEAZAR BEN JUDAH OF WORMS. Germany. ca. 1165–ca. 1230. Halakhist and mystic.

ELIEZER BEN NATHAN OF MAINZ (RaBaN). Germany, ca. 1090–ca. 1170. Early German-Jewish halakhist.

ELIJAH BEN SOLOMON OF VILNA (GRA). Lithuania. 1720–1797. Major talmudic scholar and intellectual exemplar.

ELYASHUV, SOLOMON BEN HAYYIM HAIKEL. Ukraine, Israel. 19th–20th cent. Kabbalist.

EMDEN, JACOB (YaVeTZ). Germany. 1697–1776. Halakhist, kabbalist, anti-Sabbatean polemicist.

EYBESCHUETZ, JONATHAN. Poland. 1690/5–1764. Talmudist, kabbalist.

EZRA BEN SOLOMON OF GERONA. Spain. d. 1238/45. Kabbalist, sometimes confused with Azriel of Gerona

FANO, MENAHEM AZARIAH DA. Italy. 1548–1620. Kabbalist, propagated Safed kabbalism in Europe.

GANS, DAVID BEN SOLOMON. Prague. 1541–1613. Chronicler and astronomer.

GERSONIDES (Levi ben Gershom, RaLBaG). Provence. 1288–1344. Philosopher and biblical commentator.

GIKATILLA, JOSEPH BEN ABRAHAM. Spain. 1248–ca. 1325. Kabbalist, author of *Sha'arei Orah,* influential on the Zohar.

GOMBINER, ABRAHAM ABELE BEN HAYYIM. Poland. 1637–1683. Halakhist, author of *Magen Avraham* (commentary on *Shulhan Arukh*).

HAI BEN SHERIRA GAON. Babylonia. 939–1038. Major gaonic halakhist.

HALEVI, EZEKIEL EZRA BEN JOSHUA. Iraq, Israel. 1852–1942. Scholar and poet, author of *Arugat Ha-Bosem* on the Aggadah.

HALEVI, JUDAH. Spain. ca. 1075–1141. Poet and philosopher, author of *Kuzari*.

HANANEL BEN HUSHIEL (Rabbenu Hananel). North Africa. d. 1055/6. Major early Talmudic commentator.

HAYYIM BEN ISAAC. Germany. Late 13th cent. Halakhist, called *"Or Zaru'a"* after the title of his father's (Isaac of Vienna's) work.

HEZEKIAH BEN MANOAH (Hizkuni). France. Mid-13th cent. Author of Torah commentary *Hizkuni*

HILLEL BEN SAMUEL "OF VERONA." Italy. ca. 1220–ca. 1295. Philosopher, moderately pro-Maimonidean

HOROWITZ, ISAIAH BEN ABRAHAM. Poland, Israel. 1565?–1630. Kabbalist, author of *Shnei Luhot Ha-Berit*.

HOROWITZ, PHINEHAS. Germany. 1730–1805. Halakhist with mystical tendencies, author of *Sefer Hafla'ah*.

IBN EZRA, ABRAHAM. Spain, Europe. 1089–1164. Philosopher, biblical commentator, and poet.

IBN GABBAI, MEIR. Egypt. Early 16th cent. Kabbalist, author of *Avodat Ha-Kodesh* (1531).

IBN GAON, SHEM TOV BEN ABRAHAM. Spain, Safed. 13th–14th cent. Kabbalist and halakhist; his mystical work is found in *Sefer Tagin,* ed. S. Sachs (Paris: Y. L. Bargis, 1865).

IBN HABIB, JACOB BEN SOLOMON. Spain, Salonika. 15th–16th cent. Author of *Ein Ya'akov,* the standard traditional anthology of the Aggadah from the Talmud, with occasional enlightening variants and paraphrases.

IBN SHEM TOV, SHEM TOV. Spain. ca. 1380–ca. 1441. Kabbalist and anti-Maimonidean polemicist.

IBN SHEM TOV, SHEM TOV BEN JOSEPH. Spain. Late 15th cent. Commentator on Maimonides' *Guide*.

IBN SHUAIB, JOSHUA. Spain. Early 14th cent. Wrote sermons on the Torah with mystical tendencies.

IBN ZUR, ISAAC LEON. Italy. 16th cent. Author of commentary *Megillat Esther* on Maimonides (Venice, 1592).

ISAAC BEN MOSES OF VIENNA. France, Germany. ca. 1180–ca. 1250. Halakhist, author of *Or Zarua*

ISAAC BEN SAMUEL OF ACRE. Israel, Spain. 13th–14th cent. Kabbalist.

ISAAC BEN SHESHET PERFET (RIBaSH). Spain. 1326–1408. Halakhist.

ISRAEL BEN ELIEZER BA'AL SHEM TOV (BeSHT). Ukraine. ca. 1700–1760. Charismatic leader, founder of Hasidic movement.

JACOB BEN HAYYIM IBN ADONIJAH. Italy. ca. 1470–ca. 1538. Masoretic scholar and early printer.

JACOB OF DUBNO. *See* Kranz.

JACOB OF VIENNA. Austria. 14th–15th cent. Halakhist and Torah commentator.

JAFFE, MORDECAI. Poland. ca. 1535–1612. Halakhist, kabbalist, and polymath, author of *Levush*.

JAFFE, SAMUEL BEN ISAAC ASHKENAZI. Constantinople. 16th cent. Midrashic commentator, author of *Yefeh Mareh, Yefeh To'ar*, etc.

JEHIEL MICHAEL BEN UZZIEL OF GLOINE. Germany. 18th cent. Kabbalist

JONAH BEN ABRAHAM GERONDI. Spain. ca. 1200–1263. Moralist, halakhist, and commentator.

JOSEPHUS FLAVIUS. Israel, Rome. ca. 38–100 C.E. Jewish historian of the Roman period, wrote *Jewish Antiquities* and *The Jewish War*

JUDAH BEN BARZILLAI ("of Barcelona"). Spain. 11th–12th cent. Halakhist and commentator on Sefer Yetzirah.

JUDAH BEN SAMUEL HE-HASID. Germany. 12th cent. Mystic-pietist, leader of Hasidei Ashkenaz movement.

JUDAH LOEW OF PRAGUE (MaHaRaL). Prague. 16th cent. Communal leader, mystic, polymath.

KALLIR, ELEAZAR. Israel. 6th–7th cent. (?). Greatest of the early liturgical poets (*payyetanim*).

KIMHI, DAVID (RaDaK). Provence. 1160?–1235? Biblical commentator of the philosophical-peshat type.

KIRKISANI, JOSEPH BEN JACOB. Iraq. Early 10th cent. Karaite commentator.

KRANZ, JACOB ("Maggid") OF DUBNO. Poland. 1741–1804. Popular itinerant preacher.

LEON, MOSES DE. *See* Moses ben Shem Tov de Leon.

LEVI ISAAC OF BERDITCHEV. Ukraine. ca. 1740–1810. Hasidic tzaddik and preacher.

LURIA, DAVID BEN JUDAH. Lithuania. 1798–1855. Talmudist and midrashic commentator.

LURIA, ISAAC BEN SOLOMON (ARI). Safed. 1534–1572. Kabbalist, founded "Lurianic" school of Kabbalah.

LURIA, SOLOMON BEN JEHIEL (MaHaRSHaL). Poland. 1510?–1574. Talmudist and halakhist.

MAIMON BEN JOSEPH ("the Judge"). Spain. d. 1165/70. Father of Maimonides.

MAIMONIDES, MOSES BEN MAIMON (RaMBaM). Spain, Egypt. 1135–1204. Halakhist, codifier and seminal philosopher.

MEIR SIMHA HA-KOHEN OF DVINSK. Russia. 1843–1926. Talmudist.

MEIRI, MENAHEM BEN SOLOMON. Provence. 1249–1316. Talmudic commentator.

MENAHEM BEN AARON IBN ZERAH. Spain. 1310–1385. Codifier, author of *Tzedah La-Derekh.*

MENAHEM ZIYYONI. Germany. 14th–15th cent. Kabbalist, author of *Ziyyoni,* a homiletical commentary on the Torah.

MESSER LEON, DAVID BEN JUDAH. Italy. 1470/72?–1526? Rabbi and philosopher, pro-Maimonidean.

MIZRAHI, ELIJAH. Turkey. ca. 1450–1526. Halakhist and supercommentator on Rashi.

MOELLIN, JACOB BEN MOSES (MaHaRIL). Germany. 1360?–1427. Halakhist, communal leader, codifier of customary practices.

MORDECAI BEN HILLEL HA-KOHEN. Germany. 1240?–1298. Talmudist, author of *The Mordecai* on the Talmud.

MORDECAI HA-KOHEN. Author of Torah commentary *Siftei Kohen* (Venice, 1605).

MOSES BEN JACOB OF COUCY. France. 13th cent. Talmudist and itinerant preacher.

MOSES BEN JOSHUA OF NARBONNE. Provence. d. 1362. Philosopher of Averroist tendency, commentator on Maimonides' *Guide*.

MOSES BEN SHEM TOV DE LEON. Spain. ca. 1240–1305. Kabbalist, author of the Zohar and numerous other books.

MOSES HA-DARSHAN. Provence. 11th cent. Aggadist, probably influenced the literary evolution of Genesis Rabbati.

MUELHAUSEN, YOM TOV LIPMANN. Bohemia. 14th–15th cent. Rabbinic scholar, philosopher, and kabbalist.

NAHMANIDES, MOSES BEN NAHMAN (RaMBaN). Spain. 1194–1270. Talmudist, philosopher, kabbalist, and biblical commentator.

NAJARA, JUDAH. Turkey.

NARBONI, MOSES. *See* Moses ben Joshua of Narbonne

NATHAN BEN JEHIEL OF ROME. Italy. 1035–ca. 1110. Talmudic lexicographer, author of *Arukh*

NETHANEL BEN ISAIAH. Yemen. 14th cent. Midrashist, author of *Nur al-Tzalam*.

NIETO, DAVID. England. 1654–1728. Philosopher and polemicist.

NISSIM BEN JACOB. Kairouan. ca. 990–1062. Talmudist, and author of tale-collection *Hibbur me-ha-Yeshu'ah*

NISSIM BEN REUBEN GERONDI (RaN, Rabbenu Nissim). Spain. 1310?–1375?. Talmudist, commentator on Tractate Nedarim and Alfasi's digest.

NORZI, JEDIDIAH SOLOMON RAPHAEL. Italy. 1560–1616. Biblical and masoretic scholar, author of *Minhat Shai*.

PARDO, DAVID SAMUEL BEN JACOB. Italy, Sarajevo, Israel. 1718–1790. Rabbinic scholar, standard commentator on Tosefta and Sifrei.

PHILO JUDAEUS (of Alexandria). Egypt. ca. 20 B.C.E.–50 C.E. Hellenistic philosopher, author of many works (in Greek) interpreting the Torah allegorically in the light of Greek philosophy.

RASHI (Solomon ben Isaac). France. 1040–1105. Seminal commentator on the Bible and Talmud.

RECANATI, MENAHEM BEN BENJAMIN. Italy. 13th–14th cent. Kabbalistic commentator and halakhist.

SAADIA (BEN JOSEPH) GAON. Egypt, Babylonia. 882–942. Halakhic authority, first medieval Jewish philosopher, also polemicist and biblical commentator.

SABA, ABRAHAM. Spain. d. 1508. Preacher and kabbalist, author of mystical Torah commentary *Tzeror Ha-Mor*.

SAMSON BEN ISAAC OF CHINON. France. 14th cent. Talmudist, late tosafist.

SAMUEL BEN MEIR (RaSHBaM). France. ca. 1080/85–ca. 1174. Biblical "peshat" commentator, grandson of Rashi.

SCHIFF, MEIR BEN JACOB HA-KOHEN (MaHaRaM). Germany. 1605–1641. Talmudic commentator.

SEGAL, SAMUEL BEN R. JUDAH LOEB. Poland. 18th cent. Anthologist of early Hasidism.

SFORNO, OBADIAH BEN JACOB. Italy. ca. 1470–ca. 1550. Biblical commentator.

SHNEUR ZALMAN OF LYADY. Russia. 1745–1813. Hasidic leader, founder of Habad school of Hasidism (later known as Lubavitch).

SIMHA BEN SAMUEL OF VITRI. France. 11th cent. Author of *Mahzor Vitri,* major source for development of liturgy.

SOFER, MOSES ("Hatam Sofer"). Germany, Hungary. 1762–1839. Halakhist, major leader of nineteenth-century Orthodoxy.

SPIRA, NATHAN NATA BEN SOLOMON. Poland. 1585–1633. Kabbalist, virtuoso of *gematria,* author of *Megalleh Amukkot.*

STRASHUN, SAMUEL BEN JOSEPH. Lithuania. 1794–1872. Talmudic commentator.

TAM, JACOB BEN MEIR. France. ca. 1100–1171. Grandson of Rashi, major talmudist and halakhic innovator, leader of "tosafist" school.

TEMPLO, SOLOMON JUDAH LEAO. Netherlands. d. 1733. Educator and preacher.

TOBIAS BEN ELIEZER. Balkans. Late 11th cent. Author of the midrashic commentary *Midrash Lekah Tov*

TRANI, MOSES BEN JOSEPH (MaBIT). Safed. 1500–1580. Halakhist, philosopher, moralist.

UCEDA, SAMUEL BEN ISAAC DE. Safed. b. 1540. Talmudist, preacher, kabbalist of Lurianic school.

VITAL, HAYYIM BEN JOSEPH. Safed. 1542–1620. Kabbalist, disseminator of Isaac Luria's teachings, author of *Etz Ha-Hayyim,* etc.

YEHUDAI GAON. Babylonia. 8th cent. Talmudic authority, head of Sura academy ca. 757–761, first gaon to compile responsa.

YOM TOV BEN ABRAHAM ISHBILI (= of Seville) (RITBA). Spain. 1250–1330. Talmudic commentator.

ZADOK HA-KOHEN OF LUBLIN. Poland. 1823–1900. Hasidic leader, combined interests in Halakhah, Kabbalah, and history.

ZARZA, SAMUEL IBN SENEH. Spain. 14th cent. Author of philosophic commentary *Mekor Hayyim*

Guide to Acronyms and Nicknames

ARI	Luria, Isaac ben Solomon
Baal Shem Tov	Israel ben Eliezer Ba'al Shem Tov
BeSHT	Israel ben Eliezer Ba'al Shem Tov
EPHoD	Duran, Isaac Profiat
GRA	Elijah ben Solomon of Vilna
Hakham Zevi	Ashkenazi, Zevi Hirsch
Hatam Sofer	Sofer, Moses
HIDA	Azulai, Hayyim Joseph David
Hizkuni	Hezekiah ben Manoah
MaBIT	Trani, Moses ben Joseph
MaHaRaL	Judah Loew of Prague

MaHaRaM	Schiff, Meir ben Jacob Ha-Kohen
MaHaRIL	Moellin, Jacob ben Moses
MaHaRShA	Edels, Samuel Eliezer ben Judah
MaHaRSHaL	Luria, Solomon ben Jehiel
MaHaRZU	Einhorn, Ze'ev Wolf
RaABaD	Abraham ben David of Posquieres
RaBaN	Eliezer ben Nathan of Mainz
Rabbenu Bahya	Bahya ben Asher
Rabbenu Hananel	Hananel ben Hushiel
Rabbenu Nissim	Nissim ben Reuben Gerondi
RaDaK	Kimhi, David
RaDBaZ	David ben Solomon Ibn Abi Zimra
RaLBaG	Gersonides (Levi ben Gershom)
RaMaK	Cordovero, Moses
RaMBaM	Maimonides, Moses
RaMBaN	Nahmanides, Moses
RaN	Nissim ben Reuben Gerondi
RaSHBA	Adret, Solomon ben Abraham
RaSHBaM	Samuel ben Meir
RaShBaTZ	Duran, Simeon ben Zemah
Resh Lakish	Rabbi Simeon ben Lakish (Amora of Israel)
RIBaSH	Isaac ben Sheshet Perfet
RITBA	Yom Tov ben Abraham Ishbili (= of Seville)
ROSH	Asher ben Jehiel
TaZ (< Turei Zahav)	David ben Samuel Halevi
YaVeTZ	Emden, Jacob

4. Primary Literary Sources

The following list comprises the majority of the primary sources that Heschel cites repeatedly in this work. Most are listed by title, either because they were anonymous or collective works, or because though the author or compiler is known, the work has acquired a personality and reputation of its own far overshadowing its human author. A few of the outstanding personalities whom Heschel cites (Maimonides, etc.) are listed here for the purpose of bibliographic familiarization.

Source references of many of these works are given by paragraph or chapter. Though these are not always entirely uniform in all editions, they are generally the best guide. In cases where references are by page number, they are according to the standard modern Hebrew edition of that work.

Thanks to the recent efforts of numerous scholars, the majority of primary sources that Heschel cites are now available in English translations. These are listed here so that the interested reader with little or no knowledge of Hebrew can explore further in the primary sources.

Avot. *Pirkei Avot* [Ethics of the Fathers], a short collection of ethical maxims of the Sages of the first and second centuries B.C.E. and C.E. Textual references are given according to the standard editions of the Mishnah, which differ slightly in paragraph division from the version in the traditional Jewish prayer book. There are several English editions, including *The Living Talmud: The Wisdom of the Fathers and Its Classical Commentaries, Selected and Translated with an Essay,* by Judah Goldin (New York: New American Library, 1957). *Pirkei Avot* is also included in the fourth division of any edition of the Mishnah, and in most traditional "daily" prayer books.

Avot de-Rabbi Natan. Much more discursive than *Avot,* this supplements the same and additional maxims with a wealth of anecdotes about the Tannaitic masters. The standard Hebrew edition is that of Solomon Schechter (3rd corrected edition by Feldheim in 1967), giving "A" and "B" versions. For an English edition, see Judah Goldin, *The Fathers According to Rabbi Nathan,* Yale Judaica Series 10 (New Haven: Yale University Press, 1955) (based on "A" version).

Babylonian Talmud. Edited in Babylonia in the fifth to seventh centuries, with gradual accretions for the next several centuries, this is the greatest classic of Jewish law and lore after the Bible. Pagination follows the nineteenth-century Vilna edition. The first complete English translation was *The Soncino Talmud* (London: Soncino Press, 1935–48). A compact edition was published in 1961, and facing-page editions since then. This is still a classic, but difficult for the novice. More recent English translations include those by Jacob Neusner, (*The Talmud of Babylonia* [Atlanta: Scholars Press, 1984–96]) and Adin Steinsaltz (*The Talmud* [New York: Random House, 1989–(proceeding slowly)]).

Beit Ha-Midrash. This anthology of midrashim in Hebrew, with German apparatus, was recovered from manuscript in the nineteenth century, edited by Adolph Jellinek (Jerusalem: Bamberger & Wahrman, 1938).

Ein Ya'akov. This is a compilation of the nonlegal, folkloristic passages of the Babylonian Talmud, with occasional enlightening variants and paraphrases. It was compiled by Jacob ben Solomon ibn Habib (1445–1515/16, Spain and Salonika). An archaic English edition by Rabbi S. H. Glick (5 volumes, facing English and Hebrew columns, 1916) was reprinted by Traditional Press. A newer English translation (by A. Finkel) has been published by Jason Aronson, Northvale, N.J., 1999.

Josephus. For a one-volume edition of all his extant works, see *The Works of Josephus* (Peabody, Mass.: Hendrickson Publishers, 1987).

Maimonides. There is a wealth of material available in English from the writings of this seminal medieval thinker, including the following:

> *The Guide of the Perplexed.* Edited by Shlomo Pines. 2 volumes. Chicago: University of Chicago Press, 1963.
>
> *Mishneh Torah,* Volumes 1–2, *The Book of Knowledge, The Book of Adoration.* Edited by Moses Hyamson. Jerusalem, 1965. English and Hebrew on facing pages.
>
> *Mishneh Torah: The Code of Maimonides.* Volumes 2–14. New Haven: Yale University Press, 1949–2004.
>
> *The Commandments* (*Sefer ha-Mitzvot*). Edited by Charles Chavel. 2 volumes. London: Soncino Press, 1967.
>
> *A Maimonides Reader.* Edited by Isadore Twersky. New York: Behrman House, 1972. Includes including extensive selections from the *Mishneh Torah* and abridgments of "Eight Chapters" (ethical treatise prefacing his commentary on *Avot*), and "Helek" (introduction to Sanhedrin chapter 10, enumerating his Thirteen Principles of belief).

Mekilta de-Rabbi Ishmael. This Tannaitic midrash on Exodus is attributed to the school of Rabbi Ishmael (second–third centuries). English edition, edited by Jacob Z. Lauterbach. 3 volumes. Philadelphia: Jewish Publication Society, 1933.

Mekilta de-Rabbi Simeon ben Yohai. This Tannaitic midrash on Exodus, attributed to the school of Rabbi Akiva (second–third centuries), was reconstructed by modern scholars from manuscript fragments and quotations in later works. The pagination follows the edition of J. N. Epstein. Hebrew only (Jerusalem: Shaare Rahamim, 1979).

Midrash Haggadol. This thirteenth-century anthology of earlier midrashim on the Torah, compiled by David ben Amram Adani of Aden is published in separate volumes (Hebrew only), as follows:

> Genesis. By Mordecai Margulies. Jerusalem: Mossad ha-Rav Kuk, 1947.

Exodus. By Mordecai Margulies. Jerusalem: Mossad ha-Rav Kuk, 1956.

Leviticus. Pagination follows edition by E. N. Rabinowitz. New York: Jewish Theological Seminary, 1930. There is a more recent edition by Adin Steinzaltz (Mossad ha-Rav Kuk, 1975). This is the current standard, but was later than Heschel's work.

Numbers. By Rabbi Dr. Solomon Fisch (London, 1957) (notes in English).

Deuteronomy. By Solomon Fisch. Jerusalem: Mossad ha-Rav Kuk, 1972.

Midrash on Psalms. A midrashic compendium based on the book of Psalms. English version: *Midrash on Psalms.* Edited by William Braude. 2 volumes. New Haven: Yale University Press, 1959.

Midrash Rabbah. The most famous of the classical post-Tannaitic midrashim, artificially pieced together centuries ago from diverse origins. Includes midrashim on books of the Torah and the "Five Scrolls" (Song of Songs, Ruth, Lamentations, Ecclesiastes, and Esther). English edition: *Midrash Rabbah.* 10 volumes. London: Soncino Press, 1939.

"Minor Tractates." The standard modern Hebrew editions were edited by Michael Higger. In 1965, Soncino Press published *The Minor Tractates of the Talmud* (2 volumes) including: *Soferim, Avot of Rabbi Nathan, Semahot* [Mourning], *Kallah, Kallah Rabbati, Derekh Eretz Rabbah, Derekh Eretz Zuta, Perek Ha-Shalom, Gerim, Kuthim, Abadim, Sefer Torah, Tefillin, Zizith, and Mezuzah.* In 1966, Yale University Press published *The Tractate Mourning (Semahot)*, edited by Dov Zlotnick, with critical notes.

Mishnah. This classic legal compendium, compiled around 200 C.E. by Judah the Patriarch, is the basis of the Babylonian Talmud and Talmud of the Land of Israel. English versions include the following:

Herbert Danby. Oxford: Oxford University Press, 1933.

Philip Blackman. New York: Judaica Press, 1964 (with facing Hebrew and helpful notes).

Pinhas Kehati. Magisterial Hebrew annotated version (1977) now in English (Jerusalem: Eliner Library, 1994–96).

Jacob Neusner. New Haven: Yale University Press, 1988.

Nahmanides. The principal work of this medieval mystic, cited frequently by Heschel, is available in English: Ramban (Nahmanides). *Commentary on the Torah.* Edited by Charles B. Chavel. 5 volumes. New York: Shilo, 1971.

Palestinian Talmud. *See* Talmud of the Land of Israel.

Pesikta de-Rav Kahana. Midrashic compendium organized according to the holiday sermonic calendar. Pagination follows Solomon Buber's Hebrew edition. English version: *Pesikta de-Rab Kahana.* Edited by William Braude and Israel Kapstein. Philadelphia: Jewish Publication Society, 1975.

Pesikta Rabbati. Similar to *Pesikta de-Rav Kahana.* Pagination follows Meir Ish Shalom [Friedmann]'s Hebrew edition. English version: *Pesikta Rabbati.* Edited by William Braude. 2 volumes. New Haven: Yale University Press, 1968.

Philo. His works are available in the Loeb Classical Library (Harvard University Press). In addition, several anthologies have appeared, notably *The Essential Philo,* edited by Nahum N. Glatzer (New York: Schocken Books, 1971).

Saadia Gaon. His philosophical work *Sefer Ha-Emunot veha-Deot* was the first major medieval Jewish philosophical book. English edition: *Book of Beliefs and Opinions.* Edited by Samuel Rosenblatt. New Haven: Yale University Press, 1948.

Shulhan Arukh. Code of Jewish law by Joseph Caro, with supplementary material by Moses Isserles, sixteenth century.

Sifra. Tannaitic midrash on Leviticus, attributed to the school of Rabbi Akiva (second–third centuries), with some portions apparently derived from the school of Rabbi Ishmael. Pagination follows the Hebrew edition of Isaac Hirsch Weiss. English edition: *Sifra.* Edited by Jacob Neusner. 3 volumes. Atlanta: Scholars Press & Brown University, 1988.

Sifre. Tannaitic midrash on Numbers and Deuteronomy, combining teachings of the schools of Rabbi Ishmael and Rabbi Akiva (second–third centuries). There are separate English editions per book, as follows:
> *Sifre to Numbers.* Edited by Jacob Neusner. Atlanta: Scholars Press and Brown University, 1986.
> *Sifre to Deuteronomy.* Edited by Jacob Neusner. 2 volumes. Atlanta: Scholars Press, 1987.
> *Sifre to Deuteronomy.* Edited by Reuven Hammer. New Haven: Yale University Press, 1986.

Sifre Zuta. A variant of *Sifre* on Numbers, from the Akivan school. Pagination follows the Hebrew edition of Horowitz.

Talmud of the Land of Israel. Edited in Israel in the fourth–fifth centuries, also called Talmud Yerushalmi (Jerusalem Talmud) or Palestinian Talmud, this is a parallel work to Babylonian Talmud, but less fully developed and far less influential in later Jewish thought. Pagination follows the classical Daniel Bomberg printed edition (Venice, 1523–24). English edition: *The Talmud of the Land of Israel.* Jacob Neusner, general editor. 35 volumes. Chicago: University of Chicago Press, 1982–(organized by chapter and paragraph, does not cross-reference to the Venice pagination).

Tanhuma. An early medieval midrashic collection following the order of the Torah, which exists in two substantially different forms. The one is called simply "Tanhuma," or "Tanhuma, Warsaw (printed) edition." The other was discovered in manuscript and edited by Solomon Buber and is called "Tanhuma Buber," or "Tanhuma, Buber's edition" (TB in the footnotes of this work). Ktav Publishers (Hoboken, N.J.) has published parts of both of these: *Midrash Tanhuma*, "printed" version, by Samuel A. Berman, on Genesis-Exodus (1996); *Midrash Tanhuma*, S. Buber Recension, by John T. Townsend, on Genesis (1989), on Exodus-Leviticus (1997), on Numbers-Deuteronomy (2003).

Tanna De-vei Eliyahu. A *sui-generis* freeform midrashic compendium (early medieval), purporting to emanate from the school of the prophet Elijah. Pagination follows Meir Ish Shalom [Friedmann]'s Hebrew edition. English version: *Tanna De-Be Eliyahu.* Edited by William Braude and Israel Kapstein. Philadelphia: Jewish Publication Society, 1981.

Tannaitic Midrashim. A collective term comprising both *Mekhiltas, Sifra, Sifre,* and Midrash Tannaim. See Glossary (appendix 5) for breakdown by schools.

Tosefta. A shadow work of the Mishnah, comprising variant and alternative legal traditions organized in the same rubric of "orders" and "tractates." The authoritative edition of the Tosefta was edited by Saul Lieberman (with separate exhaustive commentary *Tosefta Ki-feshuta*), covering the first three-and-one-half orders. English edition: *The Tosefta.* Translated from the Hebrew by Jacob Neusner. New York: Ktav, 1979-86.

Yalkut Shimoni. A popular comprehensive anthology of midrashim, arranged in the order of the Bible, most likely written in Germany in the thirteenth century. Hebrew only.

Zohar. The thirteenth-century classic of Jewish mysticism is today in print in many Hebrew editions. Pagination follows the nineteenth-century Vilna edition. English version: *The Zohar.* 2nd ed. London: Soncino Press, 1984. A new translation is in preparation by Daniel Matt. Two volumes covering much of Genesis have been published by Stanford University Press (2003, 2004). In addition, Isaiah Tishby's magisterial topical anthology *Mishnat Ha-Zohar* is now available in English: *The Wisdom of the Zohar,* 3 volumes (New York: Oxford University Press, 1989).

5. Glossary of Terms

a fortiori. *See kal vahomer.*

aggadah (pl. *aggadot*). (1) An exemplary or homiletic tale. (2) Aggadah (collective): The lore of the rabbis, inclusive of tales, proverbs, and obiter dicta.

Amora (pl. Amoraim). A rabbinic teacher of the period between the closure of the Mishnah and the first compilation of the Talmud, approximately 200–500 C.E.

Generations of Amoraim (according to Steinsaltz)

		Land of Israel	Babylonia
1	220–250 C.E.	Joshua ben Levi	Rav, Samuel
2	250–290 C.E.	Johanan, Resh Lakish	Huna, Judah
3	290–320 C.E.	Ammi, Assi, Zera	Rabbah, Joseph
4	320–350 C.E.	Hillel II	Abbaye, Rava
5	350–375 C.E.	Tanhuma ben Abba	Pappa
6	375–425 C.E.		Ashi, Ravina I
7	425–460 C.E.		Mar ben Rav Ashi
8	460–500 C.E.		Ravina II

apikoros (from "Epicurus," hence Epicurean). A heretic, especially one who denies active providence. The ancient Epicureans taught that the gods do not care for humankind. The term *apikoros* probably originally entered the rabbinic vocabulary from their recognition of this aspect of Epicurean philosophy. However, later Jewish teachers (who were not directly familiar with classic Epicureanism) applied the term to disbelievers in general.

Aspaklaryah. Rabbinic adaptation of Latin *specularium,* "mirror or lens." Medium through which one sees or perceives; perspective. Used by Heschel in three contexts: (1) Rabbinic contrast between "a bright speculum" and "a dark speculum," contrasting the perfect clarity of Moses' prophetic insight with the lesser clarity of the other prophets. This is identical with Paul's "now we see through a glass darkly" (1 Corinthians 13:12). The ideal mystic is supposed to overcome this barrier and see heavenly matters "through a bright speculum." The failed mystic sees only through "a dark speculum." (2) "Transcendental" and "terrestrial" perspectives (see chapter 14). (3) In the subtitle "As Refracted through the Generations": this book deals with the notion of "Torah from Heaven" reflected in the interpretations of generations of Jewish Sages, from rabbinic times to the present.

Baraita (pl. Baraitot). An orally transmitted teaching, attributed to one or more of the Tannaim (rabbis of 20–200 C.E.) but not included in the Mishnah.

B.C.E. Before Common Era, that is, before the current general or Christian calendar.

canons of interpretation (*middot sheha-Torah nidreshet bahen*). Principles used by the Rabbis in making deductive interpretations from the Torah. Especially, the "Thirteen Canons of Rabbi Ishmael," enunciated in the beginning of the *Sifra* and included in the Jewish daily prayer service.

C.E. Common Era, that is, the current general or Christian calendar.

Derash. Homilizing interpretation. (1) A nonliteral or fanciful interpretation of a single word or phrase, to elicit a moral or homiletic meaning. (2) The method of nonliteral, homiletic interpretation in general, as opposed to *Peshat.*

derekh eretz. "The Way of the World." This term is extremely broad in signification, denoting all the virtues of ordinary, worldly conduct in complementarity to the higher virtues inculcated by Torah. It includes working for a livelihood, good manners, life experience, natural ethics (as attested by non-Jewish as well as Jewish practice), and even sexual intercourse. Many sayings attest to the general rabbinic view that whoever has only Torah or only *derekh eretz* without the other, is incomplete.

Dorshei Reshumot. "Solvers of enigmas" (following W. Bacher's understanding of *rasham* in *Erkhei Midrash Tannaim,* p. 125 [see appendix 6]). Apparently a school of allegorists who were proficient at interpreting the symbolism of language. Who exactly they were is still an enigma in search of a solution.

Epicurean. *See apikoros.*

Eretz Yisrael. The Land of Israel.

get. Legal writ, especially of divorce.

gezerah shavah. Verbal analogy. Canon 2 attributed to Rabbi Ishmael. If the same word occurs in two separate passages, traditions of exegesis may apply certain aspects of the legal force of that word in the one passage (or other circumstances of the law in that case) to the law in the second passage.

Great Assembly (*Keneset Ha-gedolah*). The cadre of leadership in the period from Ezra to the conquests of Alexander. What form this leadership body took is utterly unknown. *Keneset* is equivalent to the Greek *synagōgē,* that is, "gathering, assembly." Traditions of this group indicated that they started the path of midrashic interpretation of Torah, to develop ancillary legislation that was later developed extensively by the Rabbis. Mishnah Avot 1:1 names this as a critical stage (in that they are the first quoted authorities) in the passing of the tradition of Torah, coming after Moses, Joshua, the elders and prophets, and before the Sages of the Mishnaic period.

halakhah (pl. *halakhot*). (1) The authoritative, decided law of the rabbis in a particular case. (2) Halakhah (collective): The whole body of rabbinic law, or the discipline of studying rabbinic law.

kal vahomer. A fortiori. Canon 1 attributed to Rabbi Ishmael. If a case of lesser weight (i.e., likely to be of less concern) is explicitly mentioned in a rule of the Torah, but one of greater weight (*homer*) is not mentioned, one may deduce that the law must certainly apply in the weightier case, even though it is not mentioned. Certain limitations must be observed in invoking this principle: (1) No judicial punishment may be enforced for the deduced case. (2) Even though case 2 is more severe, only the equivalent legal status of case 1 may be inferred, not a more severe status.

kavanah. Intention, specifically: (1) the intention to fulfill a mitzvah, when one happens to perform an action that falls under the category of that injunction; (2) attentiveness, especially to the meaning of prayers or other content of religious actions when engaged in them. See chapter 10, pp. 204–5.

kiddush Ha-shem. Sanctification of the (Divine) Name. This is the classic rabbinic term for laying down one's life rather than transgress Torah—what in common parlance we call martyrdom.

menorah. Lampstand. Biblical: The seven-branched lampstand that stood in the Tabernacle and Temple, with cups filled with olive oil. Not to be confused with candelabra—candles were of medieval origin. Also not to be confused with the nine-branched candelabra used in the holiday of Hanukkah.

Merkavah. Chariot. The study of divine mysteries, based on the description of the Divine Chariot in Ezekiel 1.

Midrash (pl. Midrashim). Homily. (1) A characteristic rabbinic form of teaching in which an idea or lesson is presented as growing out of an interpretation of a scriptural verse or verses. (2) An extended homiletic lesson or teaching, using one or more examples of *Derash*-interpretations of individual words or verses as building blocks to underpin its argument. (3) A compiled work of midrashim.

Mishnah. (Legal) teaching. (1) The code of legal teachings assembled from previous oral traditions by Judah the Patriarch around 200 C.E. (2) A paragraph or single teaching from that collection.

mitzvah (pl. mitzvot). Commandment. (1) Any of the positive injunctions or prohibitions held to be commanded by God in the Torah, or derived by the Rabbis in their interpretation of the Torah. (2) By extension, any action, whether ethical or ritual, performed for the sake of serving God and carrying out the divine will.

mi'ut. Limitation. The hermeneutic principle (associated with Rabbi Akiva) that certain words ("however," "only," etc.) may be interpreted as implying limitations of the extent of a law, even though these cases are not explicitly mentioned in the text. (*See also ribbui.*)

Oral Torah (*Torah shebe'al peh*). Authoritative Jewish religious teachings, supplementary to the Written Torah and originally transmitted orally, though later compiled in works such as the Mishnah and Talmud. Debates proliferated as to the origin of the Oral Torah (whether of divine origin, human origin, or a mixture of both), its chronology (whether from Sinai, or later, or both), and the nature of its authority. These debates are documented and analyzed in the current work (especially volumes 2 and 3).

Pardes. Orchard. From Latin *paradisium.* The "Orchard," or garden of mysteries; the study or practice of mysticism.

Peshat. The plain-sense or contextual understanding (more literally: surface meaning) of Scripture (as opposed to *Derash*). (1) The contextual understanding of a particular word, phrase, or verse. (2) The method of contextual interpretation in general. Note: While *Peshat* is often equated with literal interpretation, it includes also plain-sense understanding of common metaphor in a nonliteral way, such as understanding the "hand of God" to mean "the power of God," and the like. See discussion of Rabbi Ishmael's principle "the Torah speaks in human language" in chapter 13.

ribbui. Expansion. The hermeneutic principle (associated with Rabbi Akiva) that certain words ("also," "and," etc.) may be interpreted as implying enlargement of the extent of application of the law, even though these cases are not explicitly mentioned in the text. (*See also mi'ut.*)

Shekhinah. The Divine Presence or Indwelling of God in the world (based on Exodus 25:8: "Let them make Me a sanctuary that I may dwell [*veshakhanti*] in their midst"). This conception became extremely important in rabbinic and later mystical literature. In the kabbalistic system, the Shekhinah is the tenth of the Sefirot, and its feminine character is quite pronounced. See chapters 5–6.

speculum. *See Aspaklaryah.*

Sukkah (pl. Sukkot). Tabernacle, booth, especially a harvest booth erected for the Festival of Sukkot (Tabernacles) in the fall.

Talmud. Study. (1) Either of the two major corpuses of Jewish law and lore (Halakhah and Aggadah), viz., the Talmud of the Land of Israel (Palestinian or Jerusalem Talmud) and the Babylonian Talmud. Each is written in the form of extensive commentaries on the Mishnah, branching out into discussion of multiple related topics and comprising the traditions of Rabbis in the second through fifth centuries, plus later interpolations. (2) The enterprise of legal exegetical discussion represented in these works.

Tanna (pl. Tannaim). A rabbinic teacher of the period reflected in the Mishnah, i.e., approximately 20 C.E. to 200 C.E.

Generations of Tannaim

1	40–80 C.E.	Johanan ben Zakkai et al.
2	80–110 C.E.	Gamaliel II, Eliezer ben Hyrcanus,
		Joshua ben Hananiah et al.
3	110–135 C.E.	Akiva, Ishmael et al.
4	135–170 C.E.	Simeon ben Yohai, Judah ben Ilay, Meir et al.
5	170–200 C.E.	Judah the Patriarch et al.

Tannaitic Midrashim. This generic term is applied to the following exegetical works, primarily halakhic (but including much aggadic material as well), and held by modern scholars to be of two major types. D. Z. Hoffmann and others saw them as largely the product of the schools of Rabbi Ishmael and Rabbi Akiva as follows:

School of Rabbi Ishmael	*School of Rabbi Akiva*
On Exodus	
Mekhilta of Rabbi Ishmael	*Mekhilta of Rabbi Simeon ben Yohai*
On Leviticus	
(some portions of *Sifra*)	*Sifra* (of the school of Rab)
On Numbers	
Sifre on Numbers	*Sifre Zuta*
On Deuteronomy	
Midrash Tannaim on Deuteronomy	*Sifre* on Deuteronomy

Torah. Instruction. (1) The Five Books of Moses (Genesis through Deuteronomy), also called "Written Torah." (2) The totality of all authoritative Jewish religious teaching, comprising Written and Oral Torah. (See chapter 20 for more nuances of this word.)

6. Principal Secondary Works Cited

The following titles are prominent among the modern scholarly works cited by Heschel in *Heavenly Torah*. Scholarship in rabbinics has made great strides in the past thirty-five years, but many of these works are classics that still contribute to the assessment of the problems they discuss. Several of the works in German and Hebrew have no equivalent in English to this date.

Bacher: Wilhelm Bacher, *Erkei Midrash Hatannaim* [*Lexicon of Rabbinic Exegetical Terminology*] (Tel Aviv: Rabinowitz, 5683/1923). Translated from the German *Exegetische Terminologie der jüdischen Traditionsliteratur* (Leipzig, 1899/1905; reprint, Darmstadt, 1965).

Chajes: Zevi Hirsch Chajes, *The Student's Guide through the Talmud* [Hebrew *Mevo Ha-Talmud*], translated by Jacob Shachter (London: East and West Library, 1952).

Epstein: J. N. Epstein, *Mevo'ot le-sifrut ha-tannaim* [Introduction to Tannaitic Literature: Mishna, Tosephta and Halakhic Midrashim] (Jerusalem: Magnes, 1957). This, and Epstein's *Introduction to the Redaction of the Mishnah* did more than any other comparable work to set modern textual study of rabbinic literature on a scientific basis.

Finkelstein (Akiba): Louis Finkelstein, *Akiba: Scholar, Saint and Martyr* (Philadelphia: Jewish Publication Society; New York: Meridian, 1936; reprint, 1962).

Finkelstein (Avot): Louis Finkelstein, *Mavo le-masekhtot Avot ve-Avot de-Rabbi Natan* [Introduction to the Treatises Abot and Abot of Rabbi Nathan] (Hebrew with English summary) (New York: Jewish Theological Seminary, 1950).

Genizah Studies in Memory of Dr. Solomon Schechter, 3 volumes (Hebrew texts with English introductions) (New York: Jewish Theological Seminary, 1928–29). These three volumes published in the early twentieth century were representative of the thousands of texts recovered by Solomon Schechter in the Cairo Genizah in the 1890s, greatly expanding scholarly knowledge of medieval Jewish life and thought:
> Volume 1: Midrash and Haggadah, edited by Louis Ginzberg.
> Volume 2: Geonic and Early Karaite Halakhah, edited by Louis Ginzberg.
> Volume 3: Liturgical and Secular Poetry, edited by Israel Davidson.

Ginzberg: Louis Ginzberg, *Legends of the Jews,* 7 volumes (Philadelphia: Jewish Publication Society, 1909–38). Reworks midrashic tales from many sources into a continuous narrative paralleling the biblical plot, with extensive notes. A classic.

Higger: Michael Higger, *Otzar Ha-Baraitot* (in Hebrew), 10 volumes (New York: Rabbinical Assembly and Central Conference of American Rabbis, 1938-48). This exhaustive collection of Baraitot cross-indexes their occurrence in the various genres of rabbinic literature. A key tool for critical scholarship of rabbinical literature.

Hoffmann: David Zevi Hoffmann, *"Le-heker Midreshei ha-Tannaim"* [On the Study of Tannaitic Midrashim], with "Supplement" by Hayyim Saul Horowitz, translated by A. Z. Rabinowitz and included in *Mesillot le-Torat ha-Tannaim* [Pathways through Tannaitic Thought] (Tel Aviv, 1928).

Lieberman: Saul Lieberman, dean of American rabbinic scholars in Heschel's lifetime. The works of his to which Heschel refers include:
> *Tosefta* and *Tosefta Ki-feshutah.* The definitive critical edition of the first three-and-one-half orders of the Tosefta, with magisterial commentary covering parallels of the material in all rabbinic literature.
> *Hellenism in Jewish Palestine: Studies in the Literary Transmission, Beliefs, and Manners of Palestine in the I Century B.C.E. - IV Century C.E."* (New York: Jewish Theological Seminary, 1962).
> *Midreshei Teiman* [Yemenite Midrash: A Lecture] (Jerusalem: Bamberger & Vahrman, 1940).

Mann: Jacob Mann, *The Bible as Read and Preached in the Old Synagogue,* Volume 1 (Cincinnati: UAHC; Philadelphia: Jewish Publication Society, 1940; Volume 2 (J. Mann & Isaiah Sayre; Cincinnati: HUC-JIR, 1966).

Marmorstein: A. Marmorstein, *The Old Rabbinic Doctrine of God* (Farnborough: Gregg, 1969).

Melamed: Ezra Zion Melamed, *Midreshei halakhah shel ha-tannaim ba-Talmud ha-Bavli* [Halakhic Midrashim of the Tannaim in the Talmud Babli] (in Hebrew) (Jerusalem: Mosad Ha-Rav Kuk, 1943).

Neubauer: Yekutiel (Jacob) Neubauer, "Halakhah u-midrash halakhah" [Halakhah and Halakhic Midrash] (in Hebrew), *Sinai* 22 (5708/Fall 1947): 49–80.

Scholem: Gershom Scholem. This German-Jewish scholar, who moved to Palestine in the 1920s, single-handedly placed the study of Jewish mysticism on a modern scientific basis, with the following works:
> *Major Trends in Jewish Mysticism,* The Hilda Stich Stroock Lectures 1938 (Jerusalem: Schocken, 1941)
> *Origins of Kabbalah* (ed. Werblowsky; Philadelphia: Jewish Publication Society, 1987).
> *Kabbalah* (Jerusalem: Keter, 1974).
> *Sabbatai Sevi: The Mystical Messiah* (Princeton, N.J.: Princeton University Press, 1973).

Zunz: Leopold Zunz, *Gottesdienstlichen Vorträge der Juden historisch entwickelt* [Liturgical Preaching among Jews, in its Historical Development] (1832; Jerusalem: Mosad Bialik, 1954; reprint, Hildesheim, 1966). Citations in this work are to the Hebrew edition, *Ha-Derashot be-Yisrael ve-hishtalshelutan ha-historit,* edited by H. Albeck (Jerusalem: Mosad Bialik, 1946/1954).